Fifth Edition

# OPTIONS, FUTURES, & OTHER DERIVATIVES

# PRENTICE HALL FINANCE SERIES

## Personal Finance
Keown, *Personal Finance: Turning Money into Wealth, Second Edition*
Trivoli, *Personal Portfolio Management: Fundamentals & Strategies*
Winger/Frasca, *Personal Finance: An Integrated Planning Approach, Sixth Edition*

## Undergraduate Investments/Portfolio Management
Alexander/Sharpe/Bailey, *Fundamentals of Investments, Third Edition*
Fabozzi, *Investment Management, Second Edition*
Haugen, *Modern Investment Theory, Fifth Edition*
Haugen, *The New Finance, Second Edition*
Haugen, *The Beast on Wall Street*
Haugen, *The Inefficient Stock Market, Second Edition*
Holden, *Spreadsheet Modeling: A Book and CD-ROM Series*
    (Available in Graduate and Undergraduate Versions)
Nofsinger, *The Psychology of Investing*
Taggart, *Quantitative Analysis for Investment Management*
Winger/Frasca, *Investments, Third Edition*

## Graduate Investments/Portfolio Management
Fischer/Jordan, *Security Analysis and Portfolio Management, Sixth Edition*
Francis/Ibbotson, *Investments: A Global Perspective*
Haugen, *The Inefficient Stock Market, Second Edition*
Holden, *Spreadsheet Modeling: A Book and CD-ROM Series*
    (Available in Graduate and Undergraduate Versions)
Nofsinger, *The Psychology of Investing*
Sharpe/Alexander/Bailey, *Investments, Sixth Edition*

## Options/Futures/Derivatives
Hull, *Fundamentals of Futures and Options Markets, Fourth Edition*
Hull, *Options, Futures, and Other Derivatives, Fifth Edition*

## Risk Management/Financial Engineering
Mason/Merton/Perold/Tufano, *Cases in Financial Engineering*

## Fixed Income Securities
Handa, *FinCoach: Fixed Income* (software)

## Bond Markets
Fabozzi, *Bond Markets, Analysis and Strategies, Fourth Edition*

## Undergraduate Corporate Finance
Bodie/Merton, *Finance*
Emery/Finnerty/Stowe, *Principles of Financial Management*
Emery/Finnerty, *Corporate Financial Management*
Gallagher/Andrew, *Financial Management: Principles and Practices, Third Edition*
Handa, *FinCoach 2.0*
Holden, *Spreadsheet Modeling: A Book and CD-ROM Series*
    (Available in Graduate and Undergraduate Versions)
Keown/Martin/Petty/Scott, *Financial Management, Ninth Edition*
Keown/Martin/Petty/Scott, *Financial Management, 9/e activebook*[TM]
Keown/Martin/Petty/Scott, *Foundations of Finance: The Logic and Practice of Financial Management, Third Edition*
Keown/Martin/Petty/Scott, *Foundations of Finance, 3/e activebook*[TM]
Mathis, *Corporate Finance Live: A Web-based Math Tutorial*
Shapiro/Balbirer, *Modern Corporate Finance: A Multidisciplinary Approach to Value Creation*
Van Horne/Wachowicz, *Fundamentals of Financial Management, Eleventh Edition*
Mastering Finance CD-ROM

## Advanced Corporate Finance

Holden, *Spreadsheet Modeling: A Book and CD-ROM Series*
   (Available in Graduate and Undergraduate Versions)
Ogden/Jen/O'Connor, *Advanced Corporate Finance: Financing Policies and Strategies*
Van Horne, *Financial Management and Policy, Twelfth Edition*
Handa, *FinCoach 2.0*

## International Finance

Baker, *International Finance: Management, Markets, and Institutions*
Click/Coval, *The Theory and Practice of International Financial Management*
Grabbe, *International Financial Markets, Third Edition*
Rivera-Batiz/Rivera-Batiz, *International Finance and Open Economy Macroeconomics, Second Edition*

## Capital Budgeting

Aggarwal, *Capital Budgeting Under Uncertainty*
Bierman/Smidt, *The Capital Budgeting Decision, Eighth Edition*

## Mergers/Acquisitions/Takeovers

Weston/Siu/Johnson, *Takeovers, Restructuring, and Corporate Governance, Third Edition*
Weston, *Cases in Takeovers, Restructuring and Corporate Governance, Third Edition*

## Taxes

Scholes/Wolfson, *Taxes and Business Strategy: A Global Planning Approach, Second Edition*

## Insurance

Black/Skipper, *Life and Health Insurance, Thirteenth Edition*
Dorfman, *Introduction to Risk Management and Insurance, Seventh Edition*
Rejda, *Social Insurance and Economic Security, Sixth Edition*

## Financial Markets and Institutions/Capital Markets

Arshadi/Karels, *Modern Financial Intermediaries and Markets*
Dietrich, *Financial Services and Financial Institutions*
Fabozzi/Modigliani, *Capital Markets: Institutions and Instruments, Second Edition*
Fabozzi/Modigliani/Ferri/Jones, *Foundations of Financial Markets and Institutions, Third Edition*
Kaufman, *The U.S. Financial Systems*
Van Horne, *Financial Market Rates and Flows, Sixth Edition*

## Commercial Banking

Sinkey, *Commercial Bank Financial Management, Sixth Edition*

## Entrepreneurial Finance

Adelman/Marks, *Entrepreneurial Finance*
Vaughn, *Financial Planning for the Entrepreneur*

## Cases in Finance

May/May/Andrew, *Effective Writing: A Handbook for Finance People*
Weston, *Cases in Dynamic Finance: Mergers and Restructuring*

## Financial Statement Analysis

Fraser/Ormiston, *Understanding Financial Statements, Fourth Edition*

## Behavioral Finance

Nofsinger, *The Psychology of Investing*

## Financial Theory

Danthine/Donaldson, *Intermediate Financial Theory*

## Finance Center

For downloadable supplements and much more visit us at www.prenhall.com
   Please select Finance in the Discipline Finder

## Fifth Edition

# OPTIONS, FUTURES, & OTHER DERIVATIVES

### John C. Hull

*Maple Financial Group Professor of Derivatives and Risk Management*
*Director, Bonham Center for Finance*
*Joseph L. Rotman School of Management*
*University of Toronto*

PRENTICE HALL, UPPER SADDLE RIVER, NEW JERSEY 07458

**Library of Congress Cataloging-in-Publication Data**

Hull, John,

    Options, futures and other derivatives/ John C. Hull.—5 ed.

      p.  cm.

    Includes bibliographical references and index.

    **ISBN 0-13-009056-5**

    1. Futures.  2. Stock options.  3. Derivative securities.  I. Title.

HG6024.A3 H85  2002

332.63'2—dc21

2002025234

**Executive Editor:** Mickey Cox
**Editor-in-Chief:** PJ Boardman
**Managing Editor (Editorial):** Gladys Soto
**Assistant Editor:** Beth Romph
**Editorial Assistant:** Kevin Hancock
**Media Project Manager:** Victoria Anderson
**Marketing Manager:** Kathleen McLellan
**Marketing Assistant:** Christopher Bath
**Managing Editor (Production):** Cynthia Regan
**Production Editor:** Kerri M. Limpert
**Production Assistant:** Dianne Falcone
**Permissions Coordinator:** Suzanne Grappi
**Associate Director, Manufacturing:** Vincent Scelta
**Manufacturing Buyer:** Diane Peirano
**Design Manager:** Pat Smythe
**Cover Design:** John Romer
**Manager, Print Production:** Richard Bretan
**Full-Service Project Management:** The Geometric Press
**Printer/Binder:** Courier-Westford

Credits and acknowledgments borrowed from other sources and reproduced, with permission, in this textbook appear on appropriate page within text.

Pearson Education LTD.
Pearson Education Australia PTY, Limited
Pearson Education Singapore, Pte. Ltd
Pearson Education North Asia Ltd
Pearson Education, Canada, Ltd
Pearson Educación de Mexico, S.A. de C.V.
Pearson Education–Japan
Pearson Education Malaysia, Pte. Ltd

10 9 8 7 6 5 4 3 2
ISBN 0-13-009056-5

To Michelle

# CONTENTS

# PREFACE

It is sometimes hard for me to believe that the first edition of this book was only 330 pages and 13 chapters long! There have been many developments in derivatives markets over the last 15 years and the book has grown to keep up with them. The fifth edition has seven new chapters that cover new derivatives instruments and recent research advances.

Like earlier editions, the book serves several markets. It is appropriate for graduate courses in business, economics, and financial engineering. It can be used on advanced undergraduate courses when students have good quantitative skills. Also, many practitioners who want to acquire a working knowledge of how derivatives can be analyzed find the book useful.

One of the key decisions that must be made by an author who is writing in the area of derivatives concerns the use of mathematics. If the level of mathematical sophistication is too high, the material is likely to be inaccessible to many students and practitioners. If it is too low, some important issues will inevitably be treated in a rather superficial way. I have tried to be particularly careful about the way I use both mathematics and notation in the book. Nonessential mathematical material has been either eliminated or included in end-of-chapter appendices. Concepts that are likely to be new to many readers have been explained carefully, and many numerical examples have been included.

The book covers both derivatives markets and risk management. It assumes that the reader has taken an introductory course in finance and an introductory course in probability and statistics. No prior knowledge of options, futures contracts, swaps, and so on is assumed. It is not therefore necessary for students to take an elective course in investments prior to taking a course based on this book. There are many different ways the book can be used in the classroom. Instructors teaching a first course in derivatives may wish to spend most time on the first half of the book. Instructors teaching a more advanced course will find that many different combinations of the chapters in the second half of the book can be used. I find that the material in Chapters 29 and 30 works well at the end of either an introductory or an advanced course.

## What's New?

Material has been updated and improved throughout the book. The changes in this edition include:

1. A new chapter on the use of futures for hedging (Chapter 4). Part of this material was previously in Chapters 2 and 3. The change results in the first three chapters being less intense and allows hedging to be covered in more depth.

2. A new chapter on models and numerical procedures (Chapter 20). Much of this material is new, but some has been transferred from the chapter on exotic options in the fourth edition.

3. A new chapter on swaps (Chapter 25). This gives the reader an appreciation of the range of nonstandard swap products that are traded in the over-the-counter market and discusses how they can be valued.

4. There is an extra chapter on credit risk. Chapter 26 discusses the measurement of credit risk and credit value at risk while Chapter 27 covers credit derivatives.

5. There is a new chapter on real options (Chapter 28).

6. There is a new chapter on insurance, weather, and energy derivatives (Chapter 29).

7. There is a new chapter on derivatives mishaps and what we can learn from them (Chapter 30).

8. The chapter on martingales and measures has been improved so that the material flows better (Chapter 21).

9. The chapter on value at risk has been rewritten so that it provides a better balance between the historical simulation approach and the model-building approach (Chapter 16).

10. The chapter on volatility smiles has been improved and appears earlier in the book. (Chapter 15).

11. The coverage of the LIBOR market model has been expanded (Chapter 24).

12. One or two changes have been made to the notation. The most significant is that the strike price is now denoted by $K$ rather than $X$.

13. Many new end-of-chapter problems have been added.

## Software

A new version of DerivaGem (Version 1.50) is released with this book. This consists of two Excel applications: the *Options Calculator* and the *Applications Builder*. The Options Calculator consists of the software in the previous release (with minor improvements). The Applications Builder consists of a number of Excel functions from which users can build their own applications. It includes a number of sample applications and enables students to explore the properties of options and numerical procedures more easily. It also allows more interesting assignments to be designed.

The software is described more fully at the end of the book. Updates to the software can be downloaded from my website:

www.rotman.utoronto.ca/~hull

## Slides

Several hundred PowerPoint slides can be downloaded from my website. Instructors who adopt the text are welcome to adapt the slides to meet their own needs.

## Answers to Questions

As in the fourth edition, end-of-chapter problems are divided into two groups: "Questions and Problems" and "Assignment Questions". Solutions to the Questions and Problems are in *Options, Futures, and Other Derivatives: Solutions Manual*, which is published by Prentice Hall and can be purchased by students. Solutions to Assignment Questions are available only in the Instructors Manual.

## Acknowledgments

Many people have played a part in the production of this book. Academics, students, and practitioners who have made excellent and useful suggestions include Farhang Aslani, Jas Badyal, Emilio Barone, Giovanni Barone-Adesi, Alex Bergier, George Blazenko, Laurence Booth, Phelim Boyle, Peter Carr, Don Chance, J.-P. Chateau, Ren-Raw Chen, George Constantinides, Michel Crouhy, Emanuel Derman, Brian Donaldson, Dieter Dorp, Scott Drabin, Jerome Duncan, Steinar Ekern, David Fowler, Louis Gagnon, Dajiang Guo, Jrgen Hallbeck, Ian Hawkins, Michael Hemler, Steve Heston, Bernie Hildebrandt, Michelle Hull, Kiyoshi Kato, Kevin Kneafsy, Tibor Kucs, Iain MacDonald, Bill Margrabe, Izzy Nelkin, Neil Pearson, Paul Potvin, Shailendra Pandit, Eric Reiner, Richard Rendleman, Gordon Roberts, Chris Robinson, Cheryl Rosen, John Rumsey, Ani Sanyal, Klaus Schurger, Eduardo Schwartz, Michael Selby, Piet Sercu, Duane Stock, Edward Thorpe, Yisong Tian, P. V. Viswanath, George Wang, Jason Wei, Bob Whaley, Alan White, Hailiang Yang, Victor Zak, and Jozef Zemek. Huafen (Florence) Wu and Matthew Merkley provided excellent research assistance.

I am particularly grateful to Eduardo Schwartz, who read the original manuscript for the first edition and made many comments that led to significant improvements, and to Richard Rendleman and George Constantinides, who made specific suggestions that led to improvements in more recent editions.

The first four editions of this book were very popular with practitioners and their comments and suggestions have led to many improvements in the book. The students in my elective courses on derivatives at the University of Toronto have also influenced the evolution of the book.

Alan White, a colleague at the University of Toronto, deserves a special acknowledgment. Alan and I have been carrying out joint research in the area of derivatives for the last 18 years. During that time we have spent countless hours discussing different issues concerning derivatives. Many of the new ideas in this book, and many of the new ways used to explain old ideas, are as much Alan's as mine. Alan read the original version of this book very carefully and made many excellent suggestions for improvement. Alan has also done most of the development work on the Deriva-Gem software.

Special thanks are due to many people at Prentice Hall for their enthusiasm, advice, and encouragement. I would particularly like to thank Mickey Cox (my editor), P. J. Boardman (the editor-in-chief) and Kerri Limpert (the production editor). I am also grateful to Scott Barr, Leah Jewell, Paul Donnelly, and Maureen Riopelle, who at different times have played key roles in the development of the book.

I welcome comments on the book from readers. My email address is:

hull@rotman.utoronto.ca

John C. Hull
University of Toronto

# CHAPTER 1

# INTRODUCTION

In the last 20 years derivatives have become increasingly important in the world of finance. Futures and options are now traded actively on many exchanges throughout the world. Forward contracts, swaps, and many different types of options are regularly traded outside exchanges by financial institutions, fund managers, and corporate treasurers in what is termed the *over-the-counter* market. Derivatives are also sometimes added to a bond or stock issue.

A *derivative* can be defined as a financial instrument whose value depends on (or derives from) the values of other, more basic underlying variables. Very often the variables underlying derivatives are the prices of traded assets. A stock option, for example, is a derivative whose value is dependent on the price of a stock. However, derivatives can be dependent on almost any variable, from the price of hogs to the amount of snow falling at a certain ski resort.

Since the first edition of this book was published in 1988, there have been many developments in derivatives markets. There is now active trading in credit derivatives, electricity derivatives, weather derivatives, and insurance derivatives. Many new types of interest rate, foreign exchange, and equity derivative products have been created. There have been many new ideas in risk management and risk measurement. Analysts have also become more aware of the need to analyze what are known as *real options*. (These are the options acquired by a company when it invests in real assets such as real estate, plant, and equipment.) This edition of the book reflects all these developments.

In this opening chapter we take a first look at forward, futures, and options markets and provide an overview of how they are used by hedgers, speculators, and arbitrageurs. Later chapters will give more details and elaborate on many of the points made here.

## 1.1 EXCHANGE-TRADED MARKETS

A derivatives exchange is a market where individuals trade standardized contracts that have been defined by the exchange. Derivatives exchanges have existed for a long time. The Chicago Board of Trade (CBOT, www.cbot.com) was established in 1848 to bring farmers and merchants together. Initially its main task was to standardize the quantities and qualities of the grains that were traded. Within a few years the first futures-type contract was developed. It was known as a *to-arrive contract*. Speculators soon became interested in the contract and found trading the contract to be an attractive alternative to trading the grain itself. A rival futures exchange, the Chicago Mercantile Exchange (CME, www.cme.com), was established in 1919. Now futures exchanges exist all over the world.

The Chicago Board Options Exchange (CBOE, www.cboe.com) started trading call option contracts on 16 stocks in 1973. Options had traded prior to 1973 but the CBOE succeeded in creating an orderly market with well-defined contracts. Put option contracts started trading on the exchange in 1977. The CBOE now trades options on over 1200 stocks and many different stock indices. Like futures, options have proved to be very popular contracts. Many other exchanges throughout the world now trade options. The underlying assets include foreign currencies and futures contracts as well as stocks and stock indices.

Traditionally derivatives traders have met on the floor of an exchange and used shouting and a complicated set of hand signals to indicate the trades they would like to carry out. This is known as the *open outcry system*. In recent years exchanges have increasingly moved from the open outcry system to *electronic trading*. The latter involves traders entering their desired trades at a keyboard and a computer being used to match buyers and sellers. There seems little doubt that eventually all exchanges will use electronic trading.

## 1.2  OVER-THE-COUNTER MARKETS

Not all trading is done on exchanges. The *over-the-counter market* is an important alternative to exchanges and, measured in terms of the total volume of trading, has become much larger than the exchange-traded market. It is a telephone- and computer-linked network of dealers, who do not physically meet. Trades are done over the phone and are usually between two financial institutions or between a financial institution and one of its corporate clients. Financial institutions often act as market makers for the more commonly traded instruments. This means that they are always prepared to quote both a bid price (a price at which they are prepared to buy) and an offer price (a price at which they are prepared to sell).

Telephone conversations in the over-the-counter market are usually taped. If there is a dispute about what was agreed, the tapes are replayed to resolve the issue. Trades in the over-the-counter market are typically much larger than trades in the exchange-traded market. A key advantage of the over-the-counter market is that the terms of a contract do not have to be those specified by an exchange. Market participants are free to negotiate any mutually attractive deal. A disadvantage is that there is usually some credit risk in an over-the-counter trade (i.e., there is a small risk that the contract will not be honored). As mentioned earlier, exchanges have organized themselves to eliminate virtually all credit risk.

## 1.3  FORWARD CONTRACTS

A *forward contract* is a particularly simple derivative. It is an agreement to buy or sell an asset at a certain future time for a certain price. It can be contrasted with a *spot contract*, which is an agreement to buy or sell an asset today. A forward contract is traded in the over-the-counter market—usually between two financial institutions or between a financial institution and one of its clients.

One of the parties to a forward contract assumes a *long position* and agrees to buy the underlying asset on a certain specified future date for a certain specified price. The other party assumes a *short position* and agrees to sell the asset on the same date for the same price.

Forward contracts on foreign exchange are very popular. Most large banks have a "forward desk" within their foreign exchange trading room that is devoted to the trading of forward

**Table 1.1**  Spot and forward quotes for the USD–GBP exchange rate, August 16, 2001 (GBP = British pound; USD = U.S. dollar)

|                 | *Bid*  | *Offer* |
|-----------------|--------|---------|
| Spot            | 1.4452 | 1.4456  |
| 1-month forward | 1.4435 | 1.4440  |
| 3-month forward | 1.4402 | 1.4407  |
| 6-month forward | 1.4353 | 1.4359  |
| 1-year forward  | 1.4262 | 1.4268  |

contracts. Table 1.1 provides the quotes on the exchange rate between the British pound (GBP) and the U.S. dollar (USD) that might be made by a large international bank on August 16, 2001. The quote is for the number of USD per GBP. The first quote indicates that the bank is prepared to buy GBP (i.e., sterling) in the spot market (i.e., for virtually immediate delivery) at the rate of $1.4452 per GBP and sell sterling in the spot market at $1.4456 per GBP. The second quote indicates that the bank is prepared to buy sterling in one month at $1.4435 per GBP and sell sterling in one month at $1.4440 per GBP; the third quote indicates that it is prepared to buy sterling in three months at $1.4402 per GBP and sell sterling in three months at $1.4407 per GBP; and so on. These quotes are for very large transactions. (As anyone who has traveled abroad knows, retail customers face much larger spreads between bid and offer quotes than those in given Table 1.1.)

Forward contracts can be used to hedge foreign currency risk. Suppose that on August 16, 2001, the treasurer of a U.S. corporation knows that the corporation will pay £1 million in six months (on February 16, 2002) and wants to hedge against exchange rate moves. Using the quotes in Table 1.1, the treasurer can agree to buy £1 million six months forward at an exchange rate of 1.4359. The corporation then has a long forward contract on GBP. It has agreed that on February 16, 2002, it will buy £1 million from the bank for $1.4359 million. The bank has a short forward contract on GBP. It has agreed that on February 16, 2002, it will sell £1 million for $1.4359 million. Both sides have made a binding commitment.

### Payoffs from Forward Contracts

Consider the position of the corporation in the trade we have just described. What are the possible outcomes? The forward contract obligates the corporation to buy £1 million for $1,435,900. If the spot exchange rate rose to, say, 1.5000, at the end of the six months the forward contract would be worth $64,100 (= $1,500,000 − $1,435,900) to the corporation. It would enable £1 million to be purchased at 1.4359 rather than 1.5000. Similarly, if the spot exchange rate fell to 1.4000 at the end of the six months, the forward contract would have a negative value to the corporation of $35,900 because it would lead to the corporation paying $35,900 more than the market price for the sterling.

In general, the payoff from a long position in a forward contract on one unit of an asset is

$$S_T - K$$

where $K$ is the delivery price and $S_T$ is the spot price of the asset at maturity of the contract. This is because the holder of the contract is obligated to buy an asset worth $S_T$ for $K$. Similarly, the payoff from a short position in a forward contract on one unit of an asset is

$$K - S_T$$

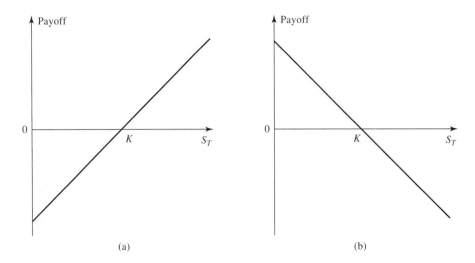

**Figure 1.1**  Payoffs from forward contracts: (a) long position, (b) short position. Delivery price = $K$; price of asset at maturity = $S_T$

These payoffs can be positive or negative. They are illustrated in Figure 1.1. Because it costs nothing to enter into a forward contract, the payoff from the contract is also the trader's total gain or loss from the contract.

### Forward Price and Delivery Price

It is important to distinguish between the forward price and delivery price. The *forward price* is the market price that would be agreed to today for delivery of the asset at a specified maturity date. The forward price is usually different from the spot price and varies with the maturity date (see Table 1.1).

In the example we considered earlier, the forward price on August 16, 2001, is 1.4359 for a contract maturing on February 16, 2002. The corporation enters into a contract and 1.4359 becomes the delivery price for the contract. As we move through time the delivery price for the corporation's contract does not change, but the forward price for a contract maturing on February 16, 2002, is likely to do so. For example, if GBP strengthens relative to USD in the second half of August the forward price could rise to 1.4500 by September 1, 2001.

### Forward Prices and Spot Prices

We will be discussing in some detail the relationship between spot and forward prices in Chapter 3. In this section we illustrate the reason why the two are related by considering forward contracts on gold. We assume that there are no storage costs associated with gold and that gold earns no income.[1]

Suppose that the spot price of gold is $300 per ounce and the risk-free interest rate for investments lasting one year is 5% per annum. What is a reasonable value for the one-year forward price of gold?

---

[1] This is not totally realistic. In practice, storage costs are close to zero, but an income of 1 to 2% per annum can be earned by lending gold.

Suppose first that the one-year forward price is $340 per ounce. A trader can immediately take the following actions:

1. Borrow $300 at 5% for one year.
2. Buy one ounce of gold.
3. Enter into a short forward contract to sell the gold for $340 in one year.

The interest on the $300 that is borrowed (assuming annual compounding) is $15. The trader can, therefore, use $315 of the $340 that is obtained for the gold in one year to repay the loan. The remaining $25 is profit. Any one-year forward price greater than $315 will lead to this arbitrage trading strategy being profitable.

Suppose next that the forward price is $300. An investor who has a portfolio that includes gold can

1. Sell the gold for $300 per ounce.
2. Invest the proceeds at 5%.
3. Enter into a long forward contract to repurchase the gold in one year for $300 per ounce.

When this strategy is compared with the alternative strategy of keeping the gold in the portfolio for one year, we see that the investor is better off by $15 per ounce. In any situation where the forward price is less than $315, investors holding gold have an incentive to sell the gold and enter into a long forward contract in the way that has been described.

The first strategy is profitable when the one-year forward price of gold is greater than $315. As more traders attempt to take advantage of this strategy, the demand for short forward contracts will increase and the one-year forward price of gold will fall. The second strategy is profitable for all investors who hold gold in their portfolios when the one-year forward price of gold is less than $315. As these investors attempt to take advantage of this strategy, the demand for long forward contracts will increase and the one-year forward price of gold will rise. Assuming that individuals are always willing to take advantage of arbitrage opportunities when they arise, we can conclude that the activities of traders should cause the one-year forward price of gold to be exactly $315. Any other price leads to an arbitrage opportunity.[2]

## 1.4 FUTURES CONTRACTS

Like a forward contract, a futures contract is an agreement between two parties to buy or sell an asset at a certain time in the future for a certain price. Unlike forward contracts, futures contracts are normally traded on an exchange. To make trading possible, the exchange specifies certain standardized features of the contract. As the two parties to the contract do not necessarily know each other, the exchange also provides a mechanism that gives the two parties a guarantee that the contract will be honored.

The largest exchanges on which futures contracts are traded are the Chicago Board of Trade (CBOT) and the Chicago Mercantile Exchange (CME). On these and other exchanges throughout the world, a very wide range of commodities and financial assets form the underlying assets in the various contracts. The commodities include pork bellies, live cattle, sugar, wool, lumber, copper, aluminum, gold, and tin. The financial assets include stock indices, currencies, and Treasury bonds.

---

[2] Our arguments make the simplifying assumption that the rate of interest on borrowed funds is the same as the rate of interest on invested funds.

One way in which a futures contract is different from a forward contract is that an exact delivery date is usually not specified. The contract is referred to by its delivery month, and the exchange specifies the period during the month when delivery must be made. For commodities, the delivery period is often the entire month. The holder of the short position has the right to choose the time during the delivery period when it will make delivery. Usually, contracts with several different delivery months are traded at any one time. The exchange specifies the amount of the asset to be delivered for one contract and how the futures price is to be quoted. In the case of a commodity, the exchange also specifies the product quality and the delivery location. Consider, for example, the wheat futures contract currently traded on the Chicago Board of Trade. The size of the contract is 5,000 bushels. Contracts for five delivery months (March, May, July, September, and December) are available for up to 18 months into the future. The exchange specifies the grades of wheat that can be delivered and the places where delivery can be made.

Futures prices are regularly reported in the financial press. Suppose that on September 1, the December futures price of gold is quoted as $300. This is the price, exclusive of commissions, at which traders can agree to buy or sell gold for December delivery. It is determined on the floor of the exchange in the same way as other prices (i.e., by the laws of supply and demand). If more traders want to go long than to go short, the price goes up; if the reverse is true, the price goes down.[3]

Further details on issues such as margin requirements, daily settlement procedures, delivery procedures, bid–offer spreads, and the role of the exchange clearinghouse are given in Chapter 2.

## 1.5  OPTIONS

Options are traded both on exchanges and in the over-the-counter market. There are two basic types of options. A *call option* gives the holder the right to buy the underlying asset by a certain date for a certain price. A *put option* gives the holder the right to sell the underlying asset by a certain date for a certain price. The price in the contract is known as the *exercise price* or *strike price*; the date in the contract is known as the *expiration date* or *maturity*. *American options* can be exercised at any time up to the expiration date. *European options* can be exercised only on the expiration date itself.[4] Most of the options that are traded on exchanges are American. In the exchange-traded equity options market, one contract is usually an agreement to buy or sell 100 shares. European options are generally easier to analyze than American options, and some of the properties of an American option are frequently deduced from those of its European counterpart.

It should be emphasized that an option gives the holder the right to do something. The holder does not have to exercise this right. This is what distinguishes options from forwards and futures, where the holder is obligated to buy or sell the underlying asset. Note that whereas it costs nothing to enter into a forward or futures contract, there is a cost to acquiring an option.

### Call Options

Consider the situation of an investor who buys a European call option with a strike price of $60 to purchase 100 Microsoft shares. Suppose that the current stock price is $58, the expiration date of

---

[3] In Chapter 3 we discuss the relationship between a futures price and the spot price of the underlying asset (gold, in this case).

[4] Note that the terms *American* and *European* do not refer to the location of the option or the exchange. Some options trading on North American exchanges are European.

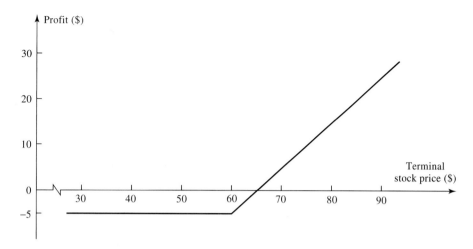

**Figure 1.2** Profit from buying a European call option on one Microsoft share.
Option price = $5; strike price = $60

the option is in four months, and the price of an option to purchase one share is $5. The initial investment is $500. Because the option is European, the investor can exercise only on the expiration date. If the stock price on this date is less than $60, the investor will clearly choose not to exercise. (There is no point in buying, for $60, a share that has a market value of less than $60.) In these circumstances, the investor loses the whole of the initial investment of $500. If the stock price is above $60 on the expiration date, the option will be exercised. Suppose, for example, that the stock price is $75. By exercising the option, the investor is able to buy 100 shares for $60 per share. If the shares are sold immediately, the investor makes a gain of $15 per share, or $1,500, ignoring transactions costs. When the initial cost of the option is taken into account, the net profit to the investor is $1,000.

Figure 1.2 shows how the investor's net profit or loss on an option to purchase one share varies with the final stock price in the example. (We ignore the time value of money in calculating the profit.) It is important to realize that an investor sometimes exercises an option and makes a loss overall. Suppose that in the example Microsoft's stock price is $62 at the expiration of the option. The investor would exercise the option for a gain of $100 \times (\$62 - \$60) = \$200$ and realize a loss overall of $300 when the initial cost of the option is taken into account. It is tempting to argue that the investor should not exercise the option in these circumstances. However, not exercising would lead to an overall loss of $500, which is worse than the $300 loss when the investor exercises. In general, call options should always be exercised at the expiration date if the stock price is above the strike price.

## Put Options

Whereas the purchaser of a call option is hoping that the stock price will increase, the purchaser of a put option is hoping that it will decrease. Consider an investor who buys a European put option to sell 100 shares in IBM with a strike price of $90. Suppose that the current stock price is $85, the expiration date of the option is in three months, and the price of an option to sell one share is $7. The initial investment is $700. Because the option is European, it will be exercised only if the stock price is below $90 at the expiration date. Suppose that the stock price is $75 on this date. The investor can

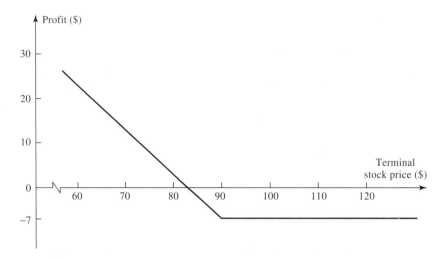

**Figure 1.3**   Profit from buying a European put option on one IBM share.
Option price = $7; strike price = $90

buy 100 shares for $75 per share and, under the terms of the put option, sell the same shares for $90 to realize a gain of $15 per share, or $1,500 (again transactions costs are ignored). When the $700 initial cost of the option is taken into account, the investor's net profit is $800. There is no guarantee that the investor will make a gain. If the final stock price is above $90, the put option expires worthless, and the investor loses $700. Figure 1.3 shows the way in which the investor's profit or loss on an option to sell one share varies with the terminal stock price in this example.

### Early Exercise

As already mentioned, exchange-traded stock options are usually American rather than European. That is, the investor in the foregoing examples would not have to wait until the expiration date before exercising the option. We will see in later chapters that there are some circumstances under which it is optimal to exercise American options prior to maturity.

### Option Positions

There are two sides to every option contract. On one side is the investor who has taken the long position (i.e., has bought the option). On the other side is the investor who has taken a short position (i.e., has sold or *written* the option). The writer of an option receives cash up front, but has potential liabilities later. The writer's profit or loss is the reverse of that for the purchaser of the option. Figures 1.4 and 1.5 show the variation of the profit or loss with the final stock price for writers of the options considered in Figures 1.2 and 1.3.

There are four types of option positions:

1. A long position in a call option.
2. A long position in a put option.
3. A short position in a call option.
4. A short position in a put option.

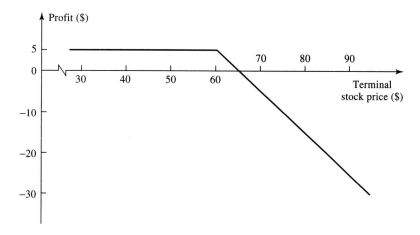

**Figure 1.4**   Profit from writing a European call option on one Microsoft share.
Option price = $5; strike price = $60

It is often useful to characterize European option positions in terms of the terminal value or payoff to the investor at maturity. The initial cost of the option is then not included in the calculation. If $K$ is the strike price and $S_T$ is the final price of the underlying asset, the payoff from a long position in a European call option is

$$\max(S_T - K, 0)$$

This reflects the fact that the option will be exercised if $S_T > K$ and will not be exercised if $S_T \leqslant K$. The payoff to the holder of a short position in the European call option is

$$-\max(S_T - K, 0) = \min(K - S_T, 0)$$

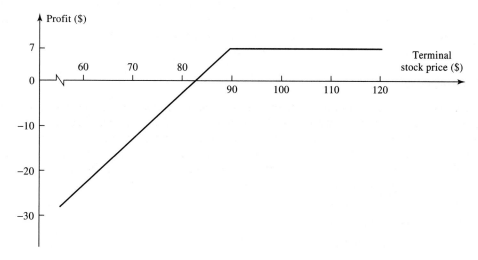

**Figure 1.5**   Profit from writing a European put option on one IBM share.
Option price = $7; strike price = $90

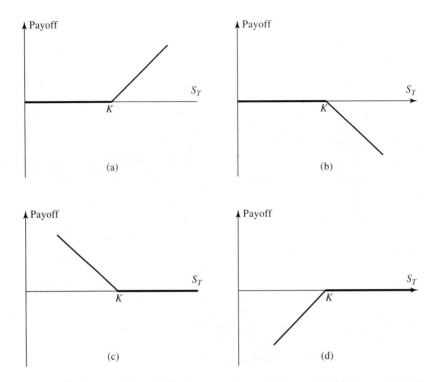

**Figure 1.6** Payoffs from positions in European options: (a) long call, (b) short call, (c) long put, (d) short put. Strike price $= K$; price of asset at maturity $= S_T$

The payoff to the holder of a long position in a European put option is

$$\max(K - S_T, 0)$$

and the payoff from a short position in a European put option is

$$-\max(K - S_T, 0) = \min(S_T - K, 0)$$

Figure 1.6 shows these payoffs.

## 1.6 TYPES OF TRADERS

Derivatives markets have been outstandingly successful. The main reason is that they have attracted many different types of traders and have a great deal of liquidity. When an investor wants to take one side of a contract, there is usually no problem in finding someone that is prepared to take the other side.

Three broad categories of traders can be identified: hedgers, speculators, and arbitrageurs. Hedgers use futures, forwards, and options to reduce the risk that they face from potential future movements in a market variable. Speculators use them to bet on the future direction of a market variable. Arbitrageurs take offsetting positions in two or more instruments to lock in a profit. In the next few sections, we consider the activities of each type of trader in more detail.

## Hedgers

We now illustrate how hedgers can reduce their risks with forward contracts and options.

Suppose that it is August 16, 2001, and ImportCo, a company based in the United States, knows that it will pay £10 million on November 16, 2001, for goods it has purchased from a British supplier. The USD–GBP exchange rate quotes made by a financial institution are given in Table 1.1. ImportCo could hedge its foreign exchange risk by buying pounds (GBP) from the financial institution in the three-month forward market at 1.4407. This would have the effect of fixing the price to be paid to the British exporter at $14,407,000.

Consider next another U.S. company, which we will refer to as ExportCo, that is exporting goods to the United Kingdom and on August 16, 2001, knows that it will receive £30 million three months later. ExportCo can hedge its foreign exchange risk by selling £30 million in the three-month forward market at an exchange rate of 1.4402. This would have the effect of locking in the U.S. dollars to be realized for the sterling at $43,206,000.

Note that if the companies choose not to hedge they might do better than if they do hedge. Alternatively, they might do worse. Consider ImportCo. If the exchange rate is 1.4000 on November 16 and the company has not hedged, the £10 million that it has to pay will cost $14,000,000, which is less than $14,407,000. On the other hand, if the exchange rate is 1.5000, the £10 million will cost $15,000,000—and the company will wish it had hedged! The position of ExportCo if it does not hedge is the reverse. If the exchange rate in September proves to be less than 1.4402, the company will wish it had hedged; if the rate is greater than 1.4402, it will be pleased it had not done so.

This example illustrates a key aspect of hedging. The cost of, or price received for, the underlying asset is ensured. However, there is no assurance that the outcome with hedging will be better than the outcome without hedging.

Options can also be used for hedging. Consider an investor who in May 2000 owns 1,000 Microsoft shares. The current share price is $73 per share. The investor is concerned that the developments in Microsoft's antitrust case may cause the share price to decline sharply in the next two months and wants protection. The investor could buy 10 July put option contracts with a strike price of $65 on the Chicago Board Options Exchange. This would give the investor the right to sell 1,000 shares for $65 per share. If the quoted option price is $2.50, each option contract would cost $100 \times \$2.50 = \$250$, and the total cost of the hedging strategy would be $10 \times \$250 = \$2,500$.

The strategy costs $2,500 but guarantees that the shares can be sold for at least $65 per share during the life of the option. If the market price of Microsoft falls below $65, the options can be exercised so that $65,000 is realized for the entire holding. When the cost of the options is taken into account, the amount realized is $62,500. If the market price stays above $65, the options are not exercised and expire worthless. However, in this case the value of the holding is always above $65,000 (or above $62,500 when the cost of the options is taken into account).

There is a fundamental difference between the use of forward contracts and options for hedging. Forward contracts are designed to neutralize risk by fixing the price that the hedger will pay or receive for the underlying asset. Option contracts, by contrast, provide insurance. They offer a way for investors to protect themselves against adverse price movements in the future while still allowing them to benefit from favorable price movements. Unlike forwards, options involve the payment of an up-front fee.

## Speculators

We now move on to consider how futures and options markets can be used by speculators. Whereas hedgers want to avoid an exposure to adverse movements in the price of an asset, speculators wish to take a position in the market. Either they are betting that the price will go up or they are betting that it will go down.

Consider a U.S. speculator who in February thinks that the British pound will strengthen relative to the U.S. dollar over the next two months and is prepared to back that hunch to the tune of £250,000. One thing the speculator can do is simply purchase £250,000 in the hope that the sterling can be sold later at a profit. The sterling once purchased would be kept in an interest-bearing account. Another possibility is to take a long position in four CME April futures contracts on sterling. (Each futures contract is for the purchase of £62,500.) Suppose that the current exchange rate is 1.6470 and the April futures price is 1.6410. If the exchange rate turns out to be 1.7000 in April, the futures contract alternative enables the speculator to realize a profit of $(1.7000 - 1.6410) \times 250,000 = \$14,750$. The cash market alternative leads to an asset being purchased for 1.6470 in February and sold for 1.7000 in April, so that a profit of $(1.7000 - 1.6470) \times 250,000 = \$13,250$ is made. If the exchange rate falls to 1.6000, the futures contract gives rise to a $(1.6410 - 1.6000) \times 250,000 = \$10,250$ loss, whereas the cash market alternative gives rise to a loss of $(1.6470 - 1.6000) \times 250,000 = \$11,750$. The alternatives appear to give rise to slightly different profits and losses. But these calculations do not reflect the interest that is earned or paid. It will be shown in Chapter 3 that when the interest earned in sterling and the interest paid in dollars are taken into account, the profit or loss from the two alternatives is the same.

What then is the difference between the two alternatives? The first alternative of buying sterling requires an up-front investment of \$411,750. As we will see in Chapter 2, the second alternative requires only a small amount of cash—perhaps \$25,000—to be deposited by the speculator in what is termed a margin account. The futures market allows the speculator to obtain leverage. With a relatively small initial outlay, the investor is able to take a large speculative position.

We consider next an example of how a speculator could use options. Suppose that it is October and a speculator considers that Cisco is likely to increase in value over the next two months. The stock price is currently \$20, and a two-month call option with a \$25 strike price is currently selling for \$1. Table 1.2 illustrates two possible alternatives assuming that the speculator is willing to invest \$4,000. The first alternative involves the purchase of 200 shares. The second involves the purchase of 4,000 call options (i.e., 20 call option contracts).

Suppose that the speculator's hunch is correct and the price of Cisco's shares rises to \$35 by December. The first alternative of buying the stock yields a profit of

$$200 \times (\$35 - \$20) = \$3,000$$

However, the second alternative is far more profitable. A call option on Cisco with a strike price

**Table 1.2**  Comparison of profits (losses) from two alternative strategies for using \$4,000 to speculate on Cisco stock in October

|                       | *December stock price* |           |
| --------------------- | :--------------------: | :-------: |
| *Investor's strategy* |          *$15*         |   *$35*   |
| Buy shares            |        ($1,000)        |  $3,000   |
| Buy call options      |        ($4,000)        |  $36,000  |

of $25 gives a payoff of $10, because it enables something worth $35 to be bought for $25. The total payoff from the 4,000 options that are purchased under the second alternative is

$$4{,}000 \times \$10 = \$40{,}000$$

Subtracting the original cost of the options yields a net profit of

$$\$40{,}000 - \$4{,}000 = \$36{,}000$$

The options strategy is, therefore, 12 times as profitable as the strategy of buying the stock.

Options also give rise to a greater potential loss. Suppose the stock price falls to $15 by December. The first alternative of buying stock yields a loss of

$$200 \times (\$20 - \$15) = \$1{,}000$$

Because the call options expire without being exercised, the options strategy would lead to a loss of $4,000—the original amount paid for the options.

It is clear from Table 1.2 that options like futures provide a form of leverage. For a given investment, the use of options magnifies the financial consequences. Good outcomes become very good, while bad outcomes become very bad!

Futures and options are similar instruments for speculators in that they both provide a way in which a type of leverage can be obtained. However, there is an important difference between the two. With futures the speculator's potential loss as well as the potential gain is very large. With options no matter how bad things get, the speculator's loss is limited to the amount paid for the options.

### *Arbitrageurs*

Arbitrageurs are a third important group of participants in futures, forward, and options markets. Arbitrage involves locking in a riskless profit by simultaneously entering into transactions in two or more markets. In later chapters we will see how arbitrage is sometimes possible when the futures price of an asset gets out of line with its cash price. We will also examine how arbitrage can be used in options markets. This section illustrates the concept of arbitrage with a very simple example.

Consider a stock that is traded on both the New York Stock Exchange (www.nyse.com) and the London Stock Exchange (www.stockex.co.uk). Suppose that the stock price is $152 in New York and £100 in London at a time when the exchange rate is $1.5500 per pound. An arbitrageur could simultaneously buy 100 shares of the stock in New York and sell them in London to obtain a risk-free profit of

$$100 \times [(\$1.55 \times 100) - \$152]$$

or $300 in the absence of transactions costs. Transactions costs would probably eliminate the profit for a small investor. However, a large investment house faces very low transactions costs in both the stock market and the foreign exchange market. It would find the arbitrage opportunity very attractive and would try to take as much advantage of it as possible.

Arbitrage opportunities such as the one just described cannot last for long. As arbitrageurs buy the stock in New York, the forces of supply and demand will cause the dollar price to rise. Similarly, as they sell the stock in London, the sterling price will be driven down. Very quickly the two prices will become equivalent at the current exchange rate. Indeed, the existence of profit-hungry arbitrageurs makes it unlikely that a major disparity between the sterling price and the dollar price could ever exist in the first place. Generalizing from this example, we can say that the very existence of arbitrageurs means that in practice only very small arbitrage opportunities are observed in the prices that are quoted in most financial markets. In this book most of the arguments concerning futures prices, forward prices, and the values of option contracts will be based on the assumption that there are no arbitrage opportunities.

## 1.7   OTHER DERIVATIVES

The call and put options we have considered so far are sometimes termed "plain vanilla" or "standard" derivatives. Since the early 1980s, banks and other financial institutions have been very imaginative in designing nonstandard derivatives to meet the needs of clients. Sometimes these are sold by financial institutions to their corporate clients in the over-the-counter market. On other occasions, they are added to bond or stock issues to make these issues more attractive to investors. Some nonstandard derivatives are simply portfolios of two or more "plain vanilla" call and put options. Others are far more complex. The possibilities for designing new interesting nonstandard derivatives seem to be almost limitless. Nonstandard derivatives are sometimes termed *exotic options* or just *exotics*. In Chapter 19 we discuss different types of exotics and consider how they can be valued.

We now give examples of three derivatives that, although they appear to be complex, can be decomposed into portfolios of plain vanilla call and put options.[5]

> **Example 1.1: Standard Oil's Bond Issue**   A bond issue by Standard Oil worked as follows. The holder received no interest. At the bond's maturity the company promised to pay $1,000 plus an additional amount based on the price of oil at that time. The additional amount was equal to the product of 170 and the excess (if any) of the price of a barrel of oil at maturity over $25. The maximum additional amount paid was $2,550 (which corresponds to a price of $40 per barrel). These bonds provided holders with a stake in a commodity that was critically important to the fortunes of the company. If the price of the commodity went up, the company was in a good position to provide the bondholder with the additional payment.

> **Example 1.2: ICON**   In the 1980s, Bankers Trust developed *index currency option notes* (ICONs). These are bonds in which the amount received by the holder at maturity varies with a foreign exchange rate. Two exchange rates, $K_1$ and $K_2$, are specified with $K_1 > K_2$. If the exchange rate at the bond's maturity is above $K_1$, the bondholder receives the full face value. If it is less than $K_2$, the bondholder receives nothing. Between $K_2$ and $K_1$, a portion of the full face value is received. Bankers Trust's first issue of an ICON was for the Long Term Credit Bank of Japan. The ICON specified that if the yen–USD exchange rate, $S_T$, is greater than 169 yen per dollar at maturity (in 1995), the holder of the bond receives $1,000. If it is less than 169 yen per dollar, the amount received by the holder of the bond is
> $$1,000 - \max\left[0,\ 1,000\left(\frac{169}{S_T} - 1\right)\right]$$
> When the exchange rate is below 84.5, nothing is received by the holder at maturity.

> **Example 1.3: Range Forward Contract**   Range forward contracts (also known as flexible forwards) are popular in foreign exchange markets. Suppose that on August 16, 2001, a U.S. company finds that it will require sterling in three months and faces the exchange rates given in Table 1.1. It

---

[5] See Problems 1.24, 1.25, and 1.30 at the end of this chapter for how the decomposition is accomplished.

could enter into a three-month forward contract to buy at 1.4407. A range forward contract is an alternative. Under this contract an exchange rate band straddling 1.4407 is set. Suppose that the chosen band runs from 1.4200 to 1.4600. The range forward contract is then designed to ensure that if the spot rate in three months is less than 1.4200, the company pays 1.4200; if it is between 1.4200 and 1.4600, the company pays the spot rate; if it is greater than 1.4600, the company pays 1.4600.

### Other, More Complex Examples

As mentioned earlier, there is virtually no limit to the innovations that are possible in the derivatives area. Some of the options traded in the over-the-counter market have payoffs dependent on maximum value attained by a variable during a period of time; some have payoffs dependent on the average value of a variable during a period of time; some have exercise prices that are functions of time; some have features where exercising one option automatically gives the holder another option; some have payoffs dependent on the square of a future interest rate; and so on.

Traditionally, the variables underlying options and other derivatives have been stock prices, stock indices, interest rates, exchange rates, and commodity prices. However, other underlying variables are becoming increasingly common. For example, the payoffs from *credit derivatives*, which are discussed in Chapter 27, depend on the creditworthiness of one or more companies; *weather derivatives* have payoffs dependent on the average temperature at particular locations; *insurance derivatives* have payoffs dependent on the dollar amount of insurance claims of a specified type made during a specified period; *electricity derivatives* have payoffs dependent on the spot price of electricity; and so on. Chapter 29 discusses weather, insurance, and energy derivatives.

## SUMMARY

One of the exciting developments in finance over the last 25 years has been the growth of derivatives markets. In many situations, both hedgers and speculators find it more attractive to trade a derivative on an asset than to trade the asset itself. Some derivatives are traded on exchanges. Others are traded by financial institutions, fund managers, and corporations in the over-the-counter market, or added to new issues of debt and equity securities. Much of this book is concerned with the valuation of derivatives. The aim is to present a unifying framework within which all derivatives—not just options or futures—can be valued.

In this chapter we have taken a first look at forward, futures, and options contracts. A forward or futures contract involves an obligation to buy or sell an asset at a certain time in the future for a certain price. There are two types of options: calls and puts. A call option gives the holder the right to buy an asset by a certain date for a certain price. A put option gives the holder the right to sell an asset by a certain date for a certain price. Forwards, futures, and options trade on a wide range of different underlying assets.

Derivatives have been very successful innovations in capital markets. Three main types of traders can be identified: hedgers, speculators, and arbitrageurs. Hedgers are in the position where they face risk associated with the price of an asset. They use derivatives to reduce or eliminate this risk. Speculators wish to bet on future movements in the price of an asset. They use derivatives to get extra leverage. Arbitrageurs are in business to take advantage of a discrepancy between prices in two different markets. If, for example, they see the futures price of an asset getting out of line with the cash price, they will take offsetting positions in the two markets to lock in a profit.

# QUESTIONS AND PROBLEMS
## (ANSWERS IN SOLUTIONS MANUAL)

1.1. What is the difference between a long forward position and a short forward position?

1.2. Explain carefully the difference between hedging, speculation, and arbitrage.

1.3. What is the difference between entering into a long forward contract when the forward price is $50 and taking a long position in a call option with a strike price of $50?

1.4. Explain carefully the difference between writing a call option and buying a put option.

1.5. A trader enters into a short forward contract on 100 million yen. The forward exchange rate is $0.0080 per yen. How much does the trader gain or lose if the exchange rate at the end of the contract is (a) $0.0074 per yen; (b) $0.0091 per yen?

1.6. A trader enters into a short cotton futures contract when the futures price is 50 cents per pound. The contract is for the delivery of 50,000 pounds. How much does the trader gain or lose if the cotton price at the end of the contract is (a) 48.20 cents per pound; (b) 51.30 cents per pound?

1.7. Suppose that you write a put contract on AOL Time Warner with a strike price of $40 and an expiration date in three months. The current stock price of AOL Time Warner is $41 and the contract is on 100 shares. What have you committed yourself to? How much could you gain or lose?

1.8. You would like to speculate on a rise in the price of a certain stock. The current stock price is $29, and a three-month call with a strike of $30 costs $2.90. You have $5,800 to invest. Identify two alternative strategies, one involving an investment in the stock and the other involving investment in the option. What are the potential gains and losses from each?

1.9. Suppose that you own 5,000 shares worth $25 each. How can put options be used to provide you with insurance against a decline in the value of your holding over the next four months?

1.10. A trader buys a European put on a share for $3. The stock price is $42 and the strike price is $40. Under what circumstances does the trader make a profit? Under what circumstances will the option be exercised? Draw a diagram showing the variation of the trader's profit with the stock price at the maturity of the option.

1.11. A trader sells a European call on a share for $4. The stock price is $47 and the strike price is $50. Under what circumstances does the trader make a profit? Under what circumstances will the option be exercised? Draw a diagram showing the variation of the trader's profit with the stock price at the maturity of the option.

1.12. A trader buys a call option with a strike price of $45 and a put option with a strike price of $40. Both options have the same maturity. The call costs $3 and the put costs $4. Draw a diagram showing the variation of the trader's profit with the asset price.

1.13. When first issued, a stock provides funds for a company. Is the same true of a stock option? Discuss.

1.14. Explain why a forward contract can be used for either speculation or hedging.

1.15. Suppose that a March call option to buy a share for $50 costs $2.50 and is held until March. Under what circumstances will the holder of the option make a profit? Under what circumstances will the option be exercised? Draw a diagram illustrating how the profit from a long position in the option depends on the stock price at maturity of the option.

1.16. Suppose that a June put option to sell a share for $60 costs $4 and is held until June. Under what circumstances will the seller of the option (i.e., the party with the short position) make a profit? Under what circumstances will the option be exercised? Draw a diagram illustrating how the profit from a short position in the option depends on the stock price at maturity of the option.

1.17. A trader writes a September call option with a strike price of $20. It is now May, the stock price is $18, and the option price is $2. Describe the trader's cash flows if the option is held until September and the stock price is $25 at that time.

1.18. A trader writes a December put option with a strike price of $30. The price of the option is $4. Under what circumstances does the trader make a gain?

1.19. A company knows that it is due to receive a certain amount of a foreign currency in four months. What type of option contract is appropriate for hedging?

1.20. A United States company expects to have to pay 1 million Canadian dollars in six months. Explain how the exchange rate risk can be hedged using (a) a forward contract; (b) an option.

1.21. The Chicago Board of Trade offers a futures contract on long-term Treasury bonds. Characterize the traders likely to use this contract.

1.22. "Options and futures are zero-sum games." What do you think is meant by this statement?

1.23. Describe the profit from the following portfolio: a long forward contract on an asset and a long European put option on the asset with the same maturity as the forward contract and a strike price that is equal to the forward price of the asset at the time the portfolio is set up.

1.24. Show that an ICON such as the one described in Section 1.7 is a combination of a regular bond and two options.

1.25. Show that a range forward contract such as the one described in Section 1.7 is a combination of two options. How can a range forward contract be constructed so that it has zero value?

1.26. On July 1, 2002, a company enters into a forward contract to buy 10 million Japanese yen on January 1, 2003. On September 1, 2002, it enters into a forward contract to sell 10 million Japanese yen on January 1, 2003. Describe the payoff from this strategy.

1.27. Suppose that sterling–USD spot and forward exchange rates are as follows:

   Spot                1.6080
   90-day forward   1.6056
   180-day forward  1.6018

   What opportunities are open to an arbitrageur in the following situations?
   a. A 180-day European call option to buy £1 for $1.57 costs 2 cents.
   b. A 90-day European put option to sell £1 for $1.64 costs 2 cents.

## ASSIGNMENT QUESTIONS

1.28. The price of gold is currently $500 per ounce. The forward price for delivery in one year is $700. An arbitrageur can borrow money at 10% per annum. What should the arbitrageur do? Assume that the cost of storing gold is zero and that gold provides no income.

1.29. The current price of a stock is $94, and three-month call options with a strike price of $95 currently sell for $4.70. An investor who feels that the price of the stock will increase is trying to decide between buying 100 shares and buying 2,000 call options (= 20 contracts). Both strategies involve an investment of $9,400. What advice would you give? How high does the stock price have to rise for the option strategy to be more profitable?

1.30. Show that the Standard Oil bond described in Section 1.7 is a combination of a regular bond, a long position in call options on oil with a strike price of $25, and a short position in call options on oil with a strike price of $40.

1.31. Use the DerivaGem software to calculate the value of the range forward contract considered in Section 1.7 on the assumption that the exchange rate volatility is 15% per annum. Adjust the upper end of the band so that the contract has zero value initially. Assume that the dollar and sterling risk-free rates are 5.0% and 6.4% per annum, respectively.

1.32. A trader owns gold as part of a long-term investment portfolio. The trader can buy gold for $250 per ounce and sell gold for $249 per ounce. The trader can borrow funds at 6% per year and invest funds at 5.5% per year. (Both interest rates are expressed with annual compounding.) For what range of one-year forward prices of gold does the trader have no arbitrage opportunities? Assume there is no bid–offer spread for forward prices.

1.33. Describe how foreign currency options can be used for hedging in the situation considered in Section 1.6 so that (a) ImportCo is guaranteed that its exchange rate will be less than 1.4600, and (b) ExportCo is guaranteed that its exchange rate will be at least 1.4200. Use DerivaGem to calculate the cost of setting up the hedge in each case assuming that the exchange rate volatility is 12%, interest rates in the United States are 3% and interest rates in Britain are 4.4%. Assume that the current exchange rate is the average of the bid and offer in Table 1.1.

1.34. A trader buys a European call option and sells a European put option. The options have the same underlying asset, strike price and maturity. Describe the trader's position. Under what circumstances does the price of the call equal the price of the put?

# CHAPTER 2

# MECHANICS OF FUTURES MARKETS

In Chapter 1 we explained that both futures and forward contracts are agreements to buy or sell an asset at a future time for a certain price. Futures contracts are traded on an organized exchange, and the contract terms are standardized by that exchange. By contrast, forward contracts are private agreements between two financial institutions or between a financial institution and one of its corporate clients.

This chapter covers the details of how futures markets work. We examine issues such as the specification of contracts, the operation of margin accounts, the organization of exchanges, the regulation of markets, the way in which quotes are made, and the treatment of futures transactions for accounting and tax purposes. We also examine forward contracts and explain the difference between the pattern of payoffs realized from futures and forward contracts.

## 2.1 TRADING FUTURES CONTRACTS

As mentioned in Chapter 1, futures contracts are now traded very actively all over the world. The two largest futures exchanges in the United States are the Chicago Board of Trade (CBOT, www.cbot.com) and the Chicago Mercantile Exchange (CME, www.cme.com). The two largest exchanges in Europe are the London International Financial Futures and Options Exchange (www.liffe.com) and Eurex (www.eurexchange.com). Other large exchanges include Bolsa de Mercadorias y Futuros (www.bmf.com.br) in São Paulo, the Tokyo International Financial Futures Exchange (www.tiffe.or.jp), the Singapore International Monetary Exchange (www.simex.com.sg), and the Sydney Futures Exchange (www.sfe.com.au). For a more complete list, see the table at the end of this book.

We examine how a futures contract comes into existence by considering the corn futures contract traded on the Chicago Board of Trade (CBOT). On March 5, an investor in New York might call a broker with instructions to buy 5,000 bushels of corn for delivery in July of the same year. The broker would immediately pass these instructions on to a trader on the floor of the CBOT. The broker would request a long position in one contract because each corn contract on the CBOT is for the delivery of exactly 5,000 bushels. At about the same time, another investor in Kansas might instruct a broker to sell 5,000 bushels of corn for July delivery. This broker would then pass instructions to short one contract to a trader on the floor of the CBOT. The two

**19**

floor traders would meet, agree on a price to be paid for the corn in July, and the deal would be done.

The investor in New York who agreed to buy has a *long futures position* in one contract; the investor in Kansas who agreed to sell has a *short futures position* in one contract. The price agreed to on the floor of the exchange is the current *futures price* for July corn. We will suppose the price is 170 cents per bushel. This price, like any other price, is determined by the laws of supply and demand. If at a particular time more traders wish to sell July corn than buy July corn, the price will go down. New buyers then enter the market so that a balance between buyers and sellers is maintained. If more traders wish to buy July corn than to sell July corn, the price goes up. New sellers then enter the market and a balance between buyers and sellers is maintained.

### Closing Out Positions

The vast majority of futures contracts do not lead to delivery. The reason is that most traders choose to close out their positions prior to the delivery period specified in the contract. Closing out a position means entering into the opposite type of trade from the original one. For example the New York investor who bought a July corn futures contract on March 5 can close out the position by selling (i.e., shorting) one July corn futures contract on April 20. The Kansas investor who sold (i.e., shorted) a July contract on March 5 can close out the position on by buying one July contract on April 20. In each case, the investor's total gain or loss is determined by the change in the futures price between March 5 and April 20.

It is important to realize that there is no particular significance to the party on the other side of a trade in a futures transaction. Consider trader A who initiates a long futures position by trading one contract. Suppose that trader B is on the other side of the transaction. At a later stage trader A might close out the position by entering into a short contract. The trader on the other side of this second transaction does not have to be, and usually is not, trader B.

## 2.2 THE SPECIFICATION OF THE FUTURES CONTRACT

When developing a new contract, the exchange must specify in some detail the exact nature of the agreement between the two parties. In particular, it must specify the asset, the contract size (exactly how much of the asset will be delivered under one contract), where delivery will be made, and when delivery will be made.

Sometimes alternatives are specified for the grade of the asset that will be delivered or for the delivery locations. As a general rule, it is the party with the short position (the party that has agreed to sell the asset) that chooses what will happen when alternatives are specified by the exchange. When the party with the short position is ready to deliver, it files a *notice of intention to deliver* with the exchange. This notice indicates selections it has made with respect to the grade of asset that will be delivered and the delivery location.

### The Asset

When the asset is a commodity, there may be quite a variation in the quality of what is available in the marketplace. When the asset is specified, it is therefore important that the exchange stipulate the grade or grades of the commodity that are acceptable. The New York Cotton Exchange has specified the asset in its orange juice futures contract as

> U.S. Grade A, with Brix value of not less than 57 degrees, having a Brix value to acid ratio of not less than 13 to 1 nor more than 19 to 1, with factors of color and flavor each scoring 37 points or higher and 19 for defects, with a minimum score 94.

The Chicago Mercantile Exchange in its random-length lumber futures contract has specified that

> Each delivery unit shall consist of nominal 2×4s of random lengths from 8 feet to 20 feet, grade-stamped Construction and Standard, Standard and Better, or #1 and #2; however, in no case may the quantity of Standard grade or #2 exceed 50%. Each delivery unit shall be manufactured in California, Idaho, Montana, Nevada, Oregon, Washington, Wyoming, or Alberta or British Columbia, Canada, and contain lumber produced from grade-stamped Alpine fir, Englemann spruce, hem-fir, lodgepole pine, and/or spruce pine fir.

For some commodities a range of grades can be delivered, but the price received depends the grade chosen. For example, in the Chicago Board of Trade corn futures contract, the standard grade is "No. 2 Yellow", but substitutions are allowed with the price being adjusted in a way established by the exchange.

The financial assets in futures contracts are generally well defined and unambiguous. For example, there is no need to specify the grade of a Japanese yen. However, there are some interesting features of the Treasury bond and Treasury note futures contracts traded on the Chicago Board of Trade. The underlying asset in the Treasury bond contract is any long-term U.S. Treasury bond that has a maturity of greater than 15 years and is not callable within 15 years. In the Treasury note futures contract, the underlying asset is any long-term Treasury note with a maturity of no less than 6.5 years and no more than 10 years from the date of delivery. In both cases, the exchange has a formula for adjusting the price received according to the coupon and maturity date of the bond delivered. This is discussed in Chapter 5.

## The Contract Size

The contract size specifies the amount of the asset that has to be delivered under one contract. This is an important decision for the exchange. If the contract size is too large, many investors who wish to hedge relatively small exposures or who wish to take relatively small speculative positions will be unable to use the exchange. On the other hand, if the contract size is too small, trading may be expensive as there is a cost associated with each contract traded.

The correct size for a contract clearly depends on the likely user. Whereas the value of what is delivered under a futures contract on an agricultural product might be $10,000 to $20,000, it is much higher for some financial futures. For example, under the Treasury bond futures contract traded on the Chicago Board of Trade, instruments with a face value of $100,000 are delivered.

In some cases exchanges have introduced "mini" contracts to attract smaller investors. For example, the CME's Mini Nasdaq 100 contract is on 20 times the Nasdaq 100 index whereas the regular contract is on 100 times the index.

## Delivery Arrangements

The place where delivery will be made must be specified by the exchange. This is particularly important for commodities that involve significant transportation costs. In the case of the Chicago

Mercantile Exchange's random-length lumber contract, the delivery location is specified as

> On track and shall either be unitized in double-door boxcars or, at no additional cost to the buyer, each unit shall be individually paper-wrapped and loaded on flatcars. Par delivery of hem-fir in California, Idaho, Montana, Nevada, Oregon, and Washington, and in the province of British Columbia.

When alternative delivery locations are specified, the price received by the party with the short position is sometimes adjusted according to the location chosen by that party. For example, in the case of the corn futures contract traded by the Chicago Board of Trade, delivery can be made at Chicago, Burns Harbor, Toledo, or St. Louis. However, deliveries at Toledo and St. Louis are made at a discount of 4 cents per bushel from the Chicago contract price.

### Delivery Months

A futures contract is referred to by its delivery month. The exchange must specify the precise period during the month when delivery can be made. For many futures contracts, the delivery period is the whole month.

The delivery months vary from contract to contract and are chosen by the exchange to meet the needs of market participants. For example, the main delivery months for currency futures on the Chicago Mercantile Exchange are March, June, September, and December; corn futures traded on the Chicago Board of Trade have delivery months of January, March, May, July, September, November, and December. At any given time, contracts trade for the closest delivery month and a number of subsequent delivery months. The exchange specifies when trading in a particular month's contract will begin. The exchange also specifies the last day on which trading can take place for a given contract. Trading generally ceases a few days before the last day on which delivery can be made.

### Price Quotes

The futures price is quoted in a way that is convenient and easy to understand. For example, crude oil futures prices on the New York Mercantile Exchange are quoted in dollars per barrel to two decimal places (i.e., to the nearest cent). Treasury bond and Treasury note futures prices on the Chicago Board of Trade are quoted in dollars and thirty-seconds of a dollar. The minimum price movement that can occur in trading is consistent with the way in which the price is quoted. Thus, it is $0.01 per barrel for the oil futures and one thirty-second of a dollar for the Treasury bond and Treasury note futures.

### Daily Price Movement Limits

For most contracts, daily price movement limits are specified by the exchange. If the price moves down by an amount equal to the daily price limit, the contract is said to be *limit down*. If it moves up by the limit, it is said to be *limit up*. A *limit move* is a move in either direction equal to the daily price limit. Normally, trading ceases for the day once the contract is limit up or limit down. However, in some instances the exchange has the authority to step in and change the limits.

The purpose of daily price limits is to prevent large price movements from occurring because of speculative excesses. However, limits can become an artificial barrier to trading when the price of the underlying commodity is increasing or decreasing rapidly. Whether price limits are, on balance, good for futures markets is controversial.

### Position Limits

Position limits are the maximum number of contracts that a speculator may hold. In the Chicago Mercantile Exchange's random-length lumber contract, for example, the position limit at the time of writing is 1,000 contracts with no more than 300 in any one delivery month. Bona fide hedgers are not affected by position limits. The purpose of the limits is to prevent speculators from exercising undue influence on the market.

## 2.3 CONVERGENCE OF FUTURES PRICE TO SPOT PRICE

As the delivery month of a futures contract is approached, the futures price converges to the spot price of the underlying asset. When the delivery period is reached, the futures price equals—or is very close to—the spot price.

To see why this is so, we first suppose that the futures price is above the spot price during the delivery period. Traders then have a clear arbitrage opportunity:

1. Short a futures contract.
2. Buy the asset.
3. Make delivery.

These steps are certain to lead to a profit equal to the amount by which the futures price exceeds the spot price. As traders exploit this arbitrage opportunity, the futures price will fall. Suppose next that the futures price is below the spot price during the delivery period. Companies interested in acquiring the asset will find it attractive to enter into a long futures contract and then wait for delivery to be made. As they do so, the futures price will tend to rise.

The result is that the futures price is very close to the spot price during the delivery period. Figure 2.1 illustrates the convergence of the futures price to the spot price. In Figure 2.1a the futures price is above the spot price prior to the delivery month, and in Figure 2.1b the futures

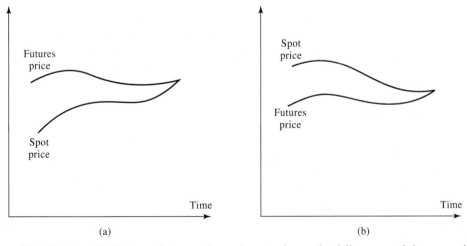

**Figure 2.1**   Relationship between futures price and spot price as the delivery month is approached. (a) Futures price above spot price; (b) futures price below spot price

price is below the spot price prior to the delivery month. The circumstances under which these two patterns are observed are discussed later in this chapter and in Chapter 3.

## 2.4  OPERATION OF MARGINS

If two investors get in touch with each other directly and agree to trade an asset in the future for a certain price, there are obvious risks. One of the investors may regret the deal and try to back out. Alternatively, the investor simply may not have the financial resources to honor the agreement. One of the key roles of the exchange is to organize trading so that contract defaults are avoided. This is where margins come in.

### *Marking to Market*

To illustrate how margins work, we consider an investor who contacts his or her broker on Thursday, June 5 to buy two December gold futures contracts on the New York Commodity Exchange (COMEX). We suppose that the current futures price is $400 per ounce. Because the contract size is 100 ounces, the investor has contracted to buy a total of 200 ounces at this price. The broker will require the investor to deposit funds in a *margin account*. The amount that must be deposited at the time the contract is entered into is known as the *initial margin*. We suppose this is $2,000 per contract, or $4,000 in total. At the end of each trading day, the margin account is adjusted to reflect the investor's gain or loss. This practice is referred to as *marking to market* the account.

Suppose, for example, that by the end of June 5 the futures price has dropped from $400 to $397. The investor has a loss of $600 (= 200 × $3), because the 200 ounces of December gold, which the investor contracted to buy at $400, can now be sold for only $397. The balance in the margin account would therefore be reduced by $600 to $3,400. Similarly, if the price of December gold rose to $403 by the end of the first day, the balance in the margin account would be increased by $600 to $4,600. A trade is first marked to market at the close of the day on which it takes place. It is then marked to market at the close of trading on each subsequent day.

Note that marking to market is not merely an arrangement between broker and client. When there is a decrease in the futures price so that the margin account of an investor with a long position is reduced by $600, the investor's broker has to pay the exchange $600 and the exchange passes the money on to the broker of an investor with a short position. Similarly, when there is an increase in the futures price, brokers for parties with short positions pay money to the exchange and brokers for parties with long positions receive money from the exchange. Later we will examine in more detail the mechanism by which this happens.

The investor is entitled to withdraw any balance in the margin account in excess of the initial margin. To ensure that the balance in the margin account never becomes negative a *maintenance margin*, which is somewhat lower than the initial margin, is set. If the balance in the margin account falls below the maintenance margin, the investor receives a *margin call* and is expected to top up the margin account to the initial margin level the next day. The extra funds deposited are known as a *variation margin*. If the investor does not provide the variation margin, the broker closes out the position by selling the contract. In the case of the investor considered earlier, closing out the position would involve neutralizing the existing contract by selling 200 ounces of gold for delivery in December.

Table 2.1 illustrates the operation of the margin account for one possible sequence of futures

**Table 2.1** Operation of margins for a long position in two gold futures contracts. The initial margin is $2,000 per contract, or $4,000 in total, and the maintenance margin is $1,500 per contract, or $3,000 in total. The contract is entered into on June 5 at $400 and closed out on June 26 at $392.30. The numbers in the second column, except the first and the last, represent the futures prices at the close of trading

| Day | Futures price ($) | Daily gain (loss) ($) | Cumulative gain (loss) ($) | Margin account balance ($) | Margin call ($) |
|---|---|---|---|---|---|
|  | 400.00 |  |  | 4,000 |  |
| June 5 | 397.00 | (600) | (600) | 3,400 |  |
| June 6 | 396.10 | (180) | (780) | 3,220 |  |
| June 9 | 398.20 | 420 | (360) | 3,640 |  |
| June 10 | 397.10 | (220) | (580) | 3,420 |  |
| June 11 | 396.70 | (80) | (660) | 3,340 |  |
| June 12 | 395.40 | (260) | (920) | 3,080 |  |
| June 13 | 393.30 | (420) | (1,340) | 2,660 | 1,340 |
| June 16 | 393.60 | 60 | (1,280) | 4,060 |  |
| June 17 | 391.80 | (360) | (1,640) | 3,700 |  |
| June 18 | 392.70 | 180 | (1,460) | 3,880 |  |
| June 19 | 387.00 | (1,140) | (2,600) | 2,740 | 1,260 |
| June 20 | 387.00 | 0 | (2,600) | 4,000 |  |
| June 23 | 388.10 | 220 | (2,380) | 4,220 |  |
| June 24 | 388.70 | 120 | (2,260) | 4,340 |  |
| June 25 | 391.00 | 460 | (1,800) | 4,800 |  |
| June 26 | 392.30 | 260 | (1,540) | 5,060 |  |

prices in the case of the investor considered earlier. The maintenance margin is assumed for the purpose of the illustration to be $1,500 per contract, or $3,000 in total. On June 13 the balance in the margin account falls $340 below the maintenance margin level. This drop triggers a margin call from the broker for additional $1,340. Table 2.1 assumes that the investor does in fact provide this margin by the close of trading on June 16. On June 19 the balance in the margin account again falls below the maintenance margin level, and a margin call for $1,260 is sent out. The investor provides this margin by the close of trading on June 20. On June 26 the investor decides to close out the position by selling two contracts. The futures price on that day is $392.30, and the investor has a cumulative loss of $1,540. Note that the investor has excess margin on June 16, 23, 24, and 25. Table 2.1 assumes that the excess is not withdrawn.

## Further Details

Many brokers allow an investor to earn interest on the balance in a margin account. The balance in the account does not therefore represent a true cost, provided that the interest rate is competitive with what could be earned elsewhere. To satisfy the initial margin requirements (but not subsequent margin calls), an investor can sometimes deposit securities with the broker. Treasury bills are usually accepted in lieu of cash at about 90% of their face value. Shares are also sometimes accepted in lieu of cash—but at about 50% of their face value.

The effect of the marking to market is that a futures contract is settled daily rather than all at the end of its life. At the end of each day, the investor's gain (loss) is added to (subtracted from) the margin account, bringing the value of the contract back to zero. A futures contract is in effect closed out and rewritten at a new price each day.

Minimum levels for initial and maintenance margins are set by the exchange. Individual brokers may require greater margins from their clients than those specified by the exchange. However, they cannot require lower margins than those specified by the exchange. Margin levels are determined by the variability of the price of the underlying asset. The higher this variability, the higher the margin levels. The maintenance margin is usually about 75% of the initial margin.

Margin requirements may depend on the objectives of the trader. A bona fide hedger, such as a company that produces the commodity on which the futures contract is written, is often subject to lower margin requirements than a speculator. The reason is that there is deemed to be less risk of default. Day trades and spread transactions often give rise to lower margin requirements than do hedge transactions. In a *day trade* the trader announces to the broker an intent to close out the position in the same day. In a *spread transaction* the trader simultaneously takes a long position in a contract on an asset for one maturity month and a short position in a contract on the same asset for another maturity month.

Note that margin requirements are the same on short futures positions as they are on long futures positions. It is just as easy to take a short futures position as it is to take a long one. The spot market does not have this symmetry. Taking a long position in the spot market involves buying the asset for immediate delivery and presents no problems. Taking a short position involves selling an asset that you do not own. This is a more complex transaction that may or may not be possible in a particular market. It is discussed further in the next chapter.

### The Clearinghouse and Clearing Margins

The *exchange clearinghouse* is an adjunct of the exchange and acts as an intermediary in futures transactions. It guarantees the performance of the parties to each transaction. The clearinghouse has a number of members. Brokers who are not clearinghouse members themselves must channel their business through a member. The main task of the clearinghouse is to keep track of all the transactions that take place during a day so that it can calculate the net position of each of its members.

Just as an investor is required to maintain a margin account with a broker, a clearinghouse member is required to maintain a margin account with the clearinghouse. This is known as a *clearing margin*. The margin accounts for clearinghouse members are adjusted for gains and losses at the end of each trading day in the same way as are the margin accounts of investors. However, in the case of the clearinghouse member, there is an original margin, but no maintenance margin. Every day the account balance for each contract must be maintained at an amount equal to the original margin times the number of contracts outstanding. Thus, depending on transactions during the day and price movements, the clearinghouse member may have to add funds to its margin account at the end of the day. Alternatively, it may find it can remove funds from the account at this time. Brokers who are not clearinghouse members must maintain a margin account with a clearinghouse member.

In determining clearing margins, the exchange clearinghouse calculates the number of contracts outstanding on either a gross or a net basis. The *gross basis* simply adds the total of all long positions entered into by clients to the total of all the short positions entered into by clients. The *net basis* allows these to be offset against each other. Suppose a clearinghouse member has two clients: one with a long position in 20 contracts, the other with a short position in 15 contracts.

Gross margining would calculate the clearing margin on the basis of 35 contracts; net margining would calculate the clearing margin on the basis of 5 contracts. Most exchanges currently use net margining.

It should be stressed that the whole purpose of the margining system is to reduce the possibility of market participants sustaining losses because of defaults. Overall the system has been very successful. Losses arising from defaults in contracts at major exchanges have been almost nonexistent.

## 2.5 NEWSPAPER QUOTES

Many newspapers carry futures quotations. The *Wall Street Journal*'s futures quotations can currently be found in the Money and Investing section. Table 2.2 shows the quotations for commodities as they appeared in the *Wall Street Journal* of Friday, March 16, 2001. The quotes refer to the trading that took place on the previous day (i.e., Thursday, March 15, 2001). The quotations for index futures and currency futures are given in Chapter 3. The quotations for interest rate futures are given in Chapter 5.

The asset underlying the futures contract, the exchange that the contract is traded on, the contract size, and how the price is quoted are all shown at the top of each section in Table 2.2. The first asset is corn, traded on the Chicago Board of Trade. The contract size is 5,000 bushels, and the price is quoted in cents per bushel. The months in which particular contracts are traded are shown in the first column. Corn contracts with maturities in May 2001, July 2001, September 2001, December 2001, March 2002, May 2002, July 2002, and December 2002 were traded on March 15, 2001.

### Prices

The first three numbers in each row show the opening price, the highest price achieved in trading during the day, and the lowest price achieved in trading during the day. The opening price is representative of the prices at which contracts were trading immediately after the opening bell. For May 2001 corn on March 15, 2001, the opening price was $217\frac{1}{2}$ cents per bushel and, during the day, the price traded between $210\frac{1}{2}$ and $217\frac{3}{4}$ cents.

### Settlement Price

The fourth number is the *settlement price*. This is the average of the prices at which the contract traded immediately before the bell signaling the end of trading for the day. The fifth number is the change in the settlement price from the previous day. In the case of the May 2001 corn futures contract, the settlement price was $210\frac{3}{4}$ cents on March 15, 2001, down 7 cents from March 14, 2001.

The settlement price is important, because it is used for calculating daily gains and losses and margin requirements. In the case of the May 2001 corn futures, an investor with a long position in one contract would find his or her margin account balance reduced by $350 (= 5,000 × 7 cents) between March 14, 2001, and March 15, 2001. Similarly, an investor with a short position in one contract would find that the margin balance increased by $350 between these two dates.

**Table 2.2**  Commodity futures quotes from the *Wall Street Journal* on March 16, 2001

# FUTURES PRICES

Thursday, March 15, 2001

**Open Interest Reflects Previous Trading Day.**

## GRAINS AND OILSEEDS

| | OPEN | HIGH | LOW | SETTLE | CHANGE | LIFETIME HIGH | LIFETIME LOW | OPEN INT. |
|---|---|---|---|---|---|---|---|---|
| **Corn (CBT) 5,000 bu.; cents per bu.** | | | | | | | | |
| May | 217½ | 217¾ | 210½ | 210¾ | − 7 | 282½ | 206½ | 186,129 |
| July | 225¼ | 225½ | 218¼ | 218¾ | − 6¾ | 287½ | 213½ | 109,750 |
| Sept | 233½ | 233½ | 226½ | 226¾ | − 7 | 276½ | 219¾ | 29,131 |
| Dec | 244½ | 244¾ | 237¼ | 237¾ | − 7 | 275 | 229¼ | 86,793 |
| Mr02 | 253¾ | 253¾ | 246¾ | 247 | − 6¾ | 270 | 246¾ | 10,285 |
| May | 258 | 259 | 253½ | 254 | − 6¼ | 266½ | 253½ | 2,165 |
| July | 263¼ | 263¾ | 257 | 257¼ | − 7 | 279½ | 242 | 2,621 |
| Dec | 263½ | 264 | 257½ | 258½ | − 6 | 272 | 245 | 3,686 |
| Est vol 103,000; vol Wed 60,060; open int 431,377, +1,845. | | | | | | | | |
| **Oats (CBT) 5,000 bu.; cents per bu.** | | | | | | | | |
| May | 108¾ | 109 | 105 | 106 | − 3¼ | 140½ | 104¼ | 9,145 |
| July | 112½ | 113 | 109¼ | 110½ | − 2½ | 131¾ | 109¼ | 3,936 |
| Sept | 113½ | 115 | 112½ | 113¼ | − 2¼ | 136½ | 112½ | 693 |
| Dec | 121¼ | 122 | 118 | 119¼ | − 2¾ | 140½ | 118 | 1,838 |
| Est vol 1,607; vol Wed 1,000; open int 15,690, +99. | | | | | | | | |
| **Soybeans (CBT) 5,000 bu.; cents per bu.** | | | | | | | | |
| May | 444 | 447¼ | 438 | 445½ | + 1½ | 604 | 438 | 71,060 |
| July | 451½ | 454 | 444 | 451¾ | + ½ | 609 | 444 | 42,238 |
| Aug | 451 | 454 | 444 | 450 | − 1 | 549 | 444 | 5,244 |
| Sept | 449½ | 451 | 441½ | 447½ | − 1¼ | 549 | 441½ | 4,018 |
| Nov | 453¾ | 455¾ | 446 | 451½ | − 2¼ | 605 | 446 | 22,257 |
| Ja02 | 463½ | 464½ | 455 | 460 | − 2½ | 537½ | 455 | 1,284 |
| Mar | 472 | 473 | 464½ | 468½ | − 3 | 546 | 464½ | 682 |
| July | 486½ | 487 | 479 | 484 | − 1 | 521 | 479 | 184 |
| Est vol 52,000; vol Wed 58,491; open int 147,411, −1,855. | | | | | | | | |
| **Soybean Meal (CBT) 100 tons; $ per ton.** | | | | | | | | |
| May | 149.90 | 152.00 | 149.50 | 151.90 | + 2.00 | 189.50 | 149.50 | 42,273 |
| July | 149.50 | 151.00 | 148.90 | 150.90 | + 1.50 | 190.00 | 148.90 | 24,434 |
| Aug | 149.40 | 149.70 | 148.10 | 149.60 | + 1.00 | 190.40 | 148.10 | 8,937 |
| Sept | 148.00 | 148.50 | 147.10 | 148.30 | + .70 | 182.80 | 147.10 | 6,311 |
| Oct | 147.90 | 148.00 | 146.30 | 147.30 | + .40 | 181.00 | 146.30 | 4,829 |
| Dec | 148.20 | 148.50 | 146.50 | 147.40 | .... | 180.00 | 146.50 | 13,704 |
| Ja02 | 148.50 | 149.30 | 147.00 | 147.70 | + .20 | 166.50 | 147.00 | 1,305 |
| Mar | 149.50 | 150.00 | 149.00 | 149.60 | + .10 | 166.50 | 149.00 | 540 |
| Est vol 16,500; vol Wed 29,151; open int 102,761, +492. | | | | | | | | |
| **Soybean Oil (CBT) 60,000 lbs.; cents per lb.** | | | | | | | | |
| May | 16.20 | 16.33 | 15.81 | 16.08 | − .11 | 20.68 | 14.72 | 55,792 |
| July | 16.55 | 16.69 | 16.15 | 16.43 | − .12 | 20.95 | 15.11 | 34,729 |
| Aug | 16.74 | 16.85 | 16.34 | 16.56 | − .13 | 20.98 | 15.30 | 8,309 |
| Sept | 16.99 | 16.99 | 16.50 | 16.72 | − .13 | 21.15 | 15.46 | 4,603 |
| Oct | 17.08 | 17.15 | 16.70 | 16.91 | − .17 | 20.35 | 15.68 | 5,260 |
| Dec | 17.33 | 17.47 | 16.95 | 17.27 | − .11 | 21.25 | 16.00 | 11,627 |
| Ja02 | 17.72 | 17.72 | 17.20 | 17.43 | − .12 | 17.88 | 16.25 | 2,151 |
| Mar | 18.03 | 18.03 | 17.50 | 17.70 | − .15 | 18.10 | 16.58 | 1,109 |
| May | .... | .... | .... | 18.00 | − .05 | 17.45 | 17.30 | 183 |
| Est vol 21,000; vol Wed 29,106; open int 124,025, −384. | | | | | | | | |
| **Wheat (CBT) 5,000 bu.; cents per bu.** | | | | | | | | |
| May | 284¾ | 285 | 271½ | 273¾ | − 10 | 326 | 268 | 70,515 |
| July | 294½ | 295¼ | 282½ | 284¾ | − 9½ | 350 | 279¼ | 47,305 |
| Sept | 305 | 305 | 292½ | 295 | − 9 | 325 | 285 | 5,420 |
| Dec | 318½ | 318½ | 307 | 309½ | − 9 | 343 | 253 | 9,840 |
| Mr02 | 329 | 329 | 318½ | 320 | − 9 | 346 | 316 | 1,416 |
| July | 334 | 334 | 325 | 327 | − 7 | 355 | 320 | 960 |
| Dec | 347 | 347 | 338 | 340 | − 8 | 365 | 331 | 294 |
| Est vol 37,000; vol Wed 27,019; open int 135,866, +2,686. | | | | | | | | |
| **Wheat (KC) 5,000 bu.; cents per bu.** | | | | | | | | |
| Mar | .... | .... | .... | 314 | − 7 | 349 | 301 | 372 |
| May | 329¾ | 330¼ | 318½ | 320¼ | − 9 | 352½ | 310 | 31,260 |
| July | 339½ | 340¼ | 328¾ | 330¼ | − 9 | 359 | 317 | 31,275 |
| Sept | 349 | 349 | 338½ | 340 | − 9 | 365½ | 328½ | 2,798 |
| Dec | 360 | 360 | 341 | 351½ | − 8½ | 375 | 339½ | 3,154 |
| Mr02 | 369 | 369 | 360 | 361 | − 9 | 383 | 353 | 565 |
| Est vol 8,418; vol Wed 7,384; open int 69,478, −669. | | | | | | | | |
| **Wheat (MPLS) 5,000 bu.; cents per bu.** | | | | | | | | |
| Mar | .... | .... | .... | 330 | − 1 | 375½ | 299 | 7 |
| May | 335 | 335½ | 325 | 328 | − 6½ | 379 | 319¾ | 14,278 |
| July | 342¾ | 343 | 332½ | 335¾ | − 6½ | 381 | 327 | 10,508 |
| Sept | 350½ | 350¾ | 341 | 343 | − 6¾ | 391 | 335½ | 1,720 |
| Dec | 361 | 361 | 352½ | 354½ | − 6 | 389 | 348 | 560 |
| Mr02 | 368 | 368 | 362½ | 363½ | − 6 | 387 | 356 | 147 |
| Est vol 5,181; vol Wed 5,117; open int 27,259, +278. | | | | | | | | |
| **Canola (WPG)-20 metric tons; Can. $ per ton** | | | | | | | | |
| Mar | .... | .... | .... | 285.00 | + 2.50 | 305.50 | 257.00 | 1,050 |
| May | 282.60 | 284.00 | 280.20 | 283.90 | + 2.30 | 305.50 | 259.20 | 38,896 |
| July | 284.00 | 284.80 | 281.30 | 284.70 | + 1.20 | 290.80 | 263.20 | 23,746 |
| Aug | .... | .... | .... | 284.00 | − 0.50 | 292.00 | 271.00 | 63 |
| Sept | .... | .... | .... | 285.50 | + 0.00 | 288.00 | 268.00 | 1,207 |
| Nov | 287.00 | 287.60 | 284.30 | 287.30 | + 1.10 | 299.00 | 271.10 | 22,434 |
| Ja02 | .... | .... | .... | 289.50 | + 0.90 | 290.80 | 277.00 | 457 |
| Est vol na; vol Wed 20,671; open int 87,853, −47. | | | | | | | | |
| **Wheat (WPG)-20 metric tons; Can. $ per ton** | | | | | | | | |
| Mar | .... | .... | .... | 145.00 | + 0.00 | 157.50 | 134.50 | 55 |
| May | 145.60 | 145.60 | 142.50 | 142.60 | − 3.30 | 159.00 | 137.50 | 4,976 |
| July | 148.00 | 148.00 | 144.50 | 144.80 | − 3.20 | 155.00 | 140.50 | 3,263 |
| Oct | 122.30 | 122.30 | 119.50 | 119.80 | − 2.80 | 123.50 | 118.10 | 1,524 |
| Dec | .... | .... | .... | 122.80 | − 2.80 | 127.00 | 121.60 | 1,234 |
| Est vol na; vol Wed 215; open int 11,052, −133. | | | | | | | | |
| **Barley-Western (WPG)-20 metric tons; Can. $ per ton** | | | | | | | | |
| Mar | .... | .... | .... | 130.00 | + 0.00 | 136.40 | 117.80 | 0 |
| May | 129.80 | 129.80 | 128.10 | 128.10 | − 1.60 | 137.50 | 120.30 | 7,242 |
| July | 130.50 | 130.60 | 129.20 | 129.20 | − 1.50 | 137.90 | 123.90 | 5,160 |
| Oct | 131.50 | 131.50 | 131.10 | 131.10 | − 0.60 | 137.90 | 129.00 | 6,035 |
| Dec | 133.50 | 133.50 | 133.50 | 133.50 | − 0.20 | 138.00 | 131.40 | 1,023 |
| Est vol na; vol Wed 586; open int 19,460, +76. | | | | | | | | |

## LIVESTOCK AND MEAT

| | OPEN | HIGH | LOW | SETTLE | CHANGE | LIFETIME HIGH | LIFETIME LOW | OPEN INT. |
|---|---|---|---|---|---|---|---|---|
| **Cattle-Feeder (CME) 50,000 lbs.; cents per lb.** | | | | | | | | |
| Mar | 85.75 | 85.80 | 85.40 | 85.45 | − .40 | 91.30 | 84.80 | 2,994 |
| Apr | 86.35 | 86.52 | 85.90 | 85.95 | − .52 | 90.80 | 85.00 | 4,588 |
| May | 86.40 | 86.65 | 86.05 | 86.07 | − .57 | 89.90 | 85.05 | 5,168 |
| Aug | 87.75 | 87.85 | 87.50 | 87.55 | − .25 | 89.90 | 86.00 | 4,552 |
| Sept | 87.35 | 87.50 | 87.15 | 87.35 | − .10 | 89.47 | 86.05 | 480 |
| Oct | 87.25 | 87.50 | 87.17 | 87.35 | − .10 | 89.47 | 86.05 | 541 |
| Nov | 87.90 | 87.90 | 87.55 | 87.85 | − .20 | 89.87 | 86.40 | 722 |
| Est vol 1,958; vol Wed 3,932; open int 19,186, −405. | | | | | | | | |
| **Cattle-Live (CME) 40,000 lbs.; cents per lb.** | | | | | | | | |
| Apr | 78.25 | 78.57 | 77.85 | 77.97 | − .72 | 81.82 | 72.17 | 55,037 |
| June | 72.80 | 73.07 | 72.40 | 72.52 | − .40 | 75.75 | 69.72 | 30,131 |
| Aug | 72.25 | 72.35 | 71.95 | 72.05 | − .32 | 75.00 | 69.97 | 23,313 |
| Oct | 74.50 | 74.60 | 74.15 | 74.17 | − .37 | 76.50 | 72.00 | 15,508 |
| Dec | 75.52 | 75.55 | 75.20 | 75.22 | − .35 | 77.20 | 73.30 | 6,268 |
| Est vol 21,158; vol Wed 26,579; open int 131,996, −4,182. | | | | | | | | |
| **Hogs-Lean (CME) 40,000 lbs.; cents per lb.** | | | | | | | | |
| Apr | 65.05 | 66.15 | 64.70 | 65.67 | + .85 | 66.15 | 48.65 | 22,330 |
| June | 70.90 | 71.45 | 70.35 | 70.92 | + .27 | 71.45 | 55.20 | 14,656 |
| July | 67.00 | 67.50 | 66.45 | 67.22 | + .07 | 67.50 | 54.77 | 3,892 |
| Aug | 63.30 | 63.87 | 62.65 | 63.00 | − .10 | 63.87 | 53.20 | 3,896 |
| Oct | 54.90 | 55.50 | 54.90 | 55.22 | + .17 | 55.50 | 46.40 | 3,407 |
| Dec | 52.00 | 53.05 | 52.00 | 52.55 | + .37 | 53.05 | 44.80 | 2,142 |
| Est vol 13,808; vol Wed 9,757; open int 50,573, +436. | | | | | | | | |
| **Pork Bellies (CME) 40,000 lbs.; cents per lb.** | | | | | | | | |
| Mar | 84.70 | 87.25 | 84.70 | 87.25 | + 3.00 | 87.25 | 58.00 | 281 |
| May | 86.00 | 88.52 | 85.55 | 88.50 | + 2.97 | 88.52 | 60.20 | 2,222 |
| July | 86.40 | 88.85 | 86.05 | 88.85 | + 3.00 | 88.85 | 60.10 | 304 |
| Est vol 1,285; vol Wed 777; open int 2,915, −72. | | | | | | | | |

## FOOD AND FIBER

| | OPEN | HIGH | LOW | SETTLE | CHANGE | LIFETIME HIGH | LIFETIME LOW | OPEN INT. |
|---|---|---|---|---|---|---|---|---|
| **Cocoa (NYBOT)-10 metric tons; $ per ton.** | | | | | | | | |
| Mar | 1,038 | 1,040 | 1,000 | 998 | − 38 | 1,362 | 707 | 22 |
| May | 1,021 | 1,033 | 1,004 | 1,015 | − 25 | 1,222 | 727 | 30,318 |
| July | 1,030 | 1,036 | 1,018 | 1,028 | − 24 | 1,245 | 753 | 21,574 |
| Sept | 1,043 | 1,047 | 1,032 | 1,040 | − 24 | 1,246 | 776 | 12,674 |
| Dec | 1,053 | 1,059 | 1,048 | 1,056 | − 23 | 1,237 | 805 | 14,910 |
| Mr02 | 1,068 | 1,070 | 1,063 | 1,074 | − 22 | 1,257 | 835 | 8,455 |
| May | .... | .... | .... | 1,088 | − 22 | 1,267 | 850 | 6,287 |
| July | .... | .... | .... | 1,100 | − 22 | 1,242 | 875 | 5,515 |
| Sept | .... | .... | .... | 1,115 | − 22 | 1,186 | 907 | 7,553 |
| Dec | .... | .... | .... | 1,135 | − 22 | 1,264 | 936 | 7,604 |
| Est vol 9,125; vol Wed 5,515; open int 114,912, −696. | | | | | | | | |
| **Coffee (NYBOT)-37,500 lbs.; cents per lb.** | | | | | | | | |
| Mar | 60.10 | 60.30 | 59.50 | 59.10 | − 1.90 | 153.85 | 59.25 | 98 |
| May | 61.25 | 62.25 | 60.90 | 61.00 | − 2.00 | 127.00 | 60.90 | 30,868 |
| July | 64.75 | 65.20 | 63.90 | 63.95 | − 1.85 | 127.00 | 63.90 | 12,405 |
| Sept | 67.50 | 67.75 | 66.65 | 66.60 | − 1.80 | 127.00 | 66.65 | 6,757 |
| Dec | 70.75 | 71.20 | 69.90 | 70.00 | − 1.60 | 127.00 | 69.90 | 4,480 |
| Mr02 | 74.25 | 74.90 | 74.05 | 73.50 | − 1.50 | 107.00 | 74.05 | 2,576 |
| May | 77.00 | 77.00 | 77.00 | 76.35 | − 1.35 | 87.00 | 77.00 | 188 |
| July | 79.75 | 79.75 | 79.75 | 79.20 | − 1.20 | 84.00 | 79.75 | 332 |
| Est vol 10,308; vol Wed 7,229; open int 57,704, +233. | | | | | | | | |
| **Sugar-World (NYBOT)-112,000 lbs.; cents per lb.** | | | | | | | | |
| May | 8.79 | 8.97 | 8.74 | 8.92 | + .19 | 10.68 | 6.10 | 81,574 |
| July | 8.35 | 8.45 | 8.26 | 8.42 | + .14 | 10.12 | 6.21 | 33,186 |

*(continued on next page)*

## Table 2.2 *(continued)*

| | Open | High | Low | Settle | Change | Lifetime High | Lifetime Low | Open Interest |
|---|---|---|---|---|---|---|---|---|
| Oct | 8.10 | 8.17 | 8.01 | 8.15 | + .13 | 9.88 | 6.27 | 24,806 |
| Mr02 | 7.90 | 7.97 | 7.82 | 7.94 | + .11 | 9.75 | 6.90 | 10,106 |
| May | 7.76 | 7.80 | 7.74 | 7.82 | + .12 | 9.64 | 7.60 | 2,856 |
| July | 7.70 | 7.70 | 7.70 | 7.74 | + .11 | 9.60 | 7.62 | 2,970 |
| Oct | 7.70 | 7.70 | 7.70 | 7.73 | + .11 | 8.50 | 7.63 | 2,471 |

Est vol 21,050; vol Wed 20,306; open int 157,969, +2,812.

**Sugar-Domestic (NYBOT)-112,000 lbs.; cents per lb.**

| | Open | High | Low | Settle | Change | High | Low | Open Int |
|---|---|---|---|---|---|---|---|---|
| May | 21.28 | 21.31 | 21.28 | 21.29 | .... | 21.65 | 18.00 | 1,265 |
| July | 21.45 | 21.45 | 21.45 | 21.45 | − .02 | 21.80 | 18.39 | 3,555 |
| Sept | 21.53 | 21.54 | 21.50 | 21.50 | − .04 | 21.99 | 18.69 | 1,529 |
| Nov | 20.86 | 20.86 | 20.86 | 20.86 | .... | 21.15 | 18.65 | 1,130 |
| Ja02 | 20.70 | 20.70 | 20.70 | 20.70 | .... | 21.25 | 18.00 | 414 |
| Mar | 20.82 | 20.82 | 20.82 | 20.82 | − .03 | 21.23 | 19.01 | 424 |
| May | 20.92 | 20.92 | 20.92 | 20.92 | − .01 | 21.20 | 20.75 | 157 |
| July | 21.05 | 21.05 | 21.05 | 21.05 | + .03 | 21.25 | 20.90 | 237 |

Est vol 178; vol Wed 1,495; open int 8,711, −785.

**Cotton (NYBOT)-50,000 lbs.; cents per lb.**

| | Open | High | Low | Settle | Change | High | Low | Open Int |
|---|---|---|---|---|---|---|---|---|
| May | 53.01 | 53.05 | 49.93 | 50.09 | − 2.56 | 70.50 | 49.93 | 35,505 |
| July | 53.90 | 54.05 | 51.05 | 51.30 | − 2.28 | 71.10 | 51.05 | 14,542 |
| Oct | 54.20 | 54.20 | 52.79 | 52.77 | − .88 | 67.20 | 52.79 | 1,117 |
| Dec | 54.30 | 54.40 | 52.90 | 53.13 | − .92 | 67.70 | 52.90 | 15,372 |
| Mr02 | 55.55 | 55.55 | 54.60 | 54.50 | − .85 | 67.10 | 54.60 | 1,628 |
| May | 55.50 | 55.50 | 54.90 | 54.95 | − .90 | 68.50 | 54.90 | 1,251 |
| July | 56.40 | 56.40 | 55.95 | 55.90 | − .85 | 68.50 | 55.95 | 1,072 |
| Oct | .... | .... | .... | 55.15 | − 1.10 | 65.50 | 59.00 | 120 |
| Dec | 55.75 | 55.75 | 55.75 | 55.15 | − 1.05 | 64.75 | 55.75 | 294 |

Est vol 15,000; vol Wed 7,514; open int 70,901, −39.

**Orange Juice (NYBOT)-15,000 lbs.; cents per lb.**

| | Open | High | Low | Settle | Change | High | Low | Open Int |
|---|---|---|---|---|---|---|---|---|
| May | 74.75 | 75.10 | 74.50 | 74.70 | − .40 | 92.15 | 74.40 | 19,984 |
| July | 78.70 | 78.90 | 78.35 | 78.45 | − .45 | 94.00 | 78.00 | 4,383 |
| Sept | 81.70 | 81.90 | 81.70 | 81.70 | − .40 | 95.85 | 80.00 | 1,356 |
| Nov | 84.70 | 85.10 | 84.70 | 84.75 | − .35 | 98.35 | 80.00 | 2,350 |
| Ja02 | .... | .... | .... | 87.75 | − .35 | 97.00 | 80.20 | 116 |

Est vol 750; vol Wed 1,398; open int 28,196, −194.

# METALS AND PETROLEUM

**Copper-High (Cmx.Div.NYM)-25,000 lbs.; cents per lb.**

| | Open | High | Low | Settle | Change | High | Low | Open Int |
|---|---|---|---|---|---|---|---|---|
| Mar | 80.50 | 80.70 | 80.25 | 80.25 | − 0.15 | 93.90 | 70.20 | 2,989 |
| Apr | 80.80 | 80.85 | 80.50 | 80.60 | − 0.20 | 93.40 | 70.65 | 3,780 |
| May | 81.40 | 81.50 | 80.75 | 81.05 | − 0.25 | 93.50 | 78.35 | 35,371 |
| June | 81.40 | 81.50 | 81.40 | 81.30 | − 0.25 | 93.00 | 80.40 | 1,697 |
| July | 81.60 | 82.05 | 81.40 | 81.55 | − 0.25 | 93.20 | 78.60 | 10,277 |
| Aug | 81.95 | 82.05 | 81.95 | 81.70 | − 0.25 | 92.50 | 80.50 | 1,173 |
| Sept | 82.20 | 82.40 | 82.10 | 81.90 | − 0.25 | 93.00 | 79.75 | 3,612 |
| Oct | .... | .... | .... | 81.95 | − 0.25 | 92.40 | 81.00 | 1,157 |
| Nov | .... | .... | .... | 82.05 | − 0.25 | 91.75 | 81.00 | 958 |
| Dec | 82.10 | 82.10 | 82.10 | 82.15 | − 0.25 | 92.00 | 79.20 | 5,425 |
| Ja02 | .... | .... | .... | 82.15 | − 0.25 | 90.80 | 81.30 | 505 |
| Feb | .... | .... | .... | 82.15 | − 0.25 | 90.00 | 81.40 | 291 |
| Mar | 82.40 | 82.40 | 82.40 | 82.15 | − 0.25 | 91.00 | 79.35 | 1,030 |
| Apr | .... | .... | .... | 82.15 | − 0.25 | 89.70 | 81.55 | 237 |
| May | .... | .... | .... | 82.10 | − 0.25 | 89.60 | 81.55 | 491 |
| June | .... | .... | .... | 82.05 | − 0.25 | 89.50 | 81.35 | 346 |
| July | .... | .... | .... | 82.05 | − 0.25 | 88.90 | 81.80 | 524 |

Est vol 8,000; vol Wed 11,151; open int 71,461, +1,582.

**Gold (Cmx.Div.NYM)-100 troy oz.; $ per troy oz.**

| | Open | High | Low | Settle | Change | High | Low | Open Int |
|---|---|---|---|---|---|---|---|---|
| Mar | .... | .... | .... | 260.00 | − 2.50 | 274.50 | 257.50 | 8 |
| Apr | 262.80 | 263.60 | 259.50 | 260.30 | − 2.60 | 305.00 | 255.10 | 64,242 |
| June | 264.90 | 265.70 | 261.30 | 262.30 | − 2.60 | 447.00 | 258.20 | 27,409 |
| Aug | 266.00 | 266.00 | 263.80 | 263.80 | − 2.70 | 322.00 | 259.50 | 5,532 |
| Oct | 266.00 | 266.50 | 265.50 | 265.10 | − 2.80 | 284.80 | 262.00 | 1,733 |
| Dec | 269.50 | 269.50 | 267.00 | 266.40 | − 2.90 | 429.50 | 264.10 | 6,560 |
| Ju02 | 272.00 | 272.00 | 272.00 | 270.20 | − 3.10 | 385.00 | 269.30 | 4,357 |
| Dec | 276.10 | 276.10 | 276.10 | 274.20 | − 3.40 | 358.00 | 276.10 | 2,097 |
| Ju03 | .... | .... | .... | 278.70 | − 3.50 | 338.00 | 281.50 | 1,032 |
| Dec | 285.00 | 285.00 | 285.00 | 283.30 | − 3.70 | 359.30 | 285.00 | 1,608 |
| Ju04 | .... | .... | .... | 288.10 | − 3.90 | 355.00 | 290.30 | 1,470 |
| Dec | .... | .... | .... | 292.90 | − 4.10 | 388.00 | 309.00 | 1,424 |

Est vol 42,000; vol Wed 42,653; open int 123,480, −3,341.

**Platinum (NYM)-50 troy oz.; $ per troy oz.**

| | Open | High | Low | Settle | Change | High | Low | Open Int |
|---|---|---|---|---|---|---|---|---|
| Apr | 582.10 | 585.00 | 578.00 | 580.40 | − 4.20 | 641.00 | 550.50 | 5,592 |
| July | 580.00 | 580.00 | 575.00 | 575.90 | − 4.20 | 630.00 | 567.00 | 1,667 |

Est vol 779; vol Wed 498; open int 7,261, −114.

**Silver (Cmx.Div.NYM)-5,000 troy oz.; cnts per troy oz.**

| | Open | High | Low | Settle | Change | High | Low | Open Int |
|---|---|---|---|---|---|---|---|---|
| Mar | 439.5 | 442.5 | 432.0 | 432.5 | − 10.3 | 552.0 | 432.0 | 124 |
| May | 447.0 | 447.0 | 434.0 | 435.3 | − 10.5 | 537.0 | 434.0 | 49,630 |
| July | 448.5 | 448.5 | 438.0 | 439.2 | − 10.5 | 574.0 | 438.0 | 9,286 |
| Dec | 456.0 | 456.0 | 447.0 | 447.0 | − 10.5 | 680.0 | 447.0 | 5,592 |
| Jl02 | 465.0 | 465.0 | 465.0 | 456.7 | − 10.3 | 559.0 | 465.0 | 511 |
| Dec | 472.0 | 472.0 | 470.0 | 463.9 | − 10.3 | 613.0 | 464.0 | 1,965 |
| Dc03 | 485.0 | 485.0 | 485.0 | 474.3 | − 10.3 | 565.0 | 485.0 | 549 |
| Dc04 | .... | .... | .... | 482.9 | − 10.3 | 560.0 | 496.5 | 741 |

Est vol 11,000; vol Wed 5,249; open int 73,524, +486.

**Crude Oil, Light Sweet (NYM) 1,000 bbls.; $ per bbl.**

| | Open | High | Low | Settle | Change | High | Low | Open Int |
|---|---|---|---|---|---|---|---|---|
| Apr | 26.46 | 26.72 | 26.12 | 26.55 | + 0.14 | 34.40 | 15.80 | 61,543 |
| May | 26.64 | 26.93 | 26.35 | 26.82 | + 0.20 | 33.50 | 15.80 | 104,734 |
| June | 26.90 | 27.10 | 26.53 | 26.97 | + 0.20 | 33.75 | 14.56 | 49,218 |
| July | 26.80 | 27.05 | 26.57 | 27.01 | + 0.26 | 32.20 | 19.05 | 26,115 |
| Aug | 26.70 | 26.90 | 26.54 | 26.90 | + 0.31 | 31.60 | 18.40 | 17,290 |
| Sept | 26.59 | 26.70 | 26.36 | 26.74 | + 0.35 | 31.00 | 17.96 | 15,444 |
| Oct | 26.25 | 26.42 | 26.25 | 26.55 | + 0.36 | 30.40 | 19.80 | 11,523 |
| Nov | 26.05 | 26.20 | 26.00 | 26.34 | + 0.38 | 30.10 | 18.20 | 14,590 |
| Dec | 26.00 | 26.10 | 25.70 | 26.12 | + 0.40 | 30.50 | 14.90 | 35,959 |
| Ja02 | 25.55 | 25.80 | 25.50 | 25.90 | + 0.42 | 29.00 | 18.90 | 12,365 |
| Feb | 25.31 | 25.60 | 25.31 | 25.68 | + 0.44 | 28.15 | 19.94 | 6,208 |
| Mar | 25.10 | 25.40 | 25.10 | 25.46 | + 0.46 | 27.90 | 18.45 | 4,247 |
| Apr | 24.98 | 25.15 | 24.98 | 25.22 | + 0.47 | 27.50 | 20.95 | 2,950 |
| May | 24.93 | 24.93 | 24.93 | 24.98 | + 0.48 | 27.35 | 20.84 | 3,021 |
| June | 24.40 | 24.60 | 24.40 | 24.74 | + 0.49 | 27.25 | 17.35 | 21,331 |
| July | .... | .... | .... | 24.54 | + 0.51 | 25.98 | 19.85 | 1,997 |
| Aug | 24.20 | 24.20 | 24.20 | 24.34 | + 0.53 | 26.77 | 20.53 | 1,118 |
| Sept | .... | .... | .... | 24.14 | + 0.55 | 24.59 | 20.43 | 5,662 |
| Oct | .... | .... | .... | 23.94 | + 0.57 | 26.36 | 22.88 | 1,254 |
| Nov | .... | .... | .... | 23.74 | + 0.59 | 25.50 | 22.77 | 1,011 |
| Dec | 23.25 | 23.35 | 23.15 | 23.53 | + 0.59 | 26.95 | 15.50 | 19,402 |
| Ja03 | .... | .... | .... | 23.36 | + 0.59 | 25.75 | 22.56 | 2,155 |
| Feb | .... | .... | .... | 23.20 | + 0.59 | 24.03 | 22.70 | 467 |
| Mar | .... | .... | .... | 23.05 | + 0.59 | 23.85 | 21.90 | 855 |
| June | 22.60 | 22.60 | 22.60 | 22.69 | + 0.59 | 25.05 | 19.82 | 8,075 |
| Sept | .... | .... | .... | 22.45 | + 0.62 | 0.00 | 0.00 | 200 |
| Dec | .... | .... | .... | 22.29 | + 0.64 | 24.44 | 15.92 | 11,882 |
| Dc04 | .... | .... | .... | 21.94 | + 0.64 | 24.00 | 16.35 | 5,814 |
| Dc05 | .... | .... | .... | 21.59 | + 0.65 | 23.00 | 17.00 | 5,054 |
| Dc06 | .... | .... | .... | 21.30 | + 0.66 | 22.55 | 19.10 | 1,052 |

Est vol 198,048; vol Wed 219,388; open int 452,586, +12,550.

**Heating Oil No. 2 (NYM) 42,000 gal; $ per gal.**

| | Open | High | Low | Settle | Change | High | Low | Open Int |
|---|---|---|---|---|---|---|---|---|
| Apr | .7040 | .7100 | .6980 | .7065 | + .0026 | .9496 | .5140 | 35,815 |
| May | .6837 | .6920 | .6780 | .6887 | + .0038 | .8900 | .5075 | 18,721 |
| June | .6835 | .6905 | .6770 | .6872 | + .0043 | .8625 | .5590 | 9,423 |
| July | .6860 | .6950 | .6830 | .6912 | + .0048 | .8430 | .5800 | 6,273 |
| Aug | .6880 | .7005 | .6880 | .6967 | + .0053 | .8430 | .5740 | 12,578 |
| Sept | .7020 | .7090 | .6980 | .7047 | + .0063 | .8430 | .5850 | 5,809 |
| Oct | .7080 | .7185 | .7080 | .7122 | + .0068 | .8030 | .5920 | 3,076 |
| Nov | .7120 | .7230 | .7120 | .7197 | + .0078 | .8425 | .6325 | 2,751 |
| Dec | .7200 | .7300 | .7175 | .7257 | + .0083 | .8426 | .6400 | 12,958 |
| Ja02 | .7210 | .7320 | .7200 | .7267 | + .0088 | .8170 | .6800 | 2,709 |
| Feb | .7150 | .7270 | .7135 | .7197 | + .0093 | .8075 | .6865 | 2,023 |
| Mar | .6950 | .7075 | .6940 | .6997 | + .0088 | .7875 | .6660 | 5,946 |
| Apr | .6794 | .6860 | .6760 | .6802 | + .0093 | .7525 | .6525 | 897 |
| May | .6594 | .6680 | .6580 | .6612 | + .0103 | .7070 | .6500 | 751 |
| June | .6479 | .6480 | .6479 | .6507 | + .0113 | .7000 | .6385 | 1,166 |
| July | .6459 | .6575 | .6459 | .6487 | + .0113 | .6700 | .6459 | 107 |
| Aug | .6494 | .6494 | .6494 | .6522 | + .0113 | .6635 | .6494 | 116 |

Est vol 42,834; vol Wed 41,457; open int 121,120, +1,283.

**Gasoline-NY Unleaded (NYM) 42,000; $ per gal.**

| | Open | High | Low | Settle | Change | High | Low | Open Int |
|---|---|---|---|---|---|---|---|---|
| Apr | .8681 | .8700 | .8530 | .8679 | + .0009 | .9959 | .6825 | 33,600 |
| May | .8626 | .8640 | .8500 | .8614 | + .0001 | .9840 | .7840 | 33,773 |
| June | .8455 | .8540 | .8430 | .8509 | − .0001 | .9745 | .7520 | 16,362 |
| July | .8325 | .8375 | .8280 | .8353 | − .0005 | .9300 | .7600 | 10,175 |
| Aug | .8140 | .8150 | .8060 | .8126 | − .0014 | .9150 | .7460 | 13,610 |
| Sept | .7780 | .7870 | .7780 | .7839 | − .0021 | .8490 | .7300 | 17,026 |
| Oct | .7490 | .7490 | .7490 | .7469 | − .0021 | .7950 | .6800 | 1,290 |
| Nov | .7275 | .7275 | .7275 | .7259 | − .0016 | .7810 | .6880 | 1,382 |
| Dec | .... | .... | .... | .7149 | − .0001 | .7470 | .6650 | 701 |

Est vol 30,025; vol Wed 32,906; open int 128,002, +2,123.

**Natural Gas (NYM) 10,000 MMBtu.; $ per MMBtu's**

| | Open | High | Low | Settle | Change | High | Low | Open Int |
|---|---|---|---|---|---|---|---|---|
| Apr | 4.900 | 4.980 | 4.870 | 4.927 | + .016 | 6.940 | 2.120 | 38,089 |
| May | 4.985 | 5.010 | 4.920 | 4.960 | + .001 | 6.220 | 2.119 | 29,702 |
| June | 5.023 | 5.070 | 4.975 | 5.000 | − .009 | 6.140 | 2.095 | 19,122 |
| July | 5.100 | 5.110 | 5.020 | 5.043 | − .016 | 6.140 | 2.095 | 15,476 |
| Aug | 5.099 | 5.130 | 5.040 | 5.068 | − .021 | 6.095 | 2.102 | 23,166 |
| Sept | 5.079 | 5.100 | 5.030 | 5.048 | − .021 | 6.040 | 2.137 | 14,964 |
| Oct | 5.089 | 5.110 | 5.030 | 5.058 | − .021 | 6.050 | 2.133 | 27,152 |
| Nov | 5.260 | 5.260 | 5.180 | 5.185 | − .019 | 6.140 | 2.275 | 12,521 |
| Dec | 5.360 | 5.360 | 5.250 | 5.305 | − .019 | 6.270 | 2.415 | 14,547 |
| Ja02 | 5.420 | 5.420 | 5.320 | 5.340 | − .019 | 6.290 | 2.450 | 10,928 |
| Feb | 5.190 | 5.190 | 5.140 | 5.145 | − .019 | 6.050 | 2.440 | 8,387 |
| Mar | 4.880 | 4.890 | 4.830 | 4.852 | − .013 | 5.730 | 2.360 | 19,059 |
| Apr | 4.440 | 4.520 | 4.440 | 4.509 | − .009 | 4.920 | 2.290 | 7,175 |
| May | 4.320 | 4.450 | 4.320 | 4.422 | − .009 | 4.775 | 2.350 | 11,249 |
| June | 4.420 | 4.460 | 4.400 | 4.439 | − .009 | 4.770 | 2.345 | 8,192 |
| July | 4.486 | 4.510 | 4.440 | 4.485 | − .011 | 4.750 | 2.365 | 5,707 |
| Aug | 4.510 | 4.520 | 4.480 | 4.499 | − .011 | 4.770 | 2.412 | 12,324 |
| Sept | 4.482 | 4.530 | 4.450 | 4.481 | − .011 | 4.770 | 2.423 | 6,387 |
| Oct | 4.477 | 4.490 | 4.457 | 4.476 | − .011 | 4.785 | 2.465 | 8,080 |
| Nov | 4.587 | 4.587 | 4.550 | 4.586 | − .011 | 4.890 | 2.610 | 3,750 |
| Dec | 4.693 | 4.693 | 4.650 | 4.692 | − .011 | 5.010 | 2.720 | 6,567 |

*(continued on next page)*

**Table 2.2**   (*continued*)

| | | | | | | | | | |
|---|---|---|---|---|---|---|---|---|---|
| Ja03 | 4.740 | 4.740 | 4.690 | 4.732 | − .011 | 5.049 | 2.730 | 11,155 |
| Feb | 4.610 | 4.610 | 4.570 | 4.601 | − .011 | 4.874 | 2.695 | 6,268 |
| Mar | .... | .... | .... | 4.438 | − .011 | 4.710 | 2.705 | 8,237 |
| Apr | .... | .... | .... | 4.247 | − .011 | 4.520 | 2.610 | 5,498 |
| May | 4.240 | 4.240 | 4.240 | 4.217 | − .011 | 4.490 | 2.630 | 4,043 |
| June | .... | .... | .... | 4.246 | − .011 | 4.400 | 2.610 | 2,173 |
| July | .... | .... | .... | 4.266 | − .011 | 4.530 | 2.550 | 4,022 |
| Aug | .... | .... | .... | 4.304 | − .011 | 4.535 | 2.970 | 4,047 |
| Sept | 4.293 | 4.293 | 4.293 | 4.302 | − .011 | 4.445 | 3.070 | 1,440 |
| Oct | 4.301 | 4.301 | 4.301 | 4.310 | − .011 | 4.455 | 3.480 | 4,198 |
| Nov | 4.423 | 4.423 | 4.423 | 4.432 | − .011 | 4.673 | 3.835 | 1,316 |
| Dec | 4.551 | 4.551 | 4.550 | 4.560 | − .011 | 4.820 | 3.960 | 1,413 |
| Ja04 | 4.590 | 4.590 | 4.590 | 4.600 | − .011 | 4.880 | 3.950 | 2,508 |
| Feb | .... | .... | .... | 4.480 | − .011 | 4.760 | 4.410 | 2,060 |
| Mar | 4.351 | 4.351 | 4.351 | 4.340 | − .011 | 4.510 | 4.351 | 130 |

Est vol 50,132; vol Wed 42,996; open int 361,052, +1,212.

**Brent Crude (IPE) 1,000 net bbls.; $ per bbl.**

| | | | | | | | | | |
|---|---|---|---|---|---|---|---|---|---|
| Apr | 24.15 | 24.54 | 23.90 | 24.19 | + 0.26 | 32.88 | 21.60 | 19,187 |
| May | 25.08 | 25.22 | 24.62 | 25.01 | + 0.17 | 31.95 | 23.18 | 61,673 |
| June | 25.35 | 25.47 | 24.88 | 25.22 | + 0.09 | 31.50 | 13.55 | 50,655 |
| July | 25.46 | 25.52 | 24.80 | 25.29 | + 0.05 | 29.95 | 23.05 | 22,558 |
| Aug | 25.35 | 25.48 | 24.79 | 25.28 | + 0.07 | 30.25 | 23.10 | 16,124 |
| Sep | 25.28 | 25.53 | 24.95 | 25.19 | + 0.10 | 28.74 | 18.35 | 10,891 |
| Oct | 25.17 | 25.17 | 24.99 | 25.05 | + 0.13 | 29.15 | 22.75 | 3,868 |
| Nov | 24.95 | 25.00 | 24.60 | 24.87 | + 0.17 | 27.04 | 23.15 | 4,057 |
| Dec | 24.80 | 24.80 | 24.42 | 24.67 | + 0.19 | 29.50 | 13.70 | 26,483 |
| Ja02 | 24.28 | 24.28 | 24.26 | 24.44 | + 0.21 | 25.55 | 22.50 | 2,617 |
| Feb | 24.01 | 24.01 | 24.01 | 24.19 | + 0.21 | 25.21 | 22.73 | 1,214 |
| Mar | .... | .... | .... | 23.99 | + 0.22 | 25.67 | 18.00 | 1,982 |
| Jun | .... | .... | .... | 23.37 | + 0.40 | 25.69 | 17.35 | 2,120 |
| Dec | 22.20 | 22.20 | 22.20 | 22.32 | + 0.45 | 25.58 | 17.35 | 8,954 |

Est vol 105,000; vol Wed 105,000; open int 232,383, +703.

**Gas Oil (IPE) 100 metric tons; $ per ton**

| | | | | | | | | | |
|---|---|---|---|---|---|---|---|---|---|
| Apr | 208.00 | 212.00 | 206.50 | 209.25 | − 4.50 | 284.50 | 161.00 | 29,838 |
| May | 208.00 | 211.50 | 206.25 | 209.00 | − 5.00 | 270.50 | 187.50 | 12,848 |
| June | 210.00 | 212.25 | 208.00 | 210.25 | − 4.50 | 269.00 | 165.00 | 11,724 |
| July | 211.50 | 213.00 | 210.50 | 211.50 | − 4.75 | 254.50 | 206.00 | 5,432 |
| Aug | 213.75 | 213.75 | 211.75 | 212.75 | − 4.25 | 248.25 | 206.75 | 3,079 |
| Sep | 214.50 | 214.75 | 213.00 | 214.00 | − 3.75 | 244.75 | 164.00 | 3,097 |
| Oct | 215.00 | 216.25 | 213.50 | 215.25 | − 3.25 | 261.50 | 168.00 | 2,238 |
| Nov | .... | .... | .... | 216.00 | − 3.00 | 244.00 | 214.00 | 2,180 |
| Dec | 215.00 | 217.50 | 214.50 | 216.50 | − 2.75 | 240.00 | 213.25 | 8,956 |
| Ja02 | 217.25 | 217.25 | 216.75 | 216.50 | − 2.75 | 240.00 | 214.00 | 2,864 |
| Feb | .... | .... | .... | 214.50 | − 2.50 | 221.00 | 214.00 | 1,916 |
| Mar | .... | .... | .... | 211.25 | − 2.25 | 245.75 | 195.00 | 351 |
| Jun | 202.50 | 202.50 | 202.00 | 202.00 | − 2.00 | 225.00 | 182.00 | 2,558 |
| Dec | 202.50 | 203.00 | 202.50 | 202.50 | − 2.50 | 210.25 | 181.00 | 530 |

Est vol 35,000; vol Wed 22,619; open int 87,611, +500.

## EXCHANGE ABBREVIATIONS

(for commodity futures and futures options)

**CANTOR**-Cantor Exchange; **CBT**-Chicago Board of Trade; **CME**-Chicago Mercantile Exchange; **CSCE**-Coffee, Sugar & Cocoa Exchange, New York; **CMX**-COMEX (Div. of New York Mercantile Exchange); **CTN**-New York Cotton Exchange; **DTB**-Deutsche Terminboerse; **FINEX**-Financial Exchange (Div. of New York Cotton Exchange; **IPE**-International Petroleum Exchange; **KC**-Kansas City Board of Trade; **LIFFE**-London International Financial Futures Exchange; **MATIF**-Marche a Terme International de France; **ME**-Montreal Exchange; **MCE**-MidAmerica Commodity Exchange; **MPLS**-Minneapolis Grain Exchange; **NYFE**-New York Futures Exchange (Sub. of New York Cotton Exchange); **NYM**-New York Mercantile Exchange; **SFE**-Sydney Futures Exchange; **SGX**-Singapore Exchange Ltd.; **WPG**-Winnipeg Commodity Exchange.

*Source*:  Reprinted by permission of Dow Jones, Inc., via copyright Clearance Center, Inc. © 2001 Dow Jones & Company, Inc. All Rights Reserved Worldwide.

### Lifetime Highs and Lows

The sixth and seventh numbers show the highest futures price and the lowest futures price achieved in the trading of the particular contract over its lifetime. The May 2001 corn contract had traded for well over a year on March 15, 2001. During this period the highest and lowest prices achieved were $282\frac{1}{2}$ cents and $206\frac{1}{2}$ cents.

### Open Interest and Volume of Trading

The final column in Table 2.2 shows the *open interest* for each contract. This is the total number of contracts outstanding. The open interest is the number of long positions or, equivalently, the number of short positions. Because of the problems in compiling the data, the open-interest information is one trading day older than the price information. Thus, in the *Wall Street Journal* of March 16, 2001, the open interest is for the close of trading on March 14, 2001. In the case of the May 2001 corn futures contract, the open interest was 186,129 contracts.

At the end of each section, Table 2.2 shows the estimated volume of trading in contracts of all maturities on March 15, 2001, and the actual volume of trading in these contracts on March 14, 2001. It also shows the total open interest for all contracts on March 14, 2001, and the change in this open interest from the previous trading day. For all corn futures contracts, the estimated trading volume was 103,000 contracts on March 15, 2001, and the actual trading volume was 60,060 contracts on March 14, 2001. The open interest for all corn futures contracts was 431,377 on March 14, 2001, up 1,845 from the previous trading day.

Sometimes the volume of trading in a day is greater than the open interest at the end of the day. This is indicative of a large number of day trades.

### Patterns of Futures Prices

A number of different patterns of futures prices can be picked out from Table 2.2. The futures price of gold on the New York Mercantile Exchange and the futures price of wheat on the Chicago Board of Trade increase as the time to maturity increases. This is known as a *normal market*. By contrast, the futures price of Sugar–World is a decreasing function of maturity. This is known as an *inverted market*. Other commodities show mixed patterns. For example, the futures price of Crude Oil first increases and then decreases with maturity.

## 2.6 KEYNES AND HICKS

We refer to the market's average opinion about what the future price of an asset will be at a certain future time as the *expected future price* of the asset at that time. Suppose that it is now June and the September futures price of corn is 200 cents. It is interesting to ask what the expected future price of corn is in September. Is it less that 200 cents, greater than 200 cents, or exactly equal to 200 cents? As illustrated in Figure 2.1, the futures price converges to the spot price at maturity. If the expected future spot price is less than 200 cents, the market must be expecting the September futures price to decline so that traders with short positions gain and traders with long positions lose. If the expected future price is greater than 200 cents the reverse must be true. The market must be expecting the September futures price to increase so that traders with long positions gain while those with short positions lose.

Economists John Maynard Keynes and John Hicks argued that if hedgers tend to hold short positions and speculators tend to hold long positions, the futures price of an asset will be below its expected future spot price. This is because speculators require compensation for the risks they are bearing. They will trade only if they can expect to make money on average. Hedgers will lose money on average, but they are likely to be prepared to accept this because the futures contract reduces their risks. If hedgers tend to hold long positions while speculators hold short positions, Keynes and Hicks argued that the futures price will be above the expected future spot price for a similar reason.

When the futures price is below the expected future spot price, the situation is known as *normal backwardation*; when the futures price is above the expected future spot price, the situation is known as *contango*. In the next chapter we will examine in more detail the relationship between futures and spot prices.

## 2.7 DELIVERY

As mentioned earlier in this chapter, very few of the futures contracts that are entered into lead to delivery of the underlying asset. Most are closed out early. Nevertheless, it is the possibility of eventual delivery that determines the futures price. An understanding of delivery procedures is therefore important.

The period during which delivery can be made is defined by the exchange and varies from contract to contract. The decision on when to deliver is made by the party with the short position, whom we shall refer to as investor A. When investor A decides to deliver, investor A's broker issues a *notice of intention to deliver* to the exchange clearinghouse. This notice states how many contracts will be delivered and, in the case of commodities, also specifies where delivery will be made and what grade will be delivered. The exchange then chooses a party with a long position to accept delivery.

Suppose that the party on the other side of investor A's futures contract when it was entered into was investor B. It is important to realize that there is no reason to expect that it will be investor B who takes delivery. Investor B may well have closed out his or her position by trading with investor C, investor C may have closed out his or her position by trading with investor D, and so on. The usual rule chosen by the exchange is to pass the notice of intention to deliver on to the party with the oldest outstanding long position. Parties with long positions must accept delivery notices. However, if the notices are transferable, long investors have a short period of time, usually half an hour, to find another party with a long position that is prepared to accept the notice from them.

In the case of a commodity, taking delivery usually means accepting a warehouse receipt in return for immediate payment. The party taking delivery is then responsible for all warehousing costs. In the case of livestock futures, there may be costs associated with feeding and looking after the animals. In the case of financial futures, delivery is usually made by wire transfer. For all contracts the price paid is usually the settlement price immediately preceding the date of the notice of intention to deliver. Where appropriate, this price is adjusted for grade, location of delivery, and so on. The whole delivery procedure from the issuance of the notice of intention to deliver to the delivery itself generally takes two to three days.

There are three critical days for a contract. These are the first notice day, the last notice day, and the last trading day. The *first notice day* is the first day on which a notice of intention to make delivery can be submitted to the exchange. The *last notice day* is the last such day. The *last trading day* is generally a few days before the last notice day. To avoid the risk of having to take delivery, an investor with a long position should close out his or her contracts prior to the first notice day.

### Cash Settlement

Some financial futures, such as those on stock indices, are settled in cash because it is inconvenient or impossible to deliver the underlying asset. In the case of the futures contract on the S&P 500, for example, delivering the underlying asset would involve delivering a portfolio of 500 stocks. When a contract is settled in cash, it is simply marked to market on the last trading day, and all positions are declared closed. To ensure that the futures price converges to the spot price, the settlement price on the last trading day is set equal to the spot price of the underlying asset at either the opening or close of trading on that day. For example, in the S&P 500 futures contract trading on the Chicago Mercantile Exchange final settlement is based on the opening price of the index on the third Friday of the delivery month.

## 2.8  TYPES OF TRADERS

There are two main types of traders executing trades: commission brokers and locals. *Commission brokers* are following the instructions of their clients and charge a commission for doing so. *Locals* are trading on their own account.

Individuals taking positions, whether locals or the clients of commission brokers, can be categorized as hedgers, speculators, or arbitrageurs, as discussed in Chapter 1. Speculators can be classified as scalpers, day traders, or position traders. *Scalpers* are watching for very short term trends and attempt to profit from small changes in the contract price. They usually hold their positions for only a few minutes. *Day traders* hold their positions for less than one trading day.

They are unwilling to take the risk that adverse news will occur overnight. *Position traders* hold their positions for much longer periods of time. They hope to make significant profits from major movements in the markets.

### Orders

The simplest type of order placed with a broker is a *market order*. It is a request that a trade be carried out immediately at the best price available in the market. However, there are many other types of orders. We will consider those that are more commonly used.

A *limit order* specifies a particular price. The order can be executed only at this price or at one more favorable to the investor. Thus, if the limit price is $30 for an investor wanting to take a long position, the order will be executed only at a price of $30 or less. There is, of course, no guarantee that the order will be executed at all, because the limit price may never be reached.

A *stop order* or *stop-loss order* also specifies a particular price. The order is executed at the best available price once a bid or offer is made at that particular price or a less-favorable price. Suppose a stop order to sell at $30 is issued when the market price is $35. It becomes an order to sell when and if the price falls to $30. In effect, a stop order becomes a market order as soon as the specified price has been hit. The purpose of a stop order is usually to close out a position if unfavorable price movements take place. It limits the loss that can be incurred.

A *stop–limit order* is a combination of a stop order and a limit order. The order becomes a limit order as soon as a bid or offer is made at a price equal to or less favorable than the stop price. Two prices must be specified in a stop–limit order: the stop price and the limit price. Suppose that at the time the market price is $35, a stop–limit order to buy is issued with a stop price of $40 and a limit price of $41. As soon as there is a bid or offer at $40, the stop–limit becomes a limit order at $41. If the stop price and the limit price are the same, the order is sometimes called a *stop-and-limit order*.

A *market-if-touched* (MIT) *order* is executed at the best available price after a trade occurs at a specified price or at a price more favorable than the specified price. In effect, an MIT order becomes a market order once the specified price has been hit. An MIT order is also known as a *board order*. Consider an investor who has a long position in a futures contract and is issuing instructions that would lead to closing out the contract. A stop order is designed to place a limit on the loss that can occur in the event of unfavorable price movements. By contrast, an MIT order is designed to ensure that profits are taken if sufficiently favorable price movements occur.

A *discretionary order* or *market-not-held order* is traded as a market order except that execution may be delayed at the broker's discretion in an attempt to get a better price.

Some orders specify time conditions. Unless otherwise stated, an order is a day order and expires at the end of the trading day. A *time-of-day order* specifies a particular period of time during the day when the order can be executed. An *open order* or a *good-till-canceled order* is in effect until executed or until the end of trading in the particular contract. A *fill-or-kill order*, as its name implies, must be executed immediately on receipt or not at all.

## 2.9 REGULATION

Futures markets in the United States are currently regulated federally by the Commodity Futures Trading Commission (CFTC, www.cftc.gov), which was established in 1974. This body is responsible for licensing futures exchanges and approving contracts. All new contracts and changes to existing contracts must be approved by the CFTC. To be approved, the contract must have some useful economic purpose. Usually this means that it must serve the needs of hedgers as well as speculators.

The CFTC looks after the public interest. It is responsible for ensuring that prices are communicated to the public and that futures traders report their outstanding positions if they are above certain levels. The CFTC also licenses all individuals who offer their services to the public in futures trading. The backgrounds of these individuals are investigated, and there are minimum capital requirements. The CFTC deals with complaints brought by the public and ensures that disciplinary action is taken against individuals when appropriate. It has the authority to force exchanges to take disciplinary action against members who are in violation of exchange rules.

With the formation of the National Futures Association (NFA, www.nfa.futures.org) in 1982, some of responsibilities of the CFTC were shifted to the futures industry itself. The NFA is an organization of individuals who participate in the futures industry. Its objective is to prevent fraud and to ensure that the market operates in the best interests of the general public. The NFA requires its members to pass an exam. It is authorized to monitor trading and take disciplinary action when appropriate. The agency has set up an efficient system for arbitrating disputes between individuals and its members.

From time to time other bodies such as the Securities and Exchange Commission (SEC, www.sec.gov), the Federal Reserve Board (www.federalreserve.gov), and the U.S. Treasury Department (www.treas.gov) have claimed jurisdictional rights over some aspects of futures trading. These bodies are concerned with the effects of futures trading on the spot markets for securities such as stocks, Treasury bills, and Treasury bonds. The SEC currently has an effective veto over the approval of new stock or bond index futures contracts. However, the basic responsibility for all futures and options on futures rests with the CFTC.

### Trading Irregularities

Most of the time futures markets operate efficiently and in the public interest. However, from time to time, trading irregularities do come to light. One type of trading irregularity occurs when an investor group tries to "corner the market".[1] The investor group takes a huge long futures position and also tries to exercise some control over the supply of the underlying commodity. As the maturity of the futures contracts is approached, the investor group does not close out its position, so that the number of outstanding futures contracts may exceed the amount of the commodity available for delivery. The holders of short positions realize that they will find it difficult to deliver and become desperate to close out their positions. The result is a large rise in both futures and spot prices. Regulators usually deal with this type of abuse of the market by increasing margin requirements, imposing stricter position limits, prohibiting trades that increase a speculator's open position, and forcing market participants to close out their positions.

Other types of trading irregularities can involve the traders on the floor of the exchange. These received some publicity early in 1989 when it was announced that the FBI had carried out a two-year investigation, using undercover agents, of trading on the Chicago Board of Trade and the Chicago Mercantile Exchange. The investigation was initiated because of complaints filed by a large agricultural concern. The alleged offenses included overcharging customers, not paying customers the full proceeds of sales, and traders using their knowledge of customer orders to trade first for themselves.

---

[1] Possibly the best known example of this involves the activities of the Hunt brothers in the silver market in 1979–80. Between the middle of 1979 and the beginning of 1980, their activities led to a price rise from $9 per ounce to $50 per ounce.

## 2.10 ACCOUNTING AND TAX

The full details of the accounting and tax treatment of futures contracts are beyond the scope of this book. A trader who wants detailed information on this should consult experts. In this section we provide some general background information.

### *Accounting*

Consider a trader who in September 2002 takes a long position in a March 2003 corn futures contract and closes out the position at the end of February 2003. Suppose that the futures prices are 150 cents per bushel when the contract is entered into, 170 cents per bushel at the end of 2002, and 180 cents per bushel when the contract is closed out. One contract is for the delivery of 5,000 bushels. If the trader is a speculator, the gains for accounting purposes are

$$5,000 \times \$0.20 = \$1,000$$

in 2002 and

$$5,000 \times \$0.10 = \$500$$

in 2003.

If the trader is hedging the purchase of 5,000 bushels of corn in February 2003, *hedge accounting* can be used. The entire \$1,500 gain then appears in the 2003 income statement. In general, hedge accounting allows the profit/loss from a hedging instrument to be recognized at the same time as the profit/loss from the item being hedged.

In June 1998, the Financial Accounting Standards Board issued FASB Statement No. 133, Accounting for Derivative Instruments and Hedging Activities (FAS 133). FAS 133 applies to all types of derivatives (including futures, forwards, swaps, and options). It requires all derivatives to be included on the balance sheet at fair market value.[2] It increases disclosure requirements. It also gives companies far less latitude in using hedge accounting. For hedge accounting to be used, the hedging instrument must be highly effective in offsetting exposures and an assessment of this effectiveness is required every three months. FAS 133 is effective for all fiscal years beginning after June 15, 2000.

### *Tax*

Under the U.S. tax rules, two key issues are the nature of a taxable gain or loss and the timing of the recognition of the gain or loss. Gains or losses are either classified as capital gains/losses or as part of ordinary income.

For a corporate taxpayer, capital gains are taxed at the same rate as ordinary income, and the ability to deduct losses is restricted. Capital losses are deductible only to the extent of capital gains. A corporation may carry back a capital loss for three years and carry it forward for up to five years.

For a noncorporate taxpayer, short-term capital gains are taxed at the same rate as ordinary income, but long-term capital gains are taxed at a lower rate than ordinary income. (Long-term capital gains are gains from the sale of a capital asset held for longer than one year; short term capital gains are the gains from the sale of a capital asset held less than one year.) The Taxpayer Relief Act of 1997 widened the rate differential between ordinary income and long-term capital gains. For a noncorporate taxpayer, capital losses are deductible to the extent of capital gains plus ordinary income up to \$3,000 and can be carried forward indefinitely.

---

[2] Previously the attraction of derivatives in some situations was that they were "off-balance-sheet" items.

Generally, positions in futures contracts are treated as if they are closed out on the last day of the tax year. Gains and losses are capital. For the noncorporate taxpayer they are considered 60% long term and 40% short term.

Hedging transactions are exempt from this rule. The definition of a hedge transaction for tax purposes is different from that for accounting purposes. The tax regulations define a hedging transaction as a transaction entered into in the normal course of business primarily for one of the following reasons:

1. To reduce the risk of price changes or currency fluctuations with respect to property that is held or to be held by the taxpayer for the purposes of producing ordinary income

2. To reduce the risk of price or interest rate changes or currency fluctuations with respect to borrowings made by the taxpayer

Gains or losses from hedging transactions are treated as ordinary income. The timing of the recognition of gains or losses from hedging transactions generally matches the timing of the recognition of income or deduction from the hedged items.

Special rules apply to foreign currency futures transactions. A taxpayer can make a binding election to treat gains and losses from all futures contracts in all foreign currencies as ordinary income, regardless of whether the contracts is entered into for hedging or speculative purposes. If a taxpayer does not make this election, then foreign currencies futures transactions are treated in the same way as other futures transactions.

## 2.11   FORWARD CONTRACTS vs. FUTURES CONTRACTS

The main differences between forward and futures contracts are summarized in Table 2.3. Both contracts are agreements to buy or sell an asset for a certain price at a certain future time. A forward contract is traded in the over-the-counter market and there is no standard contract size or standard delivery arrangements. A single delivery date is usually specified and the contract is usually held to the end of its life and then settled. A futures contract is a standardized contract traded on an exchange. A range of delivery dates is usually specified. It is settled daily and usually closed out prior to maturity.

Suppose that the sterling exchange rate for a 90-day forward contract is 1.4381 and that this rate is also the futures price for a contract that will be delivered in exactly 90 days. What is the difference between the gains and losses under the two contracts?

**Table 2.3**   Comparison of forward and futures contracts

| *Forward* | *Futures* |
| --- | --- |
| Traded on over-the-counter market | Traded on an exchange |
| Not standardized | Standardized contract |
| Usually one specified delivery date | Range of delivery dates |
| Settled at end of contract | Settled daily |
| Delivery or final cash settlement usually takes place | Contract is usually closed out prior to maturity |

Under the forward contract, the whole gain or loss is realized at the end of the life of the contract. Under the futures contract, the gain or loss is realized day by day because of the daily settlement procedures. Suppose that investor A is long £1 million in a 90-day forward contract and investor B is long £1 million in 90-day futures contracts. (Because each futures contract is for the purchase or sale of £62,500, investor B must purchase a total of 16 contracts.) Assume that the spot exchange rate in 90 days proves to be 1.4600. Investor A makes a gain of $21,900 on the 90th day. Investor B makes the same gain—but spread out over the 90-day period. On some days investor B may realize a loss, whereas on other days he or she makes a gain. However, in total, when losses are netted against gains, there is a gain of $21,900 over the 90-day period.

### Foreign Exchange Quotes

Both forward and futures contracts trade actively on foreign currencies. However, there is a difference in the way exchange rates are quoted in the two markets. Futures prices are always quoted as the number of U.S. dollars per unit of the foreign currency or as the number of U.S. cents per unit of the foreign currency. Forward prices are always quoted in the same way as spot prices. This means that for the British pound, the euro, the Australian dollar, and the New Zealand dollar, the forward quotes show the number of U.S. dollars per unit of the foreign currency and are directly comparable with futures quotes. For other major currencies, forward quotes show the number of units of the foreign currency per U.S. dollar (USD). Consider the Canadian dollar (CAD). A futures price quote of 0.7050 USD per CAD corresponds to a forward price quote of 1.4184 CAD per USD (1.4184 = 1/0.7050).

## SUMMARY

In futures markets, contracts are traded on an exchange, and it is necessary for the exchange to define carefully the precise nature of what is traded, the procedures that will be followed, and the regulations that will govern the market. Forward contracts are negotiated directly over the telephone by two relatively sophisticated individuals. As a result, there is no need to standardize the product, and an extensive set of rules and procedures is not required.

A very high proportion of the futures contracts that are traded do not lead to the delivery of the underlying asset. They are closed out before the delivery period is reached. However, it is the possibility of final delivery that drives the determination of the futures price. For each futures contract, there is a range of days during which delivery can be made and a well-defined delivery procedure. Some contracts, such as those on stock indices, are settled in cash rather than by delivery of the underlying asset.

The specification of contracts is an important activity for a futures exchange. The two sides to any contract must know what can be delivered, where delivery can take place, and when delivery can take place. They also need to know details on the trading hours, how prices will be quoted, maximum daily price movements, and so on. New contracts must be approved by the Commodity Futures Trading Commission before trading starts.

Margins are an important aspect of futures markets. An investor keeps a margin account with his or her broker. The account is adjusted daily to reflect gains or losses, and from time to time the broker may require the account to be topped up if adverse price movements have taken place. The broker either must be a clearinghouse member or must maintain a margin account with a clearinghouse member. Each clearinghouse member maintains a margin account with the exchange clearinghouse. The balance in the account is adjusted daily to reflect gains and losses on the business for which the clearinghouse member is responsible.

Information on futures prices is collected in a systematic way at exchanges and relayed within a matter of seconds to investors throughout the world. Many daily newspapers such as the *Wall Street Journal* carry a summary of the previous day's trading.

Forward contracts differ from futures contracts in a number of ways. Forward contracts are private arrangements between two parties, whereas futures contracts are traded on exchanges. There is generally a single delivery date in a forward contract, whereas futures contracts frequently involve a range of such dates. Because they are not traded on exchanges, forward contracts need not be standardized. A forward contract is not usually settled until the end of its life, and most contracts do in fact lead to delivery of the underlying asset or a cash settlement at this time.

In the next few chapters we will look at how forward and futures prices are determined. We will also examine in more detail the ways in which forward and futures contracts can be used for hedging.

## SUGGESTIONS FOR FURTHER READING

Chance, D., *An Introduction to Derivatives*, 4th edn., Dryden Press, Orlando, FL, 1997.

Duffie, D., *Futures Markets*, Prentice Hall, Upper Saddle River, NJ, 1989.

Hicks, J. R., *Value and Capital*, Clarendon Press, Oxford, 1939.

Horn, F. F., *Trading in Commodity Futures*, New York Institute of Finance, New York, 1984.

Keynes, J. M., *A Treatise on Money*, Macmillan, London, 1930.

Kolb, R., *Futures, Options, and Swaps*, 3rd edn., Blackwell, Oxford, 2000.

Schwager, J. D., *A Complete Guide to the Futures Markets*, Wiley, New York, 1984.

Teweles, R. J., and F. J. Jones, *The Futures Game*, McGraw-Hill, New York, 1987.

## QUESTIONS AND PROBLEMS
## (ANSWERS IN SOLUTIONS MANUAL)

2.1. Distinguish between the terms *open interest* and *trading volume*.

2.2. What is the difference between a *local* and a *commission broker*?

2.3. Suppose that you enter into a short futures contract to sell July silver for $5.20 per ounce on the New York Commodity Exchange. The size of the contract is 5,000 ounces. The initial margin is $4,000, and the maintenance margin is $3,000. What change in the futures price will lead to a margin call? What happens if you do not meet the margin call?

2.4. Suppose that in September 2002 you take a long position in a contract on May 2003 crude oil futures. You close out your position in March 2003. The futures price (per barrel) is $18.30 when you enter into your contract, $20.50 when you close out your position, and $19.10 at the end of December 2000. One contract is for the delivery of 1,000 barrels. What is your total profit? When is it realized? How is it taxed if you are (a) a hedger and (b) a speculator? Assume that you have a December 31 year-end.

2.5. What does a stop order to sell at $2 mean? When might it be used? What does a limit order to sell at $2 mean? When might it be used?

2.6. What is the difference between the operation of the margin accounts administered by a clearinghouse and those administered by a broker?

2.7. What differences exist in the way prices are quoted in the foreign exchange futures market, the foreign exchange spot market, and the foreign exchange forward market?

2.8. The party with a short position in a futures contract sometimes has options as to the precise asset that will be delivered, where delivery will take place, when delivery will take place, and so on. Do these options increase or decrease the futures price? Explain your reasoning.

2.9. What are the most important aspects of the design of a new futures contract?

2.10. Explain how margins protect investors against the possibility of default.

2.11. An investor enters into two long futures contracts on frozen orange juice. Each contract is for the delivery of 15,000 pounds. The current futures price is 160 cents per pound, the initial margin is $6,000 per contract, and the maintenance margin is $4,500 per contract. What price change would lead to a margin call? Under what circumstances could $2,000 be withdrawn from the margin account?

2.12. Show that if the futures price of a commodity is greater than the spot price during the delivery period there is an arbitrage opportunity. Does an arbitrage opportunity exist if the futures price is less than the spot price? Explain your answer.

2.13. Explain the difference between a market-if-touched order and a stop order.

2.14. Explain what a stop–limit order to sell at 20.30 with a limit of 20.10 means.

2.15. At the end of one day a clearinghouse member is long 100 contracts, and the settlement price is $50,000 per contract. The original margin is $2,000 per contract. On the following day the member becomes responsible for clearing an additional 20 long contracts, entered into at a price of $51,000 per contract. The settlement price at the end of this day is $50,200. How much does the member have to add to its margin account with the exchange clearinghouse?

2.16. On July 1, 2002, a company enters into a forward contract to buy 10 million Japanese yen on January 1, 2003. On September 1, 2002, it enters into a forward contract to sell 10 million Japanese yen on January 1, 2003. Describe the payoff from this strategy.

2.17. The forward price on the Swiss franc for delivery in 45 days is quoted as 1.8204. The futures price for a contract that will be delivered in 45 days is 0.5479. Explain these two quotes. Which is more favorable for an investor wanting to sell Swiss francs?

2.18. Suppose you call your broker and issue instructions to sell one July hogs contract. Describe what happens.

2.19. "Speculation in futures markets is pure gambling. It is not in the public interest to allow speculators to trade on a futures exchange." Discuss this viewpoint.

2.20. Identify the contracts with the highest open interest in Table 2.2. Consider each of the following sections separately: grains and oilseeds, livestock and meat, food and fiber, and metals and petroleum.

2.21. What do you think would happen if an exchange started trading a contract in which the quality of the underlying asset was incompletely specified?

2.22. "When a futures contract is traded on the floor of the exchange, it may be the case that the open interest increases by one, stays the same, or decreases by one." Explain this statement.

2.23. Suppose that on October 24, 2002, you take a short position in an April 2003 live-cattle futures contract. You close out your position on January 21, 2003. The futures price (per pound) is 61.20 cents when you enter into the contract, 58.30 cents when you close out your position, and 58.80 cents at the end of December 2002. One contract is for the delivery of 40,000 pounds of cattle. What is your total profit? How is it taxed if you are (a) a hedger and (b) a speculator?

2.24. A cattle farmer expects to have 120,000 pounds of live cattle to sell in three months. The live-cattle futures contract on the Chicago Mercantile Exchange is for the delivery of 40,000 pounds of cattle. How can the farmer use the contract for hedging? From the farmer's viewpoint, what are the pros and cons of hedging?

2.25. It is now July 2002. A mining company has just discovered a small deposit of gold. It will take six months to construct the mine. The gold will then be extracted on a more or less continuous basis for one year. Futures contracts on gold are available on the New York Commodity Exchange. There are delivery months every two months from August 2002 to December 2003. Each contract is for the delivery of 100 ounces. Discuss how the mining company might use futures markets for hedging.

## ASSIGNMENT QUESTIONS

2.26. A company enters into a short futures contract to sell 5,000 bushels of wheat for 250 cents per bushel. The initial margin is $3,000 and the maintenance margin is $2,000. What price change would lead to a margin call? Under what circumstances could $1,500 be withdrawn from the margin account?

2.27. Suppose that on March 15, 2001, speculators tended to be short Sugar–World futures and hedgers tended to be long Sugar–World futures. What does the Keynes and Hicks argument imply about the expected future price of sugar? Use Table 2.2. Explain carefully what is meant by the expected price of a commodity on a particular future date.

2.28. Suppose that corn can be stored for 20 cents per bushel per year and the risk-free interest rate is 5% per year. How could you make money in the corn market on March 15, 2001, by trading the May 2001 and May 2002 contracts? Use Table 2.2.

2.29. The author's Web page www.rotman.utoronto.ca/~hull contains daily closing prices for the December 2001 crude oil futures contract and the December 2001 gold futures contract. (Both contracts are traded on NYMEX.) You are required to download the data and answer the following:

  a. How high do the maintenance margin levels for oil and gold have to be set so that there is a 1% chance that an investor with a balance slightly above the maintenence margin level on a particular day has a negative balance two days later (i.e., one day after a margin call). How high do they have to be for a 0.1% chance. Assume daily price changes are normally distributed with mean zero.

  b. Imagine an investor who starts with a long position in the oil contract at the beginning of the period covered by the data and keeps the contract for the whole of the period of time covered by the data. Margin balances in excess of the initial margin are withdrawn. Use the maintenance margin you calculated in part (a) for a 1% risk level and assume that the maintenance margin is 75% of the initial margin. Calculate the number of margin calls and the number of times the investor has a negative margin balance and therefore an incentive to walk away. Assume that all margin calls are met in your calculations. Repeat the calculations for an investor who starts with a short position in the gold contract.

# CHAPTER 3

# DETERMINATION OF FORWARD AND FUTURES PRICES

In this chapter we examine how forward prices and futures prices are related to the spot price of the underlying asset. Forward contracts are easier to analyze than futures contracts because there is no daily settlement—only a single payment at maturity. Consequently, most of the analysis in the first part of the chapter is directed toward determining forward prices rather than futures prices. Luckily it can be shown that the forward price and futures price of an asset are usually very close when the maturities of the two contracts are the same. In the second part of the chapter we use this result to examine the properties of futures prices for contracts on stock indices, foreign exchange, and other assets.

## 3.1  INVESTMENT ASSETS vs. CONSUMPTION ASSETS

When considering forward and futures contracts, it is important to distinguish between investment assets and consumption assets. An *investment asset* is an asset that is held for investment purposes by significant numbers of investors. Stocks and bonds are clearly investment assets. Gold and silver are also examples of investment assets. Note that investment assets do not have to be held exclusively for investment. Silver, for example, has a number of industrial uses. However, they do have to satisfy the requirement that they are held by significant numbers of investors solely for investment. A *consumption asset* is an asset that is held primarily for consumption. It is not usually held for investment. Examples of consumption assets are commodities such as copper, oil, and pork bellies.

   As we will see later in this chapter, we can use arbitrage arguments to determine the forward and futures prices of an investment asset from its spot price and other observable market variables. We cannot do this for the forward and futures prices of consumption assets.

## 3.2  SHORT SELLING

Some of the arbitrage strategies presented in this chapter involve *short selling*. This trade, usually simply referred to as "shorting", involves selling an asset that is not owned. It is something that is possible for some—but not all—investment assets. We will illustrate how it works by considering a short sale of shares of a stock.

Suppose an investor instructs a broker to short 500 IBM shares. The broker will carry out the instructions by borrowing the shares from another client and selling them in the market in the usual way. The investor can maintain the short position for as long as desired, provided there are always shares for the broker to borrow. At some stage, however, the investor will close out the position by purchasing 500 IBM shares. These are then replaced in the account of the client from whom the shares were borrowed. The investor takes a profit if the stock price has declined and a loss if it has risen. If, at any time while the contract is open, the broker runs out of shares to borrow, the investor is *short-squeezed* and is forced to close out the position immediately even if not ready to do so.

An investor with a short position must pay to the broker any income, such as dividends or interest, that would normally be received on the securities that have been shorted. The broker will transfer this to the account of the client from whom the securities have been borrowed. Consider the position of an investor who shorts 500 IBM shares in April when the price per share is $120 and closes out the position by buying them back in July when the price per share is $100. Suppose that a dividend of $1 per share is paid in May. The investor receives $500 \times \$120 = \$60,000$ in April when the short position is initiated. The dividend leads to a payment by the investor of $500 \times \$1 = \$500$ in May. The investor also pays $500 \times \$100 = \$50,000$ when the position is closed out in July. The net gain is therefore

$$\$60,000 - \$500 - \$50,000 = \$9,500$$

Regulators in the United States currently allow a stock to be shorted only on an *uptick*—that is, when the most recent movement in the price of the stock was an increase. An exception is made when traders are shorting a basket of stocks replicating a stock index.

## 3.3 MEASURING INTEREST RATES

Before getting into the details of how forward and futures prices are determined, it is important to talk about how interest rates are measured. A statement by a bank that the interest rate on one-year deposits is 10% per annum may sound straightforward and unambiguous. In fact, its precise meaning depends on the way the interest rate is measured.

If the interest rate is quoted with annual compounding, the bank's statement that the interest rate is 10% means that $100 grows to

$$\$100 \times 1.1 = \$110$$

at the end of one year. When the interest rate is expressed with semiannual compounding, it means that we earn 5% every six months, with the interest being reinvested. In this case $100 grows to

$$\$100 \times 1.05 \times 1.05 = \$110.25$$

at the end of one year. When the interest rate is expressed with quarterly compounding, the bank's statement means that we earn 2.5% every three months, with the interest being reinvested. The $100 then grows to

$$\$100 \times 1.025^4 = \$110.38$$

at the end of one year. Table 3.1 shows the effect of increasing the compounding frequency further.

The compounding frequency defines the units in which an interest rate is measured. A rate

**Table 3.1** Effect of the compounding frequency on the value of $100 at the end of one year when the interest rate is 10% per annum

| *Compounding frequency* | *Value of $100 at end of year ($)* |
| --- | --- |
| Annually ($m = 1$) | 110.00 |
| Semiannually ($m = 2$) | 110.25 |
| Quarterly ($m = 4$) | 110.38 |
| Monthly ($m = 12$) | 110.47 |
| Weekly ($m = 52$) | 110.51 |
| Daily ($m = 365$) | 110.52 |

expressed with one compounding frequency can be converted into an equivalent rate with a different compounding frequency. For example, from Table 3.1 we see that 10.25% with annual compounding is equivalent to 10% with semiannual compounding. We can think of the difference between one compounding frequency and another to be analogous to the difference between kilometers and miles. They are two different units of measurement.

To generalize our results, suppose that an amount $A$ is invested for $n$ years at an interest rate of $R$ per annum. If the rate is compounded once per annum, the terminal value of the investment is

$$A(1 + R)^n$$

If the rate is compounded $m$ times per annum, the terminal value of the investment is

$$A\left(1 + \frac{R}{m}\right)^{mn} \tag{3.1}$$

## Continuous Compounding

The limit as $m$ tends to infinity is known as *continuous compounding*. With continuous compounding, it can be shown that an amount $A$ invested for $n$ years at rate $R$ grows to

$$Ae^{Rn} \tag{3.2}$$

where $e = 2.71828$. The function $e^x$ is built into most calculators, so the computation of the expression in equation (3.2) presents no problems. In the example in Table 3.1, $A = 100$, $n = 1$, and $R = 0.1$, so that the value to which $A$ grows with continuous compounding is

$$100e^{0.1} = \$110.52$$

This is (to two decimal places) the same as the value with daily compounding. For most practical purposes, continuous compounding can be thought of as being equivalent to daily compounding. Compounding a sum of money at a continuously compounded rate $R$ for $n$ years involves multiplying it by $e^{Rn}$. Discounting it at a continuously compounded rate $R$ for $n$ years involves multiplying by $e^{-Rn}$.

In this book interest rates will be measured with continuous compounding except where otherwise stated. Readers used to working with interest rates that are measured with annual, semiannual, or some other compounding frequency may find this a little strange at first. However, continuously compounded interest rates are used to such a great extent in pricing derivatives that it makes sense to get used to working with them now.

Suppose that $R_c$ is a rate of interest with continuous compounding and $R_m$ is the equivalent rate with compounding $m$ times per annum. From the results in equations (3.1) and (3.2), we must have

$$Ae^{R_c n} = A\left(1 + \frac{R_m}{m}\right)^{mn}$$

or

$$e^{R_c} = \left(1 + \frac{R_m}{m}\right)^{m}$$

This means that

$$R_c = m \ln\left(1 + \frac{R_m}{m}\right) \tag{3.3}$$

and

$$R_m = m(e^{R_c/m} - 1) \tag{3.4}$$

These equations can be used to convert a rate with a compounding frequency of $m$ times per annum to a continuously compounded rate and vice versa. The function ln is the natural logarithm function and is built into most calculators. It is defined so that if $y = \ln x$, then $x = e^y$.

**Example 3.1**  Consider an interest rate that is quoted as 10% per annum with semiannual compounding. From equation (3.3) with $m = 2$ and $R_m = 0.1$, the equivalent rate with continuous compounding is

$$2\ln\left(1 + \frac{0.1}{2}\right) = 0.09758$$

or 9.758% per annum.

**Example 3.2**  Suppose that a lender quotes the interest rate on loans as 8% per annum with continuous compounding, and that interest is actually paid quarterly. From equation (3.4) with $m = 4$ and $R_c = 0.08$, the equivalent rate with quarterly compounding is

$$4(e^{0.08/4} - 1) = 0.0808$$

or 8.08% per annum. This means that on a $1,000 loan, interest payments of $20.20 would be required each quarter.

## 3.4  ASSUMPTIONS AND NOTATION

In this chapter we will assume that the following are all true for some market participants:

1. The market participants are subject to no transactions costs when they trade.
2. The market participants are subject to the same tax rate on all net trading profits.
3. The market participants can borrow money at the same risk-free rate of interest as they can lend money.
4. The market participants take advantage of arbitrage opportunities as they occur.

Note that we do not require these assumptions to be true for all market participants. All that we require is that they be true—or at least approximately true—for a few key market participants such as large investment banks. This is not unreasonable. It is the trading activities of these key market participants and their eagerness to take advantage of arbitrage opportunities as they occur that determine the relationship between forward and spot prices.

The following notation will be used throughout this chapter:

$T$: Time until delivery date in a forward or futures contract (in years)

$S_0$: Price of the asset underlying the forward or futures contract today

$F_0$: Forward or futures price today

$r$: Risk-free rate of interest per annum, expressed with continuous compounding, for an investment maturing at the delivery date (i.e., in $T$ years)

The risk-free rate, $r$, is in theory the rate at which money is borrowed or lent when there is no credit risk, so that the money is certain to be repaid. It is often thought of as the Treasury rate, that is, the rate at which a national government borrows in its own currency. In practice, large financial institutions usually set $r$ equal to the London Interbank Offer Rate (LIBOR) instead of Treasury rate in the formulas in this chapter and in those in the rest of the book. LIBOR will be discussed in Chapter 5.

## 3.5 FORWARD PRICE FOR AN INVESTMENT ASSET

The easiest forward contract to value is one written on an investment asset that provides the holder with no income. Non-dividend-paying stocks and zero-coupon bonds are examples of such investment assets.[1]

### *Illustration*

Consider a long forward contract to purchase a non-dividend-paying stock in three months. Assume the current stock price is $40 and the three-month risk-free interest rate is 5% per annum. We consider strategies open to an arbitrageur in two extreme situations.

Suppose first that the forward price is relatively high at $43. An arbitrageur can borrow $40 at the risk-free interest rate of 5% per annum, buy one share, and short a forward contract to sell one share in three months. At the end of the three months, the arbitrageur delivers the share and receives $43. The sum of money required to pay off the loan is

$$40e^{0.05 \times 3/12} = \$40.50$$

By following this strategy, the arbitrageur locks in a profit of $43.00 − $40.50 = $2.50 at the end of the three-month period.

Suppose next that the forward price is relatively low at $39. An arbitrageur can short one share, invest the proceeds of the short sale at 5% per annum for three months, and take a long position in

---

[1] Some of the contracts mentioned in the first half of this chapter (e.g., forward contracts on individual stocks) do not normally arise in practice. However, they form useful examples for developing our ideas.

a three-month forward contract. The proceeds of the short sale grow to

$$40e^{0.05 \times 3/12}$$

or $40.50 in three months. At the end of the three months, the arbitrageur pays $39, takes delivery of the share under the terms of the forward contract, and uses it to close out the short position. A net gain of

$$\$40.50 - \$39.00 = \$1.50$$

is therefore made at the end of the three months.

Under what circumstances do arbitrage opportunities such as those we have just considered exist. The first arbitrage works when the forward price is greater than $40.50. The second arbitrage works when the forward price is less than $40.50. We deduce that for there to be no arbitrage the forward price must be exactly $40.50.

### A Generalization

To generalize this example, we consider a forward contract on an investment asset with price $S_0$ that provides no income. Using our notation, $T$ is the time to maturity, $r$ is the risk-free rate, and $F_0$ is the forward price. The relationship between $F_0$ and $S_0$ is

$$F_0 = S_0 e^{rT} \tag{3.5}$$

If $F_0 > S_0 e^{rT}$, arbitrageurs can buy the asset and short forward contracts on the asset. If $F_0 < S_0 e^{rT}$, they can short the asset and buy forward contracts on it.[2] In our example, $S_0 = 40$, $r = 0.05$, and $T = 0.25$, so that equation (3.5) gives

$$F_0 = 40e^{0.05 \times 0.25} = \$40.50$$

which is in agreement with our earlier calculations.

> **Example 3.3**   Consider a four-month forward contract to buy a zero-coupon bond that will mature one year from today. The current price of the bond is $930. (This means that the bond will have eight months to go when the forward contract matures.) We assume that the four-month risk-free rate of interest (continuously compounded) is 6% per annum. Because zero-coupon bonds provide no income, we can use equation (3.5) with $T = 4/12$, $r = 0.06$, and $S_0 = 930$. The forward price, $F_0$, is given by
>
> $$F_0 = 930e^{0.06 \times 4/12} = \$948.79$$
>
> This would be the delivery price in a contract negotiated today.

### What If Short Sales Are Not Possible?

Short sales are not possible for all investment assets. As it happens, this does not matter. To derive equation (3.5), we do not need to be able to short the asset. All that we require is that there be a significant number of people who hold the asset purely for investment (and by definition this is

---

[2] For another way of seeing that equation (3.5) is correct, consider the following strategy: buy one unit of the asset and enter into a short forward contract to sell it for $F_0$ at time $T$. This costs $S_0$ and is certain to lead to a cash inflow of $F_0$ at time $T$. Therefore $S_0$ must equal the present value of $F_0$; that is, $S_0 = F_0 e^{-rT}$, or equivalently $F_0 = S_0 e^{rT}$.

always true of an investment asset). If the forward price is too low, they will find it attractive to sell the asset and take a long position in a forward contract.

Suppose the underlying asset is gold and assume no storage costs or income.[3] If $F_0 > S_0 e^{rT}$, an investor can adopt the following strategy:

1. Borrow $S_0$ dollars at an interest rate $r$ for $T$ years.

2. Buy one ounce of gold.

3. Short a forward contract on one ounce of gold.

At time $T$ one ounce of gold is sold for $F_0$. An amount $S_0 e^{rT}$ is required to repay the loan at this time and the investor makes a profit of $F_0 - S_0 e^{rT}$.

Suppose next that $F_0 < S_0 e^{rT}$. In this case an investor who owns one ounce of gold can

1. Sell the gold for $S_0$.

2. Invest the proceeds at interest rate $r$ for time $T$.

3. Take a long position in a forward contract on one ounce of gold.

At time $T$ the cash invested has grown to $S_0 e^{rT}$. The gold is repurchased for $F_0$ and the investor makes a profit of $S_0 e^{rT} - F_0$ relative to the position the investor would have been in if the gold had been kept.

As in the non-dividend-paying stock example considered earlier, we can expect the forward price to adjust so that neither of the two arbitrage opportunities we have considered exists. This means that the relationship in equation (3.5) must hold.

## 3.6  KNOWN INCOME

In this section we consider a forward contract on an investment asset that will provide a perfectly predictable cash income to the holder. Examples are stocks paying known dividends and coupon-bearing bonds. We adopt the same approach as in the previous section. We first look at a numerical example and then review the formal arguments.

### *Illustration*

Consider a long forward contract to purchase a coupon-bearing bond whose current price is $900. We will suppose that the forward contract matures in one year and the bond matures in five years, so that the forward contract is a contract to purchase a four-year bond in one year. We will also suppose that coupon payments of $40 are expected after 6 months and 12 months, with the second coupon payment being immediately prior to the delivery date in the forward contract. We assume the six-month and one-year risk-free interest rates (continuously compounded) are 9% per annum and 10% per annum, respectively.

Suppose first that the forward price is relatively high at $930. An arbitrageur can borrow $900 to buy the bond and short a forward contract. The first coupon payment has a present value of $40e^{-0.09 \times 0.5} = \$38.24$. Of the $900, $38.24 is therefore borrowed at 9% per annum for six months so that it can be repaid with the first coupon payment. The remaining $861.76 is borrowed at 10% per annum for one year. The amount owing at the end of the year is $861.76e^{0.1 \times 1} = \$952.39$. The

---

[3] Section 1.3 provides a numerical example for this case.

second coupon provides \$40 toward this amount, and \$930 is received for the bond under the terms of the forward contract. The arbitrageur therefore makes a net profit of

$$\$40 + \$930 - \$952.39 = \$17.61$$

Suppose next that the forward price is relatively low at \$905. An investor who holds the bond can sell it and enter into a long forward contract. Of the \$900 realized from selling the bond, \$38.24 is invested for 6 months at 9% per annum so that it grows into an amount sufficient to equal the coupon that would have been paid on the bond. The remaining \$861.76 is invested for 12 months at 10% per annum and grows to \$952.39. Of this sum, \$40 is used to replace the coupon that would have been received on the bond, and \$905 is paid under the terms of the forward contract to replace the bond in the investor's portfolio. The investor therefore gains

$$\$952.39 - \$40.00 - \$905.00 = \$7.39$$

relative to the situation the investor would have been in by keeping the bond.

The first strategy produces a profit when the forward price is greater than \$912.39, whereas the second strategy produces a profit when the forward price is less than \$912.39. It follows that if there are no arbitrage opportunities then the forward price must be \$912.39.

### A Generalization

We can generalize from this example to argue that when an investment asset will provide income with a present value of $I$ during the life of a forward contract

$$F_0 = (S_0 - I)e^{rT} \tag{3.6}$$

In our example, $S_0 = 900.00$, $I = 40e^{-0.09 \times 0.5} + 40e^{-0.10 \times 1} = 74.433$, $r = 0.1$, and $T = 1$, so that

$$F_0 = (900.00 - 74.433)e^{0.1 \times 1} = \$912.39$$

This is in agreement with our earlier calculation. Equation (3.6) applies to any asset that provides a known cash income.

If $F_0 > (S_0 - I)e^{rT}$, an arbitrageur can lock in a profit by buying the asset and shorting a forward contract on the asset. If $F_0 < (S_0 - I)e^{rT}$ an arbitrageur can lock in a profit by shorting the asset and taking a long position in a forward contract. If short sales are not possible, investors who own the asset will find it profitable to sell the asset and enter into long forward contracts.[4]

**Example 3.4** Consider a 10-month forward contract on a stock with a price of \$50. We assume that the risk-free rate of interest (continuously compounded) is 8% per annum for all maturities. We also assume that dividends of \$0.75 per share are expected after three months, six months, and nine months. The present value of the dividends, $I$, is given by

$$I = 0.75e^{-0.08 \times 3/12} + 0.75e^{-0.08 \times 6/12} + 0.75e^{-0.08 \times 9/12} = 2.162$$

---

[4] For another way of seeing that equation (3.6) is correct, consider the following strategy: buy one unit of the asset and enter into a short forward contract to sell it for $F_0$ at time $T$. This costs $S_0$ and is certain to lead to a cash inflow of $F_0$ at time $T$ and income with a present value of $I$. The initial outflow is $S_0$. The present value of the inflows is $I + F_0e^{-rT}$. Hence, $S_0 = I + F_0e^{-rT}$, or equivalently $F_0 = (S_0 - I)e^{rT}$.

The variable $T$ is 10 months, so that the forward price, $F_0$, from equation (3.6), is given by

$$F_0 = (50 - 2.162)e^{0.08 \times 10/12} = \$51.14$$

If the forward price were less than this, an arbitrageur would short the stock spot and buy forward contracts. If the forward price were greater than this, an arbitrageur would short forward contracts and buy the stock spot.

## 3.7  KNOWN YIELD

We now consider the situation where the asset underlying a forward contract provides a known yield rather than a known cash income. This means that the income is known when expressed as a percent of the asset's price at the time the income is paid. Suppose that an asset is expected to provide a yield of 5% per annum. This could mean that income equal to 5% of the asset price is paid once a year. (The yield would then be 5% with annual compounding.) It could mean that income equal to 2.5% of the asset price is paid twice a year. (The yield would then be 5% per annum with semiannual compounding.) In Section 3.3 we explained that we will normally measure interest rates with continuous compounding. Similarly we will normally measure yields with continuous compounding. Formulas for translating a yield measured with one compounding frequency to a yield measured with another compounding frequency are the same as those given for interest rates in Section 3.3.

Define $q$ as the average yield per annum on an asset during the life of a forward contract. It can be shown (see Problem 3.22) that

$$F_0 = S_0 e^{(r-q)T} \tag{3.7}$$

**Example 3.5**   Consider a six-month forward contract on an asset that is expected to provide income equal to 2% of the asset price once during a six-month period. The risk-free rate of interest (with continuous compounding) is 10% per annum. The asset price is $25. In this case $S_0 = 25$, $r = 0.10$, and $T = 0.5$. The yield is 4% per annum with semiannual compounding. From equation (3.3) this is 3.96% per annum with continuous compounding. It follows that $q = 0.0396$, so that from equation (3.7) the forward price $F_0$ is given by

$$r_c = 2 \ln\left(1 + \frac{.04}{2}\right)$$

$$F_0 = 25e^{(0.10-0.0396) \times 0.5} = \$25.77$$

## 3.8  VALUING FORWARD CONTRACTS

The value of a forward contract at the time it is first entered into is zero. At a later stage it may prove to have a positive or negative value. Using the notation introduced earlier, we suppose $F_0$ is the current forward price for contract that was negotiated some time ago, the delivery date is in $T$ years, and $r$ is the $T$-year risk-free interest rate. We also define:

$K$:  Delivery price in the contract

$f$:  Value of a long forward contract today

A general result, applicable to all forward contracts (both those on investment assets and those on consumption assets), is

$$f = (F_0 - K)e^{-rT} \tag{3.8}$$

When the forward contract is first negotiated, $K$ is set equal to $F_0$ and $f = 0$. As time passes, both the forward price, $F_0$, and the value of the forward contract, $f$, change.

To see why equation (3.8) is correct, we compare a long forward contract that has a delivery price of $F_0$ with an otherwise identical long forward contract that has a delivery price of $K$. The difference between the two is only in the amount that will be paid for the underlying asset at time $T$. Under the first contract this amount is $F_0$; under the second contract it is $K$. A cash outflow difference of $F_0 - K$ at time $T$ translates to a difference of $(F_0 - K)e^{-rT}$ today. The contract with a delivery price $F_0$ is therefore less valuable than the contract with delivery price $K$ by an amount $(F_0 - K)e^{-rT}$. The value of the contract that has a delivery price of $F_0$ is by definition zero. It follows that the value of the contract with a delivery price of $K$ is $(F_0 - K)e^{-rT}$. This proves equation (3.8). Similarly, the value of a short forward contract with delivery price $K$ is

$$(K - F_0)e^{-rT}$$

**Example 3.6**   A long forward contract on a non-dividend-paying stock was entered into some time ago. It currently has six months to maturity. The risk-free rate of interest (with continuous compounding) is 10% per annum, the stock price is $25, and the delivery price is $24. In this case $S_0 = 25$, $r = 0.10$, $T = 0.5$, and $K = 24$. From equation (3.5) the six-month forward price, $F_0$, is given by

$$F_0 = 25e^{0.1 \times 0.5} = \$26.28$$

From equation (3.8) the value of the forward contract is

$$f = (26.28 - 24)e^{-0.1 \times 0.5} = \$2.17$$

Equation (3.8) shows that we can value a long forward contract on an asset by making the assumption that the price of the asset at the maturity of the forward contract equals the forward price $F_0$. To see this, note that when we make the assumption, a long forward contract provides a payoff at time $T$ of $F_0 - K$. This has a present value of $(F_0 - K)e^{-rT}$, which is the value of $f$ in equation (3.8). Similarly, we can value a short forward contract on the asset by assuming that the current forward price of the asset is realized.

Using equation (3.8) in conjunction with (3.5) gives the following expression for the value of a forward contract on an investment asset that provides no income:

$$f = S_0 - Ke^{-rT} \tag{3.9}$$

Similarly, using equation (3.8) in conjunction with (3.6) gives the following expression for the value of a long forward contract on an investment asset that provides a known income with present value $I$:

$$f = S_0 - I - Ke^{-rT} \tag{3.10}$$

Finally, using equation (3.8) in conjunction with (3.7) gives the following expression for the value of a long forward contract on an investment asset that provides a known yield at rate $q$:

$$f = S_0 e^{-qT} - Ke^{-rT} \tag{3.11}$$

## 3.9   ARE FORWARD PRICES AND FUTURES PRICES EQUAL?

Appendix 3A provides an arbitrage argument to show that when the risk-free interest rate is constant and the same for all maturities, the forward price for a contract with a certain delivery date is the same as the futures price for a contract with that delivery date. The argument in Appendix 3A can be extended to cover situations where the interest rate is a known function of time.

When interest rates vary unpredictably (as they do in the real world), forward and futures prices are in theory no longer the same. We can get a sense of the nature of the relationship between the two by considering the situation where the price of the underlying asset, $S$, is strongly positively correlated with interest rates. When $S$ increases, an investor who holds a long futures position makes an immediate gain because of the daily settlement procedure. The positive correlation indicates that it is likely that interest rates have also increased. The gain will therefore tend to be invested at a higher than average rate of interest. Similarly, when $S$ decreases, the investor will incur an immediate loss. This loss will tend to be financed at a lower than average rate of interest. An investor holding a forward contract rather than a futures contract is not affected in this way by interest rate movements. It follows that a long futures contract will be more attractive than a similar long forward contract. Hence, when $S$ is strongly positively correlated with interest rates, futures prices will tend to be higher than forward prices. When $S$ is strongly negatively correlated with interest rates, a similar argument shows that forward prices will tend to be higher than futures prices.

The theoretical differences between forward and futures prices for contracts that last only a few months are in most circumstances sufficiently small to be ignored. In practice, there are a number of factors not reflected in theoretical models that may cause forward and futures prices to be different. These include taxes, transactions costs, and the treatment of margins. The risk that the counterparty will default is generally less in the case of a futures contract because of the role of the exchange clearinghouse. Also, in some instances, futures contracts are more liquid and easier to trade than forward contracts. Despite all these points, for most purposes it is reasonable to assume that forward and futures prices are the same. This is the assumption we will usually make in this book. We will use the symbol $F_0$ to represent both the futures price and the forward price of an asset today.

As the life of a futures contract increases, the differences between forward and futures contracts are liable to become significant. It is then dangerous to assume that forward and futures prices are perfect substitutes for each other. This point is particularly relevant to Eurodollar futures contracts because they have maturities as long as ten years. These contracts are covered in Chapter 5.

### *Empirical Research*

Some empirical research that has been carried out comparing forward and futures contracts is listed at the end of this chapter. Cornell and Reinganum studied forward and futures prices on the British pound, Canadian dollar, German mark, Japanese yen, and Swiss franc between 1974 and 1979. They found very few statistically significant differences between the two sets of prices. Their results were confirmed by Park and Chen, who as part of their study looked at the British pound, German mark, Japanese yen, and Swiss franc between 1977 and 1981.

French studied copper and silver during the period from 1968 to 1980. The results for silver show that the futures price and the forward price are significantly different (at the 5% confidence level), with the futures price generally above the forward price. The results for copper are less clear-cut. Park and Chen looked at gold, silver, silver coin, platinum, copper, and plywood between 1977 and 1981. Their results are similar to those of French for silver. The forward and futures prices are significantly different, with the futures price above the forward price. Rendleman and Carabini studied the Treasury bill market between 1976 and 1978. They also found statistically significant differences between futures and forward prices. In all these studies, it seems likely that the differences observed are due to the factors mentioned in the previous section (taxes, transactions costs, and so on).

## 3.10   STOCK INDEX FUTURES

A *stock index* tracks changes in the value of a hypothetical portfolio of stocks. The weight of a stock in the portfolio equals the proportion of the portfolio invested in the stock. The percentage increase in the stock index over a small interval of time is set equal to the percentage increase in the value of the hypothetical portfolio. Dividends are usually not included in the calculation so that the index tracks the capital gain/loss from investing in the portfolio.[5]

If the hypothetical portfolio of stocks remains fixed, the weights assigned to individual stocks in the portfolio do not remain fixed. When the price of one particular stock in the portfolio rises more sharply than others, more weight is automatically given to that stock. Some indices are constructed from a hypothetical portfolio consisting of one of each of a number of stocks. The weights assigned to the stocks are then proportional to their market prices, with adjustments being made when there are stock splits. Other indices are constructed so that weights are proportional to market capitalization (stock price × number of shares outstanding). The underlying portfolio is then automatically adjusted to reflect stock splits, stock dividends, and new equity issues.

### Stock Indices

Table 3.2 shows futures prices for contracts on a number of different stock indices as they were reported in the *Wall Street Journal* of March 16, 2001. The prices refer to the close of trading on March 15, 2001.

The *Dow Jones Industrial Average* is based on a portfolio consisting of 30 blue-chip stocks in the United States. The weights given to the stocks are proportional to their prices. One futures contract, traded on the Chicago Board of Trade, is on $10 times the index.

The *Standard & Poor's 500* (S&P 500) *Index* is based on a portfolio of 500 different stocks: 400 industrials, 40 utilities, 20 transportation companies, and 40 financial institutions. The weights of the stocks in the portfolio at any given time are proportional to their market capitalizations. This index accounts for 80% of the market capitalization of all the stocks listed on the New York Stock Exchange. The Chicago Mercantile Exchange (CME) trades two contracts on the S&P 500. One is on $250 times the index; the other (the Mini S&P 500 contract) is on $50 times the index. The *Standard & Poor's MidCap 400 Index* is similar to the S&P 500, but based on a portfolio of 400 stocks that have somewhat lower market capitalizations.

The *Nikkei 225 Stock Average* is based on a portfolio of 225 of the largest stocks trading on the Tokyo Stock Exchange. Stocks are weighted according to their prices. One futures contract (traded on the CME) is on $5 times the index.

---

[5] An exception to this is a *total return index*. This is calculated by assuming that dividends on the hypothetical portfolio are reinvested in the portfolio.

**Table 3.2** Stock index futures quotes from the *Wall Street Journal*, March 16, 2001. (Columns show month, open, high, low, settle, change, lifetime high, lifetime low, and open interest, respectively.)

### INDEX

**DJ Industrial Average (CBOT)-$10 times average**
```
Mar   10095  10115   9980  10020  +   12  11640   9880    8,023
June  10170  10200  10060  10105  +   10  11795   9980   24,367
Sept  10260  10260  10160  10200  +    7  11330  10095      294
```
Est vol 19,000; vol Wed 45,038; open int 32,716, +1,471.
Idx prl: Hi 10097.73; Lo 9980.85; Close 10031.28, +57.82.

**S&P 500 Index (CME)-$250 times Index**
```
Mar   118000 118200 116950 117330 + 410 164260 115500  112,346
June  118080 119450 117450 118470 + 390 166660 116550  455,531
Sept  119500 120680 119300 119640 + 360 169060 117820    2,635
Dec   120700 121780 120500 120740 + 360 171460 118920      969
Mr02   ....   ....         121790 + 330 173860 120070      409
June  123500 124200 122500 123040 + 380 170550 121320      459
```
Est vol 113,148; vol Wed 209,907; open int 572,426, +8,748.
Idx prl: Hi 1182.04; Lo 1166.71; Close 1173.56, +6.85.

**Mini S&P 500 (CME)-$50 times index**
```
Mar   116950 118200 116400 117325 + 400 150000 115400   58,162
```
Vol Wed 183,181; open int 99,765, −2,471.

**S&P Midcap 400 (CME)-$500 times index**
```
Mar   475.00 477.00 471.00 471.55 − 1.90 564.00 450.50    4,347
June  480.00 484.00 475.50 476.15 − 2.10 571.00 475.00   15,905
```
Est vol 3,128; vol Wed 4,403; open int 20,262, −48.
Idx prl: Hi 479.23; Lo 471.25; Close 471.25, −2.34.

**Nikkei 225 Stock Average (CME)-$5 times index**
```
June  12080. 12175. 12030. 12130. + 735 17730. 11255.   16,825
```
Est vol 1,233; vol Wed 2,341; open int 16,846, +81.
Idx prl: Hi 12152.83; Lo 11433.88; Close 12152.83, +309.24.

**Nasdaq 100 (CME)-$100 times index**
```
Mar   181400 181800 168000 169250 − 6000 424150 168000  21,284
June  178000 184100 170800 171500 − 6100 396100 169800  47,728
```
Est vol 25,437; vol Wed 41,468; open int 69,062, −3,889.
Idx prl: Hi 1813.68; Lo 1697.61; Close 1697.92, −47.16.

**Mini Nasdaq 100 (CME)-$20 times index**
```
Mar   1761.5 1813.0 1683.0 1692.5 − 60.0 3850.0 1676.0   65,740
```
Vol Wed 146,423; open int 104,082, −771.

**GSCI (CME)-$250 times nearby index**
```
Mar   217.00 217.00 214.40   na     na  250.00 214.40    2,503
Apr   216.90 217.00 214.40 215.50 − .50 237.50 214.40   14,551
```
Est vol 3,241; vol Wed 3,807; open int 17,055, +157.
Idx prl: Hi 217.26; Lo 214.34; Close 215.58, −.52.

**Russell 2000 (CME)-$500 times index**
```
Mar   458.00 458.00 450.00 452.00 − .10 603.10 445.50    4,407
June  461.00 463.00 454.50 456.00 − .50 574.65 454.50   16,083
```
Est vol 4,190; vol Wed 4,632; open int 20,490, −40.
Idx prl: Hi 457.96; Lo 451.71; Close 452.16, −1.53.

**U.S. Dollar index (NYBOT)-$1,000 times USDX**
```
Mar   114.10 115.10 114.10 114.72 +  .96 118.72 108.04      828
June  113.73 115.38 113.55 114.87 + 1.00 118.13 108.18    5,297
```
Est vol 3,100; vol Wed 5,031; open int 8,133, +485.
Idx prl: Hi 115.19; Lo 113.43; Close 114.71, +1.01.

**Share Price index (SFE)**
**A $25 times index**
```
Mar   3261.0 3261.0 3197.0 3247.0 − 14.0 3395.0 3045.0  163,238
June  3284.0 3288.0 3228.0 3273.0 − 14.0 3410.0 3080.0   16,992
Sept   ....   ....         3289.0 − 16.0 3450.0 3303.0    1,442
Dec    ....   ....         3307.0 − 14.0 3435.0 3318.0      528
```
Est vol 28,053; vol Wed 15,314; open int 182,234, +13,838.
Index Hi 3263.9; Lo 3204.1; Close 3242.9, −21.0.

**CAC-40 Stock index (MATIF)-Euro 10.00 x index**
```
Mar   5140.0 5207.5 5069.0 5176.0 − 50.0 7102.0 4489.0  370,341
Apr   5175.0 5196.5 5100.0 5195.0 + 49.0 6022.5 5032.0   12,519
May   5145.0 5180.5 5070.5 5167.0 + 50.0 5508.5 4976.5       75
June  5119.0 5154.0 5095.0 5156.0 + 51.0 7034.0 4973.0   14,742
Sept   ....   ....         5207.0 + 51.0 6013.5 4804.0    5,930
Dec    ....   ....         5261.0 + 52.0 6162.5 5892.5      913
Mr02   ....   ....         5314.0 + 51.0   ....   ....    2,600
Sept   ....   ....         5346.0 + 52.0   ....   ....      600
```
Est vol 117,659; vol Wed 94,843; open int 407,720, +21,514.

**DAX-30 German Stock index (EUREX)**
**Euro 25 per DAX index pt.**
```
Mar   5850.0 5887.5 5768.5 5856.0 + 56.0 7699.0 5665.0  190,163
June  5876.5 5912.0 5793.0 5882.5 + 61.5 7364.0 5690.0  293,541
Sept  5888.0 5959.5 5888.0 5945.5 + 64.0 6952.5 5786.0    2,844
```
Vol Thu 125,542; open int 486,548, +49,245.
Index Hi 5889.95 Lo 5767.06 Close 5889.95, +95.83.

**FT-SE 100 index (LIFFE)-£10 per index point**
```
Mar   5667.5 5718.0 5596.5 5669.0 + 45.0 6620.0 5463.0   71,880
June  5710.0 5751.5 5640.0 5709.0 + 41.5 6398.0  618.0  260,404
Sept   ....   ....         5749.0 + 39.0 6436.0 5966.5    6,750
```
Est vol 113,700; vol Wed 151,724; open int 339,034, +10,145.

**DJ Euro Stoxx 50 index (EUREX)-Euro 10.00 x index**
```
Mar   4140.0 4189.0 4086.0 4180.0 + 63.0 5536.0 3998.0  340,951
June  4135.0 4174.0 4070.0 4166.0 + 62.0 5232.0 3984.0  434,041
Sept  4195.0 4195.0 4191.0 4202.0 + 66.0 4913.0 4058.0   24,311
```
Vol Thu 361,073; open int 799,303, +44,714.
Index Hi 4200.08; Lo 4088.84; Close 4200.08, +76.11.

**DJ Stoxx 50 index (EUREX)-Euro 10.00 x index**
```
Mar   3945.0 4000.0 3903.0 3991.0 + 51.0 5159.0 3803.0   13,901
June  3940.0 4008.0 3905.0 3999.0 + 52.0 5050.0 3811.0   14,427
```
Vol Thu 6,794; open int 28,334, +894.
Index Hi 4032.16; Lo 3908.72; Close 4032.98, +91.22.

*Source*: Reprinted by permission of Dow Jones, Inc., via copyright Clearance Center, Inc. © 2001 Dow Jones & Company, Inc. All Rights Reserved Worldwide.

The *Nasdaq 100* is based on 100 stocks using the National Association of Securities Dealers Automatic Quotations Service. The CME trades two contracts. One is on $100 times the index; the other (the Mini Nasdaq 100 contract) is on $20 times the index.

In the GSCI index futures contract shown in Table 3.2, the underlying asset is the *Goldman Sachs Commodity Index*. This is not a stock index. It is a broadly based index of commodity prices. All the major commodity groups, such as energy, livestock, grains and oilseeds, food and fiber, and metals, are represented in the GSCI. Studies by Goldman Sachs have shown that the GSCI is negatively related to the S&P 500 index, with the correlation being in the range −0.30 to −0.40.

The *Russell 2000* index is an index of small stocks in the United States. The *U.S. dollar index* is a trade-weighted index of the values of six foreign currencies (the euro, yen, pound, Canadian dollar, Swedish krona, and Swiss franc). The *Share Price Index* is the All Ordinaries Share Price Index, a broadly based index of Australian stocks. The *CAC-40 Index* is based on 40 large stocks trading in France. The *DAX-30 Index* is based on 30 stocks trading in Germany. The *FT-SE 100 Index* is based on a portfolio of 100 major U.K. stocks listed on the London Stock Exchange. The *DJ Euro Stoxx 50 Index* and the *DJ Stoxx 50 Index* are two different indices of blue chip European stocks compiled by Dow Jones and its European partners. The futures contracts on these indices trade on Eurex and are on 10 times the values of the indices measured in euros.

As mentioned in Chapter 2, futures contracts on stock indices are settled in cash, not by delivery of the underlying asset. All contracts are marked to market at either the opening price or the closing price of the index on the last trading day, and the positions are then deemed to be closed. For example, contracts on the S&P 500 are closed out at the opening S&P 500 index on the third Friday of the delivery month. Trading in the contracts continues until 8:30 a.m. on that Friday.

### Futures Prices of Stock Indices

A stock index can be regarded as the price of an investment asset that pays dividends. The investment asset is the portfolio of stocks underlying the index, and the dividends paid by the investment asset are the dividends that would be received by the holder of this portfolio. It is usually assumed that the dividends provide a known yield rather than a known cash income. If $q$ is the dividend yield rate, equation (3.7) gives the futures price, $F_0$, as

$$F_0 = S_0 e^{(r-q)T} \tag{3.12}$$

> **Example 3.7.** Consider a three-month futures contract on the S&P 500. Suppose that the stocks underlying the index provide a dividend yield of 1% per annum, that the current value of the index is 400, and that the continuously compounded risk-free interest rate is 6% per annum. In this case, $r = 0.06$, $S_0 = 400$, $T = 0.25$, and $q = 0.01$. Hence, the futures price, $F_0$, is given by
>
> $$F_0 = 400e^{(0.06-0.01)\times0.25} = \$405.03$$

In practice, the dividend yield on the portfolio underlying an index varies week by week throughout the year. For example, a large proportion of the dividends on the NYSE stocks are paid in the first week of February, May, August, and November each year. The chosen value of $q$ should represent the average annualized dividend yield during the life of the contract. The dividends used for estimating $q$ should be those for which the ex-dividend date is during the life of the futures contract. Looking at Table 3.2, we see that the futures prices for the S&P 500 Index appear to be increasing with the maturity of the futures contract at about 3.8% per annum. This corresponds to the situation where the risk-free interest rate exceeds the dividend yield by about 3.8% per annum.

### Index Arbitrage

If $F_0 > S_0 e^{(r-q)T}$, profits can be made by buying spot (i.e., for immediate delivery) the stocks underlying the index and shorting futures contracts. If $F_0 < S_0 e^{(r-q)T}$, profits can be made by doing the reverse—that is, shorting or selling the stocks underlying the index and taking a long position in futures contracts. These strategies are known as *index arbitrage*. When $F_0 < S_0 e^{(r-q)T}$, index arbitrage is often done by a pension fund that owns an indexed portfolio of stocks. When $F_0 > S_0 e^{(r-q)T}$, it is often done by a corporation holding short-term money market investments. For indices involving many stocks, index arbitrage is sometimes accomplished by trading a relatively small representative sample of stocks whose movements closely mirror those of the index. Often index arbitrage is implemented through *program trading*, with a computer system being used to generate the trades.

### October 1987

To do index arbitrage, a trader must be able to trade both the index futures contract and the portfolio of stocks underlying the index very quickly at the prices quoted in the market. In normal market conditions this is possible using program trading, and $F_0$ is very close to $S_0 e^{(r-q)T}$. Examples of days when the market was anything but normal are October 19 and 20 of 1987. On what is termed "Black Monday", October 19, 1987, the market fell by more than 20%, and the 604 million shares traded on the New York Stock Exchange easily exceeded all previous records. The exchange's systems were overloaded and if you placed an order to buy or sell a share on that day there could be a delay of up to two hours before your order was executed. For most of the day, futures prices were at a significant discount to the underlying index. For example, at the close of trading the S&P 500 Index was at 225.06 (down 57.88 on the day), whereas the futures price for December delivery on the S&P 500 was 201.50 (down 80.75 on the day). This was largely because the delays in processing orders made index arbitrage impossible. On the next day, Tuesday, October 20, 1987, the New York Stock Exchange placed temporary restrictions on the way in which program trading could be done. This also made index arbitrage very difficult, and the breakdown of the traditional linkage between stock indices and stock index futures continued. At one point the futures price for the December contract was 18% less than the S&P 500 Index. However, after a few days the market returned to normal, and the activities of arbitrageurs ensured that equation (3.12) governed the relationship between futures and spot prices of indices.

### The Nikkei Futures Contract

Equation (3.12) does not apply to the futures contract on the Nikkei 225. The reason is quite subtle. When $S$ is the value of the Nikkei 225 Index, it is the value of a portfolio measured in yen. The variable underlying the CME futures contract on the Nikkei 225 has a *dollar value* of $5S$. In other words, the futures contract takes a variable that is measured in yen and treats it as though it is dollars. We cannot invest in a portfolio whose value will always be $5S$ dollars. The best we can do is to invest in one that is always worth $5S$ yen or in one that is always worth $5QS$ dollars, where $Q$ is the dollar value of one yen. The arbitrage arguments that have been used in this chapter require the spot price underlying the futures price to be the price of an asset that can be traded by investors. The arguments are therefore not exactly correct for the Nikkei 225 contract. We will discuss this issue further in Section 21.8.

## 3.11₋ FORWARD AND FUTURES CONTRACTS ON CURRENCIES

We now move on to consider forward and futures foreign currency contracts. The underlying asset in such contracts is a certain number of units of the foreign currency. We will, therefore, define the variable $S_0$ as the current spot price in dollars of one unit of the foreign currency and $F_0$ as the forward or futures price in dollars of one unit of the foreign currency. This is consistent with the way we have defined $S_0$ and $F_0$ for other assets underlying forward and futures contracts. However, as mentioned in Chapter 2, it does not necessarily correspond to the way spot and forward exchange rates are quoted. For major exchange rates other than the British pound, euro, Australian dollar, and New Zealand dollar, a spot or forward exchange rate is normally quoted as the number of units of the currency that are equivalent to one dollar.

A foreign currency has the property that the holder of the currency can earn interest at the risk-free interest rate prevailing in the foreign country. For example, the holder can invest the currency in a foreign-denominated bond. We define $r_f$ as the value of the foreign risk-free interest rate when money is invested for time $T$. As before, $r$ is the domestic risk-free rate when money is invested for this period of time.

The relationship between $F_0$ and $S_0$ is

$$F_0 = S_0 e^{(r-r_f)T} \tag{3.13}$$

This is the well-known interest rate parity relationship from international finance. To see that it must be true, we suppose that the two-year interest rates in Australia and the United States are 5% and 7%, respectively, and the spot exchange rate between the Australian dollar (AUD) and the U.S. dollar (USD) is 0.6200 USD per AUD. From equation (3.13) the two-year forward exchange rate should be

$$0.6200 e^{(0.07-0.05) \times 2} = 0.6453$$

Suppose first the two-year forward exchange rate is less than this, say 0.6300. An arbitrageur can:

1. Borrow 1,000 AUD at 5% per annum for two years, convert to 620 USD, and invest the USD at 7% (both rates are continuously compounded).
2. Enter into a forward contract to buy 1,105.17 AUD for $1,105.17 \times 0.63 = 696.26$ USD.

The 620 USD that are invested at 7% grow to $620 e^{0.07 \times 2} = 713.17$ USD in two years. Of this, 696.26 USD are used to purchase 1,105.17 AUD under the terms of the forward contract. This is exactly enough to repay principal and interest on the 1,000 AUD that are borrowed $(1,000 e^{0.05 \times 2} = 1,105.17)$. The strategy therefore gives rise to a riskless profit of $713.17 - 696.26 = 16.91$ USD. (If this does not sound very exciting, consider following a similar strategy where you borrow 100 million AUD!)

Suppose next that the two-year forward rate is 0.6600 (greater than the 0.6453 value given by equation (3.13)). An arbitrageur can:

1. Borrow 1,000 USD at 7% per annum for two years, convert to $1,000/0.6200 = 1,612.90$ AUD, and invest the AUD at 5%.
2. Enter into a forward contract to sell 1,782.53 AUD for $1,782.53 \times 0.66 = 1,176.47$ USD.

The 1,612.90 AUD that are invested at 5% grow to $1,612.90 e^{0.05 \times 2} = 1,782.53$ AUD in two years. The forward contract has the effect of converting this to 1,176.47 USD. The amount needed to pay off the USD borrowings is $1,000 e^{0.07 \times 2} = 1,150.27$ USD. The strategy therefore gives rise to a riskless profit of $1,176.47 - 1,150.27 = 26.20$ USD.

Table 3.3 shows futures prices on March 15, 2001, for a variety of different currency futures trading on the Chicago Mercantile Exchange. In the case of the Japanese yen, prices are expressed as the number of cents per unit of foreign currency. In the case of the other currencies, prices are expressed as the number of U.S. dollars per unit of foreign currency.

When the foreign interest rate is greater than the domestic interest rate $(r_f > r)$, equation (3.13) shows that $F_0$ is always less than $S_0$ and that $F_0$ decreases as the time to maturity of the contract, $T$, increases. Similarly, when the domestic interest rate is greater than the foreign interest rate $(r > r_f)$, equation (3.13) shows that $F_0$ is always greater than $S_0$ and that $F_0$ increases as $T$ increases. On March 15, 2001, interest rates on the Japanese yen, Canadian dollar, and the euro were lower than in the interest rate on the U.S. dollar. This corresponds to the $r > r_f$ situation and explains why futures prices for these currencies increase with maturity in Table 3.3. In Australia, Britain, and

**Table 3.3** Foreign exchange futures quotes from the *Wall Street Journal* on March 16, 2001. (Columns show month, open, high, low, settle, change, lifetime high, lifetime low, and open interest, respectively.)

## CURRENCY

**Japan Yen (CME)-12.5 million yen; $ per yen (.00)**

| Month | Open | High | Low | Settle | Change | Life High | Life Low | Open Int |
|---|---|---|---|---|---|---|---|---|
| Mar | .8270 | .8297 | .8160 | .8174 | − .0094 | 1.0300 | .8160 | 41,711 |
| June | .8358 | .8398 | .8256 | .8270 | − .0095 | 1.0219 | .8256 | 87,632 |
| Sept | .8475 | .8475 | .8345 | .8363 | − .0097 | 1.0050 | .8345 | 579 |
| Dec | .8450 | .8450 | .8450 | .8455 | − .0099 | .9880 | .8450 | 431 |

Est vol 23,771; vol Wed 55,559; open int 130,445, +6,474.

**Deutschemark (CME)-125,000 marks; $ per mark**

| Month | Open | High | Low | Settle | Change | Life High | Life Low | Open Int |
|---|---|---|---|---|---|---|---|---|
| Mar | .4652 | .4652 | .4581 | .4606 | − .0061 | .4925 | .4225 | 236 |
| June | .4660 | .4661 | .4596 | .4607 | − .0058 | .4900 | .4596 | 229 |

Est vol 217; vol Wed 161; open int 467, −172.

**Canadian Dollar (CME)-100,000 dlrs.; $ per Can $**

| Month | Open | High | Low | Settle | Change | Life High | Life Low | Open Int |
|---|---|---|---|---|---|---|---|---|
| Mar | .6425 | .6431 | .6401 | .6405 | − .0018 | .7040 | .6401 | 20,442 |
| June | .6427 | .6434 | .6404 | .6408 | − .0018 | .6990 | .6404 | 56,601 |
| Sept | .6425 | .6436 | .6405 | .6412 | − .0018 | .6906 | .6405 | 2,630 |
| Dec | .6440 | .6440 | .6417 | .6416 | − .0018 | .6825 | .6417 | 1,286 |

Est vol 8,574; vol Wed 27,233; open int 81,108, +998.

**British Pound (CME)-62,500 pds.; $ per pound**

| Month | Open | High | Low | Settle | Change | Life High | Life Low | Open Int |
|---|---|---|---|---|---|---|---|---|
| Mar | 1.4448 | 1.4488 | 1.4340 | 1.4392 | − .0064 | 1.6050 | 1.4010 | 14,833 |
| June | 1.4444 | 1.4478 | 1.4330 | 1.4374 | − .0064 | 1.5304 | 1.4060 | 23,641 |

Est vol 7,361; vol Wed 15,385; open int 38,510, −2,720.

**Swiss Franc (CME)-125,000 francs; $ per franc**

| Month | Open | High | Low | Settle | Change | Life High | Life Low | Open Int |
|---|---|---|---|---|---|---|---|---|
| Mar | .5910 | .5910 | .5828 | .5858 | − .0051 | .6326 | .5541 | 20,680 |
| June | .5885 | .5951 | .5842 | .5879 | − .0052 | .6358 | .5585 | 32,622 |

Est vol 14,447; vol Wed 34,342; open int 53,337, +4,514.

**Australian Dollar (CME)-100,000 dlrs.; $ per A.$**

| Month | Open | High | Low | Settle | Change | Life High | Life Low | Open Int |
|---|---|---|---|---|---|---|---|---|
| Mar | .4960 | .4960 | .4908 | .4925 | − .0019 | .6390 | .4908 | 18,376 |
| June | .4956 | .4971 | .4898 | .4924 | − .0020 | .6083 | .4898 | 23,621 |
| Sept | .4942 | .4942 | .4917 | .4923 | − .0021 | .5622 | .4917 | 264 |

Est vol 3,212; vol Wed 8,578; open int 42,329, +313.

**Mexican Peso (CME)-500,000 new Mex. peso, $ per MP**

| Month | Open | High | Low | Settle | Change | Life High | Life Low | Open Int |
|---|---|---|---|---|---|---|---|---|
| Mar | .10438 | .10445 | .10395 | .10403 | − .00017 | .10453 | .09120 | 13,248 |
| Apr | .... | .... | .... | .10298 | − .00027 | .10353 | .09730 | 390 |
| May | .... | .... | .... | .10198 | − .00027 | .10180 | .09900 | 848 |
| June | .10155 | .10170 | .10095 | .10108 | − .00027 | .10170 | .09070 | 20,061 |
| Aug | .... | .... | .... | .09908 | − .00027 | .09800 | .09800 | 100 |
| Sept | .... | .... | .... | .09815 | − .00027 | .09880 | .09300 | 2,693 |

**Euro FX (CME)-Euro 125,000; $ per Euro**

| Month | Open | High | Low | Settle | Change | Life High | Life Low | Open Int |
|---|---|---|---|---|---|---|---|---|
| Mar | .9116 | .9120 | .8965 | .9009 | − .0089 | .9999 | .8333 | 38,657 |
| June | .9121 | .9130 | .8960 | .9010 | − .0092 | .9784 | .8358 | 59,061 |
| Sept | .9060 | .9071 | .8990 | .9013 | − .0093 | .9634 | .8379 | 1,178 |

Est vol 33,027; vol Wed 40,744; open int 99,063, −3,000.

*Source*: Reprinted by permission of Dow Jones, Inc., via copyright Clearance Center, Inc. © 2001 Dow Jones & Company, Inc. All Rights Reserved Worldwide.

Mexico interest rates were higher than in the United States. This corresponds to the $r_f > r$ situation and explains why the futures prices of these three currencies decrease with maturity.

**Example 3.8** The futures price of the Japanese yen in Table 3.3 appears to be increasing at a rate of about 4.6% per annum with the maturity of the contract. The increase suggests that short-term interest rates were about 4.6% per annum higher in the United States than in Japan on March 15, 2001.

### A Foreign Currency as an Asset Providing a Known Yield

Note that equation (3.13) is identical to equation (3.7) with $q$ replaced by $r_f$. This is not a coincidence. A foreign currency can be regarded as an investment asset paying a known yield. The yield is the risk-free rate of interest in the foreign currency.

To understand this, suppose that the one-year interest rate on British pounds is 5% per annum. (For simplicity, we assume that the interest rate is measured with annual compounding and interest is paid at the end of the year.) Consider a United States investor who buys 1 million pounds. The investor knows that £50,000 of interest will be earned at the end of one year. The value of this interest in dollars depends the exchange rate. If the exchange rate in one year is 1.5000, the interest is worth $75,000; if it is 1.4000, the interest is worth $70,000; and so on. The value in dollars of the interest earned is 5% of the value of the sterling investment. The 5% interest therefore represents a known yield to the United States investor on the sterling investment.

## 3.12 FUTURES ON COMMODITIES

We now move on to consider futures contracts on commodities. First we consider the impact of storage on the futures prices of commodities that are investment assets, such as gold and silver.[6] We assume that no income is earned on the assets.

### Storage Costs

Equation (3.5) shows that in the absence of storage costs the forward price of a commodity that is an investment asset is given by

$$F_0 = S_0 e^{rT} \qquad (3.14)$$

Storage costs can be regarded as negative income. If $U$ is the present value of all the storage costs that will be incurred during the life of a forward contract, it follows from equation (3.6) that

$$F_0 = (S_0 + U)e^{rT} \qquad (3.15)$$

> **Example 3.9** Consider a one-year futures contract on gold. Suppose that it costs $2 per ounce per year to store gold, with the payment being made at the end of the year. Assume that the spot price is $450 and the risk-free rate is 7% per annum for all maturities. This corresponds to $r = 0.07$, $S_0 = 450$, $T = 1$, and
>
> $$U = 2e^{-0.07 \times 1} = 1.865$$
>
> From equation (3.15) the futures price, $F_0$, is given by
>
> $$F_0 = (450 + 1.865)e^{0.07 \times 1} = \$484.63$$
>
> If $F_0 > 484.63$, an arbitrageur can buy gold and short one-year gold futures contracts to lock in a profit. If $F_0 < 484.63$, an investor who already owns gold can improve the return by selling the gold and buying gold futures contracts.

If the storage costs incurred at any time are proportional to the price of the commodity, they can be regarded as providing a negative yield. In this case, from equation (3.7),

$$F_0 = S_0 e^{(r+u)T} \qquad (3.16)$$

where $u$ denotes the storage costs per annum as a proportion of the spot price.

### Consumption Commodities

For commodities that are consumption assets rather than investment assets, the arbitrage arguments used to determine futures prices need to be reviewed carefully. Suppose that instead of

---

[6] Recall that for an asset to be an investment asset it need not be held solely for investment purposes. What is required is that some individuals hold it for investment purposes and that these individuals be prepared to sell their holdings and go long forward contracts, if the latter look more attractive. This explains why silver, although it has significant industrial uses, is an investment asset.

equation (3.15) we have

$$F_0 > (S_0 + U)e^{rT} \tag{3.17}$$

To take advantage of this opportunity, an arbitrageur can implement the following strategy:

1. Borrow an amount $S_0 + U$ at the risk-free rate and use it to purchase one unit of the commodity and to pay storage costs.
2. Short a forward contract on one unit of the commodity.

If we regard the futures contract as a forward contract, this strategy leads to a profit of $F_0 - (S_0 + U)e^{rT}$ at time $T$. There is no problem in implementing the strategy for any commodity. However, as arbitrageurs do so, there will be a tendency for $S_0$ to increase and $F_0$ to decrease until equation (3.17) is no longer true. We conclude that equation (3.17) cannot hold for any significant length of time.

Suppose next that

$$F_0 < (S_0 + U)e^{rT} \tag{3.18}$$

In the case of investment assets such as gold and silver, we can argue that many investors hold the commodity solely for investment. When they observe the inequality in equation (3.18), they will find it profitable to:

1. Sell the commodity, save the storage costs, and invest the proceeds at the risk-free interest rate.
2. Take a long position in a forward contract.

The result is a riskless profit at maturity of $(S_0 + U)e^{rT} - F_0$ relative to the position the investors would have been in if they had held the commodity. It follows that equation (3.18) cannot hold for long. Because neither equation (3.17) nor (3.18) can hold for long, we must have $F_0 = (S_0 + U)e^{rT}$.

For commodities that are not to any significant extent held for investment, this argument cannot be used. Individuals and companies who keep such a commodity in inventory do so because of its consumption value—not because of its value as an investment. They are reluctant to sell the commodity and buy forward contracts, because forward contracts cannot be consumed. There is therefore nothing to stop equation (3.18) from holding. All we can assert for a consumption commodity is therefore

$$F_0 \leqslant (S_0 + U)e^{rT} \tag{3.19}$$

If storage costs are expressed as a proportion $u$ of the spot price, the equivalent result is

$$F_0 \leqslant S_0 e^{(r+u)T} \tag{3.20}$$

### Convenience Yields

We do not necessarily have equality in equations (3.19) and (3.20) because users of a consumption commodity may feel that ownership of the physical commodity provides benefits that are not obtained by holders of futures contracts. For example, an oil refiner is unlikely to regard a futures contract on crude oil as equivalent to crude oil held in inventory. The crude oil in inventory can be an input to the refining process whereas a futures contract cannot be used for this purpose. In general, ownership of the physical asset enables a manufacturer to keep a production process running and perhaps profit from temporary local shortages. A futures contract does not do the same. The benefits from holding the physical asset are sometimes referred to as the *convenience yield* provided by the commodity. If the dollar amount of storage costs is known and has a present value $U$, the convenience yield, $y$, is defined so that

$$F_0 e^{yT} = (S_0 + U)e^{rT}$$

If the storage costs per unit are a constant proportion $u$ of the spot price, $y$ is defined so that

$$F_0 e^{yT} = S_0 e^{(r+u)T}$$

or

$$F_0 = S_0 e^{(r+u-y)T} \tag{3.21}$$

The convenience yield simply measures the extent to which the left-hand side is less than the right-hand side in equation (3.19) or (3.20). For investment assets the convenience yield must be zero; otherwise, there are arbitrage opportunities. Table 2.2 of Chapter 2 shows that the futures prices of some commodities such as Sugar–World tended to decrease as the time to maturity of the contract increased on March 15, 2001. This pattern suggests that the convenience yield, $y$, is greater than $r + u$ for these commodities.

The convenience yield reflects the market's expectations concerning the future availability of the commodity. The greater the possibility that shortages will occur, the higher the convenience yield. If users of the commodity have high inventories, there is very little chance of shortages in the near future and the convenience yield tends to be low. On the other hand, low inventories tend to lead to high convenience yields.

## 3.13 COST OF CARRY

The relationship between futures prices and spot prices can be summarized in terms of the *cost of carry*. This measures the storage cost plus the interest that is paid to finance the asset less the income earned on the asset. For a non-dividend-paying stock, the cost of carry is $r$, because there are no storage costs and no income is earned; for a stock index, it is $r - q$, because income is earned at rate $q$ on the asset. For a currency, it is $r - r_f$; for a commodity with storage costs that are a proportion $u$ of the price, it is $r + u$; and so on.

Define the cost of carry as $c$. For an investment asset, the futures price is

$$F_0 = S_0 e^{cT} \tag{3.22}$$

For a consumption asset, it is

$$F_0 = S_0 e^{(c-y)T} \tag{3.23}$$

where $y$ is the convenience yield.

## 3.14 DELIVERY OPTIONS

Whereas a forward contract normally specifies that delivery is to take place on a particular day, a futures contract often allows the party with the short position to choose to deliver at any time during a certain period. (Typically the party has to give a few days' notice of its intention to deliver.) The choice introduces a complication into the determination of futures prices. Should the maturity of the futures contract be assumed to be the beginning, middle, or end of the delivery period? Even though most futures contracts are closed out prior to maturity, it is important to know when delivery would have taken place in order to calculate the theoretical futures price.

If the futures price is an increasing function of the time to maturity, it can be seen from equation (3.23) that $c > y$, so that the benefits from holding the asset (including convenience yield and net of storage costs) are less than the risk-free rate. It is usually optimal in such a case for the party with the short position to deliver as early as possible, because the interest earned on the cash received outweighs the benefits of holding the asset. As a rule, futures prices in these circumstances should be calculated on the basis that delivery will take place at the beginning of the delivery period. If futures prices are decreasing as time to maturity increases ($c < y$), the reverse is true. It is then usually optimal for the party with the short position to deliver as late as possible, and futures prices should, as a rule, be calculated on this assumption.

## 3.15   FUTURES PRICES AND THE EXPECTED FUTURE SPOT PRICE

A question that is often raised is whether the futures price of an asset is equal to its expected future spot price. If you have to guess what the price of an asset will be in three months, is the futures price an unbiased estimate? Chapter 2 presented the arguments of Keynes and Hicks. These authors contend that speculators will not trade a futures contract unless their expected profit is positive. By contrast, hedgers are prepared to accept a negative expected profit because of the risk-reduction benefits they get from a futures contract. If more speculators are long than short, the futures price will tend to be less than the expected future spot price. On average, speculators can then expect to make a gain, because the futures price converges to the spot price at maturity of the contract. Similarly, if more speculators are short than long, the futures price will tend to be greater than the expected future spot price.

### Risk and Return

Another explanation of the relationship between futures prices and expected future spot prices can be obtained by considering the relationship between risk and expected return in the economy. In general, the higher the risk of an investment, the higher the expected return demanded by an investor. Readers familiar with the capital asset pricing model will know that there are two types of risk in the economy: systematic and nonsystematic. Nonsystematic risk should not be important to an investor. It can be almost completely eliminated by holding a well-diversified portfolio. An investor should not therefore require a higher expected return for bearing nonsystematic risk. Systematic risk, by contrast, cannot be diversified away. It arises from a correlation between returns from the investment and returns from the stock market as a whole. An investor generally requires a higher expected return than the risk-free interest rate for bearing positive amounts of systematic risk. Also, an investor is prepared to accept a lower expected return than the risk-free interest rate when the systematic risk in an investment is negative.

### The Risk in a Futures Position

Let us consider a speculator who takes a long futures position in the hope that the spot price of the asset will be above the futures price at maturity. We suppose that the speculator puts the present value of the futures price into a risk-free investment while simultaneously taking a long futures position. We assume that the futures contract can be treated as a forward contract. The proceeds of the risk-free investment are used to buy the asset on the delivery date. The asset is then immediately sold for its market price. The cash flows to the speculator are:

Time $0$: $-F_0 e^{-rT}$

Time $T$: $+S_T$

where $S_T$ is the price of the asset at time $T$.

The present value of this investment is

$$-F_0 e^{-rT} + E(S_T)e^{-kT}$$

where $k$ is the discount rate appropriate for the investment (i.e., the expected return required by investors on the investment) and $E$ denotes the expected value. Assuming that all investment opportunities in securities markets have zero net present value,

$$-F_0 e^{-rT} + E(S_T)e^{-kT} = 0$$

or

$$F_0 = E(S_T)e^{(r-k)T} \tag{3.24}$$

The value of $k$ depends on the systematic risk of the investment. If $S_T$ is uncorrelated with the level of the stock market, the investment has zero systematic risk. In this case $k = r$, and equation (3.24) shows that $F_0 = E(S_T)$. If $S_T$ is positively correlated with the stock market as a whole, the investment has positive systematic risk. In this case $k > r$, and equation (3.24) shows that $F_0 < E(S_T)$. Finally, if $S_T$ is negatively correlated with the stock market, the investment has negative systematic risk. In this case $k < r$, and equation (3.24) shows that $F_0 > E(S_T)$.

### Empirical Evidence

If $F_0 = E(S_T)$, the futures price will drift up or down only if the market changes its views about the expected future spot price. Over a long period of time, we can reasonably assume that the market revises its expectations about future spot prices upward as often as it does so downward. It follows that when $F_0 = E(S_T)$, the average profit from holding futures contracts over a long period of time should be zero. The $F_0 < E(S_T)$ situation corresponds to the positive systematic risk situation. Because the futures price and the spot price must be equal at maturity of the futures contract, a futures price should on average drift up, and a trader should over a long period of time make positive profits from consistently holding long futures positions. Similarly, the $F_0 > E(S_T)$ situation implies that a trader should over a long period of time make positive profits from consistently holding short futures positions.

How do futures prices behave in practice? Some of the empirical work that has been carried out is listed at the end of this chapter. The results are mixed. Houthakker's study looked at futures prices for wheat, cotton, and corn from 1937 to 1957. It showed that significant profits could be earned by taking long futures positions. This suggests that an investment in one of these assets has positive systematic risk and $F_0 < E(S_T)$. Telser's study contradicted the findings of Houthakker. His data covered the period from 1926 to 1950 for cotton and from 1927 to 1954 for wheat and gave rise to no significant profits for traders taking either long or short positions. To quote from Telser: "The futures data offer no evidence to contradict the simple...hypothesis that the futures price is an unbiased estimate of the expected future spot price." Gray's study looked at corn futures prices during the period 1921 to 1959 and resulted in similar findings to those of Telser. Dusak's study used data on corn, wheat, and soybeans from 1952 to 1967 and took a different approach. It attempted to estimate the systematic risk of an investment in these commodities by calculating the correlation of movements in the commodity prices with movements in the S&P 500. The results suggest that there is no systematic risk and lend support to the $F_0 = E(S_T)$ hypothesis. However, more recent work by Chang using the same commodities and more advanced statistical techniques supports the $F_0 < E(S_T)$ hypothesis.

## SUMMARY

For most purposes, the futures price of a contract with a certain delivery date can be considered to be the same as the forward price for a contract with the same delivery date. It can be shown that in theory the two should be exactly the same when interest rates are perfectly predictable.

For the purposes of understanding futures (or forward) prices, it is convenient to divide futures contracts into two categories: those in which the underlying asset is held for investment by a significant number of investors and those in which the underlying asset is held primarily for consumption purposes.

In the case of investment assets, we have considered three different situations:

1. The asset provides no income.
2. The asset provides a known dollar income.
3. The asset provides a known yield.

The results are summarized in Table 3.4. They enable futures prices to be obtained for contracts on stock indices, currencies, gold, and silver. Storage costs can be regarded as negative income.

In the case of consumption assets, it is not possible to obtain the futures price as a function of the spot price and other observable variables. Here the parameter known as the asset's convenience yield becomes important. It measures the extent to which users of the commodity feel that ownership of the physical asset provides benefits that are not obtained by the holders of the futures contract. These benefits may include the ability to profit from temporary local shortages or the ability to keep a production process running. We can obtain an upper bound for the futures price of consumption assets using arbitrage arguments, but we cannot nail down an equality relationship between futures and spot prices.

**Table 3.4**   Summary of results for a contract with time to maturity $T$ on an investment asset with price $S_0$ when the risk-free interest rate for a $T$-year period is $r$

| *Asset* | *Forward/futures price* | *Value of long forward contract with delivery price K* |
|---|---|---|
| Provides no income | $S_0 e^{rT}$ | $S_0 - K e^{-rT}$ |
| Provides known income with present value $I$ | $(S_0 - I) e^{rT}$ | $S_0 - I - K e^{-rT}$ |
| Provides known yield $q$ | $S_0 e^{(r-q)T}$ | $S_0 e^{-qT} - K e^{-rT}$ |

The concept of cost of carry is sometimes useful. The cost of carry is the storage cost of the underlying asset plus the cost of financing it minus the income received from it. In the case of investment assets, the futures price is greater than the spot price by an amount reflecting the cost of carry. In the case of consumption assets, the futures price is greater than the spot price by an amount reflecting the cost of carry net of the convenience yield.

If we assume the capital asset pricing model is true, the relationship between the futures price and the expected future spot price depends on whether the return on the asset is positively or negatively correlated with the return on the stock market. Positive correlation will tend to lead to a futures price lower than the expected future spot price. Negative correlation will tend to lead to a futures price higher than the expected future spot price. Only when the correlation is zero will the theoretical futures price be equal to the expected future spot price.

## SUGGESTIONS FOR FURTHER READING

### On Empirical Research Concerning Forward and Futures Prices

Cornell, B., and M. Reinganum, "Forward and Futures Prices: Evidence from Foreign Exchange Markets," *Journal of Finance*, 36 (December 1981), 1035–45.

French, K., "A Comparison of Futures and Forward Prices," *Journal of Financial Economics*, 12 (November 1983), 311–42.

Park, H. Y., and A. H. Chen, "Differences between Futures and Forward Prices: A Further Investigation of Marking to Market Effects," *Journal of Futures Markets*, 5 (February 1985), 77–88.

Rendleman, R., and C. Carabini, "The Efficiency of the Treasury Bill Futures Markets," *Journal of Finance*, 34 (September 1979), 895–914.

Viswanath, P. V., "Taxes and the Futures-Forward Price Difference in the 91-Day T-Bill Market," *Journal of Money Credit and Banking*, 21, no. 2 (May 1989), 190–205.

### On Empirical Research Concerning the Relationship Between Futures Prices and Expected Future Spot Prices

Chang, E. C., "Returns to Speculators and the Theory of Normal Backwardation," *Journal of Finance*, 40 (March 1985), 193–208.

Dusak, K., "Futures Trading and Investor Returns: An Investigation of Commodity Risk Premiums," *Journal of Political Economy*, 81 (December 1973), 1387–1406.

Gray, R. W., "The Search for a Risk Premium," *Journal of Political Economy*, 69 (June 1961), 250–60.

Houthakker, H. S., "Can Speculators Forecast Prices?" *Review of Economics and Statistics*, 39 (1957), 143–51.

Telser, L. G., "Futures Trading and the Storage of Cotton and Wheat," *Journal of Political Economy*, 66 (June 1958), 233–55.

### On the Theoretical Relationship Between Forward and Futures Prices

Cox, J. C., J. E. Ingersoll, and S. A. Ross, "The Relation between Forward Prices and Futures Prices," *Journal of Financial Economics*, 9 (December 1981), 321–46.

Jarrow, R. A., and G. S. Oldfield, "Forward Contracts and Futures Contracts," *Journal of Financial Economics*, 9 (December 1981), 373–82.

Kane, E. J., "Market Incompleteness and Divergences between Forward and Futures Interest Rates," *Journal of Finance*, 35 (May 1980), 221–34.

Richard, S., and M. Sundaresan, "A Continuous-Time Model of Forward and Futures Prices in a Multigood Economy," *Journal of Financial Economics*, 9 (December 1981), 347–72.

# QUESTIONS AND PROBLEMS
## (ANSWERS IN SOLUTIONS MANUAL)

3.1. A bank quotes you an interest rate of 14% per annum with quarterly compounding. What is the equivalent rate with (a) continuous compounding and (b) annual compounding?

3.2. Explain what happens when an investor shorts a certain share.

3.3. Suppose that you enter into a six-month forward contract on a non-dividend-paying stock when the stock price is $30 and the risk-free interest rate (with continuous compounding) is 12% per annum. What is the forward price?

3.4. A stock index currently stands at 350. The risk-free interest rate is 8% per annum (with continuous compounding) and the dividend yield on the index is 4% per annum. What should the futures price for a four-month contract be?

3.5. Explain carefully why the futures price of gold can be calculated from its spot price and other observable variables whereas the futures price of copper cannot.

3.6. Explain carefully the meaning of the terms *convenience yield* and *cost of carry*. What is the relationship between futures price, spot price, convenience yield, and cost of carry?

3.7. Is the futures price of a stock index greater than or less than the expected future value of the index? Explain your answer.

3.8. An investor receives $1,100 in one year in return for an investment of $1,000 now. Calculate the percentage return per annum with
   a. Annual compounding
   b. Semiannual compounding
   c. Monthly compounding
   d. Continuous compounding

3.9. What rate of interest with continuous compounding is equivalent to 15% per annum with monthly compounding?

3.10. A deposit account pays 12% per annum with continuous compounding, but interest is actually paid quarterly. How much interest will be paid each quarter on a $10,000 deposit?

3.11. A one-year long forward contract on a non-dividend-paying stock is entered into when the stock price is $40 and the risk-free rate of interest is 10% per annum with continuous compounding.
   a. What are the forward price and the initial value of the forward contract?
   b. Six months later, the price of the stock is $45 and the risk-free interest rate is still 10%. What are the forward price and the value of the forward contract?

3.12. The risk-free rate of interest is 7% per annum with continuous compounding, and the dividend yield on a stock index is 3.2% per annum. The current value of the index is 150. What is the six-month futures price?

3.13. Assume that the risk-free interest rate is 9% per annum with continuous compounding and that the dividend yield on a stock index varies throughout the year. In February, May, August, and November, dividends are paid at a rate of 5% per annum. In other months, dividends are paid at a rate of 2% per annum. Suppose that the value of the index on July 31, 2002, is 300. What is the futures price for a contract deliverable on December 31, 2002?

3.14. Suppose that the risk-free interest rate is 10% per annum with continuous compounding and that the dividend yield on a stock index is 4% per annum. The index is standing at 400, and the futures price for a contract deliverable in four months is 405. What arbitrage opportunities does this create?

3.15. Estimate the difference between short-term interest rates in Mexico and the United States on March 15, 2001, from the information in Table 3.3.

3.16. The two-month interest rates in Switzerland and the United States are 3% and 8% per annum, respectively, with continuous compounding. The spot price of the Swiss franc is $0.6500. The futures price for a contract deliverable in two months is $0.6600. What arbitrage opportunities does this create?

3.17. The current price of silver is $9 per ounce. The storage costs are $0.24 per ounce per year payable quarterly in advance. Assuming that interest rates are 10% per annum for all maturities, calculate the futures price of silver for delivery in nine months.

3.18. Suppose that $F_1$ and $F_2$ are two futures contracts on the same commodity with times to maturity, $t_1$ and $t_2$, where $t_2 > t_1$. Prove that

$$F_2 \leqslant F_1 e^{r(t_2 - t_1)}$$

where $r$ is the interest rate (assumed constant) and there are no storage costs. For the purposes of this problem, assume that a futures contract is the same as a forward contract.

3.19. When a known future cash outflow in a foreign currency is hedged by a company using a forward contract, there is no foreign exchange risk. When it is hedged using futures contracts, the marking-to-market process does leave the company exposed to some risk. Explain the nature of this risk. In particular, consider whether the company is better off using a futures contract or a forward contract when
    a. The value of the foreign currency falls rapidly during the life of the contract
    b. The value of the foreign currency rises rapidly during the life of the contract
    c. The value of the foreign currency first rises and then falls back to its initial value
    d. The value of the foreign currency first falls and then rises back to its initial value
       Assume that the forward price equals the futures price.

3.20. It is sometimes argued that a forward exchange rate is an unbiased predictor of future exchange rates. Under what circumstances is this so?

3.21. Show that the growth rate in an index futures price equals the excess return of the index over the risk-free rate. Assume that the risk-free interest rate and the dividend yield are constant.

3.22. Show that equation (3.7) is true by considering an investment in the asset combined with a short position in a futures contract. Assume that all income from the asset is reinvested in the asset. Use an argument similar to that in footnotes 2 and 4 and explain in detail what an arbitrageur would do if equation (3.7) did not hold.

3.23. The Value Line Index is designed to reflect changes in the value of a portfolio of over 1,600 equally weighted stocks. Prior to March 9, 1988, the change in the index from one day to the next was calculated as the *geometric* average of the changes in the prices of the stocks underlying the index. In these circumstances, does equation (3.12) correctly relate the futures price of the index to its cash price? If not, does the equation overstate or understate the futures price?

## ASSIGNMENT QUESTIONS

3.24. A stock is expected to pay a dividend of $1 per share in two months and in five months. The stock price is $50, and the risk-free rate of interest is 8% per annum with continuous compounding for all maturities. An investor has just taken a short position in a six-month forward contract on the stock.

    a. What are the forward price and the initial value of the forward contract?

    b. Three months later, the price of the stock is $48 and the risk-free rate of interest is still 8% per annum. What are the forward price and the value of the short position in the forward contract?

3.25. A bank offers a corporate client a choice between borrowing cash at 11% per annum and borrowing gold at 2% per annum. (If gold is borrowed, interest must be repaid in gold. Thus, 100 ounces borrowed today would require 102 ounces to be repaid in one year.) The risk-free interest rate is 9.25% per annum, and storage costs are 0.5% per annum. Discuss whether the rate of interest on the gold loan is too high or too low in relation to the rate of interest on the cash loan. The interest rates on the two loans are expressed with annual compounding. The risk-free interest rate and storage costs are expressed with continuous compounding. Assume that no income is earned on gold. Repeat your calculations for the situation where income of 1.5% per annum can be earned on gold.

3.26. A company that is uncertain about the exact date when it will pay or receive a foreign currency may try to negotiate with its bank a forward contract that specifies a period during which delivery can be made. The company wants to reserve the right to choose the exact delivery date to fit in with its own cash flows. Put yourself in the position of the bank. How would you price the product that the company wants?

3.27. A foreign exchange trader working for a bank enters into a long forward contract to buy one million pounds sterling at an exchange rate of 1.6000 in three months. At the same time, another trader on the next desk takes a long position in 16 three-month futures contracts on sterling. The futures price is 1.6000, and each contract is on 62,500 pounds. Within minutes of the trades being executed the forward and the futures prices both increase to 1.6040. Both traders immediately claim a profit of $4,000. The bank's systems show that the futures trader has made a $4,000 profit, but the forward trader has made a profit of only $3,900. The forward trader immediately picks up the phone to complain to the systems department. Explain what is going on here. Why are the profits different?

3.28. A company enters into a forward contract with a bank to sell a foreign currency for $K_1$ at time $T_1$. The exchange rate at time $T_1$ proves to be $S_1$ ($> K_1$). The company asks the bank if it can roll the contract forward until time $T_2$ ($> T_1$) rather than settle at time $T_1$. The bank agrees to a new delivery price, $K_2$. Explain how $K_2$ should be calculated.

# APPENDIX 3A
## Proof That Forward and Futures Prices Are Equal When Interest Rates Are Constant

This appendix demonstrates that forward and futures prices are equal when interest rates are constant. Suppose that a futures contract lasts for $n$ days and that $F_i$ is the futures price at the end of day $i$ $(0 < i < n)$. Define $\delta$ as the risk-free rate per day (assumed constant). Consider the following strategy.[7]

1. Take a long futures position of $e^\delta$ at the end of day 0 (i.e., at the beginning of the contract).
2. Increase long position to $e^{2\delta}$ at the end of day 1.
3. Increase long position to $e^{3\delta}$ at the end of day 2.

And so on.

This strategy is summarized in Table 3.5. By the beginning of day $i$, the investor has a long position of $e^{\delta i}$. The profit (possibly negative) from the position on day $i$ is

$$(F_i - F_{i-1})e^{\delta i}$$

Assume that the profit is compounded at the risk-free rate until the end of day $n$. Its value at the end of day $n$ is

$$(F_i - F_{i-1})e^{\delta i}e^{(n-i)\delta} = (F_i - F_{i-1})e^{n\delta}$$

The value at the end of day $n$ of the entire investment strategy is therefore

$$\sum_{i=1}^{n}(F_i - F_{i-1})e^{n\delta}$$

This is

$$[(F_n - F_{n-1}) + (F_{n-1} - F_{n-2}) + \cdots + (F_1 - F_0)]e^{n\delta} = (F_n - F_0)e^{n\delta}$$

Because $F_n$ is the same as the terminal asset spot price, $S_T$, the terminal value of the investment strategy can be written

$$(S_T - F_0)e^{n\delta}$$

**Table 3.5**  The investment strategy to show that futures and forward prices are equal

| Day | 0 | 1 | 2 | $\cdots$ | $n-1$ | $n$ |
|---|---|---|---|---|---|---|
| Futures price | $F_0$ | $F_1$ | $F_2$ | $\cdots$ | $F_{n-1}$ | $F_n$ |
| Futures position | $e^\delta$ | $e^{2\delta}$ | $e^{3\delta}$ | $\cdots$ | $e^{n\delta}$ | 0 |
| Gain/loss | 0 | $(F_1 - F_0)e^\delta$ | $(F_2 - F_1)e^{2\delta}$ | $\cdots$ | $\cdots$ | $(F_n - F_{n-1})e^{n\delta}$ |
| Gain/loss compounded to day $n$ | 0 | $(F_1 - F_0)e^{n\delta}$ | $(F_2 - F_1)e^{n\delta}$ | $\cdots$ | $\cdots$ | $(F_n - F_{n-1})e^{n\delta}$ |

---

[7] This strategy was proposed by J. C. Cox, J. E. Ingersoll, and S. A. Ross, "The Relation between Forward Prices and Futures Prices," *Journal of Financial Economics*, 9 (December 1981), 321–46.

An investment of $F_0$ in a risk-free bond combined with the strategy just given yields

$$F_0 e^{n\delta} + (S_T - F_0)e^{n\delta} = S_T e^{n\delta}$$

at time $T$. No investment is required for all the long futures positions described. It follows that an amount $F_0$ can be invested to give an amount $S_T e^{n\delta}$ at time $T$.

Suppose next that the forward price at the end of day 0 is $G_0$. Investing $G_0$ in a riskless bond and taking a long forward position of $e^{n\delta}$ forward contracts also guarantees an amount $S_T e^{n\delta}$ at time $T$. Thus, there are two investment strategies—one requiring an initial outlay of $F_0$ and the other requiring an initial outlay of $G_0$—both of which yield $S_T e^{n\delta}$ at time $T$. It follows that, in the absence of arbitrage opportunities,

$$F_0 = G_0$$

In other words, the futures price and the forward price are identical. Note that in this proof there is nothing special about the time period of one day. The futures price based on a contract with weekly settlements is also the same as the forward price when corresponding assumptions are made.

# C H A P T E R   4

# HEDGING STRATEGIES USING FUTURES

Many of the participants in futures markets are hedgers. Their aim is to use futures markets to reduce a particular risk that they face. This risk might relate to the price of oil, a foreign exchange rate, the level of the stock market, or some other variable. A *perfect hedge* is one that completely eliminates the risk. In practice, perfect hedges are rare. To quote one trader: "The only perfect hedge is in a Japanese garden." For the most part, therefore, a study of hedging using futures contracts is a study of the ways in which hedges can be constructed so that they perform as close to perfect as possible.

In this chapter we consider a number of general issues associated with the way hedges are set up. When is a short futures position appropriate? When is a long futures position appropriate? Which futures contract should be used? What is the optimal size of the futures position for reducing risk? At this stage, we restrict our attention to what might be termed *hedge-and-forget* strategies. We assume that no attempt is made to adjust the hedge once it has been put in place. The hedger simply takes a futures position at the beginning of the life of the hedge and closes out the position at the end of the life of the hedge. In Chapter 14 we will examine dynamic hedging strategies in which the hedge is monitored closely and frequent adjustments are made.

Throughout this chapter we will treat futures contracts as forward contracts, that is, we will ignore daily settlement. This means that we can ignore the time value of money in most situations because all cash flows occur at the time the hedge is closed out.

## 4.1  BASIC PRINCIPLES

When an individual or company chooses to use futures markets to hedge a risk, the objective is usually to take a position that neutralizes the risk as far as possible. Consider a company that knows it will gain $10,000 for each 1 cent increase in the price of a commodity over the next three months and lose $10,000 for each 1 cent decrease in the price during the same period. To hedge, the company's treasurer should take a short futures position that is designed to offset this risk. The futures position should lead to a loss of $10,000 for each 1 cent increase in the price of the commodity over the three months and a gain of $10,000 for each 1 cent decrease in the price during this period. If the price of the commodity goes down, the gain on the futures position offsets the loss on the rest of the company's business. If the price of the commodity goes up, the loss on the futures position is offset by the gain on the rest of the company's business.

### Short Hedges

A *short hedge* is a hedge, such as the one just described, that involves a short position in futures contracts. A short hedge is appropriate when the hedger already owns an asset and expects to sell it at some time in the future. For example, a short hedge could be used by a farmer who owns some hogs and knows that they will be ready for sale at the local market in two months. A short hedge can also be used when an asset is not owned right now but will be owned at some time in the future. Consider, for example, a U.S. exporter who knows that he or she will receive euros in three months. The exporter will realize a gain if the euro increases in value relative to the U.S. dollar and will sustain a loss if the euro decreases in value relative to the U.S. dollar. A short futures position leads to a loss if the euro increases in value and a gain if it decreases in value. It has the effect of offsetting the exporter's risk.

To provide a more detailed illustration of the operation of a short hedge in a specific situation, we assume that it is May 15 today and that an oil producer has just negotiated a contract to sell 1 million barrels of crude oil. It has been agreed that the price that will apply in the contract is the market price on August 15. The oil producer is therefore in the position considered above where it will gain $10,000 for each 1 cent increase in the price of oil over the next three months and lose $10,000 for each 1 cent decrease in the price during this period. Suppose that the spot price on May 15 is $19 per barrel and the August crude oil futures price on the New York Mercantile Exchange (NYMEX) is $18.75 per barrel. Because each futures contract on NYMEX is for the delivery of 1,000 barrels, the company can hedge its exposure by shorting 1,000 August futures contracts. If the oil producer closes out its position on August 15, the effect of the strategy should be to lock in a price close to $18.75 per barrel.

As an example of what might happen, suppose that the spot price on August 15 proves to be $17.50 per barrel. The company realizes $17.5 million for the oil under its sales contract. Because August is the delivery month for the futures contract, the futures price on August 15 should be very close to the spot price of $17.50 on that date. The company therefore gains approximately

$$\$18.75 - \$17.50 = \$1.25$$

per barrel, or $1.25 million in total from the short futures position. The total amount realized from both the futures position and the sales contract is therefore approximately $18.75 per barrel, or $18.75 million in total.

For an alternative outcome, suppose that the price of oil on August 15 proves to be $19.50 per barrel. The company realizes $19.50 for the oil and loses approximately

$$\$19.50 - \$18.75 = \$0.75$$

per barrel on the short futures position. Again, the total amount realized is approximately $18.75 million. It is easy to see that in all cases the company ends up with approximately $18.75 million.

### Long Hedges

Hedges that involve taking a long position in a futures contract are known as *long hedges*. A long hedge is appropriate when a company knows it will have to purchase a certain asset in the future and wants to lock in a price now.

Suppose that it is now January 15. A copper fabricator knows it will require 100,000 pounds of copper on May 15 to meet a certain contract. The spot price of copper is 140 cents per pound, and the May futures price is 120 cents per pound. The fabricator can hedge its position by taking a long position in four May futures contracts on the COMEX division of NYMEX and closing its position on May 15. Each contract is for the delivery of 25,000 pounds of copper. The strategy has the effect of locking in the price of the required copper at close to 120 cents per pound.

Suppose that the price of copper on May 15 proves to be 125 cents per pound. Because May is the delivery month for the futures contract, this should be very close to the futures price. The fabricator therefore gains approximately

$$100,000 \times (\$1.25 - \$1.20) = \$5,000$$

on the futures contracts. It pays $100,000 \times \$1.25 = \$125,000$ for the copper, making the total cost approximately $\$125,000 - \$5,000 = \$120,000$. For an alternative outcome, suppose that the futures price is 105 cents per pound on May 15. The fabricator then loses approximately

$$100,000 \times (\$1.20 - \$1.05) = \$15,000$$

on the futures contract and pays $100,000 \times \$1.05 = \$105,000$ for the copper. Again, the total cost is approximately $120,000, or 120 cents per pound.

Note that it is better for the company to use futures contracts than to buy the copper on January 15 in the spot market. If it does the latter, it will pay 140 cents per pound instead of 120 cents per pound and will incur both interest costs and storage costs. For a company using copper on a regular basis, this disadvantage would be offset by the convenience yield associated with having the copper on hand (see Section 3.12 for a discussion of convenience yields). However, for a company that knows it will not require the copper until May 15, the convenience yield has no value.

Long hedges can also be used to partially offset an existing short position. Consider an investor who has shorted a certain stock. Part of the risk faced by the investor is related to the performance of the stock market as a whole. The investor can neutralize this risk by taking a long position in index futures contracts. This type of hedging strategy is discussed further later in the chapter.

The examples we have looked at assume that the futures position is closed out in the delivery month. The hedge has the same basic effect if delivery is allowed to happen. However, making or taking delivery can be a costly business. For this reason, delivery is not usually made even when the hedger keeps the futures contract until the delivery month. As will be discussed later, hedgers with long positions usually avoid any possibility of having to take delivery by closing out their positions before the delivery period.

We have also assumed in the two examples that a futures contract is the same as a forward contract. In practice, marking to market does have a small effect on the performance of a hedge. As explained in Chapter 2, it means that the payoff from the futures contract is realized day by day throughout the life of the hedge rather than all at the end.

## 4.2  ARGUMENTS FOR AND AGAINST HEDGING

The arguments in favor of hedging are so obvious that they hardly need to be stated. Most companies are in the business of manufacturing or retailing or wholesaling or providing a service. They have no particular skills or expertise in predicting variables such as interest rates, exchange rates, and commodity prices. It makes sense for them to hedge the risks associated with these variables as they arise. The companies can then focus on their main activities—in which presumably they do have particular skills and expertise. By hedging, they avoid unpleasant surprises such as sharp rises in the price of a commodity.

In practice, many risks are left unhedged. In the rest of this section we will explore some of the reasons.

### Hedging and Shareholders

One argument sometimes put forward is that the shareholders can, if they wish, do the hedging themselves. They do not need the company to do it for them. This argument is, however, open to question. It assumes that shareholders have as much information about the risks faced by a company as does the company's management. In most instances, this is not the case. The argument also ignores commissions and other transactions costs. These are less expensive per dollar of hedging for large transactions than for small transactions. Hedging is therefore likely to be less expensive when carried out by the company than by individual shareholders. Indeed, the size of futures contracts makes hedging by individual shareholders impossible in many situations.

One thing that shareholders can do far more easily than a corporation is diversify risk. A shareholder with a well-diversified portfolio may be immune to many of the risks faced by a corporation. For example, in addition to holding shares in a company that uses copper, a well-diversified shareholder may hold shares in a copper producer, so that there is very little overall exposure to the price of copper. If companies are acting in the best interests of well-diversified shareholders, it can be argued that hedging is unnecessary in many situations. However, the extent to which managements are in practice influenced by this type of argument is open to question.

### Hedging and Competitors

If hedging is not the norm in a certain industry, it may not make sense for one particular company to choose to be different from all the others. Competitive pressures within the industry may be such that the prices of the goods and services produced by the industry fluctuate to reflect raw material costs, interest rates, exchange rates, and so on. A company that does not hedge can expect its profit margins to be roughly constant. However, a company that does hedge can expect its profit margins to fluctuate!

To illustrate this point, consider two manufacturers of gold jewelry, SafeandSure Company and TakeaChance Company. We assume that most jewelry manufacturers do not hedge against movements in the price of gold and that TakeaChance Company is no exception. However, SafeandSure Company has decided to be different from its competitors and to use futures contracts to hedge its purchases of gold over the next 18 months.

Has SafeandSure Company reduced its risks? If the price of gold goes up, economic pressures will tend to lead to a corresponding increase in the wholesale price of the jewelry, so that TakeaChance Company's profit margin is unaffected. By contrast, SafeandSure Company's profit margin will increase after the effects of the hedge have been taken into account. If the price of gold goes down, economic pressures will tend to lead to a corresponding decrease in the wholesale price of the jewelry. Again, TakeaChance Company's profit margin is unaffected. However, SafeandSure Company's profit margin goes down. In extreme conditions, SafeandSure Company's profit margin could become negative as a result of the "hedging" carried out! The situation is summarized in Table 4.1.

The foregoing example emphasizes the importance of looking at the big picture when hedging.

**Table 4.1**   Danger in hedging when competitors do not

| Change in gold price | Effect on price of gold jewelry | Effect on profits of TakeaChance Co. | Effect on profits of SafeandSure Co. |
|---|---|---|---|
| Increase | Increase | None | Increase |
| Decrease | Decrease | None | Decrease |

All the implications of price changes on a company's profitability should be taken into account in the design of a hedging strategy to protect against the price changes.

### Other Considerations

It is important to realize that a hedge using futures contracts can result in a decrease or an increase in a company's profits relative to the position it would be in with no hedging. In the example involving the oil producer considered earlier, if the price of oil goes down, the company loses money on its sale of 1 million barrels of oil and the futures position leads to an offsetting gain. The treasurer can be congratulated for having had the foresight to put the hedge in place. Clearly, the company is better off than it would be with no hedging. Other executives in the organization, it is hoped, will appreciate the contribution made by the treasurer. If the price of oil goes up, the company gains from its sale of the oil, and the futures position leads to an offsetting loss. The company is in a worse position than it would be with no hedging. Although the hedging decision was perfectly logical, the treasurer may in practice have a difficult time justifying it. Suppose that the price of oil is $21.75 at the end of the hedge, so that the company loses $3 per barrel on the futures contract. We can imagine a conversation such as the following between the treasurer and the president.

PRESIDENT:   This is terrible. We've lost $3 million in the futures market in the space of three months. How could it happen? I want a full explanation.

TREASURER:   The purpose of the futures contracts was to hedge our exposure to the price of oil—not to make a profit. Don't forget that we made about $3 million from the favorable effect of the oil price increases on our business.

PRESIDENT:   What's that got to do with it? That's like saying that we do not need to worry when our sales are down in California because they are up in New York.

TREASURER:   If the price of oil had gone down...

PRESIDENT:   I don't care what would have happened if the price of oil had gone down. The fact is that it went up. I really do not know what you were doing playing the futures markets like this. Our shareholders will expect us to have done particularly well this quarter. I'm going to have to explain to them that your actions reduced profits by $3 million. I'm afraid this is going to mean no bonus for you this year.

TREASURER:   That's unfair. I was only...

PRESIDENT:   Unfair! You are lucky not to be fired. You lost $3 million.

TREASURER:   It all depends how you look at it...

It is easy to see why many treasurers are reluctant to hedge! Hedging reduces risk for the company.

However, it may increase risks for the treasurer if others do not fully understand what is being done. The only real solution to this problem involves ensuring that all senior executives within the organization fully understand the nature of hedging before a hedging program is put in place. Ideally, hedging strategies are set by a company's board of directors and are clearly communicated to both the company's management and its shareholders.

## 4.3 BASIS RISK

The hedges in the examples considered so far have been almost too good to be true. The hedger was able to identify the precise date in the future when an asset would be bought or sold. The hedger was then able to use futures contracts to remove almost all the risk arising from the price of the asset on that date. In practice, hedging is often not quite as straightforward. Some of the reasons are as follows:

1. The asset whose price is to be hedged may not be exactly the same as the asset underlying the futures contract.

2. The hedger may be uncertain as to the exact date when the asset will be bought or sold.

3. The hedge may require the futures contract to be closed out well before its expiration date.

These problems give rise to what is termed *basis risk*. This concept will now be explained.

### The Basis

The *basis* in a hedging situation is as follows:[1]

Basis = Spot price of asset to be hedged − Futures price of contract used

If the asset to be hedged and the asset underlying the futures contract are the same, the basis should be zero at the expiration of the futures contract. Prior to expiration, the basis may be positive or negative. From the analysis in Chapter 3, when the underlying asset is a low-interest-rate currency or gold or silver, the futures price is greater than the spot price. This means that the basis is negative. For high-interest-rate currencies and many commodities, the reverse is true, and the basis is positive.

When the spot price increases by more than the futures price, the basis increases. This is referred to as a *strengthening of the basis*. When the futures price increases by more than the spot price, the basis declines. This is referred to as a *weakening of the basis*. Figure 4.1 illustrates how a basis might change over time in a situation where the basis is positive prior to expiration of the futures contract.

To examine the nature of basis risk, we will use the following notation:

$S_1$ : Spot price at time $t_1$

$S_2$ : Spot price at time $t_2$

$F_1$ : Futures price at time $t_1$

---

[1] This is the usual definition. However, the alternative definition

Basis = Futures price − Spot price

is sometimes used, particularly when the futures contract is on a financial asset.

**Figure 4.1** Variation of basis over time

$F_2$ : Futures price at time $t_2$

$b_1$ : Basis at time $t_1$

$b_2$ : Basis at time $t_2$

We will assume that a hedge is put in place at time $t_1$ and closed out at time $t_2$. As an example, we will consider the case where the spot and futures prices at the time the hedge is initiated are \$2.50 and \$2.20, respectively, and that at the time the hedge is closed out they are \$2.00 and \$1.90, respectively. This means that $S_1 = 2.50$, $F_1 = 2.20$, $S_2 = 2.00$, and $F_2 = 1.90$.

From the definition of the basis, we have

$$b_1 = S_1 - F_1$$

$$b_2 = S_2 - F_2$$

and hence, in our example, $b_1 = 0.30$ and $b_2 = 0.10$.

Consider first the situation of a hedger who knows that the asset will be sold at time $t_2$ and takes a short futures position at time $t_1$. The price realized for the asset is $S_2$ and the profit on the futures position is $F_1 - F_2$. The effective price that is obtained for the asset with hedging is therefore

$$S_2 + F_1 - F_2 = F_1 + b_2$$

In our example, this is \$2.30. The value of $F_1$ is known at time $t_1$. If $b_2$ were also known at this time, a perfect hedge would result. The hedging risk is the uncertainty associated with $b_2$ and is known as *basis risk*. Consider next a situation where a company knows it will buy the asset at time $t_2$ and initiates a long hedge at time $t_1$. The price paid for the asset is $S_2$ and the loss on the hedge is $F_1 - F_2$. The effective price that is paid with hedging is therefore

$$S_2 + F_1 - F_2 = F_1 + b_2$$

This is the same expression as before and is \$2.30 in the example. The value of $F_1$ is known at time $t_1$, and the term $b_2$ represents basis risk.

For investment assets such as currencies, stock indices, gold, and silver, the basis risk tends to be much less than for consumption commodities. The reason, as shown in Chapter 3, is that arbitrage arguments lead to a well-defined relationship between the futures price and the spot price of an investment asset. The basis risk for an investment asset arises mainly from uncertainty as to the level of the risk-free interest rate in the future. In the case of a consumption commodity, imbalances between supply and demand and the difficulties sometimes associated with storing the commodity can lead to large variations in the convenience yield. This in turn leads to a big increase in the basis risk.

The asset that gives rise to the hedger's exposure is sometimes different from the asset underlying the hedge. The basis risk is then usually greater. Define $S_2^*$ as the price of the asset underlying the futures contract at time $t_2$. As before, $S_2$ is the price of the asset being hedged at time $t_2$. By hedging, a company ensures that the price that will be paid (or received) for the asset is

$$S_2 + F_1 - F_2$$

This can be written as

$$F_1 + (S_2^* - F_2) + (S_2 - S_2^*)$$

$\beta = F - S$

The terms $S_2^* - F_2$ and $S_2 - S_2^*$ represent the two components of the basis. The $S_2^* - F_2$ term is the basis that would exist if the asset being hedged were the same as the asset underlying the futures contract. The $S_2 - S_2^*$ term is the basis arising from the difference between the two assets.

Note that basis risk can lead to an improvement or a worsening of a hedger's position. Consider a short hedge. If the basis strengthens unexpectedly, the hedger's position improves; if the basis weakens unexpectedly, the hedger's position worsens. For a long hedge, the reverse holds. If the basis strengthens unexpectedly, the hedger's position worsens; if the basis weakens unexpectedly, the hedger's position improves.

### Choice of Contract

One key factor affecting basis risk is the choice of the futures contract to be used for hedging. This choice has two components:

1. The choice of the asset underlying the futures contract
2. The choice of the delivery month

If the asset being hedged exactly matches an asset underlying a futures contract, the first choice is generally fairly easy. In other circumstances, it is necessary to carry out a careful analysis to determine which of the available futures contracts has futures prices that are most closely correlated with the price of the asset being hedged.

The choice of the delivery month is likely to be influenced by several factors. In the examples given earlier in this chapter, we assumed that when the expiration of the hedge corresponds to a delivery month, the contract with that delivery month is chosen. In fact, a contract with a later delivery month is usually chosen in these circumstances. The reason is that futures prices are in some instances quite erratic during the delivery month. Also, a long hedger runs the risk of having to take delivery of the physical asset if the contract is held during the delivery month. Taking delivery can be expensive and inconvenient.

In general, basis risk increases as the time difference between the hedge expiration and the delivery month increases. A good rule of thumb is therefore to choose a delivery month that is as close as possible to, but later than, the expiration of the hedge. Suppose delivery months are March, June, September, and December for a particular contract. For hedge expirations in December, January, and February, the March contract will be chosen; for hedge expirations in March, April, and May, the June contract will be chosen; and so on. This rule of thumb assumes that there is sufficient liquidity in all contracts to meet the hedger's requirements. In practice, liquidity tends to be greatest in short maturity futures contracts. The hedger may therefore, in some situations, be inclined to use short maturity contracts and roll them forward. This strategy is discussed later in the chapter.

**Example 4.1**  It is March 1. A U.S. company expects to receive 50 million Japanese yen at the end of July. Yen futures contracts on the Chicago Mercantile Exchange have delivery months of March, June, September, and December. One contract is for the delivery of 12.5 million yen. The company therefore shorts four September yen futures contracts on March 1. When the yen are received at the end of July, the company closes out its position. We suppose that the futures price on March 1 in cents per yen is 0.7800 and that the spot and futures prices when the contract is closed out are 0.7200 and 0.7250, respectively.

The gain on the futures contract is $0.7800 - 0.7250 = 0.0550$ cents per yen. The basis is $0.7200 - 0.7250 = -0.0050$ cents per yen when the contract is closed out. The effective price obtained in cents per yen is the final spot price plus the gain on the futures:

$$0.7200 + 0.0550 = 0.7750$$

This can also be written as the initial futures price plus the final basis:

$$0.7800 - 0.0050 = 0.7750$$

The total amount received by the company for the 50 million yen is $50 \times 0.00775$ million dollars, or $387,500.

**Example 4.2**  It is June 8 and a company knows that it will need to purchase 20,000 barrels of crude oil at some time in October or November. Oil futures contracts are currently traded for delivery every month on NYMEX and the contract size is 1,000 barrels. The company therefore decides to use the December contract for hedging and takes a long position in 20 December contracts. The futures price on June 8 is $18.00 per barrel. The company finds that it is ready to purchase the crude oil on November 10. It therefore closes out its futures contract on that date. The spot price and futures price on November 10 are $20.00 per barrel and $19.10 per barrel.

The gain on the futures contract is $19.10 - 18.00 = \$1.10$ per barrel. The basis when the contract is closed out is $20.00 - 19.10 = \$0.90$ per barrel. The effective price paid (in dollars per barrel) is the final spot price less the gain on the futures, or

$$20.00 - 1.10 = 18.90$$

This can also be calculated as the initial futures price plus the final basis:

$$18.00 + 0.90 = 18.90$$

The total price received is $18.90 \times 20,000 = \$378,000$.

## 4.4  MINIMUM VARIANCE HEDGE RATIO

The *hedge ratio* is the ratio of the size of the position taken in futures contracts to the size of the exposure. Up to now we have always used a hedge ratio of 1.0. For instance, in Example 4.2, the hedger's exposure was to 20,000 barrels of oil and futures contracts were entered into for the delivery of exactly this amount of oil. If the objective of the hedger is to minimize risk, setting the hedge ratio equal to 1.0 is not necessarily optimal.

We will use the following notation:

$\delta S$: Change in spot price, $S$, during a period of time equal to the life of the hedge

$\delta F$: Change in futures price, $F$, during a period of time equal to the life of the hedge

$\sigma_S$: Standard deviation of $\delta S$

$\sigma_F$: Standard deviation of $\delta F$

$\rho$: Coefficient of correlation between $\delta S$ and $\delta F$

$h^*$: Hedge ratio that minimizes the variance of the hedger's position

In Appendix 4A, we show that

$$h^* = \rho \frac{\sigma_S}{\sigma_F} \tag{4.1}$$

The optimal hedge ratio is the product of the coefficient of correlation between $\delta S$ and $\delta F$ and the ratio of the standard deviation of $\delta S$ to the standard deviation of $\delta F$. Figure 4.2 shows how the variance of the value of the hedger's position depends on the hedge ratio chosen.

If $\rho = 1$ and $\sigma_F = \sigma_S$, the hedge ratio, $h^*$, is 1.0. This result is to be expected, because in this case the futures price mirrors the spot price perfectly. If $\rho = 1$ and $\sigma_F = 2\sigma_S$, the hedge ratio $h^*$ is 0.5. This result is also as expected, because in this case the futures price always changes by twice as much as the spot price.

The optimal hedge ratio, $h^*$, is the slope of the best fit line when $\delta S$ is regressed against $\delta F$, as indicated in Figure 4.3. This is intuitively reasonable, because we require $h^*$ to correspond to the ratio of changes in $\delta S$ to changes in $\delta F$. The *hedge effectiveness* can be defined as the proportion of the variance that is eliminated by hedging. This is $\rho^2$, or

$$h^{*2} \frac{\sigma_F^2}{\sigma_S^2}$$

The parameters $\rho$, $\sigma_F$, and $\sigma_S$ in equation (4.1) are usually estimated from historical data on $\delta S$ and $\delta F$. (The implicit assumption is that the future will in some sense be like the past.) A number of equal nonoverlapping time intervals are chosen, and the values of $\delta S$ and $\delta F$ for each of the

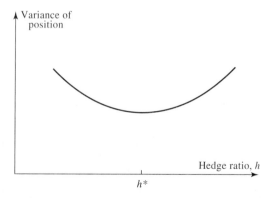

**Figure 4.2** Dependence of variance of hedger's position on hedge ratio

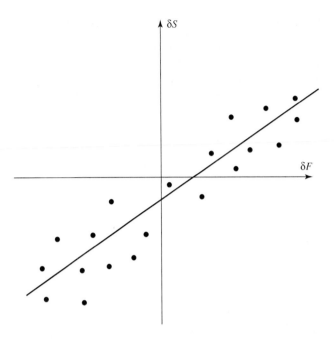

**Figure 4.3**   Regression of change in spot price against change in futures price

intervals are observed. Ideally, the length of each time interval is the same as the length of the time interval for which the hedge is in effect. In practice, this sometimes severely limits the number of observations that are available, and a shorter time interval is used.

### *Optimal Number of Contracts*

Define variables as follows:

$N_A$ : Size of position being hedged (units)

$Q_F$ : Size of one futures contract (units)

$N^*$ : Optimal number of futures contracts for hedging

The futures contracts used should have a face value of $h^* N_A$. The number of futures contracts required is therefore given by

$$N^* = \frac{h^* N_A}{Q_F} \tag{4.2}$$

**Example 4.3**   An airline expects to purchase two million gallons of jet fuel in one month and decides to use heating oil futures for hedging. (The article by Nikkhah referenced at the end of the chapter discusses this type of strategy.) We suppose that Table 4.2 gives, for 15 successive months, data on the change, $\delta S$, in the jet fuel price per gallon and the corresponding change, $\delta F$, in the futures price for the contract on heating oil that would be used for hedging price changes during the month. The number of observations, which we will denote by $n$, is 15. We will denote the $i$th

**Table 4.2**  Data to calculate minimum variance hedge ratio when heating oil futures contract is used to hedge purchase of jet fuel

| Month *i* | *Change in futures price per gallon (= $x_i$)* | *Change in fuel price per gallon (= $y_i$)* |
|---|---|---|
| 1 | 0.021 | 0.029 |
| 2 | 0.035 | 0.020 |
| 3 | −0.046 | −0.044 |
| 4 | 0.001 | 0.008 |
| 5 | 0.044 | 0.026 |
| 6 | −0.029 | −0.019 |
| 7 | −0.026 | −0.010 |
| 8 | −0.029 | −0.007 |
| 9 | 0.048 | 0.043 |
| 10 | −0.006 | 0.011 |
| 11 | −0.036 | −0.036 |
| 12 | −0.011 | −0.018 |
| 13 | 0.019 | 0.009 |
| 14 | −0.027 | −0.032 |
| 15 | 0.029 | 0.023 |

observations on $\delta F$ and $\delta S$ by $x_i$ and $y_i$, respectively. From Table 4.2,

$$\sum x_i = -0.013, \qquad \sum x_i^2 = 0.0138$$

$$\sum y_i = 0.003, \qquad \sum y_i^2 = 0.0097$$

$$\sum x_i y_i = 0.0107$$

Standard formulas from statistics give the estimate of $\sigma_F$ as

$$\sqrt{\frac{\sum x_i^2}{n-1} - \frac{(\sum x_i)^2}{n(n-1)}} = 0.0313$$

The estimate of $\sigma_S$ is

$$\sqrt{\frac{\sum y_i^2}{n-1} - \frac{(\sum y_i)^2}{n(n-1)}} = 0.0263$$

The estimate of $\rho$ is

$$\frac{n\sum x_i y_i - \sum x_i \sum y_i}{\sqrt{[n\sum x_i^2 - (\sum x_i)^2][n\sum y_i^2 - (\sum y_i)^2]}} = 0.928$$

From equation (4.1), the minimum variance hedge ratio, $h^*$, is therefore

$$0.928 \times \frac{0.0263}{0.0313} = 0.78$$

Each heating oil contract traded on NYMEX is on 42,000 gallons of heating oil. From equation (4.2), the optimal number of contracts is

$$\frac{0.78 \times 2,000,000}{42,000} = 37.14$$

or, rounding to the nearest whole number, 37.

## 4.5  STOCK INDEX FUTURES

Stock index futures can be used to hedge an equity portfolio. Define:

$P$ :  Current value of the portfolio

$A$ :  Current value of the stocks underlying one futures contract

If the portfolio mirrors the index, a hedge ratio of 1.0 is clearly appropriate, and equation (4.2) shows that the number of futures contracts that should be shorted is

$$N^* = \frac{P}{A} \tag{4.3}$$

Suppose, for example, that a portfolio worth $1 million mirrors the S&P 500. The current value of the index is 1,000, and each futures contract is on $250 times the index. In this case $P = 1,000,000$ and $A = 250,000$, so that four contracts should be shorted to hedge the portfolio.

When the portfolio does not exactly mirror the index, we can use the parameter beta ($\beta$) from the capital asset pricing model to determine the appropriate hedge ratio. Beta is the slope of the best fit line obtained when excess return on the portfolio over the risk-free rate is regressed against the excess return of the market over the risk-free rate. When $\beta = 1.0$, the return on the portfolio tends to mirror the return on the market; when $\beta = 2.0$, the excess return on the portfolio tends to be twice as great as the excess return on the market; when $\beta = 0.5$, it tends to be half as great; and so on.

Assuming that the index underlying the futures contract is a proxy for the market, it can be shown that the appropriate hedge ratio is the beta of the portfolio. From equation (4.2) this means that

$$N^* = \beta \frac{P}{A} \tag{4.4}$$

This formula assumes that the maturity of the futures contract is close to the maturity of the hedge and ignores the daily settlement of the futures contract.[2]

---

[2] A small adjustment known as *tailing the hedge* can be used to take account of the daily settlement when a futures contract is used for hedging. For a discussion of this, see D. Duffie, *Futures Markets*, Prentice Hall, Upper Saddle River, NJ, 1989; R. Rendleman, "A Reconciliation of Potentially Conflicting Approaches to Hedging with Futures," *Advances in Futures and Options Research*, 6 (1993), 81–92. Problem 4.20 deals with this issue.

We illustrate that this formula gives good results with an example. Suppose that

$$\text{Value of S\&P 500 index} = 1{,}000$$

$$\text{Value of portfolio} = \$5{,}000{,}000$$

$$\text{Risk-free interest rate} = 10\% \text{ per annum}$$

$$\text{Dividend yield on index} = 4\% \text{ per annum}$$

$$\text{Beta of portfolio} = 1.5$$

We assume that a futures contract on the S&P 500 with four months to maturity is used to hedge the value of the portfolio over the next three months. One futures contract is for delivery of $250 times the index. From equation (3.12), the current futures price should be

$$1{,}000e^{(0.10-0.04)\times4/12} = 1{,}020.20$$

From equation (4.4), the number of futures contracts that should be shorted to hedge the portfolio is

$$1.5 \times \frac{5{,}000{,}000}{250{,}000} = 30$$

Suppose the index turns out to be 900 in three months. The futures price will be

$$900e^{(0.10-0.04)\times1/12} = 904.51$$

The gain from the short futures position is therefore

$$30 \times (1{,}020.20 - 904.51) \times 250 = \$867{,}676$$

The loss on the index is 10%. The index pays a dividend of 4% per annum, or 1% per three months. When dividends are taken into account, an investor in the index would therefore earn $-9\%$ in the three-month period. The risk-free interest rate is approximately 2.5% per three months.[3] Because the portfolio has a $\beta$ of 1.5,

   Expected return on portfolio $-$ Risk-free interest rate

$$= 1.5 \times (\text{Return on index} - \text{Risk-free interest rate})$$

It follows that the expected return (%) on the portfolio is

$$2.5 + [1.5 \times (-9.0 - 2.5)] = -14.75$$

The expected value of the portfolio (inclusive of dividends) at the end of the three months is therefore

$$\$5{,}000{,}000 \times (1 - 0.1475) = \$4{,}262{,}500$$

It follows that the expected value of the hedger's position, including the gain on the hedge, is

$$\$4{,}262{,}500 + \$867{,}676 = \$5{,}130{,}176$$

---

[3] For ease of presentation, the fact that the interest rate and dividend yield are continuously compounded has been ignored. This makes very little difference.

**Table 4.3**  Performance of stock index hedge

| | | | | | |
|---|---|---|---|---|---|
| Value of index in three months | 900.00 | 950.00 | 1,000.00 | 1,050.00 | 1,100.00 |
| Futures price of index in three months | 904.51 | 954.76 | 1,005.01 | 1,055.26 | 1,105.51 |
| Gain (loss) on futures position ($000) | 867,676 | 490,796 | 113,916 | (262,964) | (639,843) |
| Value of portfolio (including dividends) in three months ($000) | 4,262,500 | 4,637,500 | 5,012,500 | 5,387,500 | 5,762,500 |
| Total value of position in three months ($000) | 5,130,176 | 5,128,296 | 5,126,416 | 5,124,537 | 5,122,657 |

Table 4.3 summarizes these calculations, together with similar calculations for other values of the index at maturity. It can be seen that the total value of the hedger's position in three months is almost independent of the value of the index.

Table 4.3 assumes that the dividend yield on the index is predictable, the risk-free interest rate remains constant, and the return on the index over the three-month period is perfectly correlated with the return on the portfolio. In practice, these assumptions do not hold perfectly, and the hedge works rather less well than is indicated by Table 4.3.

### Reasons for Hedging an Equity Portfolio

Table 4.3 shows that the hedging scheme results in a value for the hedger's position close to $5,125,000 at the end of three months. This is greater than the $5,000,000 initial value of the position by about 2.5%. There is no surprise here. The risk-free interest rate is 10% per annum, or about 2.5% per quarter. The hedge results in the hedger's position growing at the risk-free interest rate.

It is natural to ask why the hedger should go to the trouble of using futures contracts. To earn the risk-free interest rate, the hedger can simply sell the portfolio and invest the proceeds in Treasury bills.

One answer to this question is that hedging can be justified if the hedger feels that the stocks in the portfolio have been chosen well. In these circumstances, the hedger might be very uncertain about the performance of the market as a whole, but confident that the stocks in the portfolio will outperform the market (after appropriate adjustments have been made for the beta of the portfolio). A hedge using index futures removes the risk arising from market moves and leaves the hedger exposed only to the performance of the portfolio relative to the market. Another reason for hedging may be that the hedger is planning to hold a portfolio for a long period of time and requires short-term protection in an uncertain market situation. The alternative strategy of selling the portfolio and buying it back later might involve unacceptably high transaction costs.

### Changing Beta

In the example in Table 4.3, the beta of the hedger's portfolio is reduced to zero. Sometimes futures contracts are used to change the beta of a portfolio to some value other than zero. In the example, to reduce the beta of the portfolio from 1.5 to 0.75, the number of contracts shorted should be 15 rather than 30; to increase the beta of the portfolio to 2.0, a long position in 10 contracts should be taken; and so on. In general, to change the beta of the portfolio from $\beta$ to $\beta^*$, where $\beta > \beta^*$, a short position in

$$(\beta - \beta^*)\frac{P}{A}$$

contracts is required. When $\beta < \beta^*$, a long position in

$$(\beta^* - \beta)\frac{P}{A}$$

contracts is required.

### *Exposure to the Price of an Individual Stock*

Some exchanges do trade futures contracts on selected individual stocks, but in most cases a position in an individual stock can only be hedged using a stock index futures contact.

Hedging an exposure to the price of an individual stock using index futures contracts is similar to hedging a stock portfolio. The number of index futures contracts that the hedger should short into is given by $\beta P/A$, where $\beta$ is the beta of the stock, $P$ is the total value of the shares owned, and $A$ is the current value of the stocks underlying one index futures contract. Note that although the number of contracts entered into is calculated in the same way as it is when a portfolio of stocks is being hedged, the performance of the hedge is considerably worse. The hedge provides protection only against the risk arising from market movements, and this risk is a relatively small proportion of the total risk in the price movements of individual stocks. The hedge is appropriate when an investor feels that the stock will outperform the market but is unsure about the performance of the market. It can also be used by an investment bank that has underwritten a new issue of the stock and wants protection against moves in the market as a whole.

Consider an investor who in June holds 20,000 IBM shares, each worth $100. The investor feels that the market will be very volatile over the next month but that IBM has a good chance of outperforming the market. The investor decides to use the August futures contract on the S&P 500 to hedge the position during the one-month period. The $\beta$ of IBM is estimated at 1.1. The current level of the index is 900, and the current futures price for the August contract on the S&P 500 is 908. Each contract is for delivery of $250 times the index. In this case $P = 20,000 \times 100 = 2,000,000$ and $A = 900 \times 250 = 225,000$. The number of contracts that should be shorted is therefore

$$1.1 \times \frac{2,000,000}{225,000} = 9.78$$

Rounding to the nearest integer, the hedger shorts 10 contracts, closing out the position one month later. Suppose IBM rises to $125 during the month, and the futures price of the S&P 500 rises to 1080. The investor gains $20,000 \times (\$125 - \$100) = \$500,000$ on IBM while losing $10 \times 250 \times (1080 - 908) = \$430,000$ on the futures contracts.

In this example, the hedge offsets a gain on the underlying asset with a loss on the futures contracts. The offset might seem to be counterproductive. However, it cannot be emphasized often enough that the purpose of a hedge is to reduce risk. A hedge tends to make unfavorable outcomes less unfavorable and favorable outcomes less favorable.

## 4.6 ROLLING THE HEDGE FORWARD

Sometimes the expiration date of the hedge is later than the delivery dates of all the futures contracts that can be used. The hedger must then roll the hedge forward by closing out one futures contract and taking the same position in a futures contract with a later delivery date. Hedges can be rolled forward many times. Consider a company that wishes to use a short hedge to reduce the risk associated with the price to be received for an asset at time $T$. If there are futures contracts 1, 2, 3,..., $n$ (not all necessarily in existence at the present time) with progressively later delivery dates, the company can use the following strategy:

Time $t_1$: Short futures contract 1.

Time $t_2$: Close out futures contract 1.
Short futures contract 2.

Time $t_3$: Close out futures contract 2.
Short futures contract 3.

$\vdots$

Time $t_n$: Close out futures contract $n - 1$.
Short futures contract $n$.

Time $T$: Close out futures contract $n$.

In this strategy there are $n$ basis risks or sources of uncertainty. At time $T$ there is uncertainty about the difference between the futures price for contract $n$ and the spot price of the asset being hedged. In addition, on each of the $n - 1$ occasions when the hedge is rolled forward, there is uncertainty about the difference between the futures price for the contract being closed out and the futures price for the new contract being entered into. (We will refer to the latter as the *rollover basis*.) In many situations the hedger has some flexibility on the exact time when a switch is made from one contract to the next. This can be used to reduce the rollover basis risk. For example, if the rollover basis is unattractive at the beginning of the period during which the rollover must be made, the hedger can delay the rollover in the hope that the rollover basis will improve.

**Example 4.4**   In April 2002, a company realizes that it will have 100,000 barrels of oil to sell in June 2003 and decides to hedge its risk with a hedge ratio of 1.0. The current spot price is $19. Although crude oil futures are traded on the New York Mercantile Exchange with maturities up to six years, we suppose that only the first six delivery months have sufficient liquidity to meet the company's needs. The company therefore shorts 100 October 2002 contracts. In September 2002 it rolls the hedge forward into the March 2003 contract. In February 2003 it rolls the hedge forward again into the July 2003 contract.

One possible outcome is that the price of oil drops from $19 to $16 per barrel between April 2002 and June 2003. Suppose that the October 2002 futures contract is shorted at $18.20 per barrel and closed out at $17.40 per barrel for a profit of $0.80 per barrel; the March 2003 contract is shorted at $17.00 per barrel and closed out at $16.50 per barrel for a profit of $0.50 per barrel; the July 2003 contract is shorted at $16.30 per barrel and closed out at $15.90 per barrel for a profit of $0.40 per barrel. In this case the futures contracts provide a total of $1.70 per barrel compensation for the $3 per barrel oil price decline.

### Metallgesellschaft

Sometimes rolling the hedge forward can lead to cash flow pressures. The problem was illustrated dramatically by the activities of a German company, Metallgesellschaft (MG), in the early 1990s.

MG sold a huge volume of 5- to 10-year heating oil and gasoline fixed-price supply contracts to its customers at 6 to 8 cents above market prices. It hedged its exposure with long positions in short-dated futures contracts that were rolled over. As it turned out, the price of oil fell and there were margin calls on the futures position. Considerable short-term cash flow pressures were placed on MG. The members of MG who devised the hedging strategy argued that these short-term cash outflows were offset by positive cash flows that would ultimately be realized on the long-term fixed-price contracts. However, the company's senior management and its bankers became concerned about the huge cash drain. As a result, the company closed out all the hedge positions and agreed with its customers that the fixed-price contracts would be abandoned. The result was a loss to MG of $1.33 billion.[4]

## SUMMARY

This chapter has discussed various ways in which a company can take a position in futures contracts to offset an exposure to the price of an asset. If the exposure is such that the company gains when the price of the asset increases and loses when the price of the asset decreases, a short hedge is appropriate. If the exposure is the other way round (i.e., the company gains when the price of the asset decreases and loses when the price of the asset increases), a long hedge is appropriate.

Hedging is a way of reducing risk. As such, it should be welcomed by most executives. In reality, there are a number of theoretical and practical reasons that companies do not hedge. On a theoretical level, we can argue that shareholders, by holding well-diversified portfolios, can eliminate many of the risks faced by a company. They do not require the company to hedge these risks. On a practical level, a company may find that it is increasing rather than decreasing risk by hedging if none of its competitors does so. Also, a treasurer may fear criticism from other executives if the company makes a gain from movements in the price of the underlying asset and a loss on the hedge.

An important concept in hedging is basis risk. The basis is the difference between the spot price of an asset and its futures price. Basis risk is created by a hedger's uncertainty as to what the basis will be at maturity of the hedge. Basis risk is generally greater for consumption assets than for investment assets.

The hedge ratio is the ratio of the size of the position taken in futures contracts to the size of the exposure. It is not always optimal to use a hedge ratio of 1.0. If the hedger wishes to minimize the variance of a position, a hedge ratio different from 1.0 may be appropriate. The optimal hedge ratio is the slope of the best fit line obtained when changes in the spot price are regressed against changes in the futures price.

Stock index futures can be used to hedge the systematic risk in an equity portfolio. The number of futures contracts required is the beta of the portfolio multiplied by the ratio of the value of the

---

[4] For a discussion of MG, see "MG's Trial by Essay," *RISK*, October 1994, pp. 228–34; M. Miller and C. Culp, "Risk Management Lessons from Metallgesellschaft," *Journal of Applied Corporate Finance*, 7, no. 4 (Winter 1995), 62–76.

portfolio to the value of one futures contract. Stock index futures can also be used to change the beta of a portfolio without changing the stocks comprising the portfolio.

When there is no liquid futures contract that matures later than the expiration of the hedge, a strategy known as rolling the hedge forward may be appropriate. This involves entering into a sequence of futures contracts. When the first futures contract is near expiration, it is closed out and the hedger enters into a second contract with a later delivery month. When the second contract is close to expiration, it is closed out and the hedger enters into a third contract with a later delivery month; and so on. Rolling the hedge forward works well if there is a close correlation between changes in the futures prices and changes in the spot prices.

## SUGGESTIONS FOR FURTHER READING

Ederington, L. H., "The Hedging Performance of the New Futures Market," *Journal of Finance*, 34 (March 1979), 157–70.

Franckle, C. T., "The Hedging Performance of the New Futures Market: Comment," *Journal of Finance*, 35 (December 1980), 1273–79.

Johnson, L. L., "The Theory of Hedging and Speculation in Commodity Futures Markets," *Review of Economics Studies*, 27 (October 1960), 139–51.

McCabe, G. M., and C. T. Franckle, "The Effectiveness of Rolling the Hedge Forward in the Treasury Bill Futures Market," *Financial Management*, 12 (Summer 1983), 21–29.

Miller, M., and C. Culp, "Risk Management Lessons from Metallgesellschaft," *Journal of Applied Corporate Finance*, 7, no. 4 (Winter 1995), 62–76.

Nikkhah, S., "How End Users Can Hedge Fuel Costs in Energy Markets," *Futures*, October 1987, 66–67.

Stulz, R. M., "Optimal Hedging Policies," *Journal of Financial and Quantitative Analysis*, 19 (June 1984), 127–40.

## QUESTIONS AND PROBLEMS
## (ANSWERS IN SOLUTIONS MANUAL)

4.1. Under what circumstances are (a) a short hedge and (b) a long hedge appropriate?

4.2. Explain what is meant by *basis risk* when futures contracts are used for hedging.

4.3. Explain what is meant by a *perfect hedge*. Does a perfect hedge always lead to a better outcome than an imperfect hedge? Explain your answer.

4.4. Under what circumstances does a minimum variance hedge portfolio lead to no hedging at all?

4.5. Give three reasons that the treasurer of a company might not hedge the company's exposure to a particular risk.

4.6. Suppose that the standard deviation of quarterly changes in the prices of a commodity is $0.65, the standard deviation of quarterly changes in a futures price on the commodity is $0.81, and the coefficient of correlation between the two changes is 0.8. What is the optimal hedge ratio for a three-month contract? What does it mean?

4.7. A company has a $20 million portfolio with a beta of 1.2. It would like to use futures contracts on the S&P 500 to hedge its risk. The index is currently standing at 1080, and each contract is for delivery of $250 times the index. What is the hedge that minimizes risk? What should the company do if it wants to reduce the beta of the portfolio to 0.6?

4.8. In the Chicago Board of Trade's corn futures contract, the following delivery months are available: March, May, July, September, and December. State the contract that should be used for hedging when the expiration of the hedge is in (a) June, (b) July, and (c) January.

4.9. Does a perfect hedge always succeed in locking in the current spot price of an asset for a future transaction? Explain your answer.

4.10. Explain why a short hedger's position improves when the basis strengthens unexpectedly and worsens when the basis weakens unexpectedly.

4.11. Imagine you are the treasurer of a Japanese company exporting electronic equipment to the United States. Discuss how you would design a foreign exchange hedging strategy and the arguments you would use to sell the strategy to your fellow executives.

4.12. Suppose that in Example 4.2 of Section 4.3 the company decides to use a hedge ratio of 0.8. How does the decision affect the way in which the hedge is implemented and the result?

4.13. "If the minimum variance hedge ratio is calculated as 1.0, the hedge must be perfect." Is this statement true? Explain your answer.

4.14. "If there is no basis risk, the minimum variance hedge ratio is always 1.0." Is this statement true? Explain your answer.

4.15. "When the convenience yield is high, long hedges are likely to be particularly attractive." Explain this statement. Illustrate it with an example.

4.16. The standard deviation of monthly changes in the spot price of live cattle is 1.2 (in cents per pound). The standard deviation of monthly changes in the futures price of live cattle for the closest contract is 1.4. The correlation between the futures price changes and the spot price changes is 0.7. It is now October 15. A beef producer is committed to purchasing 200,000 pounds of live cattle on November 15. The producer wants to use the December live-cattle futures contracts to hedge its risk. Each contract is for the delivery of 40,000 pounds of cattle. What strategy should the beef producer follow?

4.17. A corn farmer argues: "I do not use futures contracts for hedging. My real risk is not the price of corn. It is that my whole crop gets wiped out by the weather." Discuss this viewpoint. Should the farmer estimate his or her expected production of corn and hedge to try to lock in a price for expected production?

4.18. On July 1, an investor holds 50,000 shares of a certain stock. The market price is $30 per share. The investor is interested in hedging against movements in the market over the next month and decides to use the September Mini S&P 500 futures contract. The index is currently 1,500 and one contract is for delivery of $50 times the index. The beta of the stock is 1.3. What strategy should the investor follow?

4.19. Suppose that in Example 4.4 the company decides to use a hedge ratio of 1.5. How does the decision affect the way the hedge is implemented and the result?

4.20. A U.S. company is interested in using the futures contracts traded on the CME to hedge its Australian dollar exposure. Define $r$ as the interest rate (all maturities) on the U.S. dollar and $r_f$ as the interest rate (all maturities) on the Australian dollar. Assume that $r$ and $r_f$ are constant and that the company uses a contract expiring at time $T$ to hedge an exposure at time $t$ ($T > t$).

    a. Using the results in Chapter 3, show that the optimal hedge ratio is

$$e^{(r_f - r)(T-t)}$$

    b. Show that, when $t$ is one day, the optimal hedge ratio is almost exactly $S_0/F_0$, where $S_0$ is the current spot price of the currency and $F_0$ is the current futures price of the currency for the contract maturing at time $T$.

    c. Show that the company can take account of the daily settlement of futures contracts for a hedge that lasts longer than one day by adjusting the hedge ratio so that it always equals the spot price of the currency divided by the futures price of the currency.

4.21. An airline executive has argued: "There is no point in our using oil futures. There is just as much chance that the price of oil in the future will be less than the futures price as there is that it will be greater than this price." Discuss this viewpoint.

## ASSIGNMENT QUESTIONS

4.22. The following table gives data on monthly changes in the spot price and the futures price for a certain commodity. Use the data to calculate a minimum variance hedge ratio.

| Spot price change | +0.50 | +0.61 | −0.22 | −0.35 | +0.79 |
|---|---|---|---|---|---|
| Futures price change | +0.56 | +0.63 | −0.12 | −0.44 | +0.60 |
| Spot price change | +0.04 | +0.15 | +0.70 | −0.51 | −0.41 |
| Futures price change | −0.06 | +0.01 | +0.80 | −0.56 | −0.46 |

4.23. It is July 16. A company has a portfolio of stocks worth $100 million. The beta of the portfolio is 1.2. The company would like to use the CME December futures contract on the S&P 500 to change the beta of the portfolio to 0.5 during the period July 16 to November 16. The index is currently 1,000, and each contract is on $250 times the index.

    a. What position should the company take?

    b. Suppose that the company changes its mind and decides to increase the beta of the portfolio from 1.2 to 1.5. What position in futures contracts should it take?

4.24. It is now October 2002. A company anticipates that it will purchase 1 million pounds of copper in each of February 2003, August 2003, February 2004, and August 2004. The company has decided to use the futures contracts traded in the COMEX division of the New York Mercantile Exchange to hedge its risk. One contract is for the delivery of 25,000 pounds of copper. The initial margin is $2,000 per contract and the maintenance margin is $1,500 per contract. The company's policy is to hedge 80% of its exposure. Contracts with maturities up to 13 months into the future are considered to have sufficient liquidity to meet the company's needs. Devise a hedging strategy for the company. Assume the market prices (in cents per pound) today and at future dates are as follows:

| Date | Oct 2002 | Feb 2003 | Aug 2003 | Feb 2004 | Aug 2004 |
|---|---|---|---|---|---|
| Spot price | 72.00 | 69.00 | 65.00 | 77.00 | 88.00 |
| Mar 2003 futures price | 72.30 | 69.10 | | | |
| Sept 2003 futures price | 72.80 | 70.20 | 64.80 | | |
| Mar 2004 futures price | 70.70 | 64.30 | 76.70 | | |
| Sept 2004 futures price | 64.20 | 76.50 | 88.20 | | |

What is the impact of the strategy you propose on the price the company pays for copper? What is the initial margin requirement in October 2002? Is the company subject to any margin calls?

4.25. A fund manager has a portfolio worth $50 million with a beta of 0.87. The manager is concerned about the performance of the market over the next two months and plans to use three-month futures contracts on the S&P 500 to hedge the risk. The current level of the index is 1250, one contract is on 250 times the index, the risk-free rate is 6% per annum, and the dividend yield on the index is 3% per annum.

   a. What is the theoretical futures price for the three-month futures contract?

   b. What position should the fund manager take to eliminate all exposure to the market over the next two months?

   c. Calculate the effect of your strategy on the fund manager's returns if the level of the market in two months is 1,000, 1,100, 1,200, 1,300, and 1,400.

# APPENDIX 4A
## Proof of the Minimum Variance Hedge Ratio Formula

As in Section 4.4 we define:

$\delta S$: change in spot price, $S$, during a period of time equal to the life of the hedge

$\delta F$: change in futures price, $F$, during a period of time equal to the life of the hedge

$\sigma_S$: standard deviation of $\delta S$

$\sigma_F$: standard deviation of $\delta F$

$\rho$: coefficient of correlation between $\delta S$ and $\delta F$

$h$: hedge ratio

When the hedger is long the asset and short futures, the change in the value of the hedger's position during the life of the hedge is

$$\delta S - h\,\delta F$$

for each unit of the asset held. For a long hedge the change is

$$h\,\delta F - \delta S$$

In either case the variance, $v$, of the change in value of the hedged position is given by

$$v = \sigma_S^2 + h^2\sigma_F^2 - 2h\rho\sigma_S\sigma_F$$

so that

$$\frac{\partial v}{\partial h} = 2h\sigma_F^2 - 2\rho\sigma_S\sigma_F$$

Setting this equal to zero, and noting that $\partial^2 v/\partial h^2$ is positive, we see that the value of $h$ that minimizes the variance is

$$h = \rho\frac{\sigma_S}{\sigma_F}$$

# CHAPTER 5

# INTEREST RATE MARKETS

In this chapter we cover many different aspects of interest rate markets. We explain zero rates, par yields, forward rates, and the relationships between them. We cover day count conventions and the way in which the prices of Treasury bonds, corporate bonds, and Treasury bills are quoted in the United States. We show how forward rate agreements can be valued. We discuss the duration measure and explain how it can be used to quantify a company's exposure to interest rates. We also consider interest rate futures markets. We describe in some detail the popular Treasury bond futures and Eurodollar futures contracts that trade in the United States, and we examine how they can be used for duration-based hedging.

## 5.1 TYPES OF RATES

For any given currency many different types of interest rates are regularly quoted. These include mortgage rates, deposit rates, prime borrowing rates, and so on. The interest rate applicable in a situation depends on the credit risk. The higher the credit risk, the higher the interest rate. In this section, we introduce three interest rates that are particularly important in options and futures markets.

### Treasury Rates

Treasury rates are the interest rates applicable to borrowing by a government in its own currency. For example, U.S. Treasury rates are the rates at which the U.S. government can borrow in U.S. dollars; Japanese Treasury rates are the rates at which the Japanese government can borrow in yen; and so on. It is usually assumed that there is no chance that a government will default on an obligation denominated in its own currency.[1] For this reason, Treasury rates are often termed risk-free rates.

### LIBOR Rates

Large international banks actively trade with each other 1-month, 3-month, 6-month, and 12-month deposits denominated in all of the world's major currencies. At a particular time Citibank might quote a bid rate of 6.250% and an offer rate of 6.375% to other banks for six-month deposits in Australian dollars. This means that it is prepared to pay 6.250% per annum on six-month deposits from another bank or advance deposits to another bank at the rate of 6.375% per annum. The bid rate is known as the *London Interbank Bid Rate*, or **LIBID**. The offer rate is known as the *London*

---

[1] The reason for this is that the government can always meet its obligation by printing more money.

*Interbank Offer Rate*, or LIBOR. The rates are determined in trading between banks and change as economic conditions change. If more banks want to borrow funds than lend funds, LIBID and LIBOR increase. If the reverse is true, they decrease.

LIBOR is a widely used reference rate. LIBOR rates are generally higher than the corresponding Treasury rates because they are not risk-free rates. There is always some chance (albeit small) that the bank borrowing the money will default. As mentioned in Chapter 3, banks and other large financial institutions tend to use the LIBOR rate rather than the Treasury rate as the "risk-free rate" when they evaluate derivatives transactions. The reason is that financial institutions invest surplus funds in the LIBOR market and borrow to meet their short-term funding requirements in this market. They regard LIBOR as their opportunity cost of capital.

### Repo Rate

Sometimes an investment dealer funds its trading activities with a *repo* or *repurchase agreement*. This is a contract where an investment dealer who owns securities agrees to sell them to another company now and buy them back later at a slightly higher price. The company is providing a loan to the investment dealer. The difference between the price at which the securities are sold and the price at which they are repurchased is the interest it earns. The interest rate is referred to as the *repo rate*. If structured carefully, the loan involves very little credit risk. If the original owner of the securities does not honor the agreement, the lending company simply keeps the securities. If the lending company does not keep to its side of the agreement, the original owner of the securities keeps the cash.

The most common type of repo is an *overnight repo*, in which the agreement is renegotiated each day. However, longer-term arrangements, known as *term repos*, are sometimes used.

## 5.2   ZERO RATES

The *n*-year *zero rate* (short for zero-coupon rate) is the rate of interest earned on an investment that starts today and lasts for *n* years. All the interest and principal is realized at the end of *n* years. There are no intermediate payments. The *n*-year zero rate is sometimes also referred to as the *n*-year *spot rate*. Suppose the five-year Treasury zero rate with continuous compounding is quoted as 5% per annum. This means that $100, if invested at the risk-free rate for five years, would grow to

$$100 \times e^{0.05 \times 5} = 128.40$$

Many of the interest rates we observe directly in the market are not pure zero rates. Consider a five-year government bond that provides a 6% coupon. The price of this bond does not exactly determine the five-year Treasury zero rate because some of the return on the bond is realized in the form of coupons prior to the end of year five. Later in this chapter we will discuss how we can determine Treasury zero rates from the prices of traded instruments.

## 5.3   BOND PRICING

Most bonds provide coupons periodically. The owner also receives the principal or face value of the bond at maturity. The theoretical price of a bond can be calculated as the present value of all

**Table 5.1** Treasury zero rates

| Maturity (years) | Zero rate (%) (continuously compounded) |
|---|---|
| 0.5 | 5.0 |
| 1.0 | 5.8 |
| 1.5 | 6.4 |
| 2.0 | 6.8 |

the cash flows that will be received by the owner of the bond using the appropriate zero rates as discount rates. Consider the situation where Treasury zero rates, measured with continuous compounding, are as in Table 5.1 (we explain later how these can be calculated). Suppose that a two-year Treasury bond with a principal of $100 provides coupons at the rate of 6% per annum semiannually. To calculate the present value of the first coupon of $3, we discount it at 5.0% for six months; to calculate the present value of the second coupon of $3, we discount it at 5.8% for one year; and so on. The theoretical price of the bond is therefore

$$3e^{-0.05\times0.5} + 3e^{-0.058\times1.0} + 3e^{-0.064\times1.5} + 103e^{-0.068\times2.0} = 98.39$$

or $98.39.

### Bond Yield

The yield on a coupon-bearing bond is the discount rate that equates the cash flows on the bond to its market value. Suppose that the theoretical price of the bond we have been considering, $98.39, is also its market value (i.e., the market's price of the bond is in exact agreement with the data in Table 5.1). If $y$ is the yield on the bond, expressed with continuous compounding, we must have

$$3e^{-y\times0.5} + 3e^{-y\times1.0} + 3e^{-y\times1.5} + 103e^{-y\times2.0} = 98.39$$

This equation can be solved using an iterative ("trial-and-error") procedure to give $y = 6.76\%$.[2]

### Par Yield

The *par yield* for a certain maturity is the coupon rate that causes the bond price to equal its face value. Usually the bond is assumed to provide semiannual coupons. Suppose that the coupon on a two-year bond in our example is $c$ per annum (or $\frac{1}{2}c$ per six months). Using the zero rates in Table 5.1, the value of the bond is equal to its face value of 100 when

$$\frac{c}{2}e^{-0.05\times0.5} + \frac{c}{2}e^{-0.058\times1.0} + \frac{c}{2}e^{-0.064\times1.5} + \left(100 + \frac{c}{2}\right)e^{-0.068\times2.0} = 100$$

This equation can be solved in a straightforward way to give $c = 6.87$. The two-year par yield is therefore 6.87% per annum with semiannual compounding (or 6.75% with continuous compounding).

---

[2] One way of solving nonlinear equations of the form $f(y) = 0$, such as this one, is to use the Newton–Raphson method. We start with an estimate $y_0$ of the solution and produce successively better estimates $y_1, y_2, y_3, \ldots$ using the formula $y_{i+1} = y_i - f(y_i)/f'(y_i)$, where $f'(y)$ denotes the partial derivative of $f$ with respect to $y$.

More generally, if $d$ is the present value of $1 received at the maturity of the bond, $A$ is the value of an annuity that pays one dollar on each coupon payment date, and $m$ is the number of coupon payments per year, the par yield $c$ must satisfy

$$100 = A\frac{c}{m} + 100d$$

so that

$$c = \frac{(100 - 100d)m}{A}$$

In our example, $m = 2$, $d = e^{-0.068 \times 2} = 0.87284$, and

$$A = e^{-0.05 \times 0.5} + e^{-0.058 \times 1.0} + e^{-0.064 \times 1.5} + e^{-0.068 \times 2.0} = 3.70027$$

The formula confirms that the par yield is 6.87% per annum with semiannual compounding.

## 5.4 DETERMINING TREASURY ZERO RATES

We now discuss how Treasury zero rates can be calculated from the prices of instruments that trade. One approach is known as the *bootstrap method*. To illustrate the nature of the method, consider the data in Table 5.2 on the prices of five bonds. Because the first three bonds pay no coupons, the zero rates corresponding to the maturities of these bonds can be easily calculated. The three-month bond provides a return of 2.5 in three months on an initial investment of 97.5. With quarterly compounding, the three-month zero rate is $(4 \times 2.5)/97.5 = 10.256\%$ per annum. Equation (3.3) shows that, when the rate is expressed with continuous compounding, it becomes

$$4\ln\left(1 + \frac{0.10256}{4}\right) = 0.10127$$

*(.25)*

or 10.127% per annum. The six-month bond provides a return of 5.1 in six months on an initial investment of 94.9. With semiannual compounding, the six-month rate is $(2 \times 5.1)/94.9 = 10.748\%$ per annum. Equation (3.3) shows that, when the rate is expressed with continuous compounding, it becomes

$$2\ln\left(1 + \frac{0.10748}{2}\right) = 0.10469$$

or 10.469% per annum. Similarly, the one-year rate with continuous compounding is

$$\ln\left(1 + \frac{10}{90}\right) = 0.10536$$

or 10.536% per annum.

The fourth bond lasts 1.5 years. The payments are as follows:

6 months :    $4
1 year :      $4
1.5 years :   $104

From our earlier calculations, we know that the discount rate for the payment at the end of six

**Table 5.2**  Data for bootstrap method

| Bond principal ($) | Time to maturity (years) | Annual coupon* ($) | Bond price ($) |
|:---:|:---:|:---:|:---:|
| 100 | 0.25 | 0 | 97.5 |
| 100 | 0.50 | 0 | 94.9 |
| 100 | 1.00 | 0 | 90.0 |
| 100 | 1.50 | 8 | 96.0 |
| 100 | 2.00 | 12 | 101.6 |

\* Half the stated coupon is assumed to be paid every six months.

months is 10.469%, and the discount rate for the payment at the end of one year is 10.536%. We also know that the bond's price, \$96, must equal the present value of all the payments received by the bondholder. Suppose the 1.5-year zero rate is denoted by $R$. It follows that

$$4e^{-0.10469 \times 0.5} + 4e^{-0.10536 \times 1.0} + 104e^{-R \times 1.5} = 96$$

This reduces to

$$e^{-1.5R} = 0.85196$$

or

$$R = -\frac{\ln 0.85196}{1.5} = 0.10681$$

The 1.5-year zero rate is therefore 10.681%. This is the only zero rate that is consistent with the 6-month rate, 1-year rate, and the data in Table 5.2.

The 2-year zero rate can be calculated similarly from the 6-month, 1-year, and 1.5-year zero rates and the information on the last bond in Table 5.2. If $R$ is the two-year zero rate, then

$$6e^{-0.10469 \times 0.5} + 6e^{-0.10536 \times 1.0} + 6e^{-0.10681 \times 1.5} + 106e^{-R \times 2.0} = 101.6$$

This gives $R = 0.10808$, or 10.808%.

The rates we have calculated are summarized in Table 5.3. A chart showing the zero rate as a function of maturity is known as the *zero curve*. A common assumption is that the zero curve is linear between the points determined using the bootstrap method. (This means that the 1.25-year zero rate is $0.5 \times 10.536 + 0.5 \times 10.681 = 10.6085\%$ in our example.) It is also usually assumed

**Table 5.3**  Continuously compounded zero rates determined from data in Table 5.2

| Maturity (years) | Zero rate (%) (continuously compounded) |
|:---:|:---:|
| 0.25 | 10.127 |
| 0.50 | 10.469 |
| 1.00 | 10.536 |
| 1.50 | 10.681 |
| 2.00 | 10.808 |

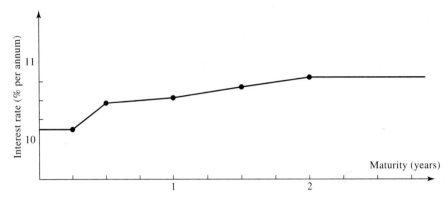

**Figure 5.1**  Zero rates given by the bootstrap method

that the zero curve is horizontal prior to the first point and horizontal beyond the last point. Figure 5.1 shows the zero curve for our data. By using longer maturity bonds, the zero curve would be more accurately determined beyond two years.

In practice, we do not usually have bonds with maturities equal to exactly 1.5 years, 2 years, 2.5 years, and so on. The approach often used by analysts is to interpolate between the bond price data before it is used to calculate the zero curve. For example, if they know that a 2.3-year bond with a coupon of 6% sells for 98 and a 2.7-year bond with a coupon of 6.5% sells for 99, they might assume that a 2.5-year bond with a coupon of 6.25% would sell for 98.5.

## 5.5  FORWARD RATES

Forward interest rates are the rates of interest implied by current zero rates for periods of time in the future. To illustrate how they are calculated, we suppose that the zero rates are as shown in the second column of Table 5.4. The rates are assumed to be continuously compounded. Thus, the 10% per annum rate for one year means that, in return for an investment of $100 today, the investor receives $100e^{0.1} = \$110.52$ in one year; the 10.5% per annum rate for two years means that, in return for an investment of $100 today, the investor receives $100e^{0.105 \times 2} = \$123.37$ in two years; and so on.

**Table 5.4**  Calculation of forward rates

| Year (n) | Zero rate for an n-year investment (% per annum) | Forward rate for n-th year (% per annum) |
|----------|--------------------------------------------------|------------------------------------------|
| 1        | 10.0                                             |                                          |
| 2        | 10.5                                             | 11.0                                     |
| 3        | 10.8                                             | 11.4                                     |
| 4        | 11.0                                             | 11.6                                     |
| 5        | 11.1                                             | 11.5                                     |

The forward interest rate in Table 5.4 for year 2 is 11% per annum. This is the rate of interest that is implied by the zero rates for the period of time between the end of the first year and the end of the second year. It can be calculated from the one-year zero interest rate of 10% per annum and the two-year zero interest rate of 10.5% per annum. It is the rate of interest for year 2 that, when combined with 10% per annum for year 1, gives 10.5% overall for the two years. To show that the correct answer is 11% per annum, suppose that $100 is invested. A rate of 10% for the first year and 11% for the second year yields

$$100e^{0.1}e^{0.11} = \$123.37$$

at the end of the second year. A rate of 10.5% per annum for two years yields

$$100e^{0.105 \times 2}$$

which is also $123.37. This example illustrates the general result that, when interest rates are continuously compounded and rates in successive time periods are combined, the overall equivalent rate is simply the average rate during the whole period. (In our example, 10% for the first year and 11% for the second year average to 10.5% for the two years.) The result is only approximately true when the rates are not continuously compounded.

The forward rate for the year 3 is the rate of interest that is implied by a 10.5% per annum two-year zero rate and a 10.8% per annum three-year zero rate. It is 11.4% per annum. The reason is that an investment for two years at 10.5% per annum combined with an investment for one year at 11.4% per annum gives an overall average return for the three years of 10.8% per annum. The other forward rates can be calculated similarly and are shown in the third column of the table. In general, if $R_1$ and $R_2$ are the zero rates for maturities $T_1$ and $T_2$, respectively, and $R_F$ is the forward interest rate for the period of time between $T_1$ and $T_2$, then

$$R_F = \frac{R_2 T_2 - R_1 T_1}{T_2 - T_1} \tag{5.1}$$

To illustrate this formula, consider the calculation of the year 4 forward rate from the data in Table 5.4: $T_1 = 3$, $T_2 = 4$, $R_1 = 0.108$, and $R_2 = 0.11$, and the formula gives $R_F = 0.116$.

Assuming that the zero rates for borrowing and investing are the same (which is not too unreasonable for a large financial institution), an investor can lock in the forward rate for a future time period. Suppose, for example, that the zero rates are as in Table 5.4. If an investor borrows $100 at 10% for one year and then invests the money at 10.5% for two years, the result is a cash outflow of $100e^{0.1} = \$110.52$ at the end of year 1 and an inflow of $100e^{0.105 \times 2} = \$123.37$ at the end of year 2. Because $123.37 = 110.52e^{0.11}$, a return equal to the forward rate (11%) is earned on $110.52 during the second year. Suppose next that the investor borrows $100 for four years at 11% and invests it for three years at 10.8%. The result is a cash inflow of $100e^{0.108 \times 3} = \$138.26$ at the end of the third year and a cash outflow of $100e^{0.11 \times 4} = \$155.27$ at the end of the fourth year. Because $155.27 = 138.26e^{0.116}$, money is being borrowed for the fourth year at the forward rate of 11.6%.

Equation (5.1) can be written

$$R_F = R_2 + (R_2 - R_1)\frac{T_1}{T_2 - T_1} \tag{5.2}$$

This shows that if the zero curve is upward sloping between $T_1$ and $T_2$, so that $R_2 > R_1$, then $R_F > R_2$. Similarly, if the zero curve is downward sloping with $R_2 < R_1$, then $R_F < R_2$.

Taking limits as $T_2$ approaches $T_1$ in equation (5.2) and letting the common value of the two be $T$, we obtain

$$R_F = R + T\frac{\partial R}{\partial T}$$

where $R$ is the zero rate for a maturity of $T$. The value of $R_F$ obtained in this way is known as the *instantaneous forward rate* for a maturity of $T$. This is the forward rate that is applicable to a very short future time period that begins at time $T$.

## 5.6  FORWARD RATE AGREEMENTS

A *forward rate agreement* (FRA) is an over-the-counter agreement that a certain interest rate will apply to a certain principal during a specified future period of time. In this section we examine how forward rate agreements can be valued in terms of forward rates.

Consider a forward rate agreement in which it is agreed that a financial institution will earn an interest rate $R_K$ for the period of time between $T_1$ and $T_2$ on a principal of $L$. Define:

$R_F$: The forward LIBOR interest rate for the period between times $T_1$ and $T_2$

$R$: The actual LIBOR interest rate observed at time $T_1$ for a maturity $T_2$

We will depart from our usual assumption of continuous compounding and assume that the rates $R_K$, $R_F$, and $R$ are all measured with a compounding frequency reflecting their maturity. This means that if $T_2 - T_1 = 0.5$, they are expressed with semiannual compounding; if $T_2 - T_1 = 0.25$, they are expressed with quarterly compounding; and so on. The forward rate agreement is an agreement to the following two cash flows:[3]

Time $T_1$: $-L$

Time $T_2$: $+L[1 + R_K(T_2 - T_1)]$

To value the FRA, we first note that it is always worth zero when $R_K = R_F$.[4] This is because, as noted in the previous section, a large financial institution can at no cost lock in the forward rate for a future time period. For example, it can ensure that it earns the forward rate for the time period between years 2 and 3 by borrowing a certain amount of money for two years and investing it for three years. Similarly, it can ensure that it pays the forward rate for the time period between years 2 and 3 by borrowing a certain amount of money for three years and investing it for two years.

We can now use an argument analogous to that used in Section 3.8 to calculate the value of the FRA for values of $R_K$ other than $R_F$. Compare two FRAs. The first promises that the forward rate $R_F$ will be earned on a principal of $L$ between times $T_1$ and $T_2$; the second promises that $R_K$ will be earned on the same principal between the same two dates. The two contracts are the same except for the interest payments received at time $T_2$. The excess of the value of the second contract over

---

[3] In practice, an FRA such as the one considered is usually settled in cash at time $T_1$. The cash settlement is the present value of the cash flows or

$$L\frac{1 + R_K(T_2 - T_1)}{1 + R(T_2 - T_1)} - L$$

[4] It is usually the case that $R_K$ is set equal to $R_F$ when the FRA is first initiated.

the first is therefore the present value of the difference between these interest payments, or

$$L(R_K - R_F)(T_2 - T_1)e^{-R_2 T_2}$$

where $R_2$ is the continously compounded zero rate for a maturity $T_2$.[5] Because the value of the FRA promising $R_F$ is zero, the value of the FRA promising $R_K$ is

$$V = L(R_K - R_F)(T_2 - T_1)e^{-R_2 T_2} \tag{5.3}$$

When an FRA specifies that the interest rate $R_K$ will be paid rather than received, its value is similarly given by

$$V = L(R_F - R_K)(T_2 - T_1)e^{-R_2 T_2} \tag{5.4}$$

**Example 5.1**   Suppose that the three-month LIBOR rate is 5% and the six-month LIBOR rate is 5.5% with continuous compounding. Consider an FRA where we will receive a rate of 7%, measured with quarterly compounding, on a principal of \$1 million between the end of month 3 and the end of month 6. In this case, the forward rate is 6% with continuous compounding or 6.0452% with quarterly compounding. From equation (5.3) it follows that the value of the FRA is

$$1,000,000 \times (0.07 - 0.060452) \times 0.25 \times e^{-0.055 \times 0.5} = \$2,322$$

### *Alternative Characterization of FRAs*

Consider again an FRA that guarantees that a rate $R_K$ will be earned between times $T_1$ and $T_2$. The principal $L$ can be borrowed at rate $R$ at time $T_1$ and repaid at time $T_2$. When this transaction is combined with the FRA, we see that the FRA is equivalent to the following cash flows:

Time $T_1$: 0
Time $T_2$: $L[1 + R_K(T_2 - T_1)]$
Time $T_2$: $-L[1 + R(T_2 - T_1)]$

Combining the two cash flows at time $T_2$, we see that the FRA is equivalent to a single cash flow of

$$L(R_K - R)(T_2 - T_1)$$

at time $T_2$. The FRA is equivalent to an agreement where at time $T_2$ interest at the predetermined rate, $R_K$, is received and interest at the market rate, $R$, is paid. Comparing this result with equation (5.3), we see that the FRA can be valued by assuming that $R = R_F$ and discounting the resultant cash flows at the risk-free rate. We have therefore shown:

1. An FRA is equivalent to an agreement where interest at a predetermined rate, $R_K$, is exchanged for interest at the market rate, $R$.
2. An FRA can be valued by assuming that forward interest rate is certain to be realized.

These two results will be useful when we consider interest rate swaps in the next chapter.

---

[5] Note that $R_K$, $R$, and $R_F$ are expressed with a compounding frequency corresponding to $T_2 - T_1$, whereas $R_2$ is expressed with continuous compounding.

## 5.7 THEORIES OF THE TERM STRUCTURE

It is natural to ask what determines the shape of the zero curve. Why is it sometimes downward sloping, sometimes upward sloping, and sometimes partly upward sloping and partly downward sloping? A number of different theories have been proposed. The simplest is *expectations theory*, which conjectures that long-term interest rates should reflect expected future short-term interest rates. More precisely, it argues that a forward interest rate corresponding to a certain future period is equal to the expected future zero interest rate for that period. Another idea, *segmentation theory*, conjectures that there need be no relationship between short-, medium-, and long-term interest rates. Under the theory, a major investor such as a large pension fund invests in bonds of a certain maturity and does not readily switch from one maturity to another. The short-term interest rate is determined by supply and demand in the short-term bond market; the medium-term interest rate is determined by supply and demand in the medium-term bond market; and so on.

The theory that is in some ways most appealing is *liquidity preference theory*, which argues that forward rates should always be higher than expected future zero rates. The basic assumption underlying the theory is that investors prefer to preserve their liquidity and invest funds for short periods of time. Borrowers, on the other hand, usually prefer to borrow at fixed rates for long periods of time. If the interest rates offered by banks and other financial intermediaries corresponded to expectations theory, long-term interest rates would equal the average of expected future short-term interest rates. In the absence of any incentive to do otherwise, investors would tend to deposit their funds for short time periods, and borrowers would tend to choose to borrow for long time periods. Financial intermediaries would then find themselves financing substantial amounts of long-term fixed-rate loans with short-term deposits. Excessive interest rate risk would result. In practice, in order to match depositors with borrowers and avoid interest rate risk, financial intermediaries raise long-term interest rates relative to expected future short-term interest rates. This strategy reduces the demand for long-term fixed-rate borrowing and encourages investors to deposit their funds for long terms.

Liquidity preference theory leads to a situation in which forward rates are greater than expected future zero rates. It is also consistent with the empirical result that yield curves tend to be upward sloping more often than they are downward sloping.

## 5.8 DAY COUNT CONVENTIONS

We now examine the day count conventions that are used when interest rates are quoted. This is a quite separate issue from the compounding frequency used to measure interest rates, which was discussed in Section 3.3. The day count defines the way in which interest accrues over time. Generally, we know the interest earned over some reference period (e.g., the time between coupon payments), and we are interested in calculating the interest earned over some other period.

The day count convention is usually expressed as $X/Y$. When we are calculating the interest earned between two dates, $X$ defines the way in which the number of days between the two dates is calculated, and $Y$ defines the way in which the total number of days in the reference period is measured. The interest earned between the two dates is

$$\frac{\text{Number of days between dates}}{\text{Number of days in reference period}} \times \text{Interest earned in reference period}$$

Three day count conventions that are commonly used in the United States are:

1. Actual/actual (in period)
2. 30/360
3. Actual/360

Actual/actual (in period) is used for U.S. Treasury bonds, 30/360 is used for U.S. corporate and municipal bonds, and actual/360 is used for U.S. Treasury bills and other money market instruments.

   The use of actual/actual (in period) for Treasury bonds indicates that the interest earned between two dates is based on the ratio of the actual days elapsed to the actual number of days in the period between coupon payments. Suppose that the bond principal is $100, coupon payment dates are March 1 and September 1, and the coupon rate is 8%. We wish to calculate the interest earned between March 1 and July 3. The reference period is from March 1 to September 1. There are 184 (actual) days in this period, and interest of $4 is earned during the period. There are 124 (actual) days between March 1 and July 3. The interest earned between March 1 and July 3 is therefore

$$\frac{124}{184} \times 4 = 2.6957$$

The use of 30/360 for corporate and municipal bonds indicates that we assume 30 days per month and 360 days per year when carrying out calculations. With 30/360, the total number of days between March 1 and September 1 is 180. The total number of days between March 1 and July 3 is $(4 \times 30) + 2 = 122$. In a corporate bond with the same terms as the Treasury bond just considered, the interest earned between March 1 and July 3 would therefore be

$$\frac{122}{180} \times 4 = 2.7111$$

The use of actual/360 for a money market instrument indicates that the reference period is 360 days. The interest earned during part of a year is calculated by dividing the actual number of elapsed days by 360 and multiplying by the rate. The interest earned in 90 days is therefore exactly one-fourth of the quoted rate. Note that the interest earned in a whole year of 365 days is 365/360 times the quoted rate.

## 5.9  QUOTATIONS

The price quoted for an interest-bearing instrument is often not the same as the cash price you would pay if you purchased it. We illustrate this by considering the way in which prices are quoted for Treasury bonds and Treasury bills in the United States.

### *Bonds*

Treasury bond prices in the United States are quoted in dollars and thirty-seconds of a dollar. The quoted price is for a bond with a face value of $100. Thus, a quote of 90-05 indicates that the quoted price for a bond with a face value of $100,000 is $90,156.25.

The quoted price is not the same as the cash price that is paid by the purchaser. In general,

Cash price = Quoted price + Accrued interest since last coupon date

To illustrate this formula, suppose that it is March 5, 2001, and the bond under consideration is an 11% coupon bond maturing on July 10, 2009, with a quoted price of 95-16 or $95.50. Because coupons are paid semiannually on government bonds, the most recent coupon date is January 10, 2001, and the next coupon date is July 10, 2001. The number of days between January 10, 2001, and March 5, 2001, is 54, whereas the number of days between January 10, 2001, and July 10, 2001, is 181. On a bond with $100 face value, the coupon payment is $5.50 on January 10 and July 10. The accrued interest on March 5, 2001, is the share of the July 10 coupon accruing to the bondholder on March 5, 2001. Because actual/actual in period is used for Treasury bonds, this is

$$\frac{54}{181} \times \$5.5 = \$1.64$$

The cash price per $100 face value for the July 10, 2001, bond is therefore

$$\$95.5 + \$1.64 = \$97.14$$

Thus, the cash price of a $100,000 bond is $97,140.

### Treasury Bills

As already mentioned, the actual/360 day count convention is used for Treasury bills in the United States. Price quotes are for a Treasury bill with a face value of $100. There is a difference between the cash price and quoted price for a Treasury bill. If $Y$ is the cash price of a Treasury bill that has a face value of $100 and $n$ days to maturity, the quoted price is

$$\frac{360}{n}(100 - Y)$$

This is referred to as the *discount rate*. It is the annualized dollar return provided by the Treasury bill expressed as a percentage of the face value. If for a 91-day Treasury bill the cash price, $Y$, were 98, then the quoted price would be $(360/91) \times (100 - 98) = 7.91$.

The discount rate or quoted price is not the same as the rate of return earned on the Treasury bill. The latter is calculated as the dollar return divided by the cost. In the example just given, the rate of return would be 2/98, or 2.04% per 91 days. This amounts to

$$\frac{2}{98} \times \frac{365}{91} = 0.08186$$

or 8.186% per annum with compounding every 91 days.

## 5.10  TREASURY BOND FUTURES

Table 5.5 shows interest rate futures quotes as they appeared in the *Wall Street Journal* on March 16, 2001. The most popular long-term interest rate futures contract is the Treasury bond futures contract traded on the Chicago Board of Trade (CBOT). In this contract, any government bond

**Table 5.5**   Interest rate futures quotes from the *Wall Street Journal* on March 16, 2001. (Columns show month, open, high, low, settle, change, lifetime high, lifetime low, and open interest, respectively.)

## INTEREST RATE

**Treasury Bonds (CBT)-$100,000; pts 32nds of 100%**
| | | | | | | | | |
|---|---|---|---|---|---|---|---|---|
| Mar | 106-15 | 106-26 | 106-03 | 106-14 | + | 3 | 106-30 | 88-06 | 47,482 |
| June | 106-06 | 106-17 | 105-24 | 106-04 | + | 3 | 106-17 | 96-21 | 474,584 |
| Sept | 105-15 | 106-02 | 105-12 | 105-22 | + | 2 | 106-04 | 96-22 | 2,818 |

Est vol 225,000; vol Wed 328,320; open int 524,994, +6,141.

**Treasury Notes (CBT)-$100,000; pts 32nds of 100%**
| Mar | 06-205 | 107-04 | 106-18 | 06-295 | + | 8.5 | 107-04 | 98-04 | 52,833 |
|---|---|---|---|---|---|---|---|---|---|
| June | 106-11 | 106-22 | 106-03 | 106-15 | + | 8.5 | 106-22 | 99-11 | 495,880 |
| Sept | 106-07 | 106-09 | 106-04 | 106-04 | + | 8.5 | 106-09 | 103-30 | 4,939 |

Est vol 226,000; vol Wed 278,130; open int 553,652, +13,722.

**10 Yr Agency Notes (CBT)-$100,000; pts 32nds of 100%**
| Mar | 101-30 | 102-12 | 01-295 | 102-07 | + | 12.0 | 102-21 | 93-25 | 10,264 |
|---|---|---|---|---|---|---|---|---|---|
| June | 101-17 | 102-02 | 101-14 | 101-27 | + | 11.5 | 02-105 | 98-22 | 46,569 |

Est vol 4,000; vol Wed 9,020; open int 56,833, +573.

**5 Yr Treasury Notes (CBT)-$100,000; pts 32nds of 100%**
| Mar | 105-05 | 05-155 | 105-01 | 05-115 | + | 8.0 | 05-155 | 100-11 | 36,713 |
|---|---|---|---|---|---|---|---|---|---|
| June | 105-15 | 05-245 | 105-09 | 105-20 | + | 9.5 | 05-245 | 101-04 | 329,523 |

Est vol 127,000; vol Wed 117,378; open int 366,236, +5,564.

**2 Yr Treasury Notes (CBT)-$200,000; pts 32nds of 100%**
| Mar | 102-24 | 102-31 | 102-24 | 102-29 | + | 5.7 | 102-31 | 11-282 | 6,647 |
|---|---|---|---|---|---|---|---|---|---|
| June | 102-28 | 03-022 | 02-252 | 103-00 | + | 6.2 | 03-022 | 101-12 | 78,842 |

Est vol 10,100; vol Wed 6,628; open int 85,489, −428.

**30 Day Federal Funds (CBT)-$5 million; pts of 100%**
| Mar | 94.740 | 94.750 | 94.730 | 94.745 | + | .010 | 95.810 | 93.205 | 21,039 |
|---|---|---|---|---|---|---|---|---|---|
| Apr | 95.18 | 95.21 | 95.16 | 95.20 | + | .04 | 95.21 | 93.21 | 28,536 |
| May | 95.30 | 95.35 | 95.29 | 95.35 | + | .06 | 95.35 | 94.02 | 6,703 |
| June | 95.44 | 95.51 | 95.42 | 95.50 | + | .07 | 95.51 | 94.38 | 5,403 |
| July | 95.62 | 95.62 | 95.55 | 95.61 | + | .08 | 95.62 | 95.02 | 2,045 |

Est vol 14,000; vol Wed 19,184; open int 63,726, −118.

**Muni Bond index (CBT)-$1,000; times Bond Buyer MBI**
| Mar | 105-15 | 105-20 | 105-14 | 105-17 | .... | | 105-27 | 98-03 | 6,532 |
|---|---|---|---|---|---|---|---|---|---|
| June | 104-21 | 104-30 | 104-16 | 104-22 | + | 1 | 105-00 | 101-30 | 11,635 |

Est vol 850; vol Wed 1,203; open int 18,167, −130.
Index: Close 104-30; Yield 5.30.

**Treasury Bills (CME)-$1 mil.; pts of 100%**
| | OPEN | HIGH | LOW | SETTLE | CHANGE | | YIELD | CHANGE | OPEN INT. |
|---|---|---|---|---|---|---|---|---|---|
| Mar | 95.59 | 95.64 | 95.59 | 95.62 | + | .05 | 4.38 | −.05 | 3,139 |
| June | 96.06 | 96.13 | 96.06 | 96.11 | + | .09 | 3.89 | −.09 | 1,491 |

Est vol 485; vol Wed 780; open int 4,630, −80.

**Libor-1 Mo. (CME)-$3,000,000; pts of 100%**
| Mar | 94.95 | 94.99 | 94.95 | 94.99 | + | .04 | 5.01 | −.04 | 29,178 |
|---|---|---|---|---|---|---|---|---|---|
| Apr | 95.15 | 95.19 | 95.13 | 95.18 | + | .05 | 4.82 | −.05 | 19,819 |
| May | 95.32 | 95.40 | 95.31 | 95.38 | + | .07 | 4.62 | −.07 | 9,811 |
| June | 95.43 | 95.60 | 95.43 | 95.53 | + | .09 | 4.47 | −.09 | 1,030 |
| July | 95.50 | 95.59 | 95.49 | 95.58 | + | .08 | 4.42 | −.08 | 464 |
| Aug | | | | 95.61 | + | .09 | 4.39 | −.08 | 204 |
| Sept | | | 95.67 | + | .10 | 4.33 | −.10 | 24 |

Est vol 5,710; vol Wed 7,033; open int 60,543, −267.

**Eurodollar (CME)-$1 Million; pts of 100%**
| Mar | 95.06 | 95.10 | 95.05 | 95.09 | + | .02 | 4.91 | −.02 | 516,751 |
|---|---|---|---|---|---|---|---|---|---|
| Apr | 95.24 | 95.29 | 95.24 | 95.28 | + | .04 | 4.72 | −.04 | 25,625 |
| May | 95.41 | 95.44 | 95.39 | 95.43 | + | .08 | 4.57 | −.08 | 3,558 |
| June | 95.43 | 95.55 | 95.43 | 95.53 | + | .08 | 4.47 | −.08 | 659,688 |
| July | 95.59 | 95.59 | 95.58 | 95.59 | + | .12 | 4.41 | −.12 | 1,012 |
| Sept | 95.50 | 95.64 | 95.50 | 95.62 | + | .10 | 4.38 | −.10 | 705,199 |
| Dec | 95.34 | 95.47 | 95.32 | 95.45 | + | .10 | 4.55 | −.10 | 391,832 |
| Mr02 | 95.26 | 95.40 | 95.25 | 95.37 | + | .09 | 4.63 | −.09 | 375,936 |
| June | 95.03 | 95.17 | 95.03 | 95.14 | + | .09 | 4.86 | −.09 | 316,329 |
| Sept | 94.84 | 94.96 | 94.83 | 94.93 | + | .09 | 5.07 | −.09 | 252,106 |
| Dec | 94.61 | 94.73 | 94.60 | 94.71 | + | .09 | 5.29 | −.09 | 163,620 |
| Mr03 | 94.57 | 94.68 | 94.57 | 94.66 | + | .08 | 5.34 | −.08 | 125,515 |
| June | 94.48 | 94.59 | 94.48 | 94.56 | + | .08 | 5.44 | −.08 | 99,406 |
| Sept | 94.40 | 94.51 | 94.40 | 94.48 | + | .08 | 5.52 | −.08 | 95,178 |
| Dec | 94.27 | 94.37 | 94.26 | 94.34 | + | .08 | 5.66 | −.08 | 79,656 |
| Mr04 | 94.27 | 94.38 | 94.26 | 94.34 | + | .08 | 5.66 | −.08 | 76,267 |
| June | 94.21 | 94.30 | 94.18 | 94.27 | + | .08 | 5.73 | −.08 | 61,145 |
| Sept | 94.12 | 94.24 | 94.12 | 94.20 | + | .08 | 5.80 | −.08 | 60,968 |
| Dec | 94.03 | 94.12 | 94.00 | 94.08 | + | .08 | 5.92 | −.08 | 51,646 |
| Mr05 | 94.01 | 94.12 | 94.01 | 94.09 | + | .08 | 5.91 | −.08 | 36,722 |
| June | 93.97 | 94.06 | 93.97 | 94.03 | + | .08 | 5.97 | −.08 | 35,002 |
| Sept | 93.91 | 94.01 | 93.91 | 93.97 | + | .07 | 6.03 | −.07 | 33,913 |
| Dec | 93.81 | 93.90 | 93.81 | 93.86 | + | .07 | 6.14 | −.07 | 25,415 |
| Mr06 | 93.82 | 93.92 | 93.82 | 93.88 | + | .06 | 6.12 | −.06 | 19,542 |
| June | 93.78 | 93.87 | 93.78 | 93.83 | + | .06 | 6.17 | −.06 | 18,291 |
| Sept | 93.75 | 93.82 | 93.74 | 93.79 | + | .06 | 6.21 | −.06 | 17,857 |
| Dec | 93.65 | 93.73 | 93.64 | 93.69 | + | .05 | 6.31 | −.05 | 13,136 |
| Mr07 | .... | .... | | 93.72 | + | .05 | 6.28 | −.05 | 11,626 |
| June | 93.64 | 93.71 | 93.63 | 93.67 | + | .04 | 6.33 | −.04 | 8,488 |
| Sept | .... | .... | | 93.63 | + | .04 | 6.37 | −.04 | 7,120 |
| Dec | .... | .... | | 93.54 | + | .04 | 6.46 | −.04 | 7,780 |
| Mr08 | 93.55 | 93.61 | 93.52 | 93.57 | + | .04 | 6.43 | −.04 | 5,289 |
| June | 93.50 | 93.57 | 93.48 | 93.53 | + | .03 | 6.47 | −.03 | 5,064 |
| Sept | 93.51 | 93.54 | 93.45 | 93.49 | + | .03 | 6.51 | −.03 | 3,976 |
| Dec | 93.42 | 93.45 | 93.36 | 93.40 | + | .03 | 6.60 | −.03 | 3,626 |
| Mr09 | .... | .... | | 93.43 | + | .02 | 6.57 | −.02 | 3,935 |
| June | .... | .... | | 93.39 | + | .02 | 6.61 | −.02 | 3,446 |
| Sept | .... | .... | | 93.35 | + | .02 | 6.65 | −.02 | 3,417 |
| Dec | .... | .... | | 93.26 | − | .01 | 6.74 | −.01 | 2,465 |
| Mr10 | .... | .... | | 93.29 | + | .01 | 6.71 | −.01 | 2,534 |
| June | .... | .... | | 93.25 | + | .01 | 6.75 | −.01 | 2,611 |
| Sept | .... | .... | | 93.22 | + | .01 | 6.78 | −.01 | 2,694 |
| Dec | .... | .... | | 93.12 | | | 6.88 | | 2,897 |

Est vol 792,400; vol Wed 950,073; open int 4,338,283, +26,797.

**Euro-Yen (CME)-Yen 100,000,000; pts of 100%**
| | | | | | | | LIFETIME | | OPEN |
| | OPEN | HIGH | LOW | SETTLE | CHANGE | | HIGH | LOW | INT. |
|---|---|---|---|---|---|---|---|---|---|
| Mar | 99.77 | 99.77 | 99.77 | 99.77 | − | .01 | 99.79 | 98.07 | 30,179 |
| June | 99.87 | 99.88 | 99.87 | 99.87 | − | .01 | 99.89 | 98.20 | 15,401 |
| Sept | 99.86 | 99.87 | 99.86 | 99.87 | − | .01 | 99.88 | 98.05 | 12,051 |
| Dec | 99.84 | 99.85 | 99.84 | 99.85 | | .... | 99.86 | 97.89 | 8,025 |
| Mr02 | 99.84 | 99.85 | 99.84 | 99.85 | − | .01 | 99.86 | 97.97 | 4,954 |
| June | 99.83 | 99.84 | 99.83 | 99.83 | − | .01 | 99.85 | 97.87 | 1,851 |
| Sept | 99.78 | 99.78 | 99.77 | 99.78 | − | .01 | 99.79 | 97.84 | 1,432 |
| Dec | 99.67 | 99.67 | 99.67 | 99.67 | − | .01 | 99.68 | 97.77 | 169 |

Est vol 4,309; vol Wed 7,187; open int 74,062, +1,498.

**Short Sterling (LIFFE)-£500,000; pts of 100%**
| Mar | 94.45 | 94.51 | 94.45 | 94.50 | + | .06 | 95.08 | 92.55 | 144,961 |
|---|---|---|---|---|---|---|---|---|---|
| June | 94.77 | 94.82 | 94.77 | 94.80 | + | .04 | 95.08 | 92.49 | 148,665 |
| Sept | 94.95 | 94.98 | 94.93 | 94.97 | + | .05 | 95.09 | 92.41 | 204,792 |
| Dec | 94.89 | 94.94 | 94.89 | 94.93 | + | .06 | 95.07 | 92.31 | 88,147 |
| Mr02 | 94.82 | 94.86 | 94.82 | 94.85 | + | .05 | 95.13 | 92.34 | 73,235 |
| June | 94.73 | 94.76 | 94.72 | 94.75 | + | .04 | 95.10 | 92.39 | 63,128 |
| Sept | 94.65 | 94.69 | 94.65 | 94.68 | + | .04 | 95.11 | 92.38 | 39,315 |
| Dec | 94.60 | 94.63 | 94.59 | 94.62 | + | .04 | 95.11 | 92.45 | 24,534 |
| Mr03 | 94.59 | 94.61 | 94.57 | 94.60 | + | .04 | 94.69 | 92.49 | 16,439 |
| June | 94.57 | 94.58 | 94.55 | 94.57 | + | .03 | 94.58 | 92.77 | 15,276 |
| Sept | 94.54 | 94.56 | 94.52 | 94.54 | + | .04 | 94.56 | 92.90 | 22,180 |
| Dec | 94.50 | 94.52 | 94.49 | 94.51 | + | .03 | 94.52 | 92.92 | 5,222 |
| Mr04 | .... | .... | | 94.48 | + | .03 | 94.43 | 93.01 | 3,759 |
| June | .... | .... | | 94.47 | + | .03 | 94.41 | 93.04 | 1,872 |
| Sept | .... | .... | | 94.45 | + | .03 | 94.16 | 93.35 | 311 |
| Dec | .... | .... | | 94.45 | + | .03 | 94.30 | 93.25 | 581 |

Est vol 154,768 vol Wed 213,500 open int 852,507 +8,941.

**Long Gilt (LIFFE) (Decimal)-£50,000; pts of 100%**
| Mar | 116.60 | 116.81 | 116.58 | 116.89 | + | .41 | 155.74 | 113.10 | 6,212 |
|---|---|---|---|---|---|---|---|---|---|
| June | 117.69 | 118.17 | 117.17 | 118.10 | + | .41 | 118.17 | 114.90 | 57,299 |

Est vol 26,977 vol Wed 32,350 open int 63,511 +3,405.

**3 Month Euribor (LIFFE) Euro 1,000,000; pts of 100%**
| Mar | 95.26 | 95.28 | 95.24 | 95.25 | − | .02 | 96.96 | 94.57 | 279,290 |
|---|---|---|---|---|---|---|---|---|---|
| Apr | .... | .... | | 95.36 | | | 95.52 | 95.31 | 615 |
| June | 95.58 | 95.60 | 95.56 | 95.59 | + | .02 | 96.85 | 94.50 | 326,977 |
| Sept | 95.80 | 95.83 | 95.78 | 95.82 | + | .04 | 96.75 | 94.44 | 341,037 |
| Dec | 95.74 | 95.76 | 95.71 | 95.75 | + | .04 | 96.58 | 92.57 | 210,373 |
| Mr02 | 95.78 | 95.81 | 95.76 | 95.80 | + | .04 | 96.48 | 94.33 | 189,331 |
| June | 95.67 | 95.71 | 95.66 | 95.70 | + | .04 | 96.37 | 94.29 | 99,203 |
| Sept | 95.60 | 95.62 | 95.56 | 95.61 | + | .04 | 96.25 | 94.24 | 63,845 |
| Dec | 95.46 | 95.47 | 95.40 | 95.46 | + | .04 | 96.06 | 94.06 | 52,546 |
| Mr03 | 95.42 | 95.46 | 95.41 | 95.44 | + | .04 | 96.01 | 94.05 | 37,455 |
| June | 95.37 | 95.39 | 95.35 | 95.38 | + | .03 | 95.95 | 93.99 | 21,445 |
| Sept | 95.31 | 95.34 | 95.30 | 95.33 | + | .03 | 95.34 | 93.91 | 16,503 |
| Dec | 95.16 | 95.21 | 95.16 | 95.19 | + | .03 | 95.21 | 93.80 | 11,770 |
| Mr04 | 95.19 | 95.19 | 95.19 | 95.19 | + | .03 | 95.19 | 93.83 | 3,667 |
| June | .... | .... | | 95.13 | + | .03 | 95.13 | 93.79 | 3,848 |
| Sept | .... | .... | | 95.08 | + | .03 | 95.07 | 93.73 | 2,162 |
| Dec | .... | .... | | 94.95 | + | .03 | 94.96 | 93.64 | 1,106 |
| Mr05 | .... | .... | | 94.94 | + | .03 | 94.95 | 94.07 | 304 |

Est vol 436,581 vol Wed 545,643 open int 1,661,500 +37,266.

**3 Month Euroswiss (LIFFE) SFr 1,000,000; pts of 100%**
| June | 96.90 | 97.00 | 96.89 | 96.96 | + | .08 | 97.47 | 95.65 | 65,688 |
|---|---|---|---|---|---|---|---|---|---|
| Sept | 97.01 | 97.12 | 97.01 | 97.09 | + | .08 | 97.12 | 95.59 | 33,796 |
| Dec | 96.96 | 97.02 | 96.94 | 97.01 | + | .07 | 97.02 | 95.45 | 15,382 |
| Mr02 | 97.03 | 97.07 | 97.00 | 97.06 | + | .07 | 97.07 | 95.50 | 8,872 |
| June | 96.97 | 96.99 | 96.97 | 96.99 | + | .05 | 96.99 | 95.82 | 5,254 |
| Sept | .... | .... | | 96.94 | + | .05 | 96.85 | 96.19 | 1,133 |
| Dec | .... | .... | | 96.86 | + | .05 | 96.81 | 96.59 | 1,623 |

Est vol 30,483 vol Wed 31,992 open int 177,670 +8,540.

**Canadian Bankers Acceptance (ME)-C$1,000,000**
| Mar | 95.28 | 95.35 | 95.28 | 95.34 | + | 0.06 | 95.35 | 93.16 | 69,439 |
|---|---|---|---|---|---|---|---|---|---|
| June | 95.56 | 95.68 | 95.55 | 95.66 | + | 0.10 | 95.68 | 93.07 | 73,299 |
| Sept | 95.63 | 95.78 | 95.62 | 95.75 | + | 0.12 | 95.78 | 93.06 | 45,109 |
| Dec | 95.47 | 95.59 | 95.46 | 95.58 | + | 0.12 | 95.59 | 92.97 | 19,261 |
| Mr02 | 95.31 | 95.38 | 95.31 | 95.38 | + | 0.08 | 95.38 | 93.25 | 14,002 |
| June | 95.17 | 95.21 | 95.15 | 95.21 | + | 0.04 | 95.21 | 92.95 | 13,095 |
| Sept | 95.01 | 95.05 | 95.01 | 95.07 | + | 0.04 | 95.05 | 93.11 | 3,736 |
| Dec | .... | .... | | 94.93 | + | 0.04 | 94.81 | 93.06 | 689 |
| Mr03 | .... | .... | | 94.83 | + | 0.04 | 94.58 | 93.98 | 278 |
| June | .... | .... | | 94.76 | + | 0.04 | 94.38 | 93.96 | 165 |
| Sept | .... | .... | | 94.69 | + | 0.04 | 94.37 | 94.32 | 145 |
| Dec | .... | .... | | 94.62 | + | 0.04 | 94.33 | 94.24 | 100 |

Est vol 29,885; vol Wed 25,957; open int 239,338, +9,450.

*(continued on next page)*

**Table 5.5**  (*continued*)

| 10 Yr. Canadian Govt. Bonds (ME)-C$100,000 | | | | | | | |
|---|---|---|---|---|---|---|---|
| Mar | .... | .... | 105.50 | + 0.10 | 105.25 | 101.80 | 5,505 |
| June | 105.10 105.33 104.91 | 105.81 | + 0.10 | 105.40 | 103.30 | | 61,851 |
| Est vol 2,838; vol Wed 3,551; open int 67,356, -723. | | | | | | | |
| **10 Yr. Euro Notional Bond (MATIF)-Euros 100,000** | | | | | | | |
| Mar | 90.32 90.40 90.13 | 90.30 | + 0.05 | 90.55 | 86.33 | | 175,093 |
| June | 90.42 90.70 90.26 | 90.45 | + 0.06 | 90.70 | 89.19 | | 28,708 |
| Est vol 221,549; vol Wed 218,960; open int 187,299, +6,100. | | | | | | | |
| **3 Month Euribor (MATIF)-Euros 1,000,000** | | | | | | | |
| Mar | .... .... .... | 95.24 | - 0.02 | 96.95 | 94.63 | | 6,053 |
| June | .... .... .... | 95.58 | + 0.02 | 96.85 | 94.55 | | 3,357 |
| Sept | .... .... .... | 95.82 | + 0.03 | 96.75 | 94.47 | | 2,021 |
| Dec | .... .... .... | 95.75 | + 0.03 | 96.58 | 94.37 | | 2,835 |
| Mr02 | .... .... .... | 95.79 | + 0.03 | 96.48 | 94.45 | | 2,617 |
| June | .... .... .... | 95.69 | + 0.03 | 96.29 | 94.35 | | 308 |
| Sept | .... .... .... | 95.60 | + 0.04 | 96.21 | 94.27 | | 475 |
| Dec | .... .... .... | 95.46 | + 0.03 | 95.97 | 94.10 | | 330 |
| Est vol 0; vol Wed 0; open int 18,059, unch. | | | | | | | |
| **3 Yr. Commonwealth T-Bonds (SFE)-A$100,000** | | | | | | | |
| Mar | 95.44 95.57 95.43 | 95.54 | + 0.09 | 95.57 | 94.25 | | 0 |
| June | 95.50 95.62 95.48 | 95.55 | + 0.05 | 95.62 | 94.94 | | 231,145 |
| Est vol 399,603; vol Wed 168,037; open int 231,145, -295,318. | | | | | | | |
| **Euro-Yen (SGX)-Yen 100,000,000 pts Of 100%** | | | | | | | |
| Mar | 99.78 99.79 99.77 | 99.77 | - 0.01 | 99.79 | 98.08 | | 98,662 |
| June | 99.88 99.88 99.87 | 99.87 | .... | 99.88 | 98.17 | | 111,646 |

| Sept | 99.88 99.88 99.87 99.87 | - 0.01 | 99.88 | 98.01 | 78,678 |
|---|---|---|---|---|---|
| Dec | 99.85 99.86 99.84 99.84 | - 0.01 | 99.86 | 97.84 | 51,494 |
| Mr02 | 99.86 99.86 99.84 99.84 | - 0.01 | 99.86 | 98.17 | 37,541 |
| June | 99.85 99.85 99.83 99.83 | - 0.02 | 99.85 | 98.11 | 33,907 |
| Sept | 99.79 99.79 99.77 99.76 | - 0.01 | 99.79 | 98.35 | 14,517 |
| Dec | 99.70 99.70 99.68 99.67 | - 0.01 | 99.70 | 98.28 | 3,264 |
| Mr03 | .... .... .... 99.60 | - 0.01 | 99.54 | 98.45 | 2,102 |
| June | .... .... .... 99.51 | .... | 99.54 | 98.40 | 2,170 |
| Sept | .... .... .... 99.37 | .... | 99.42 | 98.34 | 5,010 |
| Est vol 25,077; vol Wed 34,493; open int 439,071, +82. | | | | | |
| **5 Yr. German Euro-Govt. Bond** | | | | | |
| **(EURO-BOBL) (EUREX)-Euro 100,000; pts of 100%** | | | | | |
| June | 106.60 106.75 106.53 106.74 | + 0.08 | 106.75 | 103.50 | 465,268 |
| Sept | .... .... .... 107.02 | + 0.08 | 106.65 | 105.51 | 9,638 |
| vol Thu 456,995; open int 479,927, +46,697. | | | | | |
| **10 Yr. German Euro-Govt. Bond** | | | | | |
| **(EURO-BUND) (EUREX)-Euro 100,000; pts of 100%** | | | | | |
| June | 109.46 109.67 109.40 109.64 | + 0.08 | 109.70 | 106.00 | 687,796 |
| Sept | 109.64 109.70 109.49 109.70 | + 0.01 | 109.70 | 107.96 | 5,747 |
| vol Thu 706,063; open int 693,543, +92,384. | | | | | |
| **2 Yr. German Euro-Govt. Bond** | | | | | |
| **(EURO-SCHATZ) (EUREX)-Euro 100,000; pts of 100%** | | | | | |
| June | 103.03 103.09 102.97 103.07 | + 0.03 | 103.22 | 102.27 | 507,068 |
| Sept | .... .... 102.98 | + 0.03 | .... | .... | 4,304 |
| vol Thu 379,199; open int 511,372, +57,585. | | | | | |

*Source*: Reprinted by permission of Dow Jones, Inc., via copyright Clearance Center, Inc. © 2001 Dow Jones & Company, Inc. All Rights Reserved Worldwide.

that has more than 15 years to maturity on the first day of the delivery month and that is not callable within 15 years from that day can be delivered. As will be explained later, the CBOT has developed a procedure for adjusting the price received by the party with the short position according to the particular bond delivered.

The Treasury note and five-year Treasury note futures contract in the United States are also actively traded. In the Treasury note futures contract, any government bond (or note) with a maturity between $6\frac{1}{2}$ and 10 years can be delivered. In the five-year Treasury note futures contract, any of the four most recently auctioned Treasury notes can be delivered.

The remaining discussion in this section focuses on Treasury bond futures. Many other bond futures contracts traded in the United States and the rest of the world are designed in a similar way to CBOT Treasury bond futures, so that many of the points we will make are applicable to these contracts as well.

### Quotes

Treasury bond futures prices are quoted in the same way as the Treasury bond prices themselves (see Section 5.9). Table 5.5 shows that the settlement price on March 15, 2001 for the June 2001 contract was 106-04, or $106\frac{4}{32}$. One contract involves the delivery of $100,000 face value of the bond. Thus, a $1 change in the quoted futures price would lead to a $1,000 change in the value of the futures contract. Delivery can take place at any time during the delivery month.

### Conversion Factors

As mentioned, the Treasury bond futures contract allows the party with the short position to choose to deliver any bond that has a maturity of more than 15 years and that is not callable within 15 years. When a particular bond is delivered, a parameter known as its *conversion factor* defines the price received by the party with the short position. The quoted price applicable to the delivery is the product of the conversion factor and the quoted futures price. Taking accrued interest into account, as described in Section 5.9, the cash received for each $100 face value of bond delivered is

$$(\text{Quoted futures price} \times \text{Conversion factor}) + \text{Accrued interest}$$

Each contract is for the delivery of \$100,000 face value of bonds. Suppose the quoted futures price is 90-00, the conversion factor for the bond delivered is 1.3800, and the accrued interest on this bond at the time of delivery is \$3 per \$100 face value. The cash received by the party with the short position (and paid by the party with the long position) is then

$$(1.3800 \times 90.00) + 3.00 = \$127.20$$

per \$100 face value. A party with the short position in one contract would deliver bonds with face value of \$100,000 and receive \$127,200.

The conversion factor for a bond is equal to the value of the bond per dollar of principal on the first day of the delivery month on the assumption that the interest rate for all maturities equals 6% per annum (with semiannual compounding).[6] The bond maturity and the times to the coupon payment dates are rounded down to the nearest three months for the purposes of the calculation. The practice enables the CBOT to produce comprehensive tables. If, after rounding, the bond lasts for an exact number of six-month periods, the first coupon is assumed to be paid in six months. If, after rounding, the bond does not last for an exact number of six-month periods (i.e., there is an extra three months), the first coupon is assumed to be paid after three months and accrued interest is subtracted.

As a first example of these rules, consider a 10% coupon bond with 20 years and two months to maturity. For the purposes of calculating the conversion factor, the bond is assumed to have exactly 20 years to maturity. The first coupon payment is assumed to be made after six months. Coupon payments are then assumed to be made at six-month intervals until the end of the 20 years when the principal payment is made. Assume that the face value is \$100. When the discount rate is 6% per annum with semiannual compounding (or 3% per six months), the value of the bond is

$$\sum_{i=1}^{40} \frac{5}{1.03^i} + \frac{100}{1.03^{40}} = \$146.23$$

Dividing by the face value gives a credit conversion factor of 1.4623.

As a second example of the rules, consider an 8% coupon bond with 18 years and four months to maturity. For the purposes of calculating the conversion factor, the bond is assumed to have exactly 18 years and three months to maturity. Discounting all the payments back to a point in time three months from today at 6% per annum (compounded semiannually) gives a value of

$$\sum_{i=0}^{36} \frac{4}{1.03^i} + \frac{100}{1.03^{36}} = \$125.83$$

The interest rate for a three-month period is $\sqrt{1.03} - 1$, or 1.4889%. Hence, discounting back to the present gives the bond's value as $125.83/1.014889 = \$123.99$. Subtracting the accrued interest of 2.0, this becomes \$121.99. The conversion factor is therefore 1.2199.

---

[6] For contracts with maturities prior to March 2000, this interest rate was 8% in the CBOT conversion factor calculation.

### Cheapest-to-Deliver Bond

At any given time during the delivery month, there are many bonds that can be delivered in the CBOT Treasury bond futures contract. These vary widely as far as coupon and maturity are concerned. The party with the short position can choose which of the available bonds is "cheapest" to deliver. Because the party with the short position receives

$$(\text{Quoted futures price} \times \text{Conversion factor}) + \text{Accrued interest}$$

and the cost of purchasing a bond is

$$\text{Quoted price} + \text{Accrued interest}$$

the cheapest-to-deliver bond is the one for which

$$\text{Quoted price} - (\text{Quoted futures price} \times \text{Conversion factor})$$

is least. Once the party with the short position has decided to deliver, it can determine the cheapest-to-deliver bond by examining each of the bonds in turn.

> **Example 5.2**  The party with the short position has decided to deliver and is trying to choose among the three bonds in Table 5.6. Assume the current quoted futures price is 93-08, or 93.25. The cost of delivering each of the bonds is as follows:
> Bond 1:  $99.50 - (93.25 \times 1.0382) = \$2.69$
> Bond 2:  $143.50 - (93.25 \times 1.5188) = \$1.87$
> Bond 3:  $119.75 - (93.25 \times 1.2615) = \$2.12$
> The cheapest-to-deliver bond is bond 2.

**Table 5.6**  Deliverable bonds in Example 5.2

| Bond | Quoted price ($) | Conversion factor |
|---|---|---|
| 1 | 99.50 | 1.0382 |
| 2 | 143.50 | 1.5188 |
| 3 | 119.75 | 1.2615 |

A number of factors determine the cheapest-to-deliver bond. When bond yields are in excess of 6%, the conversion factor system tends to favor the delivery of low-coupon, long-maturity bonds. When yields are less than 6%, the system tends to favor the delivery of high-coupon, short-maturity bonds. Also, when the yield curve is upward sloping, there is a tendency for bonds with a long time to maturity to be favored, whereas when it is downward sloping, there is a tendency for bonds with a short time to maturity to be delivered.

### The Wild Card Play

Trading in the CBOT Treasury bond futures contract ceases at 2:00 p.m. Chicago time. However, Treasury bonds themselves continue trading in the spot market until 4:00 p.m. Furthermore, a trader with a short futures position has until 8:00 p.m. to issue to the clearinghouse a notice of intention to deliver. If the notice is issued, the invoice price is calculated on the basis of the settlement price that day. This is the price at which trading was conducted just before the closing bell at 2:00 p.m.

This practice gives rise to an option known as the *wild card play*. If bond prices decline after 2:00 p.m., the party with the short position can issue a notice of intention to deliver and proceed to buy cheapest-to-deliver bonds in preparation for delivery at the 2:00 p.m. futures price. If the bond price does not decline, the party with the short position keeps the position open and waits until the next day when the same strategy can be used.

As with the other options open to the party with the short position, the wild card play is not free. Its value is reflected in the futures price, which is lower than it would be without the option.

### Determining the Quoted Futures Price

An exact theoretical futures price for the Treasury bond contract is difficult to determine because the short party's options concerned with the timing of delivery and choice of the bond that is delivered cannot easily be valued. However, if we assume that both the cheapest-to-deliver bond and the delivery date are known, the Treasury bond futures contract is a futures contract on a security providing the holder with known income.[7] Equation (3.6) then shows that the futures price, $F_0$, is related to the spot price, $S_0$, by

$$F_0 = (S_0 - I)e^{rT} \tag{5.5}$$

where $I$ is the present value of the coupons during the life of the futures contract, $T$ is the time until the futures contract matures, and $r$ is the risk-free interest rate applicable to a time period of length $T$.

**Example 5.3** Suppose that, in a Treasury bond futures contract, it is known that the cheapest-to-deliver bond will be a 12% coupon bond with a conversion factor of 1.4000. Suppose also that it is known that delivery will take place in 270 days. Coupons are payable semiannually on the bond. As illustrated in Figure 5.2, the last coupon date was 60 days ago, the next coupon date is in 122 days, and the coupon date thereafter is in 305 days. The term structure is flat, and the rate of interest (with continuous compounding) is 10% per annum. Assume that the current quoted bond price is $120. The cash price of the bond is obtained by adding to this quoted price the proportion of the next coupon payment that accrues to the holder. The cash price is therefore

$$120 + \frac{60}{60 + 122} \times 6 = 121.978$$

A coupon of $6 will be received after 122 days (= 0.3342 year). The present value of this is

$$6e^{-0.1 \times 0.3342} = 5.803$$

The futures contract lasts for 270 days (0.7397 year). The cash futures price if the contract were written on the 12% bond would therefore be

$$(121.978 - 5.803)e^{0.1 \times 0.7397} = 125.094$$

---

[7] In practice, for the purposes of determining the cheapest-to-deliver in this calculation, analysts usually assume that zero rates at the maturity of the futures contract will equal today's forward rates.

**Figure 5.2**  Time chart for Example 5.3

At delivery there are 148 days of accrued interest. The quoted futures price if the contract were written on the 12% bond is calculated by subtracting the accrued interest:

$$125.094 - 6 \times \frac{148}{305 - 122} = 120.242$$

From the definition of the conversion factor, 1.4000 standard bonds are considered equivalent to each 12% bond. The quoted futures price should therefore be

$$\frac{120.242}{1.4000} = 85.887$$

## 5.11  EURODOLLAR FUTURES

Another very popular United States interest rate futures contract is the three-month Eurodollar futures contract traded on the Chicago Mercantile Exchange (CME). A Eurodollar is a dollar deposited in a U.S. or foreign bank outside the United States. The Eurodollar interest rate is the rate of interest earned on Eurodollars deposited by one bank with another bank. It is essentially the same as the London Interbank Offer Rate (LIBOR) mentioned in earlier chapters.

Three-month Eurodollar futures contracts are futures contracts on the three-month Eurodollar interest rate. The contracts have maturities in March, June, September, and December for up to 10 years into the future. In addition, as can be seen from Table 5.5, the CME trades short-maturity contracts with maturities in other months.

If $Q$ is the quoted price for a Eurodollar futures contract, the exchange defines the value of one contract as

$$10,000[100 - 0.25(100 - Q)] \tag{5.6}$$

Thus, the settlement price of 95.53 for the June 2001 contract in Table 5.5 corresponds to a contract price of

$$10,000[100 - 0.25(100 - 95.53)] = \$988,825$$

It can be seen from equation (5.6) that a change of one basis point or 0.01 in a Eurodollar futures quote corresponds to a contract price change of $25.

When the third Wednesday of the delivery month is reached the contract is settled in cash. The final marking to market sets $Q$ equal to $100 - R$, where $R$ is the actual three-month Eurodollar interest rate on that day, expressed with quarterly compounding and an actual/360 day count convention. Thus, if the three-month Eurodollar interest rate on the third Wednesday of the delivery month is 8%, the final marking to market is 92, and the final contract price, from equation (5.6), is

$$10,000[100 - 0.25(100 - 92)] = \$980,000$$

If $Q$ is a Eurodollar futures quote, $(100 - Q)\%$ is the Eurodollar futures interest rate for a three-month period beginning on the third Wednesday of the delivery month. Thus Table 5.5 indicates that on March 15, 2001, the futures interest rate for the three-month period beginning Wednesday June 20, 2001, was $100 - 95.53 = 4.47\%$. This is expressed with quarterly compounding and an actual/360 day count convention.

Other contracts similar to the CME Eurodollar futures contracts trade on interest rates in other countries. As shown in Table 5.5, CME and SGX trade Euroyen contracts, LIFFE and MATIF trade Euribor contracts (i.e., contracts on the three-month LIBOR rate for the euro), and LIFFE trades three-month Euroswiss futures (see Table 2.2 for the meaning of these exchange abbreviations).

### Forward vs. Futures Interest Rates

For short maturities (up to one year) the Eurodollar futures interest rate can be assumed to be the same as the corresponding forward interest rate. For longer-dated contracts the differences between futures and forward interest rates mentioned in Section 3.9 become important.

Analysts make what is known as a *convexity adjustment* to convert Eurodollar futures rates to forward interest rates. One way of doing this is by using the formula

$$\text{Forward rate} = \text{Futures rate} - \tfrac{1}{2}\sigma^2 t_1 t_2$$

where $t_1$ is the time to maturity of the futures contract, $t_2$ is the time to the maturity of the rate underlying the futures contract, and $\sigma$ is the standard deviation of the change in the short-term interest rate in one year. Both rates are expressed with continuous compounding.[8] A typical value for $\sigma$ is 1.2% or 0.012.

> **Example 5.4**  Consider the situation where $\sigma = 0.012$, and we wish to calculate the forward rate when the eight-year Eurodollar futures price quote is 94. In this case $t_1 = 8$, $t_2 = 8.25$, and the convexity adjustment is
>
> $$\tfrac{1}{2} \times 0.012^2 \times 8 \times 8.25 = 0.00475$$
>
> or 0.475%. The futures rate is 6% per annum on an actual/360 basis with quarterly compounding. This is $6 \times 365/360 = 6.083\%$ per annum on an actual/365 basis with quarterly compounding or 6.038% with continuous compounding. The forward rate is, therefore, $6.038 - 0.475 = 5.563\%$ per annum with continuous compounding.

The forward rate is less than the futures rate.[9] The size of the adjustment is roughly proportional to the square of the time to maturity of the futures contract. Thus the convexity adjustment for the eight-year contract is approximately 64 times that for a one-year contract.

## 5.12  THE LIBOR ZERO CURVE

The LIBOR zero curve (which is also sometimes referred to as the *swap zero curve*) is frequently used as the risk-free zero curve when derivatives are valued. Spot LIBOR rates (see Section 5.1) are

---

[8] This formula is based on an interest rate model known as the Ho–Lee model.

[9] The reason for this can be seen from the arguments in Section 3.9. The variable underlying the Eurodollar futures contracts is an interest rate and therefore is highly positively correlated to other interest rates. See Problem 5.32.

used to determine very short-term LIBOR zero rates. After that Euro futures (i.e., Eurodollar futures, Euroyen futures, Euribor futures, etc.) are frequently used. Once a convexity adjustment such as that just described is made, the Euro futures contracts define forward rates for future three-month time periods.

In the United States, March, June, September, and December Eurodollar futures are often used to determine the LIBOR zero curve out to five years. Suppose that the $i$th Eurodollar futures contract matures at time $T_i$ $(i = 1, 2, \ldots)$. We usually assume that the forward interest rate calculated from this futures contract applies to the period $T_i$ to $T_{i+1}$. (There is at most a small approximation here.) This enables a bootstrap procedure to be used to determine zero rates. Suppose that $F_i$ is the forward rate calculated from the $i$th Eurodollar futures contract and $R_i$ is the zero rate for a maturity $T_i$. From equation (5.1), we have

$$F_i = \frac{R_{i+1}T_{i+1} - R_i T_i}{T_{i+1} - T_i}$$

so that

$$R_{i+1} = \frac{F_i(T_{i+1} - T_i) + R_i T_i}{T_{i+1}} \tag{5.7}$$

**Example 5.5**  The 400-day LIBOR zero rate has been calculated as 4.80% with continuous compounding and, from a Eurodollar futures quote, it has been calculated that the forward rate for a 91-day period beginning in 400 days is 5.30% with continuous compounding. We can use equation (5.7) to obtain the 491-day rate as

$$\frac{0.053 \times 91 + 0.048 \times 400}{491} = 0.04893$$

or 4.893%.

## 5.13  DURATION

The *duration* of a bond, as its name implies, is a measure of how long on average the holder of the bond has to wait before receiving cash payments. A zero-coupon bond that matures in $n$ years has a duration of $n$ years. However, a coupon-bearing bond maturing in $n$ years has a duration of less than $n$ years, because the holder receives some of the cash payments prior to year $n$.

Suppose that a bond provides the holder with cash flows $c_i$ at time $t_i$ $(1 \leqslant i \leqslant n)$. The price, $B$, and yield, $y$ (continuously compounded), are related by

$$B = \sum_{i=1}^{n} c_i e^{-yt_i} \tag{5.8}$$

The duration, $D$, of the bond is defined as

$$D = \frac{\sum_{i=1}^{n} t_i c_i e^{-yt_i}}{B} \tag{5.9}$$

This can be written

$$D = \sum_{i=1}^{n} t_i \left[ \frac{c_i e^{-yt_i}}{B} \right]$$

The term in square brackets is the ratio of the present value of the cash flow at time $t_i$ to the bond price. The bond price is the present value of all payments. The duration is therefore a weighted average of the times when payments are made, with the weight applied to time $t_i$ being equal to the proportion of the bond's total present value provided by the cash flow at time $t_i$. The sum of the weights is 1.0. We now show why duration is a popular and widely used measure.

From equation (5.8),

$$\frac{\partial B}{\partial y} = -\sum_{i=1}^{n} c_i t_i e^{-yt_i}$$

and from equation (5.9) this can be written

$$\frac{\partial B}{\partial y} = -BD \tag{5.10}$$

If we make a small parallel shift to the yield curve, increasing all interest rates by a small amount, $\delta y$, the yields on all bonds also increase by $\delta y$. Equation (5.10) shows that the bond's price increases by $\delta B$, where

$$\frac{\delta B}{\delta y} = -BD \tag{5.11}$$

or

$$\frac{\delta B}{B} = -D\,\delta y \tag{5.12}$$

Equation (5.12) is the key duration relationship. It shows that the percentage change in a bond price is (approximately) equal to its duration multiplied by the size of the parallel shift in the yield curve.

Consider a three-year 10% coupon bond with a face value of $100. Suppose that the yield on the bond is 12% per annum with continuous compounding. This means that $y = 0.12$. Coupon payments of $5 are made every six months. Table 5.7 shows the calculations necessary to determine the bond's duration. The present values of the bond's cash flows, using the yield as the discount rate, are shown in column 3 (e.g., the present value of the first cash flow is $5e^{-0.12 \times 0.5} = 4.709$). The sum of the numbers in column 3 gives the bond's price as 94.213. The weights are calculated by dividing the numbers in column 3 by 94.213. The sum of the numbers in column 5 gives the duration as 2.653 years.

**Table 5.7** Calculation of duration

| Time (years) | Cash flow ($) | Present value | Weight | Time × weight |
|:---:|:---:|:---:|:---:|:---:|
| 0.5 | 5 | 4.709 | 0.050 | 0.025 |
| 1.0 | 5 | 4.435 | 0.047 | 0.047 |
| 1.5 | 5 | 4.176 | 0.044 | 0.066 |
| 2.0 | 5 | 3.933 | 0.042 | 0.083 |
| 2.5 | 5 | 3.704 | 0.039 | 0.098 |
| 3.0 | 105 | 73.256 | 0.778 | 2.333 |
| Total | 130 | 94.213 | 1.000 | 2.653 |

Small changes in interest rates are often measured in *basis points*. A basis point is 0.01% per annum. The following example investigates the accuracy of the duration relationship in equation (5.11).

**Example 5.6** For the bond in Table 5.7, the bond price, $B$, is 94.213 and the duration, $D$, is 2.653, so that equation (5.11) gives

$$\delta B = -94.213 \times 2.653 \, \delta y$$

or

$$\delta B = -249.95 \, \delta y$$

When the yield on the bond increases by 10 basis points ($= 0.1\%$), $\delta y = +0.001$. The duration relationship predicts that $\delta B = -249.95 \times 0.001 = -0.250$, so that the bond price goes down to $94.213 - 0.250 = 93.963$. How accurate is this? When the bond yield increases by 10 basis points to 12.1%, the bond price is

$$5e^{-0.121 \times 0.5} + 5e^{-0.121} + 5e^{-0.121 \times 1.5} + 5e^{-0.121 \times 2.0} + 5e^{-0.121 \times 2.5} + 105e^{-0.121 \times 1.5} = 93.963$$

which is (to three decimal places) the same as that predicted by the duration relationship.

### Modified Duration

The preceding analysis is based on the assumption that $y$ is expressed with continuous compounding. If $y$ is expressed with annual compounding, it can be shown that the approximate relationship in equation (5.11) becomes (see Problem 5.31)

$$\delta B = -\frac{BD \, \delta y}{1 + y}$$

More generally, if $y$ is expressed with a compounding frequency of $m$ times per year,

$$\delta B = -\frac{BD \, \delta y}{1 + y/m}$$

A variable $D^*$ defined by

$$D^* = \frac{D}{1 + y/m}$$

is sometimes referred to as the bond's *modified duration*. It allows the duration relationship to be simplified to

$$\delta B = -BD^* \, \delta y \tag{5.13}$$

when $y$ is expressed with a compounding frequency of $m$ times per year. The following example investigates the accuracy of the modified duration relationship.

**Example 5.7** The bond in Table 5.7 has a price of 94.213 and a duration of 2.653. The yield, expressed with semiannual compounding, is 12.3673%. The modified duration, $D^*$, is

$$D^* = \frac{2.653}{1 + 0.123673/2} = 2.499$$

From equation (5.13),

$$\delta B = -94.213 \times 2.4985 \, \delta y$$

or

$$\delta B = -235.39 \, \delta y$$

When the yield (semiannually compounded) increases by 10 basis points ($= 0.1\%$), $\delta y = +0.001$. The duration relationship predicts that we expect $\delta B$ to be $-235.39 \times 0.001 = -0.235$, so that the bond price to goes down to $94.213 - 0.235 = 93.978$. How accurate is this? When the bond yield (semiannually compounded) increases by 10 basis points to 12.4673% (or to 12.0941% with continuous compounding), an exact calculation similar to that in the previous example shows that the bond price becomes 93.978. This shows that the modified duration calculation gives good accuracy.

### Bond Portfolios

The duration, $D$, of a bond portfolio can be defined as a weighted average of the durations of the individual bonds in the portfolio, with the weights being proportional to the bond prices. Equations (5.11) to (5.13) then apply with $B$ being defined as the value of the bond portfolio. They estimate the change in the value of the bond portfolio for a particular change $\delta y$ in the yields of all the bonds.

It is important to realize that, when duration is used for bond portfolios, there is an implicit assumption that the yields of all bonds will change by the same amount. When the bonds have widely differing maturities, this happens only when there is a parallel shift in the zero-coupon yield curve. We should therefore interpret equations (5.11) to (5.13) as providing estimates of the impact on the price of a bond portfolio of a parallel shift, $\delta y$, in the zero curve.

The duration relationship applies only to small changes in yields. This is illustrated in Figure 5.3, which shows the relationship between the percentage change in value and change in yield for two bond portfolios having the same duration. The gradients of the two curves are the same at the origin. This means that both bond portfolios change in value by the same percentage for small yield changes and is consistent with equation (5.12). For large yield changes, the portfolios behave differently. Portfolio $X$ has more curvature in its relationship with yields than portfolio $Y$. A factor known as *convexity* measures this curvature and can be used to improve the relationship in equation (5.12).

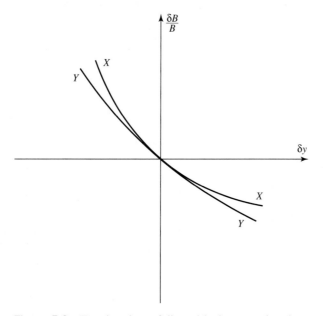

**Figure 5.3**  Two bond portfolios with the same duration

### Hedging Portfolios of Assets and Liabilities

Financial institutions frequently attempt to hedge themselves against interest rate risk by ensuring that the average duration of their assets equals the average duration of their liabilities. (The liabilities can be regarded as short positions in bonds.) This strategy is known as *duration matching* or *portfolio immunization*. When implemented, it ensures that a small parallel shift in interest rates will have little effect on the value of the portfolio of assets and liabilities. The gain (loss) on the assets should offset the loss (gain) on the liabilities.

Duration matching does not immunize a portfolio against nonparallel shifts in the zero curve. This is a weakness of the approach. In practice, short-term rates are usually more volatile than, and are not perfectly correlated with, long-term rates. Sometimes it even happens that short- and long-term rates move in opposite directions to each other. Financial institutions often try to allow for nonparallel shifts by dividing the zero-coupon yield curve up into segments and ensuring that they are hedged against a movement in each segment. Suppose that the $i$th segment is the part of the zero-coupon yield curve between maturities $t_i$ and $t_{i+1}$. A financial institution would examine the effect of a small increase $\delta y$ in all the zero rates with maturities between $t_i$ and $t_{i+1}$ while keeping the rest of the zero-coupon yield curve unchanged. If the exposure were unacceptable, further trades would be undertaken in carefully selected instruments to reduce it. In the context of a bank managing a portfolio of assets and liabilities, this approach is sometimes referred to as *GAP management*.

## 5.14  DURATION-BASED HEDGING STRATEGIES

Consider the situation where a position in an interest-rate-dependent asset such as a bond portfolio or a money market security is being hedged using an interest rate futures contract. Define:

$F_C$ : Contract price for the interest rate futures contract

$D_F$ : Duration of the asset underlying the futures contract at the maturity of the futures contract

$P$ : Forward value of the portfolio being hedged at the maturity of the hedge (in practice this is usually assumed to be the same as the value of the portfolio today)

$D_P$ : Duration of the portfolio at the maturity of the hedge

If we assume that the change in the yield, $\delta y$, is the same for all maturities, which means that only parallel shifts in the yield curve can occur, it is approximately true that

$$\delta P = -PD_P \delta y$$

To a reasonable approximation, it is also true that

$$\delta F_C = -F_C D_F \delta y$$

The number of contracts required to hedge against an uncertain $\delta y$ is therefore

$$N^* = \frac{PD_P}{F_C D_F} \tag{5.14}$$

This is the *duration-based hedge ratio*. It is sometimes also called the *price sensitivity hedge ratio*.[10] Using it has the effect of making the duration of the entire position zero.

When the hedging instrument is a Treasury bond futures contract, the hedger must base $D_F$ on an assumption that one particular bond will be delivered. This means that the hedger must estimate which of the available bonds is likely to be cheapest to deliver at the time the hedge is put in place. If, subsequently, the interest rate environment changes so that it looks as though a different bond will be cheapest to deliver, the hedge has to be adjusted, and its performance may be worse than anticipated.

When hedges are constructed using interest rate futures, it is important to bear in mind that interest rates and futures prices move in opposite directions. When interest rates go up, an interest rate futures price goes down. When interest rates go down, the reverse happens, and the interest rate futures price goes up. Thus, a company in a position to lose money if interest rates drop should hedge by taking a long futures position. Similarly, a company in a position to lose money if interest rates rise should hedge by taking a short futures position.

The hedger tries to choose the futures contract so that the duration of the underlying asset is as close as possible to the duration of the asset being hedged. Eurodollar futures tend to be used for exposures to short-term interest rates, whereas Treasury bond and Treasury note futures contracts are used for exposures to longer-term rates.

**Example 5.8**  It is August 2 and a fund manager with $10 million invested in government bonds is concerned that interest rates are expected to be highly volatile over the next three months. The fund manager decides to use the December T-bond futures contract to hedge the value of the portfolio. The current futures price is 93-02, or 93.0625. Because each contract is for the delivery of $100,000 face value of bonds, the futures contract price is $93,062.50.

We suppose that the duration of the bond portfolio in three months will be 6.80 years. The cheapest-to-deliver bond in the T-bond contract is expected to be a 20-year 12% per annum coupon bond. The yield on this bond is currently 8.80% per annum, and the duration will be 9.20 years at maturity of the futures contract.

The fund manager requires a short position in T-bond futures to hedge the bond portfolio. If interest rates go up, a gain will be made on the short futures position and a loss will be made on the bond portfolio. If interest rates decrease, a loss will be made on the short position, but there will be a gain on the bond portfolio. The number of bond futures contracts that should be shorted can be calculated from equation (5.14) as

$$\frac{10,000,000}{93,062.50} \times \frac{6.80}{9.20} = 79.42$$

Rounding to the nearest whole number, the portfolio manager should short 79 contracts.

## Convexity

For very small parallel shifts in the yield curve, the change in value of a portfolio depends solely on its duration. When moderate or large parallel shifts in interest rates are considered, a factor known as *convexity* is important. Figure 5.3 shows the relationship between the percentage change in value and change in yield, $\delta y$, for two portfolios having the same duration. The gradients of the two curves are the same when $\delta y = 0$ (and equal to the duration of the portfolio). This means that both portfolios change in value by the same percentage for small yield changes which is consistent with

---

[10] For a more detailed discussion of equation (5.14), see R. Rendleman, "Duration-Based Hedging with Treasury Bond Futures," *Journal of Fixed Income*, 9, no. 1 (June 1999), 84–91.

equation (5.11). For large interest rate changes, the portfolios behave differently. Portfolio X has more convexity (or curvature) than portfolio Y. Its value increases by a greater percentage amount than that of portfolio Y when yields decline, and its value decreases by less than that of portfolio Y when yields increase.

A measure of convexity is

$$C = \frac{1}{B} \frac{\partial^2 B}{\partial y^2} = \frac{\sum_{i=1}^{n} c_i t_i^2 e^{-yt_i}}{B}$$

The convexity of a bond portfolio tends to be greatest when the portfolio provides payments evenly over a long period of time. It is least when the payments are concentrated around one particular point in time.

When convexity is taken into account, it can be shown that equation (5.11) becomes

$$\frac{\delta B}{B} = -D \, \delta y + \tfrac{1}{2} C \, (\delta y)^2$$

By matching convexity as well as duration, a company can make itself immune to relatively large parallel shift in the zero curve. However, it is still exposed to nonparallel shifts.

## SUMMARY

Many different interest rates are quoted in financial markets and calculated by analysts. The $n$-year zero rate or $n$-year spot rate is the rate applicable to an investment lasting for $n$ years when all of the return is realized at the end. Forward rates are rates applicable to futures periods of time implied by today's zero rates. The par yield on a bond of a certain maturity is the coupon rate that causes the bond to sell for its par value.

Treasury rates should be distinguished from LIBOR rates. Treasury rates are the rates at which the government of the country borrows. LIBOR rates are the rates at which one large international bank is prepared to lend to another large international bank. LIBOR rates are often used as the risk-free rates when derivatives are valued.

Two very popular interest rate contracts are the Treasury bond and Eurodollar futures contracts that trade in the United States. In the Treasury bond futures contracts, the party with the short position has a number of interesting delivery options:

1. Delivery can be made on any day during the delivery month.
2. There are a number of alternative bonds that can be delivered.
3. On any day during the delivery month, the notice of intention to deliver at the 2:00 p.m. settlement price can be made any time up to 8:00 p.m.

These options all tend to reduce the futures price.

The Eurodollar futures contract is a contract on the three-month rate starting on the third Wednesday of the delivery month. Eurodollar futures are frequently used to estimate LIBOR forward rates for the purpose of constructing a LIBOR zero curve. When long-dated contracts are used in this way, it is important to make what is termed a convexity adjustment to allow for the marking to market in the futures contract.

The concept of duration is important in hedging interest rate risk. Duration measures how long on average an investor has to wait before receiving payments. It is a weighted average of the times until payments are received, with the weight for a particular payment time being proportional to the present value of the payment.

A key result underlying the duration-based hedging scheme described in this chapter is

$$\delta B = -BD\,\delta y$$

where $B$ is a bond price, $D$ is its duration, $\delta y$ is a small change in its yield (continuously compounded), and $\delta B$ is the resultant small change in $B$. The equation enables a hedger to assess the sensitivity of a bond price to small changes in its yield. It also enables the hedger to assess the sensitivity of an interest rate futures price to small changes in the yield of the underlying bond. If the hedger is prepared to assume that $\delta y$ is the same for all bonds, the result enables the hedger to calculate the number of futures contracts necessary to protect a bond or bond portfolio against small changes in interest rates.

The key assumption underlying the duration-based hedging scheme is that all interest rates change by the same amount. This means that only parallel shifts in the term structure are allowed for. In practice, short-term interest rates are generally more volatile than are long-term interest rates, and hedge performance is liable to be poor if the duration of the bond underlying the futures contract differs markedly from the duration of the asset being hedged.

## SUGGESTIONS FOR FURTHER READING

Allen, S. L., and A. D. Kleinstein, *Valuing Fixed-Income Investments and Derivative Securities*, New York Institute of Finance, New York, 1991.

Fabozzi, F. J., *Fixed-Income Mathematics: Analytical and Statistical Techniques*, McGraw-Hill, New York, 1996.

Fabozzi, F. J., *Duration, Convexity, and Other Bond Risk Measures*, Frank J. Fabozzi Assoc., 1999.

Figlewski, S., *Hedging with Financial Futures for Institutional Investors*, Ballinger, Cambridge, MA, 1986.

Gay, G. D., R. W. Kolb, and R. Chiang, "Interest Rate Hedging: An Empirical Test of Alternative Strategies," *Journal of Financial Research*, 6 (Fall 1983), 187–97.

Klemkosky, R. C., and D. J. Lasser, "An Efficiency Analysis of the T-bond Futures Market," *Journal of Futures Markets*, 5 (1985), 607–20.

Kolb, R. W., and R. Chiang, "Improving Hedging Performance Using Interest Rate Futures," *Financial Management*, 10 (Fall 1981), 72–79.

Resnick, B. G. "The Relationship between Futures Prices for U.S. Treasury Bonds," *Review of Research in Futures Markets*, 3 (1984), 88–104.

Resnick, B. G., and E. Hennigar, "The Relationship between Futures and Cash Prices for U.S. Treasury Bonds," *Review of Research in Futures Markets*, 2 (1983), 282–99.

Senchak, A. J., and J. C. Easterwood, "Cross Hedging CDs with Treasury Bill Futures," *Journal of Futures Markets*, 3 (1983), 429–38.

Veit, W. T., and W. W. Reiff, "Commercial Banks and Interest Rate Futures: A Hedging Survey," *Journal of Futures Markets*, 3 (1983), 283–93.

# QUESTIONS AND PROBLEMS
# (ANSWERS IN SOLUTIONS MANUAL)

5.1. Suppose that zero interest rates with continuous compounding are as follows:

| Maturity (years) | Rate (% per annum) |
| --- | --- |
| 1 | 8.0 |
| 2 | 7.5 |
| 3 | 7.2 |
| 4 | 7.0 |
| 5 | 6.9 |

Calculate forward interest rates for the second, third, fourth, and fifth years.

5.2. The term structure is upward sloping. Put the following in order of magnitude:
   a. The five-year zero rate
   b. The yield on a five-year coupon-bearing bond
   c. The forward rate corresponding to the period between 5 and 5.25 years in the future
   What is the answer to this question when the term structure is downward sloping?

5.3. The six-month and one-year zero rates are both 10% per annum. For a bond that lasts 18 months and pays a coupon of 8% per annum (with a coupon payment having just been made), the yield is 10.4% per annum. What is the bond's price? What is the 18-month zero rate? All rates are quoted with semiannual compounding.

5.4. It is January 9, 2003. The price of a Treasury bond with a 12% coupon that matures on October 12, 2009, is quoted as 102-07. What is the cash price?

5.5. The price of a 90-day Treasury bill is quoted as 10.00. What continuously compounded return (on an actual/365 basis) does an investor earn on the Treasury bill for the 90-day period?

5.6. What assumptions does a duration-based hedging scheme make about the way in which the term structure of interest rates moves?

5.7. It is January 30. You are managing a bond portfolio worth $6 million. The duration of the portfolio in six months will be 8.2 years. The September Treasury bond futures price is currently 108-15, and the cheapest-to-deliver bond will have a duration of 7.6 years in September. How should you hedge against changes in interest rates over the next six months?

5.8. Suppose that 6-month, 12-month, 18-month, 24-month, and 30-month zero rates are 4%, 4.2%, 4.4%, 4.6%, and 4.8% per annum with continuous compounding respectively. Estimate the cash price of a bond with a face value of 100 that will mature in 30 months pays a coupon of 4% per annum semiannually.

5.9. A three-year bond provides a coupon of 8% semiannually and has a cash price of 104. What is the bond yield?

5.10. Suppose that the 6-month, 12-month, 18-month, and 24-month zero rates are 5%, 6%, 6.5%, and 7%, respectively. What is the two-year par yield?

5.11. The cash prices of six-month and one-year Treasury bills are 94.0 and 89.0. A 1.5-year bond that will pay coupons of $4 every six months currently sells for $94.84. A two-year bond that will pay coupons of $5 every six months currently sells for $97.12. Calculate the 6-month, 1-year, 1.5-year, and 2-year zero rates.

5.12. Suppose that zero interest rates with continuous compounding are as follows:

| Maturity (years) | Rate (% per annum) |
|:---:|:---:|
| 1 | 12.0 |
| 2 | 13.0 |
| 3 | 13.7 |
| 4 | 14.2 |
| 5 | 14.5 |

Calculate forward interest rates for the second, third, fourth, and fifth years.

5.13. Suppose that zero interest rates with continuous compounding are as follows:

| Maturity (months) | Rate (% per annum) |
|:---:|:---:|
| 3 | 8.0 |
| 6 | 8.2 |
| 9 | 8.4 |
| 12 | 8.5 |
| 15 | 8.6 |
| 18 | 8.7 |

Calculate forward interest rates for the second, third, fourth, fifth, and sixth quarters.

5.14. A 10-year, 8% coupon bond currently sells for $90. A 10-year, 4% coupon bond currently sells for $80. What is the 10-year zero rate? (*Hint*: Consider taking a long position in two of the 4% coupon bonds and a short position in one of the 8% coupon bonds.)

5.15. Explain carefully why liquidity preference theory is consistent with the observation that the term structure tends to be upward sloping more often than it is downward sloping.

5.16. It is May 5, 2003. The quoted price of a government bond with a 12% coupon that matures on July 27, 2011, is 110-17. What is the cash price?

5.17. Suppose that the Treasury bond futures price is 101-12. Which of the following four bonds is cheapest to deliver?

| Bond | Price | Conversion factor |
|:---:|:---:|:---:|
| 1 | 125-05 | 1.2131 |
| 2 | 142-15 | 1.3792 |
| 3 | 115-31 | 1.1149 |
| 4 | 144-02 | 1.4026 |

5.18. It is July 30, 2002. The cheapest-to-deliver bond in a September 2002 Treasury bond futures contract is a 13% coupon bond, and delivery is expected to be made on September 30, 2002. Coupon payments on the bond are made on February 4 and August 4 each year. The term structure is flat, and the rate of interest with semiannual compounding is 12% per annum. The conversion factor for the bond is 1.5. The current quoted bond price is $110. Calculate the quoted futures price for the contract.

5.19. An investor is looking for arbitrage opportunities in the Treasury bond futures market. What complications are created by the fact that the party with a short position can choose to deliver any bond with a maturity of over 15 years?

5.20. Assuming that zero rates are as in Problem 5.12, what is the value of an FRA that enables the holder to earn 9.5% for a three-month period starting in one year on a principal of $1,000,000? The interest rate is expressed with quarterly compounding.

5.21. Suppose that the nine-month LIBOR interest rate is 8% per annum and the six-month LIBOR interest rate is 7.5% per annum (both with continuous compounding). Estimate the three-month Eurodollar futures price quote for a contract maturing in six months.

5.22. A five-year bond with a yield of 11% (continuously compounded) pays an 8% coupon at the end of each year.
    a. What is the bond's price?
    b. What is the bond's duration?
    c. Use the duration to calculate the effect on the bond's price of a 0.2% decrease in its yield.
    d. Recalculate the bond's price on the basis of a 10.8% per annum yield and verify that the result is in agreement with your answer to (c).

5.23. Suppose that a bond portfolio with a duration of 12 years is hedged using a futures contract in which the underlying asset has a duration of four years. What is likely to be the impact on the hedge of the fact that the 12-year rate is less volatile than the four-year rate?

5.24. Suppose that it is February 20 and a treasurer realizes that on July 17 the company will have to issue $5 million of commercial paper with a maturity of 180 days. If the paper were issued today, the company would realize $4,820,000. (In other words, the company would receive $4,820,000 for its paper and have to redeem it at $5,000,000 in 180 days' time.) The September Eurodollar futures price is quoted as 92.00. How should the treasurer hedge the company's exposure?

5.25. On August 1 a portfolio manager has a bond portfolio worth $10 million. The duration of the portfolio in October will be 7.1 years. The December Treasury bond futures price is currently 91-12 and the cheapest-to-deliver bond will have a duration of 8.8 years at maturity. How should the portfolio manager immunize the portfolio against changes in interest rates over the next two months?

5.26. How can the portfolio manager change the duration of the portfolio to 3.0 years in Problem 5.25?

5.27. Between February 28, 2002, and March 1, 2002, you have a choice between owning a government bond paying a 10% coupon and a corporate bond paying a 10% coupon. Consider carefully the day count conventions discussed in this chapter and decide which of the two bonds you would prefer to own. Ignore the risk of default.

5.28. Suppose that a Eurodollar futures quote is 88 for a contract maturing in 60 days. What is the LIBOR forward rate for the 60- to 150-day period? Ignore the difference between futures and forwards for the purposes of this question.

5.29. "When the zero curve is upward sloping, the zero rate for a particular maturity is greater than the par yield for that maturity. When the zero curve is downward sloping the reverse is true." Explain why this is so.

5.30. The three-month Eurodollar futures price for a contract maturing in six years is quoted as 95.20. The standard deviation of the change in the short-term interest rate in one year is 1.1%. Estimate the forward LIBOR interest rate for the period between 6.00 and 6.25 years in the future.

5.31. Prove equation (5.13).

5.32. Explain why the forward interest rate is less than the corresponding futures interest rate calculated from a Eurodollar futures contract.

# ASSIGNMENT QUESTIONS

5.33. Assume that a bank can borrow or lend money at the same interest rate in the LIBOR market. The 91-day rate is 10% per annum, and the 182-day rate is 10.2% per annum, both expressed with continuous compounding. The Eurodollar futures price for a contract maturing in 91 days is quoted as 89.5. What arbitrage opportunities are open to the bank?

5.34. A Canadian company wishes to create a Canadian LIBOR futures contract from a U.S. Eurodollar futures contract and forward contracts on foreign exchange. Using an example, explain how the company should proceed. For the purposes of this problem, assume that a futures contract is the same as a forward contract.

5.35. Portfolio A consists of a one-year zero-coupon bond with a face value of $2,000 and a 10-year zero-coupon bond with a face value of $6,000. Portfolio B consists of a 5.95-year zero-coupon bond with a face value of $5,000. The current yield on all bonds is 10% per annum.
   a. Show that both portfolios have the same duration.
   b. Show that the percentage changes in the values of the two portfolios for a 0.1% per annum increase in yields are the same.
   c. What are the percentage changes in the values of the two portfolios for a 5% per annum increase in yields?

5.36. The following table gives the prices of bonds:

| Bond principal ($) | Time to maturity (years) | Annual coupon* ($) | Bond price ($) |
|---|---|---|---|
| 100 | 0.50 | 0.0 | 98 |
| 100 | 1.00 | 0.0 | 95 |
| 100 | 1.50 | 6.2 | 101 |
| 100 | 2.00 | 8.0 | 104 |

\* Half the stated coupon is assumed to be paid every six months.

   a. Calculate zero rates for maturities of 6 months, 12 months, 18 months, and 24 months.
   b. What are the forward rates for the periods: 6 months to 12 months, 12 months to 18 months, 18 months to 24 months?
   c. What are the 6-month, 12-month, 18-month, and 24-month par yields for bonds that provide semiannual coupon payments?
   d. Estimate the price and yield of a two-year bond providing a semiannual coupon of 7% per annum.

5.37. It is June 25, 2002. The futures price for the June 2002 CBOT bond futures contract is 118-23.
   a. Calculate the conversion factor for a bond maturing on January 1, 2018, paying a coupon of 10%.
   b. Calculate the conversion factor for a bond maturing on October 1, 2023, paying a coupon of 7%.
   c. Suppose that the quoted prices of the bonds in (a) and (b) are 169.00 and 136.00, respectively. Which bond is cheaper to deliver?
   d. Assuming that the cheapest-to-deliver bond is actually delivered, what is the cash price received for the bond?

5.38. A portfolio manager plans to use a Treasury bond futures contract to hedge a bond portfolio over the next three months. The portfolio is worth $100 million and will have a duration of 4.0 years in three months. The futures price is 122, and each futures contract is on $100,000 of bonds. The bond that is expected to be cheapest to deliver will have a duration of 9.0 years at the maturity of the futures contract. What position in futures contracts is required?

a. What adjustments to the hedge are necessary if after one month the bond that is expected to be cheapest to deliver changes to one with a duration of seven years?

b. Suppose that all rates increase over the three months, but long-term rates increase less than short-term and medium-term rates. What is the effect of this on the performance of the hedge?

# CHAPTER 6

# SWAPS

A swap is an agreement between two companies to exchange cash flows in the future. The agreement defines the dates when the cash flows are to be paid and the way in which they are to be calculated. Usually the calculation of the cash flows involves the future values of one or more market variables.

A forward contract can be viewed as a simple example of a swap. Suppose it is March 1, 2002, and a company enters into a forward contract to buy 100 ounces of gold for $300 per ounce in one year. The company can sell the gold in one year as soon as it is received. The forward contract is therefore equivalent to a swap where the company agrees that on March 1, 2003, it will pay $30,000 and receive $100S$, where $S$ is the market price of one ounce of gold on that date.

Whereas a forward contract leads to the exchange of cash flows on just one future date, swaps typically lead to cash flow exchanges taking place on several future dates. The first swap contracts were negotiated in the early 1980s. Since then the market has seen phenomenal growth. In this chapter we examine how swaps are designed, how they are used, and how they can be valued. Our discussion centers on the two popular types of swaps: plain vanilla interest rate swaps and fixed-for-fixed currency swaps. Other types of swaps are discussed in Chapter 25.

## 6.1 MECHANICS OF INTEREST RATE SWAPS

The most common type of swap is a "plain vanilla" interest rate swap. In this, a company agrees to pay cash flows equal to interest at a predetermined fixed rate on a notional principal for a number of years. In return, it receives interest at a floating rate on the same notional principal for the same period of time.

The floating rate in many interest rate swap agreements is the London Interbank Offer Rate (LIBOR). This was introduced in Chapter 5. LIBOR is the rate of interest offered by banks on deposits from other banks in Eurocurrency markets. One-month LIBOR is the rate offered on one-month deposits, three-month LIBOR is the rate offered on three-month deposits, and so on. LIBOR rates are determined by trading between banks and change frequently so that the supply of funds in the interbank market equals the demand for funds in that market. Just as prime is often the reference rate of interest for floating-rate loans in the domestic financial market, LIBOR is a reference rate of interest for loans in international financial markets. To understand how it is used, consider a five-year loan with a rate of interest specified as six-month LIBOR plus 0.5% per annum. The life of the loan is divided into ten periods, each six months in length. For each period the rate of interest is set at 0.5% per annum above the six-month LIBOR rate at the beginning of the period. Interest is paid at the end of the period.

## *Illustration*

Consider a hypothetical three-year swap initiated on March 5, 2003, between Microsoft and Intel. We suppose Microsoft agrees to pay to Intel an interest rate of 5% per annum on a notional principal of $100 million, and in return Intel agrees to pay Microsoft the six-month LIBOR rate on the same notional principal. We assume the agreement specifies that payments are to be exchanged every six months, and the 5% interest rate is quoted with semiannual compounding. This swap is represented diagrammatically in Figure 6.1.

The first exchange of payments would take place on September 5, 2003, six months after the initiation of the agreement. Microsoft would pay Intel $2.5 million. This is the interest on the $100 million principal for six months at 5%. Intel would pay Microsoft interest on the $100 million principal at the six-month LIBOR rate prevailing six months prior to September 5, 2003—that is, on March 5, 2003. Suppose that the six-month LIBOR rate on March 5, 2003, is 4.2%. Intel pays Microsoft $0.5 \times 0.042 \times \$100 = \$2.1$ million.[1] Note that there is no uncertainty about this first exchange of payments because it is determined by the LIBOR rate at the time the contract is entered into.

The second exchange of payments would take place on March 5, 2004, one year after the initiation of the agreement. Microsoft would pay $2.5 million to Intel. Intel would pay interest on the $100 million principal to Microsoft at the six-month LIBOR rate prevailing six months prior to March 5, 2004—that is, on September 5, 2003. Suppose that the six-month LIBOR rate on September 5, 2003, is 4.8%. Intel pays $0.5 \times 0.048 \times \$100 = \$2.4$ million to Microsoft.

In total, there are six exchanges of payment on the swap. The fixed payments are always $2.5 million. The floating-rate payments on a payment date are calculated using the six-month LIBOR rate prevailing six months before the payment date. An interest rate swap is generally structured so that one side remits the difference between the two payments to the other side. In our example, Microsoft would pay Intel $0.4 million (= $2.5 million − $2.1 million) on September 5, 2003, and $0.1 million (= $2.5 million − $2.4 million) on March 5, 2004.

Table 6.1 provides a complete example of the payments made under the swap for one particular set of six-month LIBOR rates. The table shows the swap cash flows from the perspective of Microsoft. Note that the $100 million principal is used only for the calculation of interest payments. The principal itself is not exchanged. This is why it is termed the *notional principal*.

If the principal were exchanged at the end of the life of the swap, the nature of the deal would not be changed in any way. The principal is the same for both the fixed and floating payments. Exchanging $100 million for $100 million at the end of the life of the swap is a transaction that would have no financial value to either Microsoft or Intel. Table 6.2 shows the cash flows in Table 6.1 with a final exchange of principal added in. This provides an interesting way of viewing the swap. The cash flows in the third column of this table are the cash flows from a long position in a floating-rate bond. The cash flows in the fourth column of the table are the cash flows from a short position in a fixed-rate bond. The table shows that the swap can be regarded as the exchange

**Figure 6.1** Interest rate swap between Microsoft and Intel

---

[1] The calculations here are slightly inaccurate because they ignore day count conventions. This point is discussed in more detail later in the chapter.

**Table 6.1** Cash flows (millions of dollars) to Microsoft in a $100 million three-year interest rate swap when a fixed rate of 5% is paid and LIBOR is received

| Date | 6-month LIBOR rate (%) | Floating cash flow received | Fixed cash flow paid | Net cash flow |
|---|---|---|---|---|
| March 5, 2003 | 4.20 | | | |
| September 5, 2003 | 4.80 | +2.10 | −2.50 | −0.40 |
| March 5, 2004 | 5.30 | +2.40 | −2.50 | −0.10 |
| September 5, 2004 | 5.50 | +2.65 | −2.50 | +0.15 |
| March 5, 2005 | 5.60 | +2.75 | −2.50 | +0.25 |
| September 5, 2005 | 5.90 | +2.80 | −2.50 | +0.30 |
| March 5, 2006 | 6.40 | +2.95 | −2.50 | +0.45 |

of a fixed-rate bond for a floating-rate bond. Microsoft, whose position is described by Table 6.2, is long a floating-rate bond and short a fixed-rate bond. Intel is long a fixed-rate bond and short a floating-rate bond.

This characterization of the cash flows in the swap helps to explain why the floating rate in the swap is set six months before it is paid. On a floating-rate bond, interest is usually set at the beginning of the period to which it will apply and is paid at the end of the period. The calculation of the floating-rate payments in a "plain vanilla" interest rate swap, such as that in Table 6.2, reflects this.

### Using the Swap to Transform a Liability

For Microsoft, the swap could be used to transform a floating-rate loan into a fixed-rate loan. Suppose that Microsoft has arranged to borrow $100 million at LIBOR plus 10 basis points. (One basis point is one-hundredth of 1%, so the rate is LIBOR plus 0.1%.) After Microsoft has entered into the swap, it has three sets of cash flows:

1. It pays LIBOR plus 0.1% to its outside lenders.
2. It receives LIBOR under the terms of the swap.
3. It pays 5% under the terms of the swap.

**Table 6.2** Cash flows (millions of dollars) from Table 6.1 when there is a final exchange of principal

| Date | 6-month LIBOR rate (%) | Floating cash flow received | Fixed cash flow paid | Net cash flow |
|---|---|---|---|---|
| March 5, 2003 | 4.20 | | | |
| September 5, 2003 | 4.80 | +2.10 | −2.50 | −0.40 |
| March 5, 2004 | 5.30 | +2.40 | −2.50 | −0.10 |
| September 5, 2004 | 5.50 | +2.65 | −2.50 | +0.15 |
| March 5, 2005 | 5.60 | +2.75 | −2.50 | +0.25 |
| September 5, 2005 | 5.90 | +2.80 | −2.50 | +0.30 |
| March 5, 2006 | 6.40 | +102.95 | −102.50 | +0.45 |

**Figure 6.2**   Microsoft and Intel use the swap to transform a liability

These three sets of cash flows net out to an interest rate payment of 5.1%. Thus, for Microsoft, the swap could have the effect of transforming borrowings at a floating rate of LIBOR plus 10 basis points into borrowings at a fixed rate of 5.1%.

For Intel, the swap could have the effect of transforming a fixed-rate loan into a floating-rate loan. Suppose that Intel has a three-year $100 million loan outstanding on which it pays 5.2%. After it has entered into the swap, it has three sets of cash flows:

1. It pays 5.2% to its outside lenders.
2. It pays LIBOR under the terms of the swap.
3. It receives 5% under the terms of the swap.

These three sets of cash flows net out to an interest rate payment of LIBOR plus 0.2% (or LIBOR plus 20 basis points). Thus, for Intel, the swap could have the effect of transforming borrowings at a fixed rate of 5.2% into borrowings at a floating rate of LIBOR plus 20 basis points. These potential uses of the swap by Intel and Microsoft are illustrated in Figure 6.2.

### *Using the Swap to Transform an Asset*

Swaps can also be used to transform the nature of an asset. Consider Microsoft in our example. The swap could have the effect of transforming an asset earning a fixed rate of interest into an asset earning a floating rate of interest. Suppose that Microsoft owns $100 million in bonds that will provide interest at 4.7% per annum over the next three years. After Microsoft has entered into the swap, it has three sets of cash flows:

1. It receives 4.7% on the bonds.
2. It receives LIBOR under the terms of the swap.
3. It pays 5% under the terms of the swap.

These three sets of cash flows net out to an interest rate inflow of LIBOR minus 30 basis points. Thus, one possible use of the swap for Microsoft is to transform an asset earning 4.7% into an asset earning LIBOR minus 30 basis points.

Now consider Intel. The swap could have the effect of transforming an asset earning a floating rate of interest into an asset earning a fixed rate of interest. Suppose that Intel has an investment of

**Figure 6.3**   Microsoft and Intel use the swap to transform an asset

**Figure 6.4** Interest rate swap from Figure 6.2 when a financial institution is used

$100 million that yields LIBOR minus 25 basis points. After it has entered into the swap, it has three sets of cash flows:

1. It receives LIBOR minus 25 basis points on its investment.
2. It pays LIBOR under the terms of the swap.
3. It receives 5% under the terms of the swap.

These three sets of cash flows net out to an interest rate inflow of 4.75%. Thus, one possible use of the swap for Intel is to transform an asset earning LIBOR minus 25 basis points into an asset earning 4.75%. These potential uses of the swap by Intel and Microsoft are illustrated in Figure 6.3.

### Role of Financial Intermediary

Usually two nonfinancial companies such as Intel and Microsoft do not get in touch directly to arrange a swap in the way indicated in Figures 6.2 and 6.3. They each deal with a financial intermediary such as a bank or other financial institution. "Plain vanilla" fixed-for-floating swaps on U.S. interest rates are usually structured so that the financial institution earns about 3 or 4 basis points (0.03 to 0.04%) on a pair of offsetting transactions.

Figure 6.4 shows what the role of the financial institution might be in the situation in Figure 6.2. The financial institution enters into two offsetting swap transactions with Intel and Microsoft. Assuming that neither defaults, the financial institution is certain to make a profit of 0.03% (3 basis points) per year multiplied by the notional principal of $100 million. (This amounts to $30,000 per year for the three-year period.) Microsoft ends up borrowing at 5.115% (instead of 5.1%, as in Figure 6.2). Intel ends up borrowing at LIBOR plus 21.5 basis points (instead of at LIBOR plus 20 basis points, as in Figure 6.2).

Figure 6.5 illustrates the role of the financial institution in the situation in Figure 6.3. Again, the financial institution is certain to make a profit of 3 basis points if neither company defaults on the swap. Microsoft ends up earning LIBOR minus 31.5 basis points (instead of LIBOR minus 30 basis points, as in Figure 6.3). Intel ends up earning 4.735% (instead of 4.75%, as in Figure 6.3).

Note that in each case the financial institution has two separate contracts: one with Intel and the other with Microsoft. In most instances, Intel will not even know that the financial institution

**Figure 6.5** Interest rate swap from Figure 6.3 when a financial institution is used

has entered into an offsetting swap with Microsoft, and vice versa. If one of the companies defaults, the financial institution still has to honor its agreement with the other company. The 3-basis-point spread earned by the financial institution is partly to compensate it for the default risk it is bearing.

### Market Makers

In practice, it is unlikely that two companies will contact a financial institution at the same time and want to take opposite positions in exactly the same swap. For this reason, many large financial institutions act as market makers for swaps. This means that they are prepared to enter into a swap without having an offsetting swap with another counterparty. Market makers must carefully quantify and hedge the risks they are taking. Bonds, forward rate agreements, and interest rate futures are examples of the instruments that can be used for hedging by swap market makers. The way market makers provide quotes in the swap market is discussed later in this chapter.

### Day Count Conventions

The day count conventions discussed in Section 5.8 affect payments on a swap, and some of the numbers calculated in the example we have given do not exactly reflect these day count conventions. Consider, for example, the six-month LIBOR payments in Table 6.1. Because it is a money market rate, six-month LIBOR is generally quoted on an actual/360 basis. The first floating payment in Table 6.1, based on the LIBOR rate of 4.2%, is shown as \$2.10 million. Because there are 184 days between March 5, 2001, and September 5, 2001, it should be

$$100 \times 0.042 \times \frac{184}{360} = \$2.1467 \text{ million}$$

In general, a LIBOR-based floating-rate cash flow on a swap payment date is calculated as $LRn/360$, where $L$ is the principal, $R$ is the relevant LIBOR rate, and $n$ is the number of days since the last payment date.

The fixed rate that is paid in a swap transaction is similarly quoted with a particular day count basis being specified. As a result, the fixed payments may not be exactly equal on each payment date. The fixed rate is usually quoted as actual/365 or 30/360. It is not therefore directly comparable with LIBOR because it applies to a full year. To make the rates comparable, either the six-month LIBOR rate must be multiplied by 365/360 or the fixed rate must be multiplied by 360/365.

For ease of exposition we will ignore day count issues in the examples in the rest of this chapter.

### Confirmations

A *confirmation* is the legal agreement underlying a swap and is signed by representatives of the two parties. Table 6.3 could be an extract from the confirmation between Microsoft and Intel. The drafting of confirmations has been facilitated by the work of the International Swaps and Derivatives Association (ISDA) in New York. This organization has produced a number of Master Agreements that consist of clauses defining in some detail the terminology used in swap agreements, what happens in the event of default by either side, and so on. Almost certainly, the full confirmation for the swap in Table 6.3 would state that the provisions of an ISDA Master Agreement apply to the contract.

**Table 6.3**  Extract from confirmation for a hypothetical plain vanilla swap between Microsoft and Intel

| | |
|---|---|
| Trade date | 27-February-2003 |
| Effective date | 5-March-2003 |
| Business day convention (all dates) | Following business day |
| Holiday calendar | U.S. |
| Termination date | 5-March-2006 |

**Fixed Amounts**

| | |
|---|---|
| Fixed-rate payer | Microsoft |
| Fixed-rate notional principal | USD 100 million |
| Fixed rate | 5% per annum |
| Fixed-rate day count convention | Actual/365 |
| Fixed rate payment dates | Each 5-March and 5-September commencing 5-September-2003, up to and including 5-March-2006 |

**Floating Amounts**

| | |
|---|---|
| Floating-rate payer | Intel |
| Floating-rate notional principal | USD 100 million |
| Floating rate | USD 6-month LIBOR |
| Floating-rate day count convention | Actual/360 |
| Floating-rate payment dates | Each 5-March and 5-September commencing 5-September-2003, up to and including 5-March-2006 |

Table 6.3 specifies that the following business day convention is to be used and that the U.S. calendar determines which days are business days and which days are holidays. This means that, if a payment date falls on a weekend or a U.S. holiday, the payment is made on the next business day.[2] In the example in Table 6.3, September 5, 2004, is a Sunday. The payment is therefore made on Monday September 6, 2004.

## 6.2  THE COMPARATIVE-ADVANTAGE ARGUMENT

An explanation commonly put forward to explain the popularity of swaps concerns comparative advantages. Consider the use of an interest rate swap to transform a liability. Some companies, it is argued, have a comparative advantage when borrowing in fixed-rate markets, whereas other companies have a comparative advantage in floating-rate markets. To obtain a new loan, it makes sense for a company to go to the market where it has a comparative advantage. As a result, the company may borrow fixed when it wants floating, or borrow floating when it wants fixed. The swap is used to transform a fixed-rate loan into a floating-rate loan, and vice versa.

---

[2] Another business day convention that is sometimes specified is the *modified following* business day convention, which is the same as the following business day convention except that when the next business day falls in a different month from the specified day, the payment is made on the immediately preceding business day. *Preceding* and *modified preceding* business day conventions are defined analogously.

**Table 6.4**  Borrowing rates that provide a basis for the comparative-advantage argument

|          | *Fixed* | *Floating*            |
|----------|---------|-----------------------|
| AAACorp  | 10.0%   | 6-month LIBOR + 0.3%  |
| BBBCorp  | 11.2%   | 6-month LIBOR + 1.0%  |

### Illustration

Suppose that two companies, AAACorp and BBBCorp, both wish to borrow $10 million for five years and have been offered the rates shown in Table 6.4. AAACorp has a AAA credit rating; BBBCorp has a BBB credit rating. We assume that BBBCorp wants to borrow at a fixed rate of interest, whereas AAACorp wants to borrow at a floating rate of interest linked to six-month LIBOR. BBBCorp, because it has a worse credit rating than AAACorp, pays a higher rate of interest than AAACorp in both fixed and floating markets.

A key feature of the rates offered to AAACorp and BBBCorp is that the difference between the two fixed rates is greater than the difference between the two floating rates. BBBCorp pays 1.2% more than AAACorp in fixed-rate markets and only 0.7% more than AAACorp in floating-rate markets. BBBCorp appears to have a comparative advantage in floating-rate markets, whereas AAACorp appears to have a comparative advantage in fixed-rate markets.[3] It is this apparent anomaly that can lead to a swap being negotiated. AAACorp borrows fixed-rate funds at 10% per annum. BBBCorp borrows floating-rate funds at LIBOR plus 1% per annum. They then enter into a swap agreement to ensure that AAACorp ends up with floating-rate funds and BBBCorp ends up with fixed-rate funds.

To understand how the swap might work, we first assume that AAACorp and BBBCorp get in touch with each other directly. The sort of swap they might negotiate is shown in Figure 6.6. This is very similar to our example in Figure 6.2. AAACorp agrees to pay BBBCorp interest at six-month LIBOR on $10 million. In return, BBBCorp agrees to pay AAACorp interest at a fixed rate of 9.95% per annum on $10 million.

AAACorp has three sets of interest rate cash flows:

1. It pays 10% per annum to outside lenders.
2. It receives 9.95% per annum from BBBCorp.
3. It pays LIBOR to BBBCorp.

The net effect of the three cash flows is that AAACorp pays LIBOR plus 0.05% per annum. This is 0.25% per annum less than it would pay if it went directly to floating-rate markets. BBBCorp also

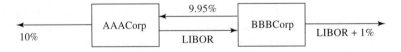

**Figure 6.6**  Swap agreement between AAACorp and BBBCorp when rates in Table 6.4 apply

---

[3] Note that BBBCorp's comparative advantage in floating-rate markets does not imply that BBBCorp pays less than AAACorp in this market. It means that the extra amount that BBBCorp pays over the amount paid by AAACorp is less in this market. One of my students summarized the situation as follows: "AAACorp pays more less in fixed-rate markets; BBBCorp pays less more in floating-rate markets."

**Figure 6.7** Swap agreement between AAACorp and BBBCorp when rates in Table 6.4 apply and a financial intermediary is involved

has three sets of interest rate cash flows:

1. It pays LIBOR + 1.0% per annum to outside lenders.
2. It receives LIBOR from AAACorp.
3. It pays 9.95% per annum to AAACorp.

The net effect of the three cash flows is that BBBCorp pays 10.95% per annum. This is 0.25% per annum less than it would pay if it went directly to fixed-rate markets.

The swap arrangement appears to improve the position of both AAACorp and BBBCorp by 0.25% per annum. The total gain is therefore 0.5% per annum. It can be shown that the total apparent gain from this type of interest rate swap arrangement is always $a - b$, where $a$ is the difference between the interest rates facing the two companies in fixed-rate markets, and $b$ is the difference between the interest rates facing the two companies in floating-rate markets. In this case, $a = 1.2\%$ and $b = 0.70\%$.

If AAACorp and BBBCorp did not deal directly with each other and used a financial institution, an arrangement such as that shown in Figure 6.7 might result. (This is very similar to the example in Figure 6.4.) In this case, AAACorp ends up borrowing at LIBOR + 0.07%, BBBCorp ends up borrowing at 10.97%, and the financial institution earns a spread of 4 basis points per year. The gain to AAACorp is 0.23%; the gain to BBBCorp is 0.23%; and the gain to the financial institution is 0.04%. The total gain to all three parties is 0.50% as before.

### Criticism of the Comparative-Advantage Argument

The comparative-advantage argument we have just outlined for explaining the attractiveness of interest rate swaps is open to question. Why, in Table 6.4, should the spreads between the rates offered to AAACorp and BBBCorp be different in fixed and floating markets? Now that the swap market has been in existence for some time, we might reasonably expect these types of differences to have been arbitraged away.

The reason that spread differentials appear to exist is due to the nature of the contracts available to companies in fixed and floating markets. The 10.0% and 11.2% rates available to AAACorp and BBBCorp in fixed-rate markets are five-year rates (e.g., the rates at which the companies can issue five-year fixed-rate bonds). The LIBOR + 0.3% and LIBOR + 1.0% rates available to AAACorp and BBBCorp in floating-rate markets are six-month rates. In the floating-rate market, the lender usually has the opportunity to review the floating rates every six months. If the creditworthiness of AAACorp or BBBCorp has declined, the lender has the option of increasing the spread over LIBOR that is charged. In extreme circumstances, the lender can refuse to roll over the loan at all. The providers of fixed-rate financing do not have the option to change the terms of the loan in this way.[4]

---

[4] If the floating rate loans are structured so that the spread over LIBOR is guaranteed in advance regardless of changes in credit rating, there is in practice little or no comparative advantage.

The spreads between the rates offered to AAACorp and BBBCorp are a reflection of the extent to which BBBCorp is more likely to default than AAACorp. During the next six months, there is very little chance that either AAACorp or BBBCorp will default. As we look further ahead, default statistics (see, for example, Table 26.6) show that the probability of a default by a company with a relatively low credit rating (such as BBBCorp) increases faster than the probability of a default by a company with a relatively high credit rating (such as AAACorp). This is why the spread between the five-year rates is greater than the spread between the six-month rates.

After negotiating a floating-rate loan at LIBOR + 1.0% and entering into the swap shown in Figure 6.7, BBBCorp appears to obtain a fixed-rate loan at 10.97%. The arguments just presented show that this is not really the case. In practice, the rate paid is 10.97% only if BBBCorp can continue to borrow floating-rate funds at a spread of 1.0% over LIBOR. If, for example, the credit rating of BBBCorp declines so that the floating-rate loan is rolled over at LIBOR + 2.0%, the rate paid by BBBCorp increases to 11.97%. Because BBBCorp's spread over six-month LIBOR is more likely to rise than to fall, BBBCorp's expected average borrowing rate when it enters into the swap is greater than 10.97%.

The swap in Figure 6.7 locks in LIBOR + 0.07% for AAACorp for the whole of the next five years, not just for the next six months. This appears to be a good deal for AAACorp. The downside is that it is bearing the risk of a default by the financial institution. If it borrowed floating-rate funds in the usual way, it would not be bearing this risk.

## 6.3  SWAP QUOTES AND LIBOR ZERO RATES

We now return to the interest rate swap in Figure 6.1. We showed in Table 6.2 that it can be characterized as the difference between two bonds. Although the principal is not exchanged, we can assume without changing the value of the swap that, at the end of the agreement, Intel pays Microsoft the notional principal of $100 million and Microsoft pays Intel the same notional principal. The swap is then the same as an arrangement in which:

1. Microsoft has lent Intel $100 million at the six-month LIBOR rate.
2. Intel has lent Microsoft $100 million at a fixed rate of 5% per annum.

To put it another way, Microsoft has purchased a $100 million floating-rate (LIBOR) bond from Intel and has sold a $100 million fixed-rate (5% per annum) bond to Intel. The value of the swap to Microsoft is therefore the difference between the values of two bonds. Define:

$B_{\text{fix}}$ : Value of fixed-rate bond underlying the swap

$B_{\text{fl}}$ : Value of floating-rate bond underlying the swap

The value of the swap to a company receiving floating and paying fixed (Microsoft in our example) is

$$V_{\text{swap}} = B_{\text{fl}} - B_{\text{fix}} \tag{6.1}$$

### Swap Rates

Many large financial institutions are market makers in the swap market. This means that they are prepared to quote, for a number of different maturities and a number of different currencies, a bid and an offer for the fixed rate they will exchange for floating. The bid is the fixed rate in a contract

**Table 6.5**  Bid and offer fixed rates in the swap market and swap rates (percent per annum); payments exchanged semiannually

| Maturity (years) | Bid (%) | Offer (%) | Swap rate (%) |
|---|---|---|---|
| 2 | 6.03 | 6.06 | 6.045 |
| 3 | 6.21 | 6.24 | 6.225 |
| 4 | 6.35 | 6.39 | 6.370 |
| 5 | 6.47 | 6.51 | 6.490 |
| 7 | 6.65 | 6.68 | 6.665 |
| 10 | 6.83 | 6.87 | 6.850 |

where the market maker will pay fixed and receive floating; the offer is the fixed rate in a swap where the market maker will receive fixed and pay floating. Table 6.5 shows typical quotes for plain vanilla U.S. dollar swaps. As mentioned earlier, the bid–offer spread is 3 to 4 basis points. The average of the bid and offer fixed rates is known as the *swap rate*. This is shown in the final column of Table 6.5.

Consider a new swap where the fixed rate equals the swap rate. We can reasonably assume that the value of this swap is zero. (Why else would a market maker choose bid–offer quotes centered on the swap rate?) From equation (6.1), it follows that

$$B_{\text{fix}} = B_{\text{fl}} \tag{6.2}$$

As mentioned in Section 5.1, banks and other financial institutions usually discount cash flows in the over-the-counter market at LIBOR rates of interest. The floating-rate bond underlying the swap pays LIBOR. As a result, the value of this bond, $B_{\text{fl}}$, equals the swap principal. It follows from equation (6.2) that the value of the fixed-rate bond, $B_{\text{fix}}$ also equals the swap principal. A swap rate is therefore a LIBOR par yield. It is the coupon rate on the LIBOR bond that causes it to be worth par.

### Determining the LIBOR Zero Curve

In Section 5.12 we showed how Eurodollar futures can be used to determine LIBOR zero rates. Swap rates also play an important role in determining LIBOR zero rates. As we have just seen, they define a series of LIBOR par yield bonds. The latter can be used to bootstrap a LIBOR zero curve in the same way that Treasury bonds are used to bootstrap the Treasury zero curve (see Section 5.4).

**Example 6.1**  Assume that the LIBOR zero curve has already been calculated out to 1.5 years (using spot LIBOR rates and Eurodollar futures) and that we wish to use the swap rates in Table 6.5 to extend the curve. The 6-month, 1-year, and 1.5-year zero rates are, respectively, 5.5%, 5.75%, and 5.9% per annum with continuous compounding. Because the swaps in Table 6.5 involve semiannual cash flows, we first interpolate between the swap rates to obtain swap rates at intervals of 0.5 years. The 2.5-year swap rate is 6.135%, the 3.5-year swap rate is 6.2975%, and so on. Next we use the bootstrap method described in Section 5.4. Because the 2-year swap rate is the 2-year par yield, a 2-year bond paying a semiannual coupon of 6.045% per annum must sell for par, so that

$$3.0225e^{-0.055\times0.5} + 3.0225e^{-0.0575\times1.0} + 3.0225e^{-0.059\times1.5} + 103.0225e^{-2R} = 100$$

where $R$ is the 2-year zero rate. This can be solved to give $R = 5.9636\%$. Similarly, a 2.5-year bond paying a semiannual coupon of 6.135% must sell for par, so that

$$3.0675e^{-0.055\times0.5} + 3.0675e^{-0.0575\times1.0} + 3.0675e^{-0.059\times1.5} + 3.0675e^{-0.059636\times2} + 103.0675e^{-2.5R} = 100$$

where $R$ is the 2.5-year zero rate. This can be solved to get $R = 6.0549\%$. Continuing in this way, the complete term structure is obtained. The 3-, 4-, 5-, 7-, and 10-year zero rates are 6.1475%, 6.2986%, 6.4265%, 6.6189%, and 6.8355%, respectively.

In the United States, spot LIBOR rates are typically used to define short-term LIBOR zero rates. Eurodollar futures are then used for maturities up to two years—and sometimes for maturities up to five years. Swap rates are used to calculate the zero curve for longer maturities. A similar procedure is followed to determine LIBOR zero rates in other countries. For example, Swiss franc LIBOR zero rates are determined from spot Swiss franc LIBOR rates, three-month Euroswiss futures, and Swiss franc swap rates.

### Nature of the LIBOR Zero Curve

The LIBOR zero curve is sometimes also referred to as the *swap zero curve*. We know that LIBOR zero rates out to one year are interbank borrowing rates. It is tempting to assume that the LIBOR zero curve beyond one year represents interbank borrowing rates. This is not completely true.

Suppose that the five-year swap rate is 5% and a bank is able to borrow for six months at six-month LIBOR. It can enter into a swap to exchange six-month LIBOR for 5%. This appears to lock in a borrowing rate of 5% for five years. However, as pointed in our criticism of the comparative-advantage argument, this rate applies only if the bank is able to continue to borrow at six-month LIBOR. In practice the bank is subject to roll-over risk. It may not be able to roll over its borrowings at six-month LIBOR. If the bank's six-month borrowing rate increases above six-month LIBOR, its five year borrowing rate will prove to be greater than 5%. The LIBOR zero curve is therefore the zero curve for interbank borrowings in a world where the a bank's interest rate roll-over risk is zero.

## 6.4  VALUATION OF INTEREST RATE SWAPS

An interest rate swap is worth zero, or close to zero, when it is first initiated. After it has been in existence for some time, its value may become positive or negative. To calculate the value we can regard the swap either as a long position in one bond combined with a short position in another bond or as a portfolio of forward rate agreements. In either case we use LIBOR zero rates for discounting.

### Valuation in Terms of Bond Prices

We saw in equation (6.1) that

$$V_{swap} = B_{fl} - B_{fix}$$

for a swap where floating is received and fixed is paid. In Section 6.3 we used this equation to show that $B_{\text{fix}}$ equals the swap's notional principal at the initiation of the swap. We now use it to value the swap some time after its initiation. To see how this equation is used, we define:

$t_i$ : Time until $i$th $(1 \leqslant i \leqslant n)$ payments are exchanged

$L$ : Notional principal in swap agreement

$r_i$ : LIBOR zero rate corresponding to maturity $t_i$

$k$ : Fixed payment made on each payment date

The fixed-rate bond, $B_{\text{fix}}$, can be valued as described in Section 5.3. The cash flows from the bond are $k$ at time $t_i$ $(1 \leqslant i \leqslant n)$ and $L$ at time $t_n$, so that

$$B_{\text{fix}} = \sum_{i=1}^{n} k e^{-r_i t_i} + L e^{-r_n t_n}$$

Consider next the floating-rate bond. Immediately after a payment date, this is identical to a newly issued floating-rate bond. It follows that $B_{\text{fl}} = L$ immediately after a payment date. Between payment dates, we can use the fact that $B_{\text{fl}}$ will equal $L$ immediately after the next payment date and argue as follows. Immediately before the next payment date, we have $B_{\text{fl}} = L + k^*$, where $k^*$ is the floating-rate payment (already known) that will be made on the next payment date. In our notation, the time until the next payment date is $t_1$. The value of the swap today is its value just before the next payment date discounted at rate $r_1$ for time $t_1$:

$$B_{\text{fl}} = (L + k^*) e^{-r_1 t_1}$$

In the situation where the company is receiving fixed and paying floating, $B_{\text{fix}}$ and $B_{\text{fl}}$ are calculated in the same way, and equation (6.1) becomes

$$V_{\text{swap}} = B_{\text{fix}} - B_{\text{fl}} \tag{6.3}$$

**Example 6.2** Suppose that a financial institution pays six-month LIBOR and receives 8% per annum (with semiannual compounding) on a swap with a notional principal of $100 million and the remaining payment dates are in 3, 9, and 15 months. The swap has a remaining life of 15 months. The LIBOR rates with continuous compounding for 3-month, 9-month, and 15-month maturities are 10%, 10.5%, and 11%, respectively. The 6-month LIBOR rate at the last payment date was 10.2% (with semiannual compounding). In this case, $k = \$4$ million and $k^* = \$5.1$ million, so that

$$B_{\text{fix}} = 4e^{-0.1 \times 3/12} + 4e^{-0.105 \times 9/12} + 104e^{-0.11 \times 15/12}$$
$$= \$98.24 \text{ million}$$
$$B_{\text{fl}} = 5.1e^{-0.1 \times 3/12} + 100e^{-0.1 \times 3/12}$$
$$= \$102.51 \text{ million}$$

Hence, the value of the swap is

$$98.24 - 102.51 = -\$4.27 \text{ million}$$

If the bank had been in the opposite position of paying fixed and receiving floating, the value of the swap would be $+\$4.27$ million. A more precise calculation would take account of day count conventions and holiday calendars in determining exact cash flows and their timing.

### Valuation in Terms of Forward Rate Agreements

We introduced forward rate agreements (FRAs) in Chapter 5. They are agreements that a certain predetermined interest rate will apply to a certain principal for a certain period of time in the future. In Section 5.6 we showed that an FRA can be characterized as an agreement where interest at the predetermined rate is exchanged for interest at the market rate of interest for the period in question. This shows that an interest rate swap is nothing more than a portfolio of forward rate agreements.

Consider again the swap agreement between Intel and Microsoft in Figure 6.1. As illustrated in Table 6.1, this commits Microsoft to six cash flow exchanges. The first exchange is known at the time the swap is negotiated. The other five exchanges can be regarded as FRAs. The exchange on March 5, 2004, is an FRA where interest at 5% is exchanged for interest at the six-month rate observed in the market on September 5, 2003; the exchange on September 5, 2004, is an FRA where interest at 5% is exchanged for interest at the six-month rate observed in the market on March 5, 2004; and so on.

As shown in Section 5.6, an FRA can be valued by assuming that forward interest rates are realized. Since it is a portfolio of forward rate agreements, a plain vanilla interest rate swap can also be valued by assuming that forward interest rates are realized. The procedure is as follows:

1. Calculate forward rates for each of the LIBOR rates that will determine swap cash flows.

2. Calculate swap cash flows assuming that the LIBOR rates will equal the forward rates.

3. Set the swap value equal to the present value of these cash flows.

**Example 6.3**  Consider again the situation in the previous example. The cash flows that will be exchanged in 3 months have already been determined. A rate of 8% will be exchanged for 10.2%. The value of the exchange to the financial institution is

$$0.5 \times 100 \times (0.08 - 0.102)e^{-0.1 \times 3/12} = -1.07$$

To calculate the value of the exchange in 9 months, we must first calculate the forward rate corresponding to the period between 3 and 9 months. From equation (5.1), this is

$$\frac{0.105 \times 0.75 - 0.10 \times 0.25}{0.5} = 0.1075$$

or 10.75% with continuous compounding. From equation (3.4), this value becomes 11.044% with semiannual compounding. The value of the FRA corresponding to the exchange in 9 months is therefore

$$0.5 \times 100 \times (0.08 - 0.11044)e^{-0.105 \times 9/12} = -1.41$$

To calculate the value of the exchange in 15 months, we must first calculate the forward rate corresponding to the period between 9 and 15 months. From equation (5.1), this is

$$\frac{0.11 \times 1.25 - 0.105 \times 0.75}{0.5} = 0.1175$$

or 11.75% with continuous compounding. From equation (3.4), this value becomes 12.102% with semiannual compounding. The value of the FRA corresponding to the exchange in 15 months is therefore

$$0.5 \times 100 \times (0.08 - 0.12102)e^{-0.11 \times 15/12} = -1.79$$

The total value of the swap is

$$-1.07 - 1.41 - 1.79 = -4.27$$

or −$4.27 million. This is in agreement with the calculation in Example 6.2 based on bond prices.

As already mentioned, the fixed rate in an interest rate swap is chosen so that the swap is worth zero initially. This means that the sum of the value of the FRAs underlying the swap is zero. It does not mean that the value of each individual FRA is zero. In general, some FRAs will have positive values, whereas others will have negative values.

Consider the FRAs underlying the swap between the financial institution and Microsoft in Figure 6.4:

Value of FRA to financial institution < 0 when forward interest rate > 5.015%

Value of FRA to financial institution = 0 when forward interest rate = 5.015%

Value of FRA to financial institution > 0 when forward interest rate < 5.015%

Suppose that the term structure of interest rates is upward sloping at the time the swap is negotiated. This means that the forward interest rates increase as the maturity of the FRA increases. Because the sum of the values of the FRAs is zero, the forward interest rate must be less than 5.015% for the early payment dates and greater than 5.015% for the later payment dates. The value to the financial

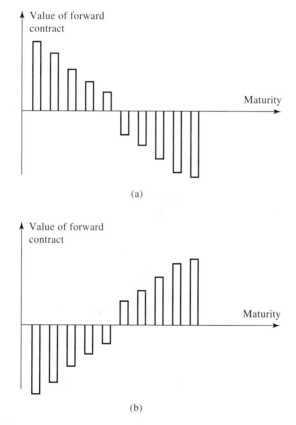

**Figure 6.8** Value of forward contracts underlying a swap as a function of maturity. In (a) the term structure of interest rates is upward sloping and we receive fixed, or the term structure of interest rates is downward sloping and we receive floating; in (b) the term structure is upward sloping and we receive floating, or the term structure is downward sloping and we receive fixed

**Figure 6.9**  A currency swap

institution of the FRAs corresponding to early payment dates is therefore positive, whereas the value of the FRAs corresponding to later payment dates is negative. If the term structure is downward sloping at the time the swap is negotiated, the reverse is true. The impact of the shape of the term structure on the values of the forward contracts underlying a swap is summarized in Figure 6.8.

## 6.5  CURRENCY SWAPS

Another popular type of swap is known as a *currency swap*. In its simplest form, this involves exchanging principal and interest payments in one currency for principal and interest payments in another currency.

A currency swap agreement requires the principal to be specified in each of the two currencies. The principal amounts are usually exchanged at the beginning and at the end of the life of the swap. Usually the principal amounts are chosen to be approximately equivalent using the exchange rate at the swap's initiation.

### Illustration

Consider a hypothetical five-year currency swap agreement between IBM and British Petroleum entered into on February 1, 2001. We suppose that IBM pays a fixed rate of interest of 11% in sterling and receives a fixed rate of interest of 8% in dollars from British Petroleum. Interest rate payments are made once a year and the principal amounts are $15 million and £10 million. This is termed a *fixed-for-fixed* currency swap because the interest rate in both currencies is fixed. The swap is shown in Figure 6.9. Initially, the principal amounts flow in the opposite direction to the arrows in Figure 6.9. The interest payments during the life of the swap and the final principal payment flow in the same direction as the arrows. Thus, at the outset of the swap, IBM pays $15 million and receives £10 million. Each year during the life of the swap contract, IBM receives $1.20 million (= 8% of $15 million) and pays £1.10 million (= 11% of £10 million). At the end of the life of the swap, it pays a principal of £10 million and receives a principal of $15 million. These cash flows are shown in Table 6.6.

**Table 6.6**  Cash flows to IBM in currency swap

| *Date* | *Dollar cash flow (millions)* | *Sterling cash flow (millions)* |
|---|---|---|
| February 1, 2001 | −15.00 | +10.00 |
| February 1, 2002 | +1.20 | −1.10 |
| February 1, 2003 | +1.20 | −1.10 |
| February 1, 2004 | +1.20 | −1.10 |
| February 1, 2005 | +1.20 | −1.10 |
| February 1, 2006 | +16.20 | −11.10 |

### Use of a Currency Swap to Transform Loans and Assets

A swap such as the one just considered can be used to transform borrowings in one currency to borrowings in another currency. Suppose that IBM can issue $15 million of U.S.-dollar-denominated bonds at 8% interest. The swap has the effect of transforming this transaction into one where IBM has borrowed £10 million pounds at 11% interest. The initial exchange of principal converts the proceeds of the bond issue from U.S. dollars to sterling. The subsequent exchanges in the swap have the effect of swapping the interest and principal payments from dollars to sterling.

The swap can also be used to transform the nature of assets. Suppose that IBM can invest £10 million pounds in the U.K to yield 11% per annum for the next five years, but feels that the U.S. dollar will strengthen against sterling and prefers a U.S.-denominated investment. The swap has the effect of transforming the U.K. investment into a $15 million investment in the U.S. yielding 8%.

### Comparative Advantage

Currency swaps can be motivated by comparative advantage. To illustrate this, we consider another hypothetical example. Suppose the five-year fixed-rate borrowing costs to General Motors and Qantas Airways in U.S. dollars (USD) and Australian dollars (AUD) are as shown in Table 6.7. The data in the table suggest that Australian rates are higher than U.S. interest rates. Also, General Motors is more creditworthy than Qantas Airways, because it is offered a more favorable rate of interest in both currencies. From the viewpoint of a swap trader, the interesting aspect of Table 6.7 is that the spreads between the rates paid by General Motors and Qantas Airways in the two markets are not the same. Qantas Airways pays 2% more than General Motors in the U.S. dollar market and only 0.4% more than General Motors in the AUD market.

This situation is analogous to that in Table 6.4. General Motors has a comparative advantage in the USD market, whereas Qantas Airways has a comparative advantage in the AUD market. In Table 6.4, where a plain vanilla interest rate swap was considered, we argued that comparative advantages were largely illusory. Here we are comparing the rates offered in two different currencies, and it is more likely that the comparative advantages are genuine. One possible source of comparative advantage is tax. General Motors's position might be such that USD borrowings lead to lower taxes on its worldwide income than AUD borrowings. Qantas Airways's position might be the reverse. (Note that we assume that the interest rates in Table 6.7 have been adjusted to reflect these types of tax advantages.)

We suppose that General Motors wants to borrow 20 million AUD and Qantas Airways wants

**Table 6.7** Borrowing rates providing basis for currency swap

|                 | USD* | AUD*  |
|-----------------|------|-------|
| General Motors  | 5.0% | 12.6% |
| Qantas Airways  | 7.0% | 13.0% |

* Quoted rates have been adjusted to reflect the differential impact of taxes.

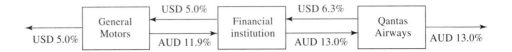

**Figure 6.10**  A currency swap motivated by comparative advantage

to borrow 12 million USD and that the current exchange rate is 0.6 USD/AUD. This creates a perfect situation for a currency swap. General Motors and Qantas Airways each borrow in the market where they have a comparative advantage; that is, General Motors borrows USD whereas Qantas Airways borrows AUD. They then use a currency swap to transform General Motors's loan into an AUD loan and Qantas Airways's loan into a USD loan.

As already mentioned, the difference between the dollar interest rates is 2%, whereas the difference between the AUD interest rates is 0.4%. By analogy with the interest rate swap case, we expect the total gain to all parties to be $2.0 - 0.4 = 1.6\%$ per annum.

There are many ways in which the swap can be organized. Figure 6.10 shows one way swaps might be entered into with a financial institution. General Motors borrows USD and Qantas Airways borrows AUD. The effect of the swap is to transform the USD interest rate of 5% per annum to an AUD interest rate of 11.9% per annum for General Motors. As a result, General Motors is 0.7% per annum better off than it would be if it went directly to AUD markets. Similarly, Qantas exchanges an AUD loan at 13% per annum for a USD loan at 6.3% per annum and ends up 0.7% per annum better off than it would be if it went directly to USD markets. The financial institution gains 1.3% per annum on its USD cash flows and loses 1.1% per annum on its AUD flows. If we ignore the difference between the two currencies, the financial institution makes a net gain of 0.2% per annum. As predicted, the total gain to all parties is 1.6% per annum.

Each year the financial institution makes a gain of USD 156,000 (= 1.3% of 12 million) and incurs a loss of AUD 220,000 (= 1.1% of 20 million). The financial institution can avoid any foreign exchange risk by buying AUD 220,000 per annum in the forward market for each year of the life of the swap, thus locking in a net gain in USD.

It is possible to redesign the swap so that the financial institution makes a 0.2% spread in USD. Figures 6.11 and 6.12 present two alternatives. These alternatives are unlikely to be used in practice

**Figure 6.11**  Alternative arrangement for currency swap:
Qantas Airways bears some foreign exchange risk

**Figure 6.12**  Alternative arrangement for currency swap:
General Motors bears some foreign exchange risk

because they do not lead to General Motors and Qantas being free of foreign exchange risk.[5] In Figure 6.11, Qantas bears some foreign exchange risk because it pays 1.1% per annum in AUD and 5.2% per annum in USD. In Figure 6.12, General Motors bears some foreign exchange risk because it receives 1.1% per annum in USD and pays 13% per annum in AUD.

## 6.6 VALUATION OF CURRENCY SWAPS

In the absence of default risk, a currency swap can be decomposed into a position in two bonds, as is the case with an interest rate swap. Consider the position of IBM in Table 6.6 some time after the initial exchange of principal. It is short a GBP bond that pays interest at 11% per annum and long a USD bond that pays interest at 8% per annum.

In general, if we define $V_{swap}$ as the value in U.S. dollars of a swap where dollars are received and a foreign currency is paid, then

$$V_{swap} = B_D - S_0 B_F$$

where $B_F$ is the value, measured in the foreign currency, of the foreign-denominated bond underlying the swap, $B_D$ is the value of the U.S. dollar bond underlying the swap, and $S_0$ is the spot exchange rate (expressed as number of units of domestic currency per unit of foreign currency). The value of a swap can therefore be determined from LIBOR rates in the two currencies, the term structure of interest rates in the domestic currency, and the spot exchange rate. Similarly, the value of a swap where the foreign currency is received and sterling is paid is

$$V_{swap} = S_0 B_F - B_D$$

**Example 6.4**  Suppose that the term structure of interest rates is flat in both Japan and the United States. The Japanese rate is 4% per annum and the U.S. rate is 9% per annum (both with continuous compounding). A financial institution has entered into a currency swap in which it receives 5% per annum in yen and pays 8% per annum in dollars once a year. The principals in the two currencies are $10 million and 1,200 million yen. The swap will last for another three years, and the current exchange rate is 110 yen = $1. In this case,

$$B_D = 0.8e^{-0.09 \times 1} + 0.8e^{-0.09 \times 2} + 10.8e^{-0.09 \times 3}$$

$$= 9.644 \text{ million dollars}$$

$$B_F = 60e^{-0.04 \times 1} + 60e^{-0.04 \times 2} + 1{,}260e^{-0.04 \times 3}$$

$$= 1{,}230.55 \text{ million yen}$$

The value of the swap in dollars is

$$\frac{1{,}230.55}{110} - 9.644 = 1.543 \text{ million}$$

If the financial institution had been paying yen and receiving dollars, the value of the swap would have been −$1.543 million.

---

[5] Usually it makes sense for the financial institution to bear the foreign exchange risk, because it is in the best position to hedge the risk.

### Decomposition into Forward Contracts

An alternative decomposition of the currency swap is into a series of forward contracts. Consider again the situation in Table 6.6. On each payment date IBM has agreed to exchange an inflow of $1.2 million and an outflow of £1.1 million. In addition, at the final payment date, it has agreed to exchange a $15 million inflow for a £10 million outflow. Each of these exchanges represents a forward contract. In Section 3.8 we saw that forward contracts can be valued on the assumption that the forward price of the underlying asset is realized. This provides a convenient way of valuing the forward contracts underlying a currency swap.

**Example 6.5**  Consider the situation in the previous example. The current spot rate is 110 yen per dollar, or 0.009091 dollar per yen. Because the difference between the dollar and yen interest rates is 5% per annum, equation (3.13) can be used to give the one-year, two-year, and three-year forward exchange rates as

$$0.009091e^{0.05 \times 1} = 0.009557$$

$$0.009091e^{0.05 \times 2} = 0.010047$$

$$0.009091e^{0.05 \times 3} = 0.010562$$

respectively. The exchange of interest involves receiving 60 million yen and paying $0.8 million. The risk-free interest rate in dollars is 9% per annum. From equation (3.8), the values of the forward contracts corresponding to the exchange of interest are (in millions of dollars)

$$(60 \times 0.009557 - 0.8)e^{-0.09 \times 1} = -0.2071$$

$$(60 \times 0.010047 - 0.8)e^{-0.09 \times 2} = -0.1647$$

$$(60 \times 0.010562 - 0.8)e^{-0.09 \times 3} = -0.1269$$

The final exchange of principal involves receiving 1,200 million yen and paying $10 million. From equation (3.8), the value of the forward contract corresponding to the exchange is (in millions of dollars)

$$(1,200 \times 0.010562 - 10)e^{-0.09 \times 3} = 2.0416$$

The total value of the swap is $2.0416 - 0.1269 - 0.1647 - 0.2071 = \$1.543$ million, which is in agreement with the result of the calculations in the previous example.

The value of a currency swap is normally zero when it is first negotiated. If the two principals are worth exactly the same using the exchange rate at the start of the swap, the value of the swap is also zero immediately after the initial exchange of principal. However, as in the case of interest rate swaps, this does not mean that each of the individual forward contracts underlying the swap has zero value. It can be shown that when interest rates in two currencies are significantly different, the payer of the low-interest-rate currency is in the position where the forward contracts corresponding to the early exchanges of cash flows have positive values, and the forward contract corresponding to final exchange of principals has a negative expected value. The payer of the high-interest-rate currency is likely to be in the opposite position; that is, the early exchanges of cash flows have negative values and the final exchange has a positive expected value.

For the payer of the low-interest-rate currency, the swap will tend to have a negative value during most of its life. The forward contracts corresponding to the early exchanges of payments have positive values, and, once these exchanges have taken place, there is a tendency for the remaining forward contracts to have, in total, a negative value. For the payer of the high-interest-rate currency, the reverse is true. The value of the swap will tend to be positive during most of its life. These results are important when the credit risk in the swap is being evaluated.

## 6.7 CREDIT RISK

Contracts such as swaps that are private arrangements between two companies entail credit risks. Consider a financial institution that has entered into offsetting contracts with two companies (see Figure 6.4, 6.5, or 6.7). If neither party defaults, the financial institution remains fully hedged. A decline in the value of one contract will always be offset by an increase in the value of the other contract. However, there is a chance that one party will get into financial difficulties and default. The financial institution then still has to honor the contract it has with the other party.

Suppose that some time after the initiation of the contracts in Figure 6.4, the contract with Microsoft has a positive value to the financial institution, whereas the contract with Intel has a negative value. If Microsoft defaults, the financial institution is liable to lose the whole of the positive value it has in this contract. To maintain a hedged position, it would have to find a third party willing to take Microsoft's position. To induce the third party to take the position, the financial institution would have to pay the third party an amount roughly equal to the value of its contract with Microsoft prior to the default.

A financial institution has credit-risk exposure from a swap only when the value of the swap to the financial institution is positive. What happens when this value is negative and the counterparty gets into financial difficulties? In theory, the financial institution could realize a windfall gain, because a default would lead to it getting rid of a liability. In practice, it is likely that the counterparty would choose to sell the contract to a third party or rearrange its affairs in some way so that its positive value in the contract is not lost. The most realistic assumption for the financial institution is therefore as follows. If the counterparty goes bankrupt, there will be a loss if the value of the swap to the financial institution is positive, and there will be no effect on the financial institution's position if the value of the swap to the financial institution is negative. This situation is summarized in Figure 6.13.

Potential losses from defaults on a swap are much less than the potential losses from defaults on a loan with the same principal. This is because the value of the swap is usually only a small fraction of the value of the loan. Potential losses from defaults on a currency swap are greater than on an interest rate swap. The reason is that, because principal amounts in two different currencies are exchanged at the end of the life of a currency swap, a currency swap can have a greater value than an interest rate swap.

Sometimes a financial institution can predict which of two offsetting contracts is more likely to have a positive value. Consider the currency swap in Figure 6.10. AUD interest rates are higher than USD interest rates. This means that, as time passes, the financial institution is likely to find that its swap with General Motors has a negative value whereas its swap with Qantas has a positive value. The creditworthiness of Qantas is therefore more important than the creditworthiness of General Motors.

It is important to distinguish between the credit risk and market risk to a financial institution in any contract. As discussed earlier, the credit risk arises from the possibility of a default by the counterparty when the value of the contract to the financial institution is positive. The market risk arises from the possibility that market variables such as interest rates and exchange rates will move in such a way that the value of a contract to the financial institution becomes negative.

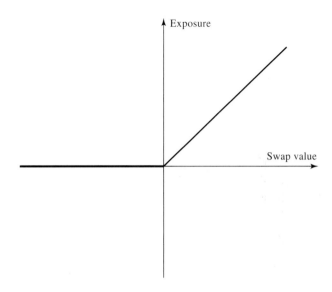

**Figure 6.13**   The credit exposure in a swap

Market risks can be hedged by entering into offsetting contracts; credit risks are less easy to hedge.

## SUMMARY

The two most common types of swaps are interest rate swaps and currency swaps. In an interest rate swap, one party agrees to pay the other party interest at a fixed rate on a notional principal for a number of years. In return, it receives interest at a floating rate on the same notional principal for the same period of time. In a currency swap, one party agrees to pay interest on a principal amount in one currency. In return, it receives interest on a principal amount in another currency.

Principal amounts are not usually exchanged in an interest rate swap. In a currency swap, principal amounts are usually exchanged at both the beginning and the end of the life of the swap. For a party paying interest in the foreign currency, the foreign principal is received, and the domestic principal is paid at the beginning of the life of the swap. At the end of the life of the swap, the foreign principal is paid and the domestic principal is received.

An interest rate swap can be used to transform a floating-rate loan into a fixed-rate loan, or vice versa. It can also be used to transform a floating-rate investment to a fixed-rate investment, or vice versa. A currency swap can be used to transform a loan in one currency into a loan in another currency. It can also be used to transform an investment denominated in one currency into an investment denominated in another currency.

There are two ways of valuing interest rate swaps and currency swaps. In the first, the swap is decomposed into a long position in one bond and a short position in another bond. In the second, it is regarded as a portfolio of forward contracts.

When a financial institution enters into a pair of offsetting swaps with different counterparties, it is exposed to credit risk. If one of the counterparties defaults when the financial institution has positive value in its swap with that counterparty, the financial institution loses money, because it still has to honor its swap agreement with the other counterparty.

The swap market is discussed further in Chapter 25.

## SUGGESTIONS FOR FURTHER READING

Bicksler, J., and A. H. Chen, "An Economic Analysis of Interest Rate Swaps," *Journal of Finance*, 41, no. 3 (1986), 645–55.

Dattatreya, R. E., and K. Hotta, *Advanced Interest Rate and Currency Swaps: State-of-the Art Products Strategies and Risk Management Applications*, Irwin, Chicago, 1993.

Hull, J., "Assessing Credit Risk in a Financial Institution's Off-Balance Sheet Commitments," *Journal of Financial and Quantitative Analysis*, 24 (December 1989), 489–502.

Hull, J., and A. White, "The Impact of Default Risk on the Prices of Options and Other Derivative Securities," *Journal of Banking and Finance*, 19 (1985), 299–322.

Hull, J., and A. White, "The Price of Default," *RISK*, September 1992, pp. 101–3.

Litzenberger, R. H., "Swaps: Plain and Fanciful," *Journal of Finance*, 47, no. 3 (1992), 831–50.

Marshall, J. F., and K. R. Kapner, *Understanding Swaps*, Wiley, New York, 1993.

Smith, C. W., C. W. Smithson, and L. M. Wakeman, "The Evolving Market for Swaps," *Midland Corporate Finance Journal*, 3 (Winter 1986), 20–32.

Turnbull, S. M., "Swaps: A Zero Sum Game," *Financial Management*, 16, no. 1 (Spring 1987), 15–21.

Wall, L. D., and J. J. Pringle, "Alternative Explanations of Interest Rate Swaps: A Theoretical and Empirical Analysis," *Financial Management*, 18, no. 2, (Summer 1989), 59–73.

## QUESTIONS AND PROBLEMS
## (ANSWERS IN SOLUTIONS MANUAL)

6.1. Companies A and B have been offered the following rates per annum on a $20 million five-year loan:

|  | Fixed rate | Floating rate |
| --- | --- | --- |
| Company A | 12.0% | LIBOR + 0.1% |
| Company B | 13.4% | LIBOR + 0.6% |

Company A requires a floating-rate loan; company B requires a fixed-rate loan. Design a swap that will net a bank, acting as intermediary, 0.1% per annum and that will appear equally attractive to both companies.

6.2. A $100 million interest rate swap has a remaining life of 10 months. Under the terms of the swap, six-month LIBOR is exchanged for 12% per annum (compounded semiannually). The average of the bid–offer rate being exchanged for six-month LIBOR in swaps of all maturities is currently 10% per annum with continuous compounding. The six-month LIBOR rate was 9.6% per annum two months ago. What is the current value of the swap to the party paying floating? What is its value to the party paying fixed?

6.3. Company X wishes to borrow U.S. dollars at a fixed rate of interest. Company Y wishes to borrow Japanese yen at a fixed rate of interest. The amounts required by the two companies are roughly the same at the current exchange rate. The companies have been quoted the following interest rates, which have been adjusted for the impact of taxes:

|  | Yen | Dollars |
|---|---|---|
| Company X | 5.0% | 9.6% |
| Company Y | 6.5% | 10.0% |

Design a swap that will net a bank, acting as intermediary, 50 basis points per annum. Make the swap equally attractive to the two companies and ensure that all foreign exchange risk is assumed by the bank.

6.4. Explain what a swap rate is. What is the relationship between swap rates and par yields?

6.5. A currency swap has a remaining life of 15 months. It involves exchanging interest at 14% on £20 million for interest at 10% on $30 million once a year. The term structure of interest rates in both the United Kingdom and the United States is currently flat, and if the swap were negotiated today the interest rates exchanged would be 8% in dollars and 11% in sterling. All interest rates are quoted with annual compounding. The current exchange rate (dollars per pound sterling) is 1.6500. What is the value of the swap to the party paying sterling? What is the value of the swap to the party paying dollars?

6.6. Explain the difference between the credit risk and the market risk in a financial contract.

6.7. Explain why a bank is subject to credit risk when it enters into two offsetting swap contracts.

6.8. Companies X and Y have been offered the following rates per annum on a $5 million 10-year investment:

|  | Fixed rate | Floating rate |
|---|---|---|
| Company X | 8.0% | LIBOR |
| Company Y | 8.8% | LIBOR |

Company X requires a fixed-rate investment; company Y requires a floating-rate investment. Design a swap that will net a bank, acting as intermediary, 0.2% per annum and will appear equally attractive to X and Y.

6.9. A financial institution has entered into an interest rate swap with company X. Under the terms of the swap, it receives 10% per annum and pays six-month LIBOR on a principal of $10 million for five years. Payments are made every six months. Suppose that company X defaults on the sixth payment date (end of year 3) when the interest rate (with semiannual compounding) is 8% per annum for all maturities. What is the loss to the financial institution? Assume that six-month LIBOR was 9% per annum halfway through year 3.

6.10. A financial institution has entered into a 10-year currency swap with company Y. Under the terms of the swap, it receives interest at 3% per annum in Swiss francs and pays interest at 8% per annum in U.S. dollars. Interest payments are exchanged once a year. The principal amounts are 7 million dollars and 10 million francs. Suppose that company Y declares bankruptcy at the end of year 6, when the exchange rate is $0.80 per franc. What is the cost to the financial institution? Assume that, at the end of year 6, the interest rate is 3% per annum in Swiss francs and 8% per annum in U.S. dollars for all maturities. All interest rates are quoted with annual compounding.

6.11. Companies A and B face the following interest rates (adjusted for the differential impact of taxes):

|                              | A            | B            |
|------------------------------|--------------|--------------|
| U.S. dollars (floating rate) | LIBOR + 0.5% | LIBOR + 1.0% |
| Canadian dollars (fixed rate)| 5.0%         | 6.5%         |

Assume that A wants to borrow U.S. dollars at a floating rate of interest and B wants to borrow Canadian dollars at a fixed rate of interest. A financial institution is planning to arrange a swap and requires a 50-basis-point spread. If the swap is equally attractive to A and B, what rates of interest will A and B end up paying?

6.12. After it hedges its foreign exchange risk using forward contracts, is the financial institution's average spread in Figure 6.10 likely to be greater than or less than 20 basis points? Explain your answer.

6.13. "Companies with high credit risks are the ones that cannot access fixed-rate markets directly. They are the companies that are most likely to be paying fixed and receiving floating in an interest rate swap." Assume that this statement is true. Do you think it increases or decreases the risk of a financial institution's swap portfolio? Assume that companies are most likely to default when interest rates are high.

6.14. Why is the expected loss from a default on a swap less than the expected loss from the default on a loan with the same principal?

6.15. A bank finds that its assets are not matched with its liabilities. It is taking floating-rate deposits and making fixed-rate loans. How can swaps be used to offset the risk?

6.16. Explain how you would value a swap that is the exchange of a floating rate in one currency for a fixed rate in another currency.

6.17. The LIBOR zero curve is flat at 5% (continuously compounded) out to 1.5 years. Swap rates for 2- and 3-year semiannual pay swaps are 5.4% and 5.6%, respectively. Estimate the LIBOR zero rates for maturities of 2.0, 2.5, and 3.0 years. (Assume that the 2.5-year swap rate is the average of the 2- and 3-year swap rates.)

## ASSIGNMENT QUESTIONS

6.18. The one-year LIBOR rate is 10%. A bank trades swaps where a fixed rate of interest is exchanged for 12-month LIBOR with payments being exchanged annually. Two- and three-year swap rates (expressed with annual compounding) are 11% and 12% per annum. Estimate the two- and three-year LIBOR zero rates.

6.19. Company X is based in the United Kingdom and would like to borrow $50 million at a fixed rate of interest for five years in U.S. funds. Because the company is not well known in the United States, this has proved to be impossible. However, the company has been quoted 12% per annum on fixed-rate five-year sterling funds. Company Y is based in the United States and would like to borrow the equivalent of $50 million in sterling funds for five years at a fixed rate of interest. It has been unable to get a quote but has been offered U.S. dollar funds at 10.5% per annum. Five-year government bonds currently yield 9.5% per annum in the United States and 10.5% in the United Kingdom. Suggest an appropriate currency swap that will net the financial intermediary 0.5% per annum.

6.20. Under the terms of an interest rate swap, a financial institution has agreed to pay 10% per annum and to receive three-month LIBOR in return on a notional principal of $100 million with payments being exchanged every three months. The swap has a remaining life of 14 months. The average of the bid and offer fixed rates currently being swapped for three-month LIBOR is 12% per annum for all maturities. The three-month LIBOR rate one month ago was 11.8% per annum. All rates are compounded quarterly. What is the value of the swap?

6.21. Suppose that the term structure of interest rates is flat in the United States and Australia. The USD interest rate is 7% per annum and the AUD rate is 9% per annum. The current value of the AUD is 0.62 USD. Under the terms of a swap agreement, a financial institution pays 8% per annum in AUD and receives 4% per annum in USD. The principals in the two currencies are $12 million USD and 20 million AUD. Payments are exchanged every year, with one exchange having just taken place. The swap will last two more years. What is the value of the swap to the financial institution? Assume all interest rates are continuously compounded.

6.22. Company A, a British manufacturer, wishes to borrow U.S. dollars at a fixed rate of interest. Company B, a U.S. multinational, wishes to borrow sterling at a fixed rate of interest. They have been quoted the following rates per annum (adjusted for differential tax effects):

|  | Sterling | U.S. Dollars |
| --- | --- | --- |
| Company A | 11.0% | 7.0% |
| Company B | 10.6% | 6.2% |

Design a swap that will net a bank, acting as intermediary, 10 basis points per annum and that will produce a gain of 15 basis points per annum for each of the two companies.

# CHAPTER 7

# MECHANICS OF OPTIONS MARKETS

We introduced options in Chapter 1. A call option is the right to buy an asset for a certain price; a put option is the right to sell an asset for a certain price. A European option can be exercised only at the end of its life; an American option can be exercised at any time during its life. The are four types of option positions: a long position in a call, a long position in a put, a short position in a call, and a short position in a put. In this chapter we explain the way that exchange-traded options markets are organized, the terminology used, how contracts are traded, how margin requirements are set, and so on. Later chapters will discuss trading strategies involving options, the pricing of options, and ways in which portfolios of options can be hedged.

Options are fundamentally different from the forward, futures, and swap contracts discussed in the last few chapters. An option gives the holder of the option the right to do something. The holder does not have to exercise this right. By contrast, in a forward, futures, or swap contract, the two parties have committed themselves to some action. It costs a trader nothing (except for the margin requirements) to enter into a forward or futures contract, whereas the purchase of an option requires an up-front payment.

## 7.1 UNDERLYING ASSETS

Exchange-traded options are currently actively traded on stocks, stock indices, foreign currencies, and futures contracts.

### Stock Options

The exchanges trading stock options in the United States are the Chicago Board Options Exchange (www.cboe.com), the Philadelphia Stock Exchange (www.phlx.com), the American Stock Exchange (www.amex.com), and the Pacific Exchange (www.pacifex.com). Options trade on more than 500 different stocks. One contract gives the holder the right to buy or sell 100 shares at the specified strike price. This contract size is convenient as the shares themselves are usually traded in lots of 100.

### Foreign Currency Options

The major exchange for trading foreign currency options is the Philadelphia Stock Exchange. It offers both European and American contracts on a variety of different currencies. The size of one contract depends on the currency. For example, in the case of the British pound, one contract gives the holder the right to buy or sell £31,250; in the case of the Japanese yen, one contract gives the holder the right to buy or sell 6.25 million yen. Foreign currency options contracts are discussed further in Chapter 13.

### Index Options

Many different index options currently trade throughout the world. The most popular contracts in the United States are those on the S&P 500 Index (SPX), the S&P 100 Index (OEX), the Nasdaq 100 Index (NDX), and the Dow Jones Industrial Index (DJX). All of these trade on the Chicago Board Options Exchange. Some index options are European and some are American. For example, the contract on the S&P 500 is European, whereas that on the S&P 100 is American. One contract is to buy or sell 100 times the index at the specified strike price. Settlement is always in cash, rather than by delivering the portfolio underlying the index. Consider, for example, one call contract on the S&P 100 with a strike price of 980. If it is exercised when the value of the index is 992, the writer of the contract pays the holder $(992 - 980) \times 100 = \$1,200$. This cash payment is based on the index value at the end of the day on which exercise instructions are issued. Not surprisingly, investors usually wait until the end of a day before issuing these instructions. Index options are discussed further in Chapter 13.

### Futures Options

In a futures option (or options on futures), the underlying asset is a futures contract. The futures contract normally matures shortly after the expiration of the option. Futures options are now available for most of the assets on which futures contracts are traded and normally trade on the same exchange as the futures contract. When a call option is exercised, the holder acquires from the writer a long position in the underlying futures contract plus a cash amount equal to the excess of the futures price over the strike price. When a put option is exercised, the holder acquires a short position in the underlying futures contract plus a cash amount equal to the excess of the strike price over the futures price. Futures options contracts are discussed further in Chapter 13.

## 7.2  SPECIFICATION OF STOCK OPTIONS

In most of the rest of this chapter, we will focus on exchange-traded stock options. As already mentioned, an exchange-traded stock option in the United States is an American-style option contract to buy or sell 100 shares of the stock. Details of the contract—the expiration date, the strike price, what happens when dividends are declared, how large a position investors can hold, and so on—are specified by the exchange.

### Expiration Dates

One of the items used to describe a stock option is the month in which the expiration date occurs. Thus, a January call trading on IBM is a call option on IBM with an expiration date in January. The precise expiration date is 10:59 p.m. Central Time on the Saturday immediately following the third Friday of the expiration month. The last day on which options trade is the third Friday of the expiration month. An investor with a long position in an option normally has until 4:30 p.m. Central Time on that Friday to instruct a broker to exercise the option. The broker then has until 10:59 p.m. the next day to complete the paperwork notifying the exchange that exercise is to take place.

Stock options are on a January, February, or March cycle. The January cycle consists of the months of January, April, July, and October. The February cycle consists of the months of February, May, August, and November. The March cycle consists of the months of March, June, September, and December. If the expiration date for the current month has not yet been reached, options trade with expiration dates in the current month, the following month, and the next two months in the cycle. If the expiration date of the current month has passed, options trade with expiration dates in the next month, the next-but-one month, and the next two months of the expiration cycle. For example, IBM is on a January cycle. At the beginning of January, options are traded with expiration dates in January, February, April, and July; at the end of January, they are traded with expiration dates in February, March, April, and July; at the beginning of May, they are traded with expiration dates in May, June, July, and October; and so on. When one option reaches expiration, trading in another is started. Longer-term options, known as LEAPS (long-term equity anticipation securities), also trade on some stocks. These have expiration dates up to three years into the future. The expiration dates for LEAPS on stocks are always in January.

### Strike Prices

The Chicago Board Options Exchange normally chooses the strike prices at which options can be written so that they are spaced $2.50, $5, or $10 apart. When the price of a stock is $12, we might see options trading with strike prices of $10, $12.50, and $15; when the stock price is $100, we might see strike prices of $90, $95, $100, $105, and $110. As will be explained shortly, stock splits and stock dividends can lead to nonstandard strike prices.

When a new expiration date is introduced, the two or three strike prices closest to the current stock price are usually selected by the exchange. If the stock price moves outside the range defined by the highest and lowest strike price, trading is usually introduced in an option with a new strike price. To illustrate these rules, suppose that the stock price is $84 when trading begins in the October options. Call and put options would probably first be offered with strike prices of $80, $85, and $90. If the stock price rose above $90, it is likely that a strike price of $95 would be offered; if it fell below $80, it is likely that a strike price of $75 would be offered; and so on.

### Terminology

For any given asset at any given time, many different option contracts may be trading. Consider a stock that has four expiration dates and five strike prices. If call and put options trade with every expiration date and every strike price, there are a total of 40 different contracts. All options of the same type (calls or puts) are referred to as an *option class*. For example, IBM calls are one class, whereas IBM puts are another class. An *option series* consists of all the options of a given class with the same expiration date and strike price. In other words, an option series refers to a particular contract that is traded. The IBM 50 October calls are an option series.

Options are referred to as *in the money, at the money,* or *out of the money.* An in-the-money option would give the holder a positive cash flow if it were exercised immediately. Similarly, an at-the-money option would lead to zero cash flow if it were exercised immediately, and an out-of-the-money option would lead to a negative cash flow if it were exercised immediately. If $S$ is the stock price and $K$ is the strike price, a call option is in the money when $S > K$, at the money when $S = K$, and out of the money when $S < K$. A put option is in the money when $S < K$, at the money when $S = K$, and out of the money when $S > K$. Clearly, an option will be exercised only when it is in the money. In the absence of transactions costs, an in-the-money option will always be exercised on the expiration date if it has not been exercised previously.

The *intrinsic value* of an option is defined as the maximum of zero and the value the option would have if it were exercised immediately. For a call option, the intrinsic value is therefore $\max(S - K, 0)$. For a put option, it is $\max(K - S, 0)$. An in-the-money American option must be worth at least as much as its intrinsic value because the holder can realize a positive intrinsic value by exercising immediately. Often it is optimal for the holder of an in-the-money American option to wait rather than exercise immediately. The option is then said to have *time value*.

The *time value* of an option is the part of the option's value that derives the possibility of future favorable movements in the stock price. Suppose that the price of a call option with two months to maturity is $3 when the stock price is $30 and the strike price is $28. The intrinsic value of the option is $30 - 28 = \$2$ and the time value is $3 - 2 = \$1$. In general, the value of an option equals the intrinsic value of the option plus the time value of the option. The time value of the option is zero when (a) the option has reached maturity or (b) it is optimal to exercise the option immediately.

### Flex Options

The Chicago Board Options Exchange offers *flex options* on equities and equity indices. These are options where the traders on the floor of the exchange agree to nonstandard terms. These nonstandard terms can involve a strike price or an expiration date that is different from what is usually offered by the exchange. It can also involve the option being European rather than American. Flex options are an attempt by option exchanges to regain business from the over-the-counter markets. The exchange specifies a minimum size for flex option trades.

### Dividends and Stock Splits

The early over-the-counter options were dividend protected. If a company declared a cash dividend, the strike price for options on the company's stock was reduced on the ex-dividend day by the amount of the dividend. Exchange-traded options are not generally adjusted for cash dividends. In other words, when a cash dividend occurs, there are no adjustments to the terms of the option contract. As we will see in Chapter 12, this has significant implications for the way in which options are valued.

Exchange-traded options are adjusted for stock splits. A stock split occurs when the existing shares are "split" into more shares. For example, in a 3-for-1 stock split, three new shares are issued to replace each existing share. Because a stock split does not change the assets or the earning ability of a company, we should not expect it to have any effect on the wealth of the company's shareholders. All else being equal, the 3-for-1 stock split should cause the stock price to go down to one-third of its previous value. In general, an $n$-for-$m$ stock split should cause the stock price to go down to $m/n$ of its previous value. The terms of option contracts are adjusted to reflect expected changes in a stock price arising from a stock split. After an $n$-for-$m$ stock split, the strike price is reduced to $m/n$ of its previous value, and the number of shares covered by one contract is increased to $n/m$ of its previous value. If the stock price declines in the way expected, the positions of both the writer and the purchaser of a contract remain unchanged.

> **Example 7.1**   Consider a call option to buy 100 shares of a company for $30 per share. Suppose that the company makes a 2-for-1 stock split. The terms of the option contract are then changed so that it gives the holder the right to purchase 200 shares for $15 per share.

Stock options are adjusted for stock dividends. A stock dividend involves a company issuing more shares to its existing shareholders. For example, a 20% stock dividend means that investors receive one new share for each five already owned. A stock dividend, like a stock split, has no effect on either the assets or the earning power of a company. The stock price can be expected to go down as a result of a stock dividend. The 20% stock dividend referred to is essentially the same as a 6-for-5 stock split. All else being equal, it should cause the stock price to decline to 5/6 of its previous value. The terms of an option are adjusted to reflect the expected price decline arising from a stock dividend in the same way as they are for that arising from a stock split.

> **Example 7.2** Consider a put option to sell 100 shares of a company for $15 per share. Suppose that the company declares a 25% stock dividend. This is equivalent to a 5-for-4 stock split. The terms of the option contract are changed so that it gives the holder the right to sell 125 shares for $12.

Adjustments are also made for rights issues. The basic procedure is to calculate the theoretical price of the rights and then to reduce the strike price by this amount.

### Position Limits and Exercise Limits

The Chicago Board Options Exchange often specifies a *position limit* for option contracts. This defines the maximum number of option contracts that an investor can hold on one side of the market. For this purpose, long calls and short puts are considered to be on the same side of the market. Also, short calls and long puts are considered to be on the same side of the market. The *exercise limit* equals the position limit. It defines the maximum number of contracts that can be exercised by any individual (or group of individuals acting together) in any period of five consecutive business days. Options on the largest and most frequently traded stocks have positions limits of 75,000 contracts. Smaller capitalization stocks have position limits of 60,000, 31,500, 22,500, or 13,500 contracts.

Position limits and exercise limits are designed to prevent the market from being unduly influenced by the activities of an individual investor or group of investors. However, whether the limits are really necessary is a controversial issue.

## 7.3 NEWSPAPER QUOTES

Many newspapers carry options quotations. In the *Wall Street Journal*, stock option quotations can currently be found under the heading "Listed Options" in the Money and Investing section. Table 7.1 shows an extract from the quotations as they appeared in the *Wall Street Journal* of Friday March 16, 2001. The quotations refer to trading that took place on the previous day (Thursday March 15, 2001).

The company on whose stock the option is written together with the closing stock price is listed in the first column of Table 7.1. The strike price and maturity month appear in the second and third columns. If a call option traded with a given strike price and maturity month, the next two columns show the volume of trading and the price at last trade for the call option. The final two columns show the same for a put option.

The quoted price is the price of an option to buy or sell one share. As mentioned earlier, one contract is for the purchase or sale of 100 shares. A contract therefore costs 100 times the price shown. Because most options are priced at less than $10 and some are priced at less than $1, investors do not have to be extremely wealthy to trade options.

**Table 7.1** Stock option quotations from the *Wall Street Journal* on March 16, 2001

# LISTED OPTIONS QUOTATIONS

| OPTION/STRIKE | | EXP | CALL VOL. | CALL LAST | PUT VOL. | PUT LAST |
|---|---|---|---|---|---|---|
| ADC Tel | 10 | May | 25 | 206 | 1035 | 131 |
| AmOnline | 30 | Mar | 608 | 1070 | ... | ... |
| 4059 | 3750 | Mar | 505 | 320 | 220 | 005 |
| 4059 | 40 | Mar | 3071 | 105 | 820 | 050 |
| 4059 | 40 | Apr | 2302 | 390 | 977 | 310 |
| 4059 | 4250 | Mar | 1270 | 020 | 487 | 2 |
| 4059 | 45 | Mar | 758 | 005 | 1456 | 450 |
| 4059 | 45 | Apr | 1136 | 170 | 597 | 610 |
| 4059 | 50 | Apr | 593 | 070 | 170 | 990 |
| 4059 | 50 | Jul | 885 | 245 | 282 | 1080 |
| ASM Intl | 1250 | Jun | 650 | 363 | 770 | 125 |
| ATT Wrls | 20 | Mar | 15 | 015 | 525 | 170 |
| 1890 | 20 | Apr | 1267 | 120 | 70 | 230 |
| 1890 | 2250 | Apr | ... | ... | 620 | 430 |
| 1890 | 25 | Mar | ... | ... | 635 | 650 |
| AT&T | 20 | Mar | 390 | 390 | 742 | 045 |
| 2335 | 2250 | Mar | 1194 | 105 | 52 | 010 |
| 2335 | 2250 | Apr | 2933 | 2 | 12689 | 110 |
| 2335 | 25 | Mar | 800 | 005 | 265 | 240 |
| 2335 | 25 | Apr | 2011 | 080 | 3891 | 250 |
| 2335 | 40 | Apr | 9 | 010 | 582 | 1670 |
| ATMI Inc | 20 | Sep | ... | ... | 1000 | 413 |
| Abbt L | 4250 | Mar | ... | ... | 521 | 025 |
| 4628 | 45 | Apr | 2228 | 280 | 324 | 180 |
| AberFitch | 35 | May | 534 | 285 | ... | ... |
| Actel | 2250 | Apr | 1046 | 150 | ... | ... |
| Adelph | 35 | Apr | 2700 | 5 | ... | ... |
| AdobeS | 25 | Mar | 612 | 156 | 1441 | 156 |
| 25 | 30 | Mar | 987 | 025 | 537 | 550 |
| AdvFibCm | 25 | Apr | 685 | 031 | ... | ... |
| A M D | 20 | Mar | 181 | 360 | 600 | 005 |
| 2356 | 2250 | Mar | 2855 | 120 | 232 | 020 |
| 2356 | 25 | Mar | 1164 | 015 | 83 | 175 |
| 2356 | 25 | Apr | 3338 | 185 | 148 | 310 |
| 2356 | 25 | Jul | 1150 | 370 | ... | ... |

| OPTION/STRIKE | | EXP. | CALL VOL. | CALL LAST | PUT VOL. | PUT LAST |
|---|---|---|---|---|---|---|
| 2356 | 25 | Oct | 1004 | 560 | ... | ... |
| Agilent | 35 | Apr | 700 | 340 | 22 | 255 |
| 3485 | 40 | Apr | 2754 | 150 | ... | ... |
| Alamosa | 1250 | Apr | 500 | 063 | ... | ... |
| AlbnyMlc | 35 | Aug | 525 | 1025 | ... | ... |
| Albtsn | 2750 | Mar | 18 | 040 | 476 | 045 |
| AliegTel | 20 | Apr | ... | ... | 2580 | 388 |
| AldWaste | 20 | Mar | ... | ... | 2128 | 520 |
| Allste | 40 | Apr | 1086 | 190 | 142 | 150 |
| 4007 | 4250 | Mar | 2750 | 010 | ... | ... |
| 4007 | 4250 | Apr | 2080 | 125 | 30 | 280 |
| Alphalnd | 1750 | Apr | 1052 | 169 | ... | ... |
| Altera | 25 | Mar | 777 | 1 | 122 | 056 |
| 2525 | 2750 | Mar | 121 | 013 | 645 | 244 |
| Amazon | 750 | Apr | 255 | 413 | 1040 | 044 |
| 11 | 45 | Mar | ... | ... | 1347 | 3375 |
| Amdocs | 65 | Apr | 20 | 3 | 2124 | 970 |
| AmExpr | 40 | Mar | 1186 | 050 | 430 | 060 |
| 3980 | 40 | Apr | 622 | 250 | 234 | 250 |
| 3980 | 4250 | Apr | 2181 | 165 | 140 | 420 |
| AmGenl | 3750 | Jul | 525 | 460 | 20 | 2 |
| 3933 | 40 | Mar | 494 | 020 | 20 | 075 |
| Am Hom | 55 | Mar | 2698 | 140 | 50 | 060 |
| 5656 | 55 | Jul | 2603 | 6 | 5 | 430 |
| AmintGp | 95 | May | ... | ... | 1700 | 1710 |
| AmStd | 45 | Jul | ... | ... | 1000 | 1 |
| Amgen | 55 | Mar | 510 | 1263 | 99 | 169 |
| 6513 | 60 | Mar | 716 | 6 | 172 | 013 |
| 6513 | 65 | Mar | 455 | 125 | 634 | 125 |
| 6513 | 70 | Apr | 737 | 313 | 225 | 7 |
| 6513 | 75 | Apr | 524 | 163 | 300 | 1050 |
| 6513 | 80 | Apr | 1299 | 088 | 2 | 15 |
| Anadrk | 55 | May | ... | ... | 500 | 180 |
| 6343 | 65 | Apr | 788 | 040 | 1020 | 220 |
| 6343 | 65 | Apr | 1113 | 320 | ... | ... |

| OPTION/STRIKE | | EXP. | CALL VOL. | CALL LAST | PUT VOL. | PUT LAST |
|---|---|---|---|---|---|---|
| 6343 | 65 | May | 505 | 460 | 34 | 580 |
| 6343 | 70 | Mar | ... | ... | 2201 | 720 |
| 6343 | 70 | Apr | 223 | 145 | 2101 | 770 |
| 6343 | 75 | Mar | 1 | 025 | 975 | 1150 |
| Analog | 40 | Mar | 532 | 195 | 564 | 075 |
| AndrxCp | 45 | Apr | 532 | 244 | 1325 | 613 |
| 3931 | 50 | Apr | 787 | 138 | 180 | 8 |
| 3931 | 65 | Apr | 490 | 050 | ... | ... |
| answthink | 5 | Mar | 507 | 031 | ... | ... |
| 528 | 5 | Apr | 510 | 113 | ... | ... |
| Apache | 65 | Mar | 23 | 010 | 2800 | 320 |
| 6166 | 65 | Apr | 24 | 235 | 2804 | 560 |
| AppleC | 15 | Apr | 36 | 588 | 3003 | 050 |
| 1969 | 1750 | Apr | 47 | 388 | 3254 | 113 |
| 1969 | 20 | Mar | 1868 | 031 | 430 | 044 |
| 1969 | 2250 | Apr | 5587 | 131 | 82 | 363 |
| 1969 | 25 | Apr | 870 | 075 | 98 | 563 |
| 1969 | 30 | Jul | 1429 | 119 | 10 | 988 |
| 1969 | 4750 | Apr | ... | ... | 1500 | 119 |
| ApdidMat | 30 | Apr | 499 | 1925 | 492 | 050 |
| 4613 | 40 | Apr | 6 | 8 | 678 | 006 |
| 4613 | 40 | Apr | 76 | 9 | 1330 | 350 |
| 4613 | 4250 | Mar | 672 | 350 | 507 | 025 |
| 4613 | 4250 | Apr | 162 | 863 | 2864 | 350 |
| 4613 | 45 | Mar | 1003 | 175 | 1618 | 081 |
| 4613 | 45 | Apr | 769 | 538 | 1467 | 425 |
| 4613 | 4750 | Mar | 675 | 063 | 1733 | 206 |
| 4613 | 50 | Apr | 2448 | 050 | 798 | 388 |
| 4613 | 50 | Apr | 3002 | 3 | 1564 | 7 |
| 4613 | 55 | Apr | 704 | 169 | 1837 | 913 |
| AMCC | 20 | Apr | 504 | 538 | 626 | 206 |
| 2363 | 35 | Mar | 6 | 006 | 557 | 1113 |
| 2363 | 4750 | Apr | ... | ... | 510 | 1 |
| Ariba | 1750 | Apr | 3080 | 063 | 10 | 6 |
| 1106 | 110 | May | ... | ... | 800 | 9863 |

*Source*: Reprinted by permission of Dow Jones, Inc., via copyright Clearance Center, Inc. © 2001 Dow Jones & Company, Inc. All Rights Reserved Worldwide.

The *Wall Street Journal* also shows the total call volume, put volume, call open interest, and put open interest for each exchange. The numbers reported in the newspaper on March 16, 2001, are shown in Table 7.2. The volume is the total number of contracts traded on the day. The open interest is the number of contracts outstanding.

From Table 7.1 it appears that there were arbitrage opportunities on March 15, 2001. For example, a March put on Amazon.com with a strike price of 45 is shown to have a price of 33.75. Because the stock price was 11, it appears that this put and the stock could have been purchased and the put exercised immediately for a profit of 0.25. In fact, these types of arbitrage opportunities

**Table 7.2** Volume and open interest reported in the *Wall Street Journal* on March 16, 2001

| Exchange | Call volume | Call open interest | Put volume | Put open interest |
|---|---|---|---|---|
| Chicago Board | 777,845 | 46,667,872 | 757,275 | 26,436,611 |
| American | 481,780 | 17,343,487 | 371,031 | 9,331,586 |
| Philadelphia | 261,970 | 27,454,323 | 226,953 | 14,051,375 |
| Pacific | 253,995 | 41,893,009 | 200,690 | 22,910,071 |
| Total | 1,775,590 | 133,358,691 | 1,555,949 | 72,729,643 |

almost certainly did not exist. For both options and stocks, Table 7.1 gives the prices at which the last trade took place on March 15, 2001. The last trade for the March Amazon.com put with a strike price of 45 probably occurred much earlier in the day than the last trade on the stock. If an option trade had been attempted at the time of the last trade on the stock, the put price would have been higher than 33.75.

## 7.4 TRADING

Traditionally, exchanges have had to provide a large open area for individuals to meet and trade options. This is changing. Eurex, the large European derivatives exchange, is fully electronic, so that traders do not have to physically meet. The Chicago Board Options Exchange launched CBOEdirect in 2001. Initially it will be used to trade certain options outside regular trading hours, but it is likely that eventually it will be used for all trading.

### Market Makers

Most options exchanges use market makers to facilitate trading. A market maker for a certain option is an individual who, when asked to do so, will quote both a bid and an offer price on the option. The bid is the price at which the market maker is prepared to buy, and the offer is the price at which the market maker is prepared to sell. At the time the bid and the offer are quoted, the market maker does not know whether the trader who asked for the quotes wants to buy or sell the option. The offer is always higher than the bid, and the amount by which the offer exceeds the bid is referred to as the bid–offer spread. The exchange sets upper limits for the bid–offer spread. For example, it might specify that the spread be no more than $0.25 for options priced at less than $0.50, $0.50 for options priced between $0.50 and $10, $0.75 for options priced between $10 and $20, and $1 for options priced over $20.

The existence of the market maker ensures that buy and sell orders can always be executed at some price without any delays. Market makers therefore add liquidity to the market. The market makers themselves make their profits from the bid–offer spread. They use some of the procedures discussed later in this book to hedge their risks.

### Offsetting Orders

An investor who has purchased an option can close out the position by issuing an offsetting order to sell the same option. Similarly, an investor who has written an option can close out the position by issuing an offsetting order to buy the same option. If, when an options contract is traded, neither investor is offsetting an existing position, the open interest increases by one contract. If one investor is offsetting an existing position and the other is not, the open interest stays the same. If both investors are offsetting existing positions, the open interest goes down by one contract.

## 7.5 COMMISSIONS

The types of orders that can be placed with a broker for options trading are similar to those for futures trading (see Section 2.8). A market order is to be executed immediately; a limit order specifies the least favorable price at which the order can be executed; and so on.

**Table 7.3**  A typical commission schedule for a discount broker

| Dollar amount of trade | Commission* |
| --- | --- |
| < $2,500 | $20 + 0.02 of dollar amount |
| $2,500 to $10,000 | $45 + 0.01 of dollar amount |
| > $10,000 | $120 + 0.0025 of dollar amount |

* Maximum commission is $30 per contract for the first five contracts plus $20 per contract for each additional contract. Minimum commission is $30 per contract for the first contract plus $2 per contract for each additional contract.

For a retail investor, commissions vary significantly from broker to broker. Discount brokers generally charge lower commissions than full-service brokers. The actual amount charged is often calculated as a fixed cost plus a proportion of the dollar amount of the trade. Table 7.3 shows the sort of schedule that might be offered by a discount broker. Thus, the purchase of eight contracts when the option price is $3 would cost $20 + (0.02 × $2,400) = $68 in commissions.

If an option position is closed out by entering into an offsetting trade, the commission must be paid again. If the option is exercised, the commission is the same as it would be if the investor placed an order to buy or sell the underlying stock. Typically, this is 1% to 2% of the stock's value.

Consider an investor who buys one call contract with a strike price of $50 when the stock price is $49. We suppose the option price is $4.50, so that the cost of the contract is $450. Under the schedule in Table 7.3, the purchase or sale of one contract always costs $30 (both the maximum and minimum commission is $30 for the first contract). Suppose that the stock price rises and the option is exercised when the stock reaches $60. Assuming that the investor pays 1.5% commission on stock trades, the commission payable when the option is exercised is

$$0.015 \times \$60 \times 100 = \$90$$

The total commission paid is therefore $120, and the net profit to the investor is

$$\$1,000 - \$450 - \$120 = \$430$$

Note that selling the option for $10 instead of exercising it would save the investor $60 in commissions. (The commission payable when an option is sold is only $30 in our example.) In general, the commission system tends to push retail investors in the direction of selling options rather than exercising them.

A hidden cost in option trading (and in stock trading) is the market maker's bid–offer spread. Suppose that, in the example just considered, the bid price was $4.00 and the offer price was $4.50 at the time the option was purchased. We can reasonably assume that a "fair" price for the option is halfway between the bid and the offer price, or $4.25. The cost to the buyer and to the seller of the market maker system is the difference between the fair price and the price paid. This is $0.25 per option, or $25 per contract.

## 7.6  MARGINS

In the United States, when shares are purchased, an investor can either pay cash or borrow using a margin account. (This is known as *buying on margin*.) The initial margin is usually 50% of the value of the shares, and the maintenance margin is usually 25% of the value of the shares. The margin account operates similarly to that for a futures contract (see Chapter 2).

When call and put options are purchased, the option price must be paid in full. Investors are not allowed to buy options on margin, because options already contain substantial leverage. Buying on margin would raise this leverage to an unacceptable level. An investor who writes options is required to maintain funds in a margin account. Both the investor's broker and the exchange want to be satisfied that the investor will not default if the option is exercised. The size of the margin required depends on the circumstances.

### Writing Naked Options

A *naked option* is an option that is not combined with an offsetting position in the underlying stock. The initial margin for a written naked call option is the greater of the following two calculations:

1. A total of 100% of the proceeds of the sale plus 20% of the underlying share price less the amount if any by which the option is out of the money
2. A total of 100% of the option proceeds plus 10% of the underlying share price

For a written naked put option it is the greater of:

1. A total of 100% of the proceeds of the sale plus 20% of the underlying share price less the amount if any by which the option is out of the money
2. A total of 100% of the option proceeds plus 10% of the exercise price

The 20% in the preceding calculations is replaced by 15% for options on a broadly based stock index, because a stock index is usually less volatile than the price of an individual stock.

> **Example 7.3**   An investor writes four naked call option contracts on a stock. The option price is $5, the strike price is $40, and the stock price is $38. Because the option is $2 out of the money, the first calculation gives
> $$400(5 + 0.2 \times 38 - 2) = \$4,240$$
> The second calculation gives
> $$400(5 + 0.1 \times 38) = \$3,520$$
>
> The initial margin requirement is therefore $4,240. Note that if the option had been a put, it would be $2 in the money and the margin requirement would be
> $$400(5 + 0.2 \times 38) = \$5,040$$
>
> In both cases the proceeds of the sale, $2,000, can be used to form part of the margin account.

A calculation similar to the initial margin calculation (but with the current market price replacing the proceeds of sale) is repeated every day. Funds can be withdrawn from the margin account when the calculation indicates that the margin required is less than the current balance in the margin account. When the calculation indicates that a significantly greater margin is required, a margin call will be made.

### Writing Covered Calls

Writing covered calls involves writing call options when the shares that might have to be delivered are already owned. Covered calls are far less risky than naked calls, because the worst that can happen is that the investor is required to sell shares already owned at below their market value. If covered call options are out of the money, no margin is required. The shares owned can be purchased using a margin account, as described previously, and the price received for the option can be used to partially fulfill this margin requirement. If the options are in the money, no margin is required for the options. However, for the purposes of calculating the investor's equity position, the share price is reduced by the extent, if any, to which the option is in the money. This may limit the amount that the investor can withdraw from the margin account if the share price increases.

> **Example 7.4** An investor in the United States decides to buy 200 shares of a certain stock on margin and to write two call option contracts on the stock. The stock price is $63, the strike price is $60, and the price of the option is $7. The margin account allows the investor to borrow 50% of the price of the stock, or $6,300. The investor is also able to use the price received for the option, $7 \times 200 = \$1,400$, to finance the purchase of the shares. The shares cost $63 \times 200 = \$12,600$. The minimum cash initially required from the investor for the trades is therefore
>
> $$\$12,600 - \$6,300 - \$1,400 = \$4,900$$

In Chapter 9, we will examine more complicated option trading strategies such as spreads, combinations, straddles, and strangles. There are special rules for determining the margin requirements when these trading strategies are used.

## 7.7 THE OPTIONS CLEARING CORPORATION

The Options Clearing Corporation (OCC) performs much the same function for options markets as the clearinghouse does for futures markets (see Chapter 2). It guarantees that options writers will fulfill their obligations under the terms of options contracts and keeps a record of all long and short positions. The OCC has a number of members, and all options trades must be cleared through a member. If a brokerage house is not itself a member of an exchange's OCC, it must arrange to clear its trades with a member. Members are required to have a certain minimum amount of capital and to contribute to a special fund that can be used if any member defaults on an option obligation.

When purchasing an option, the buyer must pay for it in full by the morning of the next business day. The funds are deposited with the OCC. The writer of the option maintains a margin account with a broker, as described earlier. The broker maintains a margin account with the OCC member that clears its trades. The OCC member in turn maintains a margin account with the OCC. The margin requirements described in the previous section are the margin requirements imposed by the OCC on its members. A brokerage house may require higher margins from its clients. However, it cannot require lower margins.

### Exercising an Option

When an investor notifies a broker to exercise an option, the broker in turn notifies the OCC member that clears its trades. This member then places an exercise order with the OCC. The OCC randomly selects a member with an outstanding short position in the same option. The member, using a procedure established in advance, selects a particular investor who has written the option. If the option is a call, this investor is required to sell stock at the strike price. If it is a put, the investor is required to buy stock at the strike price. The investor is said to be *assigned*. When an option is exercised, the open interest goes down by one.

At the expiration of the option, all in-the-money options should be exercised unless the transactions costs are so high as to wipe out the payoff from the option. Some brokerage firms will automatically exercise options for their clients at expiration when it is in their clients' interest to do so. Many exchanges also have rules for exercising options that are in the money at expiration.

## 7.8 REGULATION

Options markets are regulated in a number of different ways. Both the exchange and its Options Clearing Corporation have rules governing the behavior of traders. In addition, there are both federal and state regulatory authorities. In general, options markets have demonstrated a willingness to regulate themselves. There have been no major scandals or defaults by OCC members. Investors can have a high level of confidence in the way the market is run.

The Securities and Exchange Commission is responsible for regulating options markets in stocks, stock indices, currencies, and bonds at the federal level. The Commodity Futures Trading Commission is responsible for regulating markets for options on futures. The major options markets are in the states of Illinois and New York. These states actively enforce their own laws on unacceptable trading practices.

## 7.9 TAXATION

Determining the tax implications of options strategies can be tricky, and an investor who is in doubt about this should consult a tax specialist. In the United States, the general rule is that (unless the taxpayer is a professional trader) gains and losses from the trading of stock options are taxed as capital gains or losses. We discussed the way capital gains and losses are taxed in the United States in Section 2.10. For both the holder and the writer of a stock option, a gain or loss is recognized when (a) the option expires unexercised or (b) the option position is closed out. If the option is exercised, the gain or loss from the option is rolled into the position taken in the stock and recognized when the stock position is closed out. For example, when a call option is exercised, the party with a long position is deemed to have purchased the stock at the strike price plus the call price. This is then used as a basis for calculating this party's gain or loss when the stock is eventually sold. Similarly, the party with the short position is deemed to have sold at the call price plus the strike price. When a put option is exercised, the writer is deemed to have bought stock for the strike price less the original put price and the purchaser is deemed to have sold the stock for this price.

### Wash Sale Rule

One tax consideration in option trading in the United States is the wash sale rule. To understand this rule, imagine an investor who buys a stock when the price is $60 and plans to keep it for the long term. If the stock price drops to $40, the investor might be tempted to sell the stock and then immediately repurchase it so that the $20 loss is realized for tax purposes. To prevent this sort of thing, the tax authorities have ruled that, when the repurchase is within 30 days of the sale (i.e., between 30 days before the sale and 30 days after the sale), any loss on the sale is not deductible.

The disallowance also applies where, within the 61-day period, the taxpayer enters into an option or similar contract to acquire the stock. Thus, selling a stock at a loss and buying a call option within a 30-day period will lead to the loss being disallowed. The wash sale rule does not apply if the taxpayer is a dealer in stocks or securities and the loss is sustained in the ordinary course of business.

### Constructive Sales

Prior to 1997, if a United States taxpayer shorted a security while holding a long position in a substantially identical security, no gain or loss was recognized until the short position was closed out. This means that short positions could be used to defer recognition of a gain for tax purposes. The situation was changed by the Tax Relief Act of 1997. An appreciated property is now treated as "constructively sold" when the owner does one of the following:

1. Enters into a short sale of the same or substantially identical property
2. Enters into a futures or forward contract to deliver the same or substantially identical property
3. Enters into one or more positions that eliminate substantially all of the loss and opportunity for gain

It should be noted that transactions reducing only the risk of loss or only the opportunity for gain should not result in constructive sales. Therefore, an investor holding a long position in a stock can buy in-the-money put options on the stock without triggering a constructive sale.

### Tax Planning Using Options

Tax practitioners sometimes use options to minimize tax costs or maximize tax benefits. For example, it is sometimes advantageous to receive the income from a security in Country A and the capital gain/loss in country B. This could be the case if Country A has a tax regime that provides for a low effective tax rate on interest and dividends and a relatively high tax rate on capital gains. One can accomplish this by arranging for a company in Country A to have legal ownership of the security and for a related company in Country B to buy a call option on the security from the company in country A with the strike price of the option equal to the current value of the security. As another example, consider the position of a company with a large holding in a particular stock whose price has risen fast during the holding period. Suppose the company wants to sell the stock. If it does so in the usual way, it will be subject to capital gains tax. An alternative strategy is to borrow funds for 20 years under an agreement where the company has the option at the end of the 20 years to repay the loan with the stock. This delays the recognition of the capital gain.

Tax authorities in many jurisdictions have proposed legislation designed to combat the use of derivatives for tax purposes. Before entering into any tax-motivated transaction, a treasurer should explore in detail how the structure could be unwound in the event of legislative change and how costly this process could be.

## 7.10 WARRANTS, EXECUTIVE STOCK OPTIONS, AND CONVERTIBLES

Usually, when a call option on a stock is exercised, the party with the short position acquires shares that have already been issued and sells them to the party with the long position for the strike price. The company whose stock underlies the option is not involved in any way. Warrants and executive stock options are call options that work slightly differently. They are written by a company on its own stock. When they are exercised, the company issues more of its own stock and sells them to the option holder for the strike price. The exercise of a warrant or executive stock option therefore leads to an increase in the number of shares of the company's stock that are outstanding.

*Warrants* are call options that often come into existence as a result of a bond issue. They are added to the bond issue to make it more attractive to investors. Typically, warrants last for a number of years. Once they have been created, they sometimes trade separately from the bonds to which they were originally attached.

*Executive stock options* are call options issued to executives to motivate them to act in the best interests of the company's shareholders. They are usually at the money when they are first issued. After a period of time they become vested and can be exercised. Executive stock options cannot be traded. They often last as long as 10 or 15 years.

A *convertible bond* is a bond issued by a company that can be converted into equity at certain times using a predetermined exchange ratio. It is therefore a bond with an embedded call option on the company's stock. Convertible bonds are like warrants and executive stock options in that their exercise leads to more shares being issued by the company. We discuss convertible bonds in more detail in Chapter 27.

## 7.11 OVER-THE-COUNTER MARKETS

Most of this chapter has focused on exchange-traded options markets. The over-the-counter market for options has become increasingly important since the early 1980s and is now larger than the exchange-traded market. As explained in Chapter 1, in the over-the-counter market, financial institutions, corporate treasurers, and fund managers trade over the phone. There is a wide range of assets underlying the options. Over-the-counter options on foreign exchange and interest rates are particularly popular. The chief potential disadvantage of the over-the-counter market is that option writer may default. This means that the purchaser is subject to some credit risk. In an attempt to overcome this disadvantage, market participants are adopting a number of measures such as requiring counterparties to post collateral.

The instruments traded in the over-the-counter market are often structured by financial institutions to meet the precise needs of their clients. Sometimes this involves choosing exercise dates, strike prices, and contract sizes that are different from those traded by the exchange. In other cases the structure of the option is different from standard calls and puts. The option is then referred to as an *exotic option*. Chapter 19 covers a number of different types of exotic options.

## SUMMARY

There are two types of options: calls and puts. A call option gives the holder the right to buy the underlying asset for a certain price by a certain date. A put option gives the holder the right to sell the underlying asset by a certain date for a certain price. There are four possible positions in options markets: a long position in a call, a short position in a call, a long position in a put, and a short position in a put. Taking a short position in an option is known as writing it.

Options are currently traded on stocks, stock indices, foreign currencies, futures contracts, and other assets.

An exchange must specify the terms of the option contracts it trades. In particular, it must specify the size of the contract, the precise expiration time, and the strike price. In the United States one stock option contract gives the holder the right to buy or sell 100 shares. The expiration of a stock option contract is 10:59 p.m. Central Time on the Saturday immediately following the third Friday of the expiration month. Options with several different expiration months trade at any given time. Strike prices are at $2\frac{1}{2}$, \$5, or \$10 intervals, depending on the stock price. The strike price is generally fairly close to the current stock price when trading in an option begins.

The terms of a stock option are not normally adjusted for cash dividends. However, they are adjusted for stock dividends, stock splits, and rights issues. The aim of the adjustment is to keep the positions of both the writer and the buyer of a contract unchanged.

Most options exchanges use market makers. A market maker is an individual who is prepared to quote both a bid price (the price at which he or she is prepared to buy) and an offer price (the price at which he or she is prepared to sell). Market makers improve the liquidity of the market and ensure that there is never any delay in executing market orders. They themselves make a profit from the difference between their bid and offer prices (known as the bid–offer spread). The exchange has rules specifying upper limits for the bid–offer spread.

Writers of options have potential liabilities and are required to maintain margins with their brokers. If it is not a member of the Options Clearing Corporation, the broker will maintain a margin account with a firm that is a member. This firm will in turn maintain a margin account with the Options Clearing Corporation. The Options Clearing Corporation is responsible for keeping a record of all outstanding contracts, handling exercise orders, and so on.

Not all options are traded on exchanges. Many options are traded by phone in the over-the-counter market. An advantage of over-the-counter options is that they can be tailored by a financial institution to meet the particular needs of a corporate treasurer or fund manager.

## SUGGESTIONS FOR FURTHER READING

Chance, D. M., *An Introduction to Derivatives*, 4th edn., Dryden Press, Orlando, FL, 1998.

Cox, J. C., and M. Rubinstein, *Options Markets*, Prentice Hall, Upper Saddle River, NJ, 1985.

Kolb, R., *Futures, Options, and Swaps*, 3rd edn., Blackwell, Oxford, 1999.

McMillan, L. G., *Options as a Strategic Investment*, New York Institute of Finance, New York, 1992.

## QUESTIONS AND PROBLEMS
## (ANSWERS IN SOLUTIONS MANUAL)

7.1. Explain why brokers require margins when clients write options but not when they buy options.

7.2. A stock option is on a February, May, August, and November cycle. What options trade on (a) April 1 and (b) May 30?

7.3. A company declares a 3-for-1 stock split. Explain how the terms change for a call option with a strike price of \$60.

7.4. Explain carefully the difference between writing a put option and buying a call option.

7.5. A corporate treasurer is designing a hedging program involving foreign currency options. What are the pros and cons of using (a) the Philadelphia Stock Exchange and (b) the over-the-counter market for trading?

7.6. Explain why an American option is always worth at least as much as a European option on the same asset with the same strike price and exercise date.

7.7. Explain why an American option is always worth at least as much as its intrinsic value.

7.8. The treasurer of a corporation is trying to choose between options and forward contracts to hedge the corporation's foreign exchange risk. Discuss the relative advantages and disadvantages of each.

7.9. Consider an exchange-traded call option contract to buy 500 shares with a strike price of $40 and maturity in four months. Explain how the terms of the option contract change when there is
   a. A 10% stock dividend
   b. A 10% cash dividend
   c. A 4-for-1 stock split

7.10. "If most of the call options on a stock are in the money, it is likely that the stock price has risen rapidly in the last few months." Discuss this statement.

7.11. What is the effect of an unexpected cash dividend on (a) a call option price and (b) a put option price?

7.12. Options on General Motors stock are on a March, June, September, and December cycle. What options trade on (a) March 1, (b) June 30, and (c) August 5?

7.13. Explain why the market maker's bid–offer spread represents a real cost to options investors.

7.14. A United States investor writes five naked call option contracts. The option price is $3.50, the strike price is $60.00, and the stock price is $57.00. What is the initial margin requirement?

## ASSIGNMENT QUESTIONS

7.15. A United States investor buys 500 shares of a stock and sells five call option contracts on the stock. The strike price is $30. The price of the option is $3. What is the investor's minimum cash investment (a) if the stock price is $28 and (b) if it is $32?

7.16. The price of a stock is $40. The price of a one-year European put option on the stock with a strike price of $30 is quoted as $7 and the price of a one-year European call option on the stock with a strike price of $50 is quoted as $5. Suppose that an investor buys 100 shares, shorts 100 call options, and buys 100 put options. Draw a diagram illustrating how the investor's profit or loss varies with the stock price over the next year. How does your answer change if the investor buys 100 shares, shorts 200 call options, and buys 200 put options?

7.17. "If a company does not do better than its competitors but the stock market goes up, executives do very well from their stock options. This makes no sense." Discuss this viewpoint. Can you think of alternatives to the usual executive stock option plan that take the viewpoint into account.

7.18. Use DerivaGem to calculate the value of an American put option on a nondividend paying stock when the stock price is $30, the strike price is $32, the risk-free rate is 5%, the volatility is 30%, and the time to maturity is 1.5 years. (Choose binomial American for the "option type" and 50 time steps.)

a.  What is the option's intrinsic value?

b.  What is the option's time value?

c.  What would a time value of zero indicate? What is the value of an option with zero time value?

d.  Using a trial-and-error approach, calculate how low the stock price would have to be for the time value of the option to be zero.

# CHAPTER 8

# PROPERTIES OF STOCK OPTIONS

In this chapter we look at the factors affecting stock option prices. We use a number of different arbitrage arguments to explore the relationships between European option prices, American option prices, and the underlying stock price. The most important of these relationships is put–call parity, which is a relationship between European call option prices and European put option prices.

The chapter examines whether American options should be exercised early. It shows that it is never optimal to exercise an American call option on a non-dividend-paying stock prior to the option's expiration, but the early exercise of an American put option on such a stock can be optimal.

## 8.1 FACTORS AFFECTING OPTION PRICES

There are six factors affecting the price of a stock option:

1. The current stock price, $S_0$
2. The strike price, $K$
3. The time to expiration, $T$
4. The volatility of the stock price, $\sigma$
5. The risk-free interest rate, $r$
6. The dividends expected during the life of the option

In this section we consider what happens to option prices when one of these factors changes with all the others remaining fixed. The results are summarized in Table 8.1.

Figures 8.1 and 8.2 show how the price of a European call and put depends on the first five factors in the situation where $S_0 = 50$, $K = 50$, $r = 5\%$ per annum, $\sigma = 30\%$ per annum, $T = 1$ year, and there are no dividends. In this case the call price is 7.116 and the put price is 4.677.

### Stock Price and Strike Price

If a call option is exercised at some future time, the payoff will be the amount by which the stock price exceeds the strike price. Call options therefore become more valuable as the stock price increases and less valuable as the strike price increases. For a put option, the payoff on exercise is the amount by which the strike price exceeds the stock price. Put options therefore behave in the opposite way from call options. They become less valuable as the stock price increases and more valuable as the strike price increases. Figures 8.1a, b, c, d illustrate the way in which put and call prices depend on the stock price and strike price.

167

**Table 8.1** Summary of the effect on the price of a stock option of increasing one variable while keeping all others fixed.*

| Variable | European call | European put | American call | American put |
|---|---|---|---|---|
| Current stock price | + | − | + | − |
| Strike price | − | + | − | + |
| Time to expiration | ? | ? | + | + |
| Volatility | + | + | + | + |
| Risk-free rate | + | − | + | − |
| Dividends | − | + | − | + |

* + indicates that an increase in the variable causes the option price to increase; − indicates that an increase in the variable causes the option price to decrease; ? indicates that the relationship is uncertain.

### Time to Expiration

Consider next the effect of the expiration date. Both put and call American options become more valuable as the time to expiration increases. Consider two options that differ only as far as the expiration date is concerned. The owner of the long-life option has all the exercise opportunities open to the owner of the short-life option—and more. The long-life option must therefore always be worth at least as much as the short-life option. Figures 8.1e, f illustrate the way in which calls and puts depend on the time to expiration.

Although European put and call options usually become more valuable as the time to expiration increases, this is not always the case. Consider two European call options on a stock: one with an expiration date in one month, and the other with an expiration date in two months. Suppose that a very large dividend is expected in six weeks. The dividend will cause the stock price to decline, so that the short-life option could be worth more than the long-life option.

### Volatility

The precise way in which volatility is defined is explained in Chapters 11 and 12. Roughly speaking, the *volatility* of a stock price is a measure of how uncertain we are about future stock price movements. As volatility increases, the chance that the stock will do very well or very poorly increases. For the owner of a stock, these two outcomes tend to offset each other. However, this is not so for the owner of a call or put. The owner of a call benefits from price increases but has limited downside risk in the event of price decreases because the most the owner can lose is the price of the option. Similarly, the owner of a put benefits from price decreases, but has limited downside risk in the event of price increases. The values of both calls and puts therefore increase as volatility increases (see Figures 8.2a, b).

### Risk-Free Interest Rate

The risk-free interest rate affects the price of an option in a less clear-cut way. As interest rates in the economy increase, the expected return required by investors from the stock tends to increase. Also, the present value of any future cash flow received by the holder of the option decreases. The combined impact of these two effects is to decrease the value of put options and increase the value of call options (see Figures 8.2c, d).

It is important to emphasize that we are assuming that interest rates change while all other variables stay the same. In particular, we are assuming that interest rates change while the stock price remains the same. In practice, when interest rates rise (fall), stock prices tend to fall (rise). The net effect of an interest rate increase and the accompanying stock price decrease can be to decrease the value of a call option and increase the value of a put option. Similarly, the net effect of an

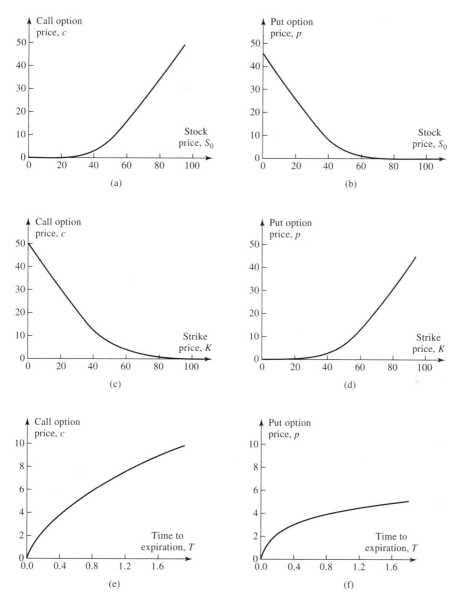

**Figure 8.1** Effect of changes in stock price, strike price, and expiration date on option prices when $S_0 = 50$, $K = 50$, $r = 5\%$, $\sigma = 30\%$, and $T = 1$.

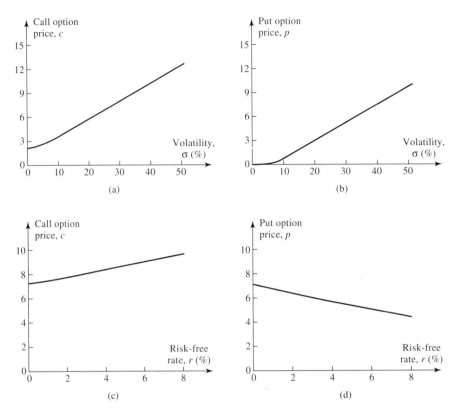

**Figure 8.2**   Effect of changes in volatility and risk-free interest rate on option prices when $S_0 = 50$, $K = 50$, $r = 5\%$, $\sigma = 30\%$, and $T = 1$.

interest rate decrease and the accompanying stock price increase can be to increase the value of a call option and decrease the value of a put option.

### Dividends

Dividends have the effect of reducing the stock price on the ex-dividend date. This is bad news for the value of call options and good news for the value of put options. The value of a call option is therefore negatively related to the size of any anticipated dividends, and the value of a put option is positively related to the size of any anticipated dividends.

## 8.2   ASSUMPTIONS AND NOTATION

In this chapter we will make assumptions similar to those made for deriving forward and futures prices in Chapter 3. We assume that there are some market participants, such as large investment banks, for which

1. There are no transactions costs.

2. All trading profits (net of trading losses) are subject to the same tax rate.

3. Borrowing and lending are possible at the risk-free interest rate.

We assume that these market participants are prepared to take advantage of arbitrage opportunities as they arise. As discussed in Chapters 1 and 3, this means that any available arbitrage opportunities disappear very quickly. For the purposes of our analyses, it is therefore reasonable to assume that there are no arbitrage opportunities.

We will use the following notation:

$S_0$ : Current stock price

$K$ : Strike price of option

$T$ : Time to expiration of option

$S_T$ : Stock price at maturity

$r$ : Continuously compounded risk-free rate of interest for an investment maturing in time $T$

$C$ : Value of American call option to buy one share

$P$ : Value of American put option to sell one share

$c$ : Value of European call option to buy one share

$p$ : Value of European put option to sell one share

It should be noted that $r$ is the nominal rate of interest, not the real rate of interest. We can assume that $r > 0$; otherwise, a risk-free investment would provide no advantages over cash. (Indeed, if $r < 0$, cash would be preferable to a risk-free investment.)

## 8.3 UPPER AND LOWER BOUNDS FOR OPTION PRICES

In this section we derive upper and lower bounds for option prices. These bounds do not depend on any particular assumptions about the factors mentioned in the previous section (except $r > 0$). If an option price is above the upper bound or below the lower bound, there are profitable opportunities for arbitrageurs.

### Upper Bounds

An American or European call option gives the holder the right to buy one share of a stock for a certain price. No matter what happens, the option can never be worth more than the stock. Hence, the stock price is an upper bound to the option price:

$$c \leqslant S_0 \quad \text{and} \quad C \leqslant S_0$$

If these relationships were not true, an arbitrageur could easily make a riskless profit by buying the stock and selling the call option.

An American or European put option gives the holder the right to sell one share of a stock for $K$. No matter how low the stock price becomes, the option can never be worth more than $K$. Hence,

$$p \leqslant K \quad \text{and} \quad P \leqslant K$$

For European options, we know that at maturity the option cannot be worth more than $K$. It follows that it cannot be worth more than the present value of $K$ today:

$$p \leqslant Ke^{-rT}$$

If this were not true, an arbitrageur could make a riskless profit by writing the option and investing the proceeds of the sale at the risk-free interest rate.

### Lower Bound for Calls on Non-Dividend-Paying Stocks

A lower bound for the price of a European call option on a non-dividend-paying stock is

$$S_0 - Ke^{-rT}$$

We first look at a numerical example and then consider a more formal argument.

Suppose that $S_0 = \$20$, $K = \$18$, $r = 10\%$ per annum, and $T = 1$ year. In this case,

$$S_0 - Ke^{-rT} = 20 - 18e^{-0.1} = 3.71$$

or $3.71. Consider the situation where the European call price is $3.00, which is less than the theoretical minimum of $3.71. An arbitrageur can buy the call and short the stock to provide a cash inflow of $20.00 - \$3.00 = \$17.00$. If invested for one year at 10% per annum, the $17.00 grows to $17e^{0.1} = \$18.79$. At the end of the year, the option expires. If the stock price is greater than $18.00, the arbitrageur exercises the option to buy the stock for $18.00, closes out the short position, and makes a profit of

$$\$18.79 - \$18.00 = \$0.79$$

If the stock price is less than $18.00, the stock is bought in the market and the short position is closed out. The arbitrageur then makes an even greater profit. For example, if the stock price is $17.00, the arbitrageur's profit is

$$\$18.79 - \$17.00 = \$1.79$$

For a more formal argument, we consider the following two portfolios:

*Portfolio A*: one European call option plus an amount of cash equal to $Ke^{-rT}$

*Portfolio B*: one share

In portfolio A, the cash, if it is invested at the risk-free interest rate, will grow to $K$ in time $T$. If $S_T > K$, the call option is exercised at maturity and portfolio A is worth $S_T$. If $S_T < K$, the call option expires worthless and the portfolio is worth $K$. Hence, at time $T$, portfolio A is worth

$$\max(S_T, K)$$

Portfolio B is worth $S_T$ at time $T$. Hence, portfolio A is always worth as much as, and can be worth more than, portfolio B at the option's maturity. It follows that in the absence of arbitrage opportunities this must also be true today. Hence,

$$c + Ke^{-rT} \geqslant S_0$$

or

$$c \geqslant S_0 - Ke^{-rT}$$

Because the worst that can happen to a call option is that it expires worthless, its value cannot be negative. This means that $c \geqslant 0$, and therefore that

$$c \geqslant \max(S_0 - Ke^{-rT}, 0) \tag{8.1}$$

**Example 8.1** Consider a European call option on a non-dividend-paying stock when the stock price is \$51, the exercise price is \$50, the time to maturity is six months, and the risk-free rate of interest is 12% per annum. In this case, $S_0 = 51$, $K = 50$, $T = 0.5$, and $r = 0.12$. From equation (8.1), a lower bound for the option price is $S_0 - Ke^{-rT}$, or

$$51 - 50e^{-0.12 \times 0.5} = \$3.91$$

### Lower Bound for European Puts on Non-Dividend-Paying Stocks

For a European put option on a non-dividend-paying stock, a lower bound for the price is

$$Ke^{-rT} - S_0$$

Again, we first consider a numerical example and then look at a more formal argument.

Suppose that $S_0 = \$37$, $K = \$40$, $r = 5\%$ per annum, and $T = 0.5$ years. In this case,

$$Ke^{-rT} - S_0 = 40e^{-0.05 \times 0.5} - 37 = \$2.01$$

Consider the situation where the European put price is \$1.00, which is less than the theoretical minimum of \$2.01. An arbitrageur can borrow \$38.00 for six months to buy both the put and the stock. At the end of the six months, the arbitrageur will be required to repay $38e^{0.05 \times 0.5} = \$38.96$. If the stock price is below \$40.00, the arbitrageur exercises the option to sell the stock for \$40.00, repays the loan, and makes a profit of

$$\$40.00 - \$38.96 = \$1.04$$

If the stock price is greater than \$40.00, the arbitrageur discards the option, sells the stock, and repays the loan for an even greater profit. For example, if the stock price is \$42.00, the arbitrageur's profit is

$$\$42.00 - \$38.96 = \$3.04$$

For a more formal argument, we consider the following two portfolios:

*Portfolio C*: one European put option plus one share

*Portfolio D*: an amount of cash equal to $Ke^{-rT}$

If $S_T < K$, the option in portfolio C is exercised at option maturity, and the portfolio becomes worth $K$. If $S_T > K$, the put option expires worthless, and the portfolio is worth $S_T$ at this time. Hence, portfolio C is worth

$$\max(S_T, K)$$

at time $T$. Assuming the cash is invested at the risk-free interest rate, portfolio D is worth $K$ at time $T$. Hence, portfolio C is always worth as much as, and can sometimes be worth more than, portfolio D at time $T$. It follows that in the absence of arbitrage opportunities portfolio C must be worth at least as much as portfolio D today. Hence,

$$p + S_0 \geqslant Ke^{-rT}$$

or

$$p \geqslant Ke^{-rT} - S_0$$

Because the worst that can happen to a put option is that it expires worthless, its value cannot be negative. This means that

$$p \geqslant \max(Ke^{-rT} - S_0, 0) \tag{8.2}$$

**Example 8.2**  Consider a European put option on a non-dividend-paying stock when the stock price is \$38, the exercise price is \$40, the time to maturity is three months, and the risk-free rate of interest is 10% per annum. In this case $S_0 = 38$, $K = 40$, $T = 0.25$, and $r = 0.10$. From equation (8.2), a lower bound for the option price is $Ke^{-rT} - S_0$, or

$$40e^{-0.1 \times 0.25} - 38 = \$1.01$$

## 8.4  PUT–CALL PARITY

We now derive an important relationship between $p$ and $c$. Consider the following two portfolios that were used in the previous section:

*Portfolio A*: one European call option plus an amount of cash equal to $Ke^{-rT}$

*Portfolio C*: one European put option plus one share

Both are worth

$$\max(S_T, K)$$

at expiration of the options. Because the options are European, they cannot be exercised prior to the expiration date. The portfolios must therefore have identical values today. This means that

$$c + Ke^{-rT} = p + S_0 \tag{8.3}$$

This relationship is known as *put–call parity*. It shows that the value of a European call with a certain exercise price and exercise date can be deduced from the value of a European put with the same exercise price and exercise date, and vice versa.

If equation (8.3) does not hold, there are arbitrage opportunities. Suppose that the stock price is \$31, the exercise price is \$30, the risk-free interest rate is 10% per annum, the price of a three-month European call option is \$3, and the price of a three-month European put option is \$2.25. In this case,

$$c + Ke^{-rT} = 3 + 30e^{-0.1 \times 3/12} = \$32.26$$

$$p + S_0 = 2.25 + 31 = \$33.25$$

Portfolio C is overpriced relative to portfolio A. The correct arbitrage strategy is to buy the securities in portfolio A and short the securities in portfolio C. The strategy involves buying the call and shorting both the put and the stock, generating a positive cash flow of

$$-3 + 2.25 + 31 = \$30.25$$

up front. When invested at the risk-free interest rate, this amount grows to $30.25e^{0.1 \times 0.25} = \$31.02$ in three months.

If the stock price at expiration of the option is greater than $30, the call will be exercised. If it is less than $30, the put will be exercised. In either case, the investor ends up buying one share for $30. This share can be used to close out the short position. The net profit is therefore

$$\$31.02 - \$30.00 = \$1.02$$

For an alternative situation, suppose that the call price is $3 and the put price is $1. In this case,

$$c + Ke^{-rT} = 3 + 30e^{-0.1 \times 3/12} = \$32.26$$
$$p + S_0 = 1 + 31 = \$32.00$$

Portfolio A is overpriced relative to portfolio C. An arbitrageur can short the securities in portfolio A and buy the securities in portfolio C to lock in a profit. The strategy involves shorting the call and buying both the put and the stock with an initial investment of

$$\$31 + \$1 - \$3 = \$29$$

When the investment is financed at the risk-free interest rate, a repayment of $29e^{0.1 \times 0.25} = \$29.73$ is required at the end of the three months. As in the previous case, either the call or the put will be exercised. The short call and long put option position therefore leads to the stock being sold for $30.00. The net profit is therefore

$$\$30.00 - \$29.73 = \$0.27$$

### American Options

Put–call parity holds only for European options. However, it is possible to derive some results for American option prices. It can be shown (see Problem 8.17) that

$$S_0 - K \leqslant C - P \leqslant S_0 - Ke^{-rT} \tag{8.4}$$

**Example 8.3** An American call option on a non-dividend-paying stock with exercise price $20.00 and maturity in five months is worth $1.50. Suppose that the current stock price is $19.00 and the risk-free interest rate is 10% per annum. From equation (8.4),

$$19 - 20 \leqslant C - P \leqslant 19 - 20e^{-0.1 \times 5/12}$$

or

$$1 \geqslant P - C \geqslant 0.18$$

showing that $P - C$ lies between $1.00 and $0.18. With $C$ at $1.50, $P$ must lie between $1.68 and $2.50. In other words, upper and lower bounds for the price of an American put with the same strike price and expiration date as the American call are $2.50 and $1.68.

## 8.5 EARLY EXERCISE: CALLS ON A NON-DIVIDEND-PAYING STOCK

This section demonstrates that it is never optimal to exercise an American call option on a non-dividend-paying stock before the expiration date. To illustrate the general nature of the argument, consider an American call option on a non-dividend-paying stock with one month to expiration when the stock price is $50 and the strike price is $40. The option is deep in the money, and the

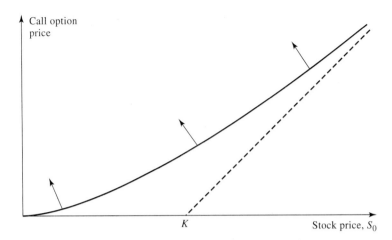

**Figure 8.3**   Variation of price of an American or European call option on a non-dividend-paying stock with the stock price, $S_0$.

investor who owns the option might well be tempted to exercise it immediately. However, if the investor plans to hold the stock for more than one month, this is not the best strategy. A better course of action is to keep the option and exercise it at the end of the month. The $40 strike price is then paid out one month later than it would be if the option were exercised immediately, so that interest is earned on the $40 for one month. Because the stock pays no dividends, no income from the stock is sacrificed. A further advantage of waiting rather than exercising immediately is that there is some chance (however remote) that the stock price will fall below $40 in one month. In this case the investor will not exercise and will be glad that the decision to exercise early was not taken!

This argument shows that there are no advantages to exercising early if the investor plans to keep the stock for the remaining life of the option (one month, in this case). What if the investor thinks the stock is currently overpriced and is wondering whether to exercise the option and sell the stock? In this case, the investor is better off selling the option than exercising it.[1] The option will be bought by another investor who does want to hold the stock. Such investors must exist; otherwise the current stock price would not be $50. The price obtained for the option will be greater than its intrinsic value of $10, for the reasons mentioned earlier.

For a more formal argument, we can use equation (8.1):

$$c \geqslant S_0 - Ke^{-rT}$$

Because the owner of an American call has all the exercise opportunities open to the owner of the corresponding European call, we must have $C \geqslant c$. Hence,

$$C \geqslant S_0 - Ke^{-rT}$$

Given $r > 0$, it follows that $C > S_0 - K$. If it were optimal to exercise early, $C$ would equal $S_0 - K$. We deduce that it can never be optimal to exercise early.

Figure 8.3 shows the general way in which the call price varies with $S_0$ and $K$. It indicates that the call price is always above its intrinsic value of $\max(S_0 - K, 0)$. As $r$ or $T$ or the volatility

---

[1] As an alternative strategy, the investor can keep the option and short the stock to lock in a better profit than $10.

increases, the line relating the call price to the stock price moves in the direction indicated by the arrows (i.e., farther away from the intrinsic value).

To summarize, there are two reasons an American call on a non-dividend-paying stock should not be exercised early. One relates to the insurance that it provides. A call option, when held instead of the stock itself, in effect insures the holder against the stock price falling below the exercise price. Once the option has been exercised and the exercise price has been exchanged for the stock price, this insurance vanishes. The other reason concerns the time value of money. From the perspective of the option holder, the later the strike price is paid out the better.

## 8.6 EARLY EXERCISE: PUTS ON A NON-DIVIDEND-PAYING STOCK

It can be optimal to exercise an American put option on a non-dividend-paying stock early. Indeed, at any given time during its life, a put option should always be exercised early if it is sufficiently deep in the money. To illustrate this, consider an extreme situation. Suppose that the strike price is $10 and the stock price is virtually zero. By exercising immediately, an investor makes an immediate gain of $10. If the investor waits, the gain from exercise might be less than $10, but it cannot be more than $10 because negative stock prices are impossible. Furthermore, receiving $10 now is preferable to receiving $10 in the future. It follows that the option should be exercised immediately.

Like a call option, a put option can be viewed as providing insurance. A put option, when held in conjunction with the stock, insures the holder against the stock price falling below a certain level. However, a put option is different from a call option in that it may be optimal for an investor to forgo this insurance and exercise early in order to realize the strike price immediately. In general, the early exercise of a put option becomes more attractive as $S_0$ decreases, as $r$ increases, and as the volatility decreases.

It will be recalled from equation (8.2) that

$$p \geqslant Ke^{-rT} - S_0$$

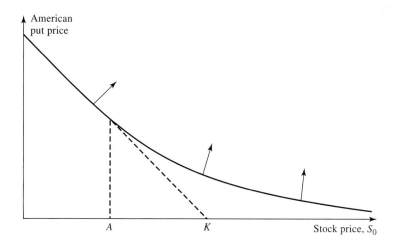

**Figure 8.4** Variation of price of an American put option with stock price, $S_0$

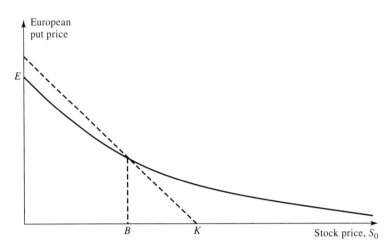

**Figure 8.5**   Variation of price of a European put option with the stock price, $S_0$

For an American put with price $P$, the stronger condition

$$P \geqslant K - S_0$$

must always hold because immediate exercise is always possible.

Figure 8.4 shows the general way in which the price of an American put varies with $S_0$. Provided that $r > 0$, it is always optimal to exercise an American put immediately when the stock price is sufficiently low. When early exercise is optimal, the value of the option is $K - S_0$. The curve representing the value of the put therefore merges into the put's intrinsic value, $K - S_0$, for a sufficiently small value of $S_0$. In Figure 8.4, this value of $S_0$ is shown as point A. The line relating the put price to the stock price moves in the direction indicated by the arrows when $r$ decreases, when the volatility increases, and when $T$ increases.

Because there are some circumstances when it is desirable to exercise an American put option early, it follows that an American put option is always worth more than the corresponding European put option. Furthermore, because an American put is sometimes worth its intrinsic value (see Figure 8.4), it follows that a European put option must sometimes be worth less than its intrinsic value. Figure 8.5 shows the variation of the European put price with the stock price. Note that point B in Figure 8.5, at which the price of the option is equal to its intrinsic value, must represent a higher value of the stock price than point A in Figure 8.4. Point E in Figure 8.5 is where $S_0 = 0$ and the European put price is $Ke^{-rT}$.

## 8.7   EFFECT OF DIVIDENDS

The results produced so far in this chapter have assumed that we are dealing with options on a non-dividend-paying stock. In this section we examine the impact of dividends. In the United States, exchange-traded stock options generally have less than eight months to maturity. The dividends payable during the life of the option can usually be predicted with reasonable accuracy. We will use $D$ to denote the present value of the dividends during the life of the option. In the calculation of $D$, a dividend is assumed to occur at the time of its ex-dividend date.

### Lower Bound for Calls and Puts

We can redefine portfolios A and B as follows:

*Portfolio A*: one European call option plus an amount of cash equal to $D + Ke^{-rT}$

*Portfolio B*: one share

A similar argument to the one used to derive equation (8.1) shows that

$$c \geqslant S_0 - D - Ke^{-rT} \tag{8.5}$$

We can also redefine portfolios C and D as follows:

*Portfolio C*: one European put option plus one share

*Portfolio D*: an amount of cash equal to $D + Ke^{-rT}$

A similar argument to the one used to derive equation (8.2) shows that

$$p \geqslant D + Ke^{-rT} - S_0 \tag{8.6}$$

### Early Exercise

When dividends are expected, we can no longer assert that an American call option will not be exercised early. Sometimes it is optimal to exercise an American call immediately prior to an ex-dividend date. It is never optimal to exercise a call at other times. This point is discussed further in Chapter 12.

### Put–Call Parity

Comparing the value at option maturity of the redefined portfolios A and C shows that, with dividends, the put–call parity result in equation (8.3) becomes

$$c + D + Ke^{-rT} = p + S_0 \tag{8.7}$$

Dividends cause equation (8.4) to be modified (see Problem 8.18) to

$$S_0 - D - K \leqslant C - P \leqslant S_0 - Ke^{-rT} \tag{8.8}$$

## 8.8 EMPIRICAL RESEARCH

Empirical research to test the results in this chapter might seem to be relatively simple to carry out once the appropriate data have been assembled. In fact, there are a number of complications:

1. It is important to be sure that option prices and stock prices are being observed at exactly the same time. For example, testing for arbitrage opportunities by looking at the price at which the last trade is done each day is inappropriate. This point was made in Chapter 7 in connection with the data in Table 7.1.

2. It is important to consider carefully whether a trader can take advantage of any observed arbitrage opportunity. If the opportunity exists only momentarily, there may in practice be no way of exploiting it.

3. Transactions costs must be taken into account when determining whether arbitrage opportunities are possible.

4. Put–call parity holds only for European options. Exchange-traded stock options are American.

5. Dividends to be paid during the life of the option must be estimated.

Some of the empirical research carried out in the early days of exchange-traded options markets is described in the papers by Bhattacharya (1983), Galai (1978), Gould and Galai (1974), Klemkosky and Resnick (1979, 1980), and Stoll (1969), all referenced at the end of this chapter. Galai and Bhattacharya test whether option prices are ever less than their theoretical lower bounds; Stoll, Gould and Galai, and the two papers by Klemkosky and Resnick test whether put–call parity holds. We will consider the results of Bhattacharya and of Klemkosky and Resnick.

Bhattacharya examined whether the theoretical lower bounds for call options applied in practice. He used data consisting of the transactions prices for options on 58 stocks over a 196-day period between August 1976 and June 1977. The first test examined whether the options satisfied the condition that price be at least as great as the intrinsic value—that is, whether $C \geqslant \max(S_0 - K, 0)$. More than 86,000 option prices were examined and about 1.3% were found to violate this condition. In 29% of the cases, the violation disappeared by the next trade, indicating that in practice traders would not have been able to take advantage of it. When transactions costs were taken into account, the profitable opportunities created by the violation disappeared. Bhattacharya's second test examined whether options sold for less than the lower bound $S_0 - D - Ke^{-rT}$ (see equation (8.5)). He found that 7.6% of his observations did in fact sell for less than this lower bound. However, when transactions costs were taken into account, these did not give rise to profitable opportunities.

Klemkosky and Resnick's tests of put–call parity used data on option prices taken from trades between July 1977 and June 1978. They subjected their data to several tests to determine the likelihood of options being exercised early, and they discarded data for which early exercise was considered probable. In doing so, they felt they were justified in treating American options as European. They identified 540 situations where the call price was too low relative to the put price and 540 situations where the reverse was true. After transactions costs were allowed for, 38 of the first set of situations and 147 of the second set of situations were still profitable. The opportunities persisted when either a 5- or a 15-minute delay between the opportunity being noted and trades being executed was assumed. Klemkosky and Resnick's conclusion was that arbitrage opportunities were available to some traders, particularly market makers, during the period they studied.

## SUMMARY

There are six factors affecting the value of a stock option: the current stock price, the strike price, the expiration date, the stock price volatility, the risk-free interest rate, and the dividends expected during the life of the option. The value of a call generally increases as the current stock price, the time to expiration, the volatility, and the risk-free interest rate increase. The value of a call decreases as the strike price and expected dividends increase. The value of a put generally increases as the strike price, the time to expiration, the volatility, and the expected dividends increase. The value of a put decreases as the current stock price and the risk-free interest rate increase.

It is possible to reach some conclusions about the value of stock options without making any assumptions about the volatility of stock prices. For example, the price of a call option on a stock must always be worth less than the price of the stock itself. Similarly, the price of a put option on a stock must always be worth less than the option's strike price.

A call option on a non-dividend-paying stock must be worth more than

$$\max(S_0 - Ke^{-rT}, 0)$$

where $S_0$ is the stock price, $K$ is the exercise price, $r$ is the risk-free interest rate, and $T$ is the time to expiration. A put option on a non-dividend-paying stock must be worth more than

$$\max(Ke^{-rT} - S_0, 0)$$

When dividends with present value $D$ will be paid, the lower bound for a call option becomes

$$\max(S_0 - D - Ke^{-rT}, 0)$$

and the lower bound for a put option becomes

$$\max(Ke^{-rT} + D - S_0, 0)$$

Put–call parity is a relationship between the price, $c$, of a European call option on a stock and the price, $p$, of a European put option on a stock. For a non-dividend-paying stock, it is

$$c + Ke^{-rT} = p + S_0$$

For a dividend-paying stock, the put–call parity relationship is

$$c + D + Ke^{-rT} = p + S_0$$

Put–call parity does not hold for American options. However, it is possible to use arbitrage arguments to obtain upper and lower bounds for the difference between the price of an American call and the price of an American put.

In Chapter 12, we will carry the analyses in this chapter further by making specific assumptions about the probabilistic behavior of stock prices. The analysis will enable us to derive exact pricing formulas for European stock options. In Chapter 18, we will see how numerical procedures can be used to price American options.

## SUGGESTIONS FOR FURTHER READING

Bhattacharya, M., "Transaction Data Tests of Efficiency of the Chicago Board Options Exchange," *Journal of Financial Economics*, 12 (1983), 161–85.

Galai, D., "Empirical Tests of Boundary Conditions for CBOE Options," *Journal of Financial Economics*, 6 (1978), 187–211.

Gould, J. P., and D. Galai, "Transactions Costs and the Relationship between Put and Call Prices," *Journal of Financial Economics*, 1 (1974), 105–29.

Klemkosky, R. C., and B. G. Resnick, "Put–Call Parity and Market Efficiency," *Journal of Finance*, 34 (December 1979), 1141–1155.

Klemkosky, R. C., and B. G. Resnick, "An Ex-Ante Analysis of Put–Call Parity," *Journal of Financial Economics*, 8 (1980), 363–78.

Merton, R. C., "The Relationship between Put and Call Prices: Comment," *Journal of Finance*, 28 (March 1973), 183–84.

Merton, R. C., "Theory of Rational Option Pricing," *Bell Journal of Economics and Management Science*, 4 (Spring 1973), 141–83.

Stoll, H. R., "The Relationship between Put and Call Option Prices," *Journal of Finance*, 31 (May 1969), 319–32.

## QUESTIONS AND PROBLEMS
## (ANSWERS IN SOLUTIONS MANUAL)

8.1. List the six factors affecting stock option prices.

8.2. What is a lower bound for the price of a four-month call option on a non-dividend-paying stock when the stock price is $28, the strike price is $25, and the risk-free interest rate is 8% per annum?

8.3. What is a lower bound for the price of a one-month European put option on a non-dividend-paying stock when the stock price is $12, the strike price is $15, and the risk-free interest rate is 6% per annum?

8.4. Give two reasons why the early exercise of an American call option on a non-dividend-paying stock is not optimal. The first reason should involve the time value of money. The second reason should apply even if interest rates are zero.

8.5. "The early exercise of an American put is a tradeoff between the time value of money and the insurance value of a put." Explain this statement.

8.6. Explain why an American call option is always worth at least as much as its intrinsic value. Is the same true of a European call option? Explain your answer.

8.7. Explain why the arguments leading to put–call parity for European options cannot be used to give a similar result for American options.

8.8. What is a lower bound for the price of a six-month call option on a non-dividend-paying stock when the stock price is $80, the strike price is $75, and the risk-free interest rate is 10% per annum?

8.9. What is a lower bound for the price of a two-month European put option on a non-dividend-paying stock when the stock price is $58, the strike price is $65, and the risk-free interest rate is 5% per annum?

8.10. A four-month European call option on a dividend-paying stock is currently selling for $5. The stock price is $64, the strike price is $60, and a dividend of $0.80 is expected in one month. The risk-free interest rate is 12% per annum for all maturities. What opportunities are there for an arbitrageur?

8.11. A one-month European put option on a non-dividend-paying stock is currently selling for $2.50. The stock price is $47, the strike price is $50, and the risk-free interest rate is 6% per annum. What opportunities are there for an arbitrageur?

8.12. Give an intuitive explanation of why the early exercise of an American put becomes more attractive as the risk-free rate increases and volatility decreases.

8.13. The price of a European call that expires in six months and has a strike price of $30 is $2. The underlying stock price is $29, and a dividend of $0.50 is expected in two months and again in five months. The term structure is flat, with all risk-free interest rates being 10%. What is the price of a European put option that expires in six months and has a strike price of $30?

8.14. Explain carefully the arbitrage opportunities in Problem 8.13 if the European put price is $3.

8.15. The price of an American call on a non-dividend-paying stock is $4. The stock price is $31, the strike price is $30, and the expiration date is in three months. The risk-free interest rate is 8%. Derive upper and lower bounds for the price of an American put on the same stock with the same strike price and expiration date.

8.16. Explain carefully the arbitrage opportunities in Problem 8.15 if the American put price is greater than the calculated upper bound.

8.17. Prove the result in equation (8.4). (*Hint*: For the first part of the relationship consider (a) a portfolio consisting of a European call plus an amount of cash equal to $K$ and (b) a portfolio consisting of an American put option plus one share.)

8.18. Prove the result in equation (8.8). (*Hint*: For the first part of the relationship consider (a) a portfolio consisting of a European call plus an amount of cash equal to $D + K$ and (b) a portfolio consisting of an American put option plus one share.)

8.19. Even when the company pays no dividends, there is a tendency for executive stock options to be exercised early (see Section 7.12 for a discussion of executive stock options). Give a possible reason for this.

8.20. Use the software DerivaGem to verify that Figures 8.1 and 8.2 are correct.

# ASSIGNMENT QUESTIONS

8.21. A European call option and put option on a stock both have a strike price of $20 and an expiration date in three months. Both sell for $3. The risk-free interest rate is 10% per annum, the current stock price is $19, and a $1 dividend is expected in one month. Identify the arbitrage opportunity open to a trader.

8.22. Suppose that $c_1$, $c_2$, and $c_3$ are the prices of European call options with strike prices $K_1$, $K_2$, and $K_3$, respectively, where $K_3 > K_2 > K_1$ and $K_3 - K_2 = K_2 - K_1$. All options have the same maturity. Show that

$$c_2 \leqslant 0.5(c_1 + c_3)$$

(*Hint*: Consider a portfolio that is long one option with strike price $K_1$, long one option with strike price $K_3$, and short two options with strike price $K_2$.)

8.23. What is the result corresponding to that in Problem 8.22 for European put options?

8.24. Suppose that you are the manager and sole owner of a highly leveraged company. All the debt will mature in one year. If at that time the value of the company is greater than the face value of the debt, you will pay off the debt. If the value of the company is less than the face value of the debt, you will declare bankruptcy and the debt holders will own the company.
   a. Express your position as an option on the value of the company.
   b. Express the position of the debt holders in terms of options on the value of the company.
   c. What can you do to increase the value of your position?

8.25. Consider an option on a stock when the stock price is $41, the strike price is $40, the risk-free rate is 6%, the volatility is 35%, and the time to maturity is one year. Assume that a dividend of $0.50 is expected after six months.

   a. Use DerivaGem to value the option assuming it is a European call.
   b. Use DerivaGem to value the option assuming it is a European put.
   c. Verify that put–call parity holds.
   d. Explore using DerivaGem what happens to the price of the options as the time to maturity becomes very large. For this purpose assume there are no dividends. Explain the results you get.

# CHAPTER 9

# TRADING STRATEGIES INVOLVING OPTIONS

We discussed the profit pattern from an investment in a single stock option in Chapter 1. In this chapter we cover more fully the range of profit patterns obtainable using options. We will assume that the underlying asset is a stock. Similar results can be obtained for other underlying assets, such as foreign currencies, stock indices, and futures contracts. We will also assume that the options used in the strategies we discuss are European. American options may lead to slightly different outcomes because of the possibility of early exercise.

In the first section we consider what happens when a position in a stock option is combined with a position in the stock itself. We then move on to examine the profit patterns obtained when an investment is made in two or more different options on the same stock. One of the attractions of options is that they can be used to create a wide range of different payoff functions. If European options were available with every single possible strike price, any payoff function could in theory be created.

For ease of exposition we ignore the time value of money when calculating the profit from a trading strategy in this chapter. The profit is calculated as the final payoff minus the initial cost, not as the present value of the final payoff minus the initial cost.

## 9.1  STRATEGIES INVOLVING A SINGLE OPTION AND A STOCK

There are a number of different trading strategies involving a single option on a stock and the stock itself. The profits from these are illustrated in Figure 9.1. In this figure and in other figures throughout this chapter, the dashed line shows the relationship between profit and the stock price for the individual securities constituting the portfolio, whereas the solid line shows the relationship between profit and the stock price for the whole portfolio.

In Figure 9.1a, the portfolio consists of a long position in a stock plus a short position in a call option. This is known as *writing a covered call*. The long stock position "covers" or protects the investor from the payoff on the short call that becomes necessary if there is a sharp rise in the stock price. In Figure 9.1b, a short position in a stock is combined with a long position in a call option. This is the reverse of writing a covered call. In Figure 9.1c, the investment strategy involves buying a put option on a stock and the stock itself. The approach is sometimes referred to as a *protective put* strategy. In Figure 9.1d, a short position in a put option is combined with a short position in the stock. This is the reverse of a protective put.

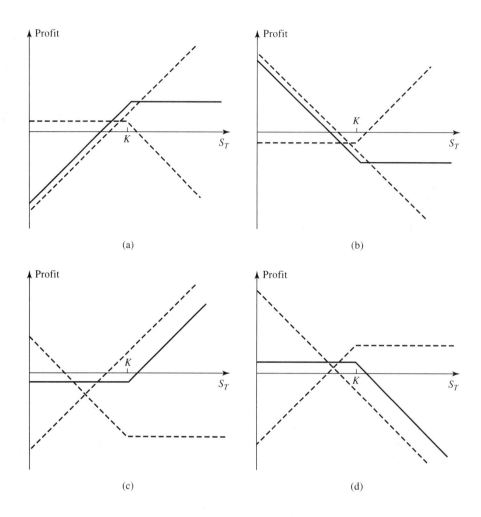

**Figure 9.1** Profit patterns (a) long position in a stock combined with short position in a call; (b) short position in a stock combined with long position in a call; (c) long position in a put combined with long position in a stock; (d) short position in a put combined with short position in a stock

The profit patterns in Figures 9.1a, b, c, d have the same general shape as the profit patterns discussed in Chapter 1 for short put, long put, long call, and short call, respectively. Put–call parity provides a way of understanding why this is so. Recall from Chapter 8 that the put–call parity relationship is

$$p + S_0 = c + Ke^{-rT} + D \tag{9.1}$$

where $p$ is the price of a European put, $S_0$ is the stock price, $c$ is the price of a European call, $K$ is the strike price of both call and put, $r$ is the risk-free interest rate, $T$ is the time to maturity of both call and put, and $D$ is the present value of the dividends anticipated during the life of the option.

Equation (9.1) shows that a long position in a put combined with a long position in the stock is equivalent to a long call position plus a certain amount ($= Ke^{-rT} + D$) of cash. This explains why the profit pattern in Figure 9.1c is similar to the profit pattern from a long call position. The position in Figure 9.1d is the reverse of that in Figure 9.1c and therefore leads to a profit pattern similar to that from a short call position.

Equation (9.1) can be rearranged to become

$$S_0 - c = Ke^{-rT} + D - p$$

In other words, a long position in a stock combined with a short position in a call is equivalent to a short put position plus a certain amount ($= Ke^{-rT} + D$) of cash. This equality explains why the profit pattern in Figure 9.1a is similar to the profit pattern from a short put position. The position in Figure 9.1b is the reverse of that in Figure 9.1a and therefore leads to a profit pattern similar to that from a long put position.

## 9.2 SPREADS

A spread trading strategy involves taking a position in two or more options of the same type (i.e., two or more calls or two or more puts).

### *Bull Spreads*

One of the most popular types of spreads is a *bull spread*. It can be created by buying a call option on a stock with a certain strike price and selling a call option on the same stock with a higher strike price. Both options have the same expiration date. The strategy is illustrated in Figure 9.2. The profits from the two option positions taken separately are shown by the dashed lines. The profit from the whole strategy is the sum of the profits given by the dashed lines and is indicated by the solid line. Because a call price always decreases as the strike price increases, the value of the option sold is always less than the value of the option bought. A bull spread, when created from calls, therefore requires an initial investment.

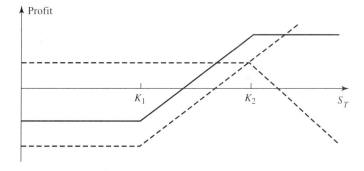

**Figure 9.2**  Bull spread created using call options

**Table 9.1**  Payoff from a bull spread

| Stock price range | Payoff from long call option | Payoff from short call option | Total payoff |
|---|---|---|---|
| $S_T \geqslant K_2$ | $S_T - K_1$ | $K_2 - S_T$ | $K_2 - K_1$ |
| $K_1 < S_T < K_2$ | $S_T - K_1$ | 0 | $S_T - K_1$ |
| $S_T \leqslant K_1$ | 0 | 0 | 0 |

Suppose that $K_1$ is the strike price of the call option bought, $K_2$ is the strike price of the call option sold, and $S_T$ is the stock price on the expiration date of the options. Table 9.1 shows the total payoff that will be realized from a bull spread in different circumstances. If the stock price does well and is greater than the higher strike price, the payoff is the difference between the two strike prices, or $K_2 - K_1$. If the stock price on the expiration date lies between the two strike prices, the payoff is $S_T - K_1$. If the stock price on the expiration date is below the lower strike price, the payoff is zero. The profit in Figure 9.2 is calculated by subtracting the initial investment from the payoff.

A bull spread strategy limits the investor's upside as well as downside risk. The strategy can be described by saying that the investor has a call option with a strike price equal to $K_1$ and has chosen to give up some upside potential by selling a call option with strike price $K_2$ ($K_2 > K_1$). In return for giving up the upside potential, the investor gets the price of the option with strike price $K_2$. Three types of bull spreads can be distinguished:

1. Both calls are initially out of the money.
2. One call is initially in the money; the other call is initially out of the money.
3. Both calls are initially in the money.

The most aggressive bull spreads are those of type 1. They cost very little to set up and have a small probability of giving a relatively high payoff ($= K_2 - K_1$). As we move from type 1 to type 2 and from type 2 to type 3, the spreads become more conservative.

**Example 9.1**  An investor buys for $3 a call with a strike price of $30 and sells for $1 a call with a strike price of $35. The payoff from this bull spread strategy is $5 if the stock price is above $35 and zero if it is below $30. If the stock price is between $30 and $35, the payoff is the amount by which the stock price exceeds $30. The cost of the strategy is $3 − $1 = $2. The profit is therefore as follows:

$ 3 → $30

| Stock price range | Profit |
|---|---|
| $S_T \leqslant 30$ | −2 |
| $30 < S_T < 35$ | $S_T - 32$ |
| $S_T \geqslant 35$ | 3 |

Bull spreads can also be created by buying a put with a low strike price and selling a put with a high strike price, as illustrated in Figure 9.3. Unlike the bull spread created from calls, bull spreads created from puts involve a positive cash flow to the investor up front (ignoring margin requirements) and a payoff that is either negative or zero.

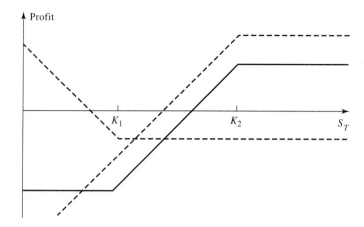

**Figure 9.3** Bull spread created using put options

### Bear Spreads

An investor who enters into a bull spread is hoping that the stock price will increase. By contrast, an investor who enters into a *bear spread* is hoping that the stock price will decline. As with a bull spread, a bear spread can be created by buying a call with one strike price and selling a call with another strike price. However, in the case of a bear spread, the strike price of the option purchased is greater than the strike price of the option sold. In Figure 9.4 the profit from the spread is shown by the solid line. A bear spread created from calls involves an initial cash inflow (when margin requirements are ignored), because the price of the call sold is greater than the price of the call purchased.

Assume that the strike prices are $K_1$ and $K_2$, with $K_1 < K_2$. Table 9.2 shows the payoff that will be realized from a bear spread in different circumstances. If the stock price is greater than $K_2$, the payoff is negative at $-(K_2 - K_1)$. If the stock price is less than $K_1$, the payoff is zero. If the stock price is between $K_1$ and $K_2$, the payoff is $-(S_T - K_1)$. The profit is calculated by adding the initial cash inflow to the payoff.

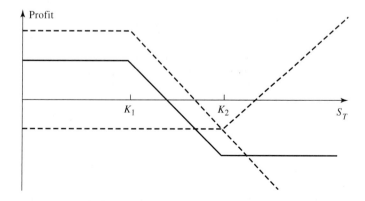

**Figure 9.4** Bear spread created using call options

**Table 9.2**  Payoff from a bear spread

| Stock price range | Payoff from long call option | Payoff from short call option | Total payoff |
|---|---|---|---|
| $S_T \geqslant K_2$ | $S_T - K_2$ | $K_1 - S_T$ | $-(K_2 - K_1)$ |
| $K_1 < S_T < K_2$ | 0 | $K_1 - S_T$ | $-(S_T - K_1)$ |
| $S_T \leqslant K_1$ | 0 | 0 | 0 |

**Example 9.2**  An investor buys for $1 a call with a strike price of $35 and sells for $3 a call with a strike price of $30. The payoff from this bear spread strategy is $-$5 if the stock price is above $35 and zero if it is below $30. If the stock price is between $30 and $35, the payoff is $-(S_T - 30)$. The investment generates $3 - $1 = $2 up front. The profit is therefore as follows:

| Stock price range | Profit |
|---|---|
| $S_T \leqslant 30$ | +2 |
| $30 < S_T < 35$ | $32 - S_T$ |
| $S_T \geqslant 35$ | $-3$ |

Like bull spreads, bear spreads limit both the upside profit potential and the downside risk. Bear spreads can be created using puts instead of calls. The investor buys a put with a high strike price and sells a put with a low strike price, as illustrated in Figure 9.5. Bear spreads created with puts require an initial investment. In essence, the investor has bought a put with a certain strike price and chosen to give up some of the profit potential by selling a put with a lower strike price. In return for the profit given up, the investor gets the price of the option sold.

### Butterfly Spreads

A *butterfly spread* involves positions in options with three different strike prices. It can be created by buying a call option with a relatively low strike price, $K_1$; buying a call option with a relatively high strike price, $K_3$; and selling two call options with a strike price, $K_2$, halfway between $K_1$ and $K_3$.

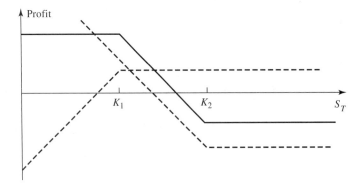

**Figure 9.5**  Bear spread created using put options

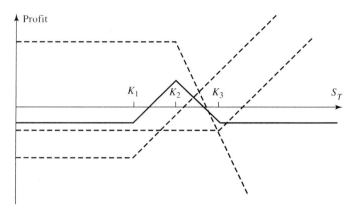

**Figure 9.6** Butterfly spread using call options

Generally $K_2$ is close to the current stock price. The pattern of profits from the strategy is shown in Figure 9.6. A butterfly spread leads to a profit if the stock price stays close to $K_2$, but gives rise to a small loss if there is a significant stock price move in either direction. It is therefore an appropriate strategy for an investor who feels that large stock price moves are unlikely. The strategy requires a small investment initially. The payoff from a butterfly spread is shown in Table 9.3.

Suppose that a certain stock is currently worth $61. Consider an investor who feels that a significant price move in the next six months is unlikely. Suppose that the market prices of six-month calls are as follows:

| Strike price ($) | Call price ($) |
|---|---|
| 55 | 10 |
| 60 | 7 |
| 65 | 5 |

The investor could create a butterfly spread by buying one call with a $55 strike price, buying one call with a $65 strike price, and selling two calls with a $60 strike price. It costs $10 + \$5 - (2 \times \$7) = \$1$ to create the spread. If the stock price in six months is greater than $65 or less than $55, the total payoff is zero, and the investor incurs a net loss of $1. If the stock price is between $56 and $64, a profit is made. The maximum profit, $4, occurs when the stock price in six months is $60.

**Table 9.3** Payoff from a butterfly spread

| Stock price range | Payoff from first long call | Payoff from second long call | Payoff from short calls | Total payoff* |
|---|---|---|---|---|
| $S_T < K_1$ | 0 | 0 | 0 | 0 |
| $K_1 < S_T < K_2$ | $S_T - K_1$ | 0 | 0 | $S_T - K_1$ |
| $K_2 < S_T < K_3$ | $S_T - K_1$ | 0 | $-2(S_T - K_2)$ | $K_3 - S_T$ |
| $S_T > K_3$ | $S_T - K_1$ | $S_T - K_3$ | $-2(S_T - K_2)$ | 0 |

* These payoffs are calculated using the relationship $K_2 = 0.5(K_1 + K_3)$.

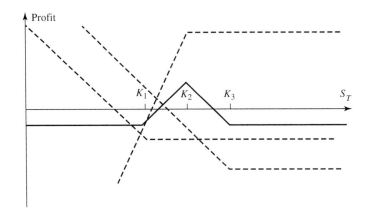

**Figure 9.7**  Butterfly spread using put options

Butterfly spreads can be created using put options. The investor buys a put with a low strike price, buys a put with a high strike price, and sells two puts with an intermediate strike price, as illustrated in Figure 9.7. The butterfly spread in the example just considered would be created by buying a put with a strike price of $55, buying a put with a strike price of $65, and selling two puts with a strike price of $60. If all options are European, the use of put options results in exactly the same spread as the use of call options. Put–call parity can be used to show that the initial investment is the same in both cases.

A butterfly spread can be sold or shorted by following the reverse strategy. Options are sold with strike prices of $K_1$ and $K_3$, and two options with the middle strike price $K_2$ are purchased. This strategy produces a modest profit if there is a significant movement in the stock price.

### Calendar Spreads

Up to now we have assumed that the options used to create a spread all expire at the same time. We now move on to *calendar spreads* in which the options have the same strike price and different expiration dates.

A calendar spread can be created by selling a call option with a certain strike price and buying a longer-maturity call option with the same strike price. The longer the maturity of an option, the more expensive it usually is. A calendar spread therefore usually requires an initial investment. Profit diagrams for calendar spreads are usually produced so that they show the profit when the short-maturity option expires on the assumption that the long-maturity option is sold at that time. The profit pattern for a calendar spread produced from call options is shown in Figure 9.8. The pattern is similar to the profit from the butterfly spread in Figure 9.6. The investor makes a profit if the stock price at the expiration of the short-maturity option is close to the strike price of the short-maturity option. However, a loss is incurred when the stock price is significantly above or significantly below this strike price.

To understand the profit pattern from a calendar spread, first consider what happens if the stock price is very low when the short-maturity option expires. The short-maturity option is worthless and the value of the long-maturity option is close to zero. The investor therefore incurs a loss that is close to the cost of setting up the spread initially. Consider next what happens if the stock price, $S_T$, is very high when the short-maturity option expires. The short-maturity option costs the

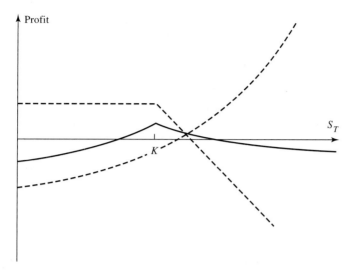

**Figure 9.8**   Calendar spread created using two calls

investor $S_T - K$, and the long-maturity option (assuming early exercise is not optimal) is worth a little more than $S_T - K$, where $K$ is the strike price of the options. Again, the investor makes a net loss that is close to the cost of setting up the spread initially. If $S_T$ is close to $K$, the short-maturity option costs the investor either a small amount or nothing at all. However, the long-maturity option is still quite valuable. In this case a significant net profit is made.

In a *neutral calendar spread*, a strike price close to the current stock price is chosen. A *bullish calendar spread* involves a higher strike price, whereas a *bearish calendar spread* involves a lower strike price.

Calendar spreads can be created with put options as well as call options. The investor buys a long-maturity put option and sells a short-maturity put option. As shown in Figure 9.9, the profit pattern is similar to that obtained from using calls.

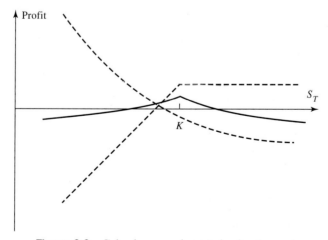

**Figure 9.9**   Calendar spread created using two puts

A *reverse calendar spread* is the opposite to that in Figures 9.8 and 9.9. The investor buys a short-maturity option and sells a long-maturity option. A small profit arises if the stock price at the expiration of the short-maturity option is well above or well below the strike price of the short-maturity option. However, a significant loss results if it is close to the strike price.

### Diagonal Spreads

Bull, bear, and calendar spreads can all be created from a long position in one call and a short position in another call. In the case of bull and bear spreads, the calls have different strike prices and the same expiration date. In the case of calendar spreads, the calls have the same strike price and different expiration dates. In a *diagonal spread* both the expiration date and the strike price of the calls are different. This increases the range of profit patterns that are possible.

## 9.3  COMBINATIONS

A *combination* is an option trading strategy that involves taking a position in both calls and puts on the same stock. We will consider straddles, strips, straps, and strangles.

### Straddle

One popular combination is a *straddle*, which involves buying a call and put with the same strike price and expiration date. The profit pattern is shown in Figure 9.10. The strike price is denoted by $K$. If the stock price is close to this strike price at expiration of the options, the straddle leads to a loss. However, if there is a sufficiently large move in either direction, a significant profit will result. The payoff from a straddle is calculated in Table 9.4.

A straddle is appropriate when an investor is expecting a large move in a stock price but does not know in which direction the move will be. Consider an investor who feels that the price of a certain stock, currently valued at $69 by the market, will move significantly in the next three months. The investor could create a straddle by buying both a put and a call with a strike price of $70 and an expiration date in three months. Suppose that the call costs $4 and the put costs $3. If the stock price stays at $69, it is easy to see that the strategy costs the investor $6. (An up-front investment of $7 is required, the call expires worthless, and the put expires worth $1.) If the stock price moves to $70, a loss of $7 is experienced. (This is the worst that can happen.) However, if the stock price

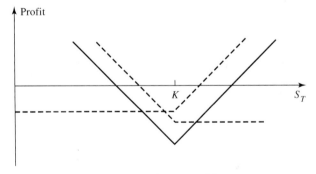

**Figure 9.10**  A straddle

**Table 9.4** Payoff from a straddle

| Range of stock price | Payoff from call | Payoff from put | Total payoff |
|---|---|---|---|
| $S_T \leqslant K$ | 0 | $K - S_T$ | $K - S_T$ |
| $S_T > K$ | $S_T - K$ | 0 | $S_T - K$ |

jumps up to $90, a profit of $13 is made; if the stock moves down to $55, a profit of $8 is made; and so on.

A straddle seems to be a natural trading strategy to use when a big jump in the price of a company's stock is expected, for example, when there is a takeover bid for the company or when the outcome of a major lawsuit is expected to be announced soon. However, this is not necessarily the case. If the general view of the market is that there will be a big jump in the stock price soon, that view will be reflected in the prices of options. An investor will find options on the stock to be significantly more expensive than options on a similar stock for which no jump is expected. For a straddle to be an effective strategy, the investor must believe that there are likely to be big movements in the stock price and these beliefs must be different from those of most other market participants.

The straddle in Figure 9.10 is sometimes referred to as a *bottom straddle* or *straddle purchase*. A *top straddle* or *straddle write* is the reverse position. It is created by selling a call and a put with the same exercise price and expiration date. It is a highly risky strategy. If the stock price on the expiration date is close to the strike price, a significant profit results. However, the loss arising from a large move in either direction is unlimited.

### Strips and Straps

A *strip* consists of a long position in one call and two puts with the same strike price and expiration date. A *strap* consists of a long position in two calls and one put with the same strike price and

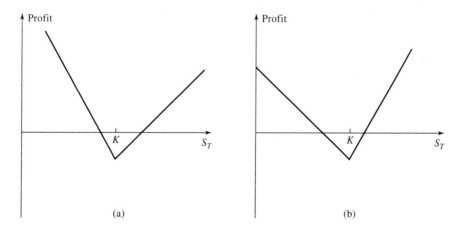

**Figure 9.11** Profit patterns from (a) a strip and (b) a strap

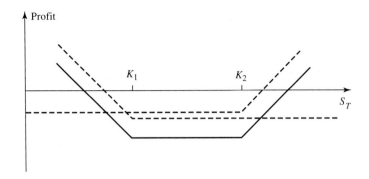

**Figure 9.12**   A strangle

expiration date. The profit patterns from strips and straps are shown in Figure 9.11. In a strip the investor is betting that there will be a big stock price move and considers a decrease in the stock price to be more likely than an increase. In a strap the investor is also betting that there will be a big stock price move. However, in this case, an increase in the stock price is considered to be more likely than a decrease.

### Strangles

In a *strangle*, sometimes called a *bottom vertical combination*, an investor buys a put and a call with the same expiration date and different strike prices. The profit pattern that is obtained is shown in Figure 9.12. The call strike price, $K_2$, is higher than the put strike price, $K_1$. The payoff function for a strangle is calculated in Table 9.5.

A strangle is a similar strategy to a straddle. The investor is betting that there will be a large price move, but is uncertain whether it will be an increase or a decrease. Comparing Figures 9.12 and 9.10, we see that the stock price has to move farther in a strangle than in a straddle for the investor to make a profit. However, the downside risk if the stock price ends up at a central value is less with a strangle.

The profit pattern obtained with a strangle depends on how close together the strike prices are. The farther they are apart, the less the downside risk and the farther the stock price has to move for a profit to be realized.

The sale of a strangle is sometimes referred to as a *top vertical combination*. It can be appropriate for an investor who feels that large stock price moves are unlikely. However, as with sale of a straddle, it is a risky strategy involving unlimited potential loss to the investor.

**Table 9.5**   Payoff from a strangle

| Range of stock price | Payoff from call | Payoff from put | Total payoff |
|---|---|---|---|
| $S_T \leqslant K_1$ | 0 | $K_1 - S_T$ | $K_1 - S_T$ |
| $K_1 < S_T < K_2$ | 0 | 0 | 0 |
| $S_T \geqslant K_2$ | $S_T - K_2$ | 0 | $S_T - K_2$ |

## 9.4 OTHER PAYOFFS

This chapter has demonstrated just a few of the ways in which options can be used to produce an interesting relationship between profit and stock price. If European options expiring at time $T$ were available with every single possible strike price, any payoff function at time $T$ could in theory be obtained. The easiest illustration of this involves a series of butterfly spreads. Recall that a butterfly spread is created by buying options with strike prices $K_1$ and $K_3$ and selling two options with strike price $K_2$ where $K_1 < K_2 < K_3$ and $K_3 - K_2 = K_2 - K_1$. Figure 9.13 shows the payoff from a butterfly spread. The pattern could be described as a spike. As $K_1$ and $K_3$ move closer together, the spike becomes smaller. Through the judicious combination of a large number of very small spikes, any payoff function can be approximated.

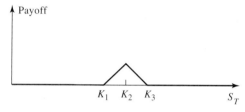

**Figure 9.13**   Payoff from a butterfly spread

## SUMMARY

A number of common trading strategies involve a single option and the underlying stock. For example, writing a covered call involves buying the stock and selling a call option on the stock; a protective put involves buying a put option and buying the stock. The former is similar to selling a put option; the latter is similar to buying a call option.

Spreads involve either taking a position in two or more calls or taking a position in two or more puts. A bull spread can be created by buying a call (put) with a low strike price and selling a call (put) with a high strike price. A bear spread can be created by buying a call (put) with a high strike price and selling a call (put) with a low strike price. A butterfly spread involves buying calls (puts) with a low and high strike price and selling two calls (puts) with some intermediate strike price. A calendar spread involves selling a call (put) with a short time to expiration and buying a call (put) with a longer time to expiration. A diagonal spread involves a long position in one option and a short position in another option such that both the strike price and the expiration date are different.

Combinations involve taking a position in both calls and puts on the same stock. A straddle combination involves taking a long position in a call and a long position in a put with the same strike price and expiration date. A strip consists of a long position in one call and two puts with the same strike price and expiration date. A strap consists of a long position in two calls and one put with the same strike price and expiration date. A strangle consists of a long position in a call and a put with different strike prices and the same expiration date. There are many other ways in which options can be used to produce interesting payoffs. It is not surprising that option trading has steadily increased in popularity and continues to fascinate investors.

## SUGGESTIONS FOR FURTHER READING

Bookstaber, R. M., *Option Pricing and Strategies in Investing*, Addison-Wesley, Reading, MA, 1981.

Degler, W. H., and H. P. Becker, "19 Option Strategies and When to Use Them," *Futures*, June 1984.

McMillan, L. G., *Options as a Strategic Investment*, New York Institute of Finance, New York, 1992.

Chaput, J. S., and L. H. Ederington, "Option Spread and Combination Trading," Working Paper, University of Otago, March 2002

Slivka, R., "Call Option Spreading," *Journal of Portfolio Management*, 7 (Spring 1981), 71–76.

Welch, W. W., *Strategies for Put and Call Option Trading*, Winthrop, Cambridge, MA, 1982.

Yates, J. W., and R. W. Kopprasch, "Writing Covered Call Options: Profits and Risks," *Journal of Portfolio Management*, 6 (Fall 1980), 74–80.

## QUESTIONS AND PROBLEMS
## (ANSWERS IN SOLUTIONS MANUAL)

9.1. What is meant by a protective put? What position in call options is equivalent to a protective put?

9.2. Explain two ways in which a bear spread can be created.

9.3. When is it appropriate for an investor to purchase a butterfly spread?

9.4. Call options on a stock are available with strike prices of $15, $17\frac{1}{2}$, and $20 and expiration dates in three months. Their prices are $4, $2, and $\frac{1}{2}$, respectively. Explain how the options can be used to create a butterfly spread. Construct a table showing how profit varies with stock price for the butterfly spread.

9.5. What trading strategy creates a reverse calendar spread?

9.6. What is the difference between a strangle and a straddle?

9.7. A call option with a strike price of $50 costs $2. A put option with a strike price of $45 costs $3. Explain how a strangle can be created from these two options. What is the pattern of profits from the strangle?

9.8. Use put–call parity to relate the initial investment for a bull spread created using calls to the initial investment for a bull spread created using puts.

9.9. Explain how an aggressive bear spread can be created using put options.

9.10. Suppose that put options on a stock with strike prices $30 and $35 cost $4 and $7, respectively. How can the options be used to create (a) a bull spread and (b) a bear spread? Construct a table that shows the profit and payoff for both spreads.

9.11. Use put–call parity to show that the cost of a butterfly spread created from European puts is identical to the cost of a butterfly spread created from European calls.

9.12. A call with a strike price of $60 costs $6. A put with the same strike price and expiration date costs $4. Construct a table that shows the profit from a straddle. For what range of stock prices would the straddle lead to a loss?

9.13. Construct a table showing the payoff from a bull spread when puts with strike prices $K_1$ and $K_2$ ($K_2 > K_1$) are used.

9.14. An investor believes that there will be a big jump in a stock price, but is uncertain as to the direction. Identify six different strategies the investor can follow and explain the differences among them.

9.15. How can a forward contract on a stock with a particular delivery price and delivery date be created from options?

9.16. A box spread is a combination of a bull call spread with strike prices $K_1$ and $K_2$ and a bear put spread with the same strike prices. The expiration dates of all options are the same. What are the characteristics of a box spread?

9.17. What is the result if the strike price of the put is higher than the strike price of the call in a strangle?

9.18. One Australian dollar is currently worth $0.64. A one-year butterfly spread is set up using European call options with strike prices of $0.60, $0.65, and $0.70. The risk-free interest rates in the United States and Australia are 5% and 4%, respectively, and the volatility of the exchange rate is 15%. Use the DerivaGem software to calculate the cost of setting up the butterfly spread position. Show that the cost is the same if European put options are used instead of European call options.

## ASSIGNMENT QUESTIONS

9.19. Three put options on a stock have the same expiration date and strike prices of $55, $60, and $65. The market prices are $3, $5, and $8, respectively. Explain how a butterfly spread can be created. Construct a table showing the profit from the strategy. For what range of stock prices would the butterfly spread lead to a loss?

9.20. A diagonal spread is created by buying a call with strike price $K_2$ and exercise date $T_2$ and selling a call with strike price $K_1$ and exercise date $T_1$ $(T_2 > T_1)$. Draw a diagram showing the profit when (a) $K_2 > K_1$ and (b) $K_2 < K_1$.

9.21. Draw a diagram showing the variation of an investor's profit and loss with the terminal stock price for a portfolio consisting of:
  a. One share and a short position in one call option
  b. Two shares and a short position in one call option
  c. One share and a short position in two call options
  d. One share and a short position in four call options
In each case, assume that the call option has an exercise price equal to the current stock price.

9.22. Suppose that the price of a non-dividend-paying stock is $32, its volatility is 30%, and the risk-free rate for all maturities is 5% per annum. Use DerivaGem to calculate the cost of setting up the following positions. In each case provide a table showing the relationship between profit and final stock price. Ignore the impact of discounting.
  a. A bull spread using European call options with strike prices of $25 and $30 and a maturity of six months
  b. A bear spread using European put options with strike prices of $25 and $30 and a maturity of six months
  c. A butterfly spread using European call options with strike prices of $25, $30, and $35 and a maturity of one year
  d. A butterfly spread using European put options with strike prices of $25, $30, and $35 and a maturity of one year
  e. A straddle using options with a strike price of $30 and a six-month maturity
  f. A strangle using options with strike prices of $30 and $35 and a six-month maturity.

# C H A P T E R   1 0

# INTRODUCTION TO BINOMIAL TREES

A useful and very popular technique for pricing a stock option involves constructing a *binomial tree*. This is a diagram that represents different possible paths that might be followed by the stock price over the life of the option. In this chapter we will take a first look at binomial trees and their relationship to an important principle known as risk-neutral valuation. The approach we adopt here is similar to that in an important paper published by Cox, Ross, and Rubinstein in 1979.

The material in this chapter is intended to be introductory. More details on the use of numerical procedures involving binomial trees are given in Chapter 18.

## 10.1   A ONE-STEP BINOMIAL MODEL

We start by supposing that we are interested in valuing a European call option to buy a stock for $21 in three months. A stock price is currently $20. We make a simplifying assumption that at the end of three months the stock price will be either $22 or $18. This means that the option will have one of two values at the end of the three months. If the stock price turns out to be $22, the value of the option will be $1; if the stock price turns out to be $18, the value of the option will be zero. The situation is illustrated in Figure 10.1.

It turns out that an elegant argument can be used to price the option in this situation. The only assumption needed is that no arbitrage opportunities exist. We set up a portfolio of the stock and

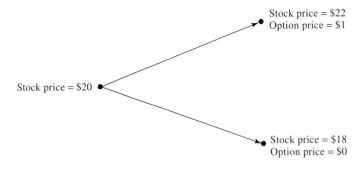

**Figure 10.1**   Stock price movements in numerical example

**200**

the option in such a way that there is no uncertainty about the value of the portfolio at the end of the three months. We then argue that, because the portfolio has no risk, the return it earns must equal the risk-free interest rate. This enables us to work out the cost of setting up the portfolio and therefore the option's price. Because there are two securities (the stock and the stock option) and only two possible outcomes, it is always possible to set up the riskless portfolio.

Consider a portfolio consisting of a long position in $\Delta$ shares of the stock and a short position in one call option. We calculate the value of $\Delta$ that makes the portfolio riskless. If the stock price moves up from $20 to $22, the value of the shares is $22\Delta$ and the value of the option is 1, so that the total value of the portfolio is $22\Delta - 1$. If the stock price moves down from $20 to $18, the value of the shares is $18\Delta$ and the value of the option is zero, so that the total value of the portfolio is $18\Delta$. The portfolio is riskless if the value of $\Delta$ is chosen so that the final value of the portfolio is the same for both alternatives. This means

$$22\Delta - 1 = 18\Delta$$

or

$$\Delta = 0.25$$

A riskless portfolio is therefore

Long: 0.25 shares

Short: 1 option

If the stock price moves up to $22, the value of the portfolio is

$$22 \times 0.25 - 1 = 4.5$$

If the stock price moves down to $18, the value of the portfolio is

$$18 \times 0.25 = 4.5$$

Regardless of whether the stock price moves up or down, the value of the portfolio is always 4.5 at the end of the life of the option.

Riskless portfolios must, in the absence of arbitrage opportunities, earn the risk-free rate of interest. Suppose that in this case the risk-free rate is 12% per annum. It follows that the value of the portfolio today must be the present value of 4.5, or

$$4.5e^{-0.12 \times 3/12} = 4.367$$

The value of the stock price today is known to be $20. Suppose the option price is denoted by $f$. The value of the portfolio today is

$$20 \times 0.25 - f = 5 - f$$

It follows that

$$5 - f = 4.367$$

or

$$f = 0.633$$

This shows that, in the absence of arbitrage opportunities, the current value of the option must be 0.633. If the value of the option were more than 0.633, the portfolio would cost less than 4.367 to set up and would earn more than the risk-free rate. If the value of the option were less than 0.633, shorting the portfolio would provide a way of borrowing money at less than the risk-free rate.

### A Generalization

We can generalize the argument just presented by considering a stock whose price is $S_0$ and an option on the stock whose current price is $f$. We suppose that the option lasts for time $T$ and that during the life of the option the stock price can either move up from $S_0$ to a new level $S_0 u$ or down from $S_0$ to a new level $S_0 d$, where $u > 1$ and $d < 1$. The proportional increase in the stock price when there is an up movement is $u - 1$; the proportional decrease when there is a down movement is $1 - d$. If the stock price moves up to $S_0 u$, we suppose that the payoff from the option is $f_u$; if the stock price moves down to $S_0 d$, we suppose the payoff from the option is $f_d$. The situation is illustrated in Figure 10.2.

As before, we imagine a portfolio consisting of a long position in $\Delta$ shares and a short position in one option. We calculate the value of $\Delta$ that makes the portfolio riskless. If there is an up movement in the stock price, the value of the portfolio at the end of the life of the option is

$$S_0 u \Delta - f_u$$

If there is a down movement in the stock price, the value becomes

$$S_0 d \Delta - f_d$$

The two are equal when

$$S_0 u \Delta - f_u = S_0 d \Delta - f_d$$

or

$$\Delta = \frac{f_u - f_d}{S_0 u - S_0 d} \tag{10.1}$$

In this case, the portfolio is riskless and must earn the risk-free interest rate. Equation (10.1) shows that $\Delta$ is the ratio of the change in the option price to the change in the stock price as we move between the nodes.

If we denote the risk-free interest rate by $r$, the present value of the portfolio is

$$(S_0 u \Delta - f_u)e^{-rT}$$

The cost of setting up the portfolio is

$$S_0 \Delta - f$$

It follows that

$$S_0 \Delta - f = (S_0 u \Delta - f_u)e^{-rT}$$

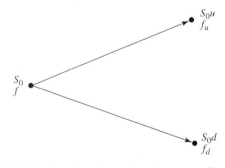

**Figure 10.2** Stock and option prices in a general one-step tree

or

$$f = S_0 \Delta - (S_0 u \Delta - f_u)e^{-rT}$$

Substituting for $\Delta$ from equation (10.1) and simplifying reduces this equation to

$$f = e^{-rT}[p f_u + (1 - p)f_d] \tag{10.2}$$

where

$$p = \frac{e^{rT} - d}{u - d} \tag{10.3}$$

Equations (10.2) and (10.3) enable an option to be priced using a one-step binomial model.

In the numerical example considered previously (see Figure 10.1), $u = 1.1$, $d = 0.9$, $r = 0.12$, $T = 0.25$, $f_u = 1$, and $f_d = 0$. From equation (10.3),

$$p = \frac{e^{0.12 \times 3/12} - 0.9}{1.1 - 0.9} = 0.6523$$

and, from equation (10.2),

$$f = e^{-0.12 \times 0.25}(0.6523 \times 1 + 0.3477 \times 0) = 0.633$$

The result agrees with the answer obtained earlier in this section.

### Irrelevance of the Stock's Expected Return

The option-pricing formula in equation (10.2) does not involve the probabilities of the stock price moving up or down. For example, we get the same option price when the probability of an upward movement is 0.5 as we do when it is 0.9. This is surprising and seems counterintuitive. It is natural to assume that, as the probability of an upward movement in the stock price increases, the value of a call option on the stock increases and the value of a put option on the stock decreases. This is not the case.

The key reason is that we are not valuing the option in absolute terms. We are calculating its value in terms of the price of the underlying stock. The probabilities of future up or down movements are already incorporated into the price of the stock. It turns out that we do not need to take them into account again when valuing the option in terms of the stock price.

## 10.2 RISK-NEUTRAL VALUATION

Although we do not need to make any assumptions about the probabilities of up and down movements in order to derive equation (10.2), it is natural to interpret the variable $p$ in equation (10.2) as the probability of an up movement in the stock price. The variable $1 - p$ is then the probability of a down movement, and the expression

$$p f_u + (1 - p)f_d$$

is the expected payoff from the option. With this interpretation of $p$, equation (10.2) then states that the value of the option today is its expected future value discounted at the risk-free rate.

We now investigate the expected return from the stock when the probability of an up movement is assumed to be $p$. The expected stock price, $E(S_T)$, at time $T$ is given by

$$E(S_T) = pS_0u + (1-p)S_0d$$

or

$$E(S_T) = pS_0(u-d) + S_0d$$

Substituting from equation (10.3) for $p$, we obtain

$$E(S_T) = S_0e^{rT} \tag{10.4}$$

showing that the stock price grows on average at the risk-free rate. Setting the probability of the up movement equal to $p$ is therefore equivalent to assuming that the return on the stock equals the risk-free rate.

In a *risk-neutral world* all individuals are indifferent to risk. In such a world investors require no compensation for risk, and the expected return on all securities is the risk-free interest rate. Equation (10.4) shows that we are assuming a risk-neutral world when we set the probability of an up movement to $p$. Equation (10.2) shows that the value of the option is its expected payoff in a risk-neutral world discounted at the risk-free rate.

This result is an example of an important general principle in option pricing known as *risk-neutral valuation*. The principle states that we can assume the world is risk neutral when pricing an option. The price we obtain is correct not just in a risk-neutral world but in the real world as well.

### The One-Step Binomial Example Revisited

We now return to the example in Figure 10.1 and illustrate that risk-neutral valuation gives the same answer as no-arbitrage arguments. In Figure 10.1, the stock price is currently $20 and will move either up to $22 or down to $18 at the end of three months. The option considered is a European call option with a strike price of $21 and an expiration date in three months. The risk-free interest rate is 12% per annum.

We define $p$ as the probability of an upward movement in the stock price in a risk-neutral world. We can calculate $p$ from equation (10.3). Alternatively, we can argue that the expected return on the stock in a risk-neutral world must be the risk-free rate of 12%. This means that $p$ must satisfy

$$22p + 18(1-p) = 20e^{0.12 \times 3/12}$$

or

$$4p = 20e^{0.12 \times 3/12} - 18$$

That is, $p$ must be 0.6523.

At the end of the three months, the call option has a 0.6523 probability of being worth 1 and a 0.3477 probability of being worth zero. Its expected value is therefore

$$0.6523 \times 1 + 0.3477 \times 0 = 0.6523$$

In a risk-neutral world this should be discounted at the risk-free rate. The value of the option today is therefore

$$0.6523e^{-0.12 \times 3/12}$$

or $0.633. This is the same as the value obtained earlier, demonstrating that no-arbitrage arguments and risk-neutral valuation give the same answer.

### Real World vs. Risk-Neutral World

It should be emphasized that $p$ is the probability of a up movement in a risk-neutral world. In general this is not the same as the probability of an up movement in the real world. In our example, $p = 0.6523$. When the probability of an up movement is 0.6523, the expected return on the stock is the risk-free rate of 12%. Suppose that in the real world the expected return on the stock is 16%, and $q$ is the probability of an up movement in the real world. It follows that

$$22q + 18(1 - q) = 20e^{0.16 \times 3/12}$$

so that $q = 0.7041$.

The expected payoff from the option in the real world is then

$$q \times 1 + (1 - q) \times 0$$

This is 0.7041. Unfortunately it is not easy to know the correct discount rate to apply to the expected payoff in the real world. A position in a call option is riskier than a position in the stock. As a result the discount rate to be applied to the payoff from a call option is greater than 16%. Without knowing the option's value, we do not know how much greater than 16% it should be.[1] The risk-neutral valuation solves this problem. We know that in a risk-neutral world the expected return on all assets (and therefore the discount rate to use for all expected payoffs) is the risk-free rate.

## 10.3 TWO-STEP BINOMIAL TREES

We can extend the analysis to a two-step binomial tree such as that shown in Figure 10.3. Here the stock price starts at $20 and in each of two time steps may go up by 10% or down by 10%. We suppose that each time step is three months long and the risk-free interest rate is 12% per annum. As before, we consider an option with a strike price of $21.

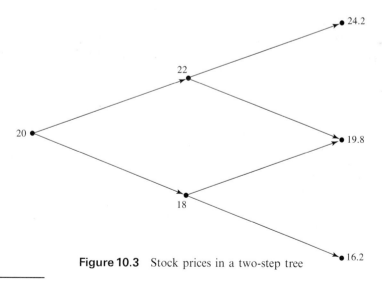

**Figure 10.3** Stock prices in a two-step tree

---

[1] Because the correct value of the option is 0.633, we can deduce that the correct discount rate is 42.6%. This is because $0.633 = 0.7041e^{-0.4258 \times 3/12}$.

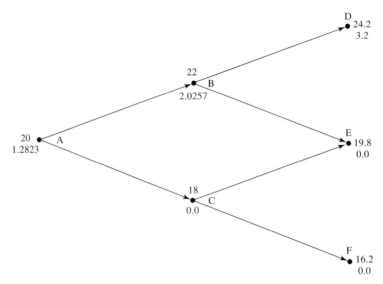

**Figure 10.4**  Stock and option prices in a two-step tree. The upper number at each node is the stock price; the lower number is the option price

The objective of the analysis is to calculate the option price at the initial node of the tree. This can be done by repeatedly applying the principles established earlier in the chapter. Figure 10.4 shows the same tree as Figure 10.3, but with both the stock price and the option price at each node. (The stock price is the upper number and the option price is the lower number.) The option prices at the final nodes of the tree are easily calculated. They are the payoffs from the option. At node D the stock price is 24.2 and the option price is $24.2 - 21 = 3.2$; at nodes E and F the option is out of the money and its value is zero.

At node C, the option price is zero, because node C leads to either node E or node F and at both nodes the option price is zero. We calculate the option price at node B by focusing our attention on the part of the tree shown in Figure 10.5. Using the notation introduced earlier in the chapter, $u = 1.1$, $d = 0.9$, $r = 0.12$, and $T = 0.25$, so that $p = 0.6523$, and equation (10.2) gives the value of the option at node B as

$$e^{-0.12 \times 3/12}(0.6523 \times 3.2 + 0.3477 \times 0) = 2.0257$$

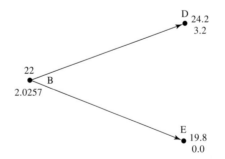

**Figure 10.5**  Evaluation of option price at node B

It remains for us to calculate to option price at the initial node A. We do so by focusing on the first step of the tree. We know that the value of the option at node B is 2.0257 and that at node C it is zero. Equation (10.2) therefore gives the value at node A as

$$e^{-0.12 \times 3/12}(0.6523 \times 2.0257 + 0.3477 \times 0) = 1.2823$$

The value of the option is $1.2823.

Note that this example was constructed so that $u$ and $d$ (the proportional up and down movements) were the same at each node of the tree and so that the time steps were of the same length. As a result, the risk-neutral probability, $p$, as calculated by equation (10.3) is the same at each node.

### A Generalization

We can generalize the case of two time steps by considering the situation in Figure 10.6. The stock price is initially $S_0$. During each time step, it either moves up to $u$ times its initial value or moves down to $d$ times its initial value. The notation for the value of the option is shown on the tree. (For example, after two up movements the value of the option is $f_{uu}$.) We suppose that the risk-free interest rate is $r$ and the length of the time step is $\delta t$ years.

Repeated application of equation (10.2) gives

$$f_u = e^{-r\delta t}[p f_{uu} + (1 - p) f_{ud}] \tag{10.5}$$

$$f_d = e^{-r\delta t}[p f_{ud} + (1 - p) f_{dd}] \tag{10.6}$$

$$f = e^{-r\delta t}[p f_u + (1 - p) f_d] \tag{10.7}$$

Substituting from equations (10.5) and (10.6) into (10.7), we get

$$f = e^{-2r\delta t}[p^2 f_{uu} + 2p(1 - p) f_{ud} + (1 - p)^2 f_{dd}] \tag{10.8}$$

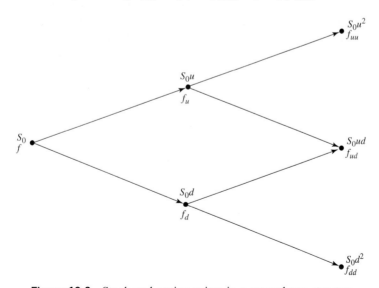

**Figure 10.6** Stock and option prices in a general two-step tree

This is consistent with the principle of risk-neutral valuation mentioned earlier. The variables $p^2$, $2p(1-p)$, and $(1-p)^2$ are the probabilities that the upper, middle, and lower final nodes will be reached. The option price is equal to its expected payoff in a risk-neutral world discounted at the risk-free interest rate.

As we add more steps to the binomial tree, the risk-neutral valuation principle continues to hold. The option price is always equal to its expected payoff in a risk-neutral world, discounted at the risk-free interest rate.

## 10.4  A PUT EXAMPLE

The procedures described in this chapter can be used to price any derivative dependent on a stock whose price changes are binomial. Consider a two-year European put with a strike price of $52 on a stock whose current price is $50. We suppose that there are two time steps of one year, and in each time step the stock price either moves up by a proportional amount of 20% or moves down by a proportional amount of 20%. We also suppose that the risk-free interest rate is 5%.

The tree is shown in Figure 10.7. The value of the risk-neutral probability, $p$, is given by

$$p = \frac{e^{0.05\times1} - 0.8}{1.2 - 0.8} = 0.6282$$

The possible final stock prices are: $72, $48, and $32. In this case $f_{uu} = 0$, $f_{ud} = 4$, and $f_{dd} = 20$. From equation (10.8),

$$f = e^{-2\times0.05\times1}(0.6282^2 \times 0 + 2 \times 0.6282 \times 0.3718 \times 4 + 0.3718^2 \times 20) = 4.1923$$

The value of the put is $4.1923. This result can also be obtained using equation (10.2) and working

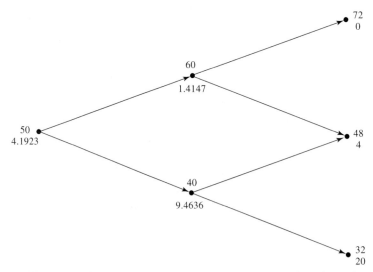

**Figure 10.7**  Use of two-step tree to value European put option. At each node, the upper number is the stock price and the lower number is the option price

back through the tree one step at a time. Figure 10.7 shows the intermediate option prices that are calculated.

## 10.5 AMERICAN OPTIONS

Up to now all the options we have considered have been European. We now move on to consider how American options can be valued using a binomial tree such as that in Figure 10.4 or 10.7. The procedure is to work back through the tree from the end to the beginning, testing at each node to see whether early exercise is optimal. The value of the option at the final nodes is the same as for the European option. At earlier nodes the value of the option is the greater of

1. The value given by equation (10.2)
2. The payoff from early exercise

Figure 10.8 shows how Figure 10.7 is affected if the option under consideration is American rather than European. The stock prices and their probabilities are unchanged. The values for the option at the final nodes are also unchanged. At node B, equation (10.2) gives the value of the option as 1.4147, whereas the payoff from early exercise is negative ($= -8$). Clearly early exercise is not optimal at node B, and the value of the option at this node is 1.4147. At node C, equation (10.2) gives the value of the option as 9.4636, whereas the payoff from early exercise is 12. In this case, early exercise is optimal and the value of the option at the node is 12. At the initial node A, the value given by equation (10.2) is

$$e^{-0.05 \times 1}(0.6282 \times 1.4147 + 0.3718 \times 12.0) = 5.0894$$

and the payoff from early exercise is 2. In this case early exercise is not optimal, and the value of

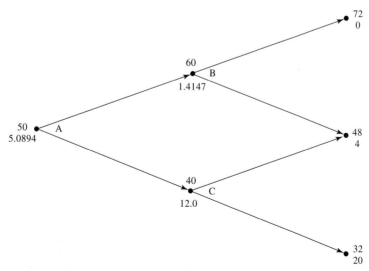

**Figure 10.8** Use of two-step tree to value American put option. At each node, the upper number is the stock price and the lower number is the option price

the option is therefore $5.0894. More details on the use of binomial trees to value American options are given in Chapter 18.

## 10.6  DELTA

At this stage it is appropriate to discuss *delta*, an important parameter in the pricing and hedging of options.

The delta of a stock option is the ratio of the change in the price of the stock option to the change in the price of the underlying stock. It is the number of units of the stock we should hold for each option shorted in order to create a riskless hedge. It is the same as the $\Delta$ introduced earlier in this chapter. The construction of a riskless hedge is sometimes referred to as *delta hedging*. The delta of a call option is positive, whereas the delta of a put option is negative.

From Figure 10.1, we can calculate the value of the delta of the call option being considered as

$$\frac{1-0}{22-18} = 0.25$$

This is because when the stock price changes from $18 to $22, the option price changes from $0 to $1.

In Figure 10.4, the delta corresponding to stock price movements over the first time step is

$$\frac{2.0257-0}{22-18} = 0.5064$$

The delta for stock price movements over the second time step is

$$\frac{3.2-0}{24.2-19.8} = 0.7273$$

if there is an upward movement over the first time step and

$$\frac{0-0}{19.8-16.2} = 0$$

if there is a downward movement over the first time step.

From Figure 10.7, delta is
$$\frac{1.4147-9.4636}{60-40} = -0.4024$$

at the end of the first time step and either

$$\frac{0-4}{72-48} = -0.1667$$

or

$$\frac{4-20}{48-32} = -1.0000$$

at the end of the second time step.

The two-step examples show that delta changes over time. (In Figure 10.4, delta changes from 0.5064 to either 0.7273 or 0; in Figure 10.7, it changes from $-0.4024$ to either $-0.1667$ or $-1.0000$.) Thus, in order to maintain a riskless hedge using an option and the underlying stock, we need to adjust our holdings in the stock periodically. This is a feature of options that we will return to in Chapter 14.

## 10.7 MATCHING VOLATILITY WITH $u$ AND $d$

In practice, when constructing a binomial tree to represent the movements in a stock price, we choose the parameters $u$ and $d$ to match the volatility of the stock price. To see how this is done, we suppose that the expected return on a stock (in the real world) is $\mu$ and its volatility is $\sigma$. Figure 10.9a shows stock price movements over the first step of a binomial tree. The step is of length $\delta t$. The stock price either moves up by a proportional amount $u$ or moves down by a proportional amount $d$. The probability of an up movement (in the real world) is assumed to be $q$.

The expected stock price at the end of the first time step is $S_0 e^{\mu \delta t}$. On the tree the expected stock price at this time is

$$q S_0 u + (1 - q) S_0 d$$

In order to match the expected return on the stock with the tree's parameters, we must therefore have

$$q S_0 u + (1 - q) S_0 d = S_0 e^{\mu \delta t}$$

or

$$q = \frac{e^{\mu \delta t} - d}{u - d} \tag{10.9}$$

As we will explain in Chapter 11, the volatility $\sigma$ of a stock price is defined so that $\sigma \sqrt{\delta t}$ is the standard deviation of the return on the stock price in a short period of time of length $\delta t$. Equivalently, the variance of the return is $\sigma^2 \delta t$. On the tree in Figure 10.9a, the variance of the stock price return is[2]

$$q u^2 + (1 - q) d^2 - [q u + (1 - q) d]^2$$

In order to match the stock price volatility with the tree's parameters, we must therefore have

$$q u^2 + (1 - q) d^2 - [q u + (1 - q) d]^2 = \sigma^2 \delta t \tag{10.10}$$

Substituting from equation (10.9) into equation (10.10), we get

$$e^{\mu \delta t} (u + d) - u d - e^{2 \mu \delta t} = \sigma^2 \delta t$$

When terms in $\delta t^2$ and higher powers of $\delta t$ are ignored, one solution to this equation is

$$u = e^{\sigma \sqrt{\delta t}} \tag{10.11}$$

$$d = e^{-\sigma \sqrt{\delta t}} \tag{10.12}$$

These are the values of $u$ and $d$ proposed by Cox, Ross, and Rubinstein (1979) for matching $u$ and $d$.

---

[2] This uses the result that the variance of a variable $Q$ equals $E(Q^2) - [E(Q)]^2$, where $E$ denotes the expected value.

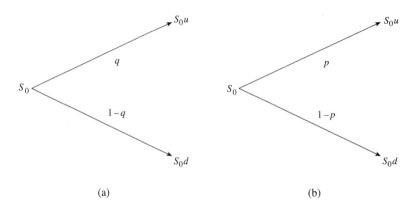

**Figure 10.9**   Change in stock price in time $\delta t$ in (a) the real world and (b) the risk-neutral world

The analysis in this chapter shows that we can replace the tree in Figure 10.9a by the tree in Figure 10.9b, where the probability of a up movement is $p$, and then behave as though the world is risk neutral. The variable $p$ is given by equation (10.3) as

$$p = \frac{e^{r\,\delta t} - d}{u - d}$$

It is the risk-neutral probability of an up movement. In Figure 10.9b, the expected stock price at the end of the time step is $S_0 e^{r\,\delta t}$, as shown in equation (10.4). The variance of the stock price return is

$$pu^2 + (1 - p)d^2 - [pu + (1 - p)d]^2 = [e^{r\,\delta t}(u + d) - ud - e^{2r\,\delta t}]$$

Substituting for $u$ and $d$ from equations (10.11) and (10.12), we find this equals $\sigma^2 \,\delta t$ when terms in $\delta t^2$ and higher powers of $\delta t$ are ignored.

This analysis shows that when we move from the real world to the risk-neutral world the expected return on the stock changes, but its volatility remains the same (at least in the limit as $\delta t$ tends to zero). This is an illustration of an important general result known as *Girsanov's theorem*. When we move from a world with one set of risk preferences to a world with another set of risk preferences, the expected growth rates in variables change, but their volatilities remain the same. We will examine the impact of risk preferences on the behavior of market variables in more detail in Chapter 21. Moving from one set of risk preferences to another is sometimes referred to as *changing the measure*.

## 10.8   BINOMIAL TREES IN PRACTICE

The binomial models presented so far have been unrealistically simple. Clearly an analyst can expect to obtain only a very rough approximation to an option price by assuming that stock price movements during the life of the option consist of one or two binomial steps.

When binomial trees are used in practice, the life of the option is typically divided into 30 or more time steps of length $\delta t$. In each time step there is a binomial stock price movement. With

30 time steps, this means that 31 terminal stock prices and $2^{30}$, or about 1 billion, possible stock price paths are considered.

The parameters $u$ and $d$ are chosen to match the stock price volatility. A popular way of doing this is by setting

$$u = e^{\sigma\sqrt{\delta t}} \quad \text{and} \quad d = e^{-\sigma\sqrt{\delta t}}$$

as indicated in the previous section. The complete set of equations defining the tree is then

$$u = e^{\sigma\sqrt{\delta t}}, \qquad d = e^{-\sigma\sqrt{\delta t}}, \qquad p = \frac{e^{r\,\delta t} - d}{u - d}$$

Chapter 18 provides a further discussion of these formulas and the practical issues involved in the construction and use of binomial trees. DerivaGem provides a way of valuing options with between 2 and 500 time steps (set the option type as Binomial European or Binomial American). Trees with up to 10 time steps can be displayed by the software.

## SUMMARY

This chapter has provided a first look at the valuation of stock options. If stock price movements during the life of an option are governed by a one-step binomial tree, it is possible to set up a portfolio consisting of a stock option and the stock that is riskless. In a world with no arbitrage opportunities, riskless portfolios must earn the risk-free interest. This enables the stock option to be priced in terms of the stock. It is interesting to note that no assumptions are required about the probabilities of up and down movements in the stock price at each node of the tree.

When stock price movements are governed by a multistep binomial tree, we can treat each binomial step separately and work back from the end of the life of the option to the beginning to obtain the current value of the option. Again only no-arbitrage arguments are used, and no assumptions are required about the probabilities of up and down movements in the stock price at each node.

Another approach to valuing stock options involves risk-neutral valuation. This very important principle states that it is permissible to assume the world is risk neutral when valuing an option in terms of the underlying stock. This chapter has shown, through both numerical examples and algebra, that no-arbitrage arguments and risk-neutral valuation are equivalent and lead to the same option prices.

The delta of a stock option, $\Delta$, considers the effect of a small change in the underlying stock price on the change in the option price. It is the ratio of the change in the option price to the change in the stock price. For a riskless position, an investor should buy $\Delta$ shares for each option sold. An inspection of a typical binomial tree shows that delta changes during the life of an option. This means that to hedge a particular option position, we must change our holding in the underlying stock periodically.

In Chapter 12 we examine the Black–Scholes analytic approach to pricing stock options. In Chapter 13 we cover the use of binomial trees for other types of options. In Chapter 18 we give a more complete discussion of how binomial trees are implemented.

## SUGGESTIONS FOR FURTHER READING

Cox, J., S. Ross, and M. Rubinstein, "Option Pricing: A Simplified Approach," *Journal of Financial Economics*, 7 (October 1979), 229–64.

Rendleman, R., and B. Bartter, "Two State Option Pricing," *Journal of Finance*, 34 (1979), 1092–1110.

## QUESTIONS AND PROBLEMS
## (ANSWERS IN SOLUTIONS MANUAL)

10.1. A stock price is currently $40. It is known that at the end of one month it will be either $42 or $38. The risk-free interest rate is 8% per annum with continuous compounding. What is the value of a one-month European call option with a strike price of $39?

10.2. Explain the no-arbitrage and risk-neutral valuation approaches to valuing a European option using a one-step binomial tree.

10.3. What is meant by the delta of a stock option?

10.4. A stock price is currently $50. It is known that at the end of six months it will be either $45 or $55. The risk-free interest rate is 10% per annum with continuous compounding. What is the the value of a six-month European put option with a strike price of $50?

10.5. A stock price is currently $100. Over each of the next two six-month periods it is expected to go up by 10% or down by 10%. The risk-free interest rate is 8% per annum with continuous compounding. What is the value of a one-year European call option with a strike price of $100?

10.6. For the situation considered in Problem 10.5, what is the value of a one-year European put option with a strike price of $100? Verify that the European call and European put prices satisfy put–call parity.

10.7. Consider the situation in which stock price movements during the life of a European option are governed by a two-step binomial tree. Explain why it is not possible to set up a position in the stock and the option that remains riskless for the whole of the life of the option.

10.8. A stock price is currently $50. It is known that at the end of two months it will be either $53 or $48. The risk-free interest rate is 10% per annum with continuous compounding. What is the value of a two-month European call option with a strike price of $49? Use no-arbitrage arguments.

10.9. A stock price is currently $80. It is known that at the end of four months it will be either $75 or $85. The risk-free interest rate is 5% per annum with continuous compounding. What is the value of a four-month European put option with a strike price of $80? Use no-arbitrage arguments.

10.10. A stock price is currently $40. It is known that at the end of three months it will be either $45 or $35. The risk-free rate of interest with quarterly compounding is 8% per annum. Calculate the value of a three-month European put option on the stock with an exercise price of $40. Verify that no-arbitrage arguments and risk-neutral valuation arguments give the same answers.

10.11. A stock price is currently $50. Over each of the next two three-month periods it is expected to go up by 6% or down by 5%. The risk-free interest rate is 5% per annum with continuous compounding. What is the value of a six-month European call option with a strike price of $51?

10.12. For the situation considered in Problem 10.11, what is the value of a six-month European put option with a strike price of $51? Verify that the European call and European put prices satisfy put–call parity. If the put option were American, would it ever be optimal to exercise it early at any of the nodes on the tree?

10.13. A stock price is currently $25. It is known that at the end of two months it will be either $23 or $27. The risk-free interest rate is 10% per annum with continuous compounding. Suppose $S_T$ is the stock price at the end of two months. What is the value of a derivative that pays off $S_T^2$ at this time?

# ASSIGNMENT QUESTIONS

10.14. A stock price is currently $50. It is known that at the end of six months it will be either $60 or $42. The risk-free rate of interest with continuous compounding is 12% per annum. Calculate the value of a six-month European call option on the stock with an exercise price of $48. Verify that no-arbitrage arguments and risk-neutral valuation arguments give the same answers.

10.15. A stock price is currently $40. Over each of the next two three-month periods it is expected to go up by 10% or down by 10%. The risk-free interest rate is 12% per annum with continuous compounding.
    a. What is the value of a six-month European put option with a strike price of $42?
    b. What is the value of a six-month American put option with a strike price of $42?

10.16. Using a "trial-and-error" approach, estimate how high the strike price has to be in Problem 10.15 for it to be optimal to exercise the option immediately.

10.17. Footnote 1 shows that the correct discount rate to use for the real-world expected payoff in the case of the call option considered in Section 10.2 is 42.6%. Show that if the option is a put rather than a call then the discount rate is $-52.5\%$. Explain why the two real-world discount rates are so different.

10.18. A stock price is currently $30. Each month for the next two months it is expected to increase by 8% or reduce by 10%. The risk-free interest rate is 5%. Use a two-step tree to calculate the value of a derivative that pays off $\max[(30 - S_T)^2, 0]$, where $S_T$ is the stock price in two months? If the derivative is American-style, should it be exercised early?

10.19. Consider a European call option on a non-dividend-paying stock where the stock price is $40, the strike price is $40, the risk-free rate is 4% per annum, the volatility is 30% per annum, and the time to maturity is six months.
    a. Calculate $u$, $d$, and $p$ for a two-step tree.
    b. Value the option using a two-step tree.
    c. Verify that DerivaGem gives the same answer.
    d. Use DerivaGem to value the option with 5, 50, 100, and 500 time steps.

C H A P T E R   1 1

# MODEL OF THE BEHAVIOR OF STOCK PRICES

Any variable whose value changes over time in an uncertain way is said to follow a *stochastic process*. Stochastic processes can be classified as *discrete time* or *continuous time*. A discrete-time stochastic process is one where the value of the variable can change only at certain fixed points in time, whereas a continuous-time stochastic process is one where changes can take place at any time. Stochastic processes can also be classified as *continuous variable* or *discrete variable*. In a continuous-variable process, the underlying variable can take any value within a certain range, whereas in a discrete-variable process, only certain discrete values are possible.

This chapter develops a continuous-variable, continuous-time stochastic process for stock prices. An understanding of this process is the first step to understanding the pricing of options and other more complicated derivatives. Note that, in practice, we do not observe stock prices following continuous-variable, continuous-time processes. Stock prices are restricted to discrete values (e.g., multiples of a cent) and changes can be observed only when the exchange is open. Nevertheless, the continuous-variable, continuous-time process proves to be a useful model for many purposes.

Many people feel that continuous-time stochastic processes are so complicated that they should be left entirely to "rocket scientists". This is not so. The biggest hurdle to understanding these processes is the notation. Here we present a step-by-step approach aimed at getting the reader over this hurdle. We also explain an important result, known as *Itô's lemma*, that is central to a full understanding of the theory underlying the pricing of derivatives.

## 11.1 THE MARKOV PROPERTY

A *Markov process* is a particular type of stochastic process where only the present value of a variable is relevant for predicting the future. The past history of the variable and the way that the present has emerged from the past are irrelevant. Stock prices are usually assumed to follow a Markov process. Suppose that the price of IBM stock is $100 now. If the stock price follows a Markov process, our predictions for the future should be unaffected by the price one week ago, one month ago, or one year ago. The only relevant piece of information is that the price is now $100.[1] Predictions for the

---

[1] Statistical properties of the stock price history of IBM may be useful in determining the characteristics of the stochastic process followed by the stock price (e.g., its volatility). The point being made here is that the particular path followed by the stock in the past is irrelevant.

**216**

future are uncertain and must be expressed in terms of probability distributions. The Markov property implies that the probability distribution of the price at any particular future time is not dependent on the particular path followed by the price in the past.

The Markov property of stock prices is consistent with the weak form of market efficiency. This states that the present price of a stock impounds all the information contained in a record of past prices. If the weak form of market efficiency were not true, technical analysts could make above-average returns by interpreting charts of the past history of stock prices. There is very little evidence that they are in fact able to do this.

It is competition in the marketplace that tends to ensure that weak-form market efficiency holds. There are many, many investors watching the stock market closely. Trying to make a profit from it leads to a situation where a stock price, at any given time, reflects the information in past prices. Suppose that it was discovered that a particular pattern in stock prices always gave a 65% chance of subsequent steep price rises. Investors would attempt to buy a stock as soon as the pattern was observed, and demand for the stock would immediately rise. This would lead to an immediate rise in its price and the observed effect would be eliminated, as would any profitable trading opportunities.

## 11.2  CONTINUOUS-TIME STOCHASTIC PROCESSES

Consider a variable that follows a Markov stochastic process. Suppose that its current value is 10 and that the change in its value during one year is $\phi(0, 1)$, where $\phi(\mu, \sigma)$ denotes a probability distribution that is normally distributed with mean $\mu$ and standard deviation $\sigma$. What is the probability distribution of the change in the value of the variable during two years?

The change in two years is the sum of two normal distributions, each of which has a mean of zero and standard deviation of 1.0. Because the variable is Markov, the two probability distributions are independent. When we add two independent normal distributions, the result is a normal distribution in which the mean is the sum of the means and the variance is the sum of the variances.[2] The mean of the change during two years in the variable we are considering is therefore zero, and the variance of this change is 2.0. The change in the variable over two years is therefore $\phi(0, \sqrt{2})$.

Consider next the change in the variable during six months. The variance of the change in the value of the variable during one year equals the variance of the change during the first six months plus the variance of the change during the second six months. We assume these are the same. It follows that the variance of the change during a six month period must be 0.5. Equivalently, the standard deviation of the change is $\sqrt{0.5}$, so that the probability distribution for the change in the value of the variable during six months is $\phi(0, \sqrt{0.5})$.

A similar argument shows that the change in the value of the variable during three months is $\phi(0, \sqrt{0.25})$. More generally, the change during any time period of length $T$ is $\phi(0, \sqrt{T})$. In particular, the change during a very short time period of length $\delta t$ is $\phi(0, \sqrt{\delta t})$.

The square root signs in these results may seem strange. They arise because, when Markov processes are considered, the variance of the changes in successive time periods are additive. The standard deviations of the changes in successive time periods are not additive. The variance of the change in the variable in our example is 1.0 per year, so that the variance of the change in two years is 2.0 and the variance of the change in three years is 3.0. The standard deviation of the

---

[2] The variance of a probability distribution is the square of its standard deviation. The variance of a one-year change in the value of the variable we are considering is therefore 1.0.

change in two and three years is $\sqrt{2}$ and $\sqrt{3}$, respectively. Strictly speaking, we should not refer to the standard deviation of the variable as 1.0 per year. It should be "1.0 per square root of years". The results explain why uncertainty is often referred to as being proportional to the square root of time.

### *Wiener Processes*

The process followed by the variable we have been considering is known as a *Wiener process*. It is a particular type of Markov stochastic process with a mean change of zero and a variance rate of 1.0 per year. It has been used in physics to describe the motion of a particle that is subject to a large number of small molecular shocks and is sometimes referred to as *Brownian motion*.

Expressed formally, a variable $z$ follows a Wiener process if it has the following two properties:

*Property* 1. The change $\delta z$ during a small period of time $\delta t$ is

$$\delta z = \epsilon \sqrt{\delta t} \tag{11.1}$$

where $\epsilon$ is a random drawing from a standardized normal distribution, $\phi(0, 1)$.

*Property* 2. The values of $\delta z$ for any two different short intervals of time $\delta t$ are independent.

It follows from the first property that $\delta z$ itself has a normal distribution with

mean of $\delta z = 0$

standard deviation of $\delta z = \sqrt{\delta t}$

variance of $\delta z = \delta t$

The second property implies that $z$ follows a Markov process.

Consider the increase in the value of $z$ during a relatively long period of time, $T$. This can be denoted by $z(T) - z(0)$. It can be regarded as the sum of the increases in $z$ in $N$ small time intervals of length $\delta t$, where

$$N = \frac{T}{\delta t}$$

Thus,

$$z(T) - z(0) = \sum_{i=1}^{N} \epsilon_i \sqrt{\delta t} \tag{11.2}$$

where the $\epsilon_i$ $(i = 1, 2, \ldots, N)$ are random drawings from $\phi(0, 1)$. From second property of Wiener processes, the $\epsilon_i$'s are independent of each other. It follows from equation (11.2) that $z(T) - z(0)$ is normally distributed with

mean of $[z(T) - z(0)] = 0$

variance of $[z(T) - z(0)] = N \, \delta t = T$

standard deviation of $[z(T) - z(0)] = \sqrt{T}$

This is consistent with the discussion earlier in this section.

**Example 11.1**  Suppose that the value, $z$, of a variable that follows a Wiener process is initially 25 and that time is measured in years. At the end of one year, the value of the variable is normally distributed with a mean of 25 and a standard deviation of 1.0. At the end of five years, it is normally distributed with a mean of 25 and a standard deviation of $\sqrt{5}$, or 2.236. Our uncertainty about the value of the variable at a certain time in the future, as measured by its standard deviation, increases as the square root of how far we are looking ahead.

In ordinary calculus it is usual to proceed from small changes to the limit as the small changes become closer to zero. Thus $\delta y/\delta x$ becomes $dy/dx$ in the limit, and so on. We can proceed similarly when dealing with stochastic processes. A Wiener process is the limit as $\delta t \to 0$ of the process described above for $z$.

Figure 11.1 illustrates what happens to the path followed by $z$ as the limit $\delta t \to 0$ is approached. Note that the path is quite "jagged". This is because the size of a movement in $z$ in time $\delta t$ is proportional to $\sqrt{\delta t}$ and, when $\delta t$ is small, $\sqrt{\delta t}$ is much bigger than $\delta t$. Two intriguing properties of Wiener processes, related to this $\sqrt{\delta t}$ property, are:

1. The expected length of the path followed by $z$ in any time interval is infinite.

2. The expected number of times $z$ equals any particular value in any time interval is infinite.

### Generalized Wiener Process

The basic Wiener process, $dz$, that has been developed so far has a drift rate of zero and a variance rate of 1.0. The drift rate of zero means that the expected value of $z$ at any future time is equal to its current value. The variance rate of 1.0 means that the variance of the change in $z$ in a time interval of length $T$ equals $T$. A *generalized Wiener process* for a variable $x$ can be defined in terms of $dz$ as follows:

$$dx = a\,dt + b\,dz \qquad (11.3)$$

where $a$ and $b$ are constants.

To understand equation (11.3), it is useful to consider the two components on the right-hand side separately. The $a\,dt$ term implies that $x$ has an expected drift rate of $a$ per unit of time. Without the $b\,dz$ term, the equation is

$$dx = a\,dt$$

which implies that

$$\frac{dx}{dt} = a$$

Integrating with respect to time, we get

$$x = x_0 + at$$

where $x_0$ is the value of $x$ at time zero. In a period of time of length $T$, the value of $x$ increases by an amount $aT$. The $b\,dz$ term on the right-hand side of equation (11.3) can be regarded as adding noise or variability to the path followed by $x$. The amount of this noise or variability is $b$ times a Wiener process. A Wiener process has a standard deviation of 1.0. It follows that $b$ times a Wiener process has a standard deviation of $b$. In a small time interval $\delta t$, the change $\delta x$ in the value of $x$ is given by equations (11.1) and (11.3) as

$$\delta x = a\,\delta t + b\epsilon\sqrt{\delta t}$$

where, as before, $\epsilon$ is a random drawing from a standardized normal distribution. Thus $\delta x$ has a

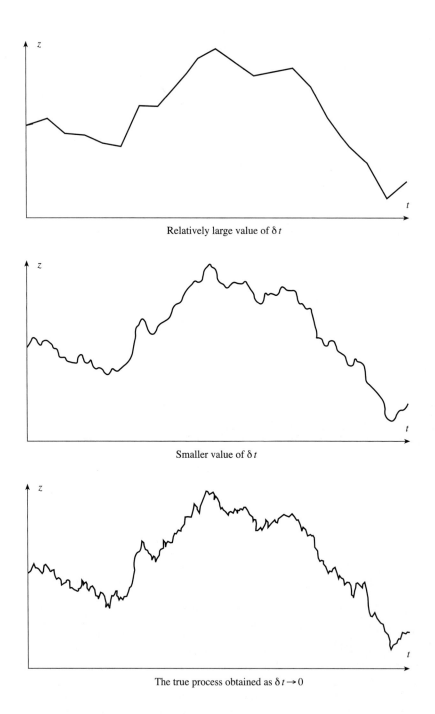

**Figure 11.1**   How a Wiener process is obtained when $\delta t \rightarrow 0$ in equation (11.1)

**Figure 11.2**   Generalized Wiener process: $a = 0.3$, $b = 1.5$

normal distribution with

$$\text{mean of } \delta x = a\,\delta t$$

$$\text{standard deviation of } \delta x = b\sqrt{\delta t}$$

$$\text{variance of } \delta x = b^2\,\delta t$$

Similar arguments to those given for a Wiener process show that the change in the value of $x$ in any time interval $T$ is normally distributed with

$$\text{mean of change in } x = aT$$

$$\text{standard deviation of change in } x = b\sqrt{T}$$

$$\text{variance of change in } x = b^2 T$$

Thus, the generalized Wiener process given in equation (11.3) has an expected drift rate (i.e., average drift per unit of time) of $a$ and a variance rate (i.e., variance per unit of time) of $b^2$. It is illustrated in Figure 11.2.

> **Example 11.2**   Consider the situation where the cash position of a company, measured in thousands of dollars, follows a generalized Wiener process with a drift of 20 per year and a variance rate of 900 per year. Initially, the cash position is 50. At the end of one year, the cash position will have a normal distribution with a mean of 70 and a standard deviation of $\sqrt{900}$, or 30. At the end of six months, it will have a normal distribution with a mean of 60 and a standard deviation of $30\sqrt{0.5} = 21.21$. Our uncertainty about the cash position at some time in the future, as measured by its standard deviation, increases as the square root of how far ahead we are looking. Note that the cash position can become negative (we can interpret this as a situation where the company is borrowing funds).

### Itô Process

A further type of stochastic process can be defined. This is known as an *Itô process*. This is a generalized Wiener process in which the parameters $a$ and $b$ are functions of the value of the underlying variable $x$ and time $t$. Algebraically, an Itô process can be written

$$dx = a(x, t)\,dt + b(x, t)\,dz \tag{11.4}$$

Both the expected drift rate and variance rate of an Itô process are liable to change over time. In a small time interval between $t$ and $t + \delta t$, the variable changes from $x$ to $x + \delta x$, where

$$\delta x = a(x, t)\,\delta t + b(x, t)\epsilon\sqrt{\delta t}$$

This relationship involves a small approximation. It assumes that the drift and variance rate of $x$ remain constant, equal to $a(x, t)$ and $b(x, t)^2$, respectively, during the time interval between $t$ and $t + \delta t$.

## 11.3  THE PROCESS FOR STOCK PRICES

In this section we discuss the stochastic process usually assumed for the price of a non-dividend-paying stock.

It is tempting to suggest that a stock price follows a generalized Wiener process, that is, that it has a constant expected drift rate and a constant variance rate. However, this model fails to capture a key aspect of stock prices. This is that the expected percentage return required by investors from a stock is independent of the stock's price. If investors require a 14% per annum expected return when the stock price is \$10, then, *ceteris paribus*, they will also require a 14% per annum expected return when it is \$50.

Clearly, the constant expected drift-rate assumption is inappropriate and needs to be replaced by the assumption that the expected return (i.e., expected drift divided by the stock price) is constant. If $S$ is the stock price at time $t$, the expected drift rate in $S$ should be assumed to be $\mu S$ for some constant parameter $\mu$. This means that in a short interval of time, $\delta t$, the expected increase in $S$ is $\mu S\,\delta t$. The parameter $\mu$ is the expected rate of return on the stock, expressed in decimal form.

If the volatility of the stock price is always zero, this model implies that

$$\delta S = \mu S\,\delta t$$

In the limit as $\delta t \to 0$,

$$dS = \mu S\,dt$$

or

$$\frac{dS}{S} = \mu\,dt$$

Integrating between time zero and time $T$, we get

$$S_T = S_0 e^{\mu T} \tag{11.5}$$

where $S_0$ and $S_T$ are the stock price at time zero and time $T$. Equation (11.5) shows that, when the variance rate is zero, the stock price grows at a continuously compounded rate of $\mu$ per unit of time.

In practice, of course, a stock price does exhibit volatility. A reasonable assumption is that the variability of the percentage return in a short period of time, $\delta t$, is the same regardless of the stock price. In other words, an investor is just as uncertain of the percentage return when the stock price is $50 as when it is $10. This suggests that the standard deviation of the change in a short period of time $\delta t$ should be proportional to the stock price and leads to the model

$$dS = \mu S\, dt + \sigma S\, dz$$

or

$$\frac{dS}{S} = \mu\, dt + \sigma\, dz \tag{11.6}$$

Equation (11.6) is the most widely used model of stock price behavior. The variable $\sigma$ is the volatility of the stock price. The variable $\mu$ is its expected rate of return.

**Example 11.3** Consider a stock that pays no dividends, has a volatility of 30% per annum, and provides an expected return of 15% per annum with continuous compounding. In this case, $\mu = 0.15$ and $\sigma = 0.30$. The process for the stock price is

$$\frac{dS}{S} = 0.15\, dt + 0.30\, dz$$

If $S$ is the stock price at a particular time and $\delta S$ is the increase in the stock price in the next small interval of time, then

$$\frac{\delta S}{S} = 0.15\, \delta t + 0.30\epsilon\sqrt{\delta t}$$

where $\epsilon$ is a random drawing from a standardized normal distribution. Consider a time interval of one week, or 0.0192 years, and suppose that the initial stock price is $100. Then $\delta t = 0.0192$, $S = 100$, and

$$\delta S = 100(0.00288 + 0.0416\epsilon)$$

or

$$\delta S = 0.288 + 4.16\epsilon$$

showing that the price increase is a random drawing from a normal distribution with mean $0.288 and standard deviation $4.16.

## 11.4 REVIEW OF THE MODEL

The model of stock price behavior developed in the previous section is known as *geometric Brownian motion*. The discrete-time version of the model is

$$\frac{\delta S}{S} = \mu\, \delta t + \sigma\epsilon\sqrt{\delta t} \tag{11.7}$$

or

$$\delta S = \mu S\, \delta t + \sigma S\epsilon\sqrt{\delta t} \tag{11.8}$$

The variable $\delta S$ is the change in the stock price $S$ in a small time interval $\delta t$, and $\epsilon$ is a random drawing from a standardized normal distribution (i.e., a normal distribution with a mean of zero and standard deviation of 1.0). The parameter $\mu$ is the expected rate of return per unit of time from the stock, and the parameter $\sigma$ is the volatility of the stock price. Both of these parameters are assumed constant.

The left-hand side of equation (11.7) is the return provided by the stock in a short period of time $\delta t$. The term $\mu \, \delta t$ is the expected value of this return, and the term $\sigma \epsilon \sqrt{\delta t}$ is the stochastic component of the return. The variance of the stochastic component (and therefore of the whole return) is $\sigma^2 \, \delta t$. This is consistent with the definition of the volatility $\sigma$ given in Section 10.7; that is, $\sigma$ is such that $\sigma \sqrt{\delta t}$ is the standard deviation of the return in a short time period $\delta t$.

Equation (11.7) shows that $\delta S / S$ is normally distributed with mean $\mu \, \delta t$ and standard deviation $\sigma \sqrt{\delta t}$. In other words,

$$\frac{\delta S}{S} \sim \phi(\mu \, \delta t, \sigma \sqrt{\delta t}) \tag{11.9}$$

### Monte Carlo Simulation

A Monte Carlo simulation of a stochastic process is a procedure for sampling random outcomes for the process. We will use it as a way of developing some understanding of the nature of the stock price process in equation (11.6).

Suppose that the expected return from a stock is 14% per annum and that the standard deviation of the return (i.e., the volatility) is 20% per annum. This means that $\mu = 0.14$ and $\sigma = 0.20$. Suppose that $\delta t = 0.01$, so that we are considering changes in the stock price in time intervals of length 0.01 years (or 3.65 days). From equation (11.8), we have

$$\delta S = 0.14 \times 0.01 S + 0.2\sqrt{0.01} \, S\epsilon$$

or

$$\delta S = 0.0014 S + 0.02 S\epsilon \tag{11.10}$$

A path for the stock price can be simulated by sampling repeatedly for $\epsilon$ from $\phi(0, 1)$ and substituting into equation (11.10). Table 11.1 shows one particular set of results from doing this.

**Table 11.1**  Simulation of stock price when $\mu = 0.14$ and $\sigma = 0.20$ during periods of length 0.01 year

| Stock price at start of period | Random sample for $\epsilon$ | Change in stock price during period |
|---|---|---|
| 20.000 | 0.52 | 0.236 |
| 20.236 | 1.44 | 0.611 |
| 20.847 | −0.86 | −0.329 |
| 20.518 | 1.46 | 0.628 |
| 21.146 | −0.69 | −0.262 |
| 20.883 | −0.74 | −0.280 |
| 20.603 | 0.21 | 0.115 |
| 20.719 | −1.10 | −0.427 |
| 20.292 | 0.73 | 0.325 |
| 20.617 | 1.16 | 0.507 |
| 21.124 | 2.56 | 1.111 |

The initial stock price is assumed to be \$20. For the first period, $\epsilon$ is sampled as 0.52. From equation (11.10), the change during the first time period is

$$\delta S = 0.0014 \times 20 + 0.02 \times 20 \times 0.52 = 0.236$$

Therefore, at the beginning of the second time period, the stock price is \$20.236. The value of $\epsilon$ sampled for the next period is 1.44. From equation (11.10), the change during the second time period is

$$\delta S = 0.0014 \times 20.236 + 0.02 \times 20.236 \times 1.44 = 0.611$$

Therefore, at the beginning of the next period, the stock price is \$20.847. And so on. Note that, because the process we are simulating is Markov, the samples for $\epsilon$ should be independent of each other.

Table 11.1 assumes that stock prices are measured to the nearest 0.001. It is important to realize that the table shows only one possible pattern of stock price movements. Different random samples would lead to different price movements. Any small time interval $\delta t$ can be used in the simulation. In the limit as $\delta t \to 0$, a perfect description of the stochastic process is obtained. The final stock price of 21.124 in Table 11.1 can be regarded as a random sample from the distribution of stock prices at the end of 10 time intervals (i.e., at the end of one-tenth of a year). By repeatedly simulating movements in the stock price, as in Table 11.1, a complete probability distribution of the stock price at the end of this time is obtained.

## 11.5 THE PARAMETERS

The process for stock prices developed in this chapter involves two parameters: $\mu$ and $\sigma$. The parameter $\mu$ is the expected continuously compounded return earned by an investor per year. Most investors require higher expected returns to induce them to take higher risks. It follows that the value of $\mu$ should depend on the risk of the return from the stock.[3] It should also depend on the level of interest rates in the economy. The higher the level of interest rates, the higher the expected return required on any given stock.

Fortunately, we do not have to concern ourselves with the determinants of $\mu$ in any detail because the value of a derivative dependent on a stock is, in general, independent of $\mu$. The parameter $\sigma$, the stock price volatility, is, by contrast, critically important to the determination of the value of most derivatives. We will discuss procedures for estimating $\sigma$ in Chapter 12. Typical values of $\sigma$ for a stock are in the range 0.20 to 0.50 (i.e., 20% to 50%).

The standard deviation of the proportional change in the stock price in a small interval of time $\delta t$ is $\sigma\sqrt{\delta t}$. As a rough approximation, the standard deviation of the proportional change in the stock price over a relatively long period of time $T$ is $\sigma\sqrt{T}$. This means that, as an approximation, volatility can be interpreted as the standard deviation of the change in the stock price in one year. In Chapter 12 we will show that the volatility of a stock price is exactly equal to the standard deviation of the continuously compounded return provided by the stock in one year.

---

[3] More precisely, $\mu$ depends on that part of the risk that cannot be diversified away by the investor.

## 11.6  ITÔ'S LEMMA

The price of a stock option is a function of the underlying stock's price and time. More generally, we can say that the price of any derivative is a function of the stochastic variables underlying the derivative and time. A serious student of derivatives must, therefore, acquire some understanding of the behavior of functions of stochastic variables. An important result in this area was discovered by the mathematician Kiyosi Itô in 1951.[4] It is known as *Itô's lemma*.

Suppose that the value of a variable $x$ follows the Itô process

$$dx = a(x, t)\,dt + b(x, t)\,dz \tag{11.11}$$

where $dz$ is a Wiener process and $a$ and $b$ are functions of $x$ and $t$. The variable $x$ has a drift rate of $a$ and a variance rate of $b^2$. Itô's lemma shows that a function $G$ of $x$ and $t$ follows the process

$$dG = \left(\frac{\partial G}{\partial x}a + \frac{\partial G}{\partial t} + \tfrac{1}{2}\frac{\partial^2 G}{\partial x^2}b^2\right)dt + \frac{\partial G}{\partial x}b\,dz \tag{11.12}$$

where the $dz$ is the same Wiener process as in equation (11.11). Thus, $G$ also follows an Itô process. It has a drift rate of

$$\frac{\partial G}{\partial x}a + \frac{\partial G}{\partial t} + \tfrac{1}{2}\frac{\partial^2 G}{\partial x^2}b^2$$

and a variance rate of

$$\left(\frac{\partial G}{\partial x}\right)^2 b^2$$

A completely rigorous proof of Itô's lemma is beyond the scope of this book. In Appendix 11A, we show that the lemma can be viewed as an extension of well-known results in differential calculus.

Earlier, we argued that

$$dS = \mu S\,dt + \sigma S\,dz \tag{11.13}$$

with $\mu$ and $\sigma$ constant, is a reasonable model of stock price movements. From Itô's lemma, it follows that the process followed by a function $G$ of $S$ and $t$ is

$$dG = \left(\frac{\partial G}{\partial S}\mu S + \frac{\partial G}{\partial t} + \tfrac{1}{2}\frac{\partial^2 G}{\partial S^2}\sigma^2 S^2\right)dt + \frac{\partial G}{\partial S}\sigma S\,dz \tag{11.14}$$

Note that both $S$ and $G$ are affected by the same underlying source of uncertainty, $dz$. This proves to be very important in the derivation of the Black–Scholes results.

### *Application to Forward Contracts*

To illustrate Itô's lemma, consider a forward contract on a non-dividend-paying stock. Assume that the risk-free rate of interest is constant and equal to $r$ for all maturities. From equation (3.5),

$$F_0 = S_0 e^{rT}$$

---

[4] See K. Itô, "On Stochastic Differential Equations," *Memoirs, American Mathematical Society*, 4 (1951), 1–51.

where $F_0$ is the forward price at time zero, $S_0$ is the spot price at time zero, and $T$ is the time to maturity of the forward contract.

We are interested in what happens to the forward price as time passes. We define $F$ and $S$ as the forward price and the stock price, respectively, at a general time $t$, with $t < T$. The relationship between $F$ and $S$ is

$$F = Se^{r(T-t)} \tag{11.15}$$

Assuming that the process for $S$ is given by equation (11.13), we can use Itô's lemma to determine the process for $F$.

From equation (11.15),

$$\frac{\partial F}{\partial S} = e^{r(T-t)}, \qquad \frac{\partial^2 F}{\partial S^2} = 0, \qquad \frac{\partial F}{\partial t} = -rSe^{r(T-t)}$$

From equation (11.14), the process for $F$ is given by

$$dF = [e^{r(T-t)}\mu S - rSe^{r(T-t)}]\,dt + e^{r(T-t)}\sigma S\,dz$$

Substituting $F = Se^{r(T-t)}$, we obtain

$$dF = (\mu - r)F\,dt + \sigma F\,dz \tag{11.16}$$

Like the stock price $S$, the forward price $F$ follows geometric Brownian motion. It has an expected growth rate of $\mu - r$ rather than $\mu$. The growth rate in $F$ is the excess return of $S$ over the risk-free rate.

## 11.7 THE LOGNORMAL PROPERTY

We now use Itô's lemma to derive the process followed by $\ln S$ when $S$ follows the process in equation (11.13). Define

$$G = \ln S$$

Because

$$\frac{\partial G}{\partial S} = \frac{1}{S}, \qquad \frac{\partial^2 G}{\partial S^2} = -\frac{1}{S^2}, \qquad \frac{\partial G}{\partial t} = 0$$

it follows from equation (11.14) that the process followed by $G$ is

$$dG = \left(\mu - \frac{\sigma^2}{2}\right)dt + \sigma\,dz \tag{11.17}$$

Because $\mu$ and $\sigma$ are constant, this equation indicates that $G = \ln S$ follows a generalized Wiener process. It has constant drift rate $\mu - \sigma^2/2$ and constant variance rate $\sigma^2$. The change in $\ln S$ between time zero and some future time, $T$, is therefore normally distributed with mean

$$\left(\mu - \frac{\sigma^2}{2}\right)T$$

and variance

$$\sigma^2 T$$

This means that

$$\ln S_T - \ln S_0 \sim \phi \left[ \left( \mu - \frac{\sigma^2}{2} \right) T, \ \sigma \sqrt{T} \right]$$  (11.18)

or

$$\ln S_T \sim \phi \left[ \ln S_0 + \left( \mu - \frac{\sigma^2}{2} \right) T, \ \sigma \sqrt{T} \right]$$  (11.19)

where $S_T$ is the stock price at a future time $T$, $S_0$ is the stock price at time zero, and $\phi(m, s)$ denotes a normal distribution with mean $m$ and standard deviation $s$.

Equation (11.19) shows that $\ln S_T$ is normally distributed. A variable has a lognormal distribution if the natural logarithm of the variable is normally distributed. The model of stock price behavior we have developed in this chapter therefore implies that a stock's price at time $T$, given its price today, is lognormally distributed. The standard deviation of the logarithm of the stock price is $\sigma \sqrt{T}$. It is proportional to the square root of how far ahead we are looking.

## SUMMARY

Stochastic processes describe the probabilistic evolution of the value of a variable through time. A Markov process is one where only the present value of the variable is relevant for predicting the future. The past history of the variable and the way in which the present has emerged from the past are irrelevant.

A Wiener process, $dz$, is a process describing the evolution of a normally distributed variable. The drift of the process is zero and the variance rate is 1.0 per unit time. This means that, if the value of the variable is $x_0$ at time zero, then at time $T$ it is normally distributed with mean $x_0$ and standard deviation $\sqrt{T}$.

A generalized Wiener process describes the evolution of a normally distributed variable with a drift of $a$ per unit time and a variance rate of $b^2$ per unit time, where $a$ and $b$ are constants. This means that if, as before, the value of the variable is $x_0$ at time zero then it is normally distributed with a mean of $x_0 + aT$ and a standard deviation of $b\sqrt{T}$ at time $T$.

An Itô process is a process where the drift and variance rate of $x$ can be a function of both $x$ itself and time. The change in $x$ in a very short period of time is, to a good approximation, normally distributed, but its change over longer periods of time is liable to be nonnormal.

One way of gaining an intuitive understanding of a stochastic process for a variable is to simulate the behavior of the variable. This involves dividing a time interval into many small time steps and randomly sampling possible paths for the variable. The future probability distribution for the variable can then be calculated. Monte Carlo simulation is discussed further in Chapter 18.

Itô's lemma is a way of calculating the stochastic process followed by a function of a variable from the stochastic process followed by the variable itself. As we will see in Chapter 12, Itô's lemma is very important in the pricing of derivatives. A key point is that the Wiener process, $dz$, underlying the stochastic process for the variable is exactly the same as the Wiener process underlying the stochastic process for the function of the variable. Both are subject to the same underlying source of uncertainty.

The stochastic process usually assumed for a stock price is geometric Brownian motion. Under this process the return to the holder of the stock in a small period of time is normally distributed and the returns in two nonoverlapping periods are independent. The value of the stock price at a future time has a lognormal distribution. The Black–Scholes model, which we cover in the next chapter, is based on the geometric Brownian motion assumption.

## SUGGESTIONS FOR FURTHER READING

### On Efficient Markets and the Markov Property of Stock Prices

Brealey, R. A., *An Introduction to Risk and Return from Common Stock*, 2nd edn., MIT Press, Cambridge, MA, 1983.

Cootner, P. H. (ed.), *The Random Character of Stock Market Prices*, MIT Press, Cambridge, MA, 1964.

### On Stochastic Processes

Cox, D. R., and H. D. Miller, *The Theory of Stochastic Processes*, Chapman & Hall, London, 1965.

Feller, W., *Probability Theory and Its Applications*, vols. 1 and 2. Wiley, New York, 1950.

Karlin, S., and H. M. Taylor, *A First Course in Stochastic Processes*, 2nd edn., Academic Press, New York, 1975.

Neftci, S., *Introduction to Mathematics of Financial Derivatives*, Academic Press, New York, 1996.

## QUESTIONS AND PROBLEMS
## (ANSWERS IN SOLUTIONS MANUAL)

11.1. What would it mean to assert that the temperature at a certain place follows a Markov process? Do you think that temperatures do, in fact, follow a Markov process?

11.2. Can a trading rule based on the past history of a stock's price ever produce returns that are consistently above average? Discuss.

11.3. A company's cash position (in millions of dollars) follows a generalized Wiener process with a drift rate of 0.5 per quarter and a variance rate of 4.0 per quarter. How high does the company's initial cash position have to be for the company to have a less than 5% chance of a negative cash position by the end of one year?

11.4. Variables $X_1$ and $X_2$ follow generalized Wiener processes with drift rates $\mu_1$ and $\mu_2$ and variances $\sigma_1^2$ and $\sigma_2^2$. What process does $X_1 + X_2$ follow if:
   a. The changes in $X_1$ and $X_2$ in any short interval of time are uncorrelated?
   b. There is a correlation $\rho$ between the changes in $X_1$ and $X_2$ in any short interval of time?

11.5. Consider a variable $S$ that follows the process

$$dS = \mu \, dt + \sigma \, dz$$

For the first three years, $\mu = 2$ and $\sigma = 3$; for the next three years, $\mu = 3$ and $\sigma = 4$. If the initial value of the variable is 5, what is the probability distribution of the value of the variable at the end of year 6?

11.6. Suppose that $G$ is a function of a stock price, $S$, and time. Suppose that $\sigma_S$ and $\sigma_G$ are the volatilities of $S$ and $G$. Show that when the expected return of $S$ increases by $\lambda \sigma_S$, the growth rate of $G$ increases by $\lambda \sigma_G$, where $\lambda$ is a constant.

11.7. Stock A and stock B both follow geometric Brownian motion. Changes in any short interval of time are uncorrelated with each other. Does the value of a portfolio consisting of one of stock A and one of stock B follow geometric Brownian motion? Explain your answer.

11.8. The process for the stock price in equation (11.8) is

$$\delta S = \mu S\, \delta t + \sigma S \epsilon \sqrt{\delta t}$$

where $\mu$ and $\sigma$ are constant. Explain carefully the difference between this model and each of the following:

$$\delta S = \mu\, \delta t + \sigma \epsilon \sqrt{\delta t}$$
$$\delta S = \mu S\, \delta t + \sigma \epsilon \sqrt{\delta t}$$
$$\delta S = \mu\, \delta t + \sigma S \epsilon \sqrt{\delta t}$$

Why is the model in equation (11.8) a more appropriate model of stock price behavior than any of these three alternatives?

11.9. It has been suggested that the short-term interest rate, $r$, follows the stochastic process

$$dr = a(b - r)\, dt + rc\, dz$$

where $a$, $b$, and $c$ are positive constants and $dz$ is a Wiener process. Describe the nature of this process.

11.10. Suppose that a stock price, $S$, follows geometric Brownian motion with expected return $\mu$ and volatility $\sigma$:

$$dS = \mu S\, dt + \sigma S\, dz$$

What is the process followed by the variable $S^n$? Show that $S^n$ also follows geometric Brownian motion.

11.11. Suppose that $x$ is the yield to maturity with continuous compounding on a zero-coupon bond that pays off \$1 at time $T$. Assume that $x$ follows the process

$$dx = a(x_0 - x)\, dt + sx\, dz$$

where $a$, $x_0$, and $s$ are positive constants and $dz$ is a Wiener process. What is the process followed by the bond price?

## ASSIGNMENT QUESTIONS

11.12. Suppose that a stock price has an expected return of 16% per annum and a volatility of 30% per annum. When the stock price at the end of a certain day is \$50, calculate the following:
   a. The expected stock price at the end of the next day
   b. The standard deviation of the stock price at the end of the next day
   c. The 95% confidence limits for the stock price at the end of the next day

11.13. A company's cash position (in millions of dollars) follows a generalized Wiener process with a drift rate of 0.1 per month and a variance rate of 0.16 per month. The initial cash position is 2.0.
   a. What are the probability distributions of the cash position after one month, six months, and one year?
   b. What are the probabilities of a negative cash position at the end of six months and one year?
   c. At what time in the future is the probability of a negative cash position greatest?

11.14. Suppose that $x$ is the yield on a perpetual government bond that pays interest at the rate of $1 per annum. Assume that $x$ is expressed with continuous compounding, that interest is paid continuously on the bond, and that $x$ follows the process

$$dx = a(x_0 - x)\,dt + sx\,dz$$

where $a$, $x_0$, and $s$ are positive constants and $dz$ is a Wiener process. What is the process followed by the bond price? What is the expected instantaneous return (including interest and capital gains) to the holder of the bond?

11.15. If $S$ follows the geometric Brownian motion process in equation (11.12), what is the process followed by:
   a. $y = 2S$?
   b. $y = S^2$?
   c. $y = e^S$?
   d. $y = e^{r(T-t)}/S$?
   In each case express the coefficients of $dt$ and $dz$ in terms of $y$ rather than $S$.

11.16. A stock price is currently 50. Its expected return and volatility are 12% and 30%, respectively. What is the probability that the stock price will be greater than 80 in two years? (*Hint*: $S_T > 80$ when $\ln S_T > \ln 80$.)

# APPENDIX 11A
## Derivation of Itô's Lemma

In this appendix, we show how Itô's lemma can be regarded as a natural extension of other, simpler results. Consider a continuous and differentiable function $G$ of a variable $x$. If $\delta x$ is a small change in $x$ and $\delta G$ is the resulting small change in $G$, a well-known result from ordinary calculus is

$$\delta G \approx \frac{dG}{dx}\,\delta x \qquad (11A.1)$$

In other words, $\delta G$ is approximately equal to the rate of change of $G$ with respect to $x$ multiplied by $\delta x$. The error involves terms of order $\delta x^2$. If more precision is required, a Taylor series expansion of $\delta G$ can be used:

$$\delta G = \frac{dG}{dx}\,\delta x + \tfrac{1}{2}\frac{d^2G}{dx^2}\,\delta x^2 + \frac{d^3G}{dx^3}\,\delta x^3 + \cdots$$

For a continuous and differentiable function $G$ of two variables $x$ and $y$, the result analogous to equation (11A.1) is

$$\delta G \approx \frac{\partial G}{\partial x}\,\delta x + \frac{\partial G}{\partial y}\,\delta y \qquad (11A.2)$$

and the Taylor series expansion of $\delta G$ is

$$\delta G = \frac{\partial G}{\partial x}\,\delta x + \frac{\partial G}{\partial y}\,\delta y + \tfrac{1}{2}\frac{\partial^2 G}{\partial x^2}\,\delta x^2 + \frac{\partial^2 G}{\partial x\,\partial y}\,\delta x\,\delta y + \tfrac{1}{2}\frac{\partial^2 G}{\partial y^2}\,\delta y^2 + \cdots \qquad (11A.3)$$

In the limit as $\delta x$ and $\delta y$ tend to zero, equation (11A.3) becomes

$$dG = \frac{\partial G}{\partial x}\,dx + \frac{\partial G}{\partial y}\,dy \qquad (11A.4)$$

We now extend equation (11A.4) to cover functions of variables following Itô processes. Suppose that a variable $x$ follows the Itô process in equation (11.4), that is,

$$dx = a(x,t)\,dt + b(x,t)\,dz \qquad (11A.5)$$

and that $G$ is some function of $x$ and of time $t$. By analogy with equation (11A.3), we can write

$$\delta G = \frac{\partial G}{\partial x}\,\delta x + \frac{\partial G}{\partial t}\,\delta t + \tfrac{1}{2}\frac{\partial^2 G}{\partial x^2}\,\delta x^2 + \frac{\partial^2 G}{\partial x\,\partial t}\,\delta x\,\delta t + \tfrac{1}{2}\frac{\partial^2 G}{\partial t^2}\,\delta t^2 + \cdots \qquad (11A.6)$$

Equation (11A.5) can be discretized to

$$\delta x = a(x,t)\,\delta t + b(x,t)\epsilon\sqrt{\delta t}$$

or, if arguments are dropped,

$$\delta x = a\,\delta t + b\epsilon\sqrt{\delta t} \qquad (11A.7)$$

This equation reveals an important difference between the situation in equation (11A.6) and the situation in equation (11A.3). When limiting arguments were used to move from equation (11A.3) to equation (11A.4), terms in $\delta x^2$ were ignored because they were second-order terms. From equation (11A.7), we have

$$\delta x^2 = b^2 \epsilon^2 \, \delta t + \text{terms of higher order in } \delta t \tag{11A.8}$$

This shows that the term involving $\delta x^2$ in equation (11A.6) has a component that is of order $\delta t$ and cannot be ignored.

The variance of a standardized normal distribution is 1.0. This means that

$$E(\epsilon^2) - [E(\epsilon)]^2 = 1$$

where $E$ denotes the expected value. Because $E(\epsilon) = 0$, it follows that $E(\epsilon^2) = 1$. The expected value of $\epsilon^2 \, \delta t$ is therefore $\delta t$. It can be shown that the variance of $\epsilon^2 \, \delta t$ is of order $\delta t^2$ and that, as a result of this, we can treat $\epsilon^2 \, \delta t$ as nonstochastic and equal to its expected value of $\delta t$ as $\delta t$ tends to zero. It follows from equation (11A.8) that $\delta x^2$ becomes nonstochastic and equal to $b^2 \, dt$ as $\delta t$ tends to zero. Taking limits as $\delta x$ and $\delta t$ tend to zero in equation (11A.6) and using this last result, we obtain

$$dG = \frac{\partial G}{\partial x} \, dx + \frac{\partial G}{\partial t} \, dt + \tfrac{1}{2} \frac{\partial^2 G}{\partial x^2} b^2 \, dt \tag{11A.9}$$

This is Itô's lemma. If we substitute for $dx$ from equation (11A.5), then equation (11A.9) becomes

$$dG = \left( \frac{\partial G}{\partial x} a + \frac{\partial G}{\partial t} + \tfrac{1}{2} \frac{\partial^2 G}{\partial x^2} b^2 \right) dt + \frac{\partial G}{\partial x} b \, dz$$

# CHAPTER 12

# THE BLACK–SCHOLES MODEL

In the early 1970s, Fischer Black, Myron Scholes, and Robert Merton made a major breakthrough in the pricing of stock options.[1] This involved the development of what has become known as the Black–Scholes model. The model has had a huge influence on the way that traders price and hedge options. It has also been pivotal to the growth and success of financial engineering in the 1980s and 1990s. In 1997, the importance of the model was recognized when Robert Merton and Myron Scholes were awarded the Nobel prize for economics. Sadly, Fischer Black died in 1995; otherwise he also would undoubtedly have been one of the recipients of this prize.

This chapter shows how the Black–Scholes model for valuing European call and put options on a non-dividend-paying stock is derived. We explain how volatility can be either estimated from historical data or implied from option prices using the model. We show how the risk-neutral valuation argument introduced in Chapter 10 can be used. We also show how the Black–Scholes model can be extended to deal with European call and put options on dividend-paying stocks and present some results on the pricing of American call options on dividend-paying stocks.

## 12.1 LOGNORMAL PROPERTY OF STOCK PRICES

The model of stock price behavior used by Black, Scholes, and Merton is the model we developed in Chapter 11. It assumes that percentage changes in the stock price in a short period of time are normally distributed. Define:

$\mu$: Expected return on stock

$\sigma$: Volatility of the stock price

The mean of the percentage change in time $\delta t$ is $\mu \, \delta t$ and the standard deviation of this percentage change is $\sigma \sqrt{\delta t}$, so that

$$\frac{\delta S}{S} \sim \phi(\mu \, \delta t, \sigma \sqrt{\delta t}) \tag{12.1}$$

where $\delta S$ is the change in the stock price $S$ in time $\delta t$, and $\phi(m, s)$ denotes a normal distribution with mean $m$ and standard deviation $s$.

---

[1] See F. Black and M. Scholes, "The Pricing of Options and Corporate Liabilities," *Journal of Political Economy*, 81 (May/June 1973), 637–659; R. C. Merton, "Theory of Rational Option Pricing," *Bell Journal of Economics and Management Science*, 4 (Spring 1973), 141–83.

As shown in Section 11.7, the model implies that

$$\ln S_T - \ln S_0 \sim \phi\left[\left(\mu - \frac{\sigma^2}{2}\right)T,\ \sigma\sqrt{T}\right]$$

From this it follows that

$$\ln\frac{S_T}{S_0} \sim \phi\left[\left(\mu - \frac{\sigma^2}{2}\right)T,\ \sigma\sqrt{T}\right] \tag{12.2}$$

and

$$\ln S_T \sim \phi\left[\ln S_0 + \left(\mu - \frac{\sigma^2}{2}\right)T,\ \sigma\sqrt{T}\right] \tag{12.3}$$

where $S_T$ is the stock price at a future time $T$ and $S_0$ is the stock price at time zero. Equation (12.3) shows that $\ln S_T$ is normally distributed. This means that $S_T$ has a lognormal distribution.

**Example 12.1**   Consider a stock with an initial price of $40, an expected return of 16% per annum, and a volatility of 20% per annum. From equation (12.3), the probability distribution of the stock price, $S_T$, in six months' time is given by

$$\ln S_T \sim \phi[\ln 40 + (0.16 - 0.2^2/2) \times 0.5,\ 0.2\sqrt{0.5}]$$
$$\ln S_T \sim \phi(3.759, 0.141)$$

There is a 95% probability that a normally distributed variable has a value within 1.96 standard deviations of its mean. Hence, with 95% confidence,

$$3.759 - 1.96 \times 0.141 < \ln S_T < 3.759 + 1.96 \times 0.141$$

This can be written

$$e^{3.759-1.96\times0.141} < S_T < e^{3.759+1.96\times0.141}$$

or

$$32.55 < S_T < 56.56$$

Thus, there is a 95% probability that the stock price in six months will lie between 32.55 and 56.56.

A variable that has a lognormal distribution can take any value between zero and infinity. Figure 12.1 illustrates the shape of a lognormal distribution. Unlike the normal distribution, it

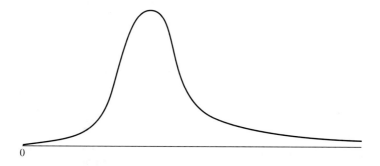

**Figure 12.1**   Lognormal distribution

is skewed so that the mean, median, and mode are all different. From equation (12.3) and the properties of the lognormal distribution, it can be shown that the expected value, $E(S_T)$, of $S_T$ is given by[2]

$$E(S_T) = S_0 e^{\mu T} \tag{12.4}$$

This fits in with the definition of $\mu$ as the expected rate of return. The variance, $\text{var}(S_T)$, of $S_T$ can be shown to be given by

$$\text{var}(S_T) = S_0^2 e^{2\mu T}(e^{\sigma^2 T} - 1) \tag{12.5}$$

**Example 12.2**  Consider a stock where the current price is $20, the expected return is 20% per annum, and the volatility is 40% per annum. The expected stock price in one year, $E(S_T)$, and the variance of the stock price in one year, $\text{var}(S_T)$, are given by

$$E(S_T) = 20e^{0.2 \times 1} = 24.43$$

$$\text{var}(S_T) = 400e^{2 \times 0.2 \times 1}(e^{0.4^2 \times 1} - 1) = 103.54$$

The standard deviation of the stock price in one year is $\sqrt{103.54}$, or 10.18.

## 12.2  THE DISTRIBUTION OF THE RATE OF RETURN

The lognormal property of stock prices can be used to provide information on the probability distribution of the continuously compounded rate of return earned on a stock between times zero and $T$. Define the continuously compounded rate of return per annum realized between times zero and $T$ as $\eta$. It follows that

$$S_T = S_0 e^{\eta T}$$

so that

$$\eta = \frac{1}{T} \ln \frac{S_T}{S_0} \tag{12.6}$$

It follows from equation (12.2) that

$$\eta \sim \phi\left(\mu - \frac{\sigma^2}{2}, \frac{\sigma}{\sqrt{T}}\right) \tag{12.7}$$

Thus, the continuously compounded rate of return per annum is normally distributed with mean $\mu - \sigma^2/2$ and standard deviation $\sigma/\sqrt{T}$.[3]

---

[2]  For a discussion of the properties of the lognormal distribution, see J. Aitchison and J. A. C. Brown, *The Lognormal Distribution*, Cambridge University Press, Cambridge, 1966.

[3]  As $T$ increases, the standard deviation of $\eta$ declines. To understand the reason for this, consider two cases: $T = 1$ and $T = 20$. We are more certain about the average return per year over 20 years than we are about the return in any one year.

**Example 12.3** Consider a stock with an expected return of 17% per annum and a volatility of 20% per annum. The probability distribution for the actual rate of return (continuously compounded) realized over three years is normal with mean

$$0.17 - \frac{0.2^2}{2} = 0.15$$

or 15% per annum and standard deviation

$$\frac{0.2}{\sqrt{3}} = 0.1155$$

or 11.55% per annum. Because there is a 95% chance that a normally distributed variable will lie within 1.96 standard deviations of its mean, we can be 95% confident that the actual return realized over three years will be between −7.6% and +37.6% per annum.

## 12.3 THE EXPECTED RETURN

The expected return, $\mu$, required by investors from a stock depends on the riskiness of the stock. The higher the risk, the higher the expected return. It also depends on the level of interest rates in the economy. The higher the level of interest rates, the higher the expected return required on any given stock. Fortunately, we do not have to concern ourselves with the determinants of $\mu$ in any detail. It turns out that the value of a stock option, when expressed in terms of the value of the underlying stock, does not depend on $\mu$ at all. Nevertheless, there is one aspect of the expected return from a stock that frequently causes confusion and is worth explaining.

Equation (12.1) shows that $\mu \, \delta t$ is the expected percentage change in the stock price in a very short period of time $\delta t$. This means that $\mu$ is the expected return in a very short period of time $\delta t$. It is natural to assume that $\mu$ is also the expected continuously compounded return on the stock over a relatively long period of time. However, this is not the case. The continuously compounded return realized over $T$ years is

$$\frac{1}{T} \ln \frac{S_T}{S_0}$$

and equation (12.7) shows that the expected value of this is $\mu - \sigma^2/2$.

The reason for the distinction between the $\mu$ in equation (12.1) and the $\mu - \sigma^2/2$ in equation (12.7) is subtle but important. We start with equation (12.4):

$$E(S_T) = S_0 e^{\mu T}$$

Taking logarithms, we get

$$\ln[E(S_T)] = \ln(S_0) + \mu T$$

It is now tempting to set

$$\ln[E(S_T)] = E[\ln(S_T)]$$

so that $E[\ln(S_T)] - \ln(S_0) = \mu T$, or $E[\ln(S_T/S_0)] = \mu T$. However, we cannot do this because ln is a nonlinear function. In fact $\ln[E(S_T)] > E[\ln(S_T)]$, so that $E[\ln(S_T/S_0)] < \mu T$. This is consistent with equation (12.7).

Suppose we consider a very large number of very short periods of time of length $\delta t$. Define $S_i$ as the stock price at the end of the $i$th interval and $\delta S_i$ as $S_{i+1} - S_i$. Under the assumptions we are making for stock price behavior, the average of the returns on the stock in each interval is close to $\mu$. In other words, $\mu$ is close to the arithmetic mean of the $\delta S_i/S_i$. However, the expected return over the whole period covered by the data, expressed with a compounding period of $\delta t$, is close to $\mu - \sigma^2/2$, not $\mu$.[4]

**Example 12.4**  Suppose that the following is a sequence of returns per annum on a stock, measured using annual compounding:

$$15\%, \quad 20\%, \quad 30\%, \quad -20\%, \quad 25\%$$

The arithmetic mean of the returns, calculated by taking the sum of the returns and dividing by 5, is 14%. However, an investor would actually earn less than 14% per annum by leaving the money invested in the stock for five years. The dollar value of $100 at the end of the five years would be

$$100 \times 1.15 \times 1.20 \times 1.30 \times 0.80 \times 1.25 = \$179.40$$

By contrast, a 14% return with annual compounding would give

$$100 \times 1.14^5 = \$192.54$$

The actual average return earned by the investor, with annual compounding, is

$$(1.7940)^{1/5} - 1 = 0.124$$

or 12.4% per annum.

The arguments in this section show that the term *expected return* is ambiguous. It can refer either to $\mu$ or to $\mu - \sigma^2/2$. Unless otherwise stated, it will be used to refer to $\mu$ throughout this book.

## 12.4  VOLATILITY

The volatility of a stock, $\sigma$, is a measure of our uncertainty about the returns provided by the stock. Stocks typically have a volatility between 20% and 50%.

From equation (12.7), the volatility of a stock price can be defined as the standard deviation of the return provided by the stock in one year when the return is expressed using continuous compounding.

When $T$ is small, equation (12.1) shows that $\sigma\sqrt{T}$ is approximately equal to the standard deviation of the percentage change in the stock price in time $T$. Suppose that $\sigma = 0.3$, or 30% per annum, and the current stock price is $50. The standard deviation of the percentage change in the stock price in one week is approximately

$$30 \times \sqrt{\frac{1}{52}} = 4.16\%$$

A one-standard-deviation move in the stock price in one week is therefore $50 \times 0.0416$, or $2.08.

Equation (12.1) shows that our uncertainty about a future stock price, as measured by its standard deviation, increases—at least approximately—with the square root of how far ahead we

---

[4]  If we define the *gross return* as one plus the regular return, the gross return over the whole period covered by the data is the geometric average of the gross returns in each time interval of length $\delta t$—not the arithmetic average. The geometric average is less than the arithmetic average.

are looking. For example, the standard deviation of the stock price in four weeks is approximately twice the standard deviation in one week.

### Estimating Volatility from Historical Data

To estimate the volatility of a stock price empirically, the stock price is usually observed at fixed intervals of time (e.g., every day, week, or month).

Define:

$n + 1$ : Number of observations

$S_i$ : Stock price at end of $i$th $(i = 0, 1, \ldots, n)$ interval

$\tau$ : Length of time interval in years

and let

$$u_i = \ln\left(\frac{S_i}{S_{i-1}}\right)$$

for $i = 1, 2, \ldots, n$.

The usual estimate, $s$, of the standard deviation of the $u_i$'s is given by

$$s = \sqrt{\frac{1}{n-1} \sum_{i=1}^{n} (u_i - \bar{u})^2}$$

or

$$s = \sqrt{\frac{1}{n-1} \sum_{i=1}^{n} u_i^2 - \frac{1}{n(n-1)} \left(\sum_{i=1}^{n} u_i\right)^2}$$

where $\bar{u}$ is the mean of the $u_i$'s.

From equation (12.2), the standard deviation of the $u_i$'s is $\sigma\sqrt{\tau}$. The variable $s$ is therefore an estimate of $\sigma\sqrt{\tau}$. It follows that $\sigma$ itself can be estimated as $\hat{\sigma}$, where

$$\hat{\sigma} = \frac{s}{\sqrt{\tau}}$$

The standard error of this estimate can be shown to be approximately $\hat{\sigma}/\sqrt{2n}$.

Choosing an appropriate value for $n$ is not easy. More data generally lead to more accuracy, but $\sigma$ does change over time and data that are too old may not be relevant for predicting the future. A compromise that seems to work reasonably well is to use closing prices from daily data over the most recent 90 to 180 days. An often-used rule of thumb is to set $n$ equal to the number of days to which the volatility is to be applied. Thus, if the volatility estimate is to be used to value a two-year option, then daily data for the last two years are used. More sophisticated approaches to estimating volatility involving GARCH models are discussed in Chapter 17.

An important issue is whether time should be measured in calendar days or trading days when volatility parameters are being estimated and used. Later in this chapter, we show that empirical research indicates that trading days should be used. In other words, days when the exchange is closed should be ignored for the purposes of the volatility calculation.

> **Example 12.5**   Table 12.1 shows a possible sequence of stock prices during 21 consecutive trading days. In this case
>
> $$\sum u_i = 0.09531 \quad \text{and} \quad \sum u_i^2 = 0.00326$$

**Table 12.1**  Computation of volatility

| Day | Closing stock price ($) | Price relative $S_i/S_{i-1}$ | Daily return $u_i = \ln(S_i/S_{i-1})$ |
|-----|-----|-----|-----|
| 0 | 20.00 | | |
| 1 | 20.10 | 1.00500 | 0.00499 |
| 2 | 19.90 | 0.99005 | −0.01000 |
| 3 | 20.00 | 1.00503 | 0.00501 |
| 4 | 20.50 | 1.02500 | 0.02469 |
| 5 | 20.25 | 0.98780 | −0.01227 |
| 6 | 20.90 | 1.03210 | 0.03159 |
| 7 | 20.90 | 1.00000 | 0.00000 |
| 8 | 20.90 | 1.00000 | 0.00000 |
| 9 | 20.75 | 0.99282 | −0.00720 |
| 10 | 20.75 | 1.00000 | 0.00000 |
| 11 | 21.00 | 1.01205 | 0.01198 |
| 12 | 21.10 | 1.00476 | 0.00475 |
| 13 | 20.90 | 0.99052 | −0.00952 |
| 14 | 20.90 | 1.00000 | 0.00000 |
| 15 | 21.25 | 1.01675 | 0.01661 |
| 16 | 21.40 | 1.00706 | 0.00703 |
| 17 | 21.40 | 1.00000 | 0.00000 |
| 18 | 21.25 | 0.99299 | −0.00703 |
| 19 | 21.75 | 1.02353 | 0.02326 |
| 20 | 22.00 | 1.01149 | 0.01143 |

and the estimate of the standard deviation of the daily return is

$$\sqrt{\frac{0.00326}{19} - \frac{0.09531^2}{380}} = 0.01216$$

or 1.216%. Assuming that there are 252 trading days per year, $\tau = 1/252$ and the data give an estimate for the volatility per annum of $0.01216\sqrt{252} = 0.193$, or 19.3%. The standard error of this estimate is

$$\frac{0.193}{\sqrt{2 \times 20}} = 0.031$$

or 3.1% per annum.

This analysis assumes that the stock pays no dividends, but it can be adapted to accommodate dividend-paying stocks. The return, $u_i$, during a time interval that includes an ex-dividend day is given by

$$u_i = \ln\frac{S_i + D}{S_{i-1}}$$

where $D$ is the amount of the dividend. The return in other time intervals is still

$$u_i = \ln\frac{S_i}{S_{i-1}}$$

However, as tax factors play a part in determining returns around an ex-dividend date, it is probably best to discard altogether data for intervals that include an ex-dividend date.

## 12.5 CONCEPTS UNDERLYING THE BLACK–SCHOLES–MERTON DIFFERENTIAL EQUATION

The Black–Scholes–Merton differential equation is an equation that must be satisfied by the price of any derivative dependent on a non-dividend-paying stock. The equation is derived in the next section. Here we consider the nature of the arguments we will use.

The arguments are similar to the no-arbitrage arguments we used to value stock options in Chapter 10 for the situation where stock price movements are binomial. They involve setting up a riskless portfolio consisting of a position in the derivative and a position in the stock. In absence of arbitrage opportunities, the return from the portfolio must be the risk-free interest rate, $r$. This leads to the Black–Scholes–Merton differential equation.

The reason a riskless portfolio can be set up is that the stock price and the derivative price are both affected by the same underlying source of uncertainty: stock price movements. In any short period of time, the price of the derivative is perfectly correlated with the price of the underlying stock. When an appropriate portfolio of the stock and the derivative is established, the gain or loss from the stock position always offsets the gain or loss from the derivative position so that the overall value of the portfolio at the end of the short period of time is known with certainty.

Suppose, for example, that at a particular point in time the relationship between a small change in the stock price, $\delta S$, and the resultant small change in the price of a European call option, $\delta c$, is given by

$$\delta c = 0.4\,\delta S$$

This means that the slope of the line representing the relationship between $c$ and $S$ is 0.4, as indicated in Figure 12.2. The riskless portfolio would consist of:

1. A long position in 0.4 share
2. A short position in one call option

There is one important difference between the Black–Scholes–Merton analysis and our analysis

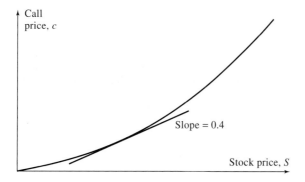

**Figure 12.2**   Relationship between $c$ and $S$

using a binomial model in Chapter 10. In the former, the position in the stock and the derivative is riskless for only a very short period of time. (In theory, it remains riskless only for an instantaneously short period of time.) To remain riskless, it must be adjusted, or *rebalanced*, frequently.[5] For example, the relationship between $\delta c$ and $\delta S$ in our example might change from $\delta c = 0.4\,\delta S$ today to $\delta c = 0.5\,\delta S$ in two weeks. This would mean that, in order to maintain the riskless position, an extra 0.1 share would have to be purchased for each call option sold. It is nevertheless true that the return from the riskless portfolio in any very short period of time must be the risk-free interest rate. This is the key element in the Black–Scholes analysis and leads to their pricing formulas.

### Assumptions

The assumptions we use to derive the Black–Scholes–Merton differential equation are as follows:

1. The stock price follows the process developed in Chapter 11 with $\mu$ and $\sigma$ constant.
2. The short selling of securities with full use of proceeds is permitted.
3. There are no transactions costs or taxes. All securities are perfectly divisible.
4. There are no dividends during the life of the derivative.
5. There are no riskless arbitrage opportunities.
6. Security trading is continuous.
7. The risk-free rate of interest, $r$, is constant and the same for all maturities.

As we discuss in later chapters, some of these assumptions can be relaxed. For example, $\sigma$ and $r$ can be a known function of $t$. We can even allow interest rates to be stochastic providing that the stock price distribution at maturity of the option is still lognormal.

## 12.6   DERIVATION OF THE BLACK–SCHOLES–MERTON DIFFERENTIAL EQUATION

The stock price process we are assuming is the one we developed in Section 11.3:

$$dS = \mu S\,dt + \sigma S\,dz \tag{12.8}$$

Suppose that $f$ is the price of a call option or other derivative contingent on $S$. The variable $f$ must be some function of $S$ and $t$. Hence, from equation (11.14),

$$df = \left(\frac{\partial f}{\partial S}\mu S + \frac{\partial f}{\partial t} + \tfrac{1}{2}\frac{\partial^2 f}{\partial S^2}\sigma^2 S^2\right)dt + \frac{\partial f}{\partial S}\sigma S\,dz \tag{12.9}$$

The discrete versions of equations (12.8) and (12.9) are

$$\delta S = \mu S\,\delta t + \sigma S\,\delta z \tag{12.10}$$

and

$$\delta f = \left(\frac{\partial f}{\partial S}\mu S + \frac{\partial f}{\partial t} + \tfrac{1}{2}\frac{\partial^2 f}{\partial S^2}\sigma^2 S^2\right)\delta t + \frac{\partial f}{\partial S}\sigma S\,\delta z \tag{12.11}$$

---

[5] We discuss the rebalancing of portfolios in more detail in Chapter 14.

where $\delta S$ and $\delta f$ are the changes in $f$ and $S$ in a small time interval $\delta t$. Recall from the discussion of Itô's lemma in Section 11.6 that the Wiener processes underlying $f$ and $S$ are the same. In other words, the $\delta z \, (= \epsilon \sqrt{\delta t})$ in equations (12.10) and (12.11) are the same. It follows that, by choosing a portfolio of the stock and the derivative, the Wiener process can be eliminated.

The appropriate portfolio is as follows:

$$-1: \quad \text{derivative}$$

$$+\frac{\partial f}{\partial S}: \quad \text{shares}$$

The holder of this portfolio is short one derivative and long an amount $\partial f / \partial S$ of shares. Define $\Pi$ as the value of the portfolio. By definition,

$$\Pi = -f + \frac{\partial f}{\partial S} S \tag{12.12}$$

The change $\delta \Pi$ in the value of the portfolio in the time interval $\delta t$ is given by

$$\delta \Pi = -\delta f + \frac{\partial f}{\partial S} \delta S \tag{12.13}$$

Substituting equations (12.10) and (12.11) into equation (12.13) yields

$$\delta \Pi = \left( -\frac{\partial f}{\partial t} - \frac{1}{2} \frac{\partial^2 f}{\partial S^2} \sigma^2 S^2 \right) \delta t \tag{12.14}$$

Because this equation does not involve $\delta z$, the portfolio must be riskless during time $\delta t$. The assumptions listed in the preceding section imply that the portfolio must instantaneously earn the same rate of return as other short-term risk-free securities. If it earned more than this return, arbitrageurs could make a riskless profit by borrowing money to buy the portfolio; if it earned less, they could make a riskless profit by shorting the portfolio and buying risk-free securities. It follows that

$$\delta \Pi = r \Pi \, \delta t$$

where $r$ is the risk-free interest rate. Substituting from equations (12.12) and (12.14), we obtain

$$\left( \frac{\partial f}{\partial t} + \frac{1}{2} \frac{\partial^2 f}{\partial S^2} \sigma^2 S^2 \right) \delta t = r \left( f - \frac{\partial f}{\partial S} S \right) \delta t$$

so that

$$\frac{\partial f}{\partial t} + r S \frac{\partial f}{\partial S} + \frac{1}{2} \sigma^2 S^2 \frac{\partial^2 f}{\partial S^2} = r f \tag{12.15}$$

Equation (12.15) is the Black–Scholes–Merton differential equation. It has many solutions, corresponding to all the different derivatives that can be defined with $S$ as the underlying variable. The particular derivative that is obtained when the equation is solved depends on the *boundary conditions* that are used. These specify the values of the derivative at the boundaries of possible values of $S$ and $t$. In the case of a European call option, the key boundary condition is

$$f = \max(S - K, \, 0) \quad \text{when } t = T$$

In the case of a European put option, it is

$$f = \max(K - S, 0) \quad \text{when } t = T$$

One point that should be emphasized about the portfolio used in the derivation of equation (12.15) is that it is not permanently riskless. It is riskless only for an infinitesimally short period of time. As $S$ and $t$ change, $\partial f/\partial S$ also changes. To keep the portfolio riskless, it is therefore necessary to frequently change the relative proportions of the derivative and the stock in the portfolio.

> **Example 12.6**   A forward contract on a non-dividend-paying stock is a derivative dependent on the stock. As such, it should satisfy equation (12.15). From equation (3.9), we know that the value of the forward contract, $f$, at a general time $t$ is given in terms of the stock price $S$ at this time by
>
> $$f = S - Ke^{-r(T-t)}$$
>
> where $K$ is the delivery price. This means that
>
> $$\frac{\partial f}{\partial t} = -rKe^{-r(T-t)}, \qquad \frac{\partial f}{\partial S} = 1, \qquad \frac{\partial^2 f}{\partial S^2} = 0$$
>
> When these are substituted into the left-hand side of equation (12.15), we obtain
>
> $$-rKe^{-r(T-t)} + rS$$
>
> This equals $rf$, showing that equation (12.15) is indeed satisfied.

### The Prices of Tradeable Derivatives

Any function $f(S, t)$ that is a solution of the differential equation (12.15) is the theoretical price of a derivative that could be traded. If a derivative with that price existed, it would not create any arbitrage opportunities. Conversely, if a function $f(S, t)$ does not satisfy the differential equation (12.15), it cannot be the price of a derivative without creating arbitrage opportunities for traders.

To illustrate this point, consider first the function $e^S$. This does not satisfy the differential equation (12.15). It is, therefore, not a candidate for being the price of a derivative dependent on the stock price. If an instrument whose price was always $e^S$ existed, there would be an arbitrage opportunity. As a second example, consider the function

$$\frac{e^{(\sigma^2 - 2r)(T-t)}}{S}$$

This does satisfy the differential equation, and so is, in theory, the price of a tradeable security. (It is the price of a derivative that pays off $1/S_T$ at time $T$.) For other examples of tradeable derivatives, see Problems 12.11, 12.12, 12.23, and 12.26.

## 12.7   RISK-NEUTRAL VALUATION

We introduced risk-neutral valuation in connection with the binomial model in Chapter 10. It is without doubt the single most important tool for the analysis of derivatives. It arises from one key property of the Black–Scholes–Merton differential equation (12.15). This property is that the equation does not involve any variable that is affected by the risk preferences of investors. The variables that do appear in the equation are the current stock price, time, stock price volatility, and the risk-free rate of interest. All are independent of risk preferences.

The Black–Scholes–Merton differential equation would not be independent of risk preferences if it involved the expected return on the stock, $\mu$. This is because the value of $\mu$ does depend on risk preferences. The higher the level of risk aversion by investors, the higher $\mu$ will be for any given stock. It is fortunate that $\mu$ happens to drop out in the derivation of the differential equation.

Because the Black–Scholes–Merton differential equation is independent of risk preferences, an ingenious argument can be used. If risk preferences do not enter the equation, they cannot affect its solution. Any set of risk preferences can, therefore, be used when evaluating $f$. In particular, the very simple assumption that all investors are risk neutral can be made.

In a world where investors are risk neutral, the expected return on all securities is the risk-free rate of interest, $r$. The reason is that risk-neutral investors do not require a premium to induce them to take risks. It is also true that the present value of any cash flow in a risk-neutral world can be obtained by discounting its expected value at the risk-free rate. The assumption that the world is risk neutral, therefore, considerably simplifies the analysis of derivatives.

Consider a derivative that provides a payoff at one particular time. It can be valued using risk-neutral valuation by using the following procedure:

1. Assume that the expected return from the underlying asset is the risk-free interest rate, $r$ (i.e., assume $\mu = r$).

2. Calculate the expected payoff from the option at its maturity.

3. Discount the expected payoff at the risk-free interest rate.

It is important to appreciate that risk-neutral valuation (or the assumption that all investors are risk neutral) is merely an artificial device for obtaining solutions to the Black–Scholes differential equation. The solutions that are obtained are valid in all worlds, not just those where investors are risk neutral. When we move from a risk-neutral world to a risk-averse world, two things happen. The expected growth rate in the stock price changes and the discount rate that must be used for any payoffs from the derivative changes. It happens that these two changes always offset each other exactly.

### Application to Forward Contracts on a Stock

We valued forward contracts on a non-dividend-paying stock in Section 3.5. In Example 12.6 we verified that the pricing formula satisfies the Black–Scholes differential equation. In this section we derive the pricing formula from risk-neutral valuation. We make the assumption that interest rates are constant and equal to $r$. This is somewhat more restrictive than the assumption in Chapter 3.

Consider a long forward contract that matures at time $T$ with delivery price $K$. As explained in Chapter 1, the value of the contract at maturity is

$$S_T - K$$

where $S_T$ is the stock price at time $T$. From the risk-neutral valuation argument, the value of the forward contract at time zero is its expected value at time $T$ in a risk-neutral world discounted at the risk-free rate of interest. If we denote the value of the forward contract at time zero by $f$, this means that

$$f = e^{-rT} \hat{E}(S_T - K) \tag{12.16}$$

where $\hat{E}$ denotes the expected value in a risk-neutral world. Because $K$ is a constant, equation (12.16) becomes

$$f = e^{-rT}\hat{E}(S_T) - Ke^{-rT} \tag{12.17}$$

The expected growth rate of the stock price, $\mu$, becomes $r$ in a risk-neutral world. Hence, from equation (12.4),

$$\hat{E}(S_T) = S_0 e^{rT} \tag{12.18}$$

Substituting equation (12.18) into equation (12.17) gives

$$f = S_0 - Ke^{-rT} \tag{12.19}$$

This is in agreement with equation (3.9).

## 12.8  BLACK–SCHOLES PRICING FORMULAS

The Black–Scholes formulas for the prices at time zero of a European call option on a non-dividend-paying stock and a European put option on a non-dividend paying stock are

$$c = S_0 N(d_1) - Ke^{-rT} N(d_2) \tag{12.20}$$

and

$$p = Ke^{-rT} N(-d_2) - S_0 N(-d_1) \tag{12.21}$$

where

$$d_1 = \frac{\ln(S_0/K) + (r + \sigma^2/2)T}{\sigma\sqrt{T}}$$

$$d_2 = \frac{\ln(S_0/K) + (r - \sigma^2/2)T}{\sigma\sqrt{T}} = d_1 - \sigma\sqrt{T}$$

The function $N(x)$ is the cumulative probability distribution function for a standardized normal distribution. In other words, it is the probability that a variable with a standard normal distribution, $\phi(0, 1)$ will be less than $x$. It is illustrated in Figure 12.3. The remaining variables should be familiar. The variables $c$ and $p$ are the European call and European put price, $S_0$ is the stock price at time zero, $K$ is the strike price, $r$ is the continuously compounded risk-free rate, $\sigma$ is the stock price volatility, and $T$ is the time to maturity of the option.

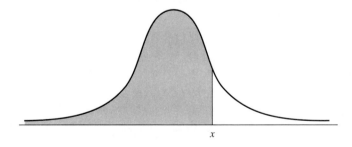

**Figure 12.3**   Shaded area represents $N(x)$

One way of deriving the Black–Scholes formulas is by solving the differential equation (12.15) subject to the boundary conditions mentioned in Section 12.6.[6] Another approach is to use risk-neutral valuation. Consider a European call option. The expected value of the option at maturity in a risk-neutral world is

$$\hat{E}[\max(S_T - K,\, 0)]$$

where, as before, $\hat{E}$ denotes the expected value in a risk-neutral world. From the risk-neutral valuation argument, the European call option price, $c$, is this expected value discounted at the risk-free rate of interest, that is,

$$c = e^{-rT}\hat{E}[\max(S_T - K,\, 0)] \tag{12.22}$$

Appendix 12A shows that this equation leads to the result in (12.20).

To provide an interpretation of the terms in equation (12.20), we note that it can be written

$$c = e^{-rT}[S_0 N(d_1)e^{rT} - KN(d_2)] \tag{12.23}$$

The expression $N(d_2)$ is the probability that the option will be exercised in a risk-neutral world, so that $KN(d_2)$ is the strike price times the probability that the strike price will be paid. The expression $S_0 N(d_1)e^{rT}$ is the expected value of a variable that equals $S_T$ if $S_T > K$ and is zero otherwise in a risk-neutral world.

Because the European price equals the American price when there are no dividends, equation (12.20) also gives the value of an American call option on a non-dividend-paying stock. Unfortunately, no exact analytic formula for the value of an American put option on a non-dividend-paying stock has been produced. Numerical procedures and analytic approximations for calculating American put values are discussed in Chapter 18.

When the Black Scholes formula is used in practice, the interest rate $r$ is set equal to the zero-coupon risk-free interest rate for a maturity $T$. As we show in later chapters, this is theoretically correct when $r$ is a known function of time. It is also theoretically correct when the interest rate is stochastic providing the stock price at time $T$ is lognormal and the volatility parameter is chosen appropriately.

### Properties of the Black–Scholes Formulas

We now show that the Black–Scholes formulas have the right general properties by considering what happens when some of the parameters take extreme values.

When the stock price, $S_0$, becomes very large, a call option is almost certain to be exercised. It then becomes very similar to a forward contract with delivery price $K$. From equation (3.9), we expect the call price to be

$$S_0 - Ke^{-rT}$$

This is, in fact, the call price given by equation (12.20) because, when $S_0$ becomes very large, both $d_1$ and $d_2$ become very large, and $N(d_1)$ and $N(d_2)$ are both close to 1.0. When the stock price becomes

---

[6] The differential equation gives the call and put prices at a general time $t$. For example, the call price that satisfies the differential equation is $c = SN(d_1) - Ke^{-r(T-t)}N(d_2)$, where

$$d_1 = \frac{\ln(S/K) + (r + \sigma^2/2)(T-t)}{\sigma\sqrt{T-t}}$$

and $d_2 = d_1 - \sigma\sqrt{T-t}$. See Problem 12.17 to prove that the differential equation is satisfied.

very large, the price of a European put option, $p$, approaches zero. This is consistent with equation (12.21) because $N(-d_1)$ and $N(-d_2)$ are both close to zero.

Consider next what happens when the volatility $\sigma$ approaches zero. Because the stock is virtually riskless, its price will grow at rate $r$ to $S_0 e^{rT}$ at time $T$ and the payoff from a call option is

$$\max(S_0 e^{rT} - K, 0)$$

If we discount at rate $r$, then the value of the call today is

$$e^{-rT} \max(S_0 e^{rT} - K, 0) = \max(S_0 - Ke^{-rT}, 0)$$

To show that this is consistent with equation (12.20), consider first the case where $S_0 > Ke^{-rT}$. This implies that $\ln(S_0/K) + rT > 0$. As $\sigma$ tends to zero, $d_1$ and $d_2$ tend to $+\infty$, so that $N(d_1)$ and $N(d_2)$ tend to 1.0 and equation (12.20) becomes

$$c = S_0 - Ke^{-rT}$$

When $S_0 < Ke^{-rT}$, it follows that $\ln(S_0/K) + rT < 0$. As $\sigma$ tends to zero, $d_1$ and $d_2$ tend to $-\infty$, so that $N(d_1)$ and $N(d_2)$ tend to zero and equation (12.20) gives a call price of zero. The call price is therefore always $\max(S_0 - Ke^{-rT}, 0)$ as $\sigma$ tends to zero. Similarly, it can be shown that the put price is always $\max(Ke^{-rT} - S_0, 0)$ as $\sigma$ tends to zero.

## 12.9 CUMULATIVE NORMAL DISTRIBUTION FUNCTION

The only problem in implementing equations (12.20) and (12.21) is in calculating the cumulative normal distribution function, $N$. Tables for $N(x)$ are provided at the end of this book. A polynomial approximation that gives six-decimal-place accuracy is[7]

$$N(x) = \begin{cases} 1 - N'(x)(a_1 k + a_2 k^2 + a_3 k^3 + a_4 k^4 + a_5 k^5) & \text{if } x \geqslant 0 \\ 1 - N(-x) & \text{if } x < 0 \end{cases}$$

where

$$k = \frac{1}{1 + \gamma x}, \quad \gamma = 0.2316419$$

$$a_1 = 0.319381530, \quad a_2 = -0.356563782, \quad a_3 = 1.781477937,$$

$$a_4 = -1.821255978, \quad a_5 = 1.330274429$$

$$N'(x) = \frac{1}{\sqrt{2\pi}} e^{-x^2/2}$$

**Example 12.7** The stock price six months from the expiration of an option is $42, the exercise price of the option is $40, the risk-free interest rate is 10% per annum, and the volatility is 20% per

---

[7] See M. Abramowitz and I. Stegun, *Handbook of Mathematical Functions*, Dover Publications, New York, 1972. The function NORMSDIST in Excel can also be used.

annum. This means that $S_0 = 42$, $K = 40$, $r = 0.1$, $\sigma = 0.2$, $T = 0.5$,

$$d_1 = \frac{\ln(42/40) + (0.1 + 0.2^2/2) \times 0.5}{0.2\sqrt{0.5}} = 0.7693$$

$$d_2 = \frac{\ln(42/40) + (0.1 - 0.2^2/2) \times 0.5}{0.2\sqrt{0.5}} = 0.6278$$

and

$$Ke^{-rT} = 40e^{-0.05} = 38.049$$

Hence, if the option is a European call, its value, $c$, is given by

$$c = 42N(0.7693) - 38.049N(0.6278)$$

If the option is a European put, its value, $p$, is given by

$$p = 38.049N(-0.6278) - 42N(-0.7693)$$

Using the polynomial approximation, we have

$$N(0.7693) = 0.7791, \quad N(-0.7693) = 0.2209, \quad N(0.6278) = 0.7349, \quad N(-0.6278) = 0.2651$$

so that

$$c = 4.76, \quad p = 0.81$$

Ignoring the time value of money, the stock price has to rise by \$2.76 for the purchaser of the call to break even. Similarly, the stock price has to fall by \$2.81 for the purchaser of the put to break even.

## 12.10 WARRANTS ISSUED BY A COMPANY ON ITS OWN STOCK

The Black–Scholes formula, with some adjustments for the impact of dilution, can be used to value European warrants issued by a company on its own stock.[8] Consider a company with $N$ outstanding shares and $M$ outstanding European warrants. Suppose that each warrant entitles the holder to purchase $\gamma$ shares from the company at time $T$ at a price of $K$ per share.

If $V_T$ is the value of the company's equity (including the warrants) at time $T$ and the warrant holders exercise, the company receives a cash inflow from the payment of the exercise price of $M\gamma K$ and the value of the company's equity increases to $V_T + M\gamma K$. This value is distributed among $N + M\gamma$ shares, so that the share price immediately after exercise becomes

$$\frac{V_T + M\gamma K}{N + M\gamma}$$

The payoff to the warrant holder if the warrant is exercised is therefore

$$\gamma\left(\frac{V_T + M\gamma K}{N + M\gamma} - K\right)$$

[8] See F. Black and M. Scholes, "The Pricing of Options and Corporate Liabilities," *Journal of Political Economy*, 81 (May/June 1973), 637–59; D. Galai and M. Schneller, "Pricing Warrants and the Value of the Firm," *Journal of Finance*, 33 (1978), 1339–42; B. Lauterbach and P. Schultz, "Pricing Warrants: An Empirical Study of the Black–Scholes Model and Its Alternatives," *Journal of Finance*, 45 (1990), 1181–1209.

or

$$\frac{N\gamma}{N + M\gamma}\left(\frac{V_T}{N} - K\right)$$

The warrants should be exercised only if this payoff is positive. The payoff to the warrant holder is therefore

$$\frac{N\gamma}{N + M\gamma}\max\left(\frac{V_T}{N} - K, 0\right)$$

This shows that the value of the warrant is the value of

$$\frac{N\gamma}{N + M\gamma}$$

regular call options on $V/N$, where $V$ is the value of the company's equity.

The value of $V$ at time zero is given by

$$V_0 = NS_0 + MW$$

where $S_0$ is the stock price at time zero and $W$ is the warrant price at that time, so that

$$\frac{V_0}{N} = S_0 + \frac{M}{N}W$$

The Black–Scholes formula in equation (12.20) therefore gives the warrant price $W$ if:

1. The stock price $S_0$ is replaced by $S_0 + (M/N)W$.
2. The volatility $\sigma$ is the volatility of the equity of the company (i.e., it is the volatility of the value of the shares plus the warrants, not just the shares).
3. The formula is multiplied by $N\gamma/(N + M\gamma)$.

When these adjustments are made, we end up with a formula for $W$ as a function of $W$. This can be solved numerically.

## 12.11   IMPLIED VOLATILITIES

The one parameter in the Black–Scholes pricing formulas that cannot be directly observed is the volatility of the stock price. In Section 12.3, we discussed how this can be estimated from a history of the stock price. In practice, traders usually work with what are known as *implied volatilities*. These are the volatilities implied by option prices observed in the market.

To illustrate how implied volatilities are calculated, suppose that the value of a call option on a non-dividend-paying stock is 1.875 when $S_0 = 21$, $K = 20$, $r = 0.1$, and $T = 0.25$. The implied volatility is the value of $\sigma$ that, when substituted into equation (12.20), gives $c = 1.875$. Unfortunately, it is not possible to invert equation (12.20) so that $\sigma$ is expressed as a function of $S_0$, $K$, $r$, $T$, and $c$. However, an iterative search procedure can be used to find the implied $\sigma$. For example, we can start by trying $\sigma = 0.20$. This gives a value of $c$ equal to 1.76, which is too low. Because $c$ is an increasing function of $\sigma$, a higher value of $\sigma$ is required. We can next try a value of 0.30 for $\sigma$. This gives a value of $c$ equal to 2.10, which is too high and means that $\sigma$ must lie between 0.20 and 0.30.

Next, a value of 0.25 can be tried for $\sigma$. This also proves to be too high, showing that $\sigma$ lies between 0.20 and 0.25. In this way, the range for $\sigma$ can be halved at each iteration and the correct value of $\sigma$ can be calculated to any required accuracy.[9] In this example, the implied volatility is 0.235, or 23.5% per annum.

Implied volatilities are used to monitor the market's opinion about the volatility of a particular stock. Traders like to calculate implied volatilities from actively traded options on a certain asset and interpolate between them to calculate the appropriate volatility for pricing a less actively traded option on the same stock. We explain this procedure in Chapter 15. It is important to note that the prices of deep-in-the-money and deep-out-of-the-money options are relatively insensitive to volatility. Implied volatilities calculated from these options tend, therefore, to be unreliable.

## 12.12   THE CAUSES OF VOLATILITY

Some analysts have claimed that the volatility of a stock price is caused solely by the random arrival of new information about the future returns from the stock. Others have claimed that volatility is caused largely by trading. An interesting question, therefore, is whether the volatility of an exchange-traded instrument is the same when the exchange is open as when it is closed.

Both Fama and K. R. French have tested this question empirically.[10] They collected data on the stock price at the close of each trading day over a long period of time, and then calculated:

1. The variance of stock price returns between the close of trading on one day and the close of trading on the next trading day when there are no intervening nontrading days

2. The variance of the stock price returns between the close of trading on Fridays and the close of trading on Mondays

If trading and nontrading days are equivalent, the variance in the second case should be three times as great as the variance in the first case. Fama found that it was only 22% higher. French's results were similar: he found that it was 19% higher.

These results suggest that volatility is far larger when the exchange is open than when it is closed. Proponents of the view that volatility is caused only by new information might be tempted to argue that most new information on stocks arrives during trading days.[11] However, studies of futures prices on agricultural commodities, which depend largely on the weather, have shown that they exhibit much the same behavior as stock prices; that is, they are much more volatile during trading hours. Presumably, news about the weather is equally likely to arise on any day. The only reasonable conclusion seems to be that volatility is largely caused by trading itself.[12]

[9] This method is presented for illustration. Other more powerful methods, such as the Newton–Raphson method, are often used in practice (see footnote 2 of Chapter 5). DerivaGem can be used to calculate implied volatilities.

[10] See E. E. Fama, "The Behavior of Stock Market Prices," *Journal of Business*, 38 (January 1965), 34–105; K. R. French, "Stock Returns and the Weekend Effect," *Journal of Financial Economics*, 8 (March 1980), 55–69.

[11] In fact, this is questionable. Frequently, important announcements (e.g., those concerned with sales and earnings) are made when exchanges are closed.

[12] For a discussion of this, see K. R. French and R. Roll, "Stock Return Variances: The Arrival of Information and the Reaction of Traders," *Journal of Financial Economics*, 17 (September 1986), 5–26. We consider one way in which trading can generate volatility when we discuss portfolio insurance schemes in Chapter 14.

What are the implications of all of this for the measurement of volatility and the Black–Scholes model? When implied volatilities are calculated, the life of an option should be measured in trading days. Furthermore, if daily data are used to provide a historical volatility estimate, days when the exchange is closed should be ignored and the volatility per annum should be calculated from the volatility per trading day using the formula

$$\text{volatility per annum} = \text{volatility per trading day} \times \sqrt{\text{number of trading days per annum}}$$

This is what we did in Example 12.5. The normal assumption in equity markets is that there are 252 trading days per year.

Although volatility appears to be a phenomenon that is related largely to trading days, interest is paid by the calendar day. This has led D. W. French to suggest that, when options are being valued, two time measures should be calculated:[13]

$$\tau_1 : \quad \frac{\text{trading days until maturity}}{\text{trading days per year}}$$

$$\tau_2 : \quad \frac{\text{calendar days until maturity}}{\text{calendar days per year}}$$

and that the Black–Scholes formulas should be adjusted to

$$c = S_0 N(d_1) - Ke^{-r\tau_2} N(d_2)$$

and

$$p = Ke^{-r\tau_2} N(-d_2) - S_0 N(-d_1)$$

where

$$d_1 = \frac{\ln(S_0/K) + r\tau_2 + \sigma^2 \tau_1/2}{\sigma\sqrt{\tau_1}}$$

$$d_2 = \frac{\ln(S_0/K) + r\tau_2 - \sigma^2 \tau_1/2}{\sigma\sqrt{\tau_1}} = d_1 - \sigma\sqrt{\tau_1}$$

In practice, this adjustment makes little difference except for very short life options.

## 12.13   DIVIDENDS

Up to now, we have assumed that the stock upon which the option is written pays no dividends. In this section, we modify the Black–Scholes model to take account of dividends. We assume that the amount and timing of the dividends during the life of an option can be predicted with certainty. For short-life options, it is usually possible to estimate dividends during the life of the option reasonably accurately. For options lasting several years, there is likely to be uncertainty about dividend growth rates making option pricing much more difficult.

A dividend-paying stock can reasonably be expected to follow the stochastic process developed in Chapter 11 except when the stock goes ex-dividend. At this point, the stock's price goes down by

---

[13] See D. W. French, "The Weekend Effect on the Distribution of Stock Prices: Implications for Option Pricing," *Journal of Financial Economics*, 13 (September 1984), 547–59.

an amount reflecting the dividend paid per share. For tax reasons, the stock price may go down by somewhat less than the cash amount of the dividend. To take account of this, the word *dividend* in this section should be interpreted as the reduction in the stock price on the ex-dividend date caused by the dividend. Thus, if a dividend of $1 per share is anticipated and the share price normally goes down by 80% of the dividend on the ex-dividend date, the dividend should be assumed to be $0.80 for the purposes of the analysis.

### European Options

European options can be analyzed by assuming that the stock price is the sum of two components: a riskless component that corresponds to the known dividends during the life of the option and a risky component. The riskless component, at any given time, is the present value of all the dividends during the life of the option discounted from the ex-dividend dates to the present at the risk-free rate. By the time the option matures, the dividends will have been paid and the riskless component will no longer exist. The Black–Scholes formula is therefore correct if $S_0$ is equal to the risky component of the stock price and $\sigma$ is the volatility of the process followed by the risky component.[14] Operationally, this means that the Black–Scholes formula can be used provided that the stock price is reduced by the present value of all the dividends during the life of the option, the discounting being done from the ex-dividend dates at the risk-free rate. A dividend is counted as being during the life of the option only if its ex-dividend date occurs during the life of the option.

**Example 12.8**   Consider a European call option on a stock when there are ex-dividend dates in two months and five months. The dividend on each ex-dividend date is expected to be $0.50. The current share price is $40, the exercise price is $40, the stock price volatility is 30% per annum, the risk-free rate of interest is 9% per annum, and the time to maturity is six months. The present value of the dividends is

$$0.5e^{-0.1667 \times 0.09} + 0.5e^{-0.4167 \times 0.09} = 0.9741$$

The option price can therefore be calculated from the Black–Scholes formula with $S_0 = 39.0259$, $K = 40$, $r = 0.09$, $\sigma = 0.3$, and $T = 0.5$. We have

$$d_1 = \frac{\ln(39.0259/40) + (0.09 + 0.3^2/2) \times 0.5}{0.3\sqrt{0.5}} = 0.2017$$

$$d_2 = \frac{\ln(39.0259/40) + (0.09 - 0.3^2/2) \times 0.5}{0.3\sqrt{0.5}} = -0.0104$$

Using the polynomial approximation in Section 12.9 gives us

$$N(d_1) = 0.5800, \quad N(d_2) = 0.4959$$

and, from equation (12.20), the call price is

$$39.0259 \times 0.5800 - 40e^{-0.09 \times 0.5} \times 0.4959 = 3.67$$

or $3.67.

---

[14] In theory this is not quite the same as the volatility of the stochastic process followed by the whole stock price. The volatility of the risky component is approximately equal to the volatility of the whole stock price multiplied by $S_0/(S_0 - D)$, where $D$ is the present value of the dividends. However, an adjustment is only necessary when volatilities are estimated using historical data. An implied volatility is calculated after the present value of dividends have been subtracted from the stock price and is the volatility of the risky component.

### American Options

Consider next American call options. In Section 8.5, we showed that in the absence of dividends American options should never be exercised early. An extension to the argument shows that, when there are dividends, it is optimal to exercise only at a time immediately before the stock goes ex-dividend. We assume that $n$ ex-dividend dates are anticipated and that $t_1, t_2, \ldots, t_n$ are moments in time immediately prior to the stock going ex-dividend, with $t_1 < t_2 < t_3 < \cdots < t_n$. The dividends corresponding to these times will be denoted by $D_1, D_2, \ldots, D_n$, respectively.

We start by considering the possibility of early exercise just prior to the final ex-dividend date (i.e., at time $t_n$). If the option is exercised at time $t_n$, the investor receives

$$S(t_n) - K$$

If the option is not exercised, the stock price drops to $S(t_n) - D_n$. As shown by equation (8.5), the value of the option is then greater than

$$S(t_n) - D_n - Ke^{-r(T-t_n)}$$

It follows that if

$$S(t_n) - D_n - Ke^{-r(T-t_n)} \geqslant S(t_n) - K$$

that is,

$$D_n \leqslant K(1 - e^{-r(T-t_n)}) \qquad (12.24)$$

it cannot be optimal to exercise at time $t_n$. On the other hand, if

$$D_n > K(1 - e^{-r(T-t_n)}) \qquad (12.25)$$

for any reasonable assumption about the stochastic process followed by the stock price, it can be shown that it is always optimal to exercise at time $t_n$ for a sufficiently high value of $S(t_n)$. The inequality in (12.25) will tend to be satisfied when the final ex-dividend date is fairly close to the maturity of the option (i.e., $T - t_n$ is small) and the dividend is large.

Next consider time $t_{n-1}$, the penultimate ex-dividend date. If the option is exercised at time $t_{n-1}$, the investor receives

$$S(t_{n-1}) - K$$

If the option is not exercised at time $t_{n-1}$, the stock price drops to $S(t_{n-1}) - D_{n-1}$ and the earliest subsequent time at which exercise could take place is $t_n$. Hence, from equation (8.5), a lower bound to the option price if it is not exercised at time $t_{n-1}$ is

$$S(t_{n-1}) - D_{n-1} - Ke^{-r(t_n-t_{n-1})}$$

It follows that if

$$S(t_{n-1}) - D_{n-1} - Ke^{-r(t_n-t_{n-1})} \geqslant S(t_{n-1}) - K$$

or

$$D_{n-1} \leqslant K(1 - e^{-r(t_n-t_{n-1})})$$

it is not optimal to exercise at time $t_{n-1}$. Similarly, for any $i < n$, if

$$D_i \leqslant K(1 - e^{-r(t_{i+1}-t_i)}) \qquad (12.26)$$

it is not optimal to exercise at time $t_i$.

The inequality in (12.26) is approximately equivalent to

$$D_i \leqslant Kr(t_{i+1} - t_i)$$

Assuming that $K$ is fairly close to the current stock price, the dividend yield on the stock would have to be either close to or above the risk-free rate of interest for this inequality not to be satisfied. This is not often the case.

We can conclude from this analysis that, in most circumstances, the only time that needs to be considered for the early exercise of an American call is the final ex-dividend date, $t_n$. Furthermore, if inequality (12.26) holds for $i = 1, 2, \ldots, n - 1$ and inequality (12.24) holds, then we can be certain that early exercise is never optimal.

### Black's Approximation

Black suggests an approximate procedure for taking account of early exercise in call options.[15] This involves calculating, as described earlier in this section, the prices of European options that mature at times $T$ and $t_n$, and then setting the American price equal to the greater of the two. This approximation seems to work well in most cases. A more exact procedure suggested by Roll (1977), Geske (1979), and Whaley (1981) is given in Appendix 12B.[16]

> **Example 12.9** Consider the situation in Example 12.8, but suppose that the option is American rather than European. In this case, $D_1 = D_2 = 0.5$, $S_0 = 40$, $K = 40$, $r = 0.09$, $t_1 = 2/12$, and $t_2 = 5/12$. Because
> $$K(1 - e^{-r(t_2 - t_1)}) = 40(1 - e^{-0.09 \times 0.25}) = 0.89$$
> is greater than 0.5, it follows (see inequality (12.26)) that the option should never be exercised immediately before the first ex-dividend date. In addition, because
> $$K(1 - e^{-r(T - t_2)}) = 40(1 - e^{-0.09 \times 0.0833}) = 0.30$$
> is less than 0.5, it follows (see inequality (12.25)) that, when it is sufficiently deep in the money, the option should be exercised immediately before the second ex-dividend date.
> We now use Black's approximation to value the option. The present value of the first dividend is
> $$0.5e^{-0.1667 \times 0.09} = 0.4926$$
> so that the value of the option, on the assumption that it expires just before the final ex-dividend date, can be calculated using the Black–Scholes formula with $S_0 = 39.5074$, $K = 40$, $r = 0.09$, $\sigma = 0.30$, and $T = 0.4167$. It is $3.52. Black's approximation involves taking the greater of this and the value of the option when it can only be exercised at the end of six months. From Example 12.8, we know that the latter is $3.67. Black's approximation therefore gives the value of the American call as $3.67.

---

[15] See F. Black, "Fact and Fantasy in the Use of Options," *Financial Analysts Journal*, 31 (July/August 1975), 36–41, 61–72.

[16] See R. Roll, "An Analytic Formula for Unprotected American Call Options on Stocks with Known Dividends," *Journal of Financial Economics*, 5 (1977), 251–58; R. Geske, "A Note on an Analytic Valuation Formula for Unprotected American Call Options on Stocks with Known Dividends," *Journal of Financial Economics*, 7 (1979), 375–80; R. Whaley, "On the Valuation of American Call Options on Stocks with Known Dividends," *Journal of Financial Economics*, 9 (June 1981), 207–11; R. Geske, "Comments on Whaley's Note," *Journal of Financial Economics*, 9 (June 1981), 213–215.

The value of the option given by the Roll, Geske, and Whaley (RGW) formula is $3.72. There are two reasons for differences between RGW and Black's approximation (BA). The first concerns the timing of the early exercise decision and tends to make RGW greater than BA. In BA, the assumption is that the holder has to decide today whether the option will be exercised after five months or after six months; RGW allows the decision on early exercise at the five-month point to depend on the stock price. The second concerns the way in which volatility is applied and tends to make BA greater than RGW. In BA, when we assume exercise takes place after five months, the volatility is applied to the stock price less the present value of the first dividend; when we assume exercise takes place after six months, the volatility is applied to the stock price less the present value of both dividends. In RGW, it is always applied to the stock price less the present value of both dividends.

Whaley[17] has empirically tested three models for the pricing of American calls on dividend-paying stocks: (1) the formula in Appendix 12B; (2) Black's model; and (3) the European option pricing model described at the beginning of this section. He used 15,582 Chicago Board options. The models produced pricing errors with means of 1.08%, 1.48%, and 2.15%, respectively. The typical bid–offer spread on a call option is greater than 2.15% of the price. On average, therefore, all three models work well and within the tolerance imposed on the options market by trading imperfections.

Up to now, our discussion has centered on American call options. The results for American put options are less clear-cut. Dividends make it less likely that an American put option will be exercised early. It can be shown that it is never worth exercising an American put for a period immediately prior to an ex-dividend date.[18] Indeed, if

$$D_i \geqslant K(1 - e^{-r(t_{i+1}-t_i)})$$

for all $i < n$ and

$$D_n \geqslant K(1 - e^{-r(T-t_n)})$$

an argument analogous to that just given shows that the put option should never be exercised early. In other cases, numerical procedures must be used to value a put.

## SUMMARY

We started this chapter by examining the properties of the process for stock prices introduced in Chapter 11. The process implies that the price of a stock at some future time, given its price today, is lognormal. It also implies that the continuously compounded return from the stock in a period of time is normally distributed. Our uncertainty about future stock prices increases as we look further ahead. The standard deviation of the logarithm of the stock price is proportional to the square root of how far ahead we are looking.

To estimate the volatility, $\sigma$, of a stock price empirically, the stock price is observed at fixed intervals of time (e.g., every day, every week, or every month). For each time period, the natural logarithm of the ratio of the stock price at the end of the time period to the stock price at the

---

[17] See R. E. Whaley, "Valuation of American Call Options on Dividend Paying Stocks: Empirical Tests," *Journal of Financial Economics*, 10 (March 1982), 29–58.

[18] See H. E. Johnson, "Three Topics in Option Pricing," Ph.D. thesis, University of California, Los Angeles, 1981, p. 42.

beginning of the time period is calculated. The volatility is estimated as the standard deviation of these numbers divided by the square root of the length of the time period in years. Usually, days when the exchanges are closed are ignored in measuring time for the purposes of volatility calculations.

The differential equation for the price of any derivative dependent on a stock can be obtained by creating a riskless position in the option and the stock. Because the derivative and the stock price both depend on the same underlying source of uncertainty, this can always be done. The position that is created remains riskless for only a very short period of time. However, the return on a riskless position must always be the risk-free interest rate if there are to be no arbitrage opportunities.

The expected return on the stock does not enter into the Black–Scholes differential equation. This leads to a useful result known as risk-neutral valuation. This result states that when valuing a derivative dependent on a stock price, we can assume that the world is risk neutral. This means that we can assume that the expected return from the stock is the risk-free interest rate, and then discount expected payoffs at the risk-free interest rate. The Black–Scholes equations for European call and put options can be derived by either solving their differential equation or by using risk-neutral valuation.

An implied volatility is the volatility that, when used in conjunction with the Black–Scholes option pricing formula, gives the market price of the option. Traders monitor implied volatilities and commonly use the implied volatilities from actively traded options to estimate the appropriate volatility to use to price a less actively traded option on the same asset. Empirical results show that the volatility of a stock is much higher when the exchange is open than when it is closed. This suggests that, to some extent, trading itself causes stock price volatility.

The Black–Scholes results can be extended to cover European call and put options on dividend-paying stocks. The procedure is to use the Black–Scholes formula with the stock price reduced by the present value of the dividends anticipated during the life of the option, and the volatility equal to the volatility of the stock price net of the present value of these dividends.

In theory, American call options are liable to be exercised early, immediately before any ex-dividend date. In practice, only the final ex-dividend date usually needs to be considered. Fischer Black has suggested an approximation. This involves setting the American call option price equal to the greater of two European call option prices. The first European call option expires at the same time as the American call option; the second expires immediately prior to the final ex-dividend date. A more exact approach involving bivariate normal distributions is explained in Appendix 12B.

## SUGGESTIONS FOR FURTHER READING

### On the Distribution of Stock Price Changes

Blattberg, R., and N. Gonedes, "A Comparison of the Stable and Student Distributions as Statistical Models for Stock Prices," *Journal of Business*, 47 (April 1974), 244–80.

Fama, E. F., "The Behavior of Stock Prices," *Journal of Business*, 38 (January 1965), 34–105.

Kon, S. J., "Models of Stock Returns—A Comparison," *Journal of Finance*, 39 (March 1984), 147–65.

Richardson, M., and T. Smith, "A Test for Multivariate Normality in Stock Returns," *Journal of Business*, 66 (1993), 295–321.

### On the Black–Scholes Analysis

Black, F., and M. Scholes, "The Pricing of Options and Corporate Liabilities," *Journal of Political Economy*, 81 (May/June 1973), 637–59.

Merton, R. C., "Theory of Rational Option Pricing," *Bell Journal of Economics and Management Science*, 4 (Spring 1973), 141–183.

### On Risk-Neutral Valuation

Cox, J. C., and S. A. Ross, "The Valuation of Options for Alternative Stochastic Processes," *Journal of Financial Economics*, 3 (1976), 145–66.

Smith, C. W., "Option Pricing: A Review," *Journal of Financial Economics*, 3 (1976), 3–54.

### On Analytic Solutions to the Pricing of American Calls

Geske, R., "Comments on Whaley's Note," *Journal of Financial Economics*, 9 (June 1981), 213–15.

Geske, R., "A Note on an Analytic Valuation Formula for Unprotected American Call Options on Stocks with Known Dividends," *Journal of Financial Economics*, 7 (1979), 375–80.

Roll, R., "An Analytical Formula for Unprotected American Call Options on Stocks with Known Dividends," *Journal of Financial Economics*, 5 (1977), 251–58.

Whaley, R., "On the Valuation of American Call Options on Stocks with Known Dividends," *Journal of Financial Economics*, 9 (1981), 207–11.

### On the Causes of Volatility

Fama, E. E., "The Behavior of Stock Market Prices," *Journal of Business*, 38 (January 1965), 34–105.

French, K. R., "Stock Returns and the Weekend Effect," *Journal of Financial Economics*, 8 (March 1980), 55–69.

French, K. R., and R. Roll, "Stock Return Variances: The Arrival of Information and the Reaction of Traders," *Journal of Financial Economics*, 17 (September 1986), 5–26.

## QUESTIONS AND PROBLEMS
## (ANSWERS IN SOLUTIONS MANUAL)

12.1. What does the Black–Scholes stock option pricing model assume about the probability distribution of the stock price in one year? What does it assume about the continuously compounded rate of return on the stock during the year?

12.2. The volatility of a stock price is 30% per annum. What is the standard deviation of the percentage price change in one trading day?

12.3. Explain the principle of risk-neutral valuation.

12.4. Calculate the price of a three-month European put option on a non-dividend-paying stock with a strike price of $50 when the current stock price is $50, the risk-free interest rate is 10% per annum, and the volatility is 30% per annum.

12.5. What difference does it make to your calculations in Problem 12.4 if a dividend of $1.50 is expected in two months?

12.6. What is *implied volatility*? How can it be calculated?

12.7. A stock price is currently $40. Assume that the expected return from the stock is 15% and that its volatility is 25%. What is the probability distribution for the rate of return (with continuous compounding) earned over a two-year period?

12.8. A stock price follows geometric Brownian motion with an expected return of 16% and a volatility of 35%. The current price is $38.
   a. What is the probability that a European call option on the stock with an exercise price of $40 and a maturity date in six months will be exercised?
   b. What is the probability that a European put option on the stock with the same exercise price and maturity will be exercised?

12.9. Prove that, with the notation in the chapter, a 95% confidence interval for $S_T$ is between

$$S_0 e^{(\mu - \sigma^2/2)T - 1.96\sigma\sqrt{T}} \quad \text{and} \quad S_0 e^{(\mu - \sigma^2/2)T + 1.96\sigma\sqrt{T}}$$

12.10. A portfolio manager announces that the average of the returns realized in each year of the last 10 years is 20% per annum. In what respect is this statement misleading?

12.11. Assume that a non-dividend-paying stock has an expected return of $\mu$ and a volatility of $\sigma$. An innovative financial institution has just announced that it will trade a security that pays off a dollar amount equal to $\ln S_T$ at time $T$, where $S_T$ denotes the value of the stock price at time $T$.
   a. Use risk-neutral valuation to calculate the price of the security at time $t$ in terms of the stock price, $S$, at time $t$.
   b. Confirm that your price satisfies the differential equation (12.15).

12.12. Consider a derivative that pays off $S_T^n$ at time $T$, where $S_T$ is the stock price at that time. When the stock price follows geometric Brownian motion, it can be shown that its price at time $t$ $(t \leqslant T)$ has the form

$$h(t, T)S^n$$

where $S$ is the stock price at time $t$ and $h$ is a function only of $t$ and $T$.
   a. By substituting into the Black–Scholes partial differential equation, derive an ordinary differential equation satisfied by $h(t, T)$.
   b. What is the boundary condition for the differential equation for $h(t, T)$?
   c. Show that

$$h(t, T) = e^{[0.5\sigma^2 n(n-1) + r(n-1)](T-t)}$$

where $r$ is the risk-free interest rate and $\sigma$ is the stock price volatility.

12.13. What is the price of a European call option on a non-dividend-paying stock when the stock price is $52, the strike price is $50, the risk-free interest rate is 12% per annum, the volatility is 30% per annum, and the time to maturity is three months?

12.14. What is the price of a European put option on a non-dividend-paying stock when the stock price is $69, the strike price is $70, the risk-free interest rate is 5% per annum, the volatility is 35% per annum, and the time to maturity is six months?

12.15. Consider an American call option on a stock. The stock price is $70, the time to maturity is eight months, the risk-free rate of interest is 10% per annum, the exercise price is $65, and the volatility is 32%. A dividend of $1 is expected after three months and again after six months. Show that it can never be optimal to exercise the option on either of the two dividend dates. Use DerivaGem to calculate the price of the option.

12.16. A call option on a non-dividend-paying stock has a market price of $2\frac{1}{2}$. The stock price is \$15, the exercise price is \$13, the time to maturity is three months, and the risk-free interest rate is 5% per annum. What is the implied volatility?

12.17. With the notation used in this chapter
   a. What is $N'(x)$?
   b. Show that $SN'(d_1) = Ke^{-r(T-t)}N'(d_2)$, where $S$ is the stock price at time $t$ and

$$d_1 = \frac{\ln(S/K) + (r + \sigma^2/2)(T-t)}{\sigma\sqrt{T-t}}$$

$$d_2 = \frac{\ln(S/K) + (r - \sigma^2/2)(T-t)}{\sigma\sqrt{T-t}}$$

   c. Calculate $\partial d_1/\partial S$ and $\partial d_2/\partial S$.
   d. Show that, when $c = SN(d_1) - Ke^{-r(T-t)}N(d_2)$,

$$\frac{\partial c}{\partial t} = -rKe^{-r(T-t)}N(d_2) - SN'(d_1)\frac{\sigma}{2\sqrt{T-t}}$$

   where $c$ is the price of a call option on a non-dividend-paying stock.
   e. Show that $\partial c/\partial S = N(d_1)$.
   f. Show that $c$ satisfies the Black–Scholes differential equation.
   g. Show that $c$ satisfies the boundary condition for a European call option, i.e., that $c = \max(S - K, 0)$ as $t \to T$.

12.18. Show that the Black–Scholes formulas for call and put options satisfy put–call parity.

12.19. A stock price is currently \$50 and the risk-free interest rate is 5%. Use the DerivaGem software to translate the following table of European call options on the stock into a table of implied volatilities, assuming no dividends:

| Strike price (\$) | Maturity (months) | | |
| --- | --- | --- | --- |
| | 3 | 6 | 12 |
| 45 | 7.0 | 8.3 | 10.5 |
| 50 | 3.7 | 5.2 | 7.5 |
| 55 | 1.6 | 2.9 | 5.1 |

Are the option prices consistent with Black–Scholes?

12.20. Explain carefully why Black's approach to evaluating an American call option on a dividend-paying stock may give an approximate answer even when only one dividend is anticipated. Does the answer given by Black's approach understate or overstate the true option value? Explain your answer.

12.21. Consider an American call option on a stock. The stock price is \$50, the time to maturity is 15 months, the risk-free rate of interest is 8% per annum, the exercise price is \$55, and the volatility is 25%. Dividends of \$1.50 are expected after 4 months and 10 months. Show that it can never be optimal to exercise the option on either of the two dividend dates. Calculate the price of the option.

12.22. Show that the probability that a European call option will be exercised in a risk-neutral world is $N(d_2)$, using the notation introduced in this chapter. What is an expression for the value of a derivative that pays off \$100 if the price of a stock at time $T$ is greater than $K$?

12.23. Show that $S^{-2r/\sigma^2}$ could be the price of a traded security.

# ASSIGNMENT QUESTIONS

12.24. A stock price is currently $50. Assume that the expected return from the stock is 18% and its volatility is 30%. What is the probability distribution for the stock price in two years? Calculate the mean and standard deviation of the distribution. Determine 95% confidence intervals.

12.25. Suppose that observations on a stock price (in dollars) at the end of each of 15 consecutive weeks are as follows:

30.2, 32.0, 31.1, 30.1, 30.2, 30.3, 30.6, 33.0, 32.9, 33.0, 33.5, 33.5, 33.7, 33.5, 33.2

Estimate the stock price volatility. What is the standard error of your estimate?

12.26. A financial institution plans to offer a security that pays off a dollar amount equal to $S_T^2$ at time $T$.
   a. Use risk-neutral valuation to calculate the price of the security at time $t$ in terms of the stock price, $S$, at time $t$. (*Hint*: The expected value of $S_T^2$ can be calculated from the mean and variance of $S_T$ given in Section 12.1.)
   b. Confirm that your price satisfies the differential equation (12.15).

12.27. Consider an option on a non-dividend-paying stock when the stock price is $30, the exercise price is $29, the risk-free interest rate is 5%, the volatility is 25% per annum, and the time to maturity is four months.
   a. What is the price of the option if it is a European call?
   b. What is the price of the option if it is an American call?
   c. What is the price of the option if it is a European put?
   d. Verify that put–call parity holds.

12.28. Assume that the stock in Problem 12.27 is due to go ex-dividend in $1\frac{1}{2}$ months. The expected dividend is 50 cents.
   a. What is the price of the option if it is a European call?
   b. What is the price of the option if it is a European put?
   c. If the option is an American call, are there any circumstances under which it will be exercised early?

12.29. Consider an American call option when the stock price is $18, the exercise price is $20, the time to maturity is six months, the volatility is 30% per annum, and the risk-free interest rate is 10% per annum. Two equal dividends are expected during the life of the option with ex-dividend dates at the end of two months and five months. Assume the dividends are 40 cents. Use Black's approximation and the DerivaGem software to value the option. How high can the dividends be without the American option being worth more than the corresponding European option?

# APPENDIX 12A
## Proof of the Black–Scholes–Merton Formula

We will prove the Black–Scholes result by first proving another key result that will also be useful in future chapters.

### Key Result

If $V$ is lognormally distributed and the standard deviation of $\ln V$ is $s$, then

$$E[\max(V - K, 0)] = E(V)N(d_1) - KN(d_2) \tag{12A.1}$$

where

$$d_1 = \frac{\ln[E(V)/K] + s^2/2}{s}$$

$$d_2 = \frac{\ln[E(V)/K] - s^2/2}{s}$$

and $E$ denotes the expected value.

### Proof of Key Result

Define $g(V)$ as the probability density function of $V$. It follows that

$$E[\max(V - K), 0] = \int_K^\infty (V - K)g(V)\,dV \tag{12A.2}$$

The variable $\ln V$ is normally distributed with standard deviation $s$. From the properties of the lognormal distribution the mean of $\ln V$ is $m$, where

$$m = \ln[E(V)] - s^2/2 \tag{12A.3}$$

Define a new variable

$$Q = \frac{\ln V - m}{s} \tag{12A.4}$$

This variable is normally distributed with a mean of zero and a standard deviation of 1.0. Denote the density function for $Q$ by $h(Q)$, so that

$$h(Q) = \frac{1}{\sqrt{2\pi}}e^{-Q^2/2}$$

Using equation (12A.4) to convert the expression on the right-hand side of equation (12A.2) from an integral over $V$ to an integral over $Q$, we get

$$E[\max(V - K, 0)] = \int_{(\ln K - m)/s}^\infty (e^{Qs+m} - K)h(Q)\,dQ$$

or

$$E[\max(V - K, 0)] = \int_{(\ln K - m)/s}^\infty e^{Qs+m}h(Q)\,dQ - K\int_{(\ln K - m)/s}^\infty h(Q)\,dQ \tag{12A.5}$$

Now

$$e^{Qs+m}h(Q) = \frac{1}{\sqrt{2\pi}}e^{(-Q^2+2Qs+2m)/2}$$

$$= \frac{1}{\sqrt{2\pi}}e^{[-(Q-s)^2+2m+s^2]/2}$$

$$= \frac{e^{m+s^2/2}}{\sqrt{2\pi}}e^{[-(Q-s)^2]/2}$$

$$= e^{m+s^2/2}h(Q-s)$$

This means that equation (12A.5) becomes

$$E[\max(V-K,0)] = e^{m+s^2/2}\int_{(\ln K-m)/s}^{\infty}h(Q-s)\,dQ - K\int_{(\ln K-m)/s}^{\infty}h(Q)\,dQ \qquad (12A.6)$$

If we define $N(x)$ as the probability that a variable with a mean of zero and a standard deviation of 1.0 is less than $x$, the first integral in equation (12A.6) is

$$1 - N[(\ln K - m)/s - s]$$

or

$$N[(-\ln K + m)/s + s]$$

Substituting for $m$ from equation (12A.3) gives

$$N\left(\frac{\ln[E(V)/K] + s^2/2}{s}\right) = N(d_1)$$

Similarly the second integral in equation (12A.6) is $N(d_2)$. Equation (12A.6) therefore becomes

$$E[\max(V-K,0)] = e^{m+s^2/2}N(d_1) - KN(d_2)$$

Substituting for $m$ from equation (12A.3) gives the key result.

### The Black–Scholes Result

We now consider a call option on a non-dividend-paying stock maturing at time $T$. The strike price is $K$, the risk-free rate is $r$, the current stock price is $S_0$, and the volatility is $\sigma$. As shown in equation (12.22), the call price, $c$, is given by

$$c = e^{-rT}\hat{E}[\max(S_T - K, 0)] \qquad (12A.7)$$

where $S_T$ is the stock price at time $T$ and $\hat{E}$ denotes the expectation in a risk-neutral world. Under the stochastic process assumed by Black–Scholes, $S_T$ is lognormal. Also from equations (12.3) and (12.4), $\hat{E}(S_T) = S_0 e^{rT}$ and the standard deviation of $\ln S_T$ is $\sigma\sqrt{T}$.

From the key result just proved, equation (12A.7) implies that

$$c = e^{-rT}[S_0 e^{rT}N(d_1) - KN(d_2)]$$

or

$$c = S_0 N(d_1) - Ke^{-rT}N(d_2)$$

where

$$d_1 = \frac{\ln[\hat{E}(S_T)/K] + \sigma^2 T/2}{\sigma\sqrt{T}}$$

$$= \frac{\ln(S_0/K) + (r + \sigma^2/2)T}{\sigma\sqrt{T}}$$

and

$$d_2 = \frac{\ln[\hat{E}(S_T)/K] - \sigma^2 T/2}{\sigma\sqrt{T}}$$

$$= \frac{\ln(S_0/K) + (r - \sigma^2/2)T}{\sigma\sqrt{T}}$$

# APPENDIX 12B
## Exact Procedure for Calculating Values of American Calls on Dividend-Paying Stocks

The Roll, Geske, and Whaley formula for the value of an American call option on a stock paying a single dividend $D_1$ at time $t_1$ is

$$C = (S_0 - D_1 e^{-rt_1})N(b_1) + (S_0 - D_1 e^{-rt_1})M\left(a_1, -b_1; -\sqrt{\frac{t_1}{T}}\right)$$

$$- Ke^{-rT}M\left(a_2, -b_2; -\sqrt{\frac{t_1}{T}}\right) - (K - D_1)e^{-rt_1}N(b_2) \quad (12B.1)$$

where

$$a_1 = \frac{\ln[(S_0 - D_1 e^{-rt_1})/K] + (r + \sigma^2/2)T}{\sigma\sqrt{T}}$$

$$a_2 = a_1 - \sigma\sqrt{T}$$

$$b_1 = \frac{\ln[(S_0 - D_1 e^{-rt_1})/S^*] + (r + \sigma^2/2)t_1}{\sigma\sqrt{t_1}}$$

$$b_2 = b_1 - \sigma\sqrt{t_1}$$

The variable $\sigma$ is the volatility of the stock price less the present value of the dividend. The function $M(a, b; \rho)$, is the cumulative probability in a standardized bivariate normal distribution that the first variable is less than $a$ and the second variable is less than $b$, when the coefficient of correlation between the variables is $\rho$. We give a procedure for calculating the $M$ function in Appendix 12C. The variable $S^*$ is the solution to

$$c(S^*) = S^* + D_1 - K$$

where $c(S^*)$ is the Black–Scholes option price given by equation (12.20) when the stock price is $S^*$ and the time to maturity is $T - t_1$. When early exercise is never optimal, $S^* = \infty$. In this case, $b_1 = b_2 = -\infty$ and equation (12B.1) reduces to the Black–Scholes equation with $S_0$ replaced by $S_0 - D_1 e^{-rt_1}$. In other situations, $S^* < \infty$ and the option should be exercised at time $t_1$ when $S(t_1) > S^* + D_1$.

When several dividends are anticipated, early exercise is normally optimal only on the final ex-dividend date (see Section 12.13). It follows that the Roll, Geske, and Whaley formula can be used with $S_0$ reduced by the present value of all dividends except the final one. The variable $D_1$ should be set equal to the final dividend and $t_1$ should be set equal to the final ex-dividend date.

# APPENDIX 12C
## Calculation of Cumulative Probability in Bivariate Normal Distribution

As in Appendix 12B, we define $M(a, b; \rho)$ as the cumulative probability in a standardized bivariate normal distribution that the first variable is less than $a$ and the second variable is less than $b$, when the coefficient of correlation between the variables is $\rho$. Drezner provides a way of calculating $M(a, b; \rho)$ to an accuracy of four decimal places.[19] If $a \leqslant 0$, $b \leqslant 0$, and $\rho \leqslant 0$, then

$$M(a, b; \rho) = \frac{\sqrt{1 - \rho^2}}{\pi} \sum_{i,j=1}^{4} A_i A_j f(B_i, B_j)$$

where

$$f(x, y) = \exp\left[a'(2x - a') + b'(2y - b') + 2\rho(x - a')(y - b')\right]$$

$$a' = \frac{a}{\sqrt{2(1 - \rho^2)}}, \qquad b' = \frac{b}{\sqrt{2(1 - \rho^2)}}$$

$$A_1 = 0.3253030, \quad A_2 = 0.4211071, \quad A_3 = 0.1334425, \quad A_4 = 0.006374323$$

$$B_1 = 0.1337764, \quad B_2 = 0.6243247, \quad B_3 = 1.3425378, \quad B_4 = 2.2626645$$

In other circumstances where the product of $a$, $b$, and $\rho$ is negative or zero, one of the following identities can be used:

$$M(a, b; \rho) = N(a) - M(a, -b; -\rho)$$

$$M(a, b; \rho) = N(b) - M(-a, b; -\rho)$$

$$M(a, b; \rho) = N(a) + N(b) - 1 + M(-a, -b; \rho)$$

In circumstances where the product of $a$, $b$, and $\rho$ is positive, the identity

$$M(a, b; \rho) = M(a, 0; \rho_1) + M(b, 0; \rho_2) - \delta$$

can be used in conjunction with the previous results, where

$$\rho_1 = \frac{(\rho a - b)\,\mathrm{sgn}(a)}{\sqrt{a^2 - 2\rho ab + b^2}}, \qquad \rho_2 = \frac{(\rho b - a)\,\mathrm{sgn}(b)}{\sqrt{a^2 - 2\rho ab + b^2}}, \qquad \delta = \frac{1 - \mathrm{sgn}(a)\,\mathrm{sgn}(b)}{4}$$

with

$$\mathrm{sgn}(x) = \begin{cases} +1 & \text{if } x \geqslant 0 \\ -1 & \text{if } x < 0 \end{cases}$$

---

[19] Z. Drezner, "Computation of the Bivariate Normal Integral," *Mathematics of Computation*, 32 (January 1978), 277–79. Note that the presentation here corrects a typo in Drezner's paper.

# C H A P T E R  1 3

# OPTIONS ON STOCK INDICES, CURRENCIES, AND FUTURES

In this chapter we tackle the problem of valuing options on stock indices, currencies, and futures contracts. As a first step, we extend the results in Chapters 8, 10, and 12 to cover European options on a stock paying a known dividend yield. We then argue that stock indices, currencies, and futures prices are analogous to stocks paying a known dividend yield. This enables the results for options on a stock paying a dividend yield to be applied to value options on these other assets.

## 13.1  RESULTS FOR A STOCK PAYING A KNOWN DIVIDEND YIELD

Consider the difference between a stock that pays a dividend yield at a rate $q$ per annum and an otherwise identical stock that pays no dividends. Both stocks should provide the same overall return (dividends plus capital gain). The payment of a dividend causes the stock price to drop by the amount of the dividend. The payment of a dividend yield at rate $q$ therefore causes the growth rate in the stock price to be less than it would otherwise be by an amount $q$. If, with a dividend yield of $q$, the stock price grows from $S_0$ at time zero to $S_T$ at time $T$, then in the absence of dividends it would grow from $S_0$ at time zero to $S_T e^{qT}$ at time $T$. Alternatively, in the absence of dividends it would grow from $S_0 e^{-qT}$ at time zero to $S_T$ at time $T$.

This argument shows that we get the same probability distribution for the stock price at time $T$ in each of the following two cases:

1. The stock starts at price $S_0$ and pays a dividend yield at rate $q$.
2. The stock starts at price $S_0 e^{-qT}$ and pays no dividend yield.

This leads to a simple rule. When valuing a European option lasting for time $T$ on a stock paying a known dividend yield at rate $q$, we reduce the current stock price from $S_0$ to $S_0 e^{-qT}$ and then value the option as though the stock pays no dividends.

### Lower Bounds for Option Prices

As a first application of this rule, consider the problem of determining bounds for the price of a European option on a stock providing a dividend yield equal to $q$. Substituting $S_0 e^{-qT}$ for $S_0$ in

**267**

equation (8.1), we see that the lower bound for the European call option price, $c$, is

$$c \geqslant \max(S_0 e^{-qT} - K e^{-rT}, \, 0) \tag{13.1}$$

We can also prove this directly (see Problem 13.40) by considering the following two portfolios:

*Portfolio A*: one European call option plus an amount of cash equal to $K e^{-rT}$

*Portfolio B*: $e^{-qT}$ shares, with dividends being reinvested in additional shares

To obtain a lower bound for a European put option, we can similarly replace $S_0$ by $S_0 e^{-qT}$ in equation (8.2) to get

$$p \geqslant \max(K e^{-rT} - S_0, \, 0) \tag{13.2}$$

This result can also be proved directly (see Problem 13.40) by considering the following two portfolios:

*Portfolio C*: one European put option plus $e^{-qT}$ shares, with dividends on the shares being reinvested in additional shares

*Portfolio D*: an amount of cash equal to $K e^{-rT}$

### Put–Call Parity

Replacing $S_0$ by $S_0 e^{-qT}$ in equation (8.3), we obtain put–call parity for a stock providing a dividend yield equal to $q$:

$$c + K e^{-rT} = p + S_0 e^{-qT} \tag{13.3}$$

This result can also be proved directly (see Problem 13.40) by considering the following two portfolios:

*Portfolio A*: one European call option plus an amount of cash equal to $K e^{-rT}$

*Portfolio C*: one European put option plus $e^{-qT}$ shares, with dividends on the shares being reinvested in additional shares

## 13.2   OPTION PRICING FORMULAS

By replacing $S_0$ by $S_0 e^{-qT}$ in the Black–Scholes formulas, equations (12.20) and (12.21), we obtain the price $c$ of a European call and the price $p$ of a European put on a stock providing a dividend yield at rate $q$ as

$$c = S_0 e^{-qT} N(d_1) - K e^{-rT} N(d_2) \tag{13.4}$$

$$p = K e^{-rT} N(-d_2) - S_0 e^{-qT} N(-d_1) \tag{13.5}$$

Since

$$\ln\left(\frac{S_0 e^{-qT}}{K}\right) = \ln\frac{S_0}{K} - qT$$

it follows that $d_1$ and $d_2$ are given by

$$d_1 = \frac{\ln(S_0/K) + (r - q + \sigma^2/2)T}{\sigma\sqrt{T}}$$

$$d_2 = \frac{\ln(S_0/K) + (r - q - \sigma^2/2)T}{\sigma\sqrt{T}} = d_1 - \sigma\sqrt{T}$$

These results were first derived by Merton.[1] As discussed in Section 12.13, the word *dividend* should be defined as the reduction of the stock price on the ex-dividend date arising from any dividends declared. If the dividend yield is not constant during the life of the option, equations (13.4) and (13.5) are still true, with $q$ equal to the average annualized dividend yield during the life of the option.

### Risk-Neutral Valuation

Appendix 13A derives, in a similar way to Section 12.6, the differential equation that must be satisfied by any derivative whose price, $f$, depends on a stock providing a dividend yield $q$. Like the Black–Scholes differential equation (12.15), it does not involve any variable affected by risk preferences. Therefore, the risk-neutral valuation procedure, described in Section 12.7, can be used. In a risk-neutral world, the total return from the stock must be $r$. The dividends provide a return of $q$. The expected growth rate in the stock price, therefore, must be $r - q$. The risk-neutral process for the stock price is

$$dS = (r - q)S\,dt + \sigma S\,dz \tag{13.6}$$

To value a derivative dependent on a stock that provides a dividend yield equal to $q$, we set the expected growth rate of the stock equal to $r - q$ and discount the expected payoff at rate $r$. To apply this approach to valuing a European call option, note that the expected stock price at time $T$ is $S_0 e^{(r-q)T}$. Equation (12A.1) gives the expected payoff from a call option as

$$e^{(r-q)T}S_0 N(d_1) - KN(d_2)$$

where $d_1$ and $d_2$ are defined as above. Discounting at rate $r$ for time $T$ leads to equation (13.4).

### Binomial Trees

We now examine the effect of a dividend yield equal to $q$ on the binomial model in Chapter 10. Consider the situation in Figure 13.1, in which a stock price starts at $S_0$ and, during time $T$, moves either up to $S_0 u$ or down to $S_0 d$. As in Chapter 10, we define $p$ as the probability of an up movement in a risk-neutral world. The total return provided by the stock in a risk-neutral world must be the risk-free interest rate, $r$. The dividends provide a return equal to $q$. The return in the form of capital gains must be $r - q$. This means that $p$ must satisfy

$$pS_0 u + (1 - p)S_0 d = S_0 e^{(r-q)T}$$

---

[1] See R. Merton, "Theory of Rational Option Pricing," *Bell Journal of Economics and Management Science*, 4 (Spring 1973), 141–83.

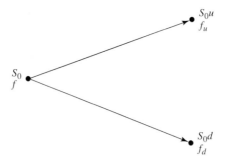

**Figure 13.1**   Stock price and option price in one-step binomial tree
when stock pays a dividend at rate $q$

or

$$p = \frac{e^{(r-q)T} - d}{u - d} \tag{13.7}$$

This is the same equation as in Chapter 10 with $r$ replaced by $r - q$. As in Chapter 10, the value of the derivative is the expected payoff in a risk-neutral world discounted at the risk-free rate, so that

$$f = e^{-rT}[pf_u + (1 - p)f_d] \tag{13.8}$$

**Example 13.1**   Suppose that the initial stock price is $30 and the stock price will move either up to $36 or down to $24 during a six-month period. The six-month risk-free interest rate is 5% and the stock is expected to provide a dividend yield of 3% during the six-month period. In this case $u = 1.2$, $d = 0.8$, and

$$p = \frac{e^{(0.05-0.03)\times 0.5} - 0.8}{1.2 - 0.8} = 0.5251$$

Consider a six-month put option on the stock with a strike price of $28. If the stock price moves up, the payoff is zero; if it moves down, the payoff is $4. The value of the option is therefore

$$e^{-0.05\times 0.5}[0.5251 \times 0 + 0.4749 \times 4] = 1.85$$

## 13.3   OPTIONS ON STOCK INDICES

Options on stock indices trade in both the over-the-counter and exchange-traded markets. As discussed in Chapter 7, some of the indices track the movement of the stock market as a whole. Others are based on the performance of a particular sector (e.g., mining, technology, or utilities).

### *Quotes*

Table 13.1 shows quotes for options on the Dow Jones Industrial Average (DJX), Nasdaq (NDX), Russell 2000 (RUT), S&P 100 (OEX), and S&P 500 (SPX) index options as they appeared in the Money and Investing section of the *Wall Street Journal* on Friday, March 16, 2001. All the options trade on the Chicago Board Options Exchange and all are European, except the contract on the S&P 100, which is American. The quotes refer to the price at which the last trade was made on Thursday, March 15, 2001. The closing prices of the DJX, NDX, RUT, OEX, and SPX on March 15, 2001, were 100.31, 1,697.92, 452.16, 600.71, and 1,173.56, respectively.

**Table 13.1**  Quotes for stock index options from *The Wall Street Journal*, March 16, 2001

Thursday, March 15, 2001

Volume, last, net change and open interest for all contracts. Volume figures are unofficial. Open interest reflects previous trading day. p-Put c-Call

### CHICAGO

#### DJ INDUS AVG(DJX)

| | STRIKE | VOL. | LAST | NET CHG. | OPEN INT. |
|---|---|---|---|---|---|
| Jun | 72 p | 57 | 030 | − 005 | 115 |
| Jun | 80 p | 10 | 065 | − 015 | 4,999 |
| Apr | 84 p | 10 | 025 | ... | ... |
| Jun | 84 p | 20 | 1 | − 010 | 1,016 |
| Jun | 88 p | 5 | 125 | − 015 | 227 |
| Apr | 90 p | 40 | 050 | ... | ... |
| Jun | 90 p | 126 | 160 | ... | 5,080 |
| Sep | 90 p | 93 | 260 | − 015 | 203 |
| Apr | 92 p | 1,787 | 085 | − 015 | 5,604 |
| Jun | 92 p | 45 | 190 | − 025 | 2,381 |
| Sep | 92 p | 59 | 3 | + 035 | 503 |
| Mar | 96 c | 8 | 450 | + 040 | 114 |
| Mar | 96 p | 170 | 005 | − 015 | 12,199 |
| Apr | 96 c | 6 | 580 | − 090 | 3 |
| Apr | 96 p | 572 | 175 | − 010 | 5,670 |
| Jun | 96 c | 3 | 780 | − 190 | 489 |
| Jun | 96 p | 628 | 310 | − 040 | 4,967 |
| Sep | 96 p | 23 | 420 | ... | 6,374 |
| Mar | 98 c | 20 | 190 | − 010 | 32 |
| Mar | 98 p | 746 | 005 | − 035 | 1,502 |
| Apr | 98 c | 49 | 440 | − 010 | 8,116 |
| Apr | 98 p | 836 | 220 | ... | 6,469 |
| Mar | 100 c | 2,323 | 070 | − 030 | 3,849 |
| Mar | 100 p | 4,550 | 030 | − 070 | 14,425 |
| Apr | 100 c | 463 | 360 | + 020 | 8,549 |
| Apr | 100 p | 1,502 | 285 | − 015 | 10,208 |
| Jun | 100 c | 1,125 | 5 | ... | 1,292 |
| Jun | 100 p | 3,119 | 410 | − 030 | 7,207 |
| Sep | 100 c | 2 | 750 | + 050 | 30 |
| Sep | 100 p | 934 | 570 | ... | 4,295 |
| Mar | 102 c | 478 | 010 | − 015 | 3,901 |
| Mar | 102 p | 1,638 | 165 | − 060 | 5,648 |
| Apr | 102 c | 148 | 260 | − 005 | 629 |
| Apr | 102 p | 103 | 380 | − 040 | 9,441 |
| Jun | 102 c | 29 | 410 | − 040 | 2,295 |
| Jun | 102 p | 513 | 5 | + 070 | 2,313 |
| Mar | 103 c | 49 | 005 | − 015 | 470 |
| Mar | 103 p | 305 | 280 | − 030 | 1,577 |
| Mar | 104 p | 740 | 380 | − 070 | 8,693 |
| Apr | 104 c | 77 | 160 | + 010 | 1,698 |
| Apr | 104 p | 197 | 510 | − 050 | 13,625 |
| Jun | 104 c | 2 | 370 | + 050 | 2,484 |
| Jun | 104 p | 230 | 620 | + 020 | 5,149 |
| Sep | 104 p | 1 | 740 | + 040 | 996 |
| Mar | 105 p | 127 | 480 | − 010 | 1,536 |
| Mar | 106 p | 181 | 6 | + 030 | 5,792 |
| Apr | 106 c | 637 | 1 | − 020 | 679 |
| Apr | 106 p | 41 | 610 | + 030 | 43,208 |
| Jun | 106 c | 82 | 250 | + 020 | 243 |
| Jun | 106 p | 61 | 730 | + 030 | 698 |
| Mar | 107 p | 2 | 660 | − 010 | 652 |
| Mar | 108 p | 214 | 8 | ... | 3,962 |
| Apr | 108 c | 15 | 095 | + 040 | 1,226 |
| Apr | 108 p | 20 | 8 | − 060 | 70,397 |
| Jun | 108 p | 53 | 840 | − 060 | 1,917 |
| Sep | 108 p | 11 | 930 | + 030 | 746 |
| Mar | 110 p | 107 | 950 | − 010 | 8,010 |
| Apr | 110 c | 1,022 | 035 | ... | 7,752 |
| Apr | 110 p | 58 | 950 | − 010 | 376 |
| Jun | 110 p | 34 | 980 | − 040 | 1,253 |
| Mar | 112 p | 11 | 12 | − 140 | 1,166 |
| Apr | 112 c | 900 | 025 | + 005 | 5,217 |
| Jun | 112 p | 1 | 1010 | − 190 | 622 |
| Sep | 112 p | 1 | 12 | − 020 | 390 |

Call Vol....9,262   Open Int....178,509
Put Vol....22,787   Open Int....361,587

#### NASDAQ-100(NDX)

| | STRIKE | VOL. | LAST | NET CHG. | OPEN INT. |
|---|---|---|---|---|---|
| Apr | 1200 p | 17 | 7 | − 110 | 980 |
| May | 1200 p | 17 | 18 | − 1 | 891 |
| Apr | 1300 p | 26 | 12 | − 6 | 144 |
| Apr | 1400 p | 62 | 2910 | − 090 | 1,827 |
| May | 1400 p | 45 | 48 | − 4 | 1,261 |
| Apr | 1500 p | 104 | 53 | + 3 | 517 |
| Mar | 1550 p | 20 | 025 | − 175 | 252 |
| Apr | 1550 p | 6 | 42 | − 1640 | 228 |
| Mar | 1600 p | 665 | 125 | − 295 | 603 |
| Apr | 1600 p | 51 | 58 | − 12 | 940 |
| Jun | 1600 p | 1 | 13040 | + 1040 | 832 |
| Mar | 1650 p | 17 | 4220 | − 4680 | ... |
| Mar | 1650 p | 388 | 15 | − 120 | 1,284 |
| Apr | 1650 p | 2 | 75 | − 12 | 597 |
| Mar | 1700 p | 217 | 20 | − 55 | 263 |
| Mar | 1700 p | 1,358 | 25 | ... | 2,149 |
| Apr | 1700 p | 10 | 133 | − 180 | 844 |
| May | 1700 p | 10 | 135 | − 10 | 21 |
| Apr | 1700 c | 2 | 203 | − 17 | 26 |
| Jun | 1700 p | 3 | 180 | ... | 799 |
| Mar | 1750 c | 105 | 4 | − 3040 | 157 |
| Mar | 1750 p | 191 | 65 | + 2320 | 541 |
| Mar | 1750 c | 6 | 110 | − 15 | 6 |
| Apr | 1750 p | 363 | 152 | + 30 | 30 |
| Mar | 1800 c | 248 | 1 | − 2090 | 330 |
| Mar | 1800 p | 209 | 100 | + 15 | 784 |
| Apr | 1800 c | 1 | 120 | + 23 | 87 |
| Apr | 1800 p | 80 | 170 | + 15 | 421 |
| Jun | 1800 p | 3 | 195 | + 15 | 36 |
| Jun | 1800 p | 16 | 230 | + 8 | 929 |
| Mar | 1850 c | 536 | 125 | − 725 | 177 |
| Mar | 1850 p | 2 | 15830 | + 3330 | 227 |
| Apr | 1850 c | 29 | 7380 | − 3820 | 118 |
| Apr | 1850 p | 6 | 199 | − 1 | 91 |
| Mar | 1900 c | 359 | 050 | − 3 | 520 |
| Mar | 1900 p | 39 | 190 | + 60 | 1,270 |
| Apr | 1900 c | 292 | 6930 | − 1850 | 838 |
| Apr | 1900 p | 56 | 241 | + 16 | 120 |
| May | 1900 c | 1 | 142 | + 3390 | 44 |
| Jun | 1900 p | 26 | 120 | − 30 | 163 |
| Mar | 1950 c | 113 | 010 | − 165 | 725 |
| Mar | 1950 p | 82 | 200 | + 30 | 1,662 |
| Apr | 1950 c | 5 | 80 | + 15 | 767 |
| Apr | 1950 p | 23 | 245 | − 5 | 525 |
| Mar | 2050 c | 10 | 025 | − 025 | 578 |
| Mar | 2050 p | 103 | 350 | + 85 | 2,315 |
| Apr | 2050 c | 280 | 30 | − 1150 | 271 |
| Apr | 2050 p | 107 | 308 | − 3450 | 52 |
| May | 2050 p | 1 | 86 | − 2 | 461 |
| Mar | 2100 p | 3 | 395 | + 45 | 1,439 |
| Apr | 2100 c | 240 | 33 | − 1 | 462 |
| Apr | 2100 p | 100 | 395 | + 15 | 305 |
| Jun | 2100 c | 1 | 7860 | − 3140 | 51 |
| Mar | 2150 p | 1 | 020 | − 030 | 425 |
| Mar | 2150 p | 98 | 370 | + 70 | 256 |
| Apr | 2150 p | 4 | 455 | + 4030 | 14 |
| Mar | 2200 c | 6 | 015 | − 035 | 1,356 |
| Mar | 2200 p | 12 | 435 | − 6030 | 579 |
| Apr | 2200 c | 3 | 1560 | − 490 | 53 |
| Apr | 2200 p | 1 | 470 | + 185 | 18 |
| May | 2200 p | 300 | 435 | − 47 | 600 |
| Jun | 2200 c | 1 | 61 | + 5 | 61 |
| Jun | 2200 p | 52 | 455 | + 240 | 283 |
| Mar | 2250 c | 15 | 005 | − 005 | 412 |
| Apr | 2250 p | 7 | 544 | + 26 | 170 |
| Apr | 2250 c | 57 | 10 | − 820 | 13 |
| Mar | 2300 p | 3 | 150 | + 1 | 1,164 |
| Apr | 2300 p | 1 | 525 | + 237 | 1,138 |
| Apr | 2300 c | 23 | 7 | − 2090 | 438 |
| Jun | 2300 p | 4 | 58310 | + 188 | 240 |
| Jun | 2300 p | 1 | 55590 | + 090 | 93 |
| Mar | 2350 p | 51 | 65940 | + 220 | 575 |
| Mar | 2400 p | 5 | 685 | + 10 | 1,338 |
| Apr | 2400 p | 2 | 860 | + 260 | 163 |
| Apr | 2400 c | 27 | 33 | − 2 | 1,016 |
| Jun | 2400 c | 4 | 61590 | − 6810 | 500 |
| Apr | 2450 c | 2 | 685 | − 25 | ... |
| Mar | 2500 p | 3 | 805 | + 5 | 542 |
| Apr | 2500 c | 12 | 270 | − 180 | 1,268 |
| May | 2500 c | 39 | 950 | ... | 2 |
| May | 2500 p | 3 | 69620 | ... | ... |
| Mar | 2600 c | 10 | 005 | − 045 | 760 |
| Mar | 2600 c | 8 | 900 | + 6680 | 785 |
| Apr | 2600 c | 5 | 170 | − 095 | 799 |
| Apr | 2600 c | 3 | 805 | − 30 | 87 |
| Mar | 2700 p | 1 | 910 | − 75 | 332 |
| Apr | 2800 c | 1 | 1 | − 030 | 2,726 |
| May | 2900 c | 7 | 3 | + 050 | 216 |
| Jun | 2900 c | 7 | 7 | + 110 | 1,067 |
| Apr | 2950 c | 12 | 070 | − 240 | 973 |
| Jun | 3050 c | 10 | 3 | + 030 | 143 |

Call Vol....2,732   Open Int....66,026
Put Vol....4,605   Open Int....52,260

#### RUSSELL 2000(RUT)

| | STRIKE | VOL. | LAST | NET CHG. | OPEN INT. |
|---|---|---|---|---|---|
| Mar | 450 c | 10 | 360 | − 3170 | 10 |
| Mar | 450 p | 460 | 140 | − 085 | 1,243 |
| Apr | 450 p | 1,644 | 17 | − 3 | 500 |
| Mar | 460 c | 15 | 190 | − 490 | 406 |
| Mar | 460 p | 29 | 910 | + 290 | 498 |
| Apr | 460 c | 100 | 1350 | − 250 | 651 |
| Apr | 460 p | 201 | 2280 | + 120 | 401 |
| Apr | 470 c | 10 | 050 | − 990 | 11 |
| Apr | 470 p | 500 | 2450 | + 1 | 1,000 |
| Apr | 500 c | 100 | 48 | + 280 | 456 |
| May | 500 c | 10 | 750 | − 110 | 298 |
| Apr | 510 c | 3 | 13 | 3 | ... |

Call Vol....158   Open Int....7,706
Put Vol....2,397   Open Int....15,139

#### S & P 100(OEX)

| | STRIKE | VOL. | LAST | NET CHG. | OPEN INT. |
|---|---|---|---|---|---|
| Apr | 500 p | 311 | 2 | − 070 | 1,515 |
| May | 500 p | 24 | 350 | − 1 | 186 |
| Jun | 500 p | 1 | 550 | − 030 | 180 |
| Apr | 510 p | 14 | 275 | − 095 | 1,233 |
| Apr | 540 c | 847 | 010 | − 015 | 3,610 |
| Apr | 540 p | 288 | 5 | − 170 | 4,208 |
| Jun | 540 p | 10 | 1110 | − 240 | 538 |
| Mar | 550 c | 5 | 52 | + 610 | 7 |
| Mar | 550 p | 749 | 005 | − 045 | 5,503 |
| Apr | 550 p | 147 | 710 | − 130 | 806 |
| Apr | 555 p | 25 | 720 | ... | ... |
| Apr | 560 c | 857 | 010 | − 070 | 8,327 |
| Apr | 560 p | 1 | 5550 | ... | ... |
| Apr | 560 p | 124 | 820 | − 110 | 2,851 |
| Jun | 560 p | 122 | 1510 | + 110 | 794 |
| Mar | 570 c | 2,136 | 030 | − 130 | 4,696 |
| Apr | 570 c | 10 | 47 | + 660 | 10 |
| Apr | 570 p | 159 | 1070 | − 180 | 1,802 |
| Apr | 575 p | 4 | 1150 | ... | ... |
| Mar | 580 c | 2,164 | 1 | − 150 | 7,552 |
| Apr | 580 p | 320 | 1340 | − 060 | 3,252 |
| May | 580 p | 14 | 1870 | − 130 | 3,418 |
| Jun | 580 c | 122 | 4850 | − 150 | 5 |
| Jun | 580 p | 123 | 21 | − 340 | 248 |
| Apr | 585 p | 1 | 1430 | ... | ... |
| Apr | 590 p | 157 | 11 | − 1 | 772 |
| Mar | 590 c | 3,264 | 170 | − 310 | 3,765 |
| Mar | 590 c | 26 | 2990 | + 140 | 34 |
| Apr | 590 c | 46 | 15 | − 350 | 1,431 |
| May | 590 p | 2 | 21 | ... | ... |
| Apr | 595 p | 27 | 1820 | ... | ... |
| Mar | 600 c | 6,508 | 570 | − 120 | 3,563 |
| Mar | 600 p | 8,644 | 470 | − 430 | 7,950 |
| Apr | 600 c | 393 | 2390 | + 290 | 465 |
| Apr | 600 p | 828 | 2050 | − 330 | 3,411 |
| May | 600 p | 105 | 24 | − 5 | 370 |
| Jun | 600 c | 1 | 3540 | + 010 | 3 |
| Jun | 600 p | 19 | 28 | − 250 | 316 |
| Mar | 605 c | 4,300 | 235 | − 195 | 2,019 |
| Mar | 605 p | 1,901 | 730 | − 470 | 2,035 |
| Apr | 605 c | 281 | 20 | + 010 | 47 |
| Apr | 605 p | 23 | 2330 | − 170 | 165 |
| Mar | 610 c | 6,920 | 175 | − 125 | 4,489 |
| Mar | 610 p | 2,738 | 10 | − 6 | 2,208 |
| Apr | 610 c | 98 | 1710 | ... | 191 |
| Apr | 610 p | 95 | 2530 | − 320 | 714 |
| May | 610 p | 4 | 3150 | ... | ... |
| Mar | 615 c | 1,773 | 060 | − 140 | 3,267 |
| Mar | 615 p | 662 | 2080 | + 080 | 2,077 |

*(continued on next page)*

**Table 13.1** (*continued*)

| Exp | Strike | Vol | Last | | Chg | Open Int |
|---|---|---|---|---|---|---|
| Apr | 615 c | 32 | 15 | + | 050 | 332 |
| Apr | 615 p | 2 | 28 | − | 5 | 315 |
| Mar | 620 c | 4,149 | 030 | − | 1 | 3,881 |
| Mar | 620 p | 1,807 | 2080 | − | 420 | 3,965 |
| Apr | 620 c | 352 | 1320 | + | 1 | 599 |
| Apr | 620 p | 131 | 2910 | − | 490 | 3,294 |
| May | 620 c | 157 | 1930 | + | 130 | 25 |
| May | 620 p | 10 | 3510 | − | 490 | 99 |
| Jun | 620 c | 6 | 26 | − | 050 | 885 |
| Jun | 620 p | 8 | 3750 | − | 340 | 1,159 |
| Mar | 625 c | 1,281 | 015 | − | 045 | 1,792 |
| Mar | 625 p | 55 | 24 | − | 5 | 810 |
| Apr | 625 c | 79 | 1120 | + | 020 | 180 |
| Apr | 625 p | 7 | 3030 | + | 430 | 182 |
| Mar | 630 c | 1,874 | 005 | − | 035 | 3,458 |
| Mar | 630 p | 928 | 29 | − | 5 | 2,106 |
| Apr | 630 c | 156 | 950 | + | 030 | 870 |
| Apr | 630 p | 146 | 3520 | − | 430 | 1,355 |
| May | 630 c | 1,187 | 16 | + | 2 | 16 |
| May | 630 p | 9 | 40 | − | 3 | 331 |
| Mar | 635 c | 1,313 | 005 | − | 015 | 2,697 |
| Mar | 635 p | 456 | 3520 | − | 280 | 735 |
| Apr | 635 c | 15 | 820 | + | 070 | 60 |
| Apr | 635 p | 5 | 3850 | + | 350 | 644 |
| Mar | 640 c | 488 | 005 | − | 010 | 4,378 |
| Mar | 640 p | 110 | 40 | − | 5 | 634 |
| Apr | 640 c | 93 | 650 | − | 020 | 951 |
| Apr | 640 p | 80 | 4340 | − | 960 | 711 |
| May | 640 c | 8 | 1110 | − | 020 | 64 |
| May | 640 p | 22 | 4730 | − | 370 | 396 |
| Jun | 640 c | 24 | 1550 | + | 1 | 164 |
| Jun | 640 p | 12 | 4850 | − | 450 | 614 |
| Mar | 645 c | 265 | 010 | − | 005 | 2,420 |
| Mar | 645 p | 147 | 4430 | − | 420 | 1,227 |
| Apr | 645 c | 41 | 5 | − | 1 | 448 |
| Apr | 645 p | 48 | 4750 | + | 9 | 166 |
| Mar | 650 c | 121 | 005 | − | 005 | 5,151 |
| Mar | 650 p | 129 | 5090 | − | 410 | 407 |
| Apr | 650 c | 300 | 420 | − | 060 | 2,160 |
| Apr | 650 p | 32 | 5250 | − | 4 | 2,016 |
| May | 650 c | 27 | 920 | + | 120 | 169 |
| Mar | 655 c | 23 | 55 | − | 5 | 108 |
| Apr | 655 c | 73 | 350 | + | 040 | 259 |
| Apr | 655 p | 9 | 54 | − | 250 | 435 |
| Mar | 660 c | 1,022 | 005 | | ... | 4,351 |
| Mar | 660 p | 42 | 59 | − | 6 | 386 |
| Apr | 660 c | 111 | 310 | − | 050 | 2,959 |
| Apr | 660 p | 169 | 6110 | − | 390 | 456 |
| May | 660 c | 220 | 650 | − | 2 | 178 |
| Mar | 665 c | 65 | 005 | | ... | 4,248 |
| Mar | 665 p | 1 | 61 | − | 9 | 94 |
| Apr | 665 c | 150 | 240 | − | 025 | 175 |
| Mar | 670 c | 95 | 005 | | ... | 4,657 |
| Mar | 670 p | 641 | 69 | − | 8 | 765 |
| Apr | 670 c | 185 | 160 | − | 040 | 704 |
| Apr | 670 p | 45 | 7250 | + | 350 | 447 |
| May | 670 p | 13 | 70 | + | 3 | 138 |
| Mar | 675 c | 401 | 005 | | ... | 3,505 |
| Mar | 675 p | 365 | 7430 | − | 670 | 706 |
| Apr | 675 c | 81 | 155 | − | 045 | 459 |
| Apr | 675 p | 50 | 71 | − | 3 | 7 |
| Mar | 680 c | 108 | 7850 | − | 650 | 150 |
| Apr | 680 c | 85 | 130 | − | 015 | 1,587 |
| Apr | 680 p | 19 | 79 | − | 820 | 533 |
| May | 680 c | 327 | 350 | + | 070 | 63 |
| Jun | 680 p | 10 | 78 | − | 9 | 503 |
| Apr | 690 c | 248 | 095 | − | 005 | 3,011 |
| Apr | 690 p | 109 | 90 | − | 10 | 353 |
| May | 690 c | 291 | 230 | − | 010 | 186 |
| May | 690 p | 10 | 90 | + | 680 | 47 |
| Mar | 700 c | 25 | 9850 | − | 450 | 66 |
| Mar | 700 c | 65 | 060 | − | 035 | 2,933 |
| Apr | 700 p | 9 | 9850 | − | 920 | 953 |
| Apr | 705 c | 30 | 055 | + | 005 | 389 |
| Apr | 705 p | 10 | 103 | | | |
| Apr | 720 c | 231 | 020 | − | 015 | 1,024 |
| Apr | 720 p | 9 | 116 | − | 580 | 149 |
| Apr | 725 p | 11 | 12010 | + | 4610 | 12 |
| Apr | 730 c | 125 | 025 | − | 020 | 837 |
| May | 730 p | 14 | 12570 | + | 48 | 25 |
| Jun | 740 p | 60 | 138 | − | 170 | 50 |
| May | 750 p | 16 | 14570 | + | 4910 | 7 |
| May | 760 c | 4 | 035 | − | 075 | 22 |
| May | 760 p | 3 | 15590 | + | 850 | 4 |
| Call Vol..........35,250 | | Open Int..........171,210 | | | | |
| Put Vol..........34,927 | | Open Int..........117,069 | | | | |

**S & P 500(SPX)**

| Exp | Strike | Vol | Last | | Chg | Open Int |
|---|---|---|---|---|---|---|
| Jun | 750 c | 300 | 432 | − | 195 | 306 |
| Jun | 750 p | 14 | 090 | − | 010 | 6,555 |
| Jun | 800 c | 161 | 140 | − | 035 | 3,039 |
| Jun | 850 p | 1 | 270 | − | 030 | 924 |
| Jun | 900 c | 1 | 291 | + | 11 | 415 |
| Jun | 900 p | 79 | 410 | − | 050 | 25,204 |
| Apr | 950 c | 391 | 220 | − | 065 | 1,974 |
| Jun | 950 p | 4 | 740 | + | 120 | 6,802 |
| Apr | 975 c | 1,225 | 310 | − | 040 | 656 |
| Jun | 995 c | 5 | 181 | − | 6010 | 11,324 |
| Mar | 995 c | 100 | 005 | − | 005 | 25,234 |
| Jun | 995 p | 955 | 198 | | ... | 914 |
| Jun | 995 p | 603 | 11 | | ... | 4,941 |
| Jun | 1005 p | 641 | 4 | − | 110 | 714 |
| Mar | 1025 c | 200 | 005 | − | 025 | 8,705 |
| Apr | 1025 p | 292 | 6 | − | 160 | 4,829 |
| Mar | 1050 p | 320 | 005 | − | 055 | 9,692 |
| Apr | 1050 c | 6 | 133 | + | 3 | 8 |
| Apr | 1050 p | 1,055 | 8 | − | 150 | 6,341 |
| Jun | 1050 p | 1,488 | 1850 | + | 160 | 6,702 |
| Jun | 1075 p | 2,394 | 11 | − | 030 | 10,504 |
| Mar | 1100 c | 842 | 010 | − | 070 | 28,705 |
| Apr | 1100 c | 1 | 9250 | + | 150 | 57 |
| Apr | 1100 p | 5,741 | 14 | − | 3 | 8,970 |
| May | 1100 p | 363 | 2250 | − | 250 | 3,078 |
| Jun | 1100 c | 301 | 11340 | − | 560 | 216 |
| Jun | 1100 p | 33 | 2830 | − | 220 | 16,096 |
| Mar | 1125 p | 1,303 | 025 | − | 175 | 4,529 |
| Apr | 1125 p | 261 | 1950 | − | 350 | 3,737 |
| May | 1125 p | 872 | 2750 | − | 450 | 3,996 |
| Jun | 1125 c | 1,000 | 9350 | + | 650 | 7 |
| Mar | 1150 c | 908 | 2280 | − | 020 | 1,801 |
| Mar | 1150 p | 4,934 | 140 | − | 460 | 12,363 |
| Apr | 1150 c | 2,755 | 55 | + | 3 | 189 |
| Apr | 1150 p | 4,247 | 2750 | − | 250 | 19,128 |
| May | 1150 c | 10 | 69 | + | 5 | 105 |
| May | 1150 p | 7,741 | 36 | − | 3 | 6,656 |
| Jun | 1150 c | 251 | 77 | − | 4 | 604 |
| Jun | 1150 p | 712 | 42 | − | 5 | 9,383 |
| Mar | 1175 c | 2,250 | 280 | − | 640 | 2,960 |
| Mar | 1175 p | 7,401 | 6 | − | 850 | 13,344 |
| Mar | 1175 c | 180 | 3870 | + | 060 | 426 |
| Apr | 1175 p | 2,735 | 3750 | − | 4 | 7,992 |
| May | 1175 c | 11 | 54 | | ... | |
| May | 1175 p | 3,716 | 4520 | − | 480 | 5,557 |
| Jun | 1175 c | 2,122 | 62 | + | 2 | 5,192 |
| Jun | 1175 p | 3,891 | 5240 | − | 060 | 7,969 |
| Mar | 1200 c | 5,969 | 1 | − | 2 | 6,286 |
| Mar | 1200 p | 3,639 | 28 | − | 8 | 16,866 |
| Apr | 1200 c | 2,131 | 2550 | − | 050 | 5,447 |
| Apr | 1200 p | 1,265 | 48 | − | 4 | 16,070 |
| May | 1200 c | 405 | 41 | + | 4 | 1,565 |
| May | 1200 p | 451 | 58 | − | 4 | 4,572 |
| Jun | 1200 c | 6,731 | 51 | + | 8 | 7,620 |
| Jun | 1200 p | 6,344 | 61 | − | 650 | 19,356 |
| Mar | 1210 c | 651 | 040 | − | 085 | 965 |
| Mar | 1210 p | 37 | 33 | + | 150 | 1,483 |
| Mar | 1220 c | 969 | 050 | − | 050 | 12,315 |
| Mar | 1220 p | 55 | 4050 | + | 1 | 1,962 |
| Mar | 1225 c | 2,365 | 015 | − | 065 | 12,754 |
| Mar | 1225 c | 1,667 | 53 | − | 5 | 13,057 |
| Apr | 1225 c | 1,497 | 16 | − | 1 | 3,307 |
| Apr | 1225 p | 2,651 | 62 | − | 15 | 6,856 |
| May | 1225 c | 1,950 | 30 | + | 510 | 120 |
| May | 1225 p | 2 | 7020 | − | 980 | 1,079 |
| Jun | 1225 c | 1,004 | 37 | − | 4 | 8,086 |
| Jun | 1225 p | 34 | 76 | − | 8 | 12,360 |
| Mar | 1230 c | 250 | 010 | − | 065 | 10,959 |
| Mar | 1230 p | 60 | 5650 | − | 1150 | 3,435 |
| Mar | 1240 c | 106 | 010 | − | 040 | 5,757 |
| Mar | 1240 p | 7 | 69 | + | 2 | 4,573 |
| Mar | 1250 c | 292 | 005 | − | 030 | 22,662 |
| Mar | 1250 p | 642 | 76 | − | 6 | 24,292 |
| Apr | 1250 c | 5,455 | 10 | − | 1 | 11,780 |
| Apr | 1250 p | 318 | 7910 | − | 890 | 19,663 |
| May | 1250 c | 1,036 | 1940 | + | 130 | 857 |
| May | 1250 p | 67 | 8450 | − | 850 | 973 |
| Jun | 1250 c | 6 | 2690 | − | 010 | 15,503 |
| Jun | 1250 p | 1 | 9250 | − | 9 | 20,443 |
| Jun | 1260 p | 55 | 8750 | + | 550 | 5,848 |
| Jun | 1270 c | 4 | 005 | − | 095 | 1,775 |
| Mar | 1275 c | 1,943 | 020 | | ... | 25,578 |
| Mar | 1275 p | 982 | 103 | − | 4 | 22,621 |
| Apr | 1275 c | 4,461 | 6 | + | 090 | 14,980 |
| Apr | 1275 p | 380 | 105 | − | 10 | 12,176 |
| May | 1275 c | 1 | 1590 | + | 5 | 4,304 |
| May | 1275 p | 3 | 103 | + | 1 | 3,811 |
| Jun | 1275 c | 1 | 19 | + | 250 | 6,297 |
| Jun | 1275 p | 331 | 110 | + | 5 | 8,895 |
| Mar | 1280 c | 2 | 005 | | ... | 3,545 |
| Mar | 1280 p | 201 | 104 | + | 8 | 700 |
| Mar | 1300 c | 188 | 12750 | − | 850 | 16,140 |
| Apr | 1300 c | 438 | 3 | − | 030 | 6,898 |
| Apr | 1300 p | 5,751 | 12360 | − | 1240 | 6,859 |
| May | 1300 c | 1,466 | 850 | + | 030 | 4,529 |
| May | 1300 p | 74 | 124 | − | 4 | 538 |
| Jun | 1300 c | 624 | 13 | + | 150 | 7,270 |
| Jun | 1300 p | 117 | 12550 | − | 580 | 13,561 |
| Mar | 1310 p | 3 | 13570 | | ... | 316 |
| Mar | 1325 c | 230 | 010 | + | 005 | 47,196 |
| Mar | 1325 p | 377 | 148 | − | 10 | 42,279 |
| Apr | 1325 c | 1,139 | 175 | − | 030 | 14,036 |
| Apr | 1325 p | 211 | 14650 | − | 1850 | 2,854 |
| May | 1325 c | 25 | 6 | | ... | 273 |
| May | 1325 p | 70 | 145 | + | 1 | 92 |
| Jun | 1325 c | 10 | 10 | + | 2 | 5,168 |
| Jun | 1325 p | 1,002 | 148 | − | 10 | 5,835 |
| Mar | 1350 c | 174 | 17720 | − | 580 | 38,269 |
| Apr | 1350 c | 490 | 1 | | | 14,129 |
| Apr | 1350 p | 6,113 | 173 | + | 350 | 1,744 |
| May | 1350 c | 114 | 310 | | | 2,434 |
| Jun | 1350 p | 505 | 590 | − | 170 | 6,873 |
| Jun | 1375 p | 132 | 201 | − | 7 | 9,898 |
| Apr | 1375 c | 140 | 050 | − | 025 | 16,347 |
| Apr | 1375 p | 51 | 196 | − | 450 | 814 |
| Jun | 1375 c | 1 | 450 | | | 3,788 |
| Mar | 1380 p | 1 | 207 | + | 12 | 1,703 |
| Apr | 1400 p | 581 | 226 | − | 14 | 11,624 |
| Apr | 1400 c | 97 | 218 | + | 3 | 837 |
| May | 1400 c | 14 | 216 | + | 4 | 512 |
| Jun | 1400 p | 79 | 20550 | − | 1550 | 8,920 |
| Apr | 1425 c | 9 | 252 | − | 5 | 10,341 |
| Apr | 1425 c | 2 | 030 | + | 005 | 9,371 |
| May | 1425 p | 2 | 241 | + | 83 | 50 |
| Jun | 1425 c | 125 | 236 | + | 4 | 6,896 |
| Apr | 1450 c | 36 | 276 | + | 7 | 6,135 |
| May | 1450 p | 3 | 269 | + | 150 | 230 |
| May | 1450 c | 26 | 050 | − | 010 | 233 |
| May | 1450 p | 4 | 265 | | | |

## LEAPS-LONG TERM

**DJ INDUS AVG - CB**

| Exp | Strike | Vol | Last | | Chg | Open Int |
|---|---|---|---|---|---|---|
| Jun 02 | 100 p | 2 | 770 | + | 050 | 243 |
| Dec 02 | 100 c | 15 | 1680 | − | 020 | 79 |
| Dec 02 | 100 c | 35 | 840 | − | 1 | 865 |
| Dec 02 | 108 c | 4 | 12 | − | 290 | 446 |
| Dec 02 | 108 p | 3 | 1280 | + | 060 | 902 |
| Call Vol.............19 | | Open Int............8,367 | | | | |
| Put Vol.............40 | | Open Int............16,890 | | | | |

**S & P 100 - CB**

| Exp | Strike | Vol | Last | | Chg | Open Int |
|---|---|---|---|---|---|---|
| Dec 01 | 190 p | 4 | 190 | + | 005 | 490 |
| Call Vol.............0 | | Open Int............1,050 | | | | |
| Put Vol.............4 | | Open Int............5,087 | | | | |

**S & P 500 - CB**

| Exp | Strike | Vol | Last | | Chg | Open Int |
|---|---|---|---|---|---|---|
| Dec 01 | 90 p | 13 | 360 | − | 050 | 2,008 |
| Dec 01 | 100 p | 3 | 310 | + | 030 | 1,324 |
| Dec 03 | 100 p | 29 | 740 | + | 040 | 3,026 |
| Dec 01 | 110 p | 9 | 550 | | | 21,879 |
| Dec 01 | 110 p | 221 | 830 | + | 020 | 27,363 |
| Dec 03 | 110 p | 10 | 950 | − | 040 | 822 |
| Dec 01 | 120 p | 50 | 850 | − | 160 | 38,210 |
| Dec 02 | 120 p | 5 | 1170 | + | 020 | 4,968 |
| Dec 03 | 120 p | 6 | 1270 | − | 090 | 9,267 |
| Dec 01 | 12750 p | 5 | 570 | | ... | 203 |
| Dec 01 | 130 p | 459 | 1370 | + | 010 | 29,336 |
| Dec 02 | 130 p | 20 | 1590 | − | 010 | 6,690 |
| Dec 03 | 130 p | 37 | 1690 | − | 070 | 12,315 |
| Dec 01 | 135 p | 45 | 1680 | − | 1 | 25,321 |
| Dec 01 | 140 c | 3 | 245 | + | 015 | 7,951 |
| Dec 01 | 140 p | 156 | 2030 | + | 010 | 42,525 |
| Dec 03 | 140 p | 1 | 2050 | | | 11,175 |
| Dec 01 | 145 p | 2 | 2370 | + | 480 | 5 |
| Dec 01 | 145 p | 40 | 2440 | + | 540 | 3,430 |
| Dec 01 | 150 p | 95 | 2870 | − | 2 | 3,743 |
| Dec 03 | 160 p | 2 | 3170 | | ... | 11,536 |
| Dec 01 | 180 p | 3 | 005 | − | 060 | 58 |
| Dec 02 | 180 p | 10 | 50 | + | 050 | 13,958 |
| Call Vol.............6 | | Open Int............405,282 | | | | |
| Put Vol.............1,218 | | Open Int............544,821 | | | | |

One index option contract is on 100 times the index. (Note that the Dow Jones index used for index options is 0.01 times the usually quoted Dow Jones index.) Index options are settled in cash. This means that, on exercise of the option, the holder of a call option receives $S - K$ in cash and the writer of the option pays this amount in cash, where $S$ is the value of the index at the close of trading on the day of the exercise and $K$ is the strike price. Similarly, the holder of a put option receives $K - S$ in cash and the writer of the option pays this amount in cash.

> **Example 13.2**  Consider the April put option contract on the S&P 100 with a strike price of 620 in Table 13.1. This is an American-style option and expires on April 21, 2001. The cost of one contract is indicated as $29.10 \times 100 = \$2,910$. The value of the index at the close of trading on March 15, 2001, is 600.71, so that the option is in the money. If the option contract were exercised, the holder would receive $(620 - 600.71) \times 100 = \$1,929$ in cash. This is less than the value of the contract— indicating that it is not optimal to exercise the contract on March 15, 2001.

Table 13.1 shows that, in addition to relatively short-dated options, the exchanges trade longer-maturity contracts known as LEAPS, which were mentioned in Chapter 7. The acronym LEAPS stands for Long-term Equity AnticiPation Securities and was originated by the CBOE. LEAPS are exchange-traded options that last up to three years. The index is divided by five for the purposes of quoting the strike price and the option price. One contract is an option on 100 times one-fifth of the index (or 20 times the index). LEAPS on indices have expiration dates in December. As mentioned in Chapter 7, the CBOE and several other exchanges also trade LEAPS on many individual stocks. These have expirations in January.

The CBOE also trades *flex options* on indices. As mentioned in Chapter 7, these are options where the trader can choose the expiration date, the strike price, and whether the option is American or European.

## Portfolio Insurance

Portfolio managers can use index options to limit their downside risk. Suppose that the value of an index today is $S_0$. Consider a manager in charge of a well-diversified portfolio whose beta is 1.0. A beta of 1.0 implies that the returns from the portfolio mirror those from the index. If the dividend yield from the portfolio is the same as the dividend yield from the index, the percentage changes in the value of the portfolio can be expected to be approximately the same as the percentage changes in the value of the index. Each contract on the S&P 500 is on 100 times the index. It follows that the value of the portfolio is protected against the possibility of the index falling below $K$ if, for each $100 S_0$ dollars in the portfolio, the manager buys one put option contract with strike price $K$. Suppose that the manager's portfolio is worth $500,000 and the value of the index is 1,000. The portfolio is worth 500 times the index. The manager can obtain insurance against the value of the portfolio dropping below $450,000 in the next three months by buying five put option contracts with a strike price of 900. To illustrate how this works, consider the situation where the index drops to 880 in three months. The portfolio will be worth about $440,000. The payoff from the options will be $5 \times (900 - 880) \times 100 = \$10,000$, bringing the total value of the portfolio up to the insured value of $450,000.

## When the Portfolio's Beta Is Not 1.0

If the portfolio's returns are not expected to equal those of an index, the capital asset pricing model can be used. This model asserts that the expected excess return of a portfolio over the risk-free

**Table 13.2** Relationship between value of index and value of portfolio for beta = 2.0

| Value of index in three months | Value of portfolio in three months ($) |
|---|---|
| 1,080 | 570,000 |
| 1,040 | 530,000 |
| 1,000 | 490,000 |
| 960 | 450,000 |
| 920 | 410,000 |
| 880 | 370,000 |

interest rate equals beta times the excess return of a market index over the risk-free interest rate. Suppose that the $500,000 portfolio just considered has a beta of 2.0 instead of 1.0. Suppose further that the current risk-free interest rate is 12% per annum, and the dividend yield on both the portfolio and the index is expected to be 4% per annum. As before, we assume that the S&P 500 index is currently 1,000. Table 13.2 shows the expected relationship between the level of the index and the value of the portfolio in three months. To illustrate the sequence of calculations necessary to derive Table 13.2, Table 13.3 shows what happens when the value of the index in three months proves to be 1,040.

Suppose that $S_0$ is the value of the index. It can be shown that, for each $100S_0$ dollars in the portfolio, a total of beta put contracts should be purchased. The strike price should be the value that the index is expected to have when the value of the portfolio reaches the insured value. Suppose that the insured value is $450,000, as in the case of beta = 1.0. Table 13.2 shows that the appropriate strike price for the put options purchased is 960. In this case, $100S_0 = \$100,000$ and beta = 2.0, so that two put contracts are required for each $100,000 in the portfolio. Because the portfolio is worth $500,000, a total of 10 contracts should be purchased.

**Table 13.3** Calculations for Table 13.2 when the value of the index is 1,040 in three months

| | |
|---|---|
| Value of index in three months | 1,040 |
| Return from change in index | 40/1,000, or 4% per three months |
| Dividends from index | $0.25 \times 4 = 1\%$ per three months |
| Total return from index | $4 + 1 = 5\%$ per three months |
| Risk-free interest rate | $0.25 \times 12 = 3\%$ per three months |
| Excess return from index over risk-free interest rate | $5 - 3 = 2\%$ per three months |
| Excess return from portfolio over risk-free interest rate | $2 \times 2 = 4\%$ per three months |
| Return from portfolio | $3 + 4 = 7\%$ per three months |
| Dividends from portfolio | $0.25 \times 4 = 1\%$ per three months |
| Increase in value of portfolio | $7 - 1 = 6\%$ per three months |
| Value of portfolio | $\$500,000 \times 1.06 = \$530,000$ |

To illustrate that the required result is obtained, consider what happens if the value of the index falls to 880. As shown in Table 13.2, the value of the portfolio is then about $370,000. The put options pay off $(960 - 880) \times 10 \times 100 = \$80,000$, and this is exactly what is necessary to move the total value of the portfolio manager's position up from $370,000 to the required level of $450,000.

### Valuation

In valuing index futures in Chapter 3, we assumed that the index could be treated as a security paying a known dividend yield. In valuing index options, we make similar assumptions. This means that equations (13.1) and (13.2) provide lower bounds for European index options; equation (13.3) is the put–call parity result for European index options; and equations (13.4) and (13.5) can be used to value European options on an index. In all cases $S_0$ is equal to the value of the index, $\sigma$ is equal to the volatility of the index, and $q$ is equal to the average annualized dividend yield on the index during the life of the option. The calculation of $q$ should include only dividends whose ex-dividend date occurs during the life of the option.

In the United States ex-dividend dates tend to occur during the first week of February, May, August, and November. At any given time, the correct value of $q$ is therefore likely to depend on the life of the option. This is even more true for some foreign indices. For example, in Japan all companies tend to use the same ex-dividend dates.

**Example 13.3** Consider a European call option on the S&P 500 that is two months from maturity. The current value of the index is 930, the exercise price is 900, the risk-free interest rate is 8% per annum, and the volatility of the index is 20% per annum. Dividend yields of 0.2% and 0.3% are expected in the first month and the second month, respectively. In this case $S_0 = 930$, $K = 900$, $r = 0.08$, $\sigma = 0.2$, and $T = 2/12$. The total dividend yield during the option's life is $0.2 + 0.3 = 0.5\%$. This is 3% per annum. Hence, $q = 0.03$ and

$$d_1 = \frac{\ln(930/900) + (0.08 - 0.03 + 0.2^2/2) \times 2/12}{0.2\sqrt{2/12}} = 0.5444$$

$$d_2 = \frac{\ln(930/900) + (0.08 - 0.03 - 0.2^2/2) \times 2/12}{0.2\sqrt{2/12}} = 0.4628$$

$$N(d_1) = 0.7069, \quad N(d_2) = 0.6782$$

so that the call price, $c$, is given by equation (13.4) as

$$c = 930 \times 0.7069 e^{-0.03 \times 2/12} - 900 \times 0.6782 e^{-0.08 \times 2/12} = 51.83$$

One contract would cost $5,183.

If the absolute amount of the dividend that will be paid on the stocks underlying the index (rather than the dividend yield) is assumed to be known, the basic Black–Scholes formula can be used with the initial stock price being reduced by the present value of the dividends. This is the approach recommended in Chapter 12 for a stock paying known dividends. However, the approach may be difficult to implement for a broadly based stock index because it requires a knowledge of the dividends expected on every stock underlying the index.

In some circumstances it is optimal to exercise American put options on an index prior to the exercise date. To a lesser extent, this is also true of American call options on an index. American stock index option prices are therefore always slightly more than the corresponding European stock index option prices. We will look at numerical procedures for valuing American index options in Chapter 18.

## 13.4  CURRENCY OPTIONS

European and American options on foreign currencies are actively traded in both the over-the-counter and exchange-traded markets. The Philadelphia Stock Exchange has been trading currency options since 1982. The currencies traded include the Australian dollar, British pound, Canadian dollar, Japanese yen, and Swiss franc. For most of the currencies the Philadelphia Exchange trades both European and American options.

For a corporation wishing to hedge a foreign exchange exposure, foreign currency options are an interesting alternative to forward contracts. A company due to receive sterling at a known time in the future can hedge its risk by buying put options on sterling that mature at that time. The strategy guarantees that the value of the sterling will not be less than the exercise price while allowing the company to benefit from any favorable exchange-rate movements. Similarly, a company due to pay sterling at a known time in the future can hedge by buying calls on sterling that mature at that time. The approach guarantees that the cost of the sterling will not exceed a certain amount while allowing the company to benefit from favorable exchange-rate movements. Whereas a forward contract locks in the exchange rate for a future transaction, an option provides a type of insurance. This insurance is, of course, not free. It costs nothing to enter into a forward transaction, whereas options require a premium to be paid up front.

### Quotes

Table 13.4 shows the closing prices of some of the currency options traded on the Philadelphia Stock Exchange on Thursday, March 15, 2001, as reported in the *Wall Street Journal* of Friday, March 16, 2001. The precise expiration date of a foreign currency option is the Saturday preceding the third Wednesday of the maturity month. The sizes of contracts are indicated at the beginning of each section of the table. The option prices are for the purchase or sale of one unit of a foreign currency with U.S. dollars. For the Japanese yen, the prices are in hundredths of a cent. For the other currencies, they are in cents. Thus, one call option contract on the euro with exercise price 90 cents and exercise month June would give the holder the right to buy 62,500 euros for 56,250 $(= 0.90 \times 62,500)$ U.S. dollars. The indicated price of the contract is 2.34 cents, so that one contract would cost $62,500 \times 0.0234 = \$1,462.50$. The spot exchange rate is shown as 88.15 cents per euro.

### Valuation

To value currency options, we define $S$ as the spot exchange rate (the value of one unit of the foreign currency measured in the domestic currency). We assume that $S$ follows a geometric Brownian motion process similar to that assume for stocks in Chapter 12. In a risk-neutral world the process is

$$dS = (r - r_f)S\,dt + \sigma S\,dz$$

where $r$ is the domestic risk-free interest rate, $r_f$ is the foreign risk-free interest rate, and $\sigma$ is the exchange rate's volatility.

**Table 13.4**   Currency option prices on the Philadelphia Exchange from the *Wall Street Journal* on March 16, 2001

### PHILADELPHIA EXCHANGE OPTIONS

| | | CALLS VOL. LAST | | PUT VOL. LAST | | | | CALLS VOL. LAST | | PUT VOL. LAST | | | | CALLS VOL. LAST | | PUT VOL. LAST |
|---|---|---|---|---|---|---|---|---|---|---|---|---|---|---|---|---|
| ADllr | | | | 54.26 | JYen | | | | 93.49 | 96 | Mar | ... | ... | 5 | 5.38 |
| 50,000 Australian Dollar EOM-European. | | | | | 6,250,000 J.Yen EOM-European style. | | | | | Euro | | | | | 88.15 |
| 51 Apr | 4 | 0.44 | ... | ... | 87⁵⁰ Mar | ... | ... | 30 | 5.55 | 62,500 Euro-cents per unit. | | | | | |
| ADollr | | | | 54.26 | JYen | | | | 93.15 | 88 | Apr | ... | ... | 10 | 0.43 |
| 50,000 Australian Dollars-European Style. | | | | | 6,250,000J.Yen-100ths of a cent per unit. | | | | | 90 | Jun | 22 | 2.34 | 1 | 2.35 |
| 52 Mar | ... | ... | 4 | 2.71 | 81⁵⁰ Mar | ... | ... | 5 | 0.30 | 94 | Mar | ... | ... | 3 | 3.65 |
| ADollr | | | | 54.26 | 82⁵⁰ Apr | 2 | 1.10 | 2 | 1.44 | 114 | Mar | ... | ... | 2 | 23.55 |
| 50,000 Australian Dollars-cents per unit | | | | | 83 Apr | ... | ... | 5 | 1.51 | SFranc | | | | | 57.83 |
| 53 Jun | 1 | 0.41 | ... | ... | JYen | | | | 92.53 | 62,500 Swiss Franc EOM-European style. | | | | | |
| CDollr | | | | 66.48 | 6,250,000J.Yen-EuropeanStyle. | | | | | 59 | Apr | 2 | 1.00 | ... | ... |
| 50,000 Canadian Dollars-European Style. | | | | | 77 Mar | 110 | 5.80 | ... | ... | SFranc | | | | | 57.83 |
| 66 Mar | ... | ... | 20 | 1.76 | 79 Sep | 110 | 6.40 | ... | ... | 62,500 Swiss Francs-European Style. | | | | | |
| 67⁵⁰ Mar | ... | ... | 20 | 3.35 | 82 Mar | 22 | 0.93 | ... | ... | 58 | Apr | 16 | 1.30 | ... | ... |
| 67⁵⁰ Sep | ... | ... | 20 | 3.37 | 84 Jun | 22 | 1.95 | ... | ... | 60 | Apr | 16 | 0.34 | ... | ... |
| CDollr | | | | 66.48 | Euro | | | | 88.15 | SFranc | | | | | 57.83 |
| 50,000 Canadian Dollars-cents per unit. | | | | | 62,500 Euro-European style | | | | | 62,500 Swiss Francs-cents per unit. | | | | | |
| 71⁵⁰ Mar | ... | ... | 20 | 7.90 | 88 Mar | ... | ... | 8 | 0.25 | 58 | Apr | 6 | 1.38 | ... | ... |
| 72⁵⁰ Mar | ... | ... | 20 | 8.40 | 94 Jun | ... | ... | 10 | 4.40 | 60 | Sep | 2 | 1.90 | ... | ... |
| 74⁵⁰ Mar | ... | ... | 20 | 10.42 | 98 Jun | ... | ... | 5 | 7.48 | Call Vol. ...........1,221 | | Open Int...........12,520 | | | |
| 75 Mar | ... | ... | 20 | 10.86 | 104 Mar | 8 | 0.55 | ... | ... | Put Vol. ...........3,926 | | Open Int...........12,955 | | | |
| CDollr | | | | 66.48 | Euro | | | | 88.15 | | | | | | |
| 50,000 Canadian Dollars-cents per unit. | | | | | 62,500 Euro-European style. | | | | | | | | | | |
| 64 Jun | 8 | 0.85 | ... | ... | 92 Apr | 2 | 0.73 | . | | | | | | | |

*Source*: Reprinted by permission of Dow Jones, Inc., via copyright Clearance Center, Inc. © 2001 Dow Jones & Company, Inc. All Rights Reserved Worldwide.

This stochastic process for an exchange rate is the same as that in equation (13.6) with $q = r_f$. This is because, as noted in Section 3.11, a foreign currency is analogous to a stock providing a known dividend yield. The owner of foreign currency receives a "dividend yield" equal to the risk-free interest rate, $r_f$, in the foreign currency. Because the stochastic process for a foreign currency is the same as that for a stock paying a dividend yield equal to the foreign risk-free rate, the formulas in Section 13.1 and 13.2 are correct with $q$ replaced by $r_f$. The European call price, $c$, and put price, $p$, are therefore given by

$$c = S_0 e^{-r_f T} N(d_1) - K e^{-rT} N(d_2) \qquad (13.9)$$

$$p = K e^{-rT} N(-d_2) - S_0 e^{-r_f T} N(-d_1) \qquad (13.10)$$

where $S_0$ is the value of the exchange rate at time zero, and

$$d_1 = \frac{\ln(S_0/K) + (r - r_f + \sigma^2/2)T}{\sigma\sqrt{T}}$$

$$d_2 = \frac{\ln(S_0/K) + (r - r_f - \sigma^2/2)T}{\sigma\sqrt{T}} = d_1 - \sigma\sqrt{T}$$

Both the domestic interest rate, $r$, and the foreign interest rate, $r_f$, are the rates for maturity $T$. Put and call options on a currency are symmetrical in that a put option to sell $X_A$ units of currency A for $X_B$ units of currency B is the same as a call option to buy $X_B$ units of currency B for $X_A$ units of currency A.

**Example 13.4**   Consider a four-month European call option on the British pound. Suppose that the current exchange rate is 1.6000, the strike price is 1.6000, the risk-free interest rate in the United States is 8% per annum, the risk-free interest rate in Britain is 11% per annum, and the option price is 4.3 cents. In this case $S_0 = 1.6$, $K = 1.6$, $r = 0.08$, $r_f = 0.11$, $T = 4/12$, and $c = 0.043$. The implied volatility can be calculated iteratively. A volatility of 20% gives an option price of 0.0639, a volatility of 10% gives an option price of 0.0285, and so on. The implied volatility is 14.1%.

From equation (3.13), the forward rate, $F_0$, for a maturity $T$ is given by

$$F_0 = S_0 e^{(r-r_f)T}$$

This enables equations (13.9) and (13.10) to be simplified to

$$c = e^{-rT}[F_0 N(d_1) - K N(d_2)] \tag{13.11}$$

$$p = e^{-rT}[K N(-d_2) - F_0 N(-d_1)] \tag{13.12}$$

where

$$d_1 = \frac{\ln(F_0/K) + \sigma^2 T/2}{\sigma \sqrt{T}}$$

$$d_2 = \frac{\ln(F_0/K) - \sigma^2 T/2}{\sigma \sqrt{T}} = d_1 - \sigma \sqrt{T}$$

Note that, for equations (13.11) and (13.12) to apply, the maturities of the forward contract and the option must be the same.

In some circumstances it is optimal to exercise American currency options prior to maturity. Thus American currency options are worth more than their European counterparts. In general, call options on high-interest currencies and put options on low-interest currencies are the most likely to be exercised prior to maturity. This is because a high-interest-rate currency is expected to depreciate relative to the U.S. dollar, and a low-interest-rate currency is expected to appreciate relative to the U.S. dollar. Unfortunately, analytic formulas do not exist for the evaluation of American currency options. We discuss numerical procedures and analytic approximations in Chapter 18.

## 13.5  FUTURES OPTIONS

Options on futures contracts, or futures options, are now traded on many different exchanges. They are American-style options and require the delivery of an underlying futures contract when exercised. If a call futures option is exercised, the holder acquires a long position in the underlying futures contract plus a cash amount equal to the most recent settlement futures price minus the strike price. If a put futures option is exercised, the holder acquires a short position in the underlying futures contract plus a cash amount equal to the strike price minus the most recent settlement futures price. As the following examples show, the effective payoff from a call futures option is the futures price at the time of exercise less the strike price; the effective payoff from a put futures option is the strike price less the futures price at the time of exercise.

**Example 13.5**  Suppose it is August 15 and an investor has one September futures call option contract on copper with a strike price of 70 cents per pound. One futures contract is on 25,000 pounds of copper. Suppose that the futures price of copper for delivery in September is currently 81 cents, and at the close of trading on August 14 (the last settlement) it was 80 cents. If the option is exercised, the investor receives a cash amount of

$$25,000 \times (80 - 70) \text{ cents} = \$2,500$$

plus a long position in a futures contract to buy 25,000 pounds of copper in September. If desired, the position in the futures contract can be closed out immediately. This would leave the investor with the $2,500 cash payoff plus an amount

$$25,000 \times (81 - 80) \text{ cents} = \$250$$

reflecting the change in the futures price since the last settlement. The total payoff from exercising the option on August 15 is $2,750, which equals $25,000(F - K)$, where $F$ is the futures price at the time of exercise and $K$ is the strike price.

**Example 13.6**  An investor has one December futures put option on corn with a strike price of 200 cents per bushel. One futures contract is on 5,000 bushels of corn. Suppose that the current futures price of corn for delivery in December is 180, and the most recent settlement price is 179 cents. If the option is exercised, the investor receives a cash amount of

$$5,000 \times (200 - 179) \text{ cents} = \$1,050$$

plus a short position in a futures contract to sell 5,000 bushels of corn in December. If desired, the position in the futures contract can be closed out. This would leave the investor with the $1,050 cash payoff minus an amount

$$5,000 \times (180 - 179) \text{ cents} = \$50$$

reflecting the change in the futures price since the last settlement. The net payoff from exercise is $1,000, which equals $5,000(K - F)$, where $F$ is the futures price at the time of exercise and $K$ is the strike price.

## Quotes

As mentioned earlier, most futures options are American. They are referred to by the month in which the underlying futures contract matures—not by the expiration month of the option. The maturity date of a futures option contract is usually on, or a few days before, the earliest delivery date of the underlying futures contract. For example, the S&P 500 index futures options expire on the same day as the underlying futures contract; the CME currency futures options expire two business days prior to the expiration of the futures contract; the CBOT Treasury bond futures option expires on the first Friday preceding by at least five business days the end of the month just prior to the futures contract expiration month. An exception is the CME mid-curve Eurodollar contract where the futures contract expires either one or two years after the options contract.

Table 13.5 shows quotes for futures options as they appeared in the *Wall Street Journal* on March 16, 2001. The most popular contracts include those on corn, soybeans, wheat, sugar, crude oil, heating oil, natural gas, gold, Treasury bonds, Treasury notes, five-year Treasury notes, Eurodollars, one-year mid-curve Eurodollars, Euribor, Eurobunds, and the S&P 500.

## Options on Interest Rate Futures

The most actively traded futures options in the United States are those on Treasury bond futures, Treasury note futures, and Eurodollar futures. A Treasury bond futures option is an option to

**Table 13.5**  Closing prices of futures options on March 15, 2001

# FUTURES OPTIONS PRICES

Thursday, March 15, 2001

## AGRICULTURAL

**Corn (CBT)**
5,000 bu.; cents per bu.

| STRIKE | CALLS-SETTLE | | | PUTS-SETTLE | | |
|---|---|---|---|---|---|---|
| PRICE | Apr | May | Jly | Apr | May | Jly |
| 190 | .... | 20¾ | .... | .... | ⅛ | 1 |
| 200 | .... | 12 | .... | ⅛ | 1¼ | 2¾ |
| 210 | .... | 5¼ | 14½ | 2 | 4¾ | 6 |
| 220 | ½ | 2¼ | 9⅝ | 9¼ | 11½ | 11⅛ |
| 230 | ⅛ | ⅞ | 6⅜ | 19¼ | 20 | 17¾ |
| 240 | ⅛ | ½ | 4½ | .... | 29½ | 25½ |

Est vol 25,000 Wd 10,993 calls 6,347 puts
Op int Wed 265,371 calls 147,975 puts

**Soybeans (CBT)**
5,000 bu.; cents per bu.

| STRIKE | CALLS-SETTLE | | | PUTS-SETTLE | | |
|---|---|---|---|---|---|---|
| PRICE | Apr | May | Jly | Apr | May | Jly |
| 400 | .... | 46 | 53¼ | .... | ½ | 2¼ |
| 420 | .... | 28 | 36⅜ | ¼ | 2¼ | 5½ |
| 440 | 8½ | 13¾ | 23⅞ | 3 | 8½ | 12¾ |
| 460 | 1⅛ | 5¾ | 15¾ | 15¾ | 20 | 24 |
| 480 | ⅛ | 2¼ | 10½ | 34½ | 36½ | 38¼ |
| 500 | ⅛ | ¾ | 6¾ | 54½ | 55 | 54¾ |

Est vol 15,000 Wd 16,691 calls 6,884 puts
Op int Wed 122,249 calls 53,376 puts

**Soybean Meal (CBT)**
100 tons; $ per ton

| STRIKE | CALLS-SETTLE | | | PUTS-SETTLE | | |
|---|---|---|---|---|---|---|
| PRICE | Apr | May | Jly | Apr | May | Jly |
| 140 | .... | .... | .... | 0.10 | 0.85 | .... |
| 145 | .... | .... | .... | 0.25 | 1.50 | 3.75 |
| 150 | .... | 5.00 | .... | .... | 3.25 | 5.75 |
| 155 | 1.00 | 2.75 | 4.75 | 4.00 | 5.85 | 8.75 |
| 160 | 0.10 | 1.50 | 3.35 | 8.25 | 9.60 | 12.40 |
| 165 | .... | 0.90 | 2.35 | .... | 13.90 | 16.40 |

Est vol 2,500 Wd 2,266 calls 3,582 puts
Op int Wed 21,870 calls 18,231 puts

**Soybean Oil (CBT)**
60,000 lbs.; cents per lb.

| STRIKE | CALLS-SETTLE | | | PUTS-SETTLE | | |
|---|---|---|---|---|---|---|
| PRICE | Apr | May | Jly | Apr | May | Jly |
| 150 | 1.100 | 1.150 | 1.590 | .030 | .090 | .160 |
| 155 | .... | .750 | 1.200 | .060 | .190 | .280 |
| 160 | .250 | .450 | .920 | .200 | .400 | .500 |
| 165 | .100 | .260 | .700 | .520 | .700 | .770 |
| 170 | .030 | .150 | .550 | .... | 1.090 | 1.120 |
| 175 | .005 | .090 | .400 | .... | .... | .... |

Est vol 1,400 Wd 598 calls 350 puts
Op int Wed 40,326 calls 16,503 puts

**Wheat (CBT)**
5,000 bu.; cents per bu.

| STRIKE | CALLS-SETTLE | | | PUTS-SETTLE | | |
|---|---|---|---|---|---|---|
| PRICE | Apr | May | Jly | Apr | May | Jly |
| 250 | .... | 24¼ | 36½ | ⅛ | ½ | 2 |
| 260 | .... | 16 | 28¾ | ¼ | 2¼ | 4 |
| 270 | 5 | 9½ | 22 | 1¼ | 5¾ | 7¼ |
| 280 | 1½ | 5½ | 16½ | 7¾ | 11¾ | 11½ |
| 290 | ½ | 2⅞ | 12 | .... | 19 | 17 |
| 300 | ⅛ | 1⅝ | 9 | .... | 28 | 24 |

Est vol 12,000 Wd 1,397 calls 1,133 puts
Op int Wed 72,666 calls 50,935 puts

**Cotton (NYBOT)**
50,000 lbs.; cents per lb.

| STRIKE | CALLS-SETTLE | | | PUTS-SETTLE | | |
|---|---|---|---|---|---|---|
| PRICE | May | Jly | Oct | May | Jly | Oct |
| 48 | .... | 4.25 | .... | 0.80 | 1.00 | .... |
| 49 | .... | .... | .... | 1.10 | 1.33 | .... |
| 50 | 1.70 | 3.01 | .... | 1.61 | 1.73 | .... |
| 51 | 1.26 | .... | .... | 2.17 | 2.18 | .... |
| 52 | 0.93 | 2.02 | .... | 2.83 | 2.71 | .... |
| 53 | 0.68 | 1.71 | .... | 3.58 | 3.38 | .... |

Est vol 8,300 Wd 3,159 calls 1,262 puts
Op int Wed 73,892 calls 39,850 puts

**Orange Juice (NYBOT)**
15,000 lbs.; cents per lb.

| STRIKE | CALLS-SETTLE | | | PUTS-SETTLE | | |
|---|---|---|---|---|---|---|
| PRICE | May | Jly | Sep | May | Jly | Sep |
| 60 | .... | .... | .... | .... | .... | .... |
| 65 | .... | .... | .... | 0.10 | .... | .... |
| 70 | 5.05 | 8.80 | .... | 0.35 | .... | 0.65 |
| 75 | 1.55 | 5.15 | 8.20 | 1.75 | 1.85 | 1.65 |
| 80 | 0.35 | 2.65 | 5.60 | 5.65 | 4.15 | 3.50 |
| 85 | 0.20 | 1.30 | .... | 10.45 | 7.70 | 6.50 |

Est vol 300 Wd 124 calls 30 puts
Op int Wed 14,097 calls 14,686 puts

**Coffee (NYBOT)**
37,500 lbs.; cents per lb.

| STRIKE | CALLS-SETTLE | | | PUTS-SETTLE | | |
|---|---|---|---|---|---|---|
| PRICE | May | Jun | Jly | May | Jun | Jly |
| 55 | 6.33 | 9.46 | 9.88 | 0.35 | 0.55 | 1.00 |
| 57.5 | 4.44 | 7.47 | 8.10 | 0.95 | 1.05 | 1.70 |
| 60 | 3.00 | 5.88 | 6.57 | 1.90 | 1.95 | 2.65 |
| 62.5 | 1.90 | 4.44 | 5.29 | 3.40 | 3.00 | 3.85 |
| 65 | 1.20 | 3.40 | 4.25 | 5.19 | 4.44 | 5.29 |
| 67.5 | 0.75 | 2.50 | 3.40 | 7.23 | 6.03 | 6.92 |

Est vol 3,176 Wd 1,898 calls 1,213 puts
Op int Wed 44,460 calls 14,659 puts

**Sugar-World (NYBOT)**
112,000 lbs.; cents per lb.

| STRIKE | CALLS-SETTLE | | | PUTS-SETTLE | | |
|---|---|---|---|---|---|---|
| PRICE | May | Jun | Jly | May | Jun | Jly |
| 800 | 0.98 | 0.70 | 0.81 | 0.06 | 0.28 | 0.39 |
| 850 | 0.58 | 0.45 | 0.56 | 0.16 | 0.53 | 0.64 |
| 900 | 0.31 | 0.27 | 0.38 | 0.39 | 0.85 | 0.96 |
| 950 | 0.14 | 0.16 | 0.25 | 0.72 | 1.23 | 1.32 |
| 1000 | 0.06 | 0.09 | 0.16 | 1.14 | 1.66 | 1.73 |
| 1050 | 0.02 | 0.05 | 0.11 | 1.60 | 2.12 | 2.18 |

Est vol 5,293 Wd 5,532 calls 1,636 puts
Op int Wed 68,646 calls 52,440 puts

**Cocoa (NYBOT)**
10 metric tons; $ per ton

| STRIKE | CALLS-SETTLE | | | PUTS-SETTLE | | |
|---|---|---|---|---|---|---|
| PRICE | May | Jun | Jly | May | Jun | Jly |
| 900 | 117 | 135 | 142 | 2 | 8 | 15 |
| 950 | 75 | 97 | 107 | 10 | 19 | 30 |
| 1000 | 42 | 67 | 81 | 27 | 39 | 53 |
| 1050 | 20 | 42 | 57 | 55 | 64 | 79 |
| 1100 | 10 | 26 | 42 | 93 | 98 | 113 |
| 1150 | 7 | 16 | 31 | 142 | 137 | 152 |

Est vol 2,376 Wd 369 calls 450 puts
Op int Wed 25,586 calls 18,254 puts

## OIL

**Crude Oil (NYM)**
1,000 bbls.; $ per bbl.

| STRIKE | CALLS-SETTLE | | | PUTS-SETTLE | | |
|---|---|---|---|---|---|---|
| PRICE | Apr | May | Jun | Apr | May | Jun |
| 2550 | 1.05 | 1.97 | 2.44 | 0.01 | 0.66 | 0.98 |
| 2600 | 0.55 | 1.66 | 2.13 | 0.01 | 0.84 | 1.17 |
| 2650 | 0.05 | 1.37 | 1.85 | 0.01 | 1.05 | 1.38 |
| 2700 | 0.01 | 1.11 | 1.57 | 0.45 | 1.29 | 1.60 |
| 2750 | 0.01 | 0.90 | 1.35 | 0.95 | 1.58 | 1.88 |
| 2800 | 0.01 | 0.69 | 1.13 | 1.45 | 1.87 | 2.15 |

Est vol 50,195 Wd 15,823 calls 23,794 puts
Op int Wed 298,568 calls 366,294 puts

**Heating Oil No.2 (NYM)**
42,000 gal.; $ per gal.

| STRIKE | CALLS-SETTLE | | | PUTS-SETTLE | | |
|---|---|---|---|---|---|---|
| PRICE | Apr | May | Jun | Apr | May | Jun |
| 69 | .0295 | .0318 | .0391 | .0130 | .0331 | .0419 |
| 70 | .0230 | .0277 | .0347 | .0165 | .0390 | .0475 |
| 71 | .0196 | .0240 | .0307 | .0231 | .0452 | .0534 |
| 72 | .0140 | .0207 | .0271 | .0275 | .0519 | .0597 |
| 73 | .0100 | .0179 | .0238 | .0335 | .0590 | .0663 |
| 74 | .0085 | .0154 | .0208 | .0419 | .0664 | .0732 |

Est vol 4,562 Wd 1,672 calls 1,373 puts
Op int Wed 37,794 calls 25,749 puts

**Gasoline-Unlead (NYM)**
42,000 gal.; $ per gal.

| STRIKE | CALLS-SETTLE | | | PUTS-SETTLE | | |
|---|---|---|---|---|---|---|
| PRICE | Apr | May | Jun | Apr | May | Jun |
| 85 | .0339 | .0474 | .0504 | .0160 | .0360 | .0495 |
| 86 | .0282 | .0424 | .0462 | .0203 | .0410 | .0553 |
| 87 | .0231 | .0380 | .0422 | .0252 | .0466 | .0612 |
| 88 | .0189 | .0340 | .0386 | .0310 | .0525 | .0675 |
| 89 | .0153 | .0304 | .0352 | .0374 | .0589 | .0740 |
| 90 | .0110 | .0270 | .0321 | .0430 | .0654 | .0808 |

Est vol 3,077 Wd 1,768 calls 676 puts
Op int Wed 77,653 calls 23,889 puts

**Natural Gas (NYM)**
10,000 MMBtu.; $ per MMBtu.

| STRIKE | CALLS-SETTLE | | | PUTS-SETTLE | | |
|---|---|---|---|---|---|---|
| PRICE | Apr | May | Jun | Apr | May | Jun |
| 485 | .202 | .... | .476 | .125 | .... | .327 |
| 490 | .174 | .331 | .451 | .147 | .271 | .351 |
| 495 | .149 | .305 | .... | .172 | .295 | .... |
| 500 | .130 | .283 | .400 | .203 | .323 | .400 |
| 505 | .112 | .258 | .377 | .235 | .348 | .... |
| 510 | .096 | .238 | .354 | .269 | .378 | .454 |

Est vol 15,918 Wd na calls na puts
Op int Wed 168,492 calls 212,884 puts

**Brent Crude (IPE)**
1,000 net bbls.; $ per bbl.

| STRIKE | CALLS-SETTLE | | | PUTS-SETTLE | | |
|---|---|---|---|---|---|---|
| PRICE | May | Jun | Jly | May | Jun | Jly |
| 2400 | 1.51 | 2.06 | 2.50 | 0.50 | 0.84 | 1.21 |
| 2450 | 1.20 | 1.78 | 2.20 | 0.69 | 1.06 | 1.41 |
| 2500 | 0.93 | 1.54 | 1.92 | 0.92 | 1.32 | 1.63 |
| 2550 | 0.71 | 1.32 | 1.66 | 1.20 | 1.60 | 1.87 |
| 2600 | 0.53 | 1.11 | 1.43 | 1.52 | 1.89 | 2.14 |
| 2650 | 0.39 | 0.92 | 1.23 | 1.88 | 2.20 | 2.44 |

Est vol 700 Wd 600 calls 0 puts
Op int Wed 8,139 calls 12,408 puts

**Gas Oil (IPE)**
100 metric tons; $ per ton

| STRIKE | CALLS-SETTLE | | | PUTS-SETTLE | | |
|---|---|---|---|---|---|---|
| PRICE | Apr | May | Jun | Apr | May | Jun |
| 20000 | 12.75 | 14.65 | 18.05 | 3.50 | 5.65 | 7.80 |
| 20500 | 9.60 | 12.00 | 15.20 | 3.53 | 8.00 | 9.95 |
| 21000 | 7.00 | 9.50 | 12.65 | 7.75 | 10.50 | 12.40 |
| 21500 | 4.85 | 7.65 | 10.45 | 10.60 | 13.65 | 15.20 |
| 22000 | 3.15 | 6.15 | 8.55 | 13.90 | 17.15 | 18.30 |
| 22500 | 2.00 | 4.70 | 6.95 | .... | 20.70 | 21.70 |

Est vol 175 Wd 1,810 calls 0 puts
Op int Wed 3,799 calls 467 puts

## LIVESTOCK

**Cattle-Feeder (CME)**
50,000 lbs.; cents per lb.

| STRIKE | CALLS-SETTLE | | | PUTS-SETTLE | | |
|---|---|---|---|---|---|---|
| PRICE | Mar | Apr | May | Mar | Apr | May |
| 8450 | .... | .... | .... | .... | .... | .... |
| 8500 | 0.65 | 1.70 | .... | 0.20 | 0.75 | .... |
| 8550 | .... | .... | .... | .... | .... | .... |
| 8600 | 0.20 | 1.15 | 1.77 | 0.75 | 1.25 | 1.70 |
| 8650 | 0.12 | .... | .... | .... | .... | .... |
| 8700 | 0.05 | .... | .... | 1.60 | 1.70 | .... |

Est vol 628 Wd 376 calls 787 puts
Op int Wed 6,063 calls 20,057 puts

**Cattle-Live (CME)**
40,000 lbs.; cents per lb.

| STRIKE | CALLS-SETTLE | | | PUTS-SETTLE | | |
|---|---|---|---|---|---|---|
| PRICE | Apr | Jun | Aug | Apr | Jun | Aug |
| 76 | 2.42 | 0.55 | 0.67 | 0.45 | 3.97 | .... |
| 77 | 1.70 | 0.32 | .... | 0.72 | .... | .... |
| 78 | 1.15 | 0.22 | 0.30 | 1.17 | .... | .... |
| 79 | 0.70 | 0.15 | .... | 1.72 | .... | .... |
| 80 | 0.40 | 0.07 | 0.22 | 2.42 | .... | .... |
| 81 | 0.22 | .... | .... | 3.25 | 8.42 | .... |

(continued on next page)

## Table 13.5 *(continued)*

Est vol 3,375 Wd 1,688 calls 2,277 puts
Op int Wed 32,648 calls 63,310 puts

**Hogs-Lean (CME)**
**40,000 lbs.; cents per lb.**

| STRIKE | CALLS-SETTLE | | | PUTS-SETTLE | | |
|---|---|---|---|---|---|---|
| PRICE | Apr | Jun | Jly | Apr | Jun | Jly |
| 64 | 3.47 | 7.92 | 5.67 | 1.80 | 1.10 | 2.50 |
| 65 | 2.87 | 7.20 | .... | 2.20 | 1.35 | .... |
| 66 | 2.32 | 6.55 | 4.45 | 2.65 | 1.70 | 3.25 |
| 67 | 1.85 | 5.97 | .... | .... | 2.10 | .... |
| 68 | 1.50 | 5.37 | 3.45 | .... | 2.50 | 4.20 |
| 69 | 1.20 | 4.80 | .... | .... | 2.90 | .... |

Est vol 1,195 Wd 491 calls 568 puts
Op int Wed 7,287 calls 5,918 puts

## METALS

**Copper (CMX)**
**25,000 lbs.; cents per lb.**

| STRIKE | CALLS-SETTLE | | | PUTS-SETTLE | | |
|---|---|---|---|---|---|---|
| PRICE | Apr | May | Jun | Apr | May | Jun |
| 76 | 4.75 | 5.80 | 6.45 | 0.15 | 0.80 | 1.20 |
| 78 | 3.05 | 4.25 | 5.00 | 0.45 | 1.25 | 1.70 |
| 80 | 1.70 | 2.95 | 3.80 | 1.10 | 1.90 | 2.50 |
| 82 | 0.80 | 1.85 | 2.80 | 2.20 | 2.80 | 3.50 |
| 84 | 0.35 | 1.15 | 2.05 | 3.70 | 4.10 | 4.70 |
| 86 | 0.10 | 0.65 | 1.40 | 5.50 | 5.60 | 6.10 |

Est vol 125 Wd 26 calls 69 puts
Op int Wed 2,926 calls 942 puts

**Gold (CMX)**
**100 troy ounces; $ per troy ounce**

| STRIKE | CALLS-SETTLE | | | PUTS-SETTLE | | |
|---|---|---|---|---|---|---|
| PRICE | May | Jun | Aug | May | Jun | Aug |
| 250 | 14.00 | 14.20 | 16.90 | 1.50 | 2.20 | 3.70 |
| 255 | 9.40 | 11.20 | 13.30 | 2.20 | 3.60 | 5.10 |
| 260 | 6.00 | 7.60 | 10.50 | 3.90 | 5.30 | 7.00 |
| 265 | 3.90 | 5.40 | 8.50 | 6.90 | 7.70 | 10.20 |
| 270 | 2.20 | 3.90 | 6.70 | 10.20 | 11.60 | 13.10 |
| 275 | 1.50 | 2.90 | 5.50 | 14.30 | 15.60 | 16.70 |

Est vol 13,000 Wd 5,232 calls 2,333 puts
Op int Wed 221,107 calls 68,332 puts

**Silver (CMX)**
**5,000 troy ounces; cts per troy ounces**

| STRIKE | CALLS-SETTLE | | | PUTS-SETTLE | | |
|---|---|---|---|---|---|---|
| PRICE | May | Jun | Jly | May | Jun | Jly |
| 375 | 60.5 | 65.2 | 65.2 | 0.3 | 1.2 | 1.0 |
| 400 | 36.3 | 41.0 | 41.7 | 1.0 | 1.8 | 2.5 |
| 425 | 13.8 | 19.5 | 22.0 | 3.5 | 5.3 | 7.8 |
| 450 | 3.3 | 6.0 | 9.5 | 18.0 | 18.8 | 20.3 |
| 475 | 1.3 | 3.4 | 5.3 | 41.0 | 39.1 | 41.1 |
| 500 | 0.8 | 2.2 | 3.2 | 65.5 | 63.0 | 64.0 |

Est vol 1,500 Wd 1,708 calls 496 puts
Op int Wed 37,475 calls 12,284 puts

## INTEREST RATE

**T-Bonds (CBT)**
**$100,000; points – 64ths of 100%**

| STRIKE | CALLS-SETTLE | | | PUTS-SETTLE | | |
|---|---|---|---|---|---|---|
| PRICE | Apr | May | Jun | Apr | May | Jun |
| 104 | 2-11 | 2-33 | 2-61 | 0-03 | 0-28 | 0-54 |
| 105 | 1-20 | 1-54 | 2-20 | 0-11 | 0-47 | 1-13 |
| 106 | 0-41 | 1-18 | 1-49 | 0-32 | 1-10 | 1-41 |
| 107 | 0-16 | 0-54 | 1-19 | 1-06 | 1-46 | .... |
| 108 | 0-05 | 0-34 | 0-60 | 1-61 | .... | 2-52 |
| 109 | 0-01 | 0-19 | 0-44 | .... | .... | 3-33 |

Est vol 53,000;
Wd 42,385 calls 34,000 puts
Op int Wed 239,691 calls 181,312 puts

**T-Notes (CBT)**
**$100,000; points – 64ths of 100%**

| STRIKE | CALLS-SETTLE | | | PUTS-SETTLE | | |
|---|---|---|---|---|---|---|
| PRICE | Apr | May | Jun | Apr | May | Jun |
| 105 | 1-34 | 1-53 | 2-10 | 0-04 | 0-23 | 0-44 |
| 106 | 0-46 | 1-11 | 1-33 | 0-16 | 0-45 | 1-04 |
| 107 | 0-16 | 0-45 | 1-04 | 0-50 | .... | 1-38 |
| 108 | 0-05 | 0-25 | 0-46 | .... | .... | 2-16 |
| 109 | 0-02 | 0-14 | 0-30 | 2-35 | .... | 2-63 |
| 110 | 0-01 | .... | 0-19 | .... | .... | 3-51 |

Est vol 65,000 Wd 44,195 calls 41,055 puts
Op int Wed 346,907 calls 249,181 puts

**5 Yr Treas Notes (CBT)**
**$100,000; points – 64ths of 100%**

| STRIKE | CALLS-SETTLE | | | PUTS-SETTLE | | |
|---|---|---|---|---|---|---|
| PRICE | Apr | May | Jun | Apr | May | Jun |
| 10450 | 1-11 | 2-13 | 1-37 | 0-03 | 0-16 | 0-30 |
| 10500 | 0-47 | .... | 1-17 | 0-07 | .... | 0-41 |
| 10550 | 0-26 | 1-23 | 0-63 | 0-18 | 0-38 | 0-55 |
| 10600 | 0-13 | 1-01 | 0-48 | .... | 0-55 | .... |
| 10650 | 0-05 | 0-46 | 0-36 | .... | .... | .... |
| 10700 | 0-03 | 0-32 | 0-26 | .... | .... | .... |

Est vol 23,000 Wd 12,507 calls 10,564 puts
Op int Wed 126,217 calls 97,191 puts

**Eurodollar (CME)**
**$ million; pts of 100%**

| STRIKE | CALLS-SETTLE | | | PUTS-SETTLE | | |
|---|---|---|---|---|---|---|
| PRICE | Mar | Apr | May | Mar | Apr | May |
| 9450 | 5.92 | 10.30 | .... | 0.00 | 0.00 | .... |
| 9475 | 3.42 | 7.80 | .... | 0.00 | 0.00 | 0.07 |
| 9500 | 0.95 | 5.30 | 5.50 | 0.02 | 0.00 | 0.22 |
| 9525 | 0.05 | 3.15 | 3.35 | 1.62 | 0.35 | .... |
| 9550 | 0.00 | 1.50 | .... | .... | 1.20 | .... |
| 9575 | 0.00 | 0.65 | .... | .... | .... | .... |

Est vol 233,398;
Wd vol 183,411 calls 101,539 puts
Op int Wed 1,845,759 calls 1,911,991 puts

**1 Yr. Mid-Curve Eurodlr (CME)**
**$1 million contract units; pts of 100%**

| STRIKE | CALLS-SETTLE | | | PUTS-SETTLE | | |
|---|---|---|---|---|---|---|
| PRICE | Mar | Apr | May | Mar | Apr | May |
| 9475 | 6.20 | 4.25 | 4.65 | 0.00 | 0.30 | .... |
| 9500 | 3.70 | 2.40 | 2.85 | 0.00 | 0.95 | 1.40 |
| 9525 | 1.30 | 1.10 | 1.65 | 0.10 | .... | .... |
| 9550 | 0.15 | 0.35 | 0.80 | .... | .... | .... |
| 9575 | 0.00 | 0.10 | .... | .... | .... | .... |
| 9600 | .... | .... | .... | .... | .... | .... |

Est vol 72,910 Wd 60,260 calls 31,975 puts
Op int Wed 671,496 calls 460,417 puts

**2 Yr. Mid-Curve Eurodlr (CME)**
**$1million contract units; pts of 100%**

| STRIKE | CALLS-SETTLE | | PUTS-SETTLE | |
|---|---|---|---|---|
| PRICE | Mar | Jun | Mar | Jun |
| 9425 | 4.10 | 4.35 | 0.00 | 1.25 |
| 9450 | 1.65 | 2.90 | 0.05 | 2.25 |
| 9475 | .... | 1.75 | .... | .... |
| 9500 | .... | .... | .... | .... |
| 9525 | .... | .... | .... | .... |
| 9550 | .... | .... | .... | .... |

Est vol 250 Wd 0 calls 0 puts
Op int Wed 16,185 calls 19,908 puts

**Euribor (LIFFE)**
**Euro 1,000,000**

| STRIKE | CALLS-SETTLE | | | PUTS-SETTLE | | |
|---|---|---|---|---|---|---|
| PRICE | Mar | Apr | May | Mar | Apr | May |
| 95000 | 0.25 | 0.58 | 0.58 | .... | .... | .... |
| 95125 | 0.12 | 0.46 | 0.46 | .... | .... | 0.00 |
| 95250 | 0.01 | 0.33 | 0.34 | 0.01 | .... | 0.01 |
| 95375 | .... | 0.22 | 0.24 | 0.12 | 0.01 | 0.03 |
| 95500 | .... | 0.12 | 0.15 | 0.25 | 0.03 | 0.06 |
| 95625 | .... | 0.05 | 0.09 | 0.37 | 0.09 | 0.13 |

Vol Th 48,655 calls 9,669 puts
Op int Wed 886,103 calls 752,794 puts

**10 Yr. German Euro Gov't Bd (Eurobund) (Eurex)100,000;pts In 100%**

| STRIKE | CALLS-SETTLE | | | PUTS-SETTLE | | |
|---|---|---|---|---|---|---|
| PRICE | Apr | May | Jun | Apr | May | Jun |
| 10850 | 1.16 | 1.33 | 1.52 | 0.02 | 0.19 | 0.38 |
| 10900 | 0.72 | 0.98 | 1.19 | 0.08 | 0.33 | 0.55 |
| 10950 | 0.37 | 0.68 | 0.90 | 0.24 | 0.53 | 0.77 |
| 11000 | 0.15 | 0.45 | 0.67 | 0.52 | 0.81 | 1.03 |
| 11050 | 0.06 | 0.28 | 0.50 | 0.92 | 1.14 | 1.36 |
| 11100 | 0.01 | 0.17 | 0.36 | 1.37 | 1.52 | 1.72 |

Vol Th 55,671 calls 28,301 puts
Op int Wed 586,672 calls 353,718 puts

## CURRENCY

**Japanese Yen (CME)**
**12,500,000 yen; cents per 100 yen**

| STRIKE | CALLS-SETTLE | | | PUTS-SETTLE | | |
|---|---|---|---|---|---|---|
| PRICE | Apr | May | Jun | Apr | May | Jun |
| 8050 | .... | .... | .... | 0.38 | .... | 1.29 |

| | | | | | | |
|---|---|---|---|---|---|---|
| 8100 | .... | .... | 3.12 | 0.51 | 0.98 | 1.44 |
| 8150 | .... | .... | .... | 0.64 | 1.13 | .... |
| 8200 | 1.54 | .... | .... | 0.84 | 1.32 | 1.80 |
| 8250 | .... | .... | .... | 1.04 | 1.54 | 2.02 |
| 8300 | 0.95 | .... | 1.96 | 1.25 | 1.78 | 2.26 |

Est vol 3,247 Wd 8,400 calls 9,234 puts
Op int Wed 39,710 calls 38,759 puts

**Deutschemark (CME)**
**125,000 marks; cents per mark**

| STRIKE | CALLS-SETTLE | | | PUTS-SETTLE | | |
|---|---|---|---|---|---|---|
| PRICE | Apr | May | Jun | Apr | May | Jun |
| 4500 | .... | .... | .... | .... | .... | .... |
| 4550 | .... | .... | .... | .... | .... | .... |
| 4600 | .... | .... | .... | .... | .... | .... |
| 4650 | .... | .... | .... | .... | .... | .... |
| 4700 | .... | .... | .... | .... | .... | .... |
| 4750 | .... | .... | .... | .... | .... | .... |

Est vol 5 Wd 1 calls 1 puts
Op int Wed 440 calls 19 puts

**Canadian Dollar (CME)**
**100,000 Can.$, cents per Can.$**

| STRIKE | CALLS-SETTLE | | | PUTS-SETTLE | | |
|---|---|---|---|---|---|---|
| PRICE | Apr | May | Jun | Apr | May | Jun |
| 6300 | .... | .... | 1.42 | .... | 0.21 | 0.35 |
| 6350 | .... | .... | .... | 0.17 | 0.33 | 0.51 |
| 6400 | .... | .... | 0.80 | 0.35 | 0.53 | 0.72 |
| 6450 | 0.22 | 0.40 | .... | 0.64 | .... | 0.98 |
| 6500 | 0.10 | 0.25 | 0.40 | 1.02 | 1.16 | 1.31 |
| 6550 | 0.05 | .... | 0.28 | 1.47 | .... | 1.68 |

Est vol 176 Wd 370 calls 376 puts
Op int Wed 15,899 calls 3,557 puts

**British Pound (CME)**
**62,500 pounds; cents per pound**

| STRIKE | CALLS-SETTLE | | | PUTS-SETTLE | | |
|---|---|---|---|---|---|---|
| PRICE | Apr | May | Jun | Apr | May | Jun |
| 1420 | .... | 3.48 | 0.62 | .... | .... | 1.76 |
| 1430 | .... | .... | 0.98 | 1.72 | .... | .... |
| 1440 | 1.24 | .... | 2.46 | 1.50 | .... | 2.72 |
| 1450 | 0.84 | 1.46 | 1.98 | 2.10 | 2.72 | 3.22 |
| 1460 | 0.52 | 1.08 | 1.58 | 2.78 | 3.22 | 3.82 |
| 1470 | 0.30 | 0.80 | 1.32 | 3.56 | 3.82 | 4.54 |

Est vol 258 Wd 68 calls 231 puts
Op int Wed 4,499 calls 3,507 puts

**Swiss Franc (CME)**
**125,000 francs; cents per franc**

| STRIKE | CALLS-SETTLE | | | PUTS-SETTLE | | |
|---|---|---|---|---|---|---|
| PRICE | Apr | May | Jun | Apr | May | Jun |
| 5750 | 1.51 | .... | .... | .... | .... | .... |
| 5800 | .... | .... | .... | .... | .... | 1.00 |
| 5850 | .... | .... | .... | 0.52 | .... | .... |
| 5900 | 0.57 | .... | 1.28 | 0.78 | .... | 1.48 |
| 5950 | 0.39 | .... | .... | 1.10 | .... | .... |
| 6000 | 0.27 | .... | 0.89 | 1.48 | .... | 2.08 |

Est vol 410 Wd 79 calls 177 puts
Op int Wed 6,888 calls 3,808 puts

## INDEX

**DJ Industrial Avg (CBOT)**
**$100 times premium**

| STRIKE | CALLS-SETTLE | | | PUTS-SETTLE | | |
|---|---|---|---|---|---|---|
| PRICE | Mar | Apr | May | Mar | Apr | May |
| 98 | .... | 49.20 | .... | 0.05 | 18.80 | .... |
| 99 | .... | .... | .... | 0.15 | 21.95 | .... |
| 100 | 2.50 | .... | .... | 2.15 | 25.60 | 36.00 |
| 101 | 0.05 | 30.20 | .... | 7.50 | 29.70 | .... |
| 102 | 0.05 | 24.85 | 35.00 | 17.50 | 34.30 | .... |
| 103 | 0.05 | 20.50 | .... | 27.50 | 39.95 | .... |

Est vol 1,100 Wd 974 calls 1,839 puts
Op int Wed 7,614 calls 11,905 puts

**S&P 500 Stock Index (CME)**
**$250 times premium**

| STRIKE | CALLS-SETTLE | | | PUTS-SETTLE | | |
|---|---|---|---|---|---|---|
| PRICE | Mar | Apr | May | Mar | Apr | May |
| 1165 | .... | .... | .... | 2.90 | 30.80 | 44.00 |
| 1170 | 7.80 | 47.30 | .... | 4.50 | 32.70 | 46.00 |
| 1175 | 5.00 | 44.30 | .... | 6.70 | 34.70 | 48.10 |
| 1180 | 3.00 | 41.50 | .... | 9.70 | 36.80 | 50.20 |
| 1185 | 1.70 | 38.70 | 47.80 | 13.40 | 39.00 | 52.20 |
| 1190 | 1.10 | 36.00 | 45.40 | 17.80 | 41.30 | 54.50 |

Est vol 22,943 Wd 10,913 calls 32,911 puts
Op int Wed 111,149 calls 220,300 puts

enter a Treasury bond futures contract. As mentioned in Chapter 5, one Treasury bond futures contract is for the delivery of Treasury bonds with a face value of $100,000. The price of a Treasury bond futures option is quoted as a percentage of the face value of the underlying Treasury bonds to the nearest $\frac{1}{64}$ of 1%. Table 13.5 gives the price of the April call futures option on Treasury bonds as 2-11 or $2\frac{11}{64}$% of the debt principal when the strike price is 104 (implying that one contract costs $2,171.87). The quotes for options on Treasury notes are similar.

An option on Eurodollar futures is an option to enter into a Eurodollar futures contract. As explained in Chapter 5, when the Eurodollar futures quote changes by one basis point, or 0.01, there is a gain or loss on a Eurodollar futures contract of $25. Similarly, in the pricing of options on Eurodollar futures, one basis point represents $25. In the shortest maturity contract, prices are quoted to the nearest quarter of a basis point. For the next two months they are quoted to the nearest half basis point. The *Wall Street Journal* quote for the CME Eurodollar futures contract in Table 13.5 should be multiplied by 10 to get the CME quote in basis points. The 5.92 quote for the CME March call futures option when the strike price is 94.50 in Table 13.5 indicates that the CME quote is 59.25 basis points and one contract costs $59.25 \times \$25 = \$1,481.25$; the 10.30 quote for the April contract indicates that the CME quote is 103 basis points; and so on.

Interest rate futures contracts work in the same way as other futures contracts. For example, the payoff from a call is $\max(F - K, 0)$, where $F$ is the futures price at the time of exercise and $K$ is the strike price. In addition to the cash payoff, the option holder obtains a long position in the futures contract at exercise and the option writer obtains a corresponding short position.

Interest rate futures prices increase when bond prices increase (i.e., when interest rates fall). They decrease when bond prices decrease (i.e., when interest rates rise). An investor who thinks that short-term interest rates will rise can speculate by buying put options on Eurodollar futures, and an investor who thinks that they will fall can speculate by buying call options on Eurodollar futures. An investor who thinks that long-term interest rates will rise can speculate by buying put options on Treasury note futures or Treasury bond futures, and an investor who thinks they will fall can speculate by buying call options on these instruments.

**Example 13.7** Suppose that it is February and the futures price for the June Eurodollar contract is 93.82. (This corresponds to a three-month Eurodollar interest rate of 6.18% per annum.) The price of a call option on this contract with a strike price of 94.00 is quoted as 0.20. This option could be attractive to an investor who feels that interest rates are likely to come down. Suppose that short-term interest rates do decline by about 100 basis points over the next three months, and the investor exercises the call when the Eurodollar futures price is 94.78. (This corresponds to a three-month Eurodollar interest rate of 5.22% per annum.) The payoff is $25 \times 78 = \$1,950$. The cost of the contract is $20 \times 25 = \$500$. The investor's profit, therefore, is $1,450.

**Example 13.8** Suppose that it is August and the futures price for the December Treasury bond contract traded on the CBOT is 96-09 (or $96\frac{9}{32} = 96.28125$). The yield on long-term government bonds is about 6.4% per annum. An investor who feels that this yield will fall by December might choose to buy December calls with a strike price of 98. Assume that the price of these calls is 1-04 (or $1\frac{4}{64} = 1.0625$% of the principal). If long-term rates fall to 6% per annum and the Treasury bond futures price rises to 100-00, the investor will make a net profit per $100 of bond futures of

$$100.00 - 98.00 - 1.0625 = 0.9375$$

Because one option contract is for the purchase or sale of instruments with a face value of $100,000, the investor would make a profit of $937.50 per option contract bought.

### Reasons for the Popularity of Futures Options

It is natural to ask why people choose to trade options on futures rather than options on the underlying asset. The main reason appears to be that a futures contract is, in many circumstances, more liquid and easier to trade than the underlying asset. Furthermore, a futures price is known immediately from trading on the futures exchange, whereas the spot price of the underlying asset may not be so readily available.

Consider Treasury bonds. The market for Treasury bond futures is much more active than the market for any particular Treasury bond. Also, a Treasury bond futures price is known immediately from trading on the CBOT. By contrast, the current market price of a bond can be obtained only by contacting one or more dealers. It is not surprising that investors would rather take delivery of a Treasury bond futures contract than Treasury bonds.

Futures on commodities are also often easier to trade than the commodities themselves. For example, it is much easier and more convenient to make or take delivery of a live-hogs futures contract than it is to make or take delivery of the hogs themselves.

An important point about a futures option is that exercising it does not usually lead to delivery of the underlying asset. This is because, in most circumstances, the underlying futures contract is closed out prior to delivery. Futures options are therefore normally eventually settled in cash. This is appealing to many investors, particularly those with limited capital who may find it difficult to come up with the funds to buy the underlying asset when an option is exercised.

Another advantage sometimes cited for futures options is that futures and futures options are traded in pits side by side in the same exchange. This facilitates hedging, arbitrage, and speculation. It also tends to make the markets more efficient.

A final point is that futures options tend to entail lower transactions costs than spot options in many situations.

### Put–Call Parity

In Chapter 8 we derived a put–call parity relationship for European stock options. We now present a similar argument to derive a put–call parity relationship for European futures options on the assumption that there is no difference between the payoffs from futures and forward contracts.

Consider European call and put futures options, both with strike price $K$ and time to expiration $T$. We can form two portfolios:

*Portfolio A*: a European call futures option plus an amount of cash equal to $Ke^{-rT}$

*Portfolio B*: a European put futures option plus a long futures contract plus an amount of cash equal to $F_0 e^{-rT}$

In portfolio A the cash can be invested at the risk-free rate, $r$, and will grow to $K$ at time $T$. Let $F_T$ be the futures price at maturity of the option. If $F_T > K$, the call option in portfolio A is exercised and portfolio A is worth $F_T$. If $F_T \leqslant K$, the call is not exercised and portfolio A is worth $K$. The value of portfolio A at time $T$ is therefore

$$\max(F_T, K)$$

In portfolio B the cash can be invested at the risk-free rate to grow to $F_0$ at time $T$. The put option provides a payoff of $\max(K - F_T, 0)$. The futures contract provides a payoff of $F_T - F_0$. The value of portfolio B at time $T$ is therefore

$$F_0 + (F_T - F_0) + \max(K - F_T, 0) = \max(F_T, K)$$

Because the two portfolios have the same value at time $T$ and there are no early exercise opportunities, it follows that they are worth the same today. The value of portfolio A today is

$$c + Ke^{-rT}$$

where $c$ is the price of the call futures option. The marking-to-market process ensures that the futures contract in portfolio B is worth zero today. Therefore portfolio B is worth

$$p + F_0e^{-rT}$$

where $p$ is the price of the put futures option. Hence

$$c + Ke^{-rT} = p + F_0e^{-rT} \qquad (13.13)$$

**Example 13.9** Suppose that the price of a European call option on silver futures for delivery in six months is $0.56 per ounce when the exercise price is $8.50. Assume that the silver futures price for delivery in six months is currently $8.00 and the risk-free interest rate for an investment that matures in six months is 10% per annum. From a rearrangement of equation (13.13), the price of a European put option on silver futures with the same maturity and exercise date as the call option is

$$0.56 + 8.50e^{-0.1 \times 0.5} - 8.00e^{-0.1 \times 0.5} = 1.04$$

For American futures the put–call parity relationship is (see Problem 13.20)

$$F_0e^{-rT} - K \leqslant C - P \leqslant F_0 - Ke^{-rT}$$

## 13.6 VALUATION OF FUTURES OPTIONS USING BINOMIAL TREES

This section uses a binomial tree approach similar to that in Chapter 10 to price futures options. The key difference between futures options and stock options is that there are no up-front costs when a futures contract is entered into.

Suppose that the current futures price is 30 and it is expected to move either up to 33 or down to 28 over the next month. We consider a one-month call option on the futures with a strike price of 29 and ignore daily settlement. The situation is shown in Figure 13.2. If the futures price proves to be 33, the payoff from the option is 4 and the value of the futures contract is 3. If the futures price proves to be 28, the payoff from the option is zero and the value of the futures contract is −2.

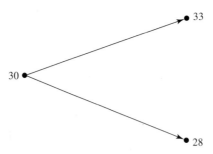

**Figure 13.2** Futures price movements in numerical example

To set up a riskless hedge, we consider a portfolio consisting of a short position in one option contract and a long position in $\Delta$ futures contracts. If the futures price moves up to 33, the value of the portfolio is $3\Delta - 4$; if it moves down to 28, the value of the portfolio is $-2\Delta$. The portfolio is riskless when these are the same—that is, when

$$3\Delta - 4 = -2\Delta$$

or $\Delta = 0.8$.

For this value of $\Delta$, we know the portfolio will be worth $3 \times 0.8 - 4 = -1.6$ in one month. Assume a risk-free interest rate of 6%. The value of the portfolio today must be

$$-1.6e^{-0.06 \times 0.08333} = -1.592$$

The portfolio consists of one short option and $\Delta$ futures contracts. Because the value of the futures contract today is zero, the value of the option today must be 1.592.

### A Generalization

We can generalize this analysis by considering a futures price that starts at $F_0$ and is anticipated to rise to $F_0 u$ or move down to $F_0 d$ over the time period $T$. We consider a derivative maturing at the end of the time period, and we suppose that its payoff is $f_u$ if the futures price moves up and $f_d$ if it moves down. The situation is summarized in Figure 13.3.

The riskless portfolio in this case consists of a short position in one option combined with a long position in $\Delta$ futures contracts, where

$$\Delta = \frac{f_u - f_d}{F_0 u - F_0 d}$$

The value of the portfolio at the end of the time period, then, is always

$$(F_0 u - F_0)\Delta - f_u$$

Denoting the risk-free interest rate by $r$, we obtain the value of the portfolio today as

$$[(F_0 u - F_0)\Delta - f_u]e^{-rT}$$

Another expression for the present value of the portfolio is $-f$, where $f$ is the value of the option today. It follows that

$$-f = [(F_0 u - F_0)\Delta - f_u]e^{-rT}$$

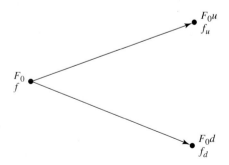

**Figure 13.3** Futures price and option price in general situation

Substituting for $\Delta$ and simplifying reduces this equation to

$$f = e^{-rT}[pf_u + (1-p)f_d] \tag{13.14}$$

where

$$p = \frac{1-d}{u-d} \tag{13.15}$$

In the numerical example in Figure 13.2, $u = 1.1$, $d = 0.9333$, $r = 0.06$, $T = 0.08333$, $f_u = 4$, and $f_d = 0$. From equation (13.15),

$$p = \frac{1 - 0.9333}{1.1 - 0.9333} = 0.4$$

and, from equation (13.14),

$$f = e^{-0.06 \times 0.08333}[0.4 \times 4 + 0.6 \times 0] = 1.592$$

This result agrees with the answer obtained earlier for this example.

## 13.7  FUTURES PRICE ANALOGY

There is a general result that makes the analysis of futures options analogous to the analysis of options on a stock paying a dividend yield. This result is that a futures price behaves in the same way as a stock paying a dividend yield at the domestic risk-free interest rate, $r$.

One clue that this might be so is given by comparing equations (13.14) and (13.15) with equations (13.7) and (13.8). The two sets of equations are identical when we set $q = r$. Another clue is that the put–call parity relationship for futures options prices are the same as those for options on a stock paying a dividend yield at rate $q$ when the stock price is replaced by the futures price and $q = r$.

We can understand the general result by noting that a futures contract requires zero investment. In a risk-neutral world the expected profit from holding a position in an investment that costs zero to set up must be zero. The expected payoff from a futures contract in a risk-neutral world must therefore be zero. It follows that the expected growth rate of the futures price in a risk-neutral world must be zero. As pointed out in Section 13.2, a stock paying a dividend at rate $q$ grows at an expected rate of $r - q$ in a risk-neutral world. If we set $q = r$, the expected growth rate of the stock price is zero, making it analogous to a futures price.

To prove the result formally, we derive in Appendix 13B the differential equation for a derivative dependent on a futures price. This differential equation is the same as that in Appendix 13A for a derivative dependent on a stock providing a known dividend yield, $q$, equal to the risk-free interest rate, $r$.

### The Expected Growth Rate of a Futures Price

The result, that the expected growth rate in a futures price in a risk-neutral world is zero, is a very general one. It is true for all futures prices. It applies in the world where interest rates are stochastic as well as the world where they are constant.[2]

---

[2] Note that the result applies in what we will refer to as the *traditional risk-neutral world*. In later chapters we will consider other risk-neutral worlds.

Because the expected growth rate of the futures price is zero,

$$F_0 = \hat{E}(F_T)$$

where $F_T$ is the futures price at the maturity of the contract, $F_0$ is the futures price at time zero, and $\hat{E}$ denotes the expected value in a risk-neutral world. Because $F_T = S_T$, where $S_T$ is the spot price at time $T$, it follows that

$$F_0 = \hat{E}(S_T) \tag{13.16}$$

This means that for all assets the futures price equals the expected future spot price in a risk-neutral world.

## 13.8 BLACK'S MODEL FOR VALUING FUTURES OPTIONS

European futures options can be valued by extending the results we have produced. Fischer Black was the first to show this in a paper published in 1976.[3] The underlying assumption is that futures prices have the same lognormal property that we assumed for stock prices in Chapter 12. The European call price, $c$, and the European put price, $p$, for a futures option are given by equations (13.4) and (13.5) with $S_0$ replaced by $F_0$ and $q = r$:

$$c = e^{-rT}[F_0 N(d_1) - K N(d_2)] \tag{13.17}$$

$$p = e^{-rT}[K N(-d_2) - F_0 N(-d_1)] \tag{13.18}$$

where

$$d_1 = \frac{\ln(F_0/K) + \sigma^2 T/2}{\sigma\sqrt{T}}$$

$$d_2 = \frac{\ln(F_0/K) - \sigma^2 T/2}{\sigma\sqrt{T}} = d_1 - \sigma\sqrt{T}$$

and $\sigma$ is the volatility of the futures price. When the cost of carry and the convenience yield are functions only of time, it can be shown that the volatility of the futures price is the same as the volatility of the underlying asset. Note that Black's model does not require the options contract and the futures contract to mature at the same time.

**Example 13.10** Consider a European put futures option on crude oil. The time to the option's maturity is four months, the current futures price is \$20, the exercise price is \$20, the risk-free interest rate is 9% per annum, and the volatility of the futures price is 25% per annum. In this case $F_0 = 20$, $K = 20$, $r = 0.09$, $T = 4/12$, $\sigma = 0.25$, and $\ln(F_0/K) = 0$, so that

$$d_1 = \frac{\sigma\sqrt{T}}{2} = 0.07216, \quad d_2 = -\frac{\sigma\sqrt{T}}{2} = -0.07216$$

$$N(-d_1) = 0.4712, \quad N(-d_2) = 0.5288$$

---

[3] See F. Black, "The Pricing of Commodity Contracts," *Journal of Financial Economics*, 3 (March 1976), 167–79.

and the put price $p$ is given by

$$p = e^{-0.09 \times 4/12}(20 \times 0.5288 - 20 \times 0.4712) = 1.12$$

or $1.12.

## 13.9 FUTURES OPTIONS vs. SPOT OPTIONS

In this section we compare options on futures and options on spot when they have the same strike price and time to maturity. An *option on a spot*, or *spot option*, is a regular option to buy or sell the underlying asset in the spot market.

The payoff from a European spot call option with strike price $K$ is

$$\max(S_T - K, 0)$$

where $S_T$ is the spot price at the option's maturity. The payoff from a European futures call option with the same strike price is

$$\max(F_T - K, 0)$$

where $F_T$ is the futures price at the option's maturity. If the European futures option matures at the same time as the futures contract, $F_T = S_T$ and the two options are in theory equivalent. If the European call futures option matures before the futures contract, it is worth more than the corresponding spot option in a normal market (where futures prices are higher than spot prices) and less than the corresponding spot option in an inverted market (where futures prices are lower than spot prices).

Similarly, a European futures put option is worth the same as its spot option counterpart when the futures option matures at the same time as the futures contract. If the European put futures option matures before the futures contract, it is worth less than the corresponding spot option in a normal market and more than the corresponding spot option in an inverted market.

### Results for American Options

Traded futures options are, in practice, usually American. If we assume that the risk-free rate of interest, $r$, is positive, then there is always some chance that it will be optimal to exercise an American futures option early. American futures options are, therefore, worth more than their European counterparts. We will look at numerical procedures for valuing futures options in Chapter 18.

It is not generally true that an American futures option is worth the same as the corresponding American spot option when the futures and options contracts have the same maturity. Suppose, for example, that there is a normal market with futures prices consistently higher than spot prices prior to maturity. This is the case with most stock indices, gold, silver, low-interest currencies, and some commodities. An American call futures option must be worth more than the corresponding American spot call option. The reason is that in some situations the futures option will be exercised early, in which case it will provide a greater profit to the holder. Similarly, an American put futures option must be worth less than the corresponding American spot put option. If there is an inverted market with futures prices consistently lower than spot prices, as is the case with high-interest currencies and some commodities, the reverse must be true. American call futures options are worth less than the corresponding American spot call option, whereas American put futures options are worth more than the corresponding American spot put option.

The differences just described between American futures options and American spot options hold true when the futures contract expires later than the options contract, as well as when the two expire at the same time. In fact, the later the futures contract expires, the greater the differences tend to be.

## SUMMARY

The Black–Scholes formula for valuing European options on a non-dividend-paying stock can be extended to cover European options on a stock providing a known dividend yield. In practice, stocks do not provide known dividend yields. However, a number of other assets on which options are written can be considered to be analogous to a stock providing a dividend yield. In particular,

1. An index is analogous to a stock providing a dividend yield. The dividend yield is the average dividend yield on the stocks composing the index.

2. A foreign currency is analogous to a stock providing a dividend yield where the dividend yield is the foreign risk-free interest rate.

3. A futures price is analogous to a stock providing a dividend yield where the dividend yield is equal to the domestic risk-free interest rate.

The extension to Black–Scholes can therefore be used to value European options on indices, foreign currencies, and futures contracts. As we will see in Chapter 18, these analogies are also useful in valuing numerically American options on indices, currencies, and futures contracts.

Index options are settled in cash. Upon exercise of an index call option, the holder receives the amount by which the index exceeds the strike price at close of trading. Similarly, upon exercise of an index put option, the holder receives the amount by which the strike price exceeds the index at close of trading. Index options can be used for portfolio insurance. If the portfolio has a $\beta$ of 1.0, it is appropriate to buy one put option for each $100S_0$ dollars in the portfolio, where $S_0$ is the value of the index; otherwise, $\beta$ put options should be purchased for each $100S_0$ dollars in the portfolio, where $\beta$ is the beta of the portfolio calculated using the capital asset pricing model. The strike price of the put options purchased should reflect the level of insurance required.

Currency options are traded both on organized exchanges and over the counter. They can be used by corporate treasurers to hedge foreign exchange exposure. For example, a U.S. corporate treasurer who knows that sterling will be received at a certain time in the future can hedge by buying put options that mature at that time. Similarly, a U.S. corporate treasurer who knows that sterling will be paid at a certain time in the future can hedge by buying call options that mature at that time.

Futures options require the delivery of the underlying futures contract upon exercise. When a call is exercised, the holder acquires a long futures position plus a cash amount equal to the excess of the futures price over the strike price. Similarly, when a put is exercised, the holder acquires a short position plus a cash amount equal to the excess of the strike price over the futures price. The futures contract that is delivered typically expires slightly later than the option. If we assume that the two expiration dates are the same, a European futures option is worth exactly the same as the corresponding European spot option. However, this is not true of American options. If the futures market is normal, an American call futures option is worth more than the corresponding American spot call option, while an American put futures option is worth less than the corresponding American spot put option. If the futures market is inverted, the reverse is true.

# SUGGESTIONS FOR FURTHER READING

### General

Merton, R. C., "Theory of Rational Option Pricing," *Bell Journal of Economics and Management Science*, 4 (Spring 1973), 141–83.

Stoll, H. R., and R. E. Whaley, "New Option Instruments: Arbitrageable Linkages and Valuation," *Advances in Futures and Options Research*, 1, pt. A (1986), 25–62.

### On options on stock indices

Chance, D. M., "Empirical Tests of the Pricing of Index Call Options," *Advances in Futures and Options Research*, 1, pt. A (1986), 141–66.

### On options on currencies

Amin, K., and R. A. Jarrow, "Pricing Foreign Currency Options under Stochastic Interest Rates," *Journal of International Money and Finance*, 10 (1991), 310–29.

Biger, N., and J. Hull, "The Valuation of Currency Options," *Financial Management*, 12 (Spring 1983), 24–28.

Bodurtha, J. N., and G. R. Courtadon, "Tests of an American Option Pricing Model on the Foreign Currency Options Market," *Journal of Financial and Quantitative Analysis*, 22 (June 1987), 153–67.

Garman, M. B., and S. W. Kohlhagen, "Foreign Currency Option Values," *Journal of International Money and Finance*, 2 (December 1983), 231–37.

Grabbe, J. O., "The Pricing of Call and Put Options on Foreign Exchange," *Journal of International Money and Finance*, 2 (December 1983), 239–53.

### On options on futures

Black, F., "The Pricing of Commodity Contracts," *Journal of Financial Economics*, 3 (March 1976), 167–79.

Brenner, M., G. Courtadon, and M. Subrahmanyam, "Options on the Spot and Options on Futures," *Journal of Finance*, 40 (December 1985), 1303–17.

Hilliard, J. E., and J. Reis, "Valuation of Commodity Futures and Options under Stochastic Convenience Yields, Interest Rates, and Jump Diffusions in the Spot," *Journal of Financial and Quantitative Analysis*, 33, no. 1 (March 1998), 61–86.

Miltersen, K. R., and E. S. Schwartz, "Pricing of Options on Commodity Futures with Stochastic Term Structures of Convenience Yields and Interest Rates," *Journal of Financial and Quantitative Analysis*, 33, no. 1 (March 1998), 33–59.

Ramaswamy, K., and S. M. Sundaresan, "The Valuation of Options on Futures Contracts," *Journal of Finance*, 40 (December 1985), 1319–40.

Wolf, A., "Fundamentals of Commodity Options on Futures," *Journal of Futures Markets*, 2 (1982), 391–408.

# QUESTIONS AND PROBLEMS
## (ANSWERS IN SOLUTIONS MANUAL)

13.1. A portfolio is currently worth $10 million and has a beta of 1.0. The S&P 100 is currently standing at 500. Explain how a put option on the S&P 100 with a strike of 480 can be used to provide portfolio insurance.

13.2. "Once we know how to value options on a stock paying a dividend yield, we know how to value options on stock indices, currencies, and futures." Explain this statement.

13.3. A stock index is currently 300, the dividend yield on the index is 3% per annum, and the risk-free interest rate is 8% per annum. What is a lower bound for the price of a six-month European call option on the index when the strike price is 290?

13.4. A currency is currently worth $0.80. Over each of the next two months it is expected to increase or decrease in value by 2%. The domestic and foreign risk-free interest rates are 6% and 8%, respectively. What is the value of a two-month European call option with a strike price of $0.80?

13.5. Explain the difference between a call option on yen and a call option on yen futures.

13.6. Explain how currency options can be used for hedging.

13.7. Calculate the value of a three-month at-the-money European call option on a stock index when the index is at 250, the risk-free interest rate is 10% per annum, the volatility of the index is 18% per annum, and the dividend yield on the index is 3% per annum.

13.8. Consider an American call futures option where the futures contract and the option contract expire at the same time. Under what circumstances is the futures option worth more than the corresponding American option on the underlying asset?

13.9. Calculate the value of an eight-month European put option on a currency with a strike price of 0.50. The current exchange rate is 0.52, the volatility of the exchange rate is 12%, the domestic risk-free interest rate is 4% per annum, and the foreign risk-free interest rate is 8% per annum.

13.10. Why are options on bond futures more actively traded than options on bonds?

13.11. "A futures price is like a stock paying a dividend yield." What is the dividend yield?

13.12. A futures price is currently 50. At the end of six months it will be either 56 or 46. The risk-free interest rate is 6% per annum. What is the value of a six-month European call option with a strike price of 50?

13.13. Calculate the value of a five-month European put futures option when the futures price is $19, the strike price is $20, the risk-free interest rate is 12% per annum, and the volatility of the futures price is 20% per annum.

13.14. A total return index tracks the return, including dividends, on a certain portfolio. Explain how you would value (a) forward contracts and (b) European options on the index.

13.15. The S&P 100 index currently stands at 696 and has a volatility of 30% per annum. The risk-free rate of interest is 7% per annum and the index provides a dividend yield of 4% per annum. Calculate the value of a three-month European put with strike price 700.

13.16. What is the put–call parity relationship for European currency options?

13.17. A foreign currency is currently worth $1.50. The domestic and foreign risk-free interest rates are 5% and 9%, respectively. Calculate a lower bound for the value of a six-month call option on the currency with a strike price of $1.40 if it is (a) European and (b) American.

13.18. Consider a stock index currently standing at 250. The dividend yield on the index is 4% per annum and the risk-free rate is 6% per annum. A three-month European call option on the index with a strike price of 245 is currently worth $10. What is the value of a three-month European put option on the index with a strike price of 245?

13.19. Show that if $C$ is the price of an American call with strike price $K$ and maturity $T$ on a stock providing a dividend yield of $q$, and $P$ is the price of an American put on the same stock with the same strike price and exercise date, then

$$S_0 e^{-qT} - K \leqslant C - P \leqslant S_0 - Ke^{-rT}$$

where $S_0$ is the stock price, $r$ is the risk-free interest rate, and $r > 0$. (*Hint*: To obtain the first half of the inequality, consider possible values of:

*Portfolio A*: a European call option plus an amount $K$ invested at the risk-free rate;
*Portfolio B*: an American put option plus $e^{-qT}$ of stock, with dividends being reinvested in the stock.

To obtain the second half of the inequality, consider possible values of:

*Portfolio C*: an American call option plus an amount $Ke^{-r(T-t)}$ invested at the risk-free rate;
*Portfolio D*: a European put option plus one stock, with dividends being reinvested in the stock.)

13.20. Show that if $C$ is the price of an American call option on a futures contract when the strike price is $K$ and the maturity is $T$, and $P$ is the price of an American put on the same futures contract with the same strike price and exercise date, then

$$F_0 e^{-rT} - K \leqslant C - P \leqslant F_0 - Ke^{-rT}$$

where $F_0$ is the futures price and $r$ is the risk-free rate. Assume that $r > 0$ and that there is no difference between forward and futures contracts. (*Hint*: Use an analogous approach to that indicated for Problem 13.19.)

13.21. If the price of currency A expressed in terms of the price of currency B follows the process

$$dS = (r_B - r_A)S\,dt + \sigma S\,dz$$

where $r_A$ is the risk-free interest rate in currency A and $r_B$ is the risk-free interest rate in currency B. What is the process followed by the price of currency B expressed in terms of currency A?

13.22. Would you expect the volatility of a stock index to be greater or less than the volatility of a typical stock? Explain your answer.

13.23. Does the cost of portfolio insurance increase or decrease as the beta of the portfolio increases? Explain your answer.

13.24. Suppose that a portfolio is worth $60 million and the S&P 500 is at 1200. If the value of the portfolio mirrors the value of the index, what options should be purchased to provide protection against the value of the portfolio falling below $54 million in one year's time?

13.25. Consider again the situation in Problem 13.24. Suppose that the portfolio has a beta of 2.0, that the risk-free interest rate is 5% per annum, and that the dividend yield on both the portfolio and the index is 3% per annum. What options should be purchased to provide protection against the value of the portfolio falling below $54 million in one year's time?

13.26. Show that the put–call parity relationship for European index options is

$$c + Ke^{-rT} = p + S_0 e^{-qT}$$

where $q$ is the dividend yield on the index, $c$ is the price of a European call option, $p$ is the price of a European put option, and both options have strike price $K$ and maturity $T$.

13.27. Suppose you buy a put option contract on October gold futures with a strike price of $400 per ounce. Each contract is for the delivery of 100 ounces. What happens if you exercise when the October futures price is $377 and the most recent settlement price is $380?

13.28. Suppose you sell a call option contract on April live-cattle futures with a strike price of 70 cents per pound. Each contract is for the delivery of 40,000 pounds. What happens if the contract is exercised when the futures price is 76 cents and the most recent settlement price is 75 cents?

13.29. Consider a two-month call futures option with a strike price of 40 when the risk-free interest rate is 10% per annum. The current futures price is 47. What is a lower bound for the value of the futures option if it is (a) European and (b) American?

13.30. Consider a four-month put futures option with a strike price of 50 when the risk-free interest rate is 10% per annum. The current futures price is 47. What is a lower bound for the value of the futures option if it is (a) European and (b) American?

13.31. A futures price is currently 60. It is known that over each of the next two three-month periods it will either rise by 10% or fall by 10%. The risk-free interest rate is 8% per annum. What is the value of a six-month European call option on the futures with a strike price of 60? If the call were American, would it ever be worth exercising it early?

13.32. In Problem 13.31, what is the value of a six-month European put option on futures with a strike price of 60? If the put were American, would it ever be worth exercising it early? Verify that the call prices calculated in Problem 13.31 and the put prices calculated here satisfy put–call parity relationships.

13.33. A futures price is currently 25, its volatility is 30% per annum, and the risk-free interest rate is 10% per annum. What is the value of a nine-month European call on the futures with a strike price of 26?

13.34. A futures price is currently 70, its volatility is 20% per annum, and the risk-free interest rate is 6% per annum. What is the value of a five-month European put on the futures with a strike price of 65?

13.35. Suppose that a futures price is currently 35. A European call option and a European put option on the futures with a strike price of 34 are both priced at 2 in the market. The risk-free interest rate is 10% per annum. Identify an arbitrage opportunity. Both options have one year to maturity.

13.36. "The price of an at-the-money European call futures option always equals the price of a similar at-the-money European put futures option." Explain why this statement is true.

13.37. Suppose that a futures price is currently 30. The risk-free interest rate is 5% per annum. A three-month American call futures option with a strike price of 28 is worth 4. Calculate bounds for the price of a three-month American put futures option with a strike price of 28.

13.38. Can an option on the yen–euro exchange rate be created from two options, one on the dollar–euro exchange rate, and the other on the dollar–yen exchange rate? Explain your answer.

13.39. A corporation knows that in three months it will have $5 million to invest for 90 days at LIBOR minus 50 basis points and wishes to ensure that the rate obtained will be at least 6.5%. What position in exchange-traded interest-rate options should the corporation take?

13.40. Prove the results in equations (13.1), (13.2), and (13.3) using Portfolios A, B, C, and D in Section 13.1.

# ASSIGNMENT QUESTIONS

13.41. A futures price is currently 40. It is known that at the end of three months the price will be either 35 or 45. What is the value of a three-month European call option on the futures with a strike price of 42 if the risk-free interest rate is 7% per annum?

13.42. A stock index currently stands at 300. It is expected to increase or decrease by 10% over each of the next two time periods of three months. The risk-free interest rate is 8% and the dividend yield on the index is 3%. What is the value of a six-month put option on the index with a strike price of 300 if it is (a) European and (b) American?

13.43. Suppose that the spot price of the Canadian dollar is U.S. $0.75 and that the Canadian dollar–U.S. dollar exchange rate has a volatility of 4% per annum. The risk-free rates of interest in Canada and the United States are 9% and 7% per annum, respectively. Calculate the value of a European call option to buy one Canadian dollar for U.S. $0.75 in nine months. Use put–call parity to calculate the price of a European put option to sell one Canadian dollar for U.S. $0.75 in nine months. What is the price of an option to buy U.S. $0.75 with one Canadian dollar in nine months?

13.44. Calculate the implied volatility of soybean futures prices from the following information concerning a European put on soybean futures:

| | |
|---|---|
| Current futures price | 525 |
| Exercise price | 525 |
| Risk-free rate | 6% per annum |
| Time to maturity | 5 months |
| Put price | 20 |

13.45. A mutual fund announces that the salaries of its fund managers will depend on the performance of the fund. If the fund loses money, the salaries will be zero. If the fund makes a profit, the salaries will be proportional to the profit. Describe the salary of a fund manager as an option. How is a fund manager motivated to behave with this type of remuneration package?

13.46. Use the DerivaGem software to calculate implied volatilities for the May options on corn futures in Table 13.5. Assume the futures prices in Table 2.2 apply and that the risk-free rate is 5% per annum. Treat the options as American and use 100 time steps. The options mature on April 21, 2001. Can you draw any conclusions from the pattern of implied volatilities you obtain?

13.47. Use the DerivaGem software to calculate implied volatilities for the June 100 call and the June 100 put on the Dow Jones Industrial Average in Table 13.1. The value of the DJX on March 15, 2001, was 100.31. Assume the risk-free rate was 4.5%, the dividend yield was 2%. The options expire on June 16, 2001. Are the quotes for the two options consistent with put–call parity?

# APPENDIX 13A
## Derivation of Differential Equation Satisfied by a Derivative Dependent on a Stock Providing a Dividend Yield

Define $f$ as the price of a derivative dependent on a stock that provides a dividend yield at rate $q$. We suppose that the stock price, $S$, follows the process

$$dS = \mu S\, dt + \sigma S\, dz$$

where $dz$ is a Wiener process. The variables $\mu$ and $\sigma$ are the expected proportional growth rate in the stock price and the volatility of the stock price, respectively. Because the stock price provides a dividend yield, $\mu$ is only part of the expected return on the stock.[4]

Because $f$ is a function of $S$ and $t$, it follows from Itô's lemma that

$$df = \left(\frac{\partial f}{\partial S}\mu S + \frac{\partial f}{\partial t} + \frac{1}{2}\frac{\partial^2 f}{\partial S^2}\sigma^2 S^2\right) dt + \frac{\partial f}{\partial S}\sigma S\, dz$$

Similarly to the procedure of Section 12.6, we can set up a portfolio consisting of

$$-1: \quad \text{derivative}$$

$$+\frac{\partial f}{\partial S}: \quad \text{stock}$$

If $\Pi$ is the value of the portfolio, then

$$\Pi = -f + \frac{\partial f}{\partial S}S \tag{13A.1}$$

and the change $\delta\Pi$ in the value of the portfolio in a time period $\delta t$ is given by equation (12.14) as

$$\delta\Pi = \left(-\frac{\partial f}{\partial t} - \frac{1}{2}\frac{\partial^2 f}{\partial S^2}\sigma^2 S^2\right)\delta t$$

In time $\delta t$, the holder of the portfolio earns capital gains equal to $\delta\Pi$ and dividends on the stock position equal to

$$qS\frac{\partial f}{\partial S}\, \delta t$$

Define $\delta W$ as the change in the wealth of the portfolio holder in time $\delta t$. It follows that

$$\delta W = \left(-\frac{\partial f}{\partial t} - \frac{1}{2}\frac{\partial^2 f}{\partial S^2}\sigma^2 S^2 + qS\frac{\partial f}{\partial S}\right)\delta t \tag{13A.2}$$

Because this expression is independent of the Wiener process, the portfolio is instantaneously riskless. Hence

$$\delta W = r\Pi\, \delta t \tag{13A.3}$$

---

[4] From equation (13.6), $\mu = r - q$ in a risk-neutral world.

Substituting from equations (13A.1) and (13A.2) into equation (13A.3) gives

$$\left(-\frac{\partial f}{\partial t} - \frac{1}{2}\frac{\partial^2 f}{\partial S^2}\sigma^2 S^2 + qS\frac{\partial f}{\partial S}\right)\delta t = r\left(-f + \frac{\partial f}{\partial S}S\right)\delta t$$

so that

$$\frac{\partial f}{\partial t} + (r - q)S\frac{\partial f}{\partial S} + \frac{1}{2}\sigma^2 S^2\frac{\partial^2 f}{\partial S^2} = rf \qquad (13A.4)$$

This is the differential equation that must be satisfied by $f$.

# APPENDIX 13B
## Derivation of Differential Equation Satisfied by a Derivative Dependent on a Futures Price

Suppose that the futures price $F$ follows the process

$$dF = \mu F\, dt + \sigma F\, dz \tag{13B.1}$$

where $dz$ is a Wiener process and $\sigma$ is constant.[5] Because $f$ is a function of $F$ and $t$, it follows from Itô's lemma that

$$df = \left(\frac{\partial f}{\partial F}\mu F + \frac{\partial f}{\partial t} + \tfrac{1}{2}\frac{\partial^2 f}{\partial F^2}\sigma^2 F^2\right)dt + \frac{\partial f}{\partial F}\sigma F\, dz \tag{13B.2}$$

Consider a portfolio consisting of

$$-1 : \quad \text{derivative}$$

$$+\frac{\partial f}{\partial F} : \quad \text{futures contracts}$$

Define $\Pi$ as the value of the portfolio and let $\delta\Pi$, $\delta f$, and $\delta F$ be the change in $\Pi$, $f$, and $F$, respectively, in time $\delta t$. Because it costs nothing to enter into a futures contract,

$$\Pi = -f \tag{13B.3}$$

In a time period $\delta t$, the holder of the portfolio earns capital gains equal to $-\delta f$ from the derivative and income of

$$\frac{\partial f}{\partial F}\delta F$$

from the futures contract. Define $\delta W$ as the total change in wealth of the portfolio holder in time $\delta t$. It follows that

$$\delta W = \frac{\partial f}{\partial F}\delta F - \delta f$$

The discrete versions of equations (13B.1) and (13B.2) are

$$\delta F = \mu F\, \delta t + \sigma F\, \delta z$$

$$\delta f = \left(\frac{\partial f}{\partial F}\mu F + \frac{\partial f}{\partial t} + \tfrac{1}{2}\frac{\partial^2 f}{\partial F^2}\sigma^2 F^2\right)\delta t + \frac{\partial f}{\partial F}\sigma F\, \delta z$$

where $\delta z = \epsilon\sqrt{\delta t}$ and $\epsilon$ is a random sample from a standardized normal distribution. It follows that

$$\delta W = \left(-\frac{\partial f}{\partial t} - \tfrac{1}{2}\frac{\partial^2 f}{\partial F^2}\sigma^2 F^2\right)\delta t \tag{13B.4}$$

---

[5] From the arguments in Section 13.7, $\mu = 0$ in a risk-neutral world.

This is riskless. Hence it must also be true that

$$\delta W = r\Pi\,\delta t \qquad\qquad (13B.5)$$

If we substitute for $\Pi$ from equation (13B.3), then equations (13B.4) and (13B.5) give

$$\left(-\frac{\partial f}{\partial t} - \frac{1}{2}\frac{\partial^2 f}{\partial F^2}\sigma^2 F^2\right)\delta t = -rf\,\delta t$$

Hence

$$\frac{\partial f}{\partial t} + \frac{1}{2}\frac{\partial^2 f}{\partial F^2}\sigma^2 F^2 = rf$$

This has the same form as equation (13A.4) with $q$ set equal to $r$. We deduce that a futures price can be treated in the same way as a stock providing a dividend yield at rate $r$ for the purpose of valuing derivatives.

# CHAPTER 14

# THE GREEK LETTERS

A financial institution that sells an option to a client in the over-the-counter markets is faced with the problem of managing its risk. If the option happens to be the same as one that is traded on an exchange, the financial institution can neutralize its exposure by buying on the exchange the same option as it has sold. But when the option has been tailored to the needs of a client and does not correspond to the standard products traded by exchanges, hedging the exposure is far more difficult.

In this chapter we discuss some of the alternative approaches to this problem. We cover what are commonly referred to as the "Greek letters" or simply the "Greeks." Each Greek letter measures a different dimension to the risk in an option position and the aim of a trader is to manage the Greeks so that all risks are acceptable. The analysis presented in this chapter is applicable to market makers in options on an exchange as well as to traders working for financial institutions.

Toward the end of the chapter we will consider the creation of options synthetically. This turns out to be very closely related to the hedging of options. Creating an option position synthetically is essentially the same task as hedging the opposite option position. For example, creating a long call option synthetically is the same as hedging a short position in the call option.

## 14.1 ILLUSTRATION

In the next few sections we use as an example the position of a financial institution that has sold for $300,000 a European call option on 100,000 shares of a non-dividend-paying stock. We assume that the stock price is $49, the strike price is $50, the risk-free interest rate is 5% per annum, the stock price volatility is 20% per annum, the time to maturity is 20 weeks (0.3846 years), and the expected return from the stock is 13% per annum.[1] With our usual notation, this means that

$$S_0 = 49, \quad K = 50, \quad r = 0.05, \quad \sigma = 0.20, \quad T = 0.3846, \quad \mu = 0.13$$

The Black–Scholes price of the option is about $240,000. The financial institution has therefore sold the option for $60,000 more than its theoretical value. But it is faced with the problem of hedging the risks.[2]

---

[1] As shown in Chapters 10 and 12, the expected return is irrelevant to the pricing of an option. It is given here because it can have some bearing on the effectiveness of a hedging scheme.

[2] Financial institutions do not normally write call options on individual stocks. However, a call option on a stock is a convenient example with which to develop our ideas. The points that will be made apply to other types of options and to other derivatives.

## 14.2  NAKED AND COVERED POSITIONS

One strategy open to the financial institution is to do nothing. This is sometimes referred to as adopting a *naked position*. It is a strategy that works well if the stock price is below $50 at the end of the 20 weeks. The option then costs the financial institution nothing and it makes a profit of $300,000. A naked position works less well if the call is exercised because the financial institution then has to buy 100,000 shares at the market price prevailing in 20 weeks to cover the call. The cost to the financial institution is 100,000 times the amount by which the stock price exceeds the strike price. For example, if after 20 weeks the stock price is $60, the option costs the financial institution $1,000,000. This is considerably greater than the $300,000 premium received.

As an alternative to a naked position, the financial institution can adopt a *covered position*. This involves buying 100,000 shares as soon as the option has been sold. If the option is exercised, this strategy works well, but in other circumstances it could lead to a significant loss. For example, if the stock price drops to $40, the financial institution loses $900,000 on its stock position. This is considerably greater than the $300,000 charged for the option.[3]

Neither a naked position nor a covered position provides a satisfactory hedge. If the assumptions underlying the Black–Scholes formula hold, the cost to the financial institution should always be $240,000 on average for both approaches.[4] But on any one occasion the cost is liable to range from zero to over $1,000,000. A perfect hedge would ensure that the cost is always $240,000. For a perfect hedge, the standard deviation of the cost of writing and hedging the option is zero.

## 14.3  A STOP-LOSS STRATEGY

One interesting hedging scheme that is sometimes proposed involves a *stop-loss strategy*. To illustrate the basic idea, consider an institution that has written a call option with strike price $K$ to buy one unit of a stock. The hedging scheme involves buying one unit of the stock as soon as its price rises above $K$ and selling it as soon as its price falls below $K$. The objective is to hold a naked position whenever the stock price is less than $K$ and a covered position whenever the stock price is greater than $K$. The scheme is designed to ensure that at time $T$ the institution owns the stock if the option closes in the money and does not own it if the option closes out of the money. The strategy appears to produce payoffs that are the same as the payoffs on the option. In the situation illustrated in Figure 14.1, it involves buying the stock at time $t_1$, selling it at time $t_2$, buying it at time $t_3$, selling it at time $t_4$, buying it at time $t_5$, and delivering it at time $T$.

As usual, we denote the initial stock price by $S_0$. The cost of setting up the hedge initially is $S_0$ if $S_0 > K$ and zero otherwise. It seems as though the total cost, $Q$, of writing and hedging the option is the option's intrinsic value, that is,

$$Q = \max(S_0 - K, 0) \tag{14.1}$$

This is because all purchases and sales subsequent to time zero are made at price $K$. If this were in fact correct, the hedging scheme would work perfectly in the absence of transactions costs.

---

[3] Put–call parity shows that the exposure from writing a covered call is the same as the exposure from writing a naked put.

[4] More precisely, the present value of the expected cost is $240,000 for both approaches, assuming that appropriate risk-adjusted discount rates are used.

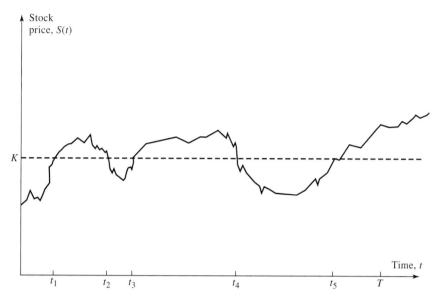

**Figure 14.1** A stop-loss strategy

Furthermore, the cost of hedging the option would always be less than its Black–Scholes price. Thus, an investor could earn riskless profits by writing options and hedging them.

There are two basic reasons why equation (14.1) is incorrect. The first is that the cash flows to the hedger occur at different times and must be discounted. The second is that purchases and sales cannot be made at exactly the same price $K$. This second point is critical. If we assume a risk-neutral world with zero interest rates, we can justify ignoring the time value of money. But we cannot legitimately assume that both purchases and sales are made at the same price. If markets are efficient, the hedger cannot know whether, when the stock price equals $K$, it will continue above or below $K$.

As a practical matter, purchases must be made at a price $K + \epsilon$ and sales must be made at a price $K - \epsilon$, for some small positive number $\epsilon$. Thus, every purchase and subsequent sale involves a cost (apart from transaction costs) of $2\epsilon$. A natural response on the part of the hedger is to monitor price movements more closely so that $\epsilon$ is reduced. Assuming that stock prices change continuously, $\epsilon$ can be made arbitrarily small by monitoring the stock prices closely. But as $\epsilon$ is made smaller, trades tend to occur more frequently. Thus, even though the cost per trade is reduced, it is offset by the increasing frequency of trading. As $\epsilon \to 0$, the expected number of trades tends to infinity.[5]

A stop-loss strategy, although superficially attractive, does not work particularly well as a hedging scheme. Consider its use for an out-of-the-money option. If the stock price never reaches the strike price of $K$, the hedging scheme costs nothing. If the path of the stock price crosses the strike price level many times, the scheme is quite expensive. Monte Carlo simulation can be used to assess the overall performance of stop-loss hedging. This involves randomly sampling paths for the stock price and observing the results of using the scheme. Table 14.1 shows the results for the option considered earlier. It assumes that the stock price is observed at the end of time intervals of

---

[5] As mentioned in Section 11.2, the expected number of times a Wiener process equals any particular value in a given time interval is infinite.

**Table 14.1**   Performance of stop-loss strategy. (The performance measure is the ratio of the standard deviation of the cost of writing the option and hedging it to the theoretical price of the option.)

| $\delta t$ (weeks) | 5 | 4 | 2 | 1 | 0.5 | 0.25 |
|---|---|---|---|---|---|---|
| Hedge performance | 1.02 | 0.93 | 0.82 | 0.77 | 0.76 | 0.76 |

length $\delta t$.[6] The hedge performance measure is the ratio of the standard deviation of the cost of hedging the option to the Black–Scholes price of the option. Each result is based on 1,000 sample paths for the stock price and has a standard error of about 2%. It appears to be impossible to produce a value for the hedge performance measure below 0.70 regardless of how small $\delta t$ is made.

## 14.4   DELTA HEDGING

Most traders use more sophisticated hedging schemes than those mentioned so far. These involve calculating measures such as delta, gamma, and vega. Here we consider the role played by delta.

The *delta* of an option, $\Delta$, was introduced in Chapter 10. It is defined as the rate of change of the option price with respect to the price of the underlying asset. It is the slope of the curve that relates the option price to the underlying asset price. Suppose that the delta of a call option on a stock is 0.6. This means that when the stock price changes by a small amount, the option price changes by about 60% of that amount. Figure 14.2 shows the relationship between a call price and the underlying stock price. When the stock price corresponds to point A, the option price corresponds to point B, and $\Delta$ is the slope of the line indicated. In general,

$$\Delta = \frac{\partial c}{\partial S}$$

where $c$ is the price of the call option and $S$ is the stock price.

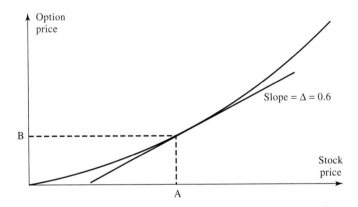

**Figure 14.2**   Calculation of delta

---

[6]  The precise hedging rule used was as follows. If the stock price moves from below $K$ to above $K$ in a time interval of length $\delta t$, it is bought at the end of the interval. If it moves from above $K$ to below $K$ in the time interval, it is sold at the end of the interval. Otherwise, no action is taken.

Suppose that in Figure 14.2 the stock price is $100 and the option price is $10. Imagine an investor who has sold 20 call option contracts—that is, options to buy 2,000 shares. The investor's position could be hedged by buying $0.6 \times 2,000 = 1,200$ shares. The gain (loss) on the option position would then tend to be offset by the loss (gain) on the stock position. For example, if the stock price goes up by $1 (producing a gain of $1,200 on the shares purchased), the option price will tend to go up by $0.6 \times \$1 = \$0.60$ (producing a loss of $1,200 on the options written); if the stock price goes down by $1 (producing a loss of $1,200 on the shares purchased), the option price will tend to go down by $0.60 (producing a gain of $1,200 on the options written).

In this example, the delta of the investor's option position is $0.6 \times (-2,000) = -1,200$. In other words, the investor loses $1,200\,\delta S$ on the short option position when the stock price increases by $\delta S$. The delta of the stock is 1.0, and the long position in 1,200 shares has a delta of $+1,200$. The delta of the investor's overall position is therefore zero. The delta of the stock position offsets the delta of the option position. A position with a delta of zero is referred to as being *delta neutral*.

It is important to realize that, because delta changes, the investor's position remains delta hedged (or delta neutral) only for a relatively short period of time. The hedge has to be adjusted periodically. This is known as *rebalancing*. In our example, at the end of three days the stock price might increase to $110. As indicated by Figure 14.2, an increase in the stock price leads to an increase in delta. Suppose that delta rises from 0.60 to 0.65. An extra $0.05 \times 2,000 = 100$ shares would then have to be purchased to maintain the hedge. The delta-hedging scheme just described is an example of a *dynamic-hedging scheme*. It can be contrasted with *static-hedging schemes*, where the hedge is set up initially and never adjusted. Static hedging schemes are sometimes also referred to as *hedge-and-forget schemes*.

Delta is closely related to the Black–Scholes–Merton analysis. As explained in Chapter 12, Black, Scholes, and Merton showed that it is possible to set up a riskless portfolio consisting of a position in an option on a stock and a position in the stock. Expressed in terms of $\Delta$, the Black–Scholes portfolio is

$$-1: \quad \text{option}$$

$$+\Delta: \quad \text{shares of the stock}$$

Using our new terminology, we can say that Black and Scholes valued options by setting up a delta-neutral position and arguing that the return on the position should be the risk-free interest rate.

### Delta of European Stock Options

For a European call option on a non-dividend-paying stock, it can be shown that

$$\Delta = N(d_1)$$

where $d_1$ is defined as in equation (12.20). Using delta hedging for a short position in a European call option therefore involves keeping a long position of $N(d_1)$ shares at any given time. Similarly, using delta hedging for a long position in a European call option involves maintaining a short position of $N(d_1)$ shares at any given time.

For a European put option on a non-dividend-paying stock, delta is given by

$$\Delta = N(d_1) - 1$$

Delta is negative, which means that a long position in a put option should be hedged with a long

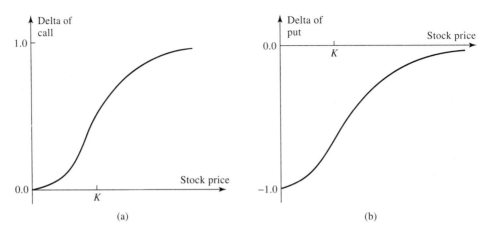

**Figure 14.3** Variation of delta with stock price: (a) call option and (b) put option on a non-dividend-paying stock

position in the underlying stock, and a short position in a put option should be hedged with a short position in the underlying stock. Figure 14.3 shows the variation of the delta of a call option and a put option with the stock price. Figure 14.4 shows the variation of delta with the time to maturity for in-the-money, at-the-money, and out-of-the-money call options.

### *Delta of Other European Options*

For European call options on an asset paying a yield $q$, we have

$$\Delta = e^{-qT} N(d_1)$$

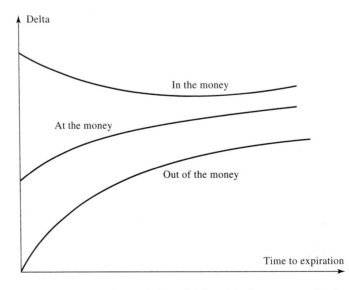

**Figure 14.4** Typical patterns for variation of delta with time to maturity for a call option

where $d_1$ is defined by equation (13.4). For European put options on the asset, we have

$$\Delta = e^{-qT}[N(d_1) - 1]$$

When the asset is a stock index, these formulas are correct with $q$ equal to the dividend yield on the index. When the asset is a currency, they are correct with $q$ equal to the foreign risk-free rate, $r_f$. When the asset is a futures contract, they are correct with $q$ equal to the domestic risk-free rate, $r$.

**Example 14.1** A U.S. bank has sold six-month put options on £1 million with a strike price of 1.6000 and wishes to make its portfolio delta neutral. Suppose that the current exchange rate is 1.6200, the risk-free interest rate in the United Kingdom is 13% per annum, the risk-free interest rate in the United States is 10% per annum, and the volatility of sterling is 15%. In this case, $S_0 = 1.6200$, $K = 1.6000$, $r = 0.10$, $r_f = 0.13$, $\sigma = 0.15$, and $T = 0.5$. The delta of a put option on a currency is

$$[N(d_1) - 1]e^{-r_f T}$$

where $d_1$ is given by equation (13.9). It can be shown that

$$d_1 = 0.0287 \quad \text{and} \quad N(d_1) = 0.5115$$

so that the delta of the put option is $-0.458$. This is the delta of a long position in one put option. (It means that when the exchange rate increases by $\delta S$, the price of the put goes down by 45.8% of $\delta S$.) The delta of the bank's total short option position is $+458,000$. To make the position delta neutral, we must therefore add a short sterling position of £458,000 to the option position. This short sterling position has a delta of $-458,000$ and neutralizes the delta of the option position.

## Delta of Forward Contracts

The concept of delta can be applied to financial instruments other than options. Consider a forward contract on a non-dividend-paying stock. Equation (3.9) shows that the value of a forward contract is $S_0 - Ke^{-rT}$, where $K$ is the delivery price and $T$ is the forward contract's time to maturity. When the price of the stock changes by $\delta S$, with all else remaining the same, the value of a forward contract on the stock also changes by $\delta S$. The delta of a forward contract on one share of the stock is therefore always 1.0. This means that a short forward contract on one share can be hedged by purchasing one share; a long forward contract on one share can be hedged by shorting one share.[7]

For an asset providing a dividend yield at rate $q$, equation (3.11) shows that the forward contract's delta is $e^{-qT}$. In the case of a stock index, $q$ is set equal to the dividend yield on the index. For a currency, it is set equal to the foreign risk-free rate, $r_f$.

## Delta of a Futures Contract

From equation (3.5), the futures price for a contract on a non-dividend-paying stock is $S_0 e^{rT}$, where $T$ is the time to maturity of the futures contract. This shows that when the price of the stock changes by $\delta S$, with all else remaining the same, the futures price changes by $\delta S\, e^{rT}$. Because futures contracts are marked to market daily, the holder of a long futures contract makes an almost immediate gain of this amount. The delta of a futures contract is therefore $e^{rT}$. For a futures contract on an asset providing a dividend yield at rate $q$, equation (3.7) shows similarly that delta is $e^{(r-q)T}$. It is interesting that the impact of marking to market is to make the deltas of futures and

---

[7] These are hedge-and-forget schemes. Because delta is always 1.0, no changes need to be made to the position in the stock during the life of the contract.

forward contracts slightly different. This is true even when interest rates are constant and the forward price equals the futures price.

Sometimes a futures contract is used to achieve a delta-neutral position. Define:

$T$:  Maturity of futures contract

$H_A$:  Required position in asset for delta hedging

$H_F$:  Alternative required position in futures contracts for delta hedging

If the underlying asset is a non-dividend-paying stock, the analysis we have just given shows that

$$H_F = e^{-rT} H_A \qquad (14.2)$$

When the underlying asset pays a dividend yield $q$, we have

$$H_F = e^{-(r-q)T} H_A \qquad (14.3)$$

For a stock index we set $q$ equal to the dividend yield on the index; for a currency we set it equal to the foreign risk-free rate, $r_f$, so that

$$H_F = e^{-(r-r_f)T} H_A \qquad (14.4)$$

**Example 14.2**  Consider the option in the previous example where hedging using the currency requires a short position of £458,000. From equation (14.4), hedging using nine-month currency futures requires a short futures position of

$$e^{-(0.10-0.13)\times 9/12} 458{,}000$$

or £468,442. Because each futures contract is for the purchase or sale of £62,500, seven contracts should be shorted (seven is the nearest whole number to 468,442/62,500).

### *Dynamic Aspects of Delta Hedging*

Tables 14.2 and 14.3 provide two examples of the operation of delta hedging for the example in Section 14.1. The hedge is assumed to be adjusted or rebalanced weekly. The initial value of delta can be calculated from the data in Section 14.1 as 0.522. This means that as soon as the option is written, $2,557,800 must be borrowed to buy 52,200 shares at a price of $49. The rate of interest is 5%. An interest cost of $2,500 is therfore incurred in the first week.

In Table 14.2 the stock price falls by the end of the first week to $48.12. The delta declines to 0.458, and 6,400 of shares are sold to maintain the hedge. The strategy realizes $308,000 in cash, and the cumulative borrowings at the end of Week 1 are reduced to $2,252,300. During the second week the stock price reduces to $47.37, delta declines again, and so on. Toward the end of the life of the option, it becomes apparent that the option will be exercised and delta approaches 1.0. By Week 20, therefore, the hedger has a fully covered position. The hedger receives $5 million for the stock held, so that the total cost of writing the option and hedging it is $263,300.

Table 14.3 illustrates an alternative sequence of events such that the option closes out of the money. As it becomes clear that the option will not be exercised, delta approaches zero. By Week 20 the hedger has a naked position and has incurred costs totaling $256,600.

In Tables 14.2 and 14.3 the costs of hedging the option, when discounted to the beginning of the period, are close to but not exactly the same as the Black–Scholes price of $240,000. If the hedging scheme worked perfectly, the cost of hedging would, after discounting, be exactly equal to the Black–Scholes price for every simulated stock price path. The reason for the variation in the cost of delta hedging is that the hedge is rebalanced only once a week. As rebalancing takes place more frequently, the variation in the cost of hedging is reduced. Of course, the examples in Tables 14.2 and 14.3 are idealized in that they assume that the volatility is constant and there are no transactions costs.

Table 14.4 shows statistics on the performance of delta hedging obtained from 1,000 random stock price paths in our example. As in Table 14.1, the performance measure is the ratio of the standard deviation of the cost of hedging the option to the Black–Scholes price of the option. Clearly delta hedging is a great improvement over a stop-loss strategy. Unlike a stop-loss strategy, the performance of a delta-hedging strategy gets steadily better as the hedge is monitored more frequently.

Delta hedging aims to keep the value of the financial institution's position as close to unchanged as possible. Initially, the value of the written option is $240,000. In the situation depicted in Table 14.2, the value of the option can be calculated as $414,500 in Week 9. Thus, the financial institution has lost $174,500 on its option position. Its cash position, as measured by the cumulative cost, is $1,442,900 worse in Week 9 than in Week 0. The value of the shares held has increased from $2,557,800 to $4,171,100. The net effect of all this is that the value of the financial institution's position has changed by only $4,100 during the nine-week period.

## Where the Cost Comes From

The delta-hedging scheme in Tables 14.2 and 14.3 in effect creates a long position in the option synthetically. This neutralizes the short position arising from the option that has been written. The scheme generally involves selling stock just after the price has gone down and buying stock just

**Table 14.2** Simulation of delta hedging (option closes in the money; cost of hedging is $263,300)

| Week | Stock price | Delta | Shares purchased | Cost of shares purchased ($000) | Cumulative cost including interest ($000) | Interest cost ($000) |
|---|---|---|---|---|---|---|
| 0 | 49.00 | 0.522 | 52,200 | 2,557.8 | 2,557.8 | 2.5 |
| 1 | 48.12 | 0.458 | (6,400) | (308.0) | 2,252.3 | 2.2 |
| 2 | 47.37 | 0.400 | (5,800) | (274.7) | 1,979.8 | 1.9 |
| 3 | 50.25 | 0.596 | 19,600 | 984.9 | 2,996.6 | 2.9 |
| 4 | 51.75 | 0.693 | 9,700 | 502.0 | 3,471.5 | 3.3 |
| 5 | 53.12 | 0.774 | 8,100 | 430.3 | 3,905.1 | 3.8 |
| 6 | 53.00 | 0.771 | (300) | (15.9) | 3,893.0 | 3.7 |
| 7 | 51.87 | 0.706 | (6,500) | (337.2) | 3,559.5 | 3.4 |
| 8 | 51.38 | 0.674 | (3,200) | (164.4) | 3,398.5 | 3.3 |
| 9 | 53.00 | 0.787 | 11,300 | 598.9 | 4,000.7 | 3.8 |
| 10 | 49.88 | 0.550 | (23,700) | (1,182.2) | 2,822.3 | 2.7 |
| 11 | 48.50 | 0.413 | (13,700) | (664.4) | 2,160.6 | 2.1 |
| 12 | 49.88 | 0.542 | 12,900 | 643.5 | 2,806.2 | 2.7 |
| 13 | 50.37 | 0.591 | 4,900 | 246.8 | 3,055.7 | 2.9 |
| 14 | 52.13 | 0.768 | 17,700 | 922.7 | 3,981.3 | 3.8 |
| 15 | 51.88 | 0.759 | (900) | (46.7) | 3,938.4 | 3.8 |
| 16 | 52.87 | 0.865 | 10,600 | 560.4 | 4,502.6 | 4.3 |
| 17 | 54.87 | 0.978 | 11,300 | 620.0 | 5,126.9 | 4.9 |
| 18 | 54.62 | 0.990 | 1,200 | 65.5 | 5,197.3 | 5.0 |
| 19 | 55.87 | 1.000 | 1,000 | 55.9 | 5,258.2 | 5.1 |
| 20 | 57.25 | 1.000 | 0 | 0.0 | 5,263.3 | |

**Table 14.3**  Simulation of delta hedging (option closes out of the money; cost of hedging is $256,600)

| Week | Stock price | Delta | Shares purchased | Cost of shares purchased ($000) | Cumulative cost including interest ($000) | Interest cost ($000) |
|------|------------|-------|------------------|-------------------------------|------------------------------------------|----------------------|
| 0 | 49.00 | 0.522 | 52,200 | 2,557.8 | 2,557.8 | 2.5 |
| 1 | 49.75 | 0.568 | 4,600 | 228.9 | 2,789.2 | 2.7 |
| 2 | 52.00 | 0.705 | 13,700 | 712.4 | 3,504.3 | 3.4 |
| 3 | 50.00 | 0.579 | (12,600) | (630.0) | 2,877.7 | 2.8 |
| 4 | 48.38 | 0.459 | (12,000) | (580.6) | 2,299.9 | 2.2 |
| 5 | 48.25 | 0.443 | (1,600) | (77.2) | 2,224.9 | 2.1 |
| 6 | 48.75 | 0.475 | 3,200 | 156.0 | 2,383.0 | 2.3 |
| 7 | 49.63 | 0.540 | 6,500 | 322.6 | 2,707.9 | 2.6 |
| 8 | 48.25 | 0.420 | (12,000) | (579.0) | 2,131.5 | 2.1 |
| 9 | 48.25 | 0.410 | (1,000) | (48.2) | 2,085.4 | 2.0 |
| 10 | 51.12 | 0.658 | 24,800 | 1,267.8 | 3,355.2 | 3.2 |
| 11 | 51.50 | 0.692 | 3,400 | 175.1 | 3,533.5 | 3.4 |
| 12 | 49.88 | 0.542 | (15,000) | (748.2) | 2,788.7 | 2.7 |
| 13 | 49.88 | 0.538 | (400) | (20.0) | 2,771.4 | 2.7 |
| 14 | 48.75 | 0.400 | (13,800) | (672.7) | 2,101.4 | 2.0 |
| 15 | 47.50 | 0.236 | (16,400) | (779.0) | 1,324.4 | 1.3 |
| 16 | 48.00 | 0.261 | 2,500 | 120.0 | 1,445.7 | 1.4 |
| 17 | 46.25 | 0.062 | (19,900) | (920.4) | 526.7 | 0.5 |
| 18 | 48.13 | 0.183 | 12,100 | 582.4 | 1,109.6 | 1.1 |
| 19 | 46.63 | 0.007 | (17,600) | (820.7) | 290.0 | 0.3 |
| 20 | 48.12 | 0.000 | (700) | (33.7) | 256.6 | |

after the price has gone up. It might be termed a buy-high, sell-low scheme! The cost of $240,000 comes from the average difference between the price paid for the stock and the price realized for it.

### Delta of a Portfolio

The delta of a portfolio of options or other derivatives dependent on a single asset whose price is $S$ is

$$\frac{\partial \Pi}{\partial S}$$

where $\Pi$ is the value of the portfolio.

The delta of the portfolio can be calculated from the deltas of the individual options in the portfolio. If a portfolio consists of a quantity $w_i$ of option $i$ ($1 \leqslant i \leqslant n$), the delta of the portfolio

**Table 14.4**  Performance of delta hedging. (The performance measure is the ratio of the standard deviation of the cost of writing the option and hedging it to the theoretical price of the option.)

| Time between hedge rebalancing (weeks) | 5 | 4 | 2 | 1 | 0.5 | 0.25 |
|----------------------------------------|------|------|------|------|------|------|
| Performance measure | 0.43 | 0.39 | 0.26 | 0.19 | 0.14 | 0.09 |

is given by

$$\Delta = \sum_{i=1}^{n} w_i \Delta_i$$

where $\Delta_i$ is the delta of $i$th option. The formula can be used to calculate the position in the underlying asset or in a futures contract on the underlying asset necessary to carry out delta hedging. When this position has been taken, the delta of the portfolio is zero, and the portfolio is referred to as being delta neutral.

Suppose a financial institution in the United States has the following three positions in options on the Australian dollar:

1. A long position in 100,000 call options with strike price 0.55 and an expiration date in three months. The delta of each option is 0.533.
2. A short position in 200,000 call options with strike price 0.56 and an expiration date in five months. The delta of each option is 0.468.
3. A short position in 50,000 put options with strike price 0.56 and an expiration date in two months. The delta of each option is −0.508.

The delta of the whole portfolio is

$$100{,}000 \times 0.533 - 200{,}000 \times 0.468 - 50{,}000 \times (-0.508) = -14{,}900$$

This means that the portfolio can be made delta neutral with a long position of 14,900 Australian dollars.

A six-month forward contract could also be used to achieve delta neutrality in this example. Suppose that the risk-free rate of interest is 8% per annum in Australia and 5% in the United States ($r = 0.05$ and $r_f = 0.08$). The delta of a forward contract maturing at time $T$ on one Australian dollar is $e^{-r_f T}$ or $e^{-0.08 \times 0.5} = 0.9608$. The long position in Australian dollar forward contracts for delta neutrality is therefore $14{,}900/0.9608 = 15{,}508$.

Another alternative is to use a six-month futures contract. From equation (14.4), the long position in Australian dollar futures for delta neutrality is

$$14{,}900 e^{-(0.05-0.08) \times 0.5} = 15{,}125$$

### Transactions Costs

Maintaining a delta-neutral position in a single option and the underlying asset, in the way that has just been described, is liable to be prohibitively expensive because of the transactions costs incurred on trades. For a large portfolio of options, delta neutrality is more feasible. Only one trade in the underlying asset is necessary to zero out delta for the whole portfolio. The hedging transactions costs are absorbed by the profits on many different trades.

## 14.5 THETA

The *theta* of a portfolio of options, $\Theta$, is the rate of change of the value of the portfolio with respect to the passage of time with all else remaining the same. Theta is sometimes referred to as the *time decay* of the portfolio. For a European call option on a non-dividend-paying stock, it can be shown from the Black–Scholes formula that

$$\Theta = -\frac{S_0 N'(d_1)\sigma}{2\sqrt{T}} - rKe^{-rT}N(d_2)$$

where $d_1$ and $d_2$ are defined as in equation (12.20) and

$$N'(x) = \frac{1}{\sqrt{2\pi}}e^{-x^2/2} \qquad (14.5)$$

For a European put option on the stock,

$$\Theta = -\frac{S_0 N'(d_1)\sigma}{2\sqrt{T}} + rKe^{-rT}N(-d_2)$$

For a European call option on an asset paying a dividend at rate $q$,

$$\Theta = -\frac{S_0 N'(d_1)\sigma e^{-qT}}{2\sqrt{T}} + qS_0 N(d_1)e^{-qT} - rKe^{-rT}N(d_2)$$

where $d_1$ and $d_2$ are defined as in equation (13.4), and, for a European put option on the asset,

$$\Theta = -\frac{S_0 N'(d_1)\sigma e^{-qT}}{2\sqrt{T}} - qS_0 N(-d_1)e^{-qT} + rKe^{-rT}N(-d_2)$$

When the asset is a stock index, these last two equations are true with $q$ equal to the dividend yield on the index. When it is a currency, they are true with $q$ equal to the foreign risk-free rate, $r_f$. When it is a futures contract, they are true with $q = r$.

In these formulas time is measured in years. Usually, when theta is quoted, time is measured in days so that theta is the change in the portfolio value when one day passes with all else remaining the same. We can either measure theta "per calendar day" or "per trading day". To obtain the theta per calendar day, the formula for theta must be divided by 365; to obtain theta per trading day, it must be divided by 252. (DerivaGem measures theta per calendar day.)

> **Example 14.3**  Consider a four-month put option on a stock index. The current value of the index is 305, the strike price is 300, the dividend yield is 3% per annum, the risk-free interest rate is 8% per annum, and the volatility of the index is 25% per annum. In this case $S_0 = 305$, $K = 300$, $q = 0.03$, $r = 0.08$, $\sigma = 0.25$, and $T = 0.3333$. The option's theta is
>
> $$-\frac{S_0 N'(d_1)\sigma e^{-qT}}{2\sqrt{T}} - qS_0 N(-d_1)e^{-qT} + rKe^{-rT}N(-d_2) = -18.15$$
>
> The theta is $-18.15/365 = -0.0497$ per calendar day or $-18.15/252 = -0.0720$ per trading day.

Theta is usually negative for an option.[8] This is because as the time to maturity decreases with all else remaining the same, the option tends to become less valuable. The variation of $\Theta$ with stock price for a call option on a stock is shown in Figure 14.5. When the stock price is very low, theta is close to zero. For an at-the-money call option, theta is large and negative. As the

---

[8] An exception to this could be an in-the-money European put option on a non-dividend-paying stock or an in-the-money European call option on a currency with a very high interest rate.

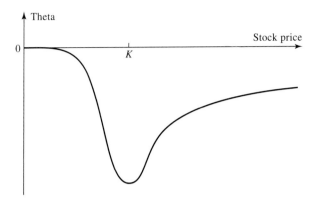

**Figure 14.5**　Variation of theta of a European call option with stock price

stock price becomes larger, theta tends to $-rKe^{-rT}$. Figure 14.6 shows typical patterns for the variation of $\Theta$ with the time to maturity for in-the-money, at-the-money, and out-of-the-money call options.

Theta is not the same type of hedge parameter as delta. There is uncertainty about the future stock price, but there is no uncertainty about the passage of time. It makes sense to hedge against changes in the price of the underlying asset, but it does not make any sense to hedge against the effect of the passage of time on an option portfolio. In spite of this, many traders regard theta as a useful descriptive statistic for a portfolio. This is because, as we will see later, in a delta-neutral portfolio theta is a proxy for gamma.

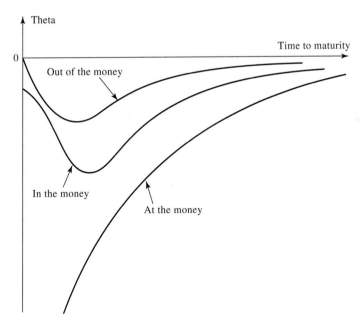

**Figure 14.6**　Typical patterns for variation of theta of a European call option
with time to maturity

## 14.6  GAMMA

The *gamma* of a portfolio of options on an underlying asset, $\Gamma$, is the rate of change of the portfolio's delta with respect to the price of the underlying asset. It is the second partial derivative of the portfolio with respect to asset price:

$$\Gamma = \frac{\partial^2 \Pi}{\partial S^2}$$

If gamma is small, delta changes slowly, and adjustments to keep a portfolio delta neutral need to be made only relatively infrequently. However, if gamma is large in absolute terms, delta is highly sensitive to the price of the underlying asset. It is then quite risky to leave a delta-neutral portfolio unchanged for any length of time. Figure 14.7 illustrates this point. When the stock price moves from $S$ to $S'$, delta hedging assumes that the option price moves from $C$ to $C'$, when in fact it moves from $C$ to $C''$. The difference between $C'$ and $C''$ leads to a hedging error. This error depends on the curvature of the relationship between the option price and the stock price. Gamma measures this curvature.[9]

Suppose that $\delta S$ is the price change of an underlying asset during a small interval of time, $\delta t$, and $\delta \Pi$ is the corresponding price change in the portfolio. If terms of higher order than $\delta t$ are ignored, Appendix 14A shows that, for a delta-neutral portfolio,

$$\delta \Pi = \Theta\, \delta t + \tfrac{1}{2}\Gamma\, \delta S^2 \tag{14.6}$$

where $\Theta$ is the theta of the portfolio. Figure 14.8 shows the nature of this relationship between $\delta \Pi$ and $\delta S$. When gamma is positive, theta tends to be negative. The portfolio declines in value if there is no change in $S$, but increases in value if there is a large positive or negative change in $S$. When gamma is negative, theta tends to be positive and the reverse is true; the portfolio increases in value if there is no change in $S$ but decreases in value if there is a large positive or negative change in $S$. As the absolute value of gamma increases, the sensitivity of the value of the portfolio to $S$ increases.

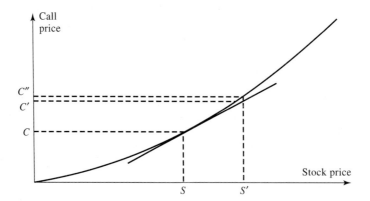

**Figure 14.7**   Hedging error introduced by curvature, or gamma

---

[9] Indeed, the gamma of an option is sometimes referred to as its *curvature* by practitioners.

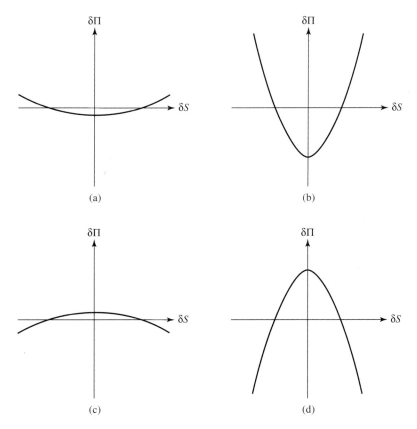

**Figure 14.8** Alternative relationships between $\delta\Pi$ and $\delta S$ for a delta-neutral portfolio: (a) slightly positive gamma, (b) large positive gamma, (c) slightly negative gamma, and (d) large negative gamma

**Example 14.4** Suppose that the gamma of a delta-neutral portfolio of options on an asset is $-10,000$. Equation (14.6) shows that if a change of $+2$ or $-2$ in the price of the asset occurs over a short period of time, there is an unexpected decrease in the value of the portfolio of approximately $0.5 \times 10,000 \times 2^2 = \$20,000$.

### Making a Portfolio Gamma Neutral

A position in the underlying asset itself or a forward contract on the underlying asset both have zero gamma and cannot be used to change the gamma of a portfolio. What is required is a position in an instrument such as an option that is not linearly dependent on the underlying asset.

Suppose that a delta-neutral portfolio has a gamma equal to $\Gamma$, and a traded option has a gamma equal to $\Gamma_T$. If the number of traded options added to the portfolio is $w_T$, the gamma of the portfolio is

$$w_T \Gamma_T + \Gamma$$

Hence, the position in the traded option necessary to make the portfolio gamma neutral is $-\Gamma/\Gamma_T$. Including the traded option is likely to change the delta of the portfolio, so the position in the underlying asset then has to be changed to maintain delta neutrality. Note that the portfolio is gamma neutral only for a short period of time. As time passes, gamma neutrality can be maintained only if the position in the traded option is adjusted so that it is always equal to $-\Gamma/\Gamma_T$.

Making a delta-neutral portfolio gamma neutral can be regarded as a first correction for the fact that the position in the underlying asset cannot be changed continuously when delta hedging is used. Delta neutrality provides protection against relatively small stock price moves between rebalancing. Gamma neutrality provides protection against larger movements in this stock price between hedge rebalancing. Suppose that a portfolio is delta neutral and has a gamma of $-3,000$. The delta and gamma of a particular traded call option are 0.62 and 1.50, respectively. The portfolio can be made gamma neutral by including in the portfolio a long position of

$$\frac{3,000}{1.5} = 2,000$$

However, the delta of the portfolio will then change from zero to $2,000 \times 0.62 = 1,240$. A quantity 1,240 of the underlying asset must therefore be sold from the portfolio to keep it delta neutral.

### Calculation of Gamma

For a European call or put option on a non-dividend-paying stock, the gamma is given by

$$\Gamma = \frac{N'(d_1)}{S_0 \sigma \sqrt{T}}$$

where $d_1$ is defined as in equation (12.20) and $N'(x)$ is as given by equation (14.5). The gamma is always positive and varies with $S_0$ in the way indicated in Figure 14.9. The variation of gamma with time to maturity for out-of-the-money, at-the-money, and in-the-money options is shown in Figure 14.10. For an at-the-money option, gamma increases as the time to maturity decreases. Short-life at-the-money options have very high gammas, which means that the value of the option holder's position is highly sensitive to jumps in the stock price.

For a European call or put option on an asset paying a continuous dividend at rate $q$,

$$\Gamma = \frac{N'(d_1)e^{-qT}}{S_0 \sigma \sqrt{T}}$$

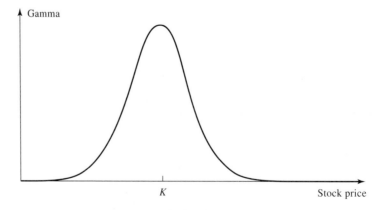

**Figure 14.9**   Variation of gamma with stock price for an option

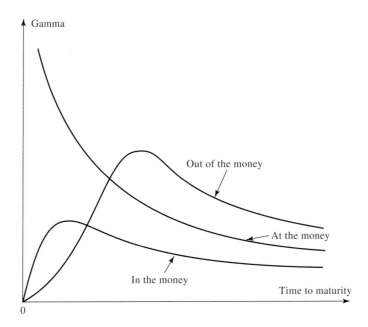

**Figure 14.10**  Variation of gamma with time to maturity for a stock option

where $d_1$ is as in equation (13.4). When the asset is a stock index, $q$ is set equal to the dividend yield on the index. When it is a currency, $q$ is set equal to the foreign risk-free rate, $r_f$. When it is a futures contract, $q = r$.

**Example 14.5**  Consider a four-month put option on a stock index. The current value of the index is 305, the strike price is 300, the dividend yield is 3% per annum, the risk-free interest rate is 8% per annum, and volatility of the index is 25% per annum. In this case, $S_0 = 305$, $K = 300$, $q = 0.03$, $r = 0.08$, $\sigma = 0.25$, and $T = 4/12$. The gamma of the index option is given by

$$\frac{N'(d_1)e^{-qT}}{S_0 \sigma \sqrt{T}} = 0.00866$$

Thus, an increase of 1 in the index (from 305 to 306) increases the delta of the option by approximately 0.00866.

## 14.7  RELATIONSHIP BETWEEN DELTA, THETA, AND GAMMA

The price of a single derivative dependent on a non-dividend-paying stock must satisfy the differential equation (12.15). It follows that the value of a portfolio of such derivatives, $\Pi$, also satisfies the differential equation

$$\frac{\partial \Pi}{\partial t} + rS\frac{\partial \Pi}{\partial S} + \tfrac{1}{2}\sigma^2 S^2 \frac{\partial^2 \Pi}{\partial S^2} = r\Pi$$

Since

$$\Theta = \frac{\partial \Pi}{\partial t}, \qquad \Delta = \frac{\partial \Pi}{\partial S}, \qquad \Gamma = \frac{\partial^2 \Pi}{\partial S^2}$$

it follows that

$$\Theta + rS\Delta + \tfrac{1}{2}\sigma^2 S^2 \Gamma = r\Pi \qquad\qquad (14.7)$$

Similar results can be produced for other underlying assets (see Problem 14.19).

For a delta-neutral portfolio, $\Delta = 0$ and

$$\Theta + \tfrac{1}{2}\sigma^2 S^2 \Gamma = r\Pi$$

This shows that, when $\Theta$ is large and positive, gamma tends to be large and negative, and vice versa. This is consistent with the way in which Figure 14.8 has been drawn and explains why theta can be regarded as a proxy for gamma in a delta-neutral portfolio.

## 14.8  VEGA

Up to now, we have implicitly assumed that the volatility of the asset underlying a derivative is constant. In practice, volatilities change over time. This means that the value of a derivative is liable to change because of movements in volatility as well as because of changes in the asset price and the passage of time.

The *vega* of a portfolio of derivatives, $\mathcal{V}$, is the rate of change of the value of the portfolio with respect to the volatility of the underlying asset:[10]

$$\mathcal{V} = \frac{\partial \Pi}{\partial \sigma}$$

If vega is high in absolute terms, the portfolio's value is very sensitive to small changes in volatility. If vega is low in absolute terms, volatility changes have relatively little impact on the value of the portfolio.

A position in the underlying asset has zero vega. However, the vega of a portfolio can be changed by adding a position in a traded option. If $\mathcal{V}$ is the vega of the portfolio and $\mathcal{V}_T$ is the vega of a traded option, a position of $-\mathcal{V}/\mathcal{V}_T$ in the traded option makes the portfolio instantaneously vega neutral. Unfortunately, a portfolio that is gamma neutral will not in general be vega neutral, and vice versa. If a hedger requires a portfolio to be both gamma and vega neutral, at least two traded derivatives dependent on the underlying asset must usually be used.

> **Example 14.6**  Consider a portfolio that is delta neutral, with a gamma of $-5{,}000$ and a vega of $-8{,}000$. A traded option has a gamma of 0.5, a vega of 2.0, and a delta of 0.6. The portfolio can be made vega neutral by including a long position in 4,000 traded options. This would increase delta to 2,400 and require that 2,400 units of the asset be sold to maintain delta neutrality. The gamma of the portfolio would change from $-5{,}000$ to $-3{,}000$.
>
> To make the portfolio gamma and vega neutral, we suppose that there is a second traded option with a gamma of 0.8, a vega of 1.2, and a delta of 0.5. If $w_1$ and $w_2$ are the quantities of the two

---

[10]  Vega is the name given to one of the "Greek letters" in option pricing, but it is not one of the letters in the Greek alphabet.

traded options included in the portfolio, we require that

$$-5{,}000 + 0.5w_1 + 0.8w_2 = 0$$
$$-8{,}000 + 2.0w_1 + 1.2w_2 = 0$$

The solution to these equations is $w_1 = 400$, $w_2 = 6{,}000$. The portfolio can therefore be made gamma and vega neutral by including 400 of the first traded option and 6,000 of the second traded option. The delta of the portfolio after the addition of the positions in the two traded options is $400 \times 0.6 + 6{,}000 \times 0.5 = 3{,}240$. Hence, 3,240 units of the asset would have to be sold to maintain delta neutrality.

For a European call or put option on a non-dividend-paying stock, vega is given by

$$\mathcal{V} = S_0 \sqrt{T}\, N'(d_1)$$

where $d_1$ is defined as in equation (12.20). The formula for $N'(x)$ is given by equation (14.5). For a European call or put option on an asset providing a dividend yield at rate $q$,

$$\mathcal{V} = S_0 \sqrt{T}\, N'(d_1)e^{-qT}$$

where $d_1$ is defined as in equation (13.4). When the asset is a stock index, $q$ is set equal to the dividend yield on the index. When it is a currency, $q$ is set equal to the foreign risk-free rate, $r_f$. When it is a futures contract, $q = r$.

The vega of a regular European or American option is always positive. The general way in which vega varies with $S_0$ is shown in Figure 14.11.

**Example 14.7**  Consider a four-month put option on a stock index. The current value of the index is 305, the strike price is 300, the dividend yield is 3% per annum, the risk-free interest rate is 8% per annum, and the volatility of the index is 25% per annum. In this case, $S_0 = 305$, $K = 300$, $q = 0.03$, $r = 0.08$, $\sigma = 0.25$, and $T = 4/12$. The option's vega is given by

$$S_0 \sqrt{T} N'(d_1)e^{-qT} = 66.44$$

Thus a 1% (0.01) increase in volatility (from 25% to 26%) increases the value of the option by approximately 0.6644 ($= 0.01 \times 66.44$).

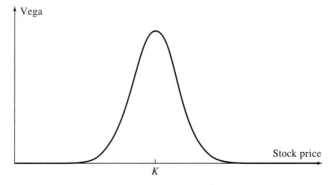

**Figure 14.11**  Variation of vega with stock price for an option

Calculating vega from the Black–Scholes model and its extensions may seem strange because one of the assumptions underlying Black–Scholes is that volatility is constant. It would be theoretically more correct to calculate vega from a model in which volatility is assumed to be stochastic. However, it turns out that the vega calculated from a stochastic volatility model is very similar to the Black–Scholes vega so the practice of calculating vega from a model in which volatility is constant works reasonably well.[11]

Gamma neutrality protects against large changes in the price of the underlying asset between hedge rebalancing. Vega neutrality protects for a variable $\sigma$. As might be expected, whether it is best to use an available traded option for vega or gamma hedging depends on the time between hedge rebalancing and the volatility of the volatility.[12]

## 14.9 RHO

The *rho* of a portfolio of options is the rate of change of the value of the portfolio with respect to the interest rate:

$$\text{rho} = \frac{\partial \Pi}{\partial r}$$

It measures the sensitivity of the value of a portfolio to interest rates. For a European call option on a non-dividend-paying stock,

$$\text{rho} = KTe^{-rT}N(d_2)$$

where $d_2$ is defined as in equation (12.20). For a European put option,

$$\text{rho} = -KTe^{-rT}N(-d_2)$$

These same formulas apply to European call and put options on stocks and stock indices paying known dividend yields when $d_2$ is as in equation (13.4).

> **Example 14.8** Consider a four-month put option on a stock index. The current value of the index is 305, the strike price is 300, the dividend yield is 3% per annum, the risk-free interest rate is 8% per annum, and the volatility of the index is 25% per annum. In this case $S_0 = 305$, $K = 300$, $q = 0.03$, $r = 0.08$, $\sigma = 0.25$, and $T = 4/12$. The option's rho is
>
> $$-KTe^{-rT}N(-d_2) = -42.6$$
>
> This means that for a 1% (0.01) change in the risk-free interest rate (from 8% to 9%) the value of the option decreases by 0.426 ($= 0.01 \times 42.6$).

In the case of currency options, there are two rhos corresponding to the two interest rates. The rho corresponding to the domestic interest rate is given by the formulas already presented, with $d_2$ as in

---

[11] See J. C. Hull and A. White, "The Pricing of Options on Assets with Stochastic Volatilities," *Journal of Finance*, 42 (June 1987), 281–300; J. C. Hull and A. White, "An Analysis of the Bias in Option Pricing Caused by a Stochastic Volatility," *Advances in Futures and Options Research*, 3 (1988), 27–61.

[12] For a discussion of this issue, see J. C. Hull and A. White, "Hedging the Risks from Writing Foreign Currency Options," *Journal of International Money and Finance*, 6 (June 1987), 131–52.

equation (13.9). The rho corresponding to the foreign interest rate for a European call on a currency is

$$\text{rho} = -Te^{-r_f T} S_0 N(d_1)$$

and for a European put it is

$$\text{rho} = Te^{-r_f T} S_0 N(-d_1)$$

where $d_1$ is given by equation (13.9).

For a European call futures option rho is $-cT$ and for a European put futures option rho is $-pT$, where $c$ and $p$ are the European call and put futures option prices, respectively.

## 14.10   HEDGING IN PRACTICE

In an ideal world, traders working for financial institutions would be able to rebalance their portfolios very frequently in order to maintain a zero delta, a zero gamma, a zero vega, and so on. In practice, this is not possible. When managing a large portfolio dependent on a single underlying asset, traders usually zero out delta at least once a day by trading the underlying asset. Unfortunately, a zero gamma and a zero vega are less easy to achieve because it is difficult to find options or other nonlinear derivatives that can be traded in the volume required at competitive prices. In most cases, gamma and vega are monitored. When they get too large in a positive or negative direction, either corrective action is taken or trading is curtailed.

There are big economies of scale in being an options trader. As noted earlier, maintaining delta neutrality for an individual option on, say, the S&P 500 by trading daily would be prohibitively expensive. But it is realistic to do this for a portfolio of several hundred options on the S&P 500. This is because the cost of daily rebalancing (either by trading the stocks underlying the index or by trading index futures) is covered by the profit on many different trades.

In many markets financial institutions find that the majority of their trades are sales of call and put options to their clients. Short calls and short puts have negative gammas and negative vegas. It follows that, as time goes by, both the gamma and vega of a financial institution's portfolio tend to become progressively more negative. Traders working for the financial institution are then always looking for ways to buy options (i.e., acquire positive gamma and vega) at competitive prices. There is one aspect of an options portfolio that mitigates this problem somewhat. Options are often close to the money when they are first sold, so that they have relatively high gammas and vegas. But after some time has elapsed, they tend to become deep out of the money or deep in the money. In such cases their gammas and vegas become very small and of little consequence. The worst situation for an options trader is that written options remain very close to the money right up until maturity.

## 14.11   SCENARIO ANALYSIS

In addition to monitoring risks such as delta, gamma, and vega, option traders often also carry out a scenario analysis. The analysis involves calculating the gain or loss on their portfolio over a specified period under a variety of different scenarios. The time period chosen is likely to depend on the liquidity of the instruments. The scenarios can be either chosen by management or generated by a model.

Consider a bank with a portfolio of options on a foreign currency. There are two main variables

**Table 14.5**  Profit or loss realized in two weeks under different scenarios (millions of dollars)

| | *Exchange rate* | | | | | | |
| --- | --- | --- | --- | --- | --- | --- | --- |
| *Volatility* | *0.94* | *0.96* | *0.98* | *1.00* | *1.02* | *1.04* | *1.06* |
| 8% | +102 | +55 | +25 | +6 | −10 | −34 | −80 |
| 10% | +80 | +40 | +17 | +2 | −14 | −38 | −85 |
| 12% | +60 | +25 | +9 | −2 | −18 | −42 | −90 |

on which the value of the portfolio depends. These are the exchange rate and the exchange rate volatility. Suppose that the exchange rate is currently 1.0000 and its volatility is 10% per annum. The bank could calculate a table such as Table 14.5 showing the profit or loss experienced during a two-week period under different scenarios. This table considers seven different exchange rates and three different volatilities. Because a one-standard-deviation move in the exchange rate during a two-week period is about 0.02, the exchange rate moves considered are approximately one, two, and three standard deviations.

In Table 14.5 the greatest loss is in the lower right corner of the table. The loss corresponds to the volatility increasing to 12% and the exchange rate moving up to 1.06. Usually the greatest loss in a table such as this occurs at one of the corners, but this is not always so. Consider, for example, the situation where a bank's portfolio consists of a reverse butterfly spread (see Section 9.2). The greatest loss will be experienced if the exchange rate stays where it is.

## 14.12  PORTFOLIO INSURANCE

A portfolio manager is often interested in acquiring a put option on his or her portfolio. This provides protection against market declines while preserving the potential for a gain if the market does well. One approach (discussed in Chapter 13) is to buy put options on a market index such as the S&P 500. An alternative is to create the option synthetically.

Creating an option synthetically involves maintaining a position in the underlying asset (or futures on the underlying asset) so that the delta of the position is equal to the delta of the required option. The position necessary to create an option synthetically is the reverse of that necessary to hedge it. This is because the procedure for hedging an option involves the creation of an equal and opposite option synthetically.

There are two reasons why it may be more attractive for the portfolio manager to create the required put option synthetically than to buy it in the market. The first is that options markets do not always have the liquidity to absorb the trades that managers of large funds would like to carry out. The second is that fund managers often require strike prices and exercise dates that are different from those available in exchange-traded options markets.

The synthetic option can be created from trading the portfolio or from trading in index futures contracts. We first examine the creation of a put option by trading the portfolio. Recall that the delta of a European put on the portfolio is

$$\Delta = e^{-qT}[N(d_1) - 1] \tag{14.8}$$

where, with our usual notation,

$$d_1 = \frac{\ln(S_0/K) + (r - q + \sigma^2/2)T}{\sigma\sqrt{T}}$$

$S_0$ is the value of the portfolio, $K$ is the strike price, $r$ is the risk-free rate, $q$ is the dividend yield on the portfolio, $\sigma$ is the volatility of the portfolio, and $T$ is the life of the option.

To create the put option synthetically, the fund manager should ensure that at any given time a proportion

$$e^{-qT}[1 - N(d_1)]$$

of the stocks in the original portfolio has been sold and the proceeds invested in riskless assets. As the value of the original portfolio declines, the delta of the put given by equation (14.8) becomes more negative and the proportion of the original portfolio sold must be increased. As the value of the original portfolio increases, the delta of the put becomes less negative and the proportion of the original portfolio sold must be decreased (i.e., some of the original portfolio must be repurchased).

Using this strategy to create portfolio insurance means that at any given time funds are divided between the stock portfolio on which insurance is required and riskless assets. As the value of the stock portfolio increases, riskless assets are sold and the position in the stock portfolio is increased. As the value of the stock portfolio declines, the position in the stock portfolio is decreased and riskless assets are purchased. The cost of the insurance arises from the fact that the portfolio manager is always selling after a decline in the market and buying after a rise in the market.

**Example 14.9**  A portfolio is worth $90 million. To protect against market downturns, the managers of the portfolio require a six-month European put option on the portfolio with a strike price of $87 million. The risk-free rate is 9% per annum, the dividend yield is 3% per annum, and the volatility of the portfolio is 25% per annum. The S&P 500 index stands at 900. As the portfolio is considered to mimic the S&P 500 fairly closely, one alternative is to buy 1,000 put option contracts on the S&P 500 with a strike price of 870. Another alternative is to create the option synthetically. In this case, $S_0 = 90$ million, $K = 87$ million, $r = 0.09$, $q = 0.03$, $\sigma = 0.25$, and $T = 0.5$, so that

$$d_1 = \frac{\ln(90/87) + (0.09 - 0.03 + 0.25^2/2)0.5}{0.25\sqrt{0.5}} = 0.4499$$

and the delta of the required option is initially

$$e^{-qT}[N(d_1) - 1] = -0.3215$$

This shows that 32.15% of the portfolio should be sold initially to match the delta of the required option. The amount of the portfolio sold must be monitored frequently. For example, if the value of the portfolio reduces to $88 million after one day, the delta of the required option changes to $-0.3679$ and a further 4.64% of the original portfolio should be sold. If the value of the portfolio increases to $92 million, the delta of the required option changes to $-0.2787$ and 4.28% of the original portfolio should be repurchased.

### Use of Index Futures

Using index futures to create options synthetically can be preferable to using the underlying stocks because the transactions costs associated with trades in index futures are generally lower than those associated with the corresponding trades in the underlying stocks. The dollar amount of the futures contracts shorted as a proportion of the value of the portfolio should from equations (14.3) and (14.8) be

$$e^{-qT}e^{-(r-q)T^*}[1 - N(d_1)] = e^{q(T^*-T)}e^{-rT^*}[1 - N(d_1)]$$

where $T^*$ is the maturity time of the futures contract. If the portfolio is worth $K_1$ times the index and each index futures contract is on $K_2$ times the index, the number of futures contracts shorted at any given time should be

$$e^{q(T^*-T)}e^{-rT^*}[1 - N(d_1)]\frac{K_1}{K_2}$$

**Example 14.10**   Suppose that in the previous example futures contracts on the S&P 500 maturing in nine months are used to create the option synthetically. In this case, initially $T = 0.5$, $T^* = 0.75$, $K_1 = 100,000$, $K_2 = 250$, and $d_1 = 0.4499$, so that the number of futures contracts shorted should be

$$e^{q(T^*-T)}e^{-rT^*}[1 - N(d_1)]\frac{K_1}{K_2} = 123.2$$

or 123 rounding to the nearest whole number. As time passes and index changes, the position in futures contracts must be adjusted.

Up to now we have assumed that the portfolio mirrors the index. As discussed in Section 13.3, the hedging scheme can be adjusted to deal with other situations. The strike price for the options used should be the expected level of the market index when the portfolio's value reaches its insured value. The number of index options used should be $\beta$ times the number of options that would be required if the portfolio had a beta of 1.0. The volatility of portfolio can be assumed to be its beta times the volatility of an appropriate well-diversified index.

### October 19, 1987

Creating put options on the index synthetically does not work well if the volatility of the index changes rapidly or if the index exhibits large jumps. On Monday, October 19, 1987, the Dow Jones Industrial Average dropped by more than 20%. Portfolio managers who had insured themselves by buying put options in the exchange-traded or over-the-counter market survived this crash well. Those who had chosen to create put options synthetically found that they were unable to sell either stocks or index futures fast enough to protect their position.

### Brady Commission Report

The report of the Brady Commission on the October 19, 1987, crash provides interesting insights into the effect of portfolio insurance on the market at that time.[13] The Brady Commission estimated that $60 billion to $90 billion of equity assets were under portfolio insurance administration in October 1987. During the period Wednesday, October 14, 1987, to Friday, October 16, 1987, the market declined by about 10%, with much of this decline taking place on Friday afternoon. The decline should have generated at least $12 billion of equity or index futures sales as a result of portfolio insurance schemes.[14] In fact, less than $4 billion were sold, which means that portfolio insurers approached the following week with huge amounts of selling already

---

[13] See "Report of the Presidential Task Force on Market Mechanisms," January 1988.

[14] To put this in perspective, on Monday, October 19, 1987, all previous records were broken when 604 million shares worth $21 billion were traded on the New York Stock Exchange. Approximately $20 billion of S&P 500 futures contracts were traded on that day.

dictated by their models. The Brady Commission estimated that on Monday, October 19 sell programs by three portfolio insurers accounted for almost 10% of the sales on the New York Stock Exchange, and that portfolio insurance sales amounted to 21.3% of all sales in index futures markets. It seems likely that portfolio insurance caused some downward pressure on the market.

Because the market declined so fast and the stock exchange systems were overloaded, many portfolio insurers were unable to execute the trades generated by their models and failed to obtain the protection they required. Needless to say, the popularity of portfolio insurance schemes based on dynamic trading in stocks and futures has declined considerably since October 1987.

## 14.13 STOCK MARKET VOLATILITY

We have already considered the issue of whether volatility is caused solely by the arrival of new information or whether trading itself generates volatility. Portfolio insurance schemes such as those just described have the potential to increase volatility. When the market declines, they cause portfolio managers either to sell stock or to sell index futures contracts. Either action may accentuate the decline. The sale of stock is liable to drive down the market index further in a direct way. The sale of index futures contracts is liable to drive down futures prices. This creates selling pressure on stocks via the mechanism of index arbitrage (see Chapter 3), so that the market index is liable to be driven down in this case as well. Similarly, when the market rises, the portfolio insurance schemes cause portfolio managers either to buy stock or to buy futures contracts. This may accentuate the rise.

In addition to formal portfolio insurance schemes, we can speculate that many investors consciously or subconsciously follow portfolio insurance schemes of their own. For example, an investor may be inclined to enter the market when it is rising but will sell when it is falling to limit the downside risk.

Whether portfolio insurance schemes (formal or informal) affect volatility depends on how easily the market can absorb the trades that are generated by portfolio insurance. If portfolio insurance trades are a very small fraction of all trades, there is likely to be no effect. As portfolio insurance becomes more popular, it is liable to have a destabilizing effect on the market.

## SUMMARY

Financial institutions offer a variety of option products to their clients. Often the options do not correspond to the standardized products traded by exchanges. The financial institutions are then faced with the problem of hedging their exposure. Naked and covered positions leave them subject to an unacceptable level of risk. One course of action that is sometimes proposed is a stop-loss strategy. This involves holding a naked position when an option is out of the money and converting it to a covered position as soon as the option moves into the money. Although superficially attractive, the strategy does not work at all well.

The delta of an option, $\Delta$, is the rate of change of its price with respect to the price of the underlying asset. Delta hedging involves creating a position with zero delta (sometimes referred to as a delta-neutral position). Because the delta of the underlying asset is 1.0, one way of hedging is to take a position of $-\Delta$ in the underlying asset for each long option being hedged.

The delta of an option changes over time. This means that the position in the underlying asset has to be frequently adjusted.

Once an option position has been made delta neutral, the next stage is often to look at its gamma. The gamma of an option is the rate of change of its delta with respect to the price of the underlying asset. It is a measure of the curvature of the relationship between the option price and the asset price. The impact of this curvature on the performance of delta hedging can be reduced by making an option position gamma neutral. If $\Gamma$ is the gamma of the position being hedged, this reduction is usually achieved by taking a position in a traded option that has a gamma of $-\Gamma$.

Delta and gamma hedging are both based on the assumption that the volatility of the underlying asset is constant. In practice, volatilities do change over time. The vega of an option or an option portfolio measures the rate of change of its value with respect to volatility. A trader who wishes to hedge an option position against volatility changes can make the position vega neutral. As with the procedure for creating gamma neutrality, this usually involves taking an offsetting position in a traded option. If the trader wishes to achieve both gamma and vega neutrality, two traded options are usually required.

Two other measures of the risk of an option position are theta and rho. Theta measures the rate of change of the value of the position with respect to the passage of time, with all else remaining constant. Rho measures the rate of change of the value of the position with respect to the short-term interest rate, with all else remaining constant.

In practice, option traders usually rebalance their portfolios at least once a day to maintain delta neutrality. It is usually not feasible to maintain gamma and vega neutrality on a regular basis. Typically a trader monitors these measures. If they get too large, either corrective action is taken or trading is curtailed.

Portfolio managers are sometimes interested in creating put options synthetically for the purposes of insuring an equity portfolio. They can do so either by trading the portfolio or by trading index futures on the portfolio. Trading the portfolio involves splitting the portfolio between equities and risk-free securities. As the market declines, more is invested in risk-free securities. As the market increases, more is invested in equities. Trading index futures involves keeping the equity portfolio intact and selling index futures. As the market declines, more index futures are sold; as it rises, fewer are sold. The strategy works well in normal market conditions. On Monday, October 19, 1987, when the Dow Jones Industrial Average dropped by more than 500 points, it worked badly. Portfolio insurers were unable to sell either stocks or index futures fast enough to protect their positions. As a result the popularity of such schemes has declined sharply.

## SUGGESTIONS FOR FURTHER READING

### On hedging option positions

Boyle, P. P., and D. Emanuel, "Discretely Adjusted Option Hedges," *Journal of Financial Economics*, 8 (1980), 259–82.

Figlewski, S., "Options Arbitrage in Imperfect Markets," *Journal of Finance*, 44 (December 1989), 1289–1311.

Galai, D., "The Components of the Return from Hedging Options against Stocks," *Journal of Business*, 56 (January 1983), 45–54.

Hull, J. C., and A. White, "Hedging the Risks from Writing Foreign Currency Options," *Journal of International Money and Finance*, 6 (June 1987), 131–52.

### On portfolio insurance

Asay, M., and C. Edelberg, "Can a Dynamic Strategy Replicate the Returns on an Option?" *Journal of Futures Markets*, 6 (Spring 1986), 63–70.

Bookstaber, R., and J. A. Langsam, "Portfolio Insurance Trading Rules," *Journal of Futures Markets*, 8 (February 1988), 15–31.

Etzioni, E. S., "Rebalance Disciplines for Portfolio Insurance," *Journal of Portfolio Insurance*, 13 (Fall 1986), 59–62.

Leland, H. E., "Option Pricing and Replication with Transactions Costs," *Journal of Finance*, 40 (December 1985), 1283–1301.

Leland, H. E., "Who Should Buy Portfolio Insurance?" *Journal of Finance*, 35 (May 1980), 581–94.

Rubinstein, M., "Alternative Paths for Portfolio Insurance," *Financial Analysts Journal*, 41 (July/August 1985), 42–52.

Rubinstein, M., and H. E. Leland, "Replicating Options with Positions in Stock and Cash," *Financial Analysts Journal*, 37 (July/August 1981), 63–72.

Tilley, J. A., and G. O. Latainer, "A Synthetic Option Framework for Asset Allocation," *Financial Analysts Journal*, 41 (May/June 1985), 32–41.

## QUESTIONS AND PROBLEMS
## (ANSWERS IN SOLUTIONS MANUAL)

14.1. Explain how a stop-loss hedging scheme can be implemented for the writer of an out-of-the-money call option. Why does it provide a relatively poor hedge?

14.2. What does it mean to assert that the delta of a call option is 0.7? How can a short position in 1,000 options be made delta neutral when the delta of each option is 0.7?

14.3. Calculate the delta of an at-the-money six-month European call option on a non-dividend-paying stock when the risk-free interest rate is 10% per annum and the stock price volatility is 25% per annum.

14.4. What does it mean to assert that the theta of an option position is −0.1 when time is measured in years? If a trader feels that neither a stock price nor its implied volatility will change, what type of option position is appropriate?

14.5. What is meant by the gamma of an option position? What are the risks in the situation where the gamma of a position is large and negative and the delta is zero?

14.6. "The procedure for creating an option position synthetically is the reverse of the procedure for hedging the option position." Explain this statement.

14.7. Why did portfolio insurance not work well on October 19, 1987?

14.8. The Black–Scholes price of an out-of-the-money call option with an exercise price of $40 is $4. A trader who has written the option plans to use a stop-loss strategy. The trader's plan is to buy at $40.10 and to sell at $39.90. Estimate the expected number of times the stock will be bought or sold.

14.9. Suppose that a stock price is currently $20 and that a call option with an exercise price of $25 is created synthetically using a continually changing position in the stock. Consider the following two scenarios:

   a. Stock price increases steadily from $20 to $35 during the life of the option
   b. Stock price oscillates wildly, ending up at $35

   Which scenario would make the synthetically created option more expensive? Explain your answer.

14.10. What is the delta of a short position in 1,000 European call options on silver futures? The options mature in eight months, and the futures contract underlying the option matures in nine months. The current nine-month futures price is $8 per ounce, the exercise price of the options is $8, the risk-free interest rate is 12% per annum, and the volatility of silver is 18% per annum.

14.11. In Problem 14.10, what initial position in nine-month silver futures is necessary for delta hedging? If silver itself is used, what is the initial position? If one-year silver futures are used, what is the initial position? Assume no storage costs for silver.

14.12. A company uses delta hedging to hedge a portfolio of long positions in put and call options on a currency. Which of the following would give the most favorable result?

   a. A virtually constant spot rate
   b. Wild movements in the spot rate

   Explain your answer.

14.13. Repeat Problem 14.12 for a financial institution with a portfolio of short positions in put and call options for a currency.

14.14. A financial institution has just sold 1,000 seven-month European call options on the Japanese yen. Suppose that the spot exchange rate is 0.80 cents per yen, the exercise price is 0.81 cents per yen, the risk-free interest rate in the United States is 8% per annum, the risk-free interest rate in Japan is 5% per annum, and the volatility of the yen is 15% per annum. Calculate the delta, gamma, vega, theta, and rho of the financial institution's position. Interpret each number.

14.15. Under what circumstances is it possible to make a European option on a stock index both gamma neutral and vega neutral by adding a position in one other European option?

14.16. A fund manager has a well-diversified portfolio that mirrors the performance of the S&P 500 and is worth $360 million. The value of the S&P 500 is 1,200, and the portfolio manager would like to buy insurance against a reduction of more than 5% in the value of the portfolio over the next six months. The risk-free interest rate is 6% per annum. The dividend yield on both the portfolio and the S&P 500 is 3%, and the volatility of the index is 30% per annum.

   a. If the fund manager buys traded European put options, how much would the insurance cost?
   b. Explain carefully alternative strategies open to the fund manager involving traded European call options, and show that they lead to the same result.
   c. If the fund manager decides to provide insurance by keeping part of the portfolio in risk-free securities, what should the initial position be?
   d. If the fund manager decides to provide insurance by using nine-month index futures, what should the initial position be?

14.17. Repeat Problem 14.16 on the assumption that the portfolio has a beta of 1.5. Assume that the dividend yield on the portfolio is 4% per annum.

14.18. Show by substituting for the various terms in equation (14.7) that the equation is true for:

   a. A single European call option on a non-dividend-paying stock
   b. A single European put option on a non-dividend-paying stock
   c. Any portfolio of European put and call options on a non-dividend-paying stock

14.19. What is the equation corresponding to equation (14.7) for (a) a portfolio of derivatives on a currency and (b) a portfolio of derivatives on a futures contract?

14.20. Suppose that $70 billion of equity assets are the subject of portfolio insurance schemes. Assume that the schemes are designed to provide insurance against the value of the assets declining by more than 5% within one year. Making whatever estimates you find necessary, use the DerivaGem software to calculate the value of the stock or futures contracts that the administrators of the portfolio insurance schemes will attempt to sell if the market falls by 23% in a single day.

14.21. Does a forward contract on a stock index have the same delta as the corresponding futures contract? Explain your answer.

14.22. A bank's position in options on the dollar–euro exchange rate has a delta of 30,000 and a gamma of −80,000. Explain how these numbers can be interpreted. The exchange rate (dollars per euro) is 0.90. What position would you take to make the position delta neutral? After a short period of time, the exchange rate moves to 0.93. Estimate the new delta. What additional trade is necessary to keep the position delta neutral? Assuming the bank did set up a delta-neutral position originally, has it gained or lost money from the exchange rate movement?

14.23. Use the put–call parity relationship to derive, for a non-dividend-paying stock, the relationship between:
   a. The delta of a European call and the delta of a European put
   b. The gamma of a European call and the gamma of a European put
   c. The vega of a European call and the vega of a European put
   d. The theta of a European call and the theta of a European put

# ASSIGNMENT QUESTIONS

14.24. Consider a one-year European call option on a stock when the stock price is $30, the strike price is $30, the risk-free rate is 5%, and the volatility is 25% per annum. Use the DerivaGem software to calculate the price, delta, gamma, vega, theta, and rho of the option. Verify that delta is correct by changing the stock price to $30.1 and recomputing the option price. Verify that gamma is correct by recomputing the delta for the situation where the stock price is $30.1. Carry out similar calculations to verify that vega, theta, and rho are correct. Use the DerivaGem Applications Builder functions to plot the option price, delta, gamma, vega, theta, and rho against the stock price for the stock option.

14.25. A financial institution has the following portfolio of over-the-counter options on sterling:

| Type | Position | Delta of option | Gamma of option | Vega of option |
|------|----------|-----------------|-----------------|----------------|
| Call | −1,000 | 0.50 | 2.2 | 1.8 |
| Call | −500 | 0.80 | 0.6 | 0.2 |
| Put | −2,000 | −0.40 | 1.3 | 0.7 |
| Call | −500 | 0.70 | 1.8 | 1.4 |

A traded option is available with a delta of 0.6, a gamma of 1.5, and a vega of 0.8.
   a. What position in the traded option and in sterling would make the portfolio both gamma neutral and delta neutral?
   b. What position in the traded option and in sterling would make the portfolio both vega neutral and delta neutral?

14.26. Consider again the situation in Problem 14.25. Suppose that a second traded option with a delta of 0.1, a gamma of 0.5, and a vega of 0.6 is available. How could the portfolio be made delta, gamma, and vega neutral?

14.27. A deposit instrument offered by a bank guarantees that investors will receive a return during a six-month period that is the greater of (a) zero and (b) 40% of the return provided by a market index. An investor is planning to put $100,000 in the instrument. Describe the payoff as an option on the index. Assuming that the risk-free rate of interest is 8% per annum, the dividend yield on the index is 3% per annum, and the volatility of the index is 25% per annum, is the product a good deal for the investor?

14.28. The formula for the price of a European call futures option in terms of the futures price, $F_0$, is from Chapter 13

$$c = e^{-rT}[F_0 N(d_1) - KN(d_2)]$$

where

$$d_1 = \frac{\ln(F_0/K) + \sigma^2 T/2}{\sigma\sqrt{T}}, \qquad d_2 = d_1 - \sigma\sqrt{T}$$

and $K$, $r$, $T$, and $\sigma$ are the strike price, interest rate, time to maturity, and volatility, respectively.
   a. Prove that $F_0 N'(d_1) = KN'(d_2)$.
   b. Prove that the delta of the call price with respect to the futures price is $e^{-rT}N(d_1)$.
   c. Prove that the vega of the call price is $F_0\sqrt{T}N'(d_1)e^{-rT}$.
   d. Prove the formula for the rho of a call futures option given at the end of Section 14.9. The delta, gamma, theta, and vega of a call futures option are the same as those for a call option on a stock paying dividends at rate $q$, with $q$ replaced by $r$ and $S_0$ replaced by $F_0$. Explain why the same is not true of the rho of a call futures option.

14.29. Use DerivaGem to check that equation (14.7) is satisfied for the option considered in Section 14.1. (*Note*: DerivaGem produces a value of theta "per calendar day". The theta in equation (14.7) is "per year".)

14.30. Use the DerivaGem Application Builder functions to reproduce Table 14.2. (Note that in Table 14.2 the stock position is rounded to the nearest 100 shares.) Calculate the gamma and theta of the position each week. Calculate the change in the value of the portfolio each week and check whether equation (14.6) is approximately satisfied. (*Note*: DerivaGem produces a value of theta "per calendar day". The theta in equation (14.6) is "per year".)

# APPENDIX 14A
## Taylor Series Expansions and Hedge Parameters

A Taylor series expansion of the change in the portfolio value in a short period of time shows the role played by different Greek letters. If the volatility of the underlying asset is assumed to be constant, the value of the portfolio, $\Pi$, is a function of the asset price $S$ and time $t$. The Taylor series expansion gives

$$\delta\Pi = \frac{\partial\Pi}{\partial S}\,\delta S + \frac{\partial\Pi}{\partial t}\,\delta t + \tfrac{1}{2}\frac{\partial^2\Pi}{\partial S^2}\,\delta S^2 + \tfrac{1}{2}\frac{\partial^2\Pi}{\partial t^2}\,\delta t^2 + \frac{\partial^2\Pi}{\partial S\,\partial t}\,\delta S\,\delta t + \cdots \qquad (14A.1)$$

where $\delta\Pi$ and $\delta S$ are the change in $\Pi$ and $S$ in a small time interval $\delta t$. Delta hedging eliminates the first term on the right-hand side. The second term is nonstochastic. The third term (which is of order $\delta t$) can be made zero by ensuring that the portfolio is gamma neutral as well as delta neutral. Other terms are of higher order than $\delta t$.

For a delta-neutral portfolio, the first term on the right-hand side of equation (14A.1) is zero, so that

$$\delta\Pi = \Theta\,\delta t + \tfrac{1}{2}\Gamma\,\delta S^2$$

when terms of higher order than $\delta t$ are ignored. This is equation (14.6).

When the volatility of the underlying asset is uncertain, $\Pi$ is a function of $\sigma$, $S$, and $t$. Equation (14A.1) then becomes

$$\delta\Pi = \frac{\partial\Pi}{\partial S}\,\delta S + \frac{\partial\Pi}{\partial \sigma}\,\delta\sigma + \frac{\partial\Pi}{\partial t}\,\delta t + \tfrac{1}{2}\frac{\partial^2\Pi}{\partial S^2}\,\delta S^2 + \tfrac{1}{2}\frac{\partial^2\Pi}{\partial \sigma^2}\,\delta\sigma^2 + \cdots$$

where $\delta\sigma$ is the change in $\sigma$ in time $\delta t$. In this case, delta hedging eliminates the first term on the right-hand side. The second term is eliminated by making the portfolio vega neutral. The third term is nonstochastic. The fourth term is eliminated by making the portfolio gamma neutral. Other Greek letters can be (and in practice are) defined to correspond to higher-order terms.

# C H A P T E R   1 5

# VOLATILITY SMILES

How close are the market prices of options to those predicted by Black–Scholes? Do traders really use Black–Scholes when determining a price for an option? Are the probability distributions of asset prices really lognormal? What research has been carried out to test the validity of the Black–Scholes formulas? In this chapter we answer these questions. We explain that traders do use the Black–Scholes model—but not in exactly the way that Black and Scholes originally intended. This is because they allow the volatility used to price an option to depend on its strike price and time to maturity.

A plot of the implied volatility of an option as a function of its strike price is known as a *volatility smile*. In this chapter we describe the volatility smiles that traders use in equity and foreign currency markets. We explain the relationship between a volatility smile and the risk-neutral probability distribution being assumed for the future asset price. We also discuss how option traders allow volatility to be a function of option maturity and how they use volatility matrices as pricing tools. The final part of the chapter summarizes some of the work researchers have carried out to test Black–Scholes.

## 15.1  PUT–CALL PARITY REVISITED

Put–call parity, which we explained in Chapter 8, provides a good starting point for understanding volatility smiles. It is an important relationship between the price, $c$, of a European call and the price, $p$, of a European put:

$$p + S_0 e^{-qT} = c + K e^{-rT} \tag{15.1}$$

The call and the put have the same strike price, $K$, and time to maturity, $T$. The variable $S_0$ is the price of the underlying asset today, $r$ is the risk-free interest rate for maturity $T$, and $q$ is the yield on the asset.

A key feature of the put–call parity relationship is that it is based on a relatively simple no-arbitrage argument. It does not require any assumption about the future probability distribution of the asset price. It is true both when the asset price distribution is lognormal and when it is not lognormal.

Suppose that, for a particular value of the volatility, $p_{BS}$ and $c_{BS}$ are the values of European put and call options calculated using the Black–Scholes model. Suppose further that $p_{mkt}$ and $c_{mkt}$ are the market values of these options. Because put–call parity holds for the Black–Scholes model, we must have

$$p_{BS} + S_0 e^{-qT} = c_{BS} + Ke^{-rT}$$

Because it also holds for the market prices, we have

$$p_{mkt} + S_0 e^{-qT} = c_{mkt} + Ke^{-rT}$$

Subtracting these two equations gives

$$p_{BS} - p_{mkt} = c_{BS} - c_{mkt} \qquad (15.2)$$

This shows that the dollar pricing error when the Black–Scholes model is used to price a European put option should be exactly the same as the dollar pricing error when it is used to price a European call option with the same strike price and time to maturity.

Suppose that the implied volatility of the put option is 22%. This means that $p_{BS} = p_{mkt}$ when a volatility of 22% is used in the Black–Scholes model. From equation (15.2), it follows that $c_{BS} = c_{mkt}$ when this volatility is used. The implied volatility of the call is therefore also 22%. This argument shows that the implied volatility of a European call option is always the same as the implied volatility of a European put option when the two have the same strike price and maturity date. To put this another way, for a given strike price and maturity, the correct volatility to use in conjunction with the Black–Scholes model to price a European call should always be the same as that used to price a European put.

This is also approximately true for American options. It follows that when traders refer to the relationship between implied volatility and strike price, or to the relationship between implied volatility and maturity, they do not need to state whether they are talking about calls or puts. The relationship is the same for both.

**Example 15.1**   The value of the Australian dollar is \$0.60. The risk-free interest rate is 5% per annum in the United States and 10% per annum in Australia. The market price of a European call option on the Australian dollar with a maturity of one year and a strike price of \$0.59 is 0.0236. DerivaGem shows that the implied volatility of the call is 14.5%. For there to be no arbitrage, the put–call parity relationship in equation (15.1) must apply with $q$ equal to the foreign risk-free rate. The price, $p$, of a European put option with a strike price of \$0.59 and maturity of one year therefore satisfies

$$p + 0.60e^{-0.10 \times 1} = 0.0236 + 0.59e^{-0.05 \times 1}$$

so that $p = 0.0419$. DerivaGem shows that, when the put has this price, its implied volatility is also 14.5%. This is what we expect from the analysis just given.

## 15.2  FOREIGN CURRENCY OPTIONS

The volatility smile used by traders to price foreign currency options has the general form shown in Figure 15.1. The volatility is relatively low for at-the-money options. It becomes progressively higher as an option moves either in the money or out of the money.

In Appendix 15A we show how to determine the risk-neutral probability distribution for an asset price at a future time from the volatility smile given by options maturing at that time. We refer to this as the *implied distribution*. The volatility smile in Figure 15.1 corresponds to the probability distribution shown by the solid line in Figure 15.2. A lognormal distribution with the

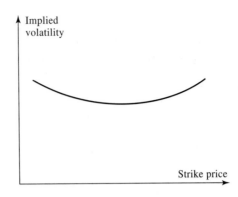

**Figure 15.1**   Volatility smile for foreign currency options

same mean and standard deviation as the implied distribution is shown by the dashed line in Figure 15.2. It can be seen that the implied distribution has heavier tails than the lognormal distribution.[1]

To see that Figure 15.1 and 15.2 are consistent with each other, consider first a deep-out-of-the-money call option with a high strike price of $K_2$. This option pays off only if the exchange rate proves to be above $K_2$. Figure 15.2 shows that the probability of this is higher for the implied probability distribution than for the lognormal distribution. We therefore expect the implied distribution to give a relatively high price for the option. A relatively high price leads to a relatively

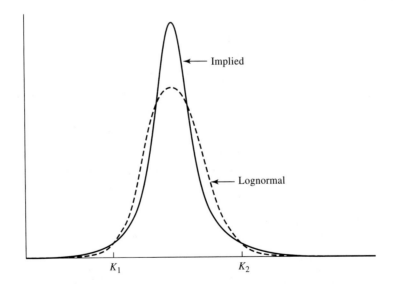

**Figure 15.2**   Implied distribution and lognormal distribution for foreign currency options

---

[1] This is known as kurtosis. Note that, in addition to having a heavier tail, the implied distribution is more "peaked". Both small and large movements in the exchange rate are more likely than with the lognormal distribution. Intermediate movements are less likely.

high implied volatility—and this is exactly what we observe in Figure 15.1 for the option. The two figures are therefore consistent with each other for high strike prices. Consider next a deep-out-of-the-money put option with a low strike price of $K_1$. This option pays off only if the exchange rate proves to be below $K_1$. Figure 15.2 shows that the probability of this is also higher for implied probability distribution than for the lognormal distribution. We therefore expect the implied distribution to give a relatively high price, and a relatively high implied volatility, for this option as well. Again, this is exactly what we observe in Figure 15.1.

### Reason for the Smile in Foreign Currency Options

We have just shown that the smile used by traders for foreign currency options implies that they consider that the lognormal distribution understates the probability of extreme movements in exchange rates. To test whether they are right, we examined the daily movements in 12 different exchange rates over a 10-year period. As a first step we calculated the standard deviation of daily percentage change in each exchange rate. We then noted how often the actual percentage change exceeded one standard deviation, two standard deviations, and so on. Finally, we calculated how often this would have happened if the percentage changes had been normally distributed. (The lognormal model implies that percentage changes are almost exactly normally distributed over a one-day time period.) The results are shown in Table 15.1.[2]

Daily changes exceed three standard deviations on 1.34% of days. The lognormal model predicts that this should happen on only 0.27% of days. Daily changes exceed four, five, and six standard deviations on 0.29%, 0.08%, and 0.03% of days, respectively. The lognormal model predicts that we should hardly ever observe this happening. The table therefore provides evidence to support the existence of heavy tails and the volatility smile used by traders.

Why are exchange rates not lognormally distributed? Two of the conditions for an asset price to have a lognormal distribution are:

1. The volatility of the asset is constant.

2. The price of the asset changes smoothly with no jumps.

In practice, neither of these conditions is satisfied for an exchange rate. The volatility of an

**Table 15.1** Percent of days when daily exchange rate moves are greater than one, two,..., six standard deviations (S.D. = standard deviation of daily change)

|  | Real world | Lognormal model |
|---|---|---|
| >1 S.D. | 25.04 | 31.73 |
| >2 S.D. | 5.27 | 4.55 |
| >3 S.D. | 1.34 | 0.27 |
| >4 S.D. | 0.29 | 0.01 |
| >5 S.D. | 0.08 | 0.00 |
| >6 S.D. | 0.03 | 0.00 |

[2] This table is taken from J. C. Hull and A. White, "Value at Risk When Daily Changes in Market Variables Are Not Normally Distributed," *Journal of Derivatives*, 5, no. 3 (Spring 1998), 9–19.

exchange rate is far from constant, and exchange rates frequently exhibit jumps.[3] It turns out that the effect of both a nonconstant volatility and jumps is that extreme outcomes become more likely.

The impact of jumps and nonconstant volatility depends on the option maturity. The percentage impact of a nonconstant volatility on prices becomes more pronounced as the maturity of the option is increased, but the volatility smile created by the nonconstant volatility usually becomes less pronounced. The percentage impact of jumps on both prices and the volatility smile becomes less pronounced as the maturity of the option is increased. When we look at sufficiently long dated options, jumps tend to get "averaged out", so that the stock price distribution when there are jumps is almost indistinguishable from the one obtained when the stock price changes smoothly.

## 15.3 EQUITY OPTIONS

The volatility smile used by traders to price equity options (both those on individual stocks and those on stock indices) has the general form shown in Figure 15.3. This is sometimes referred to as a *volatility skew*. The volatility decreases as the strike price increases. The volatility used to price a low-strike-price option (i.e., a deep-out-of-the-money put or a deep-in-the-money call) is significantly higher than that used to price a high-strike-price option (i.e., a deep-in-the-money put or a deep-out-of-the-money call).

The volatility smile for equity options corresponds to the implied probability distribution given by the solid line in Figure 15.4. A lognormal distribution with the same mean and standard

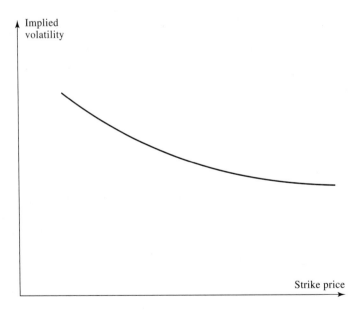

**Figure 15.3**   Volatility smile for equities

---

[3] Often the jumps are in response to the actions of central banks.

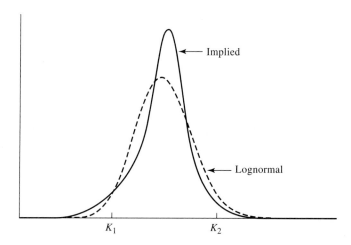

**Figure 15.4**   Implied distribution and lognormal distribution for equity options

deviation as the implied distribution is shown by the dotted line. It can be seen that the implied distribution has a heavier left tail and a less heavy right tail than the lognormal distribution.

To see that Figures 15.3 and 15.4 are consistent with each other, we proceed as for Figures 15.1 and 15.2 and consider options that are deep out of the money. From Figure 15.4 a deep-out-of-the-money call with a strike price of $K_2$ has a lower price when the implied distribution is used than when the lognormal distribution is used. This is because the option pays off only if the stock price proves to be above $K_2$, and the probability of this is lower for the implied probability distribution than for the lognormal distribution. Therefore we expect the implied distribution to give a relatively low price for the option. A relatively low price leads to a relatively low implied volatility—and this is exactly what we observe in Figure 15.3 for the option. Consider next a deep-out-of-the-money put option with a strike price of $K_1$. This option pays off only if the stock price proves to be below $K_1$. Figure 15.3 shows that the probability of this is higher for implied probability distribution than for the lognormal distribution. We therefore expect the implied distribution to give a relatively high price, and a relatively high implied volatility, for this option. Again, this is exactly what we observe in Figure 15.3.

### The Reason for the Smile in Equity Options

One possible explanation for the smile in equity options concerns leverage. As a company's equity declines in value, the company's leverage increases. As a result the volatility of its equity increases, making even lower stock prices more likely. As a company's equity increases in value, leverage decreases. As a result the volatility of its equity declines, making higher stock prices less likely. This argument shows that we can expect the volatility of equity to be a decreasing function of price and is consistent with Figures 15.3 and 15.4.

It is an interesting observation that the pattern in Figure 15.3 for equities has existed only since the stock market crash of October 1987. Prior to October 1987 implied volatilities were much less dependent on strike price. This has led Mark Rubinstein to suggest that one reason for the pattern in Figure 15.3 may be "crashophobia". Traders are concerned about the possibility of another crash similar to October 1987, and they price options accordingly. There is some empirical support for crashophobia. Whenever the market declines (increases), there is a tendency for the skew in Figure 15.3 to become more (less) pronounced.

## 15.4 THE VOLATILITY TERM STRUCTURE AND VOLATILITY SURFACES

In addition to a volatility smile, traders use a volatility term structure when pricing options. This means that the volatility used to price an at-the-money option depends on the maturity of the option. Volatility tends to be an increasing function of maturity when short-dated volatilities are historically low. This is because there is then an expectation that volatilities will increase. Similarly, volatility tends to be an decreasing function of maturity when short-dated volatilities are historically high. This is because there is then an expectation that volatilities will decrease.

Volatility surfaces combine volatility smiles with the volatility term structure to tabulate the volatilities appropriate for pricing an option with any strike price and any maturity. An example of a volatility surfaces that might be used for foreign currency options is shown in Table 15.2.

One dimension of Table 15.2 is strike price; the other is time to maturity. The main body of the table shows implied volatilities calculated from the Black–Scholes model. At any given time, some of the entries in the table are likely to correspond to options for which reliable market data are available. The implied volatilities for these options are calculated directly from their market prices and entered into the table. The rest of the table is determined using linear interpolation.

When a new option has to be valued, financial engineers look up the appropriate volatility in the table. For example, when valuing a nine-month option with a strike price of 1.05, a financial engineer would interpolate between 13.4 and 14.0 to obtain a volatility of 13.7%. This is the volatility that would be used in the Black–Scholes formula (or in the binomial tree model, which we will discuss further in Chapter 18).

The shape of the volatility smile depends on the option maturity. As illustrated in Table 15.2, the smile tends to become less pronounced as the option maturity increases. Define $T$ as the time to maturity and $F_0$ as the forward price of the asset. Some financial engineers choose to define the volatility smile as the relationship between implied volatility and

$$\frac{1}{\sqrt{T}} \ln \frac{K}{F_0}$$

**Table 15.2**  Volatility surface

| | *Strike price* | | | | |
|---|---|---|---|---|---|
| | *0.90* | *0.95* | *1.00* | *1.05* | *1.10* |
| 1 month | 14.2 | 13.0 | 12.0 | 13.1 | 14.5 |
| 3 month | 14.0 | 13.0 | 12.0 | 13.1 | 14.2 |
| 6 month | 14.1 | 13.3 | 12.5 | 13.4 | 14.3 |
| 1 year | 14.7 | 14.0 | 13.5 | 14.0 | 14.8 |
| 2 year | 15.0 | 14.4 | 14.0 | 14.5 | 15.1 |
| 5 year | 14.8 | 14.6 | 14.4 | 14.7 | 15.0 |

rather than as the relationship between the implied volatility and $K$. The smile is then usually much less dependent on the time to maturity.[4]

### *The Role of the Model*

How important is the pricing model if traders are prepared to use a different volatility for every option? It can be argued that the Black–Scholes model is no more than a sophisticated interpolation tool used by traders for ensuring that an option is priced consistently with the market prices of other actively traded options. If traders stopped using Black–Scholes and switched to another plausible model, the volatility surface would change and the shape of the smile would change. But arguably, the dollar prices quoted in the market would not change appreciably.

## 15.5  GREEK LETTERS

The volatility smile complicates the calculation of Greek letters. Derman describes a number of volatility regimes or rules of thumb than are sometimes assumed by traders.[5] The simplest of these is known as the *sticky strike rule*. This assumes that the implied volatility of an option remains constant from one day to the next. It means that Greek letters calculated using the Black–Scholes assumptions are correct provided that the volatility used for an option is its current implied volatility.

A more complicated rule is known as the *sticky delta* rule. This assumes that the relationship we observe between an option price and $S/K$ today will apply tomorrow. As the price of the underlying asset changes the implied volatility of the option is assumed to change to reflect the option's moneyness (i.e., the extent to which it is in or out of the money). If we use the sticky delta rule, the formulas for Greek letters given in the Chapter 14 are no longer correct. For example, delta of a call option is given by

$$\frac{\partial c_{BS}}{\partial S} + \frac{\partial c_{BS}}{\partial \sigma_{imp}} \frac{\partial \sigma_{imp}}{\partial S}$$

where $c_{BS}$ is the Black–Scholes price of the option expressed as a function of the asset price $S$ and the implied volatility $\sigma_{imp}$. Consider the impact of this formula on the delta of an equity call option. From Figure 15.3, volatility is a decreasing function of the strike price $K$. Alternatively it can be regarded as an increasing function of $S/K$. Under the sticky delta model, therefore, the volatility increases as the asset price increases, so that

$$\frac{\partial \sigma_{imp}}{\partial S} > 0$$

As a result, delta is higher than that given by the Black–Scholes assumptions.

It turns out that the sticky strike and sticky delta rules do not correspond to internally consistent models (except when the volatility smile is flat for all maturities). A model that can be made exactly consistent with the smiles is known as the *implied volatility function* model or the *implied tree model*. We will explain this model in Chapter 20.

---

[4] For a discussion of this approach, see S. Natenberg, *Option Pricing and Volatility: Advanced Trading Strategies and Techniques*, 2nd edn., McGraw-Hill, New York, 1994; R. Tompkins, *Options Analysis: A State of the Art Guide to Options Pricing*, Irwin, Burr Ridge, IL,1994.

[5] See E. Derman, "Regimes of Volatility," *RISK*, April 1999, pp. 54–59.

In practice many banks try to ensure that their exposure to the changes in the volatility surface that are most commonly observed is reasonably small. One technique for identifying these changes is principal components analysis, which we discuss in Chapter 16.

## 15.6   WHEN A SINGLE LARGE JUMP IS ANTICIPATED

Suppose that a stock price is currently $50 and an important news announcement in a few days is expected to either increase the stock price by $8 or reduce it by $8. (This announcement could concern the outcome of a takeover attempt or the verdict in an important lawsuit.) The probability distribution of the stock price in, say, three months might then consist of a mixture of two lognormal distributions, the first corresponding to favorable news, and the second to unfavorable news. The situation is illustrated in Figure 15.5. The solid line shows the mixtures-of-lognormals distribution for the stock price in three months; the dashed line shows a lognormal distribution with the same mean and standard deviation as this distribution. Assume that favorable news and unfavorable news are equally likely.[6] Assume also that after the news (favorable or unfavorable) the volatility will be constant at 20% for three months.

Consider a three-month European call option on the stock with a strike price of $50. We assume that the risk-free interest rate is 5% per annum. Because the news announcement is expected very soon, the value of the option assuming favorable news can be calculated from the Black–Scholes formula with $S_0 = 58$, $K = 50$, $r = 5\%$, $\sigma = 20\%$, and $T = 0.25$. It is 8.743. Similarly, the value of the option assuming unfavorable news can be calculated from the Black–Scholes formula with $S_0 = 42$, $K = 50$, $r = 5\%$, $\sigma = 20\%$, and $T = 0.25$. It is 0.101. The value of the call option today should therefore be

$$0.5 \times 8.743 + 0.5 \times 0.101 = 4.422$$

The implied volatility calculated from this option price is 41.48%.

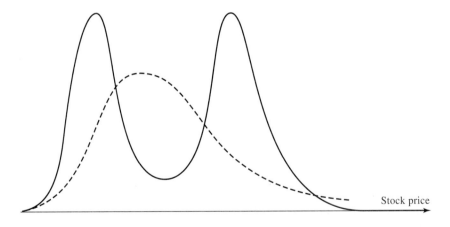

**Figure 15.5**   Effect of a single large jump: the solid line is the true distribution; the dashed line is the lognormal distribution

---

[6] Strictly speaking, we are assuming that the probabilities are equally likely in a risk-neutral world.

**Table 15.3**  Implied volatilities in a situation where an important announcement is imminent

| Strike price ($) | Call price if good news ($) | Call price if bad news ($) | Call price today ($) | Implied volatility (%) |
|---|---|---|---|---|
| 35 | 23.435 | 7.471 | 15.453 | 30.95 |
| 40 | 18.497 | 3.169 | 10.833 | 35.46 |
| 45 | 13.565 | 0.771 | 7.168 | 39.94 |
| 50 | 8.743 | 0.101 | 4.422 | 41.48 |
| 55 | 4.546 | 0.008 | 2.277 | 39.27 |
| 60 | 1.764 | 0.000 | 0.882 | 35.66 |
| 65 | 0.494 | 0.000 | 0.247 | 32.50 |

A similar calculation can be made for other strike prices and a volatility smile constructed. The results of doing this are shown in Table 15.3, and the volatility smile is shown in Figure 15.6.[7] It turns out that we are in the opposite situation to that of Figure 15.1. At-the-money options have higher volatilities than either out-of-the-money or in-the-money options.

## 15.7  EMPIRICAL RESEARCH

A number of problems arise in carrying out empirical research to test the Black–Scholes and other option pricing models.[8] The first problem is that any statistical hypothesis about how options are priced has to be a joint hypothesis to the effect that (1) the option pricing formula is

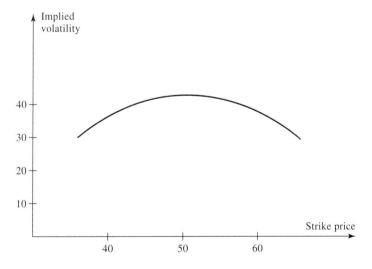

**Figure 15.6**  Volatility smile for situation in Table 15.3

---

[7] In this case, the smile is a frown!

[8] See the end-of-chapter references for citations to the studies reviewed in this section.

correct and (2) markets are efficient. If the hypothesis is rejected, it may be the case that (1) is untrue, (2) is untrue, or both (1) and (2) are untrue. A second problem is that the stock price volatility is an unobservable variable. One approach is to estimate the volatility from historical stock price data. Alternatively, implied volatilities can be used in some way. A third problem for the researcher is to make sure that data on the stock price and option price are synchronous. For example, if the option is thinly traded, it is not likely to be acceptable to compare closing option prices with closing stock prices. The closing option price might correspond to a trade at 1:00 p.m., whereas the closing stock price corresponds to a trade at 4:00 p.m.

Black and Scholes (1972) and Galai (1977) have tested whether it is possible to make excess returns above the risk-free rate of interest by buying options that are undervalued by the market (relative to the theoretical price) and selling options that are overvalued by the market (relative to the theoretical price). Black and Scholes used data from the over-the-counter options market where options are dividend protected. Galai used data from the Chicago Board Options Exchange (CBOE) where options are not protected against the effects of cash dividends. Galai used Black's approximation as described in Section 12.13 to incorporate the effect of anticipated dividends into the option price. Both studies showed that, in the absence of transactions costs, significant excess returns over the risk-free rate can be obtained by buying undervalued options and selling over-valued options. However, it is possible that these excess returns are available only to market makers and that, when transactions costs are considered, they vanish.

A number of researchers have chosen to make no assumptions about the behavior of stock prices and have tested whether arbitrage strategies can be used to make a riskless profit in options markets. Garman (1976) provides a computational procedure for finding any arbitrage possibilities that exist in a given situation. One frequently cited study by Klemkosky and Resnick (1979) tests whether the relationship in equation (8.8) is ever violated. It concludes that some small arbitrage profits are possible from using the relationship. These are due mainly to the overpricing of American calls.

Chiras and Manaster (1978) carried out a study using CBOE data to compare a weighted implied volatility from options on a stock at a point in time with the volatility calculated from historical data. They found that the former provide a much better forecast of the volatility of the stock price during the life of the option. We can conclude that option traders are using more than just historical data when determining future volatilities. Chiras and Manaster also tested to see whether it was possible to make above-average returns by buying options with low implied volatilities and selling options with high implied volatilities. The strategy showed a profit of 10% per month. The Chiras and Manaster study can be interpreted as providing good support for the Black–Scholes model and showing that the CBOE was inefficient in some respects.

MacBeth and Merville (1979) tested the Black–Scholes model using a different approach. They looked at different call options on the same stock at the same time and compared the volatilities implied by the option prices. The stocks chosen were AT&T, Avon, Kodak, Exxon, IBM, and Xerox, and the time period considered was the year 1976. They found that implied volatilities tended to be relatively high for in-the-money options and relatively low for out-of-the-money options. A relatively high implied volatility is indicative of a relatively high option price, and a relatively low implied volatility is indicative of a relatively low option price. Therefore, if it is assumed that Black–Scholes prices at-the-money options correctly, it can be concluded that out-of-the-money (high strike price) call options are overpriced by Black–Scholes and in-the-money (low strike price) call options are underpriced by Black–Scholes. These effects become more pronounced as the time to maturity increases and the degree to which the option is in or out of the money increases. MacBeth and Merville's results are consistent with Figure 15.3. The results were confirmed by Lauterbach and Schultz (1990) in a later study concerned with the pricing of warrants.

Rubinstein has done a great deal of research similar to that of MacBeth and Merville. No clear-cut pattern emerged from his early research, but the research in his 1994 paper and joint 1996 paper with Jackwerth gives results consistent with Figure 15.3. Options with low strike prices have much higher volatilities than those with high strike prices. As mentioned previously in the chapter, leverage and the resultant negative correlation between volatility and stock price may partially account for the finding. It is also possible that investors fear a repeat of the crash of 1987.

A number of authors have researched the pricing of options on assets other than stocks. For example, Shastri and Tandon (June 1986) and Bodurtha and Courtadon (1987) have examined the market prices of currency options; in another paper, Shastri and Tandon (December 1986) have examined the market prices of futures options; and Chance (1986) has examined the market prices of index options.

In most cases, the mispricing by Black–Scholes is not sufficient to present profitable opportunities to investors when transactions costs and bid–offer spreads are taken into account. When profitable opportunities are sought, it is important to bear in mind that, even for a market maker, some time must elapse between a profitable opportunity being identified and action being taken. This delay, even if it is only to the next trade, can be sufficient to eliminate the profitable opportunity.

## SUMMARY

The Black–Scholes model and its extensions assume that the probability distribution of the underlying asset at any given future time is lognormal. This assumption is not the one made by traders. They assume the probability distribution of an equity price has a heavier left tail and a less heavy right tail than the lognormal distribution. They also assume that the probability of an exchange rate has a heavier right tail and a heavier left tail than the lognormal distribution.

Traders use volatility smiles to allow for nonlognormality. The volatility smile defines the relationship between the implied volatility of an option and its strike price. For equity options, the volatility smile tends to be downward sloping. This means that out-of-the-money puts and in-the-money calls tend to have high implied volatilities, whereas out-of-the-money calls and in-the-money puts tend to have low implied volatilities. For foreign currency options, the volatility smile is U-shaped. Deep-out-of-the-money and deep-in-the-money options have higher implied volatilities than at-the-money options.

Often traders also use a volatility term structure. The implied volatility of an option then depends on its life. When volatility smiles and volatility term structures are combined, they produce a volatility surface. This defines implied volatility as a function of both the strike price and the time to maturity.

## SUGGESTIONS FOR FURTHER READING

Bakshi, G., C. Cao, and Z. Chen, "Empirical Performance of Alternative Option Pricing Models," *Journal of Finance*, 52, no. 5 (December 1997), 2004–49.

Black, F., "How to Use the Holes in Black–Scholes," *RISK*, March 1988.

Black, F., and M. Scholes, "The Valuation of Option Contracts and a Test of Market Efficiency," *Journal of Finance*, 27 (May 1972), 399–418.

Bodurtha, J. N., and G. R. Courtadon, "Tests of an American Option Pricing Model on the Foreign Currency Options Market," *Journal of Financial and Quantitative Analysis*, 22 (June 1987), 153–68.

Breeden, M., and R. Litzenberger, "Prices of State Contingent Claims Implicit in Option Prices," *Journal of Business*, 51 (1978), 621–51.

Chance, D. M., "Empirical Tests of the Pricing of Index Call Options," *Advances in Futures and Options Research*, 1, pt. A (1986), 141–66.

Chiras, D., and S. Manaster, "The Information Content of Option Prices and a Test of Market Efficiency," *Journal of Financial Economics*, 6 (September 1978), 213–34.

Derman, E., "Regimes of Volatility," *RISK*, April 1999, pp. 55–59.

Dumas, B., J. Fleming, and R. E. Whaley, "Implied Volatility Functions: Empirical Tests," *Journal of Finance* 53, 6 (December 1998), 2059–2106.

Galai, D., "Tests of Market Efficiency and the Chicago Board Options Exchange." *Journal of Business*, 50 (April 1977), 167–97.

Garman, M., "An Algebra for Evaluating Hedge Portfolios," *Journal of Financial Economics*, 3 (October 1976), 403–27.

Harvey, C. R., and R. E. Whaley, "S&P 100 Index Option Volatility," *Journal of Finance*, 46 (1991), 1551–61.

Harvey, C. R., and R. E. Whaley, "Market Volatility Prediction and the Efficiency of the S&P 100 Index Option Market," *Journal of Financial Economics*, 31 (1992), 43–73.

Harvey, C. R., and R. E. Whaley, "Dividends and S&P 100 Index Option Valuations," *Journal of Futures Markets*, 12 (1992), 123–37.

Jackwerth, J. C., and M. Rubinstein, "Recovering Probability Distributions from Option Prices," *Journal of Finance*, 51 (December 1996), 1611–31.

Klemkosky, R. C., and B. G. Resnick, "Put–Call Parity and Market Efficiency," *Journal of Finance*, 34 (December 1979), 1141–55.

Lauterbach, B., and P. Schultz, "Pricing Warrants: An Empirical Study of the Black–Scholes Model and Its Alternatives," *Journal of Finance*, 4, no. 4 (September 1990), 1181–1210.

MacBeth, J. D., and L. J. Merville, "An Empirical Examination of the Black–Scholes Call Option Pricing Model," *Journal of Finance*, 34 (December 1979), 1173–86.

Melick, W. R., and C. P. Thomas, "Recovering an Asset's Implied Probability Density Function from Option Prices: An Application to Crude Oil during the Gulf Crisis," *Journal of Financial and Quantitative Analysis*, 32, no. 1 (March 1997), 91–115.

Rubinstein, M., "Nonparametric Tests of Alternative Option Pricing Models Using All Reported Trades and Quotes on the 30 Most Active CBOE Option Classes from August 23, 1976 through August 31, 1978," *Journal of Finance*, 40 (June 1985), 455–80.

Rubinstein, M., "Implied Binomial Trees," *Journal of Finance*, 49, 3 (July 1994), 771–818.

Shastri, K., and K. Tandon, "An Empirical Test of a Valuation Model for American Options on Futures Contracts," *Journal of Financial and Quantitative Analysis*, 21 (December 1986), 377–92.

Shastri, K., and K. Tandon, "Valuation of Foreign Currency Options: Some Empirical Tests," *Journal of Financial and Quantitative Analysis*, 21 (June 1986), 145–60.

Xu, X., and S. J. Taylor, "The Term Structure of Volatility Implied by Foreign Exchange Options," *Journal of Financial and Quantitative Analysis*, 29 (1994), 57–74.

## QUESTIONS AND PROBLEMS
## (ANSWERS IN SOLUTIONS MANUAL)

15.1. What pattern of implied volatilities is likely to be observed when
   a. Both tails of the stock price distribution are less heavy than those of the lognormal distribution?
   b. The right tail is heavier, and the left tail is less heavy, than that of a lognormal distribution?

15.2. What pattern of implied volatilities is likely to be observed for six-month options when the volatility is uncertain and positively correlated to the stock price?

15.3. What pattern of implied volatilities is likely to be caused by jumps in the underlying asset price? Is the pattern likely to be more pronounced for a six-month option than for a three-month option?

15.4. A call and put option have the same strike price and time to maturity. Show that the difference between their prices should be the same for any option pricing model.

15.5. Explain carefully why Figure 15.4 is consistent with Figure 15.3.

15.6. The market price of a European call is $3.00 and its Black–Scholes price is $3.50. The Black–Scholes price of a European put option with the same strike price and time to maturity is $1.00. What should the market price of this option be? Explain the reasons for your answer.

15.7. A stock price is currently $20. Tomorrow, news is expected to be announced that will either increase the price by $5 or decrease the price by $5. What are the problems in using Black–Scholes to value one-month options on the stock?

15.8. What are the major problems in testing a stock option pricing model empirically?

15.9. Suppose that a central bank's policy is to allow an exchange rate to fluctuate between 0.97 and 1.03. What pattern of implied volatilities for options on the exchange rate would you expect to see?

15.10. Option traders sometimes refer to deep-out-of-the-money options as being options on volatility. Why do you think they do this?

15.11. A European call option on a certain stock has a strike price of $30, a time to maturity of one year, and an implied volatility of 30%. A European put option on the same stock has a strike price of $30, a time to maturity of one year, and an implied volatility of 33%. What is the arbitrage opportunity open to a trader? Does the arbitrage work only when the lognormal assumption underlying Black–Scholes holds? Explain carefully the reasons for your answer.

15.12. Suppose that the result of a major lawsuit affecting Microsoft is due to be announced tomorrow. Microsoft's stock price is currently $60. If the ruling is favorable to Microsoft, the stock price is expected to jump to $75. If it is unfavorable, the stock is expected to jump to $50. What is the risk-neutral probability of a favorable ruling? Assume that the volatility of Microsoft's stock will be 25% for six months after the ruling if the ruling is favorable and 40% if it is unfavorable. Use DerivaGem to calculate the relationship between implied volatility and strike price for six-month European options on Microsoft today. Microsoft does not pay dividends. Assume that the six-month risk-free rate is 6%. Consider call options with strike prices of 30, 40, 50, 60, 70, and 80.

15.13. An exchange rate is currently 0.8000. The volatility of the exchange rate is quoted as 12% and interest rates in the two countries are the same. Using the lognormal assumption, estimate the probability that the exchange rate in three months will be (a) less than 0.7000, (b) between 0.7000 and 0.7500, (c) between 0.7500 and 0.8000, (d) between 0.8000 and 0.8500, (e) between 0.8500 and 0.9000, and (f) greater than 0.9000. Based on the volatility smile usually observed in the market for exchange rates, which of these estimates would you expect to be too low and which would you expect to be too high?

15.14. A stock price is $40. A six-month European call option on the stock with a strike price of $30 has an implied volatility of 35%. A six-month European call option on the stock with a strike price of $50 has an implied volatility of 28%. The six-month risk-free rate is 5% and no dividends are expected. Explain why the two implied volatilities are different. Use DerivaGem to calculate the prices of the two options. Use put–call parity to calculate the prices of six-month European put options with strike prices of $30 and $50. Use DerivaGem to calculate the implied volatilities of these two put options.

15.15. "The Black–Scholes model is used by traders as an interpolation tool." Discuss this view.

## ASSIGNMENT QUESTIONS

15.16. A company's stock is selling for $4. The company has no outstanding debt. Analysts consider the liquidation value of the company to be at least $300,000 and there are 100,000 shares outstanding. What volatility smile would you expect to see?

15.17. A company is currently awaiting the outcome of a major lawsuit. This is expected to be known within one month. The stock price is currently $20. If the outcome is positive, the stock price is expected to be $24 at the end of one month. If the outcome is negative, it is expected to be $18 at this time. The one-month risk-free interest rate is 8% per annum.
    a. What is the risk-neutral probability of a positive outcome?
    b. What are the values of one-month call options with strike prices of $19, $20, $21, $22, and $23?
    c. Use DerivaGem to calculate a volatility smile for one-month call options.
    d. Verify that the same volatility smile is obtained for one-month put options.

15.18. A futures price is currently $40. The risk-free interest rate is 5%. Some news is expected tomorrow that will cause the volatility over the next three months to be either 10% or 30%. There is a 60% chance of the first outcome and a 40% chance of the second outcome. Use DerivaGem to calculate a volatility smile for three-month options.

15.19. Data for a number of foreign currencies are provided on the author's Web site:
    www.rotman.utoronto.ca/~hull
    Choose a currency and use the data to produce a table similar to Table 15.1.

15.20. Data for a number of stock indices are provided on the author's Web site:
    www.rotman.utoronto.ca/~hull
    Choose an index and test whether a three standard deviation down movement happens more often than a three standard deviation up movement.

15.21. Consider a European call and a European put with the same strike price and time to maturity. Show that they change in value by the same amount when the volatility increases from a level $\sigma_1$ to a new level $\sigma_2$ within a short period of time. (*Hint*: Use put–call parity.)

# APPENDIX 15A
## Determining Implied Risk-Neutral Distributions from Volatility Smiles

The price of a European call option on an asset with strike price $K$ and maturity $T$ is given by

$$c = e^{-rT} \int_{S_T=K}^{\infty} (S_T - K)g(S_T)\,dS_T$$

where $r$ is the interest rate (assumed constant), $S_T$ is the asset price at time $T$, and $g$ is the risk-neutral probability density function of $S_T$. Differentiating once with respect to $K$, we obtain

$$\frac{\partial c}{\partial K} = -e^{-rT} \int_{S_T=K}^{\infty} g(S_T)\,dS_T$$

Differentiating again with respect to $K$ gives

$$\frac{\partial^2 c}{\partial K^2} = e^{-rT} g(K)$$

This shows that the probability density function, $g$, is given by

$$g(K) = e^{rT} \frac{\partial^2 c}{\partial K^2}$$

This result, which is from Breeden and Litzenberger (1978), allows risk-neutral probability distributions to be estimated from volatility smiles. Suppose that $c_1$, $c_2$, and $c_3$ are the prices of European call options with maturity $T$ and strike prices are $K - \delta$, $K$, and $K + \delta$, respectively. Assuming $\delta$ is small, an estimate of $g(K)$ is

$$e^{rT} \frac{c_1 + c_3 - 2c_2}{\delta^2}$$

# CHAPTER 16

# VALUE AT RISK

In Chapter 14 we examined measures such as delta, gamma, and vega for describing different aspects of the risk in a portfolio consisting of options and other financial assets. A financial institution usually calculates each of these measures each day for every market variable to which it is exposed. Often there are hundreds, or even thousands, of these market variables. A delta–gamma–vega analysis therefore leads to a huge number of different risk measures being produced each day. These risk measures provide valuable information for a trader who is responsible for managing the part of the financial institution's portfolio that is dependent on a particular market variable, but they are of limited use to senior management.

Value at risk (VaR) is an attempt to provide a single number summarizing the total risk in a portfolio of financial assets for senior management. It has become widely used by corporate treasurers and fund managers as well as by financial institutions. Central bank regulators also use VaR in determining the capital a bank is required to keep to reflect the market risks it is bearing.[1]

In this chapter we explain the VaR measure and describe the two main approaches for calculating it. These are the *historical simulation* approach and the *model-building* approach. Both are widely used by both financial and nonfinancial companies. There is no general agreement on which of the two is better.

## 16.1 THE VaR MEASURE

When using the value-at-risk measure, the manager in charge of a portfolio of financial instruments is interested in making a statement of the following form:

"We are $X$ percent certain that we will not lose more than $V$ dollars in the next $N$ days."

The variable $V$ is the VaR of the portfolio. It is a function of two parameters: $N$, the time horizon, and $X$, the confidence level. It is the loss level over $N$ days that the manager is $X\%$ certain will not be exceeded.

In calculating a bank's capital for market risk, regulators use $N = 10$ and $X = 99$. This means that they focus on the loss level over a 10-day period that is expected to be exceeded only 1% of the time. The capital they require the bank to keep is at least three times this VaR measure.[2]

---

[1] For a discussion of this, see P. Jackson, D. J. Maude, and W. Perraudin, "Bank Capital and Value at Risk," *Journal of Derivatives*, 4, no. 3 (Spring 1997), 73–90.

[2] To be more precise, the market risk capital required for a particular bank is $k$ times the 10-day 99% VaR, where the multiplier $k$ is chosen by the regulators and is at least 3.0.

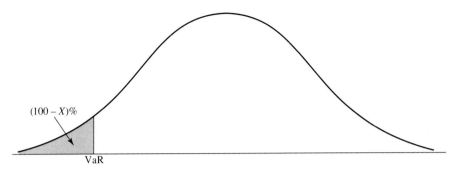

**Figure 16.1** Calculation of VaR from the probability distribution of changes in the portfolio value; confidence level is $X\%$

In general, when $N$ days is the time horizon and $X\%$ is the confidence level, VaR is the loss corresponding to the $(100 - X)$th percentile of the distribution of the change in the value of the portfolio over the next $N$ days. For example, when $N = 5$ and $X = 97$, it is the third percentile of the distribution of changes in the value of the portfolio over the next five days. Figure 16.1 illustrates VaR for the situation where the change in the value of the portfolio is approximately normally distributed.

VaR is an attractive measure because it is easy to understand. In essence, it asks the simple question "How bad can things get?" This is the question all senior managers want answered. They are very comfortable with the idea of compressing all the Greek letters for all the market variables underlying the portfolio into a single number.

If we accept that it is useful to have a single number to describe the risk of a portfolio, an interesting question is whether VaR is the best alternative. Some researchers have argued that VaR may tempt traders to choose a portfolio with a return distribution similar to that in Figure 16.2. The portfolios in Figures 16.1 and 16.2 have the same VaR, but the portfolio in Figure 16.2 is much riskier because potential losses are much larger.

A measure that deals with the problem we have just mentioned is *Conditional VaR* (C-VaR).[3] Whereas VaR asks the question "How bad can things get?", C-VaR asks "If things do get bad, how much can we expect to lose?" C-VaR is the expected loss during an $N$-day period conditional

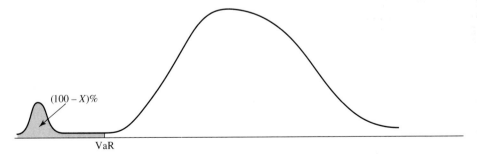

**Figure 16.2** Alternative situation to Figure 16.1; VaR is the same, but the potential loss is larger

---

[3] This measure was suggested by P. Artzner, F. Delbaen, J.-M. Eber, and D. Heath, "Coherent Measures of Risk," *Mathematical Finance*, 9 (1999), 203–28. These authors define certain properties that a good risk measure should have and show that the standard VaR measure does not have all of them.

that we are in the $(100 - X)\%$ left tail of the distribution. For example, with $X = 99$ and $N = 10$, C-VaR is the average amount we lose over a 10-day period assuming that a 1% worst-case event occurs.

In spite of its weaknesses, VaR (not C-VaR) is the most popular measure of risk among both regulators and senior management. We will therefore devote most of the rest of this chapter to how it can be measured.

### The Time Horizon

In theory, VaR has two parameters. These are $N$, the time horizon measured in days, and $X$, the confidence interval. In practice, analysts almost invariably set $N = 1$ in the first instance. This is because there is not enough data to estimate directly the behavior of market variables over periods of time longer than one day. The usual assumption is

$$N\text{-day VaR} = 1\text{-day VaR} \times \sqrt{N}$$

This formula is exactly true when the changes in the value of the portfolio on successive days have independent identical normal distributions with mean zero. In other cases it is an approximation.

We mentioned earlier that regulators require a bank's capital to be at least three times the 10-day 99% VaR. Given the way a 10-day VaR is calculated, this capital level is, to all intents and purposes, $3 \times \sqrt{10} = 9.49$ times the 1-day 99% VaR.

## 16.2  HISTORICAL SIMULATION

Historical simulation is one popular way of estimating VaR. It involves using past data in a very direct way as a guide to what might happen in the future. Suppose that we wish to calculate VaR for a portfolio using a one-day time horizon, a 99% confidence level, and 500 days of data. The first step is to identify the market variables affecting the portfolio. These will typically be exchange rates, equity prices, interest rates, and so on. We then collect data on the movements in these market variables over the most recent 500 days. This provides us with 500 alternative scenarios for what can happen between today and tomorrow. Scenario 1 is where the percentage changes in the

**Table 16.1**  Data for VaR historical simulation calculation

| Day | Market variable 1 | Market variable 2 | $\cdots$ | Market variable $N$ |
|-----|-------------------|-------------------|----------|---------------------|
| 0   | 20.33             | 0.1132            | $\cdots$ | 65.37               |
| 1   | 20.78             | 0.1159            | $\cdots$ | 64.91               |
| 2   | 21.44             | 0.1162            | $\cdots$ | 65.02               |
| 3   | 20.97             | 0.1184            | $\cdots$ | 64.90               |
| $\vdots$ | $\vdots$     | $\vdots$          | $\vdots$ | $\vdots$            |
| 498 | 25.72             | 0.1312            | $\cdots$ | 62.22               |
| 499 | 25.75             | 0.1323            | $\cdots$ | 61.99               |
| 500 | 25.85             | 0.1343            | $\cdots$ | 62.10               |

**Table 16.2** Scenarios generated for tomorrow (Day 501) using
data in Table 16.1

| Scenario number | Market variable 1 | Market variable 2 | $\cdots$ | Market variable N | Portfolio value ($ millions) |
|---|---|---|---|---|---|
| 1 | 26.42 | 0.1375 | $\cdots$ | 61.66 | 23.71 |
| 2 | 26.67 | 0.1346 | $\cdots$ | 62.21 | 23.12 |
| 3 | 25.28 | 0.1368 | $\cdots$ | 61.99 | 22.94 |
| $\vdots$ | $\vdots$ | $\vdots$ | $\vdots$ | $\vdots$ | $\vdots$ |
| 499 | 25.88 | 0.1354 | $\cdots$ | 61.87 | 23.63 |
| 500 | 25.95 | 0.1363 | $\cdots$ | 62.21 | 22.87 |

values of all variables are the same as they were on the first day for which we have collected data; scenario 2 is where they are the same as on the second day for which we have data; and so on. For each scenario we calculate the dollar change in the value of the portfolio between today and tomorrow. This defines a probability distribution for daily changes in the value of our portfolio. The fifth-worst daily change is the first percentile of the distribution. The estimate of VaR is the loss when we are at this first percentile point. Assuming that the last 500 days are a good guide to what could happen during the next day, we are 99% certain that we will not take a loss greater than our VaR estimate.

The historical simulation methodology is illustrated in Tables 16.1 and 16.2. Table 16.1 shows observations on market variables over the last 500 days. The observations are taken at some particular point in time during the day (usually the close of trading). We denote the first day for which we have data as Day 0; the second as Day 1; and so on. Today is Day 500; tomorrow is Day 501.

Table 16.2 shows the values of the market variables tomorrow if their percentage changes between today and tomorrow are the same as they were between Day $i - 1$ and Day $i$ for $1 \leqslant i \leqslant 500$. The first row in Table 16.2 shows the values of market variables tomorrow assuming their percentage changes between today and tomorrow are the same as they were between Day 0 and Day 1; the second row shows the values of market variables tomorrow assuming their percentage changes between Day 1 and Day 2 occur; and so on. The 500 rows in Table 16.2 are the 500 scenarios considered.

Define $v_i$ as the value of a market variable on Day $i$ and suppose that today is Day $m$. The $i$th scenario assumes that the value of the market variable tomorrow will be

$$v_m \frac{v_i}{v_{i-1}}$$

In our example, $m = 500$. For the first variable, the value today, $v_{500}$, is 25.85. Also $v_0 = 20.33$ and $v_1 = 20.78$. It follows that the value of the first market variable in the first scenario is

$$25.85 \times \frac{20.78}{20.33} = 26.42$$

The final column of Table 16.2 shows the value of the portfolio tomorrow for each of the 500 scenarios. The value of the portfolio today is known. Suppose this is $23.50 million. We can calculate the change in the value of the portfolio between today and tomorrow for all the different scenarios. For Scenario 1, it is +$210,000; for Scenario 2 it is −$380,000; and so on. These changes in value are then ranked. The fifth-worst loss is the one-day 99% VaR. As mentioned in the previous section, the $N$-day VaR for a 99% confidence level is calculated as $\sqrt{N}$ times the one-day VaR.

Each day the VaR estimate in our example would be updated using the most recent 500 days of data. Consider, for example, what happens on Day 501. We find out new values for all the market variables and are able to calculate a new value for our portfolio.[4] We then go through the procedure we have outlined to calculate a new VaR. We use data on the market variables from Day 1 to Day 501. (This gives us the required 500 observations on the percentage changes in market variables; the Day 0 values of the market variables are no longer used.) Similarly, on Day 502 we use data from Day 2 to Day 502 to determine VaR, and so on.

## 16.3  MODEL-BUILDING APPROACH

The main alternative to historical simulation is the model-building approach (sometimes also called the variance–covariance approach). Before getting into the details of the approach, it is appropriate to mention one issue concerned with the units for measuring volatility.

### Daily Volatilities

In option pricing we usually measure time in years, and the volatility of an asset is usually quoted as a "volatility per year". When using the model-building approach to calculate VaR, we usually measure time in days and the volatility of an asset is usually quoted as a "volatility per day".

What is the relationship between the volatility per year used in option pricing and the volatility per day used in VaR calculations? Let us define $\sigma_{yr}$ as the volatility per year of a certain asset and $\sigma_{day}$ as the equivalent volatility per day of the asset. Assuming 252 trading days in a year, we can use equation (12.2) to write the standard deviation of the continuously compounded return on the asset in one year as either $\sigma_{yr}$ or $\sigma_{day}\sqrt{252}$. It follows that

$$\sigma_{yr} = \sigma_{day}\sqrt{252}$$

or

$$\sigma_{day} = \frac{\sigma_{yr}}{\sqrt{252}}$$

so that daily volatility is about 6% of annual volatility.

As pointed out in Section 12.4, $\sigma_{day}$ is approximately equal to the standard deviation of the percentage change in the asset price in one day. For the purposes of calculating VaR, we assume exact equality. We define the daily volatility of an asset price (or any other variable) as equal to the standard deviation of the percentage change in one day.

Our discussion in the next few sections assumes that we have estimates of daily volatilities and correlations. In Chapter 17 we explain how the estimates are produced.

### Single-Asset Case

We now consider how VaR is calculated using the model-building approach in a very simple situation where the portfolio consists of a position in a single stock. The portfolio we consider is

---

[4] Note that the portfolio's composition may have changed between Day 500 and Day 501.

one consisting of $10 million in shares of Microsoft. We suppose that $N = 10$ and $X = 99$, so that we are interested in the loss level over 10 days that we are 99% confident will not be exceeded. Initially, we consider a one-day time horizon.

We assume that the volatility of Microsoft is 2% per day (corresponding to about 32% per year). Because the size of the position is $10 million, the standard deviation of daily changes in the value of the position is 2% of $10 million, or $200,000.

It is customary in the model-building approach to assume that the expected change in a market variable over the time period considered is zero. This is not exactly true, but it is a reasonable assumption. The expected change in the price of a market variable over a short time period is generally small when compared with the standard deviation of the change. Suppose, for example, that Microsoft has an expected return of 20% per annum. Over a one-day period, the expected return is 0.20/252, or about 0.08%, whereas the standard deviation of the return is 2%. Over a 10-day period, the expected return is 0.20/25.2, or about 0.8%, whereas the standard deviation of the return is $2\sqrt{10}$, or about 6.3%.

So far, we have established that the change in the value of the portfolio of Microsoft shares over a one-day period has a standard deviation of $200,000 and (at least approximately) a mean of zero. We assume that the change is normally distributed.[5] From the tables at the end of this book, we see that $N(-2.33) = 0.01$. This means that there is a 1% probability that a normally distributed variable will decrease in value by more than 2.33 standard deviations. Equivalently, it means that we are 99% certain that a normally distributed variable will not decrease in value by more than 2.33 standard deviations. The 1-day 99% VaR for our portfolio consisting of a $10 million position in Microsoft is therefore

$$2.33 \times 200,000 = \$466,000$$

As discussed earlier, the $N$-day VaR is calculated as $\sqrt{N}$ times the one-day VaR. The 10-day 99% VaR for Microsoft is therefore

$$466,000 \times \sqrt{10} = \$1,473,621$$

Consider next a portfolio consisting of a $5 million position in AT&T, and suppose the daily volatility of AT&T is 1% (approximately 16% per year). A similar calculation to that for Microsoft shows that the standard deviation of the change in the value of the portfolio in one day is

$$5,000,000 \times 0.01 = 50,000$$

Assuming the change is normally distributed, the 1-day 99% VaR is

$$50,000 \times 2.33 = \$116,500$$

and the 10-day 99% VaR is

$$116,500 \times \sqrt{10} = \$368,405$$

### Two-Asset Case

Now consider a portfolio consisting of both $10 million of Microsoft shares and $5 million of AT&T shares. We suppose that the returns on the two shares have a bivariate normal distribution with a correlation of 0.3. A standard result in statistics tells us that, if two variables $X$ and $Y$ have

---

[5] To be consistent with the option pricing assumption in Chapter 11, we could assume that the price of Microsoft is lognormal tomorrow. Because one day is such a short period of time, this is almost indistinguishable from the assumption we do make—that the change in the stock price between today and tomorrow is normal.

standard deviations equal to $\sigma_X$ and $\sigma_Y$ with the coefficient of correlation between them being equal to $\rho$, then the standard deviation of $X + Y$ is given by

$$\sigma_{X+Y} = \sqrt{\sigma_X^2 + \sigma_Y^2 + 2\rho\sigma_X\sigma_Y}$$

To apply this result, we set $X$ equal to the change in the value of the position in Microsoft over a one-day period and $Y$ equal to the change in the value of the position in AT&T over a one-day period, so that

$$\sigma_X = 200,000, \qquad \sigma_Y = 50,000$$

The standard deviation of the change in the value of the portfolio consisting of both stocks over a one-day period is therefore

$$\sqrt{200,000^2 + 50,000^2 + 2 \times 0.3 \times 200,000 \times 50,000} = 220,227$$

The mean change is assumed to be zero. The 1-day 99% VaR is therefore

$$220,227 \times 2.33 = \$513,129$$

The 10-day 99% VaR is $\sqrt{10}$ times this or $1,622,657.

### The Benefits of Diversification

In the example we have just considered:

1. The 10-day 99% VaR for the portfolio of Microsoft shares is $1,473,621.
2. The 10-day 99% VaR for the portfolio of AT&T shares is $368,405.
3. The 10-day 99% VaR for the portfolio of both Microsoft and AT&T shares is $1,622,657.

The amount

$$(1473,621 + 368,405) - 1,622,657 = \$219,369$$

represents the benefits of diversification. If Microsoft and AT&T were perfectly correlated, the VaR for the portfolio of both Microsoft and AT&T would equal the VaR for the Microsoft portfolio plus the VaR for the AT&T portfolio. Less than perfect correlation leads to some of the risk being "diversified away." [6]

## 16.4   LINEAR MODEL

The examples we have just considered are simple illustrations of the use of the linear model for calculating VaR. Suppose that we have a portfolio worth $P$ consisting of $n$ assets with an amount $\alpha_i$ being invested in asset $i$ $(1 \leqslant i \leqslant n)$. We define $\delta x_i$ as the return on asset $i$ in one day. It follows that

---

[6] Harry Markowitz was one of the first researchers to study the benefits of diversification to a portfolio manager. He was awarded a Nobel prize for this research in 1990. See H. Markowitz, "Portfolio Selection," *Journal of Finance*, 7, no. 1 (March 1952), 77–91.

the dollar change in the value of our investment in asset $i$ in one day is $\alpha_i \, \delta x_i$ and

$$\delta P = \sum_{i=1}^{n} \alpha_i \, \delta x_i \tag{16.1}$$

where $\delta P$ is the dollar change in the value of the whole portfolio in one day.

In the example considered in the previous section, $10 million was invested in the first asset (Microsoft) and $5 million was invested in the second asset (AT&T), so that (in millions of dollars) $\alpha_1 = 10$, $\alpha_2 = 5$, and

$$\delta P = 10 \, \delta x_1 + 5 \, \delta x_2$$

If we assume that the $\delta x_i$ in equation (16.1) are multivariate normal, then $\delta P$ is normally distributed. To calculate VaR, we therefore need to calculate only the mean and standard deviation of $\delta P$. We assume, as discussed in the previous section, that the expected value of each $\delta x_i$ is zero. This implies that the mean of $\delta P$ is zero.

To calculate the standard deviation of $\delta P$, we define $\sigma_i$ as the daily volatility of the $i$th asset and $\rho_{ij}$ as the coefficient of correlation between returns on asset $i$ and asset $j$. This means that $\sigma_i$ is the standard deviation of $\delta x_i$, and $\rho_{ij}$ is the coefficient of correlation between $\delta x_i$ and $\delta x_j$. The variance of $\delta P$, which we will denote by $\sigma_P^2$, is given by

$$\sigma_P^2 = \sum_{i=1}^{n} \sum_{j=1}^{n} \rho_{ij} \alpha_i \alpha_j \sigma_i \sigma_j$$

This equation can also be written

$$\sigma_P^2 = \sum_{i=1}^{n} \alpha_i^2 \sigma_i^2 + 2 \sum_{i=1}^{n} \sum_{j<i} \rho_{ij} \alpha_i \alpha_j \sigma_i \sigma_j \tag{16.2}$$

The standard deviation of the change over $N$ days is $\sigma_P \sqrt{N}$, and the 99% VaR for an $N$-day time horizon is $2.33 \sigma_P \sqrt{N}$.

In the example considered in the previous section, $\sigma_1 = 0.02$, $\sigma_2 = 0.01$, and $\rho_{12} = 0.3$. As already noted, $\alpha_1 = 10$ and $\alpha_2 = 5$, so that

$$\sigma_P^2 = 10^2 \times 0.02^2 + 5^2 \times 0.01^2 + 2 \times 10 \times 5 \times 0.3 \times 0.02 \times 0.01 = 0.0485$$

and $\sigma_P = 0.220$. This is the standard deviation of the change in the portfolio value per day (in millions of dollars). The 10-day 99% VaR is $2.33 \times 0.220 \times \sqrt{10} = \$1.623$ million. This agrees with the calculation in the previous section.

### Handling Interest Rates

It is out of the question to define a separate market variable for every single bond price or interest rate to which a company is exposed. Some simplifications are necessary. One possibility is to assume that only parallel shifts in the yield curve occur. It is then necessary to define only one market variable: the size of the parallel shift. The changes in the value of a bond portfolio can then be calculated using the duration relationship

$$\delta P = -D P \, \delta y$$

where $P$ is the value of the portfolio, $\delta P$ is the change in $P$ in one day, $D$ is the modified duration of the portfolio, and $\delta y$ is the parallel shift in one day.

This approach does not usually give enough accuracy. The procedure usually followed is to choose as market variables the prices of zero-coupon bonds with standard maturities: 1 month, 3 months, 6 months, 1 year, 2 years, 5 years, 7 years, 10 years, and 30 years. For the purposes of calculating VaR, the cash flows from instruments in the portfolio are mapped into cash flows occurring on the standard maturity dates.

Consider a \$1 million position in a Treasury bond lasting 1.2 years that pays a coupon of 6% semiannually. Coupons are paid in 0.2, 0.7, and 1.2 years, and the principal is paid in 1.2 years. This bond is therefore, in the first instance, regarded as a \$30,000 position in 0.2-year zero-coupon bond plus a \$30,000 position in a 0.7-year zero-coupon bond plus a \$1.03 million position in a 1.2-year zero-coupon bond. The position in the 0.2-year bond is then replaced by an equivalent position in 1-month and 3-month zero-coupon bonds; the position in the 0.7-year bond is replaced by an equivalent position in 6-month and 1-year zero-coupon bonds; and the position in the 1.2-year bond is replaced by an equivalent position in 1-year and 2-year zero-coupon bonds. The result is that the position in the 1.2-year coupon-bearing bond is for VaR purposes regarded as a position in zero-coupon bonds having maturities of 1 month, 3 months, 6 months, 1 year, and 2 years.

This procedure is known as *cash-flow mapping*. One way of implementing the procedure is explained in Appendix 16A.

### Applications of the Linear Model

The simplest application of the linear model is to a portfolio with no derivatives consisting of positions in stocks, bonds, foreign exchange, and commodities. In this case the change in the value of the portfolio is linearly dependent on the percentage changes in the prices of the assets comprising the portfolio. Note that, for the purposes of VaR calculations, all asset prices are measured in the domestic currency. The market variables considered by a large bank in the United States are therefore likely to include the Nikkei 225 index measured in dollars, the price of a 10-year sterling zero-coupon bond measured in dollars, and so on.

An example of a derivative that can be handled by the linear model is a forward contract to buy a foreign currency. Suppose the contract matures at time $T$. It can be regarded as the exchange of a foreign zero-coupon bond maturing at time $T$ for a domestic zero-coupon bond maturing at time $T$. For the purposes of calculating VaR, the forward contract is therefore treated as a long position in the foreign bond combined with a short position in the domestic bond. Each bond can be handled using a cash-flow mapping procedure.

Consider next an interest rate swap. As explained in Chapter 6, this can be regarded as the exchange of a floating-rate bond for a fixed-rate bond. The fixed-rate bond is a regular coupon-bearing bond. The floating-rate bond is worth par just after the next payment date. It can be regarded as a zero-coupon bond with a maturity date equal to the next payment date. The interest rate swap therefore reduces to a portfolio of long and short positions in bonds and can be handled using a cash-flow mapping procedure.

### The Linear Model and Options

We now consider how the linear model can be used when there are options. Consider first a portfolio consisting of options on a single stock whose current price is $S$. Suppose that the delta of the position (calculated in the way described in Chapter 14) is $\Delta$. Because $\Delta$ is the rate of change of the value of the portfolio with $S$, it is approximately true that

$$\Delta = \frac{\delta P}{\delta S}$$

or

$$\delta P = \Delta \, \delta S \tag{16.3}$$

where $\delta S$ is the dollar change in the stock price in one day and $\delta P$ is, as usual, the dollar change in the portfolio in one day. We define $\delta x$ as the percentage change in the stock price in one day, so that

$$\delta x = \frac{\delta S}{S}$$

It follows that an approximate relationship between $\delta P$ and $\delta x$ is

$$\delta P = S\Delta \, \delta x.$$

When we have a position in several underlying market variables that includes options, we can derive an approximate linear relationship between $\delta P$ and the $\delta x_i$'s similarly. This relationship is

$$\delta P = \sum_{i=1}^{n} S_i \Delta_i \, \delta x_i \tag{16.4}$$

where $S_i$ is the value of the $i$th market variable and $\Delta_i$ is the delta of the portfolio with respect to the $i$th market variable. This corresponds to equation (16.1):

$$\delta P = \sum_{i=1}^{n} \alpha_i \, \delta x_i \tag{16.5}$$

with $\alpha_i = S_i \, \Delta_i$. Equation (16.2) can therefore be used to calculate the standard deviation of $\delta P$.

**Example 16.1**   A portfolio consists of options on Microsoft and AT&T. The options on Microsoft have a delta of 1,000, and the options on AT&T have a delta of 20,000. The Microsoft share price is $120, and the AT&T share price is $30. From equation (16.4), it is approximately true that

$$\delta P = 120 \times 1,000 \times \delta x_1 + 30 \times 20,000 \times \delta x_2$$

or

$$\delta P = 120,000 \delta x_1 + 600,000 \delta x_2$$

where $\delta x_1$ and $\delta x_2$ are the returns from Microsoft and AT&T in one day and $\delta P$ is the resultant change in the value of the portfolio. (The portfolio is assumed to be equivalent to an investment of $120,000 in Microsoft and $600,000 in AT&T.) Assuming that the daily volatility of Microsoft is 2% and the daily volatility of AT&T is 1%, and the correlation between the daily changes is 0.3, the standard deviation of $\delta P$ (in thousands of dollars) is

$$\sqrt{(120 \times 0.02)^2 + (600 \times 0.01)^2 + 2 \times 120 \times 0.02 \times 600 \times 0.01 \times 0.3} = 7.099$$

Because $N(-1.65) = 0.05$, the 5-day 95% value at risk is

$$1.65 \times \sqrt{5} \times 7,099 = \$26,193$$

## 16.5 QUADRATIC MODEL

When a portfolio includes options, the linear model is an approximation. It does not take account of the gamma of the portfolio. As discussed in Chapter 14, delta is defined as the rate of change of the portfolio value with respect to an underlying market variable and gamma is defined as the rate of change of the delta with respect to the market variable. Gamma measures the curvature of the relationship between the portfolio value and an underlying market variable.

Figure 16.3 shows the impact of a nonzero gamma on the probability distribution of the value of the portfolio. When gamma is positive, the probability distribution tends to be positively skewed; when gamma is negative, it tends to be negatively skewed. Figures 16.4 and 16.5 illustrate the reason for this result. Figure 16.4 shows the relationship between the value of a long call option and the price of the underlying asset. A long call is an example of an option position with positive gamma. The figure shows that, when the probability distribution for the price of the underlying asset at the end of one day is normal, the probability distribution for the option price is positively skewed.[7] Figure 16.5 shows the relationship between the value of a short call position and the price of the underlying asset. A short call position has negative gamma. In this case we see that a normal distribution for the price of the underlying asset at the end of one day gets mapped into a negatively skewed distribution for the value of the option position.

The VaR for a portfolio is critically dependent on the left tail of the probability distribution of the portfolio value. For example, when the confidence level used is 99%, the VaR is calculated from the value in the left tail below which there is only 1% of the distribution. As indicated in Figures 16.3a and 16.4, a positive-gamma portfolio tends to have a less heavy left tail than the normal distribution. If we assume the distribution is normal, we will tend to calculate a VaR that is too high. Similarly, as indicated in Figures 16.3b and 16.5, a negative-gamma portfolio tends to have a heavier left tail than the normal distribution. If we assume the distribution is normal, we will tend to calculate a VaR that is too low.

For a more accurate estimate of VaR than that given by the linear model, we can use both delta and gamma measures to relate $\delta P$ to the $\delta x_i$'s. Consider a portfolio dependent on a single asset whose price is $S$. Suppose that the delta of a portfolio is $\Delta$ and its gamma is $\Gamma$. From Appendix 14A, the equation

$$\delta P = \Delta \, \delta S + \tfrac{1}{2}\Gamma \, (\delta S)^2$$

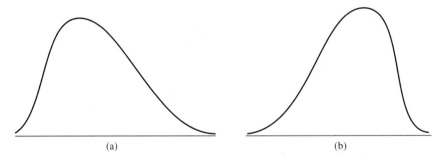

(a)                    (b)

**Figure 16.3** Probability distribution for value of portfolio: (a) positive gamma, (b) negative gamma

---

[7] As mentioned in footnote 5, we can use the normal distribution as an approximation to the lognormal distribution in VaR calculations.

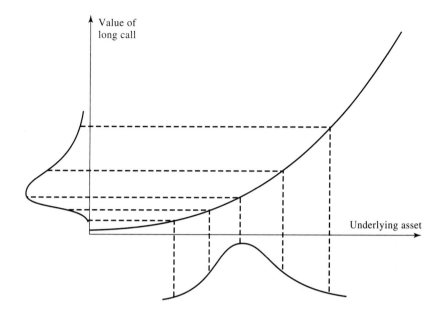

**Figure 16.4** Translation of normal probability distribution for asset into probability distribution for value of a long call on asset

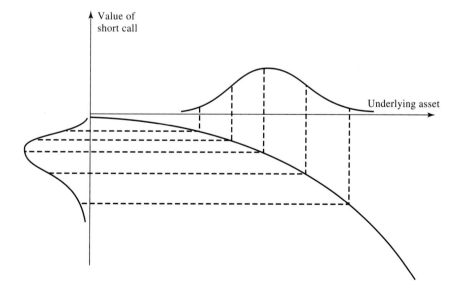

**Figure 16.5** Translation of normal probability distribution for asset into probability distribution for value of a short call on asset

is an improvement over the approximation in equation (16.3).[8] Setting

$$\delta x = \frac{\delta S}{S}$$

reduces this to

$$\delta P = S\Delta\,\delta x + \tfrac{1}{2}S^2\Gamma\,(\delta x)^2 \tag{16.6}$$

The variable $\delta P$ is not normal. Assuming that $\delta x$ is normal with mean zero and standard deviation $\sigma$, the first three moments of $\delta P$ are

$$E(\delta P) = \tfrac{1}{2}S^2\Gamma\sigma^2$$

$$E[(\delta P)^2] = S^2\Delta^2\sigma^2 + \tfrac{3}{4}S^4\Gamma^2\sigma^4$$

$$E[(\delta P)^3] = \tfrac{9}{2}S^4\Delta^2\Gamma\sigma^4 + \tfrac{15}{8}S^6\Gamma^3\sigma^6$$

The first two moments can be fitted to a normal distribution. This is better than ignoring gamma altogether, but, as already pointed out, the assumption that $\delta P$ is normal is less than ideal. An alternative approach is to use the three moments in conjunction with the Cornish–Fisher expansion as described in Appendix 16B.[9]

For a portfolio with $n$ underlying market variables, with each instrument in the portfolio being dependent on only one of the market variables, equation (16.6) becomes

$$\delta P = \sum_{i=1}^{n} S_i\Delta_i\,\delta x_i + \sum_{i=1}^{n} \tfrac{1}{2}S_i^2\Gamma_i\,(\delta x_i)^2$$

where $S_i$ is the value of the $i$th market variable, and $\Delta_i$ and $\Gamma_i$ are the delta and gamma of the portfolio with respect to the $i$th market variable. When individual instruments in the portfolio may be dependent on more than one market variable, this equation takes the more general form

$$\delta P = \sum_{i=1}^{n} S_i\Delta_i\,\delta x_i + \sum_{i=1}^{n}\sum_{j=1}^{n} \tfrac{1}{2}S_iS_j\Gamma_{ij}\,\delta x_i\,\delta x_j \tag{16.7}$$

where $\Gamma_{ij}$ is a "cross gamma" defined as

$$\Gamma_{ij} = \frac{\partial^2 P}{\partial S_i\,\partial S_j}$$

Equation (16.7) can be written as

$$\delta P = \sum_{i=1}^{n} \alpha_i\,\delta x_i + \sum_{i=1}^{n}\sum_{j=1}^{n} \beta_{ij}\,\delta x_i\,\delta x_j \tag{16.8}$$

where $\alpha_i = S_i\Delta_i$ and $\beta_{ij} = \tfrac{1}{2}S_iS_j\Gamma_{ij}$.

---

[8] The Taylor series expansion in Appendix 14A suggests the approximation

$$\delta P = \Theta\,\delta t + \Delta\,\delta S + \tfrac{1}{2}\Gamma\,(\delta S)^2$$

when terms of order higher than $\delta t$ are ignored. In practice the $\Theta\,\delta t$ term is so small that it is usually ignored.

[9] The Cornish–Fisher expansion provides a relationship between the moments of a distribution and its percentiles. For a description, see N. L. Johnson and S. Kotz, *Distributions in Statistics: Continuous Univariate Distributions 1*, Wiley, New York, 1972.

Equation (16.8) is not as easy to work with as equation (16.5), but it can be used to calculate moments for $\delta P$. Appendix 16B gives the first three moments and describes how they can be used in conjunction with the Cornish–Fisher expansion to estimate the percentiles of the probability distribution of $\delta P$ that correspond to the required VaR.

## 16.6 MONTE CARLO SIMULATION

As an alternative to the approaches described so far, we can implement the model-building approach using Monte Carlo simulation to generate the probability distribution for $\delta P$. Suppose we wish to calculate a one-day VaR for a portfolio. The procedure is as follows:

1. Value the portfolio today in the usual way using the current values of market variables.
2. Sample once from the multivariate normal probability distribution of the $\delta x_i$'s.[10]
3. Use the values of the $\delta x_i$'s that are sampled to determine the value of each market variable at the end of one day.
4. Revalue the portfolio at the end of the day in the usual way.
5. Subtract the value calculated in step 1 from the value in step 4 to determine a sample $\delta P$.
6. Repeat steps 2 to 5 many times to build up a probability distribution for $\delta P$.

The VaR is calculated as the appropriate percentile of the probability distribution of $\delta P$. Suppose, for example, that we calculate 5,000 different sample values of $\delta P$ in the way just described. The 1-day 99% VaR is the value of $\delta P$ for the 50th worst outcome; the 1-day VaR 95% is the value of $\delta P$ for the 250th worst outcome; and so on.[11] The $N$-day VaR is usually assumed to be the 1-day VaR multiplied by $\sqrt{N}$.[12]

The drawback of Monte Carlo simulation is that it tends to be slow because a company's complete portfolio (which might consist of hundreds of thousands of different instruments) has to be revalued many times.[13] One way of speeding things up is to assume that equation (16.8) describes the relationship between $\delta P$ and the $\delta x_i$'s. We can then jump straight from step 2 to step 5 in the Monte Carlo simulation and avoid the need for a complete revaluation of the portfolio. This is sometimes referred to as the *partial simulation approach*.

## 16.7 COMPARISON OF APPROACHES

We have discussed two methods for estimating VaR: the historical simulation approach and the model-building approach. The advantages of the model-building approach are that results can be

---

[10] One way of doing so is given in Chapter 18.

[11] Extreme value theory provides a way of "smoothing the tails" so that better estimates of extreme percentiles are obtained. See, for example, P. Embrechts, C. Kluppelberg, and T. Mikosch, *Modeling Extremal Events for Insurance and Finance*, Springer, New York, 1997.

[12] This is only approximately true when the portfolio includes options, but it is the assumption that is made in practice for all VaR calculation methods.

[13] An approach for limiting the number of portfolio revaluations is proposed in F. Jamshidian and Y. Zhu, "Scenario Simulation Model: Theory and Methodology," *Finance and Stochastics*, 1 (1997), 43–67.

produced very quickly and it can be used in conjunction with volatility updating schemes such as those we will describe in the next chapter. The main disadvantage of the model-building approach is that it assumes that the market variables have a multivariate normal distribution. In practice, daily changes in market variables often have distributions that are quite different from normal (see, for example, Table 15.1).

The historical simulation approach has the advantage that historical data determine the joint probability distribution of the market variables. It also avoids the need for cash-flow mapping (see Problem 16.2). The main disadvantages of historical simulation are that it is computationally slow and does not easily allow volatility updating schemes to be used.

One disadvantage of the model-building approach is that it tends to give poor results for low-delta portfolios (see Problem 16.22).

## 16.8  STRESS TESTING AND BACK TESTING

In addition to calculating a VaR, many companies carry out what is known as a *stress test* of their portfolio. Stress testing involves estimating how the portfolio would have performed under some of the most extreme market moves seen in the last 10 to 20 years.

For example, to test the impact of an extreme movement in U.S. equity prices, a company might set the percentage changes in all market variables equal to those on October 19, 1987 (when the S&P 500 moved by 22.3 standard deviations). If this is considered to be too extreme, the company might choose January 8, 1988 (when the S&P 500 moved by 6.8 standard deviations). To test the effect of extreme movements in U.K. interest rates, the company might set the percentage changes in all market variables equal to those on April 10, 1992 (when 10-year bond yields moved by 7.7 standard deviations).

Stress testing can be considered as a way of taking into account extreme events that do occur from time to time but that are virtually impossible according to the probability distributions assumed for market variables. A five-standard-deviation daily move in a market variable is one such extreme event. Under the assumption of a normal distribution, it happens about once every 7,000 years, but, in practice, it is not uncommon to see a five-standard-deviation daily move once or twice every 10 years.

Whatever the method used for calculating VaR, an important reality check is *back testing*. It involves testing how well the VaR estimates would have performed in the past. Suppose that we are calculating a 1-day 99% VaR. Back testing would involve looking at how often the loss in a day exceeded the 1-day 99% VaR calculated for that day. If this happened on about 1% of the days, we can feel reasonably comfortable with the methodology for calculating VaR. If it happened on, say, 7% of days, the methodology is suspect.

## 16.9  PRINCIPAL COMPONENTS ANALYSIS

One approach to handling the risk arising from groups of highly correlated market variables is principal components analysis. This takes historical data on movements in the market variables and attempts to define a set of components or factors that explain the movements.

The approach is best illustrated with an example. The market variables we will consider are ten U.S. Treasury rates with maturities between three months and 30 years. Tables 16.3 and 16.4 show

**Table 16.3**  Factor loadings for U.S. Treasury data

|      | PC1 | PC2 | PC3 | PC4 | PC5 | PC6 | PC7 | PC8 | PC9 | PC10 |
|------|-----|-----|-----|-----|-----|-----|-----|-----|-----|------|
| 3m   | 0.21 | −0.57 | 0.50 | 0.47 | −0.39 | −0.02 | 0.01 | 0.00 | 0.01 | 0.00 |
| 6m   | 0.26 | −0.49 | 0.23 | −0.37 | 0.70 | 0.01 | −0.04 | −0.02 | −0.01 | 0.00 |
| 12m  | 0.32 | −0.32 | −0.37 | −0.58 | −0.52 | −0.23 | −0.04 | −0.05 | 0.00 | 0.01 |
| 2y   | 0.35 | −0.10 | −0.38 | 0.17 | 0.04 | 0.59 | 0.56 | 0.12 | −0.12 | −0.05 |
| 3y   | 0.36 | 0.02 | −0.30 | 0.27 | 0.07 | 0.24 | −0.79 | 0.00 | −0.09 | −0.00 |
| 4y   | 0.36 | 0.14 | −0.12 | 0.25 | 0.16 | −0.63 | 0.15 | 0.55 | −0.14 | −0.08 |
| 5y   | 0.36 | 0.17 | −0.04 | 0.14 | 0.08 | −0.10 | 0.09 | −0.26 | 0.71 | 0.48 |
| 7y   | 0.34 | 0.27 | 0.15 | 0.01 | 0.00 | −0.12 | 0.13 | −0.54 | 0.00 | −0.68 |
| 10y  | 0.31 | 0.30 | 0.28 | −0.10 | −0.06 | 0.01 | 0.03 | −0.23 | −0.63 | 0.52 |
| 30y  | 0.25 | 0.33 | 0.46 | −0.34 | −0.18 | 0.33 | −0.09 | 0.52 | 0.26 | −0.13 |

results produced by Frye for these market variables using 1,543 daily observations between 1989 and 1995.[14] The first column in Table 16.3 shows the maturities of the rates that were considered. The remaining ten columns in the table show the ten factors (or principal components) describing the rate moves. The first factor, shown in the column labeled PC1, corresponds to a roughly parallel shift in the yield curve. When we have one unit of that factor, the three-month rate increases by 0.21 basis points, the six-month rate increases by 0.26 basis points, and so on. The second factor is shown in the column labeled PC2. It corresponds to a "twist" or "steepening" of the yield curve. Rates between 3 months and 2 years move in one direction; rates between 3 years and 30 years move in the other direction. The third factor corresponds to a "bowing" of the yield curve. Rates at the short end and long end of the yield curve move in one direction; rates in the middle move in the other direction. The interest rate move for a particular factor is known as *factor loading*. In our example, the first factor's loading for the three-month rate is 0.21.[15]

Because there are ten rates and ten factors, the interest rate changes observed on any given day can always be expressed as a linear sum of the factors by solving a set of ten simultaneous equations. The quantity of a particular factor in the interest rate changes on a particular day is known as the *factor score* for that day.

The importance of a factor is measured by the standard deviation of its factor score. The standard deviations of the factor scores in our example are shown in Table 16.4 and the factors are listed in order of their importance. The numbers in Table 16.4 are measured in basis points. A quantity of the first factor equal to one standard deviation, therefore, corresponds to the three-month rate moving by $0.21 \times 17.49 = 3.67$ basis points, the six-month rate moving by $0.26 \times 17.49 = 4.55$ basis points, and so on.

**Table 16.4**  Standard deviation of factor scores (basis points)

| PC1 | PC2 | PC3 | PC4 | PC5 | PC6 | PC7 | PC8 | PC9 | PC10 |
|-----|-----|-----|-----|-----|-----|-----|-----|-----|------|
| 17.49 | 6.05 | 3.10 | 2.17 | 1.97 | 1.69 | 1.27 | 1.24 | 0.80 | 0.79 |

---

[14] See J. Frye, "Principals of Risk: Finding VAR through Factor-Based Interest Rate Scenarios," in *VAR: Understanding and Applying Value at Risk*, Risk Publications, London, 1997, pp. 275–88.

[15] The factor loadings have the property that the sum of their squares for each factor is 1.0.

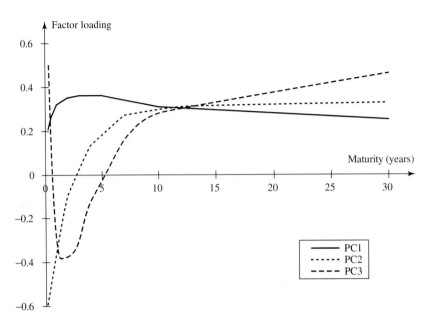

**Figure 16.6**   Three most important factors driving yield curve movements

The technical details of how the factors are determined are not covered here. It is sufficient for us to note that the factors are chosen so that the factor scores are uncorrelated. For instance, in our example, the first factor score (amount of parallel shift) is uncorrelated with the second factor score (amount of twist) across the 1,543 days.

The variances of the factor scores (i.e., the squares of the standard deviations) have the property that they add up to the total variance of the data. From Table 16.3, the total variance of the original data (i.e., the sum of the variance of the observations on the three-month rate, the variance of the observations on the six-month rate, and so on) is

$$17.49^2 + 6.05^2 + 3.10^2 + \cdots + 0.79^2 = 367.9$$

From this it can be seen that the first factor accounts for $17.49^2/367.9 = 83.1\%$ of the variation in the original data; the first two factors account for $(17.49^2 + 6.05^2)/367.9 = 93.1\%$ of the variation in the data; the third factor accounts for a further 2.8% of the variation. This shows most of the risk in interest rate moves is accounted for by the first two or three factors. It suggests that we can relate the risks in a portfolio of interest rate dependent instruments to movements in these factors instead of considering all ten interest rates. The three most important factors from Table 16.3 are plotted in Figure 16.6.[16]

### Using Principal Components Analysis to Calculate VaR

To illustrate how a principal components analysis can be used to calculate VaR, suppose we have a portfolio with the exposures shown in Table 16.5 to interest rate moves. A one-basis-point change

---

[16] Similar results to those described here, in respect of the nature of the factors and the amount of the total risk they account for, are obtained when a principal components analysis is used to explain the movements in almost any yield curve in any country.

**Table 16.5** Change in portfolio value for a one-basis-point rate move ($ millions)

| 1-year rate | 2-year rate | 3-year rate | 4-year rate | 5-year rate |
|---|---|---|---|---|
| +10 | +4 | −8 | −7 | +2 |

in the one-year rate causes the portfolio value to increase by $10 million; a one-basis-point change in the two-year rate causes it to increase by $4 million; and so on. We use the first two factors to model rate moves. (As mentioned in the preceding section, this captures over 90% of the uncertainty in rate moves.) Using the data in Table 16.3, our exposure to the first factor (measured in millions of dollars per factor score basis point) is

$$10 \times 0.32 + 4 \times 0.35 - 8 \times 0.36 - 7 \times 0.36 + 2 \times 0.36 = -0.08$$

and our exposure to the second factor is

$$10 \times (-0.32) + 4 \times (-0.10) - 8 \times 0.02 - 7 \times 0.14 + 2 \times 0.17 = -4.40$$

Suppose that $f_1$ and $f_2$ are the factor scores (measured in basis points). The change in the portfolio value is, to a good approximation, given by

$$\delta P = -0.08 f_1 - 4.40 f_2$$

The factor scores are uncorrelated and have the standard deviations given in Table 16.4. The standard deviation of $\delta P$ is therefore

$$\sqrt{0.08^2 \times 17.49^2 + 4.40^2 \times 6.05^2} = 26.66$$

The 1-day 99% VaR is therefore $26.66 \times 2.33 = 62.12$. Note that the data in Table 16.5 are such that we have very little exposure to the first factor and significant exposure to the second factor. Using only one factor would significantly understate VaR (see Problem 16.13). The duration-based method for handling interest rates, mentioned in Section 16.4, would also significantly understate VaR as it considers only parallel shifts in the yield curve.

A principal components analysis can in theory be used for market variables other than interest rates. Suppose that a financial institution has exposures to a number of different stock indices. A principal components analysis can be used to identify factors describing movements in the indices and the most important of these can be used to replace the market indices in a VaR analysis. How effective a principal components analysis is for a group of market variables depends on how closely correlated they are.

As explained earlier in the chapter, VaR is usually calculated by relating the actual changes in a portfolio to percentage changes in market variables (the $\delta x_i$'s). A principal components analysis is therefore often carried out on percentage changes in market variables rather than on their actual changes.

# SUMMARY

A value-at-risk (VaR) calculation is aimed at making a statement of the form "We are $X$ percent certain that we will not lose more than $V$ dollars in the next $N$ days." The variable $V$ is the VaR, $X$ is the confidence level, and $N$ is the time horizon.

One approach to calculating VaR is historical simulation. This involves creating a database consisting of the daily movements in all market variables over a period of time. The first simulation trial assumes that the percentage changes in each market variable are the same as those on the first day covered by the database; the second simulation trial assumes that the percentage changes are the same as those on the second day; and so on. The change in the portfolio value, $\delta P$, is calculated for each simulation trial, and the VaR is calculated as the appropriate percentile of the probability distribution of $\delta P$.

An alternative is the model-building approach. This is relatively straightforward if two assumptions can be made:

1. The change in the value of the portfolio ($\delta P$) is linearly dependent on percentage changes in market variables.
2. The percentage changes in market variables are multivariate normally distributed.

The probability distribution of $\delta P$ is then normal, and there are analytic formulas for relating the standard deviation of $\delta P$ to the volatilities and correlations of the underlying market variables. The VaR can be calculated from well-known properties of the normal distribution.

When a portfolio includes options, $\delta P$ is not linearly related to the percentage changes in market variables. From a knowledge of the gamma of the portfolio, we can derive an approximate quadratic relationship between $\delta P$ and the percentage changes in market variables. Either the Cornish–Fisher expansion or Monte Carlo simulation can then be used to estimate VaR.

In the next chapter we discuss how volatilities and correlations can be estimated for the model-building approach.

# SUGGESTIONS FOR FURTHER READING

Boudoukh, J., M. Richardson, and R. Whitelaw, "The Best of Both Worlds," *RISK*, May 1998, pp. 64–67.

Dowd, K., *Beyond Value at Risk: The New Science of Risk Management*, Wiley, New York, 1998.

Duffie, D., and J. Pan, "An Overview of Value at Risk," *Journal of Derivatives*, 4, no. 3 (Spring 1997), 7–49.

Embrechts, P., C. Kluppelberg, and T. Mikosch, *Modeling Extremal Events for Insurance and Finance*, Springer, New York, 1997.

Frye, J., "Principals of Risk: Finding VAR through Factor-Based Interest Rate Scenarios," in *VAR: Understanding and Applying Value at Risk*, Risk Publications, London, 1997, pp. 275–88.

Hendricks, D., "Evaluation of Value-at-Risk Models Using Historical Data." *Economic Policy Review*, Federal Reserve Bank of New York, 2 (April 1996), 39–69.

Hopper, G., "Value at Risk: A New Methodology for Measuring Portfolio Risk," *Business Review*, Federal Reserve Bank of Philadelphia, July/August 1996, 19–29.

Hua, P., and P. Wilmott, "Crash Courses," *RISK*, June 1997, pp. 64–67.

Hull, J. C., and A. White, "Value at Risk When Daily Changes in Market Variables Are Not Normally Distributed," *Journal of Derivatives*, 5 (Spring 1998), 9–19.

Hull, J. C., and A. White, "Incorporating Volatility Updating into the Historical Simulation Method for Value at Risk," *Journal of Risk*, 1, no. 1 (1998), 5–19.

Jackson, P., D. J. Maude, and W. Perraudin, "Bank Capital and Value at Risk," *Journal of Derivatives*, 4, no. 3 (Spring 1997), 73–90.

Jamshidian, F., and Y. Zhu, "Scenario Simulation Model: Theory and Methodology," *Finance and Stochastics*, 1 (1997), 43–67.

Jorion, P., *Value at Risk: The New Benchmark for Controlling Market Risk*, Irwin, Burr Ridge, IL, 1997.

Risk Publications, "Value at Risk," *RISK* supplement, June 1996.

## QUESTIONS AND PROBLEMS
## (ANSWERS IN SOLUTIONS MANUAL)

16.1. Consider a position consisting of a $100,000 investment in asset A and a $100,000 investment in asset B. Assume that the daily volatilities of both assets are 1% and that the coefficient of correlation between their returns is 0.3. What is the 5-day 99% value at risk for the portfolio?

16.2. Describe three alternative ways of handling interest-rate-dependent instruments when the model-building approach is used to calculate VaR. How would you handle interest-rate-dependent instruments when historical simulation is used to calculate VaR?

16.3. A financial institution owns a portfolio of options on the U.S. dollar–sterling exchange rate. The delta of the portfolio is 56.0. The current exchange rate is 1.5000. Derive an approximate linear relationship between the change in the portfolio value and the percentage change in the exchange rate. If the daily volatility of the exchange rate is 0.7%, estimate the 10-day 99% VaR.

16.4. Suppose that you know that the gamma of the portfolio in the previous question is 16.2. How does this change your estimate of the relationship between the change in the portfolio value and the percentage change in the exchange rate? Calculate a new 10-day 99% VaR based on estimates of the first two moments of the change in the portfolio value.

16.5. Suppose that the daily change in the value of a portfolio is, to a good approximation, linearly dependent on two factors, calculated from a principal components analysis. The delta of a portfolio with respect to the first factor is 6 and the delta with respect to the second factor is $-4$. The standard deviations of the factor are 20 and 8, respectively. What is the 5-day 90% VaR?

16.6. Suppose that a company has a portfolio consisting of positions in stocks, bonds, foreign exchange, and commodities. Assume there are no derivatives. Explain the assumptions underlying (a) the linear model and (b) the historical simulation model for calculating VaR.

16.7. Explain how an interest rate swap is mapped into a portfolio of zero-coupon bonds with standard maturities for the purposes of a VaR calculation.

16.8. Explain the difference between value at risk and conditional value at risk.

16.9. Explain why the linear model can provide only approximate estimates of VaR for a portfolio containing options.

16.10. Verify that the 0.3-year zero-coupon bond in the cash-flow mapping example in Appendix 16A is mapped in a $37,397 position in a three-month bond and a $11,793 position in a six-month bond.

16.11. Suppose that the 5-year rate is 6%, the seven year rate is 7% (both expressed with annual compounding), the daily volatility of a 5-year zero-coupon bond is 0.5%, and the daily volatility of a 7-year zero-coupon bond is 0.58%. The correlation between daily returns on the two bonds is 0.6. Map a cash flow of $1,000 received at time 6.5 years into a position in a five-year bond and a position in a seven-year bond. What cash flows in five and seven years are equivalent to the 6.5-year cash flow?

16.12. Some time ago a company has entered into a six-month forward contract to buy £1 million for $1.5 million. The daily volatility of a six-month zero-coupon sterling bond (when its price is translated to dollars) is 0.06% and the daily volatility of a six-month zero-coupon dollar bond is 0.05%. The correlation between returns from the two bonds is 0.8. The current exchange rate is 1.53. Calculate the standard deviation of the change in the dollar value of the forward contract in one day. What is the 10-day 99% VaR? Assume that the six-month interest rate in both sterling and dollars is 5% per annum with continuous compounding.

16.13. The text calculates a VaR estimate for the example in Table 16.5 assuming two factors. How does the estimate change if you assume (a) one factor and (b) three factors.

16.14. A bank has a portfolio of options on an asset. The delta of the options is −30 and the gamma is −5. Explain how these numbers can be interpreted. The asset price is 20 and its volatility is 1% per day. Using the quadratic model, calculate the first three moments of the change in the portfolio value. Calculate a 1-day 99% VaR using (a) the first two moments and (b) the first three moments.

16.15. Suppose that in Problem 16.14 the vega of the portfolio is −2 per 1% change in the annual volatility. Derive a model relating the change in the portfolio value in one day to delta, gamma, and vega. Explain, without doing detailed calculations, how you would use the model to calculate a VaR estimate.

# ASSIGNMENT QUESTIONS

16.16. A company has a position in bonds worth $6 million. The modified duration of the portfolio is 5.2 years. Assume that only parallel shifts in the yield curve can take place and that the standard deviation of the daily yield change (when yield is measured in percent) is 0.09. Use the duration model to estimate the 20-day 90% VaR for the portfolio. Explain carefully the weaknesses of this approach to calculating VaR. Explain two alternatives that give more accuracy.

16.17. Consider a position consisting of a $300,000 investment in gold and a $500,000 investment in silver. Suppose that the daily volatilities of these two assets are 1.8% and 1.2%, respectively, and that the coefficient of correlation between their returns is 0.6. What is the 10-day 97.5% value at risk for the portfolio? By how much does diversification reduce the VaR?

16.18. Consider a portfolio of options on a single asset. Suppose that the delta of the portfolio is 12, the value of the asset is $10, and the daily volatility of the asset is 2%. Estimate the 1-day 95% VaR for the portfolio.

16.19. Suppose that the gamma of the portfolio in Problem 16.18 is −2.6. Derive a quadratic relationship between the change in the portfolio value and the percentage change in the underlying asset price in one day.

    a. Calculate the first three moments of the change in the portfolio value.

    b. Using the first two moments and assuming that the change in the portfolio is normally distributed, calculate the 1-day 95% VaR for the portfolio.

    c. Use the third moment and the Cornish–Fisher expansion to revise your answer to (b).

16.20. A company has a long position in a two-year bond and a three-year bond as well as a short position in a five-year bond. Each bond has a principal of $100 and pays a 5% coupon annually. Calculate the company's exposure to the 1-year, 2-year, 3-year, 4-year, and 5-year rates. Use the data in Tables 16.3 and 16.4 to calculate a 20-day 95% VaR on the assumption that rate changes are explained by (a) one factor, (b) two factors, and (c) three factors. Assume that the zero-coupon yield curve is flat at 5%.

16.21. A bank has written a call option on one stock and a put option on another stock. For the first option the stock price is 50, the strike price is 51, the volatility is 28% per annum, and the time to maturity is nine months. For the second option the stock price is 20, the strike price is 19, the volatility is 25% per annum, and the time to maturity is one year. Neither stock pays a dividend, the risk-free rate is 6% per annum, and the correlation between stock price returns is 0.4. Calculate a 10-day 99% VaR:

    a. Using only delta

    b. Using delta, gamma, and the first two moments of the change in the portfolio value

    c. Using delta, gamma, and the first three moments of the change in the portfolio value

    d. Using the partial simulation approach

    e. Using the full simulation approach

16.22. A common complaint of risk managers is that the model-building approach (either linear or quadratic) does not work well when delta is close to zero. Test what happens when delta is close to zero in using Sample Application E in the DerivaGem Application Builder software. (You can do this by experimenting with different option positions and adjusting the position in the underlying to give a delta of zero.) Explain the results you get.

# APPENDIX 16A
## Cash-Flow Mapping

In this appendix we explain one procedure for mapping cash flows to standard maturity dates. We will illustrate the procedure by considering a simple example of a portfolio consisting of a long position in a single Treasury bond with a principal of $1 million maturing in 0.8 years. We suppose that the bond provides a coupon of 10% per annum payable semiannually. This means that the bond provides coupon payments of $50,000 in 0.3 years and 0.8 years. It also provides a principal payment of $1 million in 0.8 years. The Treasury bond can therefore be regarded as a position in a 0.3-year zero-coupon bond with a principal of $50,000 and a position in a 0.8-year zero-coupon bond with a principal of $1,050,000.

The position in the 0.3-year zero-coupon bond is mapped into an equivalent position in 3-month and 6-month zero-coupon bonds. The position in the 0.8-year zero-coupon bond is mapped into an equivalent position in 6-month and 1-year zero-coupon bonds. The result is that the position in the 0.8-year coupon-bearing bond is, for VaR purposes, regarded as a position in zero-coupon bonds having maturities of three months, six months, and one year.

### The Mapping Procedure

Consider the $1,050,000 that will be received in 0.8 years. We suppose that zero rates, daily bond price volatilities, and correlations between bond returns are as shown in Table 16.6.

The first stage is to interpolate between the 6-month rate of 6.0% and the 1-year rate of 7.0% to obtain a 0.8-year rate of 6.6%. (Annual compounding is assumed for all rates.) The present value of the $1,050,000 cash flow to be received in 0.8 years is

$$\frac{1,050,000}{1.066^{0.8}} = 997,662$$

We also interpolate between the 0.1% volatility for the 6-month bond and the 0.2% volatility for the 1-year bond to get a 0.16% volatility for the 0.8-year bond.

**Table 16.6**   Data to illustrate mapping procedure

| Maturity | 3-month | 6-month | 1-year |
|---|---|---|---|
| Zero rate (% with annual compounding) | 5.50 | 6.00 | 7.00 |
| Bond price volatility (% per day) | 0.06 | 0.10 | 0.20 |

| Correlation between daily returns | 3-month bond | 6-month bond | 1-year bond |
|---|---|---|---|
| 3-month bond | 1.0 | 0.9 | 0.6 |
| 6-month bond | 0.9 | 1.0 | 0.7 |
| 1-year bond | 0.6 | 0.7 | 1.0 |

**Table 16.7** The cash-flow mapping

| | $50,000 received in 0.3 years | $1,050,000 received in 0.8 years | Total |
|---|---|---|---|
| Position in 3-month bond ($) | 37,397 | | 37,397 |
| Position in 6-month bond ($) | 11,793 | 319,589 | 331,382 |
| Position in 1-year bond ($) | | 678,074 | 678,074 |

Suppose we allocate $\alpha$ of the present value to the 6-month bond and $1 - \alpha$ of the present value to the 1-year bond. Using equation (16.2) and matching variances, we obtain

$$0.0016^2 = 0.001^2\alpha^2 + 0.002^2(1 - \alpha)^2 + 2 \times 0.7 \times 0.001 \times 0.002\alpha(1 - \alpha)$$

This is a quadratic equation that can be solved in the usual way to give $\alpha = 0.320337$. This means that 32.0337% of the value should be allocated to a 6-month zero-coupon bond and 67.9663% of the value should be allocated to a 1-year zero coupon bond. The 0.8-year bond worth $997,662 is therefore replaced by a 6-month bond worth

$$997,662 \times 0.320337 = \$319,589$$

and a 1-year bond worth

$$997,662 \times 0.679663 = \$678,074$$

This cash-flow mapping scheme has the advantage that it preserves both the value and the variance of the cash flow. Also, it can be shown that the weights assigned to the two adjacent zero-coupon bonds are always positive.

For the $50,000 cash flow received at time 0.3 years, we can carry out similar calculations (see Problem 16.10). It turns out that the present value of the cash flow is $49,189. It can be mapped into a position worth $37,397 in a three-month bond and a position worth $11,793 in a six-month bond.

The results of the calculations are summarized in Table 16.7. The 0.8-year coupon-bearing bond is mapped into a position worth $37,397 in a three-month bond, a position worth $331,382 in a six-month bond, and a position worth $678,074 in a one-year bond. Using the volatilities and correlations in Table 16.6, equation (16.2) gives the variance of the change in the price of the 0.8-year bond with $n = 3$, $\alpha_1 = 37,397$, $\alpha_2 = 331,382$, $\alpha_3 = 678,074$, $\sigma_1 = 0.0006$, $\sigma_2 = 0.001$, $\sigma_3 = 0.002$, and $\rho_{12} = 0.9$, $\rho_{13} = 0.6$, $\rho_{23} = 0.7$. This variance is 2,628,518. The standard deviation of the change in the price of the bond is therefore $\sqrt{2,628,518} = 1,621.3$. Because we are assuming that the bond is the only instrument in the portfolio, the 10-day 99% VaR is

$$1621.3 \times \sqrt{10} \times 2.33 = 11,946$$

or about $11,950.

# APPENDIX 16B
## Use of the Cornish–Fisher Expansion to Estimate VaR

As shown in equation (16.8), we can approximate $\delta P$ for a portfolio containing options as

$$\delta P = \sum_{i=1}^{n} \alpha_i \, \delta x_i + \sum_{i=1}^{n} \sum_{j=1}^{n} \beta_{ij} \, \delta x_i \, \delta x_j \tag{16B.1}$$

Define $\sigma_{ij}$ as the covariance between variable $i$ and $j$:

$$\sigma_{ij} = \rho_{ij} \sigma_i \sigma_j$$

It can be shown that when the $\delta x_i$ are multivariate normal

$$E(\delta P) = \sum_{i,j} \beta_{ij} \sigma_{ij}$$

$$E[(\delta P)^2] - \sum_{i,j} \alpha_i \alpha_j \sigma_{ij} + \sum_{i,j,k,l} \beta_{ij} \beta_{kl} (\sigma_{ij}\sigma_{kl} + \sigma_{ik}\sigma_{jl} + \sigma_{il}\sigma_{jk})$$

$$E[(\delta P)^3] = 3 \sum_{i,j,k,l} \alpha_i \alpha_j \beta_{kl} (\sigma_{ij}\sigma_{kl} + \sigma_{ik}\sigma_{jl} + \sigma_{il}\sigma_{jk}) + \sum_{i_1,i_2,i_3,i_4,i_5,i_6} \beta_{i_1 i_2} \beta_{i_3 i_4} \beta_{i_5 i_6} Q$$

The variable $Q$ consists of fifteen terms of the form $\sigma_{k_1 k_2} \sigma_{k_3 k_4} \sigma_{k_5 k_6}$, where the $k_1$, $k_2$, $k_3$, $k_4$, $k_5$, $k_6$ are permutations of $i_1$, $i_2$, $i_3$, $i_4$, $i_5$, $i_6$.

Define $\mu_P$ and $\sigma_P$ as the mean and standard deviation of $\delta P$, so that

$$\mu_P = E(\delta P)$$

$$\sigma_P^2 = E[(\delta P)^2] - [E(\delta P)]^2$$

The skewness, $\xi_P$, of the probability distribution of $\delta P$ is defined as

$$\xi_P = \frac{1}{\sigma_P^3} E[(\delta P - \mu_P)^3] = \frac{E[(\delta P)^3] - 3E[(\delta P)^2]\mu_P + 2\mu_P^3}{\sigma_P^3}$$

Using the first three moments of $\delta P$, the Cornish–Fisher expansion estimates the $q$th percentile of the distribution of $\delta P$ as

$$\mu_P + w_q \sigma_P$$

where

$$w_q = z_q + \tfrac{1}{6}(z_q^2 - 1)\xi_P$$

and $z_q$ is the $q$th percentile of the standard normal distribution $\phi(0, 1)$.

**Example 16.2** Suppose that for a certain portfolio we calculate $\mu_P = -0.2$, $\sigma_P = 2.2$, and $\xi_P = -0.4$. If we assume that the probability distribution of $\delta P$ is normal, the first percentile of the probability distribution of $\delta P$ is

$$-0.2 - 2.33 \times 2.2 = -5.326$$

In other words, we are 99% certain that

$$\delta P > -5.326$$

When we use the Cornish–Fisher expansion to adjust for skewness and set $q = 0.01$, we obtain

$$w_q = -2.33 - \tfrac{1}{6}(2.33^2 - 1) \times 0.4 = -2.625$$

so that the first percentile of the distribution is

$$-0.2 - 2.625 \times 2.2 = -5.976$$

Taking account of skewness, therefore, changes the VaR from 5.326 to 5.976.

# CHAPTER 17

# ESTIMATING VOLATILITIES AND CORRELATIONS

In this chapter we explain how historical data can be used to produce estimates of the current and future levels of volatilities and correlations. The chapter is relevant both to the calculation of value at risk using the model-building approach and to the valuation of derivatives. When calculating value at risk, we are most interested in the current levels of volatilities and correlations because we are assessing possible changes in the value of a portfolio over a very short period of time. When valuing derivatives, forecasts of volatilities and correlations over the whole life of the derivative are usually required.

The chapter considers models with imposing names such as exponentially weighted moving average (EWMA), autoregressive conditional heteroscedasticity (ARCH), and generalized auto-regressive conditional heteroscedasticity (GARCH). The distinctive feature of the models is that they recognize that volatilities and correlations are not constant. During some periods a particular volatility or correlation may be relatively low, whereas during other periods it may be relatively high. The models attempt to keep track of the variations in the volatility or correlation through time.

## 17.1 ESTIMATING VOLATILITY

Define $\sigma_n$ as the volatility of a market variable on day $n$, as estimated at the end of day $n-1$. The square of the volatility, $\sigma_n^2$, on day $n$ is the *variance rate*.

We described the standard approach to estimating $\sigma_n$ from historical data in Section 12.4. Suppose that the value of the market variable at the end of day $i$ is $S_i$. The variable $u_i$ is defined as the continuously compounded return during day $i$ (between the end of day $i-1$ and the end of day $i$):

$$u_i = \ln\left(\frac{S_i}{S_{i-1}}\right)$$

An unbiased estimate of the variance rate per day, $\sigma_n^2$, using the most recent $m$ observations on the $u_i$ is

$$\sigma_n^2 = \frac{1}{m-1}\sum_{i=1}^{m}(u_{n-i} - \bar{u})^2 \tag{17.1}$$

where $\bar{u}$ is the mean of the $u_i$'s:

$$\bar{u} = \frac{1}{m} \sum_{i=1}^{m} u_{n-i}$$

For the purposes of calculating VaR, the formula in equation (17.1) is usually changed in a number of ways:

1. $u_i$ is defined as the percentage change in the market variable between the end of day $i - 1$ and the end of day $i$, so that[1]

$$u_i = \frac{S_i - S_{i-1}}{S_{i-1}} \qquad (17.2)$$

2. $\bar{u}$ is assumed to be zero.[2]
3. $m - 1$ is replaced by $m$.[3]

These three changes make very little difference to the variance estimates that are calculated, but they allow us to simplify the formula for the variance rate to

$$\sigma_n^2 = \frac{1}{m} \sum_{i=1}^{m} u_{n-i}^2 \qquad (17.3)$$

where $u_i$ is given by equation (17.2).[4]

## Weighting Schemes

Equation (17.3) gives equal weight to all $u_i^2$'s. Our objective is to estimate the current level of volatility, $\sigma_n$. It therefore makes sense to give more weight to recent data. A model that does this is

$$\sigma_n^2 = \sum_{i=1}^{m} \alpha_i u_{n-i}^2 \qquad (17.4)$$

The variable $\alpha_i$ is the amount of weight given to the observation $i$ days ago. The $\alpha$'s are positive. If we choose them so that $\alpha_i < \alpha_j$ when $i > j$, less weight is given to older observations. The weights must sum to unity, so that

$$\sum_{i=1}^{m} \alpha_i = 1$$

---

[1] This is consistent with the point made in Section 16.3 about the way that volatility is defined for the purposes of VaR calculations.

[2] As explained in Section 16.3, this assumption usually has very little effect on estimates of the variance because the expected change in a variable in one day is very small when compared with the standard deviation of changes.

[3] Replacing $m - 1$ by $m$ moves us from an unbiased estimate of the variance to a maximum likelihood estimate. Maximum likelihood estimates are discussed later in the chapter.

[4] Note that the $u$'s in this chapter play the same role as the $\delta x$'s in Chapter 16. Both are daily percentage changes in market variables. In the case of the $u$'s, the subscripts count observations made on different days on the same market variable. In the case of the $\delta x$'s, they count observations made on the same day on different market variables. The use of subscripts for $\sigma$ is similarly different between the two chapters. In this chapter, the subscripts refer to days; in Chapter 16, they referred to market variables.

An extension of the idea in equation (17.4) is to assume that there is a long-run average variance rate and that this should be given some weight. This leads to the model that takes the form

$$\sigma_n^2 = \gamma V_L + \sum_{i=1}^{m} \alpha_i u_{n-i}^2 \tag{17.5}$$

where $V_L$ is the long-run variance rate and $\gamma$ is the weight assigned to $V_L$. Because the weights must sum to unity,

$$\gamma + \sum_{i=1}^{m} \alpha_i = 1$$

This is known as an ARCH($m$) model. It was first suggested by Engle.[5] The estimate of the variance is based on a long-run average variance and $m$ observations. The older an observation, the less weight it is given. Defining $\omega = \gamma V_L$, the model in equation (17.5) can be written

$$\sigma_n^2 = \omega + \sum_{i=1}^{m} \alpha_i u_{n-i}^2 \tag{17.6}$$

This is the version of the model that is used when parameters are estimated.

In the next two sections we discuss two important approaches to monitoring volatility using the ideas in equations (17.4) and (17.5).

## 17.2  THE EXPONENTIALLY WEIGHTED MOVING AVERAGE MODEL

The exponentially weighted moving average (EWMA) model is a particular case of the model in equation (17.4) where the weights, $\alpha_i$, decrease exponentially as we move back through time. Specifically, $\alpha_{i+1} = \lambda \alpha_i$, where $\lambda$ is a constant between zero and one.

It turns out that this weighting scheme leads to a particularly simple formula for updating volatility estimates. The formula is

$$\sigma_n^2 = \lambda \sigma_{n-1}^2 + (1 - \lambda) u_{n-1}^2 \tag{17.7}$$

The estimate $\sigma_n$ of the volatility for day $n$ (made at the end of day $n-1$) is calculated from $\sigma_{n-1}$ (the estimate that was made at the end of day $n-2$ of the volatility for day $n-1$) and $u_{n-1}$ (the most recent daily percentage change in the market variable).

To understand why equation (17.7) corresponds to weights that decrease exponentially, we substitute for $\sigma_{n-1}^2$ to get

$$\sigma_n^2 = \lambda [\lambda \sigma_{n-2}^2 + (1 - \lambda) u_{n-2}^2] + (1 - \lambda) u_{n-1}^2$$

or

$$\sigma_n^2 = (1 - \lambda)(u_{n-1}^2 + \lambda u_{n-2}^2) + \lambda^2 \sigma_{n-2}^2$$

---

[5] See R. Engle, "Autoregressive Conditional Heteroscedasticity with Estimates of the Variance of UK Inflation," *Econometrica*, 50 (1982), 987–1008.

Substituting in a similar way for $\sigma^2_{n-2}$ gives

$$\sigma^2_n = (1 - \lambda)(u^2_{n-1} + \lambda u^2_{n-2} + \lambda^2 u^2_{n-3}) + \lambda^3 \sigma^2_{n-3}$$

Continuing in this way, we see that

$$\sigma^2_n = (1 - \lambda) \sum_{i=1}^{m} \lambda^{i-1} u^2_{n-i} + \lambda^m \sigma^2_{n-m}$$

For large $m$, the term $\lambda^m \sigma^2_{n-m}$ is sufficiently small to be ignored, so that equation (17.7) is the same as equation (17.4) with $\alpha_i = (1 - \lambda)\lambda^{i-1}$. The weights for the $u_i$'s decline at rate $\lambda$ as we move back through time. Each weight is $\lambda$ times the previous weight.

**Example 17.1**  Suppose that $\lambda$ is 0.90, the volatility estimated for a market variable for day $n - 1$ is 1% per day, and during day $n - 1$ the market variable increased by 2%. This means that $\sigma^2_{n-1} = 0.01^2 = 0.0001$ and $u^2_{n-1} = 0.02^2 = 0.0004$. Equation (17.7) gives

$$\sigma^2_n = 0.9 \times 0.0001 + 0.1 \times 0.0004 = 0.00013$$

The estimate of the volatility, $\sigma_n$, for day $n$ is therefore $\sqrt{0.00013}$, or 1.14% per day. Note that the expected value of $u^2_{n-1}$ is $\sigma^2_{n-1}$ or 0.0001. In this example, the realized value of $u^2_{n-1}$ is greater than the expected value, and as a result our volatility estimate increases. If the realized value of $u^2_{n-1}$ had been less than its expected value, our estimate of the volatility would have decreased.

The EWMA approach has the attractive feature that relatively little data need to be stored. At any given time, we need to remember only the current estimate of the variance rate and the most recent observation on the value of the market variable. When we get a new observation on the value of the market variable, we calculate a new daily percentage change and use equation (17.7) to update our estimate of the variance rate. The old estimate of the variance rate and the old value of the market variable can then be discarded.

The EWMA approach is designed to track changes in the volatility. Suppose that there is a big move in the market variable on day $n - 1$, so that $u^2_{n-1}$ is large. From equation (17.7) this causes our estimate of the current volatility to move upward. The value of $\lambda$ governs how responsive the estimate of the daily volatility is to the most recent daily percentage change. A low value of $\lambda$ leads to a great deal of weight being given to the $u^2_{n-1}$ when $\sigma_n$ is calculated. In this case, the estimates produced for the volatility on successive days are themselves highly volatile. A high value of $\lambda$ (i.e., a value close to 1.0) produces estimates of the daily volatility that respond relatively slowly to new information provided by the daily percentage changes.

The RiskMetrics database, which was created by J.P. Morgan and made publicly available in 1994, uses the EWMA model with $\lambda = 0.94$ for updating daily volatility estimates. The company found that, across a range of different market variables, this value of $\lambda$ gives forecasts of the variance rate that come closest to the realized variance rate.[6] The realized variance rate on a particular day was calculated as an equally weighted average of the $u^2_i$ on the subsequent 25 days. (See Problem 17.17.)

---

[6] See J.P. Morgan, *RiskMetrics Monitor*, Fourth Quarter, 1995. We will explain an alternative (maximum likelihood) approach to estimating parameters later in the chapter.

## 17.3   THE GARCH(1,1) MODEL

We now move on to discuss what is known as the GARCH(1, 1) model proposed by Bollerslev in 1986.[7] The difference between the GARCH(1, 1) model and the EWMA model is analogous to the difference between equation (17.4) and equation (17.5). In GARCH(1, 1), $\sigma_n^2$ is calculated from a long-run average variance rate, $V_L$, as well as from $\sigma_{n-1}$ and $u_{n-1}$. The equation for GARCH(1, 1) is

$$\sigma_n^2 = \gamma V_L + \alpha u_{n-1}^2 + \beta \sigma_{n-1}^2 \tag{17.8}$$

where $\gamma$ is the weight assigned to $V_L$, $\alpha$ is the weight assigned to $u_{n-1}^2$, and $\beta$ is the weight assigned to $\sigma_{n-1}^2$. Because the weights must sum to one,

$$\gamma + \alpha + \beta = 1$$

The EWMA model is a particular case of the GARCH(1, 1) model where $\gamma = 0$, $\alpha = 1 - \lambda$, and $\beta = \lambda$.

The "(1, 1)" in GARCH(1, 1) indicates that $\sigma_n^2$ is based on the most recent observation of $u^2$ and the most recent estimate of the variance rate. The more general GARCH($p, q$) model calculates $\sigma_n^2$ from the most recent $p$ observations on $u^2$ and the most recent $q$ estimates of the variance rate.[8] GARCH(1, 1) is by far the most popular of the GARCH models.

Setting $\omega = \gamma V_L$, the GARCH(1, 1) model can also be written

$$\sigma_n^2 = \omega + \alpha u_{n-1}^2 + \beta \sigma_{n-1}^2 \tag{17.9}$$

This is the form of the model that is usually used for the purposes of estimating the parameters. Once $\omega$, $\alpha$, and $\beta$ have been estimated, we can calculate $\gamma$ as $1 - \alpha - \beta$. The long-term variance $V_L$ can then be calculated as $\omega/\gamma$. For a stable GARCH(1, 1) process, we require $\alpha + \beta < 1$. Otherwise the weight applied to the long-term variance is negative.

**Example 17.2**   Suppose that a GARCH(1, 1) model is estimated from daily data as

$$\sigma_n^2 = 0.000002 + 0.13 u_{n-1}^2 + 0.86 \sigma_{n-1}^2$$

This corresponds to $\alpha = 0.13$, $\beta = 0.86$, and $\omega = 0.000002$. Because $\gamma = 1 - \alpha - \beta$, it follows that $\gamma = 0.01$. Because $\omega = \gamma V_L$, it follows that $V_L = 0.0002$. In other words, the long-run average variance per day implied by the model is 0.0002. This corresponds to a volatility of $\sqrt{0.0002} = 0.014$, or 1.4% per day.

---

[7] See T. Bollerslev, "Generalized Autoregressive Conditional Heteroscedasticity," *Journal of Econometrics*, 31 (1986), 307–27.

[8] Other GARCH models have been proposed that incorporate asymmetric news. These models are designed so that $\sigma_n$ depends on the sign of $u_{n-1}$. Arguably, the models are more appropriate for equities than GARCH(1, 1). As mentioned in Chapter 15, the volatility of an equity's price tends to be inversely related to the price so that a negative $u_{n-1}$ should have a bigger effect on $\sigma_n$ than the same positive $u_{n-1}$. For a discussion of models for handling asymmetric news, see D. Nelson, "Conditional Heteroscedasticity and Asset Returns: A New Approach," *Econometrica*, 59 (1990), 347–70; R. F. Engle and V. Ng, "Measuring and Testing the Impact of News on Volatility," *Journal of Finance*, 48 (1993), 1749–78.

Suppose that the estimate of the volatility on day $n-1$ is 1.6% per day, so that $\sigma_{n-1}^2 = 0.016^2 = 0.000256$, and that on day $n-1$ the market variable decreased by 1%, so that $u_{n-1}^2 = 0.01^2 = 0.0001$. Then

$$\sigma_n^2 = 0.000002 + 0.13 \times 0.0001 + 0.86 \times 0.000256 = 0.00023516$$

The new estimate of the volatility is therefore $\sqrt{0.00023516} = 0.0153$, or 1.53% per day.

### The Weights

Substituting for $\sigma_{n-1}^2$ in equation (17.9), we obtain

$$\sigma_n^2 = \omega + \alpha u_{n-1}^2 + \beta(\omega + \alpha u_{n-2}^2 + \beta\sigma_{n-2}^2)$$

or

$$\sigma_n^2 = \omega + \beta\omega + \alpha u_{n-1}^2 + \alpha\beta u_{n-2}^2 + \beta^2\sigma_{n-2}^2$$

Substituting for $\sigma_{n-2}^2$, we get

$$\sigma_n^2 = \omega + \beta\omega + \beta^2\omega + \alpha u_{n-1}^2 + \alpha\beta u_{n-2}^2 + \alpha\beta^2 u_{n-3}^2 + \beta^3\sigma_{n-3}^2$$

Continuing in this way, we see that the weight applied to $u_{n-i}^2$ is $\alpha\beta^{i-1}$. The weights decline exponentially at rate $\beta$. The parameter $\beta$ can be interpreted as a "decay rate". It is similar to $\lambda$ in the EWMA model. It defines the relative importance of the observations on $u$'s in determining the current variance rate. For example, if $\beta = 0.9$, $u_{n-2}^2$ is only 90% as important as $u_{n-1}^2$; $u_{n-3}^2$ is 81% as important as $u_{n-1}^2$; and so on. The GARCH(1, 1) model is similar to the EWMA model except that, in addition to assigning weights that decline exponentially to past $u^2$, it also assigns some weight to the long-run average volatility.

### Mean Reversion

The GARCH (1, 1) model recognizes that over time the variance tends to get pulled back to a long-run average level of $V_L$. The amount of weight assigned to $V_L$ is $\gamma = 1 - \alpha - \beta$. The GARCH(1, 1) is equivalent to a model where the variance $V$ follows the stochastic process

$$dV = a(V_L - V)\,dt + \xi V\,dz$$

where time is measured in days, $a = 1 - \alpha - \beta$, and $\xi = \alpha\sqrt{2}$ (see Problem 17.14). This is a mean-reverting model. The variance has a drift that pulls it back to $V_L$ at rate $a$. When $V > V_L$, the variance has a negative drift; when $V_L < V$, it has a positive drift. Superimposed on the drift is a volatility $\xi$. We will discuss this type of model further in Section 20.3.

## 17.4 CHOOSING BETWEEN THE MODELS

In practice, variance rates do tend to be mean reverting. The GARCH(1, 1) model incorporates mean reversion, whereas the EWMA model does not. GARCH (1, 1) is therefore theoretically more appealing than the EWMA model.

In the next section, we will discuss how best-fit parameters $\omega$, $\alpha$, and $\beta$ in GARCH(1, 1) can be estimated. When the parameter $\omega$ is zero, the GARCH(1, 1) reduces to EWMA. In circumstances where the best-fit value of $\omega$ turns out to be negative the GARCH(1, 1) model is not stable and it makes sense to switch to the EWMA model.

## 17.5 MAXIMUM LIKELIHOOD METHODS

It is now appropriate to discuss how the parameters in the models we have been considering are estimated from historical data. The approach used is the *maximum likelihood method.* It involves choosing values for the parameters that maximize the chance (or likelihood) of the data occurring.

To illustrate the method, we start with a very simple example. Suppose that we sample ten stocks at random on a certain day and find that the price of one of them declined on that day and the prices of the other nine either remained the same or increased. What is our best estimate of the proportion of all stocks with price declines? The natural answer is 10%. Let us see if this is what the maximum likelihood method gives.

Suppose that the proportion of stocks with price declines is $p$. The probability that one particular stock declines in price and the other nine do not is $p(1 - p)^9$. Using the maximum likelihood approach, the best estimate of $p$ is the one that maximizes $p(1 - p)^9$. Differentiating this expression with respect to $p$ and setting the result equal to zero, we find that $p = 0.1$ maximizes the expression. This shows that the maximum likelihood estimate of $p$ is 10% as expected.

### Estimating a Constant Variance

As our next example of maximum likelihood methods, we consider the problem of estimating the variance of a variable $X$ from $m$ observations on $X$ when the underlying distribution is normal with zero mean. We assume that the observations are $u_1, u_2, \ldots, u_m$ and that the mean of the underlying distribution is zero. Denote the variance by $v$. The likelihood of $u_i$ being observed is the value of the probability density function for $X$ when $X = u_i$. This is

$$\frac{1}{\sqrt{2\pi v}} \exp\left(\frac{-u_i^2}{2v}\right)$$

The likelihood of the $m$ observations occurring in the order in which they are observed is

$$\prod_{i=1}^{m}\left[\frac{1}{\sqrt{2\pi v}}\exp\left(\frac{-u_i^2}{2v}\right)\right] \tag{17.10}$$

Using the maximum likelihood method, the best estimate of $v$ is the value that maximizes this expression.

Maximizing an expression is equivalent to maximizing the logarithm of the expression. Taking logarithms of the expression in equation (17.10) and ignoring constant multiplicative factors, it can be seen that we wish to maximize

$$\sum_{i=1}^{m}\left(-\ln(v) - \frac{u_i^2}{v}\right) \tag{17.11}$$

or

$$-m\ln(v) - \sum_{i=1}^{m}\frac{u_i^2}{v}$$

Differentiating this expression with respect to $v$ and setting the result equation to zero, we see that the maximum likelihood estimator of $v$ is[9]

$$\frac{1}{m}\sum_{i=1}^{m}u_i^2.$$

### Estimating GARCH(1, 1) Parameters

We now consider how the maximum likelihood method can be used to estimate the parameters when GARCH(1, 1) or some other volatility updating scheme is used. Define $v_i = \sigma_i^2$ as the variance estimated for day $i$. We assume that the probability distribution of $u_i$ conditional on the variance is normal. A similar analysis to the one just given shows that the best parameters are the ones that maximize

$$\prod_{i=1}^{m}\left[\frac{1}{\sqrt{2\pi v_i}}\exp\left(\frac{-u_i^2}{2v_i}\right)\right]$$

Taking logarithms, we see that this is equivalent to maximizing

$$\sum_{i=1}^{m}\left(-\ln(v_i)-\frac{u_i^2}{v_i}\right) \tag{17.12}$$

This is the same as the expression in equation (17.11), except that $v$ is replaced by $v_i$. We search iteratively to find the parameters in the model that maximize the expression in equation (17.12).

The spreadsheet in Table 17.1 indicates how the calculations could be organized for the GARCH(1, 1) model. The table analyzes data on the Japanese yen exchange rate between January 6, 1988, and August 15, 1997. The numbers in the table are based on trial estimates of the three GARCH(1, 1) parameters $\omega$, $\alpha$, and $\beta$. The first column in the table records the date. The second column counts the days. The third column shows the exchange rate, $S_i$, at the end of day $i$. The fourth column shows the proportional change in the exchange rate between the end of day $i - 1$ and the end of day $i$. This is $u_i = (S_i - S_{i-1})/S_{i-1}$. The fifth column shows the estimate of the variance rate, $v_i = \sigma_i^2$, for day $i$ made at the end of day $i - 1$. On day 3, we start things off by setting the variance equal to $u_2^2$. On subsequent days equation (17.9) is used. The sixth column tabulates the likelihood measure, $-\ln(v_i) - u_i^2/v_i$. The values in the fifth and sixth columns are based on the current trial estimates of $\omega$, $\alpha$, and $\beta$. We are interested in choosing $\omega$, $\alpha$, and $\beta$ to maximize the sum of the numbers in the sixth column. This involves an iterative search procedure.[10]

In our example, the optimal values of the parameters turn out to be

$$\omega = 0.00000176, \quad \alpha = 0.0626, \quad \beta = 0.8976$$

and the maximum value of the function in equation (17.12) is 22,063.5763. The numbers shown in Table 17.1 were calculated on the final iteration of the search for the optimal $\omega$, $\alpha$, and $\beta$.

---

[9] This confirms the point made in footnote 3.

[10] A general purpose algorithm such as Solver in Microsoft's Excel is liable to provide a local rather than global maximum of the likelihood function. A special purpose algorithm, such as Levenberg–Marquardt, should ideally be used. See W. H. Press, B. P. Flannery, S. A. Teukolsky, and W. T. Vetterling, *Numerical Recipes in C: The Art of Scientific Computing*, Cambridge University Press, Cambridge, 1988.

**Table 17.1**  Estimation of parameters in GARCH(1, 1) model

| Date | Day $i$ | $S_i$ | $u_i$ | $v_i = \sigma_i^2$ | $-\ln(v_i) - u_i^2/v_i$ |
|---|---|---|---|---|---|
| 06-Jan-88 | 1 | 0.007728 | | | |
| 07-Jan-88 | 2 | 0.007779 | 0.006599 | | |
| 08-Jan-88 | 3 | 0.007746 | −0.004242 | 0.00004355 | 9.6283 |
| 11-Jan-88 | 4 | 0.007816 | 0.009037 | 0.00004198 | 8.1329 |
| 12-Jan-88 | 5 | 0.007837 | 0.002687 | 0.00004455 | 9.8568 |
| 13-Jan-88 | 6 | 0.007924 | 0.011101 | 0.00004220 | 7.1529 |
| ⋮ | ⋮ | ⋮ | ⋮ | ⋮ | ⋮ |
| 13-Aug-97 | 2421 | 0.008643 | 0.003374 | 0.00007626 | 9.3321 |
| 14-Aug-97 | 2422 | 0.008493 | −0.017309 | 0.00007092 | 5.3294 |
| 15-Aug-97 | 2423 | 0.008495 | 0.000144 | 0.00008417 | 9.3824 |
| | | | | | 22,063.5763 |

Trial estimates of GARCH parameters

| $\omega$ | $\alpha$ | $\beta$ |
|---|---|---|
| 0.00000176 | 0.0626 | 0.8976 |

The long-term variance rate, $V_L$, in our example is

$$\frac{\omega}{1 - \alpha - \beta} = \frac{0.00000176}{0.0398} = 0.00004422$$

The long-term volatility is $\sqrt{0.00004422}$, or 0.665% per day.

Figure 17.1 shows the way the GARCH (1, 1) volatility for the Japanese yen changed over the 10-year period covered by the data. Most of the time, the volatility was between 0.4% and 0.8% per day, but volatilities over 1% were experienced during some periods.

An alternative more robust approach to estimating parameters in GARCH(1, 1) is known as *variance targeting*.[11] This involves setting the long-run average variance rate, $V_L$, equal to the sample variance calculated from the data (or to some other value that is believed to be reasonable). The value of $\omega$ then equals $V_L(1 - \alpha - \beta)$ and only two parameters have to be estimated. For the data in Table 17.1, the sample variance is 0.00004341, which gives a daily volatility of 0.659%. Setting $V_L$ equal to the sample variance, the values of $\alpha$ and $\beta$ that maximize the objective function in equation (17.12) are 0.0607 and 0.8990, respectively. The value of the objective function is 22,063.5274, only marginally below the value of 22,063.5763 obtained using the earlier procedure.[12]

When the EWMA model is used, the estimation procedure is relatively simple. We set $\omega = 0$, $\alpha = 1 - \lambda$, and $\beta = \lambda$, and only one parameter has to be estimated. In the data in Table 17.1, the value of $\lambda$ that maximizes the objective function in equation (17.12) is 0.9686 and the value of the objective function is 21,995.8377.

---

[11]  See R. Engle and J. Mezrich, "GARCH for Groups," *RISK*, August 1996, pp. 36–40.

[12]  The Solver routine in Microsoft's Excel can be used to give good results when variance targeting is used.

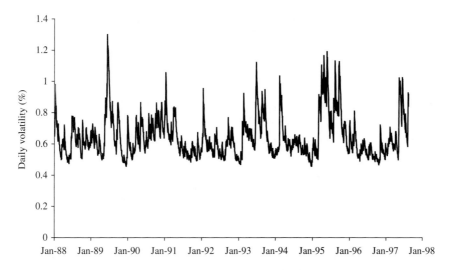

**Figure 17.1**  Daily volatility of the yen–USD exchange rate, 1987–97

### How Good Is the Model?

The assumption underlying a GARCH model is that volatility changes with the passage of time. During some periods volatility is relatively high; during other periods it is relatively low. To put this another way, when $u_i^2$ is high, there is a tendency for $u_{i+1}^2$, $u_{i+2}^2$, ... to be high; when $u_i^2$ is low, there is a tendency for $u_{i+1}^2$, $u_{i+2}^2$, ... to be low. We can test how true this is by examining the autocorrelation structure of the $u_i^2$.

Let us assume that the $u_i^2$ do exhibit autocorrelation. If a GARCH model is working well, it should remove the autocorrelation. We can test whether it has done this by considering the autocorrelation structure for the variables $u_i^2/\sigma_i^2$. If these show very little autocorrelation, our model for $\sigma_i$ has succeeded in explaining autocorrelations in the $u_i^2$.

Table 17.2 shows results for the yen–dollar exchange rate data referred to earlier. The first column shows the lags considered when the autocorrelation is calculated. The second column shows autocorrelations for $u_i^2$; the third column shows autocorrelations for $u_i^2/\sigma_i^2$.[13] The table shows that the autocorrelations are positive for $u_i^2$ for all lags between 1 and 15. In the case of $u_i^2/\sigma_i^2$, some of the autocorrelations are positive and some are negative. They are all much smaller in magnitude than the autocorrelations for $u_i^2$.

The GARCH model appears to have done a good job in explaining the data. For a more scientific test, we can use what is known as the Ljung–Box statistic. If a certain series has $m$ observations the Ljung–Box statistic is

$$m \sum_{k=1}^{K} w_k \eta_k^2$$

where $\eta_k$ is the autocorrelation for a lag of $k$ and

$$w_k = \frac{m-2}{m-k}$$

---

[13] For a series $x_i$, the autocorrelation with a lag of $k$ is the coefficient of correlation between $x_i$ and $x_{i+k}$.

**Table 17.2**  Autocorrelations before and after the use
of a GARCH model

| Time lag | Autocorrelation for $u_i^2$ | Autocorrelation for $u_i^2/\sigma_i^2$ |
|---|---|---|
| 1 | 0.072 | 0.004 |
| 2 | 0.041 | −0.005 |
| 3 | 0.057 | 0.008 |
| 4 | 0.107 | 0.003 |
| 5 | 0.075 | 0.016 |
| 6 | 0.066 | 0.008 |
| 7 | 0.019 | −0.033 |
| 8 | 0.085 | 0.012 |
| 9 | 0.054 | 0.010 |
| 10 | 0.030 | −0.023 |
| 11 | 0.038 | −0.004 |
| 12 | 0.038 | −0.021 |
| 13 | 0.057 | −0.001 |
| 14 | 0.040 | 0.002 |
| 15 | 0.007 | −0.028 |

For $k = 15$, zero autocorrelation can be rejected with 95% confidence when the Ljung–Box statistic is greater than 25.

From Table 17.2, the Ljung–Box statistic for the $u_i^2$ series is about 123. This is strong evidence of autocorrelation. For the $u_i^2/\sigma_i^2$ series the Ljung–Box statistic is 8.2, suggesting that the autocorrelation has been largely removed by the GARCH model.

## 17.6   USING GARCH(1,1) TO FORECAST FUTURE VOLATILITY

Substituting $\gamma = 1 - \alpha - \beta$ in equation (17.8), the variance rate estimated at the end of day $n - 1$ for day $n$ is

$$\sigma_n^2 = (1 - \alpha - \beta)V_L + \alpha u_{n-1}^2 + \beta\sigma_{n-1}^2$$

so that

$$\sigma_n^2 - V_L = \alpha(u_{n-1}^2 - V_L) + \beta(\sigma_{n-1}^2 - V_L)$$

On day $n + k$ in the future, we have

$$\sigma_{n+k}^2 - V_L = \alpha(u_{n+k-1}^2 - V_L) + \beta(\sigma_{n+k-1}^2 - V_L)$$

The expected value of $u_{n+k-1}^2$ is $\sigma_{n+k-1}^2$. Hence,

$$E(\sigma_{n+k}^2 - V_L) = (\alpha + \beta)E(\sigma_{n+k-1}^2 - V_L)$$

where $E$ denotes the expected value. Using this equation repeatedly yields

$$E(\sigma_{n+k}^2 - V_L) = (\alpha + \beta)^k(\sigma_n^2 - V_L)$$

or

$$E(\sigma_{n+k}^2) = V_L + (\alpha + \beta)^k(\sigma_n^2 - V_L) \qquad (17.13)$$

This equation forecasts the volatility on day $n + k$ using the information available at the end of day $n - 1$. In the EWMA model, $\alpha + \beta = 1$ and equation (17.13) shows that the expected future variance rate equals the current variance rate. When $\alpha + \beta < 1$, the final term in the equation becomes progressively smaller as $k$ increases. Figure 17.2 shows the expected path followed by the variance rate for situations where the current variance rate is different from $V_L$. As mentioned earlier, the variance rate exhibits mean reversion with a reversion level of $V_L$ and a reversion rate of $1 - \alpha - \beta$. Our forecast of the future variance rate tends towards $V_L$ as we look further and further ahead. This analysis emphasizes the point that we must have $\alpha + \beta < 1$ for a stable GARCH$(1, 1)$ process. When $\alpha + \beta > 1$, the weight given to the long-term average variance is negative and the process is "mean fleeing" rather than "mean reverting".

In the yen–dollar exchange rate example considered earlier $\alpha + \beta = 0.9602$ and $V_L = 0.00004422$. Suppose that our estimate of the current variance rate per day is 0.00006. (This corresponds to a volatility of 0.77% per day.) In 10 days the expected variance rate is

$$0.00004422 + 0.9602^{10}(0.00006 - 0.00004422) = 0.00005473$$

The expected volatility per day is 0.74%, which is only marginally below the current volatility of 0.77% per day. However, the expected variance rate in 100 days is

$$0.00004422 + 0.9602^{100}(0.00006 - 0.00004422) = 0.00004449$$

The expected volatility per day is 0.67%, very close the long-term volatility.

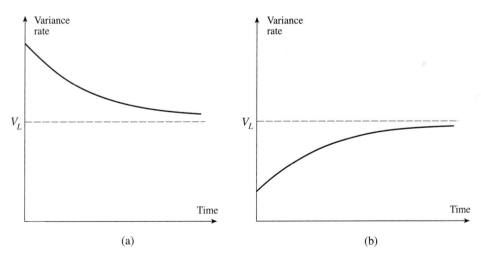

**Figure 17.2** Expected path for the variance rate when (a) current variance rate is above long-term variance rate and (b) current variance rate is below long-term variance rate

## Volatility Term Structures

Consider an option lasting between day $n$ and day $n + N$. We can use equation (17.13) to calculate the expected variance rate during the life of the option as

$$\frac{1}{N}\sum_{k=0}^{N-1} E(\sigma_{n+k}^2) \qquad (17.14)$$

The longer the life of the option, the closer this is to $V_L$.

As we discussed in Chapter 15, the market prices of different options on the same asset are often used to calculate a *volatility term structure*. This is the relationship between the implied volatilities of the options and their maturities. Equation (17.14) can be used to estimate a volatility term structure based on the GARCH(1, 1) model. The square root of the expression in equation (17.14) is an estimate of the volatility appropriate for valuing the $N$-day option. The estimated volatility term structure is not usually the same as the actual volatility term structure. However, as we will show, it is often used to predict the way that the actual volatility term structure will respond to volatility changes.

When the current volatility is above the long-term volatility, the GARCH(1, 1) model estimates a downward-sloping volatility term structure. When the current volatility is below the long-term volatility, it estimates an upward-sloping volatility term structure. Table 17.3 shows the results of using equation (17.14) to estimate a volatility term structure for options on the yen–dollar exchange rate when the current estimate of the variance rate is 0.00006. For the purposes of this table, the daily volatilities have been annualized by multiplying them by $\sqrt{252}$. Consider, for example, a 10-day option. The estimated variance rate is 0.00006 for the first day. Similar calculations to those given earlier in this section show that the estimated variance rate is

$$0.00004422 + 0.9602(0.00006 - 0.00004422) = 0.00005937$$

for the second day,

$$0.00004422 + 0.9602^2(0.00006 - 0.00004422) = 0.00005879$$

for the third day, and so on. The average variance rate over 10 days is

$$\tfrac{1}{10}(0.00006 + 0.00005937 + 0.00005879 + \cdots) = 0.00005745$$

The estimated volatility is therefore $\sqrt{0.00005745} \times \sqrt{252} = 12.03\%$.

## Impact of Volatility Changes

Table 17.4 shows the effect of a volatility change on options of varying maturities for our yen–dollar exchange rate example. We assume as before that the current variance rate is 0.00006 per day. This corresponds to a daily volatility of 0.7746% and a volatility of $0.7746\sqrt{252} = 12.30\%$ per year. We will refer to this as the instantaneous volatility. A 1% increase changes the instantaneous

**Table 17.3**  Yen–dollar volatility term structure predicted from GARCH(1, 1)

| Option life (days) | 10 | 30 | 50 | 100 | 500 |
|---|---|---|---|---|---|
| Option volatility (% per annum) | 12.03 | 11.61 | 11.35 | 11.01 | 10.65 |

**Table 17.4**   Impact of 1% change in the instantaneous volatility predicted from GARCH(1, 1)

| *Option life (days)* | *10* | *30* | *50* | *100* | *500* |
|---|---|---|---|---|---|
| Option volatility now (%) | 12.03 | 11.61 | 11.35 | 11.01 | 10.65 |
| Option volatility after change (%) | 12.89 | 12.25 | 11.83 | 11.29 | 10.71 |
| Increase in volatility (%) | 0.86 | 0.64 | 0.48 | 0.28 | 0.06 |

volatility to 13.30% per year. The daily volatility becomes $0.1330/\sqrt{252} = 0.84\%$ and the current variance rate per day becomes $0.0084^2 = 0.00007016$.

Consider the calculation of the 10-day volatility after the 1% increase in the instantaneous volatility. The variance rate is 0.00007016 for the first day. Equation (17.13) gives an estimated variance rate of

$$0.00004422 + 0.9602(0.00007016 - 0.00004422) = 0.00006913$$

for the second day,

$$0.00004422 + 0.9602^2(0.00007016 - 0.00004422) = 0.00006814$$

for the third day, and so on. The average variance rate over 10 days is, from equation (17.14),

$$\tfrac{1}{10}(0.00007016 + 0.00006913 + 0.00006814 + \cdots) = 0.00006597$$

The estimated volatility is therefore $\sqrt{0.00006597} \times \sqrt{252} = 12.89\%$. The increase in volatility for different maturities is shown in the third row of Table 17.4.

Many financial institutions use analyses such as this when determining the exposure of their books to volatility changes. Rather than consider an across-the-board increase of 1% in implied volatilities when calculating vega, they relate the size of the volatility increase that is considered to the maturity of the option. Based on Table 17.4, a 0.86% volatility increase would be considered for a 10-day option, a 0.64% increase for a 30-day option, a 0.48% increase for a 50-day option, and so on.

## 17.7   CORRELATIONS

The discussion so far has centered on the estimation and forecasting of volatility. As explained in Chapter 16, correlations also play a key role in the calculation of VaR. In this section, we show how correlation estimates can be updated in a similar way to volatility estimates.

The correlation between two variables $X$ and $Y$ can be defined as

$$\frac{\text{cov}(X, Y)}{\sigma_X \sigma_Y}$$

where $\sigma_X$ and $\sigma_Y$ are the standard deviation of $X$ and $Y$ and $\text{cov}(X, Y)$ is the covariance between $X$ and $Y$. The covariance between $X$ and $Y$ is defined as

$$E[(X - \mu_X)(Y - \mu_Y)]$$

where $\mu_X$ and $\mu_Y$ are the means of $X$ and $Y$, and $E$ denotes the expected value. Although it is easier to develop intuition about the meaning of a correlation than it is for a covariance, it is covariances that are the fundamental variables of our analysis.[14]

Define $x_i$ and $y_i$ as the percentage changes in $X$ and $Y$ between the end of day $i-1$ and the end of day $i$:

$$x_i = \frac{X_i - X_{i-1}}{X_{i-1}}, \qquad y_i = \frac{Y_i - Y_{i-1}}{Y_{i-1}}$$

where $X_i$ and $Y_i$ are the values of $X$ and $Y$ at the end of day $i$. We also define:

$\sigma_{x,n}$ : Daily volatility of variable $X$, estimated for day $n$

$\sigma_{y,n}$ : Daily volatility of variable $Y$, estimated for day $n$

$\text{cov}_n$ : Estimate of covariance between daily changes in $X$ and $Y$, calculated on day $n$

Our estimate of the correlation between $X$ and $Y$ on day $n$ is

$$\frac{\text{cov}_n}{\sigma_{x,n}\sigma_{y,n}}$$

Using an equal-weighting scheme and assuming that the means of $x_i$ and $y_i$ are zero, equation (17.3) shows that we can estimate the variance rates of $X$ and $Y$ from the most recent $m$ observations as

$$\sigma_{x,n}^2 = \frac{1}{m}\sum_{i=1}^{m} x_{n-i}^2, \qquad \sigma_{y,n}^2 = \frac{1}{m}\sum_{i=1}^{m} y_{n-i}^2$$

A similar estimate for the covariance between $X$ and $Y$ is

$$\text{cov}_n = \frac{1}{m}\sum_{i=1}^{m} x_{n-i}\, y_{n-i} \qquad (17.15)$$

One alternative is an EWMA model similar to equation (17.7). The formula for updating the covariance estimate is then

$$\text{cov}_n = \lambda\, \text{cov}_{n-1} + (1-\lambda)x_{n-1}\, y_{n-1}$$

A similar analysis to that presented for the EWMA volatility model shows that the weights given to observations on the $x_i y_i$'s decline as we move back through time. The lower the value of $\lambda$, the greater the weight that is given to recent observations.

**Example 17.3** Suppose that $\lambda = 0.95$ and that the estimate of the correlation between two variables $X$ and $Y$ on day $n-1$ is 0.6. Suppose further that the estimate of the volatilities for the $X$ and $Y$ on day $n-1$ are 1% and 2%, respectively. From the relationship between correlation and covariance, the estimate of the covariance between the $X$ and $Y$ on day $n-1$ is

$$0.6 \times 0.01 \times 0.02 = 0.00012$$

---

[14] An analogy here is that variance rates were the fundamental variables for the EWMA and GARCH schemes in first part of this chapter, even though volatilities are easier to understand.

Suppose that the percentage changes in $X$ and $Y$ on day $n-1$ are 0.5% and 2.5%, respectively. The variance and covariance for day $n$ would be updated as follows:

$$\sigma_{x,n}^2 = 0.95 \times 0.01^2 + 0.05 \times 0.005^2 = 0.00009625$$

$$\sigma_{y,n}^2 = 0.95 \times 0.02^2 + 0.05 \times 0.025^2 = 0.00041125$$

$$\text{cov}_n = 0.95 \times 0.00012 + 0.05 \times 0.005 \times 0.025 = 0.00012025$$

The new volatility of $X$ is $\sqrt{0.00009625} = 0.981\%$ and the new volatility of $Y$ is $\sqrt{0.00041125} = 2.028\%$. The new coefficient of correlation between $X$ and $Y$ is

$$\frac{0.00012025}{0.00981 \times 0.02028} = 0.6044$$

GARCH models can also be used for updating covariance estimates and forecasting the future level of covariances. For example, the GARCH(1, 1) model for updating a covariance is

$$\text{cov}_n = \omega + \alpha x_{n-1} y_{n-1} + \beta \text{cov}_{n-1}$$

and the long-term average covariance is $\omega/(1 - \alpha - \beta)$. Formulas similar to those in equations (17.13) and (17.14) can be developed for forecasting future covariances and calculating the average covariance during the life of an option.[15]

### Consistency Condition for Covariances

Once all the variances and covariances have been calculated, a variance–covariance matrix can be constructed. When $i \neq j$, the $(i, j)$ element of this matrix shows the covariance between variable $i$ and variable $j$. When $i = j$, it shows the variance of variable $i$.

Not all variance–covariance matrices are internally consistent. The condition for an $N \times N$ variance–covariance matrix, $\Omega$, to be internally consistent is

$$w^{\mathsf{T}} \Omega w \geqslant 0 \tag{17.16}$$

for all $N \times 1$ vectors $w$, where $w^{\mathsf{T}}$ is the transpose of $w$. A matrix that satisfies this property is known as *positive semidefinite*.

To understand why the condition in equation (17.16) must hold, suppose that

$$w^{\mathsf{T}} = [w_1, w_2, \ldots, w_n].$$

The expression $w^{\mathsf{T}} \Omega w$ is the variance of a portfolio consisting of $w_i$ of market variable $i$. As such, it must be positive or zero.

To ensure that a positive-semidefinite matrix is produced, variances and covariances should be calculated consistently. For example, if variances are calculated by giving equal weight to the last $m$ data items, the same should be done for covariances. If variances are updated using an EWMA model with $\lambda = 0.94$, the same should be done for covariances.

---

[15] An extension of the ideas in this chapter is to multivariate GARCH models where an entire variance–covariance matrix is updated in a consistent way. See R. Engle and J. Mezrich, "GARCH for Groups," *RISK*, August 1996, pp. 36–40, for a discussion of alternative approaches.

An example of a variance–covariance matrix that is not internally consistent is

$$\begin{bmatrix} 1 & 0 & 0.9 \\ 0 & 1 & 0.9 \\ 0.9 & 0.9 & 1 \end{bmatrix}$$

The variance of each variable is 1.0, and so the covariances are also coefficients of correlation. The first variable is highly correlated with the third variable and the second variable is highly correlated with the third variable. However, there is no correlation at all between the first and second variables. This seems strange. When we set $w$ equal to $(1, 1, -1)$, we find that the condition in equation (17.16) is not satisfied, proving that the matrix is not positive semidefinite.[16]

## SUMMARY

Most popular option pricing models, such as Black–Scholes, assume that the volatility of the underlying asset is constant. This assumption is far from perfect. In practice, the volatility of an asset, like the asset's price, is a stochastic variable. Unlike the asset price, it is not directly observable. This chapter has discussed schemes for attempting to keep track of the current level of volatility.

We define $u_i$ as the percentage change in a market variable between the end of day $i - 1$ and the end of day $i$. The variance rate of the market variable (i.e., the square of its volatility) is calculated as a weighted average of the $u_i^2$. The key feature of the schemes that have been discussed here is that they do not give equal weight to the observations on the $u_i^2$. The more recent an observation, the greater the weight assigned to it. In the EWMA model and the GARCH(1, 1) model, the weights assigned to observations decrease exponentially as the observations become older. The GARCH(1, 1) model differs from the EWMA model in that some weight is also assigned to the long-run average variance rate. Both the EWMA and GARCH(1, 1) models have structures that enable forecasts of the future level of variance rate to be produced relatively easily.

Maximum likelihood methods are usually used to estimate parameters in GARCH(1, 1) and similar models from historical data. These methods involve using an iterative procedure to determine the parameter values that maximize the chance or likelihood that the historical data will occur. Once its parameters have been determined, a model can be judged by how well it removes autocorrelation from the $u_i^2$.

For every model that is developed to track variances, there is a corresponding model that can be developed to track covariances. The procedures described here can therefore be used to update the complete variance–covariance matrix used in value-at-risk calculations.

## SUGGESTIONS FOR FURTHER READING

Bollerslev, T., "Generalized Autoregressive Conditional Heteroscedasticity," *Journal of Econometrics*, 31 (1986), 307–27.

---

[16] It can be shown that the condition for a $3 \times 3$ matrix of correlations to be internally consistent is

$$\rho_{12}^2 + \rho_{13}^2 + \rho_{23}^2 - 2\rho_{12}\rho_{13}\rho_{23} \leqslant 1$$

where $\rho_{ij}$ is the coefficient of correlation between variables $i$ and $j$.

Cumby, R., S. Figlewski, and J. Hasbrook, "Forecasting Volatilities and Correlations with EGARCH Models," *Journal of Derivatives*, 1, no. 2 (Winter 1993), 51–63.

Engle, R. F., "Autoregressive Conditional Heteroscedasticity with Estimates of the Variance of UK Inflation," *Econometrica*, 50 (1982), 987–1008.

Engle R. F., and J. Mezrich, "Grappling with GARCH," *RISK*, September 1995, pp. 112–117.

Engle, R. F., and J. Mezrich, "GARCH for Groups," *RISK*, August 1996, pp. 36–40.

Engle, R. F., and V. Ng, "Measuring and Testing the Impact of News on Volatility," *Journal of Finance*, 48 (1993), 1749–78.

Ljung, G. M., and G. E. P. Box, "On a Measure of Lack of Fit in Time Series Models," *Biometrica*, 65 (1978), 297–303.

Nelson, D., "Conditional Heteroscedasticity and Asset Returns: A New Approach," *Econometrica*, 59 (1990), 347–70.

Noh, J., R. F. Engle, and A. Kane, "Forecasting Volatility and Option Prices of the S&P 500 Index," *Journal of Derivatives*, 2 (1994), 17–30.

## QUESTIONS AND PROBLEMS
## (ANSWERS IN SOLUTIONS MANUAL)

17.1. Explain the exponentially weighted moving average (EWMA) model for estimating volatility from historical data.

17.2. What is the difference between the exponentially weighted moving average model and the GARCH(1, 1) model for updating volatilities?

17.3. The most recent estimate of the daily volatility of an asset is 1.5% and the price of the asset at the close of trading yesterday was $30.00. The parameter $\lambda$ in the EWMA model is 0.94. Suppose that the price of the asset at the close of trading today is $30.50. How will this cause the volatility to be updated by the EWMA model?

17.4. A company uses an EWMA model for forecasting volatility. It decides to change the parameter $\lambda$ from 0.95 to 0.85. Explain the likely impact on the forecasts.

17.5. The volatility of a certain market variable is 30% per annum. Calculate a 99% confidence interval for the size of the percentage daily change in the variable.

17.6. A company uses the GARCH(1, 1) model for updating volatility. The three parameters are $\omega$, $\alpha$, and $\beta$. Describe the impact of making a small increase in each of the parameters while keeping the others fixed.

17.7. The most recent estimate of the daily volatility of the USD–GBP exchange rate is 0.6% and the exchange rate at 4 p.m. yesterday was 1.5000. The parameter $\lambda$ in the EWMA model is 0.9. Suppose that the exchange rate at 4 p.m. today proves to be 1.4950. How would the estimate of the daily volatility be updated?

17.8. Assume that S&P 500 at close of trading yesterday was 1,040 and the daily volatility of the index was estimated as 1% per day at that time. The parameters in a GARCH(1, 1) model are $\omega = 0.000002$, $\alpha = 0.06$, and $\beta = 0.92$. If the level of the index at close of trading today is 1,060, what is the new volatility estimate?

17.9. Suppose that the current daily volatilities of asset A and asset B are 1.6% and 2.5%, respectively. The prices of the assets at close of trading yesterday were $20 and $40 and the estimate of the coefficient of correlation between the returns on the two assets made at that time was 0.25. The parameter $\lambda$ used in the EWMA model is 0.95.
  a. Calculate the current estimate of the covariance between the assets.
  b. On the assumption that the prices of the assets at close of trading today are $20.5 and $40.5, update the correlation estimate.

17.10. The parameters of a GARCH(1, 1) model are estimated as $\omega = 0.000004$, $\alpha = 0.05$, and $\beta = 0.92$. What is the long-run average volatility and what is the equation describing the way that the variance rate reverts to its long-run average? If the current volatility is 20% per year, what is the expected volatility in 20 days?

17.11. Suppose that the current daily volatilities of asset X and asset Y are 1.0% and 1.2%, respectively. The prices of the assets at close of trading yesterday were $30 and $50 and the estimate of the coefficient of correlation between the returns on the two assets made at this time was 0.50. Correlations and volatilities are updated using a GARCH(1, 1) model. The estimates of the model's parameters are $\alpha = 0.04$ and $\beta = 0.94$. For the correlation $\omega = 0.000001$, and for the volatilities $\omega = 0.000003$. If the prices of the two assets at close of trading today are $31 and $51, how is the correlation estimate updated?

17.12. Suppose that the daily volatility of the FTSE 100 stock index (measured in pounds sterling) is 1.8% and the daily volatility of the USD–GBP exchange rate is 0.9%. Suppose further that the correlation between the FTSE 100 and the USD–GBP exchange rate is 0.4. What is the volatility of the FTSE 100 when it is translated to U.S. dollars? Assume that the USD–GBP exchange rate is expressed as the number of U.S. dollars per pound sterling. (*Hint:* When $Z = XY$, the percentage daily change in Z is approximately equal to the percentage daily change in X plus the percentage daily change in Y.)

17.13. Suppose that in Problem 17.12 the correlation between the S&P 500 index (measured in dollars) and the FTSE 100 index (measured in sterling) is 0.7, the correlation between the S&P 500 index (measured in dollars) and the USD–GBP exchange rate is 0.3, and the daily volatility of the S&P 500 index is 1.6%. What is the correlation between the S&P 500 index (measured in dollars) and the FTSE 100 index when it is translated to dollars? (*Hint:* For three variables X, Y, and Z, the covariance between $X + Y$ and Z equals the covariance between X and Z plus the covariance between Y and Z.)

17.14. Show that the GARCH(1, 1) model

$$\sigma_n^2 = \omega + \alpha u_{n-1}^2 + \beta \sigma_{n-1}^2$$

in equation (17.9) is equivalent to the stochastic volatility model

$$dV = a(V_L - V)\, dt + \xi V\, dz$$

where time is measured in days, V is the variance of the asset price, and

$$a = 1 - \alpha - \beta, \qquad V_L = \frac{\omega}{1 - \alpha - \beta}, \qquad \xi = \alpha\sqrt{2}$$

What is the stochastic volatility model when time is measure in years? (*Hint:* The variable $u_{n-1}$ is the return on the asset price in time $\delta t$. It can be assumed to be normally distributed with mean zero and standard deviation $\sigma_{n-1}$. It follows that the means of $u_{n-1}^2$ and $u_{n-1}^4$ are $\sigma_{n-1}^2$ and $3\sigma_{n-1}^4$, respectively.)

# ASSIGNMENT QUESTIONS

17.15. Suppose that the current price of gold at close of trading yesterday was $300 and its volatility was estimated as 1.3% per day. The price at the close of trading today is $298. Update the volatility estimate using
   a. The EWMA model with $\lambda = 0.94$
   b. The GARCH(1, 1) model with $\omega = 0.000002$, $\alpha = 0.04$, and $\beta = 0.94$

17.16. Suppose that in Problem 17.15 the price of silver at the close of trading yesterday was $8, its volatility was estimated as 1.5% per day, and its correlation with gold was estimated as 0.8. The price of silver at the close of trading today is unchanged at $8. Update the volatility of silver and the correlation between silver and gold using the two models in Problem 17.15. In practice, is the $\omega$ parameter likely to be the same for gold and silver?

17.17. An Excel spreadsheet containing 500 days of daily data on a number of different exchange rates and stock indices can be downloaded from the author's Web site:
   www.rotman.utoronto.ca/˜hull
   Choose one exchange rate and one stock index. Estimate the value of $\lambda$ in the EWMA model that minimizes the value of

$$\sum_i (v_i - \beta_i)^2$$

   where $v_i$ is the variance forecast made at the end of day $i - 1$ and $\beta_i$ is the variance calculated from data between day $i$ and day $i + 25$. Use the Solver tool in Excel. Set the variance forecast at the end of the first day equal to the square of the return on that day to start the EWMA calculations.

17.18. Suppose that the parameters in a GARCH(1, 1) model are $\alpha = 0.03$, $\beta = 0.95$, and $\omega = 0.000002$.
   a. What is the long-run average volatility?
   b. If the current volatility is 1.5% per day, what is your estimate of the volatility in 20, 40, and 60 days?
   c. What volatility should be used to price 20-, 40-, and 60-day options?
   d. Suppose that there is an event that increases the current volatility by 0.5% to 2% per day. Estimate the effect on the volatility in 20, 40, and 60 days.
   e. By how much does the event increase the volatilities used to price 20-, 40-, and 60-day options?

# CHAPTER 18

# NUMERICAL PROCEDURES

This chapter discusses three numerical procedures that can be used to value derivatives when exact formulas are not available. These involve the use of binomial trees, Monte Carlo simulation, and finite difference methods, respectively. Monte Carlo simulation is used primarily for derivatives where the payoff is dependent on the history of the underlying variable or where there are several underlying variables. Binomial trees and finite difference methods are particularly useful when the holder has early exercise decisions to make prior to maturity. In addition to valuing a derivative, all the procedures can be used to calculate Greek letters such as delta, gamma, and vega.

## 18.1 BINOMIAL TREES

In Chapter 10, we introduced one- and two-step binomial trees for non-dividend-paying stocks and showed how they lead to valuations for European and American options. These trees are very imprecise models of reality. A more realistic model is one that assumes stock price movements are composed of a much larger number of small binomial movements. This is the assumption that underlies a widely used numerical procedure first proposed by Cox, Ross, and Rubinstein.[1]

Consider the evaluation of an option on a non-dividend-paying stock. We start by dividing the life of the option into a large number of small time intervals of length $\delta t$. We assume that in each time interval the stock price moves from its initial value of $S_0$ to one of two new values, $S_0 u$ and $S_0 d$. This model is illustrated in Figure 18.1. In general, $u > 1$ and $d < 1$. The movement

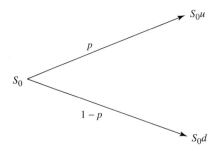

**Figure 18.1**   Stock price movements in time $\delta t$ under the binomial model

---

[1] See J. C. Cox, S. A. Ross, and M. Rubinstein, "Option Pricing: A Simplified Approach," *Journal of Financial Economics*, 7 (October 1979), 229–63.

from $S_0$ to $S_0u$ is therefore an "up" movement, and the movement from $S_0$ to $S_0d$ is a "down" movement. The probability of an up movement will be denoted by $p$. The probability of a down movement is $1 - p$.

### Risk-Neutral Valuation

The risk-neutral valuation principle, introduced in Chapters 10 and 12, states that an option (or other derivative) can be valued on the assumption that the world is risk neutral. This means that for valuation purposes we can assume the following:

1. The expected return from all traded securities is the risk-free interest rate.
2. Future cash flows can be valued by discounting their expected values at the risk-free interest rate.

We make use of this result when using binomial trees. The tree we will build for a non-dividend-paying stock represents stock price movements in a risk-neutral world.

### Determination of $p$, $u$, and $d$

The parameters $p$, $u$, and $d$ must give correct values for the mean and variance of stock price changes during a time interval of length $\delta t$. Because we are working in a risk-neutral world, the expected return from a stock is the risk-free interest rate, $r$. Hence the expected value of the stock price at the end of a time interval of length $\delta t$ is $Se^{r\delta t}$, where $S$ is the stock price at the beginning of the time interval. It follows that

$$Se^{r\delta t} = pSu + (1 - p)Sd \tag{18.1}$$

or

$$e^{r\delta t} = pu + (1 - p)d \tag{18.2}$$

The stochastic process we developed for stock prices in Chapter 11 implies that the variance of the percentage change in the stock price in a small time interval of length $\delta t$ is $\sigma^2 \delta t$. Because the variance of a variable $Q$ is defined as $E(Q^2) - [E(Q)]^2$, it follows that

$$pu^2 + (1 - p)d^2 - [pu + (1 - p)d]^2 = \sigma^2 \delta t$$

Substituting for $p$ from equation (18.2) reduces this to

$$e^{r\delta t}(u + d) - ud - e^{2r\delta t} = \sigma^2 \delta t \tag{18.3}$$

Equations (18.2) and (18.3) impose two conditions on $p$, $u$, and $d$. A third condition used by Cox, Ross, and Rubinstein is

$$u = \frac{1}{d}$$

These three conditions imply

$$p = \frac{a - d}{u - d} \tag{18.4}$$

$$u = e^{\sigma\sqrt{\delta t}} \tag{18.5}$$

$$d = e^{-\sigma\sqrt{\delta t}} \tag{18.6}$$

where

$$a = e^{r\,\delta t} \tag{18.7}$$

and terms of order higher than $\delta t$ are ignored.[2] The variable $a$ is sometimes referred to as the *growth factor*. Equations (18.4) to (18.7) are consistent with the results in Section 10.7.

### Tree of Stock Prices

Figure 18.2 illustrates the complete tree of stock prices that is considered when the binomial model is used. At time zero, the stock price, $S_0$, is known. At time $\delta t$, there are two possible stock prices, $S_0 u$ and $S_0 d$; at time $2\,\delta t$, there are three possible stock prices, $S_0 u^2$, $S_0$, and $S_0 d^2$; and so on. In general, at time $i\,\delta t$, $i+1$ stock prices are considered. These are

$$S_0 u^j d^{i-j}, \quad j = 0, 1, \ldots, i$$

Note that the relationship $u = 1/d$ is used in computing the stock price at each node of the tree in Figure 18.2. For example, $S_0 u^2 d = S_0 u$. Note also that the tree recombines in the sense that an up movement followed by a down movement leads to the same stock price as a down movement followed by an up movement.

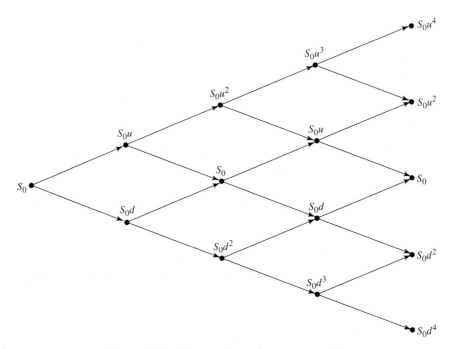

**Figure 18.2**   Tree used to value a stock option

---

[2] To see this, we note that equations (18.4) and (18.7) satisfy the condition in equation (18.2) exactly. From Taylor series expansions, when terms of order higher than $\delta t$ are ignored, equation (18.5) implies that $u = 1 + \sigma\sqrt{\delta t} + \frac{1}{2}\sigma^2\,\delta t$ and equation (18.6) implies that $d = 1 - \sigma\sqrt{\delta t} + \frac{1}{2}\sigma^2\,\delta t$, with $e^{r\,\delta t} = 1 + r\,\delta t$ and $e^{2r\,\delta t} = 1 + 2r\,\delta t$. It follows that equations (18.5) and (18.6) satisfy equation (18.3) when terms of order higher than $\delta t$ are ignored.

## Working Backward through the Tree

Options are evaluated by starting at the end of the tree (time $T$) and working backward. The value of the option is known at time $T$. For example, a put option is worth $\max(K - S_T, 0)$ and a call option is worth $\max(S_T - K, 0)$, where $S_T$ is the stock price at time $T$ and $K$ is the strike price. Because a risk-neutral world is being assumed, the value at each node at time $T - \delta t$ can be calculated as the expected value at time $T$ discounted at rate $r$ for a time period $\delta t$. Similarly, the value at each node at time $T - 2\delta t$ can be calculated as the expected value at time $T - \delta t$ discounted for a time period $\delta t$ at rate $r$, and so on. If the option is American, it is necessary to check at each node to see whether early exercise is preferable to holding the option for a further time period $\delta t$. Eventually, by working back through all the nodes, we are able to obtain the value of the option at time zero.

**Example 18.1**  Consider a five-month American put option on a non-dividend-paying stock when the stock price is $50, the strike price is $50, the risk-free interest rate is 10% per annum, and the volatility is 40% per annum. With our usual notation, this means that $S_0 = 50$, $K = 50$, $r = 0.10$, $\sigma = 0.40$, and $T = 0.4167$. Suppose that we divide the life of the option into five intervals of length one month ($= 0.0833$ year) for the purposes of constructing a binomial tree. Then $\delta t = 0.0833$ and, using equations (18.4) to (18.7),

$$u = e^{\sigma\sqrt{\delta t}} = 1.1224, \qquad d = e^{-\sigma\sqrt{\delta t}} = 0.8909$$

$$a = e^{r\delta t} = 1.0084, \qquad p = \frac{a - d}{u - d} = 0.5073$$

$$1 - p = 0.4927$$

Figure 18.3 shows the binomial tree produced by DerivaGem. At each node there are two numbers. The top one shows the stock price at the node; the lower one shows the value of the option at the node. The probability of an up movement is always 0.5073; the probability of a down movement is always 0.4927.

The stock price at the $j$th node ($j = 0, 1, \ldots, i$) at time $i\delta t$ ($i = 0, 1, \ldots, 5$) is calculated as $S_0 u^j d^{i-j}$. For example, the stock price at node A ($i = 4, j = 1$) (i.e., the second node up at the end of the fourth time step) is $50 \times 1.1224 \times 0.8909^3 = \$39.69$.

The option prices at the final nodes are calculated as $\max(K - S_T, 0)$. For example, the option price at node G is $50.00 - 35.36 = 14.64$. The option prices at the penultimate nodes are calculated from the option prices at the final nodes. First, we assume no exercise of the option at the nodes. This means that the option price is calculated as the present value of the expected option price one time step later. For example, at node E, the option price is calculated as

$$(0.5073 \times 0 + 0.4927 \times 5.45)e^{-0.10 \times 0.0833} = 2.66 \qquad P \times \qquad e^{-r\delta t}$$

whereas at node A it is calculated as

$$(0.5073 \times 5.45 + 0.4927 \times 14.64)e^{-0.10 \times 0.0833} = 9.90$$

We then check to see if early exercise is preferable to waiting. At node E, early exercise would give a value for the option of zero because both the stock price and strike price are $50. Clearly it is best to wait. The correct value for the option at node E is therefore $2.66. At node A it is a different story. If the option is exercised, it is worth $50.00 - $39.69, or $10.31. This is more than $9.90. If node A is reached, the option should therefore be exercised and the correct value for the option at node A is $10.31.

At each node:
 Upper value = Underlying Asset Price
 Lower value = Option Price
Shading indicates where option is exercised

Strike price = 50
Discount factor per step = 0.9917
Time step, dt = 0.0833 years, 30.42 days
Growth factor per step, a = 1.0084
Probability of up move, p = 0.5073
Up step size, u = 1.1224
Down step size, d = 0.8909

Node Time:
   0.0000        0.0833        0.1667        0.2500        0.3333        0.4167

**Figure 18.3**  Binomial tree from DerivaGem for American put on non-dividend-paying stock (Example 18.1)

Option prices at earlier nodes are calculated in a similar way. Note that it is not always best to exercise an option early when it is in the money. Consider node B. If the option is exercised, it is worth $50.00 − $39.69, or $10.31. However, if it is held, it is worth

$$(0.5073 \times 6.38 + 0.4927 \times 14.64)e^{-0.10 \times 0.0833} = 10.36$$

The option should therefore not be exercised at this node, and the correct option value at the node is $10.36.

Working back through the tree, the value of the option at the initial node to be $4.49. This is our numerical estimate for the option's current value. In practice, a smaller value of $\delta t$, and many more nodes, would be used. DerivaGem shows that with 30, 50, 100, and 500 time steps we get values for the option of 4.263, 4.272, 4.278, and 4.283.

### Expressing the Approach Algebraically

Suppose that the life of an American put option on a non-dividend-paying stock is divided into $N$ subintervals of length $\delta t$. We will refer to the $j$th node at time $i\,\delta t$ as the $(i, j)$ node, where $0 \leqslant i \leqslant N$ and $0 \leqslant j \leqslant i$. Define $f_{i,j}$ as the value of the option at the $(i, j)$ node. The stock price at the $(i, j)$ node is $S_0 u^j d^{i-j}$. Because the value of an American put at its expiration date is $\max(K - S_T, 0)$, we know that

$$f_{N,j} = \max(K - S_0 u^j d^{N-j}, 0), \quad j = 0, 1, \ldots, N$$

There is a probability $p$ of moving from the $(i, j)$ node at time $i\,\delta t$ to the $(i+1, j+1)$ node at time $(i+1)\,\delta t$, and a probability $1 - p$ of moving from the $(i, j)$ node at time $i\,\delta t$ to the $(i+1, j)$ node at time $(i+1)\,\delta t$. If we assume no early exercise, risk-neutral valuation gives

$$f_{i,j} = e^{-r\,\delta t}[p f_{i+1,\,j+1} + (1 - p)f_{i+1,\,j}]$$

for $0 \leqslant i \leqslant N - 1$ and $0 \leqslant j \leqslant i$. When early exercise is taken into account, this value for $f_{i,j}$ must be compared with the option's intrinsic value, and we obtain

$$f_{i,j} = \max\left\{K - S_0 u^j d^{i-j},\ e^{-r\,\delta t}[p f_{i+1,\,j+1} + (1 - p)f_{i+1,\,j}]\right\}$$

Note that, because the calculations start at time $T$ and work backward, the value at time $i\,\delta t$ captures not only the effect of early exercise possibilities at time $i\,\delta t$ but also the effect of early exercise at subsequent times.

In the limit as $\delta t$ tends to zero, an exact value for the American put is obtained. In practice, $N = 30$ usually gives reasonable results. Figure 18.4 shows the convergence of the option price in the example we have been considering. This figure was calculated using the Application Builder functions provided with the DerivaGem software (see Sample Application A).

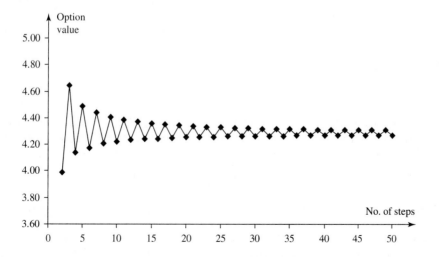

**Figure 18.4**   Convergence of the price of the option in Example 18.1 calculated from the DerivaGem Application Builder functions

### Estimating Delta and Other Greek Letters

It will be recalled that the delta, $\Delta$, of an option is the rate of change of its price with respect to a change in the underlying asset price. It can be estimated as

$$\Delta = \frac{\delta f}{\delta S}$$

where $\delta S$ is a small change in the stock price and $\delta f$ is the corresponding small change in the option price. At time $\delta t$, we have an estimate $f_{11}$ for the option price when the stock price is $S_0 u$, and an estimate $f_{10}$ for the option price when the stock price is $S_0 d$. This means that, when $\delta S = S_0 u - S_0 d$, the value of $\delta f$ is $f_{11} - f_{10}$. An estimate of $\Delta$ at time $\delta t$ is therefore

$$\Delta = \frac{f_{11} - f_{10}}{S_0 u - S_0 d} \tag{18.8}$$

To determine gamma, $\Gamma$, note that we have two estimates of $\Delta$ at time $2\,\delta t$. When $S = \frac{1}{2}(S_0 u^2 + S_0)$ (halfway between the second and third node), delta is $(f_{22} - f_{21})/(S_0 u^2 - S_0)$; when $S = \frac{1}{2}(S_0 + S_0 d^2)$ (halfway between the first and second node), delta is $(f_{21} - f_{20})/(S_0 - S_0 d^2)$. The difference between the two values of $S$ is $h$, where

$$h = 0.5(S_0 u^2 - S_0 d^2)$$

Gamma is the change in delta divided by $h$:

$$\Gamma = \frac{[(f_{22} - f_{21})/(S_0 u^2 - S_0)] - [(f_{21} - f_{20})/(S_0 - S_0 d^2)]}{h} \tag{18.9}$$

These procedures provide estimates of delta at time $\delta t$ and of gamma at time $2\,\delta t$. In practice, they are usually used as estimates of delta and gamma at time zero as well.[3]

A further hedge parameter that can be obtained directly from the tree is theta, $\Theta$. This is the rate of change of the option price with time when all else is kept constant. If the tree starts at time zero, an estimate of theta is

$$\Theta = \frac{f_{21} - f_{00}}{2\,\delta t} \tag{18.10}$$

Vega can be calculated by making a small change $\delta\sigma$ in the volatility and constructing a new tree to obtain a new value of the option. (The time step $\delta t$ should be kept the same.) The estimate of vega is

$$\mathcal{V} = \frac{f^* - f}{\delta\sigma}$$

where $f$ and $f^*$ are the estimates of the option price from the original and the new tree, respectively. Rho can be calculated similarly.

---

[3] If slightly more accuracy is required for delta and gamma, we can start the binomial tree at time $-2\,\delta t$ and assume that the stock price is $S_0$ at this time. This leads to the option price being calculated for three different stock prices at time zero.

**Example 18.2** Consider again Example 18.1. From Figure 18.3, $f_{1,0} = 6.96$ and $f_{1,1} = 2.16$. Equation (18.8) gives an estimate of delta of

$$\frac{2.16 - 6.96}{56.12 - 44.55} = -0.41$$

From equation (18.9), an estimate of the gamma of the option can be obtained from the values at nodes B, C, and F as

$$\frac{[(0.64 - 3.77)/(62.99 - 50.00)] - [(3.77 - 10.36)/(50.00 - 39.69)]}{11.65} = 0.03$$

From equation (18.10), an estimate of the theta of the option can be obtained from the values at nodes D and C as

$$\frac{3.77 - 4.49}{0.1667} = -4.3 \text{ per year}$$

or $-0.012$ per calendar day. These are, of course, only rough estimates. They become progressively better as the number of time steps on the tree is increased. Using 50 time steps, DerivaGem provides estimates of $-0.415$, $0.034$, and $-0.0117$ for delta, gamma, and theta, respectively.

## 18.2 USING THE BINOMIAL TREE FOR OPTIONS ON INDICES, CURRENCIES, AND FUTURES CONTRACTS

As shown in Section 13.2, the binomial tree approach to valuing options on non-dividend-paying stocks can be adapted to valuing American calls and puts on a stock providing a dividend yield at rate $q$.

Because the dividends provide a return of $q$, the stock price itself must, on average, in a risk-neutral world provide a return of $r - q$. Hence equation (18.1) becomes

$$Se^{(r-q)\,\delta t} = pSu + (1 - p)Sd$$

so that

$$e^{(r-q)\,\delta t} = pu + (1 - p)d$$

Equation (18.3) becomes

$$e^{(r-q)\,\delta t}(u + d) - ud - e^{2(r-q)\,\delta t} = \sigma^2\,\delta t$$

It can be shown (as in footnote 2) that equations (18.4), (18.5), and (18.6) are still correct (when terms of order higher than $\delta t$ are ignored) but with

$$a = e^{(r-q)\,\delta t} \tag{18.11}$$

Therefore, with this interpretation of $q$, the binomial tree numerical procedure can be used exactly as before except that the old value of $a$ is replaced with this new one.

Recall from Chapter 13 that stock indices, currencies, and futures contracts can, for the purposes of option evaluation, be considered as assets providing known yields. In the case of a stock index, the relevant yield is the dividend yield on the stock portfolio underlying the index; in the case of a currency, it is the foreign risk-free interest rate; in the case of a futures contract, it is the domestic risk-free interest rate. The binomial tree approach can therefore be used to value options on stock indices, currencies, and futures contracts providing $q$ in equation (18.11) is interpreted appropriately.

**Example 18.3** Consider a four-month American call option on index futures where the current futures price is 300, the exercise price is 300, the risk-free interest rate is 8% per annum, and the volatility of the index is 30% per annum. We divide the life of the option into four one-month periods for the purposes of constructing the tree. In this case, $F_0 = 300$, $K = 300$, $r = 0.08$, $\sigma = 0.3$, $T = 0.3333$, and $\delta t = 0.0833$. Because a futures contract is analogous to a stock paying dividends at a rate $r$, $q$ should be set equal to $r$ in equation (18.11). This gives $a = 1$. The other parameters necessary to construct the tree are

$$u = e^{\sigma\sqrt{\delta t}} = 1.0905, \qquad d = \frac{1}{u} = 0.9170$$

$$p = \frac{a - d}{u - d} = 0.4784, \qquad 1 - p = 0.5216$$

The tree, as produced by DerivaGem, is shown in Figure 18.5 (The upper number is the futures price; the lower number is the option price.) The estimated value of the option is 19.16. More accuracy is obtained using more steps. With 50 time steps DerivaGem gives a value of 20.18; with 100 time steps it gives 20.22.

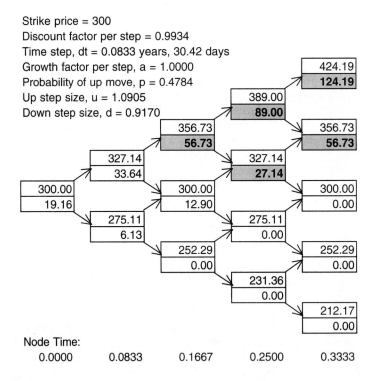

At each node:
Upper value = Underlying Asset Price
Lower value = Option Price
Shading indicates where option is exercised

Strike price = 300
Discount factor per step = 0.9934
Time step, dt = 0.0833 years, 30.42 days
Growth factor per step, a = 1.0000
Probability of up move, p = 0.4784
Up step size, u = 1.0905
Down step size, d = 0.9170

Node Time:
0.0000    0.0833    0.1667    0.2500    0.3333

**Figure 18.5**  Binomial tree produced by DerivaGem for American call option on an index futures contract (Example 18.3)

**Example 18.4** Consider a one-year American put option on the British pound. The current exchange rate is 1.6100, the strike price is 1.6000, the U.S. risk-free interest rate is 8% per annum, the sterling risk-free interest rate is 9% per annum, and the volatility of the sterling exchange rate is 12% per annum. In this case, $S_0 = 1.61$, $K = 1.60$, $r = 0.08$, $r_f = 0.09$, $\sigma = 0.12$, and $T = 1.0$. We divide the life of the option into four three-month periods for the purposes of constructing the tree, so that $\delta t = 0.25$. In this case, $q = r_f$ and equation (18.11) gives

$$a = e^{(0.08-0.09)\times 0.25} = 0.9975$$

The other parameters necessary to construct the tree are

$$u = e^{\sigma\sqrt{\delta t}} = 1.0618, \qquad d = \frac{1}{u} = 0.9418$$

$$p = \frac{a-d}{u-d} = 0.4642, \qquad 1 - p = 0.5358$$

The tree, as produced by DerivaGem, is shown in Figure 18.6. (The upper number is the exchange

At each node:
 Upper value = Underlying Asset Price
 Lower value = Option Price
 Shading indicates where option is exercised

Strike price = 1.6
Discount factor per step = 0.9802
Time step, dt = 0.2500 years, 91.25 days
Growth factor per step, a = 0.9975
Probability of up move, p = 0.4642
Up step size, u = 1.0618
Down step size, d = 0.9418

| Node Time: | | | | |
|---|---|---|---|---|
| 0.0000 | 0.2500 | 0.5000 | 0.7500 | 1.0000 |

**Figure 18.6** Binomial tree produced by DerivaGem for American put option on a currency (Example 18.4)

rate; the lower number is the option price.) The estimated value of the option is $0.0710. (Using 50 time steps, DerivaGem gives the value of the option as 0.0738; with 100 time steps, it also gives 0.0738.)

## 18.3 BINOMIAL MODEL FOR A DIVIDEND-PAYING STOCK

We now move on to the more tricky issue of how the binomial model can be used for a dividend-paying stock. As in Chapter 12, the word *dividend* will, for the purposes of our discussion, be used to refer to the reduction in the stock price on the ex-dividend date as a result of the dividend.

### Known Dividend Yield

If it is assumed that there is a single dividend, and the dividend yield (i.e., the dividend as a percentage of the stock price) is known, the tree takes the form shown in Figure 18.7 and can be analyzed in a manner similar to that just described. If the time $i\,\delta t$ is prior to the stock going ex-dividend, the nodes on the tree correspond to stock prices

$$S_0 u^j d^{i-j}, \quad j = 0, 1, \ldots, i$$

where $u$ and $d$ are defined as in equations (18.5) and (18.6). If the time $i\,\delta t$ is after the stock goes

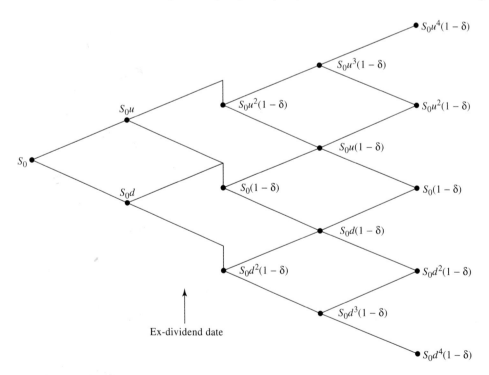

**Figure 18.7** Tree when stock pays a known dividend yield at one particular time

ex-dividend, the nodes correspond to stock prices

$$S_0(1 - \delta)u^j d^{i-j}, \quad j = 0, 1, \ldots, i$$

where $\delta$ is the dividend yield. Several known dividend yields during the life of an option can be dealt with similarly. If $\delta_i$ is the total dividend yield associated with all ex-dividend dates between time zero and time $i\,\delta t$, the nodes at time $i\,\delta t$ correspond to stock prices

$$S_0(1 - \delta_i)u^j d^{i-j}$$

### Known Dollar Dividend

In some situations, the most realistic assumption is that the dollar amount of the dividend rather than the dividend yield is known in advance. If the volatility of the stock, $\sigma$, is assumed constant, the tree then takes the form shown in Figure 18.8. It does not recombine, which means that the number of nodes that have to be evaluated, particularly if there are several dividends, is liable to become very large. Suppose that there is only one dividend, that the ex-dividend date, $\tau$, is between $k\,\delta t$ and $(k + 1)\,\delta t$, and that the dollar amount of the dividend is $D$. When $i \leqslant k$, the nodes on the tree at time $i\,\delta t$ correspond to stock prices

$$S_0 u^j d^{i-j}, \quad j = 0, 1, \ldots, i$$

as before. When $i = k + 1$, the nodes on the tree correspond to stock prices

$$S_0 u^j d^{i-j} - D, \quad j = 0, 1, \ldots, i$$

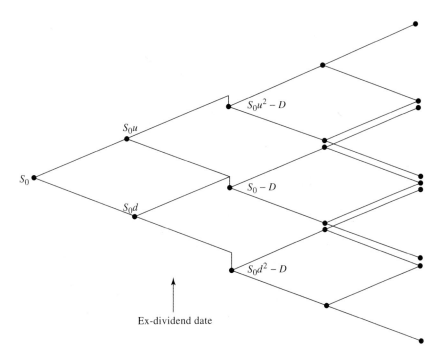

**Figure 18.8**  Tree when dollar amount of dividend is assumed known and volatility is assumed constant

When $i = k + 2$, the nodes on the tree correspond to stock prices

$$(S_0 u^j d^{i-1-j} - D)u \quad \text{and} \quad (S_0 u^j d^{i-1-j} - D)d$$

for $j = 0, 1, \ldots, i - 1$, so that there are $2i$ rather than $i + 1$ nodes. When $i = k + m$, there are $m(k + 2)$ rather than $k + m + 1$ nodes.

The problem can be simplified by assuming, as in the analysis of European options in Section 12.12, that the stock price has two components: a part that is uncertain and a part that is the present value of all future dividends during the life of the option. Suppose, as before, that there is only one ex-dividend date, $\tau$, during the life of the option and that $k\,\delta t \leqslant \tau \leqslant (k+1)\,\delta t$. The value of the uncertain component, $S^*$, at time $i\,\delta t$ is given by

$$S^* = S, \quad \text{when } i\,\delta t > \tau$$

and by

$$S^* = S - De^{-r(\tau - i\,\delta t)}, \quad \text{when } i\,\delta t \leqslant \tau$$

where $D$ is the dividend. Define $\sigma^*$ as the volatility of $S^*$ and assume that $\sigma^*$ is constant.[4] The parameters $p$, $u$, and $d$ can be calculated from equations (18.4) to (18.7) with $\sigma$ replaced by $\sigma^*$ and a tree can be constructed in the usual way to model $S^*$. By adding to the stock price at each node the present value of future dividends (if any), the tree can be converted into another tree that models $S$. Suppose that $S_0^*$ is the value of $S^*$ at time zero. At time $i\,\delta t$, the nodes on this tree correspond to the stock prices

$$S_0^* u^j d^{i-j} + De^{-r(\tau - i\,\delta t)}, \quad j = 0, 1, \ldots, i$$

when $i\,\delta t < \tau$ and

$$S_0^* u^j d^{i-j}, \quad j = 0, 1, \ldots, i$$

when $i\,\delta t > \tau$. This approach, which has the advantage of being consistent with the approach for European options in Section 12.12, succeeds in achieving a situation where the tree recombines so that there are $i + 1$ nodes at time $i\,\delta t$. It can be generalized in a straightforward way to deal with the situation where there are several dividends.

> **Example 18.5** Consider a five-month put option on a stock that is expected to pay a single dividend of \$2.06 during the life of the option. The initial stock price is \$52, the strike price is \$50, the risk-free interest rate is 10% per annum, the volatility is 40% per annum, and the ex-dividend date is in $3\frac{1}{2}$ months.
>
> We first construct a tree to model $S^*$, the stock price less the present value of future dividends during the life of the option. At time zero, the present value of the dividend is
>
> $$2.06e^{-0.2917 \times 0.1} = 2.00$$
>
> The initial value of $S^*$, therefore, is 50.00. Assuming that the 40% per annum volatility refers to $S^*$, we find that Figure 18.3 provides a binomial tree for $S^*$. (This is because $S^*$ has the same initial value and volatility as the stock price that Figure 18.3 was based upon.) Adding the present value of the dividend at each node leads to Figure 18.9, which is a binomial model for $S$. The probabilities at each node are, as in Figure 18.3, 0.5073 for an up movement and 0.4927 for a down movement. Working back through the tree in the usual way gives the option price as \$4.44. (Using 50 time steps, DerivaGem gives a value for the option of 4.202; using 100 steps, it gives 4.212.)

---

[4] As mentioned in Section 12.13, $\sigma^*$ is in theory slightly greater than $\sigma$, the volatility of $S$. In practice, the use of implied volatilities avoids the need for analysts to distinguish between $\sigma$ and $\sigma^*$.

At each node:
 Upper value = Underlying Asset Price
 Lower value = Option Price
 Shading indicates where option is exercised

Strike price = 50
Discount factor per step = 0.9917
Time step, dt = 0.0833 years, 30.42 days
Growth factor per step, a = 1.0084
Probability of up move, p = 0.5073
Up step size, u = 1.1224
Down step size, d = 0.8909

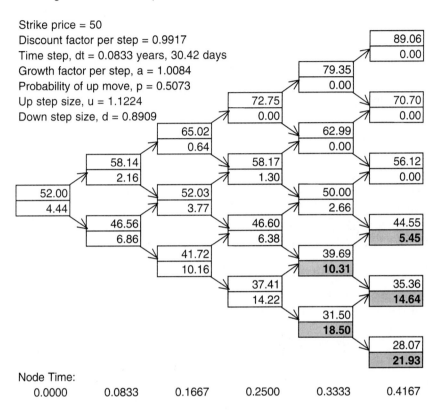

Node Time:
  0.0000      0.0833      0.1667      0.2500      0.3333      0.4167

**Figure 18.9**   Tree produced by DerivaGem for Example 18.5

## 18.4   EXTENSIONS OF THE BASIC TREE APPROACH

We now explain some ways the basic tree methodology we have described can be extended.

### Time-Dependent Interest Rates

The usual assumption when American options are being valued is that interest rates are constant. When the term structure is steeply upward or downward sloping, this may not be a satisfactory assumption. It is more appropriate to assume that the interest rate for a future period of length $\delta t$ equals the current forward interest rate for that period. We can accommodate this assumption by setting

$$a = e^{f(t)\,\delta t} \tag{18.12}$$

for nodes at time $t$, where $f(t)$ is the forward rate between times $t$ and $t + \delta t$. This does not change the geometry of the tree because $u$ and $d$ do not depend on $a$. The probabilities on the branches emanating from nodes at time $t$ are[5]

$$p = \frac{e^{f(t)\delta t} - d}{u - d} \quad \text{and} \quad 1 - p = \frac{u - e^{f(t)\delta t}}{u - d}$$

The rest of the way that we use the tree is the same as before, except that when discounting between times $t$ and $t + \delta t$ we use $f(t)$. A similar modification of the basic tree can be used to value index options, foreign exchange options, and futures options. The dividend yield on an index or a foreign risk-free rate can be made a function of time by using a similar approach to that just described.

### Control Variate Technique

A technique known as the *control variate technique* can be used for the evaluation of an American option.[6] This involves using the same tree to calculate both the value of the American option, $f_A$, and the value of the corresponding European option, $f_E$. We also calculate the Black–Scholes price of the European option, $f_{BS}$. The error given by the tree in the pricing of the European option is assumed equal to that given by the tree in the pricing of the American option. This gives the estimate of the price of the American option to be

$$f_A + f_{BS} - f_E$$

To illustrate this approach, Figure 18.10 values the option in Figure 18.3 on the assumption that it is European. The price obtained is \$4.32. From the Black–Scholes formula, the true European price of the option is \$4.08. The estimate of the American price in Figure 18.3 is \$4.49. The control variate estimate of the American price is therefore

$$4.49 + 4.08 - 4.32 = 4.25$$

A good estimate of the American price, calculated using 100 steps, is 4.278. The control variate approach, therefore, does produce a considerable improvement over the basic tree estimate of 4.49 in this case.

The control variate technique in effect involves using the tree to calculate the difference between the European and the American price rather than the American price itself. We give a further application of the control variate technique when we discuss Monte Carlo simulation later in the chapter.

## 18.5  ALTERNATIVE PROCEDURES FOR CONSTRUCTING TREES

The original Cox, Ross, and Rubinstein approach is not the only way of building a binomial tree. Instead of imposing the assumption $u = 1/d$ on equations (18.2) and (18.3), we can set $p = 0.5$.

---

[5] For a sufficiently large number of time steps, these probabilities are always positive.

[6] See J. Hull and A. White, "The Use of the Control Variate Technique in Option Pricing," *Journal of Financial and Quantitative Analysis*, 23 (September 1988), 237–51.

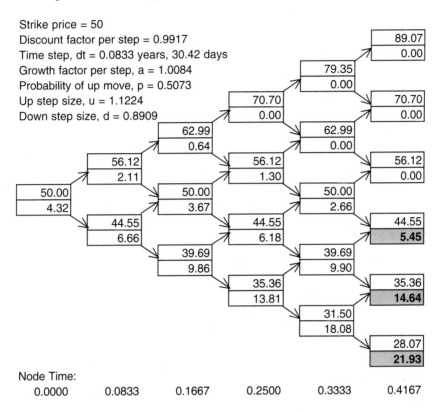

At each node:
 Upper value = Underlying Asset Price
 Lower value = Option Price
 Shading indicates where option is exercised

Strike price = 50
Discount factor per step = 0.9917
Time step, dt = 0.0833 years, 30.42 days
Growth factor per step, a = 1.0084
Probability of up move, p = 0.5073
Up step size, u = 1.1224
Down step size, d = 0.8909

| | | | | | 89.07 |
| | | | | | 0.00 |
| | | | | 79.35 | |
| | | | | 0.00 | |
| | | | 70.70 | | 70.70 |
| | | | 0.00 | | 0.00 |
| | | 62.99 | | 62.99 | |
| | | 0.64 | | 0.00 | |
| | 56.12 | | 56.12 | | 56.12 |
| | 2.11 | | 1.30 | | 0.00 |
| 50.00 | | 50.00 | | 50.00 | |
| 4.32 | | 3.67 | | 2.66 | |
| | 44.55 | | 44.55 | | 44.55 |
| | 6.66 | | 6.18 | | **5.45** |
| | | 39.69 | | 39.69 | |
| | | 9.86 | | 9.90 | |
| | | | 35.36 | | 35.36 |
| | | | 13.81 | | **14.64** |
| | | | | 31.50 | |
| | | | | 18.08 | |
| | | | | | 28.07 |
| | | | | | **21.93** |

Node Time:
 0.0000   0.0833   0.1667   0.2500   0.3333   0.4167

**Figure 18.10**  Tree, as produced by DerivaGem, for the European version of the option in Figure 18.3.
At each node, the upper number is the stock price, and the lower number is the option price

A solution to the equations when terms of order higher than $\delta t$ are ignored is then

$$u = e^{(r-\sigma^2/2)\delta t + \sigma\sqrt{\delta t}}, \qquad d = e^{(r-\sigma^2/2)\delta t - \sigma\sqrt{\delta t}}$$

When the stock provides a dividend yield at rate $q$, the variable $r$ becomes $r - q$ in these formulas. This allows trees with $p = 0.5$ to be built for options on indices, foreign exchange, and futures.

This alternative tree-building procedure has the advantage over the Cox, Ross, and Rubinstein approach that the probabilities are always 0.5 regardless of the value of $\sigma$ or the number of time steps.[7] Its disadvantage is that it is not as easy to calculate delta, gamma, and rho from the tree because the value of the underlying asset at the central node at time $2\,\delta t$ is no longer the same as at time zero.

---

[7] When time steps are so large that $\sigma < |(r-q)\sqrt{\delta t}|$, the Cox, Ross, and Rubinstein tree gives negative probabilities. The alternative procedure described here does not have that drawback.

**Example 18.6**   Consider a nine-month American call option on the Canadian dollar. The current exchange rate is 0.7900, the strike price is 0.7950, the U.S. risk-free interest rate is 6% per annum, the Canadian risk-free interest rate is 10% per annum, and the volatility of the exchange rate is 4% per annum. In this case, $S_0 = 0.79$, $K = 0.795$, $r = 0.06$, $r_f = 0.10$, $\sigma = 0.04$, and $T = 0.75$. We divide the life of the option into three-month periods for the purposes of constructing the tree, so that $\delta t = 0.25$. We set the probabilities on each branch to 0.5 and

$$u = e^{(0.06-0.10-0.0016/2)0.25+0.04\sqrt{0.25}} = 1.0098$$

$$d = e^{(0.06-0.10-0.0016/2)0.25-0.04\sqrt{0.25}} = 0.9703$$

The tree for the exchange rate is shown in Figure 18.11 and tree gives the value of the option as $0.0026.

### Trinomial Trees

Trinomial trees can be used as an alternative to binomial trees. The general form of the tree is as shown in Figure 18.12. Suppose that $p_u$, $p_m$, and $p_d$ are the probabilities of up, middle, and down

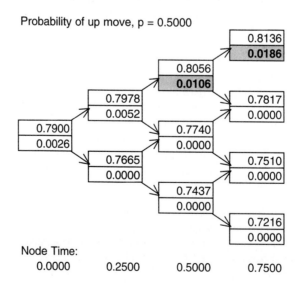

**Figure 18.11**   Binomial tree for an American call option on the Canadian dollar. At each node, the upper number is spot exchange rate, and the lower number is option price. All probabilities are 0.5

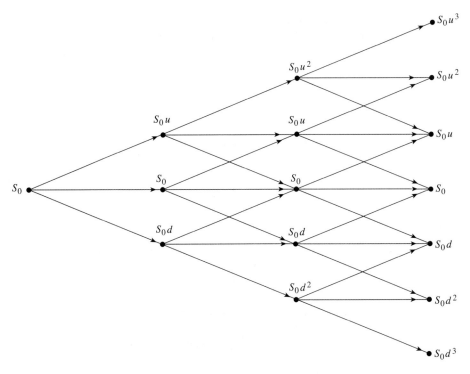

**Figure 18.12** Trinomial stock price tree

movements at each node and $\delta t$ is the length of the time step. For a non-dividend-paying stock, parameter values that match the mean and standard deviation of price changes when terms of order higher than $\delta t$ are ignored are

$$u = e^{\sigma\sqrt{3\,\delta t}}, \qquad d = \frac{1}{u}$$

$$p_d = -\sqrt{\frac{\delta t}{12\sigma^2}}\left(r - \tfrac{1}{2}\sigma^2\right) + \tfrac{1}{6}, \qquad p_m = \tfrac{2}{3}, \qquad p_u = \sqrt{\frac{\delta t}{12\sigma^2}}\left(r - \tfrac{1}{2}\sigma^2\right) + \tfrac{1}{6}$$

For a stock paying a dividend yield at rate $q$, we replace $r$ by $r - q$ in these equations. Calculations for a trinomial tree are analogous to those for a binomial tree. The trinomial tree approach proves to be equivalent to the explicit finite difference method, which will be described in Section 18.8.

### The Adaptive Mesh Model

Figlewski and Gao have proposed a method, which they call the *adaptive mesh model*, for building trees where a high-resolution (small-$\delta t$) tree is grafted on to a low-resolution (large-$\delta t$) tree.[8] It turns out that, for an American option, we need high resolution close to the strike price and close

[8] See S. Figlewski and B. Gao, "The Adaptive Mesh Model: A New Approach to Efficient Option Pricing," *Journal of Financial Economics*, 53 (1999), 313–51.

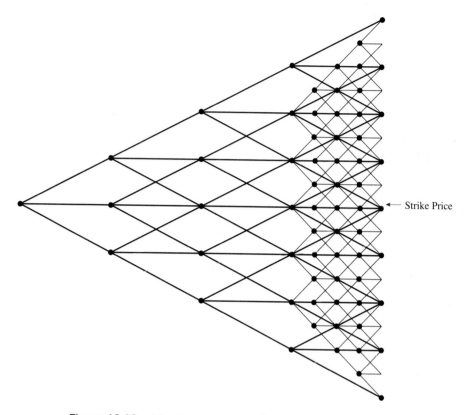

← Strike Price

**Figure 18.13**   Adaptive mesh model for an American-style option

to maturity. Figure 18.13 indicates how we can achieve this. In this figure a trinomial tree with a time step of $\delta t/4$ has been grafted on to a trinomial tree with a time step of $\delta t$. The calculation of probabilities on branches and the rollback procedure is analogous to that for a regular tree. The tree in Figure 18.13 leads to a significant improvement in numerical efficiency over a binomial or trinomial tree.

## 18.6 MONTE CARLO SIMULATION

We now move on to discuss Monte Carlo simulation. This uses the risk-neutral valuation result. The expected payoff in a risk-neutral world is calculated using a sampling procedure. It is then discounted at the risk-free interest rate.

Consider a derivative dependent on a single market variable $S$ that provides a payoff at time $T$. Assuming that interest rates are constant, we can value the derivative as follows:[9]

1. Sample a random path for $S$ in a risk-neutral world.
2. Calculate the payoff from the derivative.

---

[9] We discuss how Monte Carlo simulation can be used with stochastic interest rates in Section 21.4.

3. Repeat steps 1 and 2 to get many sample values of the payoff from the derivative in a risk-neutral world.

4. Calculate the mean of the sample payoffs to get an estimate of the expected payoff in a risk-neutral world.

5. Discount the expected payoff at the risk-free rate to get an estimate of the value of the derivative.

Suppose that the process followed by the underlying market variable in a risk-neutral world is

$$dS = \hat{\mu} S \, dt + \sigma S \, dz \qquad (18.13)$$

where $dz$ is a Weiner process, $\hat{\mu}$ is the expected return in a risk-neutral world, and $\sigma$ is the volatility.[10] To simulate the path followed by $S$, we divide the life of the derivative into $N$ short intervals of length $\delta t$ and approximate equation (18.13) as

$$S(t + \delta t) - S(t) = \hat{\mu} S(t) \, \delta t + \sigma S(t) \epsilon \sqrt{\delta t} \qquad (18.14)$$

where $S(t)$ denotes the value of $S$ at time $t$, and $\epsilon$ is a random sample from a normal distribution with mean zero and standard deviation 1.0. This enables the value of $S$ at time $\delta t$ to be calculated from the initial value of $S$, the value at time $2 \delta t$ to be calculated from the value at time $\delta t$, and so on. An illustration of the procedure is given in Section 11.4. One simulation trial involves constructing a complete path for $S$ using $N$ random samples from a normal distribution.

In practice, it is usually more accurate to simulate $\ln S$ rather than $S$. From Itô's lemma the process followed by $\ln S$ is

$$d \ln S = \left( \hat{\mu} - \frac{\sigma^2}{2} \right) dt + \sigma \, dz$$

so that

$$\ln S(t + \delta t) - \ln S(t) = \left( \hat{\mu} - \frac{\sigma^2}{2} \right) \delta t + \sigma \epsilon \sqrt{\delta t}$$

or equivalently

$$S(t + \delta t) = S(t) \exp\left[ \left( \hat{\mu} - \frac{\sigma^2}{2} \right) \delta t + \sigma \epsilon \sqrt{\delta t} \right] \qquad (18.15)$$

This equation is used to construct a path for $S$ in a similar way to equation (18.14). Whereas equation (18.14) is true only in the limit as $\delta t$ tends to zero, equation (18.15) is exactly true for all $\delta t$.

The advantage of Monte Carlo simulation is that it can be used when the payoff depends on the path followed by the underlying variable $S$ as well as when it depends only on the final value of $S$. Payoffs can occur at several times during the life of the derivative rather than all at the end. Any stochastic process for $S$ can be accommodated. As will be shown shortly, the procedure can also be extended to accommodate situations where the payoff from the derivative depends on several underlying market variables. The drawbacks of Monte Carlo simulation are that it is computationally very time-consuming and cannot easily handle situations where there are early exercise opportunities.[11]

---

[10] If $S$ is the price of a non-dividend-paying stock, $\hat{\mu} = r$; if it is an exchange rate, $\hat{\mu} = r - r_f$; and so on. Note that the volatility is the same in a risk-neutral world as in the real world, as shown in Section 10.7.

[11] A number of researchers have suggested ways Monte Carlo simulation can be extended to value American options (see Section 20.9).

In the particular case where a derivative provides a payoff at time $T$ dependent only on the value of $S$ at that time, it is not necessary to sample a whole path for $S$. Instead we can jump straight from the value of $S$ at time zero to its value at time $T$. When the process in equation (18.13) is assumed,

$$S(T) = S(0) \exp\left[\left(\hat{\mu} - \frac{\sigma^2}{2}\right)T + \sigma\epsilon\sqrt{T}\right]$$

### Derivatives Dependent on More than One Market Variable

Consider the situation where the payoff from a derivative depends on $n$ variables, $\theta_i$ ($1 \leqslant i \leqslant n$). Define $s_i$ as the volatility of $\theta_i$, $\hat{m}_i$ as the expected growth rate of $\theta_i$ in a risk-neutral world, and $\rho_{ik}$ as the instantaneous correlation between $\theta_i$ and $\theta_k$.[12] As in the single-variable case, the life of the derivative must be divided into $N$ subintervals of length $\delta t$. The discrete version of the process for $\theta_i$ is then

$$\theta_i(t + \delta t) - \theta_i(t) = \hat{m}_i \theta_i(t)\,\delta t + s_i \theta_i(t)\epsilon_i \sqrt{\delta t} \tag{18.16}$$

where $\epsilon_i$ is a random sample from a standard normal distribution. The coefficient of correlation between $\epsilon_i$ and $\epsilon_k$ is $\rho_{ik}$ for $1 \leqslant i,k \leqslant n$. One simulation trial involves obtaining $N$ samples of the $\epsilon_i$ ($1 \leqslant i \leqslant n$) from a multivariate standardized normal distribution. These are substituted into equation (18.16) to produce simulated paths for each $\theta_i$, thereby enabling a sample value for the derivative to be calculated.

### Generating the Random Samples from Normal Distributions

Most programming languages incorporate routines for sampling a random number between zero and one. An approximate sample from a univariate standardized normal distribution can be obtained from the formula

$$\epsilon = \sum_{i=1}^{12} R_i - 6 \tag{18.17}$$

where the $R_i$ ($1 \leqslant i \leqslant 12$) are independent random numbers between zero and one, and $\epsilon$ is the required sample from $\phi(0, 1)$. This approximation is satisfactory for most purposes.

When two correlated samples $\epsilon_1$ and $\epsilon_2$ from standard normal distributions are required, an appropriate procedure is as follows. Independent samples $x_1$ and $x_2$ from a univariate standardized normal distribution are obtained as just described. The required samples $\epsilon_1$ and $\epsilon_2$ are then calculated as follows:

$$\epsilon_1 = x_1$$
$$\epsilon_2 = \rho x_1 + x_2 \sqrt{1 - \rho^2}$$

where $\rho$ is the coefficient of correlation.

Consider next the situation where we require $n$ correlated samples from normal distributions where the coefficient of correlation between sample $i$ and sample $j$ is $\rho_{i,j}$. We first sample $n$ independent variables $x_i$ ($1 \leqslant i \leqslant n$), from univariate standardized normal distributions. The

---

[12] Note that $s_i$, $\hat{m}_i$, and $\rho_{ik}$ are not necessarily constant; they may depend on the $\theta_i$.

required samples are $\epsilon_i$ $(1 \leqslant i \leqslant n)$, where

$$\epsilon_i = \sum_{k=1}^{i} \alpha_{ik} x_k$$

For $\epsilon_i$ to have the correct variance and the correct correlation with the $\epsilon_j$ $(1 \leqslant j < i)$, we must have

$$\sum_{k=1}^{i} \alpha_{ik}^2 = 1$$

and, for all $j < i$,

$$\sum_{k=1}^{j} \alpha_{ik} \alpha_{jk} = \rho_{ij}$$

The first sample, $\epsilon_1$, is set equal to $x_1$. These equations for the $\alpha$'s can be solved so that $\epsilon_2$ is calculated from $x_1$ and $x_2$, $\epsilon_3$ is calculated from $x_1$, $x_2$ and $x_3$, and so on.[13] The procedure is known as the *Cholesky decomposition*.

### Number of Trials

The number of simulation trials carried out depends on the accuracy required. If $M$ independent trials are carried out as described above, it is usual to calculate the standard deviation as well as the mean of the discounted payoffs given by the simulation trials for the derivative. Denote the mean by $\mu$ and the standard deviation by $\omega$. The variable $\mu$ is the simulation's estimate of the value of the derivative. The standard error of the estimate is

$$\frac{\omega}{\sqrt{M}}$$

A 95% confidence interval for the price $f$ of the derivative is therefore given by

$$\mu - \frac{1.96\omega}{\sqrt{M}} < f < \mu + \frac{1.96\omega}{\sqrt{M}}$$

This shows that our uncertainty about the value of the derivative is inversely proportional to the square root of the number of trials. To double the accuracy of a simulation, we must quadruple the number of trials; to increase the accuracy by a factor of 10, the number of trials must increase by a factor of 100; and so on.

### Applications

Monte Carlo simulation tends to be numerically more efficient than other procedures when there are three or more stochastic variables. This is because the time taken to carry out a Monte Carlo simulation increases approximately linearly with the number of variables, whereas the time taken for most other procedures increases exponentially with the number of variables. One advantage of Monte Carlo simulation is that it can provide a standard error for the estimates that it makes. Another is that it is an approach that can accommodate complex payoffs and complex stochastic processes. It can also be used when the payoff depends on some function of the whole path

---

[13] If the equations for the $\alpha$'s do not have real solutions, the assumed correlation structure is internally inconsistent, as explained in Section 17.7.

followed by a variable, not just its terminal value. As already noted, a limitation of the Monte Carlo simulation approach is that it is difficult to use it for non-European-style derivatives.

### Calculating the Greek Letters

The Greek letters discussed in Chapter 14 can be calculated using Monte Carlo simulation. Suppose that we are interested in the partial derivative of $f$ with $x$, where $f$ is the value of the derivative and $x$ is the value of an underlying variable or a parameter. First, Monte Carlo simulation is used in the usual way to calculate an estimate, $\hat{f}$, for the value of the derivative. A small increase $\delta x$ is then made in the value of $x$, and a new value for the derivative, $\hat{f}^*$, is calculated in the same way as $\hat{f}$. An estimate for the hedge parameter is given by

$$\frac{\hat{f}^* - \hat{f}}{\delta x}$$

In order to minimize the standard error of the estimate, the number of time intervals $N$, the random number streams, and the number of trials $M$ should be the same for calculating both $\hat{f}$ and $\hat{f}^*$.

### Sampling through a Tree

Instead of implementing Monte Carlo simulation by randomly sampling from the stochastic process for an underlying variable, we can sample paths for the underlying variable using a binomial tree. Suppose we have a binomial tree where the probability of an "up" movement is 0.6. The procedure for sampling a random path through the tree is as follows. At each node, we sample a random number between zero and one. If the number is less than 0.4, we take the down path. If it is greater than 0.4, we take the up path. Once we have a complete path from the initial node to the end of the tree, we can calculate a payoff. This completes the first trial. A similar procedure is used to complete more trials. The mean of the payoffs is discounted at the risk-free rate to get an estimate of the value of the derivative.

## 18.7 VARIANCE REDUCTION PROCEDURES

If the simulation is carried out as described so far, a very large value of $M$ is usually necessary to estimate $f$ with reasonable accuracy. This is very expensive in terms of computation time. In this section, we examine a number of variance reduction procedures that can lead to dramatic savings in computation time.

### Antithetic Variable Technique

In the antithetic variable technique, a simulation trial involves calculating two values of the derivative. The first value, $f_1$, is calculated in the usual way; the second value, $f_2$, is calculated by changing the sign of all the random samples from standard normal distributions. (If $\epsilon$ is a sample used to calculate $f_1$, $-\epsilon$ is the corresponding sample used to calculate $f_2$.) The sample value of the derivative calculated from a simulation trial is the average of $f_1$ and $f_2$. This works well because when one value is above the true value, the other tends to be below, and vice versa.

Denote $\bar{f}$ as the average of $f_1$ and $f_2$:

$$\bar{f} = \frac{f_1 + f_2}{2}$$

The final estimate of the value of the derivative is the average of the $\bar{f}$'s. If $\bar{\omega}$ is the standard deviation of the $\bar{f}$'s, and $M$ is the number of simulation trials (i.e., the number of pairs of values calculated), the standard error of the estimate is $\bar{\omega}/\sqrt{M}$. This is generally much less than the standard error calculated using $2M$ random trials.

### Control Variate Technique

We have already given one example of the control variate technique in connection with the use of trees to value American options (see Section 18.4). The control variate technique is applicable when there are two similar derivatives, A and B. Derivative A is the security under consideration; derivative B is similar to derivative A and has an analytic solution available. Two simulations using the same random number streams and the same $\delta t$ are carried out in parallel. The first is used to obtain an estimate, $f_A^*$, of the value of A; the second is used to obtain an estimate, $f_B^*$, of the value of B. A better estimate, $f_A$, of the value of A is then obtained using the formula

$$f_A = f_A^* - f_B^* + f_B \tag{18.18}$$

where $f_B$ is the known true value of B. Hull and White provide an example of the use of the control variate technique when evaluating the effect of stochastic volatility on the price of a European call option.[14] In this case, $f_A$ is the estimated value of the option assuming stochastic volatility and $f_B$ is its estimated value assuming constant volatility.

### Importance Sampling

Importance sampling is best explained with an example. Suppose that we wish to calculate the price of a deep-out-of-the-money European call option with strike price $K$ and maturity $T$. If we sample values for the underlying asset price at time $T$ in the usual way, most of the paths will lead to zero payoff. This is a waste of computation time because the zero-payoff paths contribute very little to the determination of the value of the option. We therefore try to choose only important paths, that is, paths where the stock price is above $K$ at maturity.

Suppose that $F$ is the unconditional probability distribution function for the stock price at time $T$ and that the probability, $k$, of the stock price being greater than $K$ at maturity is known analytically. Then $G = F/k$ is the probability distribution of the stock price conditional on the stock price being greater than $K$. To implement importance sampling, we sample from $G$ rather than $F$. The estimate of the value of the option is the average discounted payoff multiplied by $k$.

### Stratified Sampling

Stratified sampling is a way of sampling from the probability distribution of a market variable at a future time. It involves dividing the distribution into ranges or intervals and sampling from each interval according to its probability. Suppose, for example, that there are ten equally likely intervals. We choose a sampling scheme that ensures that exactly 10% of our samples are from

[14] See J. Hull and A. White, "The Pricing of Options on Assets with Stochastic Volatilities," *Journal of Finance*, 42 (June 1987), 281–300.

the first interval, 10% from the second interval, and so on. If a large number of intervals are used, we can regard either the mean or the median value of the variable, conditional on it being in an interval, as a representative value for the interval. When sampling from an interval, we then always pick the representative value.

Curran shows results from using this procedure to value both European call options and path-dependent options.[15] In the case of a standard normal distribution when there are $n$ intervals, we can calculate the representative value for the $i$th interval as

$$N^{-1}\left(\frac{i - 0.5}{n}\right)$$

where $N^{-1}$ is the inverse cumulative normal distribution. For example, when $n = 4$ the representative values corresponding to the four intervals are $N^{-1}(0.125)$, $N^{-1}(0.375)$, $N^{-1}(0.625)$, $N^{-1}(0.875)$. The function $N^{-1}$ can be calculated iteratively using the approximation to the $N$ given in Section 12.9 (or the NORMSINV function in Excel). An alternative approach is suggested by Moro.[16]

### Moment Matching

Moment matching involves adjusting the samples taken from a standardized normal distribution so that the first, second, and possibly higher moments are matched. Suppose that the normal distribution samples used to calculate the change in the value of a particular variable over a particular time period are $\epsilon_i$ ($1 \leqslant i \leqslant n$). To match the first two moments, we calculate the mean of the samples, $m$, and the standard deviation of the samples, $s$. We then define adjusted samples $y_i$ ($1 \leqslant i \leqslant n$) as

$$y_i = \frac{\epsilon_i - m}{s}$$

These adjusted samples have the correct mean of zero and the correct standard deviation of 1.0. We use the adjusted samples for all calculations.

Moment matching saves computation time, but can lead to memory problems because every number sampled must be stored until the end of the simulation. Moment matching is sometimes termed *quadratic resampling*. It is often used in conjunction with the antithetic variable technique. Because the latter automatically matches all odd moments, the goal of moment matching then becomes that of matching the second moment and, possibly, the fourth moment.

### Using Quasi-Random Sequences

A quasi-random sequence (also called a *low-discrepancy* sequence) is a sequence of representative samples from a probability distribution.[17] Descriptions of the use of quasi-random sequences have been given by Brotherton-Ratcliffe and by Press *et al.*[18] Quasi-random sequences can have the desirable property that they lead to the standard error of an estimate being proportional to $1/M$ rather than $1/\sqrt{M}$, where $M$ is the sample size.

---

[15] See M. Curran, "Strata Gems," *RISK*, March 1994, pp. 70–71.

[16] See B. Moro, "The Full Monte," *RISK*, February 1985, pp. 57–58.

[17] The term *quasi-random* is a misnomer. A quasi-random sequence is totally deterministic.

[18] See R. Brotherton-Ratcliffe, "Monte Carlo Motoring," *RISK*, December 1994, pp. 53–58; W. H. Press, S. A. Teukolsky, W. T. Vetterling, and B. P. Flannery, *Numerical Recipes in C: The Art of Scientific Computing*, 2nd edn., Cambridge University Press, Cambridge, 1992.

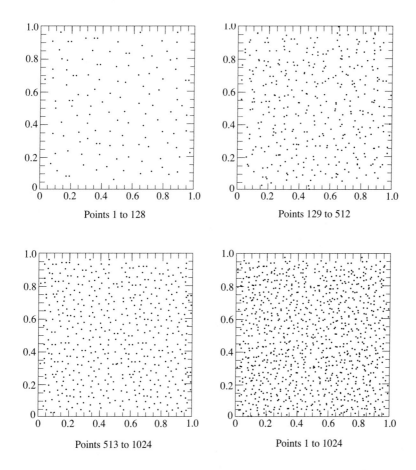

**Figure 18.14**   First 1024 points of a Sobol' sequence

Quasi-random sampling is similar to stratified sampling. The objective is to sample representative values for the underlying variables. In stratified sampling, it is assumed that we know in advance how many samples will be taken. A quasi-random sampling scheme is more flexible. The samples are taken in such a way that we are always "filling in" gaps between existing samples. At each stage of the simulation, the sampled points are roughly evenly spaced throughout the probability space.

Figure 18.14 shows points generated in two dimensions using a procedure suggested by Sobol'.[19] It can be seen that successive points do tend to fill in the gaps left by previous points.

### *Representative Sampling through a Tree*

As explained previously, we can implement Monte Carlo simulation by sampling paths through a tree. In the spirit of stratified sampling, we can choose representative paths through the tree instead

---

[19] See I. M. Sobol', *USSR Computational Mathematics and Mathematical Physics*, 7, no. 4 (1967), 86–112. A description of the Sobol' procedure is given by W. H. Press, S. A. Teukolsky, W. T. Vetterling, and B. P. Flannery, *Numerical Recipes in C: The Art of Scientific Computing*, 2nd edn., Cambridge University Press, Cambridge, 1992.

of random paths. A set of paths is representative if the proportion of paths going through any given node equals (or is close to) the probability of that node being reached. The construction of representative paths is discussed by Mintz.[20]

The first step is to choose the total number of sample paths. We can then calculate the expected number of sample paths going through each node. (This is the probability of the node being reached times the total number of sample paths.) Suppose that $u_{ij}$ is the expected number of sample paths going through node $(i, j)$. Typically the $u_{ij}$ are not integers. It is necessary to develop an algorithm for the "integerization" of each $u_{ij}$ (i.e., the decision as to whether each $u_{ij}$ is rounded up or down). The result of the algorithm should be that the correct number of sample paths leaves the initial node and that the number of sample paths entering each subsequent node equals the number of sample paths leaving the node. Once we have determined the number of sample paths that will pass along each branch, a "sampling without replacement" procedure can be used to define the sample paths.

## 18.8 FINITE DIFFERENCE METHODS

Finite difference methods value a derivative by solving the differential equation that the derivative satisfies. The differential equation is converted into a set of difference equations, and the difference equations are solved iteratively.

To illustrate the approach, we consider how it might be used to value an American put option on a non-dividend-paying stock. The differential equation that the option must satisfy is from Chapter 12:

$$\frac{\partial f}{\partial t} + rS\frac{\partial f}{\partial S} + \frac{1}{2}\sigma^2 S^2 \frac{\partial^2 f}{\partial S^2} = rf \tag{18.19}$$

Suppose that the life of the option is $T$. We divide this into $N$ equally spaced intervals of length $\delta t = T/N$. A total of $N + 1$ times are therefore considered

$$0, \delta t, 2\,\delta t, \ldots, T$$

Suppose that $S_{\max}$ is a stock price sufficiently high that, when it is reached, the put has virtually no value. We define $\delta S = S_{\max}/M$ and consider a total of $M + 1$ equally spaced stock prices:

$$0, \delta S, 2\,\delta S, \ldots, S_{\max}$$

The level $S_{\max}$ is chosen so that one of these is the current stock price.

The time points and stock price points define a grid consisting of a total of $(M + 1) \times (N + 1)$ points as shown in Figure 18.15. The $(i, j)$ point on the grid is the point that corresponds to time $i\,\delta t$ and stock price $j\,\delta S$. We will use the variable $f_{i,j}$ to denote the value of the option at the $(i, j)$ point.

### Implicit Finite Difference Method

For an interior point $(i, j)$ on the grid, $\partial f/\partial S$ can be approximated as

$$\frac{\partial f}{\partial S} = \frac{f_{i,j+1} - f_{i,j}}{\delta S} \tag{18.20}$$

---

[20] See D. Mintz, "Less is More," *RISK*, July 1997, pp. 42–45.

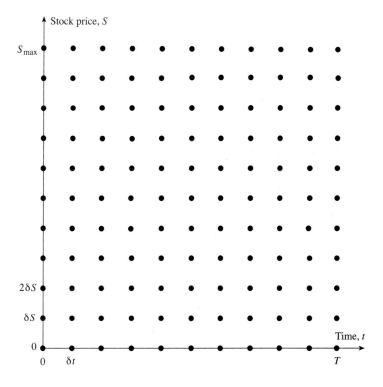

**Figure 18.15**   Grid for finite difference approach

or as

$$\frac{\partial f}{\partial S} = \frac{f_{i,j} - f_{i,j-1}}{\delta S} \tag{18.21}$$

Equation (18.20) is known as the *forward difference approximation*; equation (18.21) is known as the *backward difference approximation*. We use a more symmetrical approximation by averaging the two:

$$\frac{\partial f}{\partial S} = \frac{f_{i,j+1} - f_{i,j-1}}{2\,\delta S} \tag{18.22}$$

For $\partial f/\partial t$, we will use a forward difference approximation, so that the value at time $i\,\delta t$ is related to the value at time $(i+1)\,\delta t$:

$$\frac{\partial f}{\partial t} = \frac{f_{i+1,j} - f_{i,j}}{\delta t} \tag{18.23}$$

The backward difference approximation for $\partial f/\partial S$ at the $(i, j)$ point is given by equation (18.21). The backward difference at the $(i, j+1)$ point is

$$\frac{f_{i,j+1} - f_{i,j}}{\delta S}$$

Hence a finite difference approximation for $\partial^2 f/\partial S^2$ at the $(i, j)$ point is

$$\frac{\partial^2 f}{\partial S^2} = \left(\frac{f_{i,j+1} - f_{i,j}}{\delta S} - \frac{f_{i,j} - f_{i,j-1}}{\delta S}\right)\bigg/ \delta S$$

or

$$\frac{\partial^2 f}{\partial S^2} = \frac{f_{i,j+1} + f_{i,j-1} - 2f_{i,j}}{\delta S^2} \tag{18.24}$$

Substituting equations (18.22), (18.23), and (18.24) into the differential equation (18.19) and noting that $S = j\delta S$ gives

$$\frac{f_{i+1,j} - f_{i,j}}{\delta t} + rj\delta S \frac{f_{i,j+1} - f_{i,j-1}}{2\delta S} + \tfrac{1}{2}\sigma^2 j^2 \delta S^2 \frac{f_{i,j+1} + f_{i,j-1} - 2f_{i,j}}{\delta S^2} = rf_{i,j}$$

for $j = 1, 2, \ldots, M - 1$ and $i = 0, 1, \ldots, N - 1$. Rearranging terms, we obtain

$$a_j f_{i,j-1} + b_j f_{i,j} + c_j f_{i,j+1} = f_{i+1,j} \tag{18.25}$$

where

$$a_j = \tfrac{1}{2}rj\delta t - \tfrac{1}{2}\sigma^2 j^2 \delta t, \qquad b_j = 1 + \sigma^2 j^2 \delta t + r\delta t, \qquad c_j = -\tfrac{1}{2}rj\delta t - \tfrac{1}{2}\sigma^2 j^2 \delta t$$

The value of the put at time $T$ is $\max(K - S_T, 0)$, where $S_T$ is the stock price at time $T$. Hence,

$$f_{N,j} = \max(K - j\delta S, 0), \quad j = 0, 1, \ldots, M \tag{18.26}$$

The value of the put option when the stock price is zero is $K$. Hence,

$$f_{i,0} = K, \quad i = 0, 1, \ldots, N \tag{18.27}$$

We assume that the put option is worth zero when $S = S_{max}$, so that

$$f_{i,M} = 0, \quad i = 0, 1, \ldots, N \tag{18.28}$$

Equations (18.26), (18.27), and (18.28) define the value of the put option along the three edges of the grid in Figure 18.16, where $S = 0$, $S = S_{max}$, and $t = T$. It remains to use equation (18.25) to arrive at the value of $f$ at all other points. First the points corresponding to time $T - \delta t$ are tackled. Equation (18.25) with $i = N - 1$ gives

$$a_j f_{N-1,j-1} + b_j f_{N-1,j} + c_j f_{N-1,j+1} = f_{N,j} \tag{18.29}$$

for $j = 1, 2, \ldots, M - 1$. The right-hand sides of these equations are known from equation (18.26). Furthermore, from equations (18.27) and (18.28),

$$f_{N-1,0} = K \tag{18.30}$$

$$f_{N-1,M} = 0 \tag{18.31}$$

Equations (18.29) are therefore $M - 1$ simultaneous equations that can be solved for the $M - 1$ unknowns: $f_{N-1,1}, f_{N-1,2}, \ldots, f_{N-1,M-1}$.[21] After this has been done, each value of $f_{N-1,j}$ is

---

[21] This does not involve inverting a matrix. The $j = 1$ equation in (18.29) can be used to express $f_{N-1,2}$ in terms of $f_{N-1,1}$; the second equation can be used to express $f_{N-1,3}$ in terms of $f_{N-1,1}$; and so on. The final equation provides a value for $f_{N-1,1}$, which can then be used to determine the other $f_{N-1,j}$.

compared with $K - j\delta S$. If $f_{N-1,j} < K - j\delta S$, early exercise at time $T - \delta t$ is optimal and $f_{N-1,j}$ is set equal to $K - j\delta S$. The nodes corresponding to time $T - 2\delta t$ are handled in a similar way, and so on. Eventually, $f_{0,1}$, $f_{0,2}$,..., $f_{0,M-1}$ are obtained. One of these is the option price of interest.

The control variate technique can be used in conjunction with finite difference methods. The same grid is used to value an option that is similar to the one under consideration but for which an analytic valuation is available. Equation (18.18) is then used.

**Example 18.7** Table 18.1 shows the result of using the implicit finite difference method as just described for pricing the American put option in Example 18.1. Values of 20, 10, and 5 were chosen for $M$, $N$, and $\delta S$, respectively. Thus, the option price is evaluated at \$5 stock price intervals between \$0 and \$100 and at half-month time intervals throughout the life of the option. The option price given by the grid is \$4.07. The same grid gives the price of the corresponding European option as \$3.91. The true European price given by the Black–Scholes formula is \$4.08. The control variate estimate of the American price is therefore

$$4.07 + 4.08 - 3.91 = \$4.24$$

**Table 18.1** Grid to value option in Example 18.1 using the implicit finite difference method

| *Stock price (dollars)* | *Time to maturity (months)* | | | | | | | | | | |
|---|---|---|---|---|---|---|---|---|---|---|---|
| | *5* | *4.5* | *4* | *3.5* | *3* | *2.5* | *2* | *1.5* | *1* | *0.5* | *0* |
| 100 | 0.00 | 0.00 | 0.00 | 0.00 | 0.00 | 0.00 | 0.00 | 0.00 | 0.00 | 0.00 | 0.00 |
| 95 | 0.02 | 0.02 | 0.01 | 0.01 | 0.00 | 0.00 | 0.00 | 0.00 | 0.00 | 0.00 | 0.00 |
| 90 | 0.05 | 0.04 | 0.03 | 0.02 | 0.01 | 0.01 | 0.00 | 0.00 | 0.00 | 0.00 | 0.00 |
| 85 | 0.09 | 0.07 | 0.05 | 0.03 | 0.02 | 0.01 | 0.01 | 0.00 | 0.00 | 0.00 | 0.00 |
| 80 | 0.16 | 0.12 | 0.09 | 0.07 | 0.04 | 0.03 | 0.02 | 0.01 | 0.00 | 0.00 | 0.00 |
| 75 | 0.27 | 0.22 | 0.17 | 0.13 | 0.09 | 0.06 | 0.03 | 0.02 | 0.01 | 0.00 | 0.00 |
| 70 | 0.47 | 0.39 | 0.32 | 0.25 | 0.18 | 0.13 | 0.08 | 0.04 | 0.02 | 0.00 | 0.00 |
| 65 | 0.82 | 0.71 | 0.60 | 0.49 | 0.38 | 0.28 | 0.19 | 0.11 | 0.05 | 0.02 | 0.00 |
| 60 | 1.42 | 1.27 | 1.11 | 0.95 | 0.78 | 0.62 | 0.45 | 0.30 | 0.16 | 0.05 | 0.00 |
| 55 | 2.43 | 2.24 | 2.05 | 1.83 | 1.61 | 1.36 | 1.09 | 0.81 | 0.51 | 0.22 | 0.00 |
| 50 | 4.07 | 3.88 | 3.67 | 3.45 | 3.19 | 2.91 | 2.57 | 2.17 | 1.66 | 0.99 | 0.00 |
| 45 | 6.58 | 6.44 | 6.29 | 6.13 | 5.96 | 5.77 | 5.57 | 5.36 | 5.17 | 5.02 | 5.00 |
| 40 | 10.15 | 10.10 | 10.05 | 10.01 | 10.00 | 10.00 | 10.00 | 10.00 | 10.00 | 10.00 | 10.00 |
| 35 | 15.00 | 15.00 | 15.00 | 15.00 | 15.00 | 15.00 | 15.00 | 15.00 | 15.00 | 15.00 | 15.00 |
| 30 | 20.00 | 20.00 | 20.00 | 20.00 | 20.00 | 20.00 | 20.00 | 20.00 | 20.00 | 20.00 | 20.00 |
| 25 | 25.00 | 25.00 | 25.00 | 25.00 | 25.00 | 25.00 | 25.00 | 25.00 | 25.00 | 25.00 | 25.00 |
| 20 | 30.00 | 30.00 | 30.00 | 30.00 | 30.00 | 30.00 | 30.00 | 30.00 | 30.00 | 30.00 | 30.00 |
| 15 | 35.00 | 35.00 | 35.00 | 35.00 | 35.00 | 35.00 | 35.00 | 35.00 | 35.00 | 35.00 | 35.00 |
| 10 | 40.00 | 40.00 | 40.00 | 40.00 | 40.00 | 40.00 | 40.00 | 40.00 | 40.00 | 40.00 | 40.00 |
| 5 | 45.00 | 45.00 | 45.00 | 45.00 | 45.00 | 45.00 | 45.00 | 45.00 | 45.00 | 45.00 | 45.00 |
| 0 | 50.00 | 50.00 | 50.00 | 50.00 | 50.00 | 50.00 | 50.00 | 50.00 | 50.00 | 50.00 | 50.00 |

### Explicit Finite Difference Method

The implicit finite difference method has the advantage of being very robust. It always converges to the solution of the differential equation as $\delta S$ and $\delta t$ approach zero.[22] One of the disadvantages of the implicit finite difference method is that $M - 1$ simultaneous equations have to be solved in order to calculate the $f_{i,j}$'s from the $f_{i+1,j}$'s. The method can be simplified if the values of $\partial f / \partial S$ and $\partial^2 f / \partial S^2$ at point $(i, j)$ on the grid are assumed to be the same as at point $(i + 1, j)$. Equations (18.22) and (18.24) then become

$$\frac{\partial f}{\partial S} = \frac{f_{i+1,j+1} - f_{i+1,j-1}}{2\,\delta S}, \qquad \frac{\partial^2 f}{\partial S^2} = \frac{f_{i+1,j+1} + f_{i+1,j-1} - 2f_{i+1,j}}{\delta S^2}$$

The difference equation is

$$\frac{f_{i+1,j} - f_{i,j}}{\delta t} + rj\,\delta S \frac{f_{i+1,j+1} - f_{i+1,j-1}}{2\,\delta S} + \tfrac{1}{2}\sigma^2 j^2\,\delta S^2 \frac{f_{i+1,j+1} + f_{i+1,j-1} - 2f_{i+1,j}}{\delta S^2} = rf_{i,j}$$

or

$$f_{i,j} = a_j^* f_{i+1,j-1} + b_j^* f_{i+1,j} + c_j^* f_{i+1,j+1} \qquad (18.32)$$

where

$$a_j^* = \frac{1}{1 + r\,\delta t}(-\tfrac{1}{2}rj\,\delta t + \tfrac{1}{2}\sigma^2 j^2\,\delta t)$$

$$b_j^* = \frac{1}{1 + r\,\delta t}(1 - \sigma^2 j^2\,\delta t)$$

$$c_j^* = \frac{1}{1 + r\,\delta t}(\tfrac{1}{2}rj\,\delta t + \tfrac{1}{2}\sigma^2 j^2\,\delta t)$$

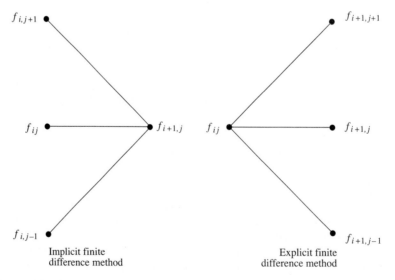

Implicit finite difference method

Explicit finite difference method

**Figure 18.16** Difference between implicit and explicit finite difference methods

[22] A general rule in finite difference methods is that $\delta S$ should be kept proportional to $\sqrt{\delta t}$ as they approach zero.

**Table 18.2**   Grid to value option in Example 18.1 using the explicit finite difference method

| Stock price (dollars) | Time to maturity (months) | | | | | | | | | | |
|---|---|---|---|---|---|---|---|---|---|---|---|
| | 5 | 4.5 | 4 | 3.5 | 3 | 2.5 | 2 | 1.5 | 1 | 0.5 | 0 |
| 100 | 0.00 | 0.00 | 0.00 | 0.00 | 0.00 | 0.00 | 0.00 | 0.00 | 0.00 | 0.00 | 0.00 |
| 95 | 0.06 | 0.00 | 0.00 | 0.00 | 0.00 | 0.00 | 0.00 | 0.00 | 0.00 | 0.00 | 0.00 |
| 90 | −0.11 | 0.05 | 0.00 | 0.00 | 0.00 | 0.00 | 0.00 | 0.00 | 0.00 | 0.00 | 0.00 |
| 85 | 0.28 | −0.05 | 0.05 | 0.00 | 0.00 | 0.00 | 0.00 | 0.00 | 0.00 | 0.00 | 0.00 |
| 80 | −0.13 | 0.20 | 0.00 | 0.05 | 0.00 | 0.00 | 0.00 | 0.00 | 0.00 | 0.00 | 0.00 |
| 75 | 0.46 | 0.06 | 0.20 | 0.04 | 0.06 | 0.00 | 0.00 | 0.00 | 0.00 | 0.00 | 0.00 |
| 70 | 0.32 | 0.46 | 0.23 | 0.25 | 0.10 | 0.09 | 0.00 | 0.00 | 0.00 | 0.00 | 0.00 |
| 65 | 0.91 | 0.68 | 0.63 | 0.44 | 0.37 | 0.21 | 0.14 | 0.00 | 0.00 | 0.00 | 0.00 |
| 60 | 1.48 | 1.37 | 1.17 | 1.02 | 0.81 | 0.65 | 0.42 | 0.27 | 0.00 | 0.00 | 0.00 |
| 55 | 2.59 | 2.39 | 2.21 | 1.99 | 1.77 | 1.50 | 1.24 | 0.90 | 0.59 | 0.00 | 0.00 |
| 50 | 4.26 | 4.08 | 3.89 | 3.68 | 3.44 | 3.18 | 2.87 | 2.53 | 2.07 | 1.56 | 0.00 |
| 45 | 6.76 | 6.61 | 6.47 | 6.31 | 6.15 | 5.96 | 5.75 | 5.50 | 5.24 | 5.00 | 5.00 |
| 40 | 10.28 | 10.20 | 10.13 | 10.06 | 10.01 | 10.00 | 10.00 | 10.00 | 10.00 | 10.00 | 10.00 |
| 35 | 15.00 | 15.00 | 15.00 | 15.00 | 15.00 | 15.00 | 15.00 | 15.00 | 15.00 | 15.00 | 15.00 |
| 30 | 20.00 | 20.00 | 20.00 | 20.00 | 20.00 | 20.00 | 20.00 | 20.00 | 20.00 | 20.00 | 20.00 |
| 25 | 25.00 | 25.00 | 25.00 | 25.00 | 25.00 | 25.00 | 25.00 | 25.00 | 25.00 | 25.00 | 25.00 |
| 20 | 30.00 | 30.00 | 30.00 | 30.00 | 30.00 | 30.00 | 30.00 | 30.00 | 30.00 | 30.00 | 30.00 |
| 15 | 35.00 | 35.00 | 35.00 | 35.00 | 35.00 | 35.00 | 35.00 | 35.00 | 35.00 | 35.00 | 35.00 |
| 10 | 40.00 | 40.00 | 40.00 | 40.00 | 40.00 | 40.00 | 40.00 | 40.00 | 40.00 | 40.00 | 40.00 |
| 5 | 45.00 | 45.00 | 45.00 | 45.00 | 45.00 | 45.00 | 45.00 | 45.00 | 45.00 | 45.00 | 45.00 |
| 0 | 50.00 | 50.00 | 50.00 | 50.00 | 50.00 | 50.00 | 50.00 | 50.00 | 50.00 | 50.00 | 50.00 |

This creates what is known as the *explicit finite difference method*.[23] Figure 18.16 shows the difference between the implicit and explicit methods. The implicit method leads to equation (18.25), which gives a relationship between three different values of the option at time $i\,\delta t$ (i.e., $f_{i,j-1}$, $f_{i,j}$, $f_{i,j+1}$) and one value of the option at time $(i+1)\,\delta t$ (i.e., $f_{i+1,j}$). The explicit method leads to equation (18.32), which gives a relationship between one value of the option at time $i\,\delta t$ (i.e., $f_{i,j}$) and three different values of the option at time $(i+1)\,\delta t$ (i.e., $f_{i+1,j-1}$, $f_{i+1,j}$, $f_{i+1,j+1}$).

**Example 18.8**   Table 18.2 shows the result of using the explicit version of the finite difference method for pricing the American put option in Example 18.1. As in Example 18.7, values of 20, 10, and 5 were chosen for $M$, $N$, and $\delta S$, respectively. The option price given by the grid is 4.26.[24]

---

[23] We also obtain the explicit finite difference method if we use the backward difference approximation instead of the forward difference approximation for $\partial f/\partial t$.

[24] The negative numbers and other inconsistencies in the top left-hand part of the grid will be explained later in the chapter.

## Change of Variable

It is computationally more efficient to use finite difference methods with $\ln S$ rather than $S$ as the underlying variable. Define $Z = \ln S$. Equation (18.19) becomes

$$\frac{\partial f}{\partial t} + (r - \sigma^2/2)\frac{\partial f}{\partial Z} + \tfrac{1}{2}\sigma^2 \frac{\partial^2 f}{\partial Z^2} = rf$$

The grid then evaluates the derivative for equally spaced values of $Z$ rather than for equally spaced values of $S$. The difference equation for the implicit method becomes

$$\frac{f_{i+1,j} - f_{i,j}}{\delta t} + (r - \sigma^2/2)\frac{f_{i,j+1} - f_{i,j-1}}{2\,\delta Z} + \tfrac{1}{2}\sigma^2 \frac{f_{i,j+1} + f_{i,j-1} - 2f_{i,j}}{\delta Z^2} = rf_{i,j}$$

or

$$\alpha_j f_{i,j-1} + \beta_j f_{i,j} + \gamma_j f_{i,j+1} = f_{i+1,j} \qquad (18.33)$$

where

$$\alpha_j = \frac{\delta t}{2\,\delta Z}(r - \sigma^2/2) - \frac{\delta t}{2\,\delta Z^2}\sigma^2$$

$$\beta_j = 1 + \frac{\delta t}{\delta Z^2}\sigma^2 + r\,\delta t$$

$$\gamma_j = -\frac{\delta t}{2\,\delta Z}(r - \sigma^2/2) - \frac{\delta t}{2\,\delta Z^2}\sigma^2$$

The difference equation for the explicit method becomes

$$\frac{f_{i+1,j} - f_{i,j}}{\delta t} + (r - \sigma^2/2)\frac{f_{i+1,j+1} - f_{i+1,j-1}}{2\,\delta Z} + \tfrac{1}{2}\sigma^2 \frac{f_{i+1,j+1} + f_{i+1,j-1} - 2f_{i+1,j}}{\delta Z^2} = rf_{i,j}$$

or

$$\alpha_j^* f_{i+1,j-1} + \beta_j^* f_{i+1,j} + \gamma_j^* f_{i+1,j+1} = f_{i,j} \qquad (18.34)$$

where

$$\alpha_j^* = \frac{1}{1 + r\,\delta t}\left(-\frac{\delta t}{2\,\delta Z}(r - \sigma^2/2) + \frac{\delta t}{2\,\delta Z^2}\sigma^2\right) \qquad (18.35)$$

$$\beta_j^* = \frac{1}{1 + r\,\delta t}\left(1 - \frac{\delta t}{\delta Z^2}\sigma^2\right) \qquad (18.36)$$

$$\gamma_j^* = \frac{1}{1 + r\,\delta t}\left(\frac{\delta t}{2\,\delta Z}(r - \sigma^2/2) + \frac{\delta t}{2\,\delta Z^2}\sigma^2\right) \qquad (18.37)$$

The change of variable approach has the property that $\alpha_j$, $\beta_j$, and $\gamma_j$, as well as $\alpha_j^*$, $\beta_j^*$, and $\gamma_j^*$, are independent of $j$. It can be shown that it is numerically most efficient to set $\delta Z = \sigma\sqrt{3\,\delta t}$.

## Relation to Trinomial Tree Approaches

The explicit finite difference method is equivalent to the trinomial tree approach.[25] In the expressions for $a_j^*$, $b_j^*$, and $c_j^*$ in equation (18.32), we can interpret terms as follows:

$-\tfrac{1}{2}rj\,\delta t + \tfrac{1}{2}\sigma^2 j^2\,\delta t$ : Probability of stock price decreasing from $j\,\delta S$ to $(j-1)\,\delta S$ in time $\delta t$

---

[25] It can also be shown that the implicit finite difference method is equivalent to a multinomial tree approach where there are $M + 1$ branches emanating from each node.

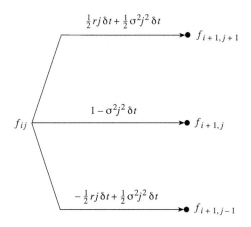

**Figure 18.17**   Interpretation of explicit finite difference method as a trinomial tree

$1 - \sigma^2 j^2 \, \delta t$ :  Probability of stock price remaining unchanged at $j \delta S$ in time $\delta t$

$\frac{1}{2} rj \, \delta t + \frac{1}{2} \sigma^2 j^2 \, \delta t$ :  Probability of stock price increasing from $j \delta S$ to $(j+1) \delta S$ in time $\delta t$

This interpretation is illustrated in Figure 18.17. The three probabilities sum to unity. They give the expected increase in the stock price in time $\delta t$ as $rj \, \delta S \, \delta t = rS \delta t$. This is the expected increase in a risk-neutral world. For small values of $\delta t$, they also give the variance of the change in the stock price in time $\delta t$ as $\sigma^2 j^2 \, \delta S^2 \, \delta t = \sigma^2 S^2 \, \delta t$. This corresponds to the stochastic process followed by $S$. The value of $f$ at time $i \, \delta t$ is calculated as the expected value of $f$ at time $(i+1) \, \delta t$ in a risk-neutral world discounted at the risk-free rate.

For the explicit version of the finite difference method to work well, the three "probabilities"

$$-\tfrac{1}{2} rj \, \delta t + \tfrac{1}{2} \sigma^2 j^2 \, \delta t, \qquad 1 - \sigma^2 j^2 \, \delta t, \qquad \tfrac{1}{2} rj \, \delta t + \tfrac{1}{2} \sigma^2 j^2 \, \delta t$$

should all be positive. In Example 18.8, $1 - \sigma^2 j^2 \, \delta t$ is negative when $j \geqslant 13$ (i.e., when $S \geqslant 65$). This explains the negative option prices and other inconsistencies in the top left-hand part of Table 18.2. This example illustrates the main problem associated with the explicit finite difference method. Because the probabilities in the associated tree may be negative, it does not necessarily produce results that converge to the solution of the differential equation.[26]

When the change-of-variable approach is used (see equations (18.34) to (18.37)), the probabilities that $Z = \ln S$ will decrease by $\delta Z$, stay the same, and increase by $\delta Z$ are, respectively,

$$-\frac{\delta t}{2 \, \delta Z}(r - \sigma^2/2) + \frac{\delta t}{2 \, \delta Z^2} \sigma^2$$

$$1 - \frac{\delta t}{\delta Z^2} \sigma^2$$

$$\frac{\delta t}{2 \, \delta Z}(r - \sigma^2/2) + \frac{\delta t}{2 \, \delta Z^2} \sigma^2$$

---

[26] J. Hull and A. White, "Valuing Derivative Securities Using the Explicit Finite Difference Method" *Journal of Financial and Quantitative Analysis*, 25 (March 1990), 87–100, show how this problem can be overcome. In the situation considered here, it is sufficient to construct the grid in $\ln S$ rather than $S$ to ensure convergence.

These movements in $Z$ correspond to the stock price changing from $S$ to $Se^{-\delta Z}$, $S$, and $Se^{\delta Z}$, respectively. If we set $\delta Z = \sigma\sqrt{3\,\delta t}$, the tree and the probabilities are identical to those for the trinomial tree approach discussed in Section 18.5.

### Other Finite Difference Methods

Many of the other finite difference methods that have been proposed have some of the features of the explicit finite difference method and some features of the implicit finite difference method.

In what is known as the *hopscotch method*, we alternate between the explicit and implicit calculations as we move from node to node. This is illustrated in Figure 18.18. At each time, we first do all the calculations at the "explicit nodes" in the usual way. We can then deal with the "implicit nodes" without solving a set of simultaneous equations because the values at the adjacent nodes have already been calculated.

The *Crank–Nicolson* scheme is an average of the explicit and implicit methods. For the implicit method equation (18.25) gives

$$f_{i,j} = a_j f_{i\ 1,j-1} + b_j f_{i-1,j} + c_j f_{i-1,j+1}$$

For the explicit method, equation (18.32) gives

$$f_{i-1,j} = a_j^* f_{i,j-1} + b_j^* f_{i,j} + c_j^* f_{i,j+1}$$

The Crank–Nicolson method averages these two equations to give

$$f_{i,j} + f_{i-1,j} = a_j f_{i-1,j-1} + b_j f_{i-1,j} + c_j f_{i-1,j+1} + a_j^* f_{i,j-1} + b_j^* f_{i,j} + c_j^* f_{i,j+1}$$

Putting

$$g_{i,j} = f_{i,j} - a_j^* f_{i,j-1} - b_j^* f_{i,j} - c_j^* f_{i,j+1}$$

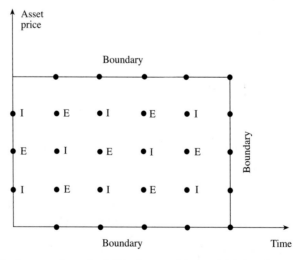

**Figure 18.18**   The hopscotch method: I indicates node at which implicit calculations are done; E indicates node at which explicit calculations are done

we obtain

$$g_{i,j} = a_j f_{i-1,j-1} + b_j f_{i-1,j} + c_j f_{i-1,j+1} - f_{i-1,j}$$

This shows that implementing the Crank–Nicolson method is similar to implementing the implicit finite difference method. The advantage of the Crank–Nicolson method is that it has faster convergence than either the explicit or implicit method.

### Applications of Finite Difference Methods

Finite difference methods can be used for the same types of derivative pricing problems as tree approaches. They can handle American-style as well as European-style derivatives, but they cannot easily be used in situations where the payoff from a derivative depends on the past history of the underlying variable. Finite difference methods can, at the expense of a considerable increase in computer time, be used when there are several state variables. The grid in Figure 18.15 then becomes multidimensional.

The method for calculating Greek letters is similar to that used for trees. Delta, gamma, and theta can be calculated directly from the $f_{i,j}$ values on the grid. For vega, it is necessary to make a small change to volatility and recalculate the value of the derivative using the same grid.

## 18.9 ANALYTIC APPROXIMATION TO AMERICAN OPTION PRICES

As an alternative to the numerical procedures described thus far, a number of analytic approximations to the valuation of American options have been suggested. The best known of these is a quadratic approximation approach originally suggested by MacMillan and extended by Barone-Adesi and Whaley.[27] It can be used to value American calls and puts on stocks, stock indices, currencies, and futures contracts. It involves estimating the difference, $v$, between the European option price and the American option price. Because both the European and American option satisfy the same differential equation, $v$ must also satisfy the differential equation. When an approximation is made, the differential equation can be solved using standard methods. More details on the approach are presented in Appendix 18A.

## SUMMARY

We have presented three different numerical procedures for valuing derivatives when no analytic solution is available. These involve the use of trees, Monte Carlo simulation, and finite difference methods.

Binomial trees assume that in each short interval of time, $\delta t$, a stock price either moves up by a percentage amount $u$ or moves down by a percentage amount $d$. The sizes of $u$ and $d$ and their associated probabilities are chosen so that the change in the stock price has the correct mean and standard deviation in a risk-neutral world. Derivative prices are calculated by starting at the end of

---

[27] See L. W. MacMillan, "Analytic Approximation for the American Put Option," *Advances in Futures and Options Research*, 1 (1986), 119–39; G. Barone-Adesi and R. E. Whaley, "Efficient Analytic Approximation of American Option Values," *Journal of Finance*, 42 (June 1987), 301–20.

the tree and working backwards. For an American option, the value at a node is the greater of the value if it is exercised immediately and the discounted expected value if it is held for a further period of time $\delta t$.

Monte Carlo simulation involves using random numbers to sample many different paths that the variables underlying the derivative could follow in a risk-neutral world. For each path, the payoff is calculated and discounted at the risk-free interest rate. The arithmetic average of the discounted payoffs is the estimated value of the derivative.

Finite difference methods solve the underlying differential equation by converting it to a difference equation. They are similar to tree approaches in that the computations work back from the end of the life of the derivative to the beginning. The explicit method is functionally the same as using a trinomial tree. The implicit finite difference method is more complicated but has the advantage that the user does not have to take any special precautions to ensure convergence.

In practice, the method that is chosen is likely to depend on the characteristics of the derivative being evaluated and the accuracy required. Monte Carlo simulation works forward from the beginning to the end of the life of a derivative. It can be used for European-style derivatives and can cope with a great deal of complexity as far as the payoffs are concerned. It becomes relatively more efficient as the number of underlying variables increases. Tree approaches and finite difference methods work from the end of the life of a security to the beginning and can accommodate American-style as well as European-style derivatives. However, they are difficult to apply when the payoffs depend on the past history of the state variables as well as on their current values. In addition, they are liable to become computationally very time-consuming when three or more variables are involved.

## SUGGESTIONS FOR FURTHER READING

### General

Clewlow, L., and C. Strickland, *Implementing Derivatives Models*, Wiley, Chichester, 1998.

### On Tree Approaches

Boyle, P. P., "A Lattice Framework for Option Pricing with Two State Variables," *Journal of Financial and Quantitative Analysis*, 23 (March 1988), 1–12.

Broadie, M., and P. Glasserman, "A Stochastic Mesh Method for Pricing High-Dimensional American Options," Working Paper, Columbia University, 1997.

Cox, J., S. Ross, and M. Rubinstein, "Option Pricing: A Simplified Approach," *Journal of Financial Economics*, 7 (October 1979), 229–64.

Figlewski, S., and B. Gao, "The Adaptive Mesh Model: A New Approach to Efficient Option Pricing," *Journal of Financial Economics*, 53 (1999), 313–51.

Hull, J. C., and A. White, "The Use of the Control Variate Technique in Option Pricing," *Journal of Financial and Quantitative Analysis*, 23 (September, 1988), 237–51.

Rendleman, R., and B. Bartter, "Two State Option Pricing," *Journal of Finance*, 34 (1979), 1092–1110.

### On Monte Carlo Simulation

Boyle, P. P., "Options: A Monte Carlo Approach," *Journal of Financial Economics*, 4 (1977), 323–38.

Broadie, M., and P. Glasserman, "Estimating Security Prices Using Simulation," *Management Science*, 42, no. 2 (February 1996), 269–85.

Broadie, M., P. Glasserman, and G. Jain, "Enhanced Monte Carlo Estimates for American Option Prices," *Journal of Derivatives*, 5 (Fall 1997), 25–44.

Brotherton-Ratcliffe, R., "Monte Carlo Motoring," *RISK*, December 1994, pp. 53–58.

Curran, M., "Strata Gems," *RISK*, March 1994, pp. 70–71.

Moro, B., "The Full Monte," *RISK*, February 1985, pp. 57–58.

Papageorgiou, A., and J. Traub, "Beating Monte Carlo," *RISK*, June 1996, 65–65.

Paskov, S. H., "New Methodologies for Valuing Derivatives", in *Mathematics Derivative Securities*, ed. M. A. H. Dempster and S. R. Pliska, Cambridge University Press, Cambridge, 1996.

Press, W. H., S. A. Teukolsky, W. T. Vetterling, and B. P. Flannery, *Numerical Recipes in C: The Art of Scientific Computing*, 2nd edn., Cambridge University Press, Cambridge, 1992.

Sobol', I. M., *USSR Computational Mathematics and Mathematical Physics*, 7, no. 4 (1967), 86–112.

### On Finite Difference Methods

Brennan, M. J., and E. S. Schwartz, "Finite Difference Methods and Jump Processes Arising in the Pricing of Contingent Claims: A Synthesis," *Journal of Financial and Quantitative Analysis*, 13 (September 1978), 462–74.

Brennan, M. J., and E. S. Schwartz, "The Valuation of American Put Options," *Journal of Finance*, 32 (May 1977), 449–62.

Courtadon, G., "A More Accurate Finite Difference Approximation for the Valuation of Options," *Journal of Financial and Quantitative Analysis*, 17 (December 1982), 697–705.

Hull, J. C., and A. White, "Valuing Derivative Securities Using the Explicit Finite Difference Method," *Journal of Financial and Quantitative Analysis*, 25 (March 1990), 87–100.

Schwartz, E. S., "The Valuation of Warrants: Implementing a New Approach," *Journal of Financial Economics*, 4 (1977), 79–94.

Wilmott, P., *Derivatives: The Theory and Practice of Financial Engineering*, Wiley, Chichester, 1998.

### On Analytic Approximations

Barone-Adesi, G., and R. E. Whaley, "Efficient Analytic Approximation of American Option Values," *Journal of Finance*, 42 (June 1987), 301–20.

Carr, P., R. Jarrow, and R. Myneni, "Alternative Characterizations of American Put Options," *Mathematical Finance*, 2 (1992), 87–106.

Geske, R., and H. E. Johnson, "The American Put Valued Analytically," *Journal of Finance*, 39 (December 1984), 1511–24.

Ho, T.-S., R. S. Stapleton, and M. G. Subrahmanyam, "The Valuation of American Options with Stochastic Interest Rates: A Generalization of the Geske–Johnson Technique," *Journal of Finance*, 52, no. 2 (June 1997), 827–40.

Johnson, H. E., "An Analytic Approximation to the American Put Price," *Journal of Financial and Quantitative Analysis*, 18 (March 1983), 141–48.

MacMillan, L. W., "Analytic Approximation for the American Put Option," *Advances in Futures and Options Research*, 1 (1986), 119–39.

## QUESTIONS AND PROBLEMS
## (ANSWERS IN SOLUTIONS MANUAL)

18.1. Which of the following can be estimated for an American option by constructing a single binomial tree: delta, gamma, vega, theta, rho?

18.2. Calculate the price of a three-month American put option on a non-dividend-paying stock when the stock price is $60, the strike price is $60, the risk-free interest rate is 10% per annum, and the volatility is 45% per annum. Use a binomial tree with a time interval of one month.

18.3. Explain how the control variate technique is implemented when a tree is used to value American options.

18.4. Calculate the price of a nine-month American call option on corn futures when the current futures price is 198 cents, the strike price is 200 cents, the risk-free interest rate is 8% per annum, and the volatility is 30% per annum. Use a binomial tree with a time interval of three months.

18.5. Consider an option that pays off the amount by which the final stock price exceeds the average stock price achieved during the life of the option. Can this be valued using the binomial tree approach? Explain your answer.

18.6. "For a dividend-paying stock, the tree for the stock price does not recombine; but the tree for the stock price less the present value of future dividends does recombine." Explain this statement.

18.7. Show that the probabilities in a Cox, Ross, and Rubinstein binomial tree are negative when the condition in footnote 7 holds.

18.8. How would you use the binomial tree approach to value an American option on a stock index when the dividend yield on the index is a function of time?

18.9. Explain why the Monte Carlo simulation approach cannot easily be used for American-style derivatives.

18.10. A nine-month American put option on a non-dividend-paying stock has a strike price of $49. The stock price is $50, the risk-free rate is 5% per annum, and the volatility is 30% per annum. Use a three-step binomial tree to calculate the option price.

18.11. Use a three-time-step tree to value a nine-month American call option on wheat futures. The current futures price is 400 cents, the strike price is 420 cents, the risk-free rate is 6%, and the volatility is 35% per annum. Estimate the delta of the option from your tree.

18.12. A three-month American call option on a stock has a strike price of $20. The stock price is $20, the risk-free rate is 3% per annum, and the volatility is 25% per annum. A dividend of $2 is expected in 1.5 months. Use a three-step binomial tree to calculate the option price.

18.13. A one-year American put option on a non-dividend-paying stock has an exercise price of $18. The current stock price is $20, the risk-free interest rate is 15% per annum, and the volatility of the stock price is 40% per annum. Use the DerivaGem software with four 3-month time steps to estimate the value of the option. Display the tree and verify that the option prices at the final and penultimate nodes are correct. Use DerivaGem to value the European version of the option. Use the control variate technique to improve your estimate of the price of the American option.

18.14. A two-month American put option on a stock index has an exercise price of 480. The current level of the index is 484, the risk-free interest rate is 10% per annum, the dividend yield on the index is 3% per annum, and the volatility of the index is 25% per annum. Divide the life of the option into four half-month periods and use the tree approach to estimate the value of the option.

18.15. How can the control variate approach improve the estimate of the delta of an American option when the tree approach is used?

18.16. Suppose that Monte Carlo simulation is being used to evaluate a European call option on a non-dividend-paying stock when the volatility is stochastic. How could the control variate and antithetic variable technique be used to improve numerical efficiency? Explain why it is necessary to calculate six values of the option in each simulation trial when both the control variate and the antithetic variable technique are used.

18.17. Explain how equations (18.25) to (18.28) change when the implicit finite difference method is being used to evaluate an American call option on a currency.

18.18. An American put option on a non-dividend-paying stock has four months to maturity. The exercise price is $21, the stock price is $20, the risk-free rate of interest is 10% per annum, and the volatility is 30% per annum. Use the explicit version of the finite difference approach to value the option. Use stock price intervals of $4 and time intervals of one month.

18.19. The spot price of copper is $0.60 per pound. Suppose that the futures prices (dollars per pound) are as follows:

| | |
|---|---|
| 3 months | 0.59 |
| 6 months | 0.57 |
| 9 months | 0.54 |
| 12 months | 0.50 |

The volatility of the price of copper is 40% per annum and the risk-free rate is 6% per annum. Use a binomial tree to value an American call option on copper with an exercise price of $0.60 and a time to maturity of one year. Divide the life of the option into four 3-month periods for the purposes of constructing the tree. (*Hint*: As explained in Section 13.7, the futures price of a variable is its expected future price in a risk-neutral world.)

18.20. Use the binomial tree in Problem 18.19 to value a security that pays off $x^2$ in one year where $x$ is the price of copper.

18.21. When do the boundary conditions for $S = 0$ and $S \rightarrow \infty$ affect the estimates of derivative prices in the explicit finite difference method?

18.22. How can finite difference methods be used when there are known dividends?

18.23. A company has issued a three-year convertible bond that has a face value of $25 and can be exchanged for two of the company's shares at any time. The company can call the issue forcing conversion when the share price is greater than or equal to $18. Assuming that the company will force conversion at the earliest opportunity, what are the boundary conditions for the price of the convertible? Describe how you would use finite difference methods to value the convertible assuming constant interest rates. Assume there is no risk of the company defaulting.

18.24. Provide formulas that can be used for obtaining three random samples from standard normal distributions when the correlation between sample $i$ and sample $j$ is $\rho_{i,j}$.

## ASSIGNMENT QUESTIONS

18.25. An American put option to sell a Swiss franc for dollars has a strike price of $0.80 and a time to maturity of one year. The volatility of the Swiss franc is 10%, the dollar interest rate is 6%, the Swiss franc interest rate is 3%, and the current exchange rate is 0.81. Use a three-time-step tree to value the option. Estimate the delta of the option from your tree.

18.26. A one-year American call option on silver futures has an exercise price of $9.00. The current futures price is $8.50, the risk-free rate of interest is 12% per annum, and the volatility of the futures price is 25% per annum. Use the DerivaGem software with four 3-month time steps to estimate the value of the option. Display the tree and verify that the option prices at the final and penultimate nodes are correct. Use DerivaGem to value the European version of the option. Use the control variate technique to improve your estimate of the price of the American option.

18.27. A six-month American call option on a stock is expected to pay dividends of $1 per share at the end of the second month and the fifth month. The current stock price is $30, the exercise price is $34, the risk-free interest rate is 10% per annum, and the volatility of the part of the stock price that will not be used to pay the dividends is 30% per annum. Use the DerivaGem software with the life of the option divided into six time steps to estimate the value of the option. Compare your answer with that given by Black's approximation (see Section 12.12).

18.28. The current value of the British pound is $1.60 and the volatility of the pound–dollar exchange rate is 15% per annum. An American call option has an exercise price of $1.62 and a time to maturity of one year. The risk-free rates of interest in the United States and the United Kingdom are 6% per annum and 9% per annum, respectively. Use the explicit finite difference method to value the option. Consider exchange rates at intervals of 0.20 between 0.80 and 2.40 and time intervals of 3 months.

18.29. Answer the following questions concerned with the alternative procedures for constructing trees in Section 18.5.
   a. Show that the binomial model in Section 18.5 is exactly consistent with the mean and variance of the change in the logarithm of the stock price in time $\delta t$.
   b. Show that the trinomial model in Section 18.5 is consistent with the mean and variance of the change in the logarithm of the stock price in time $\delta t$ when terms of order $(\delta t)^2$ and higher are ignored.
   c. Construct an alternative to the trinomial model in Section 18.5 so that the probabilities are $1/6$, $2/3$, and $1/6$ on the upper, middle, and lower branches emanating from each node. Assume that the branching is from $S$ to $Su$, $Sm$, or $Sd$, with $m^2 = ud$. Match the mean and variance of the change in the logarithm of the stock price exactly.

18.30. The DerivaGem Application Buider functions enable you to investigate how the prices of options calculated from a binomial tree converge to the correct value as the number of time steps increases (see Figure 18.4 and Sample Application A in DerivaGem). Consider a put option on a stock index where the index level is 900, the strike price is 900, the risk-free rate is 5%, the dividend yield is 2%, and the time to maturity is 2 years
   a. Produce results similar to Sample Application A on convergence for the situation where the option is European and the volatility of the index is 20%.
   b. Produce results similar to Sample Application A on convergence for the situation where the option is American and the volatility of the index is 20%.
   c. Produce a chart showing the pricing of the American option when the volatility is 20% as a function of the number of time steps when the control variate technique is used.
   d. Suppose that the price of the American option in the market is 85.0. Produce a chart showing the implied volatility estimate as a function of the number of time steps.

# APPENDIX 18A

## Analytic Approximation to American Option Prices of MacMillan and of Barone-Adesi and Whaley

Consider an option on a stock providing a dividend yield equal to $q$. We will denote the difference between the American and European option price by $v$. Because both the American and the European option prices satisfy the Black–Scholes differential equation, $v$ also does so. Hence,

$$\frac{\partial v}{\partial t} + (r-q)S\frac{\partial v}{\partial S} + \tfrac{1}{2}\sigma^2 S^2 \frac{\partial^2 v}{\partial S^2} = rv$$

For convenience, we define

$$\tau = T - t, \qquad h(\tau) = 1 - e^{-r\tau}, \qquad \alpha = \frac{2r}{\sigma^2}, \qquad \beta = \frac{2(r-q)}{\sigma^2}$$

We also write, without loss of generality,

$$v = h(\tau)\,g(S, h)$$

With appropriate substitutions and variable changes, this gives

$$S^2 \frac{\partial^2 g}{\partial S^2} + \beta S \frac{\partial g}{\partial S} - \frac{\alpha}{h}g - (1-h)\alpha\frac{\partial g}{\partial h} = 0$$

The approximation involves assuming that the final term on the left-hand side is zero, so that

$$S^2 \frac{\partial^2 g}{\partial S^2} + \beta S \frac{\partial g}{\partial S} - \frac{\alpha}{h}g = 0 \tag{18A.1}$$

The ignored term is generally fairly small. When $\tau$ is large, $1 - h$ is close to zero; when $\tau$ is small, $\partial g / \partial h$ is close to zero.

The American call and put prices at time $t$ will be denoted by $C(S, t)$ and $P(S, t)$, where $S$ is the stock price, and the corresponding European call and put prices will be denoted by $c(S, t)$ and $p(S, t)$. Equation (18A.1) can be solved using standard techniques. After boundary conditions have been applied, it is found that

$$C(S, t) = \begin{cases} c(S, t) + A_2(S/S^*)^{\gamma_2} & \text{if } S < S^* \\ S - K & \text{if } S \geqslant S^* \end{cases}$$

The variable $S^*$ is the critical price of the stock above which the option should be exercised. It is estimated by solving the equation

$$S^* - K = c(S^*, t) + \left[1 - e^{-q(T-t)}N\big(d_1(S^*)\big)\right]\frac{S^*}{\gamma_2}$$

iteratively. For a put option, the valuation formula is

$$P(S, t) = \begin{cases} p(S, t) + A_1(S/S^{**})^{\gamma_1} & \text{if } S > S^{**} \\ K - S & \text{if } S \leqslant S^{**} \end{cases}$$

The variable $S^{**}$ is the critical price of the stock below which the option should be exercised. It is estimated by solving the equation

$$K - S^{**} = p(S^{**}, t) - \left[1 - e^{-q(T-t)}N\left(-d_1(S^{**})\right)\right]\frac{S^{**}}{\gamma_1}$$

iteratively. The other variables that have been used here are as follows:

$$\gamma_1 = \tfrac{1}{2}\left(-(\beta - 1) - \sqrt{(\beta - 1)^2 + \frac{4\alpha}{h}}\right)$$

$$\gamma_2 = \tfrac{1}{2}\left(-(\beta - 1) + \sqrt{(\beta - 1)^2 + \frac{4\alpha}{h}}\right)$$

$$A_1 = -\left(\frac{S^{**}}{\gamma_1}\right)\left[1 - e^{-q(T-t)}N\left(-d_1(S^{**})\right)\right]$$

$$A_2 = \left(\frac{S^*}{\gamma_2}\right)\left[1 - e^{-q(T-t)}N\left(d_1(S^*)\right)\right]$$

$$d_1(S) = \frac{\ln(S/K) + (r - q + \sigma^2/2)(T - t)}{\sigma\sqrt{T - t}}$$

As pointed out in Chapter 13, options on stock indices, currencies, and futures contracts are analogous to options on a stock providing a constant dividend yield. Hence the quadratic approximation approach can easily be applied to all of these types of options.

# CHAPTER 19

# EXOTIC OPTIONS

The derivatives we have covered in the first 18 chapters of this book are what are termed *plain vanilla products*. They have standard well-defined properties and trade actively. Their prices or implied volatilities are quoted by exchanges or by brokers on a regular basis. One of the exciting aspects of the over-the-counter derivatives market is the number of nonstandard (or exotic) products that have been created by financial engineers. Although they are usually a relatively small part of its portfolio, these exotic products are important to an investment bank because they are generally much more profitable than plain vanilla products.

Exotic products come about for a number of reasons. Sometimes they meet a genuine hedging need in the market; sometimes there are tax, accounting, legal, or regulatory reasons why corporate treasurers find exotic products attractive; sometimes the products are designed to reflect a corporate treasurer's view on potential future movements in particular market variables; occasionally an exotic product is designed by an investment bank to appear more attractive than it is to an unwary corporate treasurer.

In this chapter we describe different types of exotic options and discuss their valuation. We use a categorization of exotic options similar to that in an excellent series of articles written by Eric Reiner and Mark Rubinstein for *RISK* magazine in 1991 and 1992. We assume that the asset provides a yield at rate $q$. As discussed in Chapter 13, for an option on a stock index we set $q$ equal to the dividend yield on the index, for an option on a currency we set $q$ equal to the foreign risk-free rate, and for an option on a futures contract we set $q$ equal to the domestic risk-free rate. Most of the options discussed in this chapter can be valued using the DerivaGem software.

## 19.1 PACKAGES

A *package* is a portfolio consisting of standard European calls, standard European puts, forward contracts, cash, and the underlying asset itself. We discussed a number of different types of packages in Chapter 9: bull spreads, bear spreads, butterfly spreads, calendar spreads, straddles, strangles, etc.

Often a package is structured by traders so that it has zero cost initially. An example is a *range forward contract*.[1] A short-range forward contract consists of a long position in a put with a low strike price, $K_1$, and a short position in a call with a high strike price, $K_2$. It guarantees that the underlying asset can be sold for a price between $K_1$ and $K_2$ at the maturity of the options. A long-range forward contract consists of a short position in a put with the low strike price, $K_1$,

---

[1] Other names used for a range forward contract are zero-cost collar, flexible forward, cylinder option, option fence, min–max, and forward band.

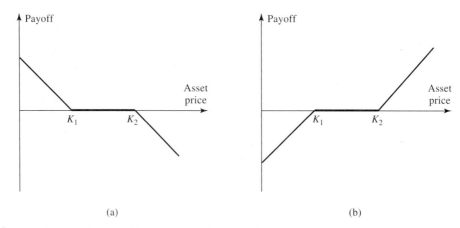

**Figure 19.1** Payoffs from (a) a short position and (b) a long position in a range forward contract

and a long position in a call with the high strike price, $K_2$. It guarantees that the underlying asset can be purchased for a price between $K_1$ and $K_2$ at the maturity of the options. The price of the call equals the price of the put when the contract is initiated. Figure 19.1 shows the payoff from short- and long-range forward contracts. As $K_1$ and $K_2$ are moved closer to each other, the price that will be received or paid for the asset at maturity becomes more certain. In the limit when $K_1 = K_2$, the range forward contract becomes a regular forward contract.

It is worth noting that any derivative can be converted into a zero-cost product by deferring payment until maturity. Consider a European call option. If $c$ is the cost of the option when payment is made at time zero, then $A = ce^{rT}$ is the cost when payment is made at time $T$, the maturity of the option. The payoff is then $\max(S_T - K, 0) - A$, or $\max(S_T - K - A, -A)$. When the strike price, $K$, equals the forward price, other names for a deferred payment option are break forward, Boston option, forward with optional exit, and cancelable forward.

## 19.2 NONSTANDARD AMERICAN OPTIONS

In a standard American option, exercise can take place at any time during the life of the option and the exercise price is always the same. In practice, the American options that are traded in the over-the-counter market sometimes have nonstandard features. For example:

1. Early exercise may be restricted to certain dates. This instrument is called a *Bermudan option*.

2. Early exercise may be allowed during only part of the life of the option. For example, there may be an initial "lock out" period with no early exercise.

3. The strike price may change during the life of the option.

The warrants issued by corporations on their own stock often have some of these features. For example, in a seven-year warrant, exercise might be possible on particular dates during years 3 to 7, with the strike price being $30 during years 3 and 4, $32 during the next two years, and $33 during the final year.

Nonstandard American options can usually be valued using a binomial tree. At each node, the test (if any) for early exercise is adjusted to reflect the terms of the option.

## 19.3  FORWARD START OPTIONS

Forward start options are options that will start at some time in the future. They are sometimes used in employee incentive schemes. The terms of the options usually specify that they will be at the money at the time they start.

Consider a forward start at-the-money European call option that will start at time $T_1$ and mature at time $T_2$. Suppose that the asset price is $S_0$ at time zero and $S_1$ at time $T_1$. To value the option, we note from the European option pricing formulas in Chapters 12 and 13 that the value of an at-the-money call option is proportional to the asset price. The value of the forward start option at time $T_1$ is therefore $cS_1/S_0$, where $c$ is the value at time zero of an at-the-money option that lasts for $T_2 - T_1$. Using risk-neutral valuation, the value of the forward start option at time zero is

$$e^{-rT_1} \hat{E}\left(c\frac{S_1}{S_0}\right)$$

where $\hat{E}$ denotes the expected value in a risk-neutral world. Because $c$ and $S_0$ are known and $\hat{E}(S_1) = S_0 e^{(r-q)T_1}$, it follows that the value of the forward start option is $ce^{-qT_1}$. For a non-dividend-paying stock, $q = 0$ and the value of the forward start option is exactly the same as the value of a regular at-the-money option with the same life as the forward start option.

## 19.4  COMPOUND OPTIONS

Compound options are options on options. There are four main types of compound option: a call on a call, a put on a call, a call on a put, and a put on a put. Compound options have two strike prices and two exercise dates. Consider, for example, a call on a call. On the first exercise date, $T_1$, the holder of the compound option is entitled to pay the first strike price, $K_1$, and receive a call option. The call option gives the holder the right to buy the underlying asset for the second strike price, $K_2$, on the second exercise date, $T_2$. The compound option will be exercised on the first exercise date only if the value of the option on that date is greater than the first strike price.

When the usual geometric Brownian motion assumption is made, European-style compound options can be valued analytically in terms of integrals of the bivariate normal distribution.[2] With our usual notation, the value at time zero of a European call option on a call option is

$$S_0 e^{-qT_2} M(a_1, b_1; \sqrt{T_1/T_2}) - K_2 e^{-rT_2} M(a_2, b_2; \sqrt{T_1/T_2}) - e^{-rT_1} K_1 N(a_2)$$

where

$$a_1 = \frac{\ln(S_0/S^*) + (r - q + \sigma^2/2)T_1}{\sigma\sqrt{T_1}}, \qquad a_2 = a_1 - \sigma\sqrt{T_1}$$

$$b_1 = \frac{\ln(S_0/K_2) + (r - q + \sigma^2/2)T_2}{\sigma\sqrt{T_2}}, \qquad b_2 = b_1 - \sigma\sqrt{T_2}$$

---

[2] See R. Geske, "The Valuation of Compound Options," *Journal of Financial Economics*, 7 (1979), 63–81; M. Rubinstein, "Double Trouble," *RISK*, December 1991/January 1992, pp. 53–56.

The function $M$ is the cumulative bivariate normal distribution function as defined in Appendix 12B. The variable $S^*$ is the asset price at time $T_1$ for which the option price at time $T_1$ equals $K_1$. If the actual asset price is above $S^*$ at time $T_1$, the first option will be exercised; if it is not above $S^*$, the option expires worthless.

With similar notation, the value of a European put on a call is

$$K_2 e^{-rT_2} M(-a_2, b_2; -\sqrt{T_1/T_2}) - S_0 e^{-qT_2} M(-a_1, b_1; -\sqrt{T_1/T_2}) + e^{-rT_1} K_1 N(-a_2)$$

The value of a European call on a put is

$$K_2 e^{-rT_2} M(-a_2, -b_2; \sqrt{T_1/T_2}) - S_0 e^{-qT_2} M(-a_1, -b_1; \sqrt{T_1/T_2}) - e^{-rT_1} K_1 N(-a_2)$$

The value of a European put on a put is

$$S_0 e^{-qT_2} M(a_1, -b_1; -\sqrt{T_1/T_2}) - K_2 e^{-rT_2} M(a_2, -b_2; -\sqrt{T_1/T_2}) + e^{-rT_1} K_1 N(a_2)$$

A procedure for computing $M$ is provided in Appendix 12C.

## 19.5 CHOOSER OPTIONS

A *chooser* option (sometimes referred to as an *as you like it* option) has the feature that, after a specified period of time, the holder can choose whether the option is a call or a put. Suppose that the time when the choice is made is $T_1$. The value of the chooser option at this time is

$$\max(c, p)$$

where $c$ is the value of the call underlying the option and $p$ is the value of the put underlying the option.

If the options underlying the chooser option are both European and have the same strike price, put–call parity can be used to provide a valuation formula. Suppose that $S_1$ is the asset price at time $T_1$, $K$ is the strike price, $T_2$ is the maturity of the options, and $r$ is the risk-free interest rate. Put–call parity implies that

$$\max(c, p) = \max(c, c + Ke^{-r(T_2-T_1)} - S_1 e^{-q(T_2-T_1)})$$
$$= c + e^{-q(T_2-T_1)} \max(0, Ke^{-(r-q)(T_2-T_1)} - S_1)$$

This shows that the chooser option is a package consisting of the following:

1. A call option with strike price $K$ and maturity $T_2$
2. $e^{-q(T_2-T_1)}$ put options with strike price $Ke^{-(r-q)(T_2-T_1)}$ and maturity $T_1$

As such, it can readily be valued.

More complex chooser options can be defined where the call and the put do not have the same strike price and time to maturity. They are then not packages and have features that are somewhat similar to compound options.

## 19.6 BARRIER OPTIONS

Barrier options are options where the payoff depends on whether the underlying asset's price reaches a certain level during a certain period of time. A number of different types of barrier options regularly trade in the over-the-counter market. They are attractive to some market participants because they are less expensive than the corresponding regular options. These barrier options can be classified as either *knock-out options* or *knock-in options*. A knock-out option ceases to exist when the underlying asset price reaches a certain barrier; a knock-in option comes into existence only when the underlying asset price reaches a barrier.

Equations (13.4) and (13.5) show that the values at time zero of a regular call and put option are

$$c = S_0 e^{-qT} N(d_1) - K e^{-rT} N(d_2)$$

$$p = K e^{-rT} N(-d_2) - S_0 e^{-qT} N(-d_1)$$

where

$$d_1 = \frac{\ln(S_0/K) + (r - q + \sigma^2/2)T}{\sigma\sqrt{T}}$$

$$d_2 = \frac{\ln(S_0/K) + (r - q - \sigma^2/2)T}{\sigma\sqrt{T}} = d_1 - \sigma\sqrt{T}$$

A *down-and-out call* is one type of knock-out option. It is a regular call option that ceases to exist if the asset price reaches a certain barrier level, $H$. The barrier level is below the initial asset price. The corresponding knock-in option is a *down-and-in call*. This is a regular call that comes into existence only if the asset price reaches the barrier level.

If $H$ is less than or equal to the strike price, $K$, the value of a down-and-in call at time zero is given by

$$c_{di} = S_0 e^{-qT}(H/S_0)^{2\lambda} N(y) - K e^{-rT}(H/S_0)^{2\lambda-2} N(y - \sigma\sqrt{T})$$

where

$$\lambda = \frac{r - q + \sigma^2/2}{\sigma^2}$$

$$y = \frac{\ln[H^2/(S_0 K)]}{\sigma\sqrt{T}} + \lambda\sigma\sqrt{T}$$

Because the value of a regular call equals the value of a down-and-in call plus the value of a down-and-out call, the value of a down-and-out call is given by

$$c_{do} = c - c_{di}$$

If $H \geqslant K$, then

$$c_{do} = S_0 N(x_1) e^{-qT} - K e^{-rT} N(x_1 - \sigma\sqrt{T}) - S_0 e^{-qT}(H/S_0)^{2\lambda} N(y_1) + K e^{-rT}(H/S_0)^{2\lambda-2} N(y_1 - \sigma\sqrt{T})$$

and

$$c_{di} = c - c_{do}$$

where

$$x_1 = \frac{\ln(S_0/H)}{\sigma\sqrt{T}} + \lambda\sigma\sqrt{T}, \qquad y_1 = \frac{\ln(H/S_0)}{\sigma\sqrt{T}} + \lambda\sigma\sqrt{T}$$

An *up-and-out call* is a regular call option that ceases to exist if the asset price reaches a barrier level, $H$, that is higher than the current asset price. An *up-and-in call* is a regular call option that comes into existence only if the barrier is reached. When $H$ is less than or equal to $K$, the value of the up-and-out call, $c_{uo}$, is zero and the value of the up-and-in call, $c_{ui}$, is $c$. When $H$ is greater than $K$,

$$c_{ui} = S_0 N(x_1) e^{-qT} - K e^{-rT} N(x_1 - \sigma\sqrt{T}) - S_0 e^{-qT} (H/S_0)^{2\lambda} [N(-y) - N(-y_1)]$$
$$+ K e^{-rT} (H/S_0)^{2\lambda-2} [N(-y + \sigma\sqrt{T}) - N(-y_1 + \sigma\sqrt{T})]$$

and

$$c_{uo} = c - c_{ui}$$

Put barrier options are defined similarly to call barrier options. An *up-and-out put* is a put option that ceases to exist when a barrier, $H$, that is greater than the current asset price is reached. An *up-and-in put* is a put that comes into existence only if the barrier is reached. When the barrier, $H$, is greater than or equal to the strike price, $K$, their prices are

$$p_{ui} = -S_0 e^{-qT} (H/S_0)^{2\lambda} N(-y) + K e^{-rT} (H/S_0)^{2\lambda-2} N(-y + \sigma\sqrt{T})$$

and

$$p_{uo} = p - p_{ui}$$

When $H$ is less than or equal to $K$,

$$p_{uo} = -S_0 N(-x_1) e^{-qT} + K e^{-rT} N(-x_1 + \sigma\sqrt{T}) + S_0 e^{-qT} (H/S_0)^{2\lambda} N(-y_1)$$
$$- K e^{-rT} (H/S_0)^{2\lambda-2} N(-y_1 + \sigma\sqrt{T})$$

and

$$p_{ui} = p - p_{uo}$$

A *down-and-out put* is a put option that ceases to exist when a barrier less than the current asset price is reached. A *down-and-in put* is a put option that comes into existence only when the barrier is reached. When the barrier is greater than the strike price, $p_{do} = 0$ and $p_{di} = p$. When the barrier is less than the strike price,

$$p_{di} = -S_0 N(-x_1) e^{-qT} + K e^{-rT} N(-x_1 + \sigma\sqrt{T}) + S_0 e^{-qT} (H/S_0)^{2\lambda} [N(y) - N(y_1)]$$
$$- K e^{-rT} (H/S_0)^{2\lambda-2} [N(y - \sigma\sqrt{T}) - N(y_1 - \sigma\sqrt{T})]$$

and

$$p_{do} = p - p_{di}$$

All of these valuations make the usual assumption that the probability distribution for the asset price at a future time is lognormal. An important issue for barrier options is the frequency that the asset price, $S$, is observed for purposes of determining whether the barrier has been reached. The analytic formulas given in this section assume that $S$ is observed continuously and sometimes this is the case.[3] Often, the terms of a contract state that $S$ is observed periodically; for example, once a day at 12 noon. Broadie, Glasserman, and Kou provide a way of adjusting the formulas we have just given for the situation where the price of the underlying is observed discretely.[4] The barrier level $H$ is replaced by $He^{0.5826\sigma\sqrt{T/m}}$ for an up-and-in or up-and-out option and by $He^{-0.5826\sigma\sqrt{T/m}}$

---

[3] One way to track whether a barrier has been reached from below (above) is to send a limit order to the exchange to sell (buy) the asset at the barrier price and see whether the order is filled.

[4] M. Broadie, P. Glasserman, and S. G. Kou, "A Continuity Correction for Discrete Barrier Options," *Mathematical Finance*, 7, no. 4 (October 1997), 325–49.

for a down-and-in or down-and-out option, where $m$ is the number of times the asset price is observed (so that $T/m$ is the time interval between observations).

Barrier options often have quite different properties from regular options. For example, sometimes vega is negative. Consider an up-and-out call option when the asset price is close to the barrier level. As volatility increases the probability that the barrier will be hit increases. As a result, a volatility increase causes a price decrease.

## 19.7 BINARY OPTIONS

Binary options are options with discontinuous payoffs. A simple example of a binary option is a *cash-or-nothing call*. This pays off nothing if the asset price ends up below the strike price at time $T$ and pays a fixed amount, $Q$, if it ends up above the strike price. In a risk-neutral world, the probability of the asset price being above the strike price at the maturity of an option is, with our usual notation, $N(d_2)$. The value of a cash-or-nothing call is therefore $Qe^{-rT}N(d_2)$. A *cash-or-nothing put* is defined analogously to a cash-or-nothing call. It pays off $Q$ if the asset price is below the strike price and nothing if it is above the strike price. The value of a cash-or-nothing put is $Qe^{-rT}N(-d_2)$.

Another type of binary option is an *asset-or-nothing call*. This pays off nothing if the underlying asset price ends up below the strike price and pays an amount equal to the asset price itself if it ends up above the strike price. With our usual notation, the value of an asset-or-nothing call is $S_0e^{-qT}N(d_1)$. An *asset-or-nothing put* pays off nothing if the underlying asset price ends up above the strike price and an amount equal to the asset price if it ends up below the strike price. The value of an asset-or-nothing put is $S_0e^{-qT}N(-d_1)$.

A regular European call option is equivalent to a long position in an asset-or-nothing call and a short position in a cash-or-nothing call where the cash payoff on the cash-or-nothing call equals the strike price. Similarly, a regular European put option is equivalent to a long position in a cash-or-nothing put and a short position in an asset-or-nothing put where the cash payoff on the cash-or-nothing put equals the strike price.

## 19.8 LOOKBACK OPTIONS

The payoffs from lookback options depend on the maximum or minimum asset price reached during the life of the option. The payoff from a European-style lookback call is the amount that the final asset price exceeds the minimum asset price achieved during the life of the option. The payoff from a European-style lookback put is the amount by which the maximum asset price achieved during the life of the option exceeds the final asset price.

Valuation formulas have been produced for European lookbacks.[5] The value of a European lookback call at time zero is

$$S_0e^{-qT}N(a_1) - S_0e^{-qT}\frac{\sigma^2}{2(r-q)}N(-a_1) - S_{min}e^{-rT}\left(N(a_2) - \frac{\sigma^2}{2(r-q)}e^{Y_1}N(-a_3)\right)$$

---

[5] See B. Goldman, H. Sosin, and M. A. Gatto, "Path-Dependent Options: Buy at the Low, Sell at the High," *Journal of Finance*, 34 (December 1979), 1111–27.; M. Garman, "Recollection in Tranquility," *RISK*, March 1989, pp. 16–19.

where

$$a_1 = \frac{\ln(S_0/S_{min}) + (r - q + \sigma^2/2)T}{\sigma\sqrt{T}},$$

$$a_2 = a_1 - \sigma\sqrt{T}$$

$$a_3 = \frac{\ln(S_0/S_{min}) + (-r + q + \sigma^2/2)T}{\sigma\sqrt{T}}$$

$$Y_1 = -\frac{2(r - q - \sigma^2/2)\ln(S_0/S_{min})}{\sigma^2}$$

and $S_{min}$ is the minimum asset price achieved to date. (If the lookback has just been originated, then $S_{min} = S_0$.)

The value of a European lookback put is

$$S_{max}e^{-rT}\left(N(b_1) - \frac{\sigma^2}{2(r-q)}e^{Y_2}N(-b_3)\right) + S_0e^{-qT}\frac{\sigma^2}{2(r-q)}N(-b_2) - S_0e^{-qT}N(b_2)$$

where

$$b_1 = \frac{\ln(S_{max}/S_0) + (-r + q + \sigma^2/2)T}{\sigma\sqrt{T}}$$

$$b_2 = b_1 - \sigma\sqrt{T}$$

$$b_3 = \frac{\ln(S_{max}/S_0) + (r - q - \sigma^2/2)T}{\sigma\sqrt{T}}$$

$$Y_2 = \frac{2(r - q - \sigma^2/2)\ln(S_{max}/S_0)}{\sigma^2}$$

and $S_{max}$ is the maximum asset price achieved to date. (If the lookback has just been originated, then $S_{max} = S_0$.)

**Example 19.1** Consider a newly issued lookback put on a non-dividend-paying stock where the stock price is 50, the stock price volatility is 40% per annum, the risk-free rate is 10% per annum, and the time to maturity is three months. In this case, $S_{max} = 50$, $S_0 = 50$, $r = 0.1$, $q = 0$, $\sigma = 0.4$, and $T = 0.25$. From the formulas just given, $b_1 = -0.025$, $b_2 = -0.225$, $b_3 = 0.025$, and $Y_2 = 0$, so that the value of the lookback put is 7.79. A newly issued lookback call on the same stock is worth 8.04.

A lookback call is a way that the holder can buy the underlying asset at the lowest price achieved during the life of the option. Similarly, a lookback put is a way that the holder can sell the underlying asset at the highest price achieved during the life of the option. The underlying asset in a lookback option is often a commodity. As with barrier options, the value of a lookback option is liable to be sensitive to the frequency that the asset price is observed for the purposes of computing the maximum or minimum. The formulas above assume that the asset price is observed continuously. Broadie, Glasserman, and Kou provide a way of adjusting the formulas we have just given for the situation where the asset price is observed discretely.[6]

---

[6] M. Broadie, P. Glasserman, and S. G. Kou, "Connecting Discrete and Continuous Path-Dependent Options," *Finance and Stochastics*, 2 (1998), 1–28.

## 19.9 SHOUT OPTIONS

A *shout option* is a European option where the holder can "shout" to the writer at one time during its life. At the end of the life of the option, the option holder receives either the usual payoff from a European option or the intrinsic value at the time of the shout, whichever is greater. Suppose the strike price is $50 and the holder of a call shouts when the price of the underlying asset is $60. If the final asset price is less than $60 the holder receives a payoff of $10. If it is greater than $60, the holder receives the excess of the asset price over $50.

A shout option has some of the same features as a lookback option, but is considerably less expensive. It can be valued by noting that if the option is shouted at a time $\tau$ when the asset price is $S_\tau$ the payoff from the option is

$$\max(0,\ S_T - S_\tau) + (S_\tau - K)$$

where, as usual, $K$ is the strike price and $S_T$ is the asset price at time $T$. The value at time $\tau$ if the option is shouted is therefore the present value of $S_\tau - K$ plus the value of a European option with strike price $S_\tau$. The latter can be calculated using Black–Scholes formulas.

We value a shout option by constructing a binomial or trinomial tree for the underlying asset in the usual way. As we roll back through the tree, we calculate at each node the value of the option if we shout and the value if we do not shout. The option's price at the node is the greater of the two. The procedure for valuing a shout option is therefore very similar to the procedure for valuing a regular American option.

## 19.10 ASIAN OPTIONS

Asian options are options where the payoff depends on the average price of the underlying asset during at least some part of the life of the option. The payoff from an *average price call* is $\max(0,\ S_{\text{ave}} - K)$ and that from an *average price put* is $\max(0,\ K - S_{\text{ave}})$, where $S_{\text{ave}}$ is the average value of the underlying asset calculated over a predetermined averaging period. Average price options are less expensive than regular options and are arguably more appropriate than regular options for meeting some of the needs of corporate treasurers. Suppose that a U.S. corporate treasurer expects to receive a cash flow of 100 million Australian dollars spread evenly over the next year from the company's Australian subsidiary . The treasurer is likely to be interested in an option that guarantees that the average exchange rate realized during the year is above some level. An average price put option can achieve this more effectively than regular put options.

Another type of Asian option is an average strike option. An *average strike call* pays off $\max(0,\ S_T - S_{\text{ave}})$ and an *average strike put* pays off $\max(0,\ S_{\text{ave}} - S_T)$. Average strike options can guarantee that the average price paid for an asset in frequent trading over a period of time is not greater than the final price. Alternatively, it can guarantee that the average price received for an asset in frequent trading over a period of time is not less than the final price.

If the underlying asset price, $S$, is assumed to be lognormally distributed and $S_{\text{ave}}$ is a geometric average of the $S$'s, analytic formulas are available for valuing European average price options.[7] This is because the geometric average of a set of lognormally distributed variables is also lognormal. Consider a newly issued option that will provide a payoff at time $T$ based on the

---

[7] See A. Kemna and A. Vorst, "A Pricing Method for Options Based on Average Asset Values," *Journal of Banking and Finance*, 14 (March 1990), 113–29.

geometric average calculated between time zero and time $T$. In a risk-neutral world, it can be shown that the probability distribution of the geometric average of a asset price over a certain period is the same as that of the asset price at the end of the period if the asset's expected growth rate is set equal to $\frac{1}{2}(r - q - \sigma^2/6)$ (rather than $r - q$) and its volatility is set equal to $\sigma/\sqrt{3}$ (rather than $\sigma$). The geometric average price option can therefore be treated like a regular option with the volatility set equal to $\sigma/\sqrt{3}$ and the dividend yield equal to

$$r - \tfrac{1}{2}\left(r - q - \frac{\sigma^2}{6}\right) = \tfrac{1}{2}\left(r + q + \frac{\sigma^2}{6}\right)$$

When, as is nearly always the case, Asian options are defined in terms of arithmetic averages, exact analytic pricing formulas are not available. This is because the distribution of the arithmetic average of a set of lognormal distributions does not have analytically tractable properties. However, the distribution is approximately lognormal and this leads to a good analytic approximation for valuing average price options. We calculate the first two moments of the probability distribution of the arithmetic average in a risk-neutral world exactly and then assume this distribution is the lognormal.[8]

Consider a newly issued Asian option that provides a payoff at time $T$ based on the arithmetic average between time zero and time $T$. The first moment, $M_1$ and the second moment, $M_2$, of the average in a risk-neutral world can be shown to be

$$M_1 = \frac{e^{(r-q)T} - 1}{(r - q)T} S_0$$

and

$$M_2 = \frac{2e^{[2(r-q)+\sigma^2]T} S_0^2}{(r - q + \sigma^2)(2r - 2q + \sigma^2)T^2} + \frac{2S_0^2}{(r - q)T^2}\left(\frac{1}{2(r - q) + \sigma^2} - \frac{e^{(r-q)T}}{r - q + \sigma^2}\right)$$

If we assume that the average asset price is lognormal, we can regard an option on the average as like an option on a futures contract and use equations (13.17) and (13.18) with

$$F_0 = M_1 \tag{19.1}$$

and

$$\sigma^2 = \frac{1}{T}\ln\left(\frac{M_2}{M_1^2}\right) \tag{19.2}$$

**Example 19.2** Consider a newly issued average price call option on a non-dividend-paying stock where the stock price is 50, the strike price is 50, the stock price volatility is 40% per annum, the risk-free rate is 10% per annum, and the time to maturity is one year. In this case, $S_0 = 50$, $K = 50$, $r = 0.1$, $q = 0$, $\sigma = 0.4$, and $T = 1$. If the average is a geometric average, we can value the option as a regular option with the volatility equal to $0.4/\sqrt{3}$, or 23.09%, and dividend yield equal to $(0.1 + 0.4^2/6)/2$, or 6.33%. The value of the option is 5.13. If the average is an arithmetic average, we first calculate $M_1 = 52.59$ and $M_2 = 2,922.76$. When we assume the average is lognormal, the option has the same value as an option on a futures contract. From equations (19.1) and (19.2), $F_0 = 52.59$ and $\sigma = 23.54\%$. DerivaGem gives the value of the option as 5.62.

The formulas just given for $M_1$ and $M_2$ assume that the average is calculated from continuous

---

[8] See S. M. Turnbull and L. M. Wakeman, "A Quick Algorithm for Pricing European Average Options," *Journal of Financial and Quantitative Analysis*, 26 (September 1991), 377–89.

observations on the asset price. Appendix 19A shows how $M_1$ and $M_2$ can be obtained when the average is calculated from observations on the asset price at discrete points in time.

We can modify the analysis to accommodate the situation where the option is not newly issued and some prices used to determine the average have already been observed. Suppose that the averaging period is composed of a period of length $t_1$ over which prices have already been observed and a future period of length $t_2$ (the remaining life of the option). Suppose that the average asset price during the first time period is $\bar{S}$. The payoff from an average price call is

$$\max\left(\frac{\bar{S}t_1 + S_{\text{ave}}t_2}{t_1 + t_2} - K, \ 0\right)$$

where $S_{\text{ave}}$ is the average asset price during the remaining part of the averaging period. This is the same as

$$\frac{t_2}{t_1 + t_2}\max(S_{\text{ave}} - K^*, \ 0)$$

where

$$K^* = \frac{t_1 + t_2}{t_2}K - \frac{t_1}{t_2}\bar{S}$$

When $K^* > 0$, the option can be valued in the same way as a newly issued Asian option provided that we change the strike price from $K$ to $K^*$ and multiply the result by $t_2/(t_1 + t_2)$. When $K^* < 0$ the option is certain to be exercised and can be valued as a forward contract. The value is

$$\frac{t_2}{t_1 + t_2}(M_1 e^{-rt_2} - K^* e^{-rt_2})$$

## 19.11 OPTIONS TO EXCHANGE ONE ASSET FOR ANOTHER

Options to exchange one asset for another (sometimes referred to as *exchange options*) arise in various contexts. An option to buy yen with Australian dollars is, from the point of view of a U.S. investor, an option to exchange one foreign currency asset for another foreign currency asset. A stock tender offer is an option to exchange shares in one stock for shares in another stock.

Consider a European option to give up an asset worth $U_T$ at time $T$ and receive in return an asset worth $V_T$. The payoff from the option is

$$\max(V_T - U_T, \ 0)$$

A formula for valuing this option was first produced by Margrabe.[9] Suppose that the asset prices $U$ and $V$ both follow geometric Brownian motion with volatilities $\sigma_U$ and $\sigma_V$. Suppose further that the instantaneous correlation between $U$ and $V$ is $\rho$, and the yields provided by $U$ and $V$ are $q_U$ and $q_V$, respectively. The value of the option at time zero is

$$V_0 e^{-q_V T} N(d_1) - U_0 e^{-q_U T} N(d_2) \tag{19.3}$$

---

[9] See W. Margrabe, "The Value of an Option to Exchange One Asset for Another," *Journal of Finance*, 33 (March 1978), 177–86.

where

$$d_1 = \frac{\ln(V_0/U_0) + (q_U - q_V + \hat{\sigma}^2/2)T}{\hat{\sigma}\sqrt{T}}$$

$$d_2 = d_1 - \hat{\sigma}\sqrt{T}$$

$$\hat{\sigma} = \sqrt{\sigma_U^2 + \sigma_V^2 - 2\rho\sigma_U\sigma_V}$$

and $U_0$ and $V_0$ are the values of $U$ and $V$ at times zero.

This result will be proved in Section 21.6. It is interesting to note that equation (19.3) is independent of the risk-free rate $r$. This is because, as $r$ increases, the growth rate of both asset prices in a risk-neutral world increases, but this is exactly offset by an increase in the discount rate. The variable $\hat{\sigma}$ is the volatility of $V/U$. Comparisons with equation (13.4) show that the option price is the same as the price of $U_0$ European call options on an asset worth $V/U$ when the strike price is 1.0, the risk-free interest rate is $q_U$, and the dividend yield on the asset is $q_V$. Mark Rubinstein shows that the American version of this option can be characterized similarly for valuation purposes.[10] It can be regarded as $U_0$ American options to buy an asset worth $V/U$ for 1.0 when the risk-free interest rate is $q_U$ and the dividend yield on the asset is $q_V$. The option can therefore be valued as described in Chapter 18 using a binomial tree.

It is worth noting that an option to obtain the better or worse of two assets can be regarded as a position in one of the assets combined with an option to exchange it for the other asset:

$$\min(U_T, V_T) = V_T - \max(V_T - U_T, 0)$$

$$\max(U_T, V_T) = U_T + \max(V_T - U_T, 0)$$

## 19.12  BASKET OPTIONS

Options involving two or more risky assets are sometimes referred to as *rainbow options*. One example is the bond futures contract traded on the CBOT described in Chapter 5. The party with the short position is allowed to choose between a large number of different bonds when making delivery. Another example is a LIBOR-contingent FX option. This is a foreign currency option whose payoff occurs only if a prespecified interest rate is within a certain range at maturity.

Possibly the most popular rainbow option is a *basket option*. This is an option where the payoff is dependent on the value of a portfolio (or basket) of assets. The assets are usually either individual stocks or stock indices or currencies. A European basket option can be valued with Monte Carlo simulation, by assuming that the assets follow correlated geometric Brownian motion processes. A much faster approach is to calculate the first two moments of the basket at the maturity of the option in a risk-neutral world and then assume that value of the basket is lognormally distributed at that time. The option can then be regarded as an option on a futures contract with the parameters shown in equations (19.1) and (19.2). Appendix 19A shows how the moments of the value of the basket at a future time can be calculated from the volatilities of, and correlations between, the assets.

---

[10]  See M. Rubinstein, "One for Another," *RISK*, July/August 1991, 30–32

## 19.13  HEDGING ISSUES

Before trading an exotic option, it is important for a financial institution to assess not only how it should be priced but also the difficulties that are likely to be experienced in hedging it. The general approach described in Chapter 14 involving the creation of a delta-neutral portfolio and the monitoring of gamma, vega, and other Greek letters can be used.

Exotic options sometimes prove to be easier to hedge using the underlying asset than the corresponding plain vanilla option. Consider for example an average price option where the averaging period is the whole life of the option. As time passes, we observe more of the asset prices that will be used in calculating the final average. This means that our uncertainty about the payoff decreases with the passage of time. As a result, the option becomes progressively easier to hedge. In the final few days, the delta of the option always approaches zero because price movements during this time have very little impact on the payoff.

Barrier options can, in certain circumstances, be significantly more difficult to hedge than regular options. Consider a down-and-out call option on a currency when the exchange rate is 0.0005 above the barrier. If the barrier is hit, the option is worth nothing. If the barrier is not hit, the option may prove to be quite valuable. The delta of the option is discontinuous at the barrier and hedging using conventional techniques is difficult. The approach in the following section is often more appropriate.

## 19.14  STATIC OPTIONS REPLICATION

Hedging an option position involves replicating the opposite position. The procedures described in Chapter 14 involve what is sometimes referred to as *dynamic options replication*. They require the position in the hedging assets to be rebalanced frequently and can be quite expensive because of the transaction costs involved.

An alternative approach that can sometimes be used to hedge a position in exotic options is *static options replication*.[11] This involves searching for a portfolio of actively traded options that approximately replicate the option position. Shorting this position provides the hedge. The basic principle underlying static options replication is as follows. If two portfolios are worth the same on a certain boundary, they are also worth the same at all interior points of the boundary.

Consider as an example a nine-month up-and-out call option on a non-dividend-paying stock where the stock price is 50, the strike price is 50, the barrier is 60, the risk-free interest rate is 10% per annum, and the volatility is 30% per annum. Suppose that $f(S, t)$ is the value of the option at time $t$ for a stock price of $S$. We can use any boundary in $(S, t)$ space for the purposes of producing the replicating portfolio. A convenient one to choose is shown in Figure 19.2. It is defined by $S = 60$ and $t = 0.75$. The values of the up-and-out option on the boundary are given by

$$f(S, 0.75) = \max(S - 50, 0) \quad \text{when } S < 60$$
$$f(60, t) = 0 \quad \text{when } 0 \leqslant t \leqslant 0.75$$

There are many ways that we can approximately match these boundary values using regular

[11] See E. Derman, D. Ergener, and I. Kani, "Static Options Replication," *Journal of Derivatives*, 2, no. 4 (Summer 1995), 78–95.

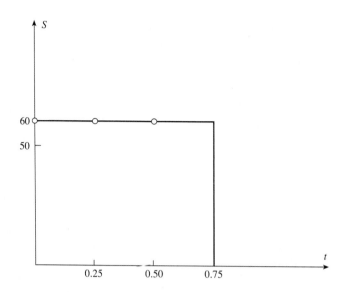

**Figure 19.2**   Boundary points used for the static options replication example

options. The natural instrument to match the first boundary is a regular nine-month European call option with a strike price of 50. The first instrument introduced into the replicating portfolio is therefore likely to be one unit of this option. (We refer to this option as option A.) One way of then proceeding is as follows. We divide the life of the option into a number of time steps and choose options that satisfy the second boundary condition at the beginning of each time step.

Suppose that we choose time steps of three months. The next instrument we choose should lead to the second boundary being matched at $t = 0.5$. In other words, it should lead to the value of the complete replicating portfolio being zero when $t = 0.5$ and $S = 60$. The option should have the property that it has zero value on the first boundary since this has already been matched. One possibility is a regular nine-month European call option with a strike price of 60. (We will refer to this as option B.) Black–Scholes formulas show that this is worth 4.33 at the six-month point when $S = 60$. They also show that the position in option A is worth 11.54 at this point. The position we require in option B, therefore, is $-11.54/4.33 = -2.66$.

We next move on to matching the second boundary condition at $t = 0.25$. The option used should have the property that it has zero value on all boundaries that have been matched thus far. One possibility is a regular six-month European call option with a strike price of 60. (We refer to this as option C.) This is worth 4.33 at the three-month point when $S = 60$. Our position in options A and B is worth $-4.21$ at this point. The position we require in option C, therefore, is $4.21/4.33 = 0.97$.

Finally, we match the second boundary condition at $t = 0$. For this we use a regular three-month European option with a strike price of 60. (We refer to this as option D.) Calculations similar to those above show that the required position in option D is 0.28.

The portfolio chosen is summarized in Table 19.1. It is worth 0.73 initially (i.e., at time zero when the stock price is 50). This compares with 0.31 given by the analytic formula for the up-and-out call earlier in this chapter. The replicating portfolio is not exactly the same as the up-and-out option because it matches the latter at only three points on the second boundary. If we use the same scheme, but match at 18 points on the second boundary (using options that mature every half

**Table 19.1**  The portfolio of European call options used to replicate an up-and-out option

| Option | Strike price | Maturity (years) | Position | Initial value |
|--------|-------|---------|----------|-------|
| A | 50 | 0.75 | 1.00 | +6.99 |
| B | 60 | 0.75 | −2.66 | −8.21 |
| C | 60 | 0.50 | 0.97 | +1.78 |
| D | 60 | 0.25 | 0.28 | +0.17 |

month), the value of the replicating portfolio reduces to 0.38. If 100 points are matched, the value reduces further to 0.32.

To hedge a derivative, we short the portfolio that replicates its boundary conditions. This has the advantage over delta hedging that it does not require frequent rebalancing. The static replication approach can be used for a wide range of derivatives. The user has a great deal of flexibility in choosing the boundary that is to be matched and the options that are to be used. The portfolio must be unwound when any part of the boundary is reached.

## SUMMARY

Exotic options are options with rules governing the payoff that are more complicated than standard options. We have discussed 13 different types of exotic option: packages, nonstandard American options, forward start options, compound options, chooser options, barrier options, binary options, lookback options, shout options, Asian options, options to exchange one asset for another, and basket options. We have discussed how these can be valued using the same assumptions as those used to derive the Black–Scholes equations in Chapter 12. Some can be valued analytically, but using much more complicated formulas than those for regular European calls and puts, some can be handled using analytic approximations, and some can be valued using extensions of the numerical procedures in Chapter 18. We will present more numerical procedures for valuing exotic options in Chapter 20.

Some exotic options are easier to hedge than the corresponding regular options; others are more difficult. In general, Asian options are easier to hedge because the payoff becomes progressively more certain as we approach maturity. Barrier options can be more difficult to hedge because delta is liable to be discontinuous at the barrier. One approach to hedging an exotic option, known as static options replication, is to find a portfolio of regular options whose value matches the value of the exotic option on some boundary. The exotic option is hedged by shorting this portfolio.

## SUGGESTIONS FOR FURTHER READING

Broadie, M., P. Glasserman, and S. G. Kou, "A Continuity Correction for Discrete Barrier Options," *Mathematical Finance*, 7, no. 4 (October 1997), 325–49.

Broadie, M., P. Glasserman, and S. G. Kou, "Connecting Discrete and Continuous Path-Dependent Options," *Finance and Stochastics*, 2 (1998), 1–28.

Clewlow, L., and C. Strickland, *Exotic Options: The State of the Art.* Thomson Business Press, London, 1997.

Curran, M., "Beyond Average Intelligence," *RISK*, October 1992, pp. 60–62.

Derman, E., D. Ergener, and I. Kani, "Static Options Replication," *Journal of Derivatives*, 2, no. 4 (Summer 1995), 78–95.

Derman, E., I. Kani, and N. Chriss, "Static Options Replication," *Journal of Derivatives*, 1, no. 4 (Summer 1994), 6–14.

Garman, M., "Recollection in Tranquility," *RISK*, March 1989, pp. 16–19.

Geske, R., "The Valuation of Compound Options," *Journal of Financial Economics*, 7 (1979), 63–81.

Goldman, B., H. Sosin, and M. A. Gatto, "Path Dependent Options: Buy at the Low, Sell at the High," *Journal of Finance*, 34 (December 1979), 1111–27.

Hudson, M., "The Value of Going Out," *RISK*, March 1991, 29–33.

Johnson, H., "Options on the Maximum and Minimum of Several Assets," *Journal of Financial and Quantitative Analysis*, 22, no. 3 (September 1987), 277–83.

Kemna, A., and A. Vorst, "A Pricing Method for Options Based on Average Asset Values," *Journal of Banking and Finance*, 14 (March 1990), 113–29.

Levy, E., "Pricing European Average Rate Currency Options," *Journal of International Money and Finance*, 11 (1992), 474–91.

Levy, E., and S. M. Turnbull, "Average Intelligence," *RISK*, February 1992, pp. 53–59.

Margrabe, W., "The Value of an Option to Exchange One Asset for Another," *Journal of Finance*, 33 (March 1978), 177–86.

Milevsky, M. A., and S. E. Posner, "Asian Options: The Sum of Lognormals and the Reciprocal Gamma Distribution," *Journal of Financial and Quantitative Analysis*, 33, no. 3 (September 1998), 409–22.

Ritchken, P., L. Sankarasubramanian, and A. M. Vijh, "The Valuation of Path Dependent Contracts on the Average," *Management Science*, 39 (1993), 1202–13.

Ritchken, P., "On Pricing Barrier Options," *Journal of Derivatives*, 3, no. 2 (Winter 1995), 19–28.

Rubinstein, M., and E. Reiner, "Breaking Down the Barriers," *RISK*, September 1991, 28–35.

Rubinstein, M., "Double Trouble," *RISK*, December 1991/January 1992, pp. 53–56.

Rubinstein, M., "One for Another," *RISK*, July/August 1991, pp. 30–32.

Rubinstein, M., "Options for the Undecided," *RISK*, April 1991, pp. 70–73.

Rubinstein, M., "Pay Now, Choose Later," *RISK*, February 1991, pp. 44–47.

Rubinstein, M., "Somewhere Over the Rainbow," *RISK*, November 1991, pp. 63–66.

Rubinstein, M., "Two in One," *RISK*, May 1991, p. 49.

Rubinstein, M., and E. Reiner, "Unscrambling the Binary Code," *RISK*, October 1991, pp. 75–83.

Stulz, R., "Options on the Minimum or Maximum of Two Assets," *Journal of Financial Economics*, 10 (1982), 161–85.

Turnbull, S. M., and L. M. Wakeman, "A Quick Algorithm for Pricing European Average Options," *Journal of Financial and Quantitative Analysis*, 26 (September 1991), 377–89.

# QUESTIONS AND PROBLEMS
## (ANSWERS IN SOLUTIONS MANUAL)

19.1. Explain the difference between a forward start option and a chooser option.

19.2. Describe the payoff from a portfolio consisting of a lookback call and a lookback put with the same maturity.

19.3. Consider a chooser option where the holder has the right to choose between a European call and a European put at any time during a two-year period. The maturity dates and strike prices for the calls and puts are the same regardless of when the choice is made. Is it ever optimal to make the choice before the end of the two-year period? Explain your answer.

19.4. Suppose that $c_1$ and $p_1$ are the prices of a European average price call and a European average price put with strike $K$ and maturity $T$, $c_2$ and $p_2$ are the prices of a European average strike call and European average strike put with maturity $T$, and $c_3$ and $p_3$ are the prices of a regular European call and a regular European put with strike price $K$ and maturity $T$. Show that

$$c_1 + c_2 - c_3 = p_1 + p_2 - p_3$$

19.5. The text derives a decomposition of a particular type of chooser option into a call maturing at time $T_2$ and a put maturing at time $T_1$. Derive an alternative decomposition into a call maturing at time $T_1$ and a put maturing at time $T_2$.

19.6. Section 19.6 gives two formulas for a down-and-out call. The first applies to the situation where the barrier, $H$, is less than or equal to the strike price, $K$. The second applies to the situation where $H \geqslant K$. Show that the two formulas are the same when $H = K$.

19.7. Explain why a down-and-out put is worth zero when the barrier is greater than the strike price.

19.8. Suppose that the strike price of an American call option on a non-dividend-paying stock grows at rate $g$. Show that if $g$ is less than the risk-free rate, $r$, it is never optimal to exercise the call early.

19.9. How can the value of a forward start put option on a non-dividend-paying stock be calculated if it is agreed that the strike price will be 10% greater than the stock price at the time the option starts?

19.10. If a stock price follows geometric Brownian motion, what process does $A(t)$ follow where $A(t)$ is the arithmetic average stock price between time zero and time $t$?

19.11. Explain why delta hedging is easier for Asian options than for regular options.

19.12. Calculate the price of a one-year European option to give up 100 ounces of silver in exchange for one ounce of gold. The current prices of gold and silver are $380 and $4, respectively, the risk-free interest rate is 10% per annum, the volatility of each commodity price is 20%, and the correlation between the two prices is 0.7. Ignore storage costs.

19.13. Is a European down-and-out option on an asset worth the same as a European down-and-out option on the asset's futures price for a futures contract maturing at the same time as the option?

19.14. Answer the following questions about compound options:
  a. What put–call parity relationship exists between the price of a European call on a call and a European put on a call? Show that the formulas given in the text satisfy the relationship.
  b. What put–call parity relationship exists between the price of a European call on a put and a European put on a put? Show that the formulas given in the text satisfy the relationship.

19.15. Does a lookback call become more valuable or less valuable as we increase the frequency with which we observe the asset price in calculating the minimum?

19.16. Does a down-and-out call become more valuable or less valuable as we increase the frequency with which we observe the asset price in determining whether the barrier has been crossed? What is the answer to the same question for a down-and-in call?

19.17. Explain why a regular European call option is the sum of a down-and-out European call and a down-and-in European call. Is the same true for American call options?

19.18. What is the value of a derivative that pays off \$100 in six months if the S&P 500 index is greater than 1,000 and zero otherwise. Assume that the current level of the index is 960, the risk-free rate is 8% per annum, the dividend yield on the index is 3% per annum, and the volatility of the index is 20%.

19.19. In a three-month down-and-out call option on silver futures, the strike price is \$20 per ounce and the barrier is \$18. The current futures price is \$19, the risk-free interest rate is 5%, and the volatility of silver futures is 40% per annum. Explain how the option works and calculate its value. What is the value of a regular call option on silver futures with the same terms? What is the value of a down-and-in call option on silver futures with the same terms?

19.20. A new European-style lookback call option on a stock index has a maturity of nine months. The current level of the index is 400, the risk-free rate is 6% per annum, the dividend yield on the index is 4% per annum, and the volatility of the index is 20%. Use DerivaGem to value the option.

19.21. Estimate the value of a new six-month European-style average price call option on a non-dividend-paying stock. The initial stock price is \$30, the strike price is \$30, the risk-free interest rate is 5%, and the stock price volatility is 30%.

19.22. Use DerivaGem to calculate the value of:
 a. A regular European call option on a non-dividend-paying stock where the stock price is \$50, the strike price is \$50, the risk-free rate is 5% per annum, the volatility is 30%, and the time to maturity is one year
 b. A down-and-out European call which is as in (a) with the barrier at \$45
 c. A down-and-in European call which is as in (a) with the barrier at \$45
Show that the option in (a) is worth the sum of the values of the options in (b) and (c).

## ASSIGNMENT QUESTIONS

19.23. What is the value in dollars of a derivative that pays off £10,000 in one year provided that the dollar–sterling exchange rate is greater than 1.5000 at that time? The current exchange rate is 1.4800. The dollar and sterling interest rates are 4% and 8% per annum, respectively. The volatility of the exchange rate is 12% per annum.

19.24. Consider an up-and-out barrier call option on a non-dividend-paying stock when the stock price is 50, the strike price is 50, the volatility is 30%, the risk-free rate is 5%, the time to maturity is one year, and the barrier at \$80. Use the software to value the option and graph the relationship between (a) the option price and the stock price, (b) the delta and the option price, (c) the option price and the time to maturity, and (d) the option price and the volatility. Provide an intuitive explanation for the results you get. Show that the delta, gamma, theta, and vega for an up-and-out barrier call option can be either positive or negative.

19.25. Sample Application F in the DerivaGem Application Builder software considers the static options replication example in Section 19.14. It shows the way a hedge can be constructed using four options (as in Section 19.14) and two ways a hedge can be constructed using 16 options.

a. Explain the difference between the two ways a hedge can be constructed using 16 options. Explain intuitively why the second method works better.

b. Improve on the four-option hedge by changing Tmat for the third and fourth options.

c. Check how well the 16-option portfolios match the delta, gamma, and vega of the barrier option.

19.26. Consider a down-and-out call option on a foreign currency. The initial exchange rate is 0.90, the time to maturity is two years, the strike price is 1.00, the barrier is 0.80, the domestic risk-free interest rate is 5%, the foreign risk-free interest rate is 6%, and the volatility is 25% per annum. Use DerivaGem to develop a static option replication strategy involving five options.

19.27. Suppose that a stock index is currently 900. The dividend yield is 2%, the risk-free rate is 5%, and the volatility is 40%. Use the results in Appendix 19A to calculate the value of a one-year average price call where the strike price is 900 and the index level is observed at the end of each quarter for the purposes of the averaging. Compare this with the price calculated by DerivaGem for a one-year average price option where the price is observed continuously. Provide an intuitive explanation for any differences between the prices.

19.28. Use the DerivaGem Application Builder software to compare the effectiveness of daily delta hedging for (a) the option considered in Tables 14.2 and 14.3 and (b) an average price call with the same parameters. Use Sample Application C. For the average price option you will find it necessary to change the calculation of the option price in cell C16, the payoffs in cells H15 and H16, and the deltas (cells G46 to G186 and N46 to N186). Carry out 20 Monte Carlo simulation runs for each option by repeatedly pressing F9. On each run, record the cost of writing and hedging the option, the volume of trading over the whole 20 weeks, and the volume of trading between weeks 11 and 20. Comment on the results.

19.29. In the DerivaGem Application Builder software, modify Sample Application D to test the effectiveness of delta and gamma hedging for a call on call compound option on a 100,000 units of a foreign currency where the exchange rate is 0.67, the domestic risk-free rate is 5%, the foreign risk-free rate is 6%, the volatility is 12%. The time to maturity of the first option is 20 weeks, and the strike price of the first option is 0.015. The second option matures 40 weeks from today and has a strike price of 0.68. Explain how you modified the cells. Comment on hedge effectiveness.

# APPENDIX 19A

## Calculation of the First Two Moments of Arithmetic Averages and Baskets

Consider first the problem of calculating the first two moments of the value of a basket of assets at a future time, $T$, in a risk-neutral world. The price of each asset in the basket is assumed to be lognormal. Define:

$n$ : The number of assets

$S_i$ : The value of the $i$th asset at time $T$

$F_i$ : The forward price[12] of the $i$th asset for a contract maturing at time $T$

$\sigma_i$ : The volatility of the $i$th asset between time zero and time $T$

$\rho_{ij}$ : Correlation between returns from the $i$th and $j$th asset

$P$ : Value of basket at time $T$

$M_1$ : First moment of $P$ in a risk-neutral world

$M_2$ : Second moment of $P$ in a risk-neutral world

Because $P = \sum_{i=1}^{n} S_i$, $\hat{E}(S_i) = F_i$, $M_1 = \hat{E}(P)$, and $M_2 = \hat{E}(P^2)$, where $\hat{E}$ denotes the expected value in a risk-neutral world, it follows that

$$M_1 = \sum_{i=1}^{n} F_i$$

Also,

$$P^2 = \sum_{i=1}^{n}\sum_{j=1}^{n} S_i S_j$$

From the properties of lognormal distributions,

$$\hat{E}(S_i S_j) = F_i F_j e^{\rho_{ij}\sigma_i\sigma_j T}$$

Hence,

$$M_2 = \sum_{i=1}^{n}\sum_{j=1}^{n} F_i F_j e^{\rho_{ij}\sigma_i\sigma_j T}$$

We now move on to the related problem of calculating the first two moments of the arithmetic average price of an asset in a risk-neutral world when the average is calculated from discrete observations. Suppose that the asset price is observed at times $T_i$ ($1 \leqslant i \leqslant m$). We redefine variables as follows:

$S_i$ : The value of the asset at time $T_i$

$F_i$ : The forward price of the asset for a contract maturing at time $T_i$

$\sigma_i$ : The implied volatility for an option on the asset with maturity $T_i$

$\rho_{ij}$ : Correlation between return on asset up to time $T_i$ and the return on the asset up to time $T_j$

[12] Strictly speaking, $F_i$ should be the futures price rather than the forward price. In practice, analysts usually assume no difference between the two when calculating moments.

$P$: Value of the arithmetic average

$M_1$: First moment of $P$ in a risk-neutral world

$M_2$: Second moment of $P$ in a risk-neutral world

In this case,

$$M_1 = \frac{1}{m} \sum_{i=1}^{m} F_i$$

Also,

$$P^2 = \frac{1}{m^2} \sum_{i=1}^{m} \sum_{j=1}^{m} S_i S_j$$

In this case,

$$\hat{E}(S_i S_j) = F_i F_j e^{\rho_{ij} \sigma_i \sigma_j \sqrt{T_i T_j}}$$

It can be shown that, when $i < j$,

$$\rho_{ij} = \frac{\sigma_i \sqrt{T_i}}{\sigma_j \sqrt{T_j}}$$

so that

$$\hat{E}(S_i S_j) = F_i F_j e^{\sigma_i^2 T_i}$$

and

$$M_2 = \frac{1}{m^2} \left( \sum_{i=1}^{m} F_i^2 e^{\sigma_i^2 T_i} + 2 \sum_{i<j} F_i F_j e^{\sigma_i^2 T_i} \right)$$

C H A P T E R   2 0

# MORE ON MODELS AND NUMERICAL PROCEDURES

Up to now the models we have used have been based on the original Black–Scholes assumptions and the numerical procedures we have used have been relatively straightforward. In this chapter we introduce a number of new models and explain how the numerical procedures can be adapted to cope with particular situations.

When the exotic option pricing formulas of Chapter 19 are used, there is no simple way of calculating the volatility that should be input from the volatility smile applicable to plain vanilla options. Sometimes the correct volatility is counterintuitive. As a result it is difficult for traders to incorporate a volatility smile into their pricing of exotic options. The first part of this chapter presents a number of alternatives to the geometric Brownian motion model that are designed to overcome this problem. The parameters of the models we will consider can be chosen so that they are approximately consistent with the volatility smile observed in the market.

The second part of the chapter extends our discussion of numerical procedures. We explain how some types of path-dependent derivatives can be valued using trees. We discuss the special problems associated with valuing barrier options numerically and how these problems can be handled. We outline alternative ways of constructing trees for two correlated variables. Finally, we show how Monte Carlo simulation can be used to value derivatives when there are early exercise opportunities.

As in Chapter 19, our results are presented for derivatives dependent on an asset providing a yield at rate $q$. For an option on a stock index $q$ should be set equal to the dividend yield on the index, for an option on a currency $q$ should be set equal to the foreign risk-free rate, and for an option on a futures contract $q$ should be set equal to the domestic risk-free rate.

## 20.1   THE CEV MODEL

The constant elasticity of variance (CEV) model assumes that the risk-neutral process for a stock price, $S$, is

$$dS = (r - q)S\,dt + \sigma S^{\alpha}\,dz$$

where $r$ is the risk-free rate, $q$ is the dividend yield, $dz$ is a Wiener process, $\sigma$ is a volatility parameter, and $\alpha$ is a positive constant.[1] The stock price has volatility $\sigma S^{\alpha-1}$. When $\alpha = 1$, the

[1] See J. C. Cox and S. A. Ross, "The Valuation of Options for Alternative Stochastic Processes," *Journal of Financial Economics*, 3 (March 1976), 145–66.

CEV model is the geometric Brownian motion model we have been using up to now. When $\alpha < 1$, the volatility increases as the stock price decreases. This creates a probability distribution similar to that observed for equities with a heavy left tail and a less heavy right tail[2] (see Figure 15.4). When $\alpha > 1$, the volatility increases as the stock price increases, giving a probability distribution with a heavy right tail and a less heavy left tail. This corresponds to a volatility smile where the implied volatility is an increasing function of the strike price. This type of volatility smile is sometimes observed for options on futures (see Assignment 13.46).

The valuation formulas for European call and put options under the CEV model is

$$c = S_0 e^{-qT}[1 - \chi^2(a, b+2, c)] - K e^{-rT} \chi^2(c, b, a)$$

$$p = K e^{-rT}[1 - \chi^2(c, b, a)] - S_0 e^{-qT} \chi^2(a, b+2, c)$$

when $0 < \alpha < 1$, and

$$c = S_0 e^{-qT}[1 - \chi^2(c, -b, a)] - K e^{-rT} \chi^2(a, 2-b, c)$$

$$p = K e^{-rT}[1 - \chi^2(a, 2-b, c)] - S_0 e^{-qT} \chi^2(c, -b, a)$$

when $\alpha > 1$, where

$$a = \frac{K^{2(1-\alpha)}}{(1-\alpha)^2 \sigma^2 T}, \qquad b = \frac{1}{1-\alpha}, \qquad c = \frac{(S e^{(r-q)T})^{2(1-\alpha)}}{(1-\alpha)^2 \sigma^2 T}$$

and $\chi^2(z, v, k)$ is the cumulative probability that a variable with a noncentral $\chi^2$ distribution with noncentrality parameter $v$ and $k$ degrees of freedom is less than $z$. An efficient procedure for computing $\chi^2(z, v, k)$ is provided by Ding.[3]

## 20.2 THE JUMP DIFFUSION MODEL

Merton has suggested a model where the asset price has jumps superimposed upon a geometric Brownian motion.[4] Define:

$\mu$ : Expected return from asset net of the dividend yield, $q$

$\lambda$ : Average number of jumps per year

$k$ : Average jump size measured as a percentage of the asset price

The percentage jump size is assumed to be drawn from a probability distribution in the model.

The probability of a jump in time $\delta t$ is $\lambda \, \delta t$. The average growth rate in the asset price from the jumps is therefore $\lambda k$. The process for the asset price is

$$\frac{dS}{S} = (\mu - \lambda k)\, dt + \sigma \, dz + dp$$

---

[2] The reason is as follows. As the stock price decreases, the volatility increases making even lower stock price more likely; when the stock price increases, the volatility decreases making higher stock prices less likely.

[3] See C. G. Ding, "Algorithm AS275: Computing the Non-central $\chi^2$ Distribution Function," *Applied Statistics*, 41 (1992), 478–82.

[4] See R. C. Merton, "Option Pricing When Underlying Stock Returns Are Discontinuous," *Journal of Financial Economics*, 3 (March 1976), 125–44.

where $dz$ is a Wiener process, $dp$ is the Poisson process generating the jumps, and $\sigma$ is the volatility of the geometric Brownian motion. The processes $dz$ and $dp$ are assumed to be independent.

The key assumption made by Merton is that the jump component of the asset's return represents nonsystematic risk (i.e., risk not priced in the economy).[5] This means that a Black–Scholes type of portfolio, which eliminates the uncertainty arising from the geometric Brownian motion (but not the jumps) must earn the riskless rate.

An important particular case of Merton's model is where the logarithm of the size of the percentage jump is normal. Assume that the standard deviation of the normal distribution is $s$. Merton shows that a European option price can then be written

$$\sum_{n=0}^{\infty} \frac{e^{-\lambda'T}(\lambda'T)^n}{n!} f_n$$

where $\lambda' = \lambda(1 + k)$. The variable $f_n$ is the Black–Scholes option price when the dividend yield is $q$, the variance rate is

$$\sigma^2 + \frac{ns^2}{T}$$

and the risk-free rate is

$$r - \lambda k + \frac{n\gamma}{T}$$

where $\gamma = \ln(1 + k)$.

The model gives rise to heavier left and heavier right tails than Black–Scholes and is consistent with the implied volatilities observed for currency options (see Section 15.2 and Problem 20.20).

## 20.3  STOCHASTIC VOLATILITY MODELS

When the instantaneous volatility is a known function of time, the risk-neutral process followed by the stock price is

$$dS = (r - q)S\,dt + \sigma(t)S\,dz \tag{20.1}$$

The Black–Scholes formulas are then correct providing the variance rate is set equal to the average variance rate during the life of the option (see Problem 20.6). The variance rate is the square of the volatility. Suppose that during a one-year period the volatility of a stock will be 20% during the first six months and 30% during the second six months. The average variance rate is

$$0.5 \times 0.20^2 + 0.5 \times 0.30^2 = 0.065$$

It is correct to use Black–Scholes with a variance rate of 0.065. This corresponds to a volatility of $\sqrt{0.065} = 0.255$, or 25.5%. We implicitly used this result in Section 17.6 when discussing how the GARCH(1, 1) model can be used to calculate volatility term structures.

Equation (20.1) assumes that the instantaneous volatility of an asset is perfectly predictable. In practice volatility varies stochastically. This has led some researchers to develop more complex models where there are two stochastic variables: the stock price and its volatility.

---

[5] This assumption is important because it turns out that we cannot apply risk-neutral valuation to situations where the size of the jump is systematic. For a discussion of this point, see E. Naik and M. Lee, "General Equilibrium Pricing of Options on the Market Portfolios with Discontinuous Returns," *Review of Financial Studies*, 3 (1990), 493–521.

Hull and White consider the following stochastic volatility model for the risk-neutral behavior of a price:

$$\frac{dS}{S} = (r - q)\,dt + \sqrt{V}\,dz_S \tag{20.2}$$

$$dV = a(V_L - V)\,dt + \xi V^\alpha\,dz_V \tag{20.3}$$

where $a$, $V_L$, $\xi$, and $\alpha$ are constants, and $dz_S$ and $dz_V$ are Wiener processes. The variable $V$ in this model is the asset's variance rate. The variance rate has a drift that pulls it back to a level $V_L$ at rate $a$. Hull and White compare the price given by this model with the price given by the Black–Scholes model when the variance rate in Black–Scholes is put equal to the expected average variance rate during the life of the option.

Hull and White show that, when volatility is stochastic but uncorrelated with the asset price, the price of a European option is the Black–Scholes price integrated over the probability distribution of the average variance rate during the life of the option.[6] Thus a European call price is

$$\int_0^\infty c(\bar{V})g(\bar{V})\,d\bar{V}$$

where $\bar{V}$ is the average value of the variance rate, $c$ is the Black–Scholes price expressed as a function of $\bar{V}$, and $g$ is the probability density function of $\bar{V}$ in a risk-neutral world. This result can be used to show that Black–Scholes overprices options that are at the money or close to the money, and underprices options that are deep in or deep out of the money. The model is consistent with the pattern of implied volatilities observed for currency options (see Section 15.2) .

The case where the asset price and volatility are correlated is more complicated. Option prices can be obtained using Monte Carlo simulation. In the particular case where $\alpha = 0.5$, Hull and White provide a series expansion and Heston gives an analytic result.[7] The pattern of implied volatilities obtained when the volatility is negatively correlated with the asset price is similar to that observed for equities[8] (see Section 15.3).

Chapter 17 discusses exponentially weighted moving average (EWMA) and GARCH(1,1) models. These are alterative approaches to characterizing a stochastic volatility model. Duan shows that it is possible to use GARCH(1,1) as the basis for an internally consistent option pricing model.[9] (See Problem 17.14 for the equivalence of GARCH(1,1) and stochastic volatility models.)

For options that last less than a year, the pricing impact of a stochastic volatility is fairly small in absolute terms (although in percentage terms it can be quite large for deep-out-of-the-money options). It becomes progressively larger as the life of the option increases.

The impact of a stochastic volatility on the performance of delta hedging is generally quite large. This can be tested by carrying out simulations of delta hedging, such as those in Section 14.4,

---

[6] See J. C. Hull and A. White, "The Pricing of Options on Assets with Stochastic Volatilities," *Journal of Finance*, 42 (June 1987), 281–300. This result is independent of the process followed by the variance rate.

[7] See J. C. Hull and A. White, "An Analysis of the Bias in Option Pricing Caused by a Stochastic Volatility," *Advances in Futures and Options Research*, 3 (1988), 27–61; S. L. Heston, "A Closed Form Solution for Options with Stochastic Volatility with Applications to Bonds and Currency Options," *Review of Financial Studies*, 6, no. 2 (1993), 327–43.

[8] The reason is given in footnote 2.

[9] See J.-C. Duan, "The GARCH Option Pricing Model," *Mathematical Finance*, 5 (1995), 13–32; and J.-C. Duan, "Cracking the Smile," *RISK*, December 1996, pp. 55–59.

assuming first a constant volatility model and then a stochastic volatility model. Delta hedging works less well when the volatility is stochastic. This emphasizes the point made in Chapter 14 that traders should monitor vega as well as delta and gamma.

## 20.4 THE IVF MODEL

A financial institution likes to use models for pricing exotic options that have the property that they price all plain vanilla options correctly.[10] The models we have looked at so far can be calibrated on any day so that they give a reasonably good fit to the prices of vanilla options, but they do not provide an exact fit. In 1994, Derman and Kani, Dupire, and Rubinstein developed what has become known as the *implied volatility function* (IVF) model or the *implied tree* model.[11] This is a model that is designed to fit exactly the prices observed today for all European option prices, regardless of the shape of the volatility surface.

The risk-neutral process for the asset price in the model has the form

$$dS = [r(t) - q(t)]S\, dt + \sigma(S, t)S\, dz$$

where $r(t)$ is the instantaneous forward interest rate for a contract maturing at time $t$ and $q(t)$ is the dividend yield as a function of time. The volatility $\sigma(S, t)$ is a function of both $S$ and $t$ and is chosen so that the model prices all European options consistently with the market. It is shown both by Dupire and by Andersen and Brotherton-Ratcliffe that $\sigma(S, t)$ can be calculated analytically:[12]

$$[\sigma(K, T)]^2 = 2\, \frac{\partial c_{\text{mkt}}/\partial T + q(T)c_{\text{mkt}} + K[r(T) - q(T)]\partial c_{\text{mkt}}/\partial K}{K^2(\partial^2 c_{\text{mkt}}/\partial K^2)} \tag{20.4}$$

where $c_{\text{mkt}}(K, T)$ is the market price of a European call option with strike price $K$ and maturity $T$. If a sufficiently large number of European call prices are available in the market, this equation can be used to estimate the $\sigma(S, t)$ function.[13]

Andersen and Brotherton-Ratcliffe implement the model by using equation (20.4) in conjunction with the implicit finite difference method. An alternative approach, known as the *implied tree* methodology, is suggested by Derman and Kani and by Rubinstein. This involves constructing a tree for the asset price that is consistent with option prices in the market. We will now describe the Derman–Kani version of the implied tree approach.

An implied tree is a binomial tree where a forward induction procedure is used to determine the positions of nodes at the end of each time step and the probabilities on branches. As in the case of the regular binomial tree, we branch from the $j$th node at time $(n - 1)\delta t$ to either the $(j + 1)$th

---

[10] There is a practical reason for this. If the bank does not use a model with this property, there is a danger that traders working for the bank will spend their time arbitraging the bank's internal models.

[11] See B. Dupire, "Pricing with a Smile," *RISK*, February 1994, pp. 18–20; E. Derman and I. Kani, "Riding on a Smile," *RISK*, February 1994, pp. 32–39; M. Rubinstein, "Implied Binomial Trees," *Journal of Finance*, 49, no. 3 (July 1994), 771–818.

[12] See B. Dupire, "Pricing with a Smile," *RISK*, February 1994, pp. 18–20; L. B. G Andersen and R. Brotherton-Ratcliffe, "The Equity Option Volatility Smile: An Implicit Finite Difference Approach," *Journal of Computational Finance*, 1, no. 2 (Winter 1997/98), 5–37. Dupire considers the case where $r$ and $q$ are zero; Andersen and Brotherton-Ratcliffe consider the more general situation.

[13] Some smoothing of the observed volatility surface is typically necessary.

node or the $j$th node at time $n\,\delta t$. It is constructed using forward induction. To understand the approach, note that there are $n+1$ nodes at time $n\,\delta t$.[14] Assume that the tree has already been constructed up to time $(n-1)\,\delta t$. The next step involves:

1. Choosing the positions of the $n+1$ nodes at time $n\,\delta t$
2. Choosing the $n$ "up" probabilities on the branches between times $(n-1)\,\delta t$ and $n\,\delta t$. (The "down" probabilities are 1 minus the "up" probabilities.)

These choices provide $2n+1$ degrees of freedom. The interest rate for the period between $(n-1)\,\delta t$ and $n\,\delta t$ is set equal to the forward rate. The expected return from the asset at each of the nodes at time $(n-1)\,\delta t$ must equal this interest rate. This uses up $n$ degrees of freedom. The tree is also constructed to ensure that $n$ European-style options maturing at time $n\,\delta t$ are priced correctly. These options have strike prices equal to the stock prices at the nodes at time $(n-1)\,\delta t$.[15] This uses up an additional $n$ degrees of freedom. The final degree of freedom is used up in ensuring that the center of the tree equals today's stock price.

The requirements just mentioned lead to $2n+1$ equations in $2n+1$ unknowns. By solving the equations, the construction of the tree is advanced by one time step. One problem with the approach is that negative probabilities do sometimes arise. When a particular probability turns out to be negative, it is necessary to introduce a rule to override the option price responsible for the negative probability.

When it is used in practice the IVF model is recalibrated daily to the prices of plain vanilla options. It is a tool to price exotic options consistently with plain vanilla options. As discussed in Chapter 15, plain vanilla options define the risk-neutral probability distribution of the asset price at all future times. It follows that the IVF model gets the risk-neutral probability distribution of the asset price at all future times correct. This means that options providing payoffs at just one time (e.g., all-or-nothing and asset-or-nothing options) are priced correctly by the IVF model. However, the model does not necessarily get the joint distribution of the asset price at two or more times correct. This means that exotic options such as compound options and barrier options may be priced incorrectly. Hull and Suo (2001) tested the IVF model by assuming that all derivative prices are determined by a stochastic volatility model.[16] They found that the model works reasonably well for compound options, but sometimes gives serious errors for barrier options.

## 20.5 PATH-DEPENDENT DERIVATIVES

A path-dependent derivative (or history-dependent derivative) is a derivative where the payoff depends on the path followed by the price of the underlying asset, and not just on its final value. Asian options and lookback options are examples of path-dependent derivatives. As explained in Chapter 19, the payoff from an Asian option depends on the average price of the underlying asset;

---

[14] The brief description of the implied tree methodology here is based on the work of E. Derman and I. Kani published in *RISK* in 1994.

[15] In practice, it is necessary to interpolate between the implied volatilities of actively traded options to determine implied volatilities for the options used in the tree construction. These implied volatilities are then converted into option prices using Black–Scholes.

[16] See J. C. Hull and W. Suo, "A Methodology for the Assessment of Model Risk and Its Application to the Implied Volatility Function Model," *Journal of Financial and Quantitative Analysis*, 37, no. 2 (June 2002).

the payoff from a lookback option depends on its maximum or minimum price. One approach to valuing path-dependent options when analytic results are not available is Monte Carlo simulation as discussed in Chapter 18. A sample value of the derivative can be calculated by sampling a random path for the underlying asset in a risk-neutral world, calculating the payoff, and discounting the payoff at the risk-free interest rate. An estimate of the value of the derivative is found by obtaining many sample values of the derivative in this way and calculating their mean.

The main problem with using Monte Carlo simulation to value path-dependent derivatives is that the computation time necessary to achieve the required level of accuracy can be unacceptably high. Also, American-style path-dependent derivatives (i.e., path-dependent derivatives where one side has exercise opportunities or other decisions to make) cannot easily be handled. In this section, we show how the binomial tree methods presented in Chapter 18 can be extended to cope with some path-dependent derivatives.[17] The procedure can handle American-style path-dependent derivatives and is computationally more efficient than Monte Carlo simulation for European-style path-dependent derivatives.

For the procedure to work, two conditions must be satisfied:

1. The payoff from the derivative must depend on a single function, $F$, of the path followed by the underlying asset.

2. It must be possible to calculate the value of $F$ at time $\tau + \delta t$ from the value of $F$ at time $\tau$ and the value of the underlying asset at time $\tau + \delta t$.

### *Illustration Using Lookback Options*

As a first illustration of the procedure, we consider an American lookback put option on a non-dividend-paying stock.[18] If exercised at time $\tau$, this pays off the amount by which the maximum stock price between time zero and time $\tau$ exceeds the current stock price. We suppose that the initial stock price is $50, the stock price volatility is 40% per annum, the risk-free interest rate is 10% per annum, the total life of the option is three months, and that stock price movements are represented by a three-step binomial tree. With our usual notation, this means that $S_0 = 50$, $\sigma = 0.4$, $r = 0.10$, $\delta t = 0.08333$, $u = 1.1224$, $d = 0.8909$, $a = 1.0084$, and $p = 0.5073$.

The tree is shown in Figure 20.1. The top number at each node is the stock price. The next level of numbers at each node shows the possible maximum stock prices achievable on paths leading to the node. The final level of numbers shows the values of the derivative corresponding to each of the possible maximum stock prices. The values of the derivative at the final nodes of the tree are calculated as the maximum stock price minus the actual stock price.

To illustrate the rollback procedure, suppose that we are at node A, where the stock price is $50. The maximum stock price achieved thus far is either 56.12 or 50. Consider first the situation where it is equal to 50. If there is an up movement, the maximum stock price becomes 56.12 and the value of the derivative is zero. If there is a down movement, the maximum stock price stays at 50 and the value of the derivative is 5.45. Assuming no early exercise, the value of the derivative at A when the maximum achieved so far is 50 is therefore

$$(0 \times 0.5073 + 5.45 \times 0.4927)e^{-0.1 \times 0.08333} = 2.66$$

---

[17] This approach was suggested by J. Hull and A. White, "Efficient Procedures for Valuing European and American Path-Dependent Options," *Journal of Derivatives*, 1, no. 1 (Fall 1993), 21–31.

[18] This example is used as a first illustration of the general procedure for handling path dependence. We present a more efficient approach to valuing American-style lookback options in the next section.

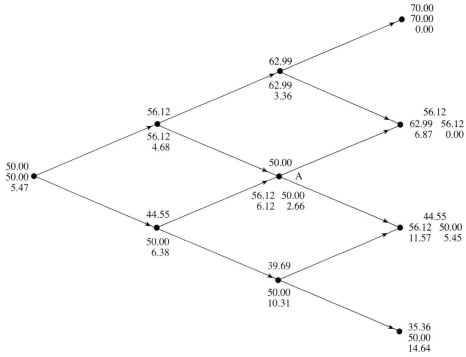

**Figure 20.1** Tree for valuing an American lookback option

Clearly, it is not worth exercising at node A in these circumstances because the payoff from doing so is zero. A similar calculation for the situation where the maximum value at node A is 56.12 gives the value of the derivative at node A, without early exercise, to be

$$(0 \times 0.5073 + 11.57 \times 0.4927)e^{-0.1 \times 0.08333} = 5.65$$

In this case, early exercise gives a value of 6.12 and is the optimal strategy. Rolling back through the tree in the way we have indicated gives the value of the American lookback as $5.47.

### Generalization

The approach just described is computationally feasible when the number of alternative values of the path function, $F$, at each node does not grow too fast as the number of time steps is increased. The example we used, a lookback option, presents no problems because the number of alternative values for the maximum asset price at a node in a binomial tree with $n$ time steps is never greater than $n$.

Luckily, the approach can be extended to cope with situations where there are a very large number of different possible values of the path function at each node. The basic idea is as follows. At a node, we carry out calculations for a small number of representative values of $F$. When the value of the derivative is required for other values of the path function, we calculate it from the known values using interpolation.

The first stage is to work forward through the tree establishing the maximum and minimum values of the path function at each node. Assuming the value of the path function at time $\tau + \delta t$ depends only on the value of the path function at time $\tau$ and the value of the underlying variable at time $\tau + \delta t$, the maximum and minimum values of the path function for the nodes at time $\tau + \delta t$ can be calculated in a straightforward way from those for the nodes at time $\tau$. The second stage is to choose representative values of the path function at each node. There are a number of approaches. A simple rule is to choose the representative values as the maximum value, the minimum value, and a number of other values that are equally spaced between the maximum and the minimum. As we roll back through the tree, we value the derivative for each of representative values of the path function.

We illustrate the nature of the calculation by considering the problem of valuing the average price call option in Example 19.2. We examine the case where the payoff depends on the arithmetic average stock price. The initial stock price is 50, the strike price is 50, the risk-free interest rate is 10%, the stock price volatility is 40%, and the time to maturity is one year. We use a tree with 20 time steps. The binomial tree parameters are $\delta t = 0.05$, $u = 1.0936$, $d = 0.9144$, $p = 0.5056$, and $1 - p = 0.4944$. The path function is the arithmetic average of the stock price.

Figure 20.2 shows the calculations that are carried out in one small part of the tree. Node X is the central node at time 0.2 year (at the end of the fourth time step). Nodes Y and Z are the two nodes at time 0.25 year that are reachable from node X. The stock price at node X is 50. Forward induction shows that the maximum average stock price that is achievable in reaching node X is 53.83. The minimum is 46.65. (We include both the initial and final stock prices when calculating the average.) From node X, we branch to one of the two nodes Y and Z. At node Y, the stock price is 54.68 and the bounds for the average are 47.99 and 57.39. At node Z, the stock price is 45.72 and the bounds for the average stock price are 43.88 and 52.48.

Suppose that we have chosen the representative values of the average to be four equally spaced values at each node. This means that, at node X, we consider the averages 46.65, 49.04, 51.44, and 53.83. At node Y, we consider the averages 47.99, 51.12, 54.26, and 57.39. At node Z, we consider the averages 43.88, 46.75, 49.61, and 52.48. We assume that backward induction has already been used to calculate the value of the option for each of the alternative values of the average at nodes Y and Z. The values are shown in Figure 20.2. For example, at node Y when the average is 51.12, the value of the option is 8.101.

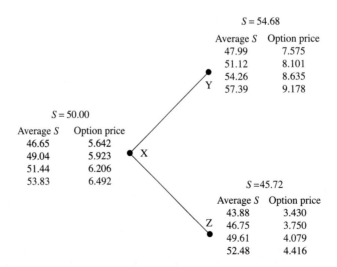

**Figure 20.2**   Part of tree for valuing option on the arithmetic average

Consider the calculations at node X for the case where the average is 51.44. If the stock price moves up to node Y, the new average will be

$$\frac{5 \times 51.44 + 54.68}{6} = 51.98$$

The value of the derivative at node Y for this average can be found by interpolating between the values when the average is 51.12 and when it is 54.26. It is

$$\frac{(51.98 - 51.12) \times 8.635 + (54.26 - 51.98) \times 8.101}{54.26 - 51.12} = 8.247$$

Similarly, if the stock price moves down to node Z, the new average will be

$$\frac{5 \times 51.44 + 45.72}{6} = 50.49$$

and by interpolation the value of the derivative is 4.182.

The value of the derivative at node X when the average is 51.44 is therefore

$$(0.5056 \times 8.247 + 0.4944 \times 4.182)e^{-0.1 \times 0.05} = 6.206$$

The other values at node X are calculated similarly. Once the values at all nodes at time 0.2 years have been calculated, we can move on to the nodes at time 0.15 years.

The value given by the full tree for the option at time zero is 7.17. As the number of time steps and the number of averages considered at each node are increased, the value of the option converges to the correct answer. With 60 time steps and 100 averages at each node, the value of the option is 5.58. The analytic approximation for the value of the option calculated in Example 19.2 is 5.62.

A key advantage of the method described here is that it can handle American options. The calculations are as we have described them except that we test for early exercise at each node for each of the alternative values of the path function at the node. (In practice, the early exercise decision is liable to depend on both the value of the path function and the value of the underlying asset.) Consider the American version of the average price call considered here. The value calculated using the 20-step tree and four averages at each node is 7.77; with 60 time steps and 100 averages, the value is 6.17.

The approach just described can be used in a wide range of different situations. The two conditions that must be satisfied were listed at the beginning of this section. Efficiency is improved somewhat if quadratic rather than linear interpolation is used at each node.

## 20.6 LOOKBACK OPTIONS

A number of researchers have suggested an interesting and instructive approach to valuing lookback options.[19] To illustrate it, we again consider the American-style lookback put in Figure 20.1. When exercised, this provides a payoff equal to the excess of the maximum stock price over the current

---

[19] The approach was proposed by Eric Reiner in a lecture at Berkeley. It is also suggested by S. Babbs, "Binomial Valuation of Lookback Options," Working Paper, Midland Global Markets, 1992; and T. H. F. Cheuk and T. C. F. Vorst, "Lookback Options and the Observation Frequency: A Binomial Approach," Working Paper, Erasmus University, Rotterdam.

stock price. We define $G(t)$ as the maximum stock price achieved up to time $t$ and set

$$Y(t) = \frac{G(t)}{S(t)}$$

We next use the Cox, Ross, and Rubinstein tree for the stock price to produce a tree for $Y$. Initially, $Y = 1$ because $G = S$ at time zero. If there is an up movement in $S$ during the first time step, both $G$ and $S$ increase by a proportional amount $u$ and $Y = 1$. If there is a down movement in $S$ during the first time step, $G$ stays the same, so that $Y = 1/d = u$. Continuing with these types of arguments, we produce the tree shown in Figure 20.3 for $Y$. (Note that in this example $u = 1.1224$, $d = 0.8909$, $a = 1.0084$, and $p = 0.5073$.) The rules defining the geometry of the tree are as follows:

1. When $Y = 1$ at time $t$, it is either $u$ or $1$ at time $t + \delta t$.
2. When $Y = u^m$ at time $t$ for $m \geqslant 1$, it is either $u^{m+1}$ or $u^{m-1}$ at time $t + \delta t$.

An up movement in $Y$ corresponds to a down movement in the stock price and vice versa. Therefore, the probability of an up movement in $Y$ is always $1 - p$, and the probability of a down movement in $Y$ is always $p$.

We use the tree to value the American lookback option in units of the stock price rather than in dollars. In dollars, the payoff from the option is

$$SY - S$$

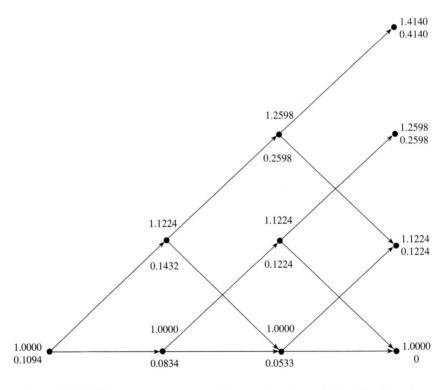

**Figure 20.3**  Efficient procedure for valuing an American-style lookback option

In stock price units, the payoff from the option, therefore, is

$$Y - 1$$

We roll back through the tree in the usual way, valuing a derivative that provides this payoff except that we adjust for the differences in the stock price (i.e., the unit of measurement) at the nodes. If $f_{i,j}$ is the value of the lookback at the $j$th node at time $i\,\delta t$ and $Y_{i,j}$ is the value of $Y$ at this node, the rollback procedure gives

$$f_{i,j} = \max\{Y_{i,j} - 1,\ e^{-r\delta t}[(1-p)f_{i+1,j+1}d + p f_{i+1,j-1}u]\}$$

when $j \geqslant 1$. Note that, in this equation, $f_{i+1,j+1}$ is multiplied by $d$, and $f_{i+1,j-1}$ is multiplied by $u$. This takes into account that the stock price at node $(i, j)$ is the unit of measurement. The stock price at node $(i + 1, j + 1)$, which is the unit of measurement for $f_{i+1,j+1}$, is $d$ times the stock price at node $(i, j)$; and the stock price at node $(i + 1, j - 1)$, which is the unit of measurement for $f_{i+1,j-1}$, is $u$ times the stock price at node $(i, j)$. Similarly, when $j = 0$, the rollback procedure gives

$$f_{i,j} = \max\{Y_{i,j} - 1,\ e^{-r\delta t}[(1-p)f_{i+1,j+1}d + p f_{i+1,j}u]\}$$

The calculations for our example are shown in Figure 20.3. The tree estimates the value of the option at time zero (in stock price units) as 0.1094. This means that the dollar value of the option is $0.1094 \times 50 = 5.47$. This is the same as the value calculated from the tree in Figure 20.1. For a given number of time steps, the two procedures are equivalent. The advantage of the procedure described here is that it considerably reduces the number of computations.

The value of the option given by the tree in Figure 20.3, when it is European, is 5.26. The exact value of the European option, as shown in Example 19.1, is 7.79. The value given by the tree converges very slowly to this as the number of time steps is increased. For example, with 100, 500, 1,000, and 5,000 time steps the values given by the tree for the European option in our example are 7.24, 7.54, 7.61, and 7.71.

## 20.7 BARRIER OPTIONS

In Chapter 19 we presented analytic results for standard barrier options. Here we consider the numerical procedures that can be used for barrier options when there are no analytic results.

In principle, a barrier option can be valued using the binomial and trinomial trees discussed in Chapter 18. Consider an up-and-out option. We can value this in the same way as a regular option except that, when we encounter a node above the barrier, we set the value of the option equal to zero.

Unfortunately, convergence is very slow when this approach is used. A large number of time steps are required to obtain a reasonably accurate result. The reason for this is that the barrier being assumed by the tree is different from the true barrier.[20] Define the *inner barrier* as the barrier formed by nodes just on the inside of the true barrier (i.e., closer to the center of the tree) and *the outer barrier* as the barrier formed by nodes just outside the true barrier (i.e., farther away from the center of the tree). Figure 20.4 shows the inner and outer barrier for a trinomial tree on the

---

[20] See P. P. Boyle and S. H. Lau, "Bumping Up Against the Barrier with the Binomial Method," *Journal of Derivatives*, 1, no. 4 (Summer 1994), 6–14, for a discussion of this.

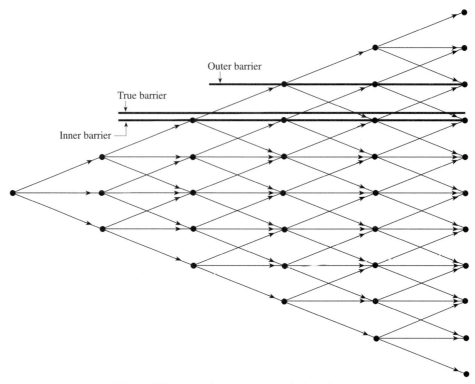

**Figure 20.4**  Barriers assumed by trinomial trees

assumption that the true barrier is horizontal. Figure 20.5 does the same for a binomial tree. The usual tree calculations implicitly assume that the outer barrier is the true barrier because the barrier conditions are first used at nodes on this barrier. When the time step is $\delta t$, the vertical spacing between the nodes is of order $\sqrt{\delta t}$. This means that errors created by the difference between the true barrier and the outer barrier also tend to be of order $\sqrt{\delta t}$.

We now present three alternative approaches for overcoming this problem. For all three approaches, it turns out to be more efficient to use a trinomial tree rather than a binomial tree.

### Positioning Nodes on the Barriers

Suppose that there are two horizontal barriers, $H_1$ and $H_2$, with $H_1 > H_2$, and that the underlying stock price follows geometric Brownian motion. In a trinomial tree, there are three possible movements in the asset's price at each node: up by a proportional amount $u$; stay the same; and down by a proportional amount $d$, where $d = 1/u$. We can always choose $u$ so that nodes lie on both barriers. The condition that must be satisfied by $u$ is

$$H_2 = H_1 u^N$$

or

$$\ln H_2 = \ln H_1 + N \ln u$$

for some integer $N$.

When discussing trinomial trees in Section 18.5, the value suggested for $u$ was $e^{\sigma\sqrt{3\,\delta t}}$, so that $\ln u = \sigma\sqrt{3\,\delta t}$. In the situation considered here, a good rule is to choose $\ln u$ as close as possible to this value, consistent with the condition given above. This means that we set

$$\ln u = \frac{\ln H_2 - \ln H_1}{N}$$

where

$$N = \text{int}\left[\frac{\ln H_2 - \ln H_1}{\sigma\sqrt{3\,\delta t}} + 0.5\right]$$

and int[$x$] is the integer part of $x$. Normally, the trinomial stock price tree is constructed so that the central node is the initial stock price. In this case, the stock price at the first node is the initial stock price. After that, we choose the central node of the tree to be $H_1 u^M$, where $M$ is the integer that makes this quantity as close as possible to the initial stock price, that is,

$$M = \text{int}\left[\frac{\ln S_0 - \ln H_1}{\ln u} + 0.5\right]$$

This leads to a tree of the form shown in Figure 20.6. The probabilities on all branches of the tree are chosen, as usual, to match the first two moments of the stochastic process followed by the asset price. The approach works well except when the initial asset price is close to a barrier.

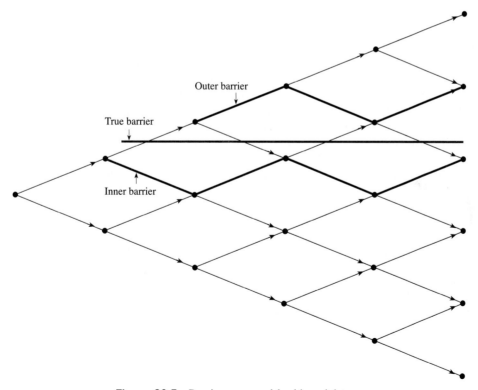

**Figure 20.5** Barriers assumed by binomial trees

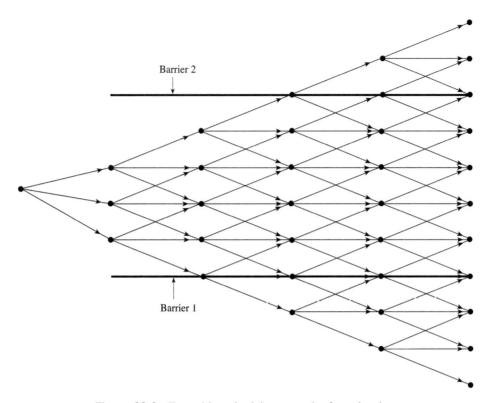

**Figure 20.6**   Tree with nodes lying on each of two barriers

### Adjusting for Nodes Not Lying on Barriers

An alternative procedure for coping with barriers is to make no changes to the tree and adjust for the fact that the barrier is specified incorrectly by the tree.[21] The first step is to calculate an inner barrier and an outer barrier, as described earlier. We then rollback through the tree, calculating two values of the derivative on the nodes that form the inner barrier. The first of these values is obtained by assuming that the inner barrier is correct; the second is obtained by assuming that the outer barrier is correct. A final estimate for the value of the derivative on the inner barrier is then obtained by interpolating between these two values. Suppose that at time $i\,\delta t$, the true barrier is 0.2 from the inner barrier and 0.6 from the outer barrier. Suppose further that the value of the derivative on the inner barrier is 0 if the inner barrier is assumed to be correct and 1.6 if the outer barrier is assumed to be correct. The interpolated value on the inner barrier is 0.4. Once we have obtained a value for the derivative at all nodes on all inner barriers, we can roll back through the tree to obtain the initial value of the derivative in the usual way.

For a single horizontal barrier, this approach is equivalent to the following:

1. Calculate the price of the derivative on the assumption that the inner barrier is the true barrier.

---

[21] The procedure we describe here is similar to that in E. Derman, I. Kani, D. Ergener, and I Bardhan, "Enhanced Numerical Methods for Options with Barriers," Working Paper, Goldman Sachs, May 1995.

2. Calculate the value of the derivative on the assumption that the outer barrier is the true barrier.

3. Interpolate between the two prices.

The method can be generalized to situations where there is more than one barrier and to situations where the barriers are nonhorizontal.

### *The Adaptive Mesh Model*

The methods we have presented so far work reasonably well when the initial asset price is not close to a barrier. When the initial asset price is close to a barrier, the adaptive mesh model, which we introduced in Section 18.5, can be used.[22] The idea behind the model is that computational efficiency can be improved by grafting a fine tree on to a coarse tree to achieve a more detailed modeling of the asset price in the regions of the tree where it is needed most.

To value a barrier option, it is useful to have a fine tree close to the barriers. Figure 20.7 illustrates the design of the tree. The geometry of the tree is arranged so that nodes lie on the barriers. The probabilities on branches are chosen, as usual, to match the first two moments of the process followed by the underlying asset.

The heavy lines in Figure 20.7 are the branches of the coarse tree. The light solid lines are the

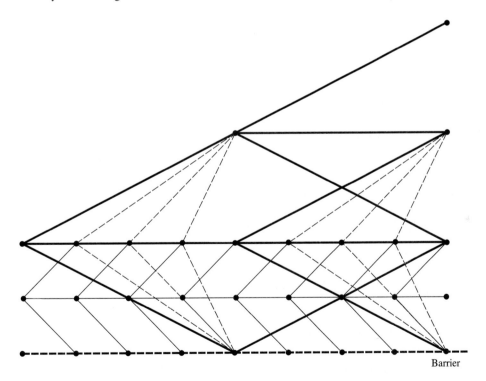

Barrier

**Figure 20.7**  The adaptive mesh model used to value barrier options

---

[22] See S. Figlewski and B. Gao, "The Adaptive Mesh Model: A New Approach to Efficient Option Pricing," *Journal of Financial Economics*, 53 (1999), 313–51.

fine tree. We first roll back through the coarse tree in the usual way. We then calculate the value at additional nodes using the branches indicated by the dotted lines. Finally we roll back through the fine tree.

## 20.8   OPTIONS ON TWO CORRELATED ASSETS

Another tricky numerical problem is that of valuing options dependent on two assets whose prices are correlated. (These are sometimes referred to as *rainbow options*.) A number of alternative approaches have been suggested. Three of these approaches are presented in this section.

### *Transforming Variables*

It is relatively easy to construct a tree in three dimensions to represent the movements of two *uncorrelated* variables. The procedure is as follows. First, we construct a two-dimensional tree for each variable. We then combine these trees into a single three-dimensional tree. The probabilities on the branches of the three-dimensional tree are the product of the corresponding probabilities on the two-dimensional trees. Suppose, for example, that the variables are stock prices $S_1$ and $S_2$. Each can be represented in two dimensions by a Cox, Ross, and Rubinstein binomial tree. Assume that $S_1$ has a probability $p_1$ of moving up by a proportional amount $u_1$ and a probability $1 - p_1$ of moving down by a proportional amount $d_1$. Suppose further that $S_2$ has a probability $p_2$ of moving up by a proportional amount $u_2$ and a probability $1 - p_2$ of moving down by a proportional amount $d_2$. In the three-dimensional tree there are four branches emanating from each node. The probabilities are:

$$p_1 p_2: \quad S_1 \text{ increases; } S_2 \text{ increases.}$$
$$p_1(1 - p_2): \quad S_1 \text{ increases; } S_2 \text{ decreases.}$$
$$(1 - p_1)p_2: \quad S_1 \text{ decreases; } S_2 \text{ increases.}$$
$$(1 - p_1)(1 - p_2): \quad S_1 \text{ decreases; } S_2 \text{ decreases.}$$

Consider next the situation where $S_1$ and $S_2$ are correlated. We suppose that the risk-neutral processes are:

$$dS_1 = (r - q_1)S_1\, dt + \sigma_1 S_1\, dz_1, \qquad dS_2 = (r - q_2)S_2\, dt + \sigma_2 S_2\, dz_2$$

and the instantaneous correlation between the Wiener processes $dz_1$ and $dz_2$ is $\rho$. This means that

$$d \ln S_1 = (r - q_1 - \sigma_1^2/2)\, dt + \sigma_1\, dz_1, \qquad d \ln S_2 = (r - q_2 - \sigma_2^2/2)\, dt + \sigma_2\, dz_2$$

We define two new uncorrelated variables:[23]

$$x_1 = \sigma_2 \ln S_1 + \sigma_1 \ln S_2, \qquad x_2 = \sigma_2 \ln S_1 - \sigma_1 \ln S_2$$

---

[23] This idea was suggested by J. Hull and A. White, "Valuing Derivative Securities Using the Explicit Finite Difference Method," *Journal of Financial and Quantitative Analysis*, 25 (1990), 87–100.

These variables follow the processes

$$dx_1 = [\sigma_2(r - q_1 - \sigma_1^2/2) + \sigma_1(r - q_2 - \sigma_2^2/2)] \, dt + \sigma_1\sigma_2\sqrt{2(1 + \rho)} \, dz_A$$

$$dx_2 = [\sigma_2(r - q_1 - \sigma_1^2/2) - \sigma_1(r - q_2 - \sigma_2^2/2)] \, dt + \sigma_1\sigma_2\sqrt{2(1 - \rho)} \, dz_B$$

where $dz_A$ and $dz_B$ are uncorrelated Wiener processes.

The variables $x_1$ and $x_2$ can be modeled using two separate binomial trees. In time $\delta t$, $x_i$ has a probability $p_i$ of increasing by $h_i$ and a probability $1 - p_i$ of decreasing by $h_i$. The variables $h_i$ and $p_i$ are chosen so that the tree gives correct values for the first two moments of the distribution of $x_1$ and $x_2$. Because they are uncorrelated, the two trees can be combined into a single three-dimensional tree, as already described.

At each node of the tree, $S_1$ and $S_2$ can be calculated from $x_1$ and $x_2$ using the inverse relationships

$$S_1 = \exp\left(\frac{x_1 + x_2}{2\sigma_2}\right) \quad \text{and} \quad S_2 = \exp\left(\frac{x_1 - x_2}{2\sigma_1}\right)$$

The procedure for rolling back through a three-dimensional tree to value a derivative is analogous to that for a two-dimensional tree.

### Using a Nonrectangular Tree

Rubinstein has suggested a way of building a three-dimensional tree for two correlated stock prices by using a nonrectangular arrangement of the nodes.[24] From a node $(S_1, S_2)$ where the first stock price is $S_1$ and the second stock price is $S_2$, we have a 0.25 chance of moving to each of the following:

$$(S_1u_1, S_2A), \quad (S_1u_1, S_2B), \quad (S_1d_1, S_2C), \quad (S_2d_1, S_2D)$$

where

$$u_1 = \exp[(r - q_1 - \sigma_1^2/2)\,\delta t + \sigma_1\sqrt{\delta t}]$$

$$d_1 = \exp[(r - q_1 - \sigma_1^2/2)\,\delta t - \sigma_1\sqrt{\delta t}]$$

$$A = \exp[(r - q_2 - \sigma_2^2/2)\,\delta t + \sigma_2\sqrt{\delta t}\,(\rho + \sqrt{1 - \rho^2}\,)]$$

$$B = \exp[(r - q_2 - \sigma_2^2/2)\,\delta t + \sigma_2\sqrt{\delta t}\,(\rho - \sqrt{1 - \rho^2}\,)]$$

$$C = \exp[(r - q_2 - \sigma_2^2/2)\,\delta t - \sigma_2\sqrt{\delta t}\,(\rho - \sqrt{1 - \rho^2}\,)]$$

$$D = \exp[(r - q_2 - \sigma_2^2/2)\,\delta t - \sigma_2\sqrt{\delta t}\,(\rho + \sqrt{1 - \rho^2}\,)]$$

When the correlation is zero, this method is equivalent to constructing separate trees for $S_1$ and $S_2$ using the alternative binomial tree construction method in Section 18.5.

### Adjusting the Probabilities

A third approach to building a three-dimensional tree for $S_1$ and $S_2$ involves first assuming no correlation and then adjusting the probabilities at each node to reflect the correlation.[25] We use the

---

[24] See M. Rubinstein, "Return to Oz," *RISK*, November 1994, pp. 67–70.

[25] This approach was suggested in the context of interest rate trees by J. Hull and A. White, "Numerical Procedures for Implementing Term Structure Models II: Two-Factor Models," *Journal of Derivatives*, Winter 1994, 37–48.

alternative binomial tree construction method for each of $S_1$ and $S_2$ in Section 18.5. This method has the property that all probabilities are 0.5. When the two binomial trees are combined on the assumption that there is no correlation, the probabilities are as follows:

| | $S_1$-move | |
|---|---|---|
| $S_2$-move | Down | Up |
| Up | 0.25 | 0.25 |
| Down | 0.25 | 0.25 |

When we adjust these probabilities to reflect the correlation, they become:

| | $S_1$-move | |
|---|---|---|
| $S_2$-move | Down | Up |
| Up | $0.25(1-\rho)$ | $0.25(1+\rho)$ |
| Down | $0.25(1+\rho)$ | $0.25(1-\rho)$ |

## 20.9 MONTE CARLO SIMULATION AND AMERICAN OPTIONS

Monte Carlo simulation is well suited to valuing path-dependent options and options where there are many stochastic variables. Trees and finite difference methods are well suited to valuing American-style options. What happens if an option is both path dependent and American? What happens if an American option depends on several stochastic variables? In Section 20.5 we explained a way in which the binomial tree approach can be modified to value path-dependent options in some situations. A number of researchers have adopted a different approach by searching for a way in which Monte Carlo simulation can be used to value American-style options.[26] Here we explain two alternative approaches ways of proceeding.

### The Least-Squares Approach

In order to value an American-style option, it is necessary to choose between exercising and continuing at each early exercise point. The value of exercising is normally easy to determine. A number of researchers including Longstaff and Schwartz provide a way of determining the value of continuing when Monte Carlo simulation is used.[27] Their approach involves using a least-squares analysis to determine the best-fit relationship between the value of continuing and the values of relevant variables at each time an early exercise decision has to be made. The approach is best illustrated with a numerical example. We use the one in the Longstaff–Schwartz paper.

Consider a three-year American put option on a non-dividend-paying stock that can be exercised

---

[26] Tilley was the first researcher to publish a solution to the problem. See J. A. Tilley, "Valuing American Options in a Path Simulation Model," *Transactions of the Society of Actuaries*, 45 (1993), 83–104.

[27] See F. A. Longstaff and E. S. Schwartz, "Valuing American Options by Simulation: A Simple Least-Squares Approach," *Review of Financial Studies*, 14, no. 1 (Spring 2001), 113–47.

**Table 20.1**   Sample paths for put option example

| Path | $t = 0$ | $t = 1$ | $t = 2$ | $t = 3$ |
|------|---------|---------|---------|---------|
| 1 | 1.00 | 1.09 | 1.08 | 1.34 |
| 2 | 1.00 | 1.16 | 1.26 | 1.54 |
| 3 | 1.00 | 1.22 | 1.07 | 1.03 |
| 4 | 1.00 | 0.93 | 0.97 | 0.92 |
| 5 | 1.00 | 1.11 | 1.56 | 1.52 |
| 6 | 1.00 | 0.76 | 0.77 | 0.90 |
| 7 | 1.00 | 0.92 | 0.84 | 1.01 |
| 8 | 1.00 | 0.88 | 1.22 | 1.34 |

at the end of year 1, the end of year 2, and the end of year 3. The risk-free rate is 6% per annum (continuously compounded). The current stock price is 1.00 and the strike price is 1.10. Assume that we sample the eight paths for the stock price shown in Table 20.1. (This example is for illustration only; in practice many more paths would be sampled.) If the option can be exercised only at the three-year point, it provides a cash flow equal to its intrinsic value at that point. This is shown in the last column of Table 20.2.

If the put option is in the money at the two-year point, the option holder must decide whether to exercise. From Table 20.1 we see that the option is in the money at the two-year point for paths 1, 3, 4, 6, and 7. For these paths we assume the approximate relationship

$$V = a + bS + cS^2$$

where $S$ is the stock price at the two-year point and $V$ is the value of continuing, discounted back to the two-year point. Our five observations on $S$ are: 1.08, 1.07, 0.97, 0.77 and 0.84. From Table 20.2 the corresponding values for $V$ are: $0.00e^{-0.06 \times 1}$, $0.07e^{-0.06 \times 1}$, $0.18e^{-0.06 \times 1}$, $0.20e^{-0.06 \times 1}$, and $0.09e^{-0.06 \times 1}$. We use this data to calculate the values of $a$, $b$, and $c$ that minimize

$$\sum_{i=1}^{5}(V_i - a - bS_i - cS_i^2)^2$$

**Table 20.2**   Cash flows if exercise only at the three-year point

| Path | $t = 1$ | $t = 2$ | $t = 3$ |
|------|---------|---------|---------|
| 1 | 0.00 | 0.00 | 0.00 |
| 2 | 0.00 | 0.00 | 0.00 |
| 3 | 0.00 | 0.00 | 0.07 |
| 4 | 0.00 | 0.00 | 0.18 |
| 5 | 0.00 | 0.00 | 0.00 |
| 6 | 0.00 | 0.00 | 0.20 |
| 7 | 0.00 | 0.00 | 0.09 |
| 8 | 0.00 | 0.00 | 0.00 |

**Table 20.3** Cash flows if exercise only possible at two- and three-year point

| Path | $t = 1$ | $t = 2$ | $t = 3$ |
|------|---------|---------|---------|
| 1 | 0.00 | 0.00 | 0.00 |
| 2 | 0.00 | 0.00 | 0.00 |
| 3 | 0.00 | 0.00 | 0.07 |
| 4 | 0.00 | 0.13 | 0.00 |
| 5 | 0.00 | 0.00 | 0.00 |
| 6 | 0.00 | 0.33 | 0.00 |
| 7 | 0.00 | 0.26 | 0.00 |
| 8 | 0.00 | 0.00 | 0.00 |

where $S_i$ and $V_i$ are the $i$th observation on $S$ and $V$, respectively. It turns out that $a = -1.070$, $b = 2.983$, and $c = -1.813$, so that the best-fit relationship is

$$V = -1.070 + 2.983S - 1.813S^2$$

This gives the value at the two-year point of continuing for paths 1, 3, 4, 6, and 7 of 0.0369, 0.0461, 0.1176, 0.1520, and 0.1565, respectively. From Table 20.1 the value of exercising is 0.02, 0.03, 0.13, 0.33, and 0.26. This means that we should exercise at the two-year point for paths 4, 6, and 7. Table 20.3 summarizes the cash flow for the eight paths assuming exercise at either the two-year point or the three-year point.

We next consider the paths that are in the money at the one-year point. These are paths 1, 4, 6, 7, and 8. From Table 20.1 the values of $S$ for the paths are 1.09, 0.93, 0.76, 0.92, and 0.88, respectively. From Table 20.3 the corresponding values of $V$ are $0.00e^{-0.06\times1}$, $0.13e^{-0.06\times1}$, $0.33e^{-0.06\times1}$, $0.26e^{-0.06\times1}$, and $0.00e^{-0.06\times1}$, respectively. The least-squares relationship is

$$V = 2.038 - 3.335S + 1.356S^2$$

This gives the value of continuing at the one-year point for paths 1, 4, 6, 7, and 8 as 0.0139, 0.1092, 0.2866, 0.1175, and 0.1533, respectively. From Table 20.1 the value of exercising is 0.01, 0.17, 0.34, 0.18, and 0.22. This means that we should exercise at the one-year point for paths 4, 6, 7, and 8.

**Table 20.4** Cash flows from option

| Path | $t = 1$ | $t = 2$ | $t = 3$ |
|------|---------|---------|---------|
| 1 | 0.00 | 0.00 | 0.00 |
| 2 | 0.00 | 0.00 | 0.00 |
| 3 | 0.00 | 0.00 | 0.07 |
| 4 | 0.17 | 0.00 | 0.00 |
| 5 | 0.00 | 0.00 | 0.00 |
| 6 | 0.34 | 0.00 | 0.00 |
| 7 | 0.18 | 0.00 | 0.00 |
| 8 | 0.22 | 0.00 | 0.00 |

Table 20.4 summarizes the cash flows assuming that early exercise is possible at all three times. The value of the option is determined by discounting each cash flow back to time zero at the risk-free rate and calculating the mean of the results. It is

$$\tfrac{1}{8}(0.07e^{-0.06\times3} + 0.17e^{-0.06\times1} + 0.34e^{-0.06\times1} + 0.18e^{-0.06\times1} + 0.22e^{-0.06\times1}) = 0.1144$$

Because this is greater than 0.10, it is not optimal to exercise the option immediately.

This method can be extended in a number of ways. If the option can be exercised at any time, we can approximate its value by considering a large number of exercise points (just as a binomial tree does). The relationship between $V$ and $S$ can be assumed to be more complicated. For example, we could assume that $V$ is a cubic rather than a quadratic function of $S$. When the early exercise decision depends on several state variables, we proceed as we did in the example just considered. A functional form for the relationship between $V$ and the variables is assumed and the parameters are estimated using the least-squares approach.

### The Exercise Boundary Parametrization Approach

A number of researchers, such as Andersen, have proposed an alternative approach in which the early exercise boundary is parametrized and the optimal values of the parameters are determined iteratively by starting at the end of the life of the option and working backward.[28] To illustrate the approach, we continue with the put option example and assume that the eight paths shown in Table 20.1 have been sampled. In this case the early exercise boundary at time $t$ can be parametrized by a critical value, $S^*(t)$, of $S$. If the asset price at time $t$ is below $S^*(t)$, we exercise at time $t$; if is above $S^*(t)$, we do not exercise at time $t$. The value of $S^*(3)$ is 1.10. If the stock price is above 1.10 when $t = 3$ (the end of the option's life), we do not exercise; if it is below 1.10, we exercise. We now consider the determination of $S^*(2)$.

Suppose that we choose a value of $S^*(2)$ less than 0.77. The option is not exercised at the two-year point for any of the paths. The value of the option at the two-year point for the eight paths is then 0.00, 0.00, $0.07e^{-0.06\times1}$, $0.18e^{-0.06\times1}$, 0.00, $0.20e^{-0.06\times1}$, $0.09e^{-0.06\times1}$, and 0.00, respectively. The average of these is 0.0636. Suppose next that $S^*(2) = 0.77$. The value of the option at the two-year point for the eight paths is then 0.00, 0.00, $0.07e^{-0.06\times1}$, $0.18e^{-0.06\times1}$, 0.00, 0.33, $0.09e^{-0.06\times1}$, and 0.00, respectively. The average of these is 0.0813. Similarly when $S^*(2)$ equals 0.84, 0.97, 1.07, and 1.08, the average value of the option at the two-year point is 0.1032, 0.0982, 0.0938, and 0.0963, respectively. This analysis shows that the optimal value of $S^*(2)$ (i.e., the one that maximizes the average value of the option) is 0.84. (More precisely, it is optimal to choose $0.84 \leqslant S^*(2) < 0.97$.) When we choose this optimal value for $S^*(2)$, the value of the option at the two-year point for the eight paths is 0.00, 0.00, 0.0659, 0.1695, 0.00, 0.33, 0.26, and 0.00, respectively. The average value is 0.1032.

We now move on to calculate $S^*(1)$. If $S^*(1) < 0.76$, the option is not exercised at the one-year point for any of the paths and the value at the option at the one-year point is $0.1032e^{-0.06\times1} = 0.0972$. If $S^*(1) = 0.76$, the value of the option for each of the eight paths at the one-year point is 0.00, 0.00, $0.0659e^{-0.06\times1}$, $0.1695e^{-0.06\times1}$, 0.0, 0.34, $0.26e^{-0.06\times1}$, and 0.00, respectively. The average value of the option is 0.1008. Similarly, when $S^*(1)$ equals 0.88, 0.92, 0.93, and 1.09, the average value of the option is 0.1283, 0.1202, 0.1215, and 0.1228, respectively. The analysis therefore shows that the optimal value of $S^*(1)$ is 0.88. (More precisely, it is optimal

---

[28] See L. Andersen, "A Simple Approach to the Pricing of Bermudan Swaptions in the Multifactor LIBOR Market Model," *Journal of Computational Finance*, 3, no. 2 (Winter 2000), 1–32.

to choose $0.88 \leqslant S^*(1) < 0.92$.) The value of the option at time zero with no early exercise is $0.1283e^{-0.06 \times 1} = 0.1208$. This is greater than the value of $0.10$ obtained by exercising at time zero.

In practice tens of thousands of simulations are carried out to determine the early exercise boundary in the way we have described. Once we have obtained the early exercise boundary, we discard the paths for the variables and carry out a new Monte Carlo simulation using the early exercise boundary to value the option.

Our American put option example is simple in that we know the early exercise boundary at a time can be defined entirely in terms of the value of the stock price at that time. In more complicated situations it is necessary to make assumptions about how the early exercise boundary should be parametrized.

### *Upper Bounds*

The two approaches we have outlined tend to underprice American-style options because they assume a suboptimal early exercise boundary. This has led Andersen and Broadie to propose a procedure that provides an upper bound to the price.[29] This procedure can be used in conjunction with any algorithm that generates a lower bound and pinpoints the true value of an American-style option more precisely than the algorithm taken on its own.

# SUMMARY

A number of models have been developed to fit the volatility smiles that are observed in practice. The constant elasticity of variance model leads to a volatility smile similar to that observed for equity options. The jump diffusion model leads to a volatility smile similar to that observed for currency options. Stochastic volatility models are more flexible in that they can lead to either the type of volatility smile observed for equity options or the type of volatility smile observed for currency options. The implied volatility function model provides even more flexibility that this. It is designed to provide an exact fit to any pattern of European option prices observed in the market.

The natural technique to use for valuing path-dependent options is Monte Carlo simulation. This has the disadvantage that it is fairly slow and unable to handle American-style derivatives easily. Luckily, trees can be used to value many types of path-dependent derivatives. The approach is to choose representative values for the underlying path function at each node of the tree and calculate the value of the derivative for each alternative value of the path function as we roll back through the tree. There is a trick for valuing lookback options using trees. Instead of valuing the option in dollars, we use the asset price as our unit of measurement.

Trees can be used to value many types of barrier options, but the convergence of the option value to the correct value as the number of time steps is increased tends to be slow. One approach for improving convergence is to arrange the geometry of the tree so that nodes always lie on the barriers. Another is to use an interpolation scheme to adjust for the fact that the barrier being assumed by the tree is different from the true barrier. A third is to design the tree so that it provides a finer representation of movements in the underlying asset price near the barrier.

One way of valuing options dependent on the prices of two correlated assets is to apply a transformation to the asset price to create two new uncorrelated variables. These two variables are

---

[29] See L. Andersen and M. Broadie, "A Primal-Dual Simulation Algorithm for Pricing Multi-Dimensional American Options," Working Paper, Columbia University, 2001.

each modeled with trees and the trees are then combined to form a single three-dimensional tree. At each node of the tree, the inverse of the transformation gives the asset prices. A second approach is to arrange the positions of nodes on the three-dimensional tree to reflect the correlation. A third approach is to start with a tree that assumes no correlation between the variables and then adjust the probabilities on the tree to reflect the correlation.

Monte Carlo simulation is not naturally suited to valuing American-style options, but there are two ways it can be adapted to handle them. The first involves using a least-squares analysis to relate the value of continuing (i.e., not exercising) to the values of relevant variables. The second involves parametrizing the early exercise boundary and determining it iteratively by working back from the end of the life of the option to the beginning.

## SUGGESTIONS FOR FURTHER READING

Andersen, L., "A simple Approach to the Pricing of Bermudan Swaptions in the Multifactor LIBOR Market Model," *Journal of Computational Finance*, 3, no. 2 (Winter 2000), 1–32.

Andersen, L. B. G., and R. Brotherton-Ratcliffe, "The Equity Option Volatility Smile: An Implicit Finite Difference Approach," *Journal of Computational Finance*, 1, no. 2 (Winter 1997/98), 3–37.

Black, F., "How to Use the Holes in Black–Scholes," *RISK*, March 1988.

Boyle, P. P., J. Evnine, and S. Gibbs, "Numerical Evaluation of Multivariate Contingent Claims," *Review of Financial Studies*, 2, no. 2 (1989), 241–50.

Boyle, P. P., and S. H. Lau, "Bumping Up Against the Barrier with the Binomial Method," *Journal of Derivatives*, 1, no. 4 (Summer 1994), 6–14.

Conze, A., and R. Viswanathan, "Path Dependent Options: The Case of Lookback Options," *Journal of Finance*, 46 (1991), 1893–1907.

Cox, J. C., and S. A. Ross, "The Valuation of Options for Alternative Stochastic Processes," *Journal of Financial Economics*, 3 (March 1976), 145–66.

Derman, E., and I. Kani, "Riding on a Smile," *RISK*, February 1994, pp. 32–39.

Duan, J.-C., "The GARCH Option Pricing Model," *Mathematical Finance*, 5 (1995), 13–32.

Duan, J.-C. "Cracking the Smile," *RISK*, December 1996, pp. 55–59.

Heston, S. L., "A Closed Form Solution for Options with Stochastic Volatility with Applications to Bonds and Currency Options," *Review of Financial Studies*, 6, no. 2 (1993), 327–43.

Dupire, B., "Pricing with a Smile," *RISK*, February 1994, pp. 18–20.

Figlewski, S., and B. Gao, "The Adaptive Mesh Model: A New Approach to Efficient Option Pricing," *Journal of Financial Economics*, 53 (1999), 313–51.

Hull, J., and A. White, "Efficient Procedures for Valuing European and American Path-Dependent Options," *Journal of Derivatives*, 1, no. 1 (Fall 1993), 21–31.

Hull, J. C., and A. White, "Finding the Keys," *RISK*, September 1993, 109–112.

Hull J. C., and A. White, "The Pricing of Options on Assets with Stochastic Volatilities," *Journal of Finance*, 42 (June 1987), 281–300.

Hull, J. C., and A. White, "An Analysis of the Bias in Option Pricing Caused by a Stochastic Volatility," *Advances in Futures and Options Research*, 3 (1988), 27–61.

Hull, J. C., and W. Suo, "A Methodology for the Assessment of Model Risk and its Application to the Implied Volatility Function Model," *Journal of Financial and Quantitative Analysis*, 37, no. 2 (June 2002).

Longstaff, F. A., and E. S. Schwartz, "Valuing American Options by Simulation: A Simple Least-Squares Approach," *Review of Financial Studies*, 14, no. 1 (Spring 2001), 113–47.

Merton, R. C., "Option Pricing When Underlying Stock Returns Are Discontinuous," *Journal of Financial Economics*, 3 (March 1976), 125–44.

Ritchken, P., and R. Trevor, "Pricing Options Under Generalized GARCH and Stochastic Volatility Processes," *Journal of Finance*, 54, no. 1 (February 1999), 377–402.

Rubinstein, M., "Implied Binomial Trees," *Journal of Finance*, 49, no. 3 (July 1994), 771–818.

Rubinstein, M., "Return to Oz," *RISK*, November 1994, pp. 67–70.

Schroder, M., "Computing the constant Elasticity of Variance Option Pricing Formula," *Journal of Finance*, 44, no. 1 (1989), 211–18.

Stutzer, M., "A Simple Nonparametric Approach to Derivative Security Valuation," *Journal of Finance*, 51 (December 1996), 1633–52.

Tilley, J. A., "Valuing American Options in a Path Simulation Model," *Transactions of the Society of Actuaries*, 45 (1993), 83–104.

## QUESTIONS AND PROBLEMS
## (ANSWERS IN SOLUTIONS MANUAL)

20.1. Confirm that the CEV model formulas satisfy put–call parity.

20.2. Explain how you would use Monte Carlo simulation to sample paths for the asset price when Merton's jump diffusion model is used.

20.3. Confirm that Merton's jump diffusion model satisfies put–call parity when the jump size is lognormal.

20.4. Suppose that the volatility of an asset will be 20% from month 0 to month 6, 22% from month 6 to month 12, and 24% from month 12 to month 24. What volatility should be used in Black–Scholes to value a two-year option?

20.5. Consider the case of Merton's jump diffusion model where jumps always reduce the asset price to zero. Assume that the average number of jumps per year is $\lambda$. Show that the price of a European call option is the same as in a world with no jumps except that the risk-free rate is $r + \lambda$ rather than $r$. Does the possibility of jumps increase or reduce the value of the call option in this case? (*Hint*: Value the option assuming no jumps and assuming one or more jumps. The probability of no jumps in time $T$ is $e^{-\lambda T}$).

20.6. At time zero the price of a non-dividend-paying stock is $S_0$. Suppose that the time interval between 0 and $T$ is divided into two subintervals of length $t_1$ and $t_2$. During the first subinterval, the risk-free interest rate and volatility are $r_1$ and $\sigma_1$, respectively. During the second subinterval, they are $r_2$ and $\sigma_2$, respectively. Assume that the world is risk neutral.
   a. Use the results in Chapter 11 to determine the stock price distribution at time $T$ in terms of $r_1$, $r_2$, $\sigma_1$, $\sigma_2$, $t_1$, $t_2$, and $S_0$.
   b. Suppose that $\bar{r}$ is the average interest rate between time zero and $T$ and that $\bar{V}$ is the average variance rate between times zero and $T$. What is the stock price distribution as a function of $T$ in terms of $\bar{r}$, $\bar{V}$, $T$, and $S_0$?

    c. What are the results corresponding to (a) and (b) when there are three subintervals with different interest rates and volatilities?

    d. Show that if the risk-free rate, $r$, and the volatility, $\sigma$, are known functions of time then the stock price distribution at time $T$ in a risk-neutral world is

$$\ln S_T \sim \phi[\ln S_0 + (\bar{r} - \tfrac{1}{2}\bar{V})T, \ \sqrt{VT}]$$

where $\bar{r}$ is the average value of $r$, $\bar{V}$ is equal to the average value of $\sigma^2$, and $S_0$ is the stock price today.

20.7. Write down the equations for simulating the path followed by the asset price in the stochastic volatility model in equation (20.2) and (20.3).

20.8. "The IVF model does not necessarily get the evolution of the volatility surface correct." Explain this statement.

20.9. "When interest rates are constant the IVF model correctly values any derivative whose payoff depends on the value of the underlying asset at only one time." Explain this statement.

20.10. Use a three-time-step tree to value an American lookback call option on a currency when the initial exchange rate is 1.6, the domestic risk-free rate is 5% per annum, the foreign risk-free interest rate is 8% per annum, the exchange rate volatility is 15%, and the time to maturity is 18 months. Use the approach in Section 20.5.

20.11. Repeat Problem 20.10 using the approach in Section 20.6.

20.12. Use a three-time-step tree to value an American put option on the geometric average of the price of a non-dividend-paying stock when the stock price is $40, the strike price is $40, the risk-free interest rate is 10% per annum, the volatility is 35% per annum, and the time to maturity is three months. The geometric average is measured from today until the option matures.

20.13. Can the approach for valuing path-dependent options in Section 20.5 be used for a two-year American-style option that provides a payoff equal to $\max(S_{\text{ave}} - K, 0)$, where $S_{\text{ave}}$ is the average asset price over the three months preceding exercise. Explain your answer.

20.14. Verify that the 6.492 number in Figure 20.2 is correct.

20.15. Examine the early exercise policy for the eight paths considered in the example in Section 20.9. What is the different between the early exercise policy given by the least-squares approach and the exercise boundary parametrization approach? Which gives a higher option price for the paths sampled?

20.16. Consider a European put option on a non-dividend-paying stock when the stock price is $100, the strike price is $110, the risk-free rate is 5% per annum, and the time to maturity is one year. Suppose that the average variance rate during the life of an option has a 0.20 probability of being 0.06, a 0.5 probability of being 0.09, and a 0.3 probability of being 0.12. The volatility is uncorrelated with the stock price. Estimate the value of the option. Use DerivaGem.

# ASSIGNMENT QUESTIONS

20.17. A new European-style lookback call option on a stock index has a maturity of nine months. The current level of the index is 400, the risk-free rate is 6% per annum, the dividend yield on the index is 4% per annum, and the volatility of the index is 20%. Use the approach in Section 20.6 to value the option and compare your answer to the result given by DerivaGem using the analytic valuation formula.

20.18. Suppose that the volatilities used to price a six-month currency option are as in Table 15.2. Assume that the domestic and foreign risk-free rates are 5% per annum and the current exchange rate is 1.00. Consider a bull spread that consists of a long position in a six-month call option with strike price 1.05 and a short position in a six-month call option with a strike price 1.10.

    a. What is the value of the option?

    b. What single volatility if used for both options gives the correct value of the bull spread? (Use the DerivaGem Application Builder in conjunction with Goal Seek or Solver.)

    c. Does your answer support the assertion at the beginning of the chapter that the correct volatility to use when pricing exotic options can be counterintuitive?

    d. Does the IVF model give the correct price for the bull spread?

20.19. Repeat the analysis in Section 20.9 for the put option example on the assumption that the strike price is 1.13. Use both the least-squares approach and the exercise boundary parametrization approach.

20.20. Consider the situation in Merton's jump diffusion model where the underlying asset is a non-dividend-paying stock. The average frequency of jumps is one per year. The average percentage jump size is 2% and the standard deviation of the logarithm of the percentage jump size is 20%. The stock price is 100, the risk-free rate is 5%, the volatility, $\sigma$, provided by the diffusion part of the process is 15%, and the time to maturity is six months. Use the DerivaGem Application Builder to calculate an implied volatility when the strike price is 80, 90, 100, 110, and 120. What does the volatility smile of skew that you obtain imply about the probability distribution of the stock price?

# CHAPTER 21

# MARTINGALES AND MEASURES

Up to now we have assumed that interest rates are constant when valuing options. In this chapter we relax this assumption in preparation for valuing interest rate derivatives in Chapters 22 to 24.

The risk-neutral valuation principle we have used up to now states that a derivative can be valued by (a) calculating the expected payoff on the assumption that the expected return from the underlying asset equals the risk-free interest rate and (b) discounting the expected payoff at the risk-free interest rate. When interest rates are constant, risk-neutral valuation provides a well-defined and unambiguous valuation tool. When interest rates are stochastic, it is less clear-cut. What does it mean to assume that the expected return on the underlying asset equals the risk-free rate? Does it mean (a) that each day the expected return is the one-day risk-free rate, or (b) that each year the expected return is the one-year risk-free rate, or (c) that over a five-year period the expected return is the five-year rate at the beginning of the period? What does it mean to discount expected payoffs at the risk-free rate? Can we, for example, discount an expected payoff realized in year 5 at today's five-year risk-free rate?

In this chapter we explain the theoretical underpinnings of risk-neutral valuation when interest rates are stochastic and show that there are many different risk-neutral worlds that can be assumed in any given situation. We first define a parameter known as the *market price of risk* and show that the excess return over the risk-free interest rate earned by any derivative in a short period of time is linearly related to the market prices of risk of the underlying stochastic variables. What we will refer to as the *traditional risk-neutral world* assumes that all market prices of risk are zero, but we will find that other assumptions about the market price of risk are useful in some situations.

*Martingales* and *measures* are critical to a full understanding of risk-neutral valuation. A martingale is a zero-drift stochastic process. A measure is the units in which we value security prices. A key result in this chapter will be the *equivalent martingale measure result*. This states that if we use the price of a traded security as the unit of measurement then there is some market price of risk for which all security prices follow martingales.

In this chapter we apply the equivalent martingale measure result to stock options when interest rates are stochastic and to the valuation of options to exchange one asset for another. We also discuss quantos, which are derivatives where an interest rate defined in one currency is applied to a principal amount in another currency. In Chapter 22 we use the result to understand the standard market models for valuing interest rate derivatives and in Chapter 24 it will assist us in developing the LIBOR market model.

## 21.1 THE MARKET PRICE OF RISK

We start by considering the properties of derivatives dependent on the value of a single variable, $\theta$. We will assume that the process followed by $\theta$ is

$$\frac{d\theta}{\theta} = m\,dt + s\,dz \tag{21.1}$$

where $dz$ is a Wiener process.

The parameters $m$ and $s$ are the expected growth rate in $\theta$ and the volatility of $\theta$, respectively. We assume that they depend only on $\theta$ and time $t$. The variable $\theta$ need not be the price of an investment asset. It could be something as far removed from financial markets as the temperature in the center of New Orleans.

Suppose that $f_1$ and $f_2$ are the prices of two derivatives dependent only on $\theta$ and $t$. These can be options or other instruments that provide a payoff equal to some function of $\theta$ at some future time. We assume that during the time period under consideration $f_1$ and $f_2$ provide no income.[1]

Suppose that the processes followed by $f_1$ and $f_2$ are

$$\frac{df_1}{f_1} = \mu_1\,dt + \sigma_1\,dz$$

and

$$\frac{df_2}{f_2} = \mu_2\,dt + \sigma_2\,dz$$

where $\mu_1$, $\mu_2$, $\sigma_1$, and $\sigma_2$ are functions of $\theta$ and $t$. The "$dz$" is the same Wiener process as in equation (21.1) because it is the only source of the uncertainty in the prices of $f_1$ and $f_2$. The discrete versions of the processes are

$$\delta f_1 = \mu_1 f_1\,\delta t + \sigma_1 f_1\,\delta z \tag{21.2}$$

$$\delta f_2 = \mu_2 f_2\,\delta t + \sigma_2 f_2\,\delta z \tag{21.3}$$

We can eliminate the $\delta z$ by forming an instantaneously riskless portfolio consisting of $\sigma_2 f_2$ of the first derivative and $-\sigma_1 f_1$ of the second derivative. If $\Pi$ is the value of the portfolio, then

$$\Pi = (\sigma_2 f_2) f_1 - (\sigma_1 f_1) f_2 \tag{21.4}$$

and

$$\delta\Pi = \sigma_2 f_2\,\delta f_1 - \sigma_1 f_1\,\delta f_2$$

Substituting from equations (21.2) and (21.3), we obtain

$$\delta\Pi = (\mu_1 \sigma_2 f_1 f_2 - \mu_2 \sigma_1 f_1 f_2)\,\delta t \tag{21.5}$$

Because the portfolio is instantaneously riskless, it must earn the risk-free rate. Hence,

$$\delta\Pi = r\Pi\,\delta t$$

Substituting into this equation from equations (21.4) and (21.5) gives

$$\mu_1 \sigma_2 - \mu_2 \sigma_1 = r\sigma_2 - r\sigma_1$$

---

[1] The analysis can be extended to derivatives that provide income (see Problem 21.7).

or

$$\frac{\mu_1 - r}{\sigma_1} = \frac{\mu_2 - r}{\sigma_2} \tag{21.6}$$

Define $\lambda$ as the value of each side in equation (21.6), so that

$$\frac{\mu_1 - r}{\sigma_1} = \frac{\mu_2 - r}{\sigma_2} = \lambda$$

Dropping subscripts, we have shown that if $f$ is the price of a derivative dependent only on $\theta$ and $t$ with

$$\frac{df}{f} = \mu \, dt + \sigma \, dz \tag{21.7}$$

then

$$\frac{\mu - r}{\sigma} = \lambda \tag{21.8}$$

The parameter $\lambda$ is known as the *market price of risk* of $\theta$. It can be dependent on both $\theta$ and $t$, but it is not dependent on the nature of the derivative $f$. At any given time, $(\mu - r)/\sigma$ must be the same for all derivatives that are dependent only on $\theta$ and $t$.

It is worth noting that $\sigma$, which we are referring to as the volatility of $f$, is defined as the coefficient of $dz$ in equation (21.7). It can be either positive or negative. If the volatility, $s$, of $\theta$ is positive and $f$ is positively related to $\theta$ (so that $\partial f / \partial \theta$ is positive), then $\sigma$ is positive. But if $f$ is negatively related to $\theta$, then $\sigma$ is negative. The volatility of $f$, as it is traditionally defined, is $|\sigma|$.

The market price of risk of $\theta$ measures the tradeoffs between risk and return that are made for securities dependent on $\theta$. Equation (21.8) can be written

$$\mu - r = \lambda \sigma \tag{21.9}$$

For an intuitive understanding of this equation, we note that the variable $\sigma$ can be loosely interpreted as the quantity of $\theta$-risk present in $f$. On the right-hand side of the equation, therefore, we are multiplying the quantity of $\theta$-risk by the price of $\theta$-risk. The left-hand side is the expected return in excess of the risk-free interest rate that is required to compensate for this risk. Equation (21.9) is analogous to the capital asset pricing model, which relates the expected excess return on a stock to its risk.

We will not be concerned with the measurement of the market price of risk in this chapter. This will be discussed in Chapter 28 in the context of the evaluation of real options.

In Chapter 3, we distinguished between investment assets and consumption assets. An investment asset is an asset that is bought or sold purely for investment purposes by a significant number of investors. It can be used as part of a trading strategy to set up a riskless portfolio. Consumption assets are held primarily for consumption and cannot be used in this way. If the variable $\theta$ is the price of an investment asset, it must be true that

$$\frac{m - r}{s} = \lambda$$

But if $\theta$ is the price of a consumption asset, this relationship is not, in general, true.

**Example 21.1** Consider a derivative whose price is positively related to the price of oil and depends on no other stochastic variables. Suppose that it provides an expected return of 12% per annum and has a volatility of 20% per annum. Assume that the risk-free interest rate is 8% per annum. It follows that the market price of risk of oil is

$$\frac{0.12 - 0.08}{0.2} = 0.2$$

Note that oil is a consumption asset rather than an investment asset. Therefore, its market price of risk cannot be calculated from equation (21.8) by setting $\mu$ equal to the expected return from an investment in oil and $\sigma$ equal to the volatility of oil prices.

**Example 21.2**  Consider two securities, both of which are positively dependent on the 90-day interest rate. Suppose that the first one has an expected return of 3% per annum and a volatility of 20% per annum, and the second one has a volatility of 30% per annum. Assume that the instantaneous risk-free rate of interest is 6% per annum. The market price of interest rate risk is, using the expected return and volatility for the first security,

$$\frac{0.03 - 0.06}{0.2} = -0.15$$

From a rearrangement of equation (21.9), the expected return from the second security is therefore

$$0.06 - 0.15 \times 0.3 = 0.015$$

or 1.5% per annum.

### Alternative Worlds

The process followed by derivative price $f$ is

$$df = \mu f \, dt + \sigma f \, dz$$

The value of $\mu$ depends on the risk preferences of investors. In a world where the market price of risk is zero, $\lambda$ equals zero. From equation (21.9), $\mu = r$, so that the process followed by $f$ is

$$df = rf \, dt + \sigma f \, dz$$

We will refer to this as the *traditional risk-neutral world.*

By making other assumptions about the market price of risk, we define other worlds that are internally consistent. In general, when the market price of risk is $\lambda$, equation (21.9) shows that

$$\mu = r + \lambda \sigma$$

so that

$$df = (r + \lambda \sigma) f \, dt + \sigma f \, dz \tag{21.10}$$

The market price of risk of a variable determines the growth rates of all securities dependent on the variable. As we move from one market price of risk to another, the expected growth rates of security prices change, but their volatilities remain the same. We illustrated this in Section 10.7. Choosing a particular market price of risk is also referred to as defining the *probability measure.* For some value of the market price of risk, we obtain the "real world" and the growth rates of security prices that are observed in practice.

## 21.2 SEVERAL STATE VARIABLES

Suppose that $n$ variables, $\theta_1, \theta_2, \ldots, \theta_n$, follow stochastic processes of the form

$$\frac{d\theta_i}{\theta_i} = m_i \, dt + s_i \, dz_i \tag{21.11}$$

for $i = 1, 2, \ldots, n$, where the $dz_i$ are Wiener processes. The parameters $m_i$ and $s_i$ are expected growth rates and volatilities and may be functions of the $\theta_i$ and time. Appendix 21A provides a version of Itô's lemma that covers functions of several variables. It shows that the process for the price, $f$, of a security that is dependent on the $\theta_i$ has the form

$$\frac{df}{f} = \mu \, dt + \sum_{i=1}^{n} \sigma_i \, dz_i \tag{21.12}$$

In this equation, $\mu$ is the expected return from the security and $\sigma_i \, dz_i$ is the component of the risk of this return attributable to $\theta_i$.

Appendix 21B shows that

$$\mu - r = \sum_{i=1}^{n} \lambda_i \sigma_i \tag{21.13}$$

where $\lambda_i$ is the market price of risk for $\theta_i$. This equation relates the expected excess return that investors require on the security to the $\lambda_i$ and $\sigma_i$. Equation (21.9) is the particular case of this equation when $n = 1$. The term $\lambda_i \sigma_i$ on the right-hand side measures the extent that the excess return required by investors on a security is affected by the dependence of the security on $\theta_i$. If $\lambda_i \sigma_i = 0$, there is no effect; if $\lambda_i \sigma_i > 0$, investors require a higher return to compensate them for the risk arising from $\theta_i$; if $\lambda_i \sigma_i < 0$, the dependence of the security on $\theta_i$ causes investors to require a lower return than would otherwise be the case. The $\lambda_i \sigma_i < 0$ situation occurs when the variable has the effect of reducing rather than increasing the risks in the portfolio of a typical investor.

> **Example 21.3** A stock price depends on three underlying variables: the price of oil, the price of gold, and the performance of a stock index. Suppose that the market prices of risk for these variables are 0.2, −0.1, and 0.4, respectively. Suppose also that the $\sigma_i$ factors in equation (21.12) corresponding to the three variables have been estimated as 0.05, 0.1, and 0.15, respectively. The excess return on the stock over the risk-free rate is
>
> $$0.2 \times 0.05 - 0.1 \times 0.1 + 0.4 \times 0.15 = 0.06$$
>
> or 6.0% per annum. If variables other than those considered affect the stock price, this result is still true provided that the market price of risk for each of these other variables is zero.

Equation (21.13) is closely related to arbitrage pricing theory, developed by Stephen Ross in 1976.[2] The continuous-time version of the capital asset pricing model (CAPM) can be regarded as a particular case of the equation. CAPM argues that an investor requires excess returns to compensate for any risk that is correlated to the risk in the return from the stock market, but requires no excess return for other risks. Risks that are correlated with the return from the stock

---

[2] See S. A. Ross, "The Arbitrage Theory of Capital Asset Pricing," *Journal of Economic Theory*, 13 (December 1976), 343–62.

market are referred to as *systematic*; other risks are referred to as *nonsystematic*. If CAPM is true, $\lambda_i$ is proportional to the correlation between changes in $\theta_i$ and the return from the market. When $\theta_i$ is uncorrelated with the return from the market, $\lambda_i$ is zero.

## 21.3  MARTINGALES

A martingale is a zero-drift stochastic process. A variable $\theta$ follows a martingale if its process has the form

$$d\theta = \sigma \, dz$$

where $dz$ is a Wiener process. The variable $\sigma$ may itself be stochastic. It can depend on $\theta$ and other stochastic variables.

A martingale has the convenient property that its expected value at any future time is equal to its value today. This means that

$$E(\theta_T) = \theta_0$$

where $\theta_0$ and $\theta_T$ denote the values of $\theta$ at times zero and $T$, respectively. To understand this result, we note that over a very small time interval the change in $\theta$ is normally distributed with zero mean. The expected change in $\theta$ over any very small time interval is therefore zero. The change in $\theta$ between time zero and time $T$ is the sum of its changes over many small time intervals. It follows that the expected change in $\theta$ between time zero and time $T$ must also be zero.

### The Equivalent Martingale Measure Result

Suppose that $f$ and $g$ are the prices of traded securities dependent on a single source of uncertainty. We assume that the securities provide no income during the time period under consideration.[3] We define

$$\phi = \frac{f}{g}$$

The variable $\phi$ is the relative price of $f$ with respect to $g$. It can be thought of as measuring the price of $f$ in units of $g$ rather than in dollars. The security price $g$ is referred to as the *numeraire*.

The *equivalent martingale measure* result shows that, when there are no arbitrage opportunities, $\phi$ is a martingale for some choice of the market price of risk. What is more, for a given numeraire security $g$, the same choice of the market price of risk makes $\phi$ a martingale for all securities $f$. This choice of the market price of risk is the volatility of $g$. In other words, when the market price of risk is set equal to the volatility of $g$, the ratio $f/g$ is a martingale for all security prices $f$.

To prove this result, we suppose that the volatilities of $f$ and $g$ are $\sigma_f$ and $\sigma_g$. From equation (21.10), in a world where the market price of risk is $\sigma_g$, we have

$$df = (r + \sigma_g \sigma_f) f \, dt + \sigma_f f \, dz$$

$$dg = (r + \sigma_g^2) g \, dt + \sigma_g g \, dz$$

---

[3] Problem 21.8 extends the analysis to situations where the securities provide income.

Using Itô's lemma gives

$$d\ln f = (r + \sigma_g\sigma_f - \sigma_f^2/2)\,dt + \sigma_f\,dz$$

$$d\ln g = (r + \sigma_g^2/2)\,dt + \sigma_g\,dz$$

so that

$$d(\ln f - \ln g) = (\sigma_g\sigma_f - \sigma_f^2/2 - \sigma_g^2/2)\,dt + (\sigma_f - \sigma_g)\,dz$$

or

$$d\left(\ln\frac{f}{g}\right) = -\frac{(\sigma_f - \sigma_g)^2}{2}\,dt + (\sigma_f - \sigma_g)\,dz$$

Using Itô's lemma to determine the process for $f/g$ from the process for $\ln(f/g)$, we obtain

$$d\left(\frac{f}{g}\right) = (\sigma_f - \sigma_g)\frac{f}{g}\,dz \tag{21.14}$$

showing that $f/g$ is a martingale.

This provides the required result. We refer to a world where the market price of risk is $\sigma_g$ as a world that is *forward risk neutral* with respect to $g$.

Because $f/g$ is a martingale in a world that is forward risk neutral with respect to $g$, it follows that

$$\frac{f_0}{g_0} = E_g\left(\frac{f_T}{g_T}\right)$$

or

$$f_0 = g_0 E_g\left(\frac{f_T}{g_T}\right) \tag{21.15}$$

where $E_g$ denotes the expected value in a world that is forward risk neutral with respect to $g$.

## 21.4 ALTERNATIVE CHOICES FOR THE NUMERAIRE

We now present a number of examples of the equivalent martingale measure result. Our first example shows that it is consistent with the traditional risk-neutral valuation result we have used up to now. The other examples prepare the way for the valuation of bond options, interest-rate caps, and swap options in Chapter 22.

### Money Market Account as the Numeraire

The dollar money market account is a security that is worth $1 at time zero and earns the instantaneous risk-free rate $r$ at any given time.[4] The variable $r$ may be stochastic. If we set $g$ equal to the money market account, it grows at rate $r$, so that

$$dg = rg\,dt \tag{21.16}$$

The drift of $g$ is stochastic, but the volatility of $g$ is zero. The world that is forward risk neutral with

---

[4] The money market account is the limit as $\delta t$ approaches zero of the following security. For the first short period of time of length $\delta t$, it is invested at the initial $\delta t$ period rate; at time $\delta t$, it is reinvested for a further period of time $\delta t$ at the new $\delta t$ period rate; at time $2\,\delta t$, it is again reinvested for a further period of time $\delta t$ at the new $\delta t$ period rate; and so on. The money market accounts in other currencies are defined analogously to the dollar money market account.

respect to $g$ is therefore a world where the market price of risk is zero. This is the world we defined earlier as the traditional risk-neutral world. It follows from equation (21.15) that

$$f_0 = g_0 \hat{E}\left(\frac{f_T}{g_T}\right) \tag{21.17}$$

where $\hat{E}$ denotes the expectation in the traditional risk-neutral world.

In this case, $g_0 = 1$ and

$$g_T = e^{\int_0^T r\,dt}$$

so that equation (21.17) reduces to

$$f_0 = \hat{E}\left(e^{-\int_0^T r\,dt} f_T\right) \tag{21.18}$$

or

$$f_0 = \hat{E}(e^{-\bar{r}T} f_T) \tag{21.19}$$

This equation shows that one way of valuing an interest rate derivative is to simulate the short-term interest rate $r$ in the traditional risk-neutral world. On each trial we calculate the expected payoff and discount at the average value of the short rate on the sampled path.

When the short-term interest rate $r$ is assumed to be constant, equation (21.19) reduces to

$$f_0 = e^{-rT} \hat{E}(f_T)$$

or the risk-neutral valuation relationship we used in earlier chapters.

### Zero-Coupon Bond Price as the Numeraire

Define $P(t, T)$ as the price at time $t$ of a zero-coupon bond that pays off \$1 at time $T$. We now explore the implications of setting $g$ equal to $P(t, T)$. We use $E_T$ to denote the expectation in a world that is forward risk neutral with respect to $P(t, T)$. Because $g_T = P(T, T) = 1$ and $g_0 = P(0, T)$, equation (21.15) gives

$$f_0 = P(0, T)E_T(f_T) \tag{21.20}$$

Notice the difference between equations (21.20) and (21.19). In equation (21.19), the discounting is inside the expectation operator. In equation (21.20), the discounting, as represented by the $P(0, T)$ term, is outside the expectation operator. By using a world that is forward risk neutral with respect to $P(t, T)$, we considerably simplify things for a security that provides a payoff solely at time $T$.

Define $F$ as the forward price of $f$ for a contract maturing at time $T$. Arbitrage arguments similar to those in Chapter 3 show that

$$F = \frac{f_0}{P(0, T)}$$

This equation and equation (21.20) jointly imply that

$$F = E_T(f_T) \tag{21.21}$$

showing that, in a world that is forward risk neutral with respect to $P(t, T)$, the forward price of $f$ is its expected future spot price.[5]

---

[5] This can be contrasted with the traditional risk-neutral world where the expected future spot price of a variable is its futures price in a continuously settled futures contract.

Equation (21.20) shows that we can value any security that provides a payoff at time $T$ by calculating its expected payoff in a world that is forward risk neutral with respect to a bond maturing at time $T$ and discounting at the risk-free rate for maturity $T$. Equation (21.21) shows that it is correct to assume that the expected value of the underlying asset equals its forward value when computing the expected payoff. These results will be critical to our understanding of the standard market model for bond options in the next chapter.

### Interest Rates When a Bond Price Is the Numeraire

For our next result, we define $R(t, T_1, T_2)$ as the forward interest rate as seen at time $t$ for the period between $T_1$ and $T_2$ expressed with a compounding period of $T_2 - T_1$ (e.g., if $T_2 - T_1 = 0.5$, the interest rate is expressed with semiannual compounding; if $T_2 - T_1 = 0.25$, it is expressed with quarterly compounding; and so on). The forward price, as seen at time $t$, of a zero-coupon bond lasting between times $T_1$ and $T_2$ is

$$\frac{P(t, T_2)}{P(t, T_1)}$$

Because a forward interest rate is the interest rate implied by the corresponding forward bond price, it follows that

$$\frac{1}{1 + (T_2 - T_1)R(t, T_1, T_2)} = \frac{P(t, T_2)}{P(t, T_1)}$$

so that

$$R(t, T_1, T_2) = \frac{1}{T_2 - T_1}\left(\frac{P(t, T_1)}{P(t, T_2)} - 1\right)$$

or

$$R(t, T_1, T_2) = \frac{1}{T_2 - T_1}\left(\frac{P(t, T_1) - P(t, T_2)}{P(t, T_2)}\right)$$

If we set

$$f = \frac{1}{T_2 - T_1}[P(t, T_1) - P(t, T_2)]$$

and $g = P(t, T_2)$, then the equivalent martingale measure result shows that $R(t, T_1, T_2)$ is a martingale in a world that is forward risk neutral with respect to $P(t, T_2)$. This means that

$$R(0, T_1, T_2) = E_2[R(T_1, T_1, T_2)] \tag{21.22}$$

where $E_2$ denotes the expectation in a world that is forward risk neutral with respect to $P(t, T_2)$.

We have shown that the forward interest rate equals the expected future interest rate in a world that is forward risk neutral with respect to a zero-coupon bond maturing at time $T_2$. This result, when combined with the result in equation (21.20), will be critical to our understanding of the standard market model for interest rate caps in the next chapter.

### Annuity Factor as the Numeraire

For our next application of equivalent martingale measure arguments, we consider a swap starting at a future time $T$ with payment dates at times $T_1, T_2, \ldots, T_N$. Define $T_0 = T$. Assume that the principal underlying the swap is \$1. Suppose that the forward swap rate (i.e., the interest rate on the fixed side that makes the swap have a value of zero) is $s(t)$ at time $t$ $(t \leqslant T)$. The value of the fixed side of the swap is

$$s(t)A(t)$$

where

$$A(t) = \sum_{i=0}^{N-1}(T_{i+1} - T_i)P(t, T_{i+1})$$

We showed in Chapter 6 that, when the principal is added to the payment on the last payment date swap, the value of the floating side of the swap on the initiation date equals the underlying principal. It follows that if we add \$1 at time $T_N$ then the floating side is worth \$1 at time $T_0$. The value at time $t$ of \$1 received at time $T_N$ is $P(t, T_N)$. The value at time $t$ of \$1 at time $T_0$ is $P(t, T_0)$. The value of the floating side at time $t$ is therefore

$$P(t, T_0) - P(t, T_N)$$

Equating the values of the fixed and floating sides, we obtain

$$s(t)A(t) = P(t, T_0) - P(t, T_N)$$

or

$$s(t) = \frac{P(t, T_0) - P(t, T_N)}{A(t)} \qquad (21.23)$$

We can apply the equivalent martingale measure result by setting $f$ equal to $P(t, T_0) - P(t, T_N)$ and $g$ equal to $A(t)$. This leads to

$$s(t) = E_A[s(T)] \qquad (21.24)$$

where $E_A$ denotes the expectation in a world that is forward risk neutral with respect to $A(t)$. In a world that is forward risk neutral with respect to $A(t)$, the expected future swap rate is therefore the current swap rate.

For any security, $f$, the result in equation (21.15) shows

$$f_0 = A(0)E_A\left(\frac{f_T}{A(T)}\right) \qquad (21.25)$$

This result, when combined with the result in equation (21.24), will be critical to our understanding of the standard market model for European swap options in the next chapter.

## 21.5  EXTENSION TO MULTIPLE INDEPENDENT FACTORS

The results presented in Sections 21.3 and 21.4 can be extended to cover the situation when there are many independent factors.[6] Assume that there are $n$ independent factors and that the processes for $f$ and $g$ in the traditional risk-neutral world are

$$df = rf \, dt + \sum_{i=1}^{n}\sigma_{f,i}f \, dz_i$$

---

[6] The independence condition is not critical. If factors are not independent, they can be orthogonalized.

and

$$dg = rg\,dt + \sum_{i=1}^{n} \sigma_{g,i} g\,dz_i$$

It follows from Section 21.2 that we can define other worlds that are internally consistent by setting

$$df = \left(r + \sum_{i=1}^{n} \lambda_i \sigma_{f,i}\right) f\,dt + \sum_{i=1}^{n} \sigma_{f,i} f\,dz_i$$

and

$$dg = \left(r + \sum_{i=1}^{n} \lambda_i \sigma_{g,i}\right) g\,dt + \sum_{i=1}^{n} \sigma_{g,i} g\,dz_i$$

where the $\lambda_i$ $(1 \leqslant i \leqslant n)$ are the $n$ market prices of risk. One of these other worlds is the real world.

We define a world that is forward risk neutral with respect to $g$ as a world where $\lambda_i = \sigma_{g,i}$. It can be shown from Itô's lemma, using the fact that the $dz_i$ are uncorrelated, that the process followed by $f/g$ in this world has zero drift (see Problem 21.12). The rest of the results in the last two sections (from equation (21.15) onward) are therefore still true.

## 21.6 APPLICATIONS

In this section we provide two applications of the forward risk-neutral valuation argument. Several others are in Chapters 22 and 24.

### The Black–Scholes Result

We can use forward risk-neutral arguments to extend the Black–Scholes result to situations where interest rates are stochastic. Consider a European call option maturing at time $T$ on a non-dividend-paying stock. From equation (21.20), the call option's price is given by

$$c = P(0, T)E_T[\max(S_T - K, 0)] \tag{21.26}$$

where $S_T$ is the stock price at time $T$, $K$ is the strike price, and $E_T$ denotes the expectation in a world that is forward risk neutral with respect to a zero-coupon bond maturing at time $T$. Define $R$ as the zero rate for maturity $T$, so that

$$P(0, T) = e^{-RT}$$

and equation (21.26) becomes

$$c = e^{-RT}E_T[\max(S_T - K, 0)] \tag{21.27}$$

If we assume that $S_T$ is lognormal in the forward risk-neutral world we are considering, with the standard deviation of $\ln(S_T)$ equal to $s$, then Appendix 12A shows that

$$E_T[\max(S_T - K, 0)] = E_T(S_T)N(d_1) - KN(d_2) \tag{21.28}$$

where

$$d_1 = \frac{\ln[E_T(S_T)/K] + s^2/2}{s}$$

$$d_2 = \frac{\ln[E_T(S_T)/K] - s^2/2}{s}$$

From equation (21.21), $E_T(S_T)$ is the forward stock price for a contract maturing at time $T$. Hence,

$$E_T(S_T) = S_0 e^{RT} \qquad (21.29)$$

Equations (21.27), (21.28), and (21.29) give

$$c = S_0 N(d_1) - K e^{-RT} N(d_2)$$

where

$$d_1 = \frac{\ln(S_0/K) + RT + s^2/2}{s}$$

$$d_2 = \frac{\ln(S_0/K) + RT - s^2/2}{s}$$

If the stock price volatility $\sigma$ is defined so that $\sigma\sqrt{T} = s$, then the expressions for $d_1$ and $d_2$ become

$$d_1 = \frac{\ln(S_0/K) + (R + \sigma^2/2)T}{\sigma\sqrt{T}}$$

$$d_2 = \frac{\ln(S_0/K) + (R - \sigma^2/2)T}{\sigma\sqrt{T}}$$

showing that the call price is given by the Black–Scholes formula with $r$ replaced by $R$. Similar results can be produced for European put options.

### Option to Exchange One Asset for Another

Consider next an option to exchange an investment asset worth $U$ for an investment asset worth $V$. This has already been discussed in Section 19.11. We suppose that the volatilities of $U$ and $V$ are $\sigma_U$ and $\sigma_V$ and the coefficient of correlation between them is $\rho$.

Suppose first that the assets provide no income. We choose the numeraire security $g$ to be $U$. Setting $f = V$ in equation (21.15), we obtain

$$V_0 = U_0 E_U\left(\frac{V_T}{U_T}\right) \qquad (21.30)$$

where $E_U$ denotes the expectation in a world that is forward risk neutral with respect to $U$.

Next we set $f$ in equation (21.15) as the value the option under consideration, so that $f_T = \max(V_T - U_T, 0)$. It follows that

$$f_0 = U_0 E_U\left(\frac{\max(V_T - U_T, 0)}{U_T}\right)$$

or

$$f_0 = U_0 \, E_U \left[ \max \left( \frac{V_T}{U_T} - 1, \, 0 \right) \right] \tag{21.31}$$

The volatility of $V/U$ is $\hat{\sigma}$, where

$$\hat{\sigma}^2 = \sigma_U^2 + \sigma_V^2 - 2\rho \sigma_U \sigma_V$$

From Appendix 12A, equation (21.31) becomes

$$f_0 = U_0 \left[ E_U \left( \frac{V_T}{U_T} \right) N(d_1) - N(d_2) \right]$$

where

$$d_1 = \frac{\ln(V_0/U_0) + \hat{\sigma}^2 T/2}{\hat{\sigma}\sqrt{T}}$$

$$d_2 = d_1 - \hat{\sigma}\sqrt{T}$$

Substituting from equation (21.30), we obtain

$$f_0 = V_0 N(d_1) - U_0 N(d_2) \tag{21.32}$$

Problem 21.8 shows that, when $f$ and $g$ provide income at rates $q_f$ and $q_g$, equation (21.15) becomes

$$f_0 = g_0 e^{(q_f - q_g)T} E_g \left( \frac{f_T}{g_T} \right)$$

This means that equations (21.30) and (21.31) become

$$E_U \left( \frac{V_T}{U_T} \right) = e^{(q_U - q_V)T} \frac{V_0}{U_0}$$

and

$$f_0 = e^{-q_U T} U_0 E_U \left[ \max \left( \frac{V_T}{U_T} - 1, \, 0 \right) \right]$$

and equation (21.32) becomes

$$f_0 = e^{-q_V T} V_0 N(d_1) - e^{-q_U T} U_0 N(d_2)$$

with $d_1$ and $d_2$ being redefined as

$$d_1 = \frac{\ln(V_0/U_0) + (q_U - q_V + \hat{\sigma}^2/2)T}{\hat{\sigma}\sqrt{T}}$$

$$d_2 = d_1 - \hat{\sigma}\sqrt{T}$$

This is the result given in equation (19.3).

## 21.7 CHANGE OF NUMERAIRE

In this section we consider the impact of a change in numeraire on the process followed by a market variable. In a world that is forward risk neutral with respect to $g$, the process followed by a traded security $f$ is

$$df = \left( r + \sum_{i=1}^{n} \sigma_{g,i}\sigma_{f,i} \right) f\, dt + \sum_{i=1}^{n} \sigma_{f,i} f\, dz_i$$

Similarly, in a world that is forward risk neutral with respect to another security $h$, the process followed by $f$ is

$$df = \left( r + \sum_{i=1}^{n} \sigma_{h,i}\sigma_{f,i} \right) f\, dt + \sum_{i=1}^{n} \sigma_{f,i} f\, dz_i$$

where $\sigma_{h,i}$ is the $i$th component of the volatility of $h$.

The effect of moving from a world that is forward risk neutral with respect to $g$ to one that is forward risk neutral with respect to $h$ (i.e., of changing the numeraire from $g$ to $h$) is therefore to increase the expected growth rate of the price of any traded security $f$ by

$$\sum_{i=1}^{n} (\sigma_{h,i} - \sigma_{g,i})\sigma_{f,i}$$

Consider next a variable $v$ that is a function of the prices of traded securities. (The variable $v$ is not necessarily the price of a traded security itself.) Define $\sigma_{v,i}$ as the $i$th component of the volatility of $v$. From Itô's lemma in Appendix 21A, we can calculate what happens to the process followed by $v$ when there is a change in numeraire causing the expected growth rate of the underlying traded securities to change. It turns out that the expected growth rate of $v$ responds to a change in numeraire in the same way as the expected growth rate of the prices of traded securities (see Problem 11.6 for the situation where there is only one stochastic variable and Problem 21.13 for the general case). It increases by

$$\alpha_v = \sum_{i=1}^{n} (\sigma_{h,i} - \sigma_{g,i})\sigma_{v,i} \tag{21.33}$$

Define $w = h/g$ and $\sigma_{w,i}$ as the $i$th component of the volatility of $w$. From Itô's lemma (see Problem 21.14),

$$\sigma_{w,i} = \sigma_{h,i} - \sigma_{g,i}$$

so that equation (21.33) becomes

$$\alpha_v = \sum_{i=1}^{n} \sigma_{w,i}\sigma_{v,i} \tag{21.34}$$

We will refer to $w$ as the *numeraire ratio*. Equation (21.34) is equivalent to

$$\alpha_v = \rho\sigma_v\sigma_w \tag{21.35}$$

where $\sigma_v$ is the total volatility of $v$, $\sigma_w$ is the total volatility of $w$, and $\rho$ is the instantaneous correlation between $v$ and $w$.[7]

---

[7] To see this, note that the changes $\delta v$ and $\delta w$ in $v$ and $w$ in a short period of time $\delta t$ are given by

$$\delta v = \cdots + \sum \sigma_{v,i} v \epsilon_i \sqrt{\delta t}, \qquad \delta w = \cdots + \sum \sigma_{w,i} w \epsilon_i \sqrt{\delta t}$$

Because the $dz_i$ are uncorrelated, $E(\epsilon_i \epsilon_j) = 0$ when $i \neq j$. Also, from the definition of $\rho$,

$$\rho v \sigma_v w \sigma_w = E(\delta v\, \delta w) - E(\delta v)E(\delta w)$$

When terms of order higher than $\delta t$ are ignored, this leads to

$$\rho \sigma_v \sigma_w = \sum \sigma_{w,i}\, \sigma_{v,i}$$

This is a surprisingly simple result. The adjustment to the expected growth rate of a variable $v$ when we change from one numeraire to another is the instantaneous covariance between the percentage change in $v$ and the percentage change in the numeraire ratio. We will apply the result to quantos in this chapter and to what are termed timing adjustments in Chapter 22.

## 21.8 QUANTOS

A *quanto* or *cross-currency derivative* is an instrument where two currencies are involved. The payoff is defined in terms of a variable that is measured in one of the currencies and the payoff is made in the other currency. One example of a quanto is the CME futures contract on the Nikkei mentioned in Section 3.10. The market variable underlying this contract is the Nikkei 225 index (which is measured in yen), but the contract is settled in U.S. dollars.

Consider a quanto that provides a payoff in currency $X$ at time $T$. We assume that the payoff depends on the value of a variable $V$ that is observed in currency $Y$ at time $T$. Define:

$F(t)$: Forward value of $V$ at time $t$ for a contract denominated in currency $Y$ and maturing at time $T$

$V_T$: Value of $V$ at time $T$

$P_X(t, T)$: Value at time $t$ in currency $X$ of a zero-coupon bond paying off 1 unit of currency $X$ at time $T$

$P_Y(t, T)$: Value at time $t$ in currency $X$ of a zero-coupon bond paying off 1 unit of currency $Y$ at time $T$

$E_X(\cdot)$: Expectation at time zero in a world that is forward risk neutral with respect to $P_X(t, T)$

$E_Y(\cdot)$: Expectation at time zero in a world that is forward risk neutral with respect to $P_Y(t, T)$

$G(t)$: Forward exchange rate at time $t$ (number of units of currency $Y$ that equal one unit of currency $X$) in a forward contract maturing at time $T$

$\sigma_F$: Volatility of $F(t)$

$\sigma_G$: Volatility of $G(t)$

$\rho$: Instantaneous correlation between $F(t)$ and $G(t)$

$S_T$: Spot exchange rate at time $T$ $(= G(T))$

We know that

$$E_Y(V_T) = F_0$$

and are interested in $E_X(V_T)$. When we change the numeraire from $P_Y(t, T)$ to $P_X(t, T)$ world, the numeraire ratio is

$$\frac{P_X(t, T)}{P_Y(t, T)} = G(t)$$

It follows from equation (21.35) that the numeraire change leads to the expected growth rate of $F(t)$ increasing by

$$\rho \sigma_F \sigma_G$$

This means that it is approximately true that

$$E_X[F(T)] = E_Y[F(T)]e^{\rho\sigma_F\sigma_G T}$$

or because $V_T = F(T)$ and $E_Y(V_T) = F(0)$

$$E_X(V_T) = F(0)e^{\rho\sigma_F\sigma_G T} \tag{21.36}$$

This relationship is in turn approximately the same as

$$E_X(V_T) = F(0)(1 + \rho\sigma_F\sigma_G T) \tag{21.37}$$

**Example 21.4** Suppose that the current value of the Nikkei stock index for a one-year contract is 15,000 yen, the one-year dollar risk-free rate is 5%, the one-year yen risk-free rate is 2%, and the yen dividend yield is 1%. The forward price of the Nikkei for a contract denominated in yen can be calculated in the usual way from equation (3.12) as

$$15,000e^{(0.02-0.01)\times 1} = 15150.75$$

Suppose that the volatility of the one-year forward price of the index is 20%, the volatility of the one-year forward yen per dollar exchange rate is 12%, and the correlation of the one-year forward Nikkei with the one-year forward exchange rate is 0.3. In this case, $F(0) = 15,150.75$, $\sigma_F = 0.20$, $\sigma_G = 0.12$, and $\rho = 0.3$. From equation (21.36), the expected value of the Nikkei in a world that is forward risk neutral with respect to a dollar bond maturing in one year is

$$15,150.75e^{0.3\times 0.2\times 0.12\times 1} = 15,260.23$$

This is the forward price of the Nikkei for a contract that provides a payoff in dollars rather than yen. (As an approximation, it is also the futures price of such a contract.)

We will apply equation (21.37) to the valuation of what are known as diff swaps in Chapter 25.

### Using Traditional Risk-Neutral Measures

The forward risk-neutral measure we have been using works well when payoffs occur at only one time. In other situations it is sometimes more appropriate to use the traditional risk-neutral measure. Suppose we know the process followed by a variable $V$ in the traditional currency-$Y$ risk-neutral world and we wish to estimate its process in the traditional currency-$X$ risk-neutral world. Define:

$\quad S$: Spot exchange rate (units of $Y$ per unit of $X$)

$\quad \sigma_S$: Volatility of $S$

$\quad \sigma_V$: Volatility of $V$

$\quad \rho$: Instantaneous correlation between $S$ and $V$.

In this case, the change of numeraire is from the money market account in currency $Y$ to the money market account in currency $X$ (with both money market accounts being denominated in currency $X$). As indicated by equation (21.16), each money market account has a stochastic growth rate, but zero volatility. It can be shown from Itô's lemma that the volatility of the numeraire ratio is $\sigma_S$ (see Problem 21.15). The change of numeraire therefore involves increasing the expected growth rate of $V$ by

$$\rho\sigma_V\sigma_S$$

The market price of risk changes from zero to $\rho\sigma_S$.

> **Example 21.5** A two-year American option provides a payoff of $\max(S - K, 0)$ pounds sterling, where $S$ is the level of the S&P 500 at the time of exercise and $K$ is the strike price. The current level of the S&P 500 is 1,200. The risk-free rates in sterling and dollars are both constant at 5% and 3%, respectively, the correlation between the dollars-per-sterling exchange rate and the S&P 500 is 0.2, the volatility of the S&P 500 is 25%, and the volatility of the exchange rate is 12%. The dividend yield on the S&P 500 is 1.5%.
>
> We can value this option by constructing a binomial tree for the S&P 500 using as the numeraire the money market account in the U.K. (i.e., using the traditional risk-neutral as seen from the perspective of a U.K. investor). We have just shown that the change in numeraire leads to an increase in the expected growth rate of
>
> $$0.2 \times 0.25 \times 0.12 = 0.006$$
>
> or 0.6%. The growth rate of the S&P 500 using a U.S. dollar numeraire is $3 - 1.5 = 1.5\%$. The growth rate using the sterling numeraire is therefore 2.1%. The risk-free interest rate in sterling is 5%. The S&P 500 therefore behaves like an asset providing a dividend yield of $5 - 2.1 = 2.9\%$ using the sterling numeraire. Using the parameter values of $S = 1,200$, $K = 1,200$, $r = 0.05$, $q = 0.029$, $\sigma = 0.25$, and $T = 2$ with 100 time steps, DerivaGem estimates the value of the option as £179.83.

## 21.9 SIEGEL'S PARADOX

An interesting application of the results in the last two sections is to what has become known as *Siegel's paradox*. Consider two currencies, $X$ and $Y$. Define $S$ as the number of units of currency $Y$ per unit of currency $X$. Because an exchange rate behaves like a stock paying a dividend yield equal to the foreign risk-free interest rate, the traditional risk-neutral process for $S$ is

$$dS = (r_Y - r_X)S\,dt + \sigma_S S\,dz \qquad (21.38)$$

where $r_X$ and $r_Y$ are the interest rates (assumed constant) in currencies $X$ and $Y$.

From Itô's lemma, equation (21.38) implies that the process for $1/S$ is

$$d(1/S) = (r_X - r_Y + \sigma_S^2)(1/S)\,dt - \sigma_S(1/S)\,dz \qquad (21.39)$$

This leads to what is known as *Siegel's paradox*. Since the expected growth rate of $S$ is $r_Y - r_X$, symmetry suggests that the expected growth rate of $1/S$ should be $r_X - r_Y$. It appears to be a paradox that the expected growth rate in equation (21.39) is $r_X - r_Y + \sigma_S^2$ rather than $r_X - r_Y$.

To understand Siegel's paradox it is necessary to appreciate that equation (21.38) is the risk-neutral process for $S$ in a world where the numeraire is the money market account in currency $Y$. Equation (21.39), because it is deduced from equation (21.38), gives the risk-neutral process for $1/S$ when this is the numeraire. Because $1/S$ is the number of units of $X$ per unit of $Y$, to be symmetrical we should measure its process in a world where the numeraire is the money market account in currency $X$. The previous section shows that when we change the numeraire, from the money market account in currency $Y$ to the money market account in currency $X$, the growth rate of $1/S$, increases by $\rho\sigma_V\sigma_S$, where $V = 1/S$ and $\rho$ is the correlation between $S$ and $1/S$. In this case, $\rho = -1$ and $\sigma_V = \sigma_S$. It follows that the change of numeraire causes the growth rate of $1/S$ to increase by $-\sigma_S^2$. From equation (21.39), therefore, the growth rate of $1/S$ in a world where the numeraire is the money market account in currency $X$ rather than currency $Y$ is

$$d(1/S) = (r_X - r_Y)(1/S)\,dt - \sigma_S(1/S)\,dz \tag{21.40}$$

This is symmetrical with the process for $S$ in equation (21.38).

## SUMMARY

The market price of risk of a variable defines the tradeoffs between risk and return for traded securities dependent on the variable. When there is one underlying variable, a derivative's excess return over the risk-free rate equals the market price of risk multiplied by the variable's volatility. When there are many underlying variables, the excess return is the sum of the market price of risk multiplied by the volatility for each variable.

A powerful tool in the valuation of derivatives is risk-neutral valuation. This was introduced in Chapters 10 and 12. The principle of risk-neutral valuation shows that, if we assume that the world is risk neutral when valuing derivatives, we get the right answer—not just in a risk-neutral world, but in all other worlds as well. In the traditional risk-neutral world, the market price of risk of all variables is zero. Furthermore, the expected price of any asset in this world is its futures price.

In this chapter we have extended the principle of risk-neutral valuation. We have shown that, when interest rates are stochastic, there are many interesting and useful alternatives to the traditional risk-neutral world. When there is only one stochastic variable, a world is defined as forward risk neutral with respect to a security price if the market price of risk for the variable is set equal to the volatility of the security price. A similar definition applies when there are many stochastic variables. We have shown that, in a world that is forward risk neutral with respect to a security price $g$, the ratio $f/g$ is a martingale for all other security prices $f$. A martingale is a zero-drift stochastic process. Any variable following a martingale has the simplifying property that its expected value at any future time equals its value today. It turns out that by appropriately choosing the numeraire security, $g$, we can simplify the valuation of many interest rate dependent derivatives.

In this chapter we have shown how our extensions of risk-neutral valuation enable quantos and options to exchange one asset for another to be valued. In Chapters 22 and 24 the extensions will be useful in valuing interest rate derivatives.

## SUGGESTIONS FOR FURTHER READING

Baxter, M., and A. Rennie, *Financial Calculus*, Cambridge University Press, Cambridge, 1996.

Cox, J. C., J. E. Ingersoll, and S. A. Ross, "An Intertemporal General Equilibrium Model of Asset Prices," *Econometrica*, 53 (1985), 363–84.

Duffie, D., *Dynamic Asset Pricing Theory*, Princeton University Press, Princeton, NJ, 1992.

Garman, M., "A General Theory of Asset Valuation under Diffusion State Processes," Working Paper 50, University of California, Berkeley, 1976.

Harrison, J. M., and D. M. Kreps, "Martingales and Arbitrage in Multiperiod Securities Markets," *Journal of Economic Theory*, 20 (1979), 381–408.

Harrison, J. M., and S. R. Pliska, "Martingales and Stochastic Integrals in the Theory of Continuous Trading," *Stochastic Processes and Their Applications*, 11 (1981), 215–260.

Hull, J. C., and A. White, "An Overview of the Pricing of Contingent Claims," *Canadian Journal of Administrative Sciences*, 5 (September 1988), 55–61.

Jamshidian, F., "Corralling Quantos," *RISK*, March 1994, pp. 71–75.

Reiner, E., "Quanto Mechanics," *RISK*, March 1992, pp. 59–63.

# QUESTIONS AND PROBLEMS
## (ANSWERS IN THE SOLUTIONS MANUAL)

21.1. How is the market price of risk defined for a variable that is not the price of an investment asset?

21.2. Suppose that the market price of risk for gold is zero. If the storage costs are 1% per annum and the risk-free rate of interest is 6% per annum, what is the expected growth rate in the price of gold? Assume that gold provides no income.

21.3. A security's price is positively dependent on two variables: the price of copper and the yen–dollar exchange rate. Suppose that the market price of risk for these variables is 0.5 and 0.1, respectively. If the price of copper were held fixed, the volatility of the security would be 8% per annum; if the yen–dollar exchange rate were held fixed, the volatility of the security would be 12% per annum. The risk-free interest rate is 7% per annum. What is the expected rate of return from the security? If the two variables are uncorrelated with each other, what is the volatility of the security?

21.4. An oil company is set up solely for the purpose of exploring for oil in a certain small area of Texas. Its value depends primarily on two stochastic variables: the price of oil and the quantity of proven oil reserves. Discuss whether the market price of risk for the second of these two variables is likely to be positive, negative, or zero.

21.5. Deduce the differential equation for a derivative dependent on the prices of two non-dividend-paying traded securities by forming a riskless portfolio consisting of the derivative and the two traded securities.

21.6. Suppose that an interest rate $x$ follows the process

$$dx = a(x_0 - x)\,dt + c\sqrt{x}\,dz$$

where $a$, $x_0$, and $c$ are positive constants. Suppose further that the market price of risk for $x$ is $\lambda$. What is the process for $x$ in the traditional risk-neutral world?

21.7. Prove that, when the security $f$ provides income at rate $q$, equation (21.9) becomes $\mu + q - r = \lambda\sigma$. (*Hint*: Form a new security, $f^*$ that provides no income by assuming that all the income from $f$ is reinvested in $f$.)

21.8. Show that when $f$ and $g$ provide income at rates $q_f$ and $q_g$, respectively, equation (21.15) becomes

$$f_0 = g_0 e^{(q_f - q_g)T} E_g\left(\frac{f_T}{g_T}\right)$$

(*Hint*: Form new securities $f^*$ and $g^*$ that provide no income by assuming that all the income from $f$ is reinvested in $f$ and all the income in $g$ is reinvested in $g$.)

21.9. "The expected future value of an interest rate in a risk-neutral world is greater than it is in the real world." What does this statement imply about the market price of risk for (a) an interest rate and (b) a bond price. Do you think the statement is likely to be true? Give reasons.

21.10. The variable $S$ is an investment asset providing income at rate $q$ measured in currency A. It follows the process

$$dS = \mu_S S\,dt + \sigma_S S\,dz$$

in the real world. Defining new variables as necessary, give the process followed by $S$, and the corresponding market price of risk, in
   a. A world that is the traditional risk-neutral world for currency A
   b. A world that is the traditional risk-neutral world for currency B
   c. A world that is forward risk neutral with respect to a zero-coupon currency-A bond maturing at time $T$
   d. A world that is forward risk neutral with respect to a zero-coupon currency-B bond maturing at time $T$

21.11. A call option provides a payoff at time $T$ of $\max(S_T - K, 0)$ yen, where $S_T$ is the dollar price of gold at time $T$ and $K$ is the strike price. Assuming that the storage costs of gold are zero and defining other variables as necessary, calculate the value of the contract.

21.12. Prove the result in Section 21.5 that when

$$df = [r + \sum_{i=1}^{n} \lambda_i \sigma_{f,i}]f\,dt + \sum_{i=1}^{n} \sigma_{f,i}f\,dz_i$$

$$dg = [r + \sum_{i=1}^{n} \lambda_i \sigma_{g,i}]g\,dt + \sum_{i=1}^{n} \sigma_{g,i}g\,dz_i$$

with the $dz_i$ uncorrelated, $f/g$ is a martingale for $\lambda_i = \sigma_{g,i}$.

21.13. Prove equation (21.33) in Section 21.7.

21.14. Show that, when $w = h/g$ and $h$ and $g$ are each dependent on $n$ Wiener processes, the $i$th component of the volatility of $w$ is the $i$th component of the volatility of $h$ minus the $i$th component of the volatility of $g$.

21.15. Suppose that $h$ is the money market account in currency $X$ and $g$ is the money market account in currency $Y$ with both money market accounts being denominated in currency $X$. Show that the volatility of $h/g$ is the volatility of the exchange rate (units of $Y$ per unit of $X$). Assume that the stochastic process for the exchange rate is geometric Brownian motion.

## ASSIGNMENT QUESTIONS

21.16. Suppose that an index of Canadian stocks currently stands at 400. The Canadian dollar is currently worth 0.70 U.S. dollars. The risk-free interest rates in Canada and the U.S. are constant at 6% and 4%, respectively. The dividend yield on the index is 3%. Define $Q$ as the number of Canadian dollars per U.S dollar and $S$ as the value of the index. The volatility of $S$ is 20%, the volatility of $Q$ is 6%, and the correlation between $S$ and $Q$ is 0.4. Use DerivaGem to determine the value of a two year American-style call option on the index if
   a. It pays off in Canadian dollars the amount by which the index exceeds 400
   b. It pays off in U.S. dollars the amount by which the index exceeds 400.

21.17. Suppose that the price of a zero-coupon bond maturing at time $T$ follows the process

$$dP(t, T) = \mu_P P(t, T) dt + \sigma_P P(t, T) dz$$

and the price of a derivative dependent on the bond follows the process

$$df = \mu_f f \, dt + \sigma_f f \, dz$$

Assume only one source of uncertainty and that $f$ provides no income.
  a. What is the forward price, $F$, of $f$ for a contract maturing at time $T$?
  b. What is the process followed by $F$ in a world that is forward risk neutral with respect to $P(t, T)$?
  c. What is the process followed by $F$ in the traditional risk-neutral world?
  d. What is the process followed by $f$ in a world that is forward risk neutral with respect to a bond maturing at time $T^*$, where $T^* \neq T$? Assume that $\sigma_P^*$ is the volatility of this bond.

21.18. Consider an instrument that will pay off $S$ dollars in two years where $S$ is the value of the Nikkei index. The index is currently 20,000. The dollar–yen exchange rate (yen per dollar) is 100. The correlation between the exchange rate and the index is 0.3 and the dividend yield on the index is 1% per annum. The volatility of the Nikkei index is 20% and the volatility of the yen–dollar exchange rate is 12%. The interest rates (assumed constant) in the U.S. and Japan are 4% and 2%, respectively.
  a. What is the value of the instrument?
  b. Suppose that the exchange rate at some point during the life of the instrument is $Q$ and the level of the index is $S$. Show that a U.S. investor can create a portfolio that changes in value by approximately $\delta S$ dollars when the index changes in value by $\delta S$ yen by investing $S$ dollars in the Nikkei and shorting $SQ$ yen.
  c. Confirm that this is correct by supposing that the index changes from 20,000 to 20,050 and the exchange rate changes from 100 to 99.7.
  d. How would you delta hedge the instrument under consideration?

# APPENDIX 21A
## Generalizations of Itô's Lemma

Itô's lemma, as presented in Appendix 11A, provides the process followed by a function of a single stochastic variable. Here we present a generalized version of Itô's lemma for the process followed by a function of several stochastic variables.

Suppose that a function $f$ depends on the $n$ variables $x_1, x_2, \ldots, x_n$ and time $t$. Suppose further that $x_i$ follows an Itô process with instantaneous drift $a_i$ and instantaneous variance $b_i^2$ ($1 \leqslant i \leqslant n$), that is,

$$dx_i = a_i \, dt + b_i \, dz_i \qquad (21A.1)$$

where $dz_i$ ($1 \leqslant i \leqslant n$) is a Wiener process. Each $a_i$ and $b_i$ may be any function of all the $x_i$'s and $t$. A Taylor series expansion of $f$ gives

$$\delta f = \sum_{i=1}^{n} \frac{\partial f}{\partial x_i} \delta x_i + \frac{\partial f}{\partial t} \delta t + \frac{1}{2} \sum_{i=1}^{n} \sum_{j=1}^{n} \frac{\partial^2 f}{\partial x_i \, \partial x_j} \delta x_i \, \delta x_j + \frac{1}{2} \sum_{i=1}^{n} \frac{\partial^2 f}{\partial x_i \, \partial t} \delta x_i \, \delta t + \cdots \qquad (21A.2)$$

Equation (21A.1) can be discretized as

$$\delta x_i = a_i \, \delta t + b_i \epsilon_i \sqrt{\delta t}$$

where $\epsilon_i$ is a random sample from a standardized normal distribution. The correlation $\rho_{ij}$ between $dz_i$ and $dz_j$ is defined as the correlation between $\epsilon_i$ and $\epsilon_j$. In Appendix 11A it was argued that

$$\lim_{\delta t \to 0} \delta x_i^2 = b_i^2 \, dt$$

Similarly,

$$\lim_{\delta t \to 0} \delta x_i \, \delta x_j = b_i b_j \rho_{ij} \, dt$$

As $\delta t \to 0$, the first three terms in the expansion of $\delta f$ in equation (21A.2) are of order $\delta t$. All other terms are of higher order. Hence,

$$df = \sum_{i=1}^{n} \frac{\partial f}{\partial x_i} dx_i + \frac{\partial f}{\partial t} dt + \frac{1}{2} \sum_{i=1}^{n} \sum_{j=1}^{n} \frac{\partial^2 f}{\partial x_i \, \partial x_j} b_i b_j \rho_{ij} \, dt$$

This is the generalized version of Itô's lemma. Substituting for $dx_i$ from equation (21A.1) gives

$$df = \left( \sum_{i=1}^{n} \frac{\partial f}{\partial x_i} a_i + \frac{\partial f}{\partial t} + \frac{1}{2} \sum_{i=1}^{n} \sum_{j=1}^{n} \frac{\partial^2 f}{\partial x_i \, \partial x_j} b_i b_j \rho_{ij} \right) dt + \sum_{i=1}^{n} \frac{\partial f}{\partial x_i} b_i \, dz_i \qquad (21A.3)$$

For an alternative generalization of Itô's lemma, suppose that $f$ depends on a single variable $x$ and that the process for $x$ involves more than one Wiener process:

$$dx = a \, dt + \sum_{i=1}^{m} b_i \, dz_i$$

In this case,

$$\delta f = \frac{\partial f}{\partial x}\,\delta x + \frac{\partial f}{\partial t}\,\delta t + \tfrac{1}{2}\frac{\partial^2 f}{\partial x^2}\,\delta x^2 + \tfrac{1}{2}\frac{\partial^2 f}{\partial x\,\partial t}\,\delta x\delta t + \cdots$$

$$\delta x = a\,\delta t + \sum_{i=1}^{m} b_i\epsilon_i\sqrt{\delta t}$$

$$\lim_{\delta t \to 0}\delta x_i^2 = \sum_{i=1}^{m}\sum_{j=1}^{m} b_i b_j \rho_{ij}\,dt$$

where as before $\rho_{ij}$ is the correlation between $dz_i$ and $dz_j$. This leads to

$$df = \left(\frac{\partial f}{\partial x}a + \frac{\partial f}{\partial t} + \tfrac{1}{2}\frac{\partial^2 f}{\partial x^2}\sum_{i=1}^{m}\sum_{j=1}^{m} b_i b_j \rho_{ij}\right)dt + \frac{\partial f}{\partial x}\sum_{i=1}^{m} b_i\,dz_i \qquad (21A.4)$$

Finally, consider the more general case where $f$ depends on variables $x_i$ ($1 \leqslant i \leqslant n$) and

$$dx_i = a_i\,dt + \sum_{k=1}^{m} b_{ik}\,dz_k$$

A similar analysis shows that

$$df = \left(\sum_{i=1}^{n}\frac{\partial f}{\partial x_i}a_i + \frac{\partial f}{\partial t} + \tfrac{1}{2}\sum_{i=1}^{n}\sum_{j=1}^{n}\frac{\partial^2 f}{\partial x_i\partial x_j}\sum_{k=1}^{m}\sum_{l=1}^{m} b_{ik}b_{jl}\rho_{kl}\right)dt + \sum_{i=1}^{n}\frac{\partial f}{\partial x_i}\sum_{k=1}^{m} b_{ik}\,dz_k \qquad (21A.5)$$

# APPENDIX 21B
## Expected Excess Return When There Are Multiple Sources of Uncertainty

This appendix proves the result in equation (21.13). Suppose there are $n$ stochastic variables following Wiener processes. Consider $n + 1$ traded securities whose prices depend on some or all of the $n$ stochastic variables. Define $f_j$ as the price of the $j$th ($1 \leqslant j \leqslant n + 1$) security. We assume that no dividends or other income is paid by the $n + 1$ traded securities.[8] It follows from Appendix 21A that the securities follow processes of the form

$$df_j = \mu_j f_j \, dt + \sum_{i=1}^{n} \sigma_{ij} f_j \, dz_i \tag{21B.1}$$

Because there are $n + 1$ traded securities and $n$ Wiener processes, it is possible to form an instantaneously riskless portfolio, $\Pi$, using the securities. Define $k_j$ as the amount of the $j$th security in the portfolio, so that

$$\Pi = \sum_{j=1}^{n+1} k_j f_j \tag{21B.2}$$

The $k_j$ must be chosen so that the stochastic components of the returns from the securities are eliminated. From equation (21B.1) this means that

$$\sum_{j=1}^{n+1} k_j \sigma_{ij} f_j = 0 \tag{21B.3}$$

for $1 \leqslant i \leqslant n$. The return from the portfolio is then given by

$$d\Pi = \sum_{j=1}^{n+1} k_j \mu_j f_j \, dt$$

The cost of setting up the portfolio is

$$\sum_{j=1}^{n+1} k_j f_j$$

If there are no arbitrage opportunities, the portfolio must earn the risk-free interest rate, so that

$$\sum_{j=1}^{n+1} k_j \mu_j f_j = r \sum_{j=1}^{n+1} k_j f_j \tag{21B.4}$$

or

$$\sum_{j=1}^{n+1} k_j f_j (\mu_j - r) = 0 \tag{21B.5}$$

---

[8] This is not restrictive. A non-dividend-paying security can always be obtained from a dividend-paying security by reinvesting the dividends in the security.

Equations (21B.3) and (21B.5) can be regarded as $n + 1$ homogeneous linear equations in the $k_j$'s. The $k_j$'s are not all zero. From a well-known theorem in linear algebra, equations (21B.3) and (21B.5) can be consistent only if, for all $j$,

$$f_j(\mu_j - r) = \sum_{i=1}^{n} \lambda_i \sigma_{ij} f_j \tag{21B.6}$$

or

$$\mu_j - r = \sum_{i=1}^{n} \lambda_i \sigma_{ij} \tag{21B.7}$$

for some $\lambda_i$ $(1 \leqslant i \leqslant n)$ that are dependent only on the state variables and time. Dropping the $j$ subscript, we see that, for any security $f$ dependent on the $n$ stochastic variables,

$$df = \mu f\, dt + \sum_{i=1}^{n} \sigma_i f\, dz_i$$

where

$$\mu - r = \sum_{i=1}^{n} \lambda_i \sigma_i$$

This proves the result in equation (21.13).

# CHAPTER 22

# INTEREST RATE DERIVATIVES: THE STANDARD MARKET MODELS

Interest rate derivatives are instruments whose payoffs are dependent in some way on the level of interest rates. In the 1980s and 1990s, the volume of trading in interest rate derivatives in both the over-the-counter and exchange-traded markets increased very quickly. Many new products were developed to meet particular needs of end-users. A key challenge for derivatives traders is to find good, robust procedures for pricing and hedging these products.

Interest rate derivatives are more difficult to value than equity and foreign exchange derivatives. There are a number of reasons for this:

1. The behavior of an individual interest rate is more complicated than that of a stock price or an exchange rate.
2. For the valuation of many products, it is necessary to develop a model describing the behavior of the entire zero-coupon yield curve.
3. The volatilities of different points on the yield curve are different.
4. Interest rates are used for discounting as well as for defining the payoff from the derivative.

In this chapter we look at the three most popular over-the-counter interest rate option products: bond options, interest rate caps/floors, and swap options. We explain the standard market models for valuing these products and use material from Chapter 21 to show that the models are internally consistent. We also explain what are known as convexity and timing adjustments. These are sometimes necessary in the valuation of nonstandard interest rate derivatives.

## 22.1 BLACK'S MODEL

Since the Black–Scholes model was first published in 1973, it has become a very popular tool. As explained in Chapter 13, the model has been extended so that it can be used to value options on foreign exchange, options on indices, and options on futures contracts. Traders have become very comfortable with both the lognormal assumption that underlies the model and the volatility measure that describes uncertainty. It is not surprising that there have been attempts to extend the model so that it covers interest rate derivatives.

In the following few sections we will discuss three of the most popular interest rate derivatives (bond options, interest rate caps, and swap options) and describe how the lognormal assumption underlying the Black–Scholes model can be used to value these instruments. The model we will use is usually referred to as Black's model because the formulas are similar to those in the model suggested by Fischer Black for valuing options on commodity futures (see Section 13.8).

We start by reviewing Black's model and showing that it provides a flexible framework for valuing a wide range of European options.

### Using Black's Model to Price European Options

Consider a European call option on a variable whose value is $V$. Define:

$T$: Time to maturity of the option

$F$: Forward price of $V$ for a contract with maturity $T$

$F_0$: Value of $F$ at time zero

$K$: Strike price of the option

$P(t, T)$: Price at time $t$ of a zero-coupon bond paying \$1 at time $T$

$V_T$: Value of $V$ at time $T$

$\sigma$: Volatility of $F$

Black's model calculates the expected payoff from the option assuming:

1. $V_T$ has a lognormal distribution with the standard deviation of $\ln V_T$ equal to $\sigma\sqrt{T}$.
2. The expected value of $V_T$ is $F_0$.

It then discounts the expected payoff at the $T$-year risk-free rate by multiplying by $P(0, T)$. The payoff from the option is $\max(V_T - K, 0)$ at time $T$. As shown in Appendix 12A, the lognormal assumption implies that the expected payoff is

$$E(V_T)N(d_1) - KN(d_2)$$

where $E(V_T)$ is the expected value of $V_T$ and

$$d_1 = \frac{\ln[E(V_T)/K] + \sigma^2 T/2}{\sigma\sqrt{T}}$$

$$d_2 = \frac{\ln[E(V_T)/K] - \sigma^2 T/2}{\sigma\sqrt{T}} = d_1 - \sigma\sqrt{T}$$

Because we are assuming that $E(V_T) = F_0$ and discounting at the risk-free rate, the value of the option is

$$c = P(0, T)[F_0 N(d_1) - KN(d_2)] \tag{22.1}$$

where

$$d_1 = \frac{\ln(F_0/K) + \sigma^2 T/2}{\sigma\sqrt{T}}$$

$$d_2 = \frac{\ln(F_0/K) - \sigma^2 T/2}{\sigma\sqrt{T}} = d_1 - \sigma\sqrt{T}$$

Similarly the value, $p$, of the corresponding put option is given by

$$p = P(0, T)[KN(-d_2) - F_0 N(-d_1)] \tag{22.2}$$

Equations (22.1) and (22.2) are equivalent to equations (13.17) and (13.18) except that $F_0$ is here defined as the forward price rather than the futures price.

We can extend Black's model to allow for the situation where the payoff is calculated from the value of the variable $V$ at time $T$, but the payoff is actually made at some later time $T^*$. The expected payoff is discounted from time $T^*$ instead of time $T$, so that equations (22.1) and (22.2) become

$$c = P(0, T^*)[F_0 N(d_1) - KN(d_2)] \tag{22.3}$$

$$p = P(0, T^*)[KN(-d_2) - F_0 N(-d_1)] \tag{22.4}$$

where

$$d_1 = \frac{\ln(F_0/K) + \sigma^2 T/2}{\sigma \sqrt{T}}$$

$$d_2 = \frac{\ln(F_0/K) - \sigma^2 T/2}{\sigma \sqrt{T}} = d_1 - \sigma \sqrt{T}$$

An important feature of Black's model is that we do not have to assume geometric Brownian motion for the evolution of either $V$ or $F$. All that we require is that $V_T$ be lognormal at time $T$. The parameter $\sigma$ is usually referred to as the volatility of $F$ or the forward volatility of $V$. However, its only role is to define the standard deviation of $\ln V_T$ by means of the relationship

$$\text{Standard deviation of } \ln V_T = \sigma \sqrt{T}$$

The volatility parameter does not necessarily say anything about the standard deviation of $\ln V$ at times other than time $T$.

### Validity of Black's Model

It is easy to see that Black's model is appropriate when interest rates are assumed to be either constant or deterministic. In this case, as explained in Chapter 3, the forward price of $V$ is equal to its futures price and the model is the same as the model in Section 13.8.

When interest rates are stochastic, there are two aspects of the derivation of equation (22.1) that are open to question.

1. Why do we set $E(V_T)$ equal to the forward price, $F_0$, of $V$? This is not the same as the futures price.

2. Why do we ignore the fact that interest rates are stochastic when discounting?

As we apply Black's model to bond options, caps/floors, and swap options, we will use the results in Section 21.4 to show that there are no approximations in equations (22.1) and (22.2) when interest rates are stochastic. It is correct to set $E(V_T)$ equal to the forward price provided that we also discount at today's $T$-year maturity zero rate. Black's model therefore has a sounder theoretical basis and wider applicability than is sometimes supposed.

## 22.2  BOND OPTIONS

A bond option is an option to buy or sell a particular bond by a certain date for a particular price. In addition to trading in the over-the-counter market, bond options are frequently embedded in bonds when they are issued to make them more attractive to either the issuer or potential purchasers.

### Embedded Bond Options

One example of a bond with an embedded bond option is a *callable bond*. This is a bond that contains provisions allowing the issuing firm to buy back the bond at a predetermined price at certain times in the future. The holder of such a bond has sold a call option to the issuer. The strike price or call price in the option is the predetermined price that must be paid by the issuer to the holder. Callable bonds cannot usually be called for the first few years of their life. (This is known as the lock out period.) After that the call price is usually a decreasing function of time. For example, in a 10-year callable bond, there might be no call privileges for the first two years. After that, the issuer might have the right to buy the bond back at a price of 110 in years 3 and 4 of its life, at a price of 107.5 in years 5 and 6, at a price of 106 in years 7 and 8, and at a price of 103 in years 9 and 10. The value of the call option is reflected in the quoted yields on bonds. Bonds with call features generally offer higher yields than bonds with no call features.

Another type of bond with an embedded option is a *puttable bond*. This contains provisions that allow the holder to demand early redemption at a predetermined price at certain times in the future. The holder of such a bond has purchased a put option on the bond as well as the bond itself. Because the put option increases the value of the bond to the holder, bonds with put features provide lower yields than bonds with no put features. A simple example of a puttable bond is a 10-year bond where the holder has the right to be repaid at the end of five years. (This is sometimes referred to as a *retractable bond*.)

Loan and deposit instruments also often contain embedded bond options. For example, a five-year fixed-rate deposit with a financial institution that can be redeemed without penalty at any time contains an American put option on a bond. (The deposit instrument is a bond that the investor has the right to put back to the financial institution at any time.) Prepayment privileges on loans and mortgages are similarly call options on bonds.

Finally, we note that a loan commitment made by a bank or other financial institution is a put option on a bond. Consider, for example, the situation where a bank quotes a five-year interest rate of 12% per annum to a potential borrower and states that the rate is good for the next two months. The client has, in effect, obtained the right to sell a five-year bond with a 12% coupon to the financial institution for its face value any time within the next two months.

### European Bond Options

Many over-the-counter bond options and some embedded bond options are European. We now consider the standard market models used to value European options.

The assumption usually made is that the bond price at the maturity of the option is lognormal. Equations (22.1) and (22.2) can be used to price the option with $F_0$ equal to the forward bond price. The variable $\sigma$ is defined so that $\sigma\sqrt{T}$ is the standard deviation of the logarithm of the bond price at the maturity of the option.

A bond is a security that provides a known cash income. From Section 3.3, $F_0$ can be calculated using the formula

$$F_0 = \frac{B_0 - I}{P(0, T)} \tag{22.5}$$

where $B_0$ is the bond price at time zero and $I$ is the present value of the coupons that will be paid during the life of the option. In this formula, both the spot bond price and the forward bond price are cash prices rather than quoted prices. The relationship between cash and quoted bond prices is explained in Section 5.9.

The strike price, $K$, in equations (22.1) and (22.2) should be the cash strike price. In choosing the correct value for $K$, the precise terms of the option are therefore important. If the strike price is defined as the cash amount that is exchanged for the bond when the option is exercised, $K$ should be put equal to this strike price. If, as is more common, the strike price is the quoted price applicable when the option is exercised, $K$ should be set equal to the strike price plus accrued interest at the expiration date of the option. Traders refer to the quoted price of a bond as the "clean price" and the cash price as the "dirty price."

> **Example 22.1**   Consider a 10-month European call option on a 9.75-year bond with a face value of $1,000. (When the option matures the bond will have 8 years and 11 months remaining.) Suppose that the current cash bond price is $960, the strike price is $1,000, the 10-month risk-free interest rate is 10% per annum, and the volatility of the forward bond price in 10 months is 9% per annum. The bond pays a semiannual coupon of 10% and coupon payments of $50 are expected in three months and nine months. (This means that the accrued interest is $25 and the quoted bond price is $935.) We suppose that the three-month and nine-month risk-free interest rates are 9.0% and 9.5% per annum, respectively. The present value of the coupon payments is therefore
>
> $$50e^{-0.25 \times 0.09} + 50e^{-0.75 \times 0.095} = 95.45$$
>
> or $95.45. From equation (22.5), the bond forward price is given by
>
> $$F_0 = (960 - 95.45)e^{0.1 \times 0.8333} = 939.68$$
>
> (a) If the strike price is the cash price that would be paid for the bond on exercise, the parameters for equation (22.1) are $F_0 = 939.68$, $K = 1000$, $P(0, T) = e^{-0.1 \times (10/12)} = 0.9200$, $\sigma = 0.09$, and $T = 10/12$. The price of the call option is $9.49.
>
> (b) If the strike price is the quoted price that would be paid for the bond on exercise, one month's accrued interest must be added to $K$ because the maturity of the option is one month after a coupon date. This produces a value for $K$ of
>
> $$1,000 + 50 \times 0.16667 = 1,008.33$$
>
> The values for the other parameters in equation (22.1) are unchanged (i.e., $F_0 = 939.68$, $P(0, T) = 0.9200$, $\sigma = 0.09$, and $T = 0.8333$). The price of the option is $7.97.

Figure 22.1 shows how the standard deviation of the logarithm of a bond's price changes with time. The standard deviation is zero today because there is no uncertainty about the bond's price today. It is also zero at the bond's maturity because we know that the bond's price will equal its face value at maturity. Between today and the maturity of the bond, the standard deviation first increases and then decreases. The volatility, $\sigma$, that should be used when a European option on the

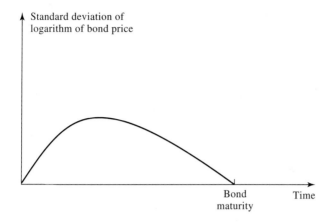

**Figure 22.1** Standard deviation of logarithm of bond price as a function of time

bond is valued is

$$\frac{\text{standard deviation of logarithm of bond price at maturity of option}}{\sqrt{\text{time to maturity of option}}}$$

Figure 22.2 shows a typical pattern for $\sigma$ as a function of the life of the option. In general, $\sigma$ declines as the life of the option increases.

### Yield Volatilities

The volatilities that are quoted for bond options are often yield volatilities rather than price volatilities. The duration concept, introduced in Chapter 5, is used by the market to convert a quoted yield volatility into a price volatility. Suppose that $D$ is the modified duration of the bond underlying the option at the option maturity, as defined in Chapter 5. The relationship between the

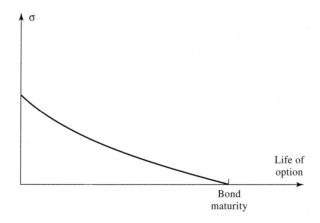

**Figure 22.2** Variation of volatility, $\sigma$, for bond with life of option

change in the forward bond price, $F$, and its forward yield, $y_F$, is

$$\frac{\delta F}{F} \approx -D\,\delta y_F$$

or

$$\frac{\delta F}{F} \approx -Dy_F \frac{\delta y_F}{y_F}$$

Volatility is a measure of the standard deviation of percentage changes in the value of a variable. This equation therefore suggests that the volatility, $\sigma$, of the forward bond price used in Black's model can be approximately related to the volatility, $\sigma_y$, of the forward bond yield by

$$\sigma = Dy_0\sigma_y \tag{22.6}$$

where $y_0$ is the initial value of $y_F$. When a yield volatility is quoted for a bond option, the implicit assumption is usually that it will be converted to a price volatility using equation (22.6), and that this volatility will then be used in conjunction with equation (22.1) or (22.2) to obtain a price. Suppose that the bond underlying a call option will have a modified duration of five years at option maturity, the forward yield is 8%, and the forward yield volatility quoted by a broker is 20%. This means that the market price of the option corresponding to the broker quote is the price given by equation (22.1) when the volatility variable, $\sigma$, is

$$5 \times 0.08 \times 0.2 = 0.08$$

or 8% per annum.

The Bond_Options worksheet of the DerivaGem software accompanying this book can be used to price European bond options using Black's model by selecting Black-European as the Pricing Model. The user inputs a yield volatility, which is handled in the way just described. The strike price can be the cash or quoted strike price.

**Example 22.2** Consider a European put option on a ten-year bond with a principal of 100. The coupon is 8% per year payable semiannually. The life of the option is 2.25 years and the strike price of the option is 115. The forward yield volatility is 20%. The zero curve is flat at 5% with continuous compounding. DerivaGem shows that the quoted price of the bond is 122.84. The price of the option when the strike price is a quoted price is 2.37. When the strike price is a cash price, the price of the option is $1.74. (Note that DerivaGem's prices may not exactly agree with manually calculated prices because DerivaGem assumes 365 days per year and rounds times to the nearest whole number of days. See Problem 22.22 for the manual calculation.)

## *Theoretical Justification for the Model*

In Section 21.4, we explored alternatives to the usual risk-neutral valuation assumption for valuing derivatives. One alternative was a world that is forward risk neutral with respect to a zero-coupon bond maturing at time $T$. We showed that:

1. The current value of any security is its expected value at time $T$ in this world multiplied by the price of a zero-coupon bond maturing at time $T$ (see equation (21.20)).

2. The expected value of any traded security at time $T$ in this world equals its forward price (see equation (21.21)).

The first of these results shows that the price of a call option with maturity $T$ years on a bond is

$$c = P(0, T)E_T[\max(B_T - K, 0)] \tag{22.7}$$

where $B_T$ is the bond price at time $T$ and $E_T$ denotes expected value in a world that is forward risk neutral with respect to a zero-coupon bond maturing at time $T$. The second result implies that

$$E_T(B_T) = F_0 \tag{22.8}$$

Assuming the bond price is lognormal with the standard deviation of the logarithm of the bond price equal to $\sigma\sqrt{T}$, Appendix 12A shows that equation (22.7) becomes

$$c = P(0, T)[E_T(B_T)N(d_1) - KN(d_2)]$$

where

$$d_1 = \frac{\ln[E_T(B_T)/K] + \sigma^2 T/2}{\sigma\sqrt{T}}$$

$$d_2 = \frac{\ln[E_T(B_T)/K] - \sigma^2 T/2}{\sigma\sqrt{T}} = d_1 - \sigma\sqrt{T}$$

Using equation (22.8), we find that this reduces to Black's model formula in equation (22.1). We have shown that we can use today's $T$-year maturity interest rate for discounting provided that we also set the expected bond price equal to the forward bond price.

## 22.3 INTEREST RATE CAPS

A popular interest rate option offered by financial institutions in the over-the-counter market is an *interest rate cap*. Interest rate caps can best be understood by first considering a floating rate note where the interest rate is periodically reset equal to LIBOR. The time between resets is known as the *tenor*. Suppose that the tenor is three months. The interest rate on the note for the first three months is the initial three-month LIBOR rate; the interest rate for the next three months is set equal to the three-month LIBOR rate prevailing in the market at the three-month point; and so on.

An interest rate cap is designed to provide insurance against the rate of interest on the floating-rate note rising above a certain level. This level is known as the *cap rate*. Suppose that the principal amount is $10 million, the tenor is three months, the life of the cap is five years, and the cap rate is 8%. (Because the payments are made quarterly, this cap rate is expressed with quarterly compounding.) The cap provides insurance against the interest on the floating rate note rising above 8%. Suppose that on a particular reset date the three-month LIBOR interest rate is 9%. The floating rate note would require

$$0.25 \times 0.09 \times \$10,000,000 = \$225,000$$

of interest to be paid three months later. With a three-month LIBOR rate of 8% the interest payment would be

$$0.25 \times 0.08 \times \$10,000,000 = \$200,000$$

The cap therefore provides a payoff of $25,000.[1] Note that the payoff does not occur on the reset date when the 9% is observed. It occurs three months later. This reflects the usual time lag between an interest rate being observed and the corresponding payment being required.

At each reset date during the life of the cap, we observe LIBOR. If LIBOR is less than 8%, there is no payoff from the cap three months later. If LIBOR is greater than 8%, the payoff is one quarter of the excess applied to the principal of $10 million. Note that caps are usually defined so that the initial LIBOR rate, even if it is greater than the cap rate, does not lead to a payoff on the first reset date. In our example the cap lasts for five years. There are, therefore, a total of 19 reset dates (at times $0.25, 0.5, 0.75, \ldots, 4.75$ years) and 19 potential payoffs from the caps (at times $0.50, 0.75, 1.00, \ldots, 5.00$ years).

### The Cap as a Portfolio of Interest Rate Options

Consider a cap with a total life of $T$, a principal of $L$, and a cap rate of $R_K$. Suppose that the reset dates are $t_1, t_2, \ldots, t_n$ and define $t_{n+1} = T$. Define $R_k$ as the interest rate for the period between time $t_k$ and $t_{k+1}$ observed at time $t_k$ ($1 \leqslant k \leqslant n$). The cap leads to a payoff at time $t_{k+1}$ ($k = 1, 2, \ldots, n$) of

$$L\delta_k \max(R_k - R_K, 0) \tag{22.9}$$

where $\delta_k = t_{k+1} - t_k$. (Both $R_k$ and $R_K$ are expressed with a compounding frequency equal to the frequency of resets.)

Equation (22.9) is a call option on the LIBOR rate observed at time $t_k$ with the payoff occurring at time $t_{k+1}$. The cap is a portfolio of $n$ such options. LIBOR rates are observed at times $t_1, t_2, \ldots, t_n$ and the corresponding payoffs occur at times $t_2, t_3, \ldots, t_{n+1}$. The $n$ call options underlying the cap are known as *caplets*.

### A Cap as a Portfolio of Bond Options

An interest rate cap can also be characterized as a portfolio of put options on zero-coupon bonds with payoffs on the puts occurring at the time they are calculated. The payoff in equation (22.9) at time $t_{k+1}$ is equivalent to

$$\frac{L\delta_k}{1 + R_k\delta_k} \max(R_k - R_K, 0)$$

at time $t_k$. A few lines of algebra show that this reduces to

$$\max\left(L - \frac{L(1 + R_K\delta_k)}{1 + \delta_k R_k}, 0\right) \tag{22.10}$$

The expression

$$\frac{L(1 + R_K\delta_k)}{1 + \delta_k R_k}$$

is the value at time $t_k$ of a zero-coupon bond that pays off $L(1 + R_K\delta_k)$ at time $t_{k+1}$. The expression in equation (22.10) is therefore the payoff from a put option with maturity $t_k$ on a zero-coupon bond with maturity $t_{k+1}$ when the face value of the bond is $L(1 + R_K\delta_k)$ and the strike price is $L$. It

---

[1] This calculation assumes exactly one quarter of a year between reset dates. In practice the calculation takes account of the exact number of days between reset dates using a specified day count convention.

follows that an interest rate cap can be regarded as a portfolio of European put options on zero-coupon bonds.

### Floors and Collars

Interest rate floors and interest rate collars (sometimes called floor–ceiling agreements) are defined analogously to caps. A *floor* provides a payoff when the interest rate on the underlying floating-rate note falls below a certain rate. With the notation already introduced, a floor provides a payoff at time $t_{k+1}$ $(k = 1, 2, \ldots, n)$ of

$$L\delta_k \max(R_K - R_k, 0)$$

Analogously to an interest rate cap, an interest rate floor is a portfolio of put options on interest rates or a portfolio of call options on zero-coupon bonds. Each of the individual options constituting a floor is known as a *floorlet*. A *collar* is an instrument designed to guarantee that the interest rate on the underlying floating-rate note always lies between two levels. A collar is a combination of a long position in a cap and a short position in a floor. It is usually constructed so that the price of the cap is initially equal to the price of the floor. The cost of entering into the collar is then zero.

There is a put–call parity relationship between the prices of caps and floors. This is

$$\text{cap price} = \text{floor price} + \text{value of swap}$$

In this relationship, the cap and floor have the same strike price, $R_K$. The swap is an agreement to receive floating and pay a fixed rate of $R_K$, with no exchange of payments on the first reset date.[2] All three instruments have the same life and the same frequency of payments. This result can be seen to be true by noting that a long position in the cap combined with a short position in the floor provides the same cash flows as the swap.

### Valuation of Caps and Floors

As shown in equation (22.9), the caplet corresponding to the rate observed at time $t_k$ provides a payoff at time $t_{k+1}$ of

$$L\delta_k \max(R_k - R_K, 0)$$

If the rate $R_k$ is assumed to be lognormal with volatility $\sigma_k$, equation (22.3) gives the value of this caplet as

$$L\delta_k P(0, t_{k+1})[F_k N(d_1) - R_K N(d_2)] \tag{22.11}$$

where

$$d_1 = \frac{\ln(F_k/R_K) + \sigma_k^2 t_k/2}{\sigma_k \sqrt{t_k}}$$

$$d_2 = \frac{\ln(F_k/R_K) - \sigma_k^2 t_k/2}{\sigma_k \sqrt{t_k}} = d_1 - \sigma_k \sqrt{t_k}$$

---

[2] Note that swaps are usually structured so that the rate at time zero determines an exchange of payments at the first reset date. As indicated earlier, caps and floors are usually structured so that there is no payoff at the first reset date. This difference explains why we have to exclude the first exchange of payments on the swap.

and $F_k$ is the forward rate for the period between time $t_k$ and $t_{k+1}$. The value of the corresponding floorlet is, from equation (22.4),

$$L\delta_k P(0, t_{k+1})[R_K N(-d_2) - F_k N(-d_1)] \tag{22.12}$$

Note that $R_K$ and $F_k$ are expressed with a compounding frequency equal to the frequency of resets in these equations.

> **Example 22.3**  Consider a contract that caps the interest rate on a $10,000 loan at 8% per annum (with quarterly compounding) for three months starting in one year. This is a caplet and could be one element of a cap. Suppose that the zero curve is flat at 7% per annum with quarterly compounding and the one-year volatility for the three-month rate underlying the caplet is 20% per annum. The continuously compounded zero rate for all maturities is 6.9394%. In equation (22.11), $F_k = 0.07$, $\delta_k = 0.25$, $L = 10,000$, $R_K = 0.08$, $t_k = 1.0$, $t_{k+1} = 1.25$, $P(0, t_{k+1}) = e^{-0.069394 \times 1.25} = 0.9169$, and $\sigma_k = 0.20$. Also,
>
> $$d_1 = \frac{\ln(0.07/0.08) + 0.2^2 \times 1/2}{0.20 \times 1} = -0.5677$$
> $$d_2 = d_1 - 0.20 = -0.7677$$
>
> so that the caplet price is
>
> $$0.25 \times 10,000 \times 0.9169[0.07N(-0.5677) - 0.08N(-0.7677)] = \$5.162$$

(Note that DerivaGem gives $5.146 for the price of this caplet. This is because it assumes 365 days per year and rounds times to the nearest whole number of days.)

Each caplet of a cap must be valued separately using equation (22.11). One approach is to use a different volatility for each caplet. The volatilities are then referred to as *spot volatilities*. An alternative approach is to use the same volatility for all the caplets constituting any particular cap but to vary this volatility according to the life of the cap. The volatilities used are then referred to as *flat volatilities*.[3] The volatilities quoted in the market are usually flat volatilities. However, many traders like to work with spot volatilities because this allows them to identify underpriced and overpriced caplets. Options on Eurodollar futures are very similar to caplets and the spot volatilities used for caplets on three-month LIBOR are frequently compared with those calculated from the prices of Eurodollar futures options.

Figure 22.3 shows a typical pattern for spot volatilities and flat volatilities as a function of maturity. (In the case of a spot volatility, the maturity is the maturity of a caplet; in the case of a flat volatility, it is the maturity of a cap.) The flat volatilities are akin to cumulative averages of the spot volatilities and therefore exhibit less variability. As indicated by Figure 22.3, we usually observe a "hump" in the volatilities. The peak of the hump is at about the two- to three-year point. This hump is observed both when the volatilities are implied from option prices and when they are calculated from historical data. There is no general agreement on the reason for the existence of the hump. One possible explanation is as follows. Rates at the short end of the zero curve are controlled by central banks. By contrast, two- and three-year interest rates are determined to a large extent by the activities of traders. These traders may be overreacting to the changes they observe in the short rate and causing the volatility of these rates to be higher than the volatility of short rates. For maturities beyond two to three years, the mean reversion of interest rates, which will be discussed in Chapter 23, causes volatilities to decline.

---

[3] Flat volatilities can be calculated from spot volatilities and vice versa. (See Problem 22.26.)

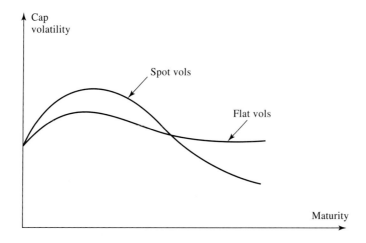

**Figure 22.3**   The volatility hump

Brokers provide tables of flat implied volatilities for caps and floors. The instruments underlying the quotes are usually at the money. This means that the cap/floor rate equals the swap rate for a swap that has the same payment dates as the cap. Table 22.1 shows typical broker quotes for the U.S. dollar market. The tenor of the cap is three months and the cap life varies from one year to ten years. The data exhibits the type of "hump" shown in Figure 22.3.

### *Theoretical Justification for the Model*

We can show that Black's model for a caplet is internally consistent by considering a world that is forward risk neutral with respect to a zero-coupon bond maturing at time $t_{k+1}$. The analysis in Section 21.4 shows that:

1. The current value of any security is its expected value at time $t_{k+1}$ in this world multiplied by the price of a zero-coupon bond maturing at time $t_{k+1}$ (see equation (21.20)).
2. The expected value of an interest rate lasting between times $t_k$ and $t_{k+1}$ equals the forward interest rate in this world (see equation (21.22)).

**Table 22.1**   Typical broker volatility quotes for U.S. dollar caps and floors (percent per annum)

| *Life* | *Cap bid* | *Cap offer* | *Floor bid* | *Floor offer* |
|---|---|---|---|---|
| 1 year | 18.00 | 20.00 | 18.00 | 20.00 |
| 2 years | 23.25 | 24.25 | 23.75 | 24.75 |
| 3 years | 24.00 | 25.00 | 24.50 | 25.50 |
| 4 years | 23.75 | 24.75 | 24.25 | 25.25 |
| 5 years | 23.50 | 24.50 | 24.00 | 25.00 |
| 7 years | 21.75 | 22.75 | 22.00 | 23.00 |
| 10 years | 20.00 | 21.00 | 20.25 | 21.25 |

The first of these results shows that, with the notation introduced earlier, the price of a caplet that provides a payoff at time $t_{k+1}$ is

$$L\delta_k P(0, t_{k+1})E_{k+1}[\max(R_k - R_K, 0)]$$

where $E_{k+1}$ denotes the expected value in a world that is forward risk neutral with respect to a zero-coupon bond maturing at time $t_{k+1}$. From Appendix 12A, this becomes

$$L\delta_k P(0, t_{k+1})[E_{k+1}(R_k)N(d_1) - R_K N(d_2)]$$

where

$$d_1 = \frac{\ln[E_{k+1}(R_k)/R_K] + \sigma_k^2 t_k/2}{\sigma_k\sqrt{t_k}}$$

$$d_2 = \frac{\ln[E_{k+1}(R_k)/R_K] - \sigma_k^2 t_k/2}{\sigma_k\sqrt{t_k}} = d_1 - \sigma\sqrt{t_k}$$

The second result implies that

$$E_{k+1}(R_k) = F_k$$

Together the results lead to the cap pricing model in equation (22.11). They show that we can discount at the $t_{k+1}$-maturity interest rate observed in the market today provided that we set the expected interest rate equal to the forward interest rate.

### Use of DerivaGem

The software DerivaGem accompanying this book can be used to price interest rate caps and floors using Black's model. In the Cap_and_Swap_Option worksheet, select Cap/Floor as the Underlying Type and Black-European as the Pricing Model. The zero curve is input using continuously compounded rates. The inputs include the start date and the end date of the period covered by the cap, the flat volatility, and the cap settlement frequency (i.e., the tenor). The software calculates the payment dates by working back from the end of period covered by the cap to the beginning. The initial caplet/floorlet is assumed to cover a period of length between 0.5 and 1.5 times a regular period. Suppose, for example, that the period covered by the cap is 1.2 years to 2.8 years and the settlement frequency is quarterly. There are six caplets covering the periods 2.55 years to 2.80 years, 2.30 years to 2.55 years, 2.05 years to 2.30 years, 1.80 years to 2.05 years, 1.55 years to 1.80 years, and 1.20 years to 1.55 years.

## 22.4 EUROPEAN SWAP OPTIONS

Swap options, or *swaptions*, are options on interest rate swaps and are another increasingly popular type of interest rate option. They give the holder the right to enter into a certain interest rate swap at a certain time in the future. (The holder does not, of course, have to exercise this right.) Many large financial institutions that offer interest rate swap contracts to their corporate clients are also prepared to sell them swaptions or buy swaptions from them.

To give an example of how a swaption might be used, consider a company that knows that in six months it will enter into a five-year floating-rate loan agreement and knows that it will wish to swap the floating interest payments for fixed interest payments to convert the loan into a fixed-rate loan (see Chapter 6 for a discussion of how swaps can be used in this way). At a cost, the company could enter into a swaption giving it the right to receive six-month LIBOR and pay a certain fixed rate of interest, say 8% per annum, for a five-year period starting in six months. If the fixed rate exchanged for floating on a regular five-year swap in six months turns out to be less than 8% per annum, the company will choose not to exercise the swaption and will enter into a swap agreement in the usual way. However, if it turns out to be greater than 8% per annum, the company will choose to exercise the swaption and will obtain a swap at more favorable terms than those available in the market.

Swaptions, when used in the way just described, provide companies with a guarantee that the fixed rate of interest they will pay on a loan at some future time will not exceed some level. They are an alternative to forward swaps (sometimes called *deferred swaps*). Forward swaps involve no up-front cost but have the disadvantage of obligating the company to enter into a swap agreement. With a swaption, the company is able to benefit from favorable interest rate movements while acquiring protection from unfavorable interest rate movements. The difference between a swaption and a forward swap is analogous to the difference between an option on foreign exchange and a forward contract on foreign exchange.

### Relation to Bond Options

It will be recalled from Chapter 6 that an interest rate swap can be regarded as an agreement to exchange a fixed-rate bond for a floating-rate bond. At the start of a swap, the value of the floating-rate bond always equals the notional principal of the swap. A swaption can, therefore, be regarded as an option to exchange a fixed-rate bond for the notional principal of the swap. If a swaption gives the holder the right to pay fixed and receive floating, it is a put option on the fixed-rate bond with strike price equal to the notional principal. If a swaption gives the holder the right to pay floating and receive fixed, it is a call option on the fixed-rate bond with a strike price equal to the principal.

### Valuation of European Swap Options

The swap rate for a particular maturity at a particular time is the fixed rate that would be exchanged for LIBOR in a newly issued swap with that maturity. The model usually used to value a European option on a swap assumes that the relevant swap rate at the maturity of the option is lognormal. Consider a swaption where we have the right to pay a rate $s_K$ and receive LIBOR on a swap that will last $n$ years starting in $T$ years. We suppose that there are $m$ payments per year under the swap and that the notional principal is $L$.

Suppose that the swap rate for an $n$-year swap at the maturity of the swap option is $s_T$. (Both $s_T$ and $s_K$ are expressed with a compounding frequency of $m$ times per year.) By comparing the cash flows on a swap where the fixed rate is $s_T$ to the cash flows on a swap where the fixed rate is $s_K$, we see that the payoff from the swaption consists of a series of cash flows equal to

$$\frac{L}{m}\max(s_T - s_K, 0)$$

The cash flows are received $m$ times per year for the $n$ years of the life of the swap. Suppose that the payment dates are $T_1, T_2, \ldots, T_{mn}$, measured in years from today (it is approximately true that $T_i = T + i/m$). Each cash flow is the payoff from a call option on $s_T$ with strike price $s_K$.

Using equation (22.3), the value of the cash flow received at time $T_i$ is

$$\frac{L}{m}P(0, T_i)[s_0 N(d_1) - s_K N(d_2)]$$

where

$$d_1 = \frac{\ln(s_0/s_K) + \sigma^2 T/2}{\sigma\sqrt{T}}$$

$$d_2 = \frac{\ln(s_0/s_K) - \sigma^2 T/2}{\sigma\sqrt{T}} = d_1 - \sigma\sqrt{T}$$

and $s_0$ is the forward swap rate.

The total value of the swaption is

$$\sum_{i=1}^{mn} \frac{L}{m} P(0, T_i)[s_0 N(d_1) - s_K N(d_2)]$$

Defining $A$ as the value of a contract that pays $1/m$ at times $T_i$ ($1 \leqslant i \leqslant mn$), the value of the swaption becomes

$$LA[s_0 N(d_1) - s_K N(d_2)] \tag{22.13}$$

where

$$A = \frac{1}{m} \sum_{i=1}^{mn} P(0, T_i)$$

If the swaption gives the holder the right to receive a fixed rate of $s_K$ instead of paying it, the payoff from the swaption is

$$\frac{L}{m} \max(s_K - s_T, 0)$$

This is a put option on $s_T$. As before, the payoffs are received at times $T_i$ ($1 \leqslant i \leqslant mn$). Equation (22.4) gives the value of the swaption as

$$LA[s_K N(-d_2) - s_0 N(-d_1)] \tag{22.14}$$

**Example 22.4** Suppose that the LIBOR yield curve is flat at 6% per annum with continuous compounding. Consider a swaption that gives the holder the right to pay 6.2% in a three-year swap starting in five years. The volatility for the swap rate is 20%. Payments are made semiannually and the principal is $100. In this case,

$$A = \tfrac{1}{2}[e^{-0.06 \times 5.5} + e^{-0.06 \times 6} + e^{-0.06 \times 6.5} + e^{-0.06 \times 7} + e^{-0.06 \times 7.5} + e^{-0.06 \times 8}] = 2.0035$$

A rate of 6% per annum with continuous compounding translates into 6.09% with semiannual compounding. It follows that, in this example, $s_0 = 0.0609$, $s_K = 0.062$, $T = 5$, $\sigma = 0.2$, so that

$$d_1 = \frac{\ln(0.0609/0.062) + 0.2^2 \times 5/2}{0.2\sqrt{5}} = 0.1836$$

$$d_2 = d_1 - 0.2\sqrt{5} = -0.2636$$

From equation (22.13), the value of the swaption is

$$100 \times 2.0035[0.0609 \times N(0.1836) - 0.062 \times N(-0.2636)] = 2.07$$

or $2.07. (This is in agreement with the price given by DerivaGem.)

Brokers provide tables of implied volatilities for European swap options. The instruments

**Table 22.2** Typical broker quotes for U.S. European swap options (mid-market volatilities percent per annum)

| Expiration | Swap length | | | | | | |
|---|---|---|---|---|---|---|---|
| | *1 year* | *2 years* | *3 years* | *4 years* | *5 years* | *7 years* | *10 years* |
| 1 month | 17.75 | 17.75 | 17.75 | 17.50 | 17.00 | 17.00 | 16.00 |
| 3 months | 19.50 | 19.00 | 19.00 | 18.00 | 17.50 | 17.00 | 16.00 |
| 6 months | 20.00 | 20.00 | 19.25 | 18.50 | 18.75 | 17.75 | 16.75 |
| 1 year | 22.50 | 21.75 | 20.50 | 20.00 | 19.50 | 18.25 | 16.75 |
| 2 years | 22.00 | 22.00 | 20.75 | 19.50 | 19.75 | 18.25 | 16.75 |
| 3 years | 21.50 | 21.00 | 20.00 | 19.25 | 19.00 | 17.75 | 16.50 |
| 4 years | 20.75 | 20.25 | 19.25 | 18.50 | 18.25 | 17.50 | 16.00 |
| 5 years | 20.00 | 19.50 | 18.50 | 17.75 | 17.50 | 17.00 | 15.50 |

underlying the quotes are usually at the money. This means that the strike swap rate equals the forward swap rate. Table 22.2 shows typical broker quotes provided for the U.S. dollar market. The tenor of the underlying swaps (i.e., the frequency of resets on the floating rate) is six months. The life of the option is shown on the vertical scale. This varies from one month to five years. The life of the underlying swap at the maturity of the option is shown on the horizontal scale. This varies from one year to ten years. The volatilities in the one-year column of the table correspond to instruments that are similar to caps. They exhibit the hump discussed earlier. As we move to the columns corresponding to options on longer-lived swaps, the hump persists but becomes less pronounced.

## Theoretical Justification for the Swap Option Model

We can show that Black's model for swap options is internally consistent by considering a world that is forward risk neutral with respect to the annuity $A$. The analysis in Section 21.4 shows that:

1. The current value of any security is the current value of the annuity multiplied by the expected value of

$$\frac{\text{security price at time } T}{\text{value of the annuity at time } T}$$

  in this world (see equation (21.25)).

2. The expected value of the swap rate at time $T$ in this world equals the forward swap rate (see equation (21.24)).

The payoff at time $T$ from a swap option where we have the right to pay $s_K$ and receive floating is the value of an annuity times

$$\frac{L}{m}\max(s_T - s_K, 0)$$

The first result shows that the value of the swaption is

$$LAE_A[\max(s_T - s_K, 0)]$$

From Appendix 12A, this is

$$LA[E_A(s_T)N(d_1) - s_K N(d_2)]$$

where

$$d_1 = \frac{\ln[E_A(s_T)/s_K] + \sigma^2 T/2}{\sigma\sqrt{T}}$$

$$d_2 = \frac{\ln[E_A(s_T)/s_K] - \sigma^2 T/2}{\sigma\sqrt{T}} = d_1 - \sigma\sqrt{T}$$

The second result shows that $E_A(s_T)$ equals $s_0$. Taken together, the results lead to the swap option pricing formula in equation (22.13). They show that we are entitled to treat interest rates as constant for the purposes of discounting provided that we also set the expected swap rate equal to the forward swap rate.

## 22.5  GENERALIZATIONS

We have presented three different versions of Black's model: one for bond options, one for caps, and one for swap options. Each of the models is internally consistent, but they are not consistent with each other. For example, when future bond prices are lognormal, future zero rates and swap rates are not; and when future zero rates are lognormal, future bond prices and swap rates are not.

These results we have produced can be generalized as follows:

1. Consider any instrument that provides a payoff at time $T$ dependent on the price of a security observed at time $T$. Its current value is $P(0, T)$ times the expected payoff provided that expectations are calculated in a world where the expected value of the underlying security equals its forward price.

2. Consider any instrument that provides a payoff at time $T_2$ dependent on the $T_2$-maturity interest rate observed at time $T_1$. Its current value is $P(0, T_2)$ times the expected payoff provided that expectations are calculated in a world where the expected value of the underlying interest rate equals the forward interest rate.

3. Consider any instrument that provides a payoff in the form of an annuity. We suppose that the size of the annuity is determined at time $T$ as a function of the swap rate for an $n$-year swap starting at time $T$. We also suppose that annuity lasts for $n$ years and payment dates for the annuity are the same as those for the swap. The value of the instrument is $A$ times the expected payoff per year, where (a) $A$ is current value of the annuity when payments are at the rate $1 per year and (b) expectations are taken in a world where the expected future swap rate equals the forward swap rate.

The first of these results is a generalization of the European bond option model; the second is a generalization of the cap/floor model; the third is a generalization of the swap option model.

## 22.6  CONVEXITY ADJUSTMENTS

This section discusses what happens when an instrument provides a payoff at time $T$ dependent on a bond yield calculated at time $T$.

The forward yield on a bond is defined as the yield implied by the forward bond price. Suppose that $B_T$ is the price of a bond at time $T$, $y_T$ is its yield, and the relationship between $B_T$ and $y_T$ is

$$B_T = G(y_T)$$

Define $F_0$ as the forward bond price at time zero for a contract maturing at time $T$ and $y_0$ as the forward bond yield at time zero. The definition of a forward bond yield means that

$$F_0 = G(y_0)$$

The function $G$ is nonlinear. This means that, when the expected future bond price equals the forward bond price (so that we are a world that is forward risk neutral with respect to a zero-coupon bond maturing at time $T$), the expected future bond yield does not equal the forward bond yield.

This is illustrated in Figure 22.4, which shows the relationship between bond prices and bond yields at time $T$. For simplicity, we suppose that there are only three possible bond prices, $B_1$, $B_2$, and $B_3$, and that they are equally likely in a world that is forward risk neutral with respect to $P(t, T)$. We assume that the bond prices are equally spaced, so that $B_2 - B_1 = B_3 - B_2$. The expected bond price is $B_2$ and this is also the forward bond price. The bond prices translate into three equally likely bond yields, $Y_1$, $Y_2$, and $Y_3$, which are not equally spaced. The variable $Y_2$ is the forward bond yield because it is the yield corresponding to the forward bond price. The expected bond yield is the average of $Y_1$, $Y_2$, and $Y_3$ and is clearly greater than $Y_2$.

Consider now a derivative that provides a payoff dependent on the bond yield at time $T$. We know from equation (21.20) that it can be valued by (a) calculating the expected payoff in a world that is forward risk neutral with respect to a zero-coupon bond maturing at time $T$ and (b) discounting at the current risk-free rate for maturity $T$. We know that the expected bond price equals the forward price in the world being considered. We therefore need to know the value of the expected bond yield when the expected bond price equals the forward bond price. The analysis in Appendix 22A shows that an approximate expression for the required expected bond yield is

$$E_T(y_T) = y_0 - \tfrac{1}{2} y_0^2 \sigma_y^2 T \frac{G''(y_0)}{G'(y_0)} \tag{22.15}$$

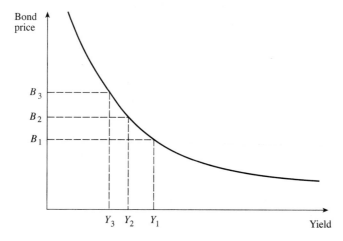

**Figure 22.4**   Relationship between bond prices and bond yields

where $G'$ and $G''$ denote the first and second partial derivatives of $G$, $E_T$ denotes expectations in a world that is forward risk neutral with respect to $P(t, T)$, and $\sigma_y$ is the forward yield volatility. It follows that we can discount expected payoffs at the current risk-free rate for maturity $T$ provided that we assume that the expected bond yield is

$$y_0 - \frac{1}{2}y_0^2\sigma_y^2 T \frac{G''(y_0)}{G'(y_0)}$$

rather than $y_0$. The difference between the expected bond yield and the forward bond yield,

$$-\frac{1}{2}y_0^2\sigma_y^2 T \frac{G''(y_0)}{G'(y_0)}$$

is known as a *convexity adjustment*. It corresponds to the difference between $Y_2$ and the expected yield in Figure 22.4. (The convexity adjustment is positive because $G'(y_0) < 0$ and $G''(y_0) > 0$.)

### Application 1: Interest Rates

As our first application of equation (22.15), we consider an instrument that provides a cash flow at time $T$ equal to the interest rate between times $T$ and $T^*$ applied to a principal of $L$. (This example will be useful when we consider LIBOR-in-arrears swaps in Chapter 25.) Note that the interest rate applicable to the time period between times $T$ and $T^*$ is normally paid $T^*$; here we are assuming that it is paid early, at time $T$.

The cash flow at time $T$ in the instrument we are considering is $LR_T\tau$, where $\tau = T^* - T$ and $R_T$ is the zero-coupon interest rate applicable to the period between $T$ and $T^*$ (expressed with a compounding period of $\tau$). The variable $R_T$ can be viewed as the yield on a zero-coupon bond maturing at time $T^*$. The relationship between the price of this bond and its yield is

$$G(y) = \frac{1}{1 + y\tau}$$

From equation (22.15),

$$E_T(R_T) = R_0 - \frac{1}{2}R_0^2\sigma_R^2 T \frac{G''(R_0)}{G'(R_0)}$$

or

$$E_T(R_T) = R_0 + \frac{R_0^2\sigma_R^2\tau T}{1 + R_0\tau} \tag{22.16}$$

where $R_0$ is the forward rate applicable to the period between $T$ and $T^*$ and $\sigma_R$ is the volatility of the forward rate.

The value of the instrument is therefore

$$P(0, T)L\tau\left(R_0 + \frac{R_0^2\sigma_R^2\tau T}{1 + R_0\tau}\right)$$

**Example 22.5**  Consider a derivative that provides a payoff in three years equal to the one-year zero-coupon rate (annually compounded) at that time multiplied by $1000. Suppose that the zero rate for all maturities is 10% per annum with annual compounding and the volatility of the forward rate applicable to the time period between year 3 and year 4 is 20%. In this case, $R_0 = 0.10$, $\sigma_R = 0.20$, $T = 3$, $\tau = 1$, and $P(0, 3) = 1/1.10^3 = 0.7513$. The value of the derivative is

$$0.7513 \times 1000 \times 1\left(0.10 + \frac{0.10^2 \times 0.20^2 \times 1 \times 3}{1 + 0.10 \times 1}\right)$$

or $75.95. (This compares with a price of $75.13 when no convexity adjustment is made.)

### Application 2: Swap Rates

Consider next a derivative providing a payoff at time $T$ equal to a swap rate observed at that time. A swap rate is a par yield. For the purposes of calculating a convexity adjustment, we make an approximation and assume that the $N$-year swap rate at time $T$ equals the yield at that time on an $N$-year bond with a coupon equal to today's forward swap rate. This enables equation (22.15) to be used.

**Example 22.6**  Consider an instrument that provides a payoff in three years equal to the three-year swap rate at that time multiplied by $100. Suppose that payments are made annually on the swap, the zero rate for all maturities is 12% per annum with annual compounding, the volatility for the three-year forward swap rate in three years (implied from swap option prices) is 22%. We approximate the swap rate as the yield on a 12% bond, so that the relevant function $G(y)$ is

$$G(y) = \frac{0.12}{1 + y} + \frac{0.12}{(1 + y)^2} + \frac{1.12}{(1 + y)^3}$$

$$G'(y) = -\frac{0.12}{(1 + y)^2} - \frac{0.24}{(1 + y)^3} - \frac{3.36}{(1 + y)^4}$$

$$G''(y) = \frac{0.24}{(1 + y)^3} + \frac{0.72}{(1 + y)^4} + \frac{13.44}{(1 + y)^5}$$

In this case the forward yield, $y_0$, is 0.12, so that $G'(y_0) = -2.4018$ and $G''(y_0) = 8.2546$. From equation (22.15),

$$E_T(y_T) = 0.12 + \tfrac{1}{2} \times 0.12^2 \times 0.22^2 \times 3 \times \frac{8.2546}{2.4018} = 0.1236$$

We should therefore assume a forward swap rate of 0.1236 (= 12.36%) rather than 0.12 when valuing the instrument. The instrument is worth

$$\frac{100 \times 0.1236}{1.12^3} = 8.80$$

or $8.80. (This compares with a price of 8.54 obtained without any convexity adjustment.)

## 22.7  TIMING ADJUSTMENTS

In this section we examine the situation where a derivative provides a payoff at time $T_2$, based on the value of a variable $v$ observed at an earlier time $T_1$. Define:

$v_1$:  Value of $v$ at time $T_1$

$F$:  Forward value of $v$ for a contract maturing at time $T_1$

$E_1(v_1)$:  Expected value of $v_1$ in a world that is forward risk neutral with respect to $P(t, T_1)$

$E_2(v_1)$: Expected value of $v_1$ in a world that is forward risk neutral with respect to $P(t, T_2)$

$G$: Forward price of a zero-coupon bond lasting between $T_1$ and $T_2$

$R$: Forward interest rate for period between $T_1$ and $T_2$, expressed with a compounding frequency of $m$

$R_0$: Value of $R$ today

$\sigma_F$: Volatility of $F$

$\sigma_G$: Volatility of $G$

$\sigma_R$: Volatility of $R$

$\rho$: Instantaneous correlation between $F$ and $R$.

When we move from a world that is forward risk neutral with respect to $P(t, T_1)$ to one that is forward risk neutral with respect to $P(t, T_2)$, the numeraire ratio is

$$G = \frac{P(t, T_2)}{P(t, T_1)}$$

From Section 21.7, the growth rate of $v$ increases by

$$\alpha_v = -\rho \sigma_G \sigma_F \qquad (22.17)$$

(The minus sign reflects the fact that, because $G$ and $R$ are instantaneously perfectly negatively correlated, the correlation between $G$ and $F$ is $-\rho$.)
   Because

$$G = \frac{1}{(1 + R/m)^{m(T_2 - T_1)}}$$

the relationship between the volatility of $G$ and the volatility of $R$ can be calculated from Itô's lemma as

$$\sigma_G = \frac{\sigma_R R(T_2 - T_1)}{1 + R/m}$$

Hence equation (22.17) becomes

$$\alpha_v = -\frac{\rho \sigma_F \sigma_R R(T_2 - T_1)}{1 + R/m}$$

As an approximation we can assume that $R$ remains constant at $R_0$ to get

$$E_2(v_1) = E_1(v_1) \exp\left(-\frac{\rho \sigma_F \sigma_R R_0 T_1 (T_2 - T_1)}{1 + R_0/m}\right) \qquad (22.18)$$

This equation shows how we can adjust the forward value of a variable to allow for a delay between the variable being observed and the payoff being made.

**Example 22.7**   Consider a derivative that provides a payoff in six years equal to the value of a stock index observed in five years. Suppose that 1,200 is the forward value of the stock index for a contract maturing in five years. Suppose that the volatility of the forward value of the index is 20%, the volatility of the forward interest rate between years five and six is 18%, and the correlation between the two is −0.4. Suppose further that the zero curve is flat at 8% with annual compounding.

We apply the results we have just produced to the situation where $v$ is equal the value of the index, $T_1 = 5$, $T_2 = 6$, $m = 1$, $R_0 = 0.08$, $\rho = -0.4$, $\sigma_F = 0.20$, and $\sigma_R = 0.18$, so that

$$E_2(v_1) = E_1(v_1)\exp\left(-\frac{-0.4 \times 0.20 \times 0.18 \times 0.08 \times 5 \times 1}{1 + 0.08}\right)$$

or $E_2(v_1) = 1.00535E_1(v_1)$. From the forward risk-neutral arguments in Chapter 21, we know that $E_1(v_1)$ is the forward price of the index, or 1,200. It follows that

$$E_2(v_T) = 1,200 \times 1.00535 = 1,206.42$$

The value of the derivative is $1,206.42 \times P(0,6)$. In this case $P(0,6) = 1/1.08^6 = 0.6302$, so that the value of the derivative is 760.25.

### Application 1 Revisited

The analysis just given provides a different way of producing the result in Application 1 of Section 22.6. Using the notation from that application, we define $R_T$ as the interest rate between $T$ and $T^*$ and $R_0$ as the forward rate for the period between time $T$ and $T^*$. In a world that is forward risk neutral with respect of $P(0, T^*)$, the expected value of $R_T$ is $R_0$. Equation (22.18) gives[4]

$$R_0 = E_T(R_T)\exp\left(-\frac{\sigma_R^2 R_0 T \tau}{1 + R_0 \tau}\right)$$

where $\tau = T^* - T$. Equivalently,

$$E_T(R_T) = R_0 \exp\left(\frac{\sigma_R^2 R_0 T \tau}{1 + R_0 \tau}\right)$$

Approximating the exponential function, we see that

$$E_T(R_T) = R_0 + \frac{R_0^2 \sigma_R^2 \tau T}{1 + R_0 \tau}$$

This is the same result as equation (22.16).

## 22.8  NATURAL TIME LAGS

The results in Sections 22.2 to 22.5 showed:

1. When the payoff from a derivative depends on the price of a traded security in a certain currency at time $T$ and is made at time $T$ in the same currency, we can value the derivative by assuming that the expected future value of the traded security equals its forward price. The expected payoff from the derivative is discounted at the risk-free rate observed in the market today for a maturity of $T$.

2. When the payoff from a derivative depends on the $T_2$-maturity interest rate observed at time $T_1$ in a certain currency and is made at time $T_2$ in the same currency, we can value the derivative by assuming that the expected future value of the interest rate equals the forward

---

[4] In this application of equation (22.18), $T_1 = T$, $T_2 = T^*$, $F = R$, so that $\sigma_F = \sigma_R$, and $\rho = 1$. Also, $m = 1/\tau$.

interest rate. The expected payoff from the derivative is discounted at the risk-free rate observed in the market today for a maturity of $T_2$.

3. When the payoff from a derivative depends on the swap rate at time $T$ in a certain currency and is an annuity in the same currency starting at time $T$, with the annuity payment dates being the swap payment dates, we can value the derivative by assuming that the expected future swap rate equals the forward swap rate. The expected payoffs from the derivatives are discounted using today's zero curve.

In each of these cases, we can say that the payoffs from the derivative incorporate natural time lags and are made in the natural currency. When we buy a traded security, we are expected to pay for it immediately. There is no time lag. When we borrow or lend money, we observe the interest rate at one time and the interest is paid (in the same currency) at the maturity of the interest rate. When we enter into a swap, the payments corresponding to the swap rate are made in the form of an annuity. In general, when a derivative is structured so that it incorporates natural time lags, no adjustments to forward rates and prices are required to value the derivative.

In Sections 22.6 and 22.7 we covered situations where payoffs from derivatives do not incorporate natural time lags and showed that adjustments to forward rates and forward prices are necessary when the derivatives are valued. This material complements the material in Section 21.8, which shows that forward rates and forward prices have to be adjusted when payoffs are not in the natural currency.

## 22.9  HEDGING INTEREST RATE DERIVATIVES

This section discusses how the material on Greek letters in Chapter 14 can be extended to cover interest rate derivatives.

In the context of interest rate derivatives, delta risk is the risk associated with a shift in the zero curve. Because there are many ways in which the zero curve can shift, many alternative deltas can be calculated. Some alternatives are:

1. Calculate the impact of a one-basis-point parallel shift in the zero curve. This is sometimes termed a DV01.

2. Calculate the impact of small changes in the quotes for each of the instruments used to construct the zero curve.

3. Divide the zero curve (or the forward curve) into a number of sections (or buckets). Calculate the impact of shifting the rates in one bucket by one basis point, keeping the rest of the initial term structure unchanged.

4. Carry out a principal components analysis as outlined in Section 16.9. Calculate a delta with respect to changes in each of the first few factors. The first delta then measures the impact of a small, approximately parallel, shift in the zero curve; the second delta measures the impact of a small twist in the zero curve; and so on.

In practice, traders tend to prefer the second approach. They argue that the only way the zero curve can change is if the quote for one of the instruments used to compute the zero curve changes. They therefore feel that it makes sense to focus on the exposures arising from changes in the prices of these instruments.

When several delta measures are calculated, there are many possible gamma measures. Suppose that ten instruments are used to compute the zero curve and that we measure deltas with respect to changes in the quotes for each of these. Gamma is a second partial derivative of the form $\partial^2\Pi/\partial x_i\,\partial x_j$, where $\Pi$ is the portfolio value. We have 10 choices for $x_i$ and 10 choices for $x_j$ and a total of 55 different gamma measures. This may be more than the trader can handle. One approach is ignore cross-gammas and focus on the 10 partial derivatives where $i = j$. Another is to calculate a single gamma measure as the second partial derivative of the value of the portfolio with respect to a parallel shift in the zero curve. A further possibility is to calculate gamma with respect to the first two factors in a principal components analysis.

The vega of a portfolio of interest rate derivatives measures its exposure to volatility changes. One approach is to calculate the impact on the portfolio of the making the same small change to the Black volatilities of all caps and European swap options. However, this assumes that one factor drives all volatilities and may be too simplistic. A better idea is to carry out a principal components analysis on the volatilities of caps and swap options and calculate vega measures corresponding to the first two or three factors.

## SUMMARY

Black's model provides a popular approach for valuing European-style interest rate options. The essence of Black's model is that the value of the variable underlying the option is assumed to be lognormal at the maturity of the option. In the case of a European bond option, Black's model assumes that the underlying bond price is lognormal at the option's maturity. For a cap, the model assumes that the interest rate underlying each of the constituent caplets is lognormally distributed. In the case of a swap option, the model assumes that the underlying swap rate is lognormally distributed. Each of these models is internally consistent, but they are not consistent with each other.

Black's model involves calculating the expected payoff based on the assumption that the expected value of a variable equal its forward price and then discounting the expected payoff at the zero rate observed in the market today. When the payoff does not incorporate a natural time lag, a convexity or timing adjustment to the forward price of the variable is necessary. For example, if an interest rate or a swap rate is observed at time $T$ and leads to a payoff at time $T$, a convexity adjustment is necessary. If a value of an investment asset is observed at time $T$ and payment is made at a later time, a timing adjustment is necessary.

## SUGGESTIONS FOR FURTHER READING

Black, F., "The Pricing of Commodity Contracts," *Journal of Financial Economics*, 3 (March 1976), 167–79.

Brotherton-Ratcliffe, R., and B. Iben, "Yield Curve Applications of Swap Products," in *Advanced Strategies in Financial Risk Management*, ed. R. Schwartz and C. Smith, New York Institute of Finance, New York, 1993.

# QUESTIONS AND PROBLEMS
# (ANSWERS IN SOLUTIONS MANUAL)

22.1. A company caps three-month LIBOR at 10% per annum. The principal amount is $20 million. On a reset date, three-month LIBOR is 12% per annum. What payment would this lead to under the cap? When would the payment be made?

22.2. Explain why a swap option can be regarded as a type of bond option.

22.3. Use Black's model to value a one-year European put option on a 10-year bond. Assume that the current value of the bond is $125, the strike price is $110, the one-year interest rate is 10% per annum, the bond's price volatility is 8% per annum, and the present value of the coupons to be paid during the life of the option is $10.

22.4. Explain how you would value a derivative that pays off $100R$ in five years, where $R$ is the one-year interest rate (annually compounded) observed in four years. What difference would it make if the payoff were in four years? What difference would it make if the payoff were in six years?

22.5. Explain whether any convexity or timing adjustments are necessary when.
   a. We wish to value a spread option that pays off every quarter the excess (if any) of the five-year swap rate over the three month LIBOR rate applied to a principal of $100. The payoff occurs 90 days after the rates are observed.
   b. We wish to value a derivative that pays off every quarter the three-month LIBOR rate minus the three-month Treasury bill rate. The payoff occurs 90 days after the rates are observed.

22.6. Explain carefully how you would use (a) spot volatilities and (b) flat volatilities to value a five-year cap.

22.7. Calculate the price of an option that caps the three-month rate, starting in 15 months time, at 13% (quoted with quarterly compounding) on a principal amount of $1,000. The forward interest rate for the period in question is 12% per annum (quoted with quarterly compounding), the 18-month risk-free interest rate (continuously compounded) is 11.5% per annum, and the volatility of the forward rate is 12% per annum.

22.8. A bank uses Black's model to price European bond options. Suppose that an implied price volatility for a five-year option on a bond maturing in 10 years is used to price a nine-year option on the bond. Would you expect the resultant price to be too high or too low? Explain.

22.9. Calculate the value of a four-year European call option on a five-year bond using Black's model. The five-year cash bond price is $105, the cash price of a four-year bond with the same coupon is $102, the strike price is $100, the four-year risk-free interest rate is 10% per annum with continuous compounding, and the volatility for the bond price in four years is 2% per annum.

22.10. If the yield volatility for a five-year put option on a bond maturing in 10 years time is specified as 22%, how should the option be valued? Assume that, based on today's interest rates, the modified duration of the bond at the maturity of the option will be 4.2 years and the forward yield on the bond is 7%.

22.11. What other instrument is the same as a five-year zero-cost collar where the strike price of the cap equals the strike price of the floor? What does the common strike price equal?

22.12. Derive a put–call parity relationship for European bond options.

22.13. Derive a put–call parity relationship for European swap options.

22.14. Explain why there is an arbitrage opportunity if the implied Black (flat) volatility of a cap is different from that of a floor. Do the broker quotes in Table 22.1 present an arbitrage opportunity?

22.15. When a bond's price is lognormal can the bond's yield be negative? Explain your answer.

22.16. Suppose that in Example 22.3 of Section 22.3 the payoff occurs after one year (i.e., when the interest rate is observed) rather than in 15 months. What difference does this make to the inputs to Black's models?

22.17. The yield curve is flat at 10% per annum with annual compounding. Calculate the value of an instrument where, in five years' time, the two-year swap rate (with annual compounding) is received and a fixed rate of 10% is paid. Both are applied to a notional principal of $100. Assume that the volatility of the swap rate is 20% per annum. Explain why the value of the instrument is different from zero.

22.18. What difference does it make in Problem 22.17 if the swap rate is observed in five years, but the exchange of payments takes place in (a) six years, and (b) seven years? Assume that the volatilities of all forward rates are 20%. Assume also that the forward swap rate for the period between years 5 and 7 has a correlation of 0.8 with the forward interest rate between years 5 and 6 and a correlation of 0.95 with the forward interest rate between years 5 and 7.

22.19. What is the value of a European swap option that gives the holder the right to enter into a three-year annual-pay swap in four years where a fixed rate of 5% is paid and LIBOR is received. The swap principal is $10 million. Assume that the yield curve is flat at 5% per annum with annual compounding and the volatility of the swap rate is 20%. Compare your answer with that given by DerivaGem.

22.20. Suppose that the yield, $R$, on a zero-coupon bond follows the process

$$dR = \mu \, dt + \sigma \, dz$$

where $\mu$ and $\sigma$ are functions of $R$ and $t$, and $dz$ is a Wiener process. Use Itô's lemma to show that the volatility of the zero-coupon bond price declines to zero as it approaches maturity.

22.21. The price of a bond at time $T$, measured in terms of its yield, is $G(y_T)$. Assume geometric Brownian motion for the forward bond yield, $y$, in a world that is forward risk neutral with respect to a bond maturing at time $T$. Suppose that the growth rate of the forward bond yield is $\alpha$ and its volatility $\sigma_y$.
   a. Use Itô's lemma to calculate the process for the forward bond price in terms of $\alpha$, $\sigma_y$, $y$, and $G(y)$.
   b. The forward bond price should follow a martingale in the world considered. Use this fact to calculate an expression for $\alpha$.
   c. Show that the expression for $\alpha$ is, to a first approximation, consistent with equation (22.15).

22.22. Carry out a manual calculation to verify the option prices in Example 22.2.

22.23. Suppose that the 1-year, 2-year, 3-year, 4-year and 5-year zero rates are 6%, 6.4%, 6.7%, 6.9%, and 7%. The price of a 5-year semiannual cap with a principal of $100 at a cap rate of 8% is $3. Use DerivaGem to determine:
   a. The 5-year flat volatility for caps and floors
   b. The floor rate in a zero-cost 5-year collar when the cap rate is 8%

22.24. Show that $V_1 + f = V_2$, where $V_1$ is the value of a swap option to pay a fixed rate of $s_K$ and receive LIBOR between times $T_1$ and $T_2$, $f$ is the value of a forward swap to receive a fixed rate of $s_K$ and pay LIBOR between times $T_1$ and $T_2$, and $V_2$ is the value of a swap option to receive a fixed rate of $s_K$ between times $T_1$ and $T_2$. Deduce that $V_1 = V_2$ when $s_K$ equals the current forward swap rate.

22.25. Suppose that zero rates are as in Problem 22.23. Use DerivaGem to determine the value of an option to pay a fixed rate of 6% and receive LIBOR on a five-year swap starting in one year. Assume that the principal is $100 million, payments are exchanged semiannually, and the swap rate volatility is 21%.

22.26. Describe how you would (a) calculate cap flat volatilities from cap spot volatilities and (b) calculate cap spot volatilities from cap flat volatilities.

# ASSIGNMENT QUESTIONS

22.27. Consider an eight-month European put option on a Treasury bond that currently has 14.25 years to maturity. The current cash bond price is $910, the exercise price is $900, and the volatility for the bond price is 10% per annum. A coupon of $35 will be paid by the bond in three months. The risk-free interest rate is 8% for all maturities up to one year. Use Black's model to determine the price of the option. Consider both the case where the strike price corresponds to the cash price of the bond and the case where it corresponds to the quoted price.

22.28. Calculate the price of a cap on the 90-day LIBOR rate in nine months' time when the principal amount is $1,000. Use Black's model and the following information:
    a. The quoted nine-month Eurodollar futures price = 92 (ignore differences between futures and forward rates)
    b. The interest rate volatility implied by a nine-month Eurodollar option = 15% per annum
    c. The current 12-month interest rate with continuous compounding = 7.5% per annum
    d. The cap rate = 8% per annum. (Assume an actual/360 day count.)

22.29. Suppose that the LIBOR yield curve is flat at 8% with annual compounding. A swaption gives the holder the right to receive 7.6% in a five-year swap starting in four years. Payments are made annually. The volatility for the swap rate is 25% per annum and the principal is $1 million. Use Black's model to price the swaption. Compare your answer with that given by DerivaGem.

22.30. Use the DerivaGem software to value a five-year collar that guarantees that the maximum and minimum interest rates on a LIBOR-based loan (with quarterly resets) are 5% and 7%, respectively. The LIBOR zero curve (continuously compounded) is currently flat at 6%. Use a flat volatility of 20%. Assume that the principal is $100.

22.31. Use the DerivaGem software to value a European swap option that gives you the right in two years to enter into a 5-year swap in which you pay a fixed rate of 6% and receive floating. Cash flows are exchanged semiannually on the swap. The 1-year, 2-year, 5-year, and 10-year zero-coupon interest rates (continuously compounded) are 5%, 6%, 6.5%, and 7%, respectively. Assume a principal of $100 and a volatility of 15% per annum. Give an example of how the swap option might be used by a corporation. What bond option is equivalent to the swap option?

22.32. Suppose that the LIBOR yield curve is flat at 8% (with continuous compounding). The payoff from a derivative occurs in four years. It is equal to the five-year rate minus the two-year rate at this time, applied to a principal of $100 with both rates being continuously compounded. (The payoff can be positive or negative.) Calculate the value of the derivative. Assume that the volatility for all rates is 25%. What difference does it make if the payoff occurs in five years instead of four years? Assume all rates are perfectly correlated.

22.33. Suppose that the payoff from a derivative will occur in ten years and will equal the three-year U.S. dollar swap rate for a semiannual-pay swap observed at that time applied to a certain principal. Assume that the yield curve is flat at 8% (semiannually compounded) per annum in dollars and 3% (semiannually compounded) in yen. The forward swap rate volatility is 18%, the volatility of the ten-year "yen per dollar" forward exchange rate is 12%, and the correlation between this exchange rate and U.S. dollar interest rates is 0.25.

    a. What is the value of the derivative if the swap rate is applied to a principal of $100 million so that the payoff is in dollars?

    b. What is its value of the derivative if the swap rate is applied to a principal of 100 million yen so that the payoff is in yen?

22.34. The payoff from a derivative will occur in 8 years. It will equal the average of the 1-year interest rates observed at times 5, 6, 7, and 8 years applied to a principal of $1,000. The yield curve is flat at 6% with annual compounding and the volatilities of all rates are 16%. Assume perfect correlation between all rates. What is the value of the derivative?

# APPENDIX 22A
## Proof of the Convexity Adjustment Formula

This appendix calculates a convexity adjustment for forward bond yields. Suppose that the payoff from a derivative at time $T$ depends on a bond yield observed at that time. Define:

$y_0$ : Forward bond yield observed today for a forward contract with maturity $T$

$y_T$ : Bond yield at time $T$

$B_T$ : Price of the bond at time $T$

$\sigma_y$ : Volatility of the forward bond yield

We suppose that

$$B_T = G(y_T)$$

Expanding $G(y_T)$ in a Taylor series about $y_T = y_0$ yields the approximation

$$B_T = G(y_0) + (y_T - y_0)G'(y_0) + 0.5(y_T - y_0)^2 G''(y_0)$$

where $G'$ and $G''$ are the first and second partial derivatives of $G$. Taking expectations in a world that is forward risk neutral with respect to a zero-coupon bond maturing at time $T$, we obtain

$$E_T(B_T) = G(y_0) + E_T(y_T - y_0)G'(y_0) + \tfrac{1}{2}E_T[(y_T - y_0)^2]G''(y_0)$$

where $E_T$ denotes expectations in this world. The expression $G(y_0)$ is by definition the forward bond price. Also, because of the particular world we are working in, $E_T(B_T)$ equals the forward bond price. Hence $E_T(B_T) = G(y_0)$, so that

$$E_T(y_T - y_0)G'(y_0) + \tfrac{1}{2}E_T[(y_T - y_0)^2]G''(y_0) = 0$$

The expression $E_T[(y_T - y_0)^2]$ is approximately $\sigma_y^2 y_0^2 T$. Hence it is approximately true that

$$E_T(y_T) = y_0 - \tfrac{1}{2}y_0^2 \sigma_y^2 T \frac{G''(y_0)}{G'(y_0)}$$

This shows that, to obtain the expected bond yield in a world that is forward risk neutral with respect to a zero-coupon bond maturing at time $T$, we should add

$$-\tfrac{1}{2}y_0^2 \sigma_y^2 T \frac{G''(y_0)}{G'(y_0)}$$

to the forward bond yield. This is the result in equation (22.15). For an alternative proof, see Problem 22.21.

# CHAPTER 23

# INTEREST RATE DERIVATIVES: MODELS OF THE SHORT RATE

The models for pricing interest rate options presented in Chapter 22 make the assumption that the probability distribution of an interest rate, a bond price, or some other variable at a future point in time is lognormal. They are widely used for valuing instruments such as caps, European bond options, and European swap options. However, they have limitations. They do not provide a description of how interest rates change through time. Consequently, they cannot be used for valuing interest rate derivatives such as American-style swap options, callable bonds, and structured notes.

This chapter and the next discuss alternative approaches for overcoming these limitations. These involve building what is known as a *term structure model*. This is a model describing the evolution of the zero curve through time. In this chapter we focus on term structure models that are constructed by specifying the behavior of the short-term interest rate, $r$.

## 23.1 EQUILIBRIUM MODELS

Equilibrium models usually start with assumptions about economic variables and derive a process for the short rate, $r$. They then explore what the process for $r$ implies about bond prices and option prices. The short rate, $r$, at time $t$ is the rate that applies to an infinitesimally short period of time at time $t$. It is sometimes referred to as the *instantaneous short rate*. It is not the process for $r$ in the real world that matters. Bond prices, option prices, and other derivative prices depend only on the process followed by $r$ in a risk-neutral world. The risk-neutral world we consider here will be the traditional risk-neutral world, where, in a very short time period between $t$ and $t + \delta t$, investors earn on average $r(t)\,\delta t$. All processes for $r$ that we present will be processes in this risk-neutral world.

From equation (21.19), the value at time $t$ of an interest rate derivative that provides a payoff of $f_T$ at time $T$ is

$$\hat{E}(e^{-\bar{r}(T-t)}f_T) \tag{23.1}$$

where $\bar{r}$ is the average value of $r$ in the time interval between $t$ and $T$, and $\hat{E}$ denotes the expected value in the traditional risk-neutral world.

As usual, we define $P(t, T)$ as the price at time $t$ of a zero-coupon bond that pays off $1 at time $T$. From equation (23.1),

$$P(t, T) = \hat{E}(e^{-\bar{r}(T-t)}) \tag{23.2}$$

**537**

If $R(t, T)$ is the continuously compounded interest rate at time $t$ for a term of $T - t$, then

$$P(t, T) = e^{-R(t,T)(T-t)} \tag{23.3}$$

so that

$$R(t, T) = -\frac{1}{T - t} \ln P(t, T) \tag{23.4}$$

and, from equation (23.2),

$$R(t, T) = -\frac{1}{T - t} \ln \hat{E}(e^{-\bar{r}(T-t)}) \tag{23.5}$$

This equation enables the term structure of interest rates at any given time to be obtained from the value of $r$ at that time and the risk-neutral process for $r$. It shows that, once we have fully defined the process for $r$, we have fully defined everything about the initial zero curve and its evolution through time.

## 23.2  ONE-FACTOR EQUILIBRIUM MODELS

In a one-factor equilibrium model, the process for $r$ involves only one source of uncertainty. Usually the risk-neutral process for the short rate is described by an Itô process of the form

$$dr = m(r) \, dt + s(r) \, dz$$

The instantaneous drift, $m$, and instantaneous standard deviation, $s$, are assumed to be functions of $r$, but are independent of time. The assumption of a single factor is not as restrictive as it might appear. A one-factor model implies that all rates move in the same direction over any short time interval, but not that they all move by the same amount. The shape of the zero curve can therefore change with the passage of time.

The next three sections consider three one-factor equilibrium models:

$m(r) = \mu r, \quad s(r) = \sigma r \quad$ (Rendleman and Bartter model)

$m(r) = a(b - r), \quad s(r) = \sigma \quad$ (Vasicek model)

$m(r) = a(b - r), \quad s(r) = \sigma\sqrt{r} \quad$ (Cox, Ingersoll, and Ross model)

## 23.3  THE RENDLEMAN AND BARTTER MODEL

In the Rendleman and Bartter model, the risk-neutral process for $r$ is[1]

$$dr = \mu r \, dt + \sigma r \, dz$$

where $\mu$ and $\sigma$ are constants. This means that $r$ follows geometric Brownian motion. The process for $r$ is of the same type as that assumed for a stock price in Chapter 12. It can be represented using a binomial tree similar to the one used for stocks in Chapter 18.[2]

---

[1] See R. Rendleman and B. Bartter, "The Pricing of Options on Debt Securities," *Journal of Financial and Quantitative Analysis*, 15 (March 1980), 11–24.

[2] The way that the interest rate tree is used is explained later in the chapter.

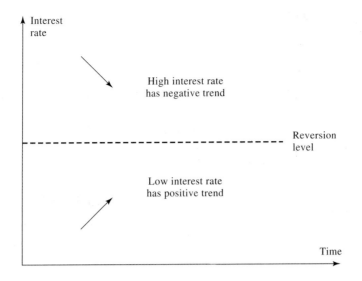

**Figure 23.1**   Mean reversion

### *Mean Reversion*

The assumption that the short-term interest rate behaves like a stock price is a natural starting point but is less than ideal. One important difference between interest rates and stock prices is that interest rates appear to be pulled back to some long-run average level over time. This phenomenon is known as *mean reversion*. When $r$ is high, mean reversion tends to cause it to have a negative drift; when $r$ is low, mean reversion tends to cause it to have a positive drift. Mean reversion is illustrated in Figure 23.1. The Rendleman and Bartter model does not incorporate mean reversion.

There are compelling economic arguments in favor of mean reversion. When rates are high, the economy tends to slow down and there is low demand for funds from borrowers. As a result, rates decline. When rates are low, there tends to be a high demand for funds on the part of borrowers and rates tend to rise.

## 23.4   THE VASICEK MODEL

In Vasicek's model, the risk-neutral process for $r$ is

$$dr = a(b - r)\,dt + \sigma\,dz$$

where $a$, $b$, and $\sigma$ are constants.[3] This model incorporates mean reversion. The short rate is pulled to a level $b$ at rate $a$. Superimposed upon this "pull" is a normally distributed stochastic term $\sigma\,dz$.

Vasicek shows that equation (23.2) can be used to obtain the following expression for the price at time $t$ of a zero-coupon bond that pays \$1 at time $T$:

$$P(t, T) = A(t, T)e^{-B(t,T)r(t)} \tag{23.6}$$

---

[3] See O. A. Vasicek, "An Equilibrium Characterization of the Term Structure," *Journal of Financial Economics*, 5 (1977), 177–88.

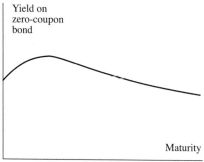

**Figure 23.2** Possible shapes of term structure when the Vasicek model is used

In this equation, $r(t)$ is the value of $r$ at time $t$,

$$B(t, T) = \frac{1 - e^{-a(T-t)}}{a} \tag{23.7}$$

and

$$A(t, T) = \exp\left(\frac{(B(t, T) - T + t)(a^2 b - \sigma^2/2)}{a^2} - \frac{\sigma^2 B(t, T)^2}{4a}\right) \tag{23.8}$$

When $a = 0$, we have $B(t, T) = T - t$, and $A(t, T) = \exp[\sigma^2(T - t)^3/6]$.

Using equation (23.4), we get

$$R(t, T) = -\frac{1}{T - t}\ln A(t, T) + \frac{1}{T - t}B(t, T)r(t) \tag{23.9}$$

showing that the entire term structure can be determined as a function of $r(t)$ once $a$, $b$, and $\sigma$ are chosen. Its shape can be upward sloping, downward sloping, or slightly "humped" (see Figure 23.2).

### Valuing European Options on Zero-Coupon Bonds

Jamshidian has shown that options on zero-coupon bonds can be valued using Vasicek's model.[4] The price at time zero of a European call option maturing at time $T$ on a zero-coupon bond with

[4] See F. Jamshidian, "An Exact Bond Option Pricing Formula," *Journal of Finance*, 44 (March 1989), 205–9.

principal $L$ is

$$LP(0, s)N(h) - KP(0, T)N(h - \sigma_P) \tag{23.10}$$

where $L$ is the bond principal, $s$ is the bond maturity,

$$h = \frac{1}{\sigma_P} \ln \frac{LP(0, s)}{P(0, T)K} + \frac{\sigma_P}{2}$$

$$\sigma_P = \frac{\sigma}{a}(1 - e^{-a(s-T)})\sqrt{\frac{1 - e^{-2aT}}{2a}}$$

and $K$ is the strike price. The price of a European put option on the bond is

$$KP(0, T)N(-h + \sigma_P) - LP(0, s)N(-h) \tag{23.11}$$

When $a = 0$, we have $\sigma_P = \sigma(s - T)\sqrt{T}$.

### Valuing European Options on Coupon-bearing Bonds

Jamshidian also shows that the prices of options on coupon-bearing bonds can be obtained from the prices of options on zero-coupon bonds in a one-factor model, such as Vasicek's, where all rates are positively related to $r$. Consider a European call option with exercise price $K$ and maturity $T$ on a coupon-bearing bond. Suppose that the bond provides a total of $n$ cash flows after the option matures. Let the $i$th cash flow be $c_i$ and occur at time $s_i$ ($1 \leqslant i \leqslant n; s_i \geqslant T$). Define:

$r_K$: Value of the short rate, $r$, at time $T$ that causes the coupon-bearing bond price to equal the strike price

$K_i$: Value at time $T$ of a zero-coupon bond paying off \$1 at time $s_i$ when $r = r_K$

When bond prices are known analytically as a function of $r$ (as they are in Vasicek's model), $r_K$ can be obtained very quickly using an iterative procedure such as the Newton–Raphson method in footnote 2 of Chapter 5.

The variable $P(T, s_i)$ is the price at time $T$ of a zero-coupon bond paying \$1 at time $s_i$. The payoff from the option is therefore

$$\max\left(0, \sum_{i=1}^{n} c_i P(T, s_i) - K\right)$$

Because all rates are increasing functions of $r$, all bond prices are decreasing functions of $r$. This means that the coupon-bearing bond is worth more than $K$ at time $T$ and should be exercised if and only if $r < r_K$. Furthermore, the zero-coupon bond maturing at time $s_i$ underlying the coupon-bearing bond is worth more than $c_i K_i$ at time $T$ if and only if $r < r_K$. It follows that the payoff from the option is

$$\sum_{i=1}^{n} c_i \max[0, P(T, s_i) - K_i]$$

This shows that the option on the coupon-bearing bond is the sum of $n$ options on the underlying zero-coupon bonds. A similar argument applies to European put options on coupon-bearing bonds.

**Example 23.1**   Suppose that $a = 0.1$, $b = 0.1$, and $\sigma = 0.02$ in Vasicek's model with the initial value of the short rate being 10% per annum. Consider a three-year European put option with a strike price of $98 on a bond that will mature in five years. Suppose that the bond has a principal of $100 and pays a coupon of $5 every six months. At the end of three years, the bond can be regarded as the sum of four zero-coupon bonds. If the short-term interest rate is $r$ at the end of the three years, the value of the bond is, from equation (23.6),

$$5A(3, 3.5)e^{-B(3,3.5)r} + 5A(3, 4)e^{-B(3,4)r} + 5A(3, 4.5)e^{-B(3,4.5)r} + 105A(3, 5)e^{-B(3,5)r}$$

Using the expressions for $A(t, T)$ and $B(t, T)$ in equations (23.7) and (23.8), we obtain

$$5 \times 0.9988e^{-0.4877r} + 5 \times 0.9952e^{-0.9516r} + 5 \times 0.9895e^{-1.3929r} + 105 \times 0.9819e^{-1.8127r}$$

To apply Jamshidian's procedure, we must find $r_K$, the value of $r$ for which this bond price equals the strike price of 98. An iterative procedure shows that $r_K = 0.10952$. When $r$ has this value, the values of the four zero-coupon bonds underlying the coupon-bearing bond are 4.734, 4.484, 4.248, and 84.535. The option on the coupon-bearing bond is therefore the sum of four options on zero-coupon bonds:

1.  A three-year option with strike price 4.734 on a 3.5-year zero-coupon bond with a principal of 5

2.  A three-year option with strike price 4.484 on a 4-year zero-coupon bond with a principal of 5

3.  A three-year option with strike price 4.248 on a 4.5-year zero-coupon bond with a principal of 5

4.  A three-year option with strike price 84.535 on a 5-year zero-coupon bond with a principal of 105

To illustrate the pricing of these options, consider the fourth. From equation (23.6), $P(0, 3) = 0.7419$ and $P(0, 5) = 0.6101$. Also, $\sigma_P = 0.05445$, $h = 0.4161$, $L = 105$, and $K = 84.535$. Equation (23.11) gives the value of the option as 0.8085. Similarly, the value of the first, second, and third options are, respectively, 0.0125, 0.0228, and 0.0314. The value of the option under consideration is therefore $0.0125 + 0.0228 + 0.0314 + 0.8085 = 0.8752$.

## 23.5   THE COX, INGERSOLL, AND ROSS MODEL

In Vasicek's model the short-term interest rate, $r$, can become negative. Cox, Ingersoll, and Ross have proposed an alternative model where rates are always nonnegative.[5] The risk-neutral process for $r$ in their model is

$$dr = a(b - r)\,dt + \sigma\sqrt{r}\,dz$$

This has the same mean-reverting drift as the Vasicek model, but the standard deviation of the change in the short rate in a short period of time is proportional to $\sqrt{r}$. This means that, as the short-term interest rate increases, its standard deviation increases.

   Cox, Ingersoll, and Ross show that, in their model, bond prices have the same general form as in Vasicek's model, that is,

$$P(t, T) = A(t, T)e^{-B(t,T)r}$$

---

[5] See J. C. Cox, J. E. Ingersoll, and S. A. Ross, "A Theory of the Term Structure of Interest Rates," *Econometrica*, 53 (1985), 385–407.

but the functions $B(t, T)$ and $A(t, T)$ are different:

$$B(t, T) = \frac{2(e^{\gamma(T-t)} - 1)}{(\gamma + a)(e^{\gamma(T-t)} - 1) + 2\gamma}$$

$$A(t, T) = \left( \frac{2\gamma e^{(a+\gamma)(T-t)/2}}{(\gamma + a)(e^{\gamma(T-t)} - 1) + 2\gamma} \right)^{2ab/\sigma^2}$$

with $\gamma = \sqrt{a^2 + 2\sigma^2}$. Upward-sloping, downward-sloping, and slightly humped yield curves are possible. As in the case of Vasicek's model, the long rate, $R(t, T)$, is linearly dependent on $r(t)$. This means that the value of $r(t)$ determines the level of the term structure at time $t$. The general shape of the term structure at time $t$ is independent of $r(t)$, but does depend on $t$.

Cox, Ingersoll, and Ross provide formulas for European call and put options on zero-coupon bonds. These involve integrals of the noncentral chi-square distribution. European options on coupon-bearing bonds can be valued using Jamshidian's approach in a similar way to that described for Vasicek's model.

## 23.6 TWO-FACTOR EQUILIBRIUM MODELS

A number of researchers have investigated the properties of two-factor equilibrium models. For example, Brennan and Schwartz have developed a model where the process for the short rate reverts to a long rate, which in turn follows a stochastic process.[6] The long rate is chosen as the yield on a perpetual bond that pays $1 per year. Because the yield on this bond is the reciprocal of its price, Itô's lemma can be used to calculate the process followed by the yield from the process followed by the price of the bond. The bond is a traded security. This simplifies the analysis because the expected return on the bond in a risk-neutral world must be the risk-free interest rate.

Another two-factor model, proposed by Longstaff and Schwartz, starts with a general equilibrium model of the economy and derives a term structure model where there is stochastic volatility.[7] The model proves to be analytically quite tractable.

## 23.7 NO-ARBITRAGE MODELS

The disadvantage of the equilibrium models presented in the preceding few sections is that they do not automatically fit today's term structure. By choosing the parameters judiciously, they can be made to provide an approximate fit to many of the term structures that are encountered in practice. But the fit is not usually an exact one and, in some cases, there are significant errors. Most traders find this unsatisfactory. Not unreasonably, they argue that they can have very little confidence in the price of a bond option when the model does not price the underlying bond correctly. A 1% error in the price of the underlying bond may lead to a 25% error in an option price.

[6] See M. J. Brennan and E. S. Schwartz, "A Continuous Time Approach to Pricing Bonds," *Journal of Banking and Finance*, 3 (July 1979), 133–55; M. J. Brennan and E. S. Schwartz, "An Equilibrium Model of Bond Pricing and a Test of Market Efficiency," *Journal of Financial and Quantitative Analysis*, 21, no. 3 (September 1982), 301–29.

[7] See F. A. Longstaff and E. S. Schwartz, "Interest Rate Volatility and the Term Structure: A Two Factor General Equilibrium Model," *Journal of Finance*, 47, no. 4 (September 1992), 1259–82.

A *no-arbitrage model* is a model designed to be exactly consistent with today's term structure of interest rates. The essential difference between an equilibrium and a no-arbitrage model is therefore as follows. In an equilibrium model, today's term structure of interest rates is an output. In a no-arbitrage model, today's term structure of interest rates is an input.

In an equilibrium model, the drift of the short rate (i.e., the coefficient of $dt$) is not usually a function of time. In a no-arbitrage model, this drift is, in general, dependent on time. This is because the shape of the initial zero curve governs the average path taken by the short rate in the future in a no-arbitrage model. If the zero curve is steeply upward sloping for maturities between $t_1$ and $t_2$, $r$ has a positive drift between these times; if it is steeply downward sloping for these maturities, $r$ has a negative drift between these times.

It turns out that some equilibrium models can be converted to no-arbitrage models by including a function of time in the drift of the short rate.

## 23.8 THE HO–LEE MODEL

Ho and Lee proposed the first no-arbitrage model of the term structure in a paper in 1986.[8] They presented the model in the form of a binomial tree of bond prices with two parameters: the short-rate standard deviation and the market price of risk of the short rate. It has since been shown that the continuous-time limit of the model is

$$dr = \theta(t)\,dt + \sigma\,dz \tag{23.12}$$

where $\sigma$, the instantaneous standard deviation of the short rate, is constant and $\theta(t)$ is a function of time chosen to ensure that the model fits the initial term structure. The variable $\theta(t)$ defines the average direction that $r$ moves at time $t$. This is independent of the level of $r$. Interestingly, Ho and Lee's parameter that concerns the market price of risk proves to be irrelevant when the model is used to price interest rate derivatives. This is analogous to risk preferences being irrelevant in the pricing of stock options.

The variable $\theta(t)$ can be calculated analytically. It is

$$\theta(t) = F_t(0, t) + \sigma^2 t \tag{23.13}$$

where the $F(0, t)$ is the instantaneous forward rate for a maturity $t$ as seen at time zero and the subscript $t$ denotes a partial derivative with respect to $t$. As an approximation $\theta(t)$ equals $F_t(0, t)$. This means that the average direction that the short rate will be moving in the future is approximately equal to the slope of the instantaneous forward curve. The Ho–Lee model is illustrated in Figure 23.3. The slope of the forward curve defines the average direction that the short rate is moving at any given time. Superimposed on this slope is the normally distributed random outcome.

In the Ho–Lee model, zero-coupon bonds and European options on zero-coupon bonds can be valued analytically. The expression for the price of a zero-coupon bond at time $t$ in terms of the short rate is

$$P(t, T) = A(t, T)e^{-r(t)(T-t)} \tag{23.14}$$

---

[8] See T. S. Y. Ho and S.-B. Lee, "Term Structure Movements and Pricing Interest Rate Contingent Claims," *Journal of Finance*, 41 (December 1986), 1011–29.

**Figure 23.3**   The Ho–Lee model

where

$$\ln A(t, T) = \ln \frac{P(0, T)}{P(0, t)} - (T - t)\frac{\partial \ln P(0, t)}{\partial t} - \tfrac{1}{2}\sigma^2 t(T - t)^2$$

In these equations, time zero is today. Times $t$ and $T$ are general times in the future with $T \geqslant t$. The equations therefore define the price of a zero-coupon bond at a future time $t$ in terms of the short rate at time $t$ and the prices of bonds today. The latter can be calculated from today's term structure.

For the remainder of this chapter, we will denote the $\delta t$-period interest rate at time $t$ by $R(t)$ or just $R$. From equation (23.14) we can show (see Problem 23.22) that

$$P(t, T) = \hat{A}(t, T)e^{-R(t)(T-t)} \tag{23.15}$$

where

$$\ln \hat{A}(t, T) = \ln \frac{P(0, T)}{P(0, t)} - \frac{T - t}{\delta t}\ln \frac{P(0, t + \delta t)}{P(0, t)} - \tfrac{1}{2}\sigma^2 t(T - t)[(T - t) - \delta t] \tag{23.16}$$

In practice, we usually compute bond prices in terms of $R$ rather than $r$ and so equation (23.15) is more useful than equation (23.14). Equations (23.15) and (23.16) involve only bond prices at time zero, not partial derivatives of these prices. They demonstrate that we do not require the initial zero curve to be differentiable in applications of the model.

The price at time zero of a call option that matures at time $T$ on a zero-coupon bond maturing at time $s$ is

$$LP(0, s)N(h) - KP(0, T)N(h - \sigma_P)$$

where $L$ is the principal of the bond, $K$ is its strike price,

$$h = \frac{1}{\sigma_P} \ln \frac{LP(0, s)}{P(0, T)K} + \frac{\sigma_P}{2}$$

and

$$\sigma_P = \sigma(s - T)\sqrt{T}$$

The price of a put option on the bond is

$$KP(0, T)N(-h + \sigma_P) - LP(0, s)N(-h)$$

This is essentially the same as Black's model for pricing bond options in Section 22.2. The bond price volatility is $\sigma(s - T)$ and the standard deviation of the logarithm of the bond price at time $T$ is $\sigma_P$. As explained in Section 22.3, an interest rate cap or floor can be expressed as a portfolio of options on zero-coupon bonds. It can therefore be valued analytically using the Ho–Lee model.

The Ho–Lee model is an analytically tractable no-arbitrage model. It is easy to apply and provides an exact fit to the current term structure of interest rates. One disadvantage of the model is that it gives the user very little flexibility in choosing the volatility structure. The changes in all spot and forward rates during a short period of time have the same standard deviation. A related disadvantage of the model is that it has no mean reversion. Equation (23.12) shows that, regardless of how high or low interest rates are at a particular point in time, the average direction in which interest rates move over the next short period of time is always the same.

## 23.9   THE HULL–WHITE MODEL

In a paper published in 1990, Hull and White explored extensions of the Vasicek model that provide an exact fit to the initial term structure.[9] One version of the extended Vasicek model that they consider is

$$dr = [\theta(t) - ar]\, dt + \sigma\, dz \tag{23.17}$$

or

$$dr = a\left(\frac{\theta(t)}{a} - r\right) dt + \sigma\, dz$$

where $a$ and $\sigma$ are constants. This is known as the Hull–White model. It can be characterized as the Ho–Lee model with mean reversion at rate $a$. Alternatively, it can be characterized as the Vasicek model with a time-dependent reversion level. At time $t$ the short rate reverts to $\theta(t)/a$ at rate $a$. The Ho–Lee model is a particular case of the Hull–White model with $a = 0$.

The model has the same amount of analytic tractability as Ho–Lee. The function $\theta(t)$ can be calculated from the initial term structure:

$$\theta(t) = F_t(0, t) + aF(0, t) + \frac{\sigma^2}{2a}(1 - e^{-2at}) \tag{23.18}$$

The last term in this equation is usually fairly small. If we ignore it, the equation implies that the drift of the process for $r$ at time $t$ is $F_t(0, t) + a[F(0, t) - r]$. This shows that, on average, $r$ follows

---

[9] See J. Hull and A. White, "Pricing Interest Rate Derivative Securities," *Review of Financial Studies*, 3, no. 4 (1990), 573–92.

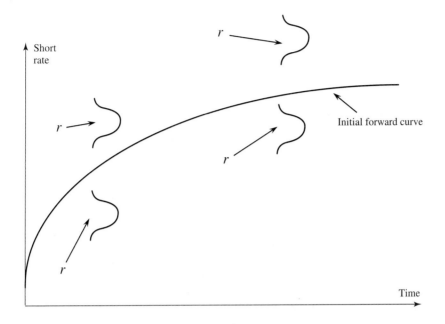

**Figure 23.4**   The Hull–White model

the slope of the initial instantaneous forward rate curve. When it deviates from that curve, it reverts back to it at rate $a$. The model is illustrated in Figure 23.4.

Bond prices at time $t$ in the Hull–White model are given by

$$P(t, T) = A(t, T)e^{-B(t,T)r(t)} \tag{23.19}$$

where

$$B(t, T) = \frac{1 - e^{-a(T-t)}}{a} \tag{23.20}$$

and

$$\ln A(t, T) = \ln \frac{P(0, T)}{P(0, t)} - B(t, T)\frac{\partial \ln P(0, t)}{\partial t} - \frac{1}{4a^3}\sigma^2(e^{-aT} - e^{-at})^2(e^{2at} - 1) \tag{23.21}$$

Equations (23.19), (23.20), and (23.21) define the price of a zero-coupon bond at a future time $t$ in terms of the short rate at time $t$ and the prices of bonds today. The latter can be calculated from today's term structure.

As in the case of the Ho–Lee model, it is more relevant to relate $P(t, T)$ to $R(t)$, the $\delta t$-period rate at time $t$. We can show (see Problem 23.23) that

$$P(t, T) = \hat{A}(t, T)e^{-\hat{B}(t,T)R(t)} \tag{23.22}$$

where

$$\ln \hat{A}(t, T) = \ln \frac{P(0, T)}{P(0, t)} - \frac{B(t, T)}{B(t, t + \delta t)}\ln \frac{P(0, t + \delta t)}{P(0, t)} - \frac{\sigma^2}{4a}(1 - e^{-2at})B(t, T)[B(t, T) - B(t, t + \delta t)]$$

$$\tag{23.23}$$

and

$$\hat{B}(t, T) = \frac{B(t, T)}{B(t, t + \delta t)} \delta t \tag{23.24}$$

As with the Ho–Lee model, these equations do not require the initial zero curve to be differentiable.

The price at time zero of a call option that matures at time $T$ on a zero-coupon bond maturing at time $s$ is

$$LP(0, s)N(h) - KP(0, T)N(h - \sigma_P) \tag{23.25}$$

where $L$ is the principal of the bond, $K$ is its strike price,

$$h = \frac{1}{\sigma_P} \ln \frac{LP(0, s)}{P(0, T)K} + \frac{\sigma_P}{2}$$

and

$$\sigma_P = \frac{\sigma}{a}[1 - e^{-a(s-T)}] \sqrt{\frac{1 - e^{-2aT}}{2a}}$$

The price of a put option on the bond is

$$KP(0, T)N(-h + \sigma_P) - LP(0, s)N(-h) \tag{23.26}$$

These option pricing formulas are the same as those given for the Vasicek model in equations (23.10) and (23.11). They are also equivalent to using Black's model as described in Section 22.2. The variable $\sigma_P$ is the standard deviation of the logarithm of the bond price at time $T$, and the volatility for the bond used in Black's model is $\sigma_P/\sqrt{T}$. As explained in Section 22.3, an interest rate cap or floor can be expressed as a portfolio of options on zero-coupon bonds. It can therefore be valued analytically using the Hull–White model.

The volatility structure in the Hull–White model is determined by both $\sigma$ and $a$. The model can represent a wider range of volatility structures than Ho–Lee. The volatility at time $t$ of the price of a zero-coupon bond maturing at time $T$ is

$$\frac{\sigma}{a}(1 - e^{-a(T-t)})$$

The instantaneous standard deviation at time $t$ of the zero-coupon interest rate maturing at time $T$ is

$$\frac{\sigma}{a(T-t)}(1 - e^{-a(T-t)})$$

and the instantaneous standard deviation of the $T$-maturity instantaneous forward rate is $\sigma e^{-a(T-t)}$. These functions are shown in Figure 23.5. The parameter $\sigma$ determines the short rate's instantaneous standard deviation. The reversion rate parameter, $a$, determines the rate at which bond price volatilities increase with maturity and the rate at which interest rate standard deviations decline with maturity. When $a = 0$, the model reduces to Ho–Lee, and zero-coupon bond price volatilities are a linear function of maturity with the instantaneous standard deviations of both spot and forward rates being constant.

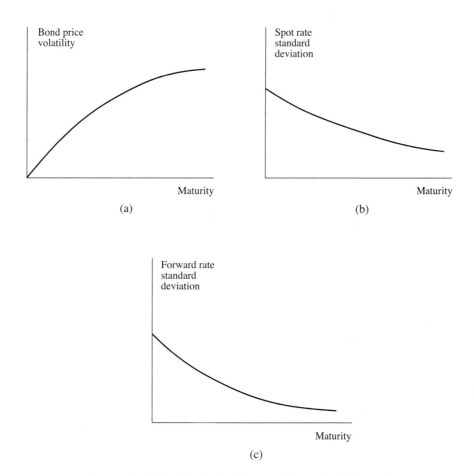

**Figure 23.5**   Volatility structure in the Hull–White model

## 23.10   OPTIONS ON COUPON-BEARING BONDS

In Section 23.4 we showed how, when the Vasicek equilibrium model is used, we can express an option on a coupon-bearing bond as a portfolio of options on zero-coupon bonds (see Example 23.1). This section shows how we can do the same for the Ho–Lee and Hull–White models.

In the case of Vasicek's model, we calculated the value of the short rate, $r = r_K$, for which the coupon-bearing bond price equaled the strike price. We then argued that the option on the coupon-bearing bond was equivalent to a portfolio of options on the zero-coupon bonds comprising the coupon-bearing bond. The strike price of each option is the value of the corresponding zero-coupon bond when $r = r_K$.

We could follow exactly the same procedure for the Ho–Lee and Hull–White models as for the Vasicek model. But it is more convenient to work with the $\delta t$-period rate, $R$, than with the instantaneous short rate, $r$. We then never need to calculate partial derivatives of $P(0, t)$ with respect to $t$.[10] A convenient choice for $\delta t$ is the time between the maturity of the option and the first subsequent coupon on the underlying bond.

We calculate a value of $R$ for which the coupon-bearing bond's price equals the strike price. Suppose this is $R_K$. The option on the coupon-bearing bond is equivalent to a portfolio of options on the zero-coupon bonds comprising the coupon-bearing bond. The strike price of each option is the value of the corresponding zero-coupon bond when $R = R_K$.

**Example 23.2**   Suppose that in the Hull–White model $a = 0.1$ and $\sigma = 0.015$ and we wish to value a 3-month European put option on a 15-month bond that pays a coupon of 12% semiannually. We suppose that both the bond principal and the strike price are 100. The continuously compounded zero rates for maturities of 3 months, 9 months, and 15 months are 9.5%, 10.5%, and 11.5%, respectively. The option under consideration is an option on a portfolio of two zero-coupon bonds. The first zero-coupon bond has a maturity of 9 months and a principal of $6. The second zero-coupon bond has a maturity of 15 months and a principal of $106.

Define $R$ as the value of the 6-month rate at the maturity of the option. The value of the first zero-coupon bond underlying the option is $6e^{-R \times 0.5}$. The value of the second zero-coupon bond is, from equation (23.22),

$$106\hat{A}(0.25, 1.25)e^{-\hat{B}(0.25, 1.25)R}$$

where the $\delta t$ in equation (23.22) equals 0.5. In this case, $B(0.25, 0.75) = 0.4877$ and $B(0.25, 1.25) = 0.9516$, so that equation (23.24) gives $\hat{B}(0.25, 1.25) = 0.9756$. Also, from equation (23.23), $\hat{A}(0.25, 1.25) = 0.9874$. Let $R_K$ be the value of $R$ for which the coupon-bearing bond price equals the strike price. It follows that

$$6e^{-0.5 \times R_K} + 106\hat{A}(0.25, 1.25)e^{-\hat{B}(0.25, 1.25)R_K} = 100$$

This can be solved using an iterative procedure such as Newton–Raphson to give $R_K = 10.675\%$. When $R$ has this value, the zero-coupon bond maturing at time 0.75 is worth 5.68814 and the zero-coupon bond maturing at time 1.25 is worth 94.31186. The option on the coupon-bearing bond is therefore equivalent to:

1. A European put option with a strike price of 5.68814 on a zero-coupon bond maturing at time 0.75 with a principal of 6; and
2. A European put option with a strike price of 94.31186 on a zero-coupon bond maturing at time 1.25 with a principal of 106.

Equation (23.26) gives the prices of these options as 0.01 and 0.43. The price of the option on the zero-coupon bond is therefore 0.44.

As explained in Section 22.4, a European swap option can be viewed as an option on a coupon-bearing bond. It can therefore be valued analytically using the Ho–Lee or Hull–White model.

## 23.11   INTEREST RATE TREES

An interest rate tree is a discrete-time representation of the stochastic process for the short rate in much the same way as a stock price tree is a discrete-time representation of the process followed by

---

[10] This emphasizes the fact that the initial zero curve does not have to be differentiable to use the Ho–Lee and Hull–White models.

a stock price. If the time step on the tree is $\delta t$, the rates on the tree are the continuously compounded $\delta t$-period rates. The usual assumption when a tree is constructed is that the $\delta t$-period rate, $R$, follows the same stochastic process as the instantaneous rate, $r$, in the corresponding continuous-time model. The main difference between interest rate trees and stock price trees is in the way that discounting is done. In a stock price tree, the discount rate is usually assumed to be the same at each node. In an interest rate tree, the discount rate varies from node to node.

It often proves to be convenient to use a trinomial rather than a binomial tree for interest rates. The main advantage of a trinomial tree is that it provides an extra degree of freedom, making it easier for the tree to represent features of the interest rate process such as mean reversion. As mentioned in Section 18.8, using a trinomial tree is equivalent to using the explicit finite difference method.

### *Illustration of Use of Trinomial Trees*

To illustrate how trinomial interest rate trees are used to value derivatives, we consider the simple example shown in Figure 23.6. This is a two-step tree with each time step equal to one year in length, so that $\delta t = 1$ year. We assume that the up, middle, and down probabilities are 0.25, 0.50, and 0.25, respectively, at each node. The assumed $\delta t$-period rate is shown as the upper number at each node.[11]

The tree is used to value a derivative that provides a payoff at the end of the second time step of

$$\max[100(R - 0.11),\ 0]$$

where $R$ is the $\delta t$-period rate. The calculated value of this derivative is the lower number at each

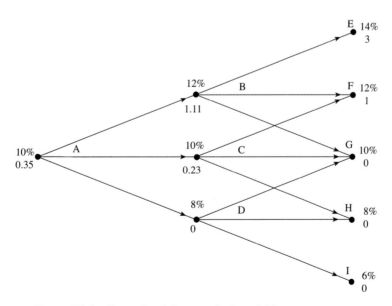

**Figure 23.6** Example of the use of trinomial interest rate trees: upper number at each node is rate; lower number is value of instrument

---

[11] We explain later how the probabilities and rates on an interest rate tree are determined.

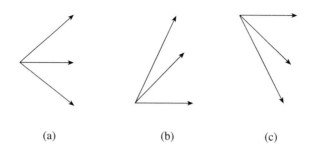

(a)                                    (b)                                    (c)

**Figure 23.7**   Alternative branching methods in a trinomial tree

node. At the final nodes, the value of the derivative equals the payoff. For example, at node E, the value is $100 \times (0.14 - 0.11) = 3$. At earlier nodes, the value of the derivative is calculated using the rollback procedure explained in Chapters 10 and 18. At node B, the one-year interest rate is 12%. This is used for discounting to obtain the value of the derivative at node B from its values at nodes E, F, and G as

$$(0.25 \times 3 + 0.5 \times 1 + 0.25 \times 0)e^{-0.12 \times 1} = 1.11$$

At node C, the one-year interest rate is 10%. This is used for discounting to obtain the value of the derivative at node C as

$$(0.25 \times 1 + 0.5 \times 0 + 0.25 \times 0)e^{-0.1 \times 1} = 0.23$$

At the initial node, A, the interest rate is also 10% and the value of the derivative is

$$(0.25 \times 1.11 + 0.5 \times 0.23 + 0.25 \times 0)e^{-0.1 \times 1} = 0.35$$

### Nonstandard Branching

It sometimes proves convenient to modify the standard branching pattern, which is used at all nodes in Figure 23.6. Three alternative branching possibilities are shown in Figure 23.7. The usual branching is shown in Figure 23.7a. It is "up one / straight along / down one". One alternative to this is "up two / up one / straight along", as shown in Figure 23.7b. This proves useful for incorporating mean reversion when interest rates are very low. A third branching pattern, shown in Figure 23.7c, is "straight along / one down / two down". This is useful for incorporating mean reversion when interest rates are very high. We illustrate the use of different branching patterns in the following section.

## 23.12   A GENERAL TREE-BUILDING PROCEDURE

Hull and White have proposed a robust two-stage procedure for constructing trinomial trees to represent a wide range of one-factor models.[12] This section first explains how the procedure can be

---

[12] See J. Hull and A. White, "Numerical Procedures for Implementing Term Structure Models I: Single-Factor Models," *Journal of Derivatives*, 2, no. 1 (1994), 7–16; J. Hull and A. White, "Using Hull–White Interest Rate Trees," *Journal of Derivatives*, Spring 1996, 26–36.

used for the Hull–White model in Section 23.9 and then shows how it can be extended to represent other models.

### First Stage

The Hull–White model for the instantaneous short rate $r$ is

$$dr = [\theta(t) - ar]\,dt + \sigma\,dz$$

For the purposes of our initial discussion, we suppose that the time step on the tree is constant and equal to $\delta t$.

We assume that the $\delta t$ rate, $R$, follows the same process as $r$.

$$dR = [\theta(t) - aR]\,dt + \sigma\,dz$$

Clearly, this is reasonable in the limit as $\delta t$ tends to zero. The first stage in building a tree for this model is to construct a tree for a variable $R^*$ that is initially zero and follows the process

$$dR^* = -aR^*\,dt + \sigma\,dz$$

This process is symmetrical about $R^* = 0$. The variable $R^*(t + \delta t) - R^*(t)$ is normally distributed. If terms of order higher than $\delta t$ are ignored, the expected value of $R^*(t + \delta t) - R^*(t)$ is $-aR^*(t)\,\delta t$ and the variance of $R^*(t + \delta t) - R^*(t)$ is $\sigma^2\,\delta t$.

We define $\delta R$ as the spacing between interest rates on the tree and set

$$\delta R = \sigma\sqrt{3\,\delta t}$$

This proves to be a good choice of $\delta R$ from the viewpoint of error minimization.

Our objective during the first stage is to build a tree similar to that shown in Figure 23.8 for $R^*$. To do this, we must resolve which of the three branching methods shown in Figure 23.7 will apply at each node. This will determine the overall geometry of the tree. Once this is done, the branching probabilities must also be calculated.

Define $(i, j)$ as the node where $t = i\,\delta t$ and $R^* = j\,\delta R$. (The variable $i$ is a positive integer and $j$ is a positive or negative integer.) The branching method used at a node must lead to the probabilities on all three branches being positive. Most of the time, the branching in Figure 23.7a is appropriate. When $a > 0$, it is necessary to switch from the branching in Figure 23.7a to the branching in Figure 23.7c for a sufficiently large $j$. Similarly, it is necessary to switch from the branching in Figure 23.7a to the branching in Figure 23.7b when $j$ is sufficiently negative. Define $j_{max}$ as the value of $j$ where we switch from the Figure 23.7a branching to the Figure 23.7c branching and $j_{min}$ as the value of $j$ where we switch from the Figure 23.7a branching to the Figure 23.7b branching. Hull and White show that probabilities are always positive if we set $j_{max}$ equal to the smallest integer greater than $0.184/(a\,\delta t)$ and $j_{min}$ equal to $-j_{max}$.[13] Define $p_u$, $p_m$, and $p_d$ as the probabilities of the highest, middle, and lowest branches emanating from the node. The probabilities are chosen to match the expected change and variance of the change in $R^*$ over the next time interval $\delta t$. The probabilities must also sum to unity. This leads to three equations in the three probabilities.

As already mentioned, the mean change in $R^*$ in time $\delta t$ is $-aR^*\,\delta t$ and the variance of the

---

[13] The probabilities are positive for any value of $j_{max}$ between $0.184/(a\,\delta t)$ and $0.816/(a\,\delta t)$ and for any value of $j_{min}$ between $-0.184/(a\,\delta t)$ and $-0.816/(a\,\delta t)$. Changing the branching at the first possible node proves to be computationally most efficient.

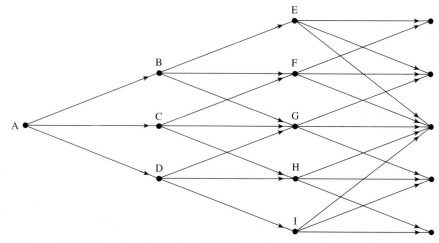

| Node: | A | B | C | D | E | F | G | H | I |
|-------|---|---|---|---|---|---|---|---|---|
| $R$ | 0.000% | 1.732% | 0.000% | −1.732% | 3.464% | 1.732% | 0.000% | −1.732% | −3.464% |
| $p_u$ | 0.1667 | 0.1217 | 0.1667 | 0.2217 | 0.8867 | 0.1217 | 0.1667 | 0.2217 | 0.0867 |
| $p_m$ | 0.6666 | 0.6566 | 0.6666 | 0.6566 | 0.0266 | 0.6566 | 0.6666 | 0.6566 | 0.0266 |
| $p_d$ | 0.1667 | 0.2217 | 0.1667 | 0.1217 | 0.0867 | 0.2217 | 0.1667 | 0.1217 | 0.8867 |

**Figure 23.8**  Tree for $R^*$ in Hull–White model (first stage)

change is $\sigma^2\,\delta t$. At node $(i, j)$, $R^* = j\,\delta R$. If the branching has the form shown in Figure 23.7a, the $p_u$, $p_m$, and $p_d$ at node $(i, j)$ must satisfy the following three equations:

$$p_u\,\delta R - p_d\,\delta R = -aj\,\delta R\,\delta t$$
$$p_u\,\delta R^2 + p_d\,\delta R^2 = \sigma^2\,\delta t + a^2 j^2\,\delta R^2\,\delta t^2$$
$$p_u + p_m + p_d = 1$$

Using $\delta R = \sigma\sqrt{3\,\delta t}$, we find that the solution to these equations is

$$p_u = \tfrac{1}{6} + \frac{a^2 j^2\,\delta t^2 - aj\,\delta t}{2}$$
$$p_m = \tfrac{2}{3} - a^2 j^2\,\delta t^2$$
$$p_d = \tfrac{1}{6} + \frac{a^2 j^2\,\delta t^2 + aj\,\delta t}{2}$$

Similarly, if the branching has the form shown in Figure 23.7b, the probabilities are

$$p_u = \tfrac{1}{6} + \frac{a^2 j^2\,\delta t^2 + aj\,\delta t}{2}$$
$$p_m = -\tfrac{1}{3} - a^2 j^2\,\delta t^2 - 2aj\,\delta t$$
$$p_d = \tfrac{7}{6} + \frac{a^2 j^2\,\delta t^2 + 3aj\,\delta t}{2}$$

Finally, if the branching has the form shown in Figure 23.7c, the probabilities are

$$p_u = \tfrac{7}{6} + \frac{a^2 j^2 \, \delta t^2 - 3aj \, \delta t}{2}$$

$$p_m = -\tfrac{1}{3} - a^2 j^2 \, \delta t^2 + 2aj \, \delta t$$

$$p_d = \tfrac{1}{6} + \frac{a^2 j^2 \, \delta t^2 - aj \, \delta t}{2}$$

To illustrate the first stage of the tree construction, suppose that $\sigma = 0.01$, $a = 0.1$, and $\delta t = 1$ year. In this case, $\delta R = 0.01\sqrt{3} = 0.0173$, $j_{max}$ is set equal to the smallest integer greater than $0.184/0.1$, and $j_{min} = -j_{max}$. This means that $j_{max} = 2$ and $j_{min} = -2$ and the tree is as shown in Figure 23.8. The probabilities on the branches emanating from each node are shown below the tree and are calculated using the equations above for $p_u$, $p_m$, and $p_d$.

Note that the probabilities at each node in Figure 23.8 depend only on $j$. For example, the probabilities at node B are the same as the probabilities at node F. Furthermore, the tree is symmetrical. The probabilities at node D are the mirror image of the probabilities at node B.

### Second Stage

The second stage in the tree construction is to convert the tree for $R^*$ into a tree for $R$. This is accomplished by displacing the nodes on the $R^*$-tree so that the initial term structure of interest rates is exactly matched. Define

$$\alpha(t) = R(t) - R^*(t)$$

Because

$$dR = [\theta(t) - aR] \, dt + \sigma \, dz$$

and

$$dR^* = -aR^* \, dt + \sigma \, dz$$

it follows that

$$d\alpha = [\theta(t) - a\alpha(t)] \, dt$$

If we ignore the distinction between $r$ and $R$, equation (23.18) shows that the solution to this is

$$\alpha(t) = F(0, t) + \frac{\sigma^2}{2a^2}(1 - e^{-at})^2 \tag{23.27}$$

As $a$ tends to zero, this becomes $\alpha(t) = F(0, t) + \sigma^2 t^2/2$.

Equation (23.27) can be used to create a tree for $R$ from the corresponding tree for $R^*$. The approach is to set the interest rates on the $R$-tree at time $i \, \delta t$ to be equal to the corresponding interest rates on the $R^*$-tree plus the value of $\alpha$ at time $i \, \delta t$ and to keep the probabilities the same.

The tree for $R$ produced using equation (23.27), although satisfactory for most purposes, is not exactly consistent with the initial term structure. An alternative procedure is to calculate the $\alpha$'s iteratively so that the initial term structure is matched exactly. We now explain this approach. It provides a tree-building procedure that can be extended to models where there are no analytic results. Furthermore it is applicable to situations where the initial zero curve is not differentiable everywhere.

Define $\alpha_i$ as $\alpha(i \, \delta t)$, the value of $R$ at time $i \, \delta t$ on the $R$-tree minus the corresponding value of $R^*$ at time $i \, \delta t$ on the $r^*$-tree. Define $Q_{i,j}$ as the present value of a security that pays off \$1 if node $(i, j)$

**Table 23.1**   Zero rates for example in Figure 23.8

| Maturity | Rate (%) |
|----------|----------|
| 0.5 | 3.430 |
| 1.0 | 3.824 |
| 1.5 | 4.183 |
| 2.0 | 4.512 |
| 2.5 | 4.812 |
| 3.0 | 5.086 |

is reached and zero otherwise. The $\alpha_i$ and $Q_{i,j}$ can be calculated using forward induction in such a way that the initial term structure is matched exactly.

### Illustration of Second Stage

Suppose that the continuously compounded zero rates in the example in Figure 23.8 are as shown in Table 23.1. The value of $Q_{0,0}$ is 1.0. The value of $\alpha_0$ is chosen to give the right price for a zero-coupon bond maturing at time $\delta t$. That is, $\alpha_0$ is set equal to the initial $\delta t$-period interest rate. Because $\delta t = 1$ in this example, $\alpha_0 = 0.03824$. This defines the position of the initial node on the $R$-tree in Figure 23.9. The next step is to calculate the values of $Q_{1,1}$, $Q_{1,0}$, and $Q_{1,-1}$. There is a probability of 0.1667 that the $(1, 1)$ node is reached and the discount rate for the first time step

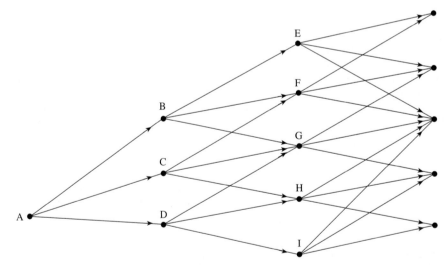

| Node: | A | B | C | D | E | F | G | H | I |
|-------|-----|-----|-----|-----|-----|-----|-----|-----|-----|
| $R$ | 3.824% | 6.937% | 5.205% | 3.473% | 9.716% | 7.984% | 6.252% | 4.520% | 2.788% |
| $p_u$ | 0.1667 | 0.1217 | 0.1667 | 0.2217 | 0.8867 | 0.1217 | 0.1667 | 0.2217 | 0.0867 |
| $p_m$ | 0.6666 | 0.6566 | 0.6666 | 0.6566 | 0.0266 | 0.6566 | 0.6666 | 0.6566 | 0.0266 |
| $p_d$ | 0.1667 | 0.2217 | 0.1667 | 0.1217 | 0.0867 | 0.2217 | 0.1667 | 0.1217 | 0.8867 |

**Figure 23.9**   Tree for $R$ in Hull–White model (the second stage)

is 3.82%. The value of $Q_{1,1}$ is therefore $0.1667e^{-0.0382} = 0.1604$. Similarly, $Q_{1,0} = 0.6417$ and $Q_{1,-1} = 0.1604$.

Once $Q_{1,1}$, $Q_{1,0}$, and $Q_{1,-1}$ have been calculated, we are in a position to determine $\alpha_1$. This is chosen to give the right price for a zero-coupon bond maturing at time $2\,\delta t$. Because $\delta R = 0.01732$ and $\delta t = 1$, the price of this bond as seen at node B is $e^{-(\alpha_1 + 0.01732)}$. Similarly, the price as seen at node C is $e^{-\alpha_1}$ and the price as seen at node D is $e^{-(\alpha_1 - 0.01732)}$. The price as seen at the initial node A is therefore

$$Q_{1,1}e^{-(\alpha_1 + 0.01732)} + Q_{1,0}e^{-\alpha_1} + Q_{1,-1}e^{-(\alpha_1 - 0.01732)} \tag{23.28}$$

From the initial term structure, this bond price should be $e^{-0.04512 \times 2} = 0.9137$. Substituting for the $Q$'s in equation (23.28), we obtain

$$0.1604e^{-(\alpha_1 + 0.0173)} + 0.6417e^{-\alpha_1} + 0.1604e^{-(\alpha_1 - 0.0173)} = 0.9137$$

or

$$e^{\alpha_1}(0.1604e^{-0.01732} + 0.6417 + 0.1604e^{0.01732}) = 0.9137$$

or

$$\alpha_1 = \ln\left(\frac{0.1604e^{-0.01732} + 0.6417 + 0.1604e^{0.01732}}{0.9137}\right) = 0.05205$$

This means that the central node at time $\delta t$ in the tree for $R$ corresponds to an interest rate of 5.205% (see Figure 23.9).

The next step is to calculate $Q_{2,2}$, $Q_{2,1}$, $Q_{2,0}$, $Q_{2,-1}$, and $Q_{2,-2}$. The calculations can be shortened by using previously determined $Q$ values. Consider $Q_{2,1}$ as an example. This is the value of a security that pays off \$1 if node F is reached and zero otherwise. Node F can be reached only from nodes B and C. The interest rates at these nodes are 6.937% and 5.205%, respectively. The probabilities associated with the B–F and C–F branches are 0.6566 and 0.1667. The value at node B of a security that pays \$1 at node F is therefore $0.6566e^{-0.06937}$. The value at node C is $0.1667e^{-0.05205}$. The variable $Q_{2,1}$ is $0.6566e^{-0.06937}$ times the present value of \$1 received at node B plus $0.1667e^{-0.05205}$ times the present value of \$1 received at node C, that is,

$$Q_{2,1} = 0.6566e^{-0.0693} \times 0.1604 + 0.1667e^{-0.05205} \times 0.6417 = 0.1998$$

Similarly, $Q_{2,2} = 0.0182$, $Q_{2,0} = 0.4736$, $Q_{2,-1} = 0.2033$, and $Q_{2,-2} = 0.0189$.

The next step in producing the $R$-tree in Figure 23.9 is to calculate $\alpha_2$. After that, the $Q_{3,j}$'s can then be computed. We can then calculate $\alpha_3$, and so on.

### Formulas for $\alpha$'s and $Q$'s

To express the approach more formally, we suppose that the $Q_{i,j}$'s have been determined for $i \leqslant m$ ($m \geqslant 0$). The next step is to determine $\alpha_m$ so that the tree correctly prices a zero-coupon bond maturing at $(m+1)\,\delta t$. The interest rate at node $(m, j)$ is $\alpha_m + j\,\delta R$, so that the price of a zero-coupon bond maturing at time $(m+1)\,\delta t$ is given by

$$P_{m+1} = \sum_{j=-n_m}^{n_m} Q_{m,j} \exp[-(\alpha_m + j\,\delta R)\,\delta t] \tag{23.29}$$

where $n_m$ is the number of nodes on each side of the central node at time $m\,\delta t$. The solution to this equation is

$$\alpha_m = \frac{\ln \sum_{j=-n_m}^{n_m} Q_{m,j} e^{-j\,\delta R\,\delta t} - \ln P_{m+1}}{\delta t}$$

Once $\alpha_m$ has been determined, the $Q_{i,j}$ for $i = m + 1$ can be calculated using

$$Q_{m+1,j} = \sum_k Q_{m,k} q(k, j) \exp[-(\alpha_m + k\,\delta R)\,\delta t]$$

where $q(k, j)$ is the probability of moving from node $(m, k)$ to node $(m + 1, j)$ and the summation is taken over all values of $k$ for which this is nonzero.

### Extension to Other Models

The procedure that has just been outlined can be extended to more general models of the form

$$df(r) = [\theta(t) - af(r)]\,dt + \sigma\,dz \qquad (23.30)$$

This family of models has the property that they can fit any term structure.[14]

As before, we assume that the $\delta t$-period rate, $R$, follows the same process as $r$:

$$df(R) = [\theta(t) - af(R)]\,dt + \sigma\,dz$$

We start by setting $x = f(R)$, so that

$$dx = [\theta(t) - ax]\,dt + \sigma\,dz$$

The first stage is to build a tree for a variable $x^*$ that follows the same process as $x$ except that $\theta(t) = 0$ and the initial value of $x$ is zero. The procedure here is identical to the procedure already outlined for building a tree such as that in Figure 23.8.

As in Figure 23.9, we then displace the nodes at time $i\,\delta t$ by an amount $\alpha_i$ to provide an exact fit to the initial term structure. The equations for determining $\alpha_i$ and $Q_{i,j}$ inductively are slightly different from those for the $f(R) = R$ case. $Q_{0,0} = 1$. Suppose that the $Q_{i,j}$'s have been determined for $i \leqslant m$ ($m \geqslant 0$). The next step is to determine $\alpha_m$ so that the tree correctly prices an $(m + 1)\,\delta t$ zero-coupon bond. Define $g$ as the inverse function of $f$ so that the $\delta t$-period interest rate at the $j$th node at time $m\,\delta t$ is

$$g(\alpha_m + j\,\delta x)$$

The price of a zero-coupon bond maturing at time $(m + 1)\,\delta t$ is given by

$$P_{m+1} = \sum_{j=-n_m}^{n_m} Q_{m,j} \exp[-g(\alpha_m + j\,\delta x)\,\delta t] \qquad (23.31)$$

---

[14] Not all no-arbitrage models have this property. For example, the extended-CIR model, considered by Cox, Ingersoll, and Ross (1985) and Hull and White (1990), which has the form

$$dr = [\theta(t) - ar]\,dt + \sigma\sqrt{r}\,dz$$

cannot fit yield curves where the forward rate declines sharply. This is because the process is not well defined when $\theta(t)$ is negative.

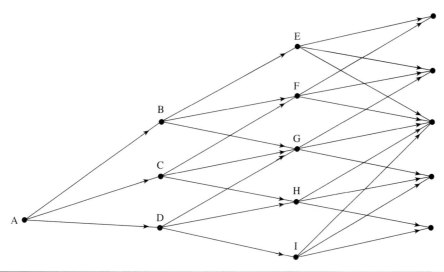

| Node: | A | B | C | D | E | F | G | H | I |
|---|---|---|---|---|---|---|---|---|---|
| $x$ | −3.373 | −2.875 | −3.181 | −3.487 | −2.430 | −2.736 | −3.042 | −3.349 | −3.655 |
| $R$ | 3.430% | 5.642% | 4.154% | 3.058% | 8.803% | 6.481% | 4.772% | 3.513% | 2.587% |
| $p_u$ | 0.1667 | 0.1177 | 0.1667 | 0.2277 | 0.8609 | 0.1177 | 0.1667 | 0.2277 | 0.0809 |
| $p_m$ | 0.6666 | 0.6546 | 0.6666 | 0.6546 | 0.0582 | 0.6546 | 0.6666 | 0.6546 | 0.0582 |
| $p_d$ | 0.1667 | 0.2277 | 0.1667 | 0.1177 | 0.0809 | 0.2277 | 0.1667 | 0.1177 | 0.8609 |

**Figure 23.10**  Tree for lognormal model

This equation can be solved using a numerical procedure such as Newton–Raphson. The value $\alpha_0$ of $\alpha$ when $m = 0$ is $f(R(0))$.

Once $\alpha_m$ has been determined, the $Q_{i,j}$ for $i = m + 1$ can be calculated using

$$Q_{m+1,j} = \sum_k Q_{m,k} q(k, j) \exp[-g(\alpha_m + k\,\delta x)\,\delta t]$$

where $q(k, j)$ is the probability of moving from node $(m, k)$ to node $(m + 1, j)$ and the summation is taken over all values of $k$ where this is nonzero.

Figure 23.10 shows the results of applying the procedure to the model

$$d\ln(r) = [\theta(t) - a\ln(r)]\,dt + \sigma\,dz$$

when $a = 0.22$, $\sigma = 0.25$, $\delta t = 0.5$, and the zero rates are as in Table 23.1.

### Choosing $f(r)$

The main alternatives when choosing a model of the short rate are $f(r) = r$ and $f(r) = \ln(r)$. In most circumstances these two models appear to perform about the same in fitting market data on actively traded instruments such as caps and European swap options. The main advantage of the $f(r) = r$ model is its analytic tractability. Its main disadvantage is that negative interest rates are possible. In most circumstances, the probability of negative interest rates occurring under the model is very small, but some analysts are reluctant to use a model where there is any chance at all of negative interest rates. The $f(r) = \ln r$ model has no analytic tractability, but has the advantage that interest rates are always positive. Another advantage is that traders naturally think in terms of $\sigma$'s arising from a lognormal model rather than $\sigma$'s arising from a normal model.

There is a problem in choosing a satisfactory model for low-interest-rate countries (At the time of writing, Japan is one such country.) The normal model is unsatisfactory because, when the initial short rate is low, the probability of negative interest rates in the future is no longer negligible. The lognormal model is unsatisfactory because the volatility of rates (i.e., the $\sigma$ parameter in the lognormal model) is usually much greater when rates are low than when they are high. (For example, a volatility of 100% might be appropriate when the short rate is less than 1%, while 20% might be appropriate when it is 4% or more.) A model that appears to work well is one where $f(r)$ is chosen so that rates are lognormal for $r$ less than 1% and normal for $r$ greater than 1%.[15]

### Using Analytic Results in Conjunction with Trees

When a tree is constructed for the $f(r) = r$ version of the Hull–White model, the analytic results in Sections 23.9 and 23.10 can be used to provide the complete term structure and European option prices at each node. It is important to recognize that the interest rate on the tree is the $\delta t$-period rate, $R$. It is not the instantaneous short rate, $r$. We should therefore calculate bond prices using equation (23.22), not equation (23.19).

**Example 23.3** As an example of the use of analytic results, we use the zero rates in Table 23.2. Rates for maturities between those indicated are generated using linear interpolation.

We will price a three-year ($= 3 \times 365$ day) European put option on a zero-coupon bond that will expire in nine years ($= 9 \times 365$ days). Interest rates are assumed to follow the Hull–White ($f(r) = r$) model. The strike price is 63, $a = 0.1$, and $\sigma = 0.01$. We constructed a three-year tree and calculated

**Table 23.2**  Zero curve with all rates continuously compounded

| *Maturity* | *Days* | *Rate (%)* |
|---|---|---|
| 3 days | 3 | 5.01772 |
| 1 month | 31 | 4.98284 |
| 2 months | 62 | 4.97234 |
| 3 months | 94 | 4.96157 |
| 6 months | 185 | 4.99058 |
| 1 year | 367 | 5.09389 |
| 2 years | 731 | 5.79733 |
| 3 years | 1,096 | 6.30595 |
| 4 years | 1,461 | 6.73464 |
| 5 years | 1,826 | 6.94816 |
| 6 years | 2,194 | 7.08807 |
| 7 years | 2,558 | 7.27527 |
| 8 years | 2,922 | 7.30852 |
| 9 years | 3,287 | 7.39790 |
| 10 years | 3,653 | 7.49015 |

[15] See J. Hull and A. White,"Taking Rates to the Limit," *RISK*, December 1997, pp. 168–69.

**Table 23.3** Value of a three-year put option on a nine-year zero-coupon bond with a strike price of 63: $a = 0.1$ and $\sigma = 0.01$; zero curve as in Table 23.2

| Steps | Tree | Analytic |
|-------|------|----------|
| 10 | 1.8658 | 1.8093 |
| 30 | 1.8234 | 1.8093 |
| 50 | 1.8093 | 1.8093 |
| 100 | 1.8144 | 1.8093 |
| 200 | 1.8097 | 1.8093 |
| 500 | 1.8093 | 1.8093 |

zero-coupon bond prices at the final nodes analytically as described in Section 23.9. As shown in Table 23.3, the results from the tree are consistent with the analytic price of the option.

This example provides a good test of the implementation of the model because the gradient of the zero curve changes sharply immediately after the expiration of the option. Small errors in the construction and use of the tree are liable to have a big effect on the option values obtained. (The example is used in Sample Application G of the DerivaGem Application Builder software.)

### Tree for American Bond Options

The DerivaGem software accompanying this book implements the normal and the lognormal model, as well as Black's model, for valuing European bond options, caps/floors, and European swap options. In addition, American-style bond options can be handled. Figure 23.11 shows the tree produced by the software when it is used to value a 1.5-year American call option on a 10-year bond using four time steps and the lognormal model. The parameters used in the lognormal model are $a = 5\%$ and $\sigma = 20\%$. The underlying bond lasts 10 years, has a principal of 100, and pays a coupon of 5% per annum semiannually. The yield curve is flat at 5% per annum. The strike price is 105. As explained in Section 22.2, the strike price can be a cash strike price or a quoted strike price. In this case it is a quoted strike price. The bond price shown on the tree is the cash bond price. The accrued interest at each node is shown below the tree. The cash strike price is calculated as the quoted strike price plus accrued interest. The quoted bond price is the cash bond price minus accrued interest. The payoff from the option is the cash bond price minus the cash strike price. Equivalently it is the quoted bond price minus the quoted strike price.

The tree gives the price of the option as 0.668. A much larger tree with 100 time steps gives the price of the option as 0.699. Two points should be noted about Figure 23.11:

1. The software measures the time to option maturity in days. When an option maturity of 1.5 years is input, the life of the option is assumed to be 1.5014 years (or 1 year and 183 days).

2. The price of the 10-year bond cannot be computed analytically when the lognormal model is assumed. It is computed numerically by rolling back through a much larger tree than that shown.

### Unequal Time Steps

In practice, it is often convenient to construct a tree with unequal time steps. Typically, we want to choose time steps so that nodes are on certain key dates (e.g., payment dates or dates when a

Bermudan option can be exercised). We can accommodate unequal time steps as follows. Suppose that the nodes are at times $t_0, t_1, \ldots, t_n$. When the $x^*$ tree is constructed, the vertical spacing between nodes at time $t_{i+1}$ is set equal to $\sigma\sqrt{3(t_{i+1} - t_i)}$. The branching method is as indicated in Figure 23.12. From any given node at time $t_i$, we branch to one of three adjacent nodes at time $t_{i+1}$. Suppose that $x_i^*$ is the value of $x^*$ at time $t_i$. The central node to which we branch at time $t_{i+1}$ is chosen to be the node closest to the expected value of $x^*$, that is, it is the node closest to $x_i^* - a(t_{i+1} - t_i)x_i^*$. The probabilities are determined so that the mean and

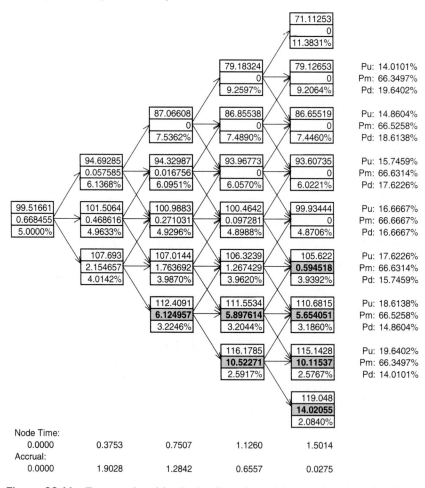

At each node:
 Upper value = Cash Bond Price
 Middle value = Option Price
 Lower value = dt-period Rate
Shaded values are as a result of early exercise

Strike price = 105
Time step, dt = 0.3753 years, 137.00 days

Node Time:
   0.0000        0.3753        0.7507        1.1260        1.5014
Accrual:
   0.0000        1.9028        1.2842        0.6557        0.0275

**Figure 23.11**   Tree, produced by DerivaGem, for valuing an American bond option

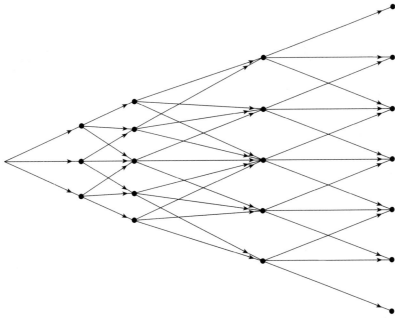

**Figure 23.12** Changing the length of the time step

standard deviation of the change in $x^*$ are matched. (This involves solving three simultaneous linear equations in the probabilities.) The tree for $x$ is constructed from the tree for $x^*$ as in the case where a constant time step is used.

## 23.13 NONSTATIONARY MODELS

The models discussed in the preceding sections have involved only one function of time, $\theta(t)$. Some authors have suggested extending the models by making $a$ or $\sigma$ (or both) functions of time. For example, in 1990, Hull and White produced analytic results for the model in equation (23.17) when $a$ and $\sigma$ are both functions of time. Also in 1990, Black, Derman, and Toy suggested a procedure for building a binomial tree that is equivalent to the model[16]

$$d \ln r = \left( \theta(t) + \frac{\sigma'(t)}{\sigma(t)} \ln(r) \right) dt + \sigma(t)\, dz$$

where $\sigma'(t)$ is the partial derivative of $\sigma$ with respect to $t$. In 1991, Black and Karasinski suggested a more general model where the reversion rate is decoupled from the volatility[17]

$$d \ln r = [\theta(t) - a(t) \ln(r)]\, dt + \sigma(t)\, dz$$

---

[16] See F. Black, E. Derman, and W. Toy, "A One-Factor Model of Interest Rates and Its Application to Treasury Bond Options," *Financial Analysts Journal*, January/February 1990, 33–39.

[17] See F. Black and P. Karasinski, "Bond and Option Pricing when Short Rates Are Lognormal," *Financial Analysts Journal*, July/August 1991, 52–59.

The trinomial tree-building procedure in Section 23.12 can be extended to accommodate models such as these where $a$ and $\sigma$ are known functions of time. As in the case of constant $a$ and $\sigma$, we first build a tree for $x^*$, where

$$dx^* = -a(t)x^* \, dt + \sigma(t) \, dz$$

The spacing between the nodes at time $t_{i+1}$ is chosen to be

$$\sigma(t_i)\sqrt{3(t_{i+1} - t_i)}$$

From any given node at time $t_i$, we branch to one of three adjacent nodes at time $t_{i+1}$. Suppose that $x_i^*$ is the value of $x^*$ at time $t_i$. The central node we branch to at time $t_{i+1}$ is chosen to be the node closest to the expected value of $x^*$, that is, it is the node closest to $x_i^* - a(t_i)(t_{i+1} - t_i)x_i^*$. The probabilities are determined similarly to the case where a constant time step is used, so that the mean and standard deviation of the change in $x^*$ are matched. The tree for $x$ is calculated from the tree for $x^*$ as in the case of constant $a$ and $\sigma$.

The advantage of making $\sigma$ or $a$ (or both) functions of time is that the model can be fitted more precisely to the prices of instruments that trade actively in the market. When we use the model to price deals that are fairly similar to actively traded deals we know that it will provide consistent prices. The disadvantage of making $a$ and $\sigma$ functions of time is that the model has a nonstationary volatility structure. The volatility term structure given by the model in the future is liable to be quite different from that existing in the market today.[18] For this reason is it usually desirable to choose $\sigma$ and $a$ as "well-behaved" functions of time that do not change too much from one time step to the next. We will discuss how this can be done in the next section.

## 23.14 CALIBRATION

Up to now, we have assumed that the volatility parameters $a$ and $\sigma$, whether constant or functions of time, are known. We now discuss how they are determined. This is known as calibrating the model.

The volatility parameters are determined from market data on actively traded options (e.g., broker quotes such as those in Tables 22.1 and 22.2). These will be referred to as the *calibrating instruments*. The first stage is to choose a "goodness-of-fit" measure. Suppose there are $n$ calibrating instruments. A popular goodness-of-fit measure is

$$\sum_{i=1}^{n}(U_i - V_i)^2$$

where $U_i$ is the market price of the $i$th calibrating instrument and $V_i$ is the price given by the model for this instrument. The objective of calibration is to choose the model parameters so that this goodness-of-fit measure is minimized.

When $a$ and $\sigma$ are constant, there are only two volatility parameters. A convenient way of making $a$ or $\sigma$ a function of time is to assume a step function. Suppose, for example, we elect to make $a$ constant and $\sigma$ a function of time. We might choose times $t_1, t_2, \ldots, t_n$ and assume $\sigma(t) = \sigma_0$ for $t \leqslant t_1$, $\sigma(t) = \sigma_i$ for $t_i < t \leqslant t_{i+1}$ ($1 \leqslant i \leqslant n-1$), and $\sigma(t) = \sigma_n$ for $t > t_n$. There would then be a

---

[18] The point made here is similar to the point we made in connection with the IVF model in Chapter 20. It is discussed further in J. Hull and A. White, "Using Hull–White Interest Rate Trees," *Journal of Derivatives*, 4, no. 3 (Spring 1996), 26–36.

total of $n + 2$ volatility parameters: $a$, $\sigma_0$, $\sigma_1, \ldots, \sigma_n$. The number of volatility parameters must always be less than the number of calibrating instruments.

The minimization of the goodness-of-fit measure is accomplished by using the Levenberg–Marquardt procedure.[19] When $a$ or $\sigma$ or both are functions of time, a penalty function is often added to the goodness-of-fit measure so that the functions are "well behaved". In the example just mentioned, where $\sigma$ is a step function we would choose the objective function as

$$\sum_{i=1}^{n}(U_i - V_i)^2 + \sum_{i=1}^{n} w_{1,i}(\sigma_i - \sigma_{i-1})^2 + \sum_{i=1}^{n-1} w_{2,i}(\sigma_{i-1} + \sigma_{i+1} - 2\sigma_i)^2$$

The second term provides a penalties for large changes in $\sigma$ between one step and the next. The third term provides a penalties for high curvature. Appropriate values for $w_{1,i}$ and $w_{2,i}$ are based on experience and are chosen to provide an appropriate level of smoothness in the $\sigma$ function.

The calibrating instruments chosen should be as similar as possible to the instrument being valued. Suppose, for example, that we wish to value a Bermudan-style swap option that lasts ten years and can be exercised on any payment date between year 5 and year 9 into a swap maturing ten years from today. The most relevant calibrating instruments are $5 \times 5$, $6 \times 4$, $7 \times 3$, $8 \times 2$, and $9 \times 1$ European swap options. (An $n \times m$ European swap option is an $n$-year option to enter into a swap lasting for $m$ years beyond the maturity of the option.)

A somewhat different approach to calibration is to use all available calibrating instruments to calculate a "global-best-fit" constant $a$ and $\sigma$ parameters. The parameter $a$ is held fixed at its best-fit value. The model can then be used in the same way as Black–Scholes. There is a one-to-one relationship between options prices and the $\sigma$ parameter. The model can be used to convert tables such as Tables 22.1 and 22.2 into tables of implied $\sigma$'s.[20] These tables can be used to assess the $\sigma$ most appropriate for pricing the instrument under consideration.

## 23.15  HEDGING USING A ONE-FACTOR MODEL

We outlined some general approaches to hedging a portfolio of interest rate derivatives in Section 22.9. They can be used with the term structure models discussed in this chapter. The calculation of deltas, gammas, and vegas involves making small changes to either the zero curve or the volatility environment and recomputing the value of the portfolio.

Note that, although we often assume there is one factor when pricing interest rate derivatives, we do not assume only one factor when hedging. For example, the deltas we calculate allow for many different movements in the yield curve, not just those that are possible under the model chosen. The practice of taking account of changes that cannot happen under the model considered, as well as those that can, is known as *outside model hedging* and is standard practice for traders.[21] The

---

[19] For a good description of this procedure, see W. H. Press, B. P. Flannery, S. A. Teukolsky, and W. T. Vetterling, *Numerical Recipes in C: The Art of Scientific Computing*, Cambridge University Press, Cambridge, 1988.

[20] Note that in a term structure model the implied $\sigma$'s are not the same as the implied volatilities calculated from Black's model in Tables 22.1 and 22.2. The procedure for computing implied $\sigma$'s is as follows. The Black volatilities are converted to prices using Black's model. An iterative procedure is then used to imply the $\sigma$ parameter in the term structure model from the price.

[21] A simple example of outside model hedging is in the way that the Black–Scholes model is used. The Black–Scholes model assumes that volatility is constant—but traders regularly calculate vega and hedge against volatility changes.

reality is that relatively simple one-factor models if used carefully usually give reasonable prices for instruments, but good hedging schemes must explicitly or implicitly assume many factors.

## 23.16 FORWARD RATES AND FUTURES RATES

In Section 5.11 we explained that a convexity adjustment is necessary when a forward interest rate is calculated from a Eurodollar futures price quote.[22]

Consider a futures contract on the interest rate lasting between times $t_1$ and $t_2$. As mentioned in Section 5.11, in the Ho–Lee model the continuously compounded forward rate for the period equals the continuously compounded futures rate minus $\sigma^2 t_1 t_2 / 2$. A typical value of $\sigma$ is 0.012. For the Eurodollar futures traded on the CME, $t_2 = t_1 + 0.25$. Typical convexity adjustments that have to be made to the rates given by these contracts when they have maturities of 2, 4, 6, 8, and 10 years are therefore 3, 12, 27, 48, and 74 basis points, respectively.

For the Hull–White model the convexity adjustment that must be subtracted from the continuously compounded futures rate to get the continuously compounded forward rate is

$$\frac{B(t_1, t_2)}{t_2 - t_1} [B(t_1, t_2)(1 - e^{-2at_1}) + 2aB(0, t_1)^2] \frac{\sigma^2}{4a} \tag{23.32}$$

where the $B$ function is as defined in equation (23.20) (see Problem 23.21).

**Example 23.4**  Consider the situation where $a = 0.05$ and $\sigma = 0.015$ and we wish to calculate a forward rate when the eight-year Eurodollar futures price is 94. In this case, $t_1 = 8$, $t_2 = 8.25$, $B(t_1, t_2) = 0.2484$, $B(0, t_1) = 6.5936$, and the convexity adjustment is

$$\frac{0.2484}{0.25} [0.2484(1 - e^{-2 \times 0.05 \times 8}) + 2 \times 0.05 \times 6.5936^2] \frac{0.015^2}{4 \times 0.05} = 0.0050$$

or 0.50%. The futures rate is 6% per annum with quarterly compounding or 5.96% with continuous compounding. The forward rate is therefore $5.96 - 0.50 = 5.46\%$ per annum with continuous compounding.

## SUMMARY

The traditional models of the term structure used in finance are known as equilibrium models. These are useful for understanding potential relationships between variables in the economy but have the disadvantage that the initial term structure is an output from the model rather than an input to it. When valuing derivatives, it is important that the model used be consistent with the initial term structure observed in the market. No-arbitrage models are designed to have this property. They take the initial term structure as given and define how it can evolve.

This chapter has provided a description of a number of one-factor no-arbitrage models of the short rate. These are very robust and can be used in conjunction with any set of initial zero rates. The simplest model is the Ho–Lee model. This has the advantage that it is analytically tractable.

---

[22] Note that the term *convexity adjustment* is overworked in derivatives. The convexity adjustment here is quite different from the one talked about in Section 22.6.

Its chief disadvantage is that it implies that all rates are equally variable at all times. The Hull–White model is a version of the Ho–Lee model that includes mean reversion. It allows a richer description of the volatility environment while preserving its analytic tractability. Lognormal one-factor models have the advantage that they avoid the possibility of negative interest rates but, unfortunately, they have no analytic tractability.

## SUGGESTIONS FOR FURTHER READING

### *Equilibrium Approaches to Modeling the Term Structure*

Brennan, M. J., and E. S. Schwartz, "An Equilibrium Model of Bond Pricing and a Test of Market Efficiency," *Journal of Financial and Quantitative Analysis*, 17, no. 3 (September 1982), 301–29.

Courtadon, G., "The Pricing of Options on Default-free Bonds," *Journal of Financial and Quantitative Analysis*, 17 (March 1982), 75–100.

Cox, J. C., J. E. Ingersoll, and S. A. Ross, "A Theory of the Term Structure of Interest Rates," *Econometrica*, 53 (1985), 385–407.

Jamshidian, F., "An Exact Bond Option Pricing Formula," *Journal of Finance*, 44 (March 1989), 205–9.

Longstaff, F. A., and E. S. Schwartz, "Interest Rate Volatility and the Term Structure: A Two Factor General Equilibrium Model," *Journal of Finance*, 47, no. 4 (September 1992), 1259–82.

Rendleman, R., and B. Bartter, "The Pricing of Options on Debt Securities," *Journal of Financial and Quantitative Analysis*, 15 (March 1980), 11–24.

Schaefer, S. M., and E. S. Schwartz, "Time-Dependent Variance and the Pricing of Options," *Journal of Finance*, 42 (December 1987), 1113–28.

Vasicek, O. A., "An Equilibrium Characterization of the Term Structure," *Journal of Financial Economics*, 5 (1977), 177–88.

### *No-Arbitrage Models*

Black, F., E. Derman, and W. Toy, "A One-Factor Model of Interest Rates and Its Application to Treasury Bond Options," *Financial Analysts Journal*, January/February 1990, 33–39.

Black, F., and P. Karasinski, "Bond and Option Pricing When Short Rates Are Lognormal," *Financial Analysts Journal*, July/August 1991, 52–59.

Burghardt, G., and B. Hoskins, "A Question of Bias," *RISK*, March 1995, pp. 63–67.

Ho, T. S. Y., and S.-B. Lee, "Term Structure Movements and Pricing Interest Rate Contingent Claims," *Journal of Finance*, 41 (December 1986), 1011–29.

Hull, J., and A. White, "Bond Option Pricing Based on a Model for the Evolution of Bond Prices," *Advances in Futures and Options Research*, 6 (1993), 1–13.

Hull, J., and A. White, "Branching Out," *RISK*, January 1994, pp. 34–37.

Hull, J., and A. White, "In the Common Interest," *RISK*, March 1992, pp. 64–68.

Hull, J., and A. White, "Numerical Procedures for Implementing Term Structure Models I: Single-Factor Models," *Journal of Derivatives*, 2, no. 1 (Fall 1994), 7–16.

Hull, J., and A. White, "One-Factor Interest Rate Models and the Valuation of Interest Rate Derivative Securities," *Journal of Financial and Quantitative Analysis*, 28 (June 1993), 235–54.

Hull, J., and A. White, "Pricing Interest Rate Derivative Securities," *The Review of Financial Studies*, 3, no. 4 (1990), 573–92.

Hull, J., and A. White, "Taking Rates to the Limit," *RISK*, December 1997, pp. 168–69.

Hull, J., and A. White, " The Pricing of Options on Interest Rate Caps and Floors Using the Hull–White Model," *Journal of Financial Engineering*, 2, no. 3 (1993), 287–96.

Hull, J., and A. White, "Using Hull–White Interest Rate Trees," *Journal of Derivatives*, Spring 1996, 26–36.

Hull, J., and A. White, "Valuing Derivative Securities Using the Explicit Finite Difference Method," *Journal of Financial and Quantitative Analysis*, 25 (March 1990), 87–100.

Kijima, M., and I. Nagayama, "Efficient Numerical Procedures for the Hull–White Extended Vasicek Model," *Journal of Financial Engineering*, 3 (September/December 1994), 275–92.

Kijima, M., and I. Nagayama, "A Numerical Procedure for the General One-Factor Interest Rate Model," *Journal of Financial Engineering*, 5 (December 1996), 317–37.

Li, A., P. Ritchken, and L. Sankarasubramanian, "Lattice Models for Pricing American Interest Rate Claims," *Journal of Finance*, 50, no. 2, June 1995, 719–37.

Pelsser, A. A. J., "Efficient Methods for Valuing and Managing Interest Rate and Other Derivative Securities," Ph.D. Dissertation, Erasmus University, Rotterdam, 1996.

Rebonato, R., *Interest Rate Option Models*, Wiley, Chichester, 1996.

## QUESTIONS AND PROBLEMS
## (ANSWERS IN SOLUTIONS MANUAL)

23.1. What is the difference between an equilibrium model and a no-arbitrage model?

23.2. If a stock price were mean reverting or followed a path-dependent process, then there would be market inefficiency. Why is there not a market inefficiency when the short-term interest rate does so?

23.3. Suppose that the short rate is currently 4% and its standard deviation is 1% per annum. What happens to the standard deviation when the short rate increases to 8% in (a) Vasicek's model; (b) Rendleman and Bartter's model; and (c) the Cox, Ingersoll, and Ross model?

23.4. Explain the difference between a one-factor and a two-factor interest rate model.

23.5. Can the approach described in Section 23.4 for decomposing an option on a coupon-bearing bond into a portfolio of options on zero-coupon bonds be used in conjunction with a two-factor model? Explain your answer.

23.6. Suppose that $a = 0.1$ and $b = 0.1$ in both the Vasicek and the Cox, Ingersoll, Ross model. In both models, the initial short rate is 10% and the initial standard deviation of the short rate change in a short time $\delta t$ is $0.02\sqrt{\delta t}$. Compare the prices given by the models for a zero-coupon bond that matures in year 10.

23.7. Suppose that $a = 0.1$, $b = 0.08$, and $\sigma = 0.015$ in Vasicek's model with the initial value of the short rate being 5%. Calculate the price of a one-year European call option on a zero-coupon bond with a principal of $100 that matures in three years when the strike price is $87.

23.8. Repeat Problem 23.7 valuing a European put option with a strike of $87. What is the put–call parity relationship between the prices of European call and put options? Show that the put and call option prices satisfy put–call parity in this case.

23.9. Suppose that $a = 0.05$, $b = 0.08$, and $\sigma = 0.015$ in Vasicek's model with the initial short-term interest rate being 6%. Calculate the price of a 2.1-year European call option on a bond that will mature in three years. Suppose that the bond pays a coupon of 5% semiannually. The principal of the bond is 100 and the strike price of the option is 99. The strike price is the cash price (not the quoted price) that will be paid for the bond.

23.10. Use the answer to Problem 23.9 and put–call parity arguments to calculate the price of a put option that has the same terms as the call option in Problem 23.9.

23.11. In the Hull–White model, $a = 0.08$ and $\sigma = 0.01$. Calculate the price of a one-year European call option on a zero-coupon bond that will mature in five years when the term structure is flat at 10%, the principal of the bond is $100, and the strike price is $68.

23.12. Suppose that $a = 0.05$ and $\sigma = 0.015$ in the Hull–White model with the initial term structure being flat at 6% with semiannual compounding. Calculate the price of a 2.1-year European call option on a bond that will mature in three years. Suppose that the bond pays a coupon of 5% per annum semiannually. The principal of the bond is 100 and the strike price of the option is 99. The strike price is the cash price (not the quoted price) that will be paid for the bond.

23.13. Using equation (23.13) and the results in Section 23.16, show that the drift rate of the short rate at time $t$ in the Ho and Lee model is $G_t(0, t)$, where $G(t, T)$ is the instantaneous futures rate as seen at time $t$ for a contract maturing at time $T$ and the subscript denotes a partial derivative.

23.14. Using equation (23.18) and the results in Section 23.16, show that the drift rate of the short rate at time $t$ in the Hull–White model is $G_t(0, t) + a[G(0, t) - r]$, where $G(t, T)$ is the instantaneous futures rate as seen at time $t$ for a contract maturing at time $T$ and the subscript denotes a partial derivative.

23.15. Suppose that $a = 0.05$, $\sigma = 0.015$, and the term structure is flat at 10%. Construct a trinomial tree for the Hull–White model where there are two time steps, each one year in length.

23.16. Calculate the price of a two-year zero-coupon bond from the tree in Figure 23.6.

23.17. Calculate the price of a two-year zero-coupon bond from the tree in Figure 23.9 and verify that it agrees with the initial term structure.

23.18. Calculate the price of an 18-month zero-coupon bond from the tree in Figure 23.10 and verify that it agrees with the initial term structure.

23.19. What does the calibration of a one-factor term structure model involve?

23.20. Use the DerivaGem software to value $1 \times 4$, $2 \times 3$, $3 \times 2$, and $4 \times 1$ European swap options to receive fixed and pay floating. Assume that the 1-, 2-, 3-, 4-, and 5-year interest rates are 6%, 5.5%, 6%, 6.5%, and 7%, respectively. The payment frequency on the swap is semiannual and the fixed rate is 6% per annum with semiannual compounding. Use the Hull–White model with $a = 3\%$ and $\sigma = 1\%$. Calculate the volatility implied by Black's model for each option.

23.21. Use equation (23.32) to calculate an expression for the difference between the instantaneous forward rate and the instantaneous futures rate. Show that it is consistent with equation (23.27).

23.22. Prove equations (23.15) and (23.16).

23.23. Prove equations (23.22), (23.23), and (23.24).

# ASSIGNMENT QUESTIONS

23.24. Construct a trinomial tree for the Ho and Lee model where $\sigma = 0.02$. Suppose that the the initial zero-coupon interest rate for maturities of 0.5, 1.0, and 1.5 years are 7.5%, 8%, and 8.5%. Use two time steps, each six months long. Calculate the value of a zero-coupon bond with a face value of $100 and a remaining life of six months at the ends of the final nodes of the tree. Use the tree to value a one-year European put option with a strike price of 95 on the bond. Compare the price given by your tree with the analytic price given by DerivaGem.

23.25. Suppose that $a = 0.1$, $\sigma = 0.02$ in the Hull–White model, and a 10-year Eurodollar futures quote is 92. What is the forward rate for the period between 10.0 years and 10.25 years?

23.26. A trader wishes to compute the price of a 1-year American call option on a 5-year bond with a face value of 100. The bond pays a coupon of 6% semiannually and the (quoted) strike price of the option is $100. The continuously compounded zero rates for maturities of 6 months, 1 year, 2 years, 3 years, 4 years, and 5 years are 4.5%, 5%, 5.5%, 5.8%, 6.1%, and 6.3%. The best-fit reversion rate for either the normal or the lognormal model has been estimated as 5%.

A 1-year European call option with a (quoted) strike price of 100 on the bond is actively traded. Its market price is $0.50. The trader decides to use this option for calibration. Use the DerivaGem software with 10 time steps to answer the following questions.

    a. Assuming a normal model, imply the parameter $\sigma$ from the price of the European option.
    b. Use the parameter $\sigma$ to calculate the price of the option when it is American.
    c. Repeat (a) and (b) for the lognormal model. Show that the model used does not significantly affect the price obtained providing it is calibrated to the known European price.
    d. Display the tree for the normal model and calculate the probability of a negative interest rate occurring.
    e. Display the tree for the lognormal model and verify that the option price is correctly calculated at the node where, with the notation of Section 23.12, $i = 9$ and $j = -1$.

23.27. Use the DerivaGem software to value $1 \times 4$, $2 \times 3$, $3 \times 2$, and $4 \times 1$ European swap options to receive floating and pay fixed. Assume that the 1-, 2-, 3-, 4-, and 5-year interest rates are 3%, 3.5%, 3.8%, 4.0%, and 4.1%, respectively. The payment frequency on the swap is semiannual and the fixed rate is 4% per annum with semiannual compounding. Use the lognormal model with $a = 5\%$, $\sigma = 15\%$, and 50 time steps. Calculate the volatility implied by Black's model for each option.

23.28. Verify that the DerivaGem software gives Figure 23.11 for the example considered. Use the software to calculate the price of the American bond option for the lognormal and normal models when the strike price is 95, 100, and 105. In the case of the normal model, assume that $a = 5\%$ and $\sigma = 1\%$. Discuss the results in the context of the heaviness of tails arguments of Chapter 15.

23.29. Modify Sample Application G in the DerivaGem Application Builder software to test the convergence of the price of the trinomial tree when it is used to price a two-year call option on a five-year bond with a face value of 100. Suppose that the strike price (quoted) is 100, the coupon rate is 7% with coupons being paid twice a year. Assume that the zero curve is as in Table 23.2. Compare results for the following cases:

    a. Option is European; normal model with $\sigma = 0.01$ and $a = 0.05$
    b. Option is European; lognormal model with $\sigma = 0.15$ and $a = 0.05$
    c. Option is American; normal model with $\sigma = 0.01$ and $a = 0.05$
    d. Option is American; lognormal model with $\sigma = 0.15$ and $a = 0.05$

C H A P T E R   2 4

# INTEREST RATE DERIVATIVES: MORE ADVANCED MODELS

The interest rate models discussed in Chapter 23 are widely used for pricing instruments when the simpler models in Chapter 22 are inappropriate. They are easy to implement and, if used carefully, can ensure that most nonstandard interest rate derivatives are priced consistently with actively traded instruments such as interest rate caps, European swap options, and European bond options. Two limitations of the models are:

1. They involve only one factor (i.e., one source of uncertainty).
2. They do not give the user complete freedom in choosing the volatility structure.

As explained in Section 23.13, an analyst can use the models so that they provide a perfect fit to volatilities observed in the market today, but there is no way of controlling future volatilities. The future pattern of volatilities is liable to be quite different from that observed in the market today.

This chapter discusses multifactor term structure models and presents some general approaches to building term structure models that give the user more flexibility in specifying the volatility environment. The models require much more computation time than the models in Chapter 23. As a result, they are often used for research and development rather than routine pricing.

This chapter also covers the mortgage-backed security market in the United States and describes how some of the ideas presented in the chapter can be used to price instruments in that market.

## 24.1  TWO-FACTOR MODELS OF THE SHORT RATE

In recent years there have been a number of attempts to extend the models introduced in Chapter 23 so that they involve two or more factors. Examples are in papers published by Duffie and Kan and Hull and White.[1] The Hull–White approach involves a similar idea to the equilibrium model suggested by Brennan and Schwartz that we described briefly in Section 23.6. It assumes that the risk-neutral process for the short rate, $r$, is

$$df(r) = [\theta(t) + u - a f(r)]\,dt + \sigma_1\,dz_1 \qquad (24.1)$$

---

[1] See D. Duffie and R. Kan, "A Yield-Factor Model of Interest Rates," *Mathematical Finance*, 6, no. 4 (1996), 379–406; J. Hull and A. White, "Numerical Procedures for Implementing Term Structure Models II: Two-Factor Models," *Journal of Derivatives*, 2, no. 2 (Winter 1994), 37–48.

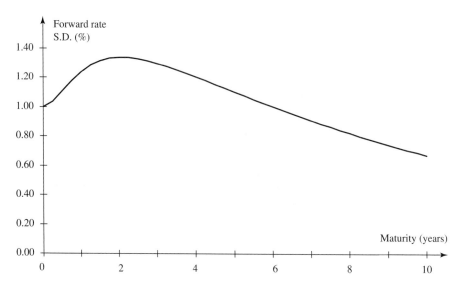

**Figure 24.1**  Example of volatility term structure that can be produced by the two-factor Hull–White model: $f(r) = r$, $a = 1$, $b = 0.1$, $\sigma_1 = 0.01$, $\sigma_2 = 0.0165$, $\rho = 0.6$

where $u$ has an initial value of zero and follows the process

$$du = -bu\,dt + \sigma_2\,dz_2$$

As in the one-factor models considered in Chapter 23, the parameter $\theta(t)$ is chosen to make the model consistent with the initial term structure. The stochastic variable $u$ is a component of the reversion level of $r$ and itself reverts to a level of zero at rate $b$. The parameters $a$, $b$, $\sigma_1$, and $\sigma_2$ are constants and $dz_1$ and $dz_2$ are Wiener processes with instantaneous correlation $\rho$.

This model provides a richer pattern of term structure movements and a richer pattern of volatility structures than the one-factor models considered in the Chapter 23. Figure 24.1 shows the forward rate standard deviations that are produced using the model when $f(r) = r$, $a = 1$, $b = 0.1$, $\sigma_1 = 0.01$, $\sigma_2 = 0.0165$, and $\rho = 0.6$. With these parameters, the model exhibits, at all times, a "humped" volatility structure similar to that observed in the market (see Figure 22.3). The correlation structure implied by the model is also plausible.

When $f(r) = r$, the model is analytically tractable. The price at time $t$ of a zero-coupon bond that provides a payoff of \$1 at time $T$ is

$$P(t, T) = A(t, T)\exp[-B(t, T)r - C(t, T)u] \tag{24.2}$$

where

$$B(t, T) = \frac{1}{a}[1 - e^{-a(T-t)}]$$

$$C(t, T) = \frac{1}{a(a - b)}e^{-a(T-t)} - \frac{1}{b(a - b)}e^{-b(T-t)} + \frac{1}{ab}$$

and $A(t, T)$ is as given in Appendix 24A.

The prices $c$ and $p$ at time zero of European call and put options on a zero-coupon bond are given by

$$c = LP(0, s)N(h) - KP(0, T)N(h - \sigma_P)$$

$$p = KP(0, T)N(-h + \sigma_P) - LP(0, s)N(-h)$$

where $T$ is the maturity of the option, $s$ is the maturity of the bond, $K$ is the strike price, $L$ is the bond's principal,

$$h = \frac{1}{\sigma_P} \ln \frac{LP(0, s)}{P(0, T)K} + \frac{\sigma_P}{2}$$

and $\sigma_P$ is as given in Appendix 24A. Because this is a two-factor model, an option on a coupon-bearing bond cannot be decomposed into a portfolio of options on zero-coupon bonds as described in Section 23.10. However, we can obtain an approximate analytic valuation by calculating the first two moments of the price of the coupon-bearing bond and assuming the price is lognormal.

### Constructing a Tree

To construct a tree for the model in equation (24.1), we simplify the notation by defining $x = f(r)$, so that

$$dx = [\theta(t) + u - ax] dt + \sigma_1 dz_1$$

with

$$du = -bu \, dt + \sigma_2 \, dz_2$$

Assuming $a \neq b$ we can eliminate the dependence of the first stochastic variable on the second by defining

$$y = x + \frac{u}{b - a}$$

so that

$$dy = [\theta(t) - ay] dt + \sigma_3 \, dz_3$$

$$du = -bu \, dt + \sigma_2 \, dz_2$$

where

$$\sigma_3^2 = \sigma_1^2 + \frac{\sigma_2^2}{(b - a)^2} + \frac{2\rho\sigma_1\sigma_2}{b - a}$$

and $dz_3$ is a Wiener process. The correlation between $dz_2$ and $dz_3$ is

$$\frac{\rho\sigma_1 + \sigma_2/(b - a)}{\sigma_3}$$

Hull and White explain how an approach similar to that in Section 20.8 can be used to develop a three-dimensional tree for $y$ and $u$ on the assumption that $\theta(t) = 0$ and the initial values of $y$ and $u$ are zero. A methodology similar to that in Section 23.12 can then be used to construct the final tree by increasing the values of $y$ at time $i \, \delta t$ by $\alpha_i$. In the case $f(r) = r$, an alternative approach is to use the analytic expression for $\theta(t)$, given in Appendix 24A.

Rebonato gives some examples of how the model can be calibrated and used in practice.[2]

---

[2] See R. Rebonato, *Interest Rate Option Models*, 2nd edn., Wiley, Chichester, 1998, pp. 306–8.

## 24.2 THE HEATH, JARROW, AND MORTON MODEL

We now present a model of the yield curve expressed in terms of the processes followed by instantaneous forward rates. We continue to use the traditional risk-neutral world.

### Notation

We will adopt the following notation:

$P(t, T)$: Price at time $t$ of a zero-coupon bond with principal \$1 maturing at time $T$

$\Omega_t$: Vector of past and present values of interest rates and bond prices at time $t$ that are relevant for determining bond price volatilities at that time

$v(t, T, \Omega_t)$: Volatility of $P(t, T)$

$f(t, T_1, T_2)$: Forward rate as seen at time $t$ for the period between time $T_1$ and time $T_2$

$F(t, T)$: Instantaneous forward rate as seen at time $t$ for a contract maturing at time $T$

$r(t)$: Short-term risk-free interest rate at time $t$

$dz(t)$: Wiener process driving term structure movements

The variable $F(t, T)$ is the limit of $f(t, T, T + \delta t)$ as $\delta t$ tends to zero.

### Processes for Zero-Coupon Bond Prices and Forward Rates

When we are assuming just one factor, the risk-neutral process for $P(t, T)$ has the form

$$dP(t, T) = r(t)P(t, T)\,dt + v(t, T, \Omega_t)P(t, T)\,dz(t) \tag{24.3}$$

The expected return is $r(t)$ because a zero-coupon bond is a traded security providing no income. As its argument $\Omega_t$ indicates, the volatility, $v$, can, in the most general form of the model, be any well-behaved function of past and present interest rates and bond prices. Because a bond's price volatility declines to zero at maturity, we must have[3]

$$v(t, t, \Omega_t) = 0$$

From equation (5.1), the forward rate, $f(t, T_1, T_2)$, can be related to zero-coupon bond prices as follows:

$$f(t, T_1, T_2) = \frac{\ln[P(t, T_1)] - \ln[P(t, T_2)]}{T_2 - T_1} \tag{24.4}$$

From equation (24.3) and Itô's lemma,

$$d\ln[P(t, T_1)] = \left(r(t) - \frac{v(t, T_1, \Omega_t)^2}{2}\right)dt + v(t, T_1, \Omega_t)\,dz(t)$$

---

[3] The $v(t, t, \Omega_t) = 0$ condition is equivalent to the assumption that all discount bonds have finite drifts at all times. If the volatility of the bond does not decline to zero at maturity, an infinite drift may be necessary to ensure that the bond's price equals its face value at maturity.

and

$$d \ln[P(t, T_2)] = \left( r(t) - \frac{v(t, T_2, \Omega_t)^2}{2} \right) dt + v(t, T_2, \Omega_t) \, dz(t)$$

so that

$$df(t, T_1, T_2) = \frac{v(t, T_2, \Omega_t)^2 - v(t, T_1, \Omega_t)^2}{2(T_2 - T_1)} dt + \frac{v(t, T_1, \Omega_t) - v(t, T_2, \Omega_t)}{T_2 - T_1} dz(t) \qquad (24.5)$$

Equation (24.5) shows that the risk-neutral process for $f$ depends solely on the $v$'s. It depends on $r$ and the $P$'s only to the extent that the $v$'s themselves depend on these variables.

When we put $T_1 = T$ and $T_2 = T + \delta T$ in equation (24.5) and then take limits as $\delta T$ tends to zero, $f(t, T_1, T_2)$ becomes $F(t, T)$, the coefficient of $dz(t)$ becomes $v_T(t, T, \Omega_t)$, and the coefficient of $dt$ becomes

$$\frac{1}{2} \frac{\partial [v(t, T, \Omega_t)^2]}{\partial T} = v(t, T, \Omega_t) v_T(t, T, \Omega_t)$$

where the subscript to $v$ denotes a partial derivative. It follows that

$$dF(t, T) = v(t, T, \Omega_t) v_T(t, T, \Omega_t) \, dt - v_T(t, T, \Omega_t) \, dz(t) \qquad (24.6)$$

Once the function $v(t, T, \Omega_t)$ has been specified, the risk-neutral processes for the $F(t, T)$'s are known.

Equation (24.6) shows that there is a link between the drift and standard deviation of an instantaneous forward rate. Heath, Jarrow, and Morton (HJM) were the first to point this out.[4] Integrating $v_\tau(t, \tau, \Omega_t)$ between $\tau = t$ and $\tau = T$, we obtain

$$v(t, T, \Omega_t) - v(t, t, \Omega_t) = \int_t^T v_\tau(t, \tau, \Omega_t) \, d\tau$$

Because $v(t, t, \Omega_t) = 0$, this becomes

$$v(t, T, \Omega_t) = \int_t^T v_\tau(t, \tau, \Omega_t) \, d\tau$$

If $m(t, T, \Omega_t)$ and $s(t, T, \Omega_t)$ are the instantaneous drift and standard deviation of $F(t, T)$, so that

$$dF(t, T) = m(t, T, \Omega_t) \, dt + s(t, T, \Omega_t) \, dz$$

it follows from equation (24.6) that

$$m(t, T, \Omega_t) = s(t, T, \Omega_t) \int_t^T s(t, \tau, \Omega_t) \, d\tau \qquad (24.7)$$

### The Process for the Short Rate

We now consider the relationship between the models we have developed in this section and the models of the short rate considered in Chapter 23. Consider the one-factor continuous-time model

---

[4] See D. Heath, R. Jarrow, and A. Morton, "Bond Pricing and the Term Structure of Interest Rates: A New Methodology," *Econometrica*, 60, no. 1 (1992), 77–105.

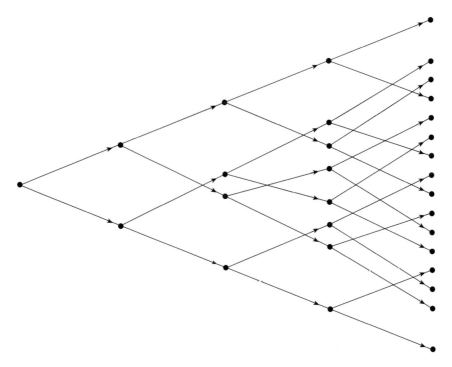

**Figure 24.2**  A nonrecombining tree such at that arising from the general HJM model

for forward rates in equation (24.6). Because

$$F(t, t) = F(0, t) + \int_0^t dF(\tau, t)$$

and $r(t) = F(t, t)$, it follows from equation (24.6) that

$$r(t) = F(0, t) + \int_0^t v(\tau, t, \Omega_\tau)v_t(\tau, t, \Omega_\tau)\, d\tau + \int_0^t v_t(\tau, t, \Omega_\tau)\, dz(\tau) \tag{24.8}$$

Differentiating with respect to $t$ and using $v(t, t, \Omega_t) = 0$, we obtain[5]

$$dr(t) = F_t(0, t)\, dt + \left( \int_0^t [v(\tau, t, \Omega_\tau)v_{tt}(\tau, t, \Omega_\tau) + v_t(\tau, t, \Omega_\tau)^2]\, d\tau \right) dt$$

$$+ \left( \int_0^t v_{tt}(\tau, t, \Omega_\tau)\, dz(\tau) \right) dt + \left[ v_t(\tau, t, \Omega_\tau)\big|_{\tau=t} \right] dz(t) \tag{24.9}$$

It is interesting to examine the terms on the right-hand side of this equation. The first and fourth terms are straightforward. The first term shows that one component of the drift in $r$ is the slope of

---

[5] The stochastic calculus in this equation may be unfamiliar to some readers. To interpret what is going on, we can replace integral signs with summation signs and $d$'s with $\delta$'s. For example, $\int_0^t v(\tau, t, \Omega_\tau)v_t(\tau, t, \Omega_\tau)\, d\tau$ becomes $\sum_{i=1}^n v(i\,\delta t, t, \Omega_i)v_t(i\,\delta t, t, \Omega_i)\,\delta t$, where $\delta t = t/n$.

the initial forward rate curve. The fourth term shows that the instantaneous standard deviation of $r$ is $v_t(\tau, t, \Omega_\tau)|_{\tau=t}$. The second and third terms are more complicated, particularly when $v$ is stochastic. The second term depends on the history of $v$ because it involves $v(\tau, t, \Omega_\tau)$ when $\tau < t$. The third term depends on the history of both $v$ and $dz$.

The second and third terms terms are liable to cause the process for $r$ to be non-Markov. The drift of $r$ between time $t$ and $t + \delta t$ is liable to depend not only on the value of $r$ at time $t$, but also on the history of $r$ prior to time $t$. This means that, when we attempt to construct a tree for $r$, it is nonrecombining as shown in Figure 24.2. An up movement followed by a down movement does not lead to the same node as a down movement followed by an up movement.

This highlights the key problem in implementing a general HJM model. We have to use Monte Carlo simulation. Trees create difficulties. When we construct a tree representing term structure movements, it is usually nonrecombining. Assuming the model has one factor and the tree is binomial as in Figure 24.2, there are $2^n$ nodes after $n$ time steps. If the model has two factors, the tree must be constructed in three dimensions and there are then $4^n$ nodes after $n$ time steps. For $n = 30$, the number of terminal nodes in a one-factor model is therefore about $10^9$; in a two-factor model it is about $10^{18}$.

### Extension to Several Factors

The HJM result can be extended to the situation where there are several independent factors. Suppose that

$$dF(t, T) = m(t, T, \Omega_t)\, dt + \sum_k s_k(t, T, \Omega_t)\, dz_k$$

A similar analysis to that just given (see Problem 24.4) shows that

$$m(t, T, \Omega_t) = \sum_k s_k(t, T, \Omega_t) \int_t^T s_k(t, \tau, \Omega_t)\, d\tau \qquad (24.10)$$

## 24.3 THE LIBOR MARKET MODEL

One drawback of the HJM model is that it is expressed in terms of instantaneous forward rates and these are not directly observable in the market. Another drawback is that it is difficult to calibrate the model to prices of actively traded instruments. This has led Brace, Gatarek, and Musiela (BGM), Jamshidian, and Miltersen, Sandmann, and Sondermann to propose an alternative.[6] It is known as the *LIBOR market model* or the *BGM model*. It is expressed in terms of the forward rates that traders are used to working with.

### The Model

Define $t_0 = 0$ and let $t_1, t_2, \ldots$ be the reset times for caps that trade in the market today. In the United States the most popular caps have quarterly resets, so that it is approximately true

---

[6] See A. Brace, D. Gatarek, and M. Musiela, "The Market Model of Interest Rate Dynamics," *Mathematical Finance*, 7, no. 2 (1997), 127–55; F. Jamshidian, "LIBOR and Swap Market Models and Measures," *Finance and Stochastics*, 1 (1997), 293–330; K. Miltersen, K. Sandmann, and D. Sondermann, "Closed Form Solutions for Term Structure Derivatives with LogNormal Interest Rate," *Journal of Finance*, 52, no. 1 (March 1997), 409–30.

that $t_1 = 0.25$, $t_2 = 0.5$, $t_3 = 0.75$, and so on. Define $\delta_k = t_{k+1} - t_k$, and:

$F_k(t)$: Forward rate between times $t_k$ and $t_{k+1}$ as seen at time $t$, expressed with a compounding period of $\delta_k$

$m(t)$: Index for the next reset date at time $t$; this means that $m(t)$ is the smallest integer such that $t \leqslant t_{m(t)}$

$\zeta_k(t)$: Volatility of $F_k(t)$ at time $t$

$v_k(t)$: Volatility of the zero-coupon bond price, $P(t, t_k)$, at time $t$

Initially, we will assume that there is only one factor. As shown in Section 21.4, in a world that is forward risk neutral with respect to $P(t, t_{k+1})$, $F_k(t)$ is a martingale and follows the process

$$dF_k(t) = \zeta_k(t)F_k(t)\,dz \tag{24.11}$$

where $dz$ is a Wiener process.

In practice, it often most convenient to value interest rate derivatives by working in a world that is always forward risk neutral with respect to a bond maturing at the next reset date. We refer to this as a *rolling forward risk-neutral world.*[7] In this world we can discount from time $t_{k+1}$ to time $t_k$ using the zero rate observed at time $t_k$ for a maturity $t_{k+1}$. We do not have to worry about what happens to interest rates between times $t_k$ and $t_{k+1}$.

The rolling forward risk-neutral world is a world that is at time $t$ forward risk neutral with respect to the bond price, $P(t, t_{m(t)})$. Equation (24.11) gives the process followed by $F_k(t)$ in a world that is forward risk neutral with respect to $P(t, t_{k+1})$. From Section 21.7, it follows that the process followed by $F_k(t)$ in the rolling forward risk-neutral world is

$$dF_k(t) = \zeta_k(t)[v_{m(t)}(t) - v_{k+1}(t)]F_k(t)\,dt + \zeta_k(t)F_k(t)\,dz \tag{24.12}$$

The relationship between forward rates and bond prices is

$$\frac{P(t, t_i)}{P(t, t_{i+1})} = 1 + \delta_i F_i(t)$$

or

$$\ln P(t, t_i) - \ln P(t, t_{i+1}) = \ln[1 + \delta_i F_i(t)]$$

Using Itô's lemma we can calculate the process followed the left-hand side and the right-hand side of this equation. Equating the coefficients of $dz$, we obtain

$$v_i(t) - v_{i+1}(t) = \frac{\delta_i F_i(t)\zeta_i(t)}{1 + \delta_i F_i(t)} \tag{24.13}$$

so that from equation (24.12) the process followed by $F_k(t)$ in the rolling forward risk-neutral world is

$$\frac{dF_k(t)}{F_k(t)} = \sum_{i=m(t)}^{k} \frac{\delta_i F_i(t)\zeta_i(t)\zeta_k(t)}{1 + \delta_i F_i(t)}\,dt + \zeta_k(t)\,dz \tag{24.14}$$

---

[7] In the terminology of Section 21.4, this world corresponds to using a "rolling CD" as the numeraire. A rolling CD is one where we start with $1, buy a bond maturing at time $t_1$, reinvest the proceeds at time $t_1$ in a bond maturing at time $t_2$, reinvest the proceeds at time $t_2$ in a bond maturing at time $t_3$, and so on. Strictly speaking, the interest rate trees we constructed in Chapter 23 are in a rolling forward risk-neutral world rather than the traditional risk-neutral world. The numeraire is a CD rolled over at the end of each time step.

The HJM result in equation (24.6) is the limiting case of this as the $\delta_i$ tend to zero. (See Problem 24.9).

### Forward Rate Volatilities

We now simplify the model by assuming that $\zeta_k(t)$ is a function only of the number of whole accrual periods between the next reset date and time $t_k$. Define $\Lambda_i$ as the value of $\zeta_k(t)$ when there are $i$ such accrual periods. This means that $\zeta_k(t) = \Lambda_{k-m(t)}$ is a step function.

The $\Lambda_i$ can (at least in theory) be estimated from the volatilities used to value caplets in Black's model (i.e., from the spot volatilities in Figure 22.3).[8] Suppose that $\sigma_k$ is the Black volatility for the caplet that corresponds to the period between times $t_k$ and $t_{k+1}$. Equating variances we must have

$$\sigma_k^2 t_k = \sum_{i=1}^{k} \Lambda_{k-i}^2 \delta_{i-1} \qquad (24.15)$$

This equation can be used to obtain the $\Lambda$'s iteratively.

**Example 24.1** Assume that the $\delta_i$ are all equal and the Black caplet spot volatilities for the first three caplets are 24%, 22%, and 20%. This means that $\Lambda_0 = 24\%$. Because

$$\Lambda_0^2 + \Lambda_1^2 = 2 \times 0.22^2$$

$\Lambda_1$ is 19.80%. Also, because

$$\Lambda_0^2 + \Lambda_1^2 + \Lambda_2^2 = 3 \times 0.20^2$$

$\Lambda_2$ is 15.23%.

**Example 24.2** Consider the data in Table 24.1 on the caplet volatilities. These exhibit the hump discussed in Section 22.3. The $\Lambda$'s are shown in the second row. Notice that the hump in the $\Lambda$'s is more pronounced than the hump in the $\sigma$'s.

### Implementation of the Model

The LIBOR market model can be implemented using Monte Carlo simulation. Expressed in terms of the $\Lambda_i$'s equation (24.14) is

$$\frac{dF_k(t)}{F_k(t)} = \sum_{i=m(t)}^{k} \frac{\delta_i F_i(t) \Lambda_{i-m(t)} \Lambda_{k-m(t)}}{1 + \delta_i F_i(t)} dt + \Lambda_{k-m(t)} dz \qquad (24.16)$$

**Table 24.1** Volatility data; accrual period = 1 year

| | Year, k | | | | | | | | | |
|---|---|---|---|---|---|---|---|---|---|---|
| | *1* | *2* | *3* | *4* | *5* | *6* | *7* | *8* | *9* | *10* |
| $\sigma_k$ (%) | 15.50 | 18.25 | 17.91 | 17.74 | 17.27 | 16.79 | 16.30 | 16.01 | 15.76 | 15.54 |
| $\Lambda_{k-1}$ (%) | 15.50 | 20.64 | 17.21 | 17.22 | 15.25 | 14.15 | 12.98 | 13.81 | 13.60 | 13.40 |

---

[8] In practice the $\Lambda$'s are determined using a least-squares calibration that we will discuss later.

or

$$d \ln F_k(t) = \left( \sum_{i=m(t)}^{k} \frac{\delta_i F_i(t) \Lambda_{i-m(t)} \Lambda_{k-m(t)}}{1 + \delta_i F_i(t)} - \frac{(\Lambda_{k-m(t)})^2}{2} \right) dt + \Lambda_{k-m(t)} \, dz \qquad (24.17)$$

If, as an approximation, we assume in the calculation of the drift of $\ln F_k(t)$ that $F_i(t) = F_i(t_j)$ for $t_j < t < t_{j+1}$, then

$$F_k(t_{j+1}) = F_k(t_j) \exp \left[ \left( \sum_{i=j+1}^{k} \frac{\delta_i F_i(t_j) \Lambda_{i-j-1} \Lambda_{k-j-1}}{1 + \delta_i F_i(t_j)} - \frac{\Lambda_{k-j-1}^2}{2} \right) \delta_j + \Lambda_{k-j-1} \epsilon \sqrt{\delta_j} \right] \qquad (24.18)$$

where $\epsilon$ is a random sample from a normal distribution with mean equal to zero and standard deviation equal to one.

### Extension to Several Factors

The LIBOR market model can be extended to incorporate several independent factors. Suppose that there are $p$ factors and $\zeta_{k,q}$ is the component of the volatility of $F_k(t)$ attributable to the $q$th factor. Equation (24.14) becomes (see Problem 24.13)

$$\frac{dF_k(t)}{F_k(t)} = \sum_{i=m(t)}^{k} \frac{\delta_i F_i(t) \sum_{q=1}^{p} \zeta_{i,q}(t) \zeta_{k,q}(t)}{1 + \delta_i F_i(t)} \, dt + \sum_{q=1}^{p} \zeta_{k,q}(t) \, dz_q \qquad (24.19)$$

Define $\lambda_{i,q}$ as the $q$th component of the volatility when there are $i$ accrual periods between the next reset date and the maturity of the forward contract. Equation (24.18) then becomes

$$F_k(t_{j+1}) = F_k(t_j) \exp \left[ \left( \sum_{i=j+1}^{k} \frac{\delta_i F_i(t_j) \sum_{q=1}^{p} \lambda_{i-j-1,q} \lambda_{k-j-1,q}}{1 + \delta_i F_i(t_j)} - \frac{\sum_{q=1}^{p} \lambda_{k-j-1,q}^2}{2} \right) \delta_j + \sum_{q=1}^{p} \lambda_{k-j-1,q} \epsilon_q \sqrt{\delta_j} \right]$$

$$(24.20)$$

where the $\epsilon_q$ are random samples from a normal distribution with mean equal to zero and standard deviation equal to one.

The approximation that the drift of a forward rate remains constant within each accrual period allows us to jump from one reset date to the next in the simulation. This is convenient because, as already mentioned, the rolling forward risk-neutral world allows us to discount from one reset date to the next. Suppose that we wish to simulate a zero curve for $N$ accrual periods. On each trial we start with the forward rates at time zero. These are $F_0(0), F_1(0), \ldots, F_{N-1}(0)$ calculated from the initial zero curve; we then use equation (24.20) to calculate $F_1(t_1), F_2(t_1), \ldots, F_{N-1}(t_1)$; we then use equation (24.20) again to calculate $F_2(t_2), F_3(t_2), \ldots, F_{N-1}(t_2)$; and so on until $F_{N-1}(t_{N-1})$ is obtained. Note that as we move through time the zero curve gets shorter and shorter. For example, suppose each accrual period is three months and $N = 40$. We start with a ten-year zero curve. At the six-year point (at time $t_{24}$) the simulation gives us information on a four-year zero curve.

Hull and White tested the drift approximation by valuing caplets using equation (24.20) and comparing the prices to those given by Black's model.[9] The value of $F_k(t_k)$ is the realized rate for

---

[9] See J. C. Hull and A. White, "Forward Rate Volatilities, Swap Rate Volatilities, and the Implementation of the LIBOR Market Model," *Journal of Fixed Income*, 10, no. 2 (September 2000), 46–62.

the time period between $t_k$ and $t_{k+1}$ and enables the caplet payoff at time $t_{k+1}$ to be calculated. This payoff is discounted back to time zero, one accrual period at a time. The caplet value is the average of the discounted payoffs. Hull and White found that the values obtained in this way are not significantly different from those given by Black's model. This is true even when the accrual periods are one year in length and a very large number of trials are used.[10] This suggests that the drift assumption is innocuous in most situations.

### Ratchet Caps, Sticky Caps, and Flexi Caps

The LIBOR market model can be used to value some types of nonstandard caps. Consider ratchet caps and sticky caps. These incorporate rules for determining how the cap rate for each caplet is set. In a *ratchet cap*, it equals the LIBOR rate at the previous reset date plus a spread. In a *sticky cap*, it equals the previous capped rate plus a spread. Suppose that the cap rate at time $t_j$ is $K_j$, the LIBOR rate at time $t_j$ is $R_j$, and the spread is $s$. In a ratchet cap, $K_{j+1} = R_j + s$. In a sticky cap, $K_{j+1} = \min(R_j, K_j) + s$.

Tables 24.2 and 24.3 provide valuations of a ratchet cap and sticky cap using the LIBOR market model with one, two, and three factors. The principal is \$100. The term structure is assumed to be flat at 5% per annum and the caplet volatilities are as in Table 24.1. The interest rate is reset annually. The spread is 25 basis points. Tables 24.4 and 24.5 show how the volatility was split into components when two- and three-factor models were used. The results are based on 100,000 Monte Carlo simulations incorporating the antithetic variable technique described in Section 18.7. The standard error of each price is about 0.001.

A third type of nonstandard cap is a *flexi cap*. This is like a regular cap except that there is a limit on the total number of caplets that can be exercised. Consider an annual-pay flexi cap when the principal is \$100, the term structure is flat at 5%, and the cap volatilities are as in Tables 24.1 (p. 579), 24.4 (p. 582), and 24.5 (p. 583). Suppose that all in-the-money caplets are exercised up to a maximum of five. With one, two, and three factors, the LIBOR market model gives the price of the instrument as 3.43, 3.58, and 3.61, respectively. (See Problem 24.17 for other types of flexi caps.)

**Table 24.2**   Valuation of ratchet caplets

| Caplet start time (years) | One factor | Two factors | Three factors |
|:---:|:---:|:---:|:---:|
| 1 | 0.196 | 0.194 | 0.195 |
| 2 | 0.207 | 0.207 | 0.209 |
| 3 | 0.201 | 0.205 | 0.210 |
| 4 | 0.194 | 0.198 | 0.205 |
| 5 | 0.187 | 0.193 | 0.201 |
| 6 | 0.180 | 0.189 | 0.193 |
| 7 | 0.172 | 0.180 | 0.188 |
| 8 | 0.167 | 0.174 | 0.182 |
| 9 | 0.160 | 0.168 | 0.175 |
| 10 | 0.153 | 0.162 | 0.169 |

---

[10] An exception is when the cap volatilities are very high.

**Table 24.3**   Valuation of sticky caplets

| Caplet start time (years) | One factor | Two factors | Three factors |
|---|---|---|---|
| 1 | 0.196 | 0.194 | 0.195 |
| 2 | 0.336 | 0.334 | 0.336 |
| 3 | 0.412 | 0.413 | 0.418 |
| 4 | 0.458 | 0.462 | 0.472 |
| 5 | 0.484 | 0.492 | 0.506 |
| 6 | 0.498 | 0.512 | 0.524 |
| 7 | 0.502 | 0.520 | 0.533 |
| 8 | 0.501 | 0.523 | 0.537 |
| 9 | 0.497 | 0.523 | 0.537 |
| 10 | 0.488 | 0.519 | 0.534 |

The pricing of a plain vanilla cap depends only on the total volatility and is independent of the number of factors. This is because the price of a plain vanilla caplet depends the behavior of only one forward rate. The prices of caplets in the nonstandard instruments we have looked at are different in that they depend on the joint probability distribution of several different forward rates. As a result they do depend on the number of factors.

### Valuing European Swap Options

As shown by Hull and White, there is an analytic approximation for valuing European swap options in the LIBOR market model.[11] Let $T_0$ be the maturity of the swap option and assume that the payment dates for the swap are $T_1, T_2, \ldots, T_N$. Define $\tau_i = T_{i+1} - T_i$. From equation (21.23), the swap rate at time $t$ is given by

$$s(t) = \frac{P(t, T_0) - P(t, T_N)}{\sum_{i=0}^{N-1} \tau_i P(t, T_{i+1})}$$

It is also true that

$$\frac{P(t, T_i)}{P(t, T_0)} = \prod_{j=0}^{i-1} \frac{1}{1 + \tau_j G_j(t)}$$

**Table 24.4**   Volatility components in two-factor model

| | Year, k | | | | | | | | | |
|---|---|---|---|---|---|---|---|---|---|---|
| | 1 | 2 | 3 | 4 | 5 | 6 | 7 | 8 | 9 | 10 |
| $\lambda_{k-1,1}$ (%) | 14.10 | 19.52 | 16.78 | 17.11 | 15.25 | 14.06 | 12.65 | 13.06 | 12.36 | 11.63 |
| $\lambda_{k-1,2}$ (%) | −6.45 | −6.70 | −3.84 | −1.96 | 0.00 | 1.61 | 2.89 | 4.48 | 5.65 | 6.65 |
| Total Vol. (%) | 15.50 | 20.64 | 17.21 | 17.22 | 15.25 | 14.15 | 12.98 | 13.81 | 13.60 | 13.40 |

[11] See J. C. Hull and A. White, "Forward Rate Volatilities, Swap Rate Volatilities, and the Implementation of the LIBOR Market Model," *Journal of Fixed Income*, 10, no. 2 (September 2000), 46–62.

**Table 24.5** Volatility components in three-factor model

| | Year, k | | | | | | | | | |
|---|---|---|---|---|---|---|---|---|---|---|
| | *1* | *2* | *3* | *4* | *5* | *6* | *7* | *8* | *9* | *10* |
| $\lambda_{k-1,1}$ (%) | 13.65 | 19.28 | 16.72 | 16.98 | 14.85 | 13.95 | 12.61 | 12.90 | 11.97 | 10.97 |
| $\lambda_{k-1,2}$ (%) | −6.62 | −7.02 | −4.06 | −2.06 | 0.00 | 1.69 | 3.06 | 4.70 | 5.81 | 6.66 |
| $\lambda_{k-1,3}$ (%) | 3.19 | 2.25 | 0.00 | −1.98 | −3.47 | −1.63 | 0.00 | 1.51 | 2.80 | 3.84 |

for $1 \leqslant i \leqslant N$, where $G_j(t)$ is the forward rate at time $t$ for the period between $T_j$ and $T_{j+1}$. These two equations together define a relationship between $s(t)$ and the $G_j(t)$'s. Applying Itô's lemma (see Problem 24.14), the variance of the swap rate, $s(t)$, is given by

$$V(t) = \sum_{q=1}^{p} \left( \sum_{k=0}^{N-1} \frac{\tau_k \beta_{k,q}(t) G_k(t) \gamma_k(t)}{1 + \tau_k G_k(t)} \right)^2$$

where

$$\gamma_k(t) = \frac{\prod_{j=0}^{N-1}[1 + \tau_j G_j(t)]}{\prod_{j=0}^{N-1}[1 + \tau_j G_j(t)] - 1} - \frac{\sum_{i=0}^{k-1} \tau_i \prod_{j=i+1}^{N-1}[1 + \tau_j G_j(t)]}{\sum_{i=0}^{N} \tau_i \prod_{j=i+1}^{N-1}[1 + \tau_j G_j(t)]}$$

and $\beta_{j,q}(t)$ is the $q$th component of the volatility of $G_j(t)$. We approximate $V(t)$ by setting $G_j(t) = G_j(0)$ for all $j$ and $t$. The swap volatility that is substituted into the standard market model for valuing a swaption is then

$$\sqrt{\frac{1}{T_0} \int_{t=0}^{T_0} V(t)\, dt}$$

or

$$\sqrt{\frac{1}{T_0} \int_{t=0}^{T_0} \sum_{q=1}^{p} \left( \sum_{k=0}^{N-1} \frac{\tau_k \beta_{k,q}(t) G_k(0) \gamma_k(0)}{1 + \tau_k G_k(0)} \right)^2 dt} \tag{24.21}$$

In the situation where the length of the accrual period for swap underlying the swaption is the same as the length of the accrual period for a cap, $\beta_{k,q}(t)$ is the $q$th component of volatility of a cap forward rate when the time to maturity is $T_k - t$. This can be looked up in Table 24.5.

The accrual periods for the swaps underlying broker quotes for European swap options do not always match the accrual periods for the caps and floors underlying broker quotes. For example, in the United States the benchmark caps and floors have quarterly resets while the swaps underlying the benchmark European swap options have semiannual resets. Fortunately, the valuation result for European swap options can be extended to the situation where the each swap accrual period includes $M$ subperiods that could be accrual periods in a typical cap. Define $\tau_{j,m}$ as the length of the $m$th subperiod in the $j$th accrual period, so that

$$\tau_j = \sum_{m=1}^{M} \tau_{j,m}$$

Define $G_{j,m}(t)$ as the forward rate observed at time $t$ for the $\tau_{j,m}$ accrual period. Because

$$1 + \tau_j G_j(t) = \prod_{m=1}^{M} [1 + \tau_{j,m} G_{j,m}(t)]$$

we can modify the analysis leading to equation (24.21) so that the volatility of $s(t)$ is obtained in terms of the volatilities of the $G_{j,m}(t)$ rather than the volatilities of the $G_j(t)$. The swap volatility to be substituted into the standard market model for valuing a swap option proves to be (see Problem 24.15)

$$\sqrt{\frac{1}{T_0} \int_{t=0}^{T_0} \sum_{q=1}^{p} \left( \sum_{k=n}^{N-1} \sum_{m=1}^{M} \frac{\tau_{k,m} \beta_{k,m,q}(t) G_{k,m}(0) \gamma_k(0)}{1 + \tau_{k,m} G_{k,m}(0)} \right)^2 dt} \qquad (24.22)$$

Here $\beta_{j,m,q}(t)$ is the $q$th component of the volatility of $G_{j,m}(t)$. It is the $q$th component of the volatility of a cap forward rate when the time to maturity is from $t$ to the beginning of the $m$th subperiod in the $(T_j, T_{j+1})$ swap accrual period.

The expressions in equations (24.21) and (24.22) for the swap volatility do involve the approximations that $G_j(t) = G_j(0)$ and $G_{j,m}(t) = G_{j,m}(0)$. Hull and White compared the prices of European swap options calculated using equations (24.21) and (24.22) with the prices calculated from a Monte Carlo simulation and found the two to be very close. Once the LIBOR market model has been calibrated, therefore, equations (24.21) and (24.22) provide a quick way of valuing European swap options. Analysts can determine whether European swap options are over- or underpriced relative to caps. As we will see shortly, they can also use the results to calibrate the model to the market prices of swap options.

### *Calibrating the Model*

To calibrate the LIBOR market model we must determine the $\Lambda_j$ and how they are split into $\lambda_{j,q}$. The first step is usually to use a principal components analysis such as that in Section 16.9 to determine the way the $\Lambda$'s are split into $\lambda$'s. The principal components model is

$$\delta F_j = \sum_{q=1}^{M} \alpha_{j,q} x_q$$

where $M$ is the total number of factors, $\delta F_j$ is the change in the forward rate for a forward contract maturing in $j$ accrual periods, $\alpha_{j,q}$ is the factor loading for the $j$th forward rate and $q$th factor, $x_q$ is the factor score for the $q$th factor, and

$$\sum_{j=1}^{M} \alpha_{j,q_1} \alpha_{j,q_2} = \begin{cases} 1 & \text{if } q_1 = q_2 \\ 0 & \text{if } q_1 \neq q_2 \end{cases}$$

Define $s_q$ as the standard deviation of the $q$th factor score. If the number of factors used in the LIBOR market model, $p$, is equal to the total number of factors, $M$, it is correct to set

$$\lambda_{j,q} = \alpha_{j,q} s_q$$

for $1 \leqslant j,q \leqslant M$. When $p < M$, the $\lambda_{j,q}$ must be scaled so that

$$\Lambda_j = \sqrt{\sum_{q=1}^{p} \lambda_{j,q}^2}$$

This involves setting

$$\lambda_{j,q} = \frac{\Lambda_j s_q \alpha_{j,q}}{\sqrt{\sum_{q=1}^{p} s_q^2 \alpha_{i,q}^2}} \tag{24.23}$$

Equation (24.15) provides one way to determine the $\Lambda$'s so that they are consistent with caplet prices. In practice it is not usually used because it often leads to wild swings in the $\Lambda$'s.[12] Also, although the LIBOR market model is designed to be consistent with the prices of caplets, analysts sometimes like to calibrate it to European swaptions. The most commonly used calibration procedure for the LIBOR market model is similar to that described for one-factor models in Section 23.14. Suppose that $U_i$ is the market price of the $i$th calibrating instrument and $V_i$ is the model price. We choose the $\Lambda$'s to minimize

$$\sum_i (U_i - V_i)^2 + P$$

where $P$ is a penalty function chosen to ensure that the $\Lambda$'s are "well behaved". Similarly to Section 23.14, $P$ has the form

$$P = \sum_i w_{1,i}(\Lambda_{i+1} - \Lambda_i)^2 + \sum_i w_{2,i}(\Lambda_{i+1} + \Lambda_{i-1} - 2\Lambda_i)^2$$

When some calibrating instruments are European swaptions the formulas in equations (24.21) and (24.22) make the minimization feasible using the Levenberg–Marquardt procedure. Equation (24.23) is used to determine the $\lambda$'s from the $\Lambda$'s.

### Volatility Skews

Brokers now provide quotes on caps that are not at the money as well as on those that are at the money. In some markets a volatility skew is observed, that is, the quoted (Black) volatility for a cap or a floor is a declining function of the strike price. This can be handled using the CEV model (see Section 20.1 for the application of the CEV model to equities). The model is

$$dF_i(t) = \cdots + \sum_{q=1}^{p} \zeta_{i,q}(t) F_i(t)^\alpha \, dz_q \tag{24.24}$$

where $\alpha$ ($0 < \alpha < 1$) is a constant . It turns out that this model can be handled in a very similar way to the lognormal model. Caps and floors can be valued analytically using the cumulative noncentral $\chi^2$ distribution. There are similar analytic approximations to those given above for the prices of European swap options.[13]

---

[12] Sometimes there is no set of $\Lambda$'s consistent with a set of cap quotes.

[13] For details, see L. Andersen and J. Andreasen, "Volatility Skews and Extensions of the LIBOR Market Model," *Applied Mathematical Finance*, 7, no. 1 (2000), 1–32; J. C. Hull and A. White, "Forward Rate Volatilities, Swap Rate Volatilities, and the Implementation of the LIBOR Market Model," *Journal of Fixed Income*, 10, no. 2 (September 2000), 46–62.

### *Bermudan Swap Options*

A popular interest rate derivative is a Bermudan swap option. This is a swap option that can be exercised on some or all of the payment dates of the underlying swap. Bermudan swap options are difficult to value using the LIBOR market model because the LIBOR market model relies on Monte Carlo simulation and it is difficult to evaluate early exercise decisions when Monte Carlo simulation is used. Fortunately the procedures described in Section 20.9 can be used. Longstaff and Schwartz apply the least-squares approach when there are a large number of factors. The value of not exercising on a particular payment date is assumed to be a polynomial function of the values of the factors.[14] Andersen shows that the optimal early exercise boundary approach can be used. He experiments with a number of ways of parametrizing the early exercise boundary and finds that good results are obtained when the early exercise decision is assumed to depend only on the intrinsic value of the option.[15] Most traders value Bermudan options using one of the one-factor no-arbitrage models discussed in Chapter 23. The accuracy of one-factor models for pricing Bermudan swap options has become a controversial issue.[16]

## 24.4  MORTGAGE-BACKED SECURITIES

One application of the models presented in this chapter is to the mortgage-backed security (MBS) market in the United States. A mortgage-backed security is created when a financial institution decides to sell part of its residential mortgage portfolio to investors. The mortgages sold are put into a pool and investors acquire a stake in the pool by buying units. The units are known as mortgage-backed securities. A secondary market is usually created for the units so that investors can sell them to other investors as desired. An investor who owns units representing $X$ percent of a certain pool is entitled to $X$ percent of the principal and interest cash flows received from the mortgages in the pool.

The mortgages in a pool are generally guaranteed by a government-related agency, such as the Government National Mortgage Association (GNMA) or the Federal National Mortgage Association (FNMA), so that investors are protected against defaults. This makes an MBS sound like a regular fixed-income security issued by the government. In fact, there is a critical difference between an MBS and a regular fixed-income investment. This difference is that the mortgages in an MBS pool have prepayment privileges. These prepayment privileges can be quite valuable to the householder. In the United States, mortgages typically last for 25 years and can be prepaid at any time. This means that the householder has a 25-year American-style option to put the mortgage back to the lender at its face value.

In practice prepayments on mortgages occur for a variety of reasons. Sometimes interest rates have fallen and the owner of the house decides to refinance at a lower rate of interest. On other

---

[14] See F. A. Longstaff and E. S. Schwartz, "Valuing American Options by Simulation: A Simple Least Squares Approach," *Review of Financial Studies*, 14, no. 1 (2001), 113–47.

[15] L. Andersen, "A simple Approach to the Pricing of Bermudan Swaptions in the Multifactor LIBOR Market Model," *Journal of Computational Finance*, 3, no. 2 (Winter 2000), 1–32.

[16] For opposing viewpoints, see "Factor Dependence of Bermudan Swaptions: Fact or Fiction," by L. Andersen and J. Andreasen, and "Throwing Away a Billion Dollars: The Cost of Suboptimal Exercise Strategies in the Swaption Market," by F. A. Longstaff, P. Santa-Clara, and E. S. Schwartz. Both are in *Journal of Financial Economics*, 62, no. 1 (October 2001).

occasions, a mortgage is prepaid simply because the house is being sold. A critical element in valuing an MBS is the determination of what is known as the *prepayment function*. This is a function describing expected prepayments on the underlying pool of mortgages at a time $t$ in terms of the yield curve at time $t$ and other relevant variables.

A prepayment function is very unreliable as a predictor of actual prepayment experience for an individual mortgage. When many similar mortgage loans are combined in the same pool, there is a "law of large numbers" effect at work and prepayments can be predicted more accurately from an analysis of historical data. As mentioned, prepayments are not always motivated by pure interest rate considerations. Nevertheless, there is a tendency for prepayments to be more likely when interest rates are low than when they are high. This means that investors require a higher rate of interest on an MBS than on other fixed-income securities to compensate for the prepayment options they have written.

### Collateralized Mortgage Obligations

The MBSs we have described so far are sometimes referred to as *pass-throughs*. All investors receive the same return and bear the same prepayment risk. Not all mortgage-backed securities work in this way. In a *collateralized mortgage obligation* (CMO) the investors are divided into a number of classes and rules are developed for determining how principal repayments are channeled to different classes.

As an example of a CMO, consider an MBS where investors are divided into three classes: class A, class B, and class C. All the principal repayments (both those that are scheduled and those that are prepayments) are channeled to class A investors until investors in this class have been completely paid off. Principal repayments are then channeled to class B investors until these investors have been completely paid off. Finally, principal repayments are channeled to class C investors. In this situation, class A investors bear the most prepayment risk. The class A securities can be expected to last for a shorter time than the class B securities, and these, in turn, can be expected to last less long than the class C securities.

The objective of this type of structure is to create classes of securities that are more attractive to institutional investors than those created by the simpler pass-through MBS. The prepayment risks assumed by the different classes depend on the par value in each class. For example, class C bears very little prepayment risk if the par values in classes A, B, and C are 400, 300, and 100, respectively. Class C bears rather more prepayment risk in the situation where the par values in the classes are 100, 200, and 500.

### IOs and POs

In what is known as a *stripped MBS*, principal payments are separated from interest payments. All principal payments are channeled to one class of security, known as a *principal only* (PO). All interest payments are channeled to another class of security known as an *interest only* (IO). Both IOs and POs are risky investments. As prepayment rates increase, a PO becomes more valuable and an IO becomes less valuable. As prepayment rates decrease, the reverse happens. In a PO, a fixed amount of principal is returned to the investor, but the timing is uncertain. A high rate of prepayments on the underlying pool leads to the principal being received early (which is, of course, good news for the holder of the PO). A low rate of prepayments on the underlying pool delays the return of the principal and reduces the yield provided by the PO. In the case of an IO, the total of the cash flows received by the investor is uncertain. The higher the rate of prepayments, the lower the total cash flows received by the investor, and vice versa.

### *Valuing Mortgage-Backed Securities*

Mortgage-backed securities are usually valued using Monte Carlo simulation. Either the HJM or LIBOR market models can be used to simulate the behavior of interest rates month by month throughout the life of an MBS. Consider what happens on one simulation trial. Each month expected prepayments are calculated from the current yield curve and the history of yield curve movements. These prepayments determine the expected cash flows to the holder of the MBS and the cash flows are discounted to time zero to obtain a sample value for the MBS. An estimate of the value of the MBS is the average of the sample values over many simulation trials.

### *Option-Adjusted Spread*

A critical input to any term structure model is the initial zero-coupon yield curve. This is a curve, generated in the way described in Chapter 5, providing the relationship between yield and maturity for zero-coupon bonds that have no embedded options.

In addition to calculating theoretical prices for mortgage-backed securities and other bonds with embedded options, traders also like to compute what is known as the *option-adjusted spread* (OAS). This is a measure of the spread over the yields on government Treasury bonds provided by the instrument when all options have been taken into account.

To calculate an OAS for an instrument, it is first priced using the zero-coupon government Treasury curve as the input to the pricing model. The price of the instrument given by the model is compared with the price in the market. A series of iterations is then used to determine the parallel shift to the input Treasury curve that causes the model price to be equal to the market price. This parallel shift is the OAS.

To illustrate the nature of the calculations, suppose that the market price is $102.00 and that the price calculated using the Treasury curve is $103.27. As a first trial we might choose to try a 60-basis-point parallel shift to the Treasury zero curve. Suppose that this gives a price of $101.20 for the instrument. This is less than the market price of $102.00 and means that a parallel shift somewhere between 0 and 60 basis points will lead to the model price being equal to the market price. We could use linear interpolation to calculate

$$60 \times \frac{103.27 - 102.00}{103.27 - 101.20} = 36.81$$

or 36.81 basis points as the next trial shift. Suppose that this gives a price of $101.95. This indicates that the OAS is slightly less than 36.81 basis points. Linear interpolation suggests that the next trial shift be

$$36.81 \times \frac{103.27 - 102.00}{103.27 - 101.95} = 35.41$$

or 35.41 basis points, and so on.

# SUMMARY

We have covered a number of advanced models for valuing interest rate derivatives. In the two-factor Hull–White model, the short rate reverts to a level dependent on another stochastic variable. This stochastic variable, in turn, reverts to zero. Unlike the models considered in Chapter 23, this model can match the volatility structure observed today in the market, not just today but at all future times.

The HJM and LIBOR market models provide approaches that give the user complete freedom in choosing the volatility term structure. The LIBOR market model has two key advantages over the HJM model. First, it is developed in terms of the forward rates that determine the pricing of caps, rather than in terms of instantaneous forward rates. Second, it is relatively easy to calibrate to the price of caps or European swap options. The HJM and LIBOR market models both have the serious disadvantage that they cannot be represented as recombining trees. In practice, this means that they must be implemented using Monte Carlo simulation.

The mortgage-backed security market in the United States has given birth to many exotic interest rate derivatives: CMOs, IOs, POs, and so on. These instruments provide cash flows to the holder that depend on the prepayments on a pool of mortgages. These prepayments depend on, among other things, the level of interest rates. Because they are heavily path dependent, mortgage-backed securities usually have to be valued using Monte Carlo simulation. These are therefore ideal candidates for applications of the HJM model and LIBOR market models.

## SUGGESTIONS FOR FURTHER READING

Amin, K., and A. Morton, "Implied Volatility Functions in Arbitrage-Free Term Structure Models," *Journal of Financial Economics*, 35 (1994), 141–80.

Andersen, L., "A Simple Approach to the Pricing of Bermudan Swaption in the Multi-Factor LIBOR Market Model," *Applied Mathematical Finance*, 7, no. 1 (2000), 1–32.

Brace, A., D. Gatarek, and M. Musiela, "The Market Model of Interest Rate Dynamics," *Mathematical Finance*, 7, no. 2 (1997), 127–55.

Buhler, W., M. Ulrig-Homberg, U. Walter, and T. Weber, "An Empirical Comparison of Forward and Spot-Rate Models for Valuing Interest Rate Options," *Journal of Finance*, 54, no. 1 (February 1999), 269–305.

Carverhill, A., "When Is the Short Rate Markovian," *Mathematical Finance*, 4 (1994), 305–12.

Cheyette, O., "Term Structure Dynamics and Mortgage Valuation," *Journal of Fixed Income*, March 1992, 28–41.

Duffie, D., and R. Kan, "A Yield-Factor Model of Interest Rates," *Mathematical Finance*, 6, no. 4 (1996), 379–406.

Heath, D., R. Jarrow, and A. Morton, "Bond Pricing and the Term Structure of Interest Rates: A Discrete Time Approximation," *Journal of Financial and Quantitative Analysis*, 25, no. 4 (December 1990), 419–40.

Heath, D., R. Jarrow, and A. Morton, "Bond Pricing and the Term Structure of the Interest Rates: A New Methodology," *Econometrica*, 60, no. 1 (1992), 77–105.

Heath, D., R. Jarrow, A. Morton, and M. Spindel, "Easier Done Than Said," *RISK*, May 1993, pp. 77–80.

Hull, J., and A. White, "Bond Option Pricing Based on a Model for the Evolution of Bond Prices," *Advances in Futures and Options Research*, 6 (1993), 1–13.

Hull, J., and A. White, "Numerical Procedures for Implementing Term Structure Models II: Two-Factor Models," *Journal of Derivatives*, 2, no. 2 (Winter 1994), 37–48.

Hull, J., and A. White, "Forward Rate Volatilities, Swap Rate Volatilities, and the Implementation of the LIBOR Market Model," *Journal of Fixed Income*, 10, no. 2 (September 2000), 46–62.

Inui, K., and M. Kijima, "A Markovian Framework in Multifactor Heath, Jarrow, and Morton Models," *Journal of Financial and Quantitative Analysis*, 33, no. 3 (September 1998), 423–40.

Jamshidian, F., "LIBOR and Swap Market Models and Measures," *Finance and Stochastics*, 1 (1977), 293–330.

Jarrow, R. A., *Modeling Fixed Income Securities and Interest Rate Options*, McGraw-Hill, New York, 1995.

Jarrow, R. A., and S. M. Turnbull, "Delta, Gamma, and Bucket Hedging of Interest Rate Derivatives," *Applied Mathematical Finance*, 1 (1994), 21–48.

Jeffrey, A., "Single Factor Heath-Jarrow-Morton Term Structure Models Based on Markov Spot Interest Rate Dynamics," *Journal of Financial and Quantitative Analysis*, 30 (1995), 619–42.

Longstaff, F. A., and E. S. Schwartz, "Valuing American Options by Simulation: A Simple Least Squares Approach," *Review of Financial Studies*, 14, no. 1 (2001), 113–47.

Miltersen, K., K. Sandmann, and D. Sondermann, "Closed Form Solutions for Term Structure Derivatives with Lognormal Interest Rates," *Journal of Finance*, 52, no. 1 (March 1997), 409–30.

Rebonato, R., *Interest Rate Option Models*, 2nd edn., Wiley, Chichester, 1998.

Ritchken, P., and L. Sankarasubramanian, "Volatility Structures of Forward Rates and the Dynamics of the Term Structure," *Mathematical Finance*, 5 (1995), 55–72.

## QUESTIONS AND PROBLEMS
## (ANSWERS IN SOLUTIONS MANUAL)

24.1. For the model in Section 24.1 when $f(r) = r$,
   a. What is the process followed by the bond price $P(t, T)$ in the traditional risk-neutral world?
   b. What is the process followed by the bond's yield in this risk-neutral world?
   c. For the parameters in Figure 24.1, what is the instantaneous correlation between the three-month and the ten-year zero rates?

24.2. For the model in Section 24.1, what are the coefficients of $dz_1$ and $dz_2$ in the process followed by the instantaneous forward rate when $f(r) = r$?

24.3. Explain the difference between a Markov and a non-Markov model of the short rate.

24.4. Prove the relationship between the drift and volatility of the forward rate for the multifactor version of HJM in equation (24.10).

24.5. Show from equation (24.9) that if the instantaneous forward rate $F(t, T)$ in the HJM model has a constant standard deviation then the process for $r$ is the same as in the Ho–Lee model.

24.6. Show that equations (23.17) and (23.18) are consistent with equations (24.8) and (24.9) when $s(t, T) = \sigma e^{-a(T-t)}$.

24.7. It can be shown that in a one-factor model where the bond price volatility $v(t, T, \Omega_t)$ is a function only of $t$ and $T$, the process for $r$ is Markov if and only if $v(t, T)$ has the form $x(t)[y(T) - y(t)]$. Use equations (24.8) and (24.9) to show that when $v(t, T)$ has this form the process for $r$ is Markov.

24.8. Provide an intuitive explanation of why a ratchet cap increases in value as the number of factors increase.

24.9. Show that equation (24.14) reduces to (24.6) as the $\delta_i$ tend to zero.

24.10. Explain why a sticky cap is more expensive than a similar ratchet cap.

24.11. Explain why IOs and POs have opposite sensitivities to the rate of prepayments.

24.12. "An option-adjusted spread is analogous to the yield on a bond." Explain this statement.

24.13. Prove equation (24.19).

24.14. Prove the formula for $V(t)$ on page 583.

24.15. Prove equation (24.22).

# ASSIGNMENT QUESTIONS

24.16. In an annual-pay cap, the Black volatilities for caplets with maturities 1, 2, 3, and 5 years are 18%, 20%, 22%, and 20%, respectively. Estimate the volatility of a one-year forward rate in the LIBOR market model when the time to maturity is (a) 0 to 1 year, (b) 1 to 2 years, (c) 2 to 3 years, and (d) 3 to 5 years. Assume that the zero curve is flat at 5% per annum (annually compounded). Use DerivaGem to estimate flat volatilities for 2-, 3-, 4-, 5-, and 6-year caps.

24.17. In the flexi cap considered in Section 24.3, the holder is obligated to exercise the first $N$ in-the-money caplets. After that, no further caplets can be exercised (in the example, $N = 5$). Two other ways that flexi caps are sometimes defined are:
   a. The holder can choose whether any caplet is exercised, but there is a limit of $N$ on the total number of caplets that can be exercised.
   b. Once the holder chooses to exercise a caplet, all subsequent in-the-money caplets must be exercised up to a maximum of $N$.

Discuss the problems in valuing these types of flexi caps. Of the three types of flexi caps, which would you expect to be most expensive? Which would you expect to be least expensive?

# APPENDIX 24A
## The $A(t, T)$, $\sigma_P$, and $\theta(t)$ Functions in the Two-Factor Hull–White Model

In this appendix, we provide some of the analytic results for the two-factor Hull–White model discussed in Section 24.1 when $f(r) = r$.

The $A(t, T)$ function is

$$\ln A(t, T) = \ln \frac{P(0, T)}{P(0, t)} + B(t, T)F(0, t) - \eta$$

where

$$\eta = \frac{\sigma_1^2}{4a}(1 - e^{-2at})B(t, T)^2 - \rho\sigma_1\sigma_2[B(0, t)C(0, t)B(t, T) + \gamma_4 - \gamma_2]$$

$$- \tfrac{1}{2}\sigma_2^2[C(0, t)^2 B(t, T) + \gamma_6 - \gamma_5]$$

$$\gamma_1 = \frac{e^{-(a+b)T}(e^{(a+b)t} - 1)}{(a + b)(a - b)} - \frac{e^{-2aT}(e^{2at} - 1)}{2a(a - b)}$$

$$\gamma_2 = \frac{1}{ab}\left(\gamma_1 + C(t, T) - C(0, T) + \tfrac{1}{2}B(t, T)^2 - \tfrac{1}{2}B(0, T)^2 + \frac{t}{a} - \frac{e^{-a(T-t)} - e^{-aT}}{a^2}\right)$$

$$\gamma_3 = -\frac{e^{-(a+b)t} - 1}{(a - b)(a + b)} + \frac{e^{-2at} - 1}{2a(a - b)}$$

$$\gamma_4 = \frac{1}{ab}\left(\gamma_3 - C(0, t) - \tfrac{1}{2}B(0, t)^2 + \frac{t}{a} + \frac{e^{-at} - 1}{a^2}\right)$$

$$\gamma_5 = \frac{1}{b}[\tfrac{1}{2}C(t, T)^2 - \tfrac{1}{2}C(0, T)^2 + \gamma_2]$$

$$\gamma_6 = \frac{1}{b}[\gamma_4 - \tfrac{1}{2}C(0, t)^2]$$

where the $B(t, T)$ and $C(t, T)$ functions are as in Section 24.1 and $F(t, T)$ is the instantaneous forward rate at time $t$ for maturity $T$.

The volatility function, $\sigma_P$, is

$$\sigma_P^2 = \int_0^t \{\sigma_1^2[B(\tau, T) - B(\tau, t)]^2 + \sigma_2^2[C(\tau, T) - C(\tau, t)]^2$$

$$+ 2\rho\sigma_1\sigma_2[B(\tau, T) - B(\tau, t)][C(\tau, T) - C(\tau, t)]\} d\tau$$

This shows that $\sigma_P^2$ has three components. Define

$$U = \frac{1}{a(a - b)}(e^{-aT} - e^{-at})$$

and

$$V = \frac{1}{b(a - b)}(e^{-bT} - e^{-bt})$$

The first component of $\sigma_P^2$ is

$$\frac{\sigma_1^2}{2a} B(t, T)^2 (1 - e^{-2at})$$

The second is

$$\sigma_2^2 \left( \frac{U^2}{2a} (e^{2at} - 1) + \frac{V^2}{2b} (e^{2bt} - 1) - 2\frac{UV}{a+b} (e^{(a+b)t} - 1) \right)$$

The third is

$$\frac{2\rho\sigma_1\sigma_2}{a} (e^{-at} - e^{-aT}) \left( \frac{U}{2a} (e^{2at} - 1) - \frac{V}{a+b} (e^{(a+b)t} - 1) \right)$$

Finally, the $\theta(t)$ function is

$$\theta(t) = F_t(0, t) + aF(0, t) + \phi_t(0, t) + a\phi(0, t)$$

where the subscript denotes a partial derivative and

$$\phi(t, T) = \tfrac{1}{2}\sigma_1^2 B(t, T)^2 + \tfrac{1}{2}\sigma_2^2 C(t, T)^2 + \rho\sigma_1\sigma_2 B(t, T)C(t, T)$$

# CHAPTER 25

# SWAPS REVISITED

Swaps have been central to the success of over-the-counter derivatives markets during the 1980s and 1990s. They have proved to be very flexible instruments for managing risk. Based on the range of different contracts that now trade and the total volume of business transacted each year, swaps are arguably one the most successful innovations in financial markets ever.

In Chapter 6 we discussed how plain vanilla interest rate swaps can be valued. The standard approach can be summarized as: "Assume forward rates will be realized." The steps are:

1. Calculate the swap's net cash flows on the assumption that LIBOR rates in the future equal today's forward LIBOR rates.

2. Set the value of the swap equal to the present value of the net cash flows using today's LIBOR zero curve for discounting.

We used this approach in Example 6.3. It involves regarding the swap as a portfolio of forward rate agreements. As discussed in Chapter 6, it is important to reflect day count conventions and business day conventions in the calculation of the cash flows and their timing. The LIBOR zero curve is calculated as described in Section 6.3 from LIBOR deposit rates, Eurodollar futures, and quoted swap rates.

In this chapter we describe a number of nonstandard swaps. Some can be valued using the "assume forward rates will be realized" approach; some require the application of the convexity, timing, and quanto adjustments we encountered in Chapters 21 and 22; and some contain embedded options.

## 25.1  VARIATIONS ON THE VANILLA DEAL

Many interest rate swaps involve relatively minor variations to the plain vanilla structure in Table 6.3. In some swaps the notional principal changes with time in a predetermined way. Swaps where the notional principal is an increasing function of time are known as *step-up swaps*. Swaps where the notional principal is a decreasing function of time are known as *amortizing swaps*. Step-up swaps could be useful for a construction company that intends to borrow increasing amounts of money at floating rates to finance a particular project and wants to swap it to fixed-rate funding. An amortizing swap could be used by a company that has fixed-rate borrowings with a certain prepayment schedule and wants to swap them to borrowings at a floating rate.

The principal, as well as the frequency of payments, can be different on the two sides of a swap. This is illustrated in Table 25.1, which shows a hypothetical swap between Microsoft and Citibank

**594**

**Table 25.1**  Extract from confirmation for a hypothetical swap where the principal and payment frequency are different on the two sides

| | |
|---|---|
| Trade date | 4-January-2001 |
| Effective date | 11-January-2001 |
| Business day convention (all dates) | Following business day |
| Holiday calendar | U.S. |
| Termination date | 11-January-2006 |
| **Fixed amounts** | |
| Fixed-rate payer | Microsoft |
| Fixed-rate notional principal | USD 100 million |
| Fixed rate | 6% per annum |
| Fixed-rate day count convention | Actual/365 |
| Fixed-rate payment dates | Each 11-July and 11-January commencing 11-July-2001 up to and including 11-January-2006 |
| **Floating amounts** | |
| Floating-rate payer | Citibank |
| Floating-rate notional principal | USD 120 million |
| Floating rate | USD 1-month LIBOR |
| Floating-rate day count convention | Actual/360 |
| Floating-rate payment dates | 11-July-2001 and the 11th of each month thereafter up to and including 11-January-2006 |

where the notional principal is $120 million on the floating side and $100 million on fixed side. Payments are made every month on the floating side and every six months on the fixed side.

These variations to the basic plain vanilla structure do not affect the valuation methodology. We can still use the "assume forward rates are realized" approach.

The floating reference rate for a swap is not always LIBOR. For example, in some swaps it is the three-month Treasury bill rate. A *basis swap* consists of exchanging cash flows calculated using one floating reference rate for cash flows calculated using another floating reference rate. An example would be a swap where the three-month Treasury bill rate plus 60 basis points is exchanged for three-month LIBOR with both being applied to a principal of $100 million. A basis swap could be used for risk management by a financial institution whose assets and liabilities are dependent on different floating reference rates.

Swaps where the floating reference rate is not LIBOR can be valued using the "assume forward rates are realized" approach. A zero curve other than LIBOR is necessary to calculate the net cash flows. However, we always discount the calculated cash flows at LIBOR.

## 25.2 COMPOUNDING SWAPS

Another variation on the plain vanilla swap is a *compounding swap*. Table 25.2 gives an example. There is only one payment date for both the floating-rate payments and the fixed-rate payments. This is at the end of the life of the swap. The floating rate of interest is LIBOR plus 20 basis points.

**Table 25.2** Extract from confirmation for a hypothetical compounding swap

| | |
|---|---|
| Trade date | 4-January-2001 |
| Effective date | 11-January-2001 |
| Holiday calendar | U.S. |
| Business day convention (all dates) | Following business day |
| Termination date | 11-January-2006 |
| **Fixed amounts** | |
| Fixed-rate payer | Microsoft |
| Fixed-rate notional principal | USD 100 million |
| Fixed rate | 6% per annum |
| Fixed-rate day count convention | Actual/365 |
| Fixed-rate payment date | 11-January-2006 |
| Fixed-rate compounding | Applicable at 6.3% |
| Fixed-rate compounding dates | Each 11-July and 11-January commencing 11-July-2001 up to and including 11-July-2005 |
| **Floating amounts** | |
| Floating-rate payer | Citibank |
| Floating-rate notional principal | USD 100 million |
| Floating rate | USD 6-month LIBOR plus 20 basis points |
| Floating-rate day count convention | Actual/360 |
| Floating-rate payment date | 11-January-2006 |
| Floating-rate compounding | Applicable at LIBOR plus 10 basis points |
| Floating-rate compounding dates | Each 11-July and 11-January commencing 11-July-2001 up to and including 11-July-2005 |

Instead of being paid, the interest is compounded forward until the end of the life of the swap at a rate of LIBOR plus 10 basis points. The fixed rate of interest is 6%. Instead of being paid, this interest is compounded forward at a fixed rate of interest of 6.3% until the end of the swap.

We can use the "assume forward rates are realized" approach for valuing a compounding swap. It is straightforward to deal with the fixed side of the swap because the payment that we will make at maturity is known with certainty. The "assume forward rates are realized" approach for the floating part is justifiable because we can devise a series of forward rate agreements (FRAs) where the floating-rate cash flows are exchanged for their values when each floating rate equals the corresponding forward rate. To explain how this is done, suppose that $t_0$ is the time of the payment date immediately preceding the valuation date and that the payment dates following the valuation date are at times $t_1, t_2, \ldots, t_n$. Define $\tau_i = t_{i+1} - t_i$ ($0 \leqslant i \leqslant n-1$) and other variables as follows:[1]

$L$: Principal on the floating side of swap

$Q_i$: Value of floating side compounded forward to time $t_i$ ($Q_0$ is known)

---

[1] All rates are here expressed with a compounding frequency reflecting their maturity. Three-month rates are expressed with quarterly compounding, six-month rates are expressed with annual compounding, and so on.

$R_i$ : LIBOR rate from $t_i$ to $t_{i+1}$ ($R_0$ is known)

$F_i$ : Forward rate applicable to period between time $t_i$ and $t_{i+1}$ for $i \geqslant 1$ (all known)

$s_1$ : Spread above LIBOR at which interest is incurred on the floating side of the swap (20 basis points in Table 25.2)

$s_2$ : Spread above LIBOR at which floating interest compounds (10 basis points in Table 25.2)

The value of the floating side of the swap at time $t_1$ is known. It is

$$Q_1 = Q_0[1 + (R_0 + s_2)\tau_0] + L(R_0 + s_1)\tau_0$$

The first term on the right-hand side is the result of compounding the floating payments from time $t_0$ to $t_1$. The second term is the floating payment at time $t_1$.

The value of the floating side at time $t_2$ is not known and depends on $R_1$. It is

$$Q_2 = Q_1[1 + (R_1 + s_2)\tau_1] + L(R_1 + s_1)\tau_1 \qquad (25.1)$$

However, we can costlessly enter into two FRAs:

1. An FRA to exchange $R_1 + s_2$ for $F_1 + s_2$ on a principal of $Q_1$
2. An FRA to exchange $R_1 + s_1$ for $F_1 + s_1$ on a principal of $L$

The first FRA shows that the first term on the right-hand side of equation (25.1) is worth $Q_1[1 + (F_1 + s_2)\tau_1]$. The second FRA shows that the second term on the right-hand side of equation (25.1) is worth $L(F_1 + s_1)\tau_1$. The value of the floating side of the swap at time $t_2$ is therefore

$$Q_2 = Q_1[1 + (F_1 + s_2)\tau_1] + L(F_1 + s_1)\tau_1$$

A similar argument gives

$$Q_{i+1} = Q_i[1 + (F_i + s_2)\tau_i) + L(F_i + s_1)\tau_i$$

for all $i$ ($1 \leqslant i \leqslant n - 1$).

**Example 25.1** A compounding swap with annual resets has a life of three years. A fixed rate is paid and a floating rate is received. The fixed interest rate is 4% and the floating interest rate is 12-month LIBOR. The fixed side compounds at 3.9% and the floating side compounds at 12-month LIBOR minus 20 basis points. The LIBOR zero curve is flat at 5% with annual compounding and the notional principal is $100 million.

On the fixed side, interest of $4 million is earned at the end of the first year. This compounds to $4 \times 1.039 = \$4.156$ million at the end of the second year. A second interest amount of $4 million is added at the end of the second year, bringing the total compounded forward amount to $8.156 million. This compounds to $8.156 \times 1.039 = \$8.474$ million by the end of the third year, when there is the third interest amount of $4 million. The cash flow at the end of the third year on the fixed side of the swap is therefore $12.474 million.

On the floating side we assume all future interest rates equal the corresponding forward LIBOR rates. Given the LIBOR zero curve, this means that we assume all future interest rates are 5% with annual compounding. The interest calculated at the end of the first year is $5 million. Compounding this forward at 4.8% (forward LIBOR minus 20 basis points) gives $5 \times 1.048 = \$5.24$ million at the end of the second year. Adding in the interest, the compounded forward amount is $10.24 million. Compounding forward to the end of the third year, we get $10.24 \times 1.048 = \$10.731$ million. Adding in the final interest gives $15.731 million.

We can value the swap by assuming that it leads to an inflow of $15.731 million and an outflow of $12.474 million at the end of year 3. The value of the swap is therefore

$$\frac{15.731 - 12.474}{1.05^3} = 2.814$$

or $2.814 million. (This analysis ignores day count issues.)

## 25.3  CURRENCY SWAPS

We introduced currency swaps in Chapter 6. These enable an interest rate exposure in one currency to be swapped for an interest rate exposure in another currency. Usually two principals are specified, one in each currency. The principals are exchanged at both the beginning and the end of the life of the swap as described in Section 6.5.

Suppose that the currencies involved in a currency swap are U.S. dollars (USD) and British pounds (GBP). In a fixed-for-fixed currency swap, a fixed rate of interest is specified in each currency. The payments on one side are determined by applying the fixed rate of interest in USD to the USD principal; the payments on the other side are determined by applying the fixed rate of interest in GBP to the GBP principal. We discussed the valuation of this type of swap in Section 6.6.

Another popular type of currency swap is floating-for-floating. In this, the payments on one side are determined by applying USD LIBOR (possibly with a spread added) to the USD principal; similarly the payments on the other side are determined by applying GBP LIBOR (possibly with a spread added) to the GBP principal. A third type of swap is a cross-currency interest rate swap, where a floating rate in one currency is exchanged for a fixed rate in another currency.

Floating-for-floating and cross-currency interest rate swaps can be valued by assuming forward rates are realized. Future LIBOR rates in each currency are assumed to equal today's forward rates. This enables the cash flows in the currencies to be determined. The USD cash flows are discounted at the USD LIBOR zero rate. The GBP cash flows are discounted at the GBP LIBOR zero rate. The current exchange rate is then used to translate the two present values to a common currency.

An adjustment to this procedure is sometimes made to reflect the realities of the market. In theory, a new floating-for-floating swap should involve exchanging LIBOR in one currency for LIBOR in another currency (with no spreads added). In practice, macroeconomic effects give rise to spreads. Financial institutions often adjust the discount rates they use to allow for this. As an example, suppose that market conditions are such that USD LIBOR is exchanged for Japanese yen (JPY) LIBOR minus 20 basis points in new floating-for-floating swaps of all maturities. In its valuations a U.S. financial institution would discount USD cash flows at USD LIBOR and it would discount JPY cash flows at JPY LIBOR minus 20 basis points.[2] It would do this in all swaps that involved both JPY and USD cash flows.

## 25.4  MORE COMPLEX SWAPS

We now move on to consider some examples of swaps where the simple rule "assume forward rates will be realized" does not work. In each case we must adjustments to forward rates.

---

[2] This adjustment is *ad hoc*, but, if it is not made, traders make an immediate profit or loss every time they trade a new JPY–USD floating-for-floating swap.

### LIBOR-in-Arrears Swap

A plain vanilla interest rate swap is designed so that the floating rate of interest observed on one payment date is paid on the next payment date. An alternative instrument that is sometimes traded is a *LIBOR-in-arrears swap*. In this, the floating rate paid on a payment date equals the rate observed on the payment date itself.

Suppose that the reset dates in the swap are $t_i$ for $i = 0, 1, \ldots, n$, with $\tau_i = t_{i+1} - t_i$. Define $R_i$ as the LIBOR rate for the period between $t_i$ and $t_{i+1}$, $F_i$ as the forward value of $R_i$, and $\sigma_i$ as the volatility of this forward rate. (The value of $\sigma_i$ is typically implied from caplet prices.) In a LIBOR-in-arrears swap, the payment on the floating side at time $t_i$ is based on $R_i$ rather than $R_{i-1}$. As explained in Section 22.6, it is necessary to make a convexity adjustment to the forward rate when the payment is valued. From equation (22.16), the valuation should be based on the assumption that the forward rate is

$$F_i + \frac{F_i^2 \sigma_i^2 \tau_i t_i}{1 + F_i \tau_i} \tag{25.2}$$

rather than $F_i$.

**Example 25.2**  In a LIBOR-in-arrears swap, the principal is \$100 million. A fixed rate of 5% is received annually and LIBOR is paid. Payments are exchanged at the ends of years 1, 2, 3, 4, and 5. The yield curve is flat at 5% per annum (measured with annual compounding). All caplet volatilities are 22% per annum.

The forward rate for each floating payment is 5%. If this were a regular swap rather than an in-arrears swap, its value would (ignoring day count conventions, etc.) be exactly zero. Because it is an in-arrears swap, we must make convexity adjustments. In equation (25.2), $F_i = 0.05$, $\sigma_i = 0.22$, and $\tau_i = 1$ for all $i$. The convexity adjustment changes the rate assumed at time $t_i$ from 0.05 to

$$0.05 + \frac{0.05^2 \times 0.22^2 \times 1 \times t_i}{1 + 0.05 \times 1} = 0.05 + 0.000105 t_i$$

The floating rates for the payments at the ends of years 1, 2, 3, 4, and 5 should therefore be assumed to be 5.0105%, 5.021%, 5.0315%, 5.0420%, and 5.0525%, respectively. The net exchange on the first payment date is equivalent to a cash outflow of 0.0105% of \$100 million or \$10,500. Equivalent net cash flows for other exchanges are calculated similarly. The value of the swap is

$$-\frac{10,500}{1.05} - \frac{21,000}{1.05^2} - \frac{31,500}{1.05^3} - \frac{42,000}{1.05^4} - \frac{52,500}{1.05^5}$$

or −\$131,947.

### CMS and CMT Swaps

A constant maturity swap (CMS) is an interest rate swap where the floating rate equals the swap rate for a swap with a certain life. For example, the floating payments on a CMS swap might be made every six months at a rate equal to the five-year swap rate. Usually there is a lag so that the payment on a particular payment date is equal to the swap rate observed on the previous payment date. Suppose that rates are set at times $t_0, t_1, t_2, \ldots$ and payments are made at times $t_1, t_2, t_3, \ldots$. The floating payment at time $t_{i+1}$ is

$$\tau_i L S_i$$

where $\tau_i = t_{i+1} - t_i$ and $S_i$ is the swap rate at time $t_i$.

Suppose that $y_i$ is the forward value of the swap rate $S_i$. To value the payment at time $t_{i+1}$, it turns out to be correct to make a convexity adjustment to the forward swap rate, so that the swap rate is assumed to be

$$y_i - \tfrac{1}{2} y_i^2 \sigma_{y,i}^2 t_i \frac{G_i''(y_i)}{G_i'(y_i)} - \frac{y_i \tau_i F_i \rho_i \sigma_{y,i} \sigma_{F,i} t_i}{1 + F_i \tau_i} \tag{25.3}$$

rather than $y_i$. In this equation, $\sigma_{y,i}$ is the volatility of the forward swap rate, $F_i$ is the current forward interest rate between times $t_i$ and $t_{i+1}$, $\sigma_{F,i}$ is the volatility of this forward rate, and $\rho_i$ is the correlation between the forward swap rate and the forward interest rate. $G_i(x)$ is the price at time $t_i$ of a bond as a function of its yield $x$. The bond pays coupons at rate $y_i$ and has the same life and payment frequency as the swap from which the CMS rate is calculated. $G_i'(x)$ and $G_i''(x)$ are the first and second partial derivatives of $G_i$ with respect to $x$. The volatilities $\sigma_{y,i}$ can be implied from swap options; the volatilities $\sigma_{F,i}$ can be implied from caplet prices; the correlation $\rho_i$ can be estimated from historical data.

Equation (25.3) involves a convexity and a timing adjustment. The term

$$-\tfrac{1}{2} y_i^2 \sigma_{y,i}^2 t_i \frac{G_i''(y_i)}{G_i'(y_i)}$$

is an adjustment similar the one we calculated in Example 22.6 of Section 22.6. It is based on the assumption that the swap rate, $S_i$, leads to only one payment at time $t_i$. The term

$$-\frac{y_i \tau_i F_i \rho_i \sigma_{y,i} \sigma_{F,i} t_i}{1 + F_i \tau_i}$$

is similar the one we calculated in equation (22.18) and allows for the fact that the payment calculated from $S_i$ is made at time $t_{i+1}$ rather than $t_i$.

**Example 25.3**  In a six-year CMS swap, the five-year swap rate is received and a fixed rate of 5% is paid on a notional principal of $100 million. The exchange of payments is semiannual (both on the underlying five-year swap and on the CMS swap itself). The exchange on a payment date is determined from the swap rate on the previous payment date. The term structure is flat at 5% per annum with semiannual compounding. All options on five-year swaps have a 15% implied volatility and all caplets with a six-month tenor have a 20% implied volatility. The correlation between each cap rate and each swap rate is 0.7.

In this case, $y_i = 0.05$, $\sigma_{y,i} = 0.15$, $\tau_i = 0.5$, $F_i = 0.05$, $\sigma_{F,i} = 0.20$, and $\rho_i = 0.7$ for all $i$. Also,

$$G_i(x) = \sum_{i=1}^{10} \frac{2.5}{(1 + x/2)^i} + \frac{100}{(1 + x/2)^{10}}$$

so that $G_i'(y_i) = -437.603$ and $G_i''(y_i) = 2261.23$. Equation (25.3) gives the total convexity/timing adjustment as $0.0001197 t_i$, or 1.197 basis points per year until the swap rate is observed. For example, for the purposes of valuing the CMS swap, the five-year swap rate in four years' time should be assumed to be 5.0479% rather than 5% and the net cash flow received at the 4.5-year point should be assumed to be $0.5 \times 0.000479 \times 100,000,000 = \$23,940$. Other net cash flows are calculated similarly. Taking their present value, we find the value of the swap to be $130,545.

A constant maturity Treasury swap (CMT swap) works similarly to a CMS swap except that the floating rate is the yield on a Treasury bond with a specified life. The analysis of a CMT swap is essentially the same as that for a CMS swap with $S_i$ defined as the par yield on a Treasury bond with the specified life.

### Differential Swaps

A *differential swap*, sometimes referred to as a *diff swap*, is an interest rate swap where the floating interest rate is observed in one currency and applied to a principal in another currency. Suppose that we observe the LIBOR rate for the period between $t_i$ and $t_{i+1}$ in currency Y and apply it to a principal in currency X with the payment taking place at time $t_{i+1}$. Define $F_i$ as the forward interest rate between $t_i$ and $t_{i+1}$ in currency Y and $G_i$ as the forward exchange rate for a contract with maturity $t_{i+1}$ (expressed as the number of units of currency Y that equal one unit of currency X). If the LIBOR rate in currency Y were applied to a principal in currency Y, we would value the cash flow on the assumption that the LIBOR rate equaled $F_i$. From the analysis in Section 21.8, a quanto adjustment is necessary when it is applied to a principal in currency X. It is correct to value the cash flow on the assumption that the LIBOR rate equals

$$F_i + F_i \rho_i \sigma_{G,i} \sigma_{F,i} t_i \tag{25.4}$$

where $\sigma_{F,i}$ is the volatility of $F_i$, $\sigma_{G,i}$ is the volatility of $G_i$, and $\rho_i$ is the correlation between $F_i$ and $G_i$.

> **Example 25.4**  Zero rates in both the United States and Britain are flat at 5% per annum with annual compounding. In a three-year diff swap agreement with annual payments, USD 12-month LIBOR is received and sterling 12-month LIBOR is paid, with both being applied to a principal of £10 million. The volatility of all one-year forward rates in the United States is estimated to be 20%, the volatility of the forward USD–sterling exchange rate (dollars per pound) is 12% for all maturities, and the correlation between the two is 0.4.
>
> In this case, $F_i = 0.05$, $\rho_i = 0.4$, $\sigma_{G,i} = 0.12$, and $\sigma_{F,i} = 0.2$. The floating-rate cash flows dependent on the one-year USD rate observed at time $t_i$ should therefore be calculated on the assumption that the rate will be
>
> $$0.05 + 0.05 \times 0.4 \times 0.12 \times 0.2 \times t_i = 0.05 + 0.00048 t_i$$

This means that the net cash flows from the swap at times one, two, and three years should be assumed to be 0, 4,800, and 9,600 pounds sterling for the purposes of valuation. The value of the swap is therefore

$$\frac{0}{1.05} + \frac{4,800}{1.05^2} + \frac{9,600}{1.05^3} = 12,647$$

or £12,647.

## 25.5  EQUITY SWAPS

In an equity swap, one party promises to pay the return on an equity index on a notional principal while the other promises to pay a fixed or floating return on a notional principal. Equity swaps enable a fund managers to increase or reduce their exposure to an index without buying and selling stock. An equity swap is a convenient way of packaging a series of forward contracts on an index to meet the needs of the market.

The equity index is usually a total return index where dividends are reinvested in the stocks comprising the index. An example of an equity swap is in Table 25.3. In this, the six-month return

**Table 25.3** Extract from confirmation for an hypothetical equity swap

| | |
|---|---|
| Trade date | 4-January-2001 |
| Effective date | 11-January-2001 |
| Business day convention (all dates) | Modified following business day |
| Holiday calendar | U.S. |
| Termination date | 11-January-2006 |

| **Equity amounts** | |
|---|---|
| Equity payer | Microsoft |
| Equity index | Total return S&P 500 index |
| Equity payment | $100(I_1 - I_0)/I_0$, where $I_1$ is the index level on the payment date and $I_0$ is the index level on the immediately preceding payment date. In the case of the first payment date, $I_0$ is the index level on 11-January-2001 |
| Equity payment dates | Each 11-July and 11-January commencing 11-July-2001 up to and including 11-January-2006 |

| **Floating amounts** | |
|---|---|
| Floating-rate payer | Intel |
| Floating-rate notional principal | USD 100 million |
| Floating rate | USD 6-month LIBOR |
| Floating-rate day count convention | Actual/360 |
| Floating-rate payment dates | Each 11-July and 11-January commencing 11-July-2001 up to and including 11-January-2006 |

on the S&P 500 is exchanged for LIBOR. The principal on either side of the swap is $100 million and payments are made every six months.

Consider an equity-for-floating swap such as that in Table 25.3. At the start of its life, it is worth zero. This is because a financial institution can arrange to costlessly replicate the cash flows to one side by borrowing the principal on each payment date at LIBOR and investing it in the index until the next payment date with any dividends being reinvested. A similar argument shows that the swap is always worth zero immediately after a payment date.

Appendix 25A shows how to value equity-for-floating swaps between payment dates. An equity-for-fixed swap can be conveniently valued by regarding it as a combination of a swap where the return on an equity index is exchanged for floating combined with a plain vanilla interest rate swap where floating is exchanged for fixed.

## 25.6 SWAPS WITH EMBEDDED OPTIONS

Some swaps contain embedded options. In this section we consider some commonly encountered examples.

### Accrual Swaps

Accrual swaps are swaps where the interest on one side accrues only when the floating reference rate is within a certain range. Sometimes the range remains fixed during the entire life of the swap; sometimes it is reset periodically.

As a simple example of an accrual swap, consider one where a fixed rate, $Q$, is exchanged for three-month LIBOR every quarter. We suppose that the fixed rate accrues only on days when three-month LIBOR is below 8% per annum. Suppose that the principal is $L$. In a normal swap the fixed-rate payer would pay $QLn_1/n_2$ on each payment date, where $n_1$ is the number of days in the preceding quarter and $n_2$ is the number of days in the year. (This assumes that the day count is actual/actual.) In an accrual swap this is changed to $QLn_3/n_2$, where $n_3$ is the number of days in the preceding quarter that the three-month LIBOR was below 8%.[3] The fixed-rate payer saves $QL/n_2$ on each day when three-month LIBOR is above 8%. The fixed-rate payer's position can therefore be considered equivalent to a regular swap plus a series of binary options, one for each day of the life of the swap. The binary options pay off $QL/n_2$ when the three-month LIBOR is above 8%.

To generalize, we suppose that the LIBOR cutoff rate (8% in the case just considered) is $R_K$ and that payments are exchanged every $\tau$ years. Consider day $i$ during the life of the swap and suppose that $t_i$ is the time until day $i$. Suppose that the $\tau$-year LIBOR rate on day $i$ is $R_i$ so that interest accrues when $R_i < R_K$. Define $F_i$ as the forward value of $R_i$ and $\sigma_i$ as the volatility of $F_i$. (The latter is estimated from spot caplet volatilities.) Using the usual lognormal assumption, the probability that LIBOR is greater than $R_K$ in a world that is forward risk neutral with respect to a zero-coupon bond maturing at time $t_i + \tau$ is $N(d_2)$, where

$$d_2 = \frac{\ln(F_i/R_K) - \sigma_i^2 t_i/2}{\sigma_i \sqrt{t_i}}$$

The payoff from the binary option is realized at the swap payment date following day $i$. We suppose that this is at time $s_i$. The probability that LIBOR is greater than $R_K$ in a world that is forward risk neutral with respect to a zero-coupon bond maturing at time $s_i$ is given by $N(d_2^*)$, where $d_2^*$ is calculated using the same formula as $d_2$, but with a small timing adjustment to $F_i$ reflecting the difference between time $t_i + \tau$ and time $s_i$.

The value of the binary option corresponding to day $i$ is

$$\frac{QL}{n_2} P(0, s_i) N(d_2^*)$$

The total value of the binary options is obtained by summing this expression for every day in the life of the swap. The timing adjustment (causing $d_1$ to be replaced by $d_1^*$) is so small that, in practice, it is frequently ignored.

### Cancelable Swap

A cancelable swap is a plain vanilla interest rate swap where one side has the option to terminate on one or more payment dates. Terminating a swap is the same as entering into the offsetting (opposite) swap. Consider a swap between Microsoft and Citibank. If Microsoft has the option to

---

[3] The usual convention is that, if a day is a holiday, the applicable rate is assumed to be the rate on the immediately preceding business day.

cancel, it can regard the swap as a regular swap plus a long position in an option to enter into the offsetting swap. If Citibank has the cancelation option, Microsoft has a regular swap plus a short position in an option to enter into the swap.

If there is only one termination date, a cancelable swap is the same as a regular swap plus a position in a European swap option. Consider, for example, a ten-year swap where Microsoft will receive 6% and pay LIBOR. Suppose that Microsoft has the option to terminate at the end of six years. The swap is a regular ten-year swap to receive 6% and pay LIBOR plus long position in a six-year European option to enter into a four-year swap where 6% is paid and LIBOR is received (the latter is referred to as a $6 \times 4$ European option). The standard market model for valuing European swap options is described in Chapter 22.

When the swap can be terminated on a number of different payment dates, it is a regular swap option plus a Bermudan-style swap option. Consider, for example, the situation where Microsoft has entered into a five-year swap with semiannual payments where 6% is received and LIBOR is paid. Suppose that the counterparty has the option to terminate on the swap on payment dates between year 2 and year 5. The swap is a regular swap plus a short position in a Bermudan-style swap option, where the Bermudan-style swap option is an option to enter into a swap that matures in five years and involves a fixed payment at 6% being received and a floating payment at LIBOR being paid. The swap can be exercised on any payment date between year 2 and year 5. We discussed methods for valuing Bermudan swap options in Chapters 23 and 24.

### Cancelable Compounding Swaps

Sometimes compounding swaps can be terminated on specified payment dates. On termination the floating-rate payer pays the compounded value of the floating amounts up to the time of termination and the fixed-rate payer pays the compounded value of the fixed payments up to the time of termination.

Some tricks can be used to value cancelable compounding swaps. Suppose first that the floating rate is LIBOR and it is compounded at LIBOR. We assume that the principal amount of the swap is paid on both the fixed and floating sides of the swap at the end of its life. This is similar to moving from Table 6.1 to Table 6.2 for a vanilla swap. It does not change the value of the swap and has the effect of ensuring that the value of the floating side is always equals the notional principal on a payment date. To make the cancelation decision, we need look only at the fixed side. We construct an interest rate tree as outlined in Chapter 23. We roll back through the tree in the usual way, valuing the fixed side. At each node where the swap can be canceled, we test whether it is optimal to keep the swap or cancel it. Canceling the swap in effect sets the value of the fixed side equal to par. If we are paying fixed and receiving floating, our objective is to minimize the value of the fixed side; if we are receiving fixed and paying floating, our objective is to maximize the value of the fixed side.

When the floating side is LIBOR plus a spread compounded at LIBOR, we can subtract cash flows corresponding to the spread rate of interest from the fixed side instead of adding them to the floating side. The option can then be valued as in the case where there is no spread.

When the compounding is at LIBOR plus a spread, an approximate approach is as follows:[4]

1. Calculate the value of the floating side of the swap at each cancelation date assuming forward rates are realized.

---

[4] This approach is not perfectly accurate in that it assumes that the decision to exercise the cancelation option is not influenced by future payments being compounded at a rate different from LIBOR.

2. Calculate the value of the floating side of the swap at each cancelation date assuming that the floating rate is LIBOR and it is compounded at LIBOR.

3. Define the excess of (1) over (2) as the "value of spreads" on a cancelation date.

4. Treat the option in the way described above. In deciding whether to exercise the cancelation option, subtract the value of the spreads from the values calculated for the fixed side.

## 25.7 OTHER SWAPS

This chapter has discussed only a few of the different types of swaps that trade. In practice the number of instruments that trade is limited only by the imagination of financial engineers and the appetite of corporate treasurers for innovative risk management tools.

A swap that was very popular in the United States in the mid-1990s is an *index amortizing rate swap* (sometimes also called an *indexed principal swap*). In this, the principal reduces in a way dependent on the level of interest rates. The lower the interest rate, the greater the reduction in the principal. The fixed side of an indexed amortizing swap was originally designed to mirror, at least approximately, the return obtained by an investor on a mortgage-backed security after prepayment options are taken into account. The swap therefore exchanged the return on a mortgage-backed security for a floating-rate return.

*Commodity swaps* are now becoming increasingly popular. A company that consumes 100,000 barrels of oil per year could agree to pay $2 million each year for the next ten years and to receive in return $100,000S$, where $S$ is the market price of oil per barrel. The agreement would in effect lock in the company's oil cost at $20 per barrel. An oil producer might agree to the opposite exchange, thereby locking in the price it realized for its oil at $20 per barrel. We will discuss energy derivatives in Chapter 29.

A recent innovation in swap markets is a *volatility swap*. In this, the payments depend on the volatility of a stock (or other asset). Suppose that the principal is $L$. On each payment date, one side pays $L\sigma$, where $\sigma$ is the historical volatility calculated in the usual way by taking daily observations on the stock during the immediately preceding accrual period and the other side pays $LK$, where $K$ is a constant prespecified volatility level. Variance swaps, correlation swaps, and covariance swaps are defined similarly.

A number of other types of swaps will be discussed later in this book. Asset swaps are covered in Chapter 26, and credit default swaps and total return swaps in Chapter 27.

## 25.8 BIZARRE DEALS

Some swaps involve the exchange of payments being calculated in quite bizarre ways. An example is provided by the so-called "5/30" swap entered into between Bankers Trust (BT) and Procter and Gamble (P&G) on November 2, 1993.[5] This was a five-year swap with semiannual exchanges of payment. The notional principal was $200 million. BT paid P&G 5.30% per annum. P&G paid BT the average 30-day commercial paper rate minus 75 basis points plus a spread. The average

---

[5] See D. J. Smith, "Aggressive Corporate Finance: A Close Look at the Procter and Gamble–Bankers Trust Leveraged Swap," *Journal of Derivatives*, 4, no. 4 (Summer 1997), 67–79.

commercial paper rate was calculated by observing the 30-day commercial paper rate each day during the preceding accrual period and averaging them.

The spread is zero for the settlement at the end of the first payment date (May 2, 1994). For the remaining nine payment dates, it is

$$\max\left(0, \frac{98.5 \times [(5\text{-year CMT}\%)/5.78\%] - (30\text{-year TSY price})}{100}\right)$$

In this, 5-year CMT is the constant maturity Treasury yield (i.e., the yield on a 5-year Treasury note, as reported by the Federal Reserve). The 30-year TSY price is the midpoint of the bid and offer cash bond prices for the 6.25% Treasury bond maturing on August 2023.

P&G were hoping that the spread would be zero and the deal would enable them to exchange fixed-rate funding at 5.30% for funding at 75 basis points less than the CP rate. As it happened, interest rates rose sharply in early 1994, bond prices fell, and the swap proved very, very expensive. We will discuss this example further in Chapter 30 (see also Problem 25.10).

## SUMMARY

Swaps have proved to be very versatile financial instruments. Many swaps can be valued using the simple assumption that LIBOR (or some other floating reference rate) will equal its forward value. These include plain vanilla interest swaps, most types of currency swaps, swaps where the principal changes in a predetermined way, swaps where the payment dates are different on each side, and compounding swaps.

Some swaps require adjustments to the forward rates when they are valued. These adjustments are termed convexity, timing, or quanto adjustments. Among the swaps that require adjustments are LIBOR-in-arrears swaps, CMS/CMT swaps, and differential swaps.

Equity swaps involve the return on an equity index being exchanged for a fixed or floating rate of interest. They are usually designed so that they are worth zero immediately after a payment date. However, some care must be exercised in valuing them between payment dates.

Some swaps involve embedded options. An accrual swap turns out to be a regular swap plus a large portfolio of binary options (one for each day of the life of the swap). A cancelable swap turns out to be a regular swap plus a Bermudan swap option.

## SUGGESTIONS FOR FURTHER READING

Chance, D., and D. Rich, "The Pricing of Equity Swap and Swaptions," *Journal of Derivatives*, 5, no. 4 (Summer 1998), 19–31.

Demeterfi, K., E. Derman, M. Kamal, and J. Zou, "A Guide to Volatility and Variance Swaps," *Journal of Derivatives*, 6, no. 4 (Summer 1999), 9–32.

Smith, D. J., "Aggressive Corporate Finance: A Close Look at the Procter and Gamble–Bankers Trust Leveraged Swap," *Journal of Derivatives*, 4, no. 4 (Summer 1997), 67–79.

# QUESTIONS AND PROBLEMS
## (ANSWERS IN SOLUTIONS MANUAL)

25.1. Calculate all the fixed cash flows and their exact timing for the swap in Table 25.1. Assume that the day count conventions are applied using target payment dates rather than actual payment dates.

25.2. Suppose that a swap specifies that a fixed rate is exchanged for twice the LIBOR rate. Can the swap be valued using the "assume forward rates are realized" rule?

25.3. What is the value of a two-year fixed-for-floating compound swap where the principal is $100 million and payments are made semiannually. Fixed interest is received and floating is paid. The fixed rate is 8% and it is compounded at 8.3% (both semiannually compounded). The floating rate is LIBOR plus 10 basis points and it is compounded at LIBOR plus 20 basis points. The LIBOR zero curve is flat at 8% with semiannual compounding.

25.4. What is the value of a five-year swap where LIBOR is paid in the usual way and in return LIBOR compounded at LIBOR is received on the other side. The principal on both sides is $100 million. Payment dates on the pay side and compounding dates on the receive side are every six months and the yield curve is flat at 5% with semiannual compounding.

25.5. Explain carefully why a bank might choose to discount cash flows on a currency swap at a rate slightly different from LIBOR.

25.6. Calculate the total convexity/timing adjustment in Example 25.3 of Section 25.4 if all cap volatilities are 18% instead of 20% and volatilities for all options on five-year swaps are 13% instead of 15%. What should the five-year swap rate in three years' time be assumed for the purpose of valuing the swap? What is the value of the swap?

25.7. Explain why a plain vanilla interest rate swap and the compounding swap in Section 25.2 can be valued using the "assume forward rates are realized" rule, but a LIBOR-in-arrears swap in Section 25.4 cannot.

25.8. In the accrual swap discussed in the text, the fixed side accrues only when the floating reference rate lies below a certain level. Discuss how the analysis can be extended to cope with a situation where the fixed side accrues only when the floating reference rate is above one level and below another.

# ASSIGNMENT QUESTIONS

25.9. LIBOR zero rates are flat at 5% in the U.S and flat at 10% in Australia (both annually compounded). In a four-year swap, Australian LIBOR is received and 9% is paid with both being applied to a USD principal of $10 million. Payments are exchanged annually. The volatility of all one-year forward rates in Australia is estimated to be 25%, the volatility of the forward USD–AUD exchange rate (AUD per USD) is 15% for all maturities, and the correlation between the two is 0.3. What is the value of the swap?

25.10. Estimate the interest rate paid by P&G on the 5/30 swap in Section 25.8 if (a) the CP rate is 6.5% and the Treasury yield curve is flat at 6% and (b) the CP rate is 7.5% and the Treasury yield curve is flat at 7% with semiannual compounding.

25.11. Suppose that you are trading a LIBOR-in-arrears swap with an unsophisticated counterparty who does not make convexity adjustments. To take advantage of the situation, should you be paying fixed or receiving fixed? How should you try to structure the swap as far as its life and payment frequencies.

Consider the situation where the yield curve is flat at 10% per annum with annual compounding. All cap volatilities are 18%. Estimate the difference between the way a sophisticated trader and an unsophisticated trader would value a LIBOR-in-arrears swap where payments are made annually and the life of the swap is (a) 5 years, (b) 10 years, and (c) 20 years. Assume a notional principal of $1 million.

25.12. Suppose that the LIBOR zero rate is flat at 5% with annual compounding. In a five-year swap, company X pays a fixed rate of 6% once a year and receives LIBOR. The volatility of the two-year swap rate in three years is 20%. The principal is $100.

    a. What is the value of the swap?

    b. Use DerivaGem to calculate the value of the swap if company X has the option to cancel after three years.

    c. Use DerivaGem to calculate the value of the swap if the counterparty has the option to cancel after three years.

    d. What is the value of the swap if either side can cancel at the end of three years?

# APPENDIX 25A
## Valuation of an Equity Swap between Payment Dates

To value an equity swap between two payment dates, we define:

$R_0$: Floating rate applicable to the next payment date (determined at the last payment date)

$L$: Principal

$\tau_0$: Time between last payment date and next payment date

$\tau$: Time between now and next payment date

$E_0$: Value of the equity index at the last reset date

$E$: Current value of the equity index

$R$: LIBOR rate for the period between now and the next payment date

If we borrow

$$\frac{E}{E_0}L$$

at rate $R$ for time $\tau$ and invest it in the index, we create an exchange of

$$\frac{E_1}{E_0}L \quad \text{for} \quad \frac{E}{E_0}L(1+R\tau) \tag{25A.1}$$

at the next payment date. Since this exchange can be created costlessly, it is worth zero. The exchange that will actually take place at the next payment date is

$$\left(\frac{E_1}{E_0}-1\right)L \quad \text{for} \quad R_0 L\tau_0$$

Adding the principal $L$ to both sides, we see the actual exchange is equivalent to

$$\frac{E_1}{E_0}L \quad \text{for} \quad L(1+R_0\tau_0) \tag{25A.2}$$

Comparing equation (25A.1) with equation (25A.2), see that value of the swap to the party receiving floating is the present value of

$$L(1+R_0\tau_0) - L\frac{E}{E_0}(1+R\tau)$$

This is

$$L\frac{1+R_0\tau_0}{1+R\tau} - L\frac{E}{E_0}$$

Similarly, the value of the swap to the party receiving the equity return is

$$L\frac{E}{E_0} - L\frac{1+R_0\tau_0}{1+R\tau}$$

# CHAPTER 26

# CREDIT RISK

Potential defaults by borrowers, counterparties in derivatives transactions, and bond issuers give rise to significant credit risk for banks and other financial institutions. As a result, most financial institutions devote considerable resources to the measurement and management of credit risk. Regulators require banks to keep capital to reflect the credit risks they are bearing.[1]

In this chapter we focus on the quantification of credit risk. We first discuss a number of different approaches to estimating the probability that a company will default. We explain the key difference between risk-neutral and real-world probabilities of default. We then move on to discuss how a bank or other financial institution can estimate its loss given that a default by a company occurs. The probability of default and the loss given default jointly determine the financial institution's expected loss. The last part of the chapter covers credit ratings migration and default correlation, and shows how the value-at-risk measure introduced in Chapter 16 can be used for credit risk as well as market risk.

In Chapter 27 we will use the material in this chapter to analyze credit derivatives. These are derivatives where the payoff is dependent in some way on the creditworthiness of one or more companies or sovereign entities.

## 26.1  BOND PRICES AND THE PROBABILITY OF DEFAULT

Rating agencies such as Moody's and S&P are in the business of providing ratings describing the creditworthiness of corporate bonds. Using the Moody's system, the best rating is Aaa. Bonds with this rating are considered to have almost no chance of defaulting. The next best rating is Aa. Following that come A, Baa, Ba, B, and Caa. Only bonds with ratings of Baa or above are considered to be *investment grade*. The S&P ratings corresponding to Moody's Aaa, Aa, A, Baa, Ba, B, and Caa are AAA, AA, A, BBB, BB, B, and CCC, respectively. To create finer rating measures, Moody's divides the Aa rating category into Aa1, Aa2, and Aa3; it divides A into A1, A2 and A3; and so on. Similarly S&P divides its AA rating category into AA+, AA, and AA−; it divides its A rating category into A+, A, and A−; and so on. (Only the Aaa category for Moody's and the AAA category for S&P are not subdivided.)

Bond traders have developed procedures for taking credit risk into account when pricing corporate bonds. They collect market data on actively traded bonds to calculate a generic zero-coupon yield curve for each credit rating category. (See Chapter 5 for a description of how zero-coupon yields can be calculated from coupon-bearing bond yields using the bootstrap

---

[1] This capital is in addition to the capital, mentioned in Chapter 16, that banks are required to keep for market risk.

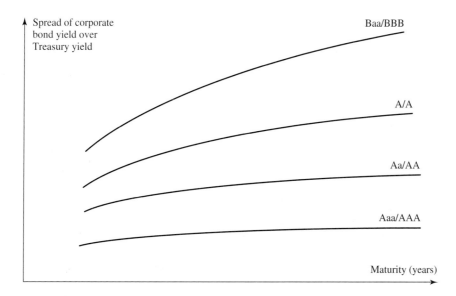

**Figure 26.1**   Spread over Treasury zero curve for corporate bond yields

method.) These zero-coupon yield curves are then used to value other bonds. For example, a newly issue A-rated bond would be priced using the zero-coupon yield curve calculated from other A-rated bonds.[2]

Figure 26.1 shows a typical pattern for the spread over the Treasury zero curve for the yields on investment grade zero-coupon bonds with different maturities and different credit ratings. The spread increases as the rating declines. It also increases with maturity. Note that the spread tends to increase faster with maturity for low credit ratings than for high credit ratings. For example, the difference between the five-year spread and the one-year spread for a BBB-rated bond is greater than that for a AAA-rated bond.[3]

### *Expected Default Losses on Bonds*

The first step in estimating default probabilities from bond prices is to calculate the expected default losses on corporate bonds of different maturities. This involves comparing the price of a corporate bond with the price of a risk-free bond that has the same maturity and pays the same coupon. The usual assumption is that the present value of the cost of defaults equals the excess of the price of the risk-free bond over the price of the corporate bond. This means that the higher yield on a corporate bond is entirely compensation for possible losses from default.[4]

The price of the risk-free bond is calculated from the risk-free zero curve. A natural choice for the risk-free zero curve is the Treasury curve and many analysts do compare corporate bond yields

---

[2] As we discuss later, there are some theoretical problems with this procedure because it relies on value additivity.

[3] This is consistent with the point made during the discussion of the comparative advantage argument for swaps in Section 6.2: that the rollover risk for a BBB issuer is greater than the rollover risk for a AAA issuer. See Problem 26.2.

[4] This is an approximation. Other factors such as liquidity influence the spread between corporate and risk-free bond yields.

**Table 26.1**  Yields and expected default losses on bonds issued by a corporation. (All rates continuously compounded.)

| Maturity (years) | Risk-free zero rate (%) | Corporate bond zero rate (%) | Expected default loss (% of no-default value) |
|---|---|---|---|
| 1 | 5.00 | 5.25 | 0.2497 |
| 2 | 5.00 | 5.50 | 0.9950 |
| 3 | 5.00 | 5.70 | 2.0781 |
| 4 | 5.00 | 5.85 | 3.3428 |
| 5 | 5.00 | 5.95 | 4.6390 |

with Treasury yields in the way indicated in Figure 26.1. However, there are sometimes factors causing Treasury bonds to have artificially low yields. For example, in the United States the interest on Treasury bonds is not taxed at the state level whereas the interest on most other bonds (including corporate bonds) is taxed at both the federal and state level. This has led most analysts to use the LIBOR zero curve as the risk-free zero curve.

We will use the data in Table 26.1 to illustrate how bond yields can be related to default losses. The table shows that zero-coupon risk-free interest rates are assumed to be 5% for all maturities. It assumes that a corporation issues zero coupon bonds with maturities between one and five years and that the yields on the bonds range from 5.25% for a one-year maturity to 5.95% for a five-year maturity.

The value of a one-year risk-free bond with a principal of 100 is $100e^{-0.05}$, or 95.1229. The value of a similar corporate bond is $100e^{-0.0525} = 94.8854$. The present value of the loss from defaults on the corporate bond is therefore $95.1229 - 94.8854 = 0.2375$. This means that we expect $0.2375/95.1229 = 0.2497\%$ of the no-default value of the corporate bond to be lost from defaults.

Consider next a two-year bond. The value of a two-year risk-free bond with a principal of 100 is $100e^{-0.05\times2} = 90.4837$. The value of a similar corporate bond is $100e^{-0.055\times2} = 89.5834$. The present value of the expected loss from defaults on the two-year corporate bond is $90.4837 - 89.5834 = 0.9003$. We therefore expect $0.9003/90.4937 = 0.9950\%$ of the no-default value of the two-year corporate bond to be lost from defaults.

These results and those for other bond maturities are shown in the final column of Table 26.1.

### Probability of Default Assuming No Recovery

Define:

$y(T)$:  Yield on a $T$-year corporate zero-coupon bond

$y^*(T)$:  Yield on a $T$-year risk-free zero-coupon bond

$Q(T)$:  Probability that corporation will default between time zero and time $T$

The value of a $T$-year risk-free zero-coupon bond with a principal of 100 is $100e^{-y^*(T)T}$ while the value of a similar corporate bond is $100e^{-y(T)T}$. The expected loss from default is therefore

$$100(e^{-y^*(T)T} - e^{-y(T)T})$$

If we assume that there is no recovery in the event of default, the calculation of $Q(T)$ is relatively easy. There is a probability $Q(T)$ that the corporate bond will be worth zero at maturity and a

**Table 26.2**   Probabilities of default in the example in Table 26.1 assuming no recovery in the event of default

| Year | Cumulative default probability (%) | Default probability in year (%) |
|------|------------------------------------|--------------------------------|
| 1 | 0.2497 | 0.2497 |
| 2 | 0.9950 | 0.7453 |
| 3 | 2.0781 | 1.0831 |
| 4 | 3.3428 | 1.2647 |
| 5 | 4.6390 | 1.2962 |

probability $1 - Q(T)$ that it will be worth 100. The value of the bond is therefore[5]

$$\{Q(T) \times 0 + [1 - Q(T)] \times 100\}e^{-y^*(T)T} = 100[1 - Q(T)]e^{-y^*(T)T}$$

The yield on the bond is $y(T)$, so that

$$100e^{-y(T)T} = 100[1 - Q(T)]e^{-y^*(T)T}$$

This means that

$$Q(T) = \frac{e^{-y^*(T)T} - e^{-y(T)T}}{e^{-y^*(T)T}}$$

or

$$Q(T) = 1 - e^{-[y(T)-y^*(T)]T} \qquad (26.1)$$

Assuming no recovery, Table 26.2 shows the cumulative probability of default and the probability of default in each year for the example in Table 26.1. The cumulative probability of default is the same as the expected percentage loss from default in the final column of Table 26.1. The probability of default in each year is obtained by subtracting consecutive cumulative defaults. For example, the probability of default in year 3 is $3.3428 - 2.0781 = 1.2647\%$.

**Example 26.1**   Suppose that the spreads over the risk-free rate for 5-year and a 10-year BBB-rated zero-coupon bonds are 130 and 170 basis points, respectively, and there is no recovery in the event of default. From equation (26.1),

$$Q(5) = 1 - e^{-0.013 \times 5} = 0.0629$$
$$Q(10) = 1 - e^{-0.017 \times 10} = 0.1563$$

It follows that the probability of default between five years and ten years is

$$0.1563 - 0.0629 = 0.0934$$

## Hazard Rates

At this stage it is appropriate to mention that there are two ways of quantifying probabilities of default. The first is in terms of what are known as *hazard rates*. The second is in terms of the *default probability density*.

---

[5] Note that we discount the expected payoff from the bond at the risk-free rate. As we will see later, this means that the probability of default, $Q(T)$, that we are estimating is a risk-neutral probability.

The hazard rate, $h(t)$, at time $t$ is defined so that $h(t)\,\delta t$ is the probability of default between time $t$ and $t + \delta t$ conditional on no earlier default (i.e., $h(t)\,\delta t$ is the probability of default between time $t$ and time $t + \delta t$ conditional on no default between time zero and time $t$). The default probability density, $q(t)$, is defined so that $q(t)\,\delta t$ is the unconditional probability of default between times $t$ and $t + \delta t$ as seen at time zero.

Either $h(t)$ or $q(t)$ can be used to describe the default probabilities. They provide equivalent information and the relationship between $h(t)$ and $q(t)$ is

$$q(t) = h(t)e^{-\int_0^t h(\tau)\,d\tau}$$

Most of our analysis in this chapter and the next will be in terms of the default probability density rather than in terms of hazard rates. Indeed we have already started to use the default probability density. The probabilities of default listed for each year in Table 26.2 are the unconditional probabilities of default as seen at time zero. Consider year 5. Table 26.2 lists the probability of default as 1.2962%. The corresponding hazard rate is the probability of default in year 5 conditional on no default up to year 4. The probability of no default prior to year 4 is $1 - 0.033428 = 0.966572\%$. The hazard rate for year 4 is therefore $0.012962/0.966572 = 1.3410\%$.

### Recovery Rates

The analysis presented so far assumes no recovery on bonds in the event of a default. This is not realistic. When a company goes bankrupt, entities that are owed money by the company file claims against the assets of the company. The assets are sold by the liquidator and the proceeds are used to meet the claims as far as possible. Some claims typically have priorities over others and are met more fully. Table 26.3 provides historical data on the amounts recovered by different categories of claims in the United States. It shows that senior secured debtholders received an average of 52.31 cents per dollar of par value while junior subordinated debtholders received an average of only 19.69 cents per dollar of par value.[6]

We define the *recovery rate* as the proportion of the "claimed amount" received in the event of a default. If we make the assumption that the claimed amount for a bond is the no-default value of the bond, the calculation of the probability of default is simplified. We use the same notation as before and suppose the expected recovery rate is $R$. In the event of a default the bondholder receives a proportion $R$ of the bond's no-default value. If there is no default, the bondholder

**Table 26.3**   Amounts recovered on corporate bonds as a percent of par value from Moody's Investor's Service (January 2000)

| Class | Mean (%) | Standard deviation (%) |
|---|---|---|
| Senior secured | 52.31 | 25.15 |
| Senior unsecured | 48.84 | 25.01 |
| Senior subordinated | 39.46 | 24.59 |
| Subordinated | 33.17 | 20.78 |
| Junior subordinated | 19.69 | 13.85 |

[6] In these statistics the amount recovered is estimated as the market value of the bond one month after default.

receives 100. The bond's no-default value is $100e^{-y^*(T)T}$ and the probability of a default is $Q(T)$. The value of the bond is therefore

$$[1 - Q(T)]100e^{-y^*(T)T} + Q(T)100Re^{-y^*(T)T}$$

so that

$$100e^{-y(T)T} = [1 - Q(T)]100e^{-y^*(T)T} + Q(T)100Re^{-y^*(T)T}$$

This gives

$$Q(T) = \frac{e^{-y^*(T)T} - e^{-y(T)T}}{(1 - R)e^{-y^*(T)T}}$$

or

$$Q(T) = \frac{1 - e^{-[y(T)-y^*(T)]T}}{1 - R} \tag{26.2}$$

### More Realistic Assumptions

Equation (26.2) is often used to provide a quick estimate of the probability of default. It is based on the assumption that the amount claimed in the event of a default equals the no-default value of the bond. This assumption is analytically convenient, but does not correspond to the way bankruptcy laws work in most countries. A more realistic assumption is that the claim made in the event of default equals the bond's face value plus accrued interest. Equation (26.2) also assumes that zero-coupon corporate bond prices are either observable or calculable. In reality probabilities of default must usually be calculated from coupon-bearing corporate bond prices, not zero coupon bond prices. We now present a way of extracting default probabilities from coupon-bearing bonds for any assumptions about the claimed amount.

Assume that we have chosen a set of $N$ coupon-bearing bonds that are either issued by the corporation being considered or by another corporation that has roughly the same probability of default as this corporation at all future times. We assume that defaults can happen on any of the bond maturity dates. (To be precise, defaults can occur immediately before each bond maturity date. Later we generalize the analysis to allow defaults to occur at any time.) Suppose that the maturity of the $i$th bond is $t_i$ with $t_1 < t_2 < \cdots < t_N$. Define:

$B_j$: Price of the $j$th bond today

$G_j$: Price of the $j$th bond today if there were no probability of default (i.e., the price of a risk-free bond promising the same cash flows as the $j$th bond)

$F_j(t)$: Forward price of the $j$th bond for a forward contract maturing at time $t$ $(t < t_j)$ assuming the bond is default-free. (Note that $F_j(t)$ is the forward value of $G_j$ not $B_j$.)

$v(t)$: Present value of \$1 received at time $t$ with certainty

$C_j(t)$: Claim made by holders of the $j$th bond if there is a default at time $t$ $(t < t_j)$

$R_j(t)$: Recovery rate for holders of the $j$th bond in the event of a default at time $t$ $(t < t_j)$

$\alpha_{ij}$: Present value of the loss from a default on the $j$th bond at time $t_i$

$p_i$: The probability of default at time $t_i$

For ease of exposition we assume that interest rates are deterministic and that both recovery rates and claim amounts are known with certainty. It can be shown that our results are still true if this assumption does not hold provided that (a) default events, (b) risk-free interest rates, and (c) recovery rates are mutually independent. (The amount claimed in the event of default can be either the no-default value of the bond or the face value plus accrued interest. The recovery rate is set equal to its expected value in a risk-neutral world.)

The price at time $t$ of the no-default value of the $j$th bond is $F_j(t)$. If there is a default at time $t$, the bondholder makes a recovery at rate $R_j(t)$ on a claim of $C_j(t)$. It follows that

$$\alpha_{ij} = v(t_i)[F_j(t_i) - R_j(t_i)C_j(t_i)]$$

There is a probability $p_i$ of the loss $\alpha_{ij}$ being incurred. The total present value of the losses on the $j$th bond is therefore given by

$$G_j - B_j = \sum_{i=1}^{j} p_i \alpha_{ij} \tag{26.3}$$

This equation allows the $p$'s to be determined inductively. The first probability, $p_1$, is $(G_1 - B_1)/\alpha_{11}$. The remaining probabilities are given by

$$p_j = \frac{G_j - B_j - \sum_{i=1}^{j-1} p_i \alpha_{ij}}{\alpha_{jj}} \tag{26.4}$$

As mentioned earlier, the $N$ bonds used in the analysis are issued either by the reference entity or by another company that is considered to have the same risk of default as the reference entity. This means that the $p_i$ should be the same for all bonds. The recovery rates can in theory vary according to the bond and the default time. From now onward we make the simplification that the expected recovery rate is the same for all bonds issued by a particular company and is independent of time. We will denote this expected recovery rate by $\hat{R}$. This means that the above equation for $\alpha_{ij}$ becomes

$$\alpha_{ij} = v(t_i)[F_j(t_i) - \hat{R}C_j(t_i)] \tag{26.5}$$

### An Illustration

Table 26.4 provides hypothetical data on six bonds issued by a particular corporation. The bonds have maturities ranging from one to ten years. The coupons are assumed to be paid semiannually, the risk-free zero curve is assumed to be flat at 5% (semiannually compounded), and the expected recovery rate is assumed to be 30%. Table 26.5 shows the default probabilities for the two alternative assumptions we have mentioned about the claim amount (see Problem 26.6 for the calculation of the first two rows of this table). The first assumption is that the claim amount equals the no-default value of the bond; the second is that it equals the bond's face value plus accrued

**Table 26.4**  Data on bonds issued by a corporation

| Bond life (years) | Coupon (%) | Bond yield (%) |
|---|---|---|
| 1 | 7.0 | 6.60 |
| 2 | 7.0 | 6.70 |
| 3 | 7.0 | 6.80 |
| 4 | 7.0 | 6.90 |
| 5 | 7.0 | 7.00 |
| 10 | 7.0 | 7.20 |

**Table 26.5** Implied probabilities of default for data in Table 26.4 assuming defaults can happen only at bond maturity dates

| Time (years) | Default probability | |
| --- | --- | --- |
| | *Claim =* No-default value | *Claim =* Face value + Accrued interest |
| 1 | 0.0224 | 0.0224 |
| 2 | 0.0249 | 0.0247 |
| 3 | 0.0273 | 0.0269 |
| 4 | 0.0297 | 0.0291 |
| 5 | 0.0320 | 0.0312 |
| 10 | 0.1717 | 0.1657 |

interest. It can be seen that the two assumptions give similar results. This is usually the case. For the probabilities to be markedly different, it would be necessary for the coupons on the bonds to be much, much greater or much, much less than the risk-free rate.

### When Defaults Can Happen at Any Time

The analysis used to derive equation (26.4) assumes that defaults can take place only on bond maturity dates. It can be extended to allow defaults at any time. As earlier, we define $q(t)$ as the default probability density. (This means that $q(t)\,\delta t$ is the probability of default between times $t$ and $t + \delta t$ as seen at time zero.)

One approach is to assume that $q(t)$ is constant and equal to $q_i$ for $t_{i-1} < t < t_i$. Setting

$$\beta_{ij} = \int_{t_{i-1}}^{t_i} v(t)[F_j(t) - \hat{R}C_j(t)]\,dt \tag{26.6}$$

a similar analysis to that used in deriving equation (26.4) gives

$$q_j = \frac{G_j - B_j - \sum_{i=1}^{j-1} q_i\beta_{ij}}{\beta_{jj}} \tag{26.7}$$

**Table 26.6** Implied default probability densities for data in Table 26.4 assuming defaults can happen at any time

| Time (years) | Default probability density | |
| --- | --- | --- |
| | *Claim =* No-default value | *Claim =* Face value + Accrued interest |
| 0–1 | 0.0220 | 0.0219 |
| 1–2 | 0.0245 | 0.0242 |
| 2–3 | 0.0269 | 0.0264 |
| 3–4 | 0.0292 | 0.0285 |
| 4–5 | 0.0315 | 0.0305 |
| 5–10 | 0.0295 | 0.0279 |

The parameters $\beta_{ij}$ can be estimated using standard procedures, such as Simpson's rule, for evaluating definite integrals. Table 26.6 shows the values of $q_j$ calculated for the example in Table 26.4.

### Claim Amounts and Value Additivity

When we make the assumption that the claim amount is the no-default value of the bond, $C_j(t) = F_j(t)$, it can be shown (see Problem 26.12) that the value of the coupon-bearing bond $B_j$ is the sum of the values of the underlying zero-coupon bonds. This property is referred to as *value additivity*. It implies that it is theoretically correct to calculate zero curves for different rating categories from actively traded bonds and use them for pricing less actively traded bonds.

When we make the more realistic assumption that $C_j(t)$ equals the face value of bond $j$ plus accrued interest at time $t$, value additivity does not apply (except in the special case where the recovery rate is zero). This means that there is in theory no zero-coupon yield curve that can be used to price corporate bonds exactly for a given set of assumptions about default probabilities and expected recovery rates.

### Asset Swaps

In practice, traders often use asset swap quotes as a way of extracting default probabilities from bond prices on the assumption that the LIBOR curve is the risk-free curve.

As explained in Chapter 6, an interest rate swap can be used to exchange a fixed return for a floating return. Suppose that an investor owns a fixed-rate five-year corporate bond that is currently worth par and pays a coupon of 6% per year. Suppose further that the LIBOR zero curve is flat at 4.5% with semiannual compounding. In a five-year plain vanilla interest rate swap, 4.5% would be exchanged for LIBOR. Equivalently 6% would be exchanged for LIBOR plus 150 basis points in a such a swap. This means that an investor can use a five-year interest rate swap to exchange the bond's coupons for LIBOR plus 150 basis points. The investor still bears the credit risk that the bond might default. The asset swap would be referred to as swapping the bond's return for a 150-basis-point spread over LIBOR.

The swap transaction shows that the investor is compensated for credit risk by receiving an extra 150 basis points per year for five years. The value of 150 basis points per year (paid semiannually) using the LIBOR curve for discounting is $6.65 per $100 of face value. It follows that, if the corporate bond had been risk-free, its value would increase $6.65 per $100 of face value. In the terminology of this section, $B_j = 100$ and $G_j = 106.65$ for this bond and equations (26.4) or (26.7) can be used for estimating default probabilities.

Suppose next that the bond is worth only $95 per $100 of par value and pays a coupon of 5% per year. We continue with our assumption that the LIBOR curve is flat at 4.5% with semiannual compounding. The asset swap would usually be structured so that the bondholder pays $5 per $100 of par value up front and then exchanges coupons for LIBOR plus a spread. Because 4.5% is swapped for LIBOR in a regular five-year swap, the coupon of 5% is swapped for LIBOR plus 50 basis points. An up-front payment of $5 is equivalent to $1.1279 per year for five years paid semiannually. The investor therefore requires a further 112.79 basis points to compensate for the up-front payment. The total floating payment should therefore be LIBOR plus 162.79 basis points. The asset swap would be referred to as exchanging the bond yield for a 162.79-basis-point spread over LIBOR. The value of 162.79 basis per year for five years is $7.22 per $100 of par value. It follows that, in this case, $B_j = 95.00$ and $G_j = 95.00 + 7.22 = 102.22$.

When asset swap spreads are known for bonds with a number of different maturities, we can

**Table 26.7** Average cumulative default rates (%)

| Rating | Term (years) | | | | | | | |
|---|---|---|---|---|---|---|---|---|
| | *1* | *2* | *3* | *4* | *5* | *7* | *10* | *15* |
| AAA | 0.00 | 0.00 | 0.04 | 0.07 | 0.12 | 0.32 | 0.67 | 0.67 |
| AA | 0.01 | 0.04 | 0.10 | 0.18 | 0.29 | 0.62 | 0.96 | 1.39 |
| A | 0.04 | 0.12 | 0.21 | 0.36 | 0.57 | 1.01 | 1.86 | 2.59 |
| BBB | 0.24 | 0.55 | 0.89 | 1.55 | 2.23 | 3.60 | 5.20 | 6.85 |
| BB | 1.08 | 3.48 | 6.65 | 9.71 | 12.57 | 18.09 | 23.86 | 27.09 |
| B | 5.94 | 13.49 | 20.12 | 25.36 | 29.58 | 36.34 | 43.41 | 48.81 |
| CCC | 25.26 | 34.79 | 42.16 | 48.18 | 54.65 | 58.64 | 62.58 | 66.12 |

*Source*: Standard & Poor's, January 2001.

use equations (26.4) or (26.7) to estimate default probabilities. The asset swap spread depends on the credit rating of the bond and its maturity. In theory, it should also be slightly dependent on the bond's coupon. In practice, because bonds are not highly liquid, the credit spread is often assumed to be the same for all coupons. A quoted asset swap spread is then assumed to apply to a corporate bond selling at par for the purposes on applying equations (26.4) or (26.7).

## 26.2 HISTORICAL DATA

We now consider how default probabilities can be estimated from historical data. Table 26.7 is typical of the information produced by rating agencies. It shows the default experience through time of companies that started with a certain credit rating. For example, a bond issue with an initial credit rating of BBB has a 0.24% chance of defaulting by the end of the first year, a 0.55% chance of defaulting by the end of the second year, and so on. The probability of a bond defaulting during a particular year can be calculated from the table. For example, the probability of a BBB-rated bond defaulting during the second year is 0.55 − 0.24 = 0.31%.

As indicated in Figure 26.1, for investment grade bonds the probability of default in a year tends to be an increasing function of time. For bonds with a poor credit rating, the reverse is often true. In Table 26.7, the probabilities, as seen at time zero, of a AA bond defaulting during year 1, 2, 3, 4, and 5 are 0.01%, 0.03%, 0.06%, 0.08%, and 0.11%, respectively. The corresponding probabilities for a CCC bond are 25.26%, 9.53%, 7.37%, 6.02%, and 6.47%.[7] For a bond with a good credit rating, some time must usually elapse for the fortunes of the issuer to decline to such an extent that a default happens. For a bond with a poor credit rating, the next year or two may be critical. If the issuer survives this period, its probability of default per year can be expected to decline.

## 26.3 BOND PRICES vs. HISTORICAL DEFAULT EXPERIENCE

The default probabilities in Table 26.7 are significantly less than we would expect from an analysis of bond prices. Consider, for example, a five-year A-rated zero-coupon bond. We suppose that the

---

[7] The hazard rates in the five years are 25.26%, 12.75%, 11.30%, 10.41%, and 12.49%, respectively.

yield on this bond is 50 basis points above the risk-free rate. Assuming a zero recovery rate, equation (26.1) gives an estimate for the probability of default during the five years of

$$1 - e^{-0.005 \times 5} = 0.0247$$

or 2.47%. By contrast, the historical probability of default over five years for an A-rated bond is from Table 26.7 only 0.57%.

The two key assumptions we have made here are: (i) A-rated bonds yield 50 basis points above the risk-free rate; and (ii) the recovery rate is zero. Both assumptions are conservative. In practice, the yield on five-year A-rated bonds is often more than 50 basis points above the risk-free rate and the recovery rate is nonzero. As we increase either the yield of A-rated bonds or the assumed recovery rate, the probability of default calculated from bond prices increases.[8]

Altman was one of the first researchers to comment on the discrepancy between bond prices and historical default data.[9] He showed that, even after taking account of the impact of defaults, an investor could expect significantly higher returns from investing in corporate bonds than from investing in risk-free bonds. As the credit rating of the corporate bonds declined, the extent of the higher returns increased.

Why do bond prices give much higher probabilities of defaults than historical data? One reason may be that investors raise the expected returns they require on corporate bonds to compensate for their relatively low liquidity. Another reason may be that bond traders are allowing in their pricing for the possibility of "depression scenarios" much worse than anything seen during the time period covered by the historical data. However, there is an important theoretical reason, which we will now explain.

## 26.4  RISK-NEUTRAL vs. REAL-WORLD ESTIMATES

We return to the five-year A-rated bond example. If the yield is 50 basis points above the risk-free rate and there is no recovery, the probability of default during the five-year life of the bond estimated from the bond price is 2.47%. This is over four times the estimate of 0.57% from historical data.

It turns out that 2.47% is an estimate of the probability of default in a risk-neutral world, whereas 0.57% is an estimate of the probability of default in the real world. To show this, we first note that the price of the corporate bond is 2.47% less than that of a risk-free bond. One way of getting this pricing difference is by assuming:

(i)   The expected cash flow from the corporate bond at the end of five years is 2.47% less than the expected cash flow from a risk-free bond at the end of the five years; and

(ii)  The discount rates appropriate for the two cash flows are the same.

The second of these two assumptions is correct in a risk-neutral world (i.e., a world where the expected return required by all investors on all investments is the risk-free interest rate). The first

---

[8]  For example, if the recovery rate is 30% and the yield above the risk-free rate is 70 basis points, bond prices predict a probability of default of about 5% during the five-year period.

[9]  See, for example, E. I. Altman, "Measuring Corporate Bond Mortality and Performance," *Journal of Finance*, 44 (1989), 902–22.

assumption corresponds to a probability of default of 2.47%. We conclude that the prices of corporate bonds are consistent with 2.47% being the probability of default in a risk-neutral world.

Approximately the same differential between the corporate bond price and the risk-free bond price is calculated if we assume:

(i) The expected cash flow from the corporate bond at the end of five years is 0.57% less than the expected cash flow from the risk-free bond at the end of the five years; and

(ii) The discount rate appropriate for the corporate bond's expected cash flow is about 0.38% higher than the discount rate appropriate for the risk-free bond cash flow.

This is because a 0.38% increase in the discount rate leads to the corporate bond price being reduced by approximately $5 \times 0.38 = 1.9\%$. When combined with the corporate bond's lower expected cash flow, we get a total difference between the corporate bond price and the risk-free bond price of approximately $1.9 + 0.57 = 2.47\%$, which is what is observed in the market.

The 0.57% estimate of the probability of default is therefore the correct estimate in the real world if the correct discount rate to use for the bond's cash flows in the real world is 0.38% higher than in the risk-neutral world. Arguably a 0.38% increase in the discount rate when we move from the risk-neutral world to the real world is not unreasonable. A-rated bonds do have some systematic (i.e., nondiversifiable) risk. (When the market does badly, they are more likely to default; when the market does well, they are less likely to default.) The excess expected return of the market over the risk-free rate is about 5%. Using the capital asset pricing model, a 0.38% excess expected return for the corporate bond is consistent with the corporate bond having a beta of about $0.38/5 = 0.076$. It is interesting that what seems to be a large discrepancy between default probability estimates translates into a relatively small adjustment to expected returns for systematic risk.[10]

This explanation of the difference between estimates calculated from bond prices and those calculated from historical data is consistent with the pattern of Altman's results, mentioned earlier. As the credit rating of a bond declines, it becomes more similar to equity and its beta increases. As a result, the excess of the expected return required by investors over the risk-free rate also increases.

At this stage, it is natural the ask whether we should use real-world or risk-neutral default probabilities in the analysis of credit risk. The answer depends on the purpose of the analysis. When valuing credit derivatives or estimating the impact of default risk on the pricing of instruments, we should use risk-neutral default probabilities. This is because we likely to be implicitly or explicitly using risk-neutral valuation in our analysis. When carrying out scenario analyses to calculate potential future losses from defaults, we should use real-world default probabilities.

## 26.5 USING EQUITY PRICES TO ESTIMATE DEFAULT PROBABILITIES

The approaches we have examined up to now for estimating a company's probability of default have relied on the company's credit rating. Unfortunately, credit ratings are revised relatively infrequently. This has led some analysts to argue that equity prices can provide more up-to-date information for estimating default probabilities.

---

[10] Note that, in this type of analysis, it is important to distinguish between the promised return on a corporate bond, which is its yield, and the expected return, which takes into account expected losses.

In 1974, Merton proposed a model where a company's equity is an option on the assets of the company.[11] Suppose, for simplicity, that a firm has one zero-coupon bond outstanding and that the bond matures at time $T$. Define:

$V_0$: Value of company's assets today

$V_T$: Value of company's assets at time $T$

$E_0$: Value of company's equity today

$E_T$: Value of company's equity at time $T$

$D$: Amount of debt interest and principal due to be repaid at time $T$

$\sigma_V$: Volatility of assets

$\sigma_E$: Volatility of equity

If $V_T < D$, it is (at least in theory) rational for the company to default on the debt at time $T$. The value of the equity is then zero. If $V_T > D$, the company should make the debt repayment at time $T$ and the value of the equity at this time is $V_T - D$. Merton's model, therefore, gives the value of the firm's equity at time $T$ as

$$E_T = \max(V_T - D, \, 0)$$

This shows that the equity is a call option on the value of the assets with a strike price equal to the repayment required on the debt. The Black–Scholes formula gives the value of the equity today as

$$E_0 = V_0 N(d_1) - De^{-rT} N(d_2) \tag{26.10}$$

where

$$d_1 = \frac{\ln V_0/D + (r + \sigma_V^2/2)T}{\sigma_V \sqrt{T}}$$

and

$$d_2 = d_1 - \sigma_V \sqrt{T}$$

The value of the debt today is $V_0 - E_0$.

The risk-neutral probability that the company will default on the debt is $N(-d_2)$. To calculate this, we require $V_0$ and $\sigma_V$. Neither of these are directly observable. However, if the company is publicly traded, we can observe $E_0$. This means that equation (26.10) provides one condition that must be satisfied by $V_0$ and $\sigma_V$. We can also estimate $\sigma_E$. From Itô's lemma,

$$\sigma_E E_0 = \frac{\partial E}{\partial V} \sigma_V V_0$$

or

$$\sigma_E E_0 = N(d_1) \sigma_V V_0 \tag{26.11}$$

This provides another equation that must be satisfied by $V_0$ and $\sigma_V$. Equations (26.10) and (26.11) provide a pair of simultaneous equations that can be solved for $V_0$ and $\sigma_V$.[12]

**Example 26.2** The value of a company's equity is $3 million and the volatility of the equity is 80%. The debt that will have to be paid in one year is $10 million. The risk-free rate is 5% per annum. In this

---

[11] See R. Merton, "On the Pricing of Corporate Debt: The Risk Structure of Interest Rates," *Journal of Finance*, 29 (1974), 449–70.

[12] To solve two nonlinear equations of the form $F(x, y) = 0$ and $G(x, y) = 0$, we can use the Solver routine in Excel to find the values of $x$ and $y$ that minimize $[F(x, y)]^2 + [G(x, y)]^2$.

case, $E_0 = 3$, $\sigma_E = 0.80$, $r = 0.05$, $T = 1$, and $D = 10$. Solving equations (26.10) and (26.11) yields $V_0 = 12.40$ and $\sigma_V = 0.2123$. The parameter $d_2$ is 1.1408, so that the probability of default is $N(-d_2) = 0.127$, or 12.7%. The market value of the debt is $V_0 - E_0$ or 9.40. The present value of the promised payment on the debt is $10e^{-0.05 \times 1} = 9.51$. The expected loss on the debt is therefore $(9.51 - 9.40)/9.51$ or about 1.2% of its no-default value. Comparing this with the probability of default gives the expected recovery in the event of a default as $(12.7 - 1.2)/12.7$, or about 91%.

Up to now, we have assumed that all of the company's debt is repayable at one time. In practice, debt repayments are likely to be required at a number of different times. This makes the model relating $V_0$ and $E_0$ more complicated than equation (26.10), but in principle it is still possible to use an option pricing approach to obtain estimates of $V_0$ and $\sigma_V$. The probability of the company defaulting at different times in the future can then be estimated.

How well do the default probabilities produced by Merton's model correspond to actual default experience? The answer is that there is a significant difference between the two, but the default probabilities produced by Merton's model can be useful for estimating actual default probabilities. KMV, a company in California, applies a transformation to the probabilities from Merton's model to produce default probability estimates.[13] Moody's Risk Management Services uses the output from Merton's model in conjunction with other financial variables to get its default probability estimates.

This completes our discussion of the estimation of default probabilities in this chapter. In the next chapter we will cover credit default swaps and explain how dealer quotes for credit default swaps provide another way to obtain default probability estimates.

## 26.6 THE LOSS GIVEN DEFAULT

Up to now in this chapter, we have focused on the estimation of the probability that a company will default at different future times. We now consider the estimation of the expected loss in the event that a default occurs. This is known as the *loss given default* and is often abbreviated LGD. The *probability of default* (often abbreviated PD) when multiplied by the LGD gives the expected loss.

The LGD on a loan made by a financial institution is usually assumed to be

$$V - R(L + A)$$

where $L$ is the outstanding principal on the loan, $A$ is the accrued interest, $R$ is the expected recovery rate, and $V$ is the no-default value of the loan. The loss given default on a long position in a bond is calculated in a similar way with $L$ equal to the face value of the bond.

For derivatives the LGD is more complicated. This is because the claim that will be made in the event of default is less certain than it is for a loan or a bond. We can distinguish three types of derivatives:

1. Those that are always a liability
2. Those that are always an asset
3. Those that can be either an asset or a liability

Derivatives in the first category have no credit risk. If the counterparty goes bankrupt, there will be

---

[13] To be more specific, KMV has two transformations: one to estimate real-world probabilities of default, the other to estimate risk-neutral probabilities of default.

no loss. Consider, for example, a company that has written an option. This derivatives position is initially a liability and stays a liability for the whole life of the option. If the counterparty (i.e., the buyer of the option) goes bankrupt, the option is one of the counterparty's assets. It is likely to be retained, closed out, or sold to a third party. In all cases, there is no loss (or gain) to the option writer.

Derivatives in the second category always have credit risk. If the counterparty goes bankrupt, a loss is likely to be experienced. Consider, for example, a company that has bought an option. This is initially an asset and remains an asset for the whole of the life of the option. If the counterparty (i.e., the writer of the option) goes bankrupt, the option holder makes a claim and may eventually receive some percentage of the value of the option.

Derivatives in the third category may or may not have credit risk. In Section 6.7 we considered swaps. When a company first enters into an interest rate swap, it has a value equal to, or very close to, zero. As time passes, interest rates change and the value of the swap may become positive or negative. If the counterparty defaults when the value of the swap is positive, a claim will be made against the assets of the counterparty and a loss is likely to be experienced. If the counterparty defaults when the value of the swap is negative, no loss is made. The swap will be retained, closed out, or sold to a third party.

In Chapter 27 we will discuss the impact of credit losses on the valuation of derivatives.

## Netting

A complication in the estimation of the losses that will be taken in the event of a counterparty default is *netting*. This is a clause in most contracts written by financial institutions. It states that if a counterparty defaults on one contract with the financial institution then it must default on all outstanding contracts with the financial institution.

Netting has been successfully tested in the courts in many jurisdictions. It can substantially reduce credit risk for a financial institution. Consider, for example, a financial institution that has three contracts outstanding with a particular counterparty. The contracts are worth +$10 million, +$30 million, and −$25 million to the financial institution. Suppose the counterparty runs into financial difficulties and defaults on its outstanding obligations. To the counterparty, the three contracts have values of −$10 million, −$30 million, and +$25 million, respectively. Without netting, the counterparty would default on the first two contracts and retain the third for a loss to the financial institution of $40 million. With netting, it is compelled to default on all three contracts for a loss to the financial institution of $15 million. (If the third contract had been worth −$45 million to the financial institution, the counterparty would choose not to default and there would be no loss to the financial institution.)

Suppose that a financial institution has a portfolio of $N$ derivative contracts with a particular counterparty. Suppose that the no-default value of the $i$th contract is $V_i$ and the recovery made in the event of default is $R$. Derivatives typically rank as unsecured claims in the event of default and the claim made in the event of default is the no-default value at the time of default. Without netting, the financial institution loses

$$(1 - R) \sum_{i=1}^{N} \max(V_i, 0)$$

With netting, it loses

$$(1 - R) \max\left(\sum_{i=1}^{N} V_i, 0\right)$$

Without netting, its loss is the payoff from a portfolio of call options on the contract values where each option has a strike price of zero. With netting, it is the payoff from a single option on the portfolio of contract values with a strike price of zero. The value of an option on a portfolio is never greater than, and is often considerably less than, the value of the corresponding portfolio of options.

### Reducing Exposure to Credit Risk

Apart from including a netting clause, there are two other ways financial institutions can reduce potential losses in the event of a default.

The first is known as *collateralization*. Consider contracts entered into between two companies A and B. Collateralization could require company A to deposit collateral with company B or with a third party. The collateralization agreement would typically state that at any given time the collateral posted should be an amount greater than the positive value (if any) that the company B has in its outstanding contracts with company A. Suppose that company B is the financial institution considered earlier, so that it has three contracts outstanding worth +$10 million, +$30 million and −$25 million with company A. It would require a collateral of at least $15 million. The collateralization agreement typically states that the collateral is adjusted periodically (e.g., every week) to reflect the value of the outstanding contracts. The collateral serves the same function as the margin in a futures contract and can significantly reduce credit risk. If company A is unable or unwilling to meet a demand for additional collateral, the collateralization agreement will state that company B has the right to close out all outstanding contracts. Collateralization requires the two parties to agree on a valuation model for the contract and to agree to a rate of interest paid on the collateral. Normally a collateralization agreement is two way. This means that company A is required to post collateral when the value of the outstanding contracts is positive to company B and company B is required to post collateral when the value of the outstanding contracts is positive to company A.[14]

The second way of reducing potential losses in the event of default is by the use of *downgrade triggers*. These are clauses in contracts with counterparties that state that if the credit rating of the counterparty falls below a certain level, say A, then the contract is closed out using a pre-determined formula with one side paying a cash amount to the other side. Downgrade triggers lead to a significant reduction in credit risk, but they do not completely eliminate all credit risk. If there is a big jump in the credit rating of the counterparty, say from A to default, in a short period of time, the financial institution will still suffer a credit loss.

Sometimes financial institutions find ways to design contracts to reduce credit risk. Consider, for example, a financial institution wishing to buy an option from a counterparty with a low credit rating. It might insist on a zero-cost package that involves the option premium being paid in arrears. This reduces the company's exposure arising from the option position.

Diversification is an important way of managing credit risk. Most large financial institutions have internal rules that limit the exposure they are allowed to have to a particular company, a particular industry, or a particular country. Traders are denied the authority to enter into a new trade if it would lead to a particular credit limit being exceeded. Credit derivatives, which will be discussed in Chapter 27, provide a way of actively managing credit risk and are sometimes used to overcome these restrictions on the activities of traders.

---

[14] Long-Term Capital Management is an example of a company that managed to avoid the need for a credit rating by entering into two-way collateralization agreements with its counterparties. After the Russian default of 1998, the value of its portfolio declined and it was unable to meet demands for additional collateral from its counterparties. See Chapter 30 for further discussion of the failure of Long-Term Capital Management.

## 26.7   CREDIT RATINGS MIGRATION

Over time, bonds are liable to move from one rating category to another. This is sometimes referred to as *credit ratings migration*. Rating agencies produce from historical data a *ratings transition matrix*. This shows the percentage probability of a bond moving from one rating to another during a certain period of time. Usually the period of time is one year. Table 26.8 shows data produced by S&P. It shows that a bond that starts with a BBB credit rating has an 89.24% chance of still being a BBB at the end of one year. It has a 0.24% chance of defaulting during the year, a 4.44% chance of dropping to BB, and so on. Appendix 26A shows how a table such as Table 26.8 can be used to calculate transition probabilities for time periods other than one year.

The probabilities in Table 26.8 are based on historical data and are therefore real-world probabilities. As we will see later, they are useful for scenario analysis and the calculation of value at risk. For valuing derivatives that depend on credit rating changes, we require a risk-neutral transition matrix. This proves to be quite difficult to estimate in practice.[15] One approach is based on bond prices. To provide a simple example, we suppose that there are three rating categories, A, B, and C, and that D is used to denote default. Table 26.9 shows hypothetical data on the cumulative risk-neutral probabilities of default. This could be calculated from bond prices as described in Section 26.1.

Suppose that $M$ is a $4 \times 4$ matrix showing the risk-neutral transition probabilities. This means that $M_{11}$ is the probability that an A-rated company stays A-rated; $M_{23}$ is the probability that a B-rated becomes C-rated; $M_{34}$ is the probability that a C-rated company defaults; and so on. Define $d_i$ as a vector that is the $i$th column of the matrix in Table 26.9. It follows that $d_2 = Md_1$, $d_3 = Md_2 = M^2d_1$, $d_4 = Md_3 = M^3d_1$, and $d_5 = Md_4 = M^4d_1$. There are nine unknown elements of $M$. These are $M_{ij}$ for $1 \leqslant i, j \leqslant 3$.[16] Table 26.9 defines 15 relationships that should hold. (These are the probabilities of A-, B-, and C-rated bonds defaulting within 1, 2, 3, 4, and 5 years.)

**Table 26.8**   One-year transition matrix of percentage probabilities

| Initial rating | Rating at year-end | | | | | | | |
|---|---|---|---|---|---|---|---|---|
|  | *AAA* | *AA* | *A* | *BBB* | *BB* | *B* | *CCC* | *Default* |
| AAA | 93.66 | 5.83 | 0.40 | 0.09 | 0.03 | 0.00 | 0.00 | 0.00 |
| AA | 0.66 | 91.72 | 6.94 | 0.49 | 0.06 | 0.09 | 0.02 | 0.01 |
| A | 0.07 | 2.25 | 91.76 | 5.18 | 0.49 | 0.20 | 0.01 | 0.04 |
| BBB | 0.03 | 0.26 | 4.83 | 89.24 | 4.44 | 0.81 | 0.16 | 0.24 |
| BB | 0.03 | 0.06 | 0.44 | 6.66 | 83.23 | 7.46 | 1.05 | 1.08 |
| B | 0.00 | 0.10 | 0.32 | 0.46 | 5.72 | 83.62 | 3.84 | 5.94 |
| CCC | 0.15 | 0.00 | 0.29 | 0.88 | 1.91 | 10.28 | 61.23 | 25.26 |
| Default | 0.00 | 0.00 | 0.00 | 0.00 | 0.00 | 0.00 | 0.00 | 100.00 |

*Source*: Standard & Poor's, January 2001.

---

[15] Fortunately relatively few credit derivatives have payoffs dependent on rating changes.

[16] Note that $M_{i,4} = 1 - M_{i,1} - M_{i,2} - M_{i,3}$, and $M_{4,j} = 1$ when $j = 4$ and zero otherwise.

**Table 26.9** Cumulative percentage probabilities of default for rating categories

| *Initial rating* | *1 year* | *2 year* | *3 year* | *4 year* | *5 year* |
|---|---|---|---|---|---|
| A | 0.67 | 1.33 | 1.99 | 2.64 | 3.29 |
| B | 1.66 | 3.29 | 4.91 | 6.50 | 8.08 |
| C | 3.29 | 6.50 | 9.63 | 12.69 | 15.67 |
| D | 100.00 | 100.00 | 100.00 | 100.00 | 100.00 |

We therefore choose the nine parameters to minimize the 15 sums of the squares of the differences between the elements of $M^{i-1}d_1$ and the corresponding elements of $d_i$ ($1 \leqslant i \leqslant 5$) in Table 26.9. The results are shown in Table 26.10. For this example the method works well. The transition probabilities are plausible and the cumulative default probabilities calculated from them are close to those in Table 26.9 (see Problem 26.13).

In practice, data on cumulative default probabilities are not always as well behaved as the data presented in Table 26.9. This has led some researchers to suggest other methods that are based on assuming that the real-world transition matrix changes in a particular way when we move from the real world to the risk-neutral world.[17]

**Table 26.10** Best-fit risk-neutral transition matrix. (Probabilities expressed as percentages.)

| *Initial rating* | Rating at year-end | | | |
|---|---|---|---|---|
| | *A* | *B* | *C* | *D* |
| A | 98.4 | 0.9 | 0.0 | 0.7 |
| B | 0.5 | 97.1 | 0.7 | 1.7 |
| C | 0.0 | 0.0 | 96.7 | 3.3 |
| Default | 0.0 | 0.0 | 0.0 | 100.0 |

## 26.8 DEFAULT CORRELATIONS

The term *default correlation* is used to describe the tendency for two companies to default at about the same time. There are a number of reasons why default correlations exist. Two companies in the same industry or the same geographic region tend to be affected similarly by external events and as a result may experience financial difficulties at the same time. Also, economic conditions generally cause average default rates to be higher in some years than in others.

---

[17] See R. A. Jarrow, D. Lando, and S. M. Turnbull, "A Markov Model for the Term Structure of Credit Spreads," *Review of Financial Studies*, 10 (1997), 481–523; M. Kijima, "A Markov Chain Model for Valuing Credit Derivatives," *Journal of Derivatives*, 6, no. 1 (Fall 1998), 97–108.

### Default Correlation Measures

Consider two companies A and B. A default correlation measure that is often calculated by rating agencies is the coefficient of correlation between:

1. A variable that equals 1 if company A defaults between times 0 and $T$ and zero otherwise; and
2. A variable that equals 1 if company B defaults between times 0 and $T$ and zero otherwise

The measure is

$$\beta_{AB}(T) = \frac{P_{AB}(T) - Q_A(T)Q_B(T)}{\sqrt{[Q_A(T) - Q_A(T)^2][Q_B(T) - Q_B(T)^2]}}$$

where $P_{AB}(T)$ is the joint probability of A and B defaulting between time zero and time $T$. As before, $Q_A(T)$ is the cumulative probability that company A will default by time $T$, and $Q_B(T)$ is the cumulative probability that company B will default by time $T$. Typically $\beta_{AB}(T)$ depends on $T$, the length of the time period considered. Usually it increases as $T$ increases.

Another correlation measure that is sometimes used is obtained from the probability distribution of the time to default. Suppose that $t_A$ and $t_B$ are the times to default of companies A and B. The variable $t_A$ and $t_B$ are not normally distributed. However,

$$u_A(t_A) = N^{-1}[Q_A(t_A)]$$

and

$$u_B(t_B) = N^{-1}[Q_B(t_B)]$$

are functions of $t_A$ and $t_B$ that are normally distributed. (As usual, $N$ is the cumulative standard normal distribution function.) We define the correlation measure as

$$\rho_{AB} = \text{corr}[u_A(t_A), u_B(t_B)]$$

We assume that the variables $u_A(t_A)$ and $u_B(t_B)$ have a bivariate normal distribution. This means that the joint probability distribution of the times to default can be described by the cumulative probability distribution $Q_A(t_A)$ of $t_A$, the cumulative probability distribution $Q_B(t_B)$ of $t_B$, and $\rho_{AB}$. The assumption is referred to as using a *Gaussian copula*.

The Gaussian copula approach can be extended to the situation where there are many companies. Suppose there are $N$ companies and $t_i$ is the time to default of company $i$. Define $Q_i(t_i)$ as the cumulative probability distribution of $t_i$ and

$$u_i(t_i) = N^{-1}[Q_i(t_i)]$$

for $1 \leqslant i \leqslant N$. We assume that the $u_i(t_i)$'s are multivariate normal.

The Gaussian copula approach is a useful way representing the correlation structure between variables that are not normally distributed. It allows the correlation structure of the variables to be estimated separately from their marginal distributions. Although the variables themselves are not multivariate normal, the approach assumes that after a transformation is applied to each variable they are multivariate normal.

**Example 26.3** Suppose that we wish to simulate defaults during the next five years in $n$ companies. For each company the cumulative probability of a default during the next 1, 2, 3, 4, and 5 years is 1%, 3%, 6%, 10%, and 15%, respectively. When a Gaussian copula is used, we sample from a multivariate normal distribution to obtain $u_i(t)$ $(1 \leqslant i \leqslant n)$. We then convert the $u_i(t)$ to $t$, a sample time to default. When the sample from the normal distribution is less than $N^{-1}(0.01) = -2.33$, a default takes place within the first year; when the sample is between $-2.33$ and $N^{-1}(0.03) = -1.88$, a default takes place during the second year; when the sample is between $-1.88$ and $N^{-1}(0.06) = -1.55$, a default takes place during the third year; when the sample is between $-1.55$ and $N^{-1}(0.03) = -1.28$, a default takes place during the fourth year; when the sample is between $-1.28$ and $N^{-1}(0.03) = -1.04$, a default takes place during the fifth year. When the sample is greater than $-1.04$, there is no default.

### Relationship between Measures

As in Appendix 12C, we define $M(a, b; \rho)$ as the probability in a standardized bivariate normal distribution that the first variable is less than $a$ and the second variable is less than $b$ when the coefficient of correlation between the variables is $\rho$. Suppose that $\rho_{AB}$ is the default correlation between A and B in the Gaussian copula model. Suppose also that $u_A(t)$ and $u_B(t)$ are the transformed times to default for companies A and B in the Gaussian copula model. It follows that

$$P_{AB}(T) = M\big(u_A(T), u_B(T); \rho_{AB}\big)$$

so that

$$\beta_{AB}(T) = \frac{M\big(u_A(T), u_B(T); \rho_{AB}\big) - Q_A(T)Q_B(T)}{\sqrt{[Q_A(T) - Q_A(T)^2][Q_B(T) - Q_B(T)^2]}} \qquad (26.12)$$

This shows that, if $Q_A(T)$ and $Q_B(T)$ are known, $\beta_{AB}(T)$ can be calculated from $\rho_{AB}$ and vice versa. Usually $\rho_{AB}$ is markedly greater than $\beta_{AB}(T)$.

> **Example 26.4** Suppose that the probability of company A defaulting in a one-year period is 1% and the probability of company B defaulting in a one-year period is also 1%. In this case, $u_A(1) = u_B(1) = -2.326$. If $\rho_{AB}$ is 0.20, then $M\big(u_A(1), u_B(1), \rho_{AB}\big) = 0.000337$ and equation (26.12) shows that $\beta_{AB}(T) = 0.024$ when $T = 1$.

### Modeling Default Correlation

Two alternative types of models of default correlation are known as *reduced-form models* and *structural models*.

Reduced-form models assume that the hazard rates for different companies follow stochastic processes and are correlated with macroeconomic variables. When the hazard rate for company A is high, there is a tendency for the hazard rate for company B to be high. This induces a default correlation between the two companies.

Reduced-form models are mathematically attractive and reflect the tendency for economic cycles to generate default correlations. They can be made consistent with either historical default probabilities or the risk-neutral probabilities of default backed out from corporate bond prices. Their main disadvantage is that the range of default correlations that can be achieved is limited. Even when there is a perfect correlation between two hazard rates, the corresponding correlation between defaults in any chosen period of time is usually very low. This is liable to be a problem in some circumstances. For example, when two companies operate in the same industry and the same country or when the financial health of one company is for some reason heavily dependent on the financial health of another company, a relatively high default correlation may be warranted. The problem can be solved by extending the model so that the hazard rate exhibits large jumps.

Structural models are based on an idea similar to that discussed in Section 26.5. A company defaults if the value of its assets is below a certain level. Default correlation between companies A and B is introduced into the model by assuming that the stochastic process followed by the assets of company A is correlated with the stochastic process followed by the assets of company B. Structural models have the advantage over reduced-form models that the correlation can be made as high as desired. Their main drawback is that they are not consistent with the probability of default calculated from historical data or bond prices.[18]

## 26.9  CREDIT VALUE AT RISK

The credit value-at-risk measure is defined similarly to the value-at-risk measure in Chapter 16. The credit VaR answers the question: What credit loss is such that we are $X$ percent certain it will not be exceeded in time $T$? The time horizon $T$ is usually longer for credit VaR than for the market risk VaR measure in Chapter 16. A typical time horizon for VaR when market risk is being considered is ten days, whereas a typical time horizon for credit VaR is one year.

Credit losses are experienced not only when a counterparty defaults. If a counterparty's credit rating reduces from, say, A to BBB, a loss is taken if all outstanding contracts with the counterparty are revalued to reflect the new rating. This section sketches out two alternative approaches to calculating credit VaR. The first is aimed at quantifying the probability distribution of the losses arising solely from counterparty defaults. The second is aimed at quantifying the probability distribution of losses arising from both credit-rating changes and defaults. In the long run, the two types of losses should be the same, but in the short run they may be different.[19] Note that we use real-world probabilities of default when calculating credit VaR. It is therefore appropriate to base default probabilities on historical data rather than on bond prices.

### Credit Risk Plus

Our first approach is based on a methodology proposed by Credit Suisse Financial Products in 1997 and has been named *Credit Risk Plus*.[20] It utilizes ideas that are well established in the insurance industry.

Suppose that a financial institution has $N$ counterparties of a certain type and the probability of default by each counterparty in time $T$ is $p$. The expected number of defaults for the whole portfolio, $\mu$, is given by $\mu = Np$. Assuming that default events are independent and $p$ is small, the probability of $n$ defaults is given by the Poisson distribution as

$$\frac{e^{-\mu}\mu^n}{n!}$$

This can be combined with a probability distribution for the losses experienced on a single

---

[18] Hull and White show how to overcome this drawback. See J. Hull and A. White, "Valuing Credit Default Swaps II: Modeling Default Correlations," *Journal of Derivatives*, 8, no. 3 (Spring 2001), 12–22.

[19] Accountants would refer to this as a *loss recognition issue*. The difference between the two approaches is really in how losses get allocated to time periods. Of course, even though the average losses are the same under both measures, the extreme tails of the probability distribution of losses (which is what determines credit VaR) may be different.

[20] See Credit Suisse Financial Products, "Credit Risk Management Framework," October, 1997.

counterparty default (taking account of the impact of netting) to obtain a probability distribution for the total default losses from the counterparties. To estimate the probability distribution for losses from a single counterparty default, we can look at the current probability distribution of our exposures to counterparties and adjust this according to historical recovery rates.

In practice, it is likely to be necessary for the financial institution to consider several categories of counterparties. This means that the analysis just described must be carried out for each category and the results combined.

Another complication is that default rates vary significantly from year to year. Data provided by Moody's shows that the default rate per year for all bonds during the 1970 to 1999 period ranged from 0.09% in 1979 to 3.52% in 1990. To account for this, we can assume a probability distribution for the overall default rate based on historical data such as that provided by Moody's. The probability of default for each category of counterparty can then be assumed to be linearly dependent on this overall default rate.

Credit Suisse Financial Products show that, if certain assumptions are made, the total loss probability distribution can be calculated analytically. To accommodate more general assumptions, Monte Carlo simulation can be used. The procedure is as follows:

1. Sample an overall default rate.
2. Calculate a probability of default for each category.
3. Sample a number of defaults for each category.
4. Sample a loss for each default.
5. Calculate total loss.
6. Repeat steps 1 to 5 many times.

The effect of assuming a probability distribution for default rates in the way just described is to build in default correlations. It has the effect of making the probability distribution of total default losses positively skewed, as indicated in Figure 26.2.

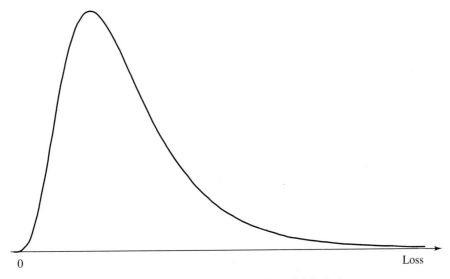

**Figure 26.2**   Probability distribution of default losses

## CreditMetrics

J.P. Morgan have developed a method for calculating credit VaR known as *CreditMetrics*. This involves estimating a probability distribution of credit losses by simulating credit rating changes for each counterparty. Suppose we are interested in determining the probability distribution of losses over a one-year period. On each simulation trial, we sample to determine the credit rating changes of all counterparties throughout the year. We also sample changes in the relevant market variables. We revalue our outstanding contracts to determine the total of credit losses from defaults and credit rating changes.[21]

This approach is clearly more complicated to implement than the Credit Risk Plus approach, where only default events are modeled. The advantage is that the precise terms of outstanding contracts can—at least in theory—be incorporated. Suppose, for example, that a particular contract with an A-rated counterparty includes a downgrade trigger stating that the contract is closed out whenever the counterparty's credit rating drops to BBB or lower. The simulation could monitor credit rating changes on a month-to-month basis to take this into account. It would incorporate the condition that a loss occurs only if the credit rating changes directly from A to default.

In sampling to determine credit losses, the credit rating changes for different counterparties should not be assumed to be independent. CreditMetrics suggests using a Gaussian copula (see Section 26.7) to model the rating changes of many different counterparties. It suggests assuming that the correlation between the normal variates corresponding to two counterparties be assumed to be the same as the correlation between their equity prices.

As an illustration of the CreditMetrics approach, suppose that we are simulating the rating change of a AAA and a BBB company over a one-year period using the trasition matrix in Table 26.8. Suppose that the correlation between the equities of the two companies is 0.2. On each simulation trial we would sample two variables $x$ and $y$ from normal distributions so that their correlation is 0.2. The variable $x$ determines the new rating of the AAA company and the variable $y$ determines the rating of the BBB company. Because

$$N^{-1}(0.9366) = 1.527$$

$$N^{-1}(0.9366 + 0.0583) = 2.569$$

$$N^{-1}(0.9366 + 0.0583 + 0.0040) = 3.062$$

the AAA company stays AAA-rated if $x < 1.527$, it becomes AA-rated if $1.527 \leqslant x < 2.569$, it becomes A-rated if $2.569 \leqslant x < 3.062$, and so on. Similarly, because

$$N^{-1}(0.0003) = -3.432$$

$$N^{-1}(0.0003 + 0.0026) = -2.759$$

$$N^{-1}(0.0003 + 0.0026 + 0.0483) = -1.633$$

the BBB company becomes AAA-rated if $y < -3.432$, it becomes AA-rated if $-3.432 \leqslant y < -2.759$, it becomes A-rated if $-2.759 \leqslant y < -1.633$, and so on. The appealing feature of the Gaussian copula approach is that it allows us to use the properties of multivariate normal distribution to jointly sample the credit migration of many companies.

---

[21] We determine losses from credit rating changes by valuing the contract at the end of the year with (i) the credit rating at the beginning of the year and (ii) the credit rating at the end of the year. The credit loss is the difference between the two.

# SUMMARY

There are a number of different ways of estimating the probability that a company will default during a particular period of time in the future. One involves bond prices, another involves historical data, and a third involves equity prices. The default probabilities backed out from bond prices are risk-neutral probabilities. The probabilities backed out from historical data are real-world probabilities. Real-world probabilities should be used for scenario analysis and the calculation of credit VaR. Risk-neutral probabilities should be used for valuing credit-sensitive instruments. In general risk-neutral default probabilities are significantly higher than real-world probabilities.

The expected loss experienced from a counterparty default is reduced by what is known as netting. This is a clause in most contracts written by financial institutions that states that if a counterparty defaults on one contract it has with a financial institution then it must default on all contracts it has with that financial institution. Losses are also reduced by collateralization and downgrade triggers. Collateralization requires counterparties to post collateral, and downgrade triggers lead to contracts being closed out when the counterparty's credit rating falls below a specified level.

A credit VaR measure can be defined as the credit loss that, with a certain probability, will not be exceeded during a certain time period. The credit VaR can be defined to take into account only losses arising from defaults. Alternatively, it can be defined so that it reflects the impact of both defaults and credit rating changes.

# SUGGESTIONS FOR FURTHER READING

Altman, E. I., "Measuring Corporate Bond Mortality and Performance," *Journal of Finance*, 44 (1989), 902–22.

Black, F., and J. Cox, "Valuing Corporate Securities: Some effects of Bond Indenture Provisions," *Journal of Finance*, 31, no. 2 (1976), 351–67.

Credit Suisse Financial Products, "Credit Risk Management Framework," October 1997.

Duffie, D., and K. Singleton, "Modeling Term Structures of Defaultable Bonds," *Review of Financial Studies*, 12 (1999), 687–720.

Finger, C. C., "A Comparison of Stochastic Default Rate Models," *RiskMetrics Journal*, 1 (November 2000), 49–73.

Group of Thirty, "Derivatives: Practices and Principles," Washington, DC, 1993.

Hull, J. C., and A. White, "Valuing Credit Default Swaps I: No Counterparty Default Risk," *Journal of Derivatives*, 8, no. 1 (Fall 2000), 29–40.

Kijima, M., "A Markov Chain Model for Valuing Credit Derivatives," *Journal of Derivatives*, 6, no. 1 (Fall 1998), 97–108.

Jarrow, R. A., D. Lando, and S. M. Turnbull, "A Markov Model for the Term Structure of Credit Spreads," *Review of Financial Studies*, 10 (1997), 481–523.

J.P. Morgan, "CreditMetrics Technical Document," April 1997.

Litterman, R., and T. Iben, "Corporate Bond Valuation and the Term Structure of Credit Spreads," *Journal of Portfolio Management*, Spring 1991, 52–64.

Merton, R. C., "On the Pricing of Corporate Debt: The Risk Structure of Interest Rates," *Journal of Finance*, 2 (1974), 449–70.

Rodriguez, R. J., "Default Risk, Yield Spreads, and Time to Maturity," *Journal of Financial and Quantitative Analysis*, 23 (1988), 111–17.

# QUESTIONS AND PROBLEMS
# (ANSWERS IN SOLUTIONS MANUAL)

26.1. Suppose that the spread between the yield on a three-year zero-coupon corporate bond and the yield on a similar risk-free bond is 50 basis points. The corresponding spread for six-year bonds is 80 basis points. Assume a zero recovery rate. What is the risk-neutral probability of default between three and six years in a risk-neutral world?

26.2. In Figure 26.1 the gradient of the curve for a Baa company is much steeper than that for a Aaa company. Explain the point made in footnote 3 that this is consistent with the comparative advantage argument.

26.3. Explain the difference between a risk-neutral and real-world default probability. Which is higher? Which should be used for (a) valuation and (b) scenario analysis?

26.4. Explain the difference between a hazard rate and a default probability density.

26.5. Suppose that the risk-neutral default probability for a one-year zero-coupon bond is 1% and the real-world default probability for the bond is 0.25%. The risk-free yield curve is flat at 6% and the excess return of the market over the risk-free rate is 5%. What does this imply about the bond's beta? Assume no recovery in the event of default.

26.6. Show that the default probabilities for year 1 and year 2 in Table 26.5 are correct for (a) the case where the claim equals the no-default value and (b) the case where the claim equals the face value plus accrued interest.

26.7. Describe how netting works. A bank already has one transaction with a counterparty on its books. Explain why a new transaction by a bank with the counterparty can have the effect of increasing or reducing the bank's credit exposure to the counterparty.

26.8. Suppose that the measure $\beta_{AB}(T)$ in Section 26.7 is the same in the real world and the risk-neutral world. Is the same true of the Gaussian copula measure, $\rho_{AB}$?

26.9. Explain the difference between Credit Risk Plus and CreditMetrics as far as the following are concerned: (a) the definition of a credit loss and (b) the way in which default correlation is modeled.

26.10. Suppose that the probability of company A defaulting during a two-year period is 0.2 and the probability of company B defaulting during this period is 0.15. If the Gaussian copula measure of default correlation is 0.3, what is $\beta_{AB}(2)$?

26.11. Suppose that the LIBOR curve is flat at 6% with continuous compounding and a three-year bond with a coupon of 5% (paid semiannually) sells for 90.00. How would an asset swap on the bond be structured? What is the asset swap spread that would be calculated in this situation?

26.12. Show that the value of a coupon-bearing corporate bond is the sum of the values of its constituent zero-coupon bonds when the claim amount is the no-default value of the bond, but that this is not so when the claim amount is the face value of the bond plus accrued interest.

26.13. Calculate the cumulative percentage probabilities of default for the transition matrix in Table 26.10.

## ASSIGNMENT QUESTIONS

26.14. The value of a company's equity is \$4 million and the volatility of its equity is 60%. The debt that will have to be repaid in two years is \$15 million. The risk-free interest rate is 6% per annum. Use Merton's model to estimate the expected loss from default, the probability of default, and the recovery rate in the event of default. Explain why Merton's model gives a high recovery rate. (*Hint*: The Solver function in Excel can be used for this question.)

26.15. Use equation (26.3) to show that

$$G_j - \sum_{i=1}^{j-1} p_i \alpha_{ij} - \alpha_{jj}\left(1 - \sum_{i=1}^{j-1} p_i\right) \leqslant B_j \leqslant G_j - \sum_{i=1}^{j-1} p_i \alpha_{ij}$$

What limits does this inequality impose on the price and yield of a 20-year bond in the example in Table 26.4 when the claim amount is the face value plus accrued interest?

26.16. Suppose that the risk-free rate is flat at 6% with annual compounding. One-, two-, and three-year bonds yield 7.2%, 7.4%, and 7.6% with annual compounding. All pay 6% coupons. Assume that defaults can happen only at the end of a year (immediately before a coupon payment date). Estimate the risk-neutral probability of default at the end of each year. Assume a recovery rate of 40% and that the claim amount equals the face value plus accrued interest.

# APPENDIX 26A
## Manipulation of the Matrices of Credit Rating Changes

Suppose that $A$ is an $N \times N$ matrix of credit rating changes in one year. This is a matrix such as the one shown in Table 26.8. The matrix of credit rating changes in $m$ years is $A^m$. This can be readily calculated using the normal rules for matrix multiplication.

The matrix corresponding to a shorter period than one year, say six months or one month is more difficult to compute. We first use standard routines to calculate eigenvectors $x_1, x_2, \ldots, x_N$ and the corresponding eigenvalues $\lambda_1, \lambda_2, \ldots, \lambda_N$. These have the property that

$$Ax_i = \lambda x_i$$

Define $X$ as a matrix whose $i$th row is $x_i$, and $\Lambda$ as a diagonal matrix where the $i$th diagonal element is $\lambda_i$. A standard result in matrix algebra shows that

$$A = X^{-1} \Lambda X$$

From this it is easy to see that the $n$th root of $A$ is

$$X^{-1} \Lambda^* X$$

where $\Lambda^*$ is a diagonal matrix where the $i$th diagonal element is $\lambda_i^{1/n}$.

Some authors such as Jarrow, Lando, and Turnbull prefer to handle this problem in terms of what is termed a *generator matrix*.[22] This is a matrix $\Gamma$ such that the transition matrix for a short period of time $\delta t$ is $1 + \Gamma \delta t$ and the transition matrix for longer period of time, $t$, is

$$\exp(t\Gamma) = \sum_{k=0}^{\infty} \frac{(t\Gamma)^k}{k!}$$

---

[22] See R. A. Jarrow, D. Lando, and S. M. Turnbull, "A Markov Model for the Term Structure of Credit Spreads," *Review of Financial Studies*, 10 (1997), 481–523.

C H A P T E R  2 7

# CREDIT DERIVATIVES

Credit derivatives are contracts where the payoff depends on the creditworthiness of one or more commercial or sovereign entities. In this chapter we explain how the most popular credit derivatives work and discuss how they can be valued. We build on the ideas introduced in Chapter 26 concerned with default probabilities, recovery rates, and default correlations.

The chapter starts by providing a detailed discussion credit default swaps. These are the most popular credit derivatives. They provide a market in which default insurance can be bought and sold. The chapter then moves on to discuss a number of other types of credit derivatives: total return swaps, credit spread options, and collateralized debt obligations. After that, it provides a general framework for taking credit risk into account in the pricing of derivatives. The final part of the chapter covers the pricing of convertible debentures. Convertible debentures are not usually thought of as credit derivatives, but it turns out to be important to take the possibility of the issuer defaulting into account in some way when a convertible debenture is valued.

## 27.1 CREDIT DEFAULT SWAPS

A credit default swap (CDS) is a contract that provides insurance against the risk of a default by particular company. The company is known as the *reference entity* and a default by the company is known as a *credit event*. The buyer of the insurance obtains the right to sell a particular bond issued by the company for its par value when a credit event occurs. The bond is known as the *reference obligation* and the total par value of the bond that can be sold is known as the swap's *notional principal*.

The buyer of the CDS makes periodic payments to the seller until the end of the life of the CDS or until a credit event occurs. A credit event usually requires a final accrual payment by the buyer. The swap is then settled by either physical delivery or in cash. If the terms of the swap require physical delivery, the swap buyer delivers the bonds to the seller in exchange for their par value. When there is cash settlement, the calculation agent polls dealers to determine the mid-market price, $Z$, of the reference obligation some specified number of days after the credit event. The cash settlement is then $(100 - Z)\%$ of the notional principal.

An example may help to illustrate how a typical deal is structured. Suppose that two parties enter into a five-year credit default swap on March 1, 2002. Assume that the notional principal is $100 million and the buyer agrees to pay 90 basis points annually for protection against default by the reference entity. If the reference entity does not default (i.e., there is no credit event), the buyer receives no payoff and pays $900,000 on March 1 of each of the years 2003, 2004, 2005, 2006,

**Figure 27.1**   Credit default swap

and 2007. If there is a credit event, a substantial payoff is likely. Suppose that the buyer notifies the seller of a credit event on September 1, 2005 (halfway through the fourth year). If the contract specifies physical settlement, the buyer has the right to sell $100 million par value of the reference obligation for $100 million. If the contract requires cash settlement, the calculation agent would poll dealers to determine the mid-market value of the reference obligation a predesignated number of days after the credit event. If the value of the reference obligation proved to be $35 per $100 of par value, the cash payoff would be $65 million. In the case of either physical or cash settlement, the buyer would be required to pay to the seller the amount of the annual payment accrued between March 1, 2005, and September 1, 2005 (approximately $450,000), but no further payments would be required. This example is illustrated in Figure 27.1.

Table 27.1 shows quotes for credit derivatives as they might have been provided by a market maker in January 2001. The second column of the table shows the Moody's and S&P credit ratings for the company (see Section 26.1 for a discussion of credit ratings). The last four columns show bid and offer quotes in basis points for credit default swaps with maturities of 3, 5, 7, and 10 years. For Toyota, the market maker is prepared to buy three-year default protection for 16 basis points per year and sell three-year default protection for 24 basis per year; it is prepared to buy five-year protection for 20 basis points per year and sell five-year protection for 30 basis points per year; and so on.

Credit derivatives allow companies to manage their credit risk actively. Suppose that a bank had several hundred million dollars of loans outstanding to Enron in January 2001 and was concerned about its exposure. It could buy a $100 million five-year CDS on Enron from the market maker in Table 27.1 for 135 basis points or $1.35 million per year. This would shift to the market maker part of the bank's Enron credit exposure.

Instead of getting rid of its credit exposure, the bank might want to exchange part of the exposure for an exposure to a company in a totally different industry, say Nissan. The bank could sell a five-year $100 million CDS on Nissan for $1.25 million per year at the same time as buying a CDS on Enron. The net cost of this strategy would be 10 basis points or $100,000 per year. The strategy

**Table 27.1**   Credit default swap quotes (basis points)

| Company | Rating | *Maturity* | | | |
|---------|--------|---------|---------|---------|----------|
| | | *3 years* | *5 years* | *7 years* | *10 years* |
| Toyota Motor Corp | Aa1/AAA | 16/24 | 20/30 | 26/37 | 32/53 |
| Merrill Lynch | Aa3/AA− | 21/41 | 40/55 | 41/83 | 56/96 |
| Ford Motor Company | A+/A | 59/80 | 85/100 | 95/136 | 118/159 |
| Enron | Baa1/BBB+ | 105/125 | 115/135 | 117/158 | 182/233 |
| Nissan Motor Co. Ltd. | Ba1/BB+ | 115/145 | 125/155 | 200/230 | 244/274 |

shows that credit default swaps can be used to diversify credit risk as well as to shift credit risk to another company.

As it happens, Enron defaulted within 12 months of January 2001. Either the risk-shifting or the risk-diversification strategy would have worked out very well!

### Valuation

We now move on to consider the valuation of a credit default swap. For convenience we assume that the notional principal is $1. We assume that default events, interest rates, and recovery rates are mutually independent. We also assume that the claim in the event of default is the face value plus accrued interest. Suppose first that default can occur only at times $t_1, t_2, \ldots, t_n$. Define:

$T$: Life of credit default swap in years

$p_i$: Risk-neutral probability of default at time $t_i$

$\hat{R}$: Expected recovery rate on the reference obligation in a risk-neutral world (this is assumed to be independent of the time of the default)

$u(t)$: Present value of payments at the rate of $1 per year on payment dates between time zero and time $t$

$e(t)$: Present value of a payment at time $t$ equal to $t - t^*$ dollars, where $t^*$ is the payment date immediately preceding time $t$ (both $t$ and $t^*$ are measured in years)

$v(t)$: Present value of $1 received at time $t$

$w$: Payments per year made by credit default swap buyer per dollar

$s$: Value of $w$ that causes the credit default swap to have a value of zero

$\pi$: The risk-neutral probability of no credit event during the life of the swap

$A(t)$: Accrued interest on the reference obligation at time $t$ as a percent face value

The value of $\pi$ is one minus the probability that a credit event will occur. It can be calculated from the $p_i$:

$$\pi = 1 - \sum_{i=1}^{n} p_i$$

The payments last until a credit event or until time $T$, whichever is sooner. The present value of the payments is therefore

$$w \sum_{i=1}^{n} [u(t_i) + e(t_i)]p_i + w\pi u(T)$$

If a credit event occurs at time $t_i$, the risk-neutral expected value of the reference obligation, as a percent of its face value, is $[1 + A(t_i)]\hat{R}$. The risk-neutral expected payoff from the CDS is therefore[1]

$$1 - [1 + A(t_i)]\hat{R} = 1 - \hat{R} - A(t_i)\hat{R}$$

---

[1] As shown by Table 26.3, rating agencies quote recovery rates as a percent of face value rather than face value plus accrued interest. Using this (less precise) definition, the risk-neutral expected payoff is $1 - \hat{R}$ rather than $1 - \hat{R} - A(t_i)\hat{R}$.

The present value of the expected payoff from the CDS is

$$\sum_{i=1}^{n}[1 - \hat{R} - A(t_i)\hat{R}]p_i v(t_i)$$

and the value of the credit default swap to the buyer is the present value of the expected payoff minus the present value of the payments made by the buyer:

$$\sum_{i=1}^{n}[1 - \hat{R} - A(t_i)\hat{R}]p_i v(t_i) - w\sum_{i=1}^{n}[u(t_i) + e(t_i)]p_i + w\pi u(T)$$

The CDS spread, $s$, is the value of $w$ that makes this expression zero:

$$s = \frac{\sum_{i=1}^{n}[1 - \hat{R} - A(t_i)\hat{R}]p_i v(t_i)}{\sum_{i=1}^{n}[u(t_i) + e(t_i)]p_i + \pi u(T)} \tag{27.1}$$

The variable $s$ is referred to as the *credit default swap spread*, or *CDS spread*. It is the payment per year, as a percent of the notional principal, for a newly issued credit default swap. (For example, in Table 27.1 the mid-market value of $s$ for Nissan for a seven-year CDS is 215 basis points, or $0.0215 per dollar of principal.)

**Example 27.1**   Suppose that the risk-free rate is 5% per annum with semiannual compounding and that, in a five-year credit default swap where payments are made semiannually, defaults can take place at the end of years 1, 2, 3, 4, and 5. The reference obligation is a five-year bond that pays a coupon semiannually of 10% per year. Default times are immediately before coupon payment dates on this bond. Assume that the probabilities of default are as in Table 26.5 (final column) and the expected recovery rate is 0.3. In this case, $A(t_i) = 0.05$ and $e(t_i) = 0$ for all $i$. Also, $v(t_1) = 0.9518$, $v(t_2) = 0.9060$, $v(t_3) = 0.8623$, $v(t_4) = 0.8207$, and $v(t_5) = 0.7812$, while $u(t_1) = 0.9637$, $u(t_2) = 1.8810$, $u(t_3) = 2.7541$, $u(t_4) = 3.5851$, and $u(t_5) = 4.3760$. From Table 26.5, it follows that $p_1 = 0.0224$, $p_2 = 0.0247$, $p_3 = 0.0269$, $p_4 = 0.0291$, $p_5 = 0.0312$, and $\pi = 0.8657$. The numerator in equation (27.1) is

$(1 - 0.3 - 0.05 \times 0.03)$

$\times (0.0224 \times 0.9518 + 0.0247 \times 0.9060 + 0.0269 \times 0.8623 + 0.0291 \times 0.8207 + 0.0312 \times 0.7812)$

or 0.07888. The denominator is

$0.0224 \times 0.9637 + 0.0247 \times 1.8810 + 0.0269 \times 2.7541$

$+ 0.0291 \times 3.5851 + 0.0312 \times 4.3760 + 0.8657 \times 4.3760$

or 4.1712. The CDS spread, $s$, is therefore $0.07888/4.1712 = 0.1891$, or 189.1 basis points. This means that payments equal to $0.5 \times 1.891 = 0.09455\%$ are made every six months.

We can extend the analysis to allow defaults at any time. Suppose that $q(t)$ is the risk-neutral default probability density at time $t$. Equation (27.1) becomes

$$s = \frac{\int_0^T [1 - \hat{R} - A(t)\hat{R}]q(t)v(t)\,dt}{\int_0^T q(t)[u(t) + e(t)]\,dt + \pi u(T)} \tag{27.2}$$

**Example 27.2**   Consider again the situation in Example 27.1. Suppose that default can take place at any time and the default probability density is as in Table 26.6 (final column). Equation (27.2) gives the swap spread as 0.01944, or 194.4 basis points. (This means that payments equal to 0.972% of the principal are required every six months.)

### Approximate No-Arbitrage Arguments

There is an approximate no-arbitrage argument that can be used to understand the determinants of $s$. If an investor buys a $T$-year par yield bond issued by the reference entity and buys a $T$-year credit default swap, the investor has eliminated most of the risks associated with default by the reference entity. Suppose that the par yield is $y$. If there is no default by the reference entity, the investor realizes a return of $y - s$ for $T$ years and receives a cash flow equal to the bond's par value at the end of the $T$ years. If there is a default, a return of $y - s$ is realized until the time of the default. There is then a payoff on the CDS so that the value of the investor's position is brought to par.

The argument just given suggests that, by combining the $T$-year par yield bond issued by the reference entity with a $T$-year CDS, the investor obtains a risk-free return of $y - s$. Suppose that $x$ is the par yield on a $T$-year risk-free bond. For no arbitrage, we should have $y - s = x$ or $s = y - x$. However, a close analysis of the argument shows that the arbitrage is less than perfect for the following reasons:

1. The credit default swap provides a payoff of par minus the post-default value of the bond. For the arbitrage to work perfectly, it would have to provide par plus accrued interest minus the post-default value of the bond.

2. For the arbitrage to work perfectly, the investor would have to be able to earn a risk-free rate of exactly $x$ between a default and time $T$. If the initial term structure is not flat or if interest rates are stochastic, the interest rate is liable to be different from $x$.

Define $s^* = y - x$. Also define $a$ as the average accrued interest on the reference bond (i.e., $a$ is the average value of $A(t)$) and $a^*$ as the average accrued interest on a par yield bond issued by the reference entity. Hull and White show that[2]

$$s = \frac{s^*(1 - \hat{R} - a\hat{R})}{(1 - \hat{R})(1 + a^*)} \tag{27.3}$$

provides a better estimate of $s$ than $s^*$.

> **Example 27.3**  Consider again the CDS in Example 27.2. In this case, the reference obligation pays a 10% coupon semiannually, so that $A(t)$ varies from 0 to 0.05 and $a = 0.025$. The five-year par yield for bonds issued by the reference entity is 7%, so that $a^* = 0.0175$. Also, $\hat{R} = 0.3$, $x = 0.05$, and $y = 0.07$, so that $s^* = 0.02$. Equation (27.3) gives
>
> $$s = \frac{0.02(1 - 0.3 - 0.025 \times 0.3)}{(1 - 0.3)(1 + 0.0175)} = 0.01945$$

or 194.5 basis points. This is very close to the 194.4 basis points calculated in Example 27.2.

### Implying Default Probabilities from CDS Swaps

The credit default swap market is now so liquid that many analysts use it to calculate implied default probabilities. This is analogous to using options markets to calculate implied volatilities from options prices.

Suppose that the CDS spreads for maturities $t_1, t_2, \ldots, t_n$ are $s_1, s_2, \ldots, s_n$. We assume a step function for the default probabilities and define $q_i$ as the default probability density between

[2] See J. C. Hull and A. White, "Valuing Credit Default Swaps I: No Counterparty Default Risk," *Journal of Derivatives*, 8, no. 1 (Fall 2000), 29–40.

times $t_{i-1}$ and $t_i$. We use the notation introduced earlier with the modification that $A_i(t)$ is the accrued interest on the $i$th reference bond at time $t$.

From equation (27.2),

$$s_i = \frac{\sum_{k=1}^{i} q_k \int_{t_{k-1}}^{t_k} [1 - \hat{R} - A_i(t)\hat{R}]v(t)\, dt}{\sum_{k=1}^{i} q_k \int_{t_{k-1}}^{t_k} [u(t) + e(t)]\, dt + u(t_i)[1 - \sum_{k=1}^{i} q_k(t_k - t_{k-1})]}$$

The $q_i$ can be calculated inductively from this equation. Define $\delta_k = t_k - t_{k-1}$ and

$$\alpha_k = \int_{t_{k-1}}^{t_k} (1 - \hat{R})v(t)\, dt$$

$$\beta_{k,i} = \int_{t_{k-1}}^{t_k} A_i(t)\hat{R}v(t)\, dt$$

$$\gamma_k = \int_{t_{k-1}}^{t_k} [u(t) + e(t)]\, dt$$

It follows that

$$q_i = \frac{s_i u(t_i) + \sum_{k=1}^{i-1} q_k[s_i \gamma_k - s_i u(t_i)\delta_k - \alpha_k + \beta_{k,i}]}{\alpha_i - \beta_{i,i} - s_i \gamma_i + s_i u(t_i)\delta_i} \tag{27.4}$$

**Example 27.4**  Suppose that the 3-, 5-, 7-, and 10-year swap spreads for a particular reference entity are 125, 155, 173, and 193 basis points, respectively. Payments are made semiannually and the reference bonds are all 7% bonds that pay coupons semiannually. The LIBOR curve is flat at 5% with continuous compounding and the expected recovery rate is 48%. Equation (27.4) shows that the default probability is 2.33% per year for the first three years, 3.63% per year for years 4 and 5, 3.73% per year for years 6 and 7, and 3.79% per year for years 8, 9, and 10.

### Recovery Rate Estimates

The only variable necessary for valuing a credit default swap that cannot be observed directly in the market is the expected recovery rate. Fortunately the pricing of a plain vanilla credit default swap depends on the recovery rate to only a small extent. This is because the expected recovery rate affects credit default swap prices in two ways. It affects the estimates of risk-neutral default probabilities and the estimates of the payoff that will be made in the event of a default. These two effects largely offset each other.[3] In Example 27.2, we calculated a five-year CDS spread based on the data in Table 26.6 as 1.944% of the principal or 194.4 basis points. This was based on an expected recovery rate of 30%. If the expected recovery rate is increased to 50%, the CDS spread changes to 191.6; if it decreases to 10%, the CDS spread changes to 196.0.[4]

### Binary Credit Default Swaps

Nonstandard credit default swaps can be quite sensitive to the expected recovery rate estimate. Consider a *binary credit default swap*. This is structured similarly to a regular credit default swap

---

[3] This is true both when the risk-neutral default probabilities are estimated from a set of bond prices, as they are in Section 26.1, and when they are estimated from a set of credit default swap spreads as in equation (27.4).

[4] Note that the probabilities of default in Table 26.6 change when these changes are made.

except that the payoff is a fixed dollar amount. In this case the expected recovery rate affects the probability of default but not the payoff. As a result the credit default spread is quite sensitive to the recovery rate. For example, a binary credit default swap spread when the expected recovery rate is 50% is typically about 80% higher than when the expected recovery rate is 10% (see Problem 27.5).

### Basket Credit Default Swaps

In a *basket credit default swap* there are a number of reference entities. An add-up basket credit default swap provides a payoff when any of the reference entities default. It is equivalent to a portfolio of credit default swaps, one on each reference entity. A first-to-default basket credit default swap provides a payoff only when the first reference entity defaults. After that, there are no further payments on the swap and it ceases to exist.

First-to-default swaps can be valued using Monte Carlo simulation. On each trial each reference entity is simulated to determine when, if ever, it defaults. We calculate (a) the present value of the payoff (if any) and (b) the present value of payments until the time of the first default or the end of the contract (whichever is earlier) at the rate of $1 per year. The swap spread is the average value of the calculations in (a) divided by the average value of the calculations in (b). First-to-default swaps are sensitive to the default correlation between reference entities. The higher the correlation, the lower the value. A conservative assumption for the seller of the swap is that all correlations are zero. Nonzero default correlations can be incorporated into the Monte Carlo simulation using the Gaussian copula model explained in Section 26.8.

### Seller Default Risk

The analysis we have presented so far assumes that there is no chance that the seller of a credit default swap will default. In this section we outline how the impact of seller default risk on CDS spreads can be estimated.

To understand the nature of seller default risk, consider the position of the buyer immediately after the seller defaults. (We assume that the reference entity has not previously defaulted.) To maintain the default protection, the buyer must immediately buy a new CDS from a new seller. The life of the new CDS will be $T - t_D$, where $T$ is the maturity of the original CDS and $t_D$ is the time at which the default occurs. The buyer will take a loss if the amount paid per annum for protection under the new contract is greater than that paid under the old contract. This is likely to be the case if the creditworthiness of the reference entity has declined significantly. Seller default risk therefore depends on:

1. The extent to which the reference entity's default probability is expected to increase with time
2. The default correlation between the reference entity and the seller

The impact of seller default risk can be quantified using Monte Carlo simulation. Define $Y$ as the present value of the payoff from the CDS and $C$ as the present value of payments made at the rate of $1 per year until either the end of the life of the CDS or until default. On each run of the simulation, we sample the times (if any) of defaults for the reference entity and the counterparty.[5] This enables sample values for $Y$ and $C$ to be obtained. If neither the reference entity nor the seller defaults, then $Y = 0$ and $C$ is the present value of the $1 annuity for the whole life of the CDS. If the reference entity defaults first, then $Y$ is the payoff from the CDS and $C$ is the present value of

---

[5] The Gaussian copula model for times to default described in Section 26.7 can be used.

the \$1 annuity until the reference entity's default. If the seller defaults first, then $Y = 0$ and $C$ is the present value of a \$1 annuity until the seller defaults.[6] The credit default swap spread is the average value of $Y$ divided by the average value of $C$.

Hull and White provide some results from this type of analysis.[7] They show that the impact of default risk on the credit default swap spread is very low when the default correlation between the seller and the reference entity is zero. As the correlation rises, the possibility of a seller default becomes more significant. Clearly it makes sense to buy a CDS from a company whose default correlation with the reference entity is as low as possible.

## 27.2 TOTAL RETURN SWAPS

A *total return swap* is an agreement to exchange the total return on a bond or other reference asset for LIBOR plus a spread. The total return includes coupons, interest, and the gain or loss on the asset over the life of the swap.

An example of a total return swap is a five-year agreement with a notional principal of \$100 million to exchange the total return on a 5% coupon bond for LIBOR plus 25 basis points. This is illustrated in Figure 27.2. On coupon payment dates, the payer pays the coupons earned on an investment of \$100 million in the bond. The receiver pays interest at a rate of LIBOR plus 25 basis points on a principal of \$100 million. (LIBOR is set on one coupon date and paid on the next as in a vanilla interest rate swap.) At the end of the life of the swap, there is a payment reflecting the change in value of the bond. For example, if the bond increases in value by 10% over the life of the swap, the payer is required to pay \$10 million (= 10% of \$100 million) at the end of the five years. Similarly, if the bond decreases in value by 15%, the receiver is required to pay \$15 million at the end of the five years. If there is a default on the bond, the swap is usually terminated and the receiver makes a final payment equal to the excess of \$100 million over the market value of the bond.

If we add the notional principal to both sides at the end of the life of the swap, we can characterize the total return swap as follows. The payer pays the cash flows on an investment of \$100 in the 5% corporate bond. The receiver pays the cash flows on a \$100 million bond paying LIBOR plus 25 basis points. If the payer owns the bond, the total return swap allows it to pass the credit risk on the bond to the receiver. If it does not own the bond, the total return swap allows it to take a short position in the bond.

Total return swaps are usually used as a financing tools. The most likely scenario leading to the swap in Figure 27.2 is as follows. The receiver wants financing to invest \$100 million in the reference bond. It approaches the payer (which is likely to be a financial institution) and agrees to the swap. The payer then invests \$100 million in the bond. This leaves the receiver in the same

**Figure 27.2** Total return swap

[6] This is somewhat conservative as the buyer of a CDS may in some circumstances be able to make a claim against the assets of the seller in the event of a default by the seller.

[7] See J. C. Hull and A. White, "Valuing Credit Default Swaps II: Modeling Default Correlations," *Journal of Derivatives*, 8, no. 3 (Spring 2001), 12–22.

position as it would have been if it had borrowed money at LIBOR plus 25 basis points to buy the bond. The payer retains ownership of the bond for the life of the swap and has much less exposure to the risk of the receiver defaulting than it would have if it had lent money to the receiver to finance the purchase of the bond. Total return swaps are similar to repos (see Section 5.1) in that they are structured to minimize credit risk when money is borrowed.

If we assume that there is no risk of a default by either the receiver or the payer, the value of the swap to the receiver at any time should be the value of the investment in the reference bond less the value of the $100 million LIBOR bond. Similarly the value of the swap to the payer should be the value of the LIBOR bond less the value of the $100 million investment in the reference bond. When it is first entered into the value of the swap should be zero. The value of the investment in the reference bond is $100 million. The value of the LIBOR bond should therefore also be $100 million. This suggests that the spread over LIBOR should be zero rather than 25 basis points.

In practice, the payer is likely to require a spread above LIBOR as compensation for bearing the risk that the receiver will default. The payer will lose money if the receiver defaults at a time when the reference bond's price has declined. The spread therefore depends on the credit quality of the receiver, the credit quality of the bond issuer, and the default correlation between the two.

There are a number of variations on the standard deal we have described. Sometimes, instead of there being a cash payment for the change in value of the bond, there is physical settlement where the payer exchanges the underlying asset for the notional principal at the end of the life of the swap. Sometimes the change-in-value payments are made periodically rather than all at the end. The swap then has similarities to an equity swap (see Section 25.5).

## 27.3 CREDIT SPREAD OPTIONS

Credit spread options are options where the payoff depends on either a particular credit spread or the price of a credit-sensitive asset. Typically the options are structured so that they cease to exist if the underlying asset defaults. If a trader wants protection against both an increase in a spread and a default, then both a credit spread option and another instrument, such as a credit default swap, are required.

One type of credit spread option is defined so that it has a payoff of

$$D \max(K - S_T, 0)$$

or

$$D \max(S_T - K, 0)$$

where $S_T$ is a particular credit spread at option maturity, $K$ is the strike spread, and $D$ is a duration used to translate the spread into a price. This can be valued using Black's model (with appropriate convexity adjustments) by assuming that the future spread conditional on no default is lognormal. The usual Black's model formula must be multiplied by the probability of no default during the life of the option.

Another type of credit spread option is a European call or put option on a credit-sensitive asset such as a floating-rate note. In this case, the payoff is either

$$\max(S_T - K, 0)$$

or

$$\max(K - S_T, 0)$$

where $S_T$ is the price of the asset at maturity and $K$ is the strike price. This can be valued using Black's model by assuming that, conditional on no default, the credit-sensitive asset price is lognormal at option maturity. As in the previous case, the usual Black's model formula must be multiplied by the probability of no default during the life of the option.

Credit spread options are sometimes embedded in other products. Examples of this are:

1. A guarantee that the spread over LIBOR in a floating-rate loan will not rise above a certain level
2. A prepayable floating-rate loan where the spread over LIBOR is fixed
3. The right to enter into an asset swap
4. The right to terminate an asset swap
5. The right to enter into a credit default swap
6. The right to terminate a credit default swap

## 27.4  COLLATERALIZED DEBT OBLIGATIONS

A collateralized debt obligation (CDO) is a way of packaging credit risk in much the same way as a collateralized mortgage obligation (see Section 24.4) is a way of packaging prepayment risk. A typical structure is shown in Figure 27.3. This involves creating four classes of securities, known as *tranches*, from a portfolio of corporate bonds or bank loans. The first tranche has 5% of the principal of the portfolio and absorbs the first 5% of the default losses. The second tranche has 10% of the principal and absorbs the next 10% of the default losses. The third tranche has 10% of the principal and absorbs the next 10% of the default losses. The fourth tranche has 75% of the bond principal and absorbs the residual default losses.

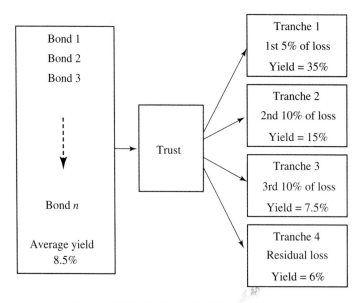

**Figure 27.3**  Collateralized debt obligation

Tranche 4 will usually be rated Aaa by Moody's and AAA by S&P, because there is very little chance of any default losses on this tranche. Default losses on the bond portfolio would have to exceed 25% of the principal before investors in tranche 4 are affected. Tranche 3 has more default risk than tranche 4, but less default risk than the original portfolio. Default risks on the original portfolio must exceed 15% of principal for the holders of tranche 3 to be affected. Tranche 2 is likely to be more risky than the original portfolio. When default losses are between 5% and 15% of the original portfolio, they are absorbed by the holders of Tranche 2. Tranche 1 is sometimes referred to as "toxic waste". It is subject to significant default risk. A default loss of 2.5% on the original portfolio translates to a default loss of 50% on tranche 1. A default loss of 5% or more on the original portfolio leads to a default loss of 100% on tranche 1. The yields in Figure 27.3, like all bond yields, are promised yields not expected yields. They do not take account of expected defaults.

The creator of the CDO normally retains tranche 1 and sells the remaining tranches in the market.[8] A CDO provides a way of creating high-quality debt from average-quality (or even low-quality) debt. The risk to the purchaser of tranches 2, 3, or 4 depends on the default correlation between the issuers of the debt instruments in the portfolio. The lower the correlation, the more highly tranches 2, 3, and 4 will be rated. Default correlation models such as the Gaussian copula model discussed in Section 26.8 are often used to analyze CDOs.

## 27.5 ADJUSTING DERIVATIVE PRICES FOR DEFAULT RISK

Suppose that you use Black–Scholes (with an appropriate volatility smile) to price a two-year European option you are planning to buy and conclude that the option is worth $6. You then discover that the counterparty selling you the option is A-rated. How do you adjust the $6 price to take account of the possibility of the counterparty defaulting?

Adjusting the pricing of a derivative such as the one we have just mentioned can be very complicated. If there are netting agreements, the adjustment should depend on the other contracts outstanding with the counterparty. The adjustment should also depend on any collateralization agreements and downgrade triggers that have been negotiated (see Section 26.6 for a discussion of this).

In this section we show how the price of a derivative should be adjusted if it is treated as a stand-alone transaction with no netting, downgrade triggers, and collateralization. This is sometimes used as a guide to the bid–offer spreads that should be negotiated. We assume that the following two sets of variables are mutually independent:

1. The variables affecting the value of the derivative value in a no-default world
2. The variables affecting the occurrence of defaults by the counterparty and the percentage recovery made in the event of a default

We also assume that the claim amount in the event of default is the no-default value of the derivative and define:

$f(t)$: Value of the derivative at time $t$ taking account of the possibility of a default by the counterparty

$f^*(t)$: Value of a similar default-free contract at time $t$

---

[8] Tranche 1 is usually difficult to sell.

### Contracts That Are Assets

We start by considering a derivative that provides a payoff at time $T$ and is always an asset to us and a liability to the counterparty. (An example is the two-year option considered earlier.) It can be shown that

$$f(0) = f^*(0)e^{-[y(T)-y^*(T)]T} \qquad (27.5)$$

In this equation, $y(T)$ is the zero-coupon yield on a $T$-year zero-coupon bond, issued by the counterparty and ranking equally with the contract under consideration, and $y^*(T)$ is the zero-coupon yield on a similar risk-free bond. To understand equation (27.5), compare the derivative with a $T$-year zero-coupon bond issued by the counterparty. Whenever a default occurs, the loss as a percent of no-default value on both the bond and option is the same. Because the no-default value of the derivative and the bond are assumed to be independent of the probability of default, the percentage reduction in the price of the derivative because of default risk is the same as that on the bond. The price of the bond is $e^{-[y(T)-y^*(T)]T}$ times its no-default price. The same must be true of the option. Equation (27.5) follows.

> **Example 27.5**  Consider a 2-year over-the-counter option with a default-free value of $3. Suppose that a 2-year bond issued by the option writer that ranks equal to the option in the event of a default yields 150 basis points over a similar risk-free bond. Default risk has the effect of reducing the option price to
>
> $$3e^{-0.015 \times 2} = 2.911$$
>
> or by about 3%.

Equation (27.5) shows that we can calculate $f(0)$ by applying a discount rate of $y - y^*$ to $f^*(0)$. Because $f^*(0)$ is itself obtained by discounting the expected payoff in a risk-neutral world at $y^*$, it follows that $f$ can be calculated by discounting the expected payoff in a risk-neutral world at $y^* + (y - y^*) = y$. One interpretation of equation (27.5), therefore, is that we should use the "risky" discount rate, $y$, instead of the risk-free discount rate, $y^*$, when discounting payoffs from a derivative contract.

Note that the risk-free interest rate enters into the valuation of a derivative in two ways. It is used to define the expected return from the underlying asset in a risk-neutral world, and it is used to discount the expected payoff. We should change the risk-free rate to the risky rate for discounting purposes, but not when determining expected returns in a risk-neutral world. For example, when using a binomial tree, the growth rate of the underlying asset should be the risk-free rate, but we should use the risky rate for discounting as we work back through the tree.

### Contracts That Can Be Assets or Liabilities

We now consider the impact of default risk on contracts such as swaps and forward contracts that can become either assets or liabilities. (As before, we assume that the transaction under consideration is subject to no netting, collateralization, or downgrade triggers.) We suppose that defaults can occur only at times $t_1, t_2, \ldots, t_n$. Define $v_i$ as value of a contract that pays off $\max[f^*(t_i), 0]$ at time $t_i$ and

$$u_i = p_i(1 - R)$$

where $p_i$ is the probability of default at time $t_i$ and $R$ is the recovery rate. From equation (26.2) an appropriate expression for $u_i$ is

$$u_i = e^{-[y(t_{i-1})-y^*(t_{i-1})]t_{i-1}} - e^{-[y(t_i)-y^*(t_i)]t_i} \qquad (27.6)$$

where $y(t)$ and $y^*(t)$ are zero-coupon yields on corporate and risk-free bonds maturing at time $t$.

Given our assumption that the claim amount on a derivative equals its no-default value, $u_i$ is the loss percentage from defaults at time $t_i$. The variable $v_i$ is the present value of the claim made in the event of a default at time $t_i$. It follows that

$$f^*(0) - f(0) = \sum_{i=1}^{n} u_i v_i \qquad (27.7)$$

## Currency Swap Example

To illustrate the use of equation (27.7), suppose that a financial institution enters into a fixed-for-fixed foreign currency swap with a counterparty, whereby it receives interest in dollars and pays interest in sterling. Principals are exchanged at the end of the life of the swap. Suppose that the swap details are as follows:

. Life of swap: five years

Frequency of payments: annual

Sterling interest exchanged: 10% per annum (compounded annually)

Dollar interest exchanged: 5% per annum (compounded annually)

Sterling principal: £50 million

Dollar principal: $100 million

Initial exchange rate: 2.0000

Volatility of exchange rate: 15%

We suppose that the sterling yield curve is flat at 10% per annum (annually compounded) and the dollar yield curve is flat at 5% per annum (annually compounded) with both interest rates constant. We also suppose that 1-, 2-, 3-, 4-, and 5-year unsecured zero-coupon bonds issued by the counterparty have yields that are spreads of 25, 50, 70, 85, and 95 basis points above the corresponding riskless rate.

We assume that defaults can occur only on payment dates (i.e., just before payments are due to be exchanged). This means that $n = 5$, $t_1 = 1$, $t_2 = 2$, $t_3 = 3$, $t_4 = 4$, and $t_5 = 5$. Because interest rates are assumed constant, we know that the value of the sterling bond underlying the swap at each possible default time is 55 million pounds. Similarly, the value of the dollar bond underlying the swap at each possible default time is 105 million dollars. The value of the swap at time $t_i$ in millions of dollars is therefore $105 - 55S(t_i)$, where $S(t)$ is the dollar–sterling exchange rate at time $t$.

The variable $v_i$ is the value of a derivative that pays off

$$\max[105 - 55S(t_i), \, 0] = 55 \max\left[\frac{105}{55} - S(t_i), \, 0\right]$$

millions of dollars at time $t_i$. This is 55 times the value of a foreign currency put option with a strike price of $105/55 = 1.90909$. The initial exchange rate is 2.0000, the domestic interest rate is 5%

**Table 27.2**  Cost of defaults in millions of dollars on a currency swap with a corporation when dollars are received and sterling is paid

| Maturity, $t_i$ | $u_i$ | $v_i$ | $u_i v_i$ |
|:---:|:---:|:---:|:---:|
| 1 | 0.002497 | 5.9785 | 0.0149 |
| 2 | 0.007453 | 10.2140 | 0.0761 |
| 3 | 0.010831 | 13.5522 | 0.1468 |
| 4 | 0.012647 | 16.2692 | 0.2058 |
| 5 | 0.012962 | 18.4967 | 0.2398 |
| Total | | | 0.6834 |

with annual compounding (or 4.879% with continuous compounding), the foreign risk-free rate is 10% with annual compounding (or 9.531% with continuous compounding), the exchange rate volatility is 15%, and the time to maturity is $t_i$. The $v_i$ can therefore be obtained from the software DerivaGem. For example, when $t_i = 3$, the value of the option is 0.246403, so that $v_3 = 55 \times 0.246403 = 13.5522$.

The $u_i$'s can be calculated from (27.6) and are shown in Table 27.2. For example, $u_3 = e^{-0.0050 \times 2} - e^{-0.0070 \times 3} = 0.010831$. Table 27.2 shows the full set of $u_i$'s and $v_i$'s for this example and the calculation of the cost of default. The total cost of defaults is 0.6834 million dollars, or 0.6834% of the principal. Table 27.3 shows a similar set of calculations for the situation where the financial institution is paying dollars and receiving sterling. In this case, $v_i$ is the price of a foreign currency call option maturing at time $t_i$. Table 27.3 shows that the expected cost of defaults is 0.2404 million dollars, or 0.2404% of the principal.

This example illustrates the general rule that a financial institution has more default risk when it is receiving a low-interest-rate currency and paying a high-interest-rate currency than the other way round. The reason is that the high-interest-rate currency is expected to depreciate relative to the low-interest-rate currency causing the low-interest-rate bond underlying the swap to appreciate in value relative to the high-interest-rate bond.

The total cost of defaults on the matched pair of swaps in Tables 27.2 and 27.3 (when there are two different counterparties) is $0.6834 + 0.2404 = 0.9238$ million dollars, or about 0.924% of the principal. Using a discount rate of 5% per annum, this is equivalent to payments of about

**Table 27.3**  Cost of defaults in millions of dollars on a currency swap with a corporation when dollars are paid and sterling is received

| Maturity, $t_i$ | $u_i$ | $v_i$ | $u_i v_i$ |
|:---:|:---:|:---:|:---:|
| 1 | 0.002497 | 5.9785 | 0.0149 |
| 2 | 0.007453 | 5.8850 | 0.0439 |
| 3 | 0.010831 | 5.4939 | 0.0595 |
| 4 | 0.012647 | 5.0169 | 0.0634 |
| 5 | 0.012962 | 4.5278 | 0.0587 |
| Total | | | 0.2404 |

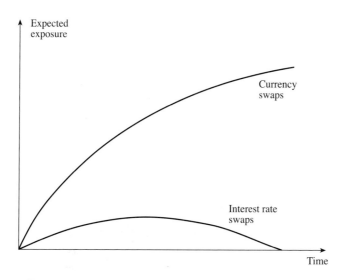

**Figure 27.4**   Expected exposure on a matched pair of interest rate swaps
and a matched pair of currency swaps

0.21 million dollars per year for five years. Because the principal is 100 million dollars, 0.21 million dollars is 21 basis points. We have therefore shown that (ignoring netting, collateralization, and downgrade triggers) the financial institution should seek a bid–offer spread of about 21 basis points on a matched pair of currency swaps to compensate for credit risk when the exchange rate volatility is 15%.[9]

### Interest Rate Swaps vs. Currency Swaps

The impact of default risk on interest rate swaps is considerably less than that on currency swaps. Using similar data to that for currency swaps, the required total spread for a matched pair of interest rate swaps is about 2 basis points. Figure 27.4 shows the reason for this. It compares the expected exposure on a matched pair of offsetting interest rate swaps with the expected exposure on a matched pair of offsetting currency swaps. The expected exposure on a matched pair of interest rate swaps starts at zero, increases, and then decreases to zero. By contrast, expected exposure on a matched pair of currency swaps increases steadily with the passage of time.[10]

### Generalization

In reality, a financial institution is likely to have several contracts outstanding with each of its counterparties and these are likely to be subject to a complicated set of netting, downgrade trigger, and collateralization agreements. The procedure we have outlined in this section provides a framework that can be used to estimate expected credit losses, but to be a practical tool it needs to be generalized. Suppose that a financial institution is calculating the present value of expected losses from defaults with a particular counterparty. The variable $u_i$ is defined as the loss percentage

---

[9] Further calculations show that the total cost of defaults, and therefore the required bid–offer spread, on a matched pair of currency swaps is relatively insensitive to the interest rates in the two currencies.

[10] This is largely because of the impact of the final exchange of principal in the currency swap.

from defaults at time $t_i$ as in Table 27.2. The variable $v_i$ must be estimated as the claim that will be made in the event of a default at time $t_i$. A precise estimate of $v_i$, as in our currency swap example, is not usually possible. An approximation based on projections of the future value of the portfolio of contracts with the counterparty and the likely effectiveness of the netting, downgrade trigger, and collateralization agreements must be used.

## 27.6 CONVERTIBLE BONDS

Convertible bonds are bonds issued by a company where the holder has the option to exchange the bonds for the company's stock at certain times in the future. The *conversion ratio* is the number of shares of stock obtained for one bond. This is usually constant but is sometimes a function of time. The bonds are almost always callable (i.e., the issuer has the right to buy them back at certain times at a predetermined prices). The holder always has the right to convert the bond once it has been called. The call feature is therefore usually a way of forcing conversion earlier than the holder would otherwise choose. Sometimes the holder's call option is conditional on the price of the company's stock being above a certain level.

Credit risk plays an important role in the valuation of convertibles. If we ignore credit risk, we will get poor prices because the coupons and principal payments on the bond, assuming no conversion, will be overvalued. This is because they will be treated as riskless and discounted at the risk-free rate.

Ingersoll provides a way of valuing convertibles using a model similar to Merton's (1974) model discussed in Section 26.5.[11] He assumes geometric Brownian motion for the issuer's total assets and models the company's equity, its convertible debt, and its other debt as claims contingent on the value of the assets. Credit risk is taken into account because the debt holders get repaid in full only if the value of the assets exceeds the amount owing to them.

A simpler model that is more widely used in practice involves modeling the issuer's stock price. A tree for the stock price is constructed in the usual way. The life of the tree is set equal to the life of the convertible bond. The value of the convertible at the final nodes of the tree is calculated based on any conversion options that the holder has at that time. We then roll back through the tree. At nodes where the terms of the instrument allow conversion, we test whether conversion is optimal. We also test whether the position of the issuer can be improved by calling the bonds. If so, we assume that the bonds are called and retest whether conversion is optimal. This is equivalent to setting the value at a node equal to

$$\max[\min(Q_1, Q_2), Q_3]$$

where $Q_1$ is the value given by the rollback (assuming that the bond is neither converted nor called at the node), $Q_2$ is the call price, and $Q_3$ is the value if conversion takes place.

One complication is the choice of the discount rate used in conjunction with the tree. Suppose first that the convertible is certain to remain a bond. It is then appropriate to use a "risky" discount rate that reflects the credit risk of the issuer. This leads to the value of the convertible being correctly calculated as the market value of a regular nonconvertible bond. Suppose next that the bond is certain to be converted. It is then appropriate to use the risk-free interest rate as the

[11] See J. E. Ingersoll, "A Contingent Claims Valuation of Convertible Securities," *Journal of Financial Economics*, 4 (May 1977), 289–322.

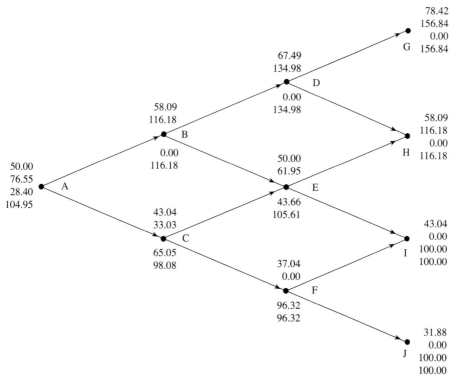

78.42
156.84
0.00
G    156.84

67.49
134.98

D

0.00
134.98

58.09
116.18

B

0.00
116.18

58.09
116.18
0.00
H    116.18

50.00
61.95

50.00
76.55
28.40
104.95

A

E

43.66
105.61

43.04
33.03

C

43.04
0.00
100.00
I    100.00

65.05
98.08

37.04
0.00

F

96.32
96.32

31.88
0.00
100.00
J    100.00

**Figure 27.5**  Tree for valuing convertible

discount rate. The value of the bond is then correctly calculated as the value of the equity underlying the bond.

In practice, we are usually uncertain as to whether the bond will be converted. We therefore arrange the calculations so that the value of the bond at each node is divided into two components: a component that arises from situations where the bond ultimately ends up as equity and a component that arises from situations where the bond ends up a debt. We apply a risk-free discount rate to the first component and a "risky" discount rate for the second component.[12]

**Example 27.6**  As a simple example of the procedure for valuing convertibles, consider a nine-month zero-coupon bond issued by company XYZ with a face value of $100. Suppose that it can be exchanged for two shares of company XYZ's stock at any time during the nine months. Assume also that it is callable for $115 at any time. The initial stock price is $50, its volatility is 30% per annum, and there are no dividends. The risk-free yield curve is flat at 10% per annum. The risky yield curve corresponding to bonds issued by company XYZ is flat at 15% per annum. Figure 27.5 shows the stock price tree that can be used to value this convertible. The top number at each node is the stock price; the second number is the component of the bond's value arising from situations where it ultimately becomes equity; the third number is the component of the bond's value arising from

---

[12] This approach is formalized in K. Tsiveriotis and C. Fernandes, "Valuing Convertible Bonds with Credit Risk," *Journal of Fixed Income*, 8, no. 2 (September 1998), 95–102.

situations where it ultimately becomes debt; the fourth number is the total value of the bond. The tree parameters are $u = 1.1618$, $d = 0.8607$, $a = 1.0253$, and $p = 0.5467$. At the final nodes, the convertible is worth $\max(100, 2S_T)$. At node G, the numbers show that the stock price is 78.42, the value of the bond is 156.84 and all of this value arises from situations where the bond ends up as equity. At node I, the stock price is 43.04, the value of the convertible is 100, and all of this arises from situations where it ends up as debt.

As we roll back through the tree, we test whether conversion is optimal and whether the bond should be called. At node D, rollback gives the value of the equity component of the convertible as

$$(0.5467 \times 156.84 + 0.4533 \times 116.18)e^{-0.1 \times 0.25} = 134.98$$

The value of the debt component is zero. Calling or converting the bond does not change its value since it is already essentially equity. At node F, the equity component of the convertible is zero and the debt component is worth $100e^{-0.15 \times 0.25}$, or 96.32. Node E is more interesting. The equity component of the convertible is worth

$$(0.5467 \times 116.18 + 0.4533 \times 0)e^{-0.1 \times 0.25} = 61.95$$

The debt component is worth

$$(0.5467 \times 0 + 0.4533 \times 100)e^{-0.15 \times 0.25} = 43.66$$

The total value of the bond is $61.95 + 43.66 = 105.61$. Clearly, the bond should be neither converted nor called.

At node B, the equity component of the convertible is worth

$$(0.5467 \times 134.98 + 0.4533 \times 61.95)e^{-0.1 \times 0.25} = 99.36$$

and the debt component is worth

$$(0.5467 \times 0 + 0.4533 \times 43.66)e^{-0.15 \times 0.25} = 19.06$$

The total value of the bond is $99.36 + 19.06 = 118.42$. It is optimal for the issuer to call the bond at node B because this will cause immediate conversion and lead to the value of the bond being reduced to $2 \times 58.09 = 116.18$ at the node. The numbers at node B recognize that this will happen. The bond is worth 116.18, all of it equity, at node B. Continuing in this way, the value of the convertible at the initial node, A, is 104.95. If the bond had no conversion or call option, its value would be

$$100e^{-0.15 \times 0.75} = 89.36.$$

The value of the conversion option (net of the issuer's call option) is therefore

$$104.95 - 89.36 = 15.59$$

When dividends on the equity or interest on the debt is paid, they must be taken into account. At each node, we first assume that the bond is debt. We include in the debt component of the value of the bond the present value of any interest payable on the bond in the next time step. Then, when testing whether the bond should be converted, we take into account the present value of any dividends that will be received during the next time step. The calculations can be made more precise by allowing the risk-free and "risky" rates to be time dependent and equal to the relevant forward rates. The tree is then built as indicated in Section 18.4. Cash flows between time $t$ and $t + \delta t$ are discounted at the appropriate forward rate applicable to the period between $t$ and $t + \delta t$.

# SUMMARY

Credit derivatives enable banks and other financial institutions to actively manage their credit risks. They can be used to transfer credit risk from one company to another and to diversify credit risk by swapping one type of exposure for another.

The most common credit derivative is a credit default swap. This is a contract where one company buys insurance against another company defaulting on its obligations. The payoff is usually the difference between the par value of a bond issued by the second company and its value immediately after a default. Credit default swaps can be analyzed by calculating the present value of the expected cost of the insurance in a risk-neutral world and the present value of the expected payoff.

A total return swap is an instrument where the total return on a portfolio of credit-sensitive assets is exchanged for LIBOR plus a spread. A total return swap can be used to exchange a corporate bond for a bond providing a LIBOR-based return. It then eliminates market risk as well as credit risk. Total return swaps are often used as financing vehicles. A company wanting to purchase a portfolio of bonds will approach a financial institution, who will buy the bonds on its behalf. The financial institution will then enter into a credit default swap where it pays the return on the bonds to the company and receives LIBOR. The advantage of this type of arrangement is that the financial institution reduces its exposure to defaults by the company.

A credit spread option is an option on a credit spread. Under one type of structure, the payoff is calculated by comparing the credit spread in the market at a future time to a strike credit spread. Under another, it is calculated by comparing the price of a floating-rate bond to a strike price.

In collateralized debt obligations a number of different securities are created from a portfolio of corporate bonds or commercial loans. There are rules for determining how credit losses are allocated to the securities. The result of the rules is that securities with both very high and very low credit ratings are created from the portfolio.

All over-the-counter derivative transactions involve some credit risk. The credit derivatives market has made market participants more conscious of the need to adjust their pricing to allow for counterparty credit risk. An option is an example of a derivative that is always an asset to one party and a liability to the other. The party for which it is an asset can adjust for credit risk by judiciously increasing the discount rate. Other derivative transactions (e.g., swaps) can be either assets or liabilities depending on movements in market variables. Usually a financial institution has several derivative transactions outstanding with a counterparty. Estimating the expected loss from defaults by the counterparty involves estimating the expected claim that will be made conditional on default at various future times.

Convertible bonds are bonds that can be converted to the issuer's equity according to pre-specified terms. Credit risk has to be considered in the valuation of a convertible bond. This is because, if the bond is not converted, the promised payments on the bond are subject to credit risk. One procedure for valuing convertible bonds is to calculate the component of the value attributable to the possibility of the bond ending up as equity separately from the component of the value attributable to the possibility of the bond ending up as debt.

# SUGGESTIONS FOR FURTHER READING

Cooper, I., and A. Mello, "The Default Risk of Swaps," *Journal of Finance*, 46 (1991), 597–620.

Das, S., *Credit Derivatives: Trading & Management of Credit & Default Risk*, Wiley, Singapore, 1998.

Duffie, D., and M. Huang, "Swap Rates and Credit Quality," *Journal of Finance*, 51, no. 3 (July 1996), 921–49.

Goldman Sachs, *Valuing Convertible Bonds as Derivatives*, Quantitative Strategies Research Notes, Goldman Sachs, November 1994.

Hull, J. C, "Assessing Credit Risk in a Financial Institution's Off-Balance-Sheet Commitments," *Journal of Financial and Quantitative Analysis*, 24 (1989), 489–501.

Hull, J. C, and A. White, "The Impact of Default Risk on the Prices of Options and Other Derivative Securities," *Journal of Banking and Finance*, 19, no. 2 (May 1995), 299–322.

Hull, J. C, and A. White, "The Price of Default," *RISK*, September 1992, pp. 101–3.

Hull, J. C., and A. White, "Valuing Credit Default Swaps I: No Counterparty Default Risk," *Journal of Derivatives*, 8, no. 1 (Fall 2000), 29–40.

Hull, J. C., and A. White, "Valuing Credit Default Swaps II: Modeling Default Correlations," *Journal of Derivatives*, 8, no. 3 (Spring 2001), 12–22.

Jarrow, R. A., and S. M. Turnbull, "Pricing Options on Derivative Securities Subject to Credit Risk," *Journal of Finance*, 50 (1995), 53–85.

Johnson, H., and R. Stulz, "The Pricing of Options Under Default Risk," *Journal of Finance*, 42 (1987), 267–80.

Tavakoli, J. M., *Credit Derivatives: A Guide to Instruments and Applications*, Wiley, New York, 1998.

Tsiveriotis, K., and C. Fernandes, "Valuing Convertible Bonds with Credit Risk," *Journal of Fixed Income*, 8, no. 2 (September 1998), 95–102.

## QUESTIONS AND PROBLEMS
## (ANSWERS IN SOLUTIONS MANUAL)

27.1. A credit default swap requires a premium of 60 basis points per year paid semiannually. The principal is $300 million and the credit default swap is settled in cash. A default occurs after four years and two months, and the calculation agent estimates that the price of the reference bond is 40% of its face value shortly after the default. List the cash flows and their timing for the seller of the credit default swap.

27.2. Suppose that the risk-free zero curve is flat at 7% per annum with continuous compounding and that defaults can occur at times 1 year, 2 years, and 3 years in a three-year credit default swap. Suppose that the recovery rate is 30% and the default probabilities are as in the final column of Table 26.5. What is the credit default swap spread? Assume that payments are made semiannually and that the accrued interest on the reference bond is always zero at the time of a default.

27.3. Suppose that the five-year risk-free yield is 4% and the five-year yield on bonds issued by a corporation is 5.6% both with semiannual compounding. Estimate the CDS spread when the corporation is the reference entity, the reference liability is an 8% coupon bond, and the expected recovery rate is 40%. Assume that semiannual payments on the CDS. Use equation (27.3)

27.4. What is the formula corresponding to equation (27.1) for valuing a binary credit default swap.

27.5. Prove the statement in the text that a binary swap spread when the expected recovery rate is 50% is typically about 80% higher than when the expected recovery rate is 10%. (*Hint*: Assume that the payoff from a regular credit default swap is the payoff from a binary credit default swap times one minus the recovery rate.)

27.6. How does a first-to-default credit default swap work. Explain why the value of a first-to-default credit default swap increases as the correlation between the reference entities in the basket decreases.

27.7. Explain why a total return swap can be an efficient financing tool.

27.8. Explain the difference between a total return swap and an asset swap.

27.9. Suppose that the spread between the yield on a three-year zero-coupon riskless bond and a three-year zero-coupon bond issued by a corporation is 1%. By how much does Black–Scholes overstate the value of a three-year option sold by the corporation?

27.10. "A long forward contract subject to credit risk is a combination of a short position in a no-default put and a long position in a call subject to credit risk." Explain this statement.

27.11. Explain why the credit exposure on a matched pair of forward contracts resembles a straddle.

27.12. Explain why the impact of credit risk on a matched pair of interest rate swaps tends to be less than that on a matched pair of currency swaps.

27.13. "When a bank is negotiating currency swaps, it should try to ensure that it is receiving the lower interest rate currency from a company with a low credit risk." Explain.

27.14. Does put–call parity hold when there is default risk? Explain your answer.

27.15. The text discusses how the price of a European option can be adjusted for credit risk. How would you adjust the price of an American option for credit risk?

27.16. Suppose that a financial institution has entered into a swap dependent on the sterling interest rate with counterparty X and an exactly offsetting swap with counterparty Y. Which of the following statements are true and which are false?

 a. The total present value of the cost of defaults is the sum of the present value of the cost of defaults on the contract with X plus the present value of the cost of defaults on the contract with Y.

 b. The expected exposure in one year on both contracts is the sum of the expected exposure on the contract with X and the expected exposure on the contract with Y.

 c. The 95% upper confidence limit for the exposure in one year on both contracts is the sum of the 95% upper confidence limit for the exposure in one year on the contract with X and the 95% upper confidence limit for the exposure in one year on the contract with Y.

 Explain your answers.

27.17. A company enters into a one-year forward contract to sell 100 U.S. dollars for 150 Australian dollars. The contract is initially at the money. In other words, the forward exchange rate is 1.50. The one-year dollar risk-free rate of interest is 5% per annum. The one-year dollar rate of interest at which the counterparty can borrow is 6% per annum. The exchange rate volatility is 12% per annum. Estimate the present value of the cost of defaults on the contract? Assume that defaults are recognized only at the end of the life of the contract.

27.18. Suppose that in Problem 27.20, the six-month forward rate is also 1.50 and the six-month dollar risk-free interest rate is 5% per annum. Suppose further that the six-month dollar rate of interest at which the counterparty can borrow is 5.5% per annum. Estimate the present value of the cost of defaults assuming that defaults can occur either at the six-month point or at the one-year point? (If a default occurs at the six-month point, the company's potential loss is the market value of the contract.)

27.19. Consider an 18-month zero-coupon bond with a face value of $100 that can be converted into five shares of the company's stock at any time during its life. Suppose that the current share price is $20, no dividends are paid on the stock, the risk-free rate for all maturities is 6% per annum with continuous compounding, and the share price volatility is 25% per annum. Assume that the yield on nonconvertible bonds issued by the company is 10% per annum for all maturities. The bond is callable at $110. Use a three-time-step tree to calculate the value of the bond. What is the value of the conversion option (net of the issuer's call option)?

# ASSIGNMENT QUESTIONS

27.20. Suppose that the risk-free zero curve is flat at 6% per annum with continuous compounding and that defaults can occur at times 1 year, 2 years, 3 years, and 4 years in a four-year plain vanilla credit default swap with semiannual payments. Suppose that the recovery rate is 20% and the probabilities of default at times 1 year, 2 years, 3 years and 4 years are 0.01, 0.015, 0.2 , and 0.25, respectively. The reference obligation is a bond paying a coupon semiannually of 8% per year. Defaults always take place immediately before coupon-payment dates on this bond. What is the credit default swap spread? What would the credit default spread be if the the instrument were a binary credit default swap?

27.21. Suppose that the 1-, 2-, 3-, 4-, and 5-year interest rates are 4%, 4.8%, 5.3%, 5.5%, and 5.6%, respectively. The volatility of all swap rates are 20%. A bank has entered into an annual-pay swap with a counterparty where the fixed rate exchanged for floating is 5.705%. The notional principal is $100 million. The spreads over the risk-free rates for 1-, 2-, 3-, 4-, and 5-year bonds issued by the counterparty are 20, 40, 55, 65, and 75 basis points, respectively. Assume that defaults can occur only on payment dates and ignore any losses arising from payments that are due to be exchanged on the date of default. Use the DerivaGem software to answer the following questions:

  a. What is the expected loss from defaults on a 5-year swap where the bank receives fixed?
  b. What is the expected loss from defaults on a 5-year swap where the bank receives floating? Explain why your answer here is higher than your answer to part (a).
  c. What is the spread required by the bank on a matched pair of interest rate swaps to compensate for credit risk?
  d. What difficulties are there in modifying your analysis to allow for losses arising from payments due to be made on the day of default?

27.22. Explain carefully the distinction between real-world and risk-neutral default probabilities. Which is higher? A bank enters into a credit derivative where it agrees to pay $100 at the end of one year if a certain company's credit rating falls from A to BBB or lower during the year. The one-year risk-free rate is 5%. Using Table 26.8, estimate a value for the derivative. What assumptions are you making? Do they tend to overstate or understate the value of the derivative?

27.23. A three-year convertible bond with a face value of $100 has been issued by company ABC. It pays a coupon of $5 at the end of each year. It can be converted into ABC's equity at the end of the first year or at the end of the second year. At the end of the first year, it can be exchanged for 3.6 shares immediately after the coupon date. At the end of the second year it can be exchanged for 3.5 shares immediately after the coupon date. The current stock price is $25 and the stock price volatility is 25%. No dividends are paid on the stock. The risk-free interest rate is 5% with continuous compounding. The yield on bonds issued by ABC is 7% with continuous compounding.

  a. Use a three-step tree to calculate the value of the bond.
  b. How much is the conversion option worth?

   c. What difference does it make to the value of the bond and the value of the conversion option if the bond is callable any time within the first two years for $115?

   d. Explain how your analysis would change if there were a dividend payment of $1 on the equity at the 6-month, 18-month, and 30-month points. Detailed calculations are not required.

27.24. You have the option to enter into a five-year credit default swap at the end of one year for a swap spread of 100 basis points. The principal is $100 million. Payments are made on the swap semiannually. The forward swap spread for the period between year 1 and year 6 is 90 basis points, and the volatility of the forward swap spread is 15%, LIBOR is flat at 5% (continously compounded). The risk-neutral probability of a default by the reference entity during the first year is 0.015. What is the value of the option? Assume that the option ceases to exist if there is a default during the first year.

# CHAPTER 28

# REAL OPTIONS

Up to now we have been almost entirely concerned with the valuation of derivatives dependent on financial assets. In this chapter we explore how the ideas we have developed can be extended to value investments in real assets. Real assets include land, buildings, plant, and so on. Often there are embedded options. Valuation is difficult because market prices are not readily available.

We start by explaining the traditional approach to evaluating investments in real assets and their shortcomings. We then move on to explain how the risk-neutral valuation principle developed in Chapters 10, 12, and 21 can be extended to value investments in real assets. After that we describe the options that are embedded in real assets and explain how the risk-neutral valuation approach can facilitate the valuation of these options.[1]

## 28.1 CAPITAL INVESTMENT APPRAISAL

The traditional approach to valuing a potential capital investment project is known as the "net present value", or NPV, approach. The NPV of a project is the present value of its expected future incremental cash inflows and outflows. The discount rate used to calculate the present value is a "risk-adjusted" discount rate, chosen to reflect the risk of the project. As the riskiness of the project increases, the discount rate also increases.

As an example consider an investment that costs $100 million and will last five years. The expected cash inflow in each year is estimated to be $25 million. If the risk-adjusted discount rate is 12%, the net present value of the investment is (in millions of dollars)

$$-100 + \frac{25}{1.12} + \frac{25}{1.12^2} + \frac{25}{1.12^3} + \frac{25}{1.12^4} + \frac{25}{1.12^5} = -9.88$$

A negative NPV, such as the one we have just calculated, indicates that the project will reduce the value of the company to its shareholders and should not be undertaken. A positive NPV indicates that the project should be undertaken because it will increase shareholder wealth.

The risk-adjusted discount rate should be the return required by the company, or the company's shareholders, on the investment. This can be calculated in a number of ways. One approach often recommended involves the capital asset pricing model. The steps are as follows:

1. Take a sample of companies whose main line of business is the same as that of the project being contemplated.

---

[1] Throughout this chapter the risk-neutral world we will consider is the traditional risk-neutral world we defined in Chapter 21.

**660**

2. Calculate the betas of the companies and average them to obtain a proxy beta for the project.
3. Set the required rate of return equal to the risk-free rate plus the proxy beta times the excess return of the market portfolio over the risk-free rate.

One problem with the traditional NPV approach is that many projects contain embedded options. Consider, for example, a company that is considering building a plant to manufacture a new product. Often the company has the option to abandon the project if things do not work out well. It may also have the option to expand the plant if demand for the output exceeds expectations. These options usually have quite different risk characteristics from the base project and require different discount rates.

To understand the problem here, return to the example at the beginning of Chapter 10. This involved a stock whose current price is $20. In three months' time the price will be either $22 or $18. Risk-neutral valuation shows that the value of a three-month call option on the stock with a strike price of 21 is 0.633. Footnote 1 of Chapter 10 shows that, if the expected return required by investors on the stock in the real world is 16%, the expected return required on the call option is 42.6%. A similar analysis shows that if the option is a put rather than a call then the expected return required on the option is −52.5%. In practice it would be very difficult to estimate these expected returns directly in order to value the options. (We know the returns only because we are able to value the options in another way.) The same point applies to options on real assets. There is no easy way of estimating the risk-adjusted discount rates appropriate for cash flows when they arise from abandonment, expansion, and other options. This is the motivation for exploring whether the risk-neutral valuation principle can be applied to options on real assets as well as to options on financial assets.

Another problem with the traditional NPV approach lies in the estimation of the appropriate risk-adjusted discount rate for the base project (i.e., the project without embedded options). The companies that are used to estimate a proxy beta for the project in the three-step procedure above have expansion options and abandonment options of their own. Their betas reflect these options and may not therefore be appropriate for estimating a beta for the base project.

In the next section we explain how the risk-neutral valuation arguments in Chapters 10, 12, and 21 can be extended to value projects dependent on multiple sources of uncertainty. The method requires estimates of market prices of risk for each source of uncertainty. Approaches for estimating market prices of risk are outlined in Section 28.3.

## 28.2 EXTENSION OF THE RISK-NEUTRAL VALUATION FRAMEWORK

Consider an asset whose price, $f$, depends on a variable $\theta$ and time $t$. (Later we will extend the analysis to the situation where there is more than one variable.) Assume that the process followed by $\theta$ is

$$\frac{d\theta}{\theta} = m \, dt + s \, dz$$

where $dz$ is a Wiener process. The parameters $m$ and $s$ are the expected growth rate in $\theta$ and the volatility of $\theta$, respectively. We assume that the parameters depend only on $\theta$ and $t$. The variable $\theta$

need not be a financial variable. It could be something as far removed from financial markets as the temperature in the center of New Orleans.

The asset price $f$ follows a process of the form

$$df = \mu f\, dt + \sigma f\, dz$$

The analysis in Section 21.1 shows that

$$\frac{\mu - r}{\sigma} = \lambda \tag{28.1}$$

where $r$ is the risk-free rate and $\lambda$ is the market price of risk for $\theta$.

Because $f$ is a function of $\theta$ and $t$ we can use Itô's lemma in Appendix 11A to express $\mu$ and $\sigma$ in terms of $m$ an $s$. The result is

$$\mu f = m\theta \frac{\partial f}{\partial \theta} + \frac{\partial f}{\partial t} + \tfrac{1}{2}s^2\theta^2 \frac{\partial^2 f}{\partial \theta^2}$$

and

$$\sigma f = s\theta \frac{\partial f}{\partial \theta}$$

Substituting into equation (28.1) leads to the following differential equation that must be satisfied by $f$:

$$\frac{\partial f}{\partial t} + \theta \frac{\partial f}{\partial \theta}(m - \lambda s) + \tfrac{1}{2}s^2\theta^2 \frac{\partial^2 f}{\partial \theta^2} = rf \tag{28.2}$$

Equation (28.2) is structurally very similar to the Black–Scholes differential equation (12.15). As we would expect, it is exactly the same as the Black–Scholes differential equation when $\theta$ is $S$, the price of a non-dividend-paying stock. This is because $\theta$ is then the price of an investment asset and from equation (28.1) must satisfy $m - r = \lambda s$, so that the second term in equation (28.2) becomes

$$r\theta \frac{\partial f}{\partial \theta}$$

Comparing equation (28.2) with equation (13A.4), we see that the differential equation for the price of an asset dependent on $\theta$ is the same as that for a derivative dependent on an asset providing a dividend yield equal to $q$, where $q = r - m + \lambda s$. This observation leads to a way of extending the traditional risk-neutral valuation result.

### Extension of Traditional Risk-Neutral Valuation

Any solution to equation (13A.4) for $S$ is a solution to equation (28.2) for $\theta$, and vice versa, when the substitution

$$q = r - m + \lambda s$$

is made. As explained in Section 13.2, we know how to solve (13A.4) using risk-neutral valuation. This involves setting the expected growth rate of $S$ equal to $r - q$ and discounting expected payoffs at the risk-free interest rate. It follows that we can solve equation (28.2) by setting the expected growth of $\theta$ equal to

$$r - (r - m + \lambda s) = m - \lambda s$$

and discounting expected payoffs at the risk-free interest rate.

In general, any asset dependent on $\theta$ can be valued by reducing the expected growth rate of $\theta$ by $\lambda s$, from $m$ to $m - \lambda s$, and then behaving as though the world is risk neutral. The procedure is to calculate expected cash flows based on the assumption that $\theta$'s expected growth rate is $m - \lambda s$ and discount these cash flows at the risk-free rate.

**Example 28.1**   The cost of renting commercial real estate in a certain city is quoted as the amount that would be paid per square foot per year in a new five-year rental agreement. The current cost is $30 per square foot. The expected growth rate in the cost is 12% per annum, its volatility is 20% per annum, and its market price of risk is 0.3. A company has the opportunity to pay $1 million now for the option to rent 100,000 square feet at $35 per square foot for a five-year period starting in two years. The risk-free rate is 5% per annum (assumed constant). Define $V$ as the quoted cost per square foot of office space in two years. We make the simplifying assumption that rent is paid annually in advance. The payoff from the option is

$$100{,}000 A \max(V - 35, \, 0)$$

where $A$ is an annuity factor:

$$A = 1 + 1 \times e^{-0.05 \times 1} + 1 \times e^{-0.05 \times 2} + 1 \times e^{-0.05 \times 3} + 1 \times e^{-0.05 \times 4} = 4.5355$$

The expected payoff in a risk-neutral world is therefore

$$100{,}000 \times 4.5355 \times \hat{E}[\max(V - 35, \, 0)] = 453{,}550 \, \hat{E}[\max(V - 35, \, 0)]$$

where $\hat{E}$ denotes the expectation in a risk-neutral world. Using the result in equation (12A.1), this is

$$453{,}550[\hat{E}(V)N(d_1) - 35N(d_2)]$$

where

$$d_1 = \frac{\ln[\hat{E}(V)/35] + 0.2^2 \times 2/2}{0.2\sqrt{2}}$$

$$d_2 = \frac{\ln[\hat{E}(V)/35] - 0.2^2 \times 2/2}{0.2\sqrt{2}}$$

The expected growth rate in the cost of commercial real estate in a risk-neutral world is $m - \lambda s$, where $m$ is the real-world growth rate, $s$ is the volatility, and $\lambda$ is the market price of risk. In this case, $m = 0.12$, $s = 0.2$, and $\lambda = 0.3$, so that the expected risk-neutral growth rate is 0.06 or 6% per year. It follows that $\hat{E}(V) = 30e^{0.06 \times 2} = 33.82$ Substituting this in the expression above gives the expected payoff in a risk-neutral world as $1.5015 million. Discounting at the risk-free rate the value of the option is $1.5015e^{-0.05 \times 2} = \$1.3586$ million. This shows that it is worth paying $1 million for the option.

The risk-neutral valuation result in Chapter 12 is a particular case of the more general result we have derived here. To see this, suppose that $\theta$ is the price of a non-dividend-paying stock. From equation (28.1),

$$m - r = \lambda s$$

or

$$m - \lambda s = r$$

which shows that changing the expected growth rate of $\theta$ to $m - \lambda s$ involves setting the return from the stock equal to the risk-free rate of interest.

It is interesting to note that our extension of the traditional risk-neutral valuation arguments in Chapters 10 and 12 is more subtle than it first appears. When $\theta$ is not the price of an investment asset, the risk-neutral valuation argument does not necessarily tell us anything about what would happen in a risk-neutral world. It simply states that changing the expected growth rate of $\theta$ from $m$ to $m - \lambda s$ and then behaving as though the world is risk neutral gives the correct values for derivatives.[2] For convenience, however, we will refer to a world where expected growth rates are changed from $m$ to $m - \lambda s$ as a risk-neutral world.

### Several Underlying Variables

We now extend the analysis by supposing that there are $n$ variables, $\theta_1, \theta_2, \ldots, \theta_n$ following stochastic processes

$$\frac{d\theta_i}{\theta_i} = m_i \, dt + s_i \, dz_i \tag{28.3}$$

for $i = 1, 2, \ldots, n$, where the $dz_i$ $(1 \leqslant i \leqslant n)$ are Wiener processes. The parameters $m_i$ and $s_i$ are expected growth rates and volatilities and may be functions of the $\theta_i$ and time $t$. The instantaneous correlation between $\theta_i$ and $\theta_j$ will be denoted by $\rho_{ij}$. The process for the price, $f$, of an asset that is dependent on the $\theta_i$ has the form

$$\frac{df}{f} = \mu \, dt + \sum_{i=1}^{n} \sigma_i \, dz_i \tag{28.4}$$

In this equation, $\mu$ is the expected return from the asset and $\sigma_i \, dz_i$ is the component of the risk of this return attributable to $\theta_i$.

Equation (21.13) shows that

$$\mu - r = \sum_{i=1}^{n} \lambda_i \sigma_i \tag{28.5}$$

where $\lambda_i$ is the market price of risk for $\theta_i$. Itô's lemma in Appendix 21A can be used to express $\mu$ and $\sigma_i$ in terms of the $m_i$ and $s_i$. Equation (28.5) then leads (see Problem 28.4) to

$$\frac{\partial f}{\partial t} + \sum_i \theta_i \frac{\partial f}{\partial \theta_i} (m_i - \lambda_i s_i) + \frac{1}{2} \sum_{i,k} \rho_{ik} s_i s_k \theta_i \theta_k \frac{\partial^2 f}{\partial \theta_i \, \partial \theta_k} = rf \tag{28.6}$$

Our risk-neutral valuation arguments presented earlier concerning differential equation (28.2) can be extended to cover the more general differential equation (28.6). As a result, we find that an asset can always be valued as if the world were risk neutral, provided that the expected growth rate of each underlying variable is assumed to be $m_i - \lambda_i s_i$ rather than $m_i$. The volatility of the variables and the coefficient of correlation between variables are not changed. This result was first developed by Cox, Ingersoll, and Ross and represents an important extension to the basic risk-neutral valuation argument.[3] The valuation methodology is valid when the asset's cash flow at a time $T$

---

[2] To illustrate this point, suppose that $\theta$ is the temperature in the center of New Orleans. The process followed by $\theta$ clearly does not depend on risk preferences (at least, not the risk preferences of human beings), but it is possible that there is a nonzero market price of risk associated with this variable because of the relationship between temperatures and agricultural production. We might, therefore, have to adjust the drift of the process when valuing derivatives dependent on $\theta$.

[3] See Lemma 4 in J. C. Cox, J. E. Ingersoll, and S. A. Ross, "An Intertemporal General Equilibrium Model of Asset Prices," *Econometrica*, 53 (1985), 363–84.

is some function of the paths followed by the $\theta_i$ up to time $T$, as well as when it is dependent only on the values of the $\theta_i$ at time $T$.

## 28.3 ESTIMATING THE MARKET PRICE OF RISK

The risk-neutral valuation approach to evaluating an investment avoids the need to estimate risk-adjusted discount rates in the way described in Section 28.1, but it does require the market price of risk parameters for all stochastic variables. When historical data are available on a particular variable, its market price of risk can be estimated using the capital asset pricing model. To show how this is done, we consider an investment asset dependent solely on the variable and define:

$\mu$ : Expected return of the investment asset

$\sigma$ : Volatility of the return of an investment asset

$\lambda$ : Market price of risk of the variable

$\rho$ : Instantaneous correlation between the percentage changes in the variable and returns on a broad index of stock market prices

$\mu_m$ : Expected return on broad index of stock market prices

$\sigma_m$ : Volatility of return on the broad index of stock market prices

$r$ : Short-term risk free rate

Because the investment asset is dependent solely on the market variable, the instantaneous correlation between its return and the broad index of stock market prices is also $\rho$. From the continuous-time version of the capital asset pricing model, we have

$$\mu - r = \frac{\rho \sigma}{\sigma_m}(\mu_m - r)$$

From equation (28.1), another expression for $\mu - r$ is

$$\mu - r = \lambda \sigma$$

It follows that

$$\lambda = \frac{\rho}{\sigma_m}(\mu_m - r) \tag{28.7}$$

This equation can be used to estimate $\lambda$.

**Example 28.2** A historical analysis of company's sales, quarter by quarter, show that percentage changes in sales have a correlation of 0.3 with returns on the S&P 500 index. The volatility of the S&P 500 is 20% per annum and, based on historical data, the expected excess return of the S&P 500 over the risk-free rate is 5%. Equation (28.7) estimates the market price of risk for the company's sales as

$$\frac{0.3}{0.2} \times 0.05 = 0.075$$

When no historical data are available for the particular variable under consideration other similar variables can sometimes be used as proxies. For example, if a plant is being constructed to manufacture a new product, data can be collected on the sales of other similar products. The correlation of the new product with the market index can then be assumed to be the same as that of these other products. In some cases the estimate of $\rho$ in equation (28.7) must be based on subjective judgment. If an analyst is convinced that a particular variable is unrelated to the performance of a market index, its market price of risk should be set to zero.

For some variables it is not necessary to estimate the market price of risk because the process followed by a variable in a risk-neutral world can be estimated directly. For example, if the variable is the price of an investment asset, its total return in a risk-neutral world is the risk-free rate. If the variable is the short-term interest rate, $r$, Chapter 23 shows how a risk-neutral process can be estimated from the initial term structure of interest rates. Later in this chapter we will show how the risk-neutral process for a commodity can be estimated from futures prices.

## 28.4 APPLICATION TO THE VALUATION OF A NEW BUSINESS

Traditional methods of business valuation, such as applying a price/earnings multiplier to current earnings, do not work well for new businesses. Typically a company's earnings are negative during its early years as it attempts to gain market share and establish relationships with customers. The company must be valued by estimating future earnings and cash flows under different scenarios.

The company's future cash flows typically depend on a number of variables such as sales, variable costs as a percent of sales, fixed costs, and so on. Single estimates should be sufficient for some of the variables. For key variables a risk-neutral stochastic process should be estimated as outlined in the previous two sections. A Monte Carlo simulation can then be carried out to generate alternative scenarios for the net cash flows per year in a risk-neutral world. It is likely that under some of these scenarios the company does very well and under others it becomes bankrupt and ceases operations. (The simulation must have a built-in rule for determining when bankruptcy happens.) The value of the company is the present value of the expected cash flow in each year using the risk-free rate for discounting.

Schwartz and Moon (2000) applied this approach to the internet start up, Amazon.com, at the end of 1999.[4] They assumed that the company's sales revenue, $R$, and its revenue growth rate, $\mu$, are stochastic.[5] Their model is

$$\frac{dR}{R} = \mu \, dt + \sigma(t) \, dz_1$$

with

$$d\mu = \kappa(\bar{\mu} - \mu) \, dt + \eta(t) \, dz_2$$

These equations show that the revenue has an expected growth rate $\mu$, which itself follows a stochastic process. The stochastic process for $\mu$ is mean reverting to a long-run average growth rate $\bar{\mu}$ at rate $\kappa$.

The volatility of revenues, $\sigma(t)$, was assumed to be deterministic and to decrease exponentially from an initial level of 10% per quarter to a long-run average level of 5% per quarter. The standard deviation of the sales growth rate, $\eta(t)$, was also assumed to be deterministic. It decreased exponentially from an initial level of 3% per quarter to zero. The initial sales level was $356 million

---

[4] E. S. Schwartz and M. Moon, "Rational Pricing of Internet Companies," *Financial Analysts Journal*, May/June 2000, 62–75.

[5] Strictly speaking, $R$ is the instantaneous rate at which revenues are generated. When discretized, the stochastic processes can be used to calculate the sample changes in the revenue and its growth rate from one quarter to the next.

per quarter and the initial sales growth rate was 11% per quarter. The values of $\kappa$ and $\bar{\mu}$ were 7% per quarter and 1.5% per quarter, respectively. The two Wiener processes $dz_1$ and $dz_2$ were assumed to be uncorrelated.

Schwartz and Moon assumed that cost of goods sold would be 75% of sales, other variable expenses would be 19% of sales, and fixed expenses would be $75 million per quarter.[6] The initial tax loss carry forward was $559 million and the tax rate was assumed to be 35%.

The market price of risk, $\lambda_R$, for $R$ was estimated from historical data using the approach described in the previous section. The market price of risk for $\mu$ was assumed to be zero. The risk-neutral stochastic process for $R$ was therefore

$$\frac{dR}{R} = (\mu - \lambda_R \sigma)\,dt + \sigma\,dz_1$$

while the risk-neutral process for $\mu$ was the same as the real-world process given above.

The time horizon for the analysis was 25 years and the terminal value of the company was assumed to be ten times pretax operating profit. The initial cash position was $906 million and the company was assumed to go bankrupt if the cash balance became negative.

Different future scenarios were generated using Monte Carlo simulation. The evaluation of the scenarios involved taking account of the possible exercise of convertible bonds and the possible exercise of employee stock options. The value of the company to the shareholders was calculated as the present value of the net cash flows discounted at the risk-free rate.

The market price of Amazon.com's shares at the end of 1999 was $76.125. The price per share given by the Monte Carlo simulation based on the assumptions we have outlined was $12.42. However, Schwartz and Moon point out that a small change in the assumption about the initial value of $\eta$ leads to a big change in the price per share. For example, when $\eta(0)$ was increased from 3% to 6%, the share price given by the Monte Carlo simulation increased to about $100.

## 28.5 COMMODITY PRICES

Many investments involve uncertainties related to future commodity prices. Often, futures prices can be used to estimate the risk-neutral stochastic process for a commodity price directly. Commodity prices are therefore similar to investment assets in that the need to estimate the market price of risk directly can be avoided.

From equation (13.16) the expected future price of the commodity in a risk-neutral world is its futures price. If we assume that the growth rate in the commodity price is dependent solely on time and that the volatility of the commodity price is constant, the risk-neutral process for the commodity price, $S$, has the form

$$\frac{dS}{S} = \mu(t)\,dt + \sigma\,dz \qquad (28.8)$$

then

$$F(t) = \hat{E}[S(t)] = S(0)e^{\int_0^t \mu(\tau)\,d\tau}$$

---

[6] This means that, in the simulation, variable costs were 94% of sales. Schwartz and Moon point out that Amazon.com's variable costs had historically been more than 100% of sales. Amazon.com's future profitability depended critically on its ability to reduce the cost of goods sold as a percent of sales, and Schwartz and Moon suggest that it could be appropriate to develop a more elaborate model where cost of goods sold is modeled stochastically.

where $F(t)$ is the futures price for a contract with maturity $t$ and $\hat{E}$ denotes the expected value in a risk-neutral world. It follows that

$$\ln F(t) = \ln S(0) + \int_0^t \mu(\tau)\, d\tau$$

Differentiating both sides with respect to time, we obtain

$$\mu(t) = \frac{\partial}{\partial t}[\ln F(t)]$$

**Example 28.3**  Suppose that the futures prices of live cattle at the end of July 2002 are (in cents per pound) as follows:

| | |
|---|---|
| August 2002 | 62.20 |
| October 2002 | 60.60 |
| December 2002 | 62.70 |
| February 2003 | 63.37 |
| April 2003 | 64.42 |
| June 2003 | 64.40 |

These can be used to estimate the expected growth rate in live cattle prices in a risk-neutral world. For example, when the model in equation (28.8) is used, the expected growth rate in live cattle prices between October and December 2002 in a risk-neutral world is

$$\ln\left(\frac{62.70}{60.60}\right) = 0.034$$

or 3.4% with continuous compounding. On an annualized basis this is 20.4% per annum.

**Example 28.4**  Suppose that the futures prices of live cattle are as in Example 28.3. A certain breeding decision would involve an investment of $100,000 now and expenditures of $20,000 in three months, six months, and nine months. The result is expected to be that extra cattle will be available for sale at the end of the year. There are two major uncertainties: the number of pounds of extra cattle that will be available for sale and the price per pound. The expected number of pounds is 300,000. The expected price of cattle in one year in a risk-neutral world is, from Example 28.3, 64.40 cents per pound. Assuming that the risk-free rate of interest is 10% per annum, the value of the investment (in thousands of dollars) is

$$-100 - 20e^{-0.1\times0.25} - 20e^{-0.1\times0.50} - 20e^{-0.1\times0.75} + 300 \times 0.644e^{-0.1\times1} = 17.729$$

This assumes that any uncertainty about the extra amount of cattle that will be available for sale has zero systematic risk and that there is no correlation between the amount of cattle that will be available for sale and the price.

### A Mean-Reverting Process

It can be argued that the process in equation (28.8) for commodity prices is too simplistic. In practice, most commodity prices follow mean-reverting processes. They tend to get pulled back to a central value. A more realistic process than equation (28.8) for the risk-neutral process followed by the commodity price, $S$, is

$$d\ln S = [\theta(t) - a\ln S]\, dt + \sigma\, dz \tag{28.9}$$

This incorporates mean reversion and is analogous to the lognormal process assumed for the short-term interest rate in Chapter 23. The trinomial tree methodology in Section 23.12 can be adapted to construct a tree for $S$ and determine the value of $\theta(t)$, so that $F(t) = \hat{E}[S(t)]$.

We will illustrate this process by building a three-step tree for oil. Suppose that the spot price of oil is $20 per barrel and the one-year, two-year, and three-year futures prices are $22, $23, and $24, respectively. Suppose that $a = 0.1$ and $\sigma = 0.2$ in equation (28.9). We first define a variable $X$ that is initially zero follows the process

$$dX = -a\,dt + \sigma\,dz \tag{28.10}$$

Using the procedure in Section 23.12, a trinomial tree can be constructed for $X$. This is shown in Figure 28.1.

The variable $\ln S$ follows the same process as $X$ except for a time-dependent drift. Analogously to Section 23.12, we can convert the tree for $X$ to a tree for $\ln S$ by displacing the positions of nodes. This tree is shown in Figure 28.2. The initial node corresponds to an oil price of 20, so the displacement for that node is $\ln 20$. Suppose that the displacements of the nodes at one year is $\alpha_1$. The values of the $X$ at the three nodes at the one-year point are $+0.3464$, $0$, and $-0.3464$. The corresponding values of $\ln S$ are $0.3464 + \alpha_1$, $\alpha_1$, and $-0.3464 + \alpha_1$. The values of $S$ are therefore $e^{0.3464+\alpha_1}$, $e^{\alpha_1}$, and $e^{-0.3464+\alpha_1}$, respectively. We require the average value of $S$ to equal the futures price. This means that

$$0.1667e^{0.3464+\alpha_1} + 0.6666e^{\alpha_1} + 0.1667e^{-0.3464+\alpha_1} = 22$$

The solution to this is $\alpha_1 = 3.071$. The values of $S$ at the one-year point are therefore 30.49, 21.56, and 15.25.

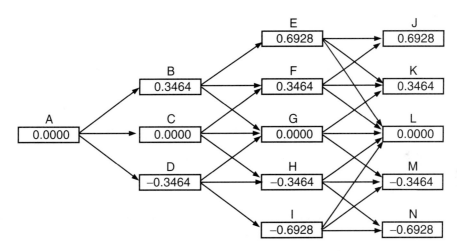

| Node: | A | B | C | D | E | F | G | H | I |
|---|---|---|---|---|---|---|---|---|---|
| $p_u$ | 0.1667 | 0.1217 | 0.1667 | 0.2217 | 0.8867 | 0.1217 | 0.1667 | 0.2217 | 0.0867 |
| $p_m$ | 0.6666 | 0.6566 | 0.6666 | 0.6566 | 0.0266 | 0.6566 | 0.6666 | 0.6566 | 0.0266 |
| $p_d$ | 0.1667 | 0.2217 | 0.1667 | 0.1217 | 0.0867 | 0.2217 | 0.1667 | 0.1217 | 0.8867 |

**Figure 28.1** Tree for $X$. Constructing this tree is the first stage in constructing a tree for the spot price of oil, $S$. Here, $p_u$, $p_m$, and $p_d$ are the probabilities of "up", "middle", and "down" movements from a node

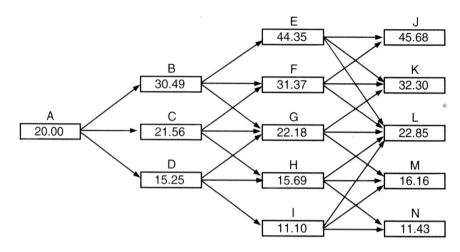

| Node: | A | B | C | D | E | F | G | H | I |
|---|---|---|---|---|---|---|---|---|---|
| $p_u$ | 0.1667 | 0.1217 | 0.1667 | 0.2217 | 0.8867 | 0.1217 | 0.1667 | 0.2217 | 0.0867 |
| $p_m$ | 0.6666 | 0.6566 | 0.6666 | 0.6566 | 0.0266 | 0.6566 | 0.6666 | 0.6566 | 0.0266 |
| $p_d$ | 0.1667 | 0.2217 | 0.1667 | 0.1217 | 0.0867 | 0.2217 | 0.1667 | 0.1217 | 0.8867 |

**Figure 28.2** Tree for spot price of oil. Here, $p_u$, $p_m$, and $p_d$ are the probabilities of "up", "middle", and "down" movements from a node

At the two-year point, we first calculate the probabilities of nodes E, F, G, H, and I being reached from the probabilities of nodes B, C, and D being reached. The probability of reaching node F is the probability of reaching node B times the probability of moving from B to F plus the probability of reaching node C times the probability of moving from C to F. This is

$$0.1667 \times 0.6566 + 0.6666 \times 0.1667 = 0.2206$$

The probabilities of reaching nodes E, F, G, H, and I are 0.0203, 0.2206, 0.5183, 0.2206, and 0.0203, respectively. The amount, $\alpha_2$, by which the nodes at time two years are displaced must satisfy

$$0.0203e^{0.6928+\alpha_2} + 0.2206e^{0.3464+\alpha_2} + 0.5183e^{\alpha_2} + 0.2206e^{-0.3464+\alpha_2} + 0.0203e^{-0.6928+\alpha_2} = 23$$

The solution to this is $\alpha_2 = 3.099$. This means that the values of $S$ at the two-year point are 44.35, 31.37, 22.18, 15.69, and 11.10, respectively. A similar calculation can be carried out at time three years. Figure 28.2 shows the resulting tree for $S$. We will illustrate how the tree can be used in the valuation of a real option in the next section.

## 28.6   EVALUATING OPTIONS IN AN INVESTMENT OPPORTUNITY

Most investment projects involve options. These options can add considerable value to the project and are often either ignored or valued incorrectly. Examples of the options embedded in projects are:

1. *Abandonment option.* This is an option to sell or close down a project. It is an American put option on the project's value. The strike price of the option is the liquidation (or resale) value of the project less any closing-down costs. When the liquidation value is low, the strike price can be negative. Abandonment options mitigate the impact of very poor investment outcomes and increase the initial valuation of a project.

2. *Expansion option.* This is the option to make further investments and increase the output if conditions are favorable. It is an American call option on the value of additional capacity. The strike price of the call option is the cost of creating this additional capacity discounted to the time of option exercise. The strike price often depends on the initial investment. If management initially chooses to build capacity in excess of the expected level of output, the strike price can be relatively small.

3. *Contraction option.* This is the option to reduce the scale of a project's operation. It is an American put option on the value of the lost capacity. The strike price is the present value of the future expenditures saved as seen at the time of exercise of the option.

4. *Option to defer.* One of the most important options open to a manager is the option to defer a project. This is an American call option on the value of the project.

5. *Option to extend.* Sometimes it is possible to extend the life of an asset by paying a fixed amount. This is a European call option on the asset's future value.

As a simple example of the evaluation of an investment with an embedded option, consider a company that has to decide whether to invest $15 million to obtain 6 million barrels of oil from a certain source at the rate of 2 million barrels per year for three years. The fixed costs of operating the equipment are $6 million per year and the variable costs are $17 per barrel. We assume that the risk-free interest rate is 10% per annum for all maturities, that the spot price of oil is $20 per barrel, and that the one-, two-, and three-year futures prices are $22, $23, and $24 per barrel, respectively. We assume that the stochastic process for oil prices has been estimated as equation (28.9) with $a = 0.1$ and $\sigma = 0.2$. This means that the tree in Figure 28.2 describes the behavior of oil prices in a risk-neutral world.

First assume that the project has no embedded options. The expected prices of oil in one, two, and three years' time in a risk-neutral world are $22, $23, and $24, respectively. The expected payoff from the project (in millions of dollars) in a risk-neutral world can be calculated from the cost data as 4.0, 6.0, and 8.0 in years 1, 2, and 3, respectively. The value of the project is therefore

$$-15.0 + 4.0e^{-0.1 \times 1} + 6.0e^{-0.1 \times 2} + 8.0e^{0.1 \times 3} = -0.54$$

This analysis indicates that the project should not be undertaken because it would reduce shareholder wealth by 0.54 million.

Figure 28.3 shows the value of the project at each node of Figure 28.2. This is calculated from Figure 28.2. Consider, for example, node H. The is a 0.2217 probability that the price of oil at the end of the third year is 22.85, so that the third-year profit is $2 \times 22.85 - 2 \times 17 - 6 = 5.70$. Similarly there is a 0.6566 probability that the price of oil at the end of the third year is 16.16, so that the profit is $-7.68$ and there is a 0.1217 probability that the price of oil at the end of the

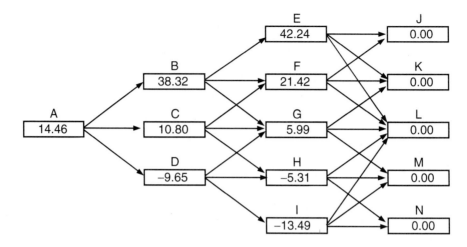

| Node: | A | B | C | D | E | F | G | H | I |
|---|---|---|---|---|---|---|---|---|---|
| $p_u$ | 0.1667 | 0.1217 | 0.1667 | 0.2217 | 0.8867 | 0.1217 | 0.1667 | 0.2217 | 0.0867 |
| $p_m$ | 0.6666 | 0.6566 | 0.6666 | 0.6566 | 0.0266 | 0.6566 | 0.6666 | 0.6566 | 0.0266 |
| $p_d$ | 0.1667 | 0.2217 | 0.1667 | 0.1217 | 0.0867 | 0.2217 | 0.1667 | 0.1217 | 0.8867 |

**Figure 28.3** Valuation of base project with no embedded options. Here, $p_u$, $p_m$, and $p_d$ are the probabilities of "up", "middle", and "down" movements from a node

third year is 11.43, so that the profit is $-17.14$. The value of the project at node H in Figure 28.3 is therefore

$$[0.2217 \times 5.70 + 0.6566 \times (-7.68) + 0.1217 \times (-17.14)]e^{-0.1 \times 1} = -5.31$$

As another example, consider node C. There is a 0.1667 chance of moving to node F where the oil price is 31.37. The second year cash flow is then $2 \times 31.37 - 2 \times 17 - 6 = 22.74$. The value of subsequent cash flows at node F is 21.42. The total value of the project if we move to node F is therefore $21.42 + 22.74 = 44.16$. Similarly, the total value of the project if we move to nodes G and H are 10.35 and $-13.93$, respectively. The value of the project at node C is therefore

$$[0.1667 \times 44.16 + 0.6666 \times 10.35 + 0.1667 \times (-13.93)]e^{-0.1 \times 1} = 10.80$$

Figure 28.3 shows that the value of the project at the initial node, A, is 14.46. When the initial investment is taken into account the value of the project is therefore $-0.54$. This is in agreement with our earlier calculations.

Suppose now that the company has the option to abandon the project at any time. We suppose that there is no salvage value and no further payments are required once the project has been abandoned. Abandonment is an American put option with a strike price of zero and is valued in Figure 28.4. The put option should not be exercised at nodes E, F, and G because the value of the project is positive at these nodes. It should be exercised at nodes H and I. The value of the put option is 5.31 and 13.49 at nodes H and I, respectively. Rolling back through the tree, we see that the value of the abandonment put option at node D, if it is not exercised, is

$$(0.1217 \times 13.49 + 0.6566 \times 5.31 + 0.2217 \times 0)e^{-0.1 \times 1} = 4.64$$

The value of exercising the put option at node D is 9.65. This is greater than 4.64, and so the put should be exercised at node D. The value of the put option at node C is

$$[0.1667 \times 0 + 0.6666 \times 0 + 0.1667 \times (5.31)]e^{-0.1 \times 1} = 0.80$$

and the value at node A is

$$(0.1667 \times 0 + 0.6666 \times 0.80 + 0.1667 \times 9.65)e^{-0.1 \times 1} = 1.94$$

The abandonment option is therefore worth $1.94 million. It increases the value of the project from −$0.54 million to +$1.40 million. A project that was previously unattractive now has a positive value to shareholders.

Suppose next that the company has no abandonment option. Instead it has the option at any time to increase the scale of the project by 20%. The cost of doing this is $2 million. Oil production increases from 2.0 to 2.4 million barrels. Variable costs remain $17 per barrel and fixed costs increase by 20% from $6.0 million to $7.2 million. This is an American call option to buy 20% of the base project in Figure 28.3 for $2 million. The option is valued in Figure 28.5. At node E, the option should be exercised. The payoff is $0.2 \times 42.24 - 2 = 6.45$. At node F, it should also be exercised for a payoff of $0.2 \times 21.42 - 2 = 2.28$. At nodes G, H, and I, the option should not be

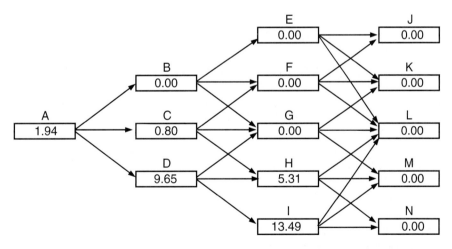

| Node: | A | B | C | D | E | F | G | H | I |
|---|---|---|---|---|---|---|---|---|---|
| $p_u$ | 0.1667 | 0.1217 | 0.1667 | 0.2217 | 0.8867 | 0.1217 | 0.1667 | 0.2217 | 0.0867 |
| $p_m$ | 0.6666 | 0.6566 | 0.6666 | 0.6566 | 0.0266 | 0.6566 | 0.6666 | 0.6566 | 0.0266 |
| $p_d$ | 0.1667 | 0.2217 | 0.1667 | 0.1217 | 0.0867 | 0.2217 | 0.1667 | 0.1217 | 0.8867 |

**Figure 28.4** Valuation of option to abandon the project. Here, $p_u$, $p_m$, and $p_d$ are the probabilities of "up", "middle", and "down" movements from a node

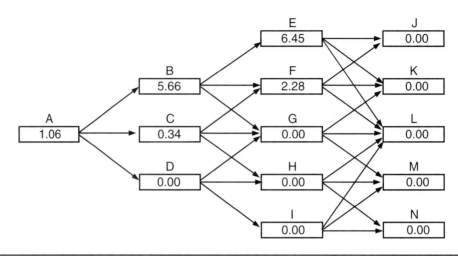

| Node: | A | B | C | D | E | F | G | H | I |
|-------|-----|-----|-----|-----|-----|-----|-----|-----|-----|
| $p_u$ | 0.1667 | 0.1217 | 0.1667 | 0.2217 | 0.8867 | 0.1217 | 0.1667 | 0.2217 | 0.0867 |
| $p_m$ | 0.6666 | 0.6566 | 0.6666 | 0.6566 | 0.0266 | 0.6566 | 0.6666 | 0.6566 | 0.0266 |
| $p_d$ | 0.1667 | 0.2217 | 0.1667 | 0.1217 | 0.0867 | 0.2217 | 0.1667 | 0.1217 | 0.8867 |

**Figure 28.5**  Valuation of option to expand the project. Here, $p_u$, $p_m$, and $p_d$ are the probabilities of "up", "middle", and "down" movements from a node

exercised. At node B, exercising is worth more than waiting and the option is worth $0.2 \times 38.32 - 2 = 5.66$. At node C, if the option is not exercised, it is worth

$$(0.1667 \times 2.28 + 0.6666 \times 0.00 + 0.1667 \times 0.00)e^{-0.1 \times 1} = 0.34$$

If the option is exercised it is worth $0.2 \times 10.80 - 2 = 0.16$. The option should therefore not be exercised at node C. At node A, the option is worth

$$(0.1667 \times 5.66 + 0.6666 \times 0.34 + 0.1667 \times 0.00)e^{-0.1 \times 1} = 1.06$$

If the option is not exercised, it is worth $0.2 \times 14.46 - 2 = 0.89$. Early exercise is therefore not optimal at node A. In this case, the option increases the value of the project from $-0.54$ to $+0.52$. Again we find that a project that previously had a negative value now has a positive value.

The expansion option in Figure 28.5 is relatively easy to value because, once the option has been exercised, all subsequent cash inflows and outflows increase by 20%. In the case where fixed costs remain the same or increase by less than 20%, it is necessary to keep track of more information at the nodes of Figure 28.3. Specifically, we need to record:

1. The present value of subsequent fixed costs
2. The present value of subsequent revenues net of variable costs

The payoff from exercising the option can then be calculated.

When a project has two or more options, they are in general not independent. The value of having both option A and option B is typically not the sum of the values of the two options. To illustrate this, suppose that the company we have been considering has both abandonment and expansion options. The project cannot be expanded if it has already be abandoned. Moreover the value of the put option to abandon depends on whether the project has been expanded.[7]

These interactions between the options in our example can be handled by defining four states at each node:

1. Not already abandoned; not already expanded
2. Not already abandoned; already expanded
3. Already abandoned; not already expanded
4. Already abandoned; already expanded

When we roll back through the tree, we calculate the combined value of the options at each node for all four alternatives. This approach to valuing path-dependent options is discussed in more detail in Section 20.5.

When there are several stochastic variables, the value of the base project is usually determined by Monte Carlo simulation. The valuation of the project's embedded options is then more difficult because a Monte Carlo simulation works from the beginning to the end of a project. When we reach a certain point, we do not have information on the present value of the project's future cash flows. However, the techniques mentioned in Section 20.9 for valuing American options using Monte Carlo simulation can sometimes be used.

As an illustration of this point, Schwartz and Moon (2000) explain how their Amazon.com analysis outlined in Section 28.4 could be extended to take account of the option to abandon (i.e., option to declare bankruptcy) when the value of future cash flows is negative.[8] At each time step, a polynomial relationship between the value of not abandoning and variables such as the current revenue, revenue growth rate, volatilities, cash balances, and loss carry forwards is assumed. Each simulation trial provides an observation for obtaining a least-squares estimate of the relationship at each time. This is the Longstaff and Schwartz approach of Section 20.9.[9]

## SUMMARY

In this chapter we have investigated how the ideas developed earlier in the book can be applied to the valuation of real assets and options on real assets. We have shown how the risk-neutral valuation principle can be used to value an asset dependent on a number of variables following diffusion processes. The drift rate of each variable is adjusted to reflect its market price of risk. The value of the asset is then the present value of its expected cash flows discounted at the risk-free rate.

Risk-neutral valuation provides an internally consistent approach to capital investment appraisal. It also makes it possible to value the options that are embedded in many of the projects that are encountered in practice. We have illustrated the approach by applying it to the valuation of Amazon.com at the end of 1999 and the valuation of an oil project.

---

[7] As it happens, the two options do not interact in Figures 28.4 and 28.5. However, the interactions between the options would become an issue if a larger tree with smaller time steps were built.

[8] The analysis in Section 28.4 assumed that bankruptcy occurs when the cash balance falls below zero, but this is not necessarily optimal for Amazon.com.

[9] F. A. Longstaff and E. S. Schwartz, "Valuing American Options by Simulation: A Simple Least-Squares Approach," *Review of Financial Studies*, 14, no. 1 (Spring 2001), 113–47.

## SUGGESTIONS FOR FURTHER READING

Amran, M., and N. Kulatilaka, *Real Options*, Harvard Business School Press, Boston, MA, 1999.

Copeland, T., T. Koller, and J. Murrin, *Valuation: Measuring and Managing the Value of Companies*, 3rd edn., Wiley, New York, 2000.

Copeland, T., and V. Antikarov, *Real Options: A Practitioners Guide*, Texere, New York, 2001.

Schwartz, E. S., and M. Moon, "Rational Pricing of Internet Companies," *Financial Analysts Journal*, May/June 2000, 62–75.

Trigeorgis, L., *Real Options: Managerial Flexibility and Strategy in Resource Allocation*, MIT Press, Cambridge, MA, 1996.

## QUESTIONS AND PROBLEMS
## (ANSWERS IN SOLUTIONS MANUAL)

28.1. Explain the difference between the net present value approach and the risk-neutral valuation approach for valuing a new capital investment opportunity. What are the advantages of the risk-neutral valuation approach for valuing real options?

28.2. The market price of risk for copper is 0.5, the volatility of copper prices is 20% per annum, the spot price is 80 cents per pound, and the six-month futures price is 75 cents per pound. What is the expected percentage growth rate in copper prices over the next six months?

28.3. Consider a commodity with constant volatility, $\sigma$, and an expected growth rate that is a function solely of time. Show that, in the traditional risk-neutral world,

$$\ln S_T \sim \phi\left(\ln F(T) - \frac{\sigma^2}{2}T, \ \sigma\sqrt{T}\right)$$

where $S_T$ is the value of the commodity at time $T$ and $F(t)$ is the futures price at time zero for a contract maturing at time $t$.

28.4. Prove equation (28.6).

28.5. Derive a relationship between the convenience yield of a commodity and its market price of risk.

28.6. The correlation between a company's gross revenue and the market index is 0.2. The excess return of the market over the risk-free rate is 6% and the volatility of the market index is 18%. What is the market price of risk for the company's revenue?

28.7. A company can buy an option for the delivery of one million barrels of oil in three years at $25 per barrel. The three-year futures price of oil is $24 per barrel. The risk-free interest rate is 5% per annum with continuous compounding and the volatility of the futures price is 20% per annum. How much is the option worth?

28.8. A driver entering into a car lease agreement can obtain the right to buy the car in four years for $10,000. The current value of the car is $30,000. The value of the car, $S$, is expected to follow the process

$$dS = \mu S\,dt + \sigma S\,dz$$

where $\mu = -0.25$, $\sigma = 0.15$, and $dz$ is a Wiener process. The market price of risk for the car price is estimated to be $-0.1$. What is the value of the option? Assume that the risk-free rate for all maturities is 6%.

## ASSIGNMENT QUESTIONS

28.9. Suppose that the spot price, 6-month futures price, and 12-month futures price for wheat are 250, 260, and 270 cents per bushel, respectively. Suppose that the price of wheat follows the process in equation (28.9) with $a = 0.05$ and $\sigma = 0.15$. Construct a two-time-step tree for the price of wheat in a risk-neutral world.

A farmer has a project that involves an expenditure of $10,000 and a further expenditure of $90,000 in six months. It will increase wheat that is harvested and sold by 40,000 bushels in one year. What is the value of the project? Suppose that the farmer can abandon the project in six months and avoid paying the $90,000 cost at that time. What is the value of the abandonment option? Assume a risk-free rate of 5% with continuous compounding.

28.10. In the oil example considered in Section 28.6:
   a. What is the value of the abandonment option if it costs $3 million rather than zero?
   b. What is the value of the expansion option if it costs $5 million rather than $2 million?

# CHAPTER 29

# INSURANCE, WEATHER, AND ENERGY DERIVATIVES

In this chapter we examine some recent innovations in derivatives markets. We explain the products that have been developed to manage weather risk, energy price risk, and insurance risks. Some of the markets that we will talk about are in the early stages of their development. As they mature, we may well see significant changes in both the products that are offered and the ways they are used.

## 29.1  REVIEW OF PRICING ISSUES

In Chapters 10 and 12 we explained the risk-neutral valuation result. This states that if we price a derivative on the assumption that investors are risk neutral then we get the right price—not just in a risk-neutral world, but in all other worlds as well. The correct approach to pricing a derivative is to calculate the expected payoff in a risk-neutral world and discount this expected payoff at the risk-free interest rate.

An alternative pricing approach, often used in the insurance industry, is sometimes referred to as the *actuarial approach*. It involves using historical data to calculate the expected payoff and discounting this expected payoff at the risk-free rate to obtain the price. Historical data give an estimate of the expected payoff in the real world. It follows that the actuarial approach is correct only when the expected payoff from the derivative is the same in both the real world and the risk-neutral world.

We showed in Section 10.7 that, when we move from the real world to the risk-neutral world, the volatilities of variables remain the same but their expected growth rates are liable to change. For example, the expected growth rate of a stock market index decreases by perhaps 4% or 5% when we move from the real world to the risk-neutral world. Our discussion in Section 28.3 shows that the expected growth rate of a variable can reasonably be assumed to be the same in both the real world and the risk-neutral world if the variable has zero systematic risk, so that percentage changes in the variable have zero correlation with stock market returns. We can deduce from this that the actuarial approach to valuing a derivative gives the right answer if all underlying variables have zero systematic risk.

A common feature of all the derivatives we will consider in this chapter is that the actuarial approach can be used. The underlying variables can reasonably be assumed to have zero systematic risk.

## 29.2   WEATHER DERIVATIVES

Many companies are in the position where their performance is liable to be adversely affected by the weather.[1] It makes sense for these companies to consider hedging their weather risk in much the same way as they hedge foreign exchange or interest rate risks.

The first over-the-counter weather derivatives were introduced in 1997. To understand how they work, we explain two variables:

HDD: Heating degree days

CDD: Cooling degree days

A day's HDD is defined as

$$HDD = \max(0,\ 65 - A)$$

and a day's CDD is defined as

$$CDD = \max(0,\ A - 65)$$

where $A$ is the average of the highest and lowest temperature during the day at a specified weather station, measured in degrees Fahrenheit. For example, if the maximum temperature during a day (midnight to midnight) is 68° Fahrenheit and the minimum temperature is 44° Fahrenheit, then $A = 56$. The daily HDD is then 9 and the daily CDD is 0.

A typical over-the-counter product is a forward or option contract providing a payoff dependent on the cumulative HDD or CDD during a period. For example, an investment dealer could in January 2002 sell a client a call option on the cumulative HDD during February 2003 at the Chicago O'Hare Airport weather station with a strike price of 700 and a payment rate of $10,000 per degree day. If the actual cumulative HDD is 820, the payoff is $1.2 million. Often contracts include a payment cap. If the payment cap in our example is $1.5 million, the contract is the equivalent of a bull spread. The client has a long call option on cumulative HDD with a strike price of 700 and a short call option with a strike price of 850.

A day's HDD is a measure of the volume of energy required for heating during the day. A day's CDD is a measure of the volume of energy required for cooling during the day. At the time of writing, most weather derivative contracts are entered into by energy producers and energy consumers. But retailers, supermarket chains, food and drink manufacturers, health service companies, agriculture companies, and companies in the leisure industry are also potential users of weather derivatives. The Weather Risk Management Association (www.wrma.org) has been formed to serve the interests of the weather risk management industry.

In September 1999 the Chicago Mercantile Exchange began trading weather futures and European options on weather futures. The contracts are on the cumulative HDD and CDD for a month observed at a weather station.[2] The contracts are settled in cash just after the end of the month once the HDD and CDD are known. One futures contract is on $100 times the cumulative HDD or CDD. The HDD and CDD are calculated by a company, Earth Satellite Corporation, using automated data-collection equipment.

The temperature at a certain location can reasonably be assumed to have zero systematic risk. It follows from Section 29.1 that weather derivatives can be priced using the actuarial approach Consider, for example, the call option on the February 2003 HDD at Chicago O'Hare airport

---

[1] The U.S. Department of Energy has estimated that one-seventh of the U.S. economy is subject to weather risk.

[2] The CME has introduced contracts for 10 different weather stations (Atlanta, Chicago, Cincinnati, Dallas, Des Moines, Las Vegas, New York, Philadelphia, Portland, and Tucson).

mentioned earlier. We could collect 50 years of data and estimate a probability distribution for the HDD. This in turn could be used to provide a probability distribution for the option payoff. Our estimate of the value of the option would be the mean of this distribution discounted at the risk-free rate. We might want to adjust the probability distribution for temperature trends. For example, a linear regression might show that the cumulative February HDD is decreasing at a rate of 10 per year on average. The output from the regression can then be used to estimate a trend-adjusted probability distribution for the HDD in February 2003.

## 29.3 ENERGY DERIVATIVES

Energy companies are among the most active and sophisticated users of derivatives. Many energy products trade in both the over-the-counter market and on exchanges. In this section we will examine the trading in crude oil, natural gas, and electricity derivatives.

### Crude Oil

Crude oil is one of the most important commodities in the world with global demand amounting to about 65 million barrels (8.9 million tonnes) daily. Ten-year fixed-price supply contracts have been commonplace in the over-the-counter market for many years. These are swaps where oil at a fixed price is exchanged for oil at a floating price.

In the 1970s the price of oil was highly volatile. The 1973 war in the Middle East led to a tripling of oil prices. The fall of the Shah of Iran in the late 1970s again increased prices. These events led oil producers and users to a realization that they needed more sophisticated tools for managing oil price risk. In the 1980s both the over-the-counter market and the exchange-traded market developed products to meet this need.

In the over-the-counter market, virtually any derivative that is available on common stocks or stock indices is now available with oil as the underlying asset. Swaps, forward contracts, and options are popular. Contracts sometimes require settlement in cash and sometimes require settlement by physical delivery (i.e., by delivery of the oil).

Exchange-traded contracts are also popular. New York Mercantile Exchange (NYMEX) and the International Petroleum Exchange (IPE) trade a number of oil futures and futures options contracts. Some of the futures contracts are settled in cash; others are settled by physical delivery. For example, the Brent crude oil futures traded on the IPE has cash settlement based on the Brent index price; the light sweet crude oil futures traded on NYMEX requires physical delivery. In both cases the amount of oil underlying one contract is 1,000 barrels. NYMEX also trades popular contracts on two refined products: heating oil and gasoline. In both cases one contract is for the delivery of 42,000 gallons.

### Natural Gas

The natural gas industry throughout the world has been going through a period of deregulation and the elimination of state monopolies. The supplier of natural gas is now not necessarily the same company as the producer of the gas. Suppliers are faced with the problem of meeting daily demand.

A typical over-the-counter contract is for the delivery of a specified amount of natural gas at a roughly uniform rate over a one-month period. Forward contracts, options, and swaps are available in the over-the-counter market. The seller of gas is usually responsible for moving the gas through pipelines to the specified location. NYMEX trades a contract for the delivery of 10,000 million British thermal units of natural gas. The contract, if not closed out, requires physical delivery to be made during the delivery month at a roughly uniform rate to a particular hub in Louisiana. The IPE trades a similar contract in London.

### Electricity

Electricity is an unusual commodity because it cannot easily be stored.[3] The maximum supply of electricity in a region at any moment is determined by the maximum capacity of all the electricity-producing plants in the region. In the United States there are 140 regions known as *control areas*. Demand and supply are first matched within a control area, and any excess power is sold to other control areas. It is this excess power that constitutes the wholesale market for electricity. The ability of one control area to sell power to another control area depends on the transmission capacity of the lines between the two areas. Transmission from one area to another involves a transmission cost, charged by the owner of the line, and there are generally some transmission or energy losses.

A major use of electricity is for air-conditioning systems. As a result the demand for electricity, and therefore its price, is much greater in the summer months than in the winter months. The nonstorability of electricity causes occasional very large movements in the spot price. Heat waves have been known to increase the spot price by as much as 1000% for short periods of time.

Like natural gas, electricity has been going through a period of deregulation and the elimination of state monopolies. This has been accompanied by the development of an electricity derivatives market. NYMEX now trades a futures contract on the price of electricity, and there is an active over-the-counter market in forward contracts, options, and swaps. A typical contract (exchange traded or over the counter) allows one side to receive a specified number of megawatt hours for a specified price at a specified location during a particular month. In a $5 \times 8$ contract, power is received for five days a week (Monday to Friday) during the off-peak period (11 p.m. to 7 a.m.) for the specified month. In a $5 \times 16$ contract, power is received five days a week during the on-peak period (7 a.m. to 11 p.m.) for the specified month. In a $7 \times 24$ contract, it is received around the clock every day during the month. Option contracts have either daily exercise or monthly exercise. In the case of daily exercise, the option holder can choose on each day of the month (by giving one day's notice) to receive the specified amount of power at the specified strike price. When there is monthly exercise a single decision on whether to receive power for the whole month at the specified strike price is made at the beginning of the month.

An interesting contract in electricity and natural gas markets is what is known as a *swing option* or *take-and-pay option*. In this a minimum and maximum for the amount of power that must be purchased at a certain price by the option holder is specified for each day during a month and for the month in total. The option holder can change (or swing) the rate at which the power is purchased during the month, but usually there is a limit on the total number of changes that can be made.

### Modeling Energy Prices

As discussed in Section 28.5 a realistic model for a energy and other commodity prices should incorporate both mean reversion and volatility. A reasonable model is equation (28.9):

$$d \ln S = [\theta(t) - a \ln S] dt + \sigma dz \qquad (29.1)$$

---

[3] Electricity producers with spare capacity often use it to pump water to the top of their hydroelectric plants so that it can be used to produce electricity at a later time. This is the closest they can get to storing this commodity.

where $S$ is the energy price, and $a$ and $\sigma$ are constant parameters. The $\theta(t)$ term captures seasonality and trends. Section 28.5 shows how to construct a trinomial tree for this model from futures prices.

The correlation between changes in energy prices and the return on the market is low. It is probably reasonable, therefore, to assume that energy prices behave in the same way in the real world and the risk-neutral world. The parameters in equation (29.1) can therefore be estimated from historical data.

The parameters are different for different sources of energy. For crude oil, the reversion rate parameter, $a$, in equation (29.1) is about 0.5 and the volatility parameter, $\sigma$, is about 20%; for natural gas, $a$ is about 1.0 and $\sigma$ is about 40%; for electricity, $a$ is typically between 10 and 20 while $\sigma$ is 100 to 200%. The seasonality of electricity prices is also greater.[4]

### How an Energy Producer Can Hedge Risks

There are two components to the risks facing an energy producer: one is the price risk; the other is the volume risk. Although prices do adjust to reflect volumes, there is a less-than-perfect relationship between the two, and energy producers have to take both into account when developing a hedging strategy. The price risk can be hedged using the energy derivative contracts discussed in this section. The volume risks can be hedged using the weather derivatives discussed in the previous section.

Define:

$Y$: Profit for a month

$P$: Average energy prices for the month

$T$: Relevant temperature variable (HDD or CDD) for the month

An energy producer can use historical data to obtain a best-fit linear regression relationship of the form

$$Y = a + bP + cT + \epsilon$$

where $\epsilon$ is the error term. The energy producer can then hedge risks for the month by taking a position of $-b$ in energy forwards or futures and a position of $-c$ in weather forwards or futures. The relationship can also be used to analyze the effectiveness of alternative option strategies.

## 29.4  INSURANCE DERIVATIVES

When derivative contracts are used for hedging purposes, they have many of the same characteristics as insurance contracts. Both types of contracts are designed to provide protection against adverse events. It is not surprising that many insurance companies have subsidiaries that trade derivatives and that many of the activities of insurance companies are becoming very similar to those of investment banks.

Traditionally the insurance industry has hedged its exposure to catastrophic (CAT) risks such as hurricanes and earthquakes using a practice known as reinsurance. Reinsurance contracts can take a number of forms. Suppose that an insurance company has an exposure of $100 million to earthquakes in California and wants to limit this to $30 million. One alternative is to enter into

---

[4] For a fuller discussion of the spot price behavior of energy products, see D. Pilipovic, *Energy Risk*, McGraw-Hill, New York, 1997.

annual reinsurance contracts that cover on a pro rata basis 70% of its exposure. If California earthquake claims in a particular year total $50 million, the costs to the company would then be only $15 million. Another more popular alternative, involving lower reinsurance premiums, is to buy a series of reinsurance contracts covering what are known as *excess cost layers*. The first layer might provide indemnification for losses between $30 million and $40 million; the next layer might cover losses between $40 million and $50 million; and so on. Each reinsurance contract is known as an *excess-of-loss* reinsurance contract. The reinsurer has written a bull spread on the total losses. It is long a call option with a strike price equal to the lower end of the layer and short a call option with a strike price equal to the upper end of the layer.[5]

The principal providers of CAT reinsurance have traditionally been reinsurance companies and Lloyds syndicates (which are unlimited liability syndicates of wealthy individuals). In recent years the industry has come to the conclusion that its reinsurance needs have outstripped what can be provided from these traditional sources. It has searched for new ways in which capital markets can provide reinsurance. One of the events that caused the industry to rethink its practices was Hurricane Andrew in 1992, which caused about $15 billion of insurance costs in Florida. This exceeded the total of relevant insurance premiums received in Florida during the previous seven years. If Hurricane Andrew had hit Miami, it is estimated that insured losses would have exceeded $40 billion. Hurricane Andrew and other catastrophes have led to increases in insurance/reinsurance premiums.

Exchange-traded insurance futures contracts have been developed by the CBOT, but have not been highly successful. The over-the-counter market has come up with a number of products that are alternatives to traditional reinsurance. The most popular is a CAT bond. This is a bond issued by a subsidiary of an insurance company that pays a higher-than-normal interest rate. In exchange for the extra interest, the holder of the bond agrees to provide an excess-of-cost reinsurance contract. Depending on the terms of the CAT bond, the interest or principal (or both) can be used to meet claims. In the example considered above where an insurance company wants protection for California earthquake losses between $30 million and $40 million, the insurance company could issue CAT bonds with a total principal of $10 million. In the event that the insurance company's California earthquake losses exceeded $30 million, bondholders would lose some or all of their principal. As an alternative, the insurance company could cover this excess cost layer by making a much bigger bond issue where only the bondholders' interest is at risk.

CAT bonds typically give a high probability of an above-normal rate of interest and a low probability of a high loss. Why would investors be interested in such instruments? The answer is that there are no statistically significant correlations between CAT risks and market returns.[6] CAT bonds are therefore an attractive addition to an investor's portfolio. They have no systematic risk so that their total risk can be completely diversified away in a large portfolio. If a CAT bond's expected return is greater than the risk-free interest rate (and typically it is), it has the potential to improve risk–return tradeoffs.

## SUMMARY

This chapter has shown that when there are risks to be managed, derivative markets have been very innovative in developing products to meet the needs of market participants.

---

[5] Reinsurance is also sometimes offered in the form of a lump sum if a certain loss level is reached. The reinsurer is then writing a cash-or-nothing binary call option on the losses.

[6] See R. H. Litzenberger, D. R. Beaglehole, and C. E. Reynolds, "Assessing Catastrophe Reinsurance-Linked Securities as a New Asset Class," *Journal of Portfolio Management*, Winter 1996, 76–86.

The market for weather derivatives is relatively new, but is already attracting a lot of attention. Two measures, HDD and CDD, have been developed to describe the temperature during a month. These are used to define the payoffs on both exchange-traded and over-the-counter derivatives. No doubt, as the weather derivatives market develops, we will see contracts on rainfall, snow, and similar variables become more commonplace.

In energy markets, oil derivatives have been important for some time and play a key role in helping oil producers and oil consumers manage their price risk. Natural gas and electricity derivatives are relatively new. They became important for risk management when these markets were deregulated and state monopolies discontinued.

Insurance derivatives are now beginning to be an alternative traditional reinsurance as a way for insurance companies to manage the risks of a catastrophic event such as a hurricane or an earthquake. No doubt we will see other sorts of insurance (e.g., life insurance and automobile insurance) being securitized in a similar way as this market develops.

Weather, energy, and insurance derivatives have the property that percentage changes in the underlying variables have negligible correlations with market returns. This means that we can use the actuarial approach for valuation. The actuarial approach for valuing a derivative involves using historical data to calculate the expected payoff and then discounting this expected payoff at the risk-free rate.

## SUGGESTIONS FOR FURTHER READING

Arditti, F., L. Cai, and M. Cao, "Whether to Hedge," *RISK Supplement on Weather Risk*, 1999, pp. 9 12.

Canter, M. S., J. B. Cole, and R. L. Sandor, "Insurance Derivatives: A New Asset Class for the Capital Markets and a New Hedging Tool for the Insurance Industry," *Journal of Applied Corporate Finance*, Autumn 1997, 69–83.

Clewlow, L., and C. Strickland, *Energy Derivatives: Pricing and Risk Management*, Lacima Group, 2000.

Eydeland, A., and H. Geman, "Pricing Power Derivatives," *RISK*, October 1998, pp. 71–73.

Geman, H., "CAT Calls," *RISK*, September 1994, pp. 86–89.

Hanley, M., "A Catastrophe Too Far," *RISK Supplement on Insurance*, July 1998.

Hunter, R., "Managing Mother Nature," *Derivatives Strategy*, February 1999.

Joskow, P. "Electricity Sectors in Transition," *The Energy Journal*, 19 (1998), 25–52.

Kendall, R., "Crude Oil: Price Shocking," *RISK Supplement on Commodity Risk*, May 1999, p. 6.

Litzenberger, R. H., D. R. Beaglehole, and C. E. Reynolds, "Assessing Catastrophe Reinsurance-linked Securities as a New Asset Class," *Journal of Portfolio Management*, Winter 1996, 76–86.

## QUESTIONS AND PROBLEMS
## (ANSWERS IN SOLUTIONS MANUAL)

29.1. Distinguish between the actuarial approach and the risk-neutral approach to valuing a derivative. Under what circumstance do they give the same answer?

29.2. Suppose that each day during July the minimum temperature is 68° Fahrenheit and the maximum temperature is 82° Fahrenheit. What is the payoff from a call option on the cumulative CDD during July with a strike of 250 and a payment rate of $5,000 per degree day?

29.3. "The CDD for a particular day is the payoff from a call option on the day's average temperature." Explain.

29.4. Suppose that you have 50 years of temperature data at your disposal. Explain carefully the analyses you would you carry out to value a forward contract on the cumulative CDD for a particular month.

29.5. Would you expect the volatility of the three-month forward price of oil to be greater than or less than the volatility of the spot price. Explain.

29.6. What are the characteristics of an energy source where the price has a very high volatility and a very high rate of mean reversion? Give an example of such an energy source.

29.7. How can a gas producer use derivative markets to hedge risks?

29.8. Explain how a $5 \times 8$ option contract for May 2003 on electricity with daily exercise works. Explain how a $5 \times 8$ option contract for May 2003 on electricity with monthly exercise works. Which is worth more?

29.9. Explain how CAT bonds work.

29.10. Consider two bonds that have the same coupon, time to maturity, and price. One is a B-rated corporate bond. The other is a CAT bond. An analysis based on historical data shows that the expected losses on the two bonds in each year of their life is the same. Which bond would you advise a portfolio manager to buy and why?

## ASSIGNMENT QUESTIONS

29.11. An insurance company's losses of a particular type are to a reasonable approximation normally distributed with a mean of $150 million and a standard deviation of $50 million. (Assume no difference between losses in a risk-neutral world and losses in the real world.) The one-year risk-free rate is 5%. Estimate the cost of the following:

   a. A contract that will pay in one year's time 60% of the insurance company's costs on a pro rata basis

   b. A contract that pays $100 million in one year's time if losses exceed $200 million.

C H A P T E R   3 0

# DERIVATIVES MISHAPS AND WHAT WE CAN LEARN FROM THEM

Since the mid-1980s there have been some spectacular losses in derivatives markets. Tables 30.1 and 30.2 provide a list of some of these losses. In Table 30.1 the losses were made by financial institutions; in Table 30.2 they were made by nonfinancial organizations. What is remarkable about the list is the number of cases where huge losses arose from the activities of a single employee. In 1995, Nick Leeson's trading brought a 200-year-old British bank, Barings, to its knees; in 1994, Robert Citron's trading led to Orange County, a municipality in California, losing about $2 billion. Joseph Jett's trading for Kidder Peabody lost $350 million. John Rusnak's losses of $700 million for Allied Irish Bank came to light in 2002. The huge losses at Daiwa, Shell, and Sumitomo were also each the result of the activities of a single individual.

The losses should not be viewed as an indictment of the whole derivatives industry. The derivatives market is a vast multitrillion-dollar market that by most measures has been outstandingly successful and has served the needs of its users well. The events described in the tables represent a tiny proportion of the total trades (both in number and value). Nevertheless, it is worth considering carefully the lessons we can learn from them. This is what we will do in this final chapter.

## 30.1  LESSONS FOR ALL USERS OF DERIVATIVES

First, we consider the lessons appropriate to all users of derivatives whether they are financial or nonfinancial companies.

### *Define Risk Limits*

It is essential that all companies define in a clear and unambiguous way limits to the financial risks that can be taken. They should then set up procedures for ensuring that the limits are obeyed. Ideally, overall risk limits should be set at board level. These should then be converted to limits applicable to the individuals responsible for managing particular risks. Daily reports should indicate the gain or loss that will be experienced for particular movements in market variables. These should be checked against the actual losses that are experienced to ensure that the valuation procedures underlying the reports are accurate.

It is particularly important that companies monitor risks carefully when derivatives are used. This is because, as we saw in Chapter 1, derivatives can be used for hedging, speculation, and

**686**

**Table 30.1**  Big losses by financial institutions

*Allied Irish Bank*

This bank lost about $700 million from speculative activities of one of its foreign exchange traders, John Rusnak, that lasted several years. Rusnak covered up his losses by creating fictitious options trades.

*Barings*

This 200-year-old British bank was wiped out in 1995 by the activities of one trader, Nick Leeson, in Singapore. The trader's mandate was to arbitrage between Nikkei 225 futures quotes in Singapore and Osaka. Instead he made big bets on the future direction of the Nikkei 225 using futures and options. The total loss was close to $1 billion.

*Chemical Bank*

This bank used an incorrect model to value interest rate caps in the late 1980s and as a result lost $33 million.

*Daiwa*

A trader working in New York for this Japanese bank lost more than $1 billion in the 1990s.

*Kidder Peabody*

The activities of a single trader, Joseph Jett, led to this New York investment dealer losing $350 million trading U.S. government securities and their strips. (Strips are created when each of the cash flows underlying a bond is sold as a separate security.) The loss arose because of a mistake in the way the company's computer system calculated profits.

*Long-Term Capital Management*

This hedge fund lost about $4 billion in 1998. The strategy followed by the fund was convergence arbitrage. This involved attempting to identify two nearly identical securities whose prices were temporarily out of line with each other. The company would buy the less-expensive security and short the more-expensive one, hedging any residual risks. In mid-1998 the company was badly hurt by widening credit spreads resulting from defaults on Russian bonds. The hedge fund was considered too large to fail. The New York Federal Reserve organized a $3.5 billion bailout by encouraging 14 banks to invest in the fund.

*Midland Bank*

This British bank lost $500 million in the early 1990s largely because of a wrong bet on the direction of interest rates. It was later taken over by the Hong Kong and Shanghai Bank.

*National Westminster Bank*

This British bank lost about $130 million from using an inappropriate model to value swap options in 1997.

*Sumitomo*

A single trader working for this Japanese bank lost about $2 billion in the copper spot, futures, and options market in the 1990s.

---

arbitrage. Without close monitoring it is impossible to know whether a derivatives trader has switched from being a hedger of the company's risks to a speculator or switched from being an arbitrageur to being a speculator. Barings is a classic example of what can go wrong. Nick Leeson's mandate was to carry out low-risk arbitrage between the Singapore and Osaka markets on Nikkei 225 futures. Unknown to his superiors in London, Leeson switched from being an arbitrageur to taking huge bets on the future direction of the Nikkei 225. Systems within Barings were so inadequate that nobody knew what he was doing.

The argument here is not that no risks should be taken. A treasurer working for a corporation or a trader in a financial institution or a fund manager should be allowed to take positions on the

---

**Table 30.2**   Big Losses by Nonfinancial Organizations

*Allied Lyons*
The treasury department of this drinks and food company lost $150 million in 1991 selling call options on the U.S. dollar–sterling exchange rate.

*Gibson Greetings*
The treasury department of this greeting card manufacturer in Cincinnati lost about $20 million in 1994 trading highly exotic interest rate derivatives contracts with Bankers Trust. They later sued Bankers Trust and settled out of court.

*Hammersmith and Fulham*
This British Local Authority lost about $600 million on sterling interest rate swaps and options in 1988. All its contracts were later declared null and void by the British courts much to the annoyance of the banks on the other side of the transactions.

*Metallgesellschaft*
This German company entered into long-term contracts to supply oil and gasoline and hedged them by rolling over short-term futures contracts (see Section 4.6). It lost $1.8 billion when it was forced to discontinue this activity.

*Orange County*
The activities of the treasurer, Robert Citron, led to this California municipality losing about $2 billion in 1994. The treasurer was using derivatives to speculate that interest rates would not rise.

*Procter and Gamble*
The treasury department of this large U.S. company lost about $90 million in 1994 trading highly exotic interest rate derivatives contracts with Bankers Trust. (One of the contracts is described in Section 25.8.) They later sued Bankers Trust and settled out of court.

*Shell*
A single employee working in the Japanese subsidiary of this company lost $1 billion dollars in unauthorized trading of currency futures.

---

future direction of relevant market variables. What we are arguing is that the sizes of the positions that can be taken should be limited and the systems in place should accurately report the risks being taken.

### Take the Risk Limits Seriously

What happens if an individual exceeds risk limits and makes a profit? This is a tricky issue for senior management. It is tempting to turn a blind eye to violations of risk limits when profits result. However, this is shortsighted. It leads to a culture where risk limits are not taken seriously, and it paves the way for a disaster. In many of the situations listed in Tables 30.1 and 30.2, the companies had become complacent about the risks they were taking because they had taken similar risks in previous years and made profits.

The classic example here is Orange County. Robert Citron's activities in 1991–93 had been very profitable for Orange County, and the municipality had come to rely on his trading for additional funding. People chose to ignore the risks he was taking because he had produced profits. Unfortunately, the losses made in 1994 far exceeded the profits from previous years.

The penalties for exceeding risk limits should be just as great when profits result as when losses result. Otherwise, traders that make losses are liable to keep increasing their bets in the hope that eventually a profit will result and all will be forgiven.

## Do Not Assume You Can Outguess the Market

Some traders are quite possibly better than others. But no trader gets it right all the time. A trader who correctly predicts the direction in which market variables will move 60% of the time is doing well. If a trader has an outstanding track record (as Robert Citron did in the early 1990s), it is likely to be a result of luck rather than superior trading skill.

Suppose that a financial institution employs 16 traders and one of those traders makes profits in every quarter of a year. Should the trader receive a good bonus? Should the trader's risk limits be increased? The answer to the first question is that inevitably the trader will receive a good bonus. The answer the second question should be no. The chance of making a profit in four consecutive quarters from random trading is $0.5^4$ or 1 in 16. This means that just by chance one of the 16 traders will "get it right" every single quarter of the year. We should not assume that the trader's luck will continue and we should not increase the trader's risk limits.

## Do Not Underestimate the Benefits of Diversification

When a trader appears good at predicting a particular market variable, there is a tendency to increase the trader's limits. We have just argued that this is a bad idea because it is quite likely that the trader has been lucky rather than clever. However, let us suppose that we are really convinced that the trader has special talents. How undiversified should we allow ourselves to become in order to take advantage of the trader's special skills? The answer is that the benefits from diversification are huge, and it is unlikely that any trader is so good that it is worth foregoing these benefits to speculate heavily on just one market variable.

An example will illustrate the point here. Suppose that there are 20 stocks, each of which has an expected return of 10% per annum and a standard deviation of returns of 30%. The correlation between the returns from any two of the stocks is 0.2. By dividing an investment equally among the 20 stocks, an investor has an expected return of 10% per annum and standard deviation of returns of 14.7%. Diversification enables the investor to reduce risks by over half. Another way of expressing this is that diversification enables an investor to double the expected return per unit of risk taken. The investor would have to be extremely good at stock picking to achieve the same result by investing in just one stock.

## Carry out Scenario Analyses and Stress Tests

The calculation of risk measures such as VaR should always be accompanied by scenario analyses and stress testing to obtain an understanding of what can go wrong. These techniques were mentioned in Chapter 16. They are very important. Human beings have an unfortunate tendency to anchor on one or two scenarios when evaluating decisions. In 1993 and 1994, for example, Procter and Gamble and Gibson Greetings were so convinced that interest rates would remain low that they ignored the possibility of a 100-basis-point increase in their decision making.

It is important to be creative in the way scenarios are generated. One approach is to look at 10 or 20 years of data and choose the most extreme events as scenarios. Sometimes there is a shortage of data on a key variable. It is then sensible to choose a similar variable for which much more data is available and use historical daily percentage changes in that variable as a proxy for possible daily percentage changes in the key variable. For example, if there is little data on the prices of bonds issued by a particular country, we can look at historical data on prices of bonds issued by other similar countries to develop possible scenarios.

## 30.2  LESSONS FOR FINANCIAL INSTITUTIONS

We now move on to consider lessons that are primarily relevant to financial institutions.

### Monitor Traders Carefully

In trading rooms there is a tendency to regard high-performing traders as "untouchable" and not to subject their activities to the same scrutiny as other traders. Apparently Joseph Jett, Kidder Peabody's star trader of Treasury instruments, was often "too busy" to answer questions and discuss his positions with the company's risk managers.

It is important that all traders—particularly those making high profits—be fully accountable. It is important for the financial institution to know whether the high profits are being made by taking unreasonably high risks. It is also important to check that the financial institution's computer systems and pricing models are correct and are not being manipulated in some way.

### Separate the Front, Middle, and Back Office

The *front office* in a financial institution consists of the traders who are executing trades, taking positions, etc. The *middle office* consists of risk managers who are monitoring the risks being taken. The *back office* is where the record keeping and accounting takes place. Some of the worst derivatives disasters have occurred because these functions were not kept separate. Nick Leeson controlled both the front and back office in Singapore and was, as a result, able to conceal the disastrous nature of his trades from his superiors in London for some time. Although full details are not available, it appears that a lack of separation of the front and back office was at least partially responsible for the huge losses experienced by Sumitomo bank in copper trading.

### Do Not Blindly Trust Models

Some of the large losses in Table 30.1 arose because of the models and computer systems being used. Perhaps the most famous systems problem was the one experienced by Kidder Peabody. Joseph Jett would buy some strips (i.e., zero-coupon bonds) and then do a forward trade to sell them in the future. The strips pay no interest and so, as explained in Chapter 3, the forward price is higher than the spot price. Kidder's system reported the difference between the forward price and the spot price as a profit at the time of the trade. Of course, the difference represented the cost of financing the strip. But, by rolling the forward contracts forward, Jett was able to prevent this financing cost from accruing to him. The result was that the system reported a profit of $100 million and Jett received a big bonus when in fact there was a loss in the region of $350 million.

Examples of incorrect models leading to losses are also provided by Chemical Bank and National Westminster Bank. Chemical Bank had an incorrect model for valuing interest rate caps and National Westminster Bank had an incorrect model for valuing swap options.

If large profits are being made by following relatively simple trading strategies, there is a good chance that the models underlying the calculation of the profits are wrong. Similarly, if a financial institution appears to be particularly competitive on its quotes for a particular type of deal, there is a good chance that it is using a different model from other market participants, and it should analyze what is going on carefully. To the head of a trading room, getting too much business of a certain type can be just as worrisome as getting too little business of that type.

### Be Conservative in Recognizing Inception Profits

When a financial institution sells a highly exotic instrument to a nonfinancial corporation, the valuation can be highly dependent on the underlying model. For example, instruments with long-dated embedded interest rate options can be highly dependent on the interest rate model used. In these circumstances, a phrase used to describe the daily marking to market of the deal is *marking to model*. This is because there are no market prices for similar deals that can be used as a benchmark.

Suppose that a financial institution manages to sell an instrument to a client for $10 million more than it is worth—or at least $10 million more than its model says it is worth. The $10 million is known as an *inception profit*. When should it be recognized? There appears to be quite a variation in what different investment banks do. Some recognize the $10 million immediately, whereas others are much more conservative and recognize it slowly over the life of the deal.

Recognizing inception profits immediately is very dangerous. It encourages traders to use aggressive models, take their bonuses, and leave before the model and the value of the deal come under close scrutiny. It is much better to recognize inception profits slowly, so that traders have the motivation to investigate the impact of several different models and several different sets of assumptions before committing themselves to a deal.

### Do Not Sell Clients Inappropriate Products

It is tempting to sell corporate clients inappropriate products, particularly when they appear to have an appetite for the underlying risks. But this is shortsighted. The most dramatic example of this is the activities of Bankers Trust (BT) in the period leading up to the spring of 1994. Many of BT's clients were persuaded to buy high-risk and totally inappropriate products. A typical product (e.g., the 5/30 swap discussed in Section 25.8) would give the client a good chance of saving a few basis points on its borrowings and a small chance of costing a large amount of money. The products worked well for BT's clients in 1992 and 1993, but blew up in 1994 when interest rates rose sharply. The bad publicity that followed hurt BT greatly. The years it had spent building up trust among corporate clients and developing an enviable reputation for innovation in derivatives were largely lost as a result of the activities of a few overly aggressive salesmen. BT was forced to pay large amounts of money to its clients to settle lawsuits out of court. It was taken over by Deutsche Bank in 1999.

### Do Not Ignore Liquidity Risk

Financial engineers usually base the pricing of exotic instruments and instruments that trade relatively infrequently on the prices of actively traded instruments. For example:

1. A financial engineer often calculates a zero curve from actively traded government bonds (known as on-the-run bonds) and uses it to price bonds that trade less frequently (off-the-run bonds).

2. A financial engineer often implies the volatility of an asset from actively traded options and uses it to price less-actively traded options.

3. A financial engineer often implies the parameters of the process for interest rates from actively traded interest rate caps and swap options and uses it to price products that are highly structured.

This practice is not unreasonable. However, it is dangerous to assume that less-actively traded instruments can always be traded at close to their theoretical price. When financial markets experience a shock of one sort or another there is often a "flight to quality". Liquidity becomes very important to investors, and illiquid instruments often sell at a big discount to their theoretical values. Trading strategies that assume large volumes of relatively illiquid instruments can be sold at short notice at close to their theoretical values are dangerous.

An example of liquidity risk is provided by Long-Term Capital Management (LTCM). This hedge fund followed a strategy known as *convergence arbitrage*. It attempted to identify two securities (or portfolios of securities) that should in theory sell for the same price. If the market price of one security was less that of the other, it would buy that security and sell the other. The strategy is based on the idea that if two securities have the same theoretical price their market prices should eventually be the same.

In the summer of 1998 LTCM made a huge loss. This was largely because a default by Russia on its debt caused a flight to quality. LTCM did not itself have a big exposure to Russian debt, but it tended to be long illiquid instruments and short the corresponding liquid instruments (e.g., it was long off-the-run bonds and short on-the-run bonds). The spreads between the prices of illiquid instruments and the corresponding liquid instruments widened sharply after the Russian default. Credit spreads also increased. LTCM was highly leveraged. It experienced huge losses and there were requirements to post collateral that it was unable to meet.

The LTCM story reinforces the importance of carrying out scenario analyses and stress testing to look at what is likely to happen in the worst of all worlds. LTCM could have tried to examine other times in history when there have been extreme flights to quality to quantify the liquidity risks it was facing.

### Beware When Everyone Is Following the Same Trading Strategy

It sometimes happens that many market participants are following essentially the same trading strategy. This creates a dangerous environment where there are liable to be big market moves, unstable markets, and large losses for the market participants.

We gave one example of this in Chapter 14 when discussing portfolio insurance and the market crash of October 1987. In the months leading up to the crash, increasing numbers of portfolio managers were attempting to insure their portfolios by creating synthetic put options. They bought stocks or stock index futures after a rise in the market and sold them after a fall. This created an unstable market. A relatively small decline in stock prices could lead to a wave of selling by portfolio insurers. The latter would lead to a further decline in the market, which could give rise to another wave of selling, and so on. There is little doubt that without portfolio insurance the crash of October 1987 would have been much less severe.

Another example is provided by LTCM in 1998. Its position was made more difficult by the fact that many other hedge funds were following similar convergence arbitrage strategies. After the Russian default and the flight to quality, LTCM tried to liquidate part of its portfolio to meet its cash needs. Unfortunately, other hedge funds were facing similar problems to LTCM and trying to do similar trades. This exacerbated the situation, causing liquidity spreads to be even higher than they would otherwise have been and reinforcing the flight to quality. Consider, for example, LTCM's position in U.S. Treasury bonds. It was long the illiquid off-the-run bonds and short the liquid on-the-run bonds. When a flight to quality caused spreads between yields on the two types of bonds to widen, LTCM had to liquidate its positions by selling off-the-run bonds and buying on-the-run bonds. Other large hedge funds were doing the same. As a result, the price of on-the-run bonds rose relative to off-the-run bonds and the spread between the two yields widened even more than it had done already.

A further example is provided by the activities of British insurance companies in the late 1990s. These insurance companies had entered into many contracts promising that the rate of interest applicable to an annuity received by an individual on retirement would be the greater of the market rate and a guaranteed rate. At about the same time, all insurance companies decided to hedge part of their risks on these contracts by buying long-dated swap options from financial institutions. The financial institutions they dealt with hedged their risks by buying huge numbers of long-dated sterling bonds. As a result, bond prices rose and long sterling rates declined. More bonds had to be bought to maintain the dynamic hedge, long sterling rates declined further, and so on. Financial institutions lost money and, because long rates declined, insurance companies found themselves in a worse position on the risks they had chosen not to hedge.

The chief lesson to be learned from these stories is that it is important to see the big picture of what is going on in financial markets and to understand the risks inherent in situations where many market participants are following the same trading strategy.

## 30.3  LESSONS FOR NONFINANCIAL CORPORATIONS

We now consider lessons primarily applicable to nonfinancial corporations.

### *Make Sure You Fully Understand the Trades You Are Doing*

Corporations should never undertake a trade or a trading strategy that they do not fully understand. This is a somewhat obvious point, but is surprising how often a trader working for a nonfinancial corporation will, after a big loss, admit to not knowing what was really going on and claim to have been misled by investment bankers. Robert Citron, the treasurer of Orange County did this. So did the traders working for Hammersmith and Fulham, who in spite of their huge positions were surprisingly uninformed about how the swaps and other interest rate derivatives they traded really worked.

If a senior manager in a corporation does not understand a trade proposed by a subordinate, the trade should not be approved. A simple rule of thumb is that if a trade and the rationale for entering into it are so complicated that they cannot be understood by the manager, it is almost certainly inappropriate for the corporation. The trades undertaken by Procter and Gamble and Gibson Greetings would have been vetoed using this criterion.

One way of ensuring that you fully understand a financial instrument is to value it. If a corporation does not have the in-house capability to value an instrument, it should not trade it. In practice, corporations often rely on their investment bankers for valuation advice. This is dangerous, as Procter and Gamble and Gibson Greetings found out when they wanted to unwind their deals. They were facing prices produced by Bankers Trust's proprietary models, which they had no way of checking.

### *Make Sure a Hedger Does Not Become a Speculator*

One of the unfortunate facts of life is that hedging is relatively dull, whereas speculation is exciting. When a company hires a trader to manage foreign exchange risk or interest rate risk there is a danger that the following happens. At first, the trader does the job diligently and earns the confidence of top management. He or she assesses the company's exposures and hedges them. As time goes by, the trader becomes convinced that he or she can outguess the market. Slowly the trader becomes a speculator. At first things go well, but then a loss is made. To recover the loss the trader doubles up the bets. Further losses are made and so on. The result is likely to be a disaster.

As mentioned earlier, clear limits to the risks that can be taken should be set by senior management. Controls should be set in place to ensure that the limits are obeyed. The trading strategy for a corporation should start with an analysis of the risks facing the corporation in foreign exchange, interest rate, commodity markets, and so on. A decision should then be taken on how the risks are to be reduced to acceptable levels. It is a clear sign that something is wrong within a corporation if the trading strategy is not derived in a very direct way from the company's exposures.

### Be Cautious about Making the Treasury Department a Profit Center

In the last 20 years there has been a tendency to make the treasury department within a corporation a profit center. This appears to have much to recommend it. The treasurer is motivated to reduce financing costs and manage risks as profitably as possible. The problem is that the potential for the treasurer to make profits is limited. When raising funds and investing surplus cash, the treasurer is facing an efficient market. The treasurer can usually improve the bottom line only by taking additional risks. The company's hedging program gives the treasurer some scope for making shrewd decisions that increase profits. But it should be remembered that the goal of a hedging program is to reduce risks, not to increase expected profits. As pointed out in Chapter 4, the decision to hedge will lead to a worse outcome than the decision not to hedge roughly 50% of the time. The danger of making the treasury department a profit center is that the treasurer is motivated to become a speculator. An Orange County, Procter and Gamble, or Gibson Greetings type of outcome is then liable to occur.

## SUMMARY

The huge losses experienced from the use of derivatives have made many treasurers very wary. Since the spate of mishaps in 1994 and 1995, some nonfinancial corporations have announced plans to reduce or even eliminate their use of derivatives. This is unfortunate because derivatives provide treasurers with very efficient ways to manage risks.

The stories behind the losses emphasize the point, made as early as Chapter 1, that derivatives can be used for either hedging or speculation; that is, they can be used either to reduce risks or to take risks. Most losses occurred because derivatives were used inappropriately. Employees who had an implicit or explicit mandate to hedge their company's risks decided instead to speculate.

The key lesson to be learned from the losses is the importance of *internal controls*. Senior management within a company should issue a clear and unambiguous policy statement about how derivatives are to be used and the extent to which it is permissible for employees to take positions on movements in market variables. Management should then institute controls to ensure that the policy is carried out. It is a recipe for disaster to give individuals authority to trade derivatives without a close monitoring of the risks being taken.

## SUGGESTIONS OR FURTHER READING

Dunbar, N., *Inventing Money: The Story of Long-Term Capital Management and the Legends Behind It*, Wiley, Chichester, 2000.

Jorion, P., *Big Bets Gone Bad: Derivatives and Bankruptcy in Orange County*, Academic Press, New York, 1995.

Jorion, P., "How Long-Term Lost Its Capital," *RISK*, September 1999.

Ju, X., and N. Pearson, "Using Value at Risk to Control Risk Taking: How Wrong Can You Be?" *Journal of Risk*, 1, no. 2 (Winter, 1998/9), 5–36.

Thomson, R., *Apocalypse Roulette: The Lethal World of Derivatives*, Macmillan, London, 1998.

Zhang, P. G., *Barings Bankruptcy and Financial Derivatives*, World Scientific, Singapore, 1995.

# GLOSSARY OF NOTATION

The following is a guide to the ways that symbols are used in this book. Symbols that appear in one small part of the book may not be listed here, but are always defined at the place when they are first used.

$a$: Growth factor per step of an underlying variable in a risk-neutral world in a binomial model during time $\delta t$. For example, when the underlying variable is a non-dividend-paying stock $a = e^{r\,\delta t}$; when it is a currency, $a = e^{(r-r_f)\,\delta t}$; and so on. The variable $a$ is also used in Chapter 11 as the drift rate in a generalized Wiener process. In Chapter 23, it is the reversion rate in an interest rate process.

$b$: In Chapter 11, $b^2$ is the variance rate in a generalized Wiener process. In Chapter 23, $b$ is the reversion level in an interest rate process.

$B$: Coupon-bearing bond price.

$c$: Price of a European call option. It is also used in Chapter 5 to denote a bond's coupon.

$C$: Price of an American call option. It is also used in Chapter 5 to denote convexity.

$d_1, d_2$: Parameters in option pricing formulas. See, for example, equations (12.20), (13.4), and (13.17).

$d$: Proportional down movement in a binomial model. If $d = 0.9$, value of variable moves to 90% of its previous value when there is a down movement.

$dz$: Wiener process.

$D$: In Chapters 8 and 12, $D$ is the present value of dividends on a stock. In Chapter 5, $D$ is used to denote duration.

$D_i$: The $i$th cash dividend payment.

$E(\cdot)$: Expected value of a variable.

$\hat{E}(\cdot)$: Expected value of a variable in a risk-neutral world. (This is the traditional risk-neutral world where the numeraire is the money market account.)

$E_T(\cdot)$: Expected value of a variable in a world where numeraire is a zero-coupon bond maturing at time $T$.

$E_A(\cdot)$: Expected value of a variable in a world where numeraire is the value of an annuity

$f$: Value of a derivative. $f_T$ is the value of a derivative at time $T$ and $f_0$ is the value of a derivative at time zero. $f_i$ is used on occasion to denote the value of the $i$th derivative.

$f_u$: Value of derivative if an up movement occurs.

$f_d$: Value of derivative if a down movement occurs.

$F$: Forward or futures price at a general time $t$.

$F_0$: Forward or futures price at time zero.

$F_T$: Forward or futures price at time $T$.

$h$: Hedge ratio in Chapter 4. The variable, $h^*$, is the optimal hedge ratio.

$H$: Barrier level in a barrier option.

$I$: Present value of income on a security.

$K$: Strike price of an option. Also the delivery price in a forward contract.

$L$: Principal amount in a derivatives contract.

$M(x, y, \rho)$: Cumulative probability in a bivariate normal distribution that the first variable is less than $x$ and the second variable is less than $y$ when the coefficient of correlation between the variables is $\rho$.

$N(x)$: Cumulative probability that a variable with a standardized normal distribution is less than $x$. A standardized normal distribution is a normal distribution has a mean of zero and standard deviation of 1.0. Tables for $N(x)$ are at the end of this book.

$p$: This is used in two important ways. The first is as the value of a European put option (e.g., in Chapter 12). The second is as the probability of an up movement in binomial models (e.g., in Chapter 18).

$P$: Value of an American put option. In Chapters 4 and 16, $P$ denotes a portfolio value.

$P(t, T)$: The price at time $t$ of a zero-coupon bond maturing at time $T$.

$q$: Dividend yield rate. In Chapter 10, $q$ denotes the probability of an up movement in the real world. (This can be contrasted with $p$ which is the probability of an up movement in the risk-neutral world.)

$r$: Risk-free interest rate. Sometimes (e.g., Chapters 3 and 8) it is the rate applicable between times 0 and $T$ and sometimes (e.g., Chapter 23) it is the instantaneous (i.e., very short term) risk-free interest rate.

$r_f$: Risk-free interest rate in a foreign country.

$\bar{r}$: Average instantaneous risk-free rate of interest during the life of a derivative.

$R$: In Chapter 23, this is the $\delta t$-period rate and should be distinguished from $r$, which is the instantaneous risk-free rate. In Chapters 26 and 27, it is the recovery rate with $\hat{R}$ defined as the expected recovery rate.

$R_c$: In Chapter 3, this is an interest rate expressed with continuous compounding

$R_m$: In Chapter 3, this is an interest rate expressed with compounding $m$ times per year

$S$: Price of asset underlying a derivative at a general time $t$. In different parts of the book, $S$ is used to refer to the price of a currency, the price of a stock, the price of a stock index, and the price of a commodity.

$S_T$: Value of $S$ at time $T$.

$S_0$: Value of $S$ at time zero.

$t$: A future point in time.

$T$: Time to end of life of option or other derivative.

$u$: Proportional up movement in a binomial model. For example, $u = 1.2$ indicates that the variable increases by 20% when an up movement occurs. In Chapter 3, $u$ is used to denote the storage costs per unit time as a proportion of the price of an asset.

$u_i$: In Chapters 12 and 17, this denotes the return provided on an asset between observation $i - 1$ and observation $i$.

$\mathcal{V}$: Vega of a derivative or a portfolio of derivatives.

$y$: Usually denotes a bond's yield. In Chapter 3, it denotes the convenience yield.

$y^*(T)$: yield on a risk-free bond maturing at time $T$ in Chapters 26 and 27; $y(T)$ is the corporate bond yield.

$\beta$: In Chapters 4 and 13, this denotes the capital asset pricing model's beta parameter.

$\Gamma$: Gamma of a derivative or a portfolio of derivatives.

$\Delta$: Delta of a derivative or a portfolio of derivatives.

$\delta x$: Small change in $x$ for any variable $x$.

$\epsilon$: Random sample from a standardized normal distribution.

$\eta$: Continuously compounded return on stock.

$\mu$: Expected return on an asset.

$\theta$: In Chapters 21 and 28, this is the value of a variable that is not necessarily the price of a traded security.

$\Theta$: Theta of a derivative or portfolio of derivatives.

$\Pi$: Value of a portfolio of derivatives.

$\rho$: Coefficient of correlation.

$\sigma$: Usually this is the volatility of an asset (i.e., $\sigma\sqrt{\delta t}$ is the standard deviation of the percentage change in the asset's price in time $\delta t$). Note that, in Chapter 4, $\sigma_F$ and $\sigma_S$ are the standard deviations of $S$ and $F$ at hedge maturity. Also, in the Hull–White and Ho–Lee models (Chapter 23), $\sigma$ is the instantaneous standard deviation (not the volatility) of the short rate.

$\sigma_n$: In Chapter 16, this is the volatility of the $n$th asset. In Chapter 17, it is the volatility of a particular asset on day $n$, estimated at the end of day $n-1$.

$\sigma_P$: Standard deviation (not volatility) of a portfolio in Chapter 16.

$\phi(m, s)$: Normal distribution with mean $m$ and standard deviation $s$.

# GLOSSARY OF TERMS

**Accrual Swap** An interest rate swap where interest on one side accrues only when a certain condition is met.

**Accrued Interest** The interest earned on a bond since the last coupon payment date.

**Adaptive Mesh Model** A model developed by Figlewski and Gao that grafts a high-resolution tree on to a low-resolution tree so that there is more detailed modeling of the asset price in critical regions.

**American Option** An option that can be exercised at any time during its life.

**Amortizing Swap** A swap where the notional principal decreases in a predetermined way as time passes.

**Analytic Result** Result where answer is in the form of an equation.

**Arbitrage** A trading strategy that takes advantage of two or more securities being mispriced relative to each other.

**Arbitrageur** An individual engaging in arbitrage.

**Asian Option** An option with a payoff dependent on the average price of the underlying asset during a specified period.

**Ask Price** *See* Offer price

**Asked Price** *See* Offer price.

**Asset-or-Nothing Call Option** An option that provides a payoff equal to the asset price if the asset price is above the strike price and zero otherwise.

**Asset-or-Nothing Put Option** An option that provides a payoff equal to the asset price if the asset price is below the strike price and zero otherwise.

**Asset Swap** Exchanges the coupon on a bond for LIBOR plus a spread.

**As-You-Like-It Option** *See* Chooser option.

**At-the-Money Option** An option in which the strike price equals the price of the underlying asset.

**Average Price Call Option** An option giving a payoff equal to the greater of zero and the amount by which the average price of the asset exceeds the strike price.

**Average Price Put Option** An option giving a payoff equal to the greater of zero and the amount by which the strike price exceeds the average price of the asset.

**Average Strike Option** An option that provides a payoff dependent on the difference between the final asset price and the average asset price.

**Back Testing** Testing a value-at-risk or other model using historical data.

**Backwards Induction** A procedure for working from the end of a tree to its beginning in order to value an option.

**Barrier Option** An option whose payoff depends on whether the path of the underlying asset has reached a barrier (i.e., a certain predetermined level).

**Basis** The difference between the spot price and the futures price of a commodity.

**Basis Point** When used to describe an interest rate, a basis point is one hundredth of one percent ($= 0.01$ percent)

**Basis Risk** The risk to a hedger arising from uncertainty about the basis at a future time.

**Basket Option** An option that provides a payoff dependent on the value of a portfolio of assets.

**Basket Credit Default Swap** Credit default swap where there are several reference entities.

**Bear Spread** A short position in a put option with strike price $K_1$ combined with a long position in a put option with strike price $K_2$, where $K_2 > K_1$. (A bear spread can also be created with call options.)

**Bermudan Option** An option that can be exercised on specified dates during its life.

**Beta** A measure of the systematic risk of an asset.

**Bid–Ask Spread** *See* Bid–offer spread.

**Bid–Offer Spread** The amount by which the offer price exceeds the bid price.

**Bid Price** The price that a dealer is prepared to pay for an asset.

**Binary Option** Option with a discontinuous payoff; for example, a cash-or-nothing option or an asset-or-nothing option.

**Binomial Model** A model where the price of an asset is monitored over successive short periods of time. In each short period it is assumed that only two price movements are possible.

**Binomial Tree** A tree that represents how an asset price can evolve under the binomial model.

**Bivariate Normal Distribution** A distribution for two correlated variables, each of which is normal.

**Black's Approximation** An approximate procedure developed by Fischer Black for valuing a call option on a dividend-paying stock.

**Black's Model** An extension of the Black–Scholes model for valuing European options on futures contracts. As described in Chapter 22, it is used extensively in practice to value European options when the distribution of the asset price at maturity is assumed to be lognormal.

**Black–Scholes Model** A model for pricing European options on stocks, developed by Fischer Black, Myron Scholes, and Robert Merton.

**Board Broker** The individual who handles limit orders in some exchanges. The board broker makes information on outstanding limit orders available to other traders.

**Bond Option** An option where a bond is the underlying asset.

**Bond Yield** Discount rate which, when applied to all the cash flows of a bond, causes the present value of the cash flows to equal the bond's market price.

**Bootstrap Method** A procedure for calculating the zero-coupon yield curve from market data.

**Boston Option** *See* Deferred payment option.

**Break Forward** *See* Deferred payment option.

**Bull Spread** A long position in a call with strike price $K_1$ combined with a short position in a call with strike price $K_2$, where $K_2 > K_1$. (A bull spread can also be created with put options.)

**Butterfly Spread** A position that is created by taking a long position in a call with strike price $K_1$, a long position in a call with strike price $K_3$, and a short position in two calls with strike price $K_2$, where $K_3 > K_2 > K_1$ and $K_2 = 0.5(K_1 + K_3)$. (A butterfly spread can also be created with put options.)

**Calendar Spread** A position that is created by taking a long position in a call option that matures at one time and a short position in a similar call option that matures at a different time. (A calendar spread can also be created using put options.)

**Calibration**   Method for implying a model's parameters from the prices of actively traded options.

**Callable bond**   A bond containing provisions that allow the issuer to buy it back at a predetermined price at certain times during its life.

**Call Option**   An option to buy an asset at a certain price by a certain date.

**Cancelable Swap**   Swap that can be canceled by one side on prespecified dates.

**Capital Asset Pricing Model**   A model relating the expected return on an asset to its beta.

**Cap**   *See* Interest rate cap.

**Caplet**   One component of an interest rate cap.

**Cap Rate**   The rate determining payoffs in an interest rate cap.

**Cash-Flow Mapping**   A procedure for representing an instrument as a portfolio of zero-coupon bonds for the purpose of calculating value at risk.

**Cash-or-Nothing Call Option**   An option that provides a fixed predetermined payoff if the final asset price is above the strike price and zero otherwise.

**Cash-or-Nothing Put Option**   An option that provides a fixed predetermined payoff if the final asset price is below the strike price an zero otherwise.

**Cash Settlement**   Procedure for settling a futures contract in cash rather than by delivering the underlying asset.

**CAT Bond**   Bond where the interest and, possibly, the principal paid are reduced if a particular category of "catastrophic" insurance claims exceed a certain amount.

**CDD**   Cooling degree days. The maximum of zero and the amount by which the daily average temperature is greater than 65° Fahrenheit. The average temperature is the

average of the highest and lowest temperatures (midnight to midnight).

**Cheapest-to-Deliver Bond**   The bond that is cheapest to deliver in the Chicago Board of Trade bond futures contract.

**Cholesky Decomposition**   Method of sampling from a multivariate normal distribution.

**Chooser Option**   An option where the holder has the right to choose whether it is a call or a put at some point during its life.

**Class of Options**   *See* Option class.

**Clean Price of Bond**   The quoted price of a bond. The cash price paid for the bond (or dirty price) is calculated by adding the accrued interest to the clean price.

**Clearinghouse**   A firm that guarantees the performance of the parties in an exchange-traded derivatives transaction. (Also referred to as a clearing corporation.)

**Clearing margin**   A margin posted by a member of a clearinghouse.

**Collar**   *See* Interest rate collar

**Collateralized Debt Obligation**   A way of packaging credit risk. Several classes of securities are created from a portfolio of bonds and there are rules for determining how defaults are allocated to classes.

**Collateralized Mortgage Obligation (CMO)**   A mortgage-backed security where investors are divided into classes and there are rules for determining how principal repayments are channeled to the classes.

**Combination**   A position involving both calls and puts on the same underlying asset.

**Commission Brokers**   Individuals who execute trades for other people and charge a commission for doing so.

**Commodity Futures Trading Commission**   A body that regulates trading in futures contracts in the United States.

**Commodity Swap**   A swap where cash flows depend on the price of a commodity.

**Compounding Frequency** This defines how an interest rate is measured.

**Compound Option** An option on an option.

**Compounding Swap** Swap where interest compounds instead of being paid.

**Conditional Value at Risk (C-VaR)** Expected loss during $N$ days conditional on being in the $(100-X)\%$ tail of the distribution of profits/losses. The variable $N$ is the time horizon and $X\%$ is the confidence level.

**Confirmation** Contract confirming verbal agreement between two parties to a trade in the over-the-counter market

**Constant Maturity Swap** A swap where a swap rate is exchanged for either a fixed rate or a floating rate on each payment date.

**Constant Maturity Treasury Swap** A swap where the yield on a Treasury bond is exchanged for either a fixed rate or a floating rate on each payment date.

**Consumption Asset** An asset held for consumption rather than investment.

**Contango** A situation where the futures price is above the expected future spot price.

**Continuous Compounding** A way of quoting interest rates. It is the limit as the assumed compounding interval is made smaller and smaller.

**Control Variate Technique** A technique that can sometimes be used for improving the accuracy of a numerical procedure.

**Convenience Yield** A measure of the benefits from ownership of an asset that are not obtained by the holder of a long futures contract on the asset.

**Conversion Factor** A factor used to determine the number of bonds that must be delivered in the Chicago Board of Trade bond futures contract.

**Convertible Bond** A corporate bond that can be converted into a predetermined amount of the company's equity at certain times during its life.

**Convexity** A measure of the curvature in the relationship between bond prices and bond yields.

**Convexity Adjustment** An overworked term. For example, it can refer to the adjustment necessary to convert a futures interest rate to a forward interest rate. It can also refer to the adjustment to a forward rate that is sometimes necessary when Black's model is used.

**Copula** A way of defining the correlation between variables with known distributions.

**Counterparty** The opposite side in a financial transaction.

**Cornish–Fisher Expansion** An approximate relationship between the fractiles of a probability distribution and its moments.

**Cost of Carry** The storage costs plus the cost of financing an asset minus the income earned on the asset.

**Coupon** Interest payment made on a bond.

**Covered Call** A short position in a call option on an asset combined with a long position in the asset.

**Credit Default Swap** An instrument that gives the holder the right to sell a bond for its face value in the event of a default by the issuer.

**Credit Derivative** A derivative whose payoff depends on the creditworthiness of one or more entities.

**Credit Rating** A measure of the creditworthiness of a bond issue.

**Credit Ratings Transition Matrix** A table showing the probability that a company will move from one credit rating to another during a certain period of time.

**Credit Risk** The risk that a loss will be experienced because of a default by the counterparty in a derivatives transaction.

**Credit Spread Option** Option whose payoff depends on the spread between the yields earned on two assets.

**Credit Value at Risk**   The credit loss that will not be exceeded at some specified confidence level.

**Cumulative Distribution Function**   The probability that a variable will be less than $x$ as a function of $x$.

**Currency Swap**   A swap where interest and principal in one currency are exchanged for interest and principal in another currency.

**Day Count**   A convention for quoting interest rates.

**Day Trade**   A trade that is entered into and closed out on the same day.

**Default Correlation**   Measures the tendency of two companies to default at about the same time.

**Default Probability Density**   Measures the unconditional probability of default in a future short period of time.

**Deferred Payment Option**   An option where the price paid is deferred until the end of the option's life.

**Deferred Swap**   An agreement to enter into a swap at some time in the future. Also called a forward swap.

**Delivery Price**   Price agreed to (possibly some time in the past) in a forward contract.

**Delta**   The rate of change of the price of a derivative with the price of the underlying asset.

**Delta Hedging**   A hedging scheme that is designed to make the price of a portfolio of derivatives insensitive to small changes in the price of the underlying asset.

**Delta-neutral Portfolio**   A portfolio with a delta of zero so that there is no sensitivity to small changes in the price of the underlying asset.

**DerivaGem**   The software accompanying this book.

**Derivative**   An instrument whose price depends on, or is derived from, the price of another asset.

**Diagonal Spread**   A position in two calls where both the strike prices and times to maturity are different. (A diagonal spread can also be created with put options.)

**Differential Swap**   A swap where a floating rate in one currency is exchanged for a floating rate in another currency and both rates are applied to the same principal.

**Diffusion Process**   Model where value of asset changes continuously (no jumps).

**Discount Bond**   *See* Zero-coupon bond.

**Discount Instrument**   An instrument, such as a Treasury bill, that provides no coupons.

**Discount Rate**   The annualized dollar return on a Treasury bill or similar instrument expressed as a percentage of the final face value.

**Dividend**   A cash payment made to the owner of a stock.

**Dividend Yield**   The dividend as a percentage of the stock price.

**Down-and-In Option**   An option that comes into existence when the price of the underlying asset declines to a prespecified level.

**Down-and-Out Option**   An option that ceases to exist when the price of the underlying asset declines to a prespecified level.

**Downgrade Trigger**   A clause in a contract that states that the contract will be terminated with a cash settlement if the credit rating of one side falls below a certain level.

**Drift rate**   The average increase per unit of time in a stochastic variable.

**Duration**   A measure of the average life a bond. It is also an approximation to the ratio of the proportional change in the bond price to the absolute change in its yield.

**Duration Matching**   A procedure for matching the durations of assets and liabilities in a financial institution.

**Dynamic Hedging**   A procedure for hedging an option position by periodically changing the position held in the underlying assets.

The objective is usually to maintain a delta-neutral position.

**Early Exercise** Exercise prior to the maturity date.

**Efficient Market Hypothesis** A hypothesis that asset prices reflect relevant information.

**Electronic Trading** System of trading where a computer is used to match buyers and sellers.

**Embedded Option** An option that is an inseparable part of another instrument.

**Empirical Research** Research based on historical market data.

**Equilibrium Model** A model for the behavior of interest rates derived from a model of the economy.

**Equity Swap** A swap where the return on an equity portfolio is exchanged for either a fixed or a floating rate of interest.

**Eurodollar** A dollar held in a bank outside the United States

**Eurodollar Futures Contract** A futures contract written on a Eurodollar deposit.

**Eurodollar Interest Rate** The interest rate on a Eurodollar deposit.

**Eurocurrency** A currency that is outside the formal control of the issuing country's monetary authorities.

**European Option** An option that can be exercised only at the end of its life.

**EWMA** Exponentially weighted moving average.

**Exchange Option** An option to exchange one asset for another.

**Ex-dividend Date** When a dividend is declared, an ex-dividend date is specified. Investors who own shares of the stock up to the ex-dividend date receive the dividend.

**Executive Stock Option** A stock option issued by company on its own stock and given to its executives as part of their remuneration.

**Exercise Limit** Maximum number of option contacts that can be exercised within a five-day period.

**Exercise Price** The price at which the underlying asset may be bought or sold in an option contract. (Also called the strike price.)

**Exotic Option** A nonstandard option.

**Expectations Theory** The theory that forward interest rates equal expected future spot interest rates.

**Expected Value of a Variable** The average value of the variable obtained by weighting the alternative values by their probabilities.

**Expiration Date** The end of life of a contract.

**Exposure** The maximum loss from default by a counterparty.

**Explicit Finite Difference Method** A method for valuing a derivative by solving the underlying differential equation. The value of the derivative at time $t$ is related to three values at time $t + \delta t$. It is essentially the same as the trinomial tree method.

**Exponentially Weighted Moving Average Model** A model where exponential weighting is used to provide forecasts for a variable from historical data. It is sometimes applied to the variance rate in value-at-risk calculations.

**Exponential Weighting** A weighting scheme where the weight given to an observation depends on how recent it is. The weight given to an observation $t$ time periods ago is $\lambda$ times the weight given to an observation $t - 1$ time periods ago where $\lambda < 1$.

**Extendable Bond** A bond whose life can be extended at the option of the holder

**Extendable Swap** A swap whose life can be extended at the option of one side to the contract.

**Factor** Source of uncertainty.

**Factor analysis** An analysis aimed at finding a small number of factors that describe most of the variation in a large number of correlated variables. (Similar to a principal components analysis.)

**FASB** Financial Accounting Standards Board.

**Financial Intermediary** A bank or other financial institution that facilitates the flow of funds between different entities in the economy.

**Finite Difference Method** A method for solving a differential equation.

**Flat Volatility** The name given to volatility used to price a cap when the same volatility is used for each caplet.

**Flex Option** An option traded on an exchange with terms that are different from the standard options traded by the exchange.

**Floor** *See* Interest rate floor.

**Floor–Ceiling Agreement** *See* Collar.

**Floorlet** One component of a floor.

**Floor Rate** The rate in an interest rate floor agreement.

**Foreign Currency Option** An option on a foreign exchange rate.

**Forward Contract** A contract that obligates the holder to buy or sell an asset for a predetermined delivery price at a predetermined future time.

**Forward Exchange Rate** The forward price of one unit of a foreign currency.

**Forward Interest Rate** The interest rate for a future period of time implied by the rates prevailing in the market today.

**Forward Price** The delivery price in a forward contract that causes the contract to be worth zero.

**Forward Rate** Rate of interest for a period of time in the future implied by today's zero rates.

**Forward Rate Agreement (FRA)** Agreement that a certain interest rate will apply to a certain principal amount for a certain time period in the future.

**Forward Risk-Neutral World** A world is forward risk-neutral with respect to a certain asset when the market price of risk equals the volatility of that asset.

**Forward Start Option** An option designed so that it will be at-the-money at some time in the future.

**Forward Swap** *See* Deferred swap.

**Futures Contract** A contract that obligates the holder to buy or sell an asset at a predetermined delivery price during a specified future time period. The contract is marked to market daily.

**Futures Option** An option on a futures contract.

**Futures Price** The delivery price currently applicable to a futures contract.

**Gamma** The rate of change of delta with respect to the asset price.

**Gamma-Neutral Portfolio** A portfolio with a gamma of zero.

**GARCH Model** A model for forecasting volatility where the variance rate follows a mean-reverting process.

**Generalized Wiener Process** A stochastic process where the change in a variable in each short time period of length $\delta t$ has a normal distribution with mean and variance, both proportional to $\delta t$.

**Geometric Average** The $n$th root of the product of $n$ numbers.

**Geometric Brownian Motion** A stochastic process often assumed for asset prices where the logarithm of the underlying variable follows a generalized Wiener process.

**Greeks** Hedge parameters such as delta, gamma, vega, theta, and rho.

**Hazard Rate** Measures probability of default in a short period of time conditional on no earlier default.

**HDD** Heating degree days. The maximum of zero and the amount by which the daily average temperature is less than 65° Fahrenheit. The average temperature is the average of the highest and lowest temperatures (midnight to midnight).

**Hedge** A trade designed to reduce risk.

**Hedger** An individual who enters into hedging trades.

**Hedge Ratio** The ratio of the size of a position in a hedging instrument to the size of the position being hedged.

**Historical Simulation** A simulation based on historical data.

**Historic Volatility** A volatility estimated from historical data.

**Holiday Calendar** Calendar defining which days are holidays for the purposes of determining payment dates in a swap.

**Implied Distribution** A distribution for a future asset price implied from option prices.

**Implied Repo Rate** The repo rate implied from the price of a Treasury bill and a Treasury bill futures price.

**Implied Tree** A tree describing the movements of an asset price that is constructed to be consistent with observed option prices.

**Implicit Finite Difference Method** A method for valuing a derivative by solving the underlying differential equation. The value of the derivative at time $t + \delta t$ is related to three values at time $t$.

**Implied Volatility** Volatility implied from an option price using the Black–Scholes or a similar model.

**Implied Volatility Function (IVF) Model** Model designed so that it matches the market prices of all European options.

**Inception Profit** Profit created by selling a derivative for more than its theoretical value.

**Index Amortizing Swap** *See* Indexed principal swap.

**Index Arbitrage** An arbitrage involving a position in the stocks comprising a stock index and a position in a futures contract on the stock index.

**Indexed Principal Swap** A swap where the principal declines over time. The reduction in the principal on a payment date depends on the level of interest rates.

**Index Futures** A futures contract on a stock index or other index.

**Index Option** An option contract on a stock index or other index.

**Initial Margin** The cash required from a futures trader at the time of the trade.

**Instantaneous Forward Rate** Forward rate for a very short period of time in the future.

**Interest Rate Cap** An option that provides a payoff when a specified interest rate is above a certain level. The interest rate is a floating rate that is reset periodically.

**Interest Rate Collar** A combination of an interest rate cap and an interest rate floor.

**Interest Rate Derivative** A derivative whose payoffs are dependent on future interest rates.

**Interest Rate Floor** An option that provides a payoff when an interest rate is below a certain level. The interest rate is a floating rate that is reset periodically.

**Interest Rate Option** An option where the payoff is dependent on the level of interest rates.

**Interest Rate Swap** An exchange of a fixed rate of interest on a certain notional principal for a floating rate of interest on the same notional principal.

**In-the-Money Option** Either (a) a call option where the asset price is greater than the strike price or (b) a put option where the asset price is less than the strike price.

**Intrinsic Value** For a call option, this is the greater of the excess of the asset price over the strike price and zero. For a put option, it is the greater of the excess of the strike price over the asset price and zero.

**Inverted Market** A market where futures prices decrease with maturity.

**Investment Asset** An asset held by at least some individuals for investment purposes.

**IO** Interest Only. A mortgage-backed security where the holder receives only interest cash flows on the underlying mortgage pool.

**Itô's Lemma** A result that enables the stochastic process for a function of a variable to be calculated from the stochastic process for the variable itself.

**Itô Process** A stochastic process where the change in a variable during each short period of time of length $\delta t$ has a normal distribution. The mean and variance of the distribution are proportional to $\delta t$ and are not necessarily constant.

**Kappa** *See* Vega.

**Kurtosis** A measure of the fatness of the tails of a distribution.

**Jump Diffusion Model** Model where asset price has jumps superimposed on to a diffusion process such as geometric Brownian motion.

**Lambda** *See* Vega.

**LEAPS** Long-term equity anticipation securities. These are relatively long-term options on individual stocks or stock indices.

**LIBID** London interbank bid rate. The rate bid by banks on Eurocurrency deposits (i.e., the rate at which a bank is willing to borrow from other banks).

**LIBOR** London interbank offer rate. The rate offered by banks on Eurocurrency deposits (i.e., the rate at which a bank is willing to lend to other banks).

**LIBOR Curve** LIBOR zero-coupon interest rates as a function of maturity.

**LIBOR-in-Arrears Swap** Swap where the interest paid on a date is determined by the interest rate observed on that date (not by the interest rate observed on the previous payment date).

**Limit Move** The maximum price move permitted by the exchange in a single trading session.

**Limit Order** An order that can be executed only at a specified price or one more favorable to the investor.

**Liquidity Preference Theory** A theory leading to the conclusion that forward interest rates are above expected future spot interest rates.

**Liquidity Premium** The amount that forward interest rates exceed expected future spot interest rates.

**Liquidity Risk** Risk that it will not be possible to sell a holding of a particular instrument at its theoretical price.

**Locals** Individuals on the floor of an exchange who trade for their own account rather than for someone else.

**Lognormal distribution** A variable has a lognormal distribution when the logarithm of the variable has a normal distribution.

**Long hedge** A hedge involving a long futures position.

**Long position** A position involving the purchase of an asset.

**Lookback Option** An option whose payoff is dependent on the maximum or minimum of the asset price achieved during a certain period.

**Low Discrepancy Sequence** *See* Quasi-random sequence.

**Maintenance Margin** When the balance in a trader's margin account falls below the maintenance margin level, the trader receives a margin call requiring the account to be topped up to the initial margin level.

**Margin** The cash balance (or security deposit) required from a futures or options trader.

**Margin Call** A request for extra margin when the balance in the margin account falls below the maintenance margin level.

**Market Maker** A trader who is willing to quote both bid and offer prices for an asset.

**Market Model** A model most commonly used by traders.

**Market Price of Risk** A measure of the trade-offs investors make between risk and return.

**Market Segmentation Theory** A theory that short interest rates are determined independently of long interest rates by the market.

**Marking to Market** The practice of revaluing an instrument to reflect the current values of the relevant market variables.

**Markov Process** A stochastic process where the behavior of the variable over a short period of time depends solely on the value of the variable at the beginning of the period, not on its past history.

**Martingale** A zero-drift stochastic process.

**Maturity Date** The end of the life of a contract.

**Maximum Likelihood Method** A method for choosing the values of parameters by maximizing the probability of a set of observations occurring.

**Mean Reversion** The tendency of a market variable (such as an interest rate) to revert back to some long-run average level.

**Measure** Sometimes also called a probability measure, it defines the market price of risk.

**Modified Duration** A modification to the standard duration measure so that it more accurately describes the relationship between proportional changes in a bond price and absolute changes in its yield. The modification takes account of the compounding frequency with which the yield is quoted.

**Money Market Account** An investment that is initially equal to $1 and, at time $t$, increases at the very short-term risk-free interest rate prevailing at that time.

**Monte Carlo Simulation** A procedure for randomly sampling changes in market variables in order to value a derivative.

**Mortgage-Backed Security** A security that entitles the owner to a share in the cash flows realized from a pool of mortgages.

**Naked Position** A short position in a call option that is not combined with a long position in the underlying asset.

**Netting** The ability to offset contracts with positive and negative values in the event of a default by a counterparty

**Newton–Raphson Method** An iterative procedure for solving nonlinear equations.

**No-arbitrage Assumption** The assumption that there are no arbitrage opportunities in market prices.

**No-arbitrage Interest Rate Model** A model for the behavior of interest rates that is exactly consistent with the initial term structure of interest rates.

**Nonstationary model** A model where the volatility parameters are a function of time.

**Nonsystematic risk** Risk that can be diversified away.

**Normal Backwardation** A situation where the futures price is below the expected future spot price.

**Normal Distribution** The standard bell-shaped distribution of statistics.

**Normal Market** A market where futures prices increase with maturity.

**Notional Principal** The principal used to calculate payments in an interest rate swap. The principal is "notional" because it is neither paid nor received.

**Numeraire** Defines the units in which security prices are measured. For example, if the price of IBM is the numeraire, all security prices are measured relative to IBM. If IBM is $80 and a particular security price is $50, the security price is 0.625 when IBM is the numeraire.

**Numerical Procedure**   A method of valuing an option when no formula is available.

**OCC**   Options Clearing Corporation. *See* Clearinghouse.

**Offer Price**   The price that a dealer is offering to sell an asset.

**Open Interest**   The total number of long positions outstanding in a futures contract (equals the total number of short positions).

**Open Outcry**   System of trading where traders meet on the floor of the exchange

**Option**   The right to buy or sell an asset.

**Option-Adjusted Spread**   The spread over the Treasury curve that makes the theoretical price of an interest rate derivative equal to the market price.

**Option Class**   All options of the same type (call or put) on a particular stock.

**Option Series**   All options of a certain class with the same strike price and expiration date.

**Order Book Official**   *See* Board broker.

**Out-of-the-Money Option**   Either (a) a call option where the asset price is less than the strike price or (b) a put option where the asset price is greater than the strike price.

**Over-the-Counter Market**   A market where traders deal by phone. The traders are usually financial institutions, corporations, and fund managers.

**Package**   A derivative that is a portfolio of standard calls and puts, possibly combined with a position in forward contracts and the asset itself.

**Parallel Shift**   A movement in the yield curve where each point on the curve changes by the same amount.

**Par Value**   The principal amount of a bond.

**Par Yield**   The coupon on a bond that makes its price equal the principal.

**Path-Dependent Option**   An option whose payoff depends on the whole path followed by the underlying variable—not just its final value.

**Payoff**   The cash realized by the holder of an option or other derivative at the end of its life.

**Plain Vanilla**   A term used to describe a standard deal.

**PO**   Principal Only. A mortgage-backed security where the holder receives only principal cash flows on the underlying mortgage pool.

**Poisson Process**   A process describing a situation where events happen at random. The probability of an event in time $\delta t$ is $\lambda \delta t$, where $\lambda$ is the intensity of the process.

**Portfolio Immunization**   Making a portfolio relatively insensitive to interest rates.

**Portfolio Insurance**   Entering into trades to ensure that the value of a portfolio will not fall below a certain level.

**Position Limit**   The maximum position a trader (or group of traders acting together) is allowed to hold.

**Premium**   The price of an option.

**Prepayment Function**   A function estimating the prepayment of principal on a portfolio of mortgages in terms of other variables.

**Principal**   The par or face value of a debt instrument.

**Principal Components Analysis**   An analysis aimed at finding a small number of factors that describe most of the variation in a large number of correlated variables. (Similar to a factor analysis.)

**Program Trading**   A procedure where trades are automatically generated by a computer and transmitted to the trading floor of an exchange.

**Protective Put**   A put option combined with a long position in the underlying asset.

**Pull-to-Par**   The reversion of a bond's price to its par value at maturity.

**Put–Call Parity**   The relationship between the price of a European call option and the price of a European put option when they have the same strike price and maturity date.

**Put Option**   An option to sell an asset for a certain price by a certain date.

**Puttable Bond**   A bond where the holder has the right to sell it back to the issuer at certain predetermined times for a predetermined price.

**Puttable Swap**   A swap where one side has the right to terminate early.

**Quanto**   A derivative where the payoff is defined by variables associated with one currency but is paid in another currency.

**Quasi-Random Sequence**   A sequence of numbers used in a Monte Carlo simulation that are representative of alternative outcomes rather than random.

**Rainbow Option**   An option whose payoff is dependent on two or more underlying variables.

**Range-Forward Contract**   The combination of a long call and short put or the combination of a short call and long put.

**Real Option**   Option involving real (as opposed to financial) assets. Real assets include land, plant, and machinery.

**Rebalancing**   The process of adjusting a trading position periodically. Usually the purpose is to maintain delta neutrality.

**Recovery Rate**   Amount recovered in the event of a default as a percent of the claim.

**Repo**   Repurchase agreement. A procedure for borrowing money by selling securities to a counterparty and agreeing to buy them back later at a slightly higher price.

**Repo Rate**   The rate of interest in a repo transaction.

**Reset Date**   The date in a swap or cap or floor when the floating rate for the next period is set.

**Reversion Level**   The level to which the value of a market variable (e.g., an interest rate) tends to revert.

**Rho**   Rate of change of the price of a derivative with the interest rate.

**Rights Issue**   An issue to existing shareholders of a security giving them the right to buy new shares at a certain price.

**Risk-Free Rate**   The rate of interest that can be earned without assuming any risks.

**Risk-Neutral Valuation**   The valuation of an option or other derivative assuming the world is risk neutral. Risk-neutral valuation gives the correct price for a derivative in all worlds, not just in a risk-neutral world.

**Risk-Neutral World**   A world where investors are assumed to require no extra return on average for bearing risks.

**Roll Back**   *See* Backwards induction.

**Scalper**   A trader who holds positions for a very short period of time.

**Scenario Analysis**   An analysis of the effects of possible alternative future movements in market variables on the value of a portfolio.

**SEC**   Securities and Exchange Commission.

**Settlement Price**   The average of the prices that a futures contract trades for immediately before the bell signaling the close of trading for a day. It is used in mark-to-market calculations.

**Short Hedge**   A hedge where a short futures position is taken.

**Short Position**   A position assumed when traders sell shares they do not own.

**Short Rate**   The interest rate applying for a very short period of time.

**Short Selling**   Selling in the market shares that have been borrowed from another investor.

**Short-Term Risk-Free Rate**   *See* Short rate.

**Shout Option**   An option where the holder has the right to lock in a minimum value for the payoff at one time during its life.

**Sigma**   *See* Vega.

**Simulation**   *See* Monte Carlo simulation.

**Specialist**   An individual responsible for managing limit orders on some exchanges. The specialist does not make the information on outstanding limit orders available to other traders.

**Speculator**   An individual who is taking a position in the market. Usually the individual is betting that the price of an asset will go up or that the price of an asset will go down.

**Spot Interest Rate**   *See* Zero-coupon interest rate.

**Spot Price**   The price for immediate delivery.

**Spot Volatilities**   The volatilities used to price a cap when a different volatility is used for each caplet.

**Spread Option**   An option where the payoff is dependent on the difference between two market variables.

**Spread Transaction**   A position in two or more options of the same type.

**Static Hedge**   A hedge that does not have to be changed once it is initiated.

**Static Options Replication**   A procedure for hedging a portfolio that involves finding another portfolio of approximately equal value on some boundary.

**Step-up Swap**   A swap where the principal increases over time in a predetermined way.

**Stochastic Process**   An equation describing the probabilistic behavior of a stochastic variable.

**Stochastic Variable**   A variable whose future value is uncertain.

**Stock Dividend**   A dividend paid in the form of additional shares.

**Stock Index**   An index monitoring the value of a portfolio of stocks.

**Stock Index Futures**   Futures on a stock index.

**Stock Index Option**   An option on a stock index.

**Stock Option**   Option on a stock.

**Stock Split**   The conversion of each existing share into more than one new share.

**Storage Costs**   The costs of storing a commodity.

**Straddle**   A long position in a call and a put with the same strike price.

**Strangle**   A long position in a call and a put with different strike prices.

**Strap**   A long position in two call options and one put option with the same strike price.

**Stress Testing**   Testing of the impact of extreme market moves on the value of a portfolio.

**Strike Price**   The price at which the asset may be bought or sold in an option contract. (Also called the exercise price.)

**Strip**   A long position in one call option and two put options with the same strike price.

**Swap**   An agreement to exchange cash flows in the future according to a prearranged formula.

**Swap Rate**   The fixed rate in an interest rate swap that causes the swap to have a value of zero.

**Swaption**   An option to enter into an interest rate swap where a specified fixed rate is exchanged for floating.

**Swing Option**   Energy option in which the rate of consumption must be between a minimum and maximum level. There is usually a limit on the number of times the option holder can change the rate at which the energy is consumed.

**Synthetic Option**   An option created by trading the underlying asset.

**Systematic Risk** Risk that cannot be diversified away.

**Take-and-Pay Option** *See Swing option.*

**Term Structure of Interest Rates** The relationship between interest rates and their maturities.

**Terminal Value** The value at maturity.

**Theta** The rate of change of the price of an option or other derivative with the passage of time.

**Time Decay** *See* Theta.

**Time Value** The value of an option arising from the time left to maturity (equals an option's price minus its intrinsic value).

**Timing Adjustment** Adjustment made to the forward value of a variable to allow for the timing of a payoff from a derivative.

**Total Return Swap** A swap where the return on an asset such as a bond is exchanged for LIBOR plus a spread. The return on the asset includes income such as coupons and the change in value of the asset.

**Transactions Costs** The cost of carrying out a trade (commissions plus the difference between the price obtained and the midpoint of the bid–offer spread).

**Treasury Bill** A short-term non-coupon-bearing instrument issued by the government to finance its debt.

**Treasury Bill Futures** A futures contract on a Treasury bill.

**Treasury Bond** A long-term coupon-bearing instrument issued by the government to finance it debt.

**Treasury Bond Futures** A futures contract on Treasury bonds.

**Treasury Note** *See* Treasury bond. (Treasury notes have maturities of less than 10 years.)

**Treasury Note Futures** A futures contract on Treasury notes.

**Tree** A representation of the evolution of the value of a market variable for the purposes of valuing an option or other derivative.

**Trinomial Tree** A tree where there are three branches emanating from each node. It is used in the same way as a binomial tree for valuing derivatives.

**Triple Witching Hour** A term given to the time when stock index futures, stock index options, and options on stock index futures all expire together.

**Underlying Variable** A variable that price of an option or other derivative depends on.

**Unsystematic risk** *See* Nonsystematic risk.

**Up-and-In Option** An option that comes into existence when the price of the underlying asset increases to a prespecified level.

**Up-and-Out Option** An option that ceases to exist when the price of the underlying asset increases to a prespecified level.

**Uptick** An increase in price.

**Value at Risk** A loss that will not be exceeded at some specified confidence level.

**Variance–covariance matrix** A matrix showing variances of, and covariances between, a number of different market variables.

**Variance Rate** The square of volatility.

**Variance Reduction Procedures** Procedures for reducing the error in a Monte Carlo simulation.

**Variation Margin** An extra margin required to bring the balance in a margin account up to the initial margin when there is a margin call.

**Vega** The rate of change in the price of an option or other derivative with volatility.

**Vega-neutral portfolio** A portfolio with a vega of zero.

**Volatility** A measure of the uncertainty of the return realized on an asset.

**Volatility Skew** A term used to describe the volatility smile when it is nonsymmetrical.

**Volatility Smile** The variation of implied volatility with strike price.

**Volatility Swap** Swap where the realized volatility during an accrual period is exchanged for a fixed volatility. Both percentage volatilities are applied to a notional principal.

**Volatility Term Structure** The variation of implied volatility with time to maturity.

**Volatility Matrix** A table showing the variation of implied volatilities with strike price and time to maturity.

**Warrant** An option issued by a company or a financial institution. Call warrants are frequently issued by companies on their own stock.

**Weather Derivatives** Derivative where the payoff depends on the weather.

**Wiener Process** A stochastic process where the change in a variable during each short period of time of length $\delta t$ has a normal distribution with a mean equal to zero and a variance equal to $\delta t$.

**Wild Card Play** The right to deliver on a futures contract at the closing price for a period of time after the close of trading.

**Writing an Option** Selling an option.

**Yield** A return provided by an instrument.

**Yield Curve** *See* Term structure.

**Zero-Coupon Bond** A bond that provides no coupons.

**Zero-Coupon Interest Rate** The interest rate that would be earned on a bond that provides no coupons.

**Zero-Coupon Yield Curve** A plot of the zero-coupon interest rate against time to maturity.

**Zero Curve** *See* Zero-coupon yield curve.

**Zero Rate** *See* Zero-coupon interest rate.

# DERIVAGEM SOFTWARE

The software accompanying this text is DerivaGem for Excel, Version 1.50. It requires Excel Version 7.0 or later. The software consists of three files: dg150.dll, DG150.xls, and DG150functions.xls To install the software you should create a directory with the name DerivGem (or some other name of your own choosing) and load DG150.xls and DG150functions.xls into the directory. You should load dg150.dll into the Windows\System directory (Windows 95 and 98 users) or the WINNT\System 32 directory (Windows 2000 and Windows NT users).[1]

Excel 2000 users should ensure that Security for Macros is set at *Medium* or *Low*. Check *Tools* followed by *Macros* in Excel to change this. While using the software you may be asked whether you want to enable macros. You should click *Enable Macros*.

Updates to the software can be downloaded from the author's website:[2]

www.rotman.utoronto.ca/~hull

There are two parts to the software: the Options Calculator (DG150.xls) and the Applications Builder (DG150functions.xls). Both parts require dg150.dll to be loaded into the Windows\System or WINNT\System32 directory. New users are advised to start with the Option Calculator.

## THE OPTIONS CALCULATOR

DG150.xls is a user-friendly options calculator. It consists of three worksheets. The first worksheet is used to carry out computations for stock options, currency options, index options, and futures options; the second is used for European and American bond options; and the third is used for caps, floors, and European swap options.

The software produces prices, Greek letters, and implied volatilities for a wide range of different instruments. It displays charts showing the way that option prices and the Greek letters depend on inputs. It also displays binomial and trinomial trees showing how the computations are carried out.

---

[1] Note that it is not uncommon for Windows Explorer to be set up so that *.dll files are not displayed. To change the setting so that the *.dll file can be seen proceed as follows. In Windows 95, click *View*, followed by *Options*, followed by *Show All Files*. In Windows 98 click *View}, followed by Folder Options, followed by View, followed by Show All Files*. *In Windows 2000, click Tools, followed by Folder Options, followed by View, followed by Show Hidden Files and Folders*.

[2] Version 1.51, which corrects a bug in the display of the binomial tree for dividend-paying stocks, is already available and should be downloaded.

### General Operation

To use the options calculator, you should choose a worksheet and click on the appropriate buttons to select Option Type, Underlying Type, and so on. You should then enter the parameters for the option you are considering, hit *Enter* on your keyboard, and click on *Calculate*. DerivaGem will then display the price or implied volatility for the option you are considering together with Greek letters. If the price has been calculated from a tree, and you are using the first or second worksheet, you can then click on *Display Tree* to see the tree. Sample displays of the tree are shown in Figures 18.3, 18.5, 18.6, 18.9, and 18.10. Many different charts can be displayed in all three worksheets. To display a chart, you must first choose the variable you require on the vertical axis, the variable you require on the horizontal axis, and the range of values to be considered on the horizontal axis. Following that you should hit *Enter* on your keyboard and click on *Draw Graph*.

Note that, whenever the values in one or more cells are changed, it is necessary to hit *Enter* on your keyboard before clicking on one of the buttons.

If you have a version of Excel later than 7.0, you will be asked whether you want to update to the new version when you first save the software. You should choose the *Yes* button.

### Options on Stocks, Currencies, Indices, and Futures

The first worksheet (Equity_FX_Index_Futures) is used for options on stocks, currencies, indices, and futures. To use it, you should first select the Underlying Type (Equity, Currency, Index, or Futures). You should then select the Option Type (Analytic European, Binomial European, Binomial American, Asian, Barrier Up and In, Barrier Up and Out, Barrier Down and In, Barrier Down and Out, Binary Cash or Nothing, Binary Asset or Nothing, Chooser, Compound Option on Call, Compound Option on Put, or Lookback). Finally, enter the data on the underlying asset and data on the option. Note that all interest rates are expressed with continuous compounding.

In the case of European and American equity options, a table pops up allowing you to enter dividends. Enter the time of each ex-dividend date (in years) in the first column and the amount of the dividend in the second column. Dividends must be entered in chronological order.

You must click on buttons to choose whether the option is a call or a put and whether you wish to calculate an implied volatility. If you do wish to calculate an implied volatility, the option price should be entered in the cell labeled Price.

Once all the data has been entered you should hit *Enter* on your keyboard and click on *Calculate*. If Implied Volatility was selected, DerivaGem displays the implied volatility in the Volatility (% per year) cell. If Implied Volatility was not selected, it uses the volatility you entered in this cell and displays the option price in the Price cell.

Once the calculations have been completed, the tree (if used) can be inspected and charts can be displayed.

When Analytic European is selected, DerivaGem uses the equations in Chapters 12 and 13 to calculate prices, and the equations in Chapter 14 to calculate Greek letters. When Binomial European or Binomial American is selected, a binomial tree is constructed as described in Sections 18.1 to 18.3. Up to 500 time steps can be used.

The input data are largely self-explanatory. In the case of an Asian option, the Current Average is the average price since inception. If the Asian option is new (Time since Inception equals zero), then the Current Average cell is irrelevant and can be left blank. In the case of a Lookback Option, the Minimum to Date is used when a Call is valued and the Maximum to Date is used when a Put is valued. For a new deal, these should be set equal to the current price of the underlying asset.

## Bond Options

The second worksheet (Bond_Options) is used for European and American options on bonds. You should first select a pricing model (Black European, Normal-Analytic European, Normal-Tree European, Normal American, Lognormal European, or Lognormal American). You should then enter the Bond Data and the Option Data. The coupon is the rate paid per year and the frequency of payments can be selected as Quarterly, Semi-Annual or Annual. The zero-coupon yield curve is entered in the table labeled Term Structure. Enter maturities (measured in years) in the first column and the corresponding continuously compounded rates in the second column. The maturities should be entered in chronological order. DerivaGem assumes a piecewise linear zero curve similar to that in Figure 5.1. Note that, when valuing interest rate derivatives, DerivaGem rounds all times to the nearest whole number of days.

When all data have been entered, hit *Enter* on your keyboard. The quoted bond price per $100 of Principal, calculated from the zero curve, is displayed when the calculations are complete. You should indicate whether the option is a call or a put and whether the strike price is a quoted (clean) strike price or a cash (dirty) strike price. (See the discussion and example in Section 22.2 to understand the difference between the two.) Note that the strike price is entered as the price per $100 of principal. You should indicate whether you are considering a call or a put option and whether you wish to calculate an implied volatility. If you select implied volatility and the normal model or lognormal model is used, DerivaGem implies the short rate volatility keeping the reversion rate fixed.

Once all the inputs are complete, you should hit *Enter* on your keyboard and click *Calculate*. After that the tree (if used) can be inspected and charts can be displayed. Note that the tree displayed lasts until the end of the life of the option. DerivaGem uses a much larger tree in its computations to value the underlying bond.

Note that, when Black's model is selected, DerivaGem uses the equations in Section 22.1. Also, the procedure in Section 22.2 is used for converting the input yield volatility into a price volatility.

## Caps and Swap Options

The third worksheet (Caps_and_Swap_Options) is used for caps and swap options. You should first select the Option Type (Swap Option or Cap/Floor) and Pricing Model (Black, Normal European, or Normal American). You should then enter data on the option you are considering. The Settlement Frequency indicates the frequency of payments and can be Annual, Semi-Annual, Quarterly, or Monthly. The software calculates payment dates by working backward from the end of the life of the cap or swap option. The initial accrual period may be a nonstandard length between 0.5 and 1.5 times a normal accrual period. The software can be used to imply either a volatility or a cap rate/swap rate from the price. When a normal model or a lognormal model is used, DerivaGem implies the short-rate volatility keeping the reversion rate fixed. The zero-coupon yield curve is entered in the table labeled Term Structure. Enter maturities (measured in years) in the first column and the corresponding continuously compounded rates in the second column. The maturities should be entered in chronological order. DerivaGem assumes a piecewise linear zero curve similar to that in Figure 5.1.

Once all the inputs are complete, you should click *Calculate*. After that, charts can be displayed.

Note that when Black's model is used, DerivaGem uses the equations in Sections 22.3 and 22.4.

### Greek Letters

In the Equity_FX_Index_Futures worksheet, the Greek letters are calculated as follows.

Delta: Change in option price per dollar increase in underlying asset

Gamma: Change in delta per dollar increase in underlying asset

Vega: Change in option price per 1% increase in volatility (e.g., volatility increases from 20% to 21%)

Rho: Change in option price per 1% increase in interest rate (e.g., interest increases from 5% to 6%)

Theta: Change in option price per calendar day passing

In the Bond_Options and Caps_and_Swap_Options worksheets the Greek letters are calculated as follows:

DV01: Change in option price per one basis point upward parallel shift in the zero curve

Gamma01: Change in DV01 per one basis point upward parallel shift in the zero curve, multiplied by 100

Vega: Change in option price when volatility parameter increases by 1% (e.g., volatility increases from 20% to 21%)

## THE APPLICATIONS BUILDER

The Applications Builder is DG150functions.xls. It is a set of 21 functions and 7 sample applications from which users can build their own applications.

### The Functions

The following is a list of the 21 functions included in the Applications Builder. Full details are on the first worksheet (FunctionSpecs).

1. Black_Scholes. This carries out Black-Scholes calculations for a European option on a stock, stock index, currency or futures contract.
2. TreeEquityOpt. This carries out binomial tree calculations for a European or American option on a stock, stock index, currency, or futures contract.
3. BinaryOption. This carries out calculations for a binary option on a stock, stock index, currency, or futures contract.
4. BarrierOption. This carries out calculations for a barrier option on a non-dividend-paying stock, stock index, currency, or futures contract.
5. AverageOption. This carries out calculations for an Asian option on a non-dividend-paying stock, stock index, currency, or futures contract.
6. ChooserOption. This carries out calculations for a chooser option on a non-dividend-paying stock, stock index, currency, or futures contract.
7. CompoundOption. This carries out calculations for compound options on non-dividend-paying stocks, stock indices, currencies, and futures.

8. LookbackOption. This carries out calculations for a lookback option on a non-dividend-paying stock, stock index, currency, or futures contract.

9. EPortfolio. This carries out calculations for a portfolio of options on a stock, stock index, currency, or futures contract.

10. BlackCap. This carries out calculations for a cap or floor using Black's model.

11. HullWhiteCap. This carries out calculations for a cap or floor using the Hull–White model.

12. TreeCap. This carries out calculations for a cap or floor using a trinomial tree.

13. BlackSwapOption. This carries out calculations for a swap option using Black's model.

14. HullWhiteSwap. This carries out calculations for a swap option using the Hull–White model.

15. TreeSwapOption. This carries out calculations for a swap option using a trinomial tree.

16. BlackBondOption. This carries out calculations for a bond option using Black's model.

17. HullWhiteBondOption. This carries out calculations for a bond option using the Hull–White model.

18. TreeBondOption. This carries out calculations for a bond option using a trinomial tree.

19. BondPrice. This values a bond.

20. SwapPrice. This values a plain vanilla interest rate swap. Note that it ignores cash flows arising from reset dates prior to start time.

21. IPortfolio. This carries out calculations for a portfolio of interest rate derivatives.

## Sample Applications

DG150functions.xls includes seven worksheets with sample applications:

A. Binomial Convergence. This investigates the convergence of the binomial model in Chapters 10 and 18.

B. Greek Letters. This provides charts showing the Greek letters in Chapter 14.

C. Delta Hedge. This investigates the performance of delta hedging as in Tables 14.2 and 14.3.

D. Delta and Gamma Hedge. This investigates the performance of delta plus gamma hedging for a position in a binary option.

E. Value and Risk. This calculates value at risk for a portfolio consisting of three options on a single stock using three different approaches.

F. Barrier Replication. This carries out calculations for the static options replication example in Section 19.4.

G. Trinomial Convergence. This investigates the convergence of the trinomial tree model in Chapter 23.

# MAJOR EXCHANGES TRADING FUTURES AND OPTIONS

| | | |
|---|---|---|
| Amsterdam Exchanges | AEX | www.aex.nl |
| American Stock Exchange | AMEX | www.amex.com |
| Australian Stock Exchange | ASX | www.asx.com.au |
| Brussels Exchanges | BXS | www.bxs.be |
| Bolsa de Mercadorias y Futuros, Brazil | BM&F | www.bmf.com.br |
| Chicago Board of Trade | CBOT | www.cbot.com |
| Chicago Board Options Exchange | CBOE | www.cboe.com |
| Chicago Mercantile Exchange | CME | www.cme.com |
| Coffee, Sugar & Cocoa Exchange, New York | CSCE | www.csce.com |
| Commodity Exchange, New York | COMEX | www.nymex.com |
| Copenhagen Stock Exchange | FUTOP | www.xcse.dk |
| Deutsche Termin Börse, Germany | DTB | www.exchange.de |
| Eurex | EUREX | www.eurexchange.com |
| Hong Kong Futures Exchange | HKFE | www.hkfe.com |
| International Petroleum Exchange, London | IPE | www.ipe.uk.com |
| Kansas City Board of Trade | KCBT | www.kcbt.com |
| Kuala Lumpur Options and Financial Futures Exchange | KLOFFE | www.kloffe.com.my |
| London International Financial Futures & Options Exchange | LIFFE | www.liffe.com |
| London Metal Exchange | LME | www.lme.co.uk |
| Marché à Terme International de France | MATIF | www.matif.fr |
| Marché des Options Négociables de Paris | MONEP | www.monep.fr |
| MEFF Renta Fija and Variable, Spain | MEFF | www.meff.es |
| MidAmerica Commodity Exchange | MidAm | www.midam.com |
| Minneapolis Grain Exchange | MGE | www.mgex.com |
| Montreal Exchange | ME | www.me.org |
| New York Board of Trade | NYBOT | www.nybot.com |
| New York Cotton Exchange | NYCE | www.nyce.com |
| New York Futures Exchange | NYFE | www.nyce.com |
| New York Mercantile Exchange | NYMEX | www.nymex.com |
| New York Stock Exchange | NYSE | www.nyse.com |
| New Zealand Futures & Options Exchange | NZFOE | www.nzfoe.com |

*(continued on next page)*

(*continued*)

| | | |
|---|---|---|
| Osaka Securities Exchange | OSA | www.ose.or.jp |
| Pacific Exchange | PXS | www.pacificex.com |
| Philadelphia Stock Exchange | PHLX | www.phlx.com |
| Singapore International Monetary Exchange | SIMEX | www.simex.com.sg |
| Stockholm Options Market | OM | www.omgroup.com |
| Sydney Futures Exchange | SFE | www.sfe.com.au |
| Tokyo Grain Exchange | TGE | www.tge.or.jp |
| Tokyo International Financial Futures Exchange | TIFFE | www.tiffe.or.jp |
| Toronto Stock Exchange | TSE | www.tse.com |
| Winnipeg Commodity Exchange | WCE | www.wce.mb.ca |

A number of exchanges have merged or formed alliances. For example:

1. Eurex is an alliance of DTB, CBOT, and exchanges in Switzerland and Finland.
2. MEFF, CME, BM&F, ME, the Paris Bourse (which includes MATIF and MONEP), and the Singapore Derivatives Exchange (part of SIMEX) have formed the GLOBEX alliance (www.globexalliance.com).
3. In September 2000, AEX, BXS, and the Paris Bourse (which includes MATIF and MONEP) announced that they were forming Euronext.

# TABLE FOR $N(x)$ WHEN $x \leqslant 0$

This table shows values of $N(x)$ for $x \leqslant 0$. The table should be used with interpolation. For example,

$$N(-0.1234) = N(-0.12) - 0.34[N(-0.12) - N(-0.13)]$$

$$= 0.4522 - 0.34 \times (0.4522 - 0.4483) = 0.4509$$

| $x$ | .00 | .01 | .02 | .03 | .04 | .05 | .06 | .07 | .08 | .09 |
|---|---|---|---|---|---|---|---|---|---|---|
| −0.0 | 0.5000 | 0.4960 | 0.4920 | 0.4880 | 0.4840 | 0.4801 | 0.4761 | 0.4721 | 0.4681 | 0.4641 |
| −0.1 | 0.4602 | 0.4562 | 0.4522 | 0.4483 | 0.4443 | 0.4404 | 0.4364 | 0.4325 | 0.4286 | 0.4247 |
| −0.2 | 0.4207 | 0.4168 | 0.4129 | 0.4090 | 0.4052 | 0.4013 | 0.3974 | 0.3936 | 0.3897 | 0.3859 |
| −0.3 | 0.3821 | 0.3783 | 0.3745 | 0.3707 | 0.3669 | 0.3632 | 0.3594 | 0.3557 | 0.3520 | 0.3483 |
| −0.4 | 0.3446 | 0.3409 | 0.3372 | 0.3336 | 0.3300 | 0.3264 | 0.3228 | 0.3192 | 0.3156 | 0.3121 |
| −0.5 | 0.3085 | 0.3050 | 0.3015 | 0.2981 | 0.2946 | 0.2912 | 0.2877 | 0.2843 | 0.2810 | 0.2776 |
| −0.6 | 0.2743 | 0.2709 | 0.2676 | 0.2643 | 0.2611 | 0.2578 | 0.2546 | 0.2514 | 0.2483 | 0.2451 |
| −0.7 | 0.2420 | 0.2389 | 0.2358 | 0.2327 | 0.2296 | 0.2266 | 0.2236 | 0.2206 | 0.2177 | 0.2148 |
| −0.8 | 0.2119 | 0.2090 | 0.2061 | 0.2033 | 0.2005 | 0.1977 | 0.1949 | 0.1922 | 0.1894 | 0.1867 |
| −0.9 | 0.1841 | 0.1814 | 0.1788 | 0.1762 | 0.1736 | 0.1711 | 0.1685 | 0.1660 | 0.1635 | 0.1611 |
| −1.0 | 0.1587 | 0.1562 | 0.1539 | 0.1515 | 0.1492 | 0.1469 | 0.1446 | 0.1423 | 0.1401 | 0.1379 |
| −1.1 | 0.1357 | 0.1335 | 0.1314 | 0.1292 | 0.1271 | 0.1251 | 0.1230 | 0.1210 | 0.1190 | 0.1170 |
| −1.2 | 0.1151 | 0.1131 | 0.1112 | 0.1093 | 0.1075 | 0.1056 | 0.1038 | 0.1020 | 0.1003 | 0.0985 |
| −1.3 | 0.0968 | 0.0951 | 0.0934 | 0.0918 | 0.0901 | 0.0885 | 0.0869 | 0.0853 | 0.0838 | 0.0823 |
| −1.4 | 0.0808 | 0.0793 | 0.0778 | 0.0764 | 0.0749 | 0.0735 | 0.0721 | 0.0708 | 0.0694 | 0.0681 |
| −1.5 | 0.0668 | 0.0655 | 0.0643 | 0.0630 | 0.0618 | 0.0606 | 0.0594 | 0.0582 | 0.0571 | 0.0559 |
| −1.6 | 0.0548 | 0.0537 | 0.0526 | 0.0516 | 0.0505 | 0.0495 | 0.0485 | 0.0475 | 0.0465 | 0.0455 |
| −1.7 | 0.0446 | 0.0436 | 0.0427 | 0.0418 | 0.0409 | 0.0401 | 0.0392 | 0.0384 | 0.0375 | 0.0367 |
| −1.8 | 0.0359 | 0.0351 | 0.0344 | 0.0336 | 0.0329 | 0.0322 | 0.0314 | 0.0307 | 0.0301 | 0.0294 |
| −1.9 | 0.0287 | 0.0281 | 0.0274 | 0.0268 | 0.0262 | 0.0256 | 0.0250 | 0.0244 | 0.0239 | 0.0233 |
| −2.0 | 0.0228 | 0.0222 | 0.0217 | 0.0212 | 0.0207 | 0.0202 | 0.0197 | 0.0192 | 0.0188 | 0.0183 |
| −2.1 | 0.0179 | 0.0174 | 0.0170 | 0.0166 | 0.0162 | 0.0158 | 0.0154 | 0.0150 | 0.0146 | 0.0143 |
| −2.2 | 0.0139 | 0.0136 | 0.0132 | 0.0129 | 0.0125 | 0.0122 | 0.0119 | 0.0116 | 0.0113 | 0.0110 |
| −2.3 | 0.0107 | 0.0104 | 0.0102 | 0.0099 | 0.0096 | 0.0094 | 0.0091 | 0.0089 | 0.0087 | 0.0084 |
| −2.4 | 0.0082 | 0.0080 | 0.0078 | 0.0075 | 0.0073 | 0.0071 | 0.0069 | 0.0068 | 0.0066 | 0.0064 |
| −2.5 | 0.0062 | 0.0060 | 0.0059 | 0.0057 | 0.0055 | 0.0054 | 0.0052 | 0.0051 | 0.0049 | 0.0048 |
| −2.6 | 0.0047 | 0.0045 | 0.0044 | 0.0043 | 0.0041 | 0.0040 | 0.0039 | 0.0038 | 0.0037 | 0.0036 |
| −2.7 | 0.0035 | 0.0034 | 0.0033 | 0.0032 | 0.0031 | 0.0030 | 0.0029 | 0.0028 | 0.0027 | 0.0026 |
| −2.8 | 0.0026 | 0.0025 | 0.0024 | 0.0023 | 0.0023 | 0.0022 | 0.0021 | 0.0021 | 0.0020 | 0.0019 |
| −2.9 | 0.0019 | 0.0018 | 0.0018 | 0.0017 | 0.0016 | 0.0016 | 0.0015 | 0.0015 | 0.0014 | 0.0014 |
| −3.0 | 0.0014 | 0.0013 | 0.0013 | 0.0012 | 0.0012 | 0.0011 | 0.0011 | 0.0011 | 0.0010 | 0.0010 |
| −3.1 | 0.0010 | 0.0009 | 0.0009 | 0.0009 | 0.0008 | 0.0008 | 0.0008 | 0.0008 | 0.0007 | 0.0007 |
| −3.2 | 0.0007 | 0.0007 | 0.0006 | 0.0006 | 0.0006 | 0.0006 | 0.0006 | 0.0005 | 0.0005 | 0.0005 |
| −3.3 | 0.0005 | 0.0005 | 0.0005 | 0.0004 | 0.0004 | 0.0004 | 0.0004 | 0.0004 | 0.0004 | 0.0003 |
| −3.4 | 0.0003 | 0.0003 | 0.0003 | 0.0003 | 0.0003 | 0.0003 | 0.0003 | 0.0003 | 0.0003 | 0.0002 |
| −3.5 | 0.0002 | 0.0002 | 0.0002 | 0.0002 | 0.0002 | 0.0002 | 0.0002 | 0.0002 | 0.0002 | 0.0002 |
| −3.6 | 0.0002 | 0.0002 | 0.0001 | 0.0001 | 0.0001 | 0.0001 | 0.0001 | 0.0001 | 0.0001 | 0.0001 |
| −3.7 | 0.0001 | 0.0001 | 0.0001 | 0.0001 | 0.0001 | 0.0001 | 0.0001 | 0.0001 | 0.0001 | 0.0001 |
| −3.8 | 0.0001 | 0.0001 | 0.0001 | 0.0001 | 0.0001 | 0.0001 | 0.0001 | 0.0001 | 0.0001 | 0.0001 |
| −3.9 | 0.0000 | 0.0000 | 0.0000 | 0.0000 | 0.0000 | 0.0000 | 0.0000 | 0.0000 | 0.0000 | 0.0000 |
| −4.0 | 0.0000 | 0.0000 | 0.0000 | 0.0000 | 0.0000 | 0.0000 | 0.0000 | 0.0000 | 0.0000 | 0.0000 |

# TABLE FOR $N(x)$ WHEN $x \geqslant 0$

This table shows values of $N(x)$ for $x \geqslant 0$. The table should be used with interpolation. For example,

$$N(0.6278) = N(0.62) + 0.78[N(0.63) - N(0.62)]$$

$$= 0.7324 + 0.78 \times (0.7357 - 0.7324) = 0.7350$$

| $x$ | .00 | .01 | .02 | .03 | .04 | .05 | .06 | .07 | .08 | .09 |
|-----|-----|-----|-----|-----|-----|-----|-----|-----|-----|-----|
| 0.0 | 0.5000 | 0.5040 | 0.5080 | 0.5120 | 0.5160 | 0.5199 | 0.5239 | 0.5279 | 0.5319 | 0.5359 |
| 0.1 | 0.5398 | 0.5438 | 0.5478 | 0.5517 | 0.5557 | 0.5596 | 0.5636 | 0.5675 | 0.5714 | 0.5753 |
| 0.2 | 0.5793 | 0.5832 | 0.5871 | 0.5910 | 0.5948 | 0.5987 | 0.6026 | 0.6064 | 0.6103 | 0.6141 |
| 0.3 | 0.6179 | 0.6217 | 0.6255 | 0.6293 | 0.6351 | 0.6368 | 0.6406 | 0.6443 | 0.6480 | 0.6517 |
| 0.4 | 0.6554 | 0.6591 | 0.6628 | 0.6664 | 0.6700 | 0.6736 | 0.6772 | 0.6808 | 0.6844 | 0.6879 |
| 0.5 | 0.6915 | 0.6950 | 0.6985 | 0.7019 | 0.7054 | 0.7088 | 0.7123 | 0.7157 | 0.7190 | 0.7224 |
| 0.6 | 0.7257 | 0.7291 | 0.7324 | 0.7357 | 0.7389 | 0.7422 | 0.7454 | 0.7486 | 0.7517 | 0.7549 |
| 0.7 | 0.7580 | 0.7611 | 0.7642 | 0.7673 | 0.7704 | 0.7734 | 0.7764 | 0.7794 | 0.7823 | 0.7852 |
| 0.8 | 0.7881 | 0.7910 | 0.7939 | 0.7967 | 0.7995 | 0.8023 | 0.8051 | 0.8078 | 0.8106 | 0.8133 |
| 0.9 | 0.8159 | 0.8186 | 0.8212 | 0.8238 | 0.8264 | 0.8289 | 0.8315 | 0.8340 | 0.8365 | 0.8389 |
| 1.0 | 0.8413 | 0.8438 | 0.8461 | 0.8485 | 0.8508 | 0.8531 | 0.8554 | 0.8577 | 0.8599 | 0.8621 |
| 1.1 | 0.8643 | 0.8665 | 0.8686 | 0.8708 | 0.8729 | 0.8749 | 0.8770 | 0.8790 | 0.8810 | 0.8830 |
| 1.2 | 0.8849 | 0.8869 | 0.8888 | 0.8907 | 0.8925 | 0.8944 | 0.8962 | 0.8980 | 0.8997 | 0.9015 |
| 1.3 | 0.9032 | 0.9049 | 0.9066 | 0.9082 | 0.9099 | 0.9115 | 0.9131 | 0.9147 | 0.9162 | 0.9177 |
| 1.4 | 0.9192 | 0.9207 | 0.9222 | 0.9236 | 0.9251 | 0.9265 | 0.9279 | 0.9292 | 0.9306 | 0.9319 |
| 1.5 | 0.9332 | 0.9345 | 0.9357 | 0.9370 | 0.9382 | 0.9394 | 0.9406 | 0.9418 | 0.9429 | 0.9441 |
| 1.6 | 0.9452 | 0.9463 | 0.9474 | 0.9484 | 0.9495 | 0.9505 | 0.9515 | 0.9525 | 0.9535 | 0.9545 |
| 1.7 | 0.9554 | 0.9564 | 0.9573 | 0.9582 | 0.9591 | 0.9599 | 0.9608 | 0.9616 | 0.9625 | 0.9633 |
| 1.8 | 0.9641 | 0.9649 | 0.9656 | 0.9664 | 0.9671 | 0.9678 | 0.9686 | 0.9693 | 0.9699 | 0.9706 |
| 1.9 | 0.9713 | 0.9719 | 0.9726 | 0.9732 | 0.9738 | 0.9744 | 0.9750 | 0.9756 | 0.9761 | 0.9767 |
| 2.0 | 0.9772 | 0.9778 | 0.9783 | 0.9788 | 0.9793 | 0.9798 | 0.9803 | 0.9808 | 0.9812 | 0.9817 |
| 2.1 | 0.9821 | 0.9826 | 0.9830 | 0.9834 | 0.9838 | 0.9842 | 0.9846 | 0.9850 | 0.9854 | 0.9857 |
| 2.2 | 0.9861 | 0.9864 | 0.9868 | 0.9871 | 0.9875 | 0.9878 | 0.9881 | 0.9884 | 0.9887 | 0.9890 |
| 2.3 | 0.9893 | 0.9896 | 0.9898 | 0.9901 | 0.9904 | 0.9906 | 0.9909 | 0.9911 | 0.9913 | 0.9916 |
| 2.4 | 0.9918 | 0.9920 | 0.9922 | 0.9925 | 0.9927 | 0.9929 | 0.9931 | 0.9932 | 0.9934 | 0.9936 |
| 2.5 | 0.9938 | 0.9940 | 0.9941 | 0.9943 | 0.9945 | 0.9946 | 0.9948 | 0.9949 | 0.9951 | 0.9952 |
| 2.6 | 0.9953 | 0.9955 | 0.9956 | 0.9957 | 0.9959 | 0.9960 | 0.9961 | 0.9962 | 0.9963 | 0.9964 |
| 2.7 | 0.9965 | 0.9966 | 0.9967 | 0.9968 | 0.9969 | 0.9970 | 0.9971 | 0.9972 | 0.9973 | 0.9974 |
| 2.8 | 0.9974 | 0.9975 | 0.9976 | 0.9977 | 0.9977 | 0.9978 | 0.9979 | 0.9979 | 0.9980 | 0.9981 |
| 2.9 | 0.9981 | 0.9982 | 0.9982 | 0.9983 | 0.9984 | 0.9984 | 0.9985 | 0.9985 | 0.9986 | 0.9986 |
| 3.0 | 0.9986 | 0.9987 | 0.9987 | 0.9988 | 0.9988 | 0.9989 | 0.9989 | 0.9989 | 0.9990 | 0.9990 |
| 3.1 | 0.9990 | 0.9991 | 0.9991 | 0.9991 | 0.9992 | 0.9992 | 0.9992 | 0.9992 | 0.9993 | 0.9993 |
| 3.2 | 0.9993 | 0.9993 | 0.9994 | 0.9994 | 0.9994 | 0.9994 | 0.9994 | 0.9995 | 0.9995 | 0.9995 |
| 3.3 | 0.9995 | 0.9995 | 0.9995 | 0.9996 | 0.9996 | 0.9996 | 0.9996 | 0.9996 | 0.9996 | 0.9997 |
| 3.4 | 0.9997 | 0.9997 | 0.9997 | 0.9997 | 0.9997 | 0.9997 | 0.9997 | 0.9997 | 0.9997 | 0.9998 |
| 3.5 | 0.9998 | 0.9998 | 0.9998 | 0.9998 | 0.9998 | 0.9998 | 0.9998 | 0.9998 | 0.9998 | 0.9998 |
| 3.6 | 0.9998 | 0.9998 | 0.9999 | 0.9999 | 0.9999 | 0.9999 | 0.9999 | 0.9999 | 0.9999 | 0.9999 |
| 3.7 | 0.9999 | 0.9999 | 0.9999 | 0.9999 | 0.9999 | 0.9999 | 0.9999 | 0.9999 | 0.9999 | 0.9999 |
| 3.8 | 0.9999 | 0.9999 | 0.9999 | 0.9999 | 0.9999 | 0.9999 | 0.9999 | 0.9999 | 0.9999 | 0.9999 |
| 3.9 | 1.0000 | 1.0000 | 1.0000 | 1.0000 | 1.0000 | 1.0000 | 1.0000 | 1.0000 | 1.0000 | 1.0000 |
| 4.0 | 1.0000 | 1.0000 | 1.0000 | 1.0000 | 1.0000 | 1.0000 | 1.0000 | 1.0000 | 1.0000 | 1.0000 |

# AUTHOR INDEX

# SUBJECT INDEX

References to items in the Glossary of Terms are bolded.

## SINGLE PC LICENSE AGREEMENT AND LIMITED WARRANTY